S0-BMA-161

Final exam:
Ch. 20, 22, 24, 25, 42

June 5th

BUSINESS AND THE LAW

BUSINESS AND THE LAW

DONALD P. LYDEN
Professor of Business Law and Former Acting Dean,
School of Business Administration and Economics
California State University, Northridge

J. DAVID REITZEL
Professor of Business Law
California State University, Fresno

NATHAN J. ROBERTS
Emeritus Professor of Law
Loyola University, Los Angeles

With contributions by
James M. Highsmith
Professor of Business Law
California State University, Fresno

NUMBER _____ SEB
YOU SEE _____ ON
THIS USED BOOK AT YOUR
SKYLINE BOOK STORE
PRICE $32.00 KB

McGraw-Hill Book Company

New York St. Louis San Francisco Auckland Bogotá Hamburg
Johannesburg London Madrid Mexico Montreal New Delhi Panama
Paris São Paulo Singapore Sydney Tokyo Toronto

BUSINESS AND THE LAW

Copyright © 1985 by McGraw-Hill, Inc. All rights reserved. Printed in the United States of America. Except as permitted under the United States Copyright Act of 1976, no part of this publication may be reproduced or distributed in any form or by any means, or stored in a data base or retrieval system, without the prior written permission of the publisher.

1234567890DOCDOC898765

ISBN 0-07-039151-3

This book was set in Caledonia by Black Dot, Inc. (ECU).
The editors were Cheryl L. Mehalik and Lisa Bernstein;
the designer was Jo Jones;
the production supervisor was Leroy A. Young.
Project supervision was done by The Total Book.
R. R. Donnelley & Sons Company was printer and binder.

Library of Congress Cataloging in Publication Data
Main entry under title:

Business and the Law.

Includes index.
1. Commercial law—United States.   I. Lyden, Donald P.
KF889.B83   1985   346.73'07   84-12533
ISBN 0-07-039151-3   347.3067

ABOUT THE AUTHORS

DONALD P. LYDEN holds a J.D. degree from the University of California, Los Angeles. He is currently Professor of Business Law, California State University, Northridge. He is a former chair of the department of business law, and was formerly acting dean of the School of Business Administration and Economics at California State University, Northridge. Dean Lyden is a member of the California Bar, and has maintained a private law practice in the Los Angeles area since 1959. He is a past president of the Pacific Southwest Business Law Association.

J. DAVID REITZEL is currently professor of business law, California State University, Fresno, and was formerly professor and chairman of the department of business law at The American College, Bryn Mawr. Before that, he taught at St. Cloud State University, St. Cloud, Minnesota. Professor Reitzel holds a J.D. from Indiana University and B.S. and M.S. degrees from Purdue University. Admitted to the Indiana and the federal bars in 1969, Professor Reitzel is currently co-editor of the *American Business Law Journal* and is the author of numerous articles and papers, many dealing with business law education.

NATHAN J. ROBERTS, emeritus professor of law at Loyola University, Los Angeles, received a J.D. degree from the Universtiy of Florida and a LL.M. from George Washington University. He has previously held positions at the University of California, Santa Barbara, and at the Army Industrial College in Washington, D.C. He is a retired Brigadier General, formerly Assistant Judge Advocate General of the Army for Civil Law. He is a member of Phi Kappa Phi.

Dean Lyden, Professor Reitzel, and Professor Roberts also are three of the authors of *Contemporary Business Law: Principles and Cases*, by Hoeber, Reitzel, Lyden, Roberts, and Severance (McGraw-Hill, 1982).

CONTENTS*

* For more detailed information about content, see the outline of content at the beginning of each chapter.

PREFACE

PURPOSE, COVERAGE, AND THE NEEDS OF STUDENTS

Many factors have affected the content and approach of *Business and the Law:* The immediate and long-term student needs that a basic law book for undergraduates should meet, the striking array of occupations our students will seek, the varying degrees of legal literacy employers will expect, and the immense variety of legal topics that contend for limited space. Our main concern is student needs. We believe that a basic course in business law—and the textbook used in it—should contribute not only to the professional and vocational aspects of a business student's education, but also to his or her awareness of the fundamental, enduring, and universal aspects of the law. The business law literature, countless discussions with colleagues, the comments of reviewers, and our own teaching experience confirm this belief.

We are addressing undergraduate students studying law for the first time: business majors primarily, but students from other programs as well—paralegal studies, nursing, vocational studies, general studies, education, journalism, political science, and pre-engineering, to mention a few. All need an orientation to the law. To that end, the opening chapters of the book and substantial portions of many other chapters focus on the nature of lawmaking, the legal processes by which law is applied to resolve disputes, the values and policy that underlie our law and legal processes, and the role of law and litigation in the conduct of everyday business affairs. The "why's" of the law are prominent throughout the book, for as Lord Coke said, "If by your studie and industrie you make not the reason of the law your owne, it is not possible for you long to retaine it in your memorie." Yet, the overwhelming emphasis of this book is on the fundamentals—both philosophical and technical—that all undergraduate business law students should receive from their courses.

Believing that a basic course in business law should contribute not only to the professional and vocational aspects of business education, but also to the process of general education, we have tried to assemble a set of instructional materials that will serve each student in both of these significant ways. Regardless of how general education is perceived—as education for citizenship, as an introduction to a basic discipline or thought process, or as a study of American culture and legal tradition—this book provides a basis for many insights.

The background and introductory chapters will help students understand the essential nature of our law and legal system. From the book as a whole, students will see how the legal system facilitates business operations and discourages or controls harmful business practices.

From that examination, students will begin to recognize that the legal system is an organic part of our social system, both shaping and being shaped by the broader society.

Another point may eventually be brought home—that every citizen has the right and the duty to evaluate the law and to contribute to its improvement. The process of evaluation requires that students be able to analyze so-called "legal" problems (which often are social problems), to detect and weigh the competing interests involved, and to judge whether a given law or judicial decision is a fair or reasonable resolution of the problem it allegedly addresses. This book, in its textual discussion of policy and functions of the law, provides a basis for the beginnings of evaluation. These qualities that make the book suitable for the general education of students are by no means out of place in a business law course attended mainly by business majors. Business students simply have additional reasons for studying business law, *viz.*, the fact that knowledge of law can enhance their professional effectiveness.

The main purpose of this book is, of course, to provide a set of instructional materials that has legal content appropriate for business majors. So, the book has the following ten parts and an appendix containing the Uniform Commercial Code:

Part One: Law and the Legal System
Part Two: Tort and Criminal Law
Part Three: Contracts
Part Four: Sales
Part Five: Agency
Part Six: Property and Estates
Part Seven: Secured Transactions and Insurance
Part Eight: Commercial Paper
Part Nine: Business Organizations
Part Ten: Government Regulation of Business

Within the framework of these ten parts, the book contains three kinds of chapters. First are those that discuss the legal foundations of business—the chapters on contracts, property, agency, torts, and crimes. These branches of law are the cornerstones upon which all business conduct rests, and students should study them for that reason, but also because those topics are the basis for understanding other foundation elements such as sales, secured transactions, commercial paper, partnerships, and corporations.

Second are the chapters dealing with the more global aspects of business law, those of special interest to future business managers. The government regulation chapters are an example. Chapter 41 sketches in broad outline the roles of the federal and state governments in the regulatory process, the central position of the United States Constitution in the regulation of business activity, the pervasive impact of administrative agencies in formulating and carrying out governmental policy, and the basic types of administrative regulation. Antitrust policy receives specific mention as an example of economic regulation; and the Federal Trade Commission is the main illustration of how administrative agencies function.

Chapters 42, 43, and 44 elaborate by focusing on key aspects of the regulatory effort: consumer protection, employment and labor law, and bankruptcy.

Third are the chapters discussing topics of interest to future technical specialists or CPA candidates. The chapter on insurance and those on the law of sales are of general interest, but also will be of vocational interest to anyone who may work in these or related areas such as banking. The parts of Chapter 23 on carriers, warehouses, and documents of title should be especially useful to persons who find employment in the distribution of goods or in the financing of sales. Likewise, the chapters on secured transactions, commercial paper, estates and wills, suretyship, limited partnership, corporate securities, and bankruptcy will help prepare students for careers in banking, financial counseling, debt collection, and other financial specialties.

COURSE FORMATS

This book has ample material for one or two courses in business law. Moreover, because of its design, the book can be used in a variety of course formats. Basic topics such as contracts, torts, and property appear relatively early in the book, while the more complex, advanced, or specialized topics appear later. Where necessary in the treatment of advanced topics, the text provides cross-references to or a review of basic material as a springboard into the new. Consequently, each part and many of the individual chapters can serve as nearly self-contained instructional units which may be assigned in a variety of orders.

By a judicious selection and sequencing of chapters, instructors can accommodate a broad spectrum of student needs. For example, an instructor could use the book as the basis for a survey course in business law by assigning, in whatever order seems appropriate, Parts One, Two, Three, Five, and Ten, together with (1) the introductory chapters of most other parts; (2) Chapters 23 and 24 on property, Chapter 26 on estates and wills, and Chapter 29 on insurance; and (3) any other chapters of interest such as Chapter 18 on product liability and Chapter 25 on checks and the relationship between bank and customer. Chapter 30, the introductory chapter on commercial paper, is especially suited to a survey course because it presents the rationale of commercial paper law in a nutshell.

This book is also well suited for use in a two-course sequence, often called Business Law I and Business Law II. Business Law I usually deals with some combination of the following basic topics: law and the legal system, tort and criminal law, contracts, property, agency, and government regulation of business. Business Law II usually covers the more advanced, technical, or specialized topics such as sales, secured transactions, commercial paper, and business organizations, together with topics of special interest to CPA candidates, such as insurance, suretyship, and bankruptcy. The formula varies, however, since property and agency often appear in Business Law II, while sales frequently appears in Business Law I as an extension of contracts. In a growing number of business programs, the topics of agency and business organizations are grouped with a treatment of employment–labor law and workers' compensation, the subjects of Chapter 43. Whatever the combination of topics in a particular course, the two-course sequence and the style of this book permit a relatively in-depth treatment of the law, and provide great flexibility in the choice and grouping of topics.

ETHICS AND BUSINESS LAW

A course in business law, provides an excellent opportunity for considering the ethical standards to which business conduct should conform. Most rules of law strike some sort of balance between or among contending interests, and it is a natural inquiry whether the balance struck is a fair, reasonable, just, or expedient one. To judge whether the law is fair—to evaluate the law—a student must be conversant with the ethical considerations that underlie it. So, although most of the ethics content of this book is expressed in terms of policy and rationale of the law, a number of review questions at the ends of the chapters focus explicitly on selected ethical issues. However, our most concerted effort at emphasizing ethics is found in the instructor's manual. There, for most chapters, the instructor will find a number of *ethics highlights*, each of which stresses the ethical implications of some rule or principle of law.

In formulating the ethics highlights, we do not subscribe to any particular school of ethical thought, nor do we try to state or develop any particular theory of ethics or jurisprudence. Rather, we focus on "ethics in practice." Consequently, in developing the ethics highlights, we have been guided by two questions: (1) Is the law as fair as it can be to the persons it affects? (2) If not, how should the law be adjusted?

PEDAGOGICAL AIDS

We are ever mindful of the futility of rote memorization as a technique for studying law. Yet the mastery of basic legal terms, principles, and concepts underlies the ability to explore the law at a more sophisticated level. The end-of-chapter review questions have been carefully designed to provide students with an opportunity systematically to review and check their comprehension of the textual materials. Many of these questions encourage students to look more deeply into a principle or topic. The end-of-chapter case problems encourage the application of legal principles in the discussion, resolution, and evaluation of legal disputes. We hope these activities will lead students to a heightened awareness of the nature, roles, limits, and suitability of the law.

Several other features of this book will also facilitate learning. They include:

1. A content outline preceding each chapter. The outline provides an overview of the chapter and a framework to aid in study, discussion, review, and retention of important terms, concepts, and principles.
2. Key terms highlighted in the text in boldface type and defined in understandable language. An extensive glossary is also provided at the end of the book.

3. Principles and rules of law, and policies underlying the law, explained in sufficient depth for accurate understanding.
4. An abundance of examples to illustrate the application of principles and rules of law, including several extended examples in particularly difficult areas.
5. Diagrams and line drawings that will help students visualize difficult abstract concepts.
6. Case briefs, in an easy-to-read format, integrated with text material and located where they best illustrate the application of the law to business situations.
7. Chapter summaries to aid in review and retention of legal concepts and principles.
8. Review questions and case problems arranged in a sequence that corresponds with the order of textual material, and worded to provide clues for locating the textual material needed to answer the questions or apply legal principles in solving the problems.
9. An index to aid in quick location of textual material.

SUPPLEMENTARY MATERIALS

Additional aids are available in three separate supplements. Each supplement is carefully integrated with text material. A Student's Study Guide and a Test Bank were prepared by Paulette Stenzel (Michigan State University) and Penny Mercurio (University of California, Northridge). The Instructor's Manual was prepared by the text authors, with the assistance of Penny Mecurio and Joerg Knipprath (University of California, Northridge) in the preparation of teaching notes and ethical highlights.

The Study Guide provides general help on how to study business law as well as providing for each chapter: introductions; summary outlines; self-test study questions consisting of fill-in, true and false, multiple-choice, and application questions (with all answers in the guide).

The Instructor's Manual features for each chapter extensive teaching notes; an outline grid keying the case briefs, review questions, and case problems to the pertinent topics in the chapter; solutions to the case problems; and transparancy masters.

The Text Bank offers approximately 2000 test items (multiple-choice, true/false, and short essay) in a chapter-by-chapter format. All test questions also are available on MICROEXAMINER, a program enabling instructors to easily produce exams using a microcomputer.

ACKNOWLEDGMENTS

In preparing *Business and the Law*, we were aided by perceptive reviews—reviews which helped us greatly in revising and adding material. We acknowledge with gratitude the work of the following reviewers:

Robert Prentice, University of Texas at Austin; Harold Schramm, Western Connecticut State University; Michael Stubbs, Joliet Junior College; Clark Wheeler, Santa Fe Community College; Jeffrey Figler, San Diego State University; Gary Schwartz, Harrisburg Area Community College; James Owens, California State University; Glen Swanson, American

River College; William Ringle, Queensborough College; Eugene Maccarrone, Hofstra University; Paulette Stenzel, Michigan State University; J. Roland Kelley, Tarrant County Junior College; Sanford Searleman, Adirondack Community College; and Benson Diamond, Suffolk University.

We are particularly indebted to Professor James M. Highsmith, California State University, Fresno, and to David I. Lippert, Judge (Retired), Workers' Compensation Appeals Board (California). Professor Highsmith prepared Chapter 12, *Form and Interpretation of Contracts; the Parol Evidence Rule;* Chapter 29, *Insurance;* and Chapter 41, *Regulating Business Conduct, Scope, and Size.* Judge Lippert, author of *Cases and Materials on Workers' Compensation,* and formerly Adjunct Professor of Law, Loyal University Law School, prepared Chapter 43, *Employment and Labor Law; Workers' Compensation.* We extend our special thanks to McGraw-Hill editor Cheryl Mehalik, general coordinator of this project; to Lisa Bernstein, our McGraw-Hill developmental editor who required us to be clear when we were not; and to editorial consultant Dr. Ethel S. Hoeber, a former university professor specializing in the language arts and education, whose patience and careful attention to detail have added immeasurably to the quality of this project.

DONALD P. LYDEN

J. DAVID REITZEL

NATHAN J. ROBERTS

PART ONE

Law
and the
Legal System

CHAPTER 1

The Background and Scope of Business Law

CHAPTER 2

The Court System; Civil Procedure; Arbitration

CHAPTER 1

THE BACKGROUND AND SCOPE OF BUSINESS LAW

Business law deals with social and economic forces that touch the lives of every one of us. As you become acquainted with its principles, you will gain insight into the reasons why, in an expanding economy, there must be rules governing the ethical conduct of business. Without such rules there would be no effective restraints upon the way people do business; people could freely take unfair advantage of one another and of the general public. The world of commerce would be a jungle. Rules that govern formation of agreements, that impose penalties upon people who do not live up to their agreements, and rules that establish equitable methods for the payment of debts all tend to ensure fair dealing in the sale of goods, products, and services, and to benefit the public as a whole.

This first chapter will introduce you to the study of business law. It defines what is meant by law, sketches the sources of law in America, and distinguishes between different fields of law. It will also comment on the direction in which business law appears to be moving, and will define the objectives which a course in business law is designed to achieve.

WHAT IS LAW?

Law is the system of rules and regulations by which society protects the community and promotes its welfare and the welfare of all its members. This is accomplished by the imposition of penalties for the violation of those rules. Law includes all the federal laws enacted (passed) by the United States Congress, state laws enacted by state legislatures, and laws passed by lesser political subdivisions such as county supervisors, boards of selectmen, and city councils. These laws frequently require **interpretation**. Interpretation of a law in the legal sense means that a judge determines the meaning intended by the enactors of the law, and how that law applies to a particular case before the court.

The philosophical basis for law or for the penalties it imposes are subjects beyond the scope of this book. Our purpose is to help you understand the fundamentals of the law governing conduct of business and business relationships, upon which the concepts of fair business dealings are based.

SOURCES OF BUSINESS LAW

Business law in America has its foundations in the English legal system. The earliest English settlers in the thirteen original colonies brought the law of their homeland to this continent. Nearly all aspects of English law applied in the new Colonies; only a few of its provisions were not carried across the Atlantic. For example, in England the eldest son automatically inherited his father's property but this rule was not followed by the colonists. Even after the American Revolution severed political ties to England, the new nation still retained English legal traditions. With the single exception of Louisiana, as new states were admitted to the union they also adopted the English system. Louisiana, having been a French colony in which French **civil law** applied, continued to follow that legal system. The civil law system is followed throughout the European continent, Japan, Egypt, and the Latin American countries. Roman Law furnishes the foundation for the civil law. Two other important legal systems are Muslim Law, based upon the Koran, and the Canon Law of the Catholic Church.

The law of England, therefore, forms the basis of American law as we see it in operation today. Superimposed upon that background are our federal and state constitutions and laws as they have been interpreted by the courts. To understand more clearly the influence of English law upon the American judicial system, we must go back in time and observe the formative period of English law.

English Sources of Law

Common Law. In English feudal society, which began in England with the Norman conquest in 1066, legal authority was centralized in the **King's Court**. Its justices "rode circuit"—that is, traveled about the country—hearing lawsuits. As the King's Court reached more and more people, its power and effect grew. This in turn diminished the authority of the older feudal courts, which had merely applied local customs as the criteria by which to settle disputes. The legal principles expressed in the decisions of the justices of the King's Court in time became a body of law effective throughout England. These accumulated decisions, based upon reason rather than upon old customs, and appropriate for all the nation, became known as the **common law** because of its acceptance countrywide—it was common to all the people.

Suits under the Common Law.   Under the common law the **plaintiff** (a person with a grievance against another person) brought suit with the objective of recovering money from the **defendant** (the one against whom the suit is brought). Under common law the *only* remedy that could be sought by an injured party was a sum of money as recompense (damages).

Proceedings in the courts under the common law were very formal. An action could be brought only if there were a **king's writ** (a letter bearing the seal of the king) allowing a grievance of that kind to be heard. Such writs were limited in number. Among types of actions for which writs existed were (1) money lent by the plaintiff to the defendant but not repaid, (2) money received by the defendant to be delivered to the plaintiff but not paid, (3) money owing for goods sold to and delivered by the plaintiff to the defendant, and (4) injury to the plaintiff or his or her property by the defendant (called an **action in trespass**). If the reason for which a plaintiff demanded payment of money from another could not be fitted into the form of some recognized king's writ, no suit could be brought.

In addition to this requirement for an appropriate writ, in a common law action the plaintiff also had to file a properly worded demand or declaration. If it were not correctly worded the defendant could file a **pleading** (a formal written document) such as a **demurrer**, claiming, in effect, that the plaintiff's declaration stated no cause of action; or a **motion to strike**, requesting that the court order the whole or part of a declaration deleted. If the court sustained either pleading, the defendant would not be required to answer the plaintiff's demand.

Although legal actions today are not nearly as formal as they were when the common law system was developing in England, demurrers and motions to strike are still used in our courts. These devices are explained in Chapter 2, where the American court system is discussed at length.

A common law case was tried in a court before a jury. If the jury found in favor of the defendant, its verdict was "not guilty." But if the jury's verdict was in favor of the plaintiff, a judgment was entered that ordered the defendant to pay the plaintiff the sum of money found to be due.

If the defendant did not pay the plaintiff, a judgment was enforced by the court at the request of the plaintiff. The court issued what was then and still is known as a **writ of execution**. This writ was an order to the sheriff "to levy upon" and take possession of any personal property owned by the defendant, such as a horse, a mill press, or merchandise in a store and, after giving public notice, sell it at a public sale. If the debtor owned real property (such as a house or farm) the sheriff levied upon that property and, after giving public notice, sold it. From the money received at the sale the judgment creditor (the person in whose favor the judgment is entered) and the court costs were paid. If any money remained, it was handed over to the debtor. If there was no property from which the court judgment could be satisfied, the debtor could be imprisoned. In America today, imprisonment for debt is not allowed and certain classes of personal property, such as implements or tools with which a person makes a living, are exempt from levy under writs of execution. Bankruptcy laws (the subject of Chapter 44) also give a debtor additional exemptions.

The Law Merchant.   During the period when common law was developing in England an increasing number of people entered commerce, and trade centers grew up. Many merchants carried on their commerce through "societies" or "companies," the members of which were legally bound by the **firma** (signatures) of their associates upon the business agreements they entered into. An organization run in this way became known as a *firm*, a word we now use for a business. These firms were the forerunners of today's partnerships and corporations—types of business organizations we will discuss in Chapters 34 through 40. Merchants developed a sophisticated system for paying for goods when the seller and the buyer were not in the same city. The procedures they developed formed the basis for our modern law of sales, a subject considered in Chapters 15 through 19, as well as for our law of commercial paper (Chapters 30 through 33).

Common law did not adequately serve these merchants, however. They required legal procedures not available to them through the common law courts, procedures which would facilitate transfer of goods and speed settlement of disputes. To satisfy these needs, merchants developed for themselves a system of law which was separate and distinct from common law. They set up their own "mercantile" courts in which the judges were themselves merchants. In England, the most important of these merchant courts was in London. A common law writ was not required for a merchant to have a dispute heard and settled. Instead, demands were made orally and the merchant-judge gave his decision immediately after hearing both sides.

Beginning about 1756 the merchants' law became part of the common law and the mercantile courts ceased to function. However, merchants were allowed to base their cases, filed in the common law courts, upon the **law merchant**, the name given to the law the merchants had themselves developed. This "law merchant" remained as part of the common law received by the American Colonies.

Force of Prior Decisions.   A cardinal rule of the common law, adopted by our American courts, is that judges will consider and take into account their own past decisions and decisions of other judges which may apply to the cases before them. This is the rule of **stare decisis** (pronounced *starry de-sy-sis*), which means "adhere to (past) decisions." The application of this rule brings continuity and certainty to the law.

An example of the rule of *stare decisis* can be seen in a case decided in 1698 which we will meet again in Chapter 21. In that case the driver of a cart carrying wine casks for his employer injured someone. The driver's *employer* was required to compensate the injured person, even though the employer was not at the scene of the accident. This was the first time a court held an employer liable for an injury inflicted by an employee, even when the employer had not ordered the act that caused the injury and was not even at the scene of the accident. Under the rule of *stare decisis* the court's decision of 1698 became the law of England—and is firmly entrenched as a principle of American law today.

In the United States today the rule of *stare decisis* applies in the following way: If a decision was rendered by a higher court of the state in which a case is being tried (or by the Supreme Court of the United States), and that decision can be applied to the case presently before the lower court, then the higher court's decision is binding upon the lower court and must be followed. However, if the decision emanated from the highest court of another state, it is taken into consideration by the judge but need not be followed. As a result, courts in different states sometimes express differing views as to the principles of law involved and, on occasion, as to their applications. Therefore, you will occasionally read in the chapters which follow that a certain principle of law expresses "the majority view," or expresses "the minority view" among the various American courts.

The rule that courts should follow prior decisions in settling cases before them does not mean that common law is so rigid that it is not subject to exception. A state court, in the absence of a decision of a higher state court or of the Supreme Court of the United States, may refuse to follow the common law in a matter if local conditions are different or if times have so changed that the common law is no longer relevant to the issues before the court. Common law is frequently changed by **statute** (another name for a law that has been enacted by a legislative body). As a United States district judge has said: ". . . the prevailing rules of common law constitute no more than rules of decision . . . binding on local courts only in the absence of local case law or statutory law to the contrary . . . . This Court has the power to deviate from prevailing rules of common law to create local laws to the contrary. . . . *Murray v. Beloit Power Systems*, 450 F. Supp. 1145 (D.C. Virgin Isl., 1979).

One practical outgrowth of the rule of *stare decisis* is that an easy way has been developed for judges and lawyers to find and study decisions of all U.S. courts of record (those which publish written opinions). These decisions are printed in several series of meticulously indexed books. The most frequently used series is the National Reporter System, which conveniently publishes decisions of courts of record by geographic area—Pacific, Atlantic, Southern, Northwestern, Southeastern, etc. This series is constantly kept current and can be found in law libraries throughout the country as well as in many law offices.

Each of the chapters which follows contains resumés of reported cases illustrating legal principles. On the line below the name of each case is its *citation*. This citation tells you where the case can be found within the National Reporter System, the state in which the case was decided, and its date. For example, the case of *Murray v. Beloit*

Power Systems, above, has this citation: 450 F. Supp. 1145 (D.C. Virgin Isl., 1979). That citation indicates that the case is published in volume 450, at page 1145, of the Federal Supplement and that it was decided in 1979 by the U.S. district court for the Virgin Islands.

Equity Law.   Because of the strict rules of common law and the limited scope of its writs—the king's permission for an action to be filed by a plaintiff—frequently there was no court to which a person could turn for help. **Equity law** developed to fill this vacuum and to provide a remedy where something other than money alone was desired.

Meaning of Equity Law.   The meaning of equity law can best be explained by an example. Suppose John wanted to stop Matthew from grazing his cattle on John's pasture. The only remedy in the common law courts was money damages, but money would not answer John's need. He wanted someone in authority to order Matthew to keep cattle off his land. John had to petition the king to secure that relief. The king would then refer the matter to his chancellor, the next most important official, who issued the order in the king's name. In this way, the court of chancery developed. The chancellor, and later the justices of the chancery court, applied their own "discretion," their "sense of justice," and "conscience" to the facts stated in the petitions which reached them, and issued their decrees accordingly.

The law applied by the chancery court was called "equity," a word implying fairness and impartiality, to distinguish it from the regular common law. The concept of equity law, as well as the precepts of common law, have come down to us as part of the American judicial system.

Courts of Equity.   Originally, courts of law and courts of equity in the United States were separate. However, although the distinction between the *functions* of law and of equity are still maintained, it is now the practice in almost all states to try equity cases and law cases in the same courts. Many states follow the English custom and designate the person (or party) who initiates a suit in equity the **complainant** and the other party to the litigation the **respondent**. There are no jury trials in equity courts. The case is heard and decided by the judge who, in some states, is called the chancellor.

American Sources of Law   Resting upon the foundation of the English legal system, the federal government and all the states, through legislative, judicial, and administrative processes, formulate laws which meet the needs of business and establish conditions under which business enterprises may operate. The underlying concept of the American political system is expressed in the Constitution of the United States and in its Amendments. These set forth the limits beyond which Congress may not legislate and beyond which the President may not act.

The federal government has only the powers that have been delegated to it by the states. All of the legislative and administrative powers which have not been delegated remain in the states. Each state, in turn, has a constitution which sets out the authorities which the people of that state have given to their state government because, ultimately, all power lies in the people. The Constitution of the United

States therefore deliniates the areas in which Congress may enact laws. State constitutions fix the authority of state legislatures to enact state laws.

Constitutional Sources. Article I, Section 8 of the Constitution gives Congress the power to legislate in several areas which affect business. Among the most important are the power to levy and collect taxes, to regulate commerce between states (the basis of the laws discussed in Chapters 41 and 42), to provide for the common defense and the general welfare of the United States, and to make all laws necessary to execute those powers. Among Congress' other powers that directly affect business are its right to establish a bankruptcy law that is effective throughout the country (Chapter 44), and its right to establish a patent and copyright system.

Legislative Sources. Primary legislative sources of law are the statutes (also called "laws" and "acts") passed by Congress and state legislatures. A state may not enact laws which are (1) inconsistent with those passed by Congress, (2) solely within the power of Congress to enact, or (3) already the subject of congressional legislation.

Judicial Sources. Courts test the validity and application of laws in the light of constitutional provisions and the intent of the Congress, legislature, local government, or agency that formulated them. The ultimate result is that, although the courts do not enact laws, they play a large part in determining how laws may be applied, what restraints laws place upon individuals and upon business, and what privileges individuals and businesses can expect to enjoy under the law. To that extent, it is frequently said that courts *make* laws. You will see examples of this throughout succeeding chapters, particularly in Chapters 41 through 43.

Administrative Sources. Day-to-day operations of government rest largely in the hands of administrative agencies such as the Internal Revenue Service, the Federal Trade Commission, and the National Labor Relations Board. The regulations of an administrative agency, when published in a government publication called the *Federal Register*, have the force and effect of law. Chapter 41 discusses administrative law emphasizing the authority of administrative agencies to regulate the conduct, scope, and size of business organizations.

CATEGORIES OF LAW

Law may be examined from a number of points of view. In this chapter we will consider substantive law, procedural law, civil law, and criminal law.

Substantive
Law

The term **substantive law** is derived from the word "substance," meaning the *subject* or *body* of the law. Substantive law is the foundation of law, establishing rights and duties. For example, a law passed by Congress establishing income tax rates, or a law passed by a state legislature defining the qualifications a person must have to practice medicine (or some other profession), or a law making kidnapping a crime, are substantive laws.

Procedural Law

Procedural law refers to the formal steps (procedures) that must be followed to enforce the rights or penalties substantive law authorizes. It is procedural law which defines, for example, (1) what papers Tom's lawyer must file at the courthouse to force Ed to pay a debt he owes Tom, (2) how Tom's lawyer directs the sheriff to seize and sell Ed's property when Ed fails to pay a judgment of the court (a writ of execution), and (3) what hearings the state must hold before a person charged with the commission of a crime may be brought to trial.

Substantive law may be said to be the body of the law itself, defining legal rights and liabilities, while procedural law determines the way in which substantive law is enforced. So that you can see the relationship between substantive law and procedural law, Chapter 2 traces a hypothetical lawsuit through the procedural steps of a typical judicial system, and Chapter 5 traces the movement of a criminal case from arrest through conviction.

Civil Law

For the most part, laws that relate to business are found within **civil law**, which has both substantive and procedural elements. In its substantive role, civil law establishes (1) property rights, and (2) the legal basis for personal and commercial transactions. For example, substantive civil law governs such matters as the settlement of all manner of disputes between people, how a business is organized, how people enter into legally binding agreements, and how contracts are enforced. In its procedural role, civil law establishes court procedures involving, for instance, how a suit is filed, how a trial is conducted, and how a judgment or decree of the court is enforced.

Most business agreements satisfy the requirements of civil law and the people involved usually carry out their promises. However, sometimes the parties to a transaction disagree about the terms or conditions of their agreement or its performance so that the differences can be settled only through some form of judicial proceeding. In that event, a lawsuit may be instituted. The one who files (brings) a civil suit against another person is called the *plaintiff*. The person against whom the suit is filed—that is, the one defending himself or herself—is called the *defendant*.

Civil Law Remedies.   A civil law suit is brought by a plaintiff to recover money damages or to secure some form of equitable relief.

Damages.   The word **damages** means money payment for injury or loss a plaintiff claims to have sustained because of a wrongful action of the defendant. Depending on the circumstances, the plaintiff may demand payment for pain and suffering, medical expenses, damage to property, loss of wages, loss of profits, or injury to reputation. Damages of this sort are **compensatory damages** and are awarded by courts in order, as is often said, to make the plaintiff "whole again."

Sometimes when a court finds that a defendant is guilty of a wrongful act, he or she is ordered by the court to pay damages in an amount far greater than the actual loss the plaintiff sustained. These additional sums are **punitive damages**. The law imposes punitive damages to punish the wrongdoer and, by example, to discourage others from committing similar wrongs. Imposition of punitive damages is justified primarily when (1) a defendant intentionally commits a wrongful act, as when Pete, to harass and annoy Sam, slashes the tires on Sam's car; or (2) when someone, in utter disregard for the rights of others, acts negligently and injures another as, for instance, if Claude, a surgeon, while under the influence of marijuana, performs an operation negligently and harms the patient. In both these assumed situations the courts would undoubtedly allow punitive damages against the defendants (Pete in the first instance, Claude in the second example) in addition to compensatory damages covering actual losses suffered by the plaintiffs.

Equitable Remedies.   If the plaintiff has a grievance which cannot be satisfied by payment of money damages alone, then an **equitable remedy** may be sought. In fact, if a sum of money is the only relief sought, a court of equity will not hear the case. Equitable remedies furnish relief in many fields of law, including contract, tort, and property law.

A court may order an **injunction** (an order prohibiting a defendant from doing something). To illustrate, suppose a factory discharges waste products into a stream and, as a result, the water becomes useless to Robert, who runs a farm downstream. Robert can sue the factory in a court of equity and **pray** (ask) not only for the value of his lost crop, but also for the court to **enjoin** (forbid) the factory from continuing to pollute the stream.

With regard to contracts, an equitable remedy may take several forms such as (1) **reformation** of a contract, that is, changing its words when the written words do not correctly express the intent of the parties; (2) **cancellation** of a contract when a person has the legal right to have the contract voided because, for instance, he or she was the victim of an unfair advantage taken by the other side in the negotiation; or (3) the **specific performance** of a contract may be ordered. An order for specific performance means that a person is directed to perform his or her contractual obligations. These equitable remedies as they apply to contracts are discussed in Chapter 14.

The scope of equitable remedies is apparent from the maxims which courts of equity apply. Among them are: "He who seeks equity must do equity"; "He who comes into equity must come with clean hands"; "Equity delights in doing justice and not by halfs"; "Equity will not suffer a wrong without a remedy"; and "Equity regards substance rather than form."

Judgments and Decrees.   After trial of a civil suit the court issues its decision. The decision, if the suit is in law, is called a **judgment** and, if the suit is in equity, is called a **decree**. As noted earlier, it is now the practice in almost all states to try law cases and equity cases (both are civil cases) in the same courts by the same judges. The formal distinction between law and equity is, however, still maintained.

If the judgment is that the defendant owes the plaintiff a stated sum of money, the person in whose favor the judgment is entered is called a **judgment creditor** and the one who must pay the money is a **judgment debtor**. A judgment creditor forces payment of the judgment by having a writ of execution issued by the clerk of the court, directing the sheriff to seize the debtor's property and sell it to satisfy the judgment.

An **equitable decree** is a court order directing one of the litigants (the parties to the suit) to do or not to do something. An equitable decree might be, for instance: (1) an order to the factory in the previous example not to dump its chemical wastes into the stream; or (2) an order prohibiting a store from using a false name on merchandise, such as labeling inferior shirts "Arrow Shirts" when, in fact, they are not that brand.

In addition to ordering some specific action, an equity court may in the same suit also grant money damages.

A decree in equity is a personal order of the court. If the person against whom it is directed fails to comply, he or she is in **contempt of court** and may be fined or imprisoned. A business concern in contempt of court may be fined. Under certain circumstances its officers may also personally be held in contempt of court.

Areas of Civil Law Relating to Business.   There is no single division of law called "business law." Every phase of civil law bears some relation to business. The composite of civil law subjects relating most directly to business and to the world of commerce are, for convenience, grouped within the informal heading of business law. The most important of these subjects are contract law and the law of business organizations.

Contract Law.   Contract law governs formation of agreements, avoidance of agreements, and the rights of one party to an agreement when the other party fails to perform as promised. Contract law also dictates circumstances under which failure of performance is excusable. Part Three of this book (Chapters 6 through 14) is devoted to the law of contracts. Part Four, "Sales" (Chapters 15 through 19), Part Five, "Agency" (Chapters 20 through 22), Part Seven, "Secured Transactions and Insurance" (Chapters 27 through 29), and Part Eight, "Commercial Paper" (Chapters 30 through 33) cover important aspects of business law which are variants of, or otherwise closely related to, contracts.

Law of Business Organizations.   Of great importance to business is that aspect of civil law concerning the relationship between employers and employees. This subject is known as the **law of agency**. An equally important subject is that dealing with types of business organizations such as partnerships and corporations. These subjects are covered in Chapters 20 through 22, and 34 through 40.

Other Law Relating to Business.   Many other areas of law relate closely to business. Among them are those dealing with insurance (Chapter 29), labor and employment laws (Chapter 43), and bankruptcy (Chapter 44). Taxation, another area of law important to business, is not included in this book because of its highly technical nature. Other specialized areas of law which sometimes affect business relations, such as admiralty law (the laws of the sea), conflicts of law (laws and legal procedures which vary between states and between the United States and foreign countries), and international law are also omitted. Two other legal areas which particularly relate to business are the law of torts and property law.

1. *The law of torts.* A **tort** is a civil wrong against property or against a person or business. A *civil wrong* may be defined as a wrong for which the injured party can secure compensation from the wrongdoer. For example, if Jane Doe shoplifts a bottle of perfume from a store, she commits a tort (a civil wrong) against the store as well as **larceny** (a crime) against the state. As we will see in Chapter 5, Jane can be both tried for the criminal offense and sued for the civil wrong, the tort. Chapters 3 and 4 discuss torts, emphasizing their effect upon business.

2. *Property law.* **Property law** deals with the ownership, purchase, and sale of (1) *immovable property*, such as land or buildings; and (2) *movable property*, such as stocks and bonds, vehicles, money, or furniture. Because of the fundamental relationship of property to all business transactions, Part Six (Chapters 23 through 26) is devoted to property law.

Criminal Law   A crime is an act punishable by the state in an action taken in the name of the state. **Criminal law** defines what actions are crimes, establishes procedures for the trial of persons charged with having committed crimes, and fixes the limits of punishments.

While a civil action involves an offense against persons or property, a crime is an offense against the public order and well-being. In a successful civil suit the plaintiff may receive compensation from the defendant in the form of money damages. In a criminal action the guilty person is punished by being required to pay a fine to the state, to serve a term of imprisonment (in some states the death penalty may be imposed), or to perform some public service. Sometimes the punishment may also involve directing the defendant to make some repayment to the victim.

Even though a victim may be physically harmed or personal property unlawfully taken in a criminal act, nonetheless the crime itself is an *offense against the state.* The person against whom the crime was committed is not the plaintiff but is only a witness in the trial of the accused. This is not to say that the victim has no right of action against the criminal. The victim may, either before or after the state brings the criminal action to trial, bring a separate civil suit for damages against the person who committed the offense.

TRENDS IN BUSINESS LAW

Law should not be viewed as something fixed and unchanging like the pyramids, for the law varies with time and with place, responding to the needs of society which itself is in ferment. Competitive pressures have grown with our expanding population. The country has outgrown the laissez faire attitude toward the conduct of business; ethical considerations must be recognized as an integral part of business life. From time to time old business practices, such as employment discrimination based on race and sex, are corrected, old laws are repealed, and new ones are enacted. Also, as time goes on, the courts adopt new legal concepts to accommodate new tools of business which spring from scientific advances. For example, new legal theories had to be formulated to protect electronically stored information from being stolen.

Business law, although of ancient lineage, is still young in spirit, ready to respond in an innovative fashion to new demands of the public and the business world. The flexibility of business law will become clearer as you read the chapters which follow.

Directions in which business law is moving are fairly well marked. Some of these trends are:

1. A lessening of technicalities in legal procedures
2. A movement toward unifying the law

3. An increase in the number of laws protecting consumers
4. An increasing emphasis upon corporate responsibility
5. An expanding use of business law in implementing government policy

Lessening of Legal Technicalities

Because of our overcrowded courts (whose procedures are the subject of Chapter 2), settling disputes through arbitration or through other abbreviated legal proceedings is being widely encouraged. In **arbitration**, parties submit their legal differences to an arbitrator rather than to a court for decision. Arbitration is explained in Chapter 2.

All states have added **small claims courts** to their legal systems. These courts are authorized to hear, in simplified proceedings, cases in which only small sums of money are sought. The limit that can be sought in a small claims court varies from state to state. Many have set the limit at $500. California permits recovery of up to $1500 in a small claims court, but some states limit recovery to only $100. Generally, the plaintiff is not represented by an attorney and a case is begun merely by filling in a short form furnished by the court. Suits in small claims courts are disposed of very quickly.

Unifying of the Law

Codification of Law.   Increasingly, states are reorganizing their laws through the process of *codification*. By that process, all currently effective state laws pertaining to a particular subject are systematically edited to eliminate duplication and inconsistencies. They are then arranged under appropriate section and subsection headings to bring all related laws into one place regardless of when they were enacted by the legislature. Thus, the codified law is a coherent statement of all currently valid law of that state on the subject, codified in such a way that all aspects of the law can be readily found.

In many states the laws relating to families, taxation, corporations, and crimes are subjects of codification. If you want to find something about taxation of property, for example, you would look under the general heading of "taxation," where you will find references to all taxes broken down into appropriate subsections.

Uniform State Laws.   There is a growing movement toward attaining uniform state laws governing commercial affairs. Uniform laws, prepared by the National Conference of Commissioners on Uniform State Laws, are particularly important when a business activity crosses state lines, for when state laws differ, a simple transaction can become most complex if subjected to differing legal rules. Over the years, many important uniform laws have been adopted, although they may be slightly modified by each state to conform with particular state policies and practices. Among these laws are the Uniform Commercial Code, the basis for Chapters 15 through 19, 27, 28, and 30 through 33; and the Uniform Partnership Act which forms the basis for Chapters 34 through 35.

Restatement of the Law.   Much of the advice given by practicing attorneys to their clients and many of the opinions handed down by judges involve application of the common law. To assist courts and lawyers in this task, the American Law Institute, composed of eminent lawyers from all over the country, has prepared sets of books called **Restatement of the Law**. Among them are *Restatement of the Law of Contracts, Restatement of the Law of Torts,* and *Restatement of the Law of Agency.*

Each *Restatement* is a systematic and authoritative exposition of the common law, covering the entire subject named in its title. These volumes unify and bring up to date the common law, based on decisions of the courts of all 50 states. Although these restatements are not official expressions of the law, they establish authoritative guidelines. There is no other comprehensive compilation of the current common law. With increasing frequency, judges quote these restatements in their opinions. As a result, they are a vital force, unifying the understanding and application of common law.

Consumer Protection Laws

Not so very many years ago a customer bought an article at his or her own risk as to whether the article would be safe and suitable for the purpose for which it was bought. The accepted expression was **caveat emptor**, meaning "let the buyer beware." Today the law has moved away from that philosophy, and emphasis is upon protecting the buyer. Now, the federal government and all states have laws to protect consumers who purchase, use, or have contact with property or services. Chapters 18 and 42 consider the application of consumer protection provisions of law. Other chapters also deal with consumer protection but primarily as aspects of other laws.

Law as a Social Tool

When you consider the trends or directions in which the law is moving, you can see that with increasing frequency business law is being used as a tool to attain broad social, economic, or political goals. Examples of laws or regulations designed primarily to attain political objectives are the Buy American Act, the regulations requiring export licenses before certain American-made products can be sold abroad, and periodic embargos against wheat exports to certain countries. Among laws which are social tools are those designed to assist small businesses to get their share of public contracts, laws controlling the sale of dangerous drugs, and laws prohibiting the sale of intoxicating liquor to minors.

ETHICAL RESPONSIBILITIES OF BUSINESS

Ever-increasing attention is being given to the ethical considerations which influence people and companies engaged in business. Throughout succeeding chapters of this book, attention will be focused upon ethical obligations of individuals and companies engaged in business. For instance, obligations of employers to employees and of employees to employers are discussed, as are the obligations of parties who have assumed the duty to perform a contract, responsibilities of partners to each other, the obligations of directors of corporations to stockholders, and the ethical obligations and responsibilities of all business to the public.

The American public is becoming ever more conscious of the social and economic impact of business upon the well-being of the country. People have become more and more aware of the dangers of pollution and of the injuries that can result from manufactured products. Thus, the public has demanded that the government take action to prevent the discharge of toxic chemicals into our streams, the manufacture of flammable clothing for children, the selling of dangerously defective cars, and the distribution of adulterated foods. As a result, Congress has enacted many laws imposing social responsibility upon business. These laws are the principal subjects of Chapters 41 through 43.

OBJECTIVES OF A COURSE IN BUSINESS LAW

A course in business law (as well as this text) has five primary objectives:

1. To present the principles of business law in a way that will help you understand the legal implications of many decisions you may be called upon to make in the course of your life, whether you are in business or not. The knowledge you acquire now should help you recognize those situations in which it would not be safe to proceed without competent legal counsel.
2. To explain the relationship between law and business and the legal processes involved in a lawsuit.
3. To show that business law is representative of the whole system of American law. You will understand not only how disputes are resolved but also how the law grows to accommodate new needs.
4. To encourage you to evaluate the social and economic purposes of laws that apply to business.
5. To highlight the ethical responsibilities of business.

SUMMARY

Law is a system of rules and regulations by which society, through imposition of penalties for their violation, seeks to control people's conduct. Business law constitutes the body of rules society has established to ensure that business affairs are conducted in an orderly and efficient way.

To understand American business law we should have a knowledge of its English roots. The accumulated decisions of the English judges came to be known as the common law. In reaching their decisions the judges relied on *stare decisis,* which means they followed decisions in prior cases involving similar questions of law. English common law and the rule of *stare decisis* have come down to us as part of our American legal system.

Because the kinds of civil cases that could be heard in the early English common law courts were limited in number and because those courts could only order the payment of money damages in civil cases, another kind of court, called a court of equity, was established. Equity law is another English root of American law. In equity the plaintiff seeks something other than, or in addition to, money. For example, a court can reform a contract or issue an injunction. In the United States the distinction between actions in law and actions in equity continues to be maintained, but in most states the same courts hear both types of cases.

Law can be divided into its substantive and procedural elements. Substantive law defines rights and duties; procedural law mandates the steps that must be taken for a court to enforce those rights and duties. Both civil law and criminal law have substantive and procedural elements. Civil law deals with property rights and personal relationships; criminal law defines the offenses punishable by the state.

Civil law directly and indirectly affects business and business relationships. Areas of civil law which pertain most to business are the law of contracts and its related subjects, the law of business organizations, the law of torts, and the law of property. Each of these subdivisions of civil law is discussed in the following chapters.

Business law is dynamic, responding to the needs of an expanding technological society. Some directions in which it is moving are (1) a lessening of legal technicalities, (2) greater uniformity throughout the country of laws governing business, and (3) growing emphasis upon laws protecting the interests of consumers.

REVIEW QUESTIONS

1. What is meant by business law?
2. Why should there be a discussion of the English legal system in a textbook setting out the fundamentals of business law in America?
3. Is there a common law in the United States? Explain.
4. What is meant by "the law merchant"?
5. Explain what is meant by the Latin phrase *stare decisis*.
6. How is *stare decisis* applied in the United States?
7. What is meant by "equity law"?
8. It was necessary to establish equity courts in England. Does the same reason for such courts exist in the United States? Why?
9. By what other name was a court of equity known in England?
10. (a) State at least three different kinds of cases you could bring in a common law court. (b) State at least three different kinds of lawsuits which involve equity law.
11. A common law case is tried before a jury but an equity case is heard by a judge alone. Why do you think this difference in procedure exists?
12. Distinguish between substantive law and procedural law.
13. Distinguish between civil law and criminal law.
14. What aspects of civil law are relevant to commercial enterprises?
15. Distinguish between contract law and property law.
16. What areas of law, other than contracts and property, also pertain to business?
17. Why is it said that "the law varies with time and place"?
18. What is meant by a codification of the law?
19. What is meant by a *Restatement of the Law?*
20. How can law be a social tool?

CHAPTER 2

THE COURT SYSTEM; CIVIL PROCEDURE; ARBITRATION

Justice and order require some system for the determination of rights and their enforcement. In the United States, the courts constitute a most important part of that system. Beginning with Chapter 3 of this book, briefs of actual court cases are presented in the chapters. To understand the background of each case, the student must be familiar with the court system and the procedure involved in the trial and appeal of a civil lawsuit.

The first part of this chapter deals with the function and jurisdiction of courts in the United States, the organization of the federal and state courts, and the work of the courts. The remainder of the chapter examines procedures related to civil lawsuits and discusses an alternative means of resolving disputes, called "arbitration."

THE COURT SYSTEM

In most states the same court system handles both criminal and civil cases. However, criminal procedure differs greatly from civil procedure. As this book deals with business law, the following discussion of the court system and court procedure centers upon civil law matters. Some aspects of criminal procedure are discussed in Chapter 5.

Function and Jurisdiction of Courts

Function of Courts.   The word "court" has various meanings. At times it means "judge," as when a judge tells an attorney to address his or her remarks "to the court and not to the opposing counsel." At other times it may be used to indicate the place where a judicial tribunal functions, as in the statement that trials must take place "in court," whereas orders may be signed "in chambers" (judge's office or anteroom). Usually, however, the word "court" is used to mean a tribunal established by the state or federal government to administer justice.

The main function of a court is to decide controversies between litigants (parties in a lawsuit). The final decision is called a "judgment." Courts ordinarily do not answer hypothetical questions. For example, a court may enforce a contract which has been breached, but it will not advise a person what his or her rights would be under a proposed contract.

Jurisdiction of Courts.   The word "jurisdiction" is used in different senses. As used here, **jurisdiction** means the authority or power a court possesses to hear and decide controversies. To process a case, a court must have two kinds of jurisdiction: jurisdiction over the subject matter (type of case) and jurisdiction over the property or the litigants in the case.

Jurisdiction over the subject matter is the authority of a court over the particular kind of case presented to it for decision. For example, a civil court may be without authority to process cases involving an amount in controversy above a certain monetary sum. (The proper tribunals to handle various types of civil suits are discussed below.)

Jurisdiction of a court may be limited also by a defined geographic area. For example, the state courts of New York have authority to handle cases involving lands lying within the state but not involving lands lying elsewhere.

Jurisdiction over the parties can be based on residency, citizenship or presence in the state. (Methods of bringing the parties before a court will be discussed in the latter part of this chapter under "Civil Procedure.")

Where only one court has the authority to hear and decide a case, the court is said to have **exclusive jurisdiction**. For example, a suit involving admiralty law (the law dealing with sailors and ocean-going vessels) can be processed only in a federal court. Where two or more courts have authority, they are said to have **concurrent jurisdiction**. In the next section on federal and state court systems, we will see that in some classes of cases the jurisdiction of the federal courts is exclusive; in other cases, the jurisdiction of the state courts is exclusive; in still others, the federal courts and the state courts have concurrent jurisdiction.

Federal and State Courts

The United States Constitution established a dual system of government—federal and state. That dual system has resulted in two sets of courts—federal and state. Most of the cases presented in this textbook are state court cases, but some are federal. A brief discussion of the federal and state court systems is necessary to understand why a case was heard in a particular tribunal.

Judicial Power of the United States.   The Constitution provides that the judicial power of the federal government shall extend to certain categories of disputes. A few of the major categories are:

1. Cases arising under the Constitution, acts of Congress, and treaties. Such cases are commonly said to involve a **federal question**.
2. Admiralty and maritime cases.
3. Cases affecting ambassadors, other public ministers, and consuls.
4. Controversies to which the United States is a party.
5. Controversies between citizens of different states. Such cases are commonly called **diversity of citizenship** cases.

Congress has extended jurisdiction of federal courts into other areas but has enacted statutes intended to restrict the number of cases filed. For example, Congress has stated that in suits between private litigants, federal courts have jurisdiction only when the matter in controversy exceeds $10,000. However, Congress has given the federal courts exclusive jurisdiction over certain classes of cases, regardless of the amount involved. For example, cases involving admiralty law, bankruptcy, patents, trademarks, copyrights, civil rights, and suits against federal officers may be brought only in federal courts. Thus, a wage earner who has only a few assets must nevertheless file for bankruptcy in a federal court.

Federal and state courts may have concurrent jurisdiction over diversity of citizenship cases (category 5 above). For example, let us suppose Paul, a resident of California, wishes to sue Diane, a resident of New York, for breach of contract and seeks $50,000 in damages. Paul may sue in either the federal court or the state court of New York.[1] Since Paul lives in California, he would likely not file suit in the state court of New York. Instead, under federal rules he is able to sue and undoubtedly

---

[1] Under the rules of civil procedure a party is generally entitled to be sued in the state where he or she resides.

would sue in the federal court in California. But when the sum involved is $10,000 or less, the state courts have exclusive jurisdiction. If Paul's damages were less than $10,000, he would have no choice but to sue Diane in the state court of New York.

The Federal Court System.   The United States Constitution provides that the "judicial power of the United States shall be vested in one Supreme Court, and in such inferior [lower] courts as the Congress may from time to time ordain and establish (Art. III., sec. 1). At present the federal court system consists of district courts, courts of appeals, the Supreme Court, and special courts, as shown in Figure 2.1. Judges who serve on a federal court are appointed for the period of their "good behavior" by the President of the United States, with the advice and consent of the Senate.

District Courts.   The **district courts** are the trial courts of the federal judicial system. Ordinarily, a litigant begins a lawsuit in a United States district court. There is one such court for each federal judicial district. In the less populous states a district covers the whole state. In the more populous states, such as California and New York, there are several federal districts.

FIGURE 2.1   The federal court system.

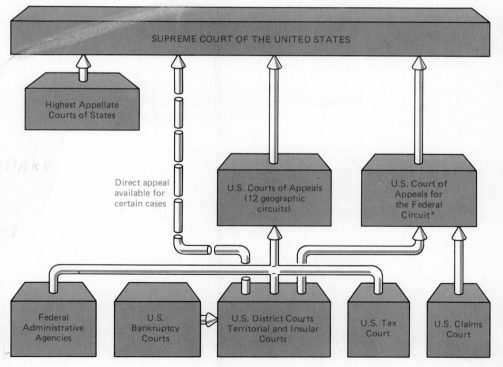

*In 1982, Congress established an additional court of appeals (based in Washington, D. C.) to review decisions of District Courts involving customs and patents, and decisions of the U.S. Claims Court.

Depending upon the volume of litigation, the court may consist of one, two, or more judges. Most cases are tried before a single judge; a few types of cases are tried before a panel of three judges.

Courts of Appeals.   If a litigant is dissatisfied with the judgment rendered by the district court, he or she may file an appeal with a higher court. The **courts of appeals** hear all appeals from district courts except for a few classes of cases where appeals may be taken directly to the Supreme Court. Courts of appeals also review orders of federal administrative agencies, such as the Consumer Product Safety Commission, the Environmental Protection Agency, and the Federal Trade Commission.

Originally judges of these courts traveled a circuit and the courts were called **circuit courts of appeals**. There are at present twelve geographic circuits serving the 50 states. Although judges of the courts of appeals no longer travel regularly, they are still referred to as "circuit judges."

Appeals are usually heard by a panel of three judges. The court of appeals does not retry a case which has been tried in a district court. Instead, the judges read a stenographic record of the trial to determine if an error of law was made in the trial. For example, a litigant may file an appeal alleging that the district court judge improperly denied a motion or gave the jury an erroneous instruction.

The Supreme Court.   The chief function of the Supreme Court is its appellate function. Most of the cases it reviews come from the courts of appeals, although a few come from other federal courts and even from the highest state courts. State decisions may be appealed when the issue in the case involves a federal question. A litigant is not entitled as a matter of right to appeal to the United States Supreme Court. This is true even if a case involves a federal question. The Supreme Court has discretion to choose the cases it deems important enough to hear.

Members of the Supreme Court are called "justices." The Constitution is silent about the size of the Supreme Court, and the number of justices has varied from six to ten. It is now, and for many years has been, nine. There is no requirement that a person be a judge, or even a lawyer, to be appointed to the Supreme Court.

Special Courts.   Congress has from time to time created special courts for limited purposes or for certain geographic areas. The more important special courts, with their jurisdictions briefly indicated, are as follows: (1) **United States Claims Court** hears nontort claims against the United States; (2) **United States Tax Court** hears cases dealing with collection of federal taxes; and (3) miscellaneous courts, including territorial courts (e.g., Guam), and United States military courts.

State Court Systems.   The state court systems vary in details but are alike in fundamentals. Every state has a series of local trial courts of original jurisdiction and a court of appeals. The dissimilarities consist primarily in the variety of local courts, in the number of levels of appellate courts, and in the titles given to some of the courts. Figure 2.2 illustrates a typical state court system.

Judges of state courts are selected in various ways. In many states judges of lower courts are elected by the citizens, but in some states the governor appoints them. In

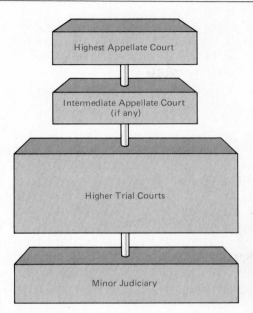

FIGURE 2.2   A typical state court system.

a few states, there is a combination of appointment and election, where judges are appointed for their first term. If a judge desires to continue in office after expiration of his or her appointive term, the judge must stand for election. Normally no other candidate's name appears on the ballot; the only decision the voters make is whether the incumbent shall be returned to office.

Trial Courts.   In most states trial courts are divided into two groups—the minor judiciary and higher trial courts.

1. *The minor judiciary.* Traditionally, legal cases of minor nature have been handled by officers called "justices of the peace." A justice of the peace is not required to be (and usually is not) a legally trained person. Typically, he or she is elected by citizens in the local community. In many states the lowest trial court is called a "city court," "police court," or "municipal court." Such courts have only limited jurisdiction. For example, in California, justice and municipal courts have jurisdiction over civil cases where the amount in controversy is $15,000 or less.

Most states have created a special division of the lowest trial court called "small claims court." This court has very limited jurisdiction; the usual maximum in civil cases is $1000 to $1500. Benefits of small claims court are low cost, speed of hearing, and informality. In some states litigants need not even be represented by lawyers. The major disadvantage of a small claims suit is the limited right to appeal. In California, for example, if the one who files the action loses, he or she has no right to appeal to a higher court. If the one who files the action wins the suit, however, the other party may appeal. In some states such as Michigan, the losing party has no right to appeal.

2. *Higher trial courts.* In every state there is a court of general and original jurisdiction for each county. It may be called the "superior court," the "district court," the "county court," or the "circuit court."[3] In California, the jurisdiction of superior courts over civil cases is limited to cases involving an amount in controversy exceeding $15,000. Superior trial courts also have limited jurisdiction to hear appeals from small claims, justice, and municipal courts. In some states, and especially in the more populous counties of some states, courts of general jurisdiction are supplemented by one or more courts of special jurisdiction. The most common courts of special jurisdiction are criminal courts, equity courts, and probate courts.[4] For example, in Los Angeles County, California, the superior court has over 200 judges and numerous special courts.

Appellate Courts.   In most states the highest appellate court is the **supreme court**.[5] Members of the court are usually called "justices." The number of justices serving in the highest state courts varies. Usually the number is either five or seven. In most states the governor appoints all supreme court justices, although in some states they are elected by the citizens.

Some states have an appellate court intermediate between the trial courts and the state supreme court. In Arizona, for example, a dissatisfied litigant may appeal to the court of appeals, alleging an error of law. As in the federal court system, appeals are heard by a panel of three justices. No new evidence is allowed; the court simply reviews the trial procedure and evidence from the stenographic record of the trial.

A litigant who is dissatisfied with the decision of the court of appeals may appeal to the state supreme court. In some states appeal to the state supreme court is allowed as a matter of right. In others, such as California, an appeal to the supreme court is largely a matter of privilege, and the practice is for the court to grant the privilege only in the most important cases.

CIVIL PROCEDURE

When disputes between individuals or business firms cannot be resolved amicably, litigation often results. This part of the chapter discusses the steps in the trial of cases, from beginning to end. Knowledge of these steps will help you understand the briefs of cases presented in later chapters. Often, an appeal is based on a defect alleged to exist in one or more steps in the trial of a case. The following discussion will familiarize you with the most common terms and procedures used in civil litigation. Figure 2.3 illustrates the steps in a civil lawsuit.

Procedures
Prior to Trial
Pleadings.   Pleadings are the initial written statements presented to the trial court by each party to a civil suit. Pleadings serve to reduce the controversy to its essential issues.

---

[3]In New York, strangely enough, it is called the "supreme court." In Ohio, it is called the "court of common pleas."
[4]Probate courts in Georgia are called "courts of the ordinary," and in Florida and some other states, "the county judge's court."
[5]In New York the highest appellate court is called the "court of appeals."

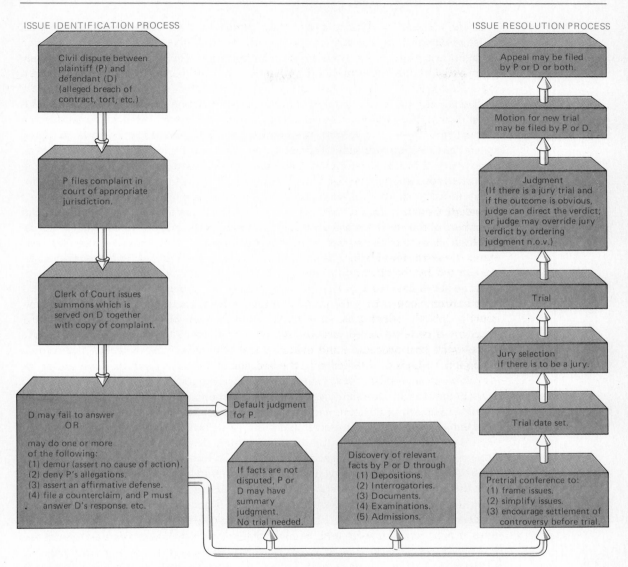

FIGURE 2.3   Flow of civil litigation.

Summons and Complaint.   The party who initiates a civil lawsuit is called the *plaintiff*. The party being sued is called the *defendant*. The plaintiff initiates a lawsuit by filing with the court a statement variously called a "complaint," "petition," or "declaration." Requirements for a complaint in California are typical of those states which have modernized their pleadings. The complaint must contain a statement of the facts constituting the cause of action, in ordinary and concise language, and a demand for the relief which the plaintiff claims. For example, the plaintiff may state, "On January 1, the defendant drove his automobile in a negligent manner and collided with the plaintiff, causing great bodily injury." The plaintiff would then request damages in a certain amount, such as $100,000. This request, called the "prayer," varies according to the nature of the action. For example, the plaintiff may "pray" that a tenant who has not paid rent be ordered to vacate an apartment owned by the plaintiff.

The plaintiff brings the defendant under the jurisdiction of the court by serving the defendant with a copy of the complaint and a document called a "summons." A **summons** is, in effect, a court order directing the defendant to appear in court within a certain time period, usually 30 days. In the summons the defendant is advised that, if no action is taken within the 30 days, the plaintiff may take a judgment against the defendant by default. The result of a judgment by default is that the plaintiff receives what is asked in the prayer (damages or other remedy) without further court proceedings. Ordinarily, "serving" a copy of the summons and complaint (called "service of process") is accomplished by handing the papers to the defendant in person. However, there are provisions in most states allowing for "substituted" service when the defendant cannot be found. Such service may be accomplished by mailing or by advertising in a newspaper.

Demurrer.   After the defendant is "served" the copy of the summons and complaint, the defendant must file with the court a responsive pleading within the required time to avoid a default judgment. The defendant may challenge the court's jurisdiction or the legal sufficiency of the plaintiff's complaint by means of a document called a "demurrer," in some states called a "motion to dismiss." A *demurrer* to a complaint challenging its legal sufficiency, says in effect: "Even if the facts alleged in the complaint be assumed to be true, still the complaint does not state a cause of action against the defendant." For example, suppose Peter alleges in his complaint that Donna promised to meet him at a certain movie theater at 7 P.M. on Saturday night and to attend the movie with him. Peter alleges that Donna failed to appear, breaching her promise, and this caused Peter great mental distress. He asks for $1000 damages. Donna would likely file a demurrer to the complaint, alleging that the complaint does not state a cause of action recognized at law.

Answer and Counterclaim.   The defendent may file an answer to a complaint. An *answer* may contain a general denial, that is, the defendant denies everything contained in the complaint; or a specific denial, in which the defendant denies the truth of one or more of the essential allegations of the complaint and admits the truth of others. For example, in the illustration above of the complaint filed by Peter, Donna may file an answer containing a general denial of all facts, or she may deny that she promised to meet Peter on the particular Saturday night stated in the complaint.

An answer may contain one or more "affirmative defenses." An *affirmative defense* is an allegation of some new matter which would prevent the plaintiff's recovery. For example, suppose that the plaintiff alleges in the complaint that on a specified date she lent the defendant the sum of $1000 and that he failed to pay it or any part of it. If the money was indeed a loan but the defendant has received a discharge in bankruptcy from all debts, he may file an answer admitting the debt, but alleging bankruptcy as an affirmative defense.

Other examples of affirmative defenses are statute of limitations and statute of frauds. These and many other defenses are presented in various chapters later in this book.

In most states the defendant as part of his or her answer may assert a counterclaim. A *counterclaim* asserts that the defendant has a claim against the plaintiff. Such a claim need not be related to the plaintiff's cause of action stated in the complaint. For example, suppose Paula sues Dennis, alleging breach of a contract. Dennis may file a counterclaim alleging that Paula made defamatory statements about him which caused him to suffer damages. The plaintiff must then file an answer to the counterclaim.

Summary Judgment.   At various points during the pleading stage of litigation, either party to the lawsuit may make a motion for a "summary judgment." The **summary judgment** procedure is designed to dispose of suits in which there is no genuine issue of fact for a judge or jury to decide. A hearing is held before the judge to review the pleadings. The parties may file affidavits (sworn statements) of witnesses who would be called by the parties to testify if a trial were held. If the pleadings and affidavits reveal no material issue of fact, the judge rules that no trial is necessary and enters a judgment for the plaintiff or defendant. Like the demurrer, the summary judgment procedure helps to avoid the expense of unnecessary trials. A judge's granting of a motion for summary judgment may be appealed to a higher court.

Discovery.   At one time there was a feeling in the legal profession that a lawsuit should be a battle of wits, with each side guarding its case jealously and making the adversary's trial preparations as difficult and onerous as possible. Often the parties did not know until the day of trial what witnesses the other would call to testify. To minimize the element of surprise, to improve and speed up the trial of cases, and to encourage settlements before trial, all states today provide for and encourage the parties to learn as much as possible about the adversary's case before trial. There are five major devices for **discovery** of facts before trial: depositions, interrogatories, inspection of documents and property, physical and mental examinations, and request for admissions.

Depositions.   A **deposition** is a statement under oath made at a hearing held out of court and after due notice to the other side. Ordinarily, each party will request permission to take the deposition of the other party and the party's key witnesses. A hearing is arranged at the office of one party's attorney. A court reporter records the questions and answers and prepares a written transcript for the witness to sign. In recent years, many courts have encouraged the use of videotape depositions. The need for a written transcript is eliminated; and if the videotape is presented at trial, the judge or jury can view the witness and better evaluate the person's credibility.

Depositions may serve various purposes: to discover what testimony to expect at the trial; to obtain testimony while it is fresh in the mind of a witness; to impeach (discredit) a person's testimony at the trial by showing that the testimony varies from the deposition; or to preserve testimony where there is danger that it may be unavailable at the trial. For example, a deposition may be desirable if a witness is elderly, has a serious illness, or is likely not to be available for the trial. Often, the deposition of an expert witness, such as a doctor or engineer, is taken and used at the trial in place of actual testimony. Expert witnesses receive large fees for testifying at trials and their schedules are often such that it may be difficult to secure their attendance at the trial.

Interrogatories.   **Interrogatories** are written questions addressed by one party in a case to the other party. Such questions might uncover information that can be used as a basis for further questions at a deposition hearing or at the trial of the case. An interrogatory may be used to demand a list of the other party's witnesses. Interrogatories are an inexpensive way to obtain information; they can be served informally (usually by mail) and answered at leisure, without the necessity of the presence of a court reporter or opposing attorney. Ordinarily, the answers must be given in writing, under penalty of perjury. As with depositions, the answers can be used for impeachment purposes at a trial.

Inspection of Documents and Property.   Either party to a case may secure a court order permitting the party or an agent to inspect, copy, or photograph documents or tangible things in the possession or control of another. For example, in a case where the plaintiff alleges personal injury the defendant may wish to inspect medical or hospital records pertaining to the injury.

Physical and Mental Examinations.   When the physical or mental condition of a person is in controversy, the court may order him or her to submit to an examination by a physician. In many lawsuits both sides will request an examination by physicians. Often, doctors' opinions as to a person's condition may conflict and the judge or jury must then weigh the credibility of each physician.

Request for Admissions.   Either party may serve upon the other (usually by mail) a request that he or she admit the genuineness of some document or the truth of some assertion described or set forth in the request. Failure to deny in writing and under oath the genuineness of the document or the truth of the assertion is deemed an admission of its genuineness or truth. The admission relieves the requesting party of the burden of producing proof on that point at the trial.

In general, information sought by discovery must be relevant to the subject matter of the lawsuit. For example, in most cases it would be improper to ask in a deposition hearing or in an interrogatory for a party or witness to disclose his or her social security number. It is not required that the information sought be used in evidence at a later trial nor that the information be admissible evidence. Thus, a plaintiff is entitled to discover the existence and scope of the defendant's insurance coverage, although such information is not admissible as evidence in a trial.

Pretrial Conference.   In most states the courts require a **pretrial conference** in civil suits. In pretrial conference, the judge and attorneys, and sometimes the parties, meet, usually two or three weeks before trial. This conference serves two purposes. One is to shorten the time of trial by refining or narrowing issues, clarifying pleadings through amendments, and placing a limit on the number of witnesses and exhibits. The second purpose of the pretrial conference is to encourage an out-of-court settlement. At the end of the conference, if no settlement is reached, the judge sets a date for the trial.

Trial of Cases   Sometime before the trial date, the plaintiff and defendant must decide whether the trial will be by judge or by jury. In some suits no jury is allowed, as in suits for equity relief. In other suits either party may request a jury but is not required to do so (i.e., they may "waive" a jury). If either side requests a jury, a deposit of jury fees ordinarily must be made in advance of the trial date. On the day of trial, if both sides still desire a jury, the first step is for the parties to select a jury. (The judge selects the jury in cases tried in federal district courts.) The remaining steps in a trial are substantially the same whether or not a jury is used.

Opening Statements of Counsel.   Ordinarily, the next step in a civil trial after a jury is selected (if there is one) consists of opening statements made by the attorneys for the plaintiff and the defendant. In some states the attorney for the defendant may elect to make an opening statement after plaintiff's evidence has been presented and before defendant presents any evidence. The purpose of the opening statements is to outline the general nature of the case and to indicate the kinds of evidence to be offered, so that the judge or jurors may understand the significance of each item of evidence as it is introduced.

Presentation of Evidence.   The plaintiff proceeds next to introduce evidence proving the allegations of the complaint. The word **evidence** is used in different senses. As used here, *evidence* means anything presented at the trial for the purpose of inducing belief in the truth or falsity of some contention. The two chief methods of inducing belief are testimony of witnesses and physical evidence. Testimony is secured by calling a witness, swearing the person in, and asking the person questions. A court reporter records all testimony in trial courts above the justice court level.

When a witness is put on the stand, the person is first examined by the attorney who called the person as a witness. This is called *direct examination* and is followed by a *cross-examination* conducted by the attorney for the other side. Ordinarily, the purpose of cross-examination is to show the witness's lack of credibility, such as by questioning his or her powers of observation. The attorney may try to impeach the witness by showing that the witness's answers to questions differ from those given in a deposition or interrogatories. The cross-examination may be followed by a redirect examination, in order to give the witness an opportunity to explain or modify answers given on cross-examination.

Physical evidence may consist of objects or documents which have been verified as authentic. Items of physical evidence are called *exhibits* and are tagged with a number for future reference (e.g., "Plaintiff's 1").

After the plaintiff has called all witnesses for his or her side and has introduced all physical evidence desired, the plaintiff "rests." At this point the defendant may make a motion for nonsuit (in some states called "a motion to dismiss"). By such a motion the defendant contends that the plaintiff has failed to prove his or her case, as outlined in the complaint and opening statements. If the judge agrees, a judgment of nonsuit is entered in favor of the defendant. If the judge does not agree, the motion will be denied and the defendant proceeds to introduce evidence to contradict the plaintiff's evidence. The defendant calls witnesses and introduces physical evidence in the same manner as did the plaintiff.

When there is a trial by jury, either side, or both, may make a motion for **directed verdict** at the close of defendant's evidence. By such a motion a party contends that the facts proven are so clear that reasonable people could not differ as to the outcome of the case. If the judge directs a verdict for a party, he or she thereby takes the case away from the jury and then enters a judgment for the party who made the motion. If neither party moves for a directed verdict, the judge may on his or her own motion order a directed verdict.

Closing Arguments of Counsel.   After all evidence is presented, the attorneys for each party make final or closing arguments. These usually take place before the judge's charge to the jury (if there is a jury). In the final argument, an attorney will usually review the evidence produced by his or her side and emphasize its adequacy and credibility, discuss the evidence produced by the other side to show its inadequacy and lack of credibility, and indicate the conclusions of fact that may reasonably be drawn from the evidence.

Charge to the Jury.   When there is a trial by jury, after closing arguments by both attorneys, the judge instructs the jurors as to the law to be applied in their deliberations. Normally the judge instructs the jury that its duty is to determine the facts of the case; to accept the law as stated by the judge; and, by applying the law so stated to the facts so determined, reach a decision for the plaintiff or the defendant. These instructions are a guide to help the jury reach a verdict. For example, the judge may say, "Negligence means the failure to exercise reasonable care to prevent harm to others. If you find that the defendant drove his car 80 miles per hour in a residential area, you must find the defendant has committed the tort of negligence."

Attorneys may, and often do, submit to the judge written instructions which they request the judge to include in the charge to the jury. The refusal to include a requested instruction or to give the instruction in the wording requested is often the basis of an appeal to a higher court.

Verdict of the Jury.   In a trial by jury, after receiving the judge's instructions, the jury retires to the jury room to consider the evidence and reach a verdict. In federal courts and in many state courts the jury verdict must be unanimous. In some states a verdict in a civil action must be reached by vote of three-fourths of the jurors. When the jury has reached its verdict, it returns to the courtroom and in the presence of the judge (and usually in the presence of the parties and their attorneys) announces its verdict.

The type of verdict just considered—that is, a verdict for plaintiff or defendant reached by applying the law as stated by the judge to the facts as found by the jury—is called a *general* verdict. If a general verdict is given for the defendant, the jurors' functions terminate. However, if the verdict is for the plaintiff in a civil action for damages, the jury must fix the amount of damages to which the plaintiff is entitled.

Another type of verdict is a *special* verdict. Such a verdict generally consists of answers to specific questions asked by the judge without any attempt to reach a decision for either party. The judge then decides the case by applying the law to the facts as given in the special verdict.

Judgment; Motions after Trial. The last step in the trial of a case is the judgment. A *judgment* is the decision of the court. Normally the judgment in jury trials is based on the verdict of the jury. Often, after the judgment in a jury trial is entered in the court records, the losing side will make a motion for judgment notwithstanding the verdict (**judgment n.o.v.**). The judge will grant the motion and enter judgment for the losing side only if there is no substantial evidence to support the decision of the jury. In some states the judge on his or her own motion may reject the jury verdict and enter a judgment for the other side. The party whose verdict is overturned usually will appeal to a higher court.

After judgment is entered, a motion for a new trial may be made by either party. If the plaintiff wins the case, the defendant may move for a new trial on the ground that the judge committed prejudicial error in the conduct of the trial, or that the damages assessed are excessive. A party may be granted a new trial if the other side, or its attorney, was guilty of prejudicial misconduct during the trial. However, a party is not entitled to a new trial if his or her own attorney was negligent or incompetent. A new trial may be granted where the losing side shows new evidence was discovered after the trial. He or she must prove that the evidence is significant and could not have been obtained before trial by due diligence. The plaintiff, although the winner, also may move for a new trial on the ground that damages awarded are insufficient, given the evidence. If a motion for a new trial is granted by the judge, the case is again put on the trial calendar. Eventually it will be set for trial before another judge or jury. If the motion is denied, the moving party may appeal.

Appeals After the entry of judgment, the party who feels dissatisfied by the outcome may file an appeal. Normally the loser appeals; sometimes the winner appeals (e.g., the plaintiff may allege that damages awarded were inadequate given the evidence); occasionally both parties appeal. The party who files an appeal is the **appellant**. The other party is the **appellee**, or the *respondent*.

Review of the Case. The appellate court does not retry the case. No new evidence is allowed. Its job is to review the case as conducted in the trial court to see if any error of law was committed. Usually the appellate court limits its review to such questions as: Did the trial judge properly exclude or admit evidence, follow proper procedure, or state or apply the law accurately? If the trial judge committed error, was the error serious enough to warrant reversal of the judge's decision?

The appellate court reviews the complete record of the trial of the case and listens to oral arguments by the attorneys for both parties. The attorneys submit written "briefs" to support their arguments.

Decision and Opinion. After considering the record and the arguments made, the appellate court announces its decision (judgment) in writing. The decision is ordinarily accompanied by a written opinion in which the court explains the basis or reasons for its decision. If the appellate justices do not agree unanimously, a dissenting opinion may be written. In that event, the court publishes both a *majority opinion* and a *minority opinion.*

If the appellate court finds that no error of law has occurred, it will affirm the judgment of the trial court. However, if prejudicial error is found, the appellate court may reverse or modify that judgment. When the evidence does not clearly justify a decision for one party or the other, the appellate court may reverse the judgment of the trial court and "remand" the case (send it back to the court) with directions to hold a new trial or take other action.

ARBITRATION AS AN ALTERNATIVE TO CIVIL LITIGATION

As can be seen from the preceding discussion, a lawsuit involves complex procedures. The courts in many states are crowded with cases, and there is a long wait for litigants to get to trial. Costs of civil litigation sometimes are staggering. Attorneys' fees, depositions, and fees of expert witnesses are but a few of the items each party to a suit must pay for. As an alternative to the costly process of civil litigation, the parties to a dispute can often avoid litigation by arbitration.

Arbitration is a nonjudicial method of resolving civil disputes. Rather than file a lawsuit, the disputing parties agree to let a neutral third party decide who is right and who is wrong. They select an arbitrator or sometimes a panel of three arbitrators. An arbitrator's decision, called an "award," is binding on the parties and is subject to only a limited judicial review. To obtain a judicial review, a party must usually show that an illegal award, fraud, or gross mistake was made.

As an alternative to litigation, arbitration of disputes has a number of advantages. It is less formal (e.g., the rules of evidence are greatly relaxed), is more efficient (the parties do not have to wait years for a courtroom), and is less expensive than litigation (there are no jury fees to pay, and attorney fees are much lower).

However, there are several disadvantages to arbitration. There is no right to a jury. The presiding officer usually is not a judge trained in the law and rules of evidence. Evidence allowed at an arbitration hearing is not subject to the same strict rules of scrutiny as in a court trial. This is a two-edged sword. For example, hearsay evidence, which may be prejudicial to a party, ordinarily is not allowed in a court of law but can be introduced at an arbitration hearing. (*Hearsay evidence* is a statement not based on personal observation, but merely a repetition of what someone else has said.) There is only a limited right to appeal an award.

In rare instances, arbitration may be imposed by law (state or federal legislation) and is called *compulsory arbitration.* It is usually limited to public-interest emergency disputes between public employees—such as police officers, fire fighters, or teachers—and their employers. The disputed issues and the award are subject to judicial review.

SUMMARY

Courts exist to decide actual controversies between parties, not to answer hypothetical questions. To process a case, a court must have jurisdiction over the subject matter and jurisdiction over the property or the parties.

In our dual system of federal and state governments, there is a federal court system and a system of state courts. The federal court system consists of district courts, courts of appeals, the Supreme Court, and various special courts. The state court systems typically include several types of trial courts, intermediate appellate courts, and a supreme court. In some classes of cases the federal courts have exclusive jurisdiction, in others the state courts have exclusive jurisdiction, and in still others federal and state courts have concurrent jurisdiction.

When a dispute is not settled by an agreement out of court and litigation results, the people involved must follow a lengthy series of civil procedures before, during, and after a court trial. However, where there is no recognized cause of action or no material question of fact for a judge or jury to decide, judgment can be awarded in the pleadings stage of litigation.

During a trial there are various times when a party may make motions to terminate the proceedings without further action. After judgment, a motion for judgment n.o.v. may be made by the losing party or a motion for a new trial may be made. Judgments at various stages of litigation can be appealed to higher courts.

The function of an appellate court, state or federal, intermediate or supreme, is to review the case as conducted by the trial court to see if any error of law was committed. The appellate court may affirm the decision of the trial court, reverse the decision, or reverse and remand the case for a new trial.

Arbitration, an alternative to litigation, is a nonjudicial method of resolving disputes by private, disinterested persons called "arbitrators." There are both advantages and disadvantages to arbitration. Compulsory arbitration is usually limited to public-interest emergency disputes.

REVIEW QUESTIONS

1. (**a**) What is the main function of a court? (**b**) Define "litigant."

2. (**a**) What is the general meaning of jurisdiction? (**b**) Describe and give an illustration of jurisdiction over the subject matter. (**c**) Distinguish between exclusive and concurrent jurisdiction.

3. (**a**) Give two examples of classes of cases over which the federal courts have exclusive jurisdiction. (**b**) To what extent do the *state* courts have jurisdiction over cases involving citizens of different states?

4. (**a**) Describe the work of the following federal courts: district courts, courts of appeals, and the Supreme Court. (**b**) Explain who appoints federal judges and the length of their terms of office.

5. (**a**) Describe the courts commonly found in a state court system. (**b**) How are vacancies filled?

6. (**a**) What is the purpose of the pleading stage of litigation? (**b**) What is the "prayer"? (**c**) Describe how process may be served on a defendant.

7. Explain the function of a demurrer.

8. (**a**) List the items a defendant may include in an answer. (**b**) What is a counterclaim? (**c**) Why do you think states allow, or even encourage, counterclaims?

9. (**a**) What is the purpose of a summary judgment? (**b**) How does a motion for summary judgment differ from a demurrer?

10. (a) What is the purpose of discovery devices? (b) Explain the purpose and use of "deposition," "interrogatory," and "request for admission of facts."

11. What are the purposes of a pretrial conference?

12. (a) Briefly describe the difference between opening and closing arguments in a trial. (b) What is an exhibit? (c) What is a motion for nonsuit? (d) What is a motion for directed verdict?

13. (a) Explain the difference between a general verdict and a special verdict. (b) What is a judgment? (c) What is a "judgment n.o.v."? (d) What are the typical grounds for a motion for a new trial?

14. (a) Explain how a plaintiff could also be an appellant; an appellee. (b) What is the function of an appellate court? (c) How does it perform this function?

PART TWO

TORT AND CRIMINAL LAW

CHAPTER 3

NATURE OF TORTS; INTENTIONAL TORTS

The law of torts is designed to give redress to individuals and business firms that sustain injury from civil wrongs other than breach of contract. The law of torts is of great importance to everyone. It is especially important to the business person, who may become the victim of a tort at one time or another, or who may intentionally or unintentionally commit a tort. As will be seen in Chapter 21, a business person may also be responsible to others for torts committed by his or her employees and agents. The proprietor of a small business, as well as the multinational corporation, continually risks being sued in tort by a customer, a fellow business person, or a member of the public.

Most torts are committed unintentionally, either because a person is not paying attention to what he or she is doing or because the person does not know that the particular act is a tort. The moral is clear: we need to acquire a basic knowledge of the nature of torts and of the law relating to the most important types of torts.

NATURE OF TORTS

Meaning of Torts

A **tort** has been defined as "a civil wrong other than breach of contract for which the court will provide a remedy in the form of an action for damages."[1] The courts and legislatures of the various states determine which civil wrongs are actionable, and the law of torts changes as values and opinions of judges and elected representatives change. New torts are recognized from time to time, and existing torts are applied to new situations. Some common law torts have been abolished. For example, a number of torts based on interference with family relations, such as breach of promise to marry and alienation of affection, are no longer recognized in many states.

Tort liability is based on conduct which is socially unreasonable.[2] What is unreasonable depends upon one's point of view. An important consideration in the minds of judges and legislators is the balance between an injured person's claim to protection of person or property and the accused person's claim to freedom of action.

Torts Distinguished from Crimes

A crime and a tort often are similar, and the student must exercise care not to confuse them. A crime may involve harm to the person or property of another or be only a violation of a statutory prohibition. A crime is an offense against the sovereign authority, usually punished by fine or imprisonment. Criminal prosecution is brought by local, state, or federal government.

A *tort* is a civil wrong, an interference with private rights, and the injured person may obtain, through a civil action against the wrongdoer (**tortfeasor**), money damages as compensation for an injury. The same act may be both a tort and a crime. For example, unjustifiably confining another person within fixed boundaries is both the tort and the crime of false imprisonment. In this chapter we are concerned solely with the civil aspects of a person's conduct.

Classes of Torts

Various kinds of civil wrongs are recognized as torts in contemporary law, and are classified generally according to the nature of the wrongdoer's conduct. The two

[1] William L. Prosser, *Handbook of the Law of Torts*, 4th ed., West Publishing Company, St. Paul, 1971, p. 2.
[2] Ibid., p. 6.

main classes are **intentional torts** and **unintentional torts.** This chapter deals with the major intentional torts, which are discussed under the following headings: intentional harm to the person, intentional harm to property, and fraud as a tort. Chapter 4 discusses negligence, liability without fault, and business torts, which involve interference with business rights.

INTENTIONAL HARM TO THE PERSON

Battery

The tort of **battery** is defined as the intentional harmful or offensive touching of another person without consent or legal justification. Harm may range from permanent disfigurement to merely removing a person's hat without permission or grabbing a plate out of someone's hand.

In an action for battery there are two major defenses available to the defendant: *consent* and *privilege.* The plaintiff's consent may be expressed by words or implied from conduct. Those participating in athletic contests such as boxing, football, and baseball are assumed to consent to the physical contact normally associated with the sport. However, the tort of battery may occur if a person exceeds the consent given. A common situation presented to the courts involves medical surgery. Let us suppose that Mrs. Abel consents to have Dr. Barr operate on her nose. While Mrs. Abel is unconscious and under an anesthetic, Dr. Barr decides she would look much better if her eyelids were also altered, and he performs this procedure. Dr. Barr may be held liable for the tort of battery.

A person's intentional touching of another without consent may be excused if such conduct is "privileged," or justified. The most common privilege asserted is self-defense, which allows one to use reasonable force to prevent personal harm. The privilege applies where the defendant reasonably believes he or she is in danger of harm. The privilege is limited to the use of force which reasonably appears to be necessary to protect against the threatened injury. Deadly force may be used only when the defendant believes he or she is threatened with death or serious physical harm. In many states the privilege of using reasonable force extends to defense of a third person who is in immediate danger of attack. The privilege may also extend to the protection of property where there is danger of immediate damage or wrongful appropriation. Ordinarily, there is no privilege to use deadly force to protect one's property. For example, a landowner is privileged to install a spiked wall or fence to keep out trespassers but may be held liable in tort if a thief is injured or killed because the landowner sets a spring gun or keeps a vicious watchdog at large.

Assault

The tort of **assault** is defined as intentionally causing someone to fear an immediate battery. However, a battery need not follow an assault for the assault to be a tort. The two torts are separate and distinct. In most states a plaintiff in a tort action for assault may not recover damages unless he or she was aware of the defendant's conduct and felt threatened. Generally, for a plaintiff to prove that he or she was apprehensive, it must be established that the defendant threatened to use force and appeared to have the ability to carry out this threat. For example, suppose Ann makes an oral threat to shoot Bill while pointing a pistol at him which he believes is loaded. Ann is liable for the tort of assault even though *she* knows the pistol is unloaded.

In an action for assault the defendant may assert the defenses of consent and privilege.

False Imprisonment

The tort of **false imprisonment** is defined generally as intentionally causing the confinement of another person without consent or legal justification. Situations involving false imprisonment include confinement caused by (1) physically restraining a person's movement, (2) threatening force to one's person or to a member of one's immediate family, (3) force or threat of force directed against a person's property, and (4) refusing to release a person from confinement when there is a duty to do so. "Confinement" ordinarily means a person is restricted to a limited area without knowledge of a reasonable means of exit.

A situation involving false imprisonment often presented to the courts is one in which a retail merchant detains a customer suspected of shoplifting. In this event, the customer may recover damages for false imprisonment if it can be proved that the customer submitted involuntarily to the merchant's restraint. Where an action is filed against a merchant for false imprisonment, ordinarily the merchant asserts the defense of "shopkeeper's privilege," alleging he or she was justified in detaining the customer. To avoid liability, the defendant must prove that he or she had reasonable grounds to believe the plaintiff committed a crime.

Limitations on the shopkeeper's privilege are discussed in the following case.

CASE 3.1   SuperX Drugs of Kentucky, Inc. v. Rice
554 S.W.2d 903 (Ky. App. 1977)

Facts:
Plaintiff, Wanda Rice, was stopped at the checkout counter of SuperX Drugs, defendant, and escorted to the employee's lounge. Mrs. Rice had three items in her shopping bag which she did not pay for. Mrs. Rice claimed she thought she had paid for the items and, in any event had no intent to steal. The sales clerk called the police, who took Mrs. Rice to the police station where she was arrested for shoplifting. Plaintiff sued for false imprisonment alleging that the store could detain her only so long as necessary to recover their goods. On the third trial of the case, plaintiff recovered a judgment in the trial court. Defendant appealed.

Question:
Assuming a merchant has probable cause to believe goods have been unlawfully taken by a person, for what length of time may the merchant legally detain the suspected shoplifter?

Answer:
A merchant is privileged to detain the person for the time necessary to make a reasonable investigation of the facts.

Reasoning:
The state of Kentucky has a fairly typical statute regarding shopkeeper's privilege. It says in part that the merchant who has probable cause may "for the purpose of attempting to effect recovery" detain a suspect "in a reasonable manner for a reasonable length of time." The court said, "If a merchant has the right to detain a person in order to recover his property, common sense dictates that the merchant should make some investigation of the facts during the period of detention. Certainly, the merchant will want to verify the

person's name and address. With this information, the merchant may find that the person has an extensive shoplifting record with the police. In other cases, the merchant may be able to ascertain that the person's failure to pay for the goods was due to inadvertence rather than criminal intent. . . . On the other hand, the person's refusal to state his or her name can justify the merchant's continued detention of that person. We conclude that a merchant's limited privilege to recover goods believed to have been stolen also includes the privilege to detain the person for the time necessary to make a reasonable investigation of the facts."

The judgment of the circuit court was reversed and a new trial ordered.

Infliction of Mental Distress

The tort of **infliction of mental distress** is defined as intentionally or recklessly causing severe mental suffering in another by means of extreme or outrageous conduct or language. Generally, extreme and outrageous misconduct means exceeding all bounds of decent behavior. For example, collection agencies have been held liable to debtors for outrageous high-pressure tactics, and landlords have been held liable to tenants for similar conduct. A person has been held liable for falsely telling a woman that her husband was seriously injured and in a hospital, thus causing the woman to suffer emotional trauma and physical injury.

The courts have been reluctant to impose liability on a defendant who uses obscene or abusive language. There are two reasons for this reluctance: a high regard for freedom of speech and the danger of encouraging groundless or trivial lawsuits. Thus, the citizen in contemporary society must be able to face insults, annoyances, profanity, and discourtesy without legal redress.

Defamation

The tort of **defamation** is defined generally as intentional or negligent unjustified publication of a false statement that tends to hold a person up to hatred, contempt, or ridicule, or to cause him or her to be shunned or avoided. Defamation harms a person's good name or reputation in the community. To constitute a tort, the statement published must reflect upon the defamed person's character or disgrace him or her. For example, it is defamatory to say falsely that a person is a drunk, a liar, or a thief. No tort is committed if a defamatory statement is published about a dead person.

Defamation includes two torts—libel and slander. **Libel** is defamation by written communication and **slander** is defamation by oral communication.

There are two major defenses to the tort of defamation: truth and privilege. In most states *truth* is a complete defense to a defamation action. For example, suppose Andrea maliciously and in bad faith publishes the statement "Charles is a criminal," and Charles actually is a convicted embezzler. Charles could not recover damages from Andrea for defamation.

The defense of *privilege* is based upon the idea that the defendant should be allowed to publish a defamatory statement to further some interest of social importance. In some instances the interest is deemed to be of such great importance that the defendant is given complete or absolute immunity regardless of motive or reasonableness of conduct.

Absolute privilege protects the following: (1) statements made in a civil or criminal action or quasi-judicial proceeding by the parties, witnesses, lawyers, judges, and jurors, as long as the statements are relevant or pertain to an issue in the proceeding; (2) statements made by federal and state legislators performing their duties and by witnesses in legislative and quasi-legislative hearings; and (3) statements made by superior officers of the executive departments and branches of the federal and state governments in the exercise of their duties.

The defense of *qualified* or *conditional privilege* can be used by a defendant under circumstances deemed to be of lesser importance than those above. To avoid liability, the defendant must prove the defamatory statement was published to protect some recognized interest in good faith and without malice. "Recognized interests" include one's own financial interest, membership in an organization, credit standing, and employment record. If a defendant abuses his or her qualified privilege, the plaintiff may hold the defendant liable in an action for defamation. The qualified privilege is lost if the defendant acts with malice or other improper purpose or has no reasonable grounds for believing the statement to be true. *Malice,* as used here, means hatred, spite, or ill will.

A qualified privilege exists to publish defamatory statements about certain public persons. This privilege is based on the constitutional protection given to freedom of speech and freedom of press. A defendant who publishes a false defamatory statement about a public official or a public figure may not be held liable unless the defendant acts with "actual malice." *Actual malice* means that the defendant knows the statement is false or shows a reckless disregard of the truth. The courts have held that public officials are those high-ranking government officers, whether executive, legislative, or judicial, who control the conduct of government. Public figures include two groups of people: (1) persons who have achieved fame and notoriety, such as sports figures and well-known entertainers; and (2) persons who voluntarily thrust or inject themselves into the forefront of public controversy to influence the outcome of issues, such as consumer advocates and environmentalists.

The following case discusses qualified privilege and the concept of malice.

CASE 3.2   **Brown v. Skaggs-Albertson's Properties, Inc.**
563 F.2d 983 (10th Cir. 1977)

Facts: Ladonna Brown gave a check to defendant's store in Oklahoma City. The check was returned to the store unpaid because Skaggs failed to indorse the check. It was sent through again without indorsement and again was returned unpaid. On April 22 the store sent a report to Check Verification Association of Central Oklahoma (CVA) mistakenly showing that Brown's check had been returned because of insufficient funds. Ladonna Brown's husband replaced the check but Skaggs did not notify CVA of the mistake and replacement until April 25. In the interim, the Browns' checks were refused because they were on the CVA list. The Browns sued for libel. Skaggs defended that it had a qualified privilege to make the report to CVA. At trial, the jury returned a verdict of $30,000 for the plaintiffs. Skaggs appealed.

Question: Did Skaggs have a qualified privilege to report to CVA?

Answer: Yes. Skaggs had a qualified privilege to report the statement which was clearly defamatory (issuing an insufficient funds check). However, Skaggs exceeded the privilege and is liable in tort.

Reasoning: A qualified privilege exists when a communication is made by a person in discharge of some public or private duty (legal or moral) or in the conduct of his or her own affairs in matters where the person's interest is concerned. However, the privilege is lost if the communication is made with malice. Here, there was no malice in the sense of ill will or an express design to inflict an injury. However, the court said, "Malice may be inferred . . . where the defendant has no reasonable basis for believing that the statement is true. This would be the case where there had been a failure to make an adequate investigation. . . . The fact that the check was stamped 'endorsement missing' and twice returned for that reason makes the case one of aggravated conduct sufficient for the jury to infer that malice was present. . . ." Skaggs' conduct may be characterized as "reckless."

The judgment was affirmed.

Invasion of Privacy   The tort of invasion of privacy usually occurs in one of four forms: (1) The wrongdoer uses a person's name or likeness without consent for business purposes. A typical example is using a public figure's name or picture without consent to advertise a commercial product. (2) The wrongdoer unreasonably intrudes upon a person's physical solitude. Examples include illegal entry of one's home, illegal wiretapping, and unauthorized investigation of one's bank account. (3) The wrongdoer publicly discloses private information about a person which is offensive and objectionable. An example is publishing the history and present identity of a reformed criminal. (4) The wrongdoer publishes information which places a person in a false light. An example is attributing to a successful poet an inferior poem which he or she did not write. When the information published is false and defamatory, the injured person may have an additional cause of action for defamation.

Several defenses are available to a defendant in an action for invasion of privacy. For example, a defendant who uses the name or photograph of a deceased public figure for commercial purposes is not liable to that person's heirs or close relatives. The courts have held that an individual has no right of privacy while in a public place, that a person by implication consents to intrusion upon personal solitude after leaving home. Thus, in the absence of special circumstances no tort is committed if a person's picture is taken while walking along a sidewalk or sitting as a spectator at a public event.

A defendant in an action for invasion of privacy may assert a constitutional privilege to give publicity to public figures or to publish news or matters of public interest. For example, a victim of a crime or a witness to a crime has no cause of action if he or she is identified in the news media and if his or her personal and family background is exposed to public view. The courts permit this invasion of a person's privacy because there is a legitimate interest in newsworthy events.

In the following case the court discussed the elements of invasion of privacy and whether the plaintiff was a public figure.

CASE 3.3   Kinsey v. Macur
165 Cal. Rptr. 608 (Cal. App. 1980)

Facts: In 1966 Bill Kinsey was charged with his wife's murder in Tanzania. He was acquitted but the case attracted some notoriety, including articles published in *Time* Magazine. In December 1971 Kinsey met Mary Macur and for the next five months they had a love affair. In April 1972 Kinsey broke off the affair for another woman. In the fall of 1972 Kinsey was married and took a job in Africa. Macur sent letters to Kinsey and his wife stating in graphic terms how Kinsey had mistreated Macur. Other letters were sent to Kinsey's parents, his wife's parents, the Kinseys' neighbors, their parents' neighbors, faculty members at Stanford (where Kinsey was a graduate student), and the President of Stanford. Some letters accused Kinsey of murdering his first wife and spending six months in jail for the crime. Kinsey filed suit for invasion of privacy and received a judgment for $5,000. Macur appealed.

Question: Did Macur commit the tort of invasion of privacy?

Answer: Yes. Macur made a public disclosure of embarrassing private facts concerning Kinsey and also placed him in a false light in the public eye.

Reasoning: Macur argued that the mailings were to only a small select group of people, perhaps twenty people at most. The court held that this was sufficient publicity to constitute mass exposure to the public, as opposed to exposure to a few people. There was a wrongful publicizing of private affairs and activities. Macur also defended that Kinsey was a public figure through his trial for murder of his first wife. The court said that the trial involuntarily thrust him into the limelight in 1966. He was acquitted and the court said, "there is a strong societal interest in allowing him 'to melt into the shadows of obscurity' once again." Little of what Macur wrote in her letters could be considered "newsworthy."

The judgment was affirmed.

INTENTIONAL HARM TO PROPERTY

Property as used in this discussion refers to things people own, such as land, furniture, and accounts receivable. The phrase "harm to property" can be used in two senses: in the sense of physical harm (i.e., injury) to the property, and in the sense of wrongful interference with the possession of property. The context will make clear in which of the senses the phrase is being used.

Trespass to Real Property   The tort of **trespass to real property** is defined generally as a person's intentionally and without consent or legal justification entering upon real property owned by another, or causing an object or third person to enter the property. Real property includes land and all things embedded in it or firmly attached to it, such as minerals, trees, fences, and buildings. Thus, one may be held liable in tort for walking across another's lawn, cutting down a neighbor's tree, or painting someone's barn without permission.

Trespass to
Personal
Property

The tort of **trespass to personal property** is defined as intentionally, and without consent or legal justification, taking or damaging personal property belonging to another. Personal property does not mean items that are "personal" to the owner, such as clothing, but means movable or portable things, such as jewelry or furniture. Thus, a person may be held liable in tort for taking another's car temporarily without permission or for unjustifiably injuring an animal that belongs to another. The tort of trespass to personal property usually involves temporary use of an item or slight harm to the item.

Conversion

The tort of **conversion** is defined generally as intentionally and without legal justification seriously interfering with possession of the personal property of another. The following illustrate acts that give rise to a cause of action for conversion: (1) wrongfully taking possession of another's property for an indefinite period, as by stealing; (2) improperly selling or transferring possession of one person's property to another person, as by delivering goods to the wrong person; (3) lawfully acquiring possession of someone's property and later wrongfully refusing to return the property upon demand to the one entitled, as when an artisan keeps goods until an exorbitant repair bill is paid; or (4) destroying another's property or substantially altering it, making it unusable, as by killing or maiming someone's animal.

In an action for conversion the plaintiff need not prove the defendant had an evil state of mind or an improper purpose in interfering with possession of the plaintiff's property. Thus, an innocent purchaser of stolen property may be liable for the tort of conversion. However, if one innocently receives lost or stolen property merely for purposes of storage or transportation, courts do not hold the warehouse or the carrier liable.

Conversion is similar in some respects to the tort of trespass to personal property, but significant differences exist between the two torts. The major difference is the *theory of recovery.* In an action for trespass, the plaintiff is compensated for the harm to property or for loss of possession. In an action for conversion, the owner recovers the full value of the property at the time and place of conversion. Upon payment of the judgment, the converter becomes the owner of the property. Thus, an action for the tort of conversion is appropriate only when the defendant has so seriously interfered with the plaintiff's possession as to justify a forced sale of the article. An action for trespass is the appropriate remedy for minor interferences resulting in little damage to the plaintiff's goods.

The owner of converted property may not wish to sue for the value of the property but may want the property returned. Property may be recovered by filing a lawsuit and, without waiting for trial of the case, having the court issue an order called a "writ of replevin." In some states the procedure is called "claim and delivery."

In the following case the court discusses the time at which conversion occurs.

CASE 3.4   Staub v. Staub
376 A.2d 1129 (Md. App. 1977)

Facts: In 1954 John C. Staub purchased $5,000 of bonds payable on his death to his grandson, John T. Staub, Jr. The grandfather died on March 9, 1954 when his grandson was 17 months old. Thereafter, John T. Staub, Sr. cashed the interest checks which accrued from the bonds. On May 19, 1955 the father signed the name of John T. Staub, Jr. on a form to reissue the bonds in the names of "John T. Staub, Jr. or John T. Staub." In November 1959 the father cashed the bonds. The son filed suit in 1975 against the father for trespass and conversion. The judge found that the father had trespassed on the interest checks between 1954 and 1959, and had converted the bonds in 1959. The son appealed, contending that the bonds were converted on May 19, 1955.

Question: When did the conversion occur?

Answer: The conversion occurred in 1959.

Reasoning: Conversion is a distinct act of ownership or dominion exerted by a person over the personal property of another which either denies the other's right or is inconsistent with it. A conversion occurs at such time as a person is deprived of property which he or she is entitled to possess. Here, although the father wrongfully added his name to the bonds in 1955, the son was not then deprived of his property. It was not until 1959, when the father cashed the bonds, that the son was deprived of his property. The trial court properly awarded the son the market value of the bonds at the time of conversion plus interest to the date of judgment as damages.

The judgment was affirmed.

FRAUD AS A TORT

When fraud occurs in a business transaction, the harm suffered is generally of a monetary nature. Fraud sometimes plays an important part in the commission of torts involving harm to the person, as where a battery is committed by inducing the injured person's consent to physical contact by means of a misrepresentation. For example, suppose that Paul consents to a blood transfusion because a doctor knowingly misrepresents that it is necessary to save his life. Because the tort of fraud may involve harm to property and harm to the person, it is discussed in a separate part of this chapter. Fraud in connection with the law of contracts is discussed in Chapter 10. A person who is fraudulently induced to enter into a contract has a variety of legal remedies available, one of which is to commence a tort action for damages.

Elements of Fraud   To recover damages in an action for the tort of fraud (sometimes called "deceit") the plaintiff must prove five elements: (1) there was a false representation of material fact, (2) the defendant knew that the representation was false, (3) intent existed to induce another to act, (4) there was justifiable reliance on the representation, and (5) the plaintiff suffered injury resulting from such reliance.

False Representation of Fact.   A person may misrepresent by means of words or actions or by concealment. A representation includes making an oral or written statement of fact and making a statement by conduct, such as turning back the odometer of a car.

Sometimes, failure to speak amounts to fraud. In recent years courts in many states have stated that a duty of disclosure exists in a sales transaction where one party has knowledge of material facts not available to the other party, and is aware that the other person is under a misapprehension as to those facts.[3] For example, in negotiating for the purchase of a residence, the buyer's decision would be affected by the fact that the house is infested with termites. If the seller knows this and the sale is completed without disclosure of this fact, the seller may be held liable for damages in tort. However, a person is not required to disclose facts that are obvious or that could be discovered by reasonable inspection.

As a general rule a person is not liable in tort for misrepresentations of opinion, value, or law, unless the individuals have a relationship of trust and confidence, as between principal and agent or between family members, or when one person claims to have superior knowledge not available to another person. Thus, most of us may be expected to rely on the opinion of a real estate broker as to the value of land or the opinion of an attorney upon a point of law, even though the parties are adversaries in a bargaining transaction.

Knowledge of Falsity.   The element of knowledge of falsity exists not only when a person falsely represents a fact with knowledge of the falsity, but also when one makes a statement without any belief as to its truth or with reckless disregard as to whether it is true or false. Thus, a person who represents something as being true of his or her own knowledge but who is in fact completely ignorant of the subject is treated in the law as knowingly making a false statement.

Intent to Induce Action.   For a plaintiff to establish a cause of action for fraud it must be proven that the defendant intended the plaintiff, or a class of persons to which plaintiff belongs, to believe and act upon the false representation. For example, a seller may be held liable not only to an immediate purchaser but also to a remote purchaser for a deliberate misrepresentation contained in a negotiable instrument or a stock certificate. Such documents are intended to be freely transferable, and the seller should reasonably have foreseen that subsequent purchasers would rely on the representation contained in the document.

Justifiable Reliance.   Justifiable reliance occurs when a person's false representation causes another person justifiably to act or to refrain from acting to his or her detriment. In a fraud action it is not necessary for the plaintiff to prove that the defendant's misrepresentation was the sole cause of the plaintiff's loss. It is sufficient for the plaintiff to prove that the misrepresentation was a substantial factor in influencing a decision.

In some situations it may be difficult to determine whether reliance was justified. Most courts hold that a person of normal intelligence, ordinary experience, and average education would not be justified in relying on representations that the average person by reasonable investigation should discover are false. On the other

[3]Ibid., p. 697.

hand, a plaintiff with special knowledge, experience, and competency may not justifiably rely on the defendant's statements, but must exercise his or her own judgment. As stated earlier, the ordinary person is not justified in relying on a defendant's statement of opinion or representation of law unless special circumstances are involved.

In the following case the element of justifiable reliance was at issue.

CASE 3.5   Butts v. Dragstrem
349 So.2d 1205 (Fla. App. 1977)

Facts: Plaintiff, John Dragstrem, purchased a mobile home subdivision from defendant Butts, relying on Butts' representation that plaintiff could easily make $1,000 per month net income. Butts stated that he had made at least that much per month for several years. Dragstrem asked to see the defendant's books and Butts stated he would bring them over in the morning. However, Butts never did supply the books. Although Dragstrem was given the name of Butts' bookkeeper, Dragstrem made no attempt to contact him. After buying the property Dragstrem was unable to make anywhere near $1,000 per month net income and filed suit for the tort of fraud. The trial court denied a motion by Butts for directed verdict and entered a judgment in favor of Dragstrem for $42,000. Butts appealed.

Question: Was the trial court correct in denying Butts' motion for directed verdict?

Answer: No. The lower court erred in denying Butts' motion since there was no fraud here as a matter of law. The jury could not reasonably reach any other conclusion.

Reasoning: Butts did misrepresent the past income of the business. However, plaintiff was required to prove that he justifiably relied on the misrepresentation. The court stated as a rule, "In the absence of a showing of a fiduciary or confidential relationship, if there is no accompanying actual deception, artifice, or misconduct, where the means of knowledge are at hand and are equally available to both parties and the subject matter is equally open to their inspection, one disregarding them will not be heard to say that he was deceived by the other's misrepresentations." Dragstrem should have inspected Butts' books. His failure to discover the truth was attributable to his own negligence.

The court reversed the judgment.

Resulting Injury. In a tort action for fraud the plaintiff must prove that the misrepresentation caused the plaintiff's loss. The damage suffered as a result of a person's false representation in a business transaction may be slight (loss of a few dollars) or serious (loss of valuable property).

Measure of Damages for Fraud

To recover damages in a tort action for fraud, the plaintiff must prove that all five elements of fraud were present in the situation involved. If fraud is proved, the judge or jury must determine what damages the plaintiff may recover. In the United States two methods are used to measure damages for fraud. The majority rule is called the "loss-of-bargain" rule. Under this rule the successful plaintiff recovers the difference between the value of the property or service received and the value it would have had if it had been as represented. For example, if the defendant, a professional antique dealer, falsely represents that the desk she sold the plaintiff was a genuine antique worth $1000 when in fact it is not genuine and is worth only $150, the plaintiff may recover $850 damages.

SUMMARY

Tort liability is based on conduct which is socially unreasonable. An important part of the determination of what is unreasonable is the balance between an injured person's claim to protection and the accused's claim to freedom of action. Various kinds of civil wrongs are recognized as torts in contemporary law, and are classified according to the nature of the wrongdoer's conduct. The two main classes are intentional torts and unintentional torts.

The major intentional torts involving harm to the person are battery, assault, false imprisonment, infliction of mental distress, defamation (libel and slander), and invasion of privacy. In an action for tort the defendant may avoid liability by proving one or more defenses, such as consent or privilege.

To constitute the tort of defamation, a false defamatory statement must be made to someone other than the one defamed. Infliction of mental distress and invasion of privacy may occur without communication to a third person. Truth is an absolute defense to an action for defamation but is no defense to an action for infliction of mental distress or invasion of privacy.

The major intentional torts involving harm to property are trespass to real property, trespass to personal property, and conversion. In an action for trespass the plaintiff is compensated for the harm to property or for loss of possession. In an action for conversion, the owner recovers the full value of his or her personal property. Replevin, or claim and delivery, is used to secure the return of property.

Fraud sometimes plays an important part in the commission of torts that harm the person, but it usually arises in connection with business transactions where money or property is involved. The tort of fraud involves intentional misrepresentation committed either by a person's actions or concealment of material facts, justifiably relied on by another to his or her injury.

REVIEW QUESTIONS

1. (a) Define the tort of battery. (b) List and explain briefly the defenses available to a defendant in an action for battery. (c) How does the privilege of self-defense differ from the privilege of protection of one's property?

2. (**a**) What is an assault? (**b**) Explain the statement, "an attempted battery is not necessarily an assault." (**c**) Give an example of a battery that is not preceded by an assault.

3. (**a**) Define false imprisonment. (**b**) Why is it important for a business person to have some knowledge of this tort?

4. (**a**) Define the tort of infliction of mental distress. (**b**) How does this tort differ from other torts involving mental distress, such as assault and false imprisonment?

5. (**a**) Define defamation. (**b**) Why do you think publication is required to recover for the tort of defamation? (**c**) Explain the difference between libel and slander.

6. (**a**) List and give examples of three types of absolute privilege. (**b**) Explain qualified privilege and how it may be lost. (**c**) Explain the difference between malice and actual malice.

7. (**a**) List and give examples of the four main forms of invasion of privacy. (**b**) How does invasion of privacy differ from defamation?

8. (**a**) List and explain briefly the defenses to an action for invasion of privacy. (**b**) Explain the legal protection given to a public figure's right of privacy.

9. (**a**) Define trespass to real property. (**b**) Define the torts of trespass to personal property and conversion. (**c**) Explain the major difference between these torts.

10. (**a**) List the five elements of the tort of fraud. (**b**) Explain how fraud may be committed by concealment. (**c**) Give an example of an opinion that may be grounds for an action in fraud.

11. Explain how a defendant who misrepresents may be held liable to someone he or she has never dealt with.

12. Explain the majority rule of measuring damages in a fraud action.

CASE PROBLEMS

1. Mrs. Turman had been treated for glaucoma for a number of years at the Eye Clinic. She owed the Eye Clinic $46 for services. She had not paid her account, and in May it was assigned to Central Billing Bureau for collection. During June, Mrs. Turman received numerous phone calls from Central informing her that someone from the sheriff's office would come to her house to serve papers on her, that unless she paid in full her husband could lose his job, and that she could lose her home and everything she owned. At one time Central's agent used profane and abusive language and said she could not "care less about Mrs. Turman's being blind" and called her "scum" and a "deadbeat." Mrs. Turman suffered severe headaches and was hospitalized because of her state of anxiety. Does Mrs. Turman have a cause of action for infliction of mental distress? Explain the reasons for your answer.

2. Dr. Corey was a vice president at the state university and acted as president while the president was away. At a meeting with a five-member faculty committee chosen to pass on the qualifications for tenure of Dr. Stukuls, Dr. Corey read a letter accusing Dr. Stukuls, a married man, of having attempted to seduce a young woman who was a student in one of his classes. Dr. Corey had taken the letter from the president's private file in the president's absence. Dr. Stukuls filed suit against the university for defamation and wished to show that Dr. Corey acted with malice. The university asserted that it was protected by an absolute privilege. Is the university entitled to an absolute privilege or a qualified privilege? Give reasons for your choice.

3. From 1953 until 1973 the Central Intelligence Agency conducted an extensive program of opening first-class mail passing in and out of the country through certain cities. Various criteria were employed in selecting letters for inspection, including the country of origin or destination. Birnbaum, MacMillen, and Avery sent letters to persons in Russia and received letters from persons in Russia, the contents of which were copied by the CIA. No judicial warrants had been obtained, and there is no evidence to suggest probable cause for a warrantless search. None of the three persons was aware until several years later that his mail had been interfered with. Do Birnbaum, MacMillen, and Avery have a cause of action against the CIA for invasion of privacy? Why or why not?

4. Willie Henderson financed the purchase of a Cadillac through Security Bank. Willie defaulted on his agreement with the bank by letting the insurance on the vehicle lapse and being delinquent in his monthly payments. The bank repossessed the car and sold it. Willie filed suit against the bank for conversion, charging that the repossessor unlawfully broke the lock on Willie's garage door to take possession of the car. The bank defended that it was entitled to take possession of the Cadillac and that it neither expressly nor impliedly authorized or ratified the unlawful breaking and entering by the repossessor. Is this a valid defense? Explain.   *NO*

5. Clark, an experienced contractor, built a house for Aenchbacher containing numerous defects. When Aenchbacher started a fire in the fireplace, the chimney did not function properly, and the room filled with smoke. When it rained, the basement floor flooded. Aenchbacher contended that Clark was guilty of fraud since he knew of the defects in construction and did not inform Aenchbacher. Also, the defects could not be discovered by the exercise of ordinary prudence and caution. Clark contended that such facts did not constitute the tort of fraud. He also defended that Aenchbacher signed a statement when he moved into the house that he had carefully inspected it and was completely satisfied with the workmanship and materials in it. Does Aenchbacher have a cause of action against Clark for fraud? Why or why not?

CHAPTER 4

UNINTENTIONAL TORTS AND BUSINESS TORTS

The contemporary world is crowded and complex. Often it seems impossible for a person to move about or engage in a business transaction without committing a civil wrong to another person. Most people do not intentionally harm others. However, an individual or business firm may unintentionally harm the person or property of another and become liable in tort for damages. There are two major areas of liability for unintentional acts: liability for the tort of negligence and liability without fault.

The first-part of this chapter discusses major legal aspects of the tort of negligence and the major defenses available. The second part of the chapter concerns two areas of liability without fault. The last part of the chapter examines torts that interfere with commercial or business rights. For convenience, these interferences are called "business torts."

NEGLIGENCE

Nature of Negligence

There is no universal definition of the tort of negligence. Many definitions have been given by legal writers, judges, and legislatures. A general definition of **negligence** for our purposes is failure to exercise due care when there is a foreseeable risk of harm to others. The tort of negligence may be illustrated simply by the following comparison. A person who intentionally drives a car into another's car commits the tort of trespass to personal property. One who carelessly drives a car too fast and cannot stop it in time to avoid a collision commits the tort of negligence.

Elements of Negligence

To establish a cause of action for negligence, the plaintiff traditionally must prove four elements: (1) the defendant owed a duty to protect the plaintiff against harm, (2) the defendant failed to exercise due care, (3) the plaintiff suffered actual loss or damage, and (4) the defendant's negligence caused the plaintiff's injury.

Duty of Care. The first element, a duty to protect the plaintiff against harm, is commonly called a "duty of care." For our purposes it can be stated that a duty of care arises whenever a person should foresee that his or her conduct will create an unreasonable risk of harm to others. For example, driving a car too fast on a deserted highway does not create a duty of care. Such conduct in a populated area, however, creates an unreasonable risk of harm to others, and the driver owes a duty of care to all persons who foreseeably may be injured.

In the following case the court expresses views regarding the duty of care owed by a state to one of its citizens.

CASE 4.1   Department of Commerce v. Glick
372 N.E.2d 479 (Ind. App. 1978)

Facts: Robert L. Johnson presented himself to the Department of Commerce, State of Indiana (defendant) as a consultant for a large Eastern concern interested in locating a laser research facility in Indiana. Hollis, assistant director of the division, assisted Johnson by mailing throughout the state a "fact sheet," referring responses to Johnson, and arranging meetings between Johnson and citizens of the Town of Hope, Indiana. In April 1972 plaintiff, Glick, provided $25,000 to Johnson to help secure a federal grant of $50 million. Shortly thereafter it was learned Johnson was a "con man" and he was convicted of theft. Prior to April 1972 Hollis had become suspicious of Johnson because he refused to identify the company he represented. Hollis made inquiries and requested a State Police report. Hollis never communicated his suspicions to Glick or other citizens of Hope. After Glick delivered the $25,000 he received the police report showing Johnson had a lengthy criminal record. Glick sued for the tort of negligence and received a judgment. The state appealed.

Questions: Did the State owe a duty of care to Glick?
Is the State of Indiana liable for negligence?

Answer: Yes. The State owed a duty of care to Glick, and is liable for the negligence of Hollis.

Reasoning: Glick proved the four elements of an action in negligence. The trial court gave the following instruction to the jury: "Every person is under a duty to exercise his senses and intelligence in his actions in order to avoid injury to others, and where a situation suggests investigation and inspection in order that its dangers may fully appear, duty to make such investigation and inspection is imposed by law." The appellate court said, "It was also reasonably foreseeable that . . . the investors . . . were in danger of losing their money, particularly where the State's suspicions were not communicated. . . ."

The judgment was affirmed.

Failure to Exercise Care.   The judge or jury in a lawsuit for negligence must determine if the defendant failed to exercise due care. To assist in this determination, the courts have established a standard of behavior, that of a hypothetical "reasonable person of ordinary prudence." Negligence is often described as the failure to do what the ordinary prudent person would do under the same or similar circumstances. The judge or jury compares the conduct of the defendant with the presumed conduct of the ordinary prudent person under the same or similar circumstances. If the defendant's conduct does not measure up to this model standard of conduct, he or she may be held liable for damages for the tort of negligence.

A person possessing or claiming to possess superior knowledge or skill is held to a higher standard of conduct than the ordinary prudent person, however. Physicians, dentists, attorneys, accountants, and other professionals present themselves to the public as having specialized skill and knowledge. In a lawsuit for professional malpractice, the defendant is presumed to have the skill and learning commonly possessed by members of the profession in good standing in the same or a similar community. Failure to possess the presumed knowledge and skill is strong evidence of negligence.

To exercise due care means to use one's presumed experience and knowledge in such a manner as to prevent an unreasonable risk of harm to others. The more probable and more serious the harm, the greater the expense and effort that must be taken to prevent that harm. Thus, the courts have held that a great amount of care must be exercised in dealing with items that are known to be dangerous such as gas, electricity, or elevators.

Injury to the Plaintiff.   The harm suffered because of another's negligence may be physical (harm to the person or property) or mental (fright, pain). In most lawsuits for negligence, the plaintiff's injury is easily shown and he or she recovers damages for any physical injury. In addition, an award may be made for mental suffering accompanying the physical injury, that is, for pain, suffering, fright, and humiliation.

Negligence the Cause of Injury.   To hold the defendant liable, the plaintiff must prove that the defendant's negligence caused the injury. Sometimes the cause is obvious, as where the defendant carelessly drives a car and collides with the plaintiff. At other times an outside event occurs that contributes to the plaintiff's injuries.

An *intervening cause* is one occuring after the defendant's negligence, which alters the consequences of the defendant's conduct. Such a contributing cause of the plaintiff's injury may be of human or natural origin. An infinite variety of possible intervening causes exists, and it is obvious that a defendant should not always be held liable for the plaintiff's injury. As a general rule the defendant is liable only if the intervening cause of plaintiff's injury is reasonably foreseeable. The courts have held that a negligent defendant should reasonably foresee the negligence of others. For example, suppose a driver injures a pedestrian and negligently leaves the person unconscious in the roadway. If a second driver negligently runs over the pedestrian and the injuries are indivisible (that is, it is impossible to tell which driver caused which injuries), both drivers may be held liable for the plaintiff's injuries. The two negligent drivers are called "joint tortfeasors."

The following case deals with negligence and an intervening cause of injury.

CASE 4.2   Ford v. Jeffries
379 A.2d 111 (Pa. 1977)

Facts: James Jeffries owned a dwelling that was located five or six feet from Mamie Ford's home. The property was vacant and in disrepair. Windows were broken, there were holes in the walls, the property harbored large rats, and dogs wandered in and out of the basement. On July 30 at 2:27 A.M. a fire started in Jeffries' house and damaged parts of it. Jeffries made no repairs. On September 26 at approximately 2 A.M., a second fire broke out in Jeffries' house. Flames spread to Ford's home, resulting in almost total destruction of her house. Ford sued Jeffries for negligence. Jeffries succeeded in having Ford's case dismissed. Ford appealed.

Question: Should Jeffries be held liable as the cause of Ford's injuries?

Answer: Yes. Jeffries should be liable for the tort of negligence.

Reasoning: A property owner can reasonably be expected to know that the visible conditions of vacant property in a state of disrepair may attract, for various purposes, children or adults, who might act, either negligently or intentionally, in a manner that would cause a fire. On the question of "causation" the court said that although some force may have intervened between Jeffries' conduct and the resulting harm to Ford, Jeffries may be held liable if he realized or should have realized that a third person might avail himself or herself of the opportunity to commit a tort or a crime on the premises. Whether or not Jeffries should have realized that such a situation had been created is a question for the jury to decide.

The order of the trial court was reversed and the case remanded for further proceedings.

Defenses to Negligence

There are three major defenses to the tort of negligence: contributory negligence, assumption of the risk, and comparative negligence.

Contributory Negligence.   The defense of **contributory negligence** can be defined as failure by the plaintiff to exercise due care for his or her own safety, which failure contributes to the plaintiff's injury. To determine whether the plaintiff exercised due care, the model of the ordinary prudent person is again utilized. Much criticism has been leveled at the defense of contributory negligence because it is a complete bar to the plaintiff's recovery. Thus, a plaintiff who is slightly negligent may not recover from a defendant who is greatly negligent. Most states have developed exceptions and modifications to the defense of contributory negligence, but the defense still is recognized in a substantial number of states.

Assumption of the Risk.   The defense of **assumption of the risk** may be defined generally as voluntary exposure to a known risk. A plaintiff's assumption of the risk may be express or implied. A common activity involving implied assumption of the risk is attending a sporting event. Suppose that a spectator at a baseball game is injured by a flying baseball. The spectator files a suit for negligence against the owner of the stadium, alleging that the owner failed to provide a protective screen for spectators. The stadium owner may assert the defense of assumption of the risk by stating that the plaintiff assumed upon entering the stadium the known risk of being hit by a bat or ball.

The defense of assumption of the risk has been criticized because it too is a complete bar to the plaintiff's recovery. As with contributory negligence, the courts have developed exceptions and modifications to this defense in an attempt to reduce the hardship resulting to the plaintiff.

Comparative Negligence.   Dissatisfaction with the absolute defenses of contributory negligence and assumption of the risk has led to the adoption of the defense of **comparative negligence** in the great majority of states.

In a lawsuit where *both* defendant and plaintiff are negligent, the defense of *comparative negligence* requires the judge or jury to apportion damages between the plaintiff and the defendant, according to the fault of each. Thus, for example, if the defendant is found to be 75 percent at fault and the plaintiff is found to be 25 percent at fault, the plaintiff's damages will be reduced by 25 percent. In addition, if the defendant is injured in the same accident, the plaintiff must pay 25 percent of his or her damages.

The effect of the adoption of the comparative negligence rule on the defense of assumption of the risk varies greatly among states. In some states express assumption of the risk remains as a complete defense, but implied assumption of the risk is treated as a form of comparative negligence, and the plaintiff's damages are reduced. In a few states assumption of the risk, whether express or implied, is retained as an absolute defense.

The following case illustrates the merger of contributory negligence and implied assumption of the risk into the doctrine of comparative negligence.

CASE 4.3   Gonzalez v. Garcia
142 Cal. Reptr. 503 (Cal. App. 1977)

Facts: Plaintiff, Juan Gonzalez, and defendant, Francisco Garcia, drank alcoholic beverages for over 3 hours. Defendant insisted on driving his car and after several attempts by plaintiff to telephone his wife, plaintiff got into the passenger seat and fell asleep. Defendant lost control of the car and caused an accident, injuring plaintiff. Defendant was unquestionably intoxicated. Plaintiff sued for damages for negligence, and defendant asserted comparative negligence and assumption of the risk as defenses. The trial judge refused to instruct the jury on assumption of the risk. The jury returned a verdict for plaintiff but found him to be 20 percent at fault. Defendant appealed, contending the trial court should have instructed the jury on the defense of assumption of the risk.

Question: Should the jury have been instructed to consider the defense of assumption of the risk?

Answer: No. In California, implied assumption of the risk has been superseded by comparative negligence.

Reasoning: The court said, "Most commentators recognize at least three kinds of assumption of risk: (1) express—where plaintiff, in advance, gives consent to relieve defendant of a legal duty and to take his chances of injury from a known risk; (2) implied—where plaintiff acts reasonably in voluntarily encountering a risk with the knowledge that defendant will not protect him; and (3) implied—where the plaintiff acts unreasonably in voluntarily exposing himself to a risk created by defendant's negligence. . . . Where the doctrine of comparative negligence has been accepted, there have been three different approaches to assumption of risk—completely abolishing it as a defense, . . . maintaining it as a complete and separate defense, . . . or merging it to some extent with contributory negligence. . . . In those states which have merged the defenses, there has frequently been a complete merger of implied assumption of risk and contributory negligence, with express assumption of risk remaining as a separate defense. . . ." Here, plaintiff knew the defendant was intoxicated and tried to call his wife. He had the alternative of calling a cab and yet he chose to ride with defendant. His conduct amounts to both contributory negligence and implied assumption of the risk, both of which are merged into the doctrine of comparative negligence.

The judgment was affirmed.

LIABILITY WITHOUT FAULT

This part of the chapter discusses **liability without fault**, sometimes called "strict liability." As the term implies, there are situations where a person may be held liable for injuring another even though he or she has no intent to injure anyone and, in fact, acts with the utmost care to prevent harm to others. In such a situation the conduct of the one causing injury is blameless, yet for reasons of social policy the law requires him or her to compensate the injured person for the loss. The social policy is based largely on the notion that one person has caused injury to another and, although no one is at fault, a system of allocating losses must be developed. The courts reason that liability for the injury should be imposed on the party who can best bear the loss; that party usually is the one who caused the injury.

Liability without fault exists in a variety of areas of contemporary law. All individuals and firms should be aware that whenever their conduct results in injury to another, there is the possibility of being required to compensate the injured person. The law regarding certain situations of strict liability, such as workers' compensation and nuisance, are too extensive to present fully here. (Workers' compensation is discussed in Chapter 43, nuisance on p. 400.) The law of product liability is discussed fully in Chapter 18. One aspect of that law is liability without fault for defective products. Two areas of strict liability have been selected for discussion here: liability for injuries by animals and liability for injuries from abnormally dangerous activities.

Liability for Injuries by Animals

Several rules of law impose liability without fault on animal owners. In most states, the owner of an animal that is likely to roam and injure the person or property of another is liable without fault for damages inflicted when the animal enters upon another's land. Such animals include cattle, horses, sheep, hogs, turkeys, chickens, and most wild animals, since their natural tendency is to escape.

Either of two rules may apply when the injury occurs on the land of the animal's owner. First, the owner may be liable without fault for injuries inflicted by an animal that is dangerous by its nature and incapable of being domesticated. Such animals include lions, tigers, bears, elephants, and wolves. As a general rule, liability is absolute though the owner has raised the animal as a pet and it has shown no outward signs of being dangerous. The second rule of law that may apply pertains to domestic animals and domesticated wild animals that normally are not likely to injure people. The owner is liable for injuries inflicted only if the owner knows, or has reason to know, of a dangerous propensity in the particular animal. Domestic animals include dogs, cats, sheep, horses, and cows. The courts have held that deer and monkeys are wild animals capable of being domesticated. In many states the legislatures have enacted special statutes which hold an owner liable for injuries from a dog bite, regardless of the owner's knowledge or prior warning.

In a lawsuit to recover damages for injuries inflicted by an animal, the defendant may assert one or more defenses. The defendant may assert assumption of the risk and prove that the plaintiff voluntarily exposed himself or herself to a known risk. In most states the defendant is not allowed to assert contributory negligence as a defense. A plaintiff's recovery may be reduced in many states that have adopted the defense of comparative negligence.

Liability for Injuries from Abnormally Dangerous Activities

As a general rule, one is liable without fault for injuring the person or property of another by an unduly dangerous activity inappropriate to the particular locality. Typical examples of such an activity are crop dusting near livestock, storing quantities of explosives in the heart of a city, and drilling an oil well in a populated area. The courts have held that the following are not considered "inappropriate to the locality": storing gasoline in a service station, maintaining an ordinary fire in a factory, and stocking a small quantity of dynamite for sale in a hardware store.

In the early decades of the twentieth century, flying an airplane was considered an abnormally dangerous activity, and aircraft operators were held strictly liable for harm to others. Today, in most states, the owner or operator of an airplane is held liable only when negligence is proven.

In a lawsuit for abnormally dangerous activities the defendant may assert the defense of assumption of the risk and prove that the plaintiff voluntarily exposed his or her person or property to a known risk. The defendant may not assert the defense of contributory negligence.

BUSINESS TORTS

In this part of the chapter we will consider two types of torts which particularly interfere with commercial or business rights. For ease of discussion, we will call such interferences "business torts." The first type to be discussed is interferences with business relations; the second is unfair trade practices.

An individual or business firm which has been injured by a business tort is entitled to compensation (damages) for the losses sustained. If the wrongdoing business does not stop its unlawful actions and the injured firm cannot be adequately compensated in money, a court may order an injunction (a prohibition or restraining order) against the continuance of the tortious activity. For example, it is normal practice for a court to enjoin (that is, to stop) a business from using a name on its products which is so similar to a name used by a competitor that a purchaser cannot easily distinguish between the products of the two companies. The manufacturer of Apple Computers could secure an injunction against a company selling a similar computer under the trade name of Pineapple Computers.

Interfering with Business Relations

The first category of business torts is that of interfering with business relations. There are two aspects of this tort: (1) interfering with contracts, and (2) interfering with employment.

Interfering with Contracts.   The understandings between business people when they buy, sell, or undertake a business activity are expressed either orally or in writing in agreements (contracts). Even when there is no explicit agreement, sometimes the existence of a contract may be implied from the actions of the parties. This principle and the nature and elements of contracts are discussed in detail in Chapters 6 through 14.

The right to engage in a contract and the right to expect its performance by the other party to it are necessary to the orderly conduct of business affairs. The law looks with great disfavor upon any interference with contractual relations by outsiders. A third person might interfere with contract relations between others at two different stages of the contracting process: (1) in the initial stages, by interfering with the *making* of a contract; or (2) after the contract is in existence, by interfering with the *performance* of the contract.

A tort is committed when an individual or a firm, acting with malice, induces another not to enter into a contract with a third party if (1) the contract would otherwise have been consummated, and (2) if the third party is damaged. As we have seen in Chapter 3, *malice* is a word not easily defined. It may have different meanings when applied to different torts. Here it means only that the interference with the making of a contract was not justified or that illegal means were used to prevent the contract from coming into existence. For example, assume that Archer, manager of the Acme Realty Company, solely to prevent a rival, the Ritter Realty Company, from earning a commission, tells Doris, who is about to buy a house through Ritter, that the property is overpriced and she should not buy it. Doris relies on Archer's advice and does not buy the property. Archer's action was intended only to harm Ritter. It follows that Archer *maliciously* caused Doris not to enter into the contract of purchase. His action constituted a business tort.

The right of an individual to expect that outsiders will not interfere with the *performance* of a contract already entered into is protected by law. A business tort occurs when a person intentionally and without legal right, makes more difficult or prevents the performance of an existing contract, or makes its performance of less value to one of the contracting parties. Let us say that Baker Company, which manufactures semiconductors, has a contract to deliver 500 semiconductors to Adams before April 1. Suppose that Crane, Baker's best customer, tells Baker, "Don't make any more deliveries to Adams until you get all our orders out to us or we'll have to get a new supplier." Baker, wanting to stay in Crane's good graces, complies and breaches its contract with Adams. Crane committed a business tort because it knowingly interfered with the Adams–Baker contract.

Bona fide competition may furnish legal justification for interfering with the *creation* of a contract. For example, if you damage your car in an accident and get bids from two body shops for its repair, the fact that AA Body Shop furnished the lower bid, thereby inducing you not to contract with Crossroads Body Shop, was lawful competition. However, competition does not furnish justification for inducing a breach of contract *already in being*. Thus, after you entered into a contract with AA Body Shop to repair your car, Crossroads Body Shop cannot lawfully induce you to breach your contract with AA by promising to do the work at a price lower than Crossroads knows you agreed to pay AA.

Interfering with Employment.   Interfering with employer–employee relations is an aspect of the broader business tort of interfering with business relations. Well-trained and experienced employees constitute a most important element of any successful business organization. If a skilled employee is induced to leave his or her job to work for a competitor, the new employer may reap a considerable economic advantage. Not only will it be saved the expense of training the employee, but the new employer may also learn some of the former employer's manufacturing processes and trade secrets and may even gain some of the former employer's customers. A contract of employment, therefore, represents a valuable property right that is given special protection by tort law.

Newspapers regularly carry advertisements for job opportunities, featuring attractive working conditions and salary scales to induce qualified persons to switch jobs. Suppose that, as a result of such an advertisement, an individual leaves his or her job and goes to work for the company placing the ad. Does this mean that the firm which advertised has committed a tort and so is liable in damages? No, unless the advertiser intentionally and without just cause or excuse interfered with the preexisting employer–employee relationship.

Contracts of employment, oral or written, are protected. An oral understanding that an employee will work *for a specified length of time* is as protected by law as is a written contract of employment. However, if the employee is not under contract or agreement for any specified length of time but is free to terminate the employment at will, no tort results if he or she switches jobs in response to an offer of higher wages or better working conditions. As one court has said, "In our free economy, social mobility is a chief characteristic. An employee who is dischargeable at will is under no obligation to treat his employer otherwise or with more consideration than he can be treated by [the employer]."[1] This does not mean, however, that a business is free to entice any employee away from a competitor if the purpose is to *injure* the former employer.

In the following case, the court deals with a competitor's attempt to entice employees to leave their employer.

CASE 4.4   **Wear-Ever Aluminum, Inc. v. Townecraft Industries, Inc.**
182 A.2d 387 (N.J. 1962)

Facts: Wear-Ever Aluminum, Inc., the plaintiff, sold cooking utensils through house-to-house sales persons. Townecraft Industries, Inc., the defendant, was in the same business. Townecraft carried on a special campaign to hire away Wear-Ever's sales people in order to increase its own sales force and to undercut Wear-Ever's sales capabilities. Wear-Ever brought suit, asking the court to enjoin (to order Townecraft to stop) this "raiding" of Wear-Ever's employees.

[1] *Sarkes Tarzian, Inc. v. Audio Devices, Inc.*, 166 F. Supp. 250 (S.D. Cal. 1958).

Question: Can a firm, by legal action, prevent a competitor from hiring away the firm's employees?

Answer: Yes. An injunction can be secured if the hiring away is intended by the competitor to injure the firm involved.

Reasoning: The court said: ". . . While a trader may lawfully engage in the sharpest competition with those in like business, by offering extraordinary inducements or by representing his own goods to be better and cheaper than those of his competitors, yet when he oversteps that line and commits an act with the malicious intent of inflicting injury upon his rival's business, his conduct is illegal, and if damage ensues from it the injured party is entitled to redress. . . . The fact that [Wear-Ever's employees'] contracts were terminable at will cannot and does not provide the basis for justification where a third party tortiously interfered with the employment relationship. The right to terminate a contract at will is one which is peculiarly personal to the contracting parties, and a stranger to the contract may not exercise his will in substitution for the will of either of the parties to the contract. . . . The conduct of the defendant was designed and intended to promote [its own] interests at the expense of the plaintiff. The injury suffered by the plaintiff, i.e., loss of man power and loss of revenue . . . was the ultimate consequence envisioned and planned for by the defendant. . . . I feel that the only effective way to prevent future irreparable injury and to protect the plaintiff . . . is a permanent injunction restraining the defendant from recruiting or attempting to recruit employees, dealers and distributors of the plaintiff."

Engaging in Unfair Trade Practices

The most far-reaching of all business torts is that of engaging in unfair trade practices directed against competitors. This tort may take many forms. Among them are fraudulent marketing; infringing another's trademark, patent, or copyright; and unlawfully appropriating another's trade secrets. Some unfair trade practices, such as an agreement among a group of manufacturers to limit the territory in which each will sell its products (called a combination in restraint of trade), are prohibited by antitrust statutes. Antitrust law is discussed in Chapter 41.

Fraudulent Marketing. Any intentional sales representation which falsifies the source of a product or its maker constitutes *fraudulent marketing*. The essence of this tort is "palming off" one product for another. Examples of this type of fraudulent marketing practice are:

• A store displays a sign, "Arrow Shirts," above a stack of shirts on a counter in such a way as to indicate that all of them are Arrow brand, whereas only one or two are Arrow shirts.

• A dress store has a sign in its window falsely claiming "Dress styles by Dior."

Such fraudulent substitution may harm the manufacturer of the genuine article because it lost a sale and because an inferior product was represented as coming from its factory. As a result, the manufacturer may be subjected to unjustified customer complaints and the loss of goodwill. The purchaser, of course, is harmed by not receiving the article that he or she intended to buy.

To retain the public benefit which free competition offers, the law does allow considerable latitude to business concerns in copying styles or designs of competitors. Assume that Amy's Dress Shop purchases couturier dresses from Paris to be sold in its dress salon. The dress styles are not patented. Betty's Ready-To-Wear, which sells popular-priced dresses, reads in the newspaper that Amy's has "original dresses fresh from Paris" for sale. Betty's sends a designer to Amy's, where she sees the Paris dresses displayed. She then returns to her own store and makes excellent copies of them. Betty's then sells the copies for one-fourth the price of Amy's original Paris dresses. Betty's Ready-To-Wear is careful, however, not to advertise or represent the dresses as original Paris models. In this situation there has been no misrepresentation and Amy's Dress Shop has no basis for a tort action against Betty's.

If we change these hypothetical facts slightly, however, and assume that Betty's designer bribed one of Amy's employees to let her examine and sketch the imported gowns, then Betty's Ready-To-Wear would have secured its copies by improper means and its privilege to imitate them would be lost. (Of course, if Betty's also represents its copies as made in Paris, thereby intentionally deceiving customers, there has been misrepresentation and the tort of falsifying the source would also be committed.)

Infringing a Trademark, Patent, or Copyright.   A **trademark** is any word, symbol, device, or design adopted and used to identify an article offered for sale. To be effective, a trademark must be placed on or affixed to an article or its container and must be registered in the U.S. Patent Office. A trademark belongs to, and may be exclusively used by, the firm which first employs it. The business tort of **trademark infringement** occurs when someone else, intentionally or unintentionally, uses a device or trademark which is so similar to another's trademark that it is likely to confuse prospective purchasers as to the source of the product. For example, another firm might use a name so similar to the trademark "Coca-Cola" that it deceives or will probably deceive purchasers and cause them to buy a product believing it to be the product of the Coca-Cola Company.

Sometimes a trademark is so commonly used that it becomes a generic or descriptive designation for that type of goods. What was formerly a trademark may then be used by anyone to describe the article, provided, of course, there is no attempt to misrepresent the new product as the original. Examples of trademarks that have become generic include aspirin, thermos, and shredded wheat.

The use of the trademark "lite" to describe a beer is the subject of the next case.

CASE 4.5   Miller Brewing Company v. G. Heileman Brewing Company
561 F.2d 75 (7th Cir. 1977)

Facts: The plaintiff, Miller Brewing Company, owned the trademark "LITE," approved by the U.S. Patent Office. Miller used that trademark to describe its low calorie beer. The defendant, G. Heileman Brewing Company, later marketed a low calorie beer which it described as "light." Miller filed a trademark infringment action against Heileman.

Question: Can a descriptive word be trademarked, thereby preventing that word from being used by a competitor to describe its competing product?

Answer: No. A word that is commonly descriptive of a product cannot be adopted or trademarked by a company as its own.

Reasoning: The court said, ". . . Miller's brand name LITE must be evaluated under the common law of trademarks without the benefit of registration [because the Patent Office trademark covered a formula for a beer of a different content from that of the beer in question that Miller was selling].

" 'Light' has been widely used in the beer industry for many years to describe beer's color, flavor, body, or alcoholic content, or a combination of these or of similar characteristics. . . . 'Light' is clearly a commonly descriptive word when used with beer. . . . Even if Miller had given its beer a characteristic not found in other light beers, it could not acquire the exclusive right to use the common descriptive word 'light' as a trademark for that beer. Other brewers whose beers have qualities that make them 'light' as that word has commonly been used remain free to call their beer 'light.' Otherwise a manufacturer could remove a common descriptive word from the public domain by investing his goods with an additional quality, thus gaining the exclusive right to call his wine 'rosé,' his whiskey 'blended,' or his bread 'white.'

"The word 'light,' including its phonetic equivalent, 'lite,' being a generic or common descriptive term as applied to beer, could not be exclusively appropriated by Miller as a trademark. . . ."

Anyone who makes or sells a patented article without the permission of the patent holder commits the business tort of **patent infringement**. The United States Constitution authorizes, and Congress has enacted, patent laws which give to inventors for an extended number of years the exclusive right to produce and market their inventions. A patent is issued by the U.S. Patent Office for an invention that is useful, novel, and "more than an obvious technical advance in the prior state of the art." A patent gives the patent holder the exclusive right to market the invention for a period of 17 years. After that span of time, the patent expires and anyone is free to use the process or to manufacture and sell the article.

A **copyright** is another means for protecting an individual's original work. Copyrights cover literary, musical, dramatic, and similar works. Recently, computer programs have been copyrighted. **Copyright infringement** occurs when a competitor publishes a work that is a clear copy of the original or so similar to it that it is likely to confuse or deceive the public. Courts often have difficulty in deciding whether infringement has occurred. To obtain a copyright, the work must be original, but it may be substantially similar to works previously written or produced by others. Many authors, for example, have written biographies of Thomas Jefferson. While each is copyrighted, that fact does not preclude other authors from writing biographies of the same man. A copyright of any work created after January 1, 1978, lasts for the lifetime of the author plus 50 years after the author's death.

Appropriating a Trade Secret.   The last type of conduct considered an unfair trade practice is violating trade secrets. A **trade secret** is any information kept secret by a firm because of its great value to the business. A trade secret may cover any aspect of a business, such as an engineering process, a chemical formula, computer software, a customer attitude survey, a list of customers, or even a cookie recipe. If a firm gains another's trade secret dishonestly, as by industrial espionage or through the abuse of a confidence, a business tort has been committed.

SUMMARY

There are two major areas of tort liability for unintentional harm to others: liability for the tort of negligence and liability without fault. Negligence is defined as the failure to exercise due care when there is a foreseeable risk of harm to others. To recover damages in a lawsuit for negligence, the plaintiff must prove four elements: (1) the defendant owed a duty of care to the plaintiff, (2) the defendant failed to exercise due care, (3) the plaintiff suffered actual loss or damage, and (4) the defendant's negligence caused the plaintiff's injury.

Three major defenses are available to a defendant in a lawsuit for negligence: contributory negligence, assumption of the risk, and comparative negligence. Comparative negligence is provided in most states and has largely replaced the two other defenses.

There are two major areas of liability without fault (strict liability): liability for injuries by animals and liability for injuries from abnormally dangerous activities. In a strict liability lawsuit the defendant may be held liable though he or she exercises all possible care to prevent harm to others. The defendant may assert the defense of assumption of the risk but ordinarily may not assert contributory negligence of the plaintiff. Some states permit the defendant to assert comparative negligence as a defense in a lawsuit involving product liability.

Business torts may be grouped into two broad categories: interfering with business relations and engaging in unfair trade practices. If a business firm intentionally and without legal justification prevents another from making a contract or interferes with the performance of a contract already in being, the business tort of interfering with business relations has been committed. Knowingly inducing an employee of one company to leave his or her job and go to work for another company is another type of interfering with business relations.

Unfair trade practices take many different forms. The most frequent is the palming off or attempted secret substitution of one article for another to a customer. This may be accomplished by imitating the physical appearance or packaging of a competitor's product and not disclosing the distinction to customers. A trademark is infringed by using a trademark so similar to another's as to confuse a customer as to the source of the product. If someone without permission sells a patented or copyrighted product, the unfair practice of patent or copyright infringement has taken place. It is also an unfair trade practice for a company, by unlawful means, to secure and use a guarded trade secret of another.

REVIEW QUESTIONS

1. (a) Define the tort of negligence. (b) List the four elements required to establish a cause of action for negligence.

2. (a) What is a "duty of care"? (b) Who owes this duty and when does it arise? (c) To whom is the duty owed?

3. Explain how a judge or jury determines if a defendant has failed to exercise due care.

4. Give examples of the types of injuries for which a plaintiff may recover damages in a negligence suit.

5. (a) Define contributory negligence. (b) How does this definition differ from the definition of the tort of negligence? (c) Define assumption of the risk. (d) Explain why, to a plaintiff, the defense of comparative negligence is more beneficial than either contributory negligence or assumption of the risk.

6. (a) Explain the social policy behind strict liability. (b) State and give examples of the three rules of law that may apply to injuries by animals. (c) In what circumstances may a person be held liable for injuring another by an abnormally dangerous activity?

7. (a) When does interference with the making of a contract become a business tort? (b) Give an example of interference with the making of a contract which is legally *justifiable* and one which is legally *unjustifiable*.

8. (a) Why is the performance of an employment contract protected by the courts from unreasonable interference by competitors? (b) Do you think that the protection of a contract of employment deserves greater, equal, or less protection from interference than does a contract involving the sale of a house? Why?

9. (a) Give examples of unlawful marketing practices which may be termed "palming off." (b) Should the courts restrain a business person from imitating the products of a competitor? Support your answer with reasons you believe would dictate the court's decision.

10. (a) What is a trademark? (b) Explain how a trademark may be infringed. (c) Explain the difference between a patent and a copyright.

11. (a) What is a trade secret? (b) Give examples of trade secrets. (c) Why might a company choose to rely on the protection afforded by a trade secret rather than on that provided by a patent?

CASE PROBLEMS

1. Galen Irby drove a cab for Cab Company. On the night of December 17, Cab Company dispatched Galen to respond to a request for a taxi at 5616 Vernon Avenue in a part of St. Louis known as a high-crime area. While at that address, Galen was

murdered. Galen's wife, Anita Irby, filed suit for negligence (wrongful death) against Cab Company, alleging that they owed a duty to exercise due care in dispatching Galen into high-crime areas and to provide means to protect him from intentional criminal acts of third persons. Cab Company filed a motion to dismiss for failure by Anita Irby to state a claim upon which relief can be granted. How should the court rule? Explain reason or reasons for answer.

2. Avis left a rental car unattended in the parking lot at Miami International Airport with the key in the ignition, the door open, and the car lights flashing. The car was subsequently stolen. The thief operated the car negligently and collided with a car driven by Charlie Vining, severely injuring him. The area around the airport had the highest incidence of auto theft in Dade County. Avis had had vehicles stolen in the past. Vining sued Avis for negligence. The trial court dismissed the complaint, stating that even if Avis were negligent it was not liable because the criminal act of stealing the car broke the chain of causation. Is Avis' negligence the cause of Vining's injuries? Explain.

3. Marcos Garcia's automobile was parked in a parallel parking space on the south side of Howard Street. Keith Howard's car was parked in the space directly in front of Garcia's car, both vehicles facing east. Garcia had obtained new license plates for his car, had returned to his car, and had begun to put the plates on his car. He had difficulty with the front license plate and spent 25 minutes trying to attach it. Howard returned to his automobile and got in, unaware that Garcia was between the rear of his car and the front of Garcia's car. Howard started his car, looked at his rearview mirror, saw only Garcia's car behind his, and slowly backed his car in the parking space. Garcia was crouching, facing his car, and was struck on the left shoulder by the rear bumper of Howard's car. Garcia sued Howard for the tort of negligence. Howard alleged Garcia was guilty of contributory negligence and assumption of the risk. Are the defenses valid? Explain.

4. Tasha, a 4½-year-old girl, visited her friend, Theresa, age 10, at the home of Theresa's grandparents, Mr. and Mrs. Yeager. The Yeagers kept a monkey, named "Mr. Jim," in a cage in the backyard. Theresa told Tasha where she could place her hand so the monkey could reach out and shake hands with her. The monkey bit Tasha's finger, causing serious injury. Mr. Jim had been a family pet for 26 years; he was regularly petted, he played with children, and had never before bitten a child. Tasha filed suit for strict liability, alleging the monkey was a wild animal. Is Tasha's allegation sufficient for her to recover damages for her injuries? Explain.

5. The plaintiff and defendant corporations both manufactured women's wearing apparel. Sonya, a noted dress designer, entered into a written contract to work for the plaintiff for a period of 5 years. The agreement required her to devote her full energies to the plaintiff's business and not to compete with it. The defendant company, knowing that Sonya was under contract to the plaintiff, offered her a job and agreed to pay her a larger salary if she would leave the plaintiff and work for the defendant. Sonya did so. The plaintiff sued the defendant for damages it claimed it sustained because the defendant induced the breach of Sonya's contract. The court held that plaintiff was entitled to recover. Do you agree with this holding? Why or why not?

6. The plaintiff manufactured and sold a pole lamp, that is, one which stands upright between the floor and ceiling of a room. The defendant, learning of the successful sale of the lamp, marketed a substantially identical one which it sold at retail at a price lower than plaintiff sold them at wholesale. The plaintiff sought to enjoin the defendant's sale of the lamps, claiming unfair competition. The lower court granted an injunction and the defendant appealed. Should the injunction have been granted? Why or why not?

7. The plaintiff cleaned private homes by mass production methods, employing crews of workers whom it had trained. The plaintiff, at considerable effort and expense, developed and screened its customers, with most of whom it had contracts. The defendant worked for the plaintiff as a house cleaner and learned the plaintiff's method of doing business. After being in plaintiff's employ for 3 years, the defendant quit his job and started the same type of business for himself. He solicited the plaintiff's customers whose names and addresses defendant had learned from his employment with the plaintiff. House cleaning is not a unique business and no trade secrets are involved. The plaintiff sought to enjoin the defendant from soliciting its customers. Should the plaintiff be successful in its suit? Why or why not?

CHAPTER 5

CRIMINAL LAW; COMPUTER AND OTHER WHITE-COLLAR CRIMES

Commercial firms may be either victims or perpetrators of criminal acts. It is, therefore, appropriate for a book on business law to discuss criminal law—what it is, how it works, and how it applies to the conduct of business. This chapter begins with an overview of that branch of the law called "criminal law." It discusses the nature of crimes, traces the procedures of a criminal prosecution, comparing them with those of civil courts, and briefly discusses the imposition of punishment for criminal acts. Lastly, it pays particular attention to computer and other **white-collar** crimes.

As explained in Chapters 3 and 4, a single wrongful act may be at the same time both a *civil* wrong (a tort) and a *public* wrong (a crime). Recovery of damages from a defendant for a tort does not bar punishment for the act in its criminal aspect. Thus, if Arthur breaks into the Olympic warehouse and steals six stereo sets, Olympic can bring a civil action against Arthur, seeking payment for the value of the sets and for any damage he did to the building. These are private wrongs. At the same time and without regard to the outcome of that tort action, the state may arrest Arthur and prosecute him for the criminal offenses (public wrongs) of breaking and entering the building and of larceny—unlawfully taking the property of another without intending to return it. Under some statutes, the offense of burglary may also have been committed.

NATURE OF CRIMES

What Is a Crime?

A **crime** is the commission of an act which the law forbids, or the omission to perform an act which the law commands, either of which can be punished by the state in a criminal proceeding in its own name. Unlike torts, which are often created through court decisions, statutes define what acts or omissions are criminal offenses.

Most acts recognized as crimes in today's society have been outlawed since ancient times. However, as social standards and ethics change, our views as to what actions constitute offenses against society have also changed. Not quite 400 years ago, in at least one American colony, a woman could be charged with practicing witchcraft, tried for that offense, and, if found guilty, burned at the stake. Today, of course, there is no such offense and no such punishment. Before the invention of the automobile it would have been physically impossible to commit the "popular" offense of taking someone else's car to go joy-riding, and the offense of cheating by credit card was unknown only a few years ago.

Elements of a Crime

A crime is (1) a socially blameworthy act, (2) committed by a mentally competent person, (3) with the requisite intent.

The Act.   A criminal act is doing something the law forbids, or failing to do something the law requires. For example, the law *forbids* a person to steal another's property; the law *requires* the filing of income tax returns.

A criminal act must be a physical happening or a breach of a legal duty. If Angus intends to steal a car sometime but does nothing to carry out that intention, no crime has been committed. If a mental state alone were enough to constitute commission of a crime, how could the offense be proved?

An act that is only *preparatory* to the commission of a crime is not a crime. Any time during the preparation stage the individual may change his or her mind and commit no crime at all. Consider these facts: Ralph, a member of the computer programming staff of the New Bank, decides secretly to program the bank's computer to credit other people's money to a hidden account he will establish. Ralph works out the details of his scheme and next day opens an account under an assumed name at a branch of the New Bank where he is not known. Ralph still is only in the preparation stage. But later, when Ralph directs the computer to transfer funds from other depositors' accounts into the account he has opened, he passes beyond preparation and has now committed a criminal act. The theft will be dubbed a "white-collar crime" since it involves some kind of business transaction.

How a court distinguishes *preparation* from *commission* of a criminal offense is revealed in the following case.

CASE 5.1   **State v. Otto**
629 P.2d 646 (Idaho 1981)

Facts: Defendant Otto paid Watts $250 and agreed to pay him $750 more after Watts killed Captain Ailor of the Police Department. Watts was an undercover police officer who did nothing to carry out Otto's scheme. Instead, Otto was arrested, charged with, tried for, and convicted of attempted first degree murder. (First degree murder is the intentional, deliberate, and unlawful killing of another). Otto appealed, contending that the facts did not amount to an *attempt.*

Question: Were the facts sufficient to establish the offense of attempted murder?

Answer: No. Conviction reversed.

Reasoning: No one can be convicted for having a criminal *intent* alone. The intent must be accompanied by some act which is part of the *commission* of the offense. Some criminal act is essential. The crime of *attempt* consists of (1) an intent to do an act and (2) an act in furtherance of that intent which goes beyond a mere preparation.

Preparation is setting up the means necessary for the commission of an offense; attempt is the direct movement toward its commission *after* the preparations are made. Most courts hold that only to solicit someone to commit a crime is the crime of solicitation, but something more is required to establish the offense of attempt.

Here, no one ever took any steps in the actual commission of the offense the defendant planned. When Otto paid the policeman to commit the killing, this was only a preparatory act. Otto therefore did not commit an attempted murder but only a solicitation of the offense. However, he was not charged with solicitation and he was not tried for that offense.

Mental Capacity.   A person may be so young or so mentally unsound as not to have the mental capacity to be responsible for a criminal act. It is generally thought that an insane person should be hospitalized rather than punished.

Youthful Offenders.   Most states, adopting the common law formula, hold that a child under 7 years of age does not have the mental capacity to commit a crime; one between 7 and 14 years may be proved to have criminal capacity; and one over 14 years has the same criminal capacity as an adult.

However, to protect people from having to bear the stigma of a criminal conviction for a youthful caper, all states have adopted some form of juvenile offender law. A youthful offender (depending on the state, usually someone under 16 to 21 years of age) accused of a criminal act normally is not charged with the commission of a specific crime but only with being a juvenile delinquent. If the charge is proved, the youth may be held in a juvenile detention center for a limited period and usually is treated as a person who requires help and guidance rather than punishment.

Insanity.   A person may be so mentally unsound because of disease, accident, alcohol, or drugs, as not to be legally responsible for what he or she does. Insanity as defined in criminal law is not the same as the mental condition which makes a person incapable of entering into a contract (see pp. 424 to 425) or incapable of making a valid will (see pp. 424 to 425).

A frequently used criminal law test of insanity is the M'Naghten rule, named after the accused person in an 1843 English case in which insanity was the issue. The M'Naghten rule (also known as the right and wrong test) is that an individual did not have the mental capacity to commit a crime if he or she suffered from such a defect of reason (1) as not to know what he or she was doing; or (2) if, knowing what he or she was doing, nonetheless did not know that the act was wrong. To preserve the integrity of our judicial system, the use of a finding of "guilty but insane," or "guilty but mentally incompetent" has been proposed. However, such a finding has opponents who assert that anyone who is insane cannot be guilty. Obviously, any test of sanity cannot be applied with precision, and psychiatrists who give expert testimony during criminal trials frequently express contrary opinions. Formerly, in federal cases when insanity was the defense, the government had to prove that the defendant was sane. However, the Comprehensive Crime Control Act of 1984 instead places upon the defendant the burden of proving insanity.

Determination of the mental capacity necessary to commit a criminal act is made even more complex in those states which permit an accused person to show that he or she, although not insane, had a diminished mental capacity when the criminal act occurred. If such a defense is proved in those states, the accused person usually is found guilty only of some lesser offense than the one charged. For example, for a person to be convicted of murder there must be proof that the act was intended. If diminished mental capacity is established, it may be impossible to prove intent, and the accused may be found guilty not of murder but only of the lesser homicide of voluntary manslaughter. The diminished capacity rule is the subject of the next case.

CASE 5.2   Commonwealth v. Walzack
360 A.2d 914 (Pa. 1976)

Facts: Walzack was tried for first degree murder—a willful, deliberate and premeditated killing. During the trial, Walzack admitted that he committed the fatal shooting and that he was sane. He offered, but was not permitted, to introduce the testimony of a psychiatrist to show that, as a result of a lobotomy (the surgical severing of a portion of the brain) which Walzack had undergone, he did not have sufficient mental capacity to form the specific intent required to establish first degree murder. Walzack was convicted of first degree murder. He appealed.

Question: Should diminished capacity be allowed as a defense to a specific intent crime such as first degree murder?

Answer: Yes. The conviction is reversed.

Reasoning: The defense of diminished capacity is not the same as insanity under the M'Naghten rule or the broader insanity test of irresistible impulse. Under those defenses, a person may avoid *all* criminal responsibility. When diminished responsibility is offered, the accused concedes a general criminal liability and claims only that he cannot be guilty of a crime of the *degree* charged.

The Commonwealth [Pennsylvania] must prove beyond a reasonable doubt each element of a crime charged. Where intent is an element, intent must be proved. Therefore, the defendant has the right, without pleading insanity, to establish that he does not have the mental capacity to form the specific intent essential to first degree murder. The psychiatrist's offered testimony was material and relevant and should have been allowed to be presented to the jury.

Criminal Intent.   To establish that an offense has been committed, it must be proved that the person accused of the act (the "actor") had an evil purpose or a blameworthy or person-endangering state of mind, identified by such words as "knowingly," "wrongfully," "corruptly," "willfully," "fraudulently," "intentionally," "maliciously," "feloniously," "negligently," or "wantonly." In general, for a person to be convicted of a criminal offense the wrongful act must have been accompanied by an unlawful intent.

Classification of Crimes by Degree of Wrongfulness   Criminal offenses are of two kinds: (1) those involving moral turpitude, that is, those involving a base or depraved act; and (2) those which do not involve moral turpitude but are wrong only because they are prohibited by law.

Moral Turpitude Offenses.   Most crimes involve moral turpitude. In these offenses the actor (or person who commits the crime) must have a criminal intent. These offenses include, but certainly are not limited to, such wrongs as murder, rape, arson, robbery, and larceny.

At this point it might be well to recognize that criminal negligence may also involve moral turpitude. Criminal negligence is a careless act resulting in injury or death which is so reckless that it reflects heedless indifference to the safety and rights of others. It is something more than the negligence which will support a tort action for damages as discussed in Chapter 4. An example of criminal negligence would be manufacturing and selling a baby's rattle without the testing which would ensure that its surface coating is safe for babies to ingest when, in fact, it is poisonous. Another example would be firing a gun in a residential area.

Prohibited Acts.   These are illegal acts (often relating to business conduct) which are not naturally evil, but which are prohibited because they violate laws enacted for the safety, health, or well-being of the community. The penal provisions of the Federal Food, Drug and Cosmetic Act and of the Truth in Lending Laws (discussed on pp. 81 and 732) are examples. Their violation does not involve moral turpitude, and offenders are punishable *without* proof of criminal intent. Assume, for instance, that John owns a bar in a state which, as a matter of public policy, makes it a criminal offense to sell liquor to minors. John knows that his bartender, Bill, occasionally sells liquor to minors, and John has instructed him to stop doing so. Nevertheless, Bill knowingly sells intoxicating liquor to a minor when the boss is away. Even though John was not present when the offense was committed, *both* he and Bill may be guilty of an offense arising out of the unlawful sale. The fact that John may be held guilty of something he did not do may seem harsh, but the law obligates him to make certain that his bar is run in a law-abiding manner. Our society takes this position because it is easier for the owner of a business to see that the public interest is protected by his or her employees than for the police to keep continuous watch over the manner in which the business is conducted.

Classification of Crimes by Degree of Punishment   When classified according to degree of permissible punishment, there are two categories of criminal offenses: felonies and misdemeanors. (Treason, a betraying or breach of allegiance, is a constitutional crime and usually is not included within the common categories of criminal acts.)

Felonies.   **Felonies** are all serious offenses for which society has authorized punishment (1) under federal law by imprisonment for more than 1 year, and (2) in most states by incarceration in a state prison rather than in a county jail. A fine may also be imposed upon conviction of a felony. In states which authorize the death sentence, certain felonies may be punishable by execution.

Misdemeanors.   A **misdemeanor** is a lesser crime, such as striking someone with the hand or stealing property worth an amount less than that required to constitute a felony (in most states less than $100). A misdemeanor is punishable by fine and possibly by imprisonment for no more than 1 year in other than a state prison.

An **infraction** is a minor wrong and in almost all states is not considered to be a criminal offense. Infractions involve such departures from community standards as minor traffic offenses and parking violations.

CRIMINAL PROCEDURE

Criminal procedure is the descriptive term for the various steps required to prosecute a person accused of having committed a crime. These procedures are entirely different from the civil law procedures discussed in Chapter 2 for the enforcement of contract rights or for collecting damages for injuries resulting from a tort.

Let us return to the assumed situation which opened this chapter, where Arthur broke into the Olympic warehouse and stole the stereo sets. Besides committing one or more torts against the Olympic Company, for which it may seek redress in a civil suit, Arthur violated at least one *public* law. Therefore, a criminal prosecution against him is brought by the *state* as plaintiff in its own name, not by Olympic, the victim of the crime. In the criminal case, Olympic will only be one of the witnesses for the prosecution.

Throughout the entire criminal process the accused person is presumed innocent until proven guilty, and his or her constitutional rights are carefully protected by the court. These rights are stated in Amendments Four, Five, and Six of the Constitution. Under these amendments, any person within the United States is protected from unreasonable searches and seizures (Fourth Amendment). No warrant can be issued without probable cause (Fourth Amendment), nor can a person be deprived of life, liberty, or property without due process of law (Fifth Amendment). An accused person is entitled to be informed of the accusation against him or her (Sixth Amendment); and if a felony is charged there must be an indictment by a grand jury, or an information (Fifth Amendment). The accused is entitled to a speedy public trial (Sixth Amendment), and cannot be compelled to be a witness against himself or herself (Fifth Amendment). Each accused person is entitled to be confronted by the witnesses against him or her (Sixth Amendment), and is entitled to compel his or her own witnesses to be present at the trial (Sixth Amendment). Furthermore, if a criminal trial ends in an acquittal, there cannot be another trial for the same offense (Fifth Amendment). The Constitution also assures an accused of the right to have the assistance of counsel (Sixth Amendment). If he or she cannot afford a lawyer, competent counsel will be designated to defend him or her, the costs being paid by the state. Most jurisdictions maintain a staff of **public defenders**, attorneys whose sole occupation is to defend those who cannot afford to pay for legal counsel.

Arrest An arrest, normally by a police officer, is the first step in criminal prosecution. The Supreme Court of the United States, in the landmark case of *Miranda v. State of Arizona* [384 U.S. 436 (1966)], held that an arrested person must not be questioned by the police unless first warned of his or her rights, among them the right to remain silent, to be represented by an attorney, and to have the attorney present during questioning. If the accused is not given these so-called "Miranda warnings" when he or she is taken into police custody, any statement (for example, a confession) he or she makes may not be used in evidence against the accused at trial. However, such a statement made by a person *not* in police custody may be used as evidence.

Except in unusual circumstances, an arrested person is entitled to be released on bail or on his or her "own recognizance." *Bail* is security, usually a sum of money or the obligation of a bonding company, given to guarantee that the accused will be present for trial. One's *own recognizance* is a personal assurance (promise) to be present for trial. The Comprehensive Crime Control Act of 1984 permits the denial of bail to federal defendants who are deemed a danger to society.

Prosecution To bring the accused to trial, the state must follow certain successive procedures.

Information or Indictment. To charge an individual with the commission of a felony, either the prosecuting (district) attorney files an **information**, or a grand jury brings an **indictment** against the accused. An information and an indictment are both formal written statements describing in detail the commission of a specific crime. If the offense is a misdemeanor, the prosecuting attorney files an information; there is no action by a grand jury in misdemeanor cases.

Arraignment. In an **arraignment**, a judicial officer reads the information or indictment to the accused, who then enters a plea either of guilty, not guilty, or (as permitted in most states) nolo contendere. **Nolo contendere**, although not technically a guilty plea, is an implied admission of guilt, the meaning of the words being, "I do not wish to contest" the accusation. This type of plea is frequently used by companies or individuals prominent in public life, since it is not such an admission of guilt that it may be used against the accused in any subsequent civil suit.

An arraignment is not a trial. If the accused pleads guilty or nolo contendere, the case is sent to a court which imposes an appropriate sentence. If the arraignment follows an indictment, and the accused pleads not guilty, the case is sent to the court for trial. But if the arraignment follows an information, a preliminary hearing is held since a grand jury has not determined that the accused probably committed the crime. At this time the prosecuting attorney presents evidence as to the commission of the crime. If the evidence establishes that there is reasonable cause to believe the accused committed the crime or crimes charged, the case is sent to the court for trial.

Trial. In the trial of a criminal case, rules as to what evidence may be presented to the jury are strictly followed. In order to convict, the jury must determine that the accused committed the criminal act charged while harboring the intent required by statute to be guilty of that particular offense. Criminal intent is almost always proven by inference; people are presumed to intend the natural consequences of their voluntary acts. So, if Barry secretly took a hand tool owned by his employer and pawned it, the jury, in Barry's trial for the crime of larceny, may presume that he had the intent to deprive the employer of its property permanently, a necessary ingredient of larceny.

The jury in a criminal case must determine *beyond a reasonable doubt* that the accused was guilty of the offense. This burden of proof is far greater than that applied in civil cases. In a civil trial the jury brings a verdict for the plaintiff or the defendant based only upon a *preponderance* of the evidence (greater weight or more convincing evidence). In a criminal case the jury must reach its verdict by a *unanimous* agreement of its members, while in a civil case the verdict may be based upon the concurrence of three-fourths of the jury, and in some jurisdictions an even smaller majority is permitted.

Criminal Penalties

When a jury has found an accused person guilty of a criminal offense, the next step is for the judge to impose a penalty (sentence) upon the accused. In imposing a sentence the judge exercises a good deal of discretion, but the punishment ordered must be within the limits fixed by law for that crime. Efforts to establish rules assuring uniformity of sentences imposed by different judges for similar criminal acts have not been very successful. The purpose of punishment, and therefore the kind and degree of punishment which fits the crime, have long been debated. A criminal penalty may be retributive, that is, intended "to make a criminal 'pay' for his or her crime"; or it may be preventive, that is, intended to restrict the individual from opportunity to commit other crimes; or the penalty may be intended to serve as an example to deter others from committing like offenses.

Let us return to Arthur and the Olympic warehouse and assume that Arthur has been tried and found guilty of stealing the stereo sets. We can expect that he will be sentenced to some term of confinement and perhaps pay a fine. In some circumstances the judge may then suspend the sentence in whole or in part, placing Arthur on probation. Arthur pays his fine (if one is imposed) *to the state* and not to Olympic, for in a criminal action no damages are awarded to the victim of an offense. Whether Arthur must pay damages to Olympic would be decided in a civil court if Olympic brings a civil suit against Arthur. However, a judge may order the sentence suspended if restitution (repayment) is made to the victim. Sometimes a judge, instead of sending the guilty person to jail, may simply sentence him or her to perform some public work. The Comprehensive Crime Control Act of 1984 phases out the granting of parole in the federal penal system.

If Arthur, the defendant, is found guilty, he may appeal to a higher court to reconsider his conviction, but a verdict of not guilty ends the case. In a civil action, either of the litigants may appeal a judgment of the court.

COMPUTER AND OTHER WHITE-COLLAR CRIMES

Certain criminal activities peculiar to the world of commerce have come to be known as business or white-collar crimes. It has been estimated that the public suffers losses of at least 40 billion dollars annually from white-collar crimes. Their direct cost to the public surpasses the combined cost of conventional crimes of larceny, robbery, burglary, and auto theft.

Losses suffered by companies because of white-collar crimes, and the resulting high cost of business insurance premiums are all ultimately passed on to the consumer. In the end it is we, the public, who pay the bill.

What Are White-Collar Crimes?

Neither the federal penal code nor state penal statutes characterize any criminal act as such as a business crime or as a white-collar crime. These are simply colloquial terms that, in general, characterize those illegal acts committed (1) by nonviolent means, (2) in relation to a legitimate occupation or endeavor, (3) by an individual or a firm, (4) to obtain a business or personal advantage.

White-collar crimes usually involve some sort of fraud, guile, misrepresentation, or evasion of laws designed to protect the public.

Computer Crimes

Computers handle the financial transactions of government, of practically all large business enterprises, and of a growing number of smaller ones. Some computers print out checks; others enter bank and savings and loan credits; or store trade secrets, accounting and financial information, and other valuable data which can be misused in the hands of people not entitled to possess it. The temptation to manipulate a computer for personal gain is heightened by the impersonality of the machine and the difficulty of detection, even by careful auditing. Thefts running into millions of dollars have been committed through computer manipulation. The Wells Fargo Bank of California in 1981 suffered a multimillion dollar loss by computer fraud. In another case a consultant used consumer codes to transfer $10.2 million from the Security Pacific Bank to a personal account he had set up in a Swiss bank. In the notorious Equity Funding case [*U.S. v. Weiner,* 578 F. 2d 757 (9th Cir. 1978)], a computer was programmed to make fraudulent printouts listing more than 50,000 insurance policies that had never actually been written. The Equity Funding insurance company, crediting itself with owning these nonexistent policies, sold them to unsuspecting insurance companies (which relied on the authentic appearance of the printouts) to spread the risk—normally a perfectly legitimate business transaction when the assets sold really exist. Here, however, where thousands of policies were merely the figment of the computer's masters' imaginations, the buying insurance companies were swindled out of millions of dollars when they bought nothing at all.

Rapid growth of computer use in businesses has been accompanied by an invasion of computers' privacy and misuse of information stored in computers. Because of this, the Comprehensive Crime Control Act of 1984 makes the improper accessing of a federal computer a federal offense. It has been said that no one knows how much computer "con artists" are raking in, but it is a fantastic amount. Federal officials estimate that the average loss in a bank robbery is $3200. A typical embezzlement by nonelectronic means comes to about $23,500. The average computer fraud is estimated at $340,000.

Other White-Collar Crimes

In a 1966 case [*American Cyanamid Co. v. Federal Trade Commission*, 363 F. 2d 757 (6th Cir.)] in a federal court, Judge Phillips, quoting from a Report of the House of Representatives, said, "It is impossible to frame definitions which embrace all unfair [business] practices. There is no limit to human inventiveness in this field. Even if all known unfair practices were specifically defined and prohibited, it would be at once necessary to begin all over again." The remainder of this chapter will briefly discuss a sampling of other white-collar crimes.

Bribery.   Attempting to influence a public servant to handle an official matter in a way that serves a private interest is *bribery*. The bribe may be intended, for example, to thwart official interference with an illicit activity, to secure a building permit, or to defeat or effect passage of an ordinance or statute. Even if the bribe is not accepted, and even if the intended recipient does not agree to perform the action sought, the person who made the corrupt offer may still be guilty of the crime of bribery.

Although payments in the form of bribes to officials may be a way of life in some foreign countries, bribery of government officials is contrary to the law of practically every country of the world. Because of the widespread bribery of foreign officials by U.S. businesses which came to light during the Watergate investigations, Congress in 1977 enacted the Foreign Corrupt Practices Act. It makes illegal giving anything of value to any foreign government official to influence an official act for business purposes. The penalties are severe.

Commercial Bribery.   Giving under-the-table payoffs to business people or their employees to gain an advantage over competitors is *commercial bribery*. Motives for such illegal acts may be, for example, to secure new business, cover up inferior products or services, obtain confidential information about competing bids, acquire secret information, or prevent work stoppages. Thus, to take trade away from a competitor, a business concern might induce an employee of a competing firm, by money or other gifts, to reveal the competitor's pricing schedules or other trade secrets; or a store manager might be bribed by a supplier not to stock a competing supplier's merchandise.

Commercial bribery is not recognized as a crime in all states. In those where it is not a crime, the injured company's only recourse is a civil suit against the offender for money damages, or for an injunction (a court order) against repetition of the act. There are some specific federal acts but no general federal laws punishing commercial bribery.

The following case expresses the views of one court in a state where commercial bribery is a crime.

CASE 5.3 North Carolina v. Brewer
129 S.E.2d 262 (N.C. 1963)

Facts: Brewer, who was employed by a company which manufactured signs, learned that the North Carolina State Highway Commission was purchasing highway signs. He offered to pay an employee of the Commission a sum of money if the employee would write specifications for the signs in such a way that Brewer's company would get the contracts. Brewer was convicted of violating North Carolina's commercial bribery statute. Brewer appealed, claiming that the law is unconstitutional.

Question: May commercial bribery be a criminal offense?

Answer: Yes. Conviction sustained.

Reasoning: Commercial bribery statutes are designed to prohibit an employee from being disloyal or unfaithful to his or her employer. The offense is committed without violence and usually there are no third-party witnesses. Therefore, it is difficult to prove that commercial bribery has occurred and few commercial bribery cases have reached the courts. Under the strenuous competitive conditions that now exist, *offering* a bribe lures an employee of another firm to assume conflicting interests—interests on behalf of the third party against the interests of the employer. *Accepting* such a bribe violates an employee's obligations to his or her employer. To assume such conflicting positions is contrary to accepted business practices and is harmful to the public at large. Sound public policy demands that there be laws prohibiting these actions and twenty-nine states have enacted commercial bribery statutes. The law is constitutional and should be upheld.

Consumer Frauds.   The law has a growing interest in consumer protection—that is, protecting the public against fraud by business concerns. Chapter 42 is devoted to that subject. We as consumers are so often the victims of business crimes that this type of crime has come to be called simply "consumer fraud." Increasingly, federal and state laws are being enacted to protect consumers from suppliers of goods and services who may take advantage of us. The following case illustrates a form of business crime commonly called "bait and switch."

CASE 5.4   People v. Block and Kleaver
427 N.Y.S.2d 133 (N.Y. 1980)

Facts: Defendant, Block and Kleaver, advertised beef for sale at prices lower than it had itself paid for the meat. When customers asked to buy the advertised meat they were shown fatty and discolored sides of beef. They were also shown better-looking, pre-trimmed meat at higher prices. This meat was represented as subject to less shrinkage and a better buy. Customers were thereby induced to purchase the more expensive beef. Defendant was found guilty of the offense of misleading advertising. The defendant appealed, claiming that the meat the customers actually purchased had not been misrepresented.

Question: May advertising one article with the intent to induce customers to buy another article constitute misleading advertising?

Answer: Yes. The conviction is sustained.

Reasoning: There is a sales practice known as "bait and switch advertising," "bait advertising," or "fictitious bargain claims." This practice consists of advertising a product at a very low price, then discouraging the customer from purchasing the advertised article, and lastly, inviting the customer to buy a more expensive product than the one advertised—that is, to "switch."

When a company advertises, it impliedly states that it wants to sell the product advertised. Here the initial advertisement was false because the store did not intend to induce the purchase of the advertised meat but, instead, intended to induce those who responded to the ad to buy some entirely different product at a higher price. The fact that the defendant made no false representation about the meat to which the customers were "switched" or that this meat was worth the money the customers paid for it, does not negate the false advertising used to accomplish the sale.

False Claims against the Government. To discourage filing a false claim against the federal government (a white-collar crime), the **False Claims Act** was originally enacted in 1863. A violator of the act may be subject to both civil and criminal penalties. The following two hypothetical cases illustrate the wide range of situations in which false claims may be made:

The Able Company has a contract with the government to supply engines manufactured with all new parts. But the company delivers engines with bearings that have been re-worked to be "as good as new." The Able Company bills the government at the price for engines with all new parts.

The Baker Company has a contract with the government which provides that the government will repay the company for all labor performed. The company falsely pads its payroll.

Federal Food, Drug, and Cosmetic Act Offenses.   We as consumers have no control over the quality of the food nor the effectiveness of the medicines we buy. To protect our health, Congress enacted the **Federal Food, Drug and Cosmetic Act**, administered by the Food and Drug Administration. Violations of the Food and Drug Administration's regulations are business crimes. A first offense is punishable as a misdemeanor, but if the offender is again convicted of any violation of the act, or if there was an intent to defraud or mislead, the crime is a felony.

The very liberal interpretation given to the criminal provisions of the Federal Food, Drug and Cosmetic Act is shown by the next case.

CASE 5.5   United States v. Hohensee
243 F.2d 367 (3rd Cir. 1957)

Facts: Hohensee was the president of El Rancho Adolphus Products, Inc., which manufactured and sold health foods. Hohensee gave lectures in Phoenix, Arizona, and distributed literature in which he recommended Adolphus peppermint tea for many different complaints from gallstones, high blood pressure, and tuberculosis to tapeworms. The lectures were given some weeks *after* the Adolphus tea had been shipped from Scranton, Pennsylvania, to Phoenix. When the packages of tea arrived, they were labeled only as "a delicious table beverage." Hohensee was convicted of having shipped in interstate commerce misbranded products intended to be used as a drug. He appealed because the statements as to the tea's use were not made until *after* the tea had already entered interstate commerce.

Question: Should the Federal Food, Drug and Cosmetic Act be given a strict or liberal interpretation?

Answer: A liberal interpretation. Conviction sustained.

Reasoning: The Federal Act imposes criminal penalties in order to regulate activities that are dangerous to the public welfare. Exceptions from the Act for good faith ignorance or for technical reasons should not be allowed.

The literature and statements of the defendant were designed to make users of the tea believe that it had medicinal properties, in other words, that it was a drug. The fact that the tea was shipped in interstate commerce *before* those statements were made is only a technical objection to the enforcement of the Act's provisions and wholly irrelevant when the purpose of the defendant's entire transaction is considered. The shipment of the tea and the description of its uses must be considered as an integrated transaction.

Violations of Securities Laws.   The issuance, sale, and purchase of securities (stocks and bonds) furnish a fertile field for white-collar crimes. Securities offenses involve fraudulent schemes to purchase or sell stocks or bonds, or the intentional failure to disclose vital information which an average investor would want to know before entering into a transaction. For example, Isabel, a stockbroker, breaks the law if she fails to tell a prospective customer that she (or her firm) has a financial interest in the company whose stock she is "pushing." Or, assume that John, a company director, knows that a medicine his firm manufactures is about to be withdrawn from the market because it produces harmful side effects. Knowing that the price of his company's stock will fall when news of the withdrawal of the highly profitable product is released, John sells his own stock in the company. Such a stock sale, based upon inside information, is illegal.

Monopolies and Antitrust Offenses.   A business that fixes prices in agreement with its competitors or engages in monopolistic practices or other restraints on commerce would unlawfully get away with charging the public unreasonably high prices. For example, it would break the law if several competing companies whose products dominate the market meet and agree among themselves what prices they will charge; or if each agreed to sell its products only in a prearranged area of the country.

Penalties for violating antitrust laws may be severe. Damaged parties may secure triple damages and litigation costs in civil suits. Not only may fines be imposed upon the corporations involved, but upon individual wrongdoers, such as company managers, as well.

Larceny and Embezzlement.   Any consideration of white-collar crimes must recognize that a business may also be the *victim* of criminal offenses. Computer offenses, discussed above, frequently are directed by employees against employers. Larceny and embezzlement by employees from their employers are all too common. **Larceny** is wrongfully taking the property of another with the intent to deprive the owner permanently of its possession. **Embezzlement** is wrongfully withholding the property of another which a person came into possession of rightfully.

In many firms the internal theft of cash, tools, spare parts, office supplies, and other materials is a very real business problem. All consumers pay for these white-collar crimes because the companies affected include amounts sufficient to cover their losses in the prices they charge.

There is almost no limit to the manner in which white-collar crimes can be committed. When a salesperson charges a friend or relative less than the correct price for an article, when a salesperson fails to ring up a sale and pockets the payment made by a customer, when a supermarket butcher takes home meats, or when an employee inflates an expense account, all these so-called "little things" are white-collar crimes.

SUMMARY

A crime is an unlawful act punishable by the state. For an act to be a crime it must be committed by a mentally competent person having the requisite criminal intent. It involves more than the mere intention to do a wrong or to prepare to do one.

A person under 7 years of age or one who is insane, as defined under criminal law, does not have sufficient mental capacity to commit a crime.

A criminal act that involves moral turpitude is a felony. To be convicted of a felony the actor must, at trial, be determined to have had a criminal intent. Upon conviction he or she may be imprisoned in a state prison. Lesser crimes are called misdemeanors, and conviction of a misdemeanor does not justify imprisonment in a state prison. An offense which is a wrong merely because it is prohibited does not involve moral turpitude, and proof of criminal intent is not required for conviction.

The process by which a person is convicted and punished for the commission of a crime is called criminal procedure. First, there is an arrest, followed by a prosecution in the name of the state, begun either by an indictment by a grand jury or an information by the prosecuting attorney. Then, at an arraignment the accused pleads either guilty, not guilty, or nolo contendere to the offense charged. If there is probable cause to believe the accused has committed the offense, a trial follows. At the trial the accused is presumed innocent until proven guilty beyond a reasonable doubt. One found guilty can appeal the verdict, but the state may not appeal a verdict of not guilty.

White-collar crime is the popular name given to nonviolent crimes committed in relation to a legitimate business by individuals or business concerns. White-collar crimes take many forms. Among them are computer crimes, bribery, consumer frauds, false claims against the government, Federal Food, Drug, and Cosmetic Act offenses, and securities, monopolies, and antitrust offenses.

REVIEW QUESTIONS

1. Using ordinary language instead of the technical terms of law books, would it be correct to say that "every immoral act is a crime"?

2. What is the M'Naghten rule?

3. Give an example of a criminal act for which a person can be imprisoned in a state prison even though he or she had no intent to commit the crime charged.

4. What is the distinction between a felony and a misdemeanor?

5. What is an infraction?

6. What is the distinction between an indictment and an information?

7. (a) What different pleas may a person make to a criminal charge? (b) What is the difference between them?

8. Assume that a person is tried for a criminal offense and that, although the proof is clear that the accused is guilty, the jury returns a verdict of not guilty. If you are the prosecuting attorney what do you do next?

9. What kinds of criminal acts may be called white-collar crimes?

10. Give three illustrations of white-collar crimes in which a computer is involved.

11. Give illustrations of other white-collar crimes in which a business is (a) the victim; (b) the culprit.

12. Distinguish between: (a) bribery and commercial bribery; (b) larceny and embezzlement.

CASE PROBLEMS

1. Gerdine bought and sold used cars. Reuben left his car with Gerdine to be sold. Some time later Reuben noticed that his car was no longer on Gerdine's sales lot and demanded payment or return of his car. Gerdine said that a customer had the car "on approval" and refused to pay Reuben for the car. Reuben brought a civil action against Gerdine to recover its value. While that action was pending, Gerdine was arrested and charged with the theft of the car. Should the district attorney attempt to have the civil action withdrawn so that the criminal action can go forward? Discuss.

2. Sisneros drank a great quantity of liquor, becoming so drunk that he staggered, but he was coherent, understood questions, and followed directions. He broke into a warehouse and was apprehended there. He was charged with burglary of a nondwelling, an offense that involves breaking and entry of a building with the intent to commit larceny. Sisneros claimed he could not be guilty of that offense because drunkenness prevented him from having a specific intent. Was he correct in stating that drunkenness in itself prevents a person from forming a specific intent? Why?

3. Assume that Congress enacts a law which makes engaging in a racketeering enterprise illegal, permits guilt to be established without proof of criminal intent, and authorizes imprisonment in a federal prison for anyone found guilty. Horace, charged with a violation of this law, claims that he cannot be guilty because, to be guilty of a criminal act, an accused must have a criminal intent, and therefore the law is unconstitutional. Is Horace's statement correct? Why or why not?

4. A fight took place which resulted in a killing. Philbrick, one of the participants in the fight, went to the hospital for treatment of superficial cuts. While in the treatment room he blurted out to a policeman guarding another patient that he, Philbrick, thought he had shot a man. This led to Philbrick's arrest. He was charged with commission of a homicide. Discuss the statement Philbrick made to the police officer with relation to the Miranda rule.

5. Mrs. Healy was a member of the town board. A man named Feld had lunch at her home and left an envelope containing $500 at his plate. No mention of money was made at the luncheon. Some time later Feld asked Mrs. Healy to introduce a resolution concerning zoning at the town board meeting. She refused to do so and soon returned the money to Feld. Was Feld guilty of bribing a public official? Why or why not?

PART THREE

CONTRACTS

CHAPTER 6

INTRODUCTION TO THE LAW OF CONTRACTS

The contract is one of the most important legal devices ever developed in the quest for economic security and a stable society. Contracts constitute "binding arrangements for the future," and it is largely by means of such arrangements that the processes of production, exchange, and distribution are carried on in a free enterprise economy. Individuals enter into contracts when, for example, they buy a home, visit the dentist, or buy an automobile on the installment plan. Business firms enter into contracts with suppliers of raw materials and parts; with banks, utility companies, and other service institutions; and with employees, investors, and customers. Although governments have considerable power to command obedience, much of their work is accomplished by means of contracts entered into voluntarily.

Freedom of individuals and organizations to contract as they think best is one of the basic elements of a free enterprise system. However, freedom of contract is not absolute. Courts and legislatures alike curtail freedom of contract when in their view the public good so requires. Courts are especially likely to control contract provisions where there is considerable inequality of bargaining power between the people involved, as, for example, there often is between adults and minors, creditors and borrowers, sellers and consumers. As our study of contract law proceeds, we shall encounter numerous examples of limitations on freedom of contract.

NATURE AND IMPORTANCE OF CONTRACT LAW

Contract law is a body of rules regarding formation, avoidance, discharge, and enforcement of contracts. A major purpose of contract law is to provide guidance for persons interested in forming binding contracts. A second major purpose of contract law is to assure that contracts properly formed are binding on and enforceable by the parties. To carry out this second purpose, the law provides procedures by which a wronged party can force compliance with the terms of a binding contract or can obtain damages when there is lack of compliance.

Contract law deserves attention not only because it governs contractual arrangements but also because it is basic to other areas of law. Much of the law governing sales of goods, commercial paper ("negotiable instruments"), agency, partnerships, corporations, landlord and tenant, and so on is but the application of general contract principles to specialized situations. An understanding of the concepts, principles, and technical vocabulary presented in the chapters on contracts will help you understand other areas of business law.

NATURE OF CONTRACTS

Meaning of Contract

There are various definitions of contract given by legal writers. For our purposes, **contract** may be defined as a promise or set of promises that the courts will enforce.

Widespread breach of business or commercial promises can create serious economic instability. For example, manufacturers rely on commitments from suppliers to deliver a steady stream of raw materials. The refusal by one supplier to honor a promise of delivery would cause serious disruption to the entire manufacturing process. To reduce economic uncertainty and to protect a person's reasonable expectations, the law makes certain kinds of commercial promises legally enforceable.

Meaning of Promise

Since promises are a vital part of contracting, let us consider the legal meaning of promise. A **promise** may be defined as a manifestation of *commitment* to act or to refrain from acting in a specified way. The person who makes a promise is the **promisor**. The one to whom the promise is made is the **promisee**.

The above definition stresses the expectations of the promisee and the need for stability. When appropriate language is used by a promisor the promisee expects performance and may expend time or money relying on that expectation. For example, suppose a manufacturer negotiates with a supplier for a particular part. The supplier says "I will deliver the part within 30 days." The manufacturer is entitled to rely on such language of commitment in making plans to use the part in the manufacturing process.

A promise may be expressed either in language or in conduct. When expressed in language, the word "promise" is not always necessary. Expressions such as "I will pay," "I hereby offer to pay," and "It is understood that I am to pay" are promises to pay.

A promise may be inferred from conduct. For example, at an auction, a promise to pay may be inferred from the bidder's act of raising a hand or a card. This is so regardless of any secret intention of the bidder not to pay. In dealing with others, people are usually entitled to rely on external manifestations of intention and are not bound by unexpressed internal intentions.

Requirements for a Contract

Legal writers have stated the requirements for a contract in various ways. It is helpful at the outset if we focus on the purpose or objective of people entering into contracts. The usual objective of contracting parties is a bargained-for exchange: money for goods, services for money, goods for services, and so on. Thus, ordinarily a contract involves a transaction in which one person performs an act or makes a promise in exchange for a return performance or promise.

Typically, a period of negotiation between the promisor and promisee precedes formation of a contract. The parties may "dicker" back and forth over price and terms until they reach a final agreement. In contract law an **agreement** is defined as a manifestation of mutual assent reached through offer and acceptance. In addition to mutual assent, the law requires that the promise or promises must be supported by consideration. Other requirements have been stated by various legal writers and we can list the requirements for a contract as follows: (1) offer; (2) acceptance; (3) consideration; (4) parties with legal capacity to contract; and (5) a legal object. Each of these requirements is discussed in detail in the following chapters.

In succeeding chapters we will see that some contracts which appear to meet these requirements are not enforceable, however. There are various defenses to enforcement that may be asserted by one party or the other to the contract. For example, a person may enter into an agreement because of fear, unfair persuasion, or deception on the part of the other person. One party, or both parties, may be laboring under a mistaken assumption that affects the bargaining process. Chapter 10 discusses the various grounds for avoidance of a contract. A person may refuse to perform his or her part of a contract because it is the type of contract that the law states must be evidenced by a writing. This defense is discussed in Chapter 12.

Contracts of Adhesion

A traditional assumption underlying contract law is that each of the parties to a contract has sufficient bargaining power that one cannot take undue advantage of the other. In many situations involving contracts, the negotiating parties are so well matched in terms of bargaining power that each can look out for his or her own interests. Often, however, one party, usually the borrower or buyer, has no meaningful choice in some or all the terms of the contract. These terms are usually embodied in a standard-form contract, called a **contract of adhesion**, or **adhesion contract**. Rather than permit the form to be varied, the firm imposing it will simply not deal with anyone who will not accept its terms. Most contracts for consumer goods, insurance, mortgages, automobiles, and a host of other goods and services are contracts of adhesion.

Standard-form contracts are essential to businesses that market large quantities of mass-produced goods or services. Such businesses could not function efficiently on a large scale if the terms of each transaction had to be negotiated individually. Transaction costs for inexpensive goods and services could become prohibitive. The insurance industry, which must be able to limit and calculate risk, would be unable to do so if the terms of insurance contracts varied with each customer. Yet, people upon whom contracts of adhesion are imposed are vulnerable to exploitation. Most consumers sign standard-form contracts without reading all the provisions. Often, important terms are in small print or on the back of the form. Because of the lack of equal bargaining power and true mutual assent in adhesion contracts, some provisions of such contracts may be unenforceable. Chapter 11 discusses adhesion contracts and points out that if a provision of the contract is oppressive, the court will strike down that provision as being unconscionable or contrary to public policy.

CLASSIFICATION OF CONTRACTS

Contracts may be classified on various bases. The following paragraphs describe some common types of contracts and their characteristics. Note that a given contract may fit into more than one category.

Formal and Informal Contracts

A **formal** contract is one to which the law gives special effect because of the form used in creating it. An example of a formal contract is a negotiable instrument such as a check. To create a negotiable instrument, a person must use a particular form or style of language. A negotiable instrument has legal characteristics which differ from those of ordinary contracts. For example, a negotiable instrument is freely transferable and is used as a substitute for money. (Negotiable instruments are discussed in Chapters 30 to 33.)

Informal contracts are those for which the law does not require a particular set of formalities. The five requirements for a contract must be met, but the parties to an informal (ordinary) contract may use any style of language they please. The contract may be oral or may even result from conduct, in the absence of a special statute. Many cases in the coming chapters involve contracts that resulted from the exchange of letters or telegrams. Often the parties were not represented by lawyers and did not realize that a contract could result from such an informal exchange. Informal contracts are sometimes called "simple" contracts, although they may in fact be very complicated. Most contracts we enter into are informal.

Unilateral and Bilateral Contracts

A **unilateral contract** is one in which only one party (promisor) makes a promise. Ordinarily, the promisor promises to pay money if the promisee performs an act. For example, "I'll pay you $5 if you mow my lawn on Friday," is an offer for a unilateral contract. The offer can be accepted by the promisee's mowing the lawn. Prior to the mowing of the lawn there is no contract, but merely an offer by the promisor. Thus, the promisor has no recourse if the promisee chooses not to mow the lawn.

In contrast, a **bilateral contract** is one in which both parties make promises. For example, suppose Hilda says to Ralph, "I will pay you $5 to mow my lawn. Will you mow it Friday for that price?" Hilda has made an offer for a bilateral contract because she wants a return promise from Ralph. If Ralph wishes to accept, he need only let Hilda know that he will mow the lawn on Friday. To Hilda, such a bilateral contract is more desirable than a unilateral contract. She has a commitment from Ralph that is enforceable. She can make plans in advance. Another advantage to her is that Ralph cannot raise the price. If Hilda makes an offer for a unilateral contract, she must wait until Friday to learn if Ralph will accept and mow the lawn for $5, or whether he will demand a higher price before mowing the lawn. To Ralph, the benefit of a bilateral contract is that Hilda is committed to pay him for mowing the lawn. If Hilda makes an offer for a unilateral contract she could change her mind before Friday and revoke the offer.

In analyzing a contract problem of this nature, it should be noted that the promisor determines whether the offer is unilateral or bilateral. The promisor indicates what is wanted from the promisee—an act or a promise to act. Thus, if Hilda offers to pay Ralph $5 if he mows the lawn on Friday, Ralph cannot create a contract by promising to mow the lawn. Hilda made an offer for a unilateral contract and Ralph cannot convert it into an offer for a bilateral contract.

Executory and Executed Contracts

An **executory contract** is one that is yet to be performed. Suppose Omar says to Mary, "I'll pay you $5 to mow my lawn. Will you mow it tomorrow?" Mary says "Yes." Omar and Mary have entered into a bilateral contract. However, the contract is executory because neither party to it has carried out the promised performance. The contract remains executory until the lawn is mowed and the $5 is paid.

An **executed** contract is one that has been performed. There are two types of executed contracts: partially executed and fully executed. If Mary mows the lawn and Omar pays the $5, the contract is *fully executed* (performed). If Mary mows the lawn but Omar fails to pay, the contract is *partially executed.* The contract could also be said to be *partially executory,* since one party has performed but the other has not.

Express and Implied Contracts

An **express contract** is one in which the terms of the contract are stated in words, either written or spoken. An **implied contract** (sometimes called "implied-in-fact") is one in which the terms of the contract are wholly or partly inferred from conduct or surrounding circumstances. When Jane, on passing a market where she has an account, picks up a bag of oranges marked "98 cents," holds up the bag, and waits until the clerk nods, a promise to pay 98 cents is implied by the conduct of the parties. In legal effect there is no difference between an express and an implied contract. They differ merely in the manner in which assent is manifested. In the above example Jane cannot refuse to pay for the oranges by asserting that she did not "expressly" promise to pay for them.

QUASI CONTRACTS

Nature and Elements of Quasi Contracts

Quasi contracts (sometimes called "implied-in-law" contracts) are not contracts at all; they are obligations imposed by law to prevent unjust enrichment of one person at another's expense. The obligation is created by law, not by mutual assent, and in fact is often imposed contrary to one's wishes.

Suppose, for example, a homeowner requests Ajax Company to deliver heating oil to the house. By mistake, Ajax delivers the oil next door. The neighbor uses the oil but refuses to pay Ajax. To prevent "unjust enrichment" Ajax may recover the price of the oil from the neighbor.

To recover in a lawsuit for quasi contract, the plaintiff must prove four elements: (1) the plaintiff conferred a benefit on the defendant, (2) the plaintiff expected to be paid for the benefit, (3) the plaintiff was not an intermeddler, and (4) to allow the defendant to retain the benefit conferred without compensating the plaintiff would result in unjust enrichment.

Recovery under Quasi Contract

Quasi-contract recovery is available in a wide variety of situations. Two parties may negotiate a contract which turns out to be unenforceable for one or more reasons. If one party has begun performance and conferred a benefit on the other, it would be unjust to allow retention of the benefits without compensation. The benefits received by the defendant could be money, property, or services rendered.

There are occasions when one person will confer benefits on another by mistake. For example, suppose Ben pays Alice, whom he mistakes for his creditor, Carla. If Alice keeps the money, it would constitute unjust enrichment. To prevent this result, the law allows debtor Ben to recover payment under quasi-contractual principles.

There are situations where the courts deny quasi-contract recovery although the defendant receives a benefit. If the plaintiff did not reasonably expect to be paid for the services or property, the court will deny recovery. For example, a physician who treats a member of his immediate family ordinarily would not be allowed quasi-contract recovery for services rendered. An intermeddler, one who tried to force benefits upon another, would not be allowed quasi-contract recovery. For example, suppose Jenny leaves her car at a service station for an oil change. When she returns, the manager states that the car has also been given a tune up. The station would not be allowed to recover in quasi contract for the benefits conferred.

Ordinarily, for a plaintiff to avoid being characterized as an intermeddler he or she must prove that the defendant knowingly and voluntarily accepted benefits from the plaintiff. However, one situation where quasi contract is applied without such proof involves emergency care. For example, suppose a physician comes upon an unconscious person lying on the highway and renders emergency medical services. The physician would be entitled to recover in quasi contract.

The amount of recovery in quasi contract is the reasonable value of services rendered or property expended (money or goods). Thus, the physician above is entitled to the customary rate in the community for the emergency procedures performed.

The following case illustrates liability for services rendered during and after an emergency.

CASE 6.1   Nursing Care Services, Inc. v. Dobos
380 So. 2d 516 (Fla. App. 1980)

Facts: Mary Dobos, defendant, became seriously ill and was hospitalized. Her doctor ordered around-the-clock nursing care. The hospital called upon the plaintiff, Nursing Care Services, Inc., to provide the services in the hospital and, following her release, at Mrs. Dobos' home. She refused to pay plaintiff for the services, arguing that she never signed a written contract nor orally agreed to be liable. She thought Medicare would take care of the payment. The trial court denied quasi-contract recovery to plaintiff, stating that there was no evidence Mrs. Dobos knew she would be responsible for the services rendered. Plaintiff appealed.

Question: Is Mrs. Dobos liable for the value of services rendered for her benefit without her consent or request?

Answer: Yes. The plaintiff is not an intermeddler and may recover for emergency care while the defendant was hospitalized. The defendant is also liable for the at-home care since she was aware of the services and readily accepted the benefits conferred.

Reasoning: The court stated that the "emergency aid rule" covered services rendered without the defendant's knowledge or consent when necessary to prevent serious bodily harm or pain, and it was impossible for the defendant to give consent. It is unclear whether Mrs. Dobos, during the period of in-hospital care, understood or intended that compensation be paid. Her condition was grave. She had been placed in an intensive care unit. Under the circumstances the services fall within the emergency aid rule. Mrs. Dobos acceptance of the at-home care falls within the usual rules of quasi contract. It is no defense that she believed the cost of services would be paid by Medicare.

The case was remanded to the trial court with instructions to enter a judgment for the plaintiff in the sum of $3,723.90 plus interest and court costs.

SUMMARY

By means of contracts, individuals and organizations make binding arrangements for the future. Freedom of people to contract as they think best is one of the basic elements of a free enterprise system, but courts and legislatures curtail freedom of contract when they think the public good so requires.

Contract law is a body of rules and procedures regarding the formation, avoidance, discharge, and enforcement of contracts. The two major purposes of contract law are to provide guidance in forming binding contracts, and to assure that contracts properly formed are binding on and enforceable by the parties.

Most people think of a contract as a bargained-for exchange. Requirements for a contract are offer and acceptance, consideration, parties with legal capacity to contract, and a legal object.

Much of the discussion of contracts in this book presupposes parties of roughly equivalent bargaining power who can fend for themselves when negotiating a contract. However, there is a vast number of contracts, called "contracts of adhesion," in which one of the parties has no meaningful choice regarding some or all terms of the contract. Contracts of adhesion serve legitimate economic functions and are usually enforced despite the weaker party's inability to bargain some of the terms. Yet, people upon whom contracts of adhesion are imposed are vulnerable to exploitation and are therefore given protection by the law.

There are various types of contracts, the significance of which will become more apparent in later chapters of this book. Quasi contracts are not contracts at all. They are obligations imposed by law to prevent unjust enrichment of one person at another person's expense.

REVIEW QUESTIONS

1. (a) Why is the contract of great importance to individuals and business firms? To a free enterprise economy? (b) Give examples of situations where restricting freedom of contract might be necessary.

2. What are the two major purposes of contract law?

3. John Doe's Aunt Martha invited John to a family reunion, promising to serve an expensive tropical fruit which was John's favorite. John promised to attend but did not arrive. Do you think John would be liable for breach of contract? Explain.

4. (a) Explain the meaning of "promise" as used in the law of contracts. (b) Define promisor. (c) Define promisee. (d) Give an example of a promise expressed by conduct.

5. What requirements must a bargained-for exchange ordinarily meet in order to constitute a contract?

6. What is a contract of adhesion?

7. On September 1, Seller and Buyer signed a written agreement which provides that Seller is to deliver certain specified merchandise on September 20 and that Buyer is to pay the specified price on or before October 10. Seller delivers the merchandise as promised. It is October 5 and Buyer has not yet paid for it. Is the contract: (a) Formal or informal? (b) Bilateral or unilateral? (c) Executory or executed? (d) Express or implied? Justify each answer.

8. (a) Quasi contracts are not contracts at all. Explain. (b) What is the underlying purpose of the law of quasi contracts? (c) Give examples of situations where quasi-contract principles would apply. (d) List the four elements required for quasi-contractual recovery.

CASE PROBLEMS

1. Warner, an unemployed woman on welfare, had a checking account with Citibank. The balance in the account was $30. The bank, which was supposed to credit the account of another of its depositors, mistakenly credited Warner's account with $23,715. Upon receiving a bank statement dated January 2 showing a balance of $23,655 in her account, Warner wrote checks exceeding $125,000. The bank honored some of the checks, but it was not until March 4 that it became aware of its mistake and transferred Warner's then remaining balance to its rightful owner. The bank sued to recover $10,446 for checks which were improperly paid out. Warner asserted that she believed the money had been deposited in her account by the sponsor of one of the contests she regularly entered, although she had never been notified by anyone of such a windfall. She also asserted that she relied to her detriment upon the negligent acts of the bank. Is Warner liable in quasi contract for the $10,446? Explain the reason (or reasons) for your answer.

2. David Johnson suffered a stroke while on the job and was hospitalized. He entered Doctor's Memorial Hospital and received treatment until his death. Prudential, under an employees' group health insurance policy, paid the hospital $5857, leaving a balance owed of $2004. Viola Johnson, the surviving widow, filed a claim against Aetna for workers' compensation death benefits. According to a compromise settlement, Aetna paid the hospital $7196. The hospital then refunded the overpayment of $5192 to Prudential. Viola claimed that the refund should have been paid to her, and she sued the hospital in quasi contract for the amount of the overpayment. Is Viola entitled to the $5192 overpayment received by the hospital? Explain reason(s).

3. Davis was a salesperson working for Brodie on a commission basis. There was no written contract, but it was understood that he would receive commissions on sales made to customers in his assigned territory. Davis discovered that on many of his invoices his customer numbers had been crossed out and changed to the house cash sales number or to a number representing a salesperson other than himself. Davis filed an action in quasi contract for commissions not paid on about 400 sales and received a judgment for $6195. Brodie appealed, arguing that recovering a payment *made* is not the same as recovering a payment *withheld*. Should the judgment for Davis be upheld? Why or why not?

CHAPTER 7

OFFER

In order to have a contract there must be an agreement, that is, a manifestation of mutual assent, reached through offer and acceptance. **Manifestation of mutual assent** is an outward expression of agreement by words or acts.

The process of reaching an agreement normally begins when one person, the "offeror," makes an offer to another person, the "offeree." The offeree may accept the offer as presented, or may make a counterproposal. Often the parties dicker back and forth over the terms of the proposed contract before reaching final agreement. Thus, there may be a series of "counteroffers" or "conditional acceptances" submitted by both parties. The present chapter deals with offer and counteroffer; Chapter 8 deals with acceptance.

NATURE OF OFFER

Meaning of Offer

An **offer** is a communication by which the **offeror** confers upon the **offeree** a legal power to accept the offer and thereby to create a contract. Usually an offer does two things:

1. It expresses or implies a promise by the offeror to do or refrain from doing some stated act.
2. It requests from the offeree a return promise of performance, or an act.

If the offeror wants a return promise from the offeree (e.g., promise to pay) the offer is for a bilateral contract. If the offeree is requested to perform an act (e.g., mow the lawn) the offer is for a unilateral contract.

Requirements for an Offer

To be a legally sufficient offer, a proposal must meet four requirements: (1) It must contain language of commitment; (2) it must be made with serious intent, or appear to be so made; (3) it must be reasonably definite and complete; and (4) it must be communicated to the offeree.

Language of Commitment. As stated previously, an offer to enter into a contract contains a promise by the offeror to do or refrain from doing some stated act. A promise involves an undertaking or commitment (e.g., "I will buy your car for $3000). Often the parties will exchange communications over a period of time, and it is necessary to analyze each communication to determine if the offeror's language was legally sufficient to constitute an offer. An offer must contain a promise or some other language of commitment.

Language of commitment must be carefully distinguished from statements of intention, negotiatory statements, and invitations to submit offers. Suppose, for example, that Alice says to Ben, "I am going to sell my camera for $100," and Ben replies, "I'll take it; here's the $100." Is there a contract? No, because a reasonable person would conclude that Alice's statement was not a promise. It was nothing more than a statement of fact. Reasonably interpreted, the statement means: "It is my present *intention* to make an offer at some time in the future."

Statements which are not in themselves proposals of conduct (promises) but preliminary to them are called *negotiatory statements* to distinguish them from offers. People use negotiatory statements for a variety of purposes—for example, to sound out the other person before making an offer, to maneuver him or her into making the first commitment, or to invite bids. Thus, a car owner does not make an offer by saying, "My car is worth $3000," or, "I should get at least $3000 for my car." The following statement would be an offer: "I will sell you my car for $3000 cash."

Circulars, catalogs, newspaper advertisements, posters, and price tags are usually mere *invitations to submit offers*. There are at least three reasons why such items usually are not offers: (1) Ordinarily, the items do not contain words of promise. (2) These items are addressed to the public and, if considered to be offers, the number of people who accept could exceed the quantity of goods for sale. (3) It is believed that the sellers ought to be able to choose those with whom they wish to contract. However, suppose that a newspaper advertisement reads, "To the first ten customers taking advantage of this offer we will sell a Model X Sure-View Television for $199.50 cash." A court would probably conclude that the advertisement was an offer, since it has three features ordinarily lacking in advertisements for the sale of goods: (1) It professes to be an offer ("this offer"). This feature by itself is of little significance, but when considered in connection with other features of the advertisement, the word "offer" assumes added significance. (2) The advertisement contains language of commitment ("we will sell"). (3) The advertisement specifies a quantity ("ten").

In deciding controversies, the courts will of course consider the language used. But words of themselves are not determinative. Thus, "We quote you a price of $4.50" usually means no more than a willingness to consider an offer to buy at $4.50; but under certain circumstances "quote" may constitute an offer to sell at the quoted price, as in the Fairmount Glass Works case (see Case 7.1).

A communication addressed to a group or to the public at large is less likely to be an offer than is one addressed to an individual. Included in this category are advertisements made by individuals and by government agencies soliciting bids from contractors or subcontractors. The advertiser has not made an offer because he or she has made no promise (i.e., commitment) to award a contract to any particular person, such as the low bidder. Each bidder promises to perform at a certain price and is thus an offeror. The one who advertises becomes the offeree and may accept whichever offer (bid) he or she wishes. Unlike advertisements, notices of reward, although addressed to the public, usually contain an express or implied promise to pay money and are held to be offers.

An advertisement of a public auction usually is not an offer but an invitation for offers. Again, the advertiser ordinarily does not promise to do any particular thing. A bidder at the auction makes an implied promise to pay a certain sum by raising his or her hand. Thus, the bidder is the offeror and the auctioneer is the offeree. An acceptance occurs when the auctioneer strikes the gavel. Prior to acceptance the bid may be withdrawn or the auctioneer may withdraw the article. However, occasionally an auction is advertised to be "without reserve." An auction without reserve means that a commitment is made not to withdraw an article and the auctioneer must accept the highest bid.

The following case illustrates that under proper circumstances a price quote may be considered an offer.

CASE 7.1   **Fairmount Glass Works v. Grunden-Martin Woodenware Co.**
51 S.W. 196 (Ky. 1899)

Facts: Grunden-Martin received the following letter:
"Fairmount, Ind., April 23, 1895. Gentlemen: Replying to your favor of April 20, we quote you Mason fruit jars, complete, in one-dozen boxes, delivered East St. Louis, Ill.: Pints $4.50, quarts $5.00, half gallons $6.50, per gross, for immediate acceptance, and shipment not later than May 15, 1895; sixty days acceptance, or 2 off, cash in ten days. Yours truly, Fairmount Glass Works."

Grunden-Martin asserted the letter constituted an offer and attempted to accept. Fairmount refused to sell any jars to Grunden-Martin and a suit for breach of contract was filed. The trial court gave judgment for the plaintiff and the defendant, Fairmount, appealed.

Question: Is the letter of April 23 a legally sufficient offer?

Answer: Yes. Under the circumstances the letter is an offer which Grunden-Martin can accept and thereby create a binding contract.

Reasoning: Ordinarily, a price quote is not an offer. However, in this case the letter was in response to an inquiry by Grunden-Martin on April 20. It was not an invitation to the general public. The words "for immediate acceptance" constitute language of commitment and indicate an offer to sell on the terms indicated.

Serious Proposal.   To constitute an offer, a proposal must be made with apparent serious intent. The offeror's subjective intent is not considered; the test is whether an ordinary reasonable person would consider the offeror's proposal to be a serious one. For example, suppose Bette bids $500 for an antique clock at an auction. It is of no consequence that she thinks to herself that she does not have $500 and secretly hopes someone else will make a higher bid and relieve her of her foolish action. The auctioneer is justified in treating Bette's bid as a serious proposal, that is, an offer. Statements obviously or apparently made in jest or under the stress of great excitement or as bravado or bluff are not offers. If Adams makes a proposal to Brown, and if Brown should realize that the proposal was made in jest or under the stress of great excitement or as bravado or bluff, the proposal would not constitute a legally effective offer.

The classic case involving a proposal made under the stress of great excitement is *Higgins v. Lessig.*[1] An old harness worth about $15 had presumably been stolen. When the defendant, Lessig, discovered the loss he became "much excited" and using "rough language and epithets" said he would give $100 to any person who found out who the thief was. Plaintiff, who had been present when Lessig made the

[1] 49 Ill. App. 459 (1893).

statement, furnished the information and sought to recover the reward. The trial court found for the plaintiff. However, the appellate court reversed the judgment on the ground that the defendant's language was not to be regarded as a serious proposal but "as the extravagant exclamation of an excited man."

In the following case, the court was called upon to determine whether the plaintiff was justified in interpreting as a serious proposal of conduct a statement which the defendant contended had been meant as a joke.

CASE 7.2

Barnes v. Treece
549 P.2d 1152 (Wash. App. 1976)

Facts: Treece was vice president and a major stockholder of Vend-A-Win, Inc., a corporation that distributed punchboards (a gambling device). On July 24 Treece spoke before the Gambling Commission and stated in effect: "I'll pay a hundred thousand dollars to anyone to find a crooked board. If they find it, I'll pay it." The statement brought laughter from the audience. The next morning Barnes observed Treece's statement on a television news report. On July 26 Barnes telephoned Treece, announced that he had two crooked punchboards and asked Treece if his earlier statement had been made seriously. Treece assured Barnes that it was and further informed him that $100,000 was being held in escrow. Barnes produced the boards but Treece refused to pay, maintaining the statement was made in jest. Barnes filed suit and the trial court held Treece liable. Treece appealed.

Question: Did Treece make an offer which Barnes accepted?

Answer: Yes. The statements and surrounding circumstances showed an objective manifestation of intent by Treece to make an offer.

Reasoning: The court stated the general rule that expressions intended as a joke and which would be understood by a reasonable person as being so intended, cannot be construed as an offer to form a contract. Treece's original statement drew laughter from the audience, but his subsequent statements, conduct, and the circumstances show an intent to lead one to believe the statements were made seriously. On July 26 Treece reaffirmed his offer to Barnes and also stated $100,000 was in escrow. The court also stated that gambling generates a great deal of income and that large sums are spent on advertising and promotion. In that atmosphere, it was a credible statement that $100,000 would be paid to promote punchboards.

The judgment was affirmed.

Definite and Complete Terms.   To be enforceable, a contract must contain reasonably definite and complete terms. The essential terms usually include the names of the parties, the subject matter involved (description, quantity), the price, and the time and place for performance. Sometimes the offer contains all the essential terms. If the offer by itself does not meet the requirement of reasonable definiteness but requires definite terms in the acceptance, the offer and acceptance together may meet the requirement that the terms of a contract must be reasonably certain.

An example of an offer requiring "such definite terms in the acceptance" was contained in the case of *Minneapolis & St. Louis Railway* (plaintiff) *v. Columbus Rolling Mill* (defendant).[2] The defendant, by letter of December 8, offerred to sell plaintiff 2000 to 5000 tons of iron rails at a specified price. The plaintiff replied, "Please enter our order for 1200 tons rails." Since the order was below the minimum quantity specified in the offer, there was no contract. In so deciding, the court said: "This offer [of December 8] would authorize the plaintiff to take at his election any number of tons not less than two thousand nor more than five thousand, on the terms specified." If the plaintiff had ordered, say, three thousand tons, there would have been a contract, although considered alone the offer was not reasonably definite as to quantity.

It should be noted that the requirement is not one of absolute definiteness but only of reasonable definiteness. Promises of performance to be rendered "immediately" or "at once" or "promptly" or "as soon as possible" have been held to meet this requirement. Similarly, quantities and prices have been held to be reasonably definite even though qualified by such expressions as "about" or "more or less" or "approximately." But proposals to pay "a fair share of my profits" and to erect "a permanent first-class hotel" have been held not to meet the requirements of reasonable definiteness.

A proposal may fail to meet the requirement of reasonably definite and complete terms if some term vital to the proposed agreement has been omitted. As stated above, the essential terms usually include the names of the parties, description of the subject matter, the price, and the time and place for performance. Courts have many times held that if the parties fail to make an enforceable agreement, the courts will not make one for them. Thus, if Henry and Carol agree that Carol is to make Henry a suit for $150, but there is no agreement concerning the material from which the suit is to be made, a court would refuse to supply the missing term.

It does not follow, however, that all the terms of an offer must necessarily be expressed. Some of them may be implied. For example, if a contract fails to mention the time of performance, courts will hold that performance within a reasonable time is implied in the offer. When a contract for the sale of land fails to mention the price to be paid for the property, there is no basis on which a court could enforce the agreement. Courts are less strict when asked to enforce contracts for services or for the sale of goods. In such contracts, if no price is specified but it is clear that the parties intended to conclude a contract and there is some objective basis for determining what is a reasonable price, courts will imply a reasonable price in the offer. In such cases if a market price for the specified goods or service exists, that price will be taken as the reasonable price. In the following case the court analyzed a communication made by a college to one of its students.

[2] 119 U.S. 149 (1866); see also Case 7.1, p. 99.

CASE 7.3   **Abrams v. Illinois College of Podiatric Medicine**
395 N.E.2d 1061 (Ill. App. 1979)

Facts: Abrams, a student at Illinois College of Podiatric Medicine, failed Physiology 101 and was placed on probation. The College informed him that "he should not worry . . . that everything would be done to assist him, including figuring out some way to help him." Abrams failed two more courses and was dismissed from school. He filed suit for breach of oral contract and sought reinstatement. The trial court dismissed his complaint. Abrams appealed.

Question: Did the College make an offer to enter into a contract?

Answer: No. The statement made by the College was too vague and indefinite to constitute an offer.

Reasoning: An offer must be so definite as to its material terms that the promises and performances to be rendered by each party are reasonably certain. The court stated the reason for the rule: "A court cannot enforce a contract unless it can determine what it is . . . Vagueness of expression, indefiniteness and uncertainty as to any of the essential terms of an agreement, have often been held to prevent the creation of an enforceable contract."

The judgment was affirmed.

Communication to Offeree.   An offer does not become legally effective until communicated to the person or persons for whom it was intended. "Communicated" literally means "brought to the attention of." Ordinarily, the offeror will communicate to the offeree by telephone, letter, or telegram.

In rare instances, the courts hold that an offeree can assent to a proposal which he or she does not know about if, under the circumstances, the offeree should have realized that a proposal was made. For example, proposals sometimes are printed on claim checks (such as those issued in parking lots, checkrooms, or repair shops), and on invoices. In any such situation the test of whether communication has occurred is that of reasonableness. Could the customer reasonably be expected to know that an offer was being made to him or her? If so, the offer has been communicated to him or her; if not, there has been *no* communication. For example, suppose a business issues claim checks which contain provisions in small print or on the reverse side of the form. In such instances courts generally hold that the ordinary person would not read such material and thus no offer is communicated to the customer (offeree).

DURATION AND TERMINATION OF OFFERS

A legally effective offer gives to the offeree the power to create a contract by accepting the offer. This "power of acceptance" continues until the offer is terminated by some legally recognized method. Offers may be terminated by: (1) lapse of time, (2) revocation by the offeror, (3) rejection or counteroffer by the offeree, (4) death or incapacity of the offeror or offeree, (5) loss or destruction of the subject matter of the offer, or (6) illegality arising subsequently to the offer ("supervening illegality").

Termination by Lapse of Time

Specified Time Limitation. An offer may be so worded as to terminate on a specified date. An example is: "This offer remains open until 5 P.M., October 10." Difficulty arises when the limitation is worded ambiguously. Suppose that an offeror mails a letter which gives the offeree "ten days to accept or reject this offer." Is the offeror's intention to have the 10-day period measured from the date the letter is sent or from the date it is received? Although there is some conflict in court decisions, the usual ruling is that the time runs from the day of receipt by the offeree.

Implied Time Limitation. Where an offeror does not specify a time limitation, the offer remains open for a reasonable period of time. What constitutes a reasonable period of time is a question of fact to be determined on the basis of all relevant circumstances, including the subject matter of the offer, the market price situation, the distance between the parties, any special objective the offeror had in making the offer where that objective is known to the offeree, and the method of communication chosen by the offeror. Thus, an offer to buy or sell eggs terminates sooner than an offer to buy or sell land; an offer to sell corporate stock during a period of rapidly fluctuating stock prices terminates sooner than an offer to sell the same stock during periods of relative price stability; an offer which the offeree knows has been made to meet an emergency situation terminates sooner than one not so made; and an offer sent by telegram normally terminates sooner than one sent by letter. An attempt by the offeree to accept an offer after a specified time or a reasonable time has expired may be considered a counteroffer.

The following case involves an offer that did not contain a time limitation.

CASE 7.4 Modern Pool Products, Inc. v. Rudel Machinery Co.
294 N.Y.S.2d 426 (Civ. Ct. City of N.Y. 1968)

Facts: On September 16, 1964 Rudel (offeror) submitted a letter to Modern Pool Products (offeree) offering to repair a machine for $1,600 plus freightage. Rudel was located in New York City; Pool Products was located in Greenwich, Connecticut. The price was subject to change without notice. Rudel stated the work would have to be done in Illinois and they were currently very busy in their shop. Rudel indicated that the work would have to be scheduled perhaps 6–8 weeks ahead. Pool Products replied January 14, 1965 that the machine would be shipped to the Illinois plant by January 20. On February 10, 1965 Rudel wrote to Pool Products that the machine had arrived but that more extensive repairs were required than originally contemplated. Rudel estimated the cost of repairs at $3,300 and stated it would await instructions. Pool Products sued Rudel for breach of contract to repair the machine at the original price.

Question: Was Rudel's offer of September 16, 1964 open on January 14, 1965, so that Pool Products' letter constituted an acceptance?

Answer: No. The offeror did not specify a time limitation and under the circumstances 114 days was not considered a reasonable time for the offer to remain open.

Reasoning: A reasonable time for acceptance varies with the circumstances. The court stated: the price quoted was subject to change without notice; the parties were not separated by vast distances; and the work required advance scheduling. Thus, the offer required a prompt reply.

Judgment for defendant.

Termination by Revocation

Power of Revocation.   As a general rule, an offeror has the power to revoke (withdraw) an offer any time before acceptance, even though he or she has promised not to do so . Thus, for example, if the offeror specifies "This offer will remain open until October 10," the offeror may revoke the offer on October 5. A revocation under these circumstances may be unethical or immoral, but is not in violation of the law.

Irrevocable Offers: Options; Promissory Estoppel.   There are several exceptions to the general rule that offers are revocable. If the offeree gives consideration (money, property, etc.) to the offeror to keep the offer open, the offer is irrevocable for the agreed period of time. Such an arrangement is called an "option" or "option contract." Thus, in the example above, if the offeree gives $10 to the offeror to keep the offer open, the offeror can no longer revoke the offer before October 10.

➤Many courts hold that an offer becomes irrevocable in cases where the offeror should reasonably expect the offer will induce the offeree to change his or her position based on the offer and, in fact, the offeree does change position based on the offer. This holding of the courts has been called the theory or doctrine of **detrimental reliance** or **promissory estoppel**. The word "estoppel" means that one is stopped, or prevented, from denying a certain statement or event. "Change of position" means acting or promising to act in a way the person would not otherwise have done. Thus, if the circumstances are appropriate, the offeror is not allowed to revoke his or her offer.

The following case presents a typical illustration of the use of promissory estoppel.

CASE 7.5   Lyon Metal Products v. Hagerman Construction Corp.
391 N.E.2d 1152 (Ind. App. 1979)

Facts: On Feb. 12, Lyon (offeror) submitted a bid to Hagerman (offeree) to sell athletic lockers in the amount of $16,824. Lyon's bid was the lowest of four received by Hagerman and was used by Hagerman in computing its bid for the construction of a school. Hagerman was the lowest bidder on the school project. Lyon learned of this three or four days after submitting its bid. In addition, Hagerman sent Lyon a letter of intent stating a formal contract would be sent about June 10. No contract was ever signed and on Sept. 6 Lyon withdrew its bid and submitted a new price of $28,750. Hagerman filed suit. The trial court entered judgment for Hagerman based upon the doctrine of promissory estoppel. Defendant appealed.

Question: Should Lyon's bid (offer) be held to be irrevocable under the doctrine of promissory estoppel?

Answer: Yes. Under the circumstances Lyon should be held liable.

Reasoning: The elements of promissory estoppel are present: (1) Lyon made a definite promise to Hagerman with the reasonable expectation that the promise would induce action of a definite and substantial character on the part of Hagerman (Lyon knew that if its bid was the lowest, Hagerman would use the bid in computing its own bid); (2) the promise induced such action (Hagerman did use Lyon's bid); (3) Hagerman acted in justifiable reliance upon the promise to its detriment (Hagerman won the bid for the school project); and (4) injustice can be avoided only by enforcement of Lyon's promise (Hagerman will suffer a loss unless Lyon is held to the original offer price).

Other Irrevocable Offers. Some types of offers are made irrevocable by statute. Among such offers are "firm offers" of merchants under Section 2–205 of the Uniform Commercial Code. A *firm offer* is a written and signed offer of a merchant to buy or sell goods, where the writing gives assurance that the offer will be held open. Such an offer is not revocable within the time-period provisions of Section 2–205, even though the offeror was not paid to keep the offer open. (Firm offers and the provisions of the UCC, Section 2–205, are discussed in Chapter 15.)

A difficult problem arises where the offeror asks for an act which requires time to perform and then, after the requested performance has begun, serves notice of revocation. For example, suppose Clyde offers to pay Debbie $500 if she will wallpaper his apartment. If Clyde attempts to revoke his offer when Debbie has papered half the apartment, what is Debbie's legal position? Where an offer is made for a unilateral contract, acceptance does not take place until the act has been substantially, i.e., almost fully, performed. But to allow revocation after part performance may cause serious hardship to an offeree who has started performance. Many courts utilize a variant of the detrimental reliance (promissory estoppel) theory to prevent such hardship to the offeree. They take the view that the offer becomes irrevocable as soon as the offeree begins performance. Thus, in the example above, Clyde is not allowed to revoke his offer. The theory behind this view is that beginning the invited performance creates an option contract. Note that the offeror is not bound to perform the other side of the bargain unless the offeree completes performance within the time stated in the offer, or if no time is stated, within a reasonable time.

What Constitutes Revocation. The usual method of revocation is for the offeror to notify the offeree that he or she is withdrawing the offer. No special form of notice is required. Anything suffices which lets the offeree know that the offeror has reconsidered and no longer intends to enter into the proposed contract. The notice may be given face to face, over the telephone, or by letter or telegram. The general rule is that a written revocation becomes effective when received.[3]

There is one situation in which the law recognizes revocation as having occurred even though the offeror's change of mind is not known by the offeree. Where an offer was made to the public generally, as in a published offer to pay a reward, the offer may be withdrawn by giving public notice of revocation. If the same amount of publicity is given to the revocation as was given to the offer, revocation is effective even against a member of the public who knew of the offer but not the publication of notice of revocation.

Termination by Rejection or Counteroffer

A *rejection* is a manifestation by the offeree of his or her intention not to accept the offer. A rejection may be express or implied by words or conduct. Thus, the offeree can reject an offer by saying, "Your offer is not acceptable," or by tearing a written offer into pieces and throwing them in the wastebasket. At that point the offer terminates and the offeree may not change his or her mind later and accept. There is no offer to accept.

A *counteroffer* is an offer made by the offeree to an offeror relating to the same matter as the original offer but differing from the original offer in one or more particulars. A counteroffer is an implied rejection and terminates the original offer. For example, suppose Arnold offers to sell his car to Barbara for $1500 and Barbara replies, "I will give you $1000 for the car." Barbara has made a counteroffer. Arnold has the choice of accepting the counteroffer, rejecting it outright, or making a counteroffer to Barbara.

A form of counteroffer is a conditional acceptance. For example, if Arnold offers to sell his car to Barbara for $1500 and Barbara says, "I accept your offer of $1500 and I will pay you in three equal monthly installments," Barbara has impliedly rejected the offer. However, Arnold becomes an offeree and is free to accept the counteroffer (conditional acceptance).

Rejections and counteroffers should be distinguished from requests for information. Suppose an offer is made to sell a house for $40,000. The offeree says, "I am considering your offer, although I think the price is high. Would you be willing to scale it down to $37,500?" Such a response to the offer is not a rejection; on the contrary, it tells the offeror the offer is being kept under advisement. Neither is the response a counteroffer because it contains no promise. It is merely an inquiry.

Termination by Death or Incapacity of Offeror or Offeree

Death or incapacity of the offeror or offeree ends the ordinary offer whether or not the other party is aware of the occurrence. Probably the most usual kind of legal incapacity terminating an offer is insanity. In some states conviction of a felony results in a person's being deprived of the capacity to enter into contracts.

Death or incapacity does not terminate a *contract* (that is, where there has been both an offer and an acceptance). The contract is binding on the estate of the deceased or incapacitated person.

---

[3]By statute in California and a few other states, a written revocation becomes effective when posted or put into the course of transmission by any reasonable mode.

Termination by Loss of Subject Matter; Termination by Supervening Illegality

The loss or destruction of the subject matter of a proposed contract terminates the offer. Thus, if the offer concerns the purchase or sale of a horse and the horse dies before the offer is accepted, the offer is terminated.

If a proposed contract or performance becomes illegal after an offer has been made but *before* it is accepted, the offer is terminated. This method of termination is usually referred to as *supervening illegality*. Suppose that Arnold offers to sell a quantity of salmon to the Baker Cannery. Before Baker accepts the offer, the state legislature enacts a law prohibiting further sales of salmon for the current year. If the statute takes effect before the offer is accepted, it terminates the offer.

SUMMARY

One of the requirements for a contract is a manifestation of mutual assent, which is an outward expression of assent by words or acts. Mutual assent is reached by means of offer and acceptance. This chapter dealt with offer.

An offer is a statement or other conduct by which the offeror confers upon the offeree a legal power to accept and thereby to create a contract. To constitute a legally effective offer, a proposal must meet four requirements:

1. The proposal must contain language of commitment. Offers contain promises and are to be distinguished from negotiatory statements. Negotiatory statements are those which lay the groundwork for or invite the submission of offers. Advertisements, circulars, catalogs, and price tags are usually invitations for offers, rather than offers.
2. The proposal must appear to be made with serious intent.
3. The proposal must be so definite and complete in its terms, or require such definite terms in the acceptance, that the parties will know their rights and duties and that in the event of litigation a court will be able to determine the extent of the obligations assumed.
4. The proposal must be communicated to the offeree. An offeree may be bound by terms contained in an invoice, a claim check, or other printed document if the offeree should reasonably be expected to know an offer was being made under the circumstances.

An offeree may accept an offer at any time before termination of the offer. An offer may be terminated or ended by: (1) lapse of time, (2) revocation, (3) rejection or counteroffer, (4) death or incapacity of offeror or offeree, (5) loss or destruction of the subject matter of the offer, or (6) illegality arising after the making of the offer.

The offeror may state a time when the offer will terminate. In the absence of a specified time, an offer remains open for a reasonable time. As a general rule, offers may be revoked at any time before acceptance. There are several exceptions to this rule. An offer will be irrevocable for a stated time, or for a reasonable time when no date for termination is specified, if (1) the offeree gives consideration to the offeror ("option contract"), (2) the promissory estoppel (detrimental reliance) doctrine applies, (3) a special statute declares the offer to be irrevocable, or (4) the offer is for a unilateral contract and the offeree begins performance. An offer is terminated when the offeree rejects the offer, expressly or impliedly, or submits a counteroffer or conditional acceptance.

REVIEW QUESTIONS

1. What is meant by "manifestation of mutual assent" as a requirement for a contract?

2. (a) Define "offer." (b) Define "negotiatory statement." (c) How do the two differ in legal effect?

3. What four requirements must a promise meet to constitute an offer?

4. What test do courts apply in determining whether a proposal of conduct is seriously intended?

5. (a) How should the following statement be qualified to make it accurate? "An offer must be so definite in its terms that the promises and the performances to be tendered by each party are reasonably certain." (b) What terms are essential to meet this requirement?

6. (a) Explain how terms of a written offer may be communicated without the offeree reading those terms. (b) How should an offeror protect himself or herself when he or she intends to include in a written offer a condition or term printed on the stationery?

7. (a) What is the rule as to termination of offer by lapse of time when a time limitation is specified? (b) When no time limitation is specified?

8. What is the general rule as to the power of an offeror to revoke his or her offer?

9. (a) What is an option contract? (b) Explain the doctrine of promissory estoppel.

10. When does a written notice of revocation become effective?

11. (a) Define "rejection." What effect does rejection have on the offeree's power of acceptance? (b) Define "counteroffer." What effect does a counteroffer have on the offeree's power of acceptance? (c) What is a conditional acceptance?

12. (a) Give an original illustration of termination of offer by loss or destruction of subject matter. (b) What is meant by "supervening illegality" as a method of terminating offers?

CASE PROBLEMS

1. Adams invited various brokers to submit proposals for fire and theft insurance. Brown submitted a proposal. In response to Adams' requests, Brown revised his proposal several times at the cost of considerable effort and some expense. (a) Is Adams free to reject all of Brown's proposals and to place the insurance with Campbell, another broker? (b) Would the answer differ if, on expert analysis, Campbell's proposal were found to be less favorable to Adams than Brown's proposal? Explain reason(s) for your answer.

2. Joseph Sidran offered to sell piece goods for the Tanenbaum Textile Company

for a commission "of 1 percent of the sale price of said merchandise." The offer made no mention of the duration of the proposed contract nor of the time and place of payment. Were the terms of the offer reasonably definite? Explain.

3. Roy Key and Michael Haitchi signed a "Contract" which stated that Key agreed to buy "a house to be built on Lot 9 Lambert Drive Dunmovin S/D Plan No. 603 W. D. Farmer." The contract further provided that it constituted "the sole and entire agreement between the parties." Was the agreement sufficiently definite to constitute a contract? Why or why not?

4. The plaintiff checked a package in a parcel room of a railway station, paid the 10-cent checking charge, and received a claim check which he put into his pocket without reading. In error the package was given out on another claim check. The package contained valuable furs, and the plaintiff sued for $1000. The evidence showed that at the bottom of the claim check, printed in large red letters, was an identifying number, and at the top, in smaller red letters, was the word "Contract." In between the two lines were eighty-eight words, in fine black type, purporting to contain the terms of contract, one of which limited liability for loss to $25. No sign containing notice of limitation was posted in the parcel room. Should plaintiff's recovery be limited to $25? Why or why not?

5. Cline sent Caldwell a letter offering to sell a tract of land for $6000. The letter was dated January 29 and gave Caldwell "eight days in which" to accept or reject the offer. Caldwell received the letter February 2. He sent notification of acceptance on February 8. Had the offer terminated before February 8? Why or why not?

6. Beach offered to contribute $2000 to a church building fund of $10,000 on condition that the church raise the remaining $8000. The church raised the $8000, but before it did so, Beach was adjudged insane, and conservators of his estate were appointed. Can the church recover the promised amount from the estate? Justify your answer.

CHAPTER 8

ACCEPTANCE

A s we have seen, a contract requires a manifestation of mutual assent, which is normally reached by offer and acceptance. The previous chapter dealt with offer; the present chapter deals with acceptance. The first part of this chapter examines legal principles which apply to acceptance of offers in general. The next two parts discuss principles which apply primarily to acceptance in situations involving (1) unilateral contracts and (2) bilateral contracts. The last part of the chapter deals with the problem of determining when a contract comes into being where the parties mutually understood that the agreement would be put into writing.

ACCEPTANCE IN GENERAL

In very general terms, **acceptance** is the offeree's manifestation of assent to the terms of the offer in the manner requested by the offeror. If the offeror requests the offeree to perform an act (e.g., mow the lawn), the offer is to enter into a unilateral contract. Such offers are often referred to as "unilateral offers." If the offeror requests the offeree to make a return promise (e.g., promise to mow the lawn), the offer is to enter into a bilateral contract. Such offers are often referred to as "bilateral offers."

An offer may be addressed to a specified person, or to one or more of a specified group of persons, or to the general public. Where an offer is addressed to a specified person, only that person can accept the offer. A person has a right to select and determine with whom he or she will contract. Thus, if Angela sends Bill an order for goods made by Bill, only Bill can accept that offer. If Bill hands the order to another manufacturer (Carl) who fills it without disclosing that Carl (and not Bill) made the goods, there is no contract.

When an offer is addressed to one or more of a specified group of persons, the acceptance is not complete until assent has been manifested by the specified person or persons. When an offer is directed to the general public, there may be any number of acceptances or only one acceptance, depending on the intent of the offeror. For example, an offer to pay $100 to anyone who fails to get relief after using a certain remedy is an offer to pay every user who fails to get relief. An offer to sell "to the first person who answers this advertisement" is limited to a single acceptance. When the wording of an offer does not clearly indicate the intent of the offeror, the offer is construed (interpreted) as a reasonable person would construe it under all the surrounding circumstances. For example, an offer to pay a reward for certain information should be construed as an offer to pay the first person who furnishes that information. The reasonable supposition is that the offeror does not intend to pay several times for the same information.

ACCEPTANCE OF UNILATERAL OFFER

A unilateral offer asks for an *act* of performance in exchange for the offeror's promise, whereas a bilateral offer asks for a *promise* of performance in exchange for the offeror's promise. Three questions merit special attention concerning acceptance of unilateral offers: (1) Is complete performance a requirement for acceptance of a unilateral offer? (2) Is knowledge of the offer a requirement for acceptance? (3) Is notification of performance a requirement?

Extent of Performance Required for Acceptance

The offeree accepts an offer for a unilateral contract by performing the act requested with intent to accept. For example, if David says to Mary, "I will pay you $1000 to paint my house," Mary must paint the entire house to receive the $1000.

Many courts take the view that an offer for a unilateral contract may be accepted by substantial performance of the requested act, unless the offer provides otherwise. Under this view David's promise would be enforceable when Mary "substantially" finished painting the house. If Mary refused to finish, David could deduct from the $1000 the cost to have another painter finish the job.

What constitutes "substantial performance" depends on the facts of each case. Twenty-five percent or even 50 percent completion would not be sufficient, but 95 percent completion would ordinarily be accepted as substantial performance.

Knowledge of Offer as a Requirement for Acceptance

Since, as a general rule, the offeree must perform the act requested with intent to accept, knowledge of the existence of an offer is essential. Thus, an offer to pay a reward creates a power of acceptance in a person only if that person knew of the offer at the time he or she performed the requested service. Suppose, for example, that Arthur advertises in a newspaper that he will pay a reward to any person who finds his lost wallet and returns it and its contents to him. Barbara finds the wallet, discovers that Arthur is the owner, and delivers the wallet and contents to him. If Barbara had no knowledge of the offer at the time she returned the wallet, a court would hold that she has no contractual claim against Arthur.

Notification of Performance as a Requirement for Acceptance

As a general rule, when the offer is for a unilateral contract the offeree is not required to notify the offeror that performance of the requested act is complete. For example, if Georgia offers to pay Henry $5 to mow her lawn, and Henry mows the lawn, he is not required to notify Georgia. In most instances the offeror will learn of the performance either by observation or by the offeree requesting payment.

The offeree is required to give notice only if the offeror has included notification as part of the offer. However, a number of courts state that if the offeree has reason to believe that the performance will not come to the offeror's attention within a reasonable time, the offeree must exercise reasonable diligence to notify the offeror. Thus, notice might be required if the offeree performs the act requested in a remote area far from the offeror.

ACCEPTANCE OF BILATERAL OFFER

A bilateral offer is accepted by the offeree's communicating the return promise requested by the offeror. Usually bilateral offers are so worded or are made under such circumstances that the requested promise must be expressed in words. Sometimes, however, the requested promise must be manifested by the performance of some act. In certain limited situations acceptance of a bilateral offer takes place even though the offeree remains silent and inactive. Each of these three methods of manifesting assent to an offer for a bilateral contract is discussed in the following pages.

Acceptance by Words Expressing Assent

Language by Which Assent May Be Expressed.   No particular words are required to express assent to a bilateral offer. A desirable way to indicate assent is to identify the offer and then add "I hereby accept your offer" (or other words indicating unequivocal acceptance). Ambiguous expressions, such as "Your order will receive our prompt and careful attention," lead to controversy over whether there actually has been an acceptance.

To constitute an acceptance, the offeree must comply exactly with the offeror's request. At common law the courts called this "the mirror-image rule," stating that the return promise must be a mirror image of the offer. Not infrequently an offeree will appear to accept the offer but will include a term or terms additional to or different from those in the offer. As stated in Chapter 7, such a variation may be a counteroffer or a conditional acceptance and thus a rejection of the offer. A major exception to this rule is discussed in the following case.

CASE 8.1

Burkhead v. Farlow
146 S.E.2d 802 (N.C. 1966)

Facts: Mr. and Mrs. Farlow, defendants, offered to sell a parcel of land to Burkhead, plaintiff, for $15,000. Burkhead agreed to buy the property and told defendants he would pay the purchase price as soon as title examination had been completed. He engaged an attorney to do a title check and told the Farlows it would be two or three weeks before the examination could be completed. After approximately two weeks, the defendants notified Burkhead they had decided not to sell the property. Plaintiff sued for specific performance of an alleged contract of sale. Defendants were successful and plaintiff appealed.

Question: Did Burkhead accept the offer or did he, by adding the language about title examination, make a counteroffer and impliedly reject the Farlows' offer?

Answer: In this case Burkhead made a valid acceptance and a binding bilateral contract resulted.

Reasoning: The court stated the general rule that "an acceptance must be unconditional and must not change, add to, or qualify the terms of the offer. It is also the general rule that the [offeree's] insertion in his acceptance of a condition which merely expresses that which 'would be implied in fact or in law by the offer does not preclude the consummation of the contract.'" In a contract to sell land the law implies an obligation by the seller to convey a good title to the buyer. Burkhead had a right to get a lawyer's opinion as to the quality of the title. Plaintiff specified no more than the law automatically implied. His acceptance was unconditional.

The judgment was reversed.

Communication of Acceptance.   The general rule is that the offeree's acceptance of an offer for a bilateral contract must be communicated to the offeror.

It is often said that the offeror is master of the offer. The offeror may specify that acceptance is to be communicated face to face or by telephone, by mail, by telegraph, or by some other medium, and that acceptance is to be effective only upon timely receipt. For example, if Steel Corporation in its offer to sell steel to a customer, says, "You must accept this offer by letter received at our home office by October 1," the offeree may not accept by any other medium. Thus, an attempt by the customer to accept by telephone is ineffective as an acceptance but amounts to a counteroffer. Steel Corporation then has the choice of accepting or rejecting the counteroffer.

The offeror may dispense with the requirement of communication of acceptance. Suppose that a salesperson for the Able Company takes an order (offer) from a customer on the Able Company's (offeree's) order form and the form contains the statement, "This offer will become a contract when signed and approved (i.e., accepted) by an executive officer of the Able Company." The customer—fully aware of the statement—signs the order. By signing the order without requiring notice of Able's acceptance, the customer (offeror) may be held to have dispensed with the requirement of communication of acceptance.

Medium of Acceptance; When and Where Acceptance Becomes Effective.   Usually an offeror does not specify how acceptance is to be made or is to take effect. Often courts are faced with controversies involving such a situation and must decide when and where an acceptance becomes effective.

Earlier, the courts were often faced with that problem when the offer was made by mail. The prevailing rule was that the offeree had power to accept the offer by mailing a letter of acceptance, properly stamped and addressed, within a reasonable time. The contract was regarded as made at the time and place that the letter of acceptance was put into possession of the post office. The rule was often referred to as the "deposited acceptance," or "mailbox" rule. One rationale for the rule at common law was that the offeror, by using the mail, made the post office his or her "agent." Thus, delivery of an acceptance to the post office was the same as delivery to the offeror. For example, if an offeror in California mailed an offer to an offeree in Arizona who promptly mailed an acceptance, a contract would be made in Arizona at the moment the letter was posted.

There was considerable confusion in the law as to when acceptance became effective where the offer was by mail and the acceptance by telegraph, or where the offer was by telegraph and the acceptance was by mail.

Acceptance by Reasonable Medium.   The general rule today is that unless otherwise specified, an offer to make a contract can be accepted by any medium reasonable under the circumstances. A medium of acceptance is reasonable if: (1) It is the one used by the offeror; (2) it is customary in similar transactions at the time and place the offer is received; or (3) it is appropriate in view of the speed and reliability of the medium used, prior dealings between offeror and offeree, and trade custom.

If the offeree uses a "reasonable medium" to accept, the acceptance becomes effective when and where the acceptance is properly dispatched, provided the offer is still open. An acceptance sent by mail is properly dispatched if it is properly addressed and stamped and deposited in a mailbox where regular pickups are made.

Note that the "proper dispatch" or "deposited acceptance" rule places the risk of a lost acceptance on the offeror. The rationale is that the offeree needs to know right away that there is a contract, and the offeror, having initiated the contractual relationship, is in a better position than the offeree to detect a loss or lateness of communication. An offeror who wishes to avoid the risk of a delayed or lost acceptance should of course specify that the acceptance must be received by the offeror at the offeror's place of business on or before a certain date.

The following case involves an unusual application of the rule that an offeree may use the same medium of communication as the offeror.

CASE 8.2

Froling v. Braun
235 N.W.2d 168 (Mich. App. 1975)

Facts: Braun owned a piece of real estate. He engaged Disner, a real estate agent, to show the property and receive offers. Disner received a written offer of $165,000 from Froling. Braun rejected the offer but through Disner, made a counteroffer of $185,000. Within a few days, Froling notified Disner that he accepted the counteroffer. Disner neglected to tell Braun and before receiving notice of acceptance, Braun told Froling that the deal was off. Froling sued for specific performance. There was a judgment for Froling and Braun appealed.

Question: Did the communication by Froling to Disner constitute communication of acceptance to the offeror?

Answer: Yes. Communication to the offeror's agent had the effect of communication to the offeror.

Reasoning: The court stated that Braun used Disner to transmit the counteroffer to Froling. Absent any contrary indications from Braun, Froling had the power to accept in the same manner. If the acceptance is made in the manner expressly or impliedly indicated by the offeror, the offeror takes the risk as to effectiveness of communication.

The judgment was affirmed.

Acceptance by Other Medium. As a general rule, acceptance by an unreasonable medium is not effective on dispatch, but only upon receipt by the offeror (if the offer is still open). For example, suppose the offeror sends a telegram to the offeree offering to sell a perishable item. Under the circumstances, if the offeree mailed a letter of acceptance, a court would likely hold that the offeree used an unreasonable medium and there was no acceptance until and unless the letter was received by the offeror. Thus, if an offeree uses an unreasonable medium of communication, the risk of loss or delay in the acceptance falls on the offeree.

A difficult problem is presented where the offeree accepts by an unreasonable medium and the offeror revokes the offer. As discussed in Chapter 7, the general rule is that if the offeror sends a revocation, it is effective when received by the offeree. Thus, if the offeror mails a revocation and the offeree attempts to accept by an unreasonable medium, it must be determined whether the offeree received the revocation before the offeror received the acceptance.

No acceptance occurs if the offeror has specified that a particular medium must be used by the offeree to communicate an acceptance, and the offeree uses a different medium. In such circumstances an attempt by the offeree to accept by a different medium amounts to a counteroffer. Therefore, in analyzing a factual situation, it is critical to determine whether the offeror has required (specified) a particular medium for acceptance.

Effect of Acceptance Plus Rejection.   There is an important exception to the general rule that a timely acceptance by any reasonable medium becomes effective on proper dispatch. The rule does not apply where the notice of acceptance was preceded by a notice of rejection sent by the offeree. The reason for the exception is that the notice of rejection might be the first to reach the offeror, who should be entitled to rely on a notice of rejection as soon as it is received. To protect the offeror, the law provides that an acceptance sent after a rejection has been sent is not effective until received and will not take effect even then unless the offer is still open. In short, when a notice of rejection is followed by a notice of acceptance promptly sent, the notice which first reaches the offeror is effective.

Suppose that instead of sending a notice of rejection followed by a notice of acceptance, the offeree sends a notice of acceptance followed by a notice of rejection. In such a situation, courts apply the general rule that a notice of acceptance becomes effective at the time it is properly dispatched. However, if the notice of rejection reaches the offeror first, and the offeror changes his or her position because of it, the offeree is estopped (barred) from enforcing the contract.

Acceptance by Act Indicating Assent

Acceptance of an offer to enter into a bilateral contract may at times properly be expressed by an act which implies a promise. A nod of the head, the raising of a hand, and the fall of an auctioneer's hammer are common examples. In addition, the courts have held that taking possession of, or exercising dominion over, something may constitute acceptance. To illustrate: Curtis, a contractor, has a pile of lumber stored on a vacant lot. Curtis tells Don, "Take a look at the lumber. If it's worth $80 to you, haul it away." Don hauls it away. The act of taking possession of the lumber is an acceptance of the offer and an implied promise to pay the $80. The offeree who objectively demonstrates an intent to accept cannot testify that his or her secret intent was otherwise. In the above example, hauling away the lumber is held to be an acceptance, regardless of Don's subjective intention.

In the following case the court considered the offeree's objective acts and not the subjective intent.

CASE 8.3

Crouch v. Marrs
430 P.2d 204 (Kans. 1967)

Facts: Crouch wrote to Purex Corporation offering to buy an old building and its contents for $500. He enclosed a check for $500 with the letter. An employee of Purex received the check on April 23. The check was indorsed and deposited in the Purex bank account. On April 27 Purex sent Crouch a telegram saying the check was mistakenly deposited and would be returned to him, or a Purex check would be issued if his check could not be located. A follow-up letter of May 16 stated that Purex was enclosing its check for $500 to reimburse Crouch and that the reason they could not accept Crouch's offer of $500 was because they had accepted an offer from another party, Asche, prior to April 23. Crouch filed suit against Marrs and Purex. Judgment for defendants and plaintiff appealed.

Question: Did cashing of the check by Purex constitute an acceptance?

Answer: Yes. Indorsing and depositing Crouch's check constituted an acceptance of a bilateral offer.

Reasoning: The court stated that an offer (for a bilateral contract) may be accepted by performing a specified act as well as by an affirmative answer. Also, where the offeree exercises dominion over the thing offered him or her—in this instance the check—such exercise constitutes an acceptance of the offer. Purex contended that Crouch's check was cashed through inadvertence or an error in office procedure. The court held that the act of depositing the check indicated acceptance (objectively). There was no evidence at the trial as to why the check was cashed.

The judgment was reversed.

Acceptance by Silence and Inaction

As a general rule, silence of the offeree does not constitute acceptance. For example, if Able Company sends an offer to Barbara and states, "If we do not hear from you by June 1, we shall assume you accept our offer," Barbara need not reply. A problem could arise, however, if Barbara uses or disposes of merchandise received with such an offer. As stated previously, if the offeree exercises dominion over an article offered (by taking possession of it), such is treated as an acceptance. To prevent unscrupulous merchants from taking advantage of unsuspecting offerees, various statutes have been passed. Several states and the federal government have enacted legislation providing that unordered merchandise received by mail may be treated as a gift. Thus, the recipient may use or dispose of the merchandise without liability.

There can be an acceptance of a bilateral offer, even though the offeree remains silent, if the circumstances warrant such a result. Following are two examples of situations in which silence and inaction operate as acceptance.

1. Silence and inaction operate as acceptance where the offeror has stated that

silence will operate as acceptance and the offeree in remaining silent and inactive intends to accept the offer. Suppose that Alan's horse is temporarily in Barbara's possession, and that Alan sends Barbara an offer to sell the horse for $250. In the letter Alan says, "I am so sure that you will accept that you need not trouble to write me. Your silence alone will operate as acceptance." *With the intention* of accepting, Barbara makes no reply and remains inactive. There is a contract.

2. Silence and inaction operate as acceptance where because of previous dealings or otherwise, it is reasonable that the offeree should notify the offeror if he or she does not intend to accept. For example, suppose the offeree sends out a salesperson to solicit offers "subject to acceptance by the home office." If, in the past, the offeree had invariably filled the customer's orders or informed the customer promptly that it was unable to fill a particular order, the offeree's silence will be treated as an acceptance. Some courts hold that the firm has the duty of rejection even in the absence of a past course of conduct. These courts believe that the initiative taken by the firm in soliciting an order warrants any customer in believing that the order is accepted unless the customer is promptly notified to the contrary so that he or she may place an order elsewhere.

The following case illustrates a situation where silence and inaction by the offeree did *not* constitute acceptance.

CASE 8.4   Corbin-Dykes Electric Co. v. Burr
500 P.2d 632 (Ariz. App. 1972)

Facts: General Motors Corporation requested bids from general contractors to construct a central air-conditioning plant. The defendant, Burr, was interested in obtaining the contract and he invited bids for the electrical subcontract. Corbin-Dykes Electric Company, the plaintiff, submitted a bid which Burr incorporated into his general contract bid. Burr was awarded the general contract but he accepted another bid for the electric subcontract. Corbin-Dykes objected to the selection of another as the subcontractor and sued Burr for breach of contract. Burr received a judgment and Corbin-Dykes appealed.

Question: Did Burr accept the offer (bid) of Corbin-Dykes?

Answer: No. There was no manifestation of mutual assent here. Burr's use of the bid did not constitute an acceptance.

Reasoning: Corbin-Dykes contended that a trade custom exists that a contractor who is listed in the general contractor's bid will receive the subcontract, if the general contractor is awarded the general contract. The court stated that evidence of custom and usage in the trade does not establish an acceptance. The law requires an actual voluntary acceptance. The acts by which mutual assent is manifested must show that they intended those acts. The inclusion of Corbin-Dykes' bid as part of the general contract bid did not constitute such an acceptance, and the offer never was accepted by Burr in any other manner.

The judgment was affirmed.

AGREEMENT LOOKING FORWARD TO A WRITING

Often those negotiating for a bilateral contract decide at some point in the process that when they reach agreement it will be put into writing and signed. If the parties reach an agreement, does a contract come into being as soon as they agree orally, or not until the agreement is put into writing and signed? The question is easily answered if the parties made clear their intentions.

Where one party files suit and the parties have not made clear what their intention was, the court will determine intention from all the surrounding circumstances. Such circumstances would include prior dealings between the parties, the complexity and number of terms, the amount of money involved in the contract, and whether the contract is of a type customarily put into writing. For example, where the contract involves a large sum, has many details, and is of a type usually put into writing, the court might conclude the intention was that there was to be no binding obligation until the writing was completed and signed.

If the parties orally agree on all the details and the transaction involves a relatively small amount of money, the court might conclude that the parties intended to be bound when the oral agreement was reached and that the writing was to serve merely as a "memorial" (record) of the agreement. For example, suppose Ken and Barbara negotiate for the sale of a stereo. They orally agree on a price of $250, delivery to take place in 1 week, and agree to have a written agreement prepared. Ken refuses to deliver the stereo until a written agreement is signed by both parties. A court would hold that the writing is merely a memorial and that Barbara may enforce the oral agreement.

The following case illustrates the use of a written agreement as a memorial.

CASE 8.5   Mohler v. Park County School District
515 P.2d 112 (Colo. App. 1973)

Facts: Mohler was employed by Park County School District as superintendent of schools for the 1970–71 school year. At the June 14, 1971 meeting of the board of education, a motion was made and carried that Mohler be offered a contract for the 1971–72 school year. Mohler was present and responded to the motion, as he had in July of the previous year, by saying, "Thank you." On July 12, 1971 the board passed a resolution to rescind its motion of June 14 to employ Mohler. Mohler sued for breach of contract and received a judgment for $14,600. Defendants (the school district and the board of education) appealed, arguing that no contract was intended prior to signing of a written agreement.

Question: Was there an offer and acceptance prior to preparation of a written contract?

Answer: Yes. In this case a written agreement would be merely a memorial. The parties were bound by the oral agreement of June 14.

Reasoning: In the prior year Mohler had accepted a verbal offer of employment. A written contract was prepared by defendants' attorney but was not signed until August 10, 1970, which was ten days after Mohler's term of employment began. The board member who made the motion at the June 14, 1971 meeting testified that he intended the motion to be an offer on the same terms as the previous year. Mohler testified that he intended his reply, "Thank you," to be an acceptance. Whether the parties to an oral agreement become bound prior to the drafting and execution of a contemplated formal writing is a question of intent on their part.

The judgment was affirmed.

SUMMARY

Acceptance is the offeree's expression of assent to the terms of an offer proposed by the offeror. Where an offer is addressed to a specified offeree, only that person may accept the offer. Where the offer is addressed to the public, there may be one acceptance or a number of acceptances, depending on the expressed intent of the offeror.

Most courts hold that substantial performance by the offeree with intent to accept is required for the acceptance of a unilateral offer. The offeree is not required to notify the offeror that performance is complete unless the offeror has so specified in the offer, or if the performance will not come to the offeror's attention within a reasonable time.

Usually bilateral offers are so worded that the acceptance (promise) must be expressed in words. Where acceptance is to be by words, any language suffices so long as it identifies the offer and clearly expresses acceptance of the offer. If the offeror requires that the acceptance be communicated by a particular medium, an attempt by the offeree to accept by a different medium is treated as a counteroffer.

Normally an offer for a bilateral contract invites communication of the acceptance by any medium reasonable in the circumstances. Acceptance by a reasonable medium becomes effective when and where notification is properly sent, provided the offer is still open. If the offeree uses an unreasonable medium, acceptance is effective on receipt.

An acceptance of a bilateral offer may be implied by the offeree's conduct. Here, the offeree's secret intent is immaterial. As a general rule, silence or inaction of the offeree does not constitute acceptance. The offeree's silence may constitute acceptance if the offeree intends to accept or if a previous course of dealing between the parties imposes an obligation to deny acceptance.

Often, parties negotiating a bilateral contract decide at some point in the process that when agreement is reached it will be put into writing and signed. Later the question may arise as to whether the oral agreement was legally binding as soon as it was reached, or not until it was put into writing. The answer depends on what the intent of the parties was. A court may determine intent from observing prior dealings between parties, the complexity and quantity of terms, the amount of money involved in the contract, and whether the contract is of a type customarily put into writing.

REVIEW QUESTIONS

1. (a) What is meant by "acceptance?" (b) What determines the number of acceptances there may be of an offer addressed to the general public? Illustrate how there could be multiple acceptances.

2. (a) What degree of performance is required for acceptance of a unilateral offer? (b) How does the law prevent hardship to the offeror where an offeree does not complete performance?

3. (a) Why is notification of performance not usually required in unilateral contracts? (b) Under what circumstances is notification of performance required?

4. When must an acceptance be actually communicated to the offeror? Explain and give an example.

5. (a) Define "reasonable medium" of acceptance. (b) Explain how the "proper dispatch" rule works. (c) Under the proper dispatch rule, who bears the risk of a lost communication? Why that person?

6. If an offeree uses an unreasonable medium, when and where is the acceptance effective?

7. What is the effect of a rejection preceding a properly and timely dispatched acceptance?

8. In what kind of situation may an act operate as an acceptance of a bilateral offer?

9. Illustrate a situation where silence and inaction might operate as acceptance of a bilateral offer.

10. (a) When does an agreement looking forward to a writing become legally effective? (b) Where an agreement becomes legally effective before it is put into writing, of what value is the writing?

CASE PROBLEMS

1. Mullaly sent Grieve an offer to lease him certain land. Grieve, without Mullaly's consent, turned the offer over to Adams. Adams sent Mullaly a lease based

No   on the terms of the offer, but naming himself as tenant. Was there an acceptance of the offer? Explain reasons for your answer.

2. Certain private individuals offered a reward for information leading to the arrest of an accused person. There were two claimants for the reward: Adams, who gave correct information to the proper officers but whose information did not lead to the arrest; and Barnes, who gave information leading to the arrest but who did not know about the reward. Is either of the claimants entitled to the reward? State reasons.

3. H. M. Johnson stated in writing that in return for a designated compensation he would assist Star Iron and Steel Co. (Star Iron) to secure short-term financing from a bank of Johnson's choice. By letter dated October 3, 1969, Star Iron indicated its willingness to accept the terms of Johnson's offer, subject to the condition that Johnson's statement, "bank of my choice," be changed to read "Bank of Tacoma." On October 8, Star Iron withdrew its conditional acceptance. Johnson brought suit for compensation under the theory that Star Iron's letter of October 3 constituted an acceptance of Johnson's offer. Did Star Iron's letter of October 3 constitute an acceptance? Explain.

→   4. On November 2, Thomas submitted to a bank a written offer to buy a certain piece of land. The offer specified that acceptance "must be in writing" and must be approved by the executive committee of the bank. While the offer was in the possession of the bank, a notation was placed on it reading: "Approved by the Executive Committee—Nov. 9—A. R. Murray." Later the notation was crossed out and another added: "Reconsidered and rejected—A. R. Murray, Minute Clerk—Date Nov. 17." No notification of acceptance had been sent to Thomas. Was there a contract? State reasons.

No comm. of acceptance

5. Plaintiff and defendant exchanged a series of letters concerning the possible sale of certain land by plaintiff to defendant. After "the terms were pretty well agreed upon," the plaintiff, at defendant's suggestion, made a draft of the agreement and mailed it to defendant. Defendant returned the draft unsigned and with certain amendments written on it. He accompanied the draft with a letter in which he said: "I believe you will find this as near as possible to the conditions which I wrote you in the possible purchase of the land by contract." The letter suggested that if the revised draft was satisfactory to plaintiff, he should have two copies made, sign them, and send them to defendant for his signature. The letter concluded: "I see no reason why we can't close it right up." Plaintiff did as defendant had suggested but defendant refused to sign. Action was brought for breach of contract. Was there a contract? Why or why not?

6. After preliminary negotiations, plaintiff and defendant reached an agreement by the terms of which plaintiff would buy a half interest in defendant's business and become partner in the operation of it. The two parties agreed that the terms of the agreement were to be reduced to writing, even though the law does not require a partnership agreement to be in writing. They also agreed they would meet on July 1 to sign the writing; and that plaintiff was to pay the purchase price at that time. Plaintiff prepared the writing and appeared at the appointed time and place with the purchase money, but defendant did not appear. Learning that defendant had sold his business to others, plaintiff brought action for breach of contract. Was there a contract? Explain.

CHAPTER 9

CONSIDERATION

Not all promises are legally enforceable. Purely social promises, such as a promise to love someone, are not enforceable, and some promises made in a commercial context are not.

To be enforceable under early common law, a promise had to be in writing, and had to bear the seal or insignia of the promisor. The writing and the seal were evidence of a serious undertaking by the promisor, and the courts were willing to enforce a promise that had been so elaborately and formally prepared.

As trade and commerce increased, a need arose for a broader range of promise enforcement. A rural and largely illiterate population conducted much of its business informally and had little time for or understanding of elaborate contractual formalities. By the early fourteenth century, courts were enforcing some kinds of unsealed promises and were seeking some basis—some underlying idea or theory—to determine which unsealed promises should be enforceable.

The courts now recognize three bases for the enforcement of unsealed (i.e., "informal") commercial promises:

- Consideration
- Promissory estoppel
- Statutes and decisional law which impose liability.

Consideration is by far the most common basis for enforcement of promises. Many judges and legal writers list consideration as one of three requirements for a contract (the first two being *offer* and *acceptance*). Thus, promissory estoppel and special laws are designated as "substitutes" for consideration and are utilized only in exceptional cases.

THE REQUIREMENT OF CONSIDERATION

The doctrine of consideration arose out of the desire to enforce promises made as part of a bargained-for exchange. A person usually rendered a performance or promised to do so because someone else promised a return performance such as payment of money. Each person's promise was made "in consideration of" (i.e., in exchange for) the other person's promise, and each promise created an expectation of performance. To protect those expectations, the courts long ago began to enforce informal promises which had been induced by consideration.

By contrast, courts generally do not enforce promises made by a promisor who does not bargain for something in return. For example, suppose a father says to his son, "I am going to buy a new car next month. I promise to give you my old car at that time." The father's promise is unenforceable. There is no consideration here, no bargained-for exchange.

Nature of Consideration   Various definitions of consideration are given by judges and legal writers. For our purposes, **consideration** may be defined as legal detriment to the promisee bargained for by the promisor. As explained below, legal detriment is doing or promising to do that which one was not previously obligated to do.

Where the offer is for a unilateral contract there is one promisor and one promisee. Where the offer is for a bilateral contract, the parties are at the same time promisors and promisees. As a general rule, in bilateral contracts both parties must incur **legal detriment**. However, for purposes of analysis it is easiest to focus on one party to a bilateral contract. First, it must be determined who is refusing to perform his or her part of the bargain. That person is designated as the promisor, for purposes of analysis. The other party to the bargain is the promisee. In order to enforce the promisor's promise, the promisee must prove that he or she incurred *legal detriment bargained for by the promisor.*

Usually the legal detriment incurred by the promisee will be a legal benefit to the promisor but this is not required.

Elements of Consideration.   Consideration consists of two elements. One element is the "bargained-for" aspect of consideration. The second element is referred to as "legal detriment."

Bargained-for Exchange.   Section 71 of the *Restatement (Second) of the Law of Contracts* provides in part:

(1)   To constitute consideration, a performance or a return promise must be bargained for.

(2)   A performance or return promise is bargained for if it is sought by the promisor in exchange for his promise and is given by the promisee in exchange for that promise.

These statements indicate that there must be a reciprocal relationship between the offeror's promise and the offeree's performance or return promise. The offeror's promise must *induce* the offeree's performance or return promise.

Legal Detriment.   The second element of consideration is that the promisee must incur legal detriment. Legal detriment does not mean "detrimental" or harmful. Legal detriment means the promisee gives up or promises to give up a legal right, or assumes or promises to assume a legal burden. A simple example will illustrate legal detriment. Suppose Sally agrees to sell her car to Tom, who agrees to buy it for $3000. But Sally changes her mind and refuses to transfer ownership of the car. For purposes of analysis, Sally is the promisor. Tom, the promisee, incurred legal detriment by promising to pay $3000. The legal detriment consists of giving up his right to spend or to invest his $3000 in some other manner.

Note that legal detriment does not necessarily mean *actual* detriment. The word "detriment" does not mean the promisee must suffer a loss or hardship but means only that he or she must give up some legal right or assume some legal burden. The often-cited case of *Hamer v. Sidway*[1] involved a promise by an uncle to pay his nephew $5000 if he would "refrain from . . . using tobacco" until he was 21. The nephew refrained from doing so. The uncle did not pay, and the nephew sued. The court held that the nephew had a legal right to use tobacco and that when he gave up

---

[1]121 N.Y. App. 538 (1891).

that right he suffered a legal detriment, even though abstaining might have constituted an actual physical benefit.

By defining consideration in terms of legal rather than actual detriment, courts accomplish two things: (1) The problem of economic valuation is left to the parties to the contract, and (2) the difficulty of finding actual detriment is avoided in those cases where the promisee is actually benefited, as in *Hamer v. Sidway*.

The following case illustrates the concept of "legal detriment."

CASE 9.1 Graphic Arts Finishers, Inc. v. Boston Redevelopment Authority
255 N.E.2d 793 (Mass. 1970)

Facts: Boston Redevelopment Authority (BRA) bought certain buildings occupied by Graphic Arts. To induce Graphic Arts to leave the premises without legal action, BRA promised to pay Graphic Arts relocation expenses of approximately $130,000. Graphic Arts agreed to move and not to liquidate its business. BRA did not pay all the relocation expenses and Graphic Arts sued for breach of contract. BRA defended that there was no consideration and thus no enforceable contract.

Question: Was there consideration, that is, was there legal detriment to the promisee (Graphic Arts) bargained for by the promisor (BRA)?

Answer: Yes. Graphic Arts incurred legal detriment by promising to relocate.

Reasoning: Legal detriment means giving up something the promisee was privileged to retain, or doing something the promisee was privileged not to do. Graphic Arts' promise to relocate its business and not liquidate clearly is the "doing something which it was privileged not to do." BRA argued that since no definite time period was specified during which Graphic Arts would remain in business there was no valid consideration. The court said that Graphic Arts bound itself to do something, namely, to relocate and open its business elsewhere. If after having done so, it decided to liquidate, it cannot be said there was a lack of consideration. The law does not concern itself with the adequacy of consideration; it is enough if it is valuable.

Movement of Consideration. The consideration (i.e., performance or return promise) demanded by a promisor usually moves from the promisee to the promisor. But it need not necessarily do so. The performance or the return promise may be given to some person other than the promisor if he or she so requires. Suppose that Brenda Buyer promises to pay $200 for a guitar to be delivered to her son. Susan Seller's promise (made to Brenda) to deliver the guitar to Brenda's son is consideration to Brenda even though her son actually receives the guitar.

Past Consideration—No Consideration. The term "past consideration," which is sometimes used, is self-contradictory. Consideration, by its definition, is something given in exchange for a promise and to induce it. Accordingly, anything which has occurred *before* a promise was made cannot be consideration. Suppose a father writes his son and daughter-in-law: "I am so happy you named your son after me. In consideration of that fact, I promise to pay you $1000 on the tenth of next month." The promise is unenforceable because the naming of the child was not something bargained for. The fact that a past event cannot be something bargained for has given rise to the statement, "Past consideration is no consideration."

Consideration Distinguished from Motives.   Consideration should not be confused with *motives*. "Love and affection" may be compelling motives for making a promise, but they are not words of bargaining. Thus, an uncle may write his nephew: "In consideration of my love and affection, I promise to send you a check for $1000 on your twenty-first birthday." The uncle bargained for nothing in exchange for his promise. His promise is therefore unsupported by consideration. The promise is a promise only to make a gift and is revocable at any time.

Illusory Promise   Whether a bargained-for promise from an offeree constitutes consideration for the offeror's promise depends on the *content* of the promise. As explained earlier in this chapter, a promise to give up a legal right or a promise to assume a legal burden constitutes consideration. However, certain words of promise do not obligate the person to any performance. Such words of promise are called *illusory* promises. Suppose, for example, that Sam offers to deliver to Barbara at a stated price per bushel as many bushels of wheat, not exceeding 5000, as Barbara may order within the next 30 days. Barbara "accepts," agreeing to buy at that price as many bushels as she shall order from Sam within the 30-day period. Although Barbara seems to have made a promise, in fact she has not committed herself to purchase any wheat. Her promise is illusory and is not consideration.

A promise may be rendered illusory if the person has an unrestricted right to cancel the contract, such as a right to cancel without notice. If the right to terminate the agreement is restricted in any way, the promise is not illusory. A right to cancel might be conditioned on the happening of some event such as a strike or a war or might require the person to give notice, such as 30 days. In such events the person incurs detriment. The person must perform for some period of time and thus the promise is not illusory.

Adequacy of Consideration   As a general rule, any detriment, no matter how small, may constitute consideration. If courts were to substitute their ideas of relative values for those of the parties as expressed in their agreement, endless litigation, delay, and uncertainty would result. Besides, courts believe that it would be unwarranted interference with freedom of contract if they were to relieve a party from a bad bargain.

Although the requirement of consideration may be met despite great differences in values exchanged, gross inadequacy of consideration may be relevant in the application of other rules. Such inadequacy (for example, $10,000 in exchange for $3 worth of foreign currency) may help to justify rescission (cancellation) of the contract on the grounds of duress, undue influence, or fraud (discussed in Chapter 10) or on the ground that the agreement is unconscionable (discussed in Chapter 11).

Occasionally an agreement states "In consideration of $1 the promisor agrees to. . . ." Generally the $1 is neither bargained for nor paid by the promisee, it is a sham or pretense. Such an amount, called "nominal" consideration, does not satisfy the requirement of consideration unless it is shown the parties did bargain for the $1. For example, if a father promises to sell his car to his daughter for $1, the promise is not enforceable. This is an ineffective attempt to disguise a gift to the daughter.

In the following case the court discusses adequacy of consideration.

CASE 9.2   Osborne v. Locke Steel Chain Co.
218 A.2d 526 (Conn. 1966)

Facts: Osborne worked for Locke Steel Chain Co. for 48 years. In 1960 a retirement agreement was signed that the company would pay Osborne $20,000 the first year and $15,000 a year thereafter for the remainder of his life. Osborne agreed to hold himself available for consultation and advice with the company and its officers and not to compete with the company in its domestic or foreign markets. The company made a few payments under the agreement and then repudiated it. Osborne sued for breach of contract. The trial court rendered judgment in favor of the company and Osborne appealed.

Question: Was there consideration to make the agreement enforceable?

Answer: Yes. Osborne (the promisee) incurred legal detriment bargained for by the company (the promisor).

Reasoning: Osborne assumed the legal burden of being available exclusively to the company and of not competing with the company. The company argued that the consideration was inadequate for a lifetime income of $15,000 per year. The court stated,

> " 'That which is bargained-for by the promisor and given in exchange for the promise by the promisee is not made insufficient as a consideration by the fact that its value in the market is not equal to that which is promised. Consideration in fact bargained for is not required to be adequate in the sense of equality in value.' 1 Corbin, Contracts sec. 127. . . .
>
> "In the absence of fraud or other unconscionable circumstances, a contract will not be rendered unenforceable at the behest of one of the contracting parties merely because of an inadequacy of consideration. The courts do not unmake bargains unwisely made. The contractual obligation of the defendant in the present case, whether wise or unwise, was supported by consideration, in the form of the plaintiff's promise to give advice and not to compete with the defendant. . . ."

The judgment is set aside.

PROBLEMS RELATING TO CONSIDERATION

The courts must deal with a variety of problems relating to consideration. For example, in some cases the issue is whether there is any consideration to support a promise to accept a lesser performance than that already owed because of an existing duty or obligation. In other cases the question is whether a promise to pay more than already owed is enforceable. These and other problems are discussed in the following paragraphs.

Performance of Existing Legal Duty or Obligation

In general, performing or promising to perform an act which a person is already under a legal obligation to perform is not consideration for a new promise. There are two situations involving existing obligation which call for some discussion: (1) where the promisee is already under contractual duty to the promisor, and (2) where the existing obligation is the result of statutory or common law rule.

Existing Contractual Duty. · Performing or promising to perform a contractual duty which is still in effect is *not* consideration. Suppose that Robert was under contract with Ann to build an asphalt road along one side of Ann's farm for a stated sum, that after partial performance Robert discovered he would lose money on the job, and that he threatened to quit. To persuade Robert to complete the job, Ann promised to pay him an additional $10,000. Robert completed the job. Nearly all courts would hold that there was no consideration given by Robert and he cannot enforce Ann's promise. Robert suffered no legal detriment in completing a job he was already under contractual duty to perform. He did not give up "a legal right"; he had no right to threaten to quit the job even though he would lose money. Such threats are a form of blackmail.

There are exceptions to the general rule of unenforceability, and occasionally courts find legal detriment by the promisee. If the parties to a contract mutually and voluntarily rescind or cancel the contract and one party promises to pay a bonus to the other for performing the same duties called for in the original contract, the courts will enforce the promise. **Rescission** (cancellation) of a contract excuses both parties from further performance. Thus, performing or promising to perform the same acts called for in the original contract is "assuming a legal burden" and constitutes consideration. Another exception to the rule of unenforceability is where the promisee encounters unforeseen difficulties. The courts are reluctant to enforce promises to pay bonuses in such situations and the difficulty must be truly unanticipated. For example, if Robert in the illustration above would lose money on the job because of a labor strike, increase in cost of materials, or bad weather, Ann's promise would still not be enforceable. A court might find consideration by Robert if the cause of his losing money was an unforeseeable flash flood that destroyed all work done to that time.

The following case discusses both unforeseen hardship and mutual rescission.

CASE 9.3   Owens v. City of Bartlett
528 P.2d 1235 (Kan. 1974)

Facts: Owens, a plumbing contractor, was hired by the City of Bartlett to install a water distribution system. Owens encountered unexpected rock. The city ran short of money and fell behind in payments required by the contract. Owens stopped work for three weeks to discuss the payment and rock removal situation. The city agreed to pay for extra work but after the project was completed refused to pay for some of the work.

Owens sued to recover for the extra work and received a judgment from the trial court. The city appealed.

Question: Was the promise of the city to pay for rock removal supported by consideration?

Answer: Yes. Owens (the promisee) did incur legal detriment by continuing the project.

Reasoning: The city argued that the ditching and removal of the rock was an obligation of the contractor under the original contract. Performance of an act the person is already bound to do does not constitute consideration. "However," the court stated,

> "If the original provisions of the contract are mutually rescinded by agreement of the parties, the contractor is then free of any obligation to obtain an order in writing for extra work or materials and is no longer obligated to perform the work for the amount specified in the original contract. Rescission depends upon the intention of the parties as shown by their words, acts, or agreement."

In the present case the evidence showed mutual rescission. In addition, the city was in default in its payments. Thus, Owens was justified in shutting down until payments were made. The city's promise to pay additional compensation was enforceable on the additional ground that Owens gave consideration by giving up the legal right to continue the shutdown.

The judgment was affirmed.

Existing Statutory or Common Law Obligation. Performance or promise of performance (or forbearance) of an act which a person is under legal obligation to perform (or forbear) because of some statutory or common law rule is *not* consideration. Everyone is obligated not to commit torts and crimes. A witness at a trial is required to tell the truth. The holder of a public office has an obligation to perform the duties of the office. There is therefore no consideration for a promise to pay for immunity from assault, to reward a witness for telling the truth, or to pay a sheriff for making an arrest that comes within the scope of the sheriff's duties. In each instance the promisee is not giving up a legal right or assuming a legal burden.

Part Payment of
a Liquidated
Claim

A debt (or claim) is said to be liquidated when there is no dispute about the existence of the debt or its amount. For example, if you purchase a couch from a department store for $550, your obligation to the store is called a "liquidated debt."

The general rule is that part payment of a liquidated debt, made when the debt is due or past due, is not consideration for the creditor's promise to accept the part payment as payment in full. There is no consideration because the debtor has incurred no legal detriment in doing what he or she was already bound to do. For example, suppose Harry is behind $225 in the rent he owes his landlord, Wanda. Harry offers to pay $150 if Wanda agrees to accept that amount as payment in full for the $225 debt owed. Wanda agrees and accepts the $150. A court would hold that there is an offer and an acceptance here, but no consideration to support Wanda's promise (to accept $150 as payment in full). Harry suffered no detriment by paying the $150 and Wanda may collect the balance owed of $75. This is merely an application of the existing-contractual-duty rule discussed previously. Since the debtor gives no consideration, a creditor can recover the unpaid part of the debt *even after promising to accept the part payment as payment in full.*

The general rule has been criticized as tending to defeat fair dealing and the rightful expectations of the debtor. Consequently, the courts have been "astute to find consideration" if the debtor had done anything at all in connection with the payment that he or she was not under obligation to do. Thus, courts will find that there is consideration if the debtor (1) gives some inconsequential thing in addition to making the part payment, (2) pays at a place other than that required by the contract, (3) pays in a medium other than required by the contract, or (4) pays a lesser sum before the due date in the contract. The widespread feeling regarding the undesirable results of the general rule has caused some state legislatures to modify or abolish it. For example, in California and a few other states, a debtor may enforce a written release by the creditor (of the balance owed) even though no new consideration is given.

Settlement of an Unliquidated Claim

The rule that a part payment does not discharge the debt applies only where the debt is liquidated. A claim is *unliquidated* when there is an honest dispute about the actual existence of an indebtedness or, more commonly, about the amount of the indebtedness. Suppose that a home owner orders a certain plumbing job without any agreement as to price. After the plumber completes the job he submits a bill for $300. The owner protests that the size of the bill is unreasonable. She suggests a price of $200. The plumber states that $300 is the "going price" for such a job but that to get the dispute settled, he will accept $250 as payment in full. The owner pays that amount. The agreement to accept $250 is called an "accord." Payment of the amount is called "satisfaction." The plumber may not recover the remaining $50 of his bill. By accepting the settlement he impliedly promises to cancel the balance claimed. The same result occurs if there is no agreement as to price, and the homeowner sends a check for $250 marked "payment in full." There is an accord and satisfaction *if* the plumber cashes the check. The result is the same even if, before cashing the check, the plumber crosses out the notation.

The creditor's promise to cancel the balance is supported by consideration, since the debtor suffered a legal detriment in paying more than a court might have required the debtor to pay. However, this reasoning applies only where the debtor asserts his or her objection in good faith. If a court believes that the debtor is trying to take advantage of the creditor, the court will not enforce the creditor's promise.

The following case involves both a liquidated debt and an unliquidated debt.

CASE 9.4

Field Lumber Co. v. Petty
512 P.2d 764 (Wash. App. 1973)

Facts: Petty made numerous purchases from Field Lumber Co. Field's ledger statement showed a balance due of $1,752.21. Petty acknowledged a balance of $1,091.96 but disputed the difference of $660.25 which represented an allegedly unauthorized

$292.60 purchase by an employee and a 1 percent per month finance charge. Petty mailed a check for $500 to Field with a letter stating the check must be accepted in full settlement of all claims or returned. Field cashed the check and filed suit for the sum alleged to be due ($1,252.21). The trial court held for Petty and Field appealed.

Question: Do the circumstances show an accord and satisfaction?

Answer: No. There is no accord and satisfaction; the payment of $500 was a payment on account.

Reasoning: Petty acknowledged a debt of $1,091.96. Payment of an amount admitted to be due can furnish no consideration for an accord and satisfaction of the entire claim. The court recognized "the general rule that where a sum is unliquidated or disputed and a remittance of an amount less than that claimed is sent to the creditor with a statement explaining that it is in full satisfaction of the claim, the acceptance of such a remittance by the creditor constitutes an accord and satisfaction." However, the rule does not apply here. "A debtor cannot unilaterally tender a lesser sum than that which it is agreed is due and owing and rely upon the retention of that sum as full settlement of the debt unless there is some additional consideration given."

Judgment reversed.

Composition Agreement

A **composition agreement** is an arrangement between a debtor and two or more creditors whereby the debtor, who is unable to pay the full amount owed, agrees to turn his or her assets over to the creditors, and the creditors agree to accept their pro rata portions in *full* satisfaction of their claims. Suppose that David owes $10,000 to Arnold, $6,000 to Bette, and $4,000 to Cynthia. David offers to enter into a composition agreement whereby each creditor will be paid 50 percent of his or her claim. If David turns over his assets to the creditors and they agree to cancel the balances owed, a composition results, and David will be discharged from his obligation to each of the participating creditors.

A composition agreement applies only to the creditors who enter into the agreement. If in the example above, Bette had refused to enter into the agreement, she would not have shared in the distribution of David's assets; but Bette would also not be precluded from attempting later on to collect the full $6,000 owed to her.

Forbearance to Sue on a Claim

Every person has a legal right to litigate or take to court a valid claim. Giving up the right to sue on a valid claim is a legal detriment, and if bargained for, constitutes consideration. Suppose that Peter and Donna are driving their cars and collide in an intersection. There is some doubt as to who is at fault. Donna promises not to sue Peter if Peter agrees to pay her $2500. Peter agrees but later changes his mind and refuses to pay the money. Donna sues Peter for the $2500. Peter's defense is that Donna gave no consideration for his promise. A court would hold that Donna's promise to forbear from suing is giving up a legal right and constitutes legal detriment.

One who agrees not to assert a clearly unfounded claim incurs no legal detriment and cannot enforce a return promise to pay money. In most cases there is doubt as to who is at fault, whether the situation involves an alleged tort or breach of contract. The general rule is that forbearance to sue is consideration if the promisee's claim is doubtful because of uncertainty as to the facts or the law, or if the promisee honestly believes that his or her claim is valid.

The following case illustrates a forbearance to sue an attorney for malpractice.

CASE 9.5   Frasier v. Carter
437 P.2d 32 (Ida. 1968)

Facts: Lena Frasier's husband died leaving a will under which Lena would receive certain bequests. D. L. Carter, her attorney and brother, advised Lena improperly and Lena received a smaller share of her husband's estate than she otherwise would have been entitled to. Carter wrote the following letter to Lena:

"Déar Lena:
   This is to advise and confirm our agreement—that in the event the J. W. Frasier estate case now on appeal is not terminated so that you will receive settlement equal to your share of the estate as you would have done if your waiver had been filed in the estate in proper time, that I will make up any balance to you in payments as suits my convenience and will pay interest on your loss at 6%."

Lena brought suit to enforce Carter's promise. A jury returned a verdict for Lena and Carter appealed.

Question: Was there consideration to make Carter's promise enforceable?

Answer: Yes. Lena (the promisee) incurred legal detriment. She agreed not to prosecute an action against Carter for his negligence in failing to advise her properly.

Reasoning: The court stated, "Waiver of, or forbearance to exercise, a right which is not utterly groundless is sufficient consideration to support a contract made in reliance thereon."

   Judgment affirmed.

PROMISES ENFORCEABLE WITHOUT REGARD TO CONSIDERATION

As we have seen, promises generally are enforceable only if they are supported by consideration. The rule produces unfortunate results in certain kinds of situations, and so the courts recognize some exceptions to the rule. Those exceptions are discussed in the following pages.

**Promises
Enforceable
Because of
Prior Legal
Duty**

As previously indicated, a past transaction cannot constitute consideration. However, where a person had a contractual duty of performance which was barred by operation of law, a subsequent promise to perform is enforceable, even if the promisor receives nothing in exchange for the new promise. Such a situation may occur where the promise was made (1) following bar of the original duty by operation of the statute of limitations, or (2) during bankruptcy.

Promise Following Bar by Statute of Limitations.   All states have statutes of limitations. Such statutes prescribe time limits within which legal action must be started. For example, in some states the time limitation for bringing an action to recover a debt may be 5 years from the maturity date of the debt if the debt involves an oral promise, and 10 years if the debt is evidenced by a writing or by a document under seal. A prescribed time limit starts running from the time a cause of action arises.

A well-recognized rule of law is that a new promise by a debtor to pay a debt which has been barred by the statute of limitations is enforceable, provided the new promise is in writing. A voluntary part payment or an unqualified acknowledgment of indebtedness is usually interpreted as an implied promise to pay, and so comes under the rule just stated.

Promise during Bankruptcy.   Prior to the federal Bankruptcy Reform Act of 1978, a promise to pay a debt which had been discharged in bankruptcy required no new consideration to make it binding. The new Bankruptcy Code discourages debtors from reaffirming debts since a major purpose of bankruptcy is a "fresh start," free from the burden of debts. The code imposes a number of conditions to have an enforceable promise, including court approval of a debtor's reaffirmation. It is clear that in the future promises to pay debts in bankruptcy will virtually disappear. The federal requirements are discussed in Chapter 44 under "Discharge hearing; reaffirmation; protection of discharge," p. 779.

**Promises
Enforceable
Because of
Promissory
Estoppel**

Promissory estoppel is an alternative to the contract doctrine of consideration as a basis for promise enforcement. Under the doctrine of promissory estoppel, the promisor is "estopped" (prevented by the law) from avoiding liability for the consequences of the promise. We discussed promissory estoppel in Chapter 7. Case 7.5 on p. 104 lists the following elements of the doctrine of promissory estoppel:

1. There must be a promise which the promisor should reasonably expect to induce action on the part of the promisee.
2. The promise must induce such action.
3. The promissee must act in justifiable reliance on the promise.
4. The situation must be such that injustice can be avoided only by enforcement of the promise.

The doctrine of promissory estoppel is of growing importance in the enforcement of promises. It is not usual, for example, for a general contractor to make contracts with subcontractors before obtaining the prime contract. Yet, as indicated in Chapter 7, Case 7.5, general contractors often rely on bids (offers) from subcontractors as the general contractors prepare their own bids and enter into contractual arrangements. If nothing more than traditional contract law were available to protect general contractors, they would be unable to enforce the promises (offers) from subcontractors. Promissory estoppel fills a gap in contract law.

Persons other than building contractors may benefit from the doctrine of promissory estoppel. In the case of *Hoffman v. Red Owl Stores, Inc.*,[2] the plaintiff sold his business, moved his family to another town, and purchased business property there in reliance on the defendant's assurance that the plaintiff would become the operator of one of the defendant's retail grocery stores. When the deal did not materialize, the plaintiff successfully invoked the doctrine of promissory estoppel, even though the defendant's representations did not meet the requirements for a contractual offer because many of the terms were missing. The elements of promissory estoppel were present: the promisor should have reasonably expected action by the promisee, the promisee did act, and injustice could only be avoided by enforcement of the defendant's promise. The court awarded plaintiff the amounts he had lost and expended in reliance on the promise.

Promises to make gifts of land have been enforced under the promissory estoppel doctrine. In the decided cases the promisee usually proved that he or she, with the knowledge of the promisor, took possession of the land in reliance on the promise of a gift and made improvements.

SUMMARY

Not all promises are enforceable. A promise may be enforceable because:

1. It was given in exchange for consideration.
2. The promise arose out of a prior legal duty which had been discharged by operation of law.
3. The promisee justifiably relied on the promise to his or her detriment.

Consideration is the most common basis of promise enforcement. Consideration may be defined as legal detriment to the promisee bargained for by the promisor. Legal detriment means the promisee gives up or promises to give up a legal right, or assumes or promises to assume a legal burden. The detriment may have little if any monetary value. Usually the legal detriment incurred by the promisee will be a legal benefit to the promisor, but this is not required. A promise is illusory if the party is not obligated to any performance or has an unrestricted right to cancel the contract.

The courts must deal with a variety of problems relating to consideration. Performing or promising to perform a contractual duty which is still in effect is not consideration. If the parties to a contract mutually rescind the contract and one party promises to pay a bonus to the other for performing the same duties called for in the original contract, the courts will enforce the promise. A promise to pay a bonus is enforceable if the promisee has encountered unforeseen difficulties in performing the

[2]133 N.W.2d 267 (Wis. 1965).

contractual duties. A debtor who makes a part payment of a liquidated debt incurs no legal detriment and may not enforce the creditor's promise to cancel the balance of the debt. The creditor's promise is enforceable if the debtor gives some new consideration or if the debt is unliquidated. Settlement of an unliquidated debt is called "accord and satisfaction." A composition agreement is enforceable by the courts even though the agreement involves liquidated debts. A promise to forbear from suing another person is legal detriment if the one forbearing has a valid claim, has a doubtful claim, or honestly believes that his or her claim is valid.

Some classes of promises are enforceable despite a lack of consideration. Where a person makes a written promise to pay a debt which has been barred by a statute of limitations, the new promise may be enforceable even though the creditor gives no consideration for the new promise. Finally, under the doctrine of promissory estoppel, a promise not supported by consideration may nevertheless be enforceable where the promisee justifiably relied on the promise to his or her detriment.

REVIEW QUESTIONS

1. What is the purpose of consideration?

2. (a) With regard to consideration, explain the meaning and purpose of "bargained-for exchange." (b) Why do the courts define consideration in terms of "legal" rather than "actual" detriment?

3. (a) Illustrate how the consideration demanded by a promisor can move to someone other than the promisor. (b) Why does "past consideration" not constitute consideration?

4. Distinguish between "consideration" and "motive."

5. (a) Why does an "illusory" promise not constitute consideration? (b) Does a person's right to cancel a contract always make the promise illusory? Explain.

6. (a) Why will courts usually not look into the adequacy of consideration? (b) Under what circumstances will courts look into the adequacy of consideration? (c) Define "nominal consideration." Explain its use in a written agreement.

7. (a) Is the performance of an act which a person is already under a legal obligation to perform consideration for a promise to pay more for the performance? Explain in terms of legal detriment. (b) For what reasons might a court enforce a promise to pay extra compensation for the performance of an existing contractual obligation?

8. (a) Is part payment of a liquidated debt consideration for the creditor's promise to accept the part payment as payment in full? Explain in terms of legal detriment. (b) Under what circumstances will a promise to accept part payment of a liquidated debt be binding on the creditor?

9. Explain how consideration theory is applied to the settlement of an unliquidated claim.

10. (a) Does forbearance to sue on a claim constitute consideration? Explain in terms of legal detriment. (b) Under what circumstances will forbearance to sue not constitute consideration?

11. A promise to pay a debt barred by the running of the statute of limitations may be enforceable without consideration. Under what circumstances will such a promise be enforced?

12. What is required for a promise to be enforced under the doctrine of promissory estoppel?

CASE PROBLEMS

1. In 1958, the mother of plaintiff Robert Adair and defendant Ralph Adair deeded a farm to Ralph and his wife Elsie. The mother received $5890 and gave approximately $3500 of that amount to Robert. Ralph gave Robert a note for $3000 and a mortgage on the property to secure the note. In 1972 the note was unpaid and Robert brought an action to foreclose the mortgage. Ralph died before the trial. Defendant Elsie contended that there was no consideration given by Robert for the note and mortgage. Was there consideration for the note and mortgage? Explain reasons for your answer.

2. Hill, as representative of the Oertel family, agreed to pay Thomas a "finder's fee" of $25,000 for procuring the sale of the controlling stock of the Oertel Brewing Co. Thomas, a director and executive vice president of the company, did arrange the sale of the stock to Brown-Forman Distillers, Inc. However, Hill refused to pay the finder's fee. Hill contended that there was no consideration for the agreement because Thomas's employment as executive vice president, for which he was being paid a salary of $25,000 per year, included the duty to find a buyer for the brewery. Was Thomas entitled to the finder's fee in addition to his salary? Why or why not?

3. Rhoades was divorced in 1971 and promised to pay $80 per week for child support. He later quit his job and accepted another position at a sharply reduced salary. In litigation relating to child support, Rhoades testified that his former wife agreed to accept payments of $50 per week instead of the $80 per week originally promised. Assume that the former wife agreed to accept the smaller payments. Is her agreement binding on her? Explain.

4. Rhea sold land to Smith, who executed a note for $12,000 in part payment. Smith had a right to pay the amount before the due date of the note, and after making payments for four years, he decided to pay off the note. He asked for a discount on the amount owed, which Rhea refused. When Smith asked the bank handling the matter to state the payoff amount, the note teller made an error. Smith paid $2363.88 less than was owed, and Rhea signed a release before anyone discovered the mistake. Smith refused to make further payment, and Rhea brought suit for the balance of the account. The trial court held that the note was discharged by an accord and satisfaction, and rendered judgment for Smith. Rhea appealed. Was there an accord and satisfaction? Give reasons.

5. British Overseas Airways Corp. (BOAC) decided to construct a new cargo building at Kennedy International Airport and awarded the general contract to Thatcher Construction Co. Thatcher awarded the structural steel subcontract to Bethlehem Fabricators, Inc., which, because of unhappy prior dealings with

Thatcher, insisted on a payment bond. BOAC at first promised Bethlehem that it would require Thatcher to obtain a payment bond, but then, to save itself the $4250 bond premium, later decided not to require the payment bond of Thatcher. Bethlehem performed its contract not knowing of this decision. Thatcher failed to pay Bethlehem and eventually filed a petition in bankruptcy, leaving a total of $78,115.98 due Bethelehem. Bethelehem sued BOAC for that amount, asserting the doctrine of promissory estoppel. Which party should prevail? Explain.

CHAPTER 10

CONTRACTUAL CAPACITY; AVOIDANCE OF CONTRACTS

Previous chapters dealt with the first three requirements for a contract: offer, acceptance, and consideration. This chapter examines the fourth requirement for a contract—parties with legal capacity to contract—and discusses a number of situations in which a party to a contract has a right to have a court set the contract aside or modify its terms.

Ordinarily, it is assumed that the parties to a contract have sufficient mental capacity to bargain effectively and that they act freely in assenting to the bargain. A party may challenge these assumptions by asserting lack of capacity to contract or by asserting the existence of a defect in negotiations preceding contract formation. Some persons have no legal capacity to contract; some have full contractual capacity. In between these two extremes are persons having limited contractual power. Most of their contracts are voidable, but some are fully enforceable.

The first two parts of this chapter examine the contractual capacity of minors, mentally incompetent persons, and those under the influence of alcohol or drugs. The last two parts of the chapter discuss a number of other grounds to avoid a contract, and the remedies associated with avoidance.

CONTRACTUAL CAPACITY OF MINORS

At common law, persons under 21 years were called "infants." The term is still widely used in the United States to refer to underage persons. However, the modern trend is to refer to such persons as "minors."

From early common law days to the present, the law has protected minors from being bound by their contracts. Several reasons have been advanced for providing this protection.

- Minors need to be protected from their immaturity, their inexperience, and their tendency to do impulsive buying.
- They are especially likely to be the victims of unscrupulous adults.
- Minors may not understand the nature and consequences of contracts which they enter into.

Period of Minority

In most states the age of majority for contract purposes has been lowered from 21 to 18. However, the age of majority is not the same for all purposes, and states often set a higher age for legally purchasing liquor. When asked to set aside a contract entered into by a minor, the court does not investigate the experience or maturity of the particular minor. It is assumed that all minors are incapable of bargaining on an equal basis with an adult.

Disaffirmance of Minors' Voidable Contracts

The general rule is that a minor's contract is "voidable" by the minor. A **voidable contract** is one that a person may avoid or may perform, as he or she chooses. A minor's exercise of the power of avoidance is commonly referred to as the **disaffirmance** of the contract.

The power of disaffirmance is personal to the minor. During his or her lifetime, only the minor or a legally appointed guardian may exercise that power; and upon the minor's death the minor's heirs or a personal representative may exercise it. An adult party to a contract with a minor has no similar power of disaffirmance; the adult is bound to the contract unless the minor disaffirms it. Where both parties to the contract are minors, each has the power of disaffirmance.

Requisites for Disaffirmance.   If the minor chooses to avoid a particular contract, he or she may assert minority as a defense in a lawsuit filed by the adult to enforce the contract, or may file a suit to disaffirm. Most states impose prerequisites to granting relief. In most states, in order to disaffirm, the person must: (1) return or offer to return any goods or property received; (2) demand the return of money or goods, if any, transferred to the other party; and (3) act during minority or within a reasonable time after attaining majority.

Upon disaffirmance, the minor must return whatever was received if it is still in his or her possession. The courts do not agree on whether the minor can disaffirm when unable to return the property received, or when able to return it only in damaged condition. The majority view is that the minor may disaffirm even though the property received has been lost, destroyed, or damaged.

As stated above, a person may disaffirm the contract during minority or within a reasonable time after reaching majority. What constitutes a "reasonable time" for disaffirmance is a question of fact and depends on the circumstances. In most states a minor may not disaffirm his or her conveyance of land until after reaching majority. In a few states, such as California, a minor's contract involving land is void, rather than voidable. Thus, in those states no time limit is imposed on disaffirmance. A void contract is never binding on either party.

The following case involves the prerequisites to disaffirmance.

CASE 10.1   Terrace Co. v. Calhoun
347 N.E.2d 315 (Ill. App. 1976)

Facts: When she was thirteen years old, Marilyn Calhoun signed a confession-of-judgment promissory note in the amount of $1,944.72 payable to L. C. Wesley Funeral Home. Her father had died and the funeral director requested her to sign the note and an assignment of Marilyn's interest in an insurance policy on her father's life. These documents were assigned to the Terrace Company. Terrace took the note to court and had judgment entered against Marilyn. In 1973, when Marilyn was 19 years old, a prospective employer informed her that because of the Terrace Co. judgment her credit record was impaired. She filed a motion to set aside the judgment but was unsuccessful. Marilyn appealed.

Question: Did Marilyn satisfy the prerequisites for disaffirmance?

Answer: Yes. Under the circumstances, Marilyn did satisfy the prerequisites for disaffirmance.

Reasoning:	Marilyn was not advised of the nature and effect of the documents she signed at age 13. Marilyn first learned of the judgment by confession when she was 19 years old. Within two months thereafter she filed a motion to open the judgment. Under these circumstances, the court said, Marilyn disaffirmed within a reasonable time after attaining majority (age 18). Ordinarily, a minor must return to the other party what the minor received. Here, the promissory note was for the funeral of the minor's father. The court said a funeral service is an intangible which is incapable of being returned.

The judgment was reversed.

Effect of Misrepresentation of Age.   Most courts hold that a minor who has intentionally misrepresented his or her age is not thereby prevented from avoiding the contract. However, there is conflict of authority on whether the minor is liable in tort for that misrepresentation. It is well established that minors are liable for their torts generally, and the view of most courts is that the minor is liable for the tort of fraud. (See Chapter 3, pp. 46–49 for discussion of fraud.)

Ratification of Minors' Voidable Contracts

Meaning of Ratification.   When used in connection with minors' contracts, **ratification** means a manifestation of an intention to be bound by a contract entered into during the period of minority. The minor cannot ratify a contract until he or she becomes of age. Any purported ratification during minority is ineffective.

How Contracts May Be Ratified.   A contract may be ratified in one of three ways: by express ratification, by implied ratification, or by failure to make a timely disaffirmance. An *express ratification* is one in which the intention to be bound by a contract previously made is expressed in words. No particular form of expression is required. Any wording suffices as long as it indicates an intention to be bound.

An *implied ratification* is one in which an intention to be bound is inferred from the person's conduct. For example, suppose that Brenda enters into a contract three months before reaching her majority. Under the terms of the contract she receives some diving gear for which she is to pay later. Two months after reaching her majority, she sells the gear. Disposal of the gear is an act inconsistent with an intent to disaffirm and thus may be held to constitute ratification. Other conduct from which ratification may be inferred includes using property purchased for more than a reasonable time after majority, and part payment or other performance of contract terms after reaching majority.

It was stated earlier that one of the requisites for disaffirming a minor's contract is to act during minority or within a reasonable time after attaining majority. Failure to disaffirm within a reasonable time after attaining majority results in a ratification. In determining a reasonable time some courts consider whether the contract is executory or executed. These courts permit a person to wait much longer to disaffirm an executory contract than an executed one, provided the delay does not prejudice the other party to the contract.

Contracts Which Minors Cannot Disaffirm

The general rule that minors may avoid their contracts is subject to certain exceptions. In some states such as California there are statutes requiring a court to approve certain minors' contracts, including contracts of employment as an entertainer or professional athlete, and contracts compromising tort claims. The minor may not later disaffirm a court-approved contract. Where a minor owns property a court may, upon petition, appoint a guardian to manage the estate of the minor. The guardian may sell the minor's property when appropriate and the sale is not subject to disaffirmance.

Liability of Minors for Necessaries

Ordinarily, a minor's parents or guardian will provide the minor with food, clothing, and housing. If the parent or guardian is unable or unwilling to supply such items, the law makes it possible for the minor to purchase them.

Nature of Liability for Necessaries. A minor who enters into a contract for necessaries may disaffirm the contract in accordance with the general rule regarding minors' contracts. However, he or she may be liable in quasi contract to the provider of the necessaries for the reasonable value of the necessaries provided (see Chapter 6, pp. 92–93 for discussion of quasi contract). The law places this liability upon minors mainly for their protection. If minors could avoid all obligation to pay, they might have difficulty securing necessaries.

Goods and Services Recognized as Necessaries. Courts have held that food, clothing, shelter, medical services, tools of a trade, and some degree of education can be classifed as necessaries.

"Necessaries" is a relative term. The same goods and services may be recognized as necessaries in one situation and not in another. One of the determinants of whether a good or service is a necessary is the minor's *station in life*. Clothing of high quality and fashion may be a necessary for a minor whose father is a diplomat, but not for one whose father works in a fish cannery. Perhaps the most important test is the *need* of the minor for the particular article or service at the time it is supplied. For example, food is not a necessary for a minor who has an adequate supply. A minor is not liable for necessaries so long as the parent or guardian is able and willing to supply them. Broad discretion is granted the parent or guardian in determining how to meet the needs of the minor.

CONTRACTUAL CAPACITY OF CERTAIN OTHER CLASSES OF PERSONS

Mentally Incompetent Persons

Ordinarily, a contract made by a mentally incompetent person is voidable, just as a contract made by a minor is voidable and for the same reason—to protect persons unable to protect themselves against imposition.

Test of Mental Incompetency. The general test for determining whether a person is so mentally incompetent as to justify a court in holding his or her contract to be voidable may be stated thus: Did the party have, at the time of entering into the contract, sufficient mental capacity to understand the nature and consequences of the transaction? Mental incompetency is not the same as insanity. There are various degrees and types of mental incompetency. Among the causes of incompetency are birth defects, senility, brain damage caused by accident, and mental illness.

A person suffering from mental illness may have lucid intervals. A contract made during such an interval is binding on both parties.

Effect of Mental Incompetency.   If a person at the time of entering into a contract lacks sufficient mental capacity, the contract is voidable and may be rescinded. The person, or a guardian or conservator, must (1) act promptly, (2) demand the return of money or goods, and (3) return or offer to return goods or property received. Mental incompetency may be raised as a defense in a lawsuit filed by the other party to enforce the contract.

In some instances a person may be adjudicated incompetent by a court, which will appoint a guardian or conservator to care for the person's assets. Thereafter, any contracts made by the person are void, not voidable.

One who is mentally incompetent is liable in quasi contract for the reasonable value of necessaries.

Persons under the Influence of Alcohol or Other Drugs

In most respects the law treats the contracts of persons acting under the influence of alcohol or other drugs the same way it treats the contracts of mentally incompetent persons. For example, where a guardian or conservator has been appointed for the property of a chronic alcoholic, any transaction entered into thereafter by the person is void. Where no guardian has been appointed, an intoxicated person's transactions are usually held to be voidable. Relief will be granted only if the person is so intoxicated or so under the influence of drugs that he or she does not understand the nature and consequences of the contract entered into.

A person who lacks understanding as a result of using alcohol or other drugs is liable in quasi contract for the reasonable value of necessaries.

AVOIDANCE OF CONTRACTS

A contract may be formed between two adults who are sane and sober, and yet that contract may be defective. Following is a discussion of five recognized grounds to avoid a contract: duress, undue influence, fraud, misrepresentation, and mistake.

Duress

Meaning of Duress.   Duress may be defined as wrongful coercion by which a person is induced to do something he or she otherwise would not do. Typically, the threatening party gains money or property to which he or she is not entitled and the underlying contract is voidable by the innocent party.

Elements of Duress.   The elements which must be present to constitute duress are (1) a wrongful threat, and (2) the overcoming of a person's free will.

Wrongful Threat.   Various kinds of threats constitute duress. The most common kinds are threats to the person, threats to property, and threats to business or to means of earning a living.

Threats to the *person* include a threat of physical injury to the person threatened, or to the person's spouse, child, or other near relative.

Threats to *a person's business* or to means of earning a livelihood may, under certain circumstances, result in duress. This kind of duress by threat is commonly referred to as *economic duress* or *business compulsion.* The importance of economic duress has greatly increased because of the ever-increasing extent of economic interdependence. Ordinarily a court will not hold that there has been economic duress unless the plaintiff seeking to rescind a contract can prove that irreparable injury to his or her business or to chances of gaining an adequate livelihood would result if the defendant were to carry out the wrongful threat. As illustrated in Case 10.2, the threat made by the defendant may consist of threatening to breach a contract under circumstances where the defendant knows the plaintiff would suffer severe economic hardship. Many courts stress the plaintiff's lack of a reasonable alternative as a necessary part of proving duress.

Overcoming of Free Will. To constitute duress, the threat must produce fear sufficient to overcome a party's free will. The test in most states is the reaction of the particular individual threatened. The particular individual need not be as brave as the "ordinary reasonable person."

CASE 10.2 Litten v. Jonathan Logan, Inc.
286 A.2d 913 (Pa. Super. 1971)

Facts: In November 1960 Bernard Litten and others (plaintiffs) entered into an oral contract with Jonathan Logan, Inc. In exchange for all the stock of two corporations owned by plaintiffs, Logan agreed to pay off certain bank loans, to employ plaintiffs for one year and to give plaintiffs an option to purchase 5000 shares of Logan stock. Litten transferred all the stock to Logan, but Logan refused to pay the creditors in full and the creditors threatened the plaintiffs with bankruptcy. On January 9, 1961 Logan insisted that plaintiffs sign a new agreement which did not include a stock option nor an employment clause. Plaintiffs could not afford to pay a $5,000 retainer fee demanded by their lawyer in order to file suit against Logan. Later, this suit was filed and plaintiffs received a judgment for damages based on the oral contract of November 1960. Logan appealed.

Question: Was the written agreement of January 9, 1961 entered into under duress and thus subject to avoidance by plaintiffs?

Answer: Yes. Plaintiffs were subjected to economic duress, and the written contract may be avoided.

Reasoning: The court said,

"The important elements in the applicability of the doctrine of economic duress or business compulsion are that (1) there exists such pressure of circumstances which compels the injured party to involuntarily or against his will execute an agreement which results in economic loss, and (2) the injured party does not have an immediate legal remedy."

Ordinarily, a threatened breach of contract is not in itself coercive but duress may occur if the breach will cause irreparable injury to a party's business. Here, once the plaintiffs had turned over all the stock in their two corporations they lost independence of decision. Logan had placed them in a position of inescapable economic peril.

The judgment was affirmed.

Undue Influence

Undue influence occurs when one party overcomes the free will of the other party by *unfair persuasion.* Many cases involve persons making gifts of money or property or making wills which include large bequests to persons outside one's immediate family. Thus, in the usual case of undue influence there is an unnatural enrichment of one party at the expense of the other party or the other's family.

Unfair persuasion is most likely to occur in situations in which

1. A person is under the domination of another person.
2. There is such a relationship of trust and confidence (often called a "fiduciary relationship") between two persons that one is justified in assuming that his or her best interests will be protected by the other.

In the first category, a person may be under the *domination of another person* because of mental weakness, ignorance, lack of experience, old age, poor health, physical handicap, emotional strain, or financial distress.

The second category embraces *relationships of trust and confidence,* such as parent and child, guardian and ward, husband and wife, physician and patient, attorney and client, or pastor and parishioner. Most courts take the position that if it is established that a confidential relationship existed when a transaction was entered into that benefited the trusted person, the burden of proof is on that person to prove the transaction was not procured by undue influence. For example, if an attorney prepares a will for a client in which the attorney is to receive a large sum of money in preference to the client's legal heirs, a court would require the attorney to prove he or she did not exercise undue influence over the client.

Fraud

Fraud as a tort was discussed in detail in Chapter 3 (see pp. 46–49), to which you may wish to refer. The five elements of fraud were each analyzed in that chapter. The following discussion assumes knowledge and familiarity with the elements of fraud, and is devoted mainly to fraud in contract situations.

Elements of Fraud in Contract Situations.   In contract law, four elements must be proved for fraud to exist: (1) a false representation of fact (not of opinion or of law, unless made by an expert), (2) knowledge that the representation was false, (3) intent to induce another to act, and (4) justifiable reliance on the representation. A fifth element, resulting injury, is required in a tort action but need not be proved in a contract case. Thus, a person who is fraudulently induced to enter a contract may get what he or she bargained for and suffer no economic loss, yet may still rescind the transaction.

Often, contracts contain exculpatory or disclaimer clauses. For example, a clause might provide: "It is agreed that there are no representations of any kind between the parties other than contained in this written contract." Most courts ignore such provisions and allow a party to introduce evidence that he or she was defrauded.

Types of Fraud in Contract Situations.   There are two types of fraud relating to contracts: (1) fraud in the *inducement*, and (2) fraud in the *execution*. If all the elements of the tort of fraud exist in the inducement of a contract, remedies are available which are not available in other contract situations.

Fraud in the Inducement: Remedies if Tort.   Fraud in the inducement of a contract is a common type of fraud. In the typical situation the fraud relates to the nature or quality of goods or services exchanged, rather than the content of an agreement or the nature of the document signed.

When a party has been fraudulently induced to enter a contract, he or she has a choice of remedies. If the five elements of fraud are established, the defrauded party may (1) raise fraud as a defense in a lawsuit filed by the promisee to enforce the contract, (2) rescind the contract entered into, or (3) file an action against the promisee for the tort of fraud. If only the elements of contract fraud are proved, the defrauded party may not file an action in tort. The remedy of rescission is discussed in the last part of this chapter. As illustrated in the following case, where a party elects to sue in tort, he or she chooses to affirm the contract, keep what he or she has received, and seek damages to compensate for the injury suffered.

CASE 10.3   Slater v. KFC Corp.
621 F.2d 932 (8th Cir. 1980)

Facts: Thomas J. Slater filed a tort action alleging that KFC Corporation fraudulently induced him to purchase two franchises for the operation of seafood restaurants. KFC counter-claimed for the cost of equipment supplied to Slater and for royalty and advertising fees owing under the franchise agreement.

The franchise agreements set out the following disclaimer in large type:

NO STATEMENT, REPRESENTATION OR OTHER ACT, EVENT OR COMMUNICATION, EXCEPT AS SET FORTH HEREIN, IS BINDING ON THE FRANCHISOR IN CONNECTION WITH THE SUBJECT MATTER OF THIS AGREEMENT.

Following a trial the jury awarded Slater $256,000 in actual and $100,000 in punitive damages and awarded KFC $141,000 on its equipment counterclaim but denied recovery on the counterclaim for royalty and advertising fees. Both parties appealed.

Question: Does the disclaimer clause prevent Slater from recovering damages for fraud, and was the court correct in denying KFC's counterclaim for royalty and advertising fees?

Answer: No. The disclaimer clause does not bar a suit for fraud. The court should have allowed KFC's counterclaim.

Reasoning: The court stated that under Missouri law "a party simply may not, by disclaimer or otherwise, contractually exclude liability for fraud in inducing that contract." As to the counterclaim, the court stated the usual rule that a fraud victim has an option: he or she may retain whatever he or she has received and sue in tort, or may return what was received and sue for recission. By electing to sue in tort Slater affirmed the contractual terms. Thus, KFC may be entitled to recover for royalty and advertising fees.

The court remanded the case for a new trial.

Fraud in the Execution.   Occasionally, a person is defrauded as to the nature of a document he or she is asked to sign. Such fraud is called "fraud in the execution" or "fraud in the factum." For example, suppose a salesperson demonstrates a vacuum cleaner to a homeowner and at the conclusion of the demonstration has the owner sign a document the salesperson describes as "an acknowledgment of the demonstration." If in fact the document is a contract obligating the homeowner to buy a vacuum cleaner, the contract is void (of no effect whatsoever). Many courts will find fraud in the execution only if the document signed is entirely different from that which the party is led to believe he or she is signing, and if the party was not negligent in signing the document under the circumstances. Void contracts are discussed in the last part of this chapter.

Innocent Misrepresentation
There are similarities between the elements of fraud and the guidelines developed for cases involving innocent misrepresentation (often referred to merely as "misrepresentation"). There are, however, two important differences between the elements of fraud and innocent misrepresentation.

1. As the word "innocent" indicates, knowledge of falsity is not an element of innocent misrepresentation.
2. To be of legal consequence, an innocent misrepresentation must be of a material fact, whereas materiality of a representation is not generally required for recission based on fraud (i.e., contract fraud).

Innocent misrepresentation is not a tort. However, an individual who is induced to enter a contract in reliance on an innocent misrepresentation may either (1) raise misrepresentation as a defense in a lawsuit filed by the promisee to enforce the contract, or (2) rescind the contract entered into.

Mistake
Mistake as used in this discussion means a self-induced error, that is, one not induced by the fraud or misrepresentation of the other contracting party. Some frequently recurring mistakes are:

- Mistake in connection with words used
- Mutual mistake of fact
- Unilateral mistake of fact

Mistake in Connection with Words Used.   The law usually takes an objective approach toward expressions of assent. If John, who owns a Ford and a Dodge, means to offer his Ford for sale but inadvertently says, "I'll sell you my Dodge for $495," and Bill replies in good faith, "I accept your offer," there is a contract for the sale of the Dodge.

Sometimes an offer contains a latent (not yet obvious) ambiguity. In the above illustration there was only one possible meaning of "my Dodge." Suppose, however, that John owned two Dodges, one a 1970 model and one a 1973 model. If John thought he was selling the 1970 Dodge and Bill thought he was buying the 1973 Dodge, there is no contract. Only if both parties actually intended the same subject matter (either car) of the sale would there be a contract.

Another type of mistake may occur in connection with words used and be of such a nature that the court will correct it. An error in transcription occurs where the parties have made an oral agreement and, while putting it in writing, a mistake is made with the result that the writing does not correctly state the terms of the oral agreement. Suppose, for example, that Paula orally agrees to sell a parcel of land to Don. The legal description of Paula's land is "Lot 6 of the Blackacre Tract." When a written document is prepared to incorporate all the terms of sale the parcel is described as "Lot 9 of the Blackacre Tract." In this situation either party may seek the remedy of **reformation** through court action. *Reformation* means the court will order that the written document be corrected to conform to the terms of the oral agreement.

Mutual Mistake of Fact.   At times both parties to a contract assume the existence of a vital fact and on the basis of that assumption enter into the contract. If they later discover the assumption is false, either may (1) raise the mistake as a defense in a lawsuit filed by the other to enforce the contract, or (2) rescind the contract.

A mutual mistake of fact usually means both parties have a false assumption about some *aspect of the subject matter* of the contract (identity or quality, quantity or extent). As illustrated in the following case, the existence or nonexistence of the aspect must be vital and basic to the parties' bargain and must not be a matter of opinion.

CASE 10.4   Beachcomber Coins, Inc. v. Boskett
400 A.2d 78 (N.J. Super. 1979)

Facts: Beachcomber Coins, Inc. (plaintiff), a retail dealer in coins, purchased from Boskett for $500 a dime purportedly minted in 1916 at Denver. It was later discovered that the "D" on the coin signifying Denver mintage was counterfeited. Boskett had acquired this coin and two others of minor value for a total of $450 and believed the dime to be a genuine rarity. A representative of plaintiff spent from 15 to 45 minutes in close examination of the coin before purchasing it. Upon discovery that the coin was a counterfeit, plaintiff brought an action for rescission, asserting mutual mistake of fact. The trial judge held for Boskett on the ground that customary coin dealing procedures were for a dealer to make his own investigation of the genuineness of the coin and to "assume the risk" of his purchase if his investigation is faulty. Plaintiff appealed to the Superior Court, Appellate Division.

Question: Was there mutual mistake of fact entitling the plaintiff to rescind the sale?

Answer: Yes. This is a classic case of mutual mistake of fact.

Reasoning: Both parties believed the coin was a genuine Denver-minted one. The price asked and paid was directly based on that assumption. The court said, "That plaintiff may have been negligent in his inspection of the coin (a point not expressly found but implied by the trial judge) does not, as noted above, bar its claim for rescission."

The judgment was affirmed.

Unilateral Mistake of Fact.   Generally, when one party to an agreement assents on the basis of his or her own mistake, the mistake is not ground for relief. Suppose, for example, that Bob Brown, a bidder on a construction project, forgets to include a very expensive item, so that his bid (offer) is materially less than it otherwise would have been. A contract is formed by the acceptance of an offer even though the offer is made under a mistake. However, if a bid is so low that the offeree should realize that a mistake has been made, the offeree would not be entitled to "snap up" the offer. Thus, if several bids around $750,000 and one bid of $570,000 were submitted, the offeree should realize that the low bid, being approximately 25 percent below the average of the other bids, probably was based on an error. When the offeree knows or should know of the offeror's mistake, the mistake is said to be "palpable" (or obvious), and no contract is formed by an attempted acceptance. The rule regarding palpable mistake does not apply to errors in judgment or opinion. Thus, for example, if Roger offers to sell his car for $500 and Sally accepts, knowing the car is a classic and worth $5000 and that Roger is unaware of this fact, a contract is formed and no relief is available to Roger.

Under certain conditions a person may be granted relief on the basis of that person's own mistake, even though the other party had no reason to suppose that a mistake had been made. The conditions essential to such relief are: (1) The mistake is significant (material), (2) enforcement of the contract would be unconscionable, (3) the party making the mistake was not negligent, (4) it is possible to rescind the contract without serious prejudice to the other party (except loss of the bargain), and (5) prompt notice of the mistake is given.

REMEDIES ASSOCIATED WITH AVOIDANCE

Remedies When Contract Is Voidable

A contract entered into where the assent of one or both parties is defective is said to be "voidable." The defect may be duress, undue influence, fraud, misrepresentation, or mistake. A *voidable* contract means that a party has the option to rescind the contract. The contract is not automatically avoided. Today in most states in order to rescind, the party seeking rescission must (1) act promptly upon discovering the defect, (2) return or offer to return the goods or property received, and (3) demand the return of money or goods transferred to the other party.

Failure to act promptly amounts to ratification of the contract. Where an individual has assented to a contract under duress or undue influence, he or she (or sometimes a guardian or executor) must act with reasonable promptness after the coercion or domination ceases. Where a person is induced to assent to a contract through fraud or misrepresentation, the truth may not be discovered until some time later. In such an event, if the person chooses to rescind he or she must act within a reasonable time after the discovery is made. The same rule applies in situations where a unilateral mistake of fact or a mutual mistake of fact is discovered after a contract is entered into.

Occasionally one party or the other is not able to return goods received. At times the contract calls for performance of a service and the party has partially performed part of the bargain. In such instances the court will grant relief in quasi contract to prevent unjust enrichment. The amount of recovery is the reasonable value of services performed or property consumed.

Remedies When Contract Is Void

In rare cases a contract is said to be "void." Although the term seems logically contradictory, in law a *void contract* is one that is of no effect and never will be. Void contracts take many forms. One form resulting from fraud in the execution is illustrated on p. 148. Generally the prerequisites to rescission do not apply where a contract is void. Thus, a person need not act promptly, and failure to act promptly does not amount to ratification. To prevent unjust enrichment, a party may recover in quasi contract the money paid under a void contract, or the reasonable value of services performed or property consumed.

Remedies When Third Persons Are Involved

The difference between voidable and void agreements may be of great importance when the rights of third persons are involved. Suppose that Bill buys goods from Sally and resells them to Tom, a bona fide (good faith) purchaser. If the original transfer of goods from Sally to Bill was merely voidable by Sally (as where Sally transferred the goods to him on the basis of Bill's innocent misrepresentation), Tom obtains good title and may retain the goods without any further obligation to Sally. Her only remedy is to sue Bill and to obtain from him damages in quasi contract. On the other hand, if a transfer by Sally was void (as where she had previously been declared insane by a court), Sally would be entitled to recover the goods from Tom, even though he is a good faith purchaser. The legal theory is that where a transaction is void, the purchaser receives no title to the goods.

SUMMARY

Minors, mentally incompetent persons, and persons under the influence of alcohol or other drugs have limited capacity to contract. Depending on the degree of incapacity and other factors, the contracts of such persons may be void, voidable, or enforceable.

The law seeks to protect minors from imprudent contracts. As a general rule, therefore, a minor's contract is voidable. A minor may disaffirm a contract while still a minor or within a reasonable time thereafter. Generally, upon disaffirmance of a contract, the minor must return whatever he or she received if still in possession of it. Upon disaffirmance a minor is entitled to the return of money or property from the other party. A minor who intentionally misrepresents his or her age may still disaffirm a contract. However, the minor may be liable for the tort of fraud.

Upon reaching the age of majority, a person may ratify contracts made as a minor. Ratification is a manifestation of an intention to be bound by a contract entered into during the period of minority. Ratification may be express or implied, or may result from not disaffirming within a reasonable time after attaining majority.

Minors cannot avoid certain kinds of contracts. For example, minors cannot avoid court-approved contracts, such as contracts of employment as entertainers or professional athletes, and contracts compromising tort claims. In most states a minor may disaffirm a contract for necessaries but is liable in quasi contract for their reasonable value. Necessaries include food, clothing, medical care, shelter, tools of a trade, and education. The item supplied must be appropriate to the minor's station in life and not be supplied by the parent or guardian in order for the minor to be held.

Where a person has been adjudged mentally incompetent and is in the care of a guardian, a contract made by the incompetent person is void. Where there is no guardian, the contract of such a person is voidable if, when it was made, he or she lacked the capacity to understand the nature and consequences of the transaction. The rules regarding the contracts of persons under the influence of alcohol or other drugs are similar.

A person lacking in understanding is liable in quasi contract for the reasonable value of necessaries furnished.

Where circumstances warrant, the courts permit competent adults to avoid their contracts. A contract may be voidable on grounds of duress, undue influence, fraud, innocent misrepresentation, or mistake.

Duress is a wrongful threat, by words or conduct, that induces such fear on the part of the person threatened as overcomes his or her free will. The wrongful threat may be to harm a person or a person's property, or the threat may consist of economic duress.

Undue influence involves overcoming freedom of will through unfair persuasion. Contracts induced by duress or undue influence are voidable.

Fraud requires (1) a false representation of fact, (2) knowledge that the representation was false, (3) intent to induce another to act, and (4) justifiable reliance on the representation. Agreements resulting from fraud in the inducement of a contract are voidable. If the elements of the tort of fraud are present, the party has the option of affirming the contract and suing in tort to recover damages. Agreements resulting from fraud in the execution of a contract are void.

Innocent misrepresentation involves neither knowledge of falsity nor intent to deceive. To be of legal consequence, the misrepresentation must be of a material fact.

Courts may give relief on the ground of *mistake*. A mutual mistake sometimes prevents the formation of a contract, as where each party attaches a different meaning to an ambiguous word in the agreement. Where there is a mistake in transcribing an oral agreement, the court will grant reformation and enforce the contract as corrected. More often a mutual mistake results in a voidable contract, as where the parties are mutually mistaken about the quality of the subject matter or some other fact basic to the agreement. A mutual mistake of opinion or judgment is not grounds for rescission. Ordinarily, unilateral mistake is not grounds for relief. If the mistake is palpable (obvious), no contract is formed by an attempted acceptance. Even when the mistake is not palpable, relief may be granted where enforcement of the contract would be unconscionable, the party making the mistake was not negligent, and the other party would not suffer serious prejudice. Mistake may be asserted as a defense or the mistaken party may rescind the agreement.

A *voidable* contract is one that a person has the option to rescind, or cancel. Rescission requires that a party, or a party's representative (1) act promptly, (2) return or offer to return goods or property received, and (3) demand the return of money or goods transferred. A *void* contract is one that is of no effect and never will be. In cases of either void or voidable contracts, quasi contract may be available to prevent unjust enrichment.

REVIEW QUESTIONS

1. For what reasons does the law permit minors to avoid their contracts?

2. (**a**) What is meant by "disaffirmance" of a contract? (**b**) Who may exercise a minor's power of disaffirmance?

3. (**a**) What are the requisites for disaffirmance of a contract by a minor? (**b**) When may a minor disaffirm a contract? (**c**) When may a minor disaffirm his or her conveyance of land?

4. (**a**) With regard to minors' contracts, explain the meaning and legal effect of ratification. (**b**) When may a minor's contract be ratified? (**c**) Illustrate the three ways in which a minor's contract may be ratified.

5. (**a**) For what practical reason is a minor liable for necessaries? (**b**) Give illustrations of necessaries. (**c**) State a general guide for deciding what constitutes a necessary.

6. (**a**) The contract of a mentally incompetent person may be voidable. Why? (**b**) What is the general test for determining whether a person is sufficiently competent mentally for his or her contract to be enforced? (**c**) What is the effect of the appointment of a guardian on contracts made thereafter?

7. (**a**) How do courts define "duress"? (**b**) What is meant by "economic duress"?

8. "Undue influence is closely related to duress." (**a**) What is the similarity? (**b**) What is the difference? (**c**) State the two kinds of situations in which undue influence is most likely to occur, and give an example of each.

9. Differentiate between "fraud in the inducement" and "fraud in the execution."

10. Explain the two differences between the elements of contract fraud and innocent misrepresentation.

11. (**a**) What is reformation? (**b**) Under what circumstances is reformation available?

12. Under what two circumstances will courts grant relief from a contract entered into under a unilateral mistake?

13. (**a**) List the prerequisites to rescind a voidable contract. (**b**) What effect would a failure to act promptly have on a void contract?

CASE PROBLEMS

1. Bristol County Stadium, Inc. (defendant) owned and operated an automobile racetrack. To enter a "novice race," Del Santo (plaintiff) had to sign several documents, one of which was a release for any injury he might sustain on the track. A release is a type of contract in which a person promises not to sue for future injury or loss. In his entry application, Del Santo misrepresented his age to conceal the fact that he was a minor.

During the race, Del Santo's car overturned. Del Santo was not injured then, but he sustained serious injuries when his car was run into by another car a short time later. A few months after attaining his majority, Del Santo sued the defendant for alleged negligence in conducting the race. In bringing suit, Del Santo disaffirmed the release contract on the ground that he was a minor when he signed the release. Should Del Santo be allowed to proceed against the defendant? Explain reasons for your answer.

2. In February 1966, Joseph Fuld contracted to sell to Virgil McPheters a commercial lot which Fuld owned. When Fuld signed the contract, he was in his late eighties and had recently been widowed. Fuld was unable to care for himself and at times appeared unaware that his wife had died prior to the signing of the contract. Once an alert businessman, Fuld had become confused as to business matters, and the contract for the sale of the real estate contained unusual terms. The purchase price was $14,000, although the same property had been appraised in his wife's estate at more than $26,000. Fuld died, and the executor of his estate refused performance of the contract on the ground that on the date of the signing Fuld was incompetent to contract. McPheters brought suit seeking performance of the contract to convey the property. *(a)* What test and guidelines should the court apply in determining whether Fuld was competent to contract? *(b)* Was McPheters entitled to performance of the contract? Explain in terms of the test stated in your answer to *(a)*.

3. Margaret Gahr and her husband Charles were considering a divorce. They met in a tavern and agreed to meet later at the office of a local lawyer to work out details of a property settlement. They had agreed to divide their property equally. At the meeting, they reviewed their holdings. To accomplish an equal division of their property, they executed a deed to certain real estate. Before the divorce could take place, Charles Gahr died. Margaret then filed an action in equity to set aside the deed, alleging that she was intoxicated during the meeting with the lawyer. The trial court refused to set aside the deed, and Margaret appealed. Should the deed be set aside? Why or why not?

4. J. J. Ansley and his son, E. C. Ansley, were partners who owned and operated a construction firm. They wanted to rent a heavy John Deere scraper from a certain equipment company. Thomas Clay, an authorized agent of the equipment company, drew up a lease, using for that purpose a printed lease form. The son inquired whether the lease included credit life insurance [on the father] and was told that it did, in the amount of $25,000. Thereupon the son signed the lease without reading it. Actually the lease did *not* include credit life insurance. Instead, the lease contained a provision reading, "Notice: Liability insurance coverage for bodily injury and property damage caused to others and life insurance on Lessee are not included." The father died and the son was unable to collect the $25,000. The son brought an action against the equipment company for damages growing out of the "false and fraudulent representations of [the company's] authorized agent." Is the son entitled to recover on the basis of fraud in the execution? Give reasons.

5. The school district of Scottsbluff advertised for bids for the construction of a school building. Just before closing time for filing of bids, the Olson Construction Company filed a bid of $68,400. The only other bid was for $89,905. The Olson Company's bid was accepted, and the company was notified of the acceptance. When Olson's vice president learned of the variation in the two bids, he examined the company's estimate sheets. He discovered that an experienced clerk had made a serious error while using an adding machine. The company had been forced to prepare its bid in a great hurry because of slowness of subcontractors in submitting *their* bids. The vice president informed the school district of the error as soon as he discovered and accounted for the error. The school district refused to allow Olson Company to withdraw its bid and eventually sued the company. Which party should win? Explain.

CHAPTER 11

ILLEGAL AGREEMENTS

The fifth and last requirement for a valid contract is that there must be a legal object. A contract which is wholly illegal is unenforceable by one or both parties. A contract which contains only a part or clause considered to be illegal may be unenforceable or partly enforceable, as will be explained later. The first part of this chapter examines illegal agreements in general; the second part, the various types of illegal agreements.

ILLEGAL AGREEMENTS IN GENERAL

Nature and Effect of Illegal Agreements

The term "illegal" as used here is not limited to violation of a criminal law. An agreement is illegal if it comes within a class of agreements made illegal by statute or if it is otherwise opposed to public policy. The illegality may be in the nature of the performance promised, in the consideration for the promise, or in the formation of the agreement (that is, in the act of entering into the agreement).

As stated above and as will be illustrated in the following pages, a contract which is wholly illegal is unenforceable by one or both parties. For example, a contract to bribe a public official is wholly illegal, and neither party can enforce the agreement. A contract which contains only a part or clause considered to be illegal (such as an agreement not to compete) may be unenforceable or partly enforceable. A court may refuse to enforce the entire contract, may strike out the illegal part and enforce the remainder of the contract, or may limit the application of the clause, in order to achieve legality and prevent serious injustice.

Agreements Illegal by Statute

Whether a certain class of agreements is made illegal by statute depends upon the intention of the legislature which enacted it. The intention is occasionally expressed in words, as where the statute states that a certain type of agreement is "illegal," "unlawful," "void," or "against public policy." For example, many states have statutes that declare gambling agreements to be illegal.

A contract may be obviously illegal from a cursory reading of the contents. Often, however, an agreement that appears to be legal is held to violate a statute when the court considers the circumstances surrounding the agreement. The following case illustrates such a situation.

CASE 11.1   National Labor Relations Board v. Bratten Pontiac Corp.
406 F.2d 349 (4th Cir. 1969)

Facts: In March 1966 nine of twelve automobile salesmen employed by Bratten Pontiac Corp. signed authorization cards granting the Teamsters Union the right to act as their collective bargaining agent. The salesmen then requested a meeting with George W. Bratten, president of the company. During the meeting Bratten said, "Why pay someone to negotiate for you when you are grown men? You can negotiate yourself with me." A day or two later the company and the entire sales staff signed a "Pay Plan" increasing a number of fringe benefits and bonuses. The plan contained an agreement that for two years the sales staff "will not enter into any combination or association with the intent or purpose of injuring the company." The salesmen then withdrew their union authorization cards.

The union filed objections and the National Labor Relations Board issued an unfair labor practices complaint. Section 8 (a) (1) of the National Labor Relations Act states it is an unfair labor practice for an employer to interfere with the pursuit by employees of their right "to form, join, or assist labor organizations."

Question: Did the pay plan violate the statute?

Answer: Yes. The agreement was considered to be illegal when the circumstances surrounding the agreement were considered.

Reasoning: The court stated that the company went beyond permissible limits in extracting a two-year agreement not to enter into any association with the intent of injuring the company. The language used was a thinly disguised attempt at preventing salesmen from joining a union or engaging in any union activity. Such an agreement is unenforceable

Agreements Which May Be Contrary to Public Policy   In the absence of legislation revealing that an agreement is against public policy, the courts may determine which kinds of agreements are so contrary to public policy that they should not be enforced. The concept of "public policy" is a changing one. A panel of judges or a judge decides, on the basis of the judge's conception of what is ethical or moral, whether an agreement is contrary to public policy. Obviously, this determination changes over time. For example, in 1976 the California Supreme Court held for the first time that an agreement between an unmarried man and woman regarding property acquired while they lived together may be enforceable. Previous to that decision, such an agreement was considered to be against public policy and unenforceable.   Some kinds of agreements are so threatening to the public welfare that virtually all agreements of the class, if challenged in court, would be held unenforceable as against public policy. Agreements to commit a crime are an example. Other kinds of agreements and clauses, such as contracts of adhesion and exculpatory clauses, are not necessarily harmful and will be denied enforcement only if misused.

Contracts of Adhesion.   A *contract of adhesion* ("standard-form" contract) is one in which there is so great a disparity of bargaining power that the weaker party has no choice but to accept the terms imposed by the stronger party or forego the transaction. As was pointed out in Chapter 6, contracts of adhesion serve legitimate functions in our economy and usually are enforced despite the weaker party's possible lack of consent to some or most terms. Yet, because of the great disparity of bargaining power which characterizes contracts of adhesion, people upon whom they are imposed are vulnerable to exploitation.

Ordinarily, one who signs a contract without reading it is bound to the terms contained in the agreement. There are, however, exceptions to this so-called "duty to read" rule. The courts have invalidated some contracts or clauses of adhesion in a variety of ways, for example, by (1) holding that because of a lack of communication, no contract arose; or (2) finding that a contract or a clause was contrary to public policy. The concept of unconscionability, discussed later in this chapter, has also been applied to invalidate clauses of adhesion. The leading cases have involved contracts containing small print, clauses on the reverse side, disparity of bargaining power, and terms that would impose severe hardship on the weaker party.

Exculpatory Clauses.   **Exculpatory clauses** are contractual provisions whose aim is to exempt a contracting party from the payment of damages for his or her own misconduct. Such clauses frequently are challenged in court as being contrary to public policy, but not all the challenged clauses are illegal.

Ordinarily, the courts will not enforce exculpatory clauses which relieve a contracting party of responsibility for his or her own criminal conduct, intentional torts, or "gross" negligence. As the following case indicated, however, a clause which exempts a person from liability for his or her own "simple" negligence might or might not be upheld. If the clause is freely consented to by parties of substantially equal bargaining power, it ordinarily will be upheld. In contrast, if the clause is part of a *contract of adhesion* so that the weaker party has no choice but to bear the consequences of the other party's simple negligence, the clause might be invalidated.

CASE 11.2

Winterstein v. Wilcom
293 A.2d 821 (Md. Ct. Spec. App., 1972)

Facts: Wilcom operated a "drag strip" where, for a fee, persons could engage in automobile timing and acceleration runs. After Winterstein and his wife each signed a document purporting to release Wilcom from liability for any injuries Winterstein might suffer while participating in drag-strip activities, Winterstein paid the fee and entered a speed contest. Near the end of his run, his car hit a 100-pound cylinder head lying on the track, and Winterstein sustained permanent injuries. The cylinder head was not visible to him when he commenced the race, but it was visible to Wilcom's employees who were stationed in a tower to watch for any hazards on the track. Alleging negligence on the part of Wilcom's employees, Winterstein sued Wilcom for damages. The trial court entered a summary judgment in favor of Wilcom, and Winterstein appealed.

Question: Was the release signed by Mr. and Mrs. Winterstein enforceable?

Answer: Yes. The release was not against public policy.

Reasoning: The court discussed several factors to be considered in determining whether a transaction was "affected with a public interest," thus making an exculpatory clause against public policy. The factors were: (1) the business is of a type generally thought suitable for public regulation; (2) the party seeking protection is performing a service of great importance which is often a practical necessity for some members of the public; (3) the party holds himself out as willing to perform this service for anyone; (4) the party invoking the exculpatory clause has a decisive advantage of bargaining strength against any member of the public seeking his or her services; (5) the party utilizes a standardized adhesion contract of exculpation; (6) the person or property of the purchaser is placed under the control of the seller; and (7) the defendant violated a safety statute enacted for the protection of the public. The court held that none of the characteristics applied to this transaction and that the release was valid.

Judgment was affirmed.

COMMON TYPES OF ILLEGAL AGREEMENTS

Because of the great variety of agreements which can be made that violate statutes and rules of the common law, only a few types of illegal agreements can be discussed here. Those discussed are representative of the more common types of such agreements.

Unconscionable Agreements

For many years, the courts have been developing legal concepts and techniques for combatting undesirable business practices that fall short of traditional wrongs such as fraud and duress. Out of those efforts has emerged the concept of "unconscionability."

Because unconscionability can take so many forms, there is no rigid definition of it. Instead, the courts apply guidelines such as "oppression" and "unfair surprise" on a case-by-case basis. Any contract or contractual term that oppresses or unfairly surprises a contracting party may be unenforceable, even though the practice involved does not constitute fraud or some other traditional variety of illegal conduct.

Throughout the years the courts have identified a number of practices which may be held unconscionable if circumstances warrant. These practices have been classified as either "procedural" or "substantive" unconscionability.

Procedural unconscionability has to do with an unfair or deceptive process of contract formation. Procedural unconscionability may occur, for example, where a seller, by means of a fine-print clause near the end of a complex contract, seeks secretly to deprive a semiliterate buyer of rights which buyers normally would not wish to give up if the topic were discussed. Procedural unconscionability may also take the form of high-pressure salesmanship.

Substantive unconscionability has more to do with unreasonably harsh terms of a contract than with a deceptive process of contract formation. An excessively high price might be held unconscionable. Substantive unconscionability also occurs where a seller-creditor in an installment sale of goods unduly expands the creditor's own remedial rights. Suppose that a furniture seller, by means of a fine-print clause in an installment-sale contract, retains a security interest in all items sold over a period of years to the buyer, and then seeks to repossess all of the furniture because the buyer missed a payment on the last item. If the value of the furniture to be repossessed greatly exceeds the amount of the unpaid debt, or the buyer did not understand the rather stringent consequences of missing a payment, the clause which provides for repossession is likely to be held substantively unconscionable, especially where the agreement is a contract of adhesion.

Agreements Not to Compete

Types of Agreements Not to Compete.   This discussion is limited to the two most common types of agreements not to compete: (1) an agreement by the seller of a business not to compete with the buyer, and (2) an agreement by an employee not to compete with the employer after the termination of employment.

Agreement by Seller of a Business.   Where the owner of a business sells it as a "going concern," the buyer purchases the "goodwill" of the business. Goodwill consists of the willingness of customers to deal with the firm. The buyer rightfully expects to receive the continued patronage of the seller's customers (that is, the goodwill) free from the seller's interference, at least until the buyer has had a reasonable opportunity to establish his or her own business reputation. To protect goodwill, the buyer might require the seller to sign an agreement not to compete with the buyer.

At times, courts have faced the question of whether an agreement not to compete (sometimes called "covenant not to compete") is against public policy. The courts hold that such an agreement is enforceable if it imposes no more than a reasonable restraint of the seller. Usually a restraint is reasonable if it protects a legitimate business interest, and is reasonable in time (duration) and in area (territory covered). For example, a covenant by the seller of a small delicatessen not to compete for 6 months anywhere within the city might be unduly restrictive and unenforceable, while a covenant by the seller of a firm doing a statewide business not to compete for 3 years throughout the state might be a reasonable restriction.

Agreement by Employee.   Employees are sometimes required to sign employment contracts which contain covenants not to compete. In such a contract, the employee usually promises that upon the termination of employment, he or she will not compete with the former employer, either by setting up a business or by entering the employment of a competitor. Tt be enforceable, such covenants not to compete must be reasonable in duration and in territory covered.

Enforcement of Agreements Not to Compete.   Suppose that Bob Brown buys a small delicatessen whose business extends for a twelve-block radius and requires the seller to agree not to compete within a radius of 20 miles for 3 years. Shortly after the sale, the seller announces that within the next few days she will open a delicatessen three blocks from her former location.

The situation just described presents a dilemma. Most courts would agree that the buyer had demanded an unreasonably broad restriction on the seller's right to conduct a business (20 miles). They would also agree that the seller threatens to unreasonably interfere with the goodwill of the buyer's new business. Whom should the courts protect?

Some courts refuse to enforce overly broad restrictions, and thus would deny the buyer any protection. Other courts would hold that because a twelve-block' limitation would have been reasonable, the restrictive agreement is enforceable at least to that extent. They would prevent the seller from opening a delicatessen three blocks away. In effect, such courts rewrite the covenant contained in the agreement so that it no longer violates the court's concept of public policy.

A similar problem arises—and a similar split of opinion occurs—where an agreement not to compete specifies a time limit greater than necessary to protect the purchaser. The case which follows involves both a time and a geographic limitation.

CASE 11.3   Boldt Machinery & Tools, Inc. v. Wallace
366 A.2d 902 (Pa. 1976)

Facts: Glen Wallace was employed by Boldt Machinery & Tools, Inc. as a salesman and covered parts of Pennsylvania and New York. In 1973 Wallace quit and was employed by Tri-State Machinery Co., a competitor of Boldt, in roughly the same territory he had covered for Boldt. Wallace's employment contract with Boldt provided that:

"Upon termination of employment . . . Employee . . . shall not engage directly or indirectly in the sale or distribution of any items regularly sold by Employer in the territory covered by Employer for a period of five years."

Boldt sold machinery and tools in Pennsylvania, New York and Ohio. They sued to enforce the covenant and the trial court prohibited Wallace from selling or distributing for 5 years in the parts of Pennsylvania, New York, and Ohio serviced by Boldt. Wallace appealed.

Question: Is the covenant not to compete enforceable in whole, in part, or not at all?

Answer: The covenant is enforceable in part.

Reasoning: The court stated the general rule that "a post-employment restraint on competition is enforceable if it is ancillary to an employment relationship between the parties, is designed to protect a legitimate business interest of the employer, and is reasonably limited in duration and area." In view of the infrequency of customer contact, the court held that 5 years was a reasonable time restraint. However, the court said the trial court erred in prohibiting Wallace from working in eastern Ohio. The restraint contained in the agreement should be enforceable no farther than the sales territory to which the employee was assigned (Pennsylvania and New York).

The case was remanded for entry of a revised decree. *Note:* One justice dissented, stating that the covenant was illegal as written and should not be enforced.

Agreements Involving Usury

To discourage charging exorbitant interest, almost every state has a statute specifying the highest rate of interest which may be charged for a loan of money. **Usury** is the charging of any rate of interest in excess of that permitted by law.

Statutes usually specify a maximum rate of interest for "normal" loans and a series of higher maximum rates for other kinds of loans, for example, loans by pawnbrokers and small loan companies. The higher rates are justified by the lender's higher costs of collection and the doubtful creditworthiness of many of the borrowers.

Maximum interest rates imposed by legislatures frequently lag behind the market price of credit. When this happens, lenders often divert their funds to more lucrative markets. To encourage lenders to provide businesses with an adequate supply of credit, the laws of many states exempt loans to corporations, real estate loans, automobile purchase loans, and installment loans made by banks from the limits imposed by the usury statutes.

The states differ in their treatment of usurious agreements. In some states usurious agreements are void, and the overreaching lender forfeits interest *and* principal. In other states a usurious agreement is voidable, but only as to the amount of interest in excess of the amount permitted by law. In still other states the agreement is voidable as to the usurious amount, and the injured party may recover a penalty of double or triple the usurious amount.

The following case discusses a seller's finance charge which is not considered "interest" but is a "time-price differential."

CASE 11.4   Overbeck v. Sears, Roebuck and Co.
349 N.E.2d 286 (Ind. App. 1976)

Facts: Karl Overbeck brought a class action seeking recovery of $6 million in allegedly usurious "interest" collected from Indiana credit card customers of defendant Sears, Roebuck & Co. The "Sears Revolving Charge Account" imposed a "finance charge" at an annual percentage rate of 18 percent on unpaid account balances.

The Indiana usury statute provided that interest on "loans or forbearance of money" shall be 8%. The trial court granted Sears' motion for summary judgment and Overbeck appealed.

Question: Does Sears' finance charge on revolving charge accounts violate the Indiana usury statute?

Answer: No. The finance charge is not considered "interest."

Reasoning: The court stated that the statute applies only to a loan of money or to the forbearance of a debt. Sears imposes a "time price differential" when a customer buys on credit. Part of the justification for this charge is that extension of consumer credit is significantly more expensive than extension of normal business credit. The court noted that if retailers were forced to reduce their rates to "non-usurious" levels, restrictions of credit would presumably result. Many middle and lower income families would probably be excluded from an important avenue of consumer credit.

The judgment was affirmed.

Agreements Violating Licensing Statutes

In all states there are numerous statutes requiring a person to obtain a license or certificate before carrying on various occupations. Thus, licenses are required of doctors, dentists, lawyers, public accountants, and those engaged in various other professions. Electricians, plumbers, contractors, beauty operators, barbers, and those in various other skilled occupations must be licensed. Licenses are also required of pawnbrokers, wholesalers and retailers of liquor, and operators of restaurants and hotels.

Usually licensing statutes provide that any person who carries on one of the designated occupations or businesses without the required license is subject to a fine. However, most licensing statutes do not state whether an unlicensed person may enforce his or her contracts. To decide this question, courts look to the character of the statute.

Some licensing statutes are regulatory in character. They are designed to protect the public against unprincipled and unqualified persons. Other licensing statutes are revenue-raising measures. The general rule is that if a statute is regulatory, unlicensed persons cannot recover for services rendered or goods delivered. For example, a building contractor who does not have a state regulatory license is not allowed to recover compensation for services performed in constructing improvements on someone's land. The rationale behind denying recovery where the statute is regulatory is that the denial of compensation will encourage an unlicensed practitioner to withhold services until he or she has demonstrated (by compliance with the statute) possession of the minimum qualifications thought necessary for public safety.

One who violates a revenue-raising statute, such as a city or county business license tax ordinance, may be fined by the municipality but may enforce contracts and recover compensation for services rendered.

Agreements Involving Interference with Governmental Processes

Any agreement which interferes with the orderly processes of government is against public policy. This statement is true whether the level of government is federal, state, or local; whether the interference consists of corrupting a public official or misleading the official's judgment; or whether the official is in the legislative, executive, or judicial branch of government. Two representative examples of the kinds of agreements which tend to interfere with the orderly processes of government are: (1) agreements involving interference with the legislative process, and (2) agreements involving interference with the administration of justice.

Interference with the Legislative Process.   Interference with the legislative process occurs most frequently through lobbying. However, not all lobbying is illegal. Anyone has the right to employ a person whose duty is to keep the employer informed about pending legislation which might affect the employer's interest, and who will try in good faith to persuade legislators to vote for or against proposed legislation. On the other hand, a person does not have the right to employ an agent whose duties include persuasion by bribery, threats, or other improper means. A lobbying agreement of this kind is illegal and thus void.

As illustrated in the next case, when the legality of a lobbying agreement is challenged in court, the court has the difficult task of scrutinizing the agreement and all relevant evidence to make sure that nothing was contemplated by the parties other than the presentation of facts and arguments in an open and aboveboard manner.

CASE 11.5 — Troutman v. Southern Railway Co.
441 F.2d 586 (5th Cir. 1971)

Facts: In 1963 the Interstate Commerce Commission (ICC) issued an order directing Southern Railway Co. to increase certain rates on grain shipments from the Midwest to the Southeast by approximately 16 percent. The order created a difficult situation for Southern. If allowed to stand, the order, according to Southern, would result in its losing a $13 million investment in "Big John" railroad cars plus a "tremendous" loss of revenue in the future. Wilbanks, a vice president of Southern, turned for help to Robert B. Troutman, an Atlanta attorney (plaintiff).

Troutman had no experience in ICC matters, but he was known to Wilbanks as a personal friend and political ally of President John F. Kennedy. Wilbanks told Troutman that Southern was filing suit in a federal district court in Ohio to enjoin the order of the ICC. He asked Troutman to persuade the President and the Department of Justice to "ditch" the ICC and to enter the case on the side of Southern. Troutman did so, and in the Ohio lawsuit, the ICC order was struck down. Southern failed to compensate Troutman in the agreed manner, and he filed suit for the reasonable value of his services. A jury awarded Troutman the sum of $175,000, and Southern appealed.

Question: Was the agreement between Southern and Troutman against public policy?

Answer: No. The agreement did not call for the improper exercise of personal influence upon a public official.

Reasoning: The court stated that all citizens have the right to petition the government for redress of their grievances. To that end, one may employ an agent or attorney to use his influence to gain access to a public official. Once having obtained an audience, the attorney may fairly present to the official the merits of his or her client's case and urge the official's support for that position. A contract is illegal and unenforceable when it contemplates the use of personal or political influence rather than an appeal on the merits of the case. This is a question for the jury. In this case the jury concluded that Troutman had agreed to use his influence merely to gain access to the President and present him the merits of Southern's case.

The judgment was affirmed.

Interference with the Administration of Justice. Any agreement which interferes with the administration of justice is illegal. The most direct form of such interference is bribing a witness, juror, or judge.

An agreement which does not directly interfere with the administration of justice will nevertheless be illegal if it tends to interfere with justice. Thus, an agreement to pay a witness who is in the jurisdiction and subject to subpoena an amount greater than permitted by statute is illegal. Statutes limitimg payment of fees to witnesses commonly exempt expert witnesses from the fee limitation, however. An agreement to pay an expert any reasonable compensation is legal, provided it does not make payment contingent on the outcome of the case.

The general principle that an agreement which interferes or tends to interfere with the administration of justice is illegal applies not only to civil proceedings but also to criminal proceedings. For example, where a male employee has stolen funds from his employer, a promise by the employee's father to restore the funds if the employer will not press charges against the son is contrary to public policy as an interference with the enforcement of the criminal law. The father's promise is therefore unenforceable by the employer. For the same reason, a promise by the employer not to press charges if the father will restore the stolen funds is unenforceable by the father.

SUMMARY

A contract which is wholly illegal is unenforceable by one or both parties. A contract containing only an illegal clause may be unenforceable or partly enforceable.

The term "illegal" as used here is not limited to violation of a criminal law. An agreement is illegal if it comes within a class of agreements made illegal by statute or if it is held by a court to be against public policy.

Contracts of adhesion and exculpatory clauses may or may not be against public policy, depending on the circumstances. The courts have refused to enforce small-print clauses in contracts imposed by a party with superior bargaining power where the terms would impose severe hardship on the weaker party. An unconscionable agreement is illegal even though the practice involved is not a traditional variety of illegal conduct, such as fraud or duress.

Agreements not to compete are restraints on trade, and the courts are reluctant to enforce them except for compelling reasons. Many such restraints are enforceable if properly limited. For example, an agreement by the seller of a business not to compete with the buyer is usually enforceable if the territory covered by the agreement and its duration is limited and protects only the interest purchased.

Many other kinds of agreements are illegal. Among them are agreements to pay a usurious rate of interest, agreements violating those licensing laws which protect the public against unqualified persons, and agreements interfering with governmental processes.

REVIEW QUESTIONS

1. (**a**) Define a contract of adhesion. (**b**) If challenged in court, will a contract of adhesion be held void as against public policy? Explain.

2. Is a clause which exempts a contracting party from the payment of damages for his or her own negligence enforceable? Explain.

3. What is the difference between procedural and substantive unconscionability? Give an illustration of each.

4. Agreements not to compete may be enforceable. **(a)** For what reasons might a court enforce such an agreement? **(b)** Even though there might be justification for enforcing an agreement not to compete, the agreement will not be enforced unless the restraint it imposes is reasonable. In general, under what circumstances will the restraint be held reasonable?

5. (a) What is usury? **(b)** Why might a state provide for different maximum rates for different categories of loans?

6. (a) What was the effect of the older usury limits on the availability of consumer credit? **(b)** What measures did the legislatures take to nullify that effect?

7. Suppose a person is required to obtain a license before rendering services. Under what circumstances will a person who fails to obtain the required license be denied the right to enforce an agreement to compensate him or her for services rendered? Why?

8. Give an example of an agreement which interferes with the legislative process.

9. Give an example of an agreement which interferes with the administration of justice.

CASE PROBLEMS

1. Graham leased the land on which his business was situated from the Chicago, R.I. & P. Railway Co. One of its trains derailed because of negligent operation of the railroad. Graham's business was damaged, and the means of public access was impaired for a substantial time. Graham sued the railroad for damages. The railroad filed a motion for summary judgment on the basis of the following clause in the lease: "The Lessee [Graham] releases the Lessor, its agents, and employees from all liability for loss or damage caused by fire or other casualty by reason of any injury to or destruction of any real or personal property, of any kind, owned by the Lessee, or in which the Lessee is interested, which now is or may hereafter be placed on any part of the leased premises." Should the railroad's motion for summary judgment be granted? Explain reasons for your answer.

2. Wanda Whittington was participating in a field trip required of members of the senior nursing class at Sowela Technical Institute. There were 18 persons occupying a 15-passenger van being driven by Jean Teel, a member of the class. Jean was negligent in her operation of the van, lost control, and the van overturned killing Wanda and another student. Sowela denied liability for the deaths, alleging that each student nurse signed a release prior to the trip. The document read, "I, Wanga Whittington, voluntarily agree to participate in the following activity . . . and hereby relieve Sowela Technical Institute of any and all liability associated with the above." Is Sowela relieved of liability for Jean Teel's negligence? Give reasons for your answer.

3. Scott, a long-term employee of General Iron and Welding Co. (General), signed a contract of employment as chief engineer. In this capacity he had access to General's design and engineering knowledge, and access to the company's customer list. Scott solicited business from customers located throughout Connecticut. General did business in not less than 25 nor more than 75 Connecticut towns in any one year. In 1972, after a salary dispute, Scott left General and took employment with a competitor as a welder. Later he wished to participate in the management of the competitor despite a restrictive clause in his contract with General. The clause forbade him for a period of 5 years from managing a competitor in Connecticut. Scott brought an action for a judgment to determine the validity of the restrictive covenant. Should the covenant be upheld? Explain.

4. Kot had a franchise from Rita Personnel Services International, Inc. (Rita). The franchise agreement provided that upon termination of the agreement, Kot would not compete with Rita in three designated counties in Georgia nor in "any territorial areas in which a franchise has been granted." The franchise agreement was terminated, and Kot began operating a personnel employment service under his own name. Rita sought an injunction to enforce the restrictive clause. Should the injunction be granted? Give reasons.

5. Cagle signed a mortgage note to finance the construction of a residence. The note bore a 10 percent annual interest rate as permitted by law. However, the lender mailed Cagle computerized monthly statements which, as a result of compounding interest and the use of a daily interest factor based on a 360-day year, produced a simple interest rate of 10.6235296 percent per annum. Cagle objected to the interest charges and made no payments. The lender brought a civil lawsuit to recover the principal and interest. Cagle sought to cancel the note and mortgage on the basis of usury. Was the transaction usurious? Explain.

CHAPTER 12

FORM AND INTERPRETATION OF CONTRACTS; PAROL EVIDENCE RULE

Earlier chapters concerning contracts considered elements of a legally binding contract. This chapter will explore (1) why some contracts should be in writing, (2) why and when a contractual agreement *must* be in writing to be enforceable, and (3) how courts interpret contracts to settle lawsuits.

The form (oral or written) an agreement takes is important because the law requires certain kinds of contracts to be written. Without a "writing" (or some acceptable substitute), these certain kinds of contracts, although they exist orally, will not be enforced in court. Even with a written contract, arguments may still arise between contracting parties, especially if the contract is poorly drafted. So it is important also to understand how a court will interpret (read) a contract to decide what the parties have agreed to, and thus what promises can be enforced.

FORM OF CONTRACTS; STATUTES OF FRAUDS

Under early English common law, only written contracts could be enforced. In the 1300s the English courts began to enforce oral promises as well. Enforcement was based on testimony of witnesses who were not parties to the contract in question. If these witnesses could be persuaded to testify falsely, a person could be held to a "contract" never actually made. In 1677, to prevent such "frauds and perjuries," the English Parliament enacted the original "Statute of Frauds," as it has come to be known. This law required that certain important classes of contracts must be proved by a writing to be enforceable. In the United States, all states have adopted statutes of frauds roughly modeled on the English original or, in a few states, have adopted the concept by court decisions. The writing requirements of the statutes of frauds apply only to those classes of contracts thought to be so significant or burdensome to a contracting party as to justify requiring written evidence of contractual intent. For example, contracts involving the sale of land have always been considered very important and, to be enforceable, must be evidenced by a writing.

The various classes of contracts requiring written proof are said to be "within the statute of frauds." All other contracts are "outside the statute"; that is, no written evidence is necessary for enforcement. So, *except where a statute of frauds* (or some other special statute) *requires a writing* for the formation or enforcement of a contract, *an oral contract is as enforceable as a written one.*

Why Many Contracts Should Be in Writing

Whether or not a statute of frauds requires a written agreement, there are several practical reasons for putting many contracts in writing. Of course, it would be impractical and foolish to try to put every contract in writing. Imagine what would happen if you demanded a written contract when you bought groceries or got a haircut or carwash. These routine transactions, usually for cash, would be unnecessarily cumbersome and expensive if written contracts were used to reach agreement. But in any agreement involving performance in the future, or containing many or complex terms and conditions, a writing may be not only wise but also necessary for the people involved to know exactly what promises are being exchanged. Agreements of this kind would include personal and professional service contracts, employment agreements, credit card contracts, real estate mortgages, and other bank loans.

Some advantages of reducing a contract to writing are obvious. Some are not. If a person should ever have to prove the existence of the contract or its specific terms, a writing simplifies the task. A writing is far superior to the faded, incomplete, or contradictory memories of the parties. A less obvious advantage of a writing is that it may lead those involved to consider more fully the consequences of their contract. For example, contingencies such as delays in performance may be discussed and provided for, where they might be left to chance in an oral agreement. Further, a written agreement may give the parties a clearer picture of what each must do under the contract, thus decreasing the likelihood of a later misunderstanding. Writings also reduce the opportunities any party has to claim the terms of the contract are different from those originally agreed to. Thus, fraudulent or bad faith attempts to change agreements, as well as honest misunderstandings, are avoided.

A writing sometimes provides the parties with an additional benefit: It tells them that they have passed the negotiation stage and that a firm understanding has been reached. In the give and take of negotiations, one side may genuinely believe agreement has been reached when the other side does not. If each side insists on a formal written agreement, signed by both, both will know a contract exists. Without a formal signed agreement, the parties may quarrel about the contract's existence and a court may have to decide whether they orally or informally (for example, in an exchange of letters, telegrams, or memos) have assented to a binding contract.

Why and When a Contract Must Be in Writing	**Why a Writing Is Required for Some Contracts.** As suggested earlier, the purpose of any statute of frauds is to prevent frauds by making it difficult to lie about the existence of a contract that would have a great impact on the parties. Clear and objective evidence—beyond mere oral statements of a party—is required for such a contract to be recognized and enforced by a court. This evidence is especially needed where one person claims, but the other denies, that a contract arose. Traditionally, the requirement of objective evidence has been satisfied by a writing, that is, either (1) a written contract, or (2) some memorandum or note referring to the contract and its terms while identifying the contract parties and the subject matter. But sometimes other evidence is acceptable, and these exceptions will be discussed later.

When a Writing Is Required: The General Rule.   The general rule is that contracts within (covered by) the statute of frauds are not enforceable in court unless (or until) evidenced by a writing. The modern statutes of frauds are not intended to impose an unfair hardship on the parties who want and expect their oral agreement to be given effect. Therefore, courts have softened the impact of a lack of a writing by *strictly limiting* what contracts must be evidenced by a writing, and by *creating exceptions* to each class. In this way, courts permit most oral agreements to be enforced. Even where enforcement of an oral contract is not permitted, courts often grant quasi-contractual remedies to prevent unjust enrichment by one party.

Classes of Contracts Required to Be in Writing

Nearly every state has statute-of-frauds provisions covering the same basic classes of contracts. The four major classes are:

1. Contracts not performable within 1 year (the long-term provision)
2. Contracts transferring an interest in land (the land contract provision)
3. Promises to answer for another's debt (the guaranty provision)
4. Contracts for the sale of goods at a price of $500 or more (the sale-of-goods statute of frauds in the Uniform Commercial Code)

Some states have statute-of-frauds provisions which include one or more additional classes of contracts. Some examples are contracts to pay a commission to a real estate agent for the sale of land (listing agreement), promises in consideration of marriage (property settlements), contracts for the sale of stocks or bonds, contracts for life insurance, promises by an estate executor to personally pay a deceased person's debt, and promises to pay a debt whose collection has been barred by operation of law (such as the running of a statute of limitations).

The discussion immediately following is limited to the four commonly recognized classes of contracts that have the most significance to business in the 1980s.

Contracts Not Performable within 1 Year.   Long-term contracts—contracts in which performance cannot be completed within 1 year—must be in writing. A commitment to perform a contract obligation over an extended definite period (to support a relative, for example) is considered burdensome even though a similar contract obligation over a short time might not be. And since contract disputes are likely to arise long after agreement is reached, a writing provides the means for accurately determining what the parties promised each other.

Limitations on the Writing Requirement.   The "long-term" statute-of-frauds requirement applies only to executory (unperformed) bilateral contracts—those under which *both* parties promise to perform in the future. It does not apply to unilateral contracts, that is, where only one party makes a promise and the other party completes performance when the agreement is made. For example, assume that Sarah lends Dan $2500 to buy a car, and Dan orally promises to repay the money in 24 equal monthly installments. This contract is unilateral—a promise is made by only one party. Sarah can enforce the oral loan contract against Dan even though his performance would take 2 years. Since Sarah has completely performed her part of the bargain at the time the contract is made, it would be unfair to refuse enforcement and deny her recovery.

Although 1 year is the dividing line, deciding whether a contract is long-term or short-term is not always easy. Courts often enforce oral contracts which appear to be long-term, basing a decision on the actual performance terms agreed to. Can the terms of the agreement possibly be carried out within 1 year from the day the contract is made? If the terms of an oral agreement can possibly be performed within 1 year, the court will enforce it. Otherwise, a writing will be required for enforcement.

Courts measure the "1 year" from the time the contract is *made*, not from the time performance is to begin. Suppose you orally agreed to work as a typist for Bob over the next 6 months. The terms of this oral agreement are obviously possible to complete within 1 year from the day you agreed, so no writing is necessary for enforcement. This first contract is not within the statute of frauds. But if you had agreed instead to work for the next 18 months, a writing would be necessary for enforcement if, contrary to the understanding, Bob refused to allow you to begin work or ended your employment early. This second oral contract has terms ("I promise to work 18 months") which cannot be satisfied within 1 year from the date of the agreement. Suppose finally that you had orally agreed in January to work for 10 months beginning in May. A written contract would also be necessary for enforcement because complete performance of your contract would not be possible within 1 year from January when the contract arose. Since the time between making the contract in January and starting performance in May is counted in the 1-year limit, there is no possibility that the agreed terms can be performed before the 14 months pass.

The rule is that an oral contract is unenforceable unless performance could be completed within a year. Performance means carrying out the acts that the parties actually agreed to do. Although a person's death could end a contract, it would nevertheless remain unperformed, as where Bob agrees to sell cars for Jones Auto "for 2 years" but dies (or could die) before completing the agreed 2-year performance. The courts ordinarily will ignore the possibility of such an occurrence (death of a party), as this results merely in a contract termination and not a performance of the terms agreed to.

If any possibility exists for performing the agreement's terms within 1 year, a court will not require a writing. A court is not concerned with what will actually happen or the eventual length of actual performance. The determining factor is only what *could* happen—whether the agreement's terms could possibly be completed in 1 year. Suppose Jim orally promises to support his father for his father's lifetime in exchange for his father's promise to name Jim the beneficiary of his life insurance policy. The "father's lifetime" is an indefinite period. The father could live for 20 years or he could die the next day. Thus, it is possible that Jim's performance (supporting his father for the rest of the father's life) could be completed within 1 year.

There are other situations where the parties agree to an indefinite length of performance ("for life," "as long as required," "until completion of the project") and the courts will treat the contract as short-term even though the duration of performance might normally last longer than 1 year. Suppose you had agreed to work "as long as Bob needs" a typist. Though you both may expect the work to continue for longer than a year—maybe even indefinitely—your oral agreement is enforceable as a short-term contract. According to the contract's terms, work is to continue as long as Bob needs typing done. Since it is possible that his "need" may end at any time, it is *possible* for you to complete the agreed performance within 1 year. The same result would be reached if you had agreed to work "for the rest of my life" or "as long as I can type," because your death or incapacity, which marks the end of the performance you agreed to, *could* occur within a year.

The following case concerning an employment contract illustrates the importance of the contract's performance terms in determining if a contract is "long-term."

CASE 12.1   Gilliland v. Allstate Insurance Co.
388 N.E.2d 68 (Ill. App. 1979)

Facts: Allstate orally agreed in March, 1954, to employ Gilliland until his retirement at age 62 if he carried out Allstate's lawful directions. Gilliland soon began participating in the company's profit-sharing, pension, and savings plans. In 1972 Allstate fired Gilliland without good cause. Gilliland sued Allstate for breach of contract, claiming losses of earnings, profits and anticipated pension benefits. Allstate asserted the contract was not enforceable because it was oral and could not be completed within one year. The trial court dismissed the case. Gilliland appealed.

Question: Was this an oral long-term contract, and therefore unenforceable?

Answer: Yes. The contract could not be performed within one year.

Reasoning: Allstate orally agreed to employ Gilliland until he reached the age of 62—a term of 36 years. Gilliland argued that the oral contract was enforceable because it could have been performed within one year if he had died or resigned. The court rejected this argument. To be outside the Statute of Frauds, the contract must be capable of being *fully performed* within one year, not simply *ended* by a contingency such as the death of a party. This contract would not have been "fully performed" if some contingency such as Gilliland's death had terminated the agreement in its first year. Therefore, the court decided the oral agreement was not enforceable.

Exceptions to the Rule.   To prevent injustice, most courts will enforce an oral bilateral, long-term contract once one of the parties has fully performed his or her side of the agreement, even though the performance is completed some time *after* the contract was made. Otherwise, the person receiving performance could use the statute of frauds to escape any obligation to perform in return. For example, a company and a management consultant orally agree that the consultant will make a 2-year study of ways to improve working conditions in the company's factories. If the company fully pays the agreed compensation before the consultant completes the study, a court will treat the oral long-term contract as enforceable. A writing is necessary for enforcement only if the long-term agreement remains executory on both sides, that is, only until either party fully completes what he or she had promised to do. However, *part* performance by one party will not render a long-term contract enforceable. (But the person who partly performs—for example, 6 months of an oral 5-year services contract—could recover the value of the part performance in quasi contract.)

Contracts Transferring an Interest in Land.   Because real estate transactions often involve large sums of money and complex terms, the law requires a writing to enforce such agreements. The statute of frauds applies to any contract transferring an *interest in land.*

Kinds of Contracts Required to Be in Writing.   The most common examples of kinds of land contracts required to be in writing are:

1. A contract to buy or sell land or buildings
2. A real estate mortgage (by means of which land is used as security for a loan, with the lender acquiring an interest in the land until the loan is repaid)
3. A contract to create an easement (a right of way that permits a person to use the land of another for a limited purpose, such as for a driveway, for laying utility pipe, or for stringing utility wires)
4. A long-term lease of land

Short-term leases ordinarily are exempt from the land contract provision of the statute of frauds. A lease is usually considered short-term if it is for a term of a year or less. In most states an oral lease for a 1-year term is enforceable no matter when the tenant's term begins.

A contract for the sale of *oil, gas, or other minerals* still in the ground may be a contract for the sale of an interest in land. Likewise, a contract for the sale of a *structure*, such as a house, to be removed from the land may fall under this section of the statute of frauds. If the *buyer* is to "sever" (remove) the minerals or structure from the land, the contract is one transferring an "interest in land" and is within the land contract statute-of-frauds provision. If the *seller* is to do the severing, the contract is for the sale of goods, and the UCC statute of frauds discussed later in the chapter may apply. A contract for the sale, *separate from the land,* of timber, growing crops, or other things attached to realty which can be removed without significant harm to the land is not a contract for the sale of an "interest in land." Regardless of who cuts the timber or harvests the crop, the contract is for the sale of goods and therefore is subject to the UCC statute of frauds, not the land provision.

Contracts for *construction on* real estate are not within the statute of frauds and therefore do not require a writing to be enforceable. Although the performance of a construction agreement will affect the land, the agreement is not a contract to transfer an *interest in* the land.

The Part Performance Exception. The courts have created an exception to the general rule that contracts transferring an interest in land must be in writing. This exception is known as the *part performance* doctrine. Where the buyer in an oral contract to purchase land has partly performed the agreement, a court may enforce the oral contract to avoid injustice to the buyer. However, the parties' actions must remove any doubt that a contract for sale was made. The usual situations where part performance justifies enforcement of an oral contract involve the buyer's taking possession of the land coupled with making significant improvements, a substantial payment, or both. For example, the seller transfers possession of a residence to the purchaser, who installs a lawn, fencing, and swimming pool. Such conduct provides ample objective proof that the parties have a contract for sale unless the conduct is contradicted by other clear evidence. If the purchaser has possession of the owner's land and does not make a substantial payment (for example, pays the owner $300 per month), a court will not invoke the part performance doctrine because the performance appears to prove a rental, not a sale.

The following case illustrates the difficulty of using the part performance doctrine to enforce an oral land contract.

CASE 12.2 **Gene Hancock Construction Co. v. Kempton and Snedigar Dairy**
510 P.2d 752 (Ariz. App. 1973)

Facts: Dairy, through its authorized agent Snedigar, made an oral agreement to sell a parcel of land to Hancock. Snedigar assured Hancock that the oral agreement could be relied upon. Thereafter, Hancock arranged a loan to cover the purchase and contracted for engineering studies to be made of the property. Hancock sued Dairy when it refused to transfer the land. Dairy asserted the statute of frauds prevented enforcement of an oral contract transferring an interest in land. Hancock claimed that his "part performance" in reliance on the oral agreement made it enforceable. Hancock appealed from a judgment in favor of Dairy.

Question: Did Hancock's actions amount to "part performance" making the oral land contract enforceable?

Answer: No. Hancock's "performance" did not clearly prove a contract for sale of land between the parties.

Reasoning: If part performance is to make enforceable an otherwise unenforceable oral contract within the statute of frauds, the performance must unequivocally show that a contract was made. Obtaining financing and having engineering studies done does not clearly prove that a contract for purchase of land has already been made. These actions, unlike a purchaser making valuable improvements on the land, can be explained without reference to the alleged oral contract. For example, these things might be done by someone prior to entering a contract. The oral contract is not enforceable.

Promises to Answer for Another's Debt. Promises to answer for the "debt or default of another" are within the statute of frauds and must be evidenced by a writing. Suppose Dave wants to buy some expensive stereo components like those his wealthy friend, Rich, owns. Outasight Sound, an audio store, won't sell the equipment to Dave on credit because he does not have an acceptable credit history. Rich tells the owner: "Let Dave buy the stereo he wants on credit, and if he doesn't pay you, I will." Knowing that Rich is financially able to make good on his promise, the store owner extends Dave credit for his stereo purchase. Dave is a debtor and the store is a creditor. Dave's promise to pay is called "original" or "primary" because he owes Outasight for the stereo he bought. Rich's promise to pay *if Dave doesn't* is called "secondary" or "collateral" because it is a promise to be liable to Outasight *only if* the primary party (Dave) defaults (fails to pay when the debt is due). By making a secondary promise, Rich is acting as a guarantor of Dave's primary promise. Dave receives the stereo equipment and has the benefit of Rich's guaranty, whereas Rich receives no real benefit from the transaction. Such a guaranty is burdensome because the guarantor gets no actual benefit in exchange for it. Accordingly, the law requires such secondary promises to be in writing to be enforceable. The primary promise may be oral unless it falls under the sale-of-goods statute of frauds in the Uniform Commercial Code (UCC).

Limitations on the Writing Requirement. The statute of frauds guaranty provision applies only to a guaranty promise made to the creditor of a primary debtor. An oral guaranty made directly to the debtor is not within the statute. For example, if Rich had promised Dave he would pay Dave's monthly installment whenever Dave couldn't, the promises would not be covered by the statute of frauds. Such an oral promise directly to a debtor, if supported by consideration, would be enforceable.

Not all contractual situations involving three persons involve a secondary obligation. Suppose Rich had said to the Outasight owner: "Let Dave have the stereo he wants and I'll pay for it." There is only one promise in this instance. Rich is promising to pay for the stereo; he is the debtor and Dave is a third-person beneficiary of the contract between Rich and Outasight. The guaranty provision does not apply and Rich's oral promise is enforceable (if the price is under $500). Or suppose, instead, that Dave and Rich buy the stereo together (each saying "I'll pay" rather than one saying "I'll pay if he doesn't"). In this case they are joint debtors and both are primarily liable to Outasight.

The Main Purpose Exception.   The courts have created an exception to the writing requirement for guaranty promises. It is known as the "main purpose" or "leading object" rule. When a guarantor's main purpose is to gain some personal economic or business advantage, the guaranty does not have to be in writing. Since the guarantor is receiving a benefit, it is more likely that the oral guaranty was actually made. Also under these circumstances, if a court refused to enforce the oral guaranty, the guarantor could obtain a benefit while unfairly avoiding any obligation to perform in return. Suppose Aram contracts to build a house for June. Aram begins the house and contracts to buy the building materials on credit from Beth's lumberyard. Then Aram gets into financial trouble and fails to pay for the materials furnished. Beth justifiably refuses to furnish Aram further materials until she receives payment for the materials already supplied. June fears that a delay may cause her hardship and unexpected cost. Faced with this possibility, June telephones Beth and promises to pay for any materials supplied to build the house if Aram doesn't pay. June's guaranty promise is enforceable even though it is not in writing. The main purpose of the guaranty was to get the house built on schedule for her benefit, not Aram's. June receives an actual benefit—the completed house.

The following case further explains when the main purpose rule permits enforcement of an oral guaranty.

CASE 12.3   Howard M. Schoor Associates v. Holmdel Heights Construction Co.
343 A.2d 401 (N.J. 1975)

Facts: Holmdel was developing a tract of land for which it had hired Schoor to do surveying and engineering work. Schoor's initial bills were not paid and it suspended work. Sugarman was Holmdel's attorney as well as an investor owning 18 per cent of Holmdel's capital stock. Holmdel owed Sugarman substantial attorney's fees, and as an investor, Sugarman would profit handsomely if the land development were successful. Holmdel needed further engineering work from Schoor to secure additional financing for the project. Sugarman orally agreed to pay Schoor all that Holmdel owed if Schoor would continue its work. Schoor completed the work but was not paid. Schoor sued Holmdel, which became insolvent, and Sugarman, on the basis of his oral promise. The trial court's judgment in favor of Schoor was overturned on appeal to an intermediate court. Schoor appealed to reinstate the judgment in its favor.

Question: Was Sugarman's oral promise to pay Holmdel's debt to Schoor unenforceable as a guaranty within the statute of frauds?

Answer: No. Sugarman's promise was made primarily to benefit himself.

Reasoning: Sugarman's oral promise fell within the "main purpose" or "leading object" exception to the writing requirement for guaranty promises. If Schoor completed engineering work needed to get financing necessary for the project's success, Sugarman stood to receive substantial profits and fees. Sugarman, in committing his personal assets to pay Schoor, mainly desired to benefit himself rather than Holmdel. His oral guaranty promise is enforceable.

Contracts for the Sale of Goods at a Price of $500 or More.   Article 2 of the Uniform Commercial Code, enacted in all states except Louisiana, has a statute-of-frauds provision which requires that sales contracts for goods having *a total price of $500 or more* be evidenced by a writing. (Article 2 of the UCC is analyzed at length in Chapters 15 through 19.) The term "goods" means most tangible personal property, including such common examples as automobiles, clothes, animals, works of art, home computers, shop tools, sailboats, and furniture. For example, if you agreed to buy a motorcycle for $750 from a fellow student, the contract would not be enforceable unless there were a signed writing. The Article 2 statute of frauds is satisfied by any signed writing which indicates a contract has been made and which states the quantity of goods. Only the party against whom enforcement is sought needs to have signed.

Exceptions to the Writing Requirement.   The UCC provides several exceptions to the signed writing requirement. An oral agreement for the sale of goods costing $500 or more can be enforced if the party resisting enforcement *admits the existence of the contract in court.* Also, if the goods are *specially manufactured* for the buyer (such as personalized or monogrammed items), the seller would be able to hold the purchaser to an oral agreement if the goods are difficult to resell.

Furthermore, *part performance* of an oral contract by *both* parties substitutes for written proof that a contract exists, and a court will enforce the oral agreement to the extent that it has been performed. Specifically, a court will enforce the oral contract (1) to the extent payment for goods has been made by the buyer and accepted by the seller, or (2) to the extent goods have been received and accepted by the buyer.

For example, suppose Jennifer orally orders fifty televisions at $300 each from Sun Distributors for her appliance store. The total value of the goods under this oral contract is $15,000. If Sun accepts a down payment of $3000 from Jennifer, a court will enforce the contract to the extent payment has been accepted (for ten televisions). If, on the other hand, Sun had shipped twenty-five televisions which Jennifer accepted upon their arrival, a court would enforce the contract to that extent and Jennifer would owe Sun $7500. In the first instance the seller, Sun, would be breaching an enforceable contract for ten televisions if it did not supply goods that have been paid for. In the second instance the buyer, Jennifer, would be breaching an enforceable contract for twenty-five televisions if she did not pay for goods sent and accepted. A court will not enforce the entire oral contract; only that part proved by the parties' actions is enforceable.

Exception for Merchants Only.   There is one exception to the UCC statute of frauds that applies only to merchants. (A merchant is one who deals in the kind of goods involved in the transaction or who has knowledge or skill peculiar to those goods.) If one merchant sends a written confirmation of an oral contract to the other, the confirmation will bind *both* merchants even though signed only by the sender, if the recipient gets the writing and does not object to its terms within 10 days after receipt. For example, in the prior illustration of Jennifer and Sun, both happened to be television merchants. If Sun has sent Jennifer a written, signed confirmation of her order for fifty televisions, both would have an enforceable contract if Jennifer did not object to the contents of the confirmation within 10 days of its receipt. In situations where it applies, this exception has the legal effect of holding the receiving merchant to a legally sufficient writing signed by the sending merchant. Thus, this provision eases the formation of a binding contract between merchants without unnecessary formality. Merchants cannot ignore such confirmations sent by other merchants.

Contract Changes and the Writing Requirement

Occasionally parties modify a contract. To avoid difficulties enforcing the modification, the people involved should ensure that not only the original contract but also the later modifications satisfy the statute of frauds. The general rule is that when a contract as modified falls within the statute of frauds, there must be a sufficient writing for court enforcement. This is true whether or not the original contract had to be (or was) in writing. For example, assume Andy hires Ben for 6 months. After 3 months, they agree to a 12-month extension of their original contract. Altering the 6-month employment agreement to one for 18 months means the statute of frauds must be complied with if the new agreement is to be enforceable. Unless there is a writing, Andy can fire Ben before the 18 months ends. Similarly, assume the parties to a written contract for the sale of farmland agree to an increase in the purchase price in exchange for an easement permitting the buyer to drive his farm vehicles on roads on the seller's property. The modification promising conveyance of an additional interest in land (the easement) cannot be enforced without a writing sufficient to satisfy the statute of frauds.

Of course when the contract as modified is *not* within the statute of frauds, no writing is necessary for enforcement of the modified agreement. For example, when an 18-month written employment contract is orally altered by agreement to a 6-month term, the oral modification is enforceable. Nevertheless, a written modification may be wise protection for each party, especially when an original written agreement still exists and appears enforceable. "Getting it in writing" may prevent a surprise attempt to enforce the original contract.

What Satisfies the Writing Requirement

The general rule is that to satisfy the statute of frauds there must be a "memorandum signed by the party to be charged." The primary purpose of the statute of frauds is to require reliable evidence that an alleged contract was indeed entered into. The statute of frauds may be satisfied either by a highly detailed, formal contract or by informal letters or memoranda. Most states require only "some memorandum or note" of the agreement sufficiently detailed to reveal an actual agreement, not necessarily what all its major terms are. In a few states the law *does* demand that "the contract" shall be in writing. In those few states the writing must state all the major terms of the contract; a sketchy memorandum is not enough. All states require the writing to be signed at least by the party charged with breach of contract.

Content and Form.   There is no exact formula stating what content must be present before a court will find a memorandum sufficient to enforce a contract. At a minimum, though, a memorandum must:

1. Identify with reasonable certainty the parties and the subject matter of the contract
2. Indicate that a contract has been made between the parties regarding that subject matter
3. State with reasonable certainty the essential terms of unperformed promises in the contract

The law does not require that the subject matter and the parties be identified with precise formality. For instance, it would not be necessary to refer to a person by his full name (Chester William Bates) if Chet Bates or C. Bates is sufficient to identify him. A memorandum that describes the subject matter of the contract as "my lot on the corner of Wall Street and Fifth Avenue in the city of Brownsville, state of Wisconsin" is definite enough if the seller owns only one of the four lots at that intersection. Similarly, "my Ford" adequately identifies the subject matter in the sale of a car if the seller has but one Ford. What is an "essential term" depends upon the type of contract made, but common examples include the price in a sale of land, and the quantity in a sale of goods.

In most states the "memorandum" does not have to be in any particular form. It may be a letter, a telegram, a receipt, an order form, an invoice, a check, or an entry in an account book or diary. It may even consist of several "writings," if one of them is signed and the writings are physically connected or have adequate internal references to indicate clearly that they all relate to the same transaction. Thus, a contract might be outlined in a signed telegram and detailed in separate correspondence or unsigned documents. Taken together, the separate writings are the "memorandum" if they clearly involve the same agreement.

Time and Signature.   The memorandum does not have to be made or signed at the time the contract arises. People often reach agreement orally and later create "writings" (formal agreements, letters, and so on) which satisfy the statute of frauds. All courts will recognize a memorandum made and signed before a suit is instituted to enforce the contract.

Most states require a signature only of the "party to be charged" with breach of contract. All parties' signatures are not needed because the party suing readily admits the existence of the contract. It is the party being sued—usually the defendant who denies the agreement or resists enforcement of it—whose signature is necessary for enforcement. But when people make a contract, they cannot be certain which party may later breach it. For his or her own protection, each party should make sure the other party signs the agreement or some adequate memorandum. The signature may consist of the signer's initials, thumbprint, or any other "symbol" actually or apparently intended to authenticate the writing as that of the signer. Under the proper circumstances, even a preprinted name on the stationery used could be considered a signature. An authorized agent may effectively sign, initial, use a signature stamp, or the like to authenticate a writing. As the following case illustrates, a business manager or secretary with proper authority can bind an employer by "signing" a writing on behalf of the employer. Signatures ordinarily need not appear at any particular place on the memorandum. However, the more uncommon the "symbol" used or the more unusual its placement on a writing, the more difficult it will be to prove it was intended as a signature.

CASE 12.4   McMahan Construction Co. v. Wegehoft Brothers, Inc.
354 N.E.2d 278 (Ind. App. 1976)

Facts: McMahan Construction was building a highway and needed dirt fill for the project. McMahan was taking some fill from its own property at 4404 Bluff Road but needed more. Wegehoft, the owner of the adjoining land, orally agreed to sell McMahan some fill from his land on condition that McMahan would sell the 4404 tract to Wegehoft at a future date for $5000. Koch, McMahan's project manager, and Wegehoft later signed a handwritten "Memorandum of Agreement" identifying the parties and stating the terms of the agreement including the price of the fill and the land. The land was described only by its common mailing address, 4404 Bluff Road. Koch said he would have an official contract prepared but he never did. McMahan removed dirt fill for three years from Wegehoft's property. Wegehoft later sued to enforce McMahan's agreement to sell the 4404 Bluff Road property. McMahan denied there was an agreement for the sale of the land. The trial court found in favor of Wegehoft, and McMahan appealed.

Question: Did the handwritten "Memorandum of Agreement" satisfy the requirements of the statute of frauds?

Answer: Yes. Wegehoft may enforce the contract for the sale of the land.

Reasoning: The memorandum required by the statute of frauds can be formal or informal, must be signed by the party charged with breaching the contract or an agent, and must state with reasonable certainty the parties, the subject matter, and the terms and conditions of the promises. The "Memorandum of Agreement" satisfied the requirements. The property to be sold was adequately identified by its mailing address and the writing was specific enough as to the parties and promises made. The writing was signed by the "party to be charged," McMahan. Koch, as project manager, had the authority to sign on behalf of McMahan.

Consequences of Lack of a Writing

General Rule.   Contracts within the statute of frauds are "unenforceable" unless proved by a writing. An "unenforceable contract" is one that lacks some formality (such as a writing) required by the law and, therefore, may not be enforced in court by direct legal proceedings. An unenforceable contract should be distinguished from a "voidable contract," which may be enforced unless avoided at one party's option, and from a "void contract," where no contract is present because an essential element is missing.

An unenforceable oral agreement may, of course, be voluntarily performed by the parties. Since full performance is satisfactory proof that a contract was made, a court would leave the parties where they are. Lack of a required writing may not be used as a basis for rescinding (canceling) a completely performed contract.

When an alleged oral contract is executory (unperformed), lack of a required writing may be used as a defense in a breach of contract suit. If the defense of lack of a writing (the "statute-of-frauds defense") is not raised by the defendant, it is *waived* and a court will normally enforce the agreement.

Usual Exceptions.   There is a danger that a person who knows about the statute of frauds may make an oral agreement intending later to use the lack of a writing as a means to avoid contractual responsibility. Thus, the statute of frauds can be used as an instrument of fraud and oppression against people who do not know the requirement or who lack the bargaining power to demand a writing. Both the courts and legislatures have created ways to prevent injustices arising from the misuse of the statute-of-frauds requirement. We have seen that there is an exception for each class of contracts discussed in this chapter. For example, the *part performance exception* (found in the UCC for sales of goods contracts and judicially recognized for land-sales contracts) permits a court to enforce an oral contract to the extent it is objectively proved by the performance of the parties.

If a party cannot bring his or her case within one of the exceptions, courts may avoid the potential hardship of an unenforceable oral agreement by allowing a *quasi-contractual remedy* if one party to the oral contract would otherwise be unjustly enriched. For example, although an oral lease of an apartment for 13 months is unenforceable, the landlord may recover the reasonable rental value in quasi contract for the time the tenant lives there.

Equitable Estoppel Exception.   Another method the courts have used to avoid serious injustice is to invoke the *doctrine of equitable estoppel* (sometimes referred to as "promissory estoppel" or "justifiable reliance") to enforce oral agreements. Courts recognize that the writing requirement meant to discourage fraud may sometimes actually be used to achieve unfair or fraudulent results. If one party to an unenforceable oral contract is threatened with or suffers serious loss or harm (detriment) due to reliance on the promises or misrepresentations of the other party, a court can enforce the contract by prohibiting (estopping) the use of the statute-of-frauds defense.

To illustrate, suppose Jethro, a consumer, orders $1000 worth of ordinary tiles over the phone from Zed's Supply. Zed doesn't have the tiles on hand and is reluctant to order them until he gets something in writing from Jethro. Jethro claims he has prepared, signed, and sent a letter stating their oral agreement, when in fact he has not done so. If Zed substantially changes his position in reliance on Jethro's misrepresentation, perhaps by ordering the tiles, Jethro will be estopped (legally prevented) from using the statute-of-frauds defense to avoid the contract. Equitable estoppel is often employed to enforce an oral contract where the result would otherwise be unconscionable or fraudulent to the party detrimentally relying. Moreover, substantial detrimental reliance by one party tends to prove that promises were made by the other.

Equitable estoppel will not have to be used by the court if there is some other legal basis for enforcing the contract. For example, if the tiles had been specially manufactured for Jethro and are unfit for other buyers, that fact would permit Zed to enforce the oral agreement under the UCC statute-of-frauds exception regarding specially manufactured goods. Neither would equitable estoppel be used to enforce the oral agreement if Jethro sent the following *signed* note to Zed: "I've decided not to buy the $1000 worth of tiles I ordered. Our agreement wasn't in writing so it's not enforceable anyway." Jethro's note, in which he admits the existence of the agreement, fulfills all the requirements of a "memorandum" satisfying the statute of frauds. Zed can use this note to enforce the contract.

The following case provides another example of injustice being prevented by invoking equitable estoppel to enforce an oral contract within the statute of frauds.

CASE 12.5   Lucas v. Whittaker Corporation
470 F.2d 326 (10th Cir. 1972)

Facts: Whittaker entered into an oral contract to employ Lucas for a two-year period. In reliance on the oral contract, Lucas resigned from his secure job of nine years, sacrificing substantial employee benefits and stock options, sold his new custom-built home, gave up his business and social contacts in California, and moved his family to Colorado. Lucas was fired apparently without cause after only thirteen months of employment, and he sued for breach of the two-year agreement. In addition to denying the contract existed, Whittaker asserted the statute of frauds prevented the enforcement of an oral two-year contract. The trial court, finding in favor of Lucas, invoked the equitable estoppel doctrine to prohibit Whittaker's use of the statute of frauds defense. Whittaker appealed.

Question: Should this long-term oral contract be enforced because of Lucas' detrimental reliance on Whittaker's promise?

Answer: Yes. The trial court was correct in enforcing the oral contract to prevent unconscionable injury to Lucas.

Reasoning: The doctrine of equitable estoppel may be used to prohibit the use of the statute of frauds where it is necessary to prevent fraud or unconscionable injury that would result if the oral contract were not enforced. Lucas was induced seriously to change his position in reliance on the oral contract, suffering more than he would have in an ordinary change of jobs. The court properly determined that unconscionable injury to Lucas should be avoided by enforcing the oral two-year agreement.

INTERPRETATION OF CONTRACTS; PAROL EVIDENCE RULE

Why Interpretation Is Needed
Even when a contract is written, the people involved may have disagreements about what the contract means or requires them to do. Many times a court will be called on to determine what the terms of the contract are, that is, what statements are to be

considered part of the contract. In this situation, the **parol evidence rule** will be useful to the court. At other times a court will need only to interpret unclear language. After deciphering such statements of the parties, a court will decide whether the contract has been breached and, if so, what remedy should be granted the wronged party.

When and How the Parol Evidence Rule Is Applied

When the Rule Is Applied.   Suppose the parties to a negotiated agreement put it in writing. Their signed contract, if it represents their final decision about the terms of the agreement, is known as an **integration** because it incorporates (integrates) and replaces any prior and contemporaneous negotiations the parties may have had. Under the parol evidence rule, the written integration, not any other evidence of their prior discussions or agreements, is what the court will consider in deciding what the parties have agreed to. "Parol evidence" is any *prior or contemporaneous oral statements* or *prior writings* outside of (not a part of) the integration. The parol evidence rule is intended to prevent any party from using parol evidence to contradict or alter the terms found in the signed integration. However, there are numerous exceptions, and in a lawsuit much parol evidence is allowed.

How the Rule Is Applied.   The purpose of the parol evidence rule is to help the court sift through various oral statements and writings to decide what words are part of "the contract." Once the parties' last signed contract is determined to be the final expression of their agreement, a court will normally ignore contemporaneous oral statements and any earlier oral agreements, oral discussions, and written matter, including prior contracts, which would *contradict or change* the terms of the integration; that is, binding effect is given to a writing signed as the final expression of an agreement.

There are two kinds of writings to which the parol evidence rule applies—the partial integration and the complete integration. A **partial integration** contains only part of the agreement between the parties but is intended as the "final expression" as to the terms included. Oral or written evidence of prior negotiations or agreements may not be used to vary or contradict the terms in the partial integration. But such evidence of prior dealings may be used to *supplement* the agreement, as long as the additional terms are consistent with the partial integration. In addition, unstated common practices of the parties or the particular industry involved (for example, standard delivery terms) may be held to be part of the agreement if they do not contradict what the parties have agreed to in the partial integration.

A **complete integration** is meant to be the parties' complete and exclusive statement of all the contract terms. For this reason, evidence of negotiations or prior agreements may neither contradict the writing nor add to it. Even terms which appear consistent with the writing will be excluded if the court determines that it is a complete integration.

Determining whether the parties intend a writing to be the final expression or integration of their agreement is not always an easy task for a court. Generally, a written agreement which is so detailed that it appears complete will be found to be an integration if there is no contrary evidence. If those involved include a declaration in the writing that this is their complete agreement, courts will often recognize the writing as an integration. However, where such a declaration is merely standard language printed on a form contract, especially a contract of adhesion, courts have frequently refused to recognize the writing as an integration and have permitted parol evidence of prior dealings to be introduced.

Exceptions to the Rule.   The parol evidence rule has numerous exceptions. The most important limitation is that the rule applies only to what happened between the parties *prior* to the integration. The parol evidence rule is not intended to prevent them from changing or canceling a contract that has been committed to writing. Evidence of later agreements which affect the integration, modifications of the integration, or even cancellation of the integration can be freely admitted by the court.

The parol evidence rule does not prevent the parties from replacing or canceling the agreement *later*. Consequently, a court faced with a series of written integrated contracts will give effect to the latest one. Moreover, the parol evidence rule would not prevent the parties from proving an oral modification was agreed to *after* the latest integration, but as discussed earlier in the chapter, the enforceability of such a later oral modification would depend upon whether the statute of frauds applies to it.

Parol evidence can be freely admitted for several other reasons even though it concerns what happened *prior* to the integration. Parol evidence may be used to clear up an ambiguity in any integration (complete or partial) since this does not change the agreement but rather explains it. Parol evidence may also be used to prove a defense to enforcement of a contract, such as fraud, duress, mistake, lack of consideration, incapacity, or illegality. Parol evidence may be introduced to show that a drafting error was made in the written agreement or that the parties agreed to an unwritten condition preventing the integration from becoming effective. Parol evidence may even be used to resolve whether the writing is a complete integration or only a partial integration.

Because of the parol evidence rule, the parties who reduce an agreement to writing should realize the risks involved and the potential disadvantages, as well as benefits, of the writing. A court may view the writing as an integration and disallow any attempt by a party to claim that a different agreement was reached. Even when one party had little bargaining power or little choice in signing an agreement, the terms of the integration may be enforced unless they are grossly unfair. So if a person signing a form contract doesn't intend to be bound by each of the terms, the objectionable terms should be removed prior to signing, in order to prevent later arguments.

How to Interpret a Contract

Although it is known (or a court has determined) what words are part of the contract, it may not be clear what the words mean. They may have to be interpreted. To decide what the parties meant, a court will apply some generally accepted rules of interpretation.

The following are some well-recognized rules used by the courts. The agreement is read as a whole, rather than as separate parts, to understand what those involved hoped to achieve. The separate parts are then interpreted in light of the parties' general goal. Each clause assists in understanding others. The parties are presumed to have intended a rational and lawful agreement, so the language whenever possible is read to avoid absurdities and illegal or unreasonable requirements. Words in the contract are given their ordinary meanings unless it is clear from the context that special or technical meanings were intended. A particular or specific term prevails over (modifies) a more general requirement. Where printed contract forms are used, any typing or handwriting takes precedence over the printed terms. Handwriting generally controls either typing or print. When the drafting party causes an uncertainty about what the contract demands, the ambiguity is interpreted in favor of the other party. Courts often supply apparently missing terms when they are common practice in the parties' business or profession, so long as they are consistent with the agreement and it is likely that the parties intended to include them.

In discovering or interpreting terms a court is not writing a new agreement for the parties. It is merely settling a dispute by declaring what appears to the court to have been originally intended. The best insurance against misinterpretation by a court is to make an agreement as clear and complete as possible. Doing so not only will assist court interpretation, but also will tend to prevent disputes from arising.

SUMMARY

The statute of frauds applies to classes of contracts thought to be so significant or burdensome to a contracting party that a writing should be required to prove the contract exists. Except where a statute of frauds or another special statute requires a writing, an oral contract is as enforceable as a written one.

The classes of contracts most commonly covered by state statutes of frauds are:

1. A contract not performable within 1 year
2. A contract transferring an interest in land
3. A promise to answer for another's debt
4. A contract for the sale of goods for $500 or more

The main purpose of a statute of frauds is to require reliable evidence that an alleged contract was actually agreed to. To satisfy the statute, some memorandum of the agreement must be in writing and be signed by the person to be charged with breach of contract in any later legal proceeding.

The statute of frauds can itself be used as an instrument of fraud or oppression against persons ignorant of the writing requirement, or too lacking in bargaining power to demand a writing. To prevent injustice which might arise from misuse of the writing requirement, the courts use the part performance, main purpose, and equitable estoppel exceptions to enforce some oral contracts which the statute of frauds would otherwise require to be in writing. Under the sale-of-goods statute of frauds, a writing is only one of several ways to evidence a contract. Other ways include part performance, specially manufactured goods, and in-court admissions. If a contract is modified and as modified is within the statute of frauds, the modified contract must satisfy the requirements of the statute.

A statute of frauds indicates what evidence is required for enforcing a contract. The parol evidence rule indicates what evidence a court will consider in determining the content of a contract. The parol evidence rule in lawsuits prevents admission of evidence of an oral or written agreement made prior to an integrated agreement if the evidence is introduced to contradict or change the terms of the integration. However, parol evidence may be admitted to explain the integration or to determine its validity, as well as for other reasons.

REVIEW QUESTIONS

1. Explain why the statute of frauds doesn't apply to all contracts.
2. List some of the advantages of putting a contract in writing.
3. (a) How do courts distinguish between contracts that are performable within 1 year and those that are not? (b) Al makes an oral contract to support Bo for the rest of Bo's life. Under the statute of frauds, is the contract enforceable? Explain.
4. When a party to a long-term oral contract has completely performed his or her part of the bargain, can that party enforce the agreement against the other party who has not yet completely performed? Explain.
5. (a) To which of the following contracts does the land provision of the statute of frauds apply? Purchase of land; lease of land; mortgage; contract for the sale of oil in the ground; contract for sale of a building to be removed from the land; contract for sale of growing crops. (b) Is an agreement to build a house covered by the statute of frauds? Explain.
6. Under what circumstances might a court enforce an oral contract for the sale of real estate?
7. (a) When must a guaranty to pay another's debt be in writing to be enforceable? (b) Explain the "main purpose" rule and what its effect is.
8. (a) What contracts for the sale of goods are covered by the statute-of-frauds provision of UCC Article 2? (b) What are the UCC Article 2 exceptions to the requirement of a writing signed by the party against whom enforcement is sought?
9. Explain when contract changes must be in writing to be enforced.
10. (a) What kind of writing will satisfy the statute of frauds? (b) What constitutes a signature on a writing?
11. (a) What are the consequences of not complying with the statute of frauds? (b) May a completely performed oral contract within the statute of frauds be rescinded for lack of a writing? Explain.
12. What is the purpose of the parol evidence rule?
13. List the rules that guide a court's interpretation of a contract.

CASE PROBLEMS

1. Kiyose was a university lecturer in a department of East Asian Languages. While he was a lecturer, the university orally assured him that upon obtaining his Ph.D. he would receive perpetual lifetime appointments at the university, commencing with a 3-year appointment as an assistant professor. After obtaining his Ph.D. and being appointed to the rank of assistant professor, Kiyose was notified that

Lifetime = Short term agreement

he would not be reappointed. Kiyose brought suit for breach of the oral agreement. The university contended that the agreement was not enforceable. Was Kiyose's action barred by the statute of frauds? Explain the reasons for your answer.

2. Hilda Anderson worked for Erik Skoglund as his housekeeper for about 7 years until Skoglund's death in 1960. She received no wages. In a suit against Skoglund's estate for the reasonable value of her services, Anderson claimed that she worked for Skoglund in reliance on his oral promise that if anything happened to him, she would receive his house. Skoglund died without a will, and Anderson, who was not related to him, received nothing. Was Anderson entitled to the house? Why or why not? Is there another way she can recover for her services?

3. Sylvia owned some mortgaged real estate. He defaulted on mortgage payments, and to avoid foreclosure of the mortgage, he agreed orally to sell the property to Weale. Weale secured a bank commitment to finance the purchase, paid an attorney $150 for examining the title and doing other legal work related to the property, and spent $2860 for a land survey. In the meantime, Cole learned of the proposed sale, visited the property, and saw the survey work. He then offered to purchase the land, and he and Sylvia signed a contract of sale. Weale and Cole brought separate actions against Sylvia for specific performance. In a single hearing, the trial court granted specific performance to Weale and ordered Cole to file a release of his recorded written purchase agreement. Cole appealed. Was Weale entitled to specific performance? Explain.

4. Jim and Slim's Tool Supply, Inc., furnished building materials to a subcontractor who was using them in constructing apartment buildings. The subcontractor defaulted in payment. The owner of the apartments orally agreed to guarantee payment for materials, and Tool Supply agreed to continue furnishing materials and to refrain from filing a claim of lien against the owner's real property. Later the owner refused to make payment, and Tool Supply brought suit for breach of the agreement. The trial court dismissed the complaint on the ground that enforcement of the agreement was barred by the statute of frauds. Tool Supply appealed. Should the trial court's ruling be upheld? Why or why not?

5. Emery, a farm owner, agreed in writing to sell landfill from his farm to the Caledonia Sand & Gravel Co., a road contractor. Under the written agreement, Caledonia was obliged to restore the excavation area "with the original topsoil or with some other material capable of supporting vegetation, to fertilize and seed the pit area, and to clean up all areas disturbed by the operation to the owner's specifications." Emery was paid for the landfill, but was dissatisfied with the restoration. He brought suit to recover damages for breach of the restoration agreement. In awarding damages to Emery, the trial court considered parol evidence relating to Emery's understanding that the land would be restored for use as a hayfield. The written agreement made no mention of the use of the land as a hayfield. Was the court in error in considering the parol evidence? Why or why not?

CHAPTER 13

RIGHTS AND DUTIES OF THIRD PARTIES

So far in our discussion of contracts we have emphasized the personal relationship between contracting parties. Contracts, such as one in which you sell your car to Joan, formed the basis upon which contracting obligations were considered in preceding chapters. In day-to-day business life, however, contractual relations may be much more complex.

Contracts may in several different ways involve third parties who are not directly parties to an agreement. For instance, Art works for you. You agree at his request to pay directly to Ben, to whom Art owes money, the wages Art earns next week. Ben, who is to receive Art's wages, is the *third-party beneficiary* of the contract between you and Art. Or, Crown Motors sells an automobile on credit to Dave, who signs a purchase agreement by which he promises to make installment payments. Crown then *assigns* (turns over) that agreement to a finance company. From that time on, Dave makes his payments to the finance company, which is the *assignee* of the contact. Or, you as director of a flying school agree to teach Sue how to fly a plane. You *delegate* the duty, that is, you designate Peg to be her instructor. Peg is a *delegatee* of your duty.

In this chapter we consider third-party beneficiary contracts, assignment of contract rights, and delegation to another person of duties to be performed under a contract.

THIRD-PARTY BENEFICIARY CONTRACTS

Who Is a Third-Party Beneficiary?

Those who enter into a contract normally expect personally to enjoy the benefits of the contract's performance. For instance, Mary receives a catalog from the Unique mail order house, advertising the latest clothing fashions for sale. Mary accepts a catalog offer by ordering a dress for herself and sending her check in payment. Mary and Unique now have a contract and Mary expects to receive performance (the dress).

Someone who is not a party to a contract may also benefit, either directly or indirectly, from its performance. Such an individual is a **third-party beneficiary**. For example, if Mary had ordered the dress to be delivered to her sister, Jane, rather than to herself, Jane would have been a third-party beneficiary of the contract between Mary and Unique.

Sometimes a person not specifically intended by the contracting parties to receive performance or to benefit from it, nonetheless indirectly benefits. For instance, you may contract with Edward to tear down a disreputable tenement house Edward owns and to erect for him in its place a landscaped shopping mall. The contract, if carried out, will enhance the value of all properties in the neighborhood. In a sense, the owners of all the nearby properties are beneficiaries of the contract between you and Edward. However, the *purpose* of that contract was not to benefit other property owners. They were merely incidental beneficiaries. Individuals of this class are *not* included within the term "third-party beneficiary" as that term is here used.

Figure 13.1 represents a third-party beneficiary contract. In that figure, Art (the promisor) promises Ben (the promisee) at Ben's request to render performance of the contract to Carl (the third-party beneficiary). The figure shows that Art made the promise to pay Carl in exchange for a consideration paid by Ben to Art.

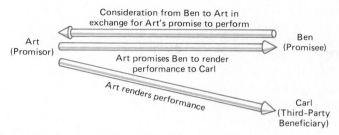

FIGURE 13.1   Third-party beneficiary contract.

It is not essential that a third-party beneficiary be identified by name or even that the beneficiary be specifically known to the contracting parties at the time of the agreement. A third-party beneficiary is entitled to the contract performance if he or she can be identified *at the time the performance is due.* Thus, if you promise your daughter Sue that upon her graduation from college you will "pay all her then creditors," you have sufficiently described the intended beneficiaries to give Sue's creditors rights of action against you under the agreement.

The following case considers whether the facts before the court are sufficient to make the plaintiff, Knickelbein, a third-person beneficiary of a contract.

CASE 13.1   Schell v. Knickelbein
252 N.W.2d 921 (Wis. 1977)

Facts: Mr. and Mrs. Knickelbein made mortgage payments on their home to Security Savings & Loan. The payments included funds to cover the premiums on a home owners' insurance policy. Security allowed the policy to lapse (expire). Schell, a third person, died as the result of having been attacked by Knickelbein's dog. Schell's widow sued Knickelbein and Security, claiming that, as third-person beneficiary of the contract between the two defendants, she could recover from Security to the extent that Knickelbein would have been covered by the insurance policy if it had not been allowed to lapse.

Question: Can an unnamed third person be a beneficiary of an agreement made by two other parties?

Answer: Yes, if in this case the policy would have covered the type of injury the plaintiff suffered.

Reasoning: The court said, "A third party cannot maintain an action as third party beneficiary if, under the contract, his was only an indirect benefit merely incidental to the contract between the parties." However, Schell would be entitled to recover: (1) if the policy had not been allowed to lapse, and (2) if it would have insured Knickelbein against liability for the dog's actions. In that event, Schell would have been entitled to claim compensation from the insurance company as a beneficiary of the agreement between Knickelbein and Security.

Types of Third-Party Beneficiary Contracts

There are two types of third-party beneficiaries: a **donee beneficiary** and a **creditor beneficiary**. In both types, the original promisee (the party to whom performance was originally owed), *intends* that a third party will have the benefit of that performance. However, the two types differ in the reasons why the promisee wants the third party to be benefited.

Third-Party Donee Beneficiary Contracts.   Where the purpose of the original promisee is to make a *gift* of the promised performance to the third party, the contract is a *third-party donee beneficiary contract*. The following would be such a contract. Dan lends Bill $1000, and it is agreed that Bill (the promisor) will repay the loan by sending the money to the American Cancer Society as a donation from Dan. The American Cancer Society is a third-party *donee* beneficiary of the contract between Dan and Bill because the payment to be made by Bill to the Society was intended by Dan as a *gift* to the Society. The American Cancer Society has the legal right to demand performance by Bill.

Third-Party Creditor Beneficiary Contracts.   A third-party creditor beneficiary contract is similar to a third-party donee beneficiary contract except that the individual who assigns the right to receive performance (Dan, in the above example) does so not as a gift, but to discharge a debt. In that example, if Dan owed the American Cancer Society the $1000 to satisfy a pledge he had made, a third-party creditor beneficiary contract would have been established. The following additional example should make this concept clear.

Tom borrows $1000 from Helen and promises to repay it to her or to anyone she designates. Helen owes her sorority $1000. Helen tells Tom to pay his debt to her sorority instead of to her. As Helen's direction to Tom was to satisfy a debt, the sorority is a third-party creditor beneficiary. The sorority, as a third-party creditor beneficiary, has the right not only to collect the money owed to it by Helen, but also to collect from Helen's debtor, Tom. Of course, the sorority cannot collect more than once for the same debt.

Promisor's Defenses against a Third-Party Beneficiary

A third-party donee beneficiary or third-party creditor beneficiary has a right to require performance by the person obligated to perform the contract. However, the promisor may assert against the beneficiary any defense which he or she could have asserted against the promisee had the latter sought to enforce the performance. To illustrate, Art (the promisor) agrees to pay Ben (the promisee) $300 within 60 days for barbed wire Ben delivers to Art. Ben assigns to Thelma (to whom he is indebted) the right to receive the payment from Art. Thelma is a third-party creditor beneficiary of the Art–Ben contract. If 60 days go by and Art fails to make the required payment, Thelma has a cause of action against Art. Art, however, may assert against Thelma any defense that he could have asserted against Ben had Ben brought the action. Therefore, the promisee is no worse off than if the assignment had not been made.

ASSIGNMENT OF CONTRACT RIGHTS

A person who has a contract right may wish to convey (assign) it to someone else. This right is frequently used by business concerns to supplement their working capital by

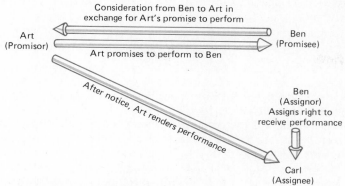

FIGURE 13.2   Assignment of contract rights.

selling or by pledging as security for loans some or all of the accounts receivable owed to them. Accounts receivable are customers' obligations to pay for articles or services received.

Nature of Assignment

A party who assigns an account or some other contract right is the **assignor**; the recipient of the account or contract right is the **assignee**.

Meaning of Assignment.   An assignment is the transfer to a third party, *after* a contract has been entered into, of a right to receive contract performance. A third-party beneficiary contract, on the other hand, establishes the third party's interest as a part of the original contract. The assignment of a contract extinguishes or ends the assignor's right to receive performance; the assignee alone has the right to receive it.

Figure 13.2 illustrates the assignment of a contract right by a party to a contract to whom performance is due. Ben (the assignor) assigns to Carl his (Ben's) right to receive the performance and Ben gives up the right to receive it. The assignment may be made either for a consideration or as a gift. In either event, the assignee is entitled to the contract performance.

The case which follows deals with the assignment of a contract right.

CASE 13.2   The Evening News Association v. Peterson
477 F. Supp. 77 (D.C., D.C. 1979)

Facts: Peterson was under contract with Post-Newsweek to serve as its TV newscaster-anchorman. The contract was to run until June 30, 1980. In June 1978, Post-Newsweek sold its TV operating license to the Evening News Association. The purchase agreement included an assignment of the Peterson contract to the Evening News. In August 1979, Peterson secured employment as a TV newscaster-anchorman with another TV station and he tendered his resignation from his position with the Evening News. Evening News thereupon brought suit to enjoin (prevent) Peterson from violating his employment contract. The question arose as to whether the right to receive Peterson's services could be assigned by Post-Newsweek to Evening News.

Question: Was Post-Newsweek's contract right to receive Peterson's services assignable?

Answer: Yes. The contract established assignable rights.

Reasoning: Duties under a personal services contract involving special skills generally are not delegable *by the one obligated to perform the services*. The issue here is not whether Peterson's personal services were delegable, but whether the right of Post-Newsweek to *receive* those services is assignable.

Contract rights as a general rule are assignable. This is subject to the exception that there may be no assignment where it would materially vary the duties to be performed by the obligor (Peterson), would materially increase a risk imposed by the contract, or would materially impair the obligor's chance of obtaining return performance (his pay, etc.). The sale of the TV station did not in any material way change Peterson's functions, duties, or obligations. The Evening News carried on Peterson's position without change. The right to receive his services was assignable.

Requirements for Assignment.   In the absence of a statute to the contrary, an assignment may be made in any form. An act or statement, written or oral, indicating an intention to transfer a legal right is sufficient. However, statutes in nearly every state require a writing and sometimes witnesses or an acknowledgment before a notary public for the assignment of wage claims or corporate shares.

A consideration moving from the assignee to the assignor is not necessary to make an assignment valid. But the courts do not regard a gift assignment as being effective until the intended recipient secures a substantial measure of control over the right assigned. Such control would be possession of appropriate documents plus notice to the party who owes the basic debt. If the right to be assigned is represented by a document such as a life insurance policy or a bank savings account book, the policy or bank book would have to be surrendered to the assignee for the assignment to be effective.

For an assignment of a right to receive performance to be effective, the party who is required to perform must be given notice of the assignment. Assume that you owe $500 to Ben, and that Ben assigns his right to receive payment to Carl and notifies you of the assignment. Thereafter, you must render performance, that is, pay, Carl. When you pay the $500 to Carl you satisfy both your debt to Ben and Ben's debt to Carl. However, until you receive notice of Ben's assignment to Carl, you owe no duty to Carl. Your only duty is to Ben.

Legal Position of the Assignee.   It is often said that an assignee stands in the shoes of the assignor. This statement means two things, as illustrated in Figure 13.2:

1. The assignee, Carl, succeeds to (acquires) any rights that the assignor, Ben, may have had against Art, the other party in the contract between Art and Ben, including Carl's right to receive Art's performance.
2. Any rights Ben had against Art have been assigned to Carl, subject to whatever

defenses Art could have asserted against Ben. Such defenses, among others, might be failure of the consideration which Ben was supposed to have given in exchange for Art's promise, fraud by Ben, or the fact that Art is a minor. Art could also assert any defense which arose *after* the assignment from Ben to Carl but before Art knew of it. Such a defense might be, among others, that payment had already been made, or that Art's obligation had been released or waived by Ben, or that the contract between them had been mutually rescinded.

The next case illustrates that someone who is obligated to perform may assert against an assignee a waiver of the contract obligation.

CASE 13.3   Chimney Hill Owners' Assoc., Inc. v. Eastern Woodworking Co.
392 A.2d 423 (Vt. 1978)

Facts: Chimney Hill Corporation owned a large housing and recreational area. The property was sold subject to an annual charge upon each lot for the right to use the swimming pools, tennis courts, etc. Eastern purchased eleven lots. Its purchase agreement stated that there would be only one charge per year upon the eleven lots as though they constituted only one lot, and, when each of the lots was improved it would become subject to the annual charge. Chimney Hill Corporation conveyed all the common land and recreational areas to the Chimney Hill Owners' Association. The Association billed Eastern for the annual charge for each of the eleven lots it owned, although not one of them was improved. Eastern paid only one assessment and the Association brought suit to collect the assessments on each of the eleven lots. Eastern claims that the Corporation had waived all but one assessment and that the Association, the Corporation's assignee, was bound by the waiver.

Question: Could Eastern assert a waiver by the Chimney Hill Corporation as a defense against the Association?

Answer: Yes. Eastern is entitled to that defense.

Reasoning: When the Association received the common land from the Corporation, it took the property subject to all defenses that Eastern had against the Corporation. A waiver is the intentional relinquishment of a known right. The Corporation had waived its right to impose individual assessments against Eastern until its properties were improved. Eastern may therefore assert the waiver against the Association just as it could have asserted it against the Corporation.

Assignments Which Are Not Legally Effective

The law allows most types of contract rights to be assigned. However, to protect a contracting party, an assignment of a contract right by one of the parties is not legally effective if the assignment would materially affect the other party to the contract by (1) changing his or her duty under the contract, (2) increasing the burden or risk imposed by the contract, or (3) impairing the chances of obtaining performance of the contract by either the assignor or the assignee.

Of course, there can be no effective assignment of contract rights where (1) the assignment is forbidden by statute—for example, claims against the United States normally may not be assigned; (2) the assignment is against public policy—for instance, assignment by a public official of funds not yet earned; or (3) the assignment is precluded by the terms of the contract—the courts generally enforce a contractual provision against assignment of a contract without the consent of the other party.

Assignments Varying Obligor's Duty or Risk.   A contract assignment which results in a substantial change in the nature or quantity of the performance required by the other party constitutes a material change in his or her duty and the terms are no longer enforceable. For example, suppose Luxury Steamship Line contracted with Eggsville Farms to buy all the eggs Luxury needs for its cruise ships. Because Luxury buys eggs in great numbers, Eggsville has contracted to furnish all Luxury's needs at the very low price of 40 cents per dozen. Luxury Steamship Lines is absorbed by Container Shipping Company and the Eggsville contract is assigned to it. Container Shipping carries no passengers and needs only about one-fourth as many eggs as did Luxury. Eggsville would lose money at the original large-quantity price if the contract price were to be enforced for the much smaller quantity. Because of the material change in circumstances brought about by the assignment, the contract cannot be enforced by Container against Eggsville.

Where the change of the duty of the obligor is only in slight and unimportant details, there can be an assignment without the obligor's consent. For example, if a sales contract requires the seller to deliver merchandise COD to the purchaser's home, the purchaser can effectively assign his or her rights under the contract to a nearby neighbor, because only a slight and unimportant detail is involved. But if the assignee lived in another city, the change in the seller's required performance might be so substantial as to make the assignment ineffective.

An assignor may not, without the obligor's consent, increase the obligor's risk. An increased risk might come about in a situation such as the following. Jill's building is insured by Fidelity Fire Insurance Company. Jill sells the building to Jack and wants to assign the fire insurance policy to him. Jack may intend to use the building for purposes that involve more risk of fire than was the case when Jill owned it. In addition, Jack's other properties may have been involved in several fires in the past. Therefore, Fidelity may not be willing to insure Jack against fires, or it may issue a policy to him only at a higher premium. It follows that Jill cannot effectively assign her insurance policy to Jack unless Fidelity first consents to the assignment.

When all that remains to be done under a contract is for one of the parties to pay money to the other, a direction to the party owing the money (the obligor) by the one to whom the money is owed (the obligee) to make the payment to an assignee imposes no additional burden upon the obligor. Therefore, the assignment is effective. For example, suppose you have entered into a contract with Johnson Heating Company to repair your furnace. When the work is finished and you are about to write a check paying Johnson's bill, he tells you to make the check payable to the American Radiator Company because he owes money to that company. The receipt Johnson gives you will reflect your payment according to his direction.

Assignments Forbidden by Statute or Public Policy.   Federal and state statutes prohibit assignment of certain types of claims and regulate assignment of others. For example, an assignment of a claim against the federal government is void unless the assignment is made to a bank or financing institution. This law serves to minimize vexatious litigation. Most states have statutes regulating the percentage of future wages that can be assigned, and if assignment is authorized, the method by which it can be accomplished. These statutes tend to protect low-income families from pressures to commit their incomes far in advance of receipt.

Assignments Prohibited by Contract.   A contract may contain a clause purporting to prohibit assignment of any rights accruing under the contract. Such a clause is called a *nonassignability clause.* In deciding whether to enforce such a restrictive clause, the courts weigh the principle that there should be freedom of contract (which would support enforcing the clause) against the policy that there should be free transfer of property (which might justify invalidating the clause).

Modern courts recognize that an assignment may facilitate a business transaction. Therefore, where possible, courts interpret a contract stipulation not to assign a contract as merely a promise not to assign, rather than as an absolute prohibition of assignment. If Art and Betty stipulated that "Neither party shall assign his or her rights under this contract," most courts would interpret such language as a promise not to assign. Under that interpretation, if Betty assigns the contract to Carl, the assignment is valid and Carl can require Art to perform under it, but Betty has breached her contract with Art, who can sue her for the breach if he so desires.

In contrast, a clause stating "No assignment of rights arising under this contract shall be valid" is too clearly a prohibition against assignment to be interpreted as only a *promise* not to assign. Such a clear prohibition will be enforced unless it is against public policy (as, for instance, certain assignments of wages), or it is otherwise illegal.

Successive (Dual) Assignments

Sometimes, through mistake, negligence, or dishonesty, a person sells the same contract right to two (or more) assignees. Which of the assignees has priority? The answer would depend upon (1) whether there is an applicable statute for recording assignments as a public record, and (2) the law applied in the jurisdiction where the question arises. If there is no applicable recording statute, the majority rule is that, under normal conditions, the *first assignment made* is the one that is effective.

The minority rule is that the assignee who *first notifies the obligor* that he or she has received the assignment has priority.

Partial Assignments

Sometimes a creditor sells part of a claim to one assignee and later sells the rest of the claim to another. For example, Dick owes Christie $1000 and Christie assigns $600 of that claim to Nell. Later, Christie assigns the remaining $400 claim to Peter.

Partial assignments are effective provided the claim is divisible—that is, can be performed in parts as in the above example—and the contract under which the obligation arises does not prohibit partial assignments. However, no legal proceeding can be maintained against the obligor unless all the persons who hold partial assignments of a claim are joined in (made plaintiffs in) the proceedings. For example, in the illustration immediately above, neither Nell nor Peter, acting alone, can bring an action against Dick; but if they join together they may do so.

Warranties of an Assignor

Suppose that an assignee tries to collect payment from the obligor but is met with a valid defense. What recourse has the assignee against the assignor? If the assignment is made for a consideration, the assignor impliedly warrants that (1) the right assigned actually exists, (2) it is subject to no limitations or defenses other than those stated in the instrument of assignment or apparent at the time of assignment, and (3) the assignor will do nothing to defeat or impair the value of the assignment.

An assignment of a nonexistent claim is a breach of warranty (1) above. Assignment of a claim that is subject to the defense of fraud is a breach of warranty (2). Unauthorized collection of the debt by the assignor would be a breach of (3).

It will be noted that the assignor does not warrant that the debtor is solvent. In the example above involving Dick, Christie, Peter, and Nell, if either Peter or Nell is unwilling to assume the risk that Dick may be unable to perform, they should require Christie to make an express warranty that Dick is financially able to perform his part of the contract obligation. Then, if Dick fails, Christie herself is liable.

DELEGATION OF CONTRACT DUTIES

Meaning of Delegation

Delegation of a contract duty is not the same as assignment of a contract right. An *assignment of a right* is a transfer that ends the assignor's interest in the right transferred. On the other hand, a *delegation of a duty* means that the person required to perform a certain duty under a contract transfers its actual performance to another. For example, assume your computer software company has contracted to write a computer program for the Russell Accounting Office. You may delegate to someone in your office the duty to write the program unless the contract requires your personal performance. If the contract requires your personal performance, it is a personal contract and performance by a substitute is not acceptable.

It is a policy of the law that a person who undertakes to perform a duty should not be able casually to put it aside. When personal performance is not required in a contract, the delegation of a duty does *not* free the contracting party from his or her obligation *either* to perform the contract personally or to have it done in accordance with the contract requirements. Thus, if you contract with Amy, an upholsterer, to re-cover your armchair, she may delegate the actual work to an assistant, but if the work is poorly done Amy herself is responsible and may be forced to correct it.

Figure 13.3 illustrates the movement of duties when there is a delegation of a duty.

In Figure 13.3, Ben gives a consideration to Art, who assumes obligations to perform under the contract. Art (the delegator) delegates his duty of performance to Carl (the delegatee). In such a situation, Art remains liable for the contract even though Carl has assumed the duty to perform it.

It is possible for the party entitled to performance of a contract to release the other party from the obligation and substitute someone else in his or her place. In that event the remaining party and the new party enter into a new contract, known as a **contract of novation**, which is substituted for the original contract.

The difference between an assignment and a delegation is illustrated in the next case.

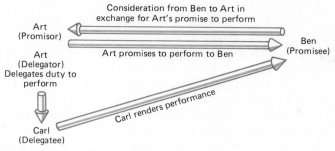

Figure 13.3   Delegation of Duty to Perform.

CASE 13.4 Contemporary Mission, Inc. v. Famous Music Corp.
557 F.2d 918 (2d Cir. 1977)

Facts: Contemporary Mission, which wrote musical compositions and recordings, contracted with Famous Music to manufacture and sell its recordings. Famous' record division was sold to ABC Records, and Contemporary was told to look to ABC for the performance of their contract. ABC refused to perform, and Contemporary desires to hold Famous for the breach.

Question: When there is a delegation of contract duties, is the contracting party who delegated the duty free from all further obligations under the contract?

Answer: No. The obligation to perform generally remains.

Reasoning: The assignment of a bilateral contract includes both an assignment of rights and a delegation of duties. When there is assignment of rights, generally the interest of the assignor in those rights comes to an end. However, one who owes a performance cannot by his or her own act, except when agreed to by the other party to the contract, divest himself or herself of the duty and substitute another to perform it. The obligation to perform may be delegated, but that does not relieve the delegator of the ultimate responsibility to see that the obligation is performed. If the delegatee fails to perform, as in this case, the delegator remains liable.

Delegable and Nondelegable Duties   Suppose that Jane agrees to do certain work for Harriet. Jane's authority to delegate the performance of the work is not mentioned. Whether Jane's duty must be performed by Jane herself or by someone to whom she delegates it (a delegatee) depends upon the nature of the work involved. The general rule is that a duty may be delegated where performance by the delegatee (the person to whom the duty is delegated) would be substantially the same to the receiver of the performance as if there had been no delegation. Duties such as the following normally may be delegated: to pay money, to deliver standard merchandise, to manufacture ordinary goods, and to build according to a set of plans and specifications.

In contrast, a duty is nondelegable if its performance requires a unique ability or the personal attention of the person who enters into the original contract. The following are illustrations of duties which may not be delegated without the consent of the other party to the contract: To manufacture a special class of high quality goods, to render a service required to be performed by a particular individual, or to farm on shares (meaning that the farmer and landowner share in the value of the products produced).

To protect the individual who contracts to receive performance, courts enforce contract clauses which forbid delegation of duties even if the act to be performed would be delegable were it not for the prohibitory clause.

Case 13.5, which follows, deals with delegable duties.

CASE 13.5   Macke Co. v. Pizza of Gaithersburg, Inc.
270 A.2d 645 (Md. 1970)

Facts: Pizza Shops contracted with Virginia Coffee Services for Virginia to install cold-drink vending machines in their stores. Macke purchased Virginia's assets and Virginia assigned the vending machine contracts to Macke. Pizza then terminated the contracts claiming that they were personal contracts to be performed by Virginia itself. Macke then brought suit for Pizza's breach of contract.

Question: Were the contracts personal and not assignable?

Answer: No. The contracts were assignable.

Reasoning: Rights and duties, where both parties have yet to render performances under a contract, may be assigned. However, duties under a contract can never be delegated to the extent of freeing a party to the contract from the obligation to perform his or her contract obligations. Pizza had chosen Virginia to install the vending machines because of the way Virginia conducted its business. It kept the machines in working order; paid commissions in cash; and permitted Pizza to retain the keys so that it could make minor necessary adjustments to the machines. These conditions, however, were a part of the contract between Pizza and Virginia. The quality of the service Pizza had received from Virginia and what it was getting from Macke were not so different as to amount to a change in performance. The performance remained substantially the same. No rare or extraordinary skill was involved. Therefore the delegation of the duty was not a breach of contract.

A contract sometimes contains a clause prohibiting "the assignment of this contract." Such a phrase is ambiguous. It is not clear whether the parties intend to prohibit the *assignment of rights* or to prohibit the *delegation of a duty to perform,* or both. Unless circumstances indicate the contrary, a prohibition against "assignment of this contract" is construed to mean that the *duty to perform* may not be delegated, but that the right to receive performance may be assigned. This rule is consistent with the policy of the law that rights should be freely transferrable, but that the transfer of duties should be limited.

Liability of the Delegatee

Suppose that Ben has agreed to supply Art with oil and that Art will pay Ben on receipt of the oil. But then Ben delegates to Charles (the delegatee) the duty to supply the oil and also assigns to him the right to receive payment. In this situation the delegation of Ben's duty to perform is accompanied by his assignment to Charles of the right to receive payment. That right furnishes Charles with consideration for his duty to deliver the oil and Art can force him to perform the contract.

SUMMARY

A person who is not a promisee to a contract may acquire rights in the contract in two ways: (1) by being made a third-party beneficiary, or (2) by being made an assignee of one of the parties to the contract.

When a third-party beneficiary contract is entered into, it designates someone other than the promisee as the one to receive the promised performance. If the purpose of the promisee is to confer a gift upon the third party, the latter is a donee beneficiary. If the purpose of the promisee is to secure discharge of an obligation he or she owes to a third party, the third party is a creditor beneficiary. In most states a third-party beneficiary has the right to enforce the obligor's promise.

The assignment of a contract is the transfer of a contract right by the owner of that right to someone else. The individual to whom the right is transferred has any right to performance which the assignor had. He or she (the assignee) takes the transferred right subject to: (1) any defense inherent in the original contract, or (2) any defense arising before the party obligated under the contract has notice that the transfer was made.

A contract right can be effectively assigned to another unless such assignment would (1) materially affect the duty of the other party to the contract (the obligor), (2) increase the obligor's risk under the contract, or (3) impair the obligor's chances of obtaining return performance. In addition, an assignment may, under certain circumstances, be forbidden by law or it may be prohibited by the contract.

Where a person sells the same claim to two or more parties, the first assignee generally has priority. A person to whom a claim is due (the obligee) may make partial assignments of the claim to several people. If the obligor objects to making a number of fractional payments when the contract requires only one, and if suit is brought, it must be in the joint name of all the assignees.

An assignor for value impliedly warrants (1) that the right assigned actually exists; (2) that it is subject to no limitations or defenses, other than those stated or apparent at the time of the assignment; and (3) that the assignor will do nothing to defeat or impair the value of the assignment.

Duties cannot be assigned, but certain duties can be delegated. A duty can be delegated unless performance by the delegatee would differ materially from performance by the delegator, or unless delegation of that duty is forbidden by law or contract.

A contract clause which prohibits "the assignment of this contract" generally bars only the delegation of the *duties* to be performed under the contract, but not the assignment of any rights under the contract.

REVIEW QUESTIONS

1. Under what circumstances may a person who is not a party to a contract be a beneficiary of performance due under that contract?

2. Distinguish between a third-party donee beneficiary contract and a third-party creditor beneficiary contract.

3. What defenses may a contract promisor assert against a suit by a third-party beneficiary under that contract?

4. Compare the rights of an assignor and an assignee against the other party to a contract.

5. What are the legal requirements for an effective assignment of a contract right?

6. A contract provides for the promisor to send goods to the promisee by parcel post at a certain address. The promisee assigns the right to receive the goods to someone who lives in another city. Has this so increased the promisor's obligation as to make the assignment void? Explain.

7. A contract states, "This contract may not be assigned." One of the parties assigns the contract. Is there any legal basis upon which the contract may be held valid? Explain.

8. If there are successive assignments of the same contract by the promisee, which asignee is entitled to the benefit of the contract?

9. What warranties does the law assume when a contracting party assigns his or her interest in a contract?

10. What is the distinction between "assignment" and "delegation" with relation to contracts?

11. (a) Where the parties to a contract say nothing about the delegation of duties, under what circumstances may the duties be delegated? (b) Not delegated?

12. Under what circumstances will a delegatee under a contract be liable for his or her failure to perform the delegated duties?

CASE PROBLEMS

1. Niagara Power Corp. contracted to supply uninterrupted electric power to a Chevrolet plant. Because of an explosion in another manufacturer's plant nearby, no power was delivered for several hours. As a result, 600 Chevrolet hourly-paid employees were out of work for 1 day. They claimed that they were the beneficiaries of the power contract and sued Niagara for their lost wages. Should they succeed? Why or why not?

2. Chevron received an exclusive franchise to operate service stations along the New York State Thruway. As part of the franchise, Chevron obligated itself to provide roadside automotive service within 30 minutes after a call for help was received. Kornblut's car had a flat tire on the Thruway. The highway patrol called Chevron. After 2½ hours had elapsed with no help having arrived, Kornblut, a heavy man not accustomed to physical exercise, changed the tire himself. He suffered a heart attack and died. Is Kornblut's widow entitled to recover from Chevron for her husband's death? Why or why not?

3. A lumber and supply corporation obtained a bank loan. As security the corporation assigned to the bank the corporation's rights under certain of its construction contracts. The corporation applied the proceeds of those contracts to other corporate debts. When the corporation failed to repay its loan to the bank, the bank sued the corporation for converting money to which the bank was entitled. (**Conversion** is the unlawful use of funds acquired in a lawful manner.) Did the corporation convert the bank's funds? Explain.

4. Bea owned an apartment house. She leased an apartment to John for 1 year at a monthly rental of $500. The lease contained a provision stating that it could not be assigned. Notwithstanding that prohibition, John assigned the lease to Hazel with the understanding that Hazel would pay the $500 per month rent directly to Bea. Hazel did so for 2 months and then moved out. She refused to pay any additional rent and John sued her for the rent due for the remaining months of the lease. Hazel's defense was that as John had no right to assign the lease, she (Hazel) was not obligiated to pay any of the rent after her departure. Was Hazel correct? Why?

5. Smith sold a taxicab company to Wrehe. Wrehe made a partial payment but still owed Smith $15,000 under the contract. With Smith's consent Wrehe then assigned the contract to a corporation. The assignee, after making some payments, defaulted on the contract. Smith sued Wrehe for the balance due. Wrehe contended that only the corporation was liable to Smith. Who was correct? Why?

CHAPTER 14

PERFORMANCE, BREACH, AND DISCHARGE; REMEDIES IN CONTRACT ACTIONS

When people enter into contracts they usually expect to *perform* (carry out) the obligations they have undertaken. When a contracting party without legal justification fails to perform as promised, he or she has *breached* (broken) the contract and must in some way compensate the other party to the contract. But the party who breached the contract may be *discharged* (relieved) from his or her obligation to perform as promised, either (1) by agreement of the other party, or (2) under certain circumstances, by operation of law.

This chapter considers (1) conditions which bring about a discharge of the obligation to perform a contract, (2) remedies available to a contracting party if there is a breach of the agreement, and (3) other contract rights.

PERFORMANCE, BREACH, AND DISCHARGE OF CONTRACTS

Meaning of "Performance," "Breach," and "Discharge"

Performance of a contract means the carrying out of contractual obligations (promises) by one or both parties.

Breach is any failure of a contracting party to perform a duty imposed by a contract. Breach occurs even if the other party to a contract benefited by the nonperformance. For example, Tom contracts with Ephram Builders to deliver lumber on a certain day, but Tom fails to do so. He has breached his contract even though Ephram engaged in other highly profitable work while waiting for the lumber to arrive.

Discharge means the termination of a contractual obligation, either by (1) the parties performing the contract as agreed, (2) the mutual agreement of the parties, (3) the obligated performance becoming illegal, (4) the purpose of the contract becoming impossible or impracticable to fulfill, or (5) the performance being frustrated.

Performance Limited by Conditions

A party to a contract may state that he or she will be obligated to perform only upon the occurrence or nonoccurrence of some specified circumstance or event. If that circumstance or event does not occur, then the party who set up that condition is discharged from performance. For example, Lars, a resident of Minnesota, agrees to work at Kirsten's dairy in Nebraska on condition that he can find a place to live near the dairy at least 1 week before his employment is to begin. Lars' duty to perform the contract (that is, to work for Kirsten in Nebraska) will not become effective unless that condition is met or is waived by him. If Lars is unable to find living quarters within the agreed time, there has been a failure of the condition and he is discharged from his obligation to work for Kirsten.

Another example of a condition in a contract might be where a contractor agrees to dig a tunnel to be completed within 18 months. However, the contractor includes in the contract the condition that any time lost because of labor disputes or strikes will not be counted against the 18 months and the completion date will be extended accordingly.

As these examples indicate, conditions add flexibility to contractual agreements and establish circumstances under which a contractual duty may be discharged. The following case involves a contract dealing with a condition precedent.

CASE 14.1   Roush v. Dan Vaden Chevrolet, Inc.
270 S.E.2d 902 (Ga. 1980)

Facts: Roush had his van towed to the Dan Vaden garage so that it could be inspected by a representative of General Motors Corp. to see why the engine would not run and then to make necessary repairs upon it. After considerable time, the garage owner sued Roush for the work it had performed on the van and for storage charges because Roush did not respond to its demand to move the van away. Roush claims that before he must pay the charges, he is supposed to receive information from General Motors about the engine failure. Roush has never received that information.

Question: May a contract provide that a condition must be satisfied before performance by the other party is required?

Answer: Yes. A contract may require performance of a condition precedent before performance by the other contracting party is required.

Reasoning: A condition—the happening of an event or of some other action—may be made precedent, that is, must be performed before a contract becomes absolute and obligatory on a contracting party. Under the terms of the agreement between Roush and the garage, his obligation to pay was conditioned upon General Motors examining the van and finding why its engine would not operate. The receipt of this information was therefore a condition precedent to Roush being required to perform his side of the contract, namely, to pay the garage. As the information has not been received, Roush is not yet required to pay the garage.

Discharge of Contracts by Performance

Each party to a contract undertakes to perform all the obligations he or she assumes under the contract in the manner agreed and within the established time limits.

Tender of Performance.   In some situations a party to a contract discharges his or her obligations by *offering* to do what the contract requires. Such an offer is a **tender of performance**. For example, suppose Tim has contracted with Edith to repair the roof of her house. The agreement says that "the work will be done in a good and workmanlike manner." Tim thereby, in effect, tells Edith that he will do the work according to the standard practices of the roofing industry in that locality. However, Edith does not approve of the way Tim is setting out to do the work and tells him that he "absolutely may not put a ladder against the house." Tim replies that he is ready, able, and willing to do the work in a way that is recognized by the trade to be proper but that he cannot get on the roof without using a ladder. Edith still does not let him proceed. Tim has made a tender of performance which discharges him from any further duty of performance. Under the circumstances, Tim is entitled to (1) payment for any work he has performed so far (such as purchasing and preparing his roofing materials), and (2) damages in the amount of the profits he was not permitted to earn because he was unjustifiably prevented from performing the contract.

Effect of Defective Performance (Breach). The nature and effect of a breach of contract can be considered from two points of view. First, the *extent* of the performance is considered—that is, has there been a substantial (considerable but not complete) performance, or a nonsubstantial performance (a failure to perform fundamental obligations of the contract)? Second, the *quality* of the nonperformance is considered—that is, was the breach (the nonperformance) material or nonmaterial?

The principles underlying these two views of breach of contract are the same. Therefore, for convenience, only the designations *material* breach or *nonmaterial* breach will be used in this chapter.

Material or Nonmaterial Breach. If you enter into a contract with someone who so seriously fails to perform his or her side of the bargain that you do not receive the benefits expected from performance of the agreement, that person has committed a *material breach* and you may be excused from performance of your own obligations under the contract. A *nonmaterial breach*, as the name implies, is less serious. If someone with whom you have entered into a contract commits a nonmaterial breach, you will not have been deprived of the benefits of the agreement although you may be caused inconvenience, annoyance, or extra expense for which you should be compensated. In other words, you received something less of a performance than you bargained for, but you are not discharged from your own obligation to perform as agreed.

The distinction between a material and a nonmaterial breach becomes apparent in the following example: Assume that Oscar contracted to build a house for Jim. Oscar pours the foundation but does nothing further and leaves town. Oscar has committed a material breach of the contract and Jim is discharged from his duty to pay. In contrast, if Oscar completes the house according to plans and specifications, except that he installs cheap doorknobs and hinges, quite different from the type the contract calls for, Oscar has substantially performed his part of the contract. He has breached the contract but the breach is nonmaterial. Jim is *not* discharged from his duty to pay Oscar, but because of Oscar's nonmaterial breach, Jim may subtract from the contract price his cost of securing and installing the specified hardware.

From the above examples it can be seen that a party to whom a contractual duty is owed has a cause of action for *any* breach of duty, whether it is material or not. If a breach is material, there having been a lack of substantial performance, the aggrieved party has grounds to cancel the contract. If the breach is nonmaterial, there having been substantial performance, the other party to the contract may sue for the damages he or she sustained but *may not* cancel the contract.

Breach Made Material by Contract Terms. Most contracts which call for a party to make something or to do some act will impose upon that party several conditions or areas of performance. Such conditions might be, for example, the use of certain materials or methods of manufacture, specific inspections or tests, a particular manner of crating and shipping, and delivery on a specified date. To avoid misunderstanding as to whether failure of any of these obligations would amount to a material breach, contracts use phrases such as "Time is of the essence of this contract" with respect to delivery date. Within limits, the courts permit the parties to incorporate such conditions in their contracts and will give effect to them. A contract in which time was of the essence is illustrated by the following case.

CASE 14.2   Allan v. Martin
574 P.2d 457 (Ariz. 1978)

Facts: Allan entered into a contract to purchase Martin's home. Martin told Allan that he had to have the purchase money by July 31 as he needed it to complete another house. The contract of sale provided that the escrow had to be "closed" (the money paid and the title papers exchanged) by July 31st. The contract stated that time was of the essence. The time for closing was orally extended by Martin 15 days (until August 15th). The purchase money was not paid by that date and Martin sent Allan a telegram saying that the home would no longer be sold to Allan under the contract.

Question: Was the time for the performance sufficiently material as to justify cancellation of the contract?

Answer: Yes. Time was of the essence of the contract.

Reasoning: The seller, Martin, told the purchaser, Allan, that the money payment had to be received on a certain date and the contract stated that time was of the essence. When the time for the performance of a contract is material and one of the parties fails to perform by the contract deadline date, the other party to the contract may treat it as ended. This Martin did by telegram to Allan.

Martin is entitled to cancellation and rescission of the contract.

Breach Made Material by Court Action.   On many occasions disputes arise between parties to a contract as to whether a breach is or is not material, and a court decision is required. Normally, a court will find that a breach of the following kind is material: unreasonable delay in performance, delivery of seriously defective goods, or substantial failure to render services bargained for.

Anticipatory Breach of Contract.   If, during the performance of a contract, one of the parties repudiates the agreement and refuses to proceed with the work, the repudiation would normally constitute an immediate breach of contract obligations. However, if the repudiation occurs *before the time for work to begin*, it is called an *anticipatory breach of contract*, because refusal to perform is announced before time for performance is due. Anticipatory repudiation does not necessarily constitute a breach for which the other party can bring immediate legal action. However, almost all courts allow the aggrieved party to suspend his or her own performance and also to change position (such as hiring another contractor to do the work) without giving up any right to sue for the breach when the time for performance arrives and the promised performance is not forthcoming.

Discharge by Other Than Performance

Contractual obligations may be discharged if the parties enter into a subsequent agreement by which each discharges the other, if the court determines that performance of the contract is impossible or impracticable, or if a court determines that the reason for performance has disappeared.

Discharge by Subsequent Agreement.   There are several kinds of agreements by which the parties to a contract can effectively end their contractual obligations.

Rescission.   The parties can enter into a mutual rescission agreement whereby each voluntarily ends the contract. If performance by one or both has already begun, normally there is included some formula for the return of the partial performance in the rescission agreement, if that is possible, or for payment.

Mutual Agreement.   One or both parties can terminate or give up rights each may have against the other by means of other agreements. In an **accord and satisfaction** the parties reach an understanding for the settlement of their differences. By a *release* one or both parties may free the other from contractual obligations. In a *contract not to sue* they would agree not to sue to enforce a particular right.

Novation.   If the parties agree to substitute someone else for one of the contracting parties, the three parties then enter into a **novation agreement**. By such an agreement the new party takes over, assuming the obligations of a departing contractor who consents to the substitution. For example, Leo enters into a contract with Baker to develop a program for Baker's computer. Leo is unable to do the work. Leo, Baker, and Madge agree that Madge will assume all Leo's obligations under the contract; that Madge will be paid in the manner Leo was to be paid; that Leo will have no further duty to perform under the contract; and that Leo will be due no further compensation from Baker. This new arrangement is a *novation* under which Leo is discharged from the original contract obligations.

Discharge Because of Impossibility or Impracticability of Performance, or Frustration of Purpose.   A party to a contract may be discharged from performance on the ground that (1) it is impossible to perform the contract, (2) that it is impracticable to perform it, or (3) that the *purpose* for which the contract was entered into is "frustrated"—in other words, the purpose for which it was entered into no longer exists.

Impossibility of Performance.   Sometimes parties enter into a contract which requires knowhow so far beyond the current state of scientific knowledge that it is impossible to perform the contract. For example, Maury, an inventor, claims to have perfected a carburetor which will utilize and separate water into its chemical elements in such a way that any automobile using it can run all day on 5 gallons of water. One of the principal automobile manufacturing companies enters into a contract with Maury for a quantity of these carburetors. As it turns out, however, neither Maury nor anyone else is able to produce such a device. Therefore, the purpose of the contract was impossible to achieve and the obligations entered into by both parties are discharged.

Performance may also be impossible when the circumstances surrounding a contract have so changed that a previously possible performance is no longer attainable. For instance, a contract may require the services of a particular person who dies before performance can be completed, or a certain material which is no longer procurable.

Impracticability of Performance.   Performance of a contract may be possible but, if carried out, may be so burdensome that one of the contracting parties would lose a great deal of money. In that event, the party so burdened may seek to be discharged from performance on the ground that it is commercially or economically impracticable to perform. If, for instance, because of unforeseen economic conditions, the price of canvas rises so high that the Outdoor Tent Company would lose $10 on each tent if it were to fulfill its contract with a retailer, Outdoor might seek to be discharged from its contract obligations because of commercial impracticability.

However, as a general rule, courts have been reluctant to discharge a contract because of commercial or economic impracticability when the contract is actually *possible* to perform, even at a great financial loss to the contractor. Instead, in the absence of agreement between parties, or unless other reasons to assert impracticability exist, the one promising to deliver goods or services generally is considered to have assumed the risks, difficulties, and burdensome costs of the contract.

 Frustration of Purpose.   When performance is legally possible but, because circumstances have so changed that the object for which one of the parties entered into the contract can no longer be attained, there is said to be a *frustration* of the purpose of the contract, and all obligations under it are discharged. For example, suppose that José owns an apartment overlooking the route of the Rose Bowl Parade. José agrees to rent his apartment to Flora for the day of the parade so that she and her friends can view it in comfort. If some disaster causes cancellation of the parade, it is not impossible for Flora to rent the apartment, but the purpose for which she contracted to rent the apartment is *frustrated*. Unless the agreement between José and Flora imposed on Flora the risk that the parade might be canceled, she is discharged from the rental contract without having to pay José. The concept of frustration of contract is illustrated by the following case.

CASE 14.3   **Brenner v. Little Red School House, Inc.**
274 S.E.2d 206 (N.C. 1981)

Facts: Brenner and his wife were divorced. Mrs. Brenner was given custody of their minor son and Brenner made payments for the child's support, including the tuition costs for sending him to the Little Red Schoolhouse, a private school. Prior to the 1978–79 school term, Brenner paid the school more than a thousand dollars for the son's tuition costs for the ensuing school year. The agreement with the school provided that the tuition was payable in advance and that no portion was refundable. Brenner's former wife did not allow the boy to attend the school and Brenner sued the school to secure return of the tuition money, claiming the purpose of the contract was frustrated.

Question: Is frustration of contract purpose a defense to failure of contract performance?

Answer: Yes. Frustration is a defense but it is not applicable under these facts.

Reasoning: In all contracts the law implies that if a condition arises which causes destruction of the expected value to be derived from its performance, there is a failure of consideration. Such a supervening condition is called frustration of the contract purpose. It is like impossibility of performance but it is not a form of impossibility. Frustration relates only to the consideration for the performance.

    If the frustrating event was reasonably foreseeable by a contracting party, then he or she cannot assert it as a defense. Also, if parties have contracted with reference to the risk involved, they may not assert the doctrine of frustration to escape their obligations. Here, Brenner made the contract with the possibility that his former wife might refuse to let the boy attend the school. In addition, the contract clause providing that the tuition was payable in advance and that no portion would be refundable allocates the risk to Brenner that the child would not attend and prevents the application of the principle of frustration.

REMEDIES IN SUITS BASED ON CONTRACTS

Lawsuits involving contracts fall within two categories: (1) actions in which money damages are sought, and (2) actions in which remedies other than money are sought.

Actions Seeking Money Damages (Breach of Contract) When a breach of contract occurs, the aggrieved party (the plaintiff) may seek money damages for the losses sustained. The basis of the lawsuit is the failure of the other party (the defendant) to perform the contract, or failure to perform it in the manner required by its terms. Because money damages are sought, the action is one "at law" as distinguished from an action "in equity." The differences between these two types of legal actions were discussed in Chapter 1, pp. 10–12.

An example of money damages as compensation for a breach of contract might be the following: You contract to sell 5000 tons of No. 1 wheat to Carl at an agreed price. Before the wheat is delivered its price rises 5 percent above the contract price. Therefore, instead of delivering the wheat to Carl, you sell it to Sam at the higher price. You have breached your contract with Carl. As wheat is readily available on the open market, Carl's remedy is to recover money damages from you for the extra amount he had to pay for buying the same kind of wheat from another source, plus any extra expenses he had to pay to procure it.

Interests Protected by Legal Action. A breach of contract action is brought to protect three interests of the plaintiff: (1) the expectation interest, (2) the reliance interest, or (3) the restitution interest.

The Expectation Interest. Each party entering into a contract expects to get something for his or her participation. For instance, a seller expects to receive the money a buyer promises to pay, and a buyer expects to receive the property the seller promises to deliver. To protect this expectation interest a court allows a plaintiff to recover damages which, in the event of breach, will place the innocent party in as good a position as he or she would have been if the contract had been performed. The measure of damages necessary to satisfy the expectation interest varies according to the circumstances surrounding the breach of contract.

The concept of damages to compensate for an unsatisfied expectation interest can be illustrated as follows. Sam, a dealer in construction equipment, sells you a tractor for $10,000 and promises to deliver it March 1. One of the following situations might arise.

1. Sam fails to deliver the tractor. You are forced to pay another dealer $11,000 for the same kind of machine. To get the benefit of your bargain (contract) with Sam, and to satisfy your expectation to pay only $10,000 for the tractor, you should recover from Sam the $1000 extra you had to pay. This is an example of a type of damages called "general damages," because they result directly from a party's breach without reference to any special circumstances. General contract damages typically consist of the difference between the contract price and the market price at the time performance is due. If the market price is lower, then no general damages were suffered.

2. At the time you and Sam entered into your contract, you told Sam that you had to have the tractor no later than March 1. Otherwise, you would incur a penalty on a grading job you promised to do. When Sam failed to deliver your tractor March 1, you bought a tractor from another dealer at the current market price of $11,000—but it was not delivered to you until March 8. As a result, you suffered a penalty in the form of reduced pay for your grading job. Sam is liable to you not only for the $1000 difference in price you had to pay (general damages), but also for the penalty you incurred on your grading job as that risk was foreseeable by Sam. This additional amount constitutes *special* or *consequential* damages. Since you told Sam, and he knew that you would have to pay a penalty if the grading job was not done on time, Sam is liable for the special damages.

The Reliance Interest.   A party who enters into a contract to be performed at some future time may, relying on the other party's expected performance of the contract, expend funds in anticipation of that performance. For example, a seller buys goods or hires people needed to perform his or her contract with a purchaser, or a purchaser may spend money to make his or her premises ready to receive promised goods or equipment. In either event, the funds are spent *in reliance upon* the other party performing the contract as agreed. Thus, a *reliance interest* is involved and, if the costs of preparation are reasonable, they may be recovered as "incidental damages" in the event the other party breaches the contact.

The Restitution Interest.   Either party to a contract may partially perform his or her obligation before the other party breaches the contract. When such a breach occurs, the innocent party should be able to secure, in protection of the *restitution interest*, a court order for the return (restitution) of his or her part performance, if that is possible, or, if not, for "substitutional restitution," meaning the money value of that partial performance.

Limits on Damages for Breach of Contract. To protect the party charged with a breach of contract, allowable damages are subject to certain limitations. With respect to *general damages*, the plaintiff must prove the amount of damages with reasonable certainty.

With respect to *special damages* (for extraordinary loss in addition to general damages) the plaintiff must prove (1) that the damages were indeed suffered, (2) that the breach was the primary and chief cause of the damages suffered, and (3) that when the contract was entered into the defaulting party foresaw or should have foreseen that special damages might arise.

Mitigation of Damages. A party who claims to be entitled to damages for breach of contract should not intentionally add to the amount of damage he or she sustained. Instead, the aggrieved party should make reasonable efforts to reduce the damages, for otherwise he or she may be unjustly enriched. Thus, for example, if a property owner has rented an apartment to Brian for 1 year with the rent payable monthly, and Brian moves out after 1 month, the landlord cannot sit idly by and expect to collect the whole year's rent from Brian. The landlord must make reasonable efforts to rent the apartment to someone else. At the end of the year, he would recover from Brian the yearly rental *less what was received* from the subsequent tenant or tenants, but would take into consideration additional expenses he may have had connected with the rental, such as cleaning and real estate agency fees.

Liquidated Damages. A contract may include a clause which states the amount of damages one of the parties will owe to the other in the event of breach, or which has a formula for calculating such damages. This type of clause is called a *liquidated damages clause*, that is, one where the amount of damage in the event of a subsequent breach is agreed to when the contract is entered into. Thus, if a breach later occurs, no proof of actual damages sustained by the other party is required. The innocent party is entitled to receive the sum stated in the contract's liquidated damages clause, regardless of the amount of actual damages sustained.

A liquidated damages clause is enforceable if (1) the actual damages which might be caused by a breach cannot be or would be difficult to estimate accurately, (2) the parties intend to provide for damages, and (3) the amount they fix in the clause is a reasonable pre-estimate of probable loss in the event of breach. If any of these conditions is absent, the liquidated damages clause will not be enforceable. However, if all these conditions are present, then the clause will be enforced even if damages actually sustained turn out to be greater or less than the agreed amount of liquidated damages.

Remedies Other Than Money Damages

Up to this point we have been considering actions in which the plaintiff seeks money damages to compensate for breach of contract. But under certain circumstances a contracting party may feel that payment of money in any amount will not make him or her "whole" again. In that event, an aggrieved party may file suit in a court of equity, where relief is granted in forms other than money. A plaintiff may secure, instead of money, a **reformation** of the contract, a **rescission** of the contract, or **specific performance** of the contract.

Reformation.   It may be that a party to a contract believes that the contract as written does not express the agreement that was entered into and that it should be corrected. For instance, Mary believes that The Art Gallery had contracted to pay her $5000 for her painting, but the written contract showed the price to be $500. Mary therefore brings an action in equity for the *reformation* (modification) of the contract so that it will express the true agreement of the parties.

Rescission.   Another example of an equitable action where damages other than for money are sought is the following: Betsy is convinced that she was fraudulently induced by Paul to sign a contract for the sale to him of her home and she wants the contract rescinded (canceled). She brings an equitable action for *rescission* of the contract and, at the same time, offers to return to Paul the money he paid her for the house. If Betsy is successful, she is discharged from the contract and Paul is repaid the money he expended.

 Specific Performance.   A third important equitable remedy in contract cases is *specific performance,* whereby a party to the contract refuses to perform and the other party seeks a court order directing the defaulting party to perform the contract as it is written, because damages would not be an adequate remedy. For example, assume that you entered into a contract to purchase from Fred a corner lot across the street from the courthouse. When the day arrives for Fred to pass title to you, you tender to him the purchase price, but he refuses to go through with the sale. You really want that unique lot and you would not be satisfied with money damages because of Fred's default. You therefore bring an action in equity for *specific performance,* meaning that you ask the court to order Fred to convey the property to you upon your payment of the purchase price according to the terms of your contract.

Under certain circumstances a court of equity will not direct specific performance even if the person bringing the suit (the plaintiff) cannot be fully compensated in damages by a money payment. Instead, the equity court leaves the plaintiff to find his or her remedy in the money damages a law court will allow, even though they may be inadequate. For example, an equity court will not enforce a contract by directing an unwilling individual to work for another as they had agreed in a contract for personal services, because for a court to make such an order would be tantamount to ordering an involuntary servitude. Nor will a court specifically enforce a contract to marry or a contract to enter into a partnership.

Courts also refuse to grant specific performance where judicial supervision of the performance is impractical or if it would be beyond the ability of the court to supervise the enforcement of its decree. For instance, a large-scale construction contract or a contract requiring delivery of goods over a long term would be especially difficult for a court to supervise. In such circumstances an injured party to such a contract is not granted specific performance but is left, instead, to seek money damages.

Application of the remedy of specific performance is demonstrated in the next case.

CASE 14.4 **First Nat'l State Bank of New Jersey v.Commonwealth Federal S & L Assoc.**
610 F.2d 164 (3rd Cir. 1980)

Facts: Commonwealth Savings and Loan issued a commitment to Matheman Developer promising to place a permanent mortgage upon a shopping center when Matheman completed building it. Matheman then secured a temporary construction loan from First National Bank upon the same property, the bank taking an assignment of the S&L's commitment to make the permanent loan. When the project was substantially completed and it was evident that it was an economic failure, the S&L refused to make the loan. The bank then brought suit against the S&L for specific performance to force the S&L to perform its commitment. Commonwealth S&L contends that specific performance may not be ordered to force a lender to lend money.

Question: Was the bank entitled to specific performance?

Answer: Yes, because the bank had no adequate remedy at law.

Reasoning: The right to specific performance turns upon the absence of an adequate remedy at law. Generally, a remedy at law is not adequate (1) when the subject matter of the contract is of such special nature that it cannot be translated into dollar terms, or (2) where it is impossible to arrive at a measure of damages with a sufficient degree of certainty.

Traditionally, courts have been reluctant to grant specific performance of an agreement to lend or to borrow money as all money is alike and the loan could be secured elsewhere. However, where construction loans are concerned, the courts recognize that specific performance may be justified. A contract to finance a large property is unique. The land for the project is unavailable elsewhere in similar form. As the shopping center was not economically successful, there was no hope of obtaining financing from another source. Furthermore, an accurate calculation of damages was impracticable since experts appraised the property at from $2,500,000 to $3,500,000.

As between the construction lender and the permanent lender, the primary duty to evaluate the business risks involved and the possibility of its success or failure rested upon the permanent lender. In addition, the construction lender relied upon the commitment made by the permanent lender. Therefore, specific performance is appropriate.

REMEDIES IN QUASI CONTRACT

In Chapter 6, where the law of contracts was first introduced, we said that in certain situations the law implies the existence of a contract although none is present. These situations are called "quasi contracts" because a contract in the normal sense is not present, but contractual-type remedies are available to prevent one party from becoming unjustly enriched at the expense of the other. However, as no actual contract is involved, the extraordinary contract remedies of reformation, rescission, and specific performance are neither appropriate nor available.

Quasi contracts may be illustrated by the two following examples.

1. Sarah spends money to improve a house she has *orally* agreed to buy. Fred, the owner, refuses to go through with the sale. Sarah cannot secure specific performance, that is, she cannot force the owner of the house to convey its title to her, because an oral agreement to purchase real property is unenforceable. Under a quasi-contract theory, however, Sarah is entitled to be reimbursed for the money she expended for improvements; otherwise Fred would be unjustly enriched.

2. Axel steals a television set from the Busy Bee Motel. By that wrongful act, Axel has committed the crime of larceny, for which he may be punished in a criminal action brought by the state. His wrongful act also constituted a trespass (a tort) against the property of the motel. Instead of suing Axel for damages in a tort action, the motel may sue him in an action founded on quasi contract, the theory being that by taking the television set, Axel had impliedly obligated himself to pay for it.

A quasi contract remedy for an unlawful holding of another person's property is the subject of the next case.

CASE 14.5 Cato Enterprises, Inc. v. Fine
271 N.E.2d 146 (Ind. 1971)

Facts: Cato operated a large outdoor motion picture theater. He wanted the area black-topped and asked Fine to do the work. Fine agreed. Cato purchased a used asphalt plant which he installed on his property near the theater. Fine agreed to repair the equipment and, with it, to pave the drive-in theater property on week-ends. Fine also placed some of his own equipment on Cato's property. During the ensuing weeks Fine manufactured and sold asphalt, using Cato's materials and paying Cato for them. Later, a disagreement arose between the two men and Cato prevented Fine from going onto Cato's property. Fine, unable to remove his own property, demanded to be paid for its reasonable value even though he could not establish that Cato had agreed to buy that equipment.

Question: Can a person secure payment for his or her personal property which, without his or her consent, is being held by someone else?

Answer: Yes. There can be recovery under quasi contract.

Reasoning: Even though an oral contract cannot be proved, an implied promise to pay for property and for services rendered can be established when the circumstances justify. Such an implied promise, resting solely upon a legal fiction, arises when there is a legal duty to pay for something belonging to another. The law will clothe the situation with the semblance of a contract for the purpose of effecting a remedy to prevent unjust enrichment from taking place.

Under the facts here, Cato was unjustly retaining Fine's property and so a quasi contract was found which the law will use as a basis to require Cato to pay for its value.

SUMMARY

A party to a contract is *discharged* when his or her contractual obligations are terminated. *Performance* is the normal way in which a contract is discharged, and is accomplished by doing what the contract requires. Under certain circumstances a tender of performance discharges a contractual obligation. When one party to a contract commits a material breach of the contract which cannot be cured, the other party to the contract is discharged. Among other means of discharging are by failure of a condition; by subsequent agreement; and by impossibility, frustration, or impracticability of performance.

Remedies for breach of contract protect three interests of the nonbreaching party: the expectation, the reliance, and the restitution interests.

Within limits, a party in a suit for contract damages may recover damages for any loss which results from a breach by the other party. The damages must be proved with reasonable certainty, establishing the causation and the foreseeability of any special damages claimed. Where money would not adequately compensate a contracting party for damages resulting from a failure of the other party to perform, or for the other party's breach of performance, the equitable remedies of reformation, rescission, or specific performance of the contract may be available.

This chapter brings to a close the discussion of general contract law. However, special applications of contract law appear in Part Four, Sales; Part Five, Agency; Part Seven, Secured Transactions and Insurance; Part Eight, Commercial Paper; and Part Ten, Government Regulation of Business.

REVIEW QUESTIONS

1. (a) What is the meaning of "discharge of a contract"? Of "performance of a contract"? (b) What is the legal effect of a discharge on contractual obligations?

2. Why are *conditions* sometimes included in contracts?

3. (a) In what ways may a party discharge a duty of contract performance? (b) To what does performance entitle the performing party?

4. What is meant by "a tender of performance"?

5. What is the difference between a material and a nonmaterial breach of contract? Give examples.

6. Why would one insert in a contract the phrase, "Time is of the essence of this contract"?

7. What is meant by "anticipatory breach" of contract?

8. Explain the use of a novation agreement.

9. Distinguish between a discharge by impossibility and a discharge by impracticability of purpose.

10. What is meant by an "expectation interest"; a "reliance interest"; a "restitution interest"?

11. (a) What is the difference between "general" and "special" damages for breach of contract? (b) Which type of damages is easier to prove? Why?

12. What is meant by "reformation" of a contract? Why would a party desire to invoke that remedy?

CASE PROBLEMS

1. Ward hired Denison to build a house on Ward's land. Ward made payments to Denison while the work was progressing. When the work was finished Ward still owed Denison $48,000. Because there were defects in Denison's workmanship, Ward claimed that he was discharged from paying the balance of the contract price. Estimates were received from others that the defects could be corrected for $2000. (a) Did Denison breach his obligation to Ward? (b) Is Ward discharged from performance? Explain. SUBSTANTIAL PERFORMANCE

2. In August 1941, Lloyd leased to Murphy a certain corner lot in Los Angeles. The lease was to run for 5 years. Murphy was going to use the property to repair and sell automobiles and also to sell petroleum products. In the spring of 1942 the federal government ordered, as a wartime measure, that new automobiles could be sold only under a preferential system. Thereafter, Murphy moved out of the premises. A few months later Lloyd leased the property to others and then brought suit against Murphy to recover the rent for the time the premises were vacant. Murphy claimed that the purpose for which the premises had been leased to him was frustrated by the restrictions imposed by the federal government and therefore his duties under the lease were terminated. Were the obligations of Murphy's lease terminated as a result of the actions of the federal government? Explain. NO FRUSTRATION OF PURPOSE

3. DuPre, a farmer, had an engine which ran his irrigation pumps. The engine used oil excessively and DuPre called Tri-Parish, an engine repair company. Tri-Parish installed new piston rings in the engine but it still used too much oil. DuPre complained to Tri-Parish and was told to use the pump until the end of the irrigation season when the engine could be taken to the Tri-Parish shop for repairs. DuPre used the engine to run his pumps until it broke down completely. He sued Tri-Parish for the loss of his engine and for the partial loss of his rice crop. (a) Had DuPre failed in his duty to mitigate his damages? (b) What damages did DuPre sustain? (c) Was Tri-Parish entitled to payment for the repair work it has performed? Why or why not?

4. D.M.H. Industries leased a large warehouse. It made a security deposit equal to 2 months' rent. The lease provided that the owner had the right to retain the

deposit if D.M.H. breached the lease. D.M.H. did not move into or take possession of the premises nor did it pay any further rent. The owner, therefore, terminated the lease, keeping the deposit. In subsequent litigation, D.M.H. claimed that it was entitled to a return of the security deposit because its retention by the landlord did not qualify as liquidated damages. What should the court hold? Why?

5. Fonda subcontracted to Southern for work on a fire sprinkler system. When Southern began performance it was evident that it and Fonda had entirely different ideas as to what kind of system was supposed to be installed and that their contract had been entered into under a mutual mistake of fact. Fonda, declaring that no contract existed between himself and Southern, entered into a contract with another company to do the work. Southern sued Fonda to recover money it had spent on the system which it believed to have been a necessary part of the contract. To what remedy, if any, is Southern entitled?

SALES

CHAPTER 15

INTRODUCTION TO THE LAW OF SALES; THE SALES CONTRACT

People need or want goods of immense variety: food, clothing, raw materials of every description, office equipment, inventory for resale—the list is endless. A department, grocery, or hardware store of modest size makes hundreds of sales each day, and our national system for the marketing of goods must handle billions of transactions daily. The principal means for channeling this vast bulk of goods from producers to consumers is the contract for the sale of goods.

Much of our commercial law is found in the Uniform Commercial Code (UCC), which has been adopted by all the states except Louisiana.[1] The Code has eleven parts called "articles," many of which set forth law that affects the sale, financing, and delivery of goods. Suppose that you sell lamps and lighting fixtures at retail and need to purchase 100 floor lamps from a manufacturer. The contract for the sale of those goods will be governed by Article 2 of the Code. But the application of the Code does not stop with the contract of sale. If the lamps are delivered by a common carrier such as a railroad or trucking company, ownership of the lamps will be transferred to you by means of a document of title called a "bill of lading." Many documents of title are governed by Article 7. You might pay for the lamps with a check (governed by Article 3) that will be cashed by the seller in accordance with the banking rules of Article 4. Or, if you arrange a credit rather than a cash purchase, the seller probably will reserve an Article 9 "security interest" in the goods so that he or she can repossess them if you fail to pay for them. If you arrange a credit purchase from a foreign manufacturer, the seller might require you to provide an Article 5 "letter of credit." Thus, a business deal may involve a number of Code transactions. (The text of the Code is reprinted in the Appendix to this volume.)

The law of sales under Article 2 is a variation of the "general" law of contracts discussed in Chapters 5 through 14 of this volume. The general law of contracts (sometimes referred to as the "common" law of contracts) applies to contracts for real estate, personal services, and so on. In contrast, the contract rules of Article 2 apply only to contracts involving *goods*—office equipment, cars, boats, clothing, food, and similar things. We have these two bodies of contract law because some rules of the general law of contracts are unsuitable for sales of goods. Some Article 2 rules differ greatly from their counterparts in the general law of contracts. Consequently, business people must keep in mind that a rule of contract law that applies to a sale of land will not necessarily apply to a sale of goods.

The first part of this chapter deals with the purposes, key concepts, and coverage of Article 2, entitled "Sales." The second part deals with the sales contract itself.

PURPOSES, KEY CONCEPTS, AND COVERAGE OF ARTICLE 2

Purposes of the Law of Sales   Before the development of the UCC, the law governing commercial transactions differed substantially from state to state. Because so many goods moved in interstate commerce, this variation in commercial law was a great inconvenience and a barrier to a national trade in goods. The UCC is designed to simplify, clarify, and modernize

---

[1]Louisiana, being of French background, adopted Roman civil law in its French form as the basis of its legal system. Therefore, Louisiana has a body of commercial law older than but much like the UCC.

the law of commercial transactions; to permit continued expansion of commercial practices through custom, usage, and agreement of the contracting parties; and to make the law among the various jurisdictions uniform. Perfect uniformity has not been achieved because each state, in adopting the Code, has a right to amend it as that state sees fit. However, despite a rather large number of nonuniform amendments, considerable uniformity has been achieved.

Actual performance of the millions of sales contracts entered into daily is especially important for the smooth operation of our national commerce and for the success of individual businesses. Therefore, many Code rules of contracting have departed from rules of the general law of contracts that could enable a contracting party to delay his or her promised performance or to escape contractual obligations without good reason. *Performance* of sales contracts, with a minimum of litigation, is a major goal of Article 2.

The emphasis of Article 2 on performance is but one aspect of a basic policy of the Code—to encourage sound business practices and *ethical* business conduct. That the Code stresses both the practical and the ethical will be apparent as we review some key concepts of the law of sales.

Key Concepts of the Law of Sales

Merchant.   Article 2 applies to sales of goods without regard to whether the parties to the sales contract are merchants or nonmerchants. However, merchants are subject to special rules of Article 2.

In one sense, **merchant** means a person who deals in goods of the kind involved in the transaction [2-104].[2] The merchant as so defined is the professional trader or dealer in goods so familiar to us in our day-to-day transactions, and is referred to later in this chapter as a "dealer-merchant."

But the meaning of merchant under Article 2 is not limited to dealers in goods. The word "merchant" also applies to persons who, though not personally dealing in goods in the manner of a professional trader, nevertheless by their occupations are expected to have knowledge or skill peculiar to the business practices or goods involved. An insurance company that buys office equipment and supplies is a merchant as to the ordinary business practices (such as ordering and taking delivery of goods) that ought to be familiar to any person in business. "Merchant" includes even those persons or organizations that employ someone to conduct business activities. Thus, a college or university can be classified as a merchant if it has a regular purchasing department, or business personnel familiar with business practices.

Dealer-merchants are subject to sales rules that do not apply to other merchants. For example, only dealer-merchants make certain warranties (guarantees) concerning the quality of goods they sell. (These and other warranties are discussed in Chapter 18.) In contrast, *all* merchants are subject to those rules of Article 2 designed to make the contracting process more efficient and fair. Many of these rules will be discussed later in this chapter. And all merchants are subject to higher standards of commercial conduct than those that apply to nonmerchants. An example is found in the next paragraph, which deals with the good faith requirement.

[2]The hyphenated numbers in brackets refer to sections of the Uniform Commercial Code reprinted in the Appendix to this volume. The number "2-104" means "Article 2, section 104" and is commonly read as "Section 2-104."

Good Faith.   All persons who engage in transactions covered by the UCC must use good faith in performing their contracts and in enforcing obligations owed to them. There are two meanings of "good faith." The first meaning is "honesty in fact" (actual honesty even though the person might have been careless) in the conduct or the transaction concerned [1-201]. This meaning applies to all persons subject to the Code. The second meaning, which applies to *merchants*, is "honesty in fact" *and* the "observance of reasonable commercial standards of fair dealing in the trade" [2-103]. Thus, merchants and nonmerchants alike must be honest in their dealings, but merchants must be especially careful not to take unfair advantage of those with whom they deal or to cause them loss. For example, sometimes a merchant-buyer has the right to reject delivered goods. If the seller has no agent or place of business where the rejection occurs, the merchant-buyer meets the obligation of good faith by disposing of the rejected goods in accordance with reasonable instructions of the seller or, *in the absence of instructions*, by selling *perishable* goods for the seller's account. A merchant-buyer who leaves rejected tomatoes on a loading dock to rot may be honest in fact but he or she would not be observing reasonable commercial standards of fair dealing with the distant seller and therefore would not be acting in good faith.

Identification (of Goods) to the Contract.   The parties to a sale may need to know precisely when the sale occurred, the earliest moment at which the buyer may insure undelivered goods against loss, or what rights the buyer has to demand delivery of particular goods. Answers to such questions may depend in part on whether goods have been "identified" (i.e., designated) as the subject of a *particular* contract of sale.

The parties may make an "explicit" (clearly stated) agreement as to when the goods will be identified to the contract [2-501]. In the absence of an explicit agreement, Article 2 provides the rules. Where the contract is for the sale of goods "already existing and identified" (e.g., particular goods owned or possessed by the seller), identification *to the contract between the seller and the buyer* occurs as soon as the contract is made. If the contract is for crops or for the unborn young of animals, identification to the contract usually occurs when the crops are planted or when the animals are conceived. If the contract is for the sale of "future goods" other than crops or animals (e.g., goods yet to be manufactured or acquired by a supplier for a retailer), identification occurs when the goods are shipped, marked, or otherwise designated as the goods to which the contract refers.

One important consequence of identifying goods to a contract is that the buyer immediately obtains a "special property" (a limited right) and an "insurable interest"[3] in the goods even though the buyer might not yet be the owner. Suppose that Bill orders 1000 radios from Sarah. Sarah then manufactures 2000 radios and marks 1000 of them as the radios to be shipped to Bill the next day. Bill does not yet have title to (ownership of) the radios. However, because the 1000 radios have been identified to the contract, Bill has a Code-created "special property" in the radios and therefore

---

[3]An insurable interest is a financial stake in property or in someone's life that will justify the person who has that stake in insuring the property or life against loss. If there never was an insurable interest, a contract of insurance is not enforceable against the insurance company.

may insure them against loss, as he may wish to do if he pays for them in advance or makes contracts for their resale before receiving them. Furthermore, if Sarah becomes insolvent before delivering the radios, Bill is entitled to those in which he has a special property *and* for which he has made arrangements for payment. Bill is thus protected from the claims of Sarah's creditors.

This section on key concepts closes with a case illustrating the meaning of good faith.

CASE 15.1   **Baker v. Ratzlaff**
564 P.2d 153 (Kan. App. 1977)

Facts: Ratzlaff contracted to sell to Baker the 1974 crop of popcorn grown on Ratzlaff's farm, for $4.75 per hundredweight (cwt.) Ratzlaff was authorized to cancel the contract if Baker for any reason failed to pay for the popcorn at the time of delivery. Ratzlaff delivered two loads of popcorn but did not demand immediate payment. Baker ordinarily made payment within a few days after delivery. During the following week Baker requested more deliveries. Ratzlaff did not make the deliveries, saying his driver was ill and some equipment had broken down. A week after the first deliveries, Ratzlaff sent Baker a written notice of contract termination and soon afterward sold the undelivered popcorn to another buyer for $8.00 per cwt. Baker sued Ratzlaff for breach of contract and was awarded $52,000 in damages. Ratzlaff appealed.

Question: Did Ratzlaff have a right to cancel the contract?

Answer: No. Ratzlaff had no right to terminate the contract.

Reasoning: Ratzlaff, a seller of goods, was subject to and breached the UCC obligation of good faith. Ratzlaff's knowledge of Baker's customary payment practice, together with Ratzlaff's failure to insist on immediate payment and his hasty resale of the popcorn to another buyer provided ample evidence of an absence of good faith. The appellate court agreed with the trial court that "the parties are under a duty to deal fairly with each other in good faith and that [Ratzlaff] breached this duty by declaring a termination of the contract upon a technical pretense. . . ."

Transactions Covered by Article 2   Article 2 applies to *transactions* in goods, but especially to *sales* of goods or to *contracts to sell* goods. A *sale* is the passing of title to (ownership of) goods from the seller to the buyer, in return for a consideration called the price. The price can be payable in money, goods, or realty, *or in some other way*. Thus, a legally binding *promise* to pay (whether with money, goods, realty, or otherwise) is another way of paying the price.

If title (ownership) passes when the sale transaction occurs, the transaction is a *present sale*. A purchase at a supermarket is a present sale executed (performed) by an exchange of goods and money across a counter. However, a purchase of goods on credit rather than for cash can also be a present sale. Suppose you buy a used car and agree to make twelve monthly payments. The seller probably will retain a "security interest" (often called "title") so that the seller can repossess the car if you fail to make the payments. However, at the time of the sale, *you* receive basic ownership rights in the car—the right to use, enjoy, and sell it—subject only to your seller's right to be paid. These basic ownership rights constitute the kind of title referred to in the definition of "present sale."

In a **contract to sell** goods, the seller agrees to transfer title (ownership) to the buyer at some future time. This kind of contract is used, for example, where the seller does not yet own existing goods or where they have not yet been produced. Article 2 covers both *present sales* of goods and *contracts to sell* goods at a future time. For convenience, Article 2 uses the term "contract for sale" in reference to both types of transactions.

Article 2 applies only to transactions in goods. In general, *goods* are things that are movable at the time they are identified to the contract for sale [2-105]. "Goods" includes the unborn young of animals, growing crops, and minerals (including gas and oil) to be removed from realty by the seller. "Goods" does *not* include real estate or personal services. Sales of real estate, personal services, and other kinds of nongoods are subject to the general law of contracts, whose rules often differ from those of the law of sales.

The courts do not agree on how to treat transactions involving a combination of goods and services. What is the nature of an automobile tune-up in which a mechanic replaces parts and adjusts the engine? Is it a sale of goods or a sale of services? The distinction is very important where the goods are defective and cause injury. If the transaction is classified as a sale of goods, an Article 2 warranty (assurance that the goods are not defective) often is available to the injured plaintiff as a basis for a lawsuit. If the transaction is classified as a sale of services, the general law of contracts applies. Under that law warranties often are *not* available where the service is improperly performed. Many courts settle the matter by deciding whether the sale is *predominantly* for goods or for services. If the amount or value of the goods is relatively insignificant in the transaction, these courts will hold that it is a sale of services for which a warranty might not be available.

But the relative amount or value of goods is not the only factor that courts consider in deciding how to treat mixed transactions. A court may place more importance on the question of who should bear the loss resulting from the use of defective goods. A transfusion of contaminated blood traditionally has been treated as an aspect of medical services and thus as not subject to sales warranties. Courts adopting this position believe that persons who provide essential medical services should be held liable only for negligence or intentional misconduct. More recently, some courts have held that blood and other medical supplies are the subject of sales of goods, and that Article 2 warranties should apply. These courts believe that a person injured by a defective product should not have to bear the loss, even where the service aspect of the transaction predominates. Have beauticians or electricians made a sale of goods to which Article 2 warranty or other rules should apply? Some courts recognize a sale (and a warranty) as to the goods. Other courts will consider the mixed contract to be one for services, but will recognize non-Code warranties, as in Case 15.2. A few courts recognize non-Code warranties, even in purely services contracts.

CASE 15.2   **Ellibee v. Dye**
15 UCC Rep. 361 (Pa. Com. Pleas, 1973)

Facts: Dye, a hairdresser, applied "French Perm" to Ellibee's hair. Shortly after the treatment, Ellibee's hair began to fall out when washed by one of Dye's employees. Alleging that the "French Perm" was defective, Ellibee sued Dye for damages resulting from breach of an implied warranty that the "French Perm" was merchantable and thus fit for its ordinary purposes.

Question: Was Dye subject to warranty liability in the application of defective "French Perm"?

Answer: Yes. Despite the fact that the transaction between Dye and Ellibee technically might not have been a sale of goods, Dye was subject to an implied warranty against injurious defects.

Reasoning: According to a Comment by the drafters of the UCC, the warranty sections of the Code were not intended to disturb that line of case-law growth which has recognized that warranties need not be confined to sales of goods. The trend in Pennsylvania law has been to extend warranties in new directions and for situations where warranties previously have been denied. A supplier of a defective product over the counter would be liable to plaintiff under a warranty theory. A beauty shop operator should also be liable in warranty if a product supplied by the operator is defective, since the supplying of the product was a vital part of the performance of the service.

THE SALES CONTRACT

Unless displaced by particular provisions of the UCC, rules of law that apply to contracts generally apply as well to contracts for the sale of goods [1-103]. So, a contract for the sale of goods must meet the usual requirements for the *formation* of a contract: mutual assent (offer and acceptance), an exchange of consideration, parties having legal capacity to contract, and a legal objective (purpose). In connection with contract formation, the word "offer" has the same meaning in the law of sales that it has in the general law of contracts. Contracts for the sale of goods are also subject to many general legal principles relating to the form and interpretation of contracts. However, the UCC modifies most of these aspects of general contract law to adjust them to sales transactions and contemporary business needs.

Formation of the Sales Contract   **Article 2 Standard for Contract Formation.**   People create sales contracts in a wide variety of ways. Some spell out the terms of the contract in great detail, as in the purchase of a new car. Others say very little or nothing, as in the purchase of goods at a supermarket. On occasion, what is said or done is so vague and sketchy that no contract arises. Consequently, the courts sometimes are faced with the question of what minimum conduct is required to create a sales contract.

Article 2 provides the standard by which the courts are to decide the question: A contract for the sale of goods may be made in any manner sufficient to show agreement, including conduct by both parties which recognizes the existence of a contract. The contract may arise even though the exact moment at which agreement arose cannot be determined. Furthermore, even though one or more terms are left open, there can still be a contract for sale if the parties have intended to make a contract and there is a reasonably certain basis for a court to give an appropriate remedy for breach of the contract [2-204].

Acts Required for Contract Formation.   Specifically, then, what minimum acts of contracting does Article 2 require of the buyer and the seller? First, before there can be a sales contract, the *parties* to it must be identified. Suppose you have recently opened a bakery and need some flour. You phone a local supplier and say, without identifying yourself, "Please send some wheat flour right away." The supplier's employee says, "OK." As of this moment there is no contract because you and the supplier have not said enough to enable a court to give an appropriate remedy to either of you if called upon to do so. The supplier does not even know with whom it is dealing.

Suppose now that you identify yourself so that the supplier can make a delivery. There still is no contract because you have not said how much flour you want. To have an enforceable sales contract you ordinarily must specify the *quantity* of the goods you seek.[4] Must you specify the *kind* of wheat flour as well? A statement of kind would be helpful but is not always necessary for a contract to arise. If you have had prior transactions with this supplier, the supplier might know from this past experience what you mean by "wheat flour." As to *price*, the Code provides that the parties can make a contract even though the price is not specified. Where the parties intend to make a contract but state no price, the price is a "reasonable" price as of the time set for delivery [2-305]. A reasonable price might be the current market price if there is one. Thus, as a practical matter, no sales contract is likely to arise unless the parties to it and the quantity of goods have been spelled out somehow. The other term essential for a contract to exist, the price, may be supplied by law.

Where the parties to a contract fail to state a term such as price, time, or place of delivery, the term is said to have been left *open*. Costs of production might not be known at the time of the sale, the market price might be subject to considerable variation, or the parties might simply have forgotten to state a price or some other term. The drafters of Article 2 recognized that it is normal and necessary for business people to contract with a minimum of detail, often on the basis of a phone call across state lines. By permitting open terms, and by providing rules of law to "fill the gaps" left by the open terms, the Code accomplishes two things: It enables the parties to contract quickly where price or other information is not immediately available, and it fosters performance of agreements that under nonsales law might have been considered too indefinite to enforce.

We turn now to some particular aspects of contract formation under Article 2—the offer and the acceptance.

---

[4]Except, for example, in a "requirements" contract. An agreement to buy "all the wheat flour I shall need in my business next year" is a requirements contract whose quantity term has been left open to be filled in later as the buyer's needs dictate.

Offer under Article 2.   Some of the common law rules governing contract offers in *non*sales transactions are unsuitable for sales of goods and have been replaced by Code rules. The common law rules governing offers for certain types of unilateral contracts and offers promised to be held open for a fixed time are examples. In contrast, the law governing sales at auctions has not been changed but instead has been codified and made part of Article 2.

Offer Seeking Prompt or Current Shipment of Goods.   Suppose a retail fish dealer needs an emergency supply of sardines and places the following order: "Ship me 50 cases of X grade sardines at once." This is an offer for a unilateral contract because the dealer expects the sardine seller to accept the offer by performing the act requested by the dealer. Under the common law rules of offer and acceptance, such an offer can be accepted *only* by the seller-offeree's performing the requested act, here, a *shipment* made at once. An attempt by the offeree to accept by making an immediate *promise* to ship promptly would be ineffective, and the offeror would be free to revoke (withdraw) the offer. The ability to revoke gives the offeror the opportunity to "play the market," often to the surprise and injury of the shipper, who is in fact making a prompt shipment just a few minutes or hours after the promise was sent. To prevent this kind of injurious surprise, Article 2 provides that an offeree may accept an offer for prompt or current shipment by making *either* a prompt shipment *or* a prompt promise to ship, unless the offeror has made it very clear that the offer can be accepted only by a prompt shipment [2-206].

Firm Offer.   Under the general law of contracts, a person who has promised to hold an offer open for a fixed time is not required to honor that promise unless he or she has received consideration for it. Suppose that Sarah offers to sell a certain piece of real estate to Ben for $50,000, giving Ben 10 days to decide whether to buy. Sarah will not be held to her promise to hold the main offer open unless she asked for and received consideration for that promise. In sales of goods, however, if a merchant states in a signed writing that the offer to buy or sell goods will be held open, this statement cannot be revoked merely because the merchant received no consideration for it [2-205]. The promise to hold the offer open is binding for the time stated or, if no time is stated, for a reasonable time not to exceed 3 months. Thus merchants who make firm offers can no longer upset the reasonable expectations of offerees that such offers will remain open for the promised time.

Offers in Auctions.   Auctions may be either "with reserve" or "without reserve." These terms indicate whether the auctioneer (who acts on behalf of the seller) has reserved (retained) the privilege of withdrawing the goods from sale during the bidding process. In an auction *with reserve* the auctioneer is the offeree, has the power of acceptance, and as offeree may withdraw the goods by rejecting all bids. In an auction *without reserve* the auctioneer is much like an offeror, with bidders competing to determine who will win the power of acceptance. After the auctioneer calls for bids in an auction without reserve, he or she cannot withdraw the goods from sale unless no bid is made within a reasonable time. In either type of auction (with or without reserve), a bidder may withdraw his or her bid until the auctioneer announces the completion of the sale by the fall of the hammer or in some other customary way.

Unless goods are "in explicit terms" put up without reserve (as where advertising says, "This auction is without reserve"), an auction is with reserve [2-328]. An auction with reserve tends to produce a fair market value because the seller, as offeree, may reject all bids and await a more favorable market. In contrast, an auction without reserve tends to produce lower prices because the seller has no power to reject low bids. However, the auction without reserve may be useful for moving goods quickly.

Acceptance under Article 2.   Much of the law concerning the acceptance of offers is the same under the UCC as under the general law of contracts, but the UCC departs from some common law rules of acceptance that unreasonably obstruct contract formation.

Authorized Medium of Acceptance.   The UCC rules as to how an offeree must accept an offer differ little from the rules of the general law of contracts. These rules may be summarized as follows:

1. Under the "deposited acceptance rule" of the general law of contracts, the acceptance is effective at the point of dispatch if the offeree has used an *authorized medium* of acceptance. This rule applies also to contracts for the sale of goods [1-103].

2. Where the offeror stipulates that a particular medium of acceptance must be used, only the stipulated medium is authorized. Suppose that Sam offers to sell goods to Brenda and stipulates in the offer that "This offer may be accepted only by a letter addressed to me at my place of business." Brenda immediately mails a letter of acceptance to Sam's business address. The acceptance is effective (i.e., a contract arises) when Brenda mails the letter. If Brenda uses a medium other than the one Sam stipulated, there is no acceptance. Brenda's use of a different medium does not necessarily destroy her power of acceptance, however, because unless otherwise indicated by the offeror (Sam), an offer is open for a reasonable time. Brenda therefore may have time remaining to use the required medium of acceptance, but runs the risk that Sam will revoke his offer (or that it will otherwise be terminated) before she can do so.

Under Article 2, the offeror will not be held to have required a particular medium of acceptance unless the requirement has been "unambiguously indicated" to the offeree [2-206(1)]. So, a court may hold that the words "Please respond by letter" do not make the letter the sole permitted medium of acceptance, but instead indicate that an acceptance by another medium may be effective, at least when received.

3. Where an offeror says nothing regarding the medium of acceptance, the offer may be accepted in any manner and by any medium reasonable under the circumstances [2-206]. Some courts have ruled that offerors impliedly authorize only those acceptance media that are at least as fast as the medium used to make the offer. The Code position is that a slower medium may in some circumstances be reasonable and therefore effective upon dispatch.

Often the beginning of performance by the offeree is an appropriate method of acceptance, as where Ben Buyer (the offeror) telegraphs Sam Seller (the offeree) in a distant state to begin manufacturing and shipping goods immediately. If Sam begins the requested performance but does not inform Ben of that fact, Ben is faced with uncertainty. To reduce this uncertainty, Article 2 requires Sam to give Ben notice within a reasonable time that the performance has begun. If Sam does not give the notice, Ben (the offeror) may treat the offer as having expired before acceptance. Thus, Ben will be free to acquire the goods from another source without liability to Sam even though Sam may in fact have begun performance.

Effect of Acceptance That Differs from the Offer.   The general law of contracts of most states requires that the offeree respond exactly to the terms of the offer. Under that law, an offeree who departs from the terms of the offer in even a relatively small way is held to have rejected the offer and to have substituted the offeree's own counteroffer. Thus, no contract will arise under the general law of contracts unless the original offeror (now the offeree of the counteroffer) accepts the counteroffer. This rule—that the original offeree's acceptance must be a "mirror image" of the offer for a contract to arise—is still widely applied in contracts for real estate and services, for example.

However, the "mirror image" rule is inconsistent with modern business practices in the sale of goods. Each day millions of contracts for goods are arranged by an exchange of preprinted forms, one prepared by the lawyer for the buyer and the other by the lawyer for the seller. Each lawyer is hired to serve the interests of his or her own client and will draft the form in a way that gives the client the most advantage. Since it is unlikely that the forms of buyers and sellers will match exactly, an offeree could never be sure that a contract arose until the offeror actually performed by, for example, accepting goods that the offeree-seller sent. But one purpose of a bilateral contract (one created by an exchange of promises) is to assure the offeree at the earliest possible moment that the offeror will be bound if the offeree accepts. If the offeror may escape contractual liability just because the offeree departed from the offer in some minor way as a result of the forms used, the offeree is faced with uncertainty as to whether a contract arose and with the expense of preparing to render (or receive) a performance that the offeror has a legal right not to accept (or deliver).

To reduce delay and harmful surprise in the formation of sales contracts, the drafters of Article 2 abandoned the mirror image rule. The offeree is still permitted under the Code to make a counteroffer by *stating* his or her intention not to be bound to a contract unless the offeror assents to whatever additional or different terms the offeree has introduced [2-207(1)]. Suppose Sam offers to sell Brenda a computer for $5000, and Brenda responds with the statement, "I accept your offer, but only on condition that you agree to arbitrate any dispute arising out of this sale instead of going to court." Brenda has made a counteroffer, and there is no contract unless Sam agrees to arbitration.

But if Brenda makes a timely statement of acceptance that introduces different or additional terms, and does so without *expressly* conditioning her acceptance on Sam's assent to the new terms, they are to be treated by the court as mere proposals for addition to the contract [2-207(2)]. Suppose that Sam made his offer to Brenda on his preprinted sales form that said nothing about arbitration, and Brenda responded by using her acceptance form that contained on its reverse side a printed clause stating, "Disputes relating to this transaction shall be resolved by arbitration." Although Brenda's form contains an arbitration clause, she has not used language expressly requiring Sam's assent to the clause. So, since the offer and acceptance forms reveal agreement as to the minimum terms necessary for a contract (computer for $5000, and identification of the parties to the sale), a contract arises despite the fact that the acceptance does not mirror the offer.

The proposed new terms may or may not become part of the contract, depending on the application of Article 2 rules governing the fate of the proposed terms. Whether a proposed new term becomes part of the contract depends, in part, on whether the term would "materially alter" the obligation that the offeror expected to undertake. The rules pertaining to proposed new terms may be summarized as follows:

1. If the new term is a major departure from or addition to the offer (i.e., if the new term "materially alters" the offer), it will not become a part of the contract unless the offeror actually consents to the (major) new term. Whether a term is material is for a court to decide. An offeree-buyer's substituting a lower price than the one offered would be a material alteration, no matter how slight the price change. Most courts consider the offeree's adding an arbitration clause to be a material matter. Offerors normally expect to have access to an impartial court if troubles develop rather than being forced into an arbitration proceeding that may occur in another state under law that favors the other party.
2. *Between merchants,* a *minor* new term (such as an insignificant variation as to method or time of delivery) will become a part of the contract unless the merchant-offeror does one of two things to prevent the minor term from being included: (*a*) When first making the offer, the merchant-offeror *expressly limits* the offeree's acceptance to the terms of the offer; or (*b*), having failed to so limit the offer, the merchant-offeror later gives the offeree notice of the offeror's objection to the minor new term and does so within a reasonable time after the term has been communicated to the offeror.

In summary, then, under Article 2 a sales contract arises if the parties agree on the basic terms necessary for a contract, and no major alterations may be imposed on any offeror (whether merchant or nonmerchant) without that person's consent. However, a *merchant*-offeror must take action to prevent a proposed *minor* term from becoming a part of the sales contract. In contrast, not even a minor new term can be imposed on a *non*merchant without the nonmerchant's consent.

Consider now a situation somewhat different from the ones just discussed: Brenda and Sam are merchants. Brenda phones Sam an order for goods, Sam ships them, and Brenda receives and begins using them. *Later* Brenda sends Sam a letter confirming her order and Sam sends Brenda a letter correctly stating the terms of the oral agreement but adding a term stating that any dispute arising from the contract will be submitted to arbitration. The goods prove defective and Brenda sues Sam for damages. He asks the court to require Brenda to submit her claim to arbitration. Must she? Here we have a situation involving an agreement followed by "confirmatory memoranda," one of which adds a new term. The courts will treat the situation in the same way they treat an acceptance that departs from the terms of the offer. If the new term is material, it is not binding on Brenda without her consent.

Sometimes the writings of buyer and seller are so much in conflict that no contract results from the exchange of writings. Yet, because the seller shipped goods and the buyer accepted and paid for them, a contract of some sort arose. In the event of a dispute between buyer and seller about the quality of the goods, their price, or other matters, what are the terms of the contract? The contract actually arrived at will include any terms on which the writings of the parties agree, together with any terms that can be inferred from other conduct of the parties and any terms supplied by the UCC: delivery terms, warranties, and so on [2-207(3)].

The case that follows involves a material alteration of an offer.

CASE 15.3

P.P.G. Industries, Inc. v. Alwinseal, Inc.
29 UCC Rep. 1162 (N.Y. App. Term 1980)

Facts: Alwinseal ordered goods from PPG for $65,000. PPG shipped them and sent Alwinseal an acknowledgment of the offer. PPG also sent a price list indicating a higher price than Alwinseal had offered to pay. PPG billed Alwinseal for $72,977.04, in accordance with PPG's new price list. Alwinseal paid the bill, claimed it had been overcharged by $7,977.04, and sought the return of that amount.

Question: Had PPG overcharged Alwinseal by $7,977.04?

Answer: Yes. Alwinseal should have been charged only $65,000.

Reasoning: The acknowledgment (acceptance) of Alwinseal's offer was not expressly made conditional on Alwinseal's assent to a higher price. Therefore PPG's price list was merely a proposal for a different price term and not a counteroffer. A departure by the offeree (here, PPG, the seller) from the price stated in the original offer of purchase is a material alteration. Since Alwinseal did not assent to the material alteration of its offer, the contract price was $65,000.

Shipment of Nonconforming Goods as an Acceptance.   Sometimes a seller fills an order by shipping goods that differ from what was ordered. The seller may have done so by accident, or intentionally. If the nonconforming shipment was intentional, the seller's motive may have been bad, as where the seller attempts to substitute slow-moving goods in the hope that the buyer will not notice the substitution. Or the seller's motive may have been good, as where the seller knows that the buyer needs the goods immediately and, lacking the exact goods ordered, ships similar goods as an accommodation to the buyer.

Suppose Bob orders for prompt shipment 100 bolts of white silk cloth from Sue for manufacture into ladies' scarfs. Sue ships 100 bolts of white nylon cloth instead. Sue has not performed the requested act. At common law, a judge would have held that Sue has not accepted Bob's offer and therefore cannot be liable for breach of contract even though her shipping nonconforming goods might have caused Bob much inconvenience or loss. Under Article 2, if Sue ships the nylon *without giving Bob notice* that the goods are nonconforming, the shipment *is* an acceptance and at the same time a breach of contract. This rule will tend to discourage sellers from negligently filling orders or deceiving buyers by intentionally substituting nonconforming goods. However, where Sue gives Bob *timely notice* that the goods are nonconforming, the shipment is *not* an acceptance, and Sue will not be liable for breach of contract. This notice is especially important if Bob receives mail at his business office but the goods are delivered to employees elsewhere. If Bob has notice that the cloth is nylon but uses it anyway, there is a contract. If Bob decides not to use the goods, he may ship them back to Sue at her expense. This rule encourages sellers to accommodate buyers who may need substitute goods for maintaining production schedules, and to act reasonably in doing so.

Interpretation
of the Sales
Contract

Where a sales agreement is so sketchy or poorly worded that its terms are in doubt, a court may have to interpret it. Interpretation is the process by which a judge decides what legal obligations each party to the agreement undertook and whether the agreement amounts to an enforceable contract. Part of the judge's task might be to determine *which* of the parties' written and oral statements are included in the contract, and *what meaning* the parties' words should have. Contractual interpretation is largely beyond the scope of this book. However, business people can benefit from knowing generally how the Code and the courts approach the problem of interpretation.

Meaning of "Contract."   Since interpretation may be viewed as a judicial search for a contract, the meaning of "contract" becomes important. Under the Code, *contract* means the total legal obligation that results from the parties' agreement, as that agreement is affected by the Code and any other applicable rules of law. *Agreement* means the actual bargain of the parties, as revealed by their language and other circumstances surrounding the transaction. Since a sales contract includes obligations imposed by the Code and other law, the parties must at least act in good faith and avoid unconscionable (harshly unfair) conduct. As was discussed earlier in this chapter, the Code and other law also fill in certain terms left open by the parties. Thus, the "sales contract" consists of the agreement of the parties as that agreement is limited and supplemented by law.

The Parol Evidence Rule.   Often parties to a sales contract make a variety of written and oral statements while negotiating the terms of the contract and then they sign a writing called an "integration" that supposedly represents their final decision as to the terms of the contract. What happens if one of the parties alleges that one of these prior statements (called "parol evidence"), and not the term that appears in the integration, truly states the parties' agreement? The court will apply the *parol evidence rule.* Under that rule the court ordinarily will not admit into evidence any parol statement that directly contradicts an unambiguous term in the integration. The unambiguous term, and not the contradictory earlier statement, will be taken by the court as an accurate statement of the parties' agreement. But parol evidence *is* admissible to clear up vague or ambiguous language, to supply missing terms, to settle allegations of fraud, and so on. Thus the court sorts through the many conflicting statements that the parties might make and arrives at the selection of words that the court will then hold to be the language of the contract.

Course of Performance, Course of Dealing, Usage of Trade.   After deciding what statements are to be considered part of the contract, the court may have to determine the meaning of unclear language. The meaning intended by the parties is to be determined by their language and conduct, read and interpreted in light of commercial practices and other relevant circumstances.

To aid interpretation, the Code gives special prominence to "course of performance," "course of dealing," and "usage of trade." **Course of performance** refers to how a particular transaction is carried out. There can be no course of performance unless there are repeated occasions for performance, such as several deliveries of oil to be made under a single contract of sale. Suppose that a contract for the delivery of oil says nothing about how large each delivery shall be. The buyer's acceptance of a series of small deliveries could establish a course of performance that would bind the buyer as to the next delivery.

Course of dealing refers to a series of transactions, not just the performance of one transaction. A course of dealing (i.e., a pattern of prior contracts) can establish a background for the interpretation of the immediate transaction. Suppose that for each of five previous winters a buyer of home heating oil has always paid the delivery person in cash. The seller's acceptance of this practice establishes a course of dealing upon which the buyer may rely, even though the driver absconds with the cash, until notified differently.

A **usage of trade** is any practice or method of dealing that is so regularly observed in a place, vocation, or trade that a party to a sales contract is justified in expecting that the practice will be observed in this contract too. It is a usage of trade in the seed corn business that sellers of seed corn make no guarantees of yield. A buyer who knew nothing of this usage of trade could nevertheless be bound by it.

UCC Grounds for Avoiding the Sales Contract

As indicated in Chapter 9, a party to a contract may avoid (cancel) it because of wrongdoing by the other party such as fraud, misrepresentation, or duress. The UCC makes these and other common law grounds for avoidance also available to the parties to a sales contract.

The elements of common law grounds for avoidance have been rather clearly worked out in long lines of cases. However, the courts have had difficulty combating many harmful business practices that fall short of fraud and other established wrongs. So, to deal with these harmful practices, the courts have developed the concept of **unconscionability**, which is specifically recognized by Article 2 as an additional ground for avoiding a sales contract.

A contract or a contractual clause is unconscionable if it is so one-sided as to "oppress" or "unfairly surprise" the party upon whom it is imposed. An unconscionable contract or clause is unenforceable even though the practice involved does not constitute fraud or some other traditional variety of wrongdoing. A court may refuse to enforce an unconscionable sales contract, may delete any unconscionable term and enforce the remainder of the contract, or may so limit the application of an unconscionable term as to avoid an unconscionable result [2-302].

The courts have identified a number of practices that may be held unconscionable if circumstances warrant. Suppose that a seller, by means of a clause in fine print placed in the middle of a complicated contract form, seeks secretly to deprive the buyer of a right that he or she normally would not agree to give up if the topic were discussed, such as a warranty (guarantee) that the goods are fit for their ordinary purposes. Such a clause is unconscionable. High-pressure sales tactics may be a form of unconscionability, as may tricky or deceptive business practices. Furthermore, as illustrated in Case 15.4 an excessively high price might be held unconscionable, as might a seller's unduly restricting the buyer's remedies for the seller's breach of contract or unduly expanding the seller's own remedies. For example, suppose that a furniture seller, by means of a clause in an installment-sale contract, retains for as long as the buyer's account is not fully paid a security interest in all items sold to the buyer over a period of years. Then the seller seeks to repossess the whole houseful of furniture because the buyer missed a payment on the last small item. If the value of the furniture to be repossessed greatly exceeds the amount of the unpaid debt, or the buyer did not understand the unusual consequences of missing a payment (losing all the furniture instead of only the item on which a payment was missed), the clause that provides for repossession is likely to be held unconscionable. However, while such a clause might be unconscionable in a contract between a merchant and a semiliterate customer, the same clause might be enforceable where buyer and seller are large corporations. This is so because people who have business experience presumably are in a better position to bargain with regard to contract terms, or at least to understand them.

CASE 15.4   Jones v. Star Credit Corp.
298 N.Y.S.2d 264 (N.Y. Sup. Ct. 1969)

Facts: The Joneses, who were welfare recipients, were visited by a salesman and they agreed to purchase a home freezer unit for $900. The freezer unit had a maximum retail value of $300. With time credit charges, credit life insurance, credit property insurance, and sales tax charges added, the purchase price totaled $1,234.80. Additional credit charges raised the total to $1,439.69. The Joneses sought to be released from the contract.

Question: Should the Joneses be allowed to avoid the contract?

Answer: Yes. Because the contract is unconscionable, it will be avoided.

Reasoning: The principle underlying the concept of unconscionability is that of preventing oppression and unfair surprise. While it is important to preserve the integrity of agreements and the fundamental right of parties to bargain and contract, the courts are also concerned for the uneducated and often illiterate individual who is the victim of gross inequality of bargaining power. A retail merchant who extends credit is expected to establish a price that will protect him against the risk of selling to those who are default prone. But here the price was far in excess of the legitimate needs of the seller. The $900 price was in itself exorbitant. Another factor to consider is that the seller knew at the time of the sale of the very limited financial resources of the purchaser and still took advantage. The plaintiffs have already paid more than $600, are hereby relieved of further payments, and may keep the freezer unit.

Form of the Sales Contract

The parties to a sales contract are not required to use any particular form of contract. As long as they provide the minimum amount of information required for a contract to arise, they may say as little or as much as they like about its terms, in whatever language and sequence of clauses they prefer. Yet, some rules of law do affect the form of some sales contracts. The Article 2 statute of frauds requires that specified kinds of sales contracts be evidenced by a *writing* or by some *legally acceptable substitute*.

The purpose of a statute of frauds is to require clear evidence—beyond mere oral statements of the parties—that a contract actually arose. This evidence is especially important where one person insists, but the other person denies, that a contract arose. As discussed in Chapter 12, statute-of-frauds requirements apply only to the more significant or more burdensome kinds of contracts. The Article 2 requirements apply only to sales contracts involving a price of $500 or more.

Under the basic Article 2 rule, such a contract is not enforceable unless the party against whom enforcement is sought has signed some writing sufficient to indicate that a contract for sale has been made between the parties. Article 2 does *not* require that all the terms of the contract be stated. The writing is sufficient if it is signed by the party to be charged with breach of contract, specifies a quantity of goods, and indicates that the parties intended to enter into a contract [2-201]. The quantity need not be accurately stated, but the contract is not enforceable for more than the quantity stated in the writing.

Two classes of sales transactions are enforceable even though the party against whom enforcement is sought has signed nothing. Both classes of transactions involve situations where one party would be subjected to unfair surprise if the other party were permitted to cancel an agreement merely because the canceling party has signed nothing.

The first class consists of contracts "between merchants" in which a writing exists but has not been signed by the person against whom enforcement is sought. Suppose that merchant Brown telephones an offer to dealer Smith to buy a particular cash register for $1000; that Smith replies over the phone, "I accept your offer"; and that Smith immediately sends Brown a written confirmation of the contract. Three weeks later, Brown, pointing out that she signed nothing, denies that the oral contract binds her. The statute of frauds is satisfied *without* Brown's signature if the following things happen: (1) Within a reasonable time after the oral transaction, Brown receives a writing confirming the contract and it is sufficiently detailed to be enforceable against the sender, Smith. (2) Brown has reason to know the contents of the writing. And (3)

Brown does not give written notice of her objection to the contents of the writing within 10 days after receiving it.

In the second class of sales transactions there usually is no writing, but there may be convincing alternative evidence that the parties made a contract. If a party *admits in court* that a contract for sale was made, the oral contract can be enforced as to the quantity of goods admitted. If an oral contract has been *partially performed,* it is enforceable as to the goods for which the seller accepted payment, or as to goods that the buyer received and accepted. Oral contracts for goods to be *specially manufactured* for the buyer may also be enforceable—if the manufacturer has begun to make or procure them and if they are not suitable for sale in the ordinary course of the seller's business.

Alteration of the Sales Contract

After forming a sales contract, the parties may wish to modify it. They may want to change the time or place of delivery, specifications in goods ordered, warranty obligations, or even price. Under the general law of contracts, such modifications may not be enforceable unless both parties receive new consideration. Yet it is common practice for honest people to agree to, and to rely on, modifications that are not supported by consideration. Under Article 2, an agreement modifying a sales contract needs no consideration to be binding [2-209].

However, sometimes a party to a sale forces a modification on the other party by, for example, threatening to withhold delivery of essential goods unless the purchaser "agrees" to pay more. Article 2 provides protections against such misconduct. One protection is the UCC requirement that any party to a Code transaction must act in good faith. In applying the good faith rule, a court may require the person seeking a modification to prove that there is a real need for it—for example, that the higher price to which the buyer agreed is justified by an actual increase in the price of raw materials. Another protection is the fact that the statute of frauds must be satisfied if the contract, as modified, will be for a price of $500 or more. Thus, there will be evidence (beyond the modification-seeker's allegations) that the other party actually agreed to the modification. There is a third protection. The parties to a signed agreement may require in their agreement that any modification or cancellation of the contract must be evidenced by a signed writing for the change to be enforceable, i.e., that there will be no oral modifications. However, where a "no oral modifications" clause is supplied by a merchant to a nonmerchant, the clause will not be binding on the nonmerchant unless he or she signs it separately.

What happens when the parties fail to provide a required writing and agree to an oral modification anyway? If one party *materially changes his or her position in reliance on* the oral modification, the other party has *waived* (given up) the protection of the required writing. Suppose Sam agrees in writing to sell Brenda a $1000 copier to be delivered in 10 days, and the contract requires any modifications to be made in writing. On the third day Brenda phones Sam to tell him delivery will have to be postponed for another 15 days because she will not have room for the copier until then. Sam agrees to the postponement. At this point in the transaction, the 15-day oral postponement agreement is not binding on either party, since the contract requires that modifications be in writing. Now suppose that Sam has only this one copier in his store and will not receive another like it for 12 days. Believing he need not deliver a copier to Brenda for 15 days, Sam sells the copier to Tom. Because Sam has *relied* on the oral agreement, Brenda has lost (waived) her right to cancel the oral agreement, and she cannot insist on the original delivery date.

SUMMARY

The law governing sales of goods is found in Article 2 of the Uniform Commercial Code, together with other aspects of commercial law. The general purpose of the Code is to simplify, unify, and modernize the law of commercial transactions. The Code encourages sound business practices, ethical business conduct, and performance of sales contracts. Merchants generally have greater duties than do nonmerchants, and all parties to Code transactions must use good faith in carrying them out. The Code concept of identification of goods to the contract enables a party to know, for example, when the buyer may insure the goods.

Article 2 applies to present sales of goods and to contracts to sell goods at a future time. In general, *goods* means all things that are movable at the time of identification to the contract. Article 2 does not apply to contracts for such nongoods as real estate and personal services. Courts differ in their application of the Code to contracts for a mixture of goods and services.

A sales contract must meet traditional requirements for the formation of a contract, but most of these requirements have been modified by Article 2 to adjust them to contemporary business needs. A sales contract may be made in any manner sufficient to show agreement. Many terms may be left open, but ordinarily the parties and the quantity of goods must be identified.

Unilateral offers to buy goods for prompt shipment may be accepted either by a prompt shipment or by a prompt promise to ship. Certain firm offers made by a merchant are irrevocable even though the merchant receives no consideration for the promise to hold the offer open. Offers may be accepted by any reasonable means; and Article 2 treats some counteroffers as acceptances. Between merchants, minor new terms can become part of the contract, but a new term that materially alters the offer will not bind the offeror without his or her actual consent.

A shipment of nonconforming goods is both an acceptance and a breach of contract. However, if the shipper gives timely notice that the goods are nonconforming, the shipment will be considered an accommodation and not an acceptance and breach.

Where a sales agreement is sketchy or poorly worded, a court may have to interpret it. The parol evidence rule helps a judge decide what statements should be held to be the language of the contract. The meaning of unclear language may be determined in part by reference to course of performance, course of dealing, and usage of trade.

A party to a sales contract may avoid it because of wrongdoing by the other party such as fraud, misrepresentation, or duress. Article 2 provides an additional ground for avoidance: unconscionability. The parties are not required to use any particular form of contract, but the Article 2 statute of frauds requires that sales contracts involving a price of $500 or more be evidenced by a writing or by some legally acceptable alternative such as admissions in court or part performance. An agreement modifying a sales contract needs no consideration to be binding.

REVIEW QUESTIONS

1. A sale of goods may involve other UCC transactions, too. Explain or illustrate.

2. Why is it necessary to have a body of sales law apart from the general law of contracts?

3. A basic policy of the UCC is to encourage sound and ethical business practices. Explain how the following Code concepts contribute to carrying out that policy: (a) merchant, (b) good faith, and (c) identification of goods to the contract.

4. (a) To what transactions does Article 2 apply? (b) How might a court treat a contract involving a mixture of goods and services?

5. Explain whether the following statement is true: "Before there can be a sales contract, the parties, the price, and the quantity and kind of goods must be identified."

6. (a) How and why does Article 2 depart from common law rules with regard to an offer for a unilateral contract? A firm offer? (b) What difference does it make whether an auction is with reserve or without reserve?

7. (a) What is the effect of using a medium of acceptance that has been authorized by the offeror? (b) How does an offeree know what medium of acceptance has been authorized?

8. How and why does Article 2 depart from common law rules with regard to (a) counteroffers, and (b) a shipment of nonconforming goods as an acceptance?

9. Explain generally how a court will interpret a sales contract whose terms are in doubt.

10. (a) On what grounds may a party to a sales contract avoid it? (b) In what main way does unconscionability differ from other, traditional, grounds for avoiding a sales contract?

11. (a) How may the Article 2 statute of frauds be satisfied? (b) If a writing is used, what must the writing contain?

12. An agreement modifying a sales contract needs no consideration to be binding. How, then, may a buyer be protected if the seller forces the buyer to agree to a higher price by threatening to withhold delivery of essential goods?

CASE PROBLEMS

1. Milau Associates, a general contractor, built a warehouse and turned it over to its owner. The owner then leased it to Baum Textile Mill Co. A few months later a large underground section of pipe burst and caused substantial water damage to bolts of textiles stored in the warehouse. The break in the pipe resulted from a "water hammer" caused by a sudden, unpredictable interruption in the flow of water from the city water main, followed by a sudden buildup of extreme water pressure when

the flow of water resumed. Baum brought suit against Milau and the subcontractor who had installed the pipe, alleging that it was defective and that the defendants had therefore breached a warranty that the pipe was fit for its intended purpose. The defendants contended that the pipe was not defective, but even if it was, no warranty arose because the installation of the pipe was a service and not a sale of goods. Explain whether the transaction was a sale or a service.

2. The First National Bank of Scottsboro posted a public notice of its intention to sell repossessed cars "at public outcry to the highest, best and last bidder." Mr. Sly bid highest on a Chevrolet Monte Carlo, but the bank later refused to accept Sly's bid, as the auctioneer told Sly might happen. Sly brought suit, alleging breach of contract. Whether there was a contract between Sly and the bank depended on whether the auction was with or without reserve. Was the auction one "without reserve"? Explain.

3. Michel, Inc., made seven oral agreements to purchase yarn fiom Anabasis Toade, Inc. In each of the seven transactions, Anabasis (seller) sent Michel a written confirmation containing an arbitration clause. Michel signed and returned the first confirmation. Michel knew that the form contained the arbitration clause but never objected to it. Michel did object to the inclusion of a 30-day rather than a 60-day credit term contained in the second and third confirmations, and these terms were changed to suit Michel. Later Michel discovered that the yarn did not conform to the contract specifications. Anabasis insisted that the dispute be submitted to arbitration. Michel brought an action to stay (stop) arbitration proceedings. The trial court held that the arbitration clause did not become part of the contract unless both parties explicitly agreed to it. Was the trial court correct? Explain.

4. Posttapes Associates used defective Kodak film in an attempt to produce a documentary film and suffered substantial losses as a result. Posttapes sued for damages. Kodak defended on the ground that a clause printed on the film boxes limited its liability to the replacement of the defective film, and that the limitation was accepted in the film industry as a usage of trade. Posttapes denied that the limitation was a usage of trade. Even if it was such a usage, Posttapes contended, the limitation was unconscionable. (a) Was the limitation of Kodak's liability a usage of trade? (b) Was the limitation unconscionable? Explain.

5. Sebasty, a farmer, made an oral agreement to sell 14,000 bushels of wheat to Perschke Hay and Grain for $1.95 per bushel. Perschke immediately sent Sebasty a written confirmation of the agreement, which Sebasty received. Under the agreement, Perschke was to pick up the wheat about 6 months later. In the meantime, the price of wheat rose, and when the time for performance arrived, Sebasty refused to provide the wheat. Alleging breach of contract, Perschke sued Sebasty for more than $14,000 in damages. Sebasty contended that the oral agreement was not enforceable because it did not comply with the statute of frauds. Part of Sebasty's defense rested on his allegation that he was not a merchant. (a) On what statute of frauds rule was plaintiff Perschke relying? (b) For the purpose of that rule, was Sebasty a merchant? Explain.

CHAPTER 16

DISTRIBUTION OF GOODS; TRANSFER OF TITLE AND RISK OF LOSS

The preceding chapter discussed the sales contract—how it is formed, what its terms are, and how it may be altered. We turn now to legal questions that may arise during the process of moving goods from the seller to the buyer. When does the buyer actually acquire title to (ownership of) goods? When goods are lost or damaged during delivery, what are the rights of buyer and seller? What are the rights of a buyer whose seller wrongfully acquired goods or sold the goods belonging to someone else? These questions will be answered in the second and third parts of this chapter. But because the answers often vary according to the method of delivery the seller used, we must first consider methods sellers commonly use to get goods to buyers.

DISTRIBUTION OF GOODS

Distribution of goods may involve three major elements: (1) some method of transporting goods; (2) a place to store goods before, during, or after delivery; and (3) paperwork necessary to ensure that goods get to the right person.

How Goods Are Transported

Delivery by Common and Private Carriers.   A seller may ship goods by means of a **carrier**, an individual or business firm engaged in transporting passengers or goods for hire. Where goods are transported, the carriage transaction is a bailment[1] in which the bailor (owner or other shipper) places goods in the custody of the bailee (the carrier) for the purpose of safe transport to a person or firm authorized by the shipper to receive them. Carriers of property include railroads, barge and ship lines, airlines, trucking companies, pipeline companies that transport oil or natural gas, and express companies whose business is the speedy delivery of small packages of goods or money.

A carrier has a "lien" on (claim against) goods in its possession for any unpaid transportation and related charges [7-307]. The carrier may enforce the lien by selling the amount of goods necessary to pay its legitimate charges [7-308]. A carrier loses its lien on any goods it voluntarily delivers or unjustifiably refuses to deliver.

Carriers are classified as "common" or "private." A **common carrier** offers its services to the public and must carry for all who apply, as long as there is room and no legal excuse for refusing to render the service. An express company, which by definition hauls only small packages, would have a legal excuse for refusing to haul passengers.

A common carrier has extensive liability for damage to or loss of goods being transported. Like any other bailee, a common carrier is liable for loss caused by its negligence and intentional torts such as *conversion* of the bailor's goods.[2] In most states common carriers also are liable for loss due to causes beyond the carrier's

---

[1]As noted in Chapter 23, a bailment is the legal relationship that results where one person (the bailor) transfers possession of personal property to another person (the bailee) under such circumstances that the bailee is under a duty to return the item to the bailor or to dispose of it as directed by the bailor.
[2]As noted in Chapter 3, conversion is the act of taking or using someone else's personal property as one's own, without legal justification. A thief is a converter. So is a carrier or other bailee that delivers goods to the wrong person, uses the bailed goods as the bailee's own, or wrongfully refuses to release the goods to the bailor or to release them in accordance with the bailor's instructions..

control, such as fires, wrecks, theft, and violent mobs. The English courts began imposing this broader "insurer's" liability in the 1500s because common carriers or their employees could easily steal the goods, sell them, and pretend that the goods had been lost. Today the common carrier's liability as an insurer is based on additional factors: the great total value of goods being shipped, vast distances involved, and difficulty a shipper would have in proving a carrier's negligence or fraud.

However, there are limits to the liability of a common carrier. It is not liable, for example, for losses caused solely by an "act of God" such as a tornado or earthquake, an act or fault of the shipper, or the dangerous or perishable nature of the goods themselves. Furthermore, unless forbidden by law to do so, a common carrier may limit its liability as an *insurer* (i.e., for loss from causes beyond the carrier's control), if the limitation is reasonable and actually consented to by the shipper. Although a common carrier may *not* exempt itself from liability for its own negligence, it may limit the amount of damages recoverable by the shipper—for example, by stating a maximum amount of liability in the contract of carriage [7-309]. But a carrier may *not* limit its liability for converting the bailee's goods to its own use. Any other rule would reward wrongdoing by allowing the converter to keep the difference between the actual value of the converted property and any limited amount stated in the contract of carriage.

Private carriers (including "contract" carriers) ordinarily are used to meet the special needs of shippers who find access to a common carrier lacking or its service unsatisfactory. An isolated rancher might hire a private carrier to haul cattle to market or to a loading yard to await the arrival of a common carrier. A manufacturer or a wholesaler might use a private carrier for deliveries to remote regions or to local areas not served by common carriers.

Private carriers differ considerably from common carriers. They do not hold themselves out as ready to serve the public generally and are not required to do so. Rather, they carry goods only for those persons with whom they choose to contract. Unlike common carriers, private carriers are *not* liable as insurers of goods. They are liable only as bailees, for loss caused by (1) their own negligence (including that of their employees), and (2) their intentional misconduct (and that of their employees), such as conversion of goods. Thus, a private carrier would be liable for theft committed by its employees but not for thefts committed by strangers unless the carrier or its employees failed to use ordinary care to prevent the thefts. Private carriers are freer than common carriers to exclude liability for negligence. Private carriers usually may enforce contract clauses that exempt them from liability for ordinary negligence, but usually may not enforce clauses that purport to exempt them from liability for "gross" negligence or for intentional misconduct.

As the preceding discussion indicates, a common or private carrier may be liable for loss of goods in its custody, but sometimes the carrier is not liable. So, either the buyer or seller must absorb the loss. The Uniform Commercial Code (UCC) provides "risk-of-loss" rules, discussed later in this chapter, that determine who—buyer or seller—must absorb the loss or, if a carrier is liable, who must seek compensation from the carrier. UCC risk-of-loss rules apply also to the noncarrier and pickup deliveries discussed in the following paragraphs.

Noncarrier and Pickup Deliveries.   Especially in the retail sale of bulky goods such as furniture, sellers commonly deliver goods to buyers by means of the sellers' own delivery vehicles. This kind of delivery is called a "noncarrier" delivery because the seller does not use a common or a private carrier. Sellers of many other kinds of goods—dairy products, fuels for home or commercial use, soft drinks, baked goods, small hand tools, and so on—make noncarrier deliveries to customers for resale or for customers' own use.

Many buyers use their own vehicles to pick up goods at the seller's premises. For example, a building contractor might have a fleet of trucks for pickup of gravel, lumber, and other building materials. Customers of local supermarkets and department stores ordinarily pick up the goods at the store rather than have the store make a noncarrier delivery. In the sale of automobiles and the like, the customer may visit the seller's premises several times to work out the terms of the sale and then return a few days later to pick up the car after it has been prepared by the seller for use.

Storage in Warehouses

Often an owner of goods must store them in a warehouse until they are sold. A *warehouse* is a building or other enclosed area used to hold goods temporarily or for an indefinite time. When a person stores goods at a warehouse, a bailment relationship is created. The owner or other depositor of the goods is the bailor. The *warehouser,* a person or firm engaged in the business of receiving and storing goods for hire, is the bailee.

A warehouse may be "public" or "private." A *public* warehouse stores goods for any member of the public who pays for the storage service. Grain elevators buy grain from farmers willing to sell, but also store grain for any farmer who wishes to wait for a higher price. Because they store for anyone seeking that service, grain elevators are public warehouses. In contrast, a *private* warehouse stores goods only for those persons with whom it chooses to contract.

A public warehouse is subject to more governmental regulation than a private warehouse is. Aside from this difference, the distinction between a public and a private warehouse is not very significant, since neither kind is liable as an insurer of stored goods unless by special agreement or under an occasional state statute imposing such liability on a public warehouse. Rather, public and private warehouses usually are liable only *as bailees* for loss of or damage to goods during storage, i.e., for loss due to their negligence or intentional misconduct in caring for goods.

Like carriers, warehouses may limit their liability for negligence during storage. As noted in Case 16.1, this liability may be limited in the contract of storage to a specific amount per item, subject to the bailor's right to increase the valuation. If the bailor declares a higher value, the warehouse has a right to charge a higher rate for storage [7-204]. Like a carrier, a warehouse has a possessory lien on goods for storage charges [7-209].

CASE 16.1   I.C.C. Metals, Inc. v. Municipal Warehouse Co.
409 N.E.2d 849 (N.Y. 1980)

Facts: I.C.C. Metals (Metals) delivered three separate lots of indium, a valuable industrial metal, to Municipal Warehouse Co. for storage. The three lots weighed a total of 845 pounds and were worth $100,000. Each warehouse receipt (contract of storage) contained a clause limiting Warehouse's liability to $50 per lot. Metals did not inform Warehouse of the value of the metal nor seek a higher valuation. Two years later when Metals requested the return of the indium, Warehouse could not find it. Alleging that Warehouse took the indium as its own property, Metals sued Warehouse in conversion for $100,000. Warehouse alleged that the indium had been stolen, and that the clause in the warehouse receipt limited Warehouse's liability, if any, to $50 per lot.

Question: Was the clause of limitation effective to limit Warehouse's liability to $150?

Answer: Yes, as to negligence; *no,* as to conversion. Warehouse is liable to Metals for the full value of the indium.

Reasoning: A warehouse, like a common carrier, may limit its liability for negligence resulting in loss of stored goods, so long as it provides the bailor with an opportunity to increase the bailee's potential liability by payment of a higher storage fee. Metals had this opportunity but chose not to use it. However, where a warehouse fails to return bailed goods, it must show with reasonable certainty how the loss occurred. Then the bailor (Metals) would have to prove that the bailee actually converted the goods. But here the warehouse merely alleged, without offering proof, that an outsider stole the metal. Under these circumstances, conversion is presumed.

Documents of Title

Documents of title are an important part of the paperwork necessary for getting goods from sellers to buyers. A **document of title** is any writing that in the *regular course of business or financing* (i.e., in normal business transactions) is treated by business people as adequate proof that the person who holds it is entitled to receive and sell or otherwise dispose of the document and the goods it covers [1-201(15)]. To be a document of title, the writing must purport to be (must indicate that it is) issued by or addressed to a bailee (i.e., a carrier or a warehouser), and must purport to cover identified goods in the bailee's possession.

A document of title serves three practical functions. First, it is a receipt—a written acknowledgment given by a bailee that the depositor or shipper left the specified goods with the bailee for storage or shipment. Second, it is a contract between the bailor and the bailee for storage or transport (carriage) of goods. Third, as indicated in the previous paragraph, it is *evidence of title to (ownership of) goods.*

Kinds of Documents.   The two principal documents of title are the warehouse receipt and the bill of lading. A **warehouse receipt** is a writing issued by a warehouser to the person or firm that deposits goods at the warehouse for storage. The depositor is the bailor; the warehouser is the bailee.

A **bill of lading** is a writing, issued by a carrier, evidencing the carrier's receipt of goods for shipment. The person delivering the goods to the carrier for shipment is the shipper and also the bailor; the carrier is the bailee. The shipper-bailor's act of delivering goods to a carrier for transport is called a **consignment**. The shipper (bailor) is the **consignor**. The person to whom the carrier is to deliver the goods at their destination is the consignee. Suppose Sam delivers goods to XYZ Railroad in Atlanta for transport to Brenda in Denver. Sam is the shipper, the bailor, and the consignor; the railroad is the carrier and the bailee; and Brenda is the consignee.

A **through bill of lading** is one issued by a carrier (to the shipper-bailor) for the transport of goods over the carrier's own lines for a certain distance, and then over connecting lines to the destination. A through bill would be used, for example, where a railroad in the consignor's city does not go to the consignee's city, but a connecting railroad does. A carrier that issues a through bill is liable not only for its own breach of the carriage contract, but also for any breach of the contract by the connecting carrier such as failure to deliver the goods to the proper person. The connecting carrier must honor the terms of the through bill even though the connecting carrier did not issue the bill [7-302].[3]

Where a seller ships goods by truck or air and then mails the bill of lading to the buyer, the goods often arrive at their destination before the bill of lading does. This is inconvenient for buyers who need the goods right away and for carriers that have little storage space at the point of destination. So, the seller may use a **destination bill of lading**. A destination bill is issued *at the destination* by the carrier or its agent so that the buyer (consignee) may take possession of the goods immediately upon their arrival. Suppose that Sue, a Los Angeles seller, delivers goods to an airline for shipment to Ben, a New York buyer, and instructs the airline to issue the "airbill" (bill of lading) *in New York* to a bank named by Sue. The airline may issue the airbill even before the goods arrive. In accordance with Sue's advance instructions, the New York bank collects payment from Ben and hands the airbill over to him. Ben can immediately use the airbill to get the goods from the airline rather than having to wait for the airbill to arrive in the mail while the goods remain in storage.

Principle of Negotiability. Documents of title may be either negotiable or nonnegotiable in form. The distinction can be of great importance to persons who use or are affected by such documents.

Negotiable Form; Its Effect on Who Is Entitled to Goods. For a warehouse receipt or a bill of lading to be in *negotiable* form, the document must contain "order" or "bearer" language. That is, the document must state that the goods are to be delivered to the bearer of the document or to the order of a person named in the document to receive the goods. A document reading "Deliver 5 desks to bearer" or "Deliver 5 desks to Sam or order" is in negotiable form.

The form of a document, negotiable versus nonnegotiable, tells us who is entitled to have the goods from the bailee. A bailee who issues a negotiable document of title must deliver the goods described in the document to any "holder" who surrenders it to the bailee. As explained in greater detail later in this chapter, a holder is any person, even a stranger to the bailee, who seems to be rightfully in possession of a negotiable document (one containing the required order or bearer language).

---

[3]Article 7 of the UCC governs documents of title where goods are shipped within a state. Where goods are transported in interstate or foreign commerce, federal law applies. For example, the federal Bills of Lading Act applies to interstate shipments of goods by common carrier. Although state law (Article 7) differs in some ways from the federal law governing documents of title, there is little difference as to the general principles discussed in this chapter.

Suppose that Sam, intending to sell certain goods when a buyer can be found, delivers the goods to Walt's Warehouse for storage. At Sam's request, Walt makes the warehouse receipt out to "Sam or [Sam's] order" and hands it to Sam. The receipt is negotiable in form and Sam is its holder. When Sam finds a buyer (Brenda), Sam needs merely to "indorse" the receipt (sign it on the back or in some other appropriate place, much as one would indorse a check) and deliver it to Brenda. Brenda is now the holder, and as such has the right, upon surrendering the document to Walt, to have the goods.

In contrast, a document that lacks order or bearer language is nonnegotiable in form. A bailee who issues a nonnegotiable document must deliver the goods only to the person specifically named in the document to receive them, or in accordance with that person's written instructions. Suppose that Sam in the preceding paragraph had instructed Walt to make the receipt out to Sam personally ("to Sam"). The receipt would be nonnegotiable in form. Such a receipt obligates Walt to deliver the goods to Sam and no one else, unless Sam gives Walt a contrary delivery instruction in writing. Sam might do this by means of a separate document called a "delivery order," or by writing on the warehouse receipt itself a statement of assignment ("I, Sam, hereby assign all my rights under this document to Brenda") and delivering the receipt to Brenda (the assignee).

Legal Rights Acquired by a Transferee of the Document.   Whether a document of title is negotiable or nonnegotiable helps determine what rights to the goods a buyer (or other transferee) of the document acquires from the seller (or other transferor). The purchaser of a *non*negotiable document is merely an assignee and as such receives only the rights that the seller had. (The law of assignments is discussed in Chapter 13.) Suppose that Tom delivers goods to Walt, who issues to Tom a nonnegotiable warehouse receipt (one made out "to Tom"). Then Sam, by use of fraud, induces Tom to assign the receipt to Sam. Sam sells the document (and, of course, the goods it represents) to Brenda, a retailer of such goods who knows nothing of Sam's fraud. Brenda has purchased the document in good faith, but being merely an assignee of Sam's rights, Brenda takes the document *subject to* Tom's claim of fraud. Sam was liable to Tom for fraud. Brenda, Sam's assignee, is in no better position than Sam was. Tom has a right to recover the goods or their value from Brenda. If Tom chooses to hold Brenda liable, she will have to get the value of the goods from Sam, absorb the loss, or pass it on to others such as an insurance company.

In contrast, a good faith purchaser of a *negotiable* document may, in proper circumstances, take the document (and the goods) *free from* many (but not all) defenses or claims of others to the goods. Suppose that Tom in the preceding paragraph had received a warehouse receipt made out to "Tom or order" and that because of Sam's fraud Tom indorsed and delivered the receipt to Sam, who then sold it to Brenda. Knowing nothing of Sam's fraud, Brenda is a "holder to whom the document has been duly negotiated" (Article 7's version of a good faith purchaser), and as such takes the document and the goods free from Tom's claim of fraud. Tom may recover the value of the goods from *Sam* (the defrauder), but Brenda (the good faith purchaser) keeps the goods and is not liable to Tom for their value. In this way, the law frees good faith purchasers from a variety of risks, and persons like Tom who are in a better position to protect themselves must pursue the wrongdoer, absorb any loss, or pass it on to others. The protection of good faith purchasers, widely known in the business community, encourages buyers to pay higher market values than they would if the chances of loss were greater.

Good faith purchaser protection exists only where the transferee of the document takes it by a "due negotiation." For there to be a due negotiation, five requirements must be met [7-501]:

1. The document must be *negotiable* in form, i.e., issued "to bearer" or "to [Sam] or order."

2. The negotiable document must be in the possession of a *holder*. A holder is a person in possession of a bearer document, a person in possession of an order document issued to that person, or a person in possession of an order document issued to someone else and properly indorsed to the possessor. A document issued "to Sam or order" and merely signed on the back by Sam is indorsed "in blank." By indorsing "in blank," Sam converts the order document into a bearer document. A finder or a thief of a bearer document is a holder and has the power to transfer it, because the finder or thief appears to be rightfully in possession of the lost or stolen document. If Sam indorses an order document by writing "Deliver to Brenda, [signed] Sam," the indorsement is "special," and Brenda must also indorse before a person to whom Brenda transfers the document can be a holder.

3. The holder must give *value* for the negotiable document, i.e., must purchase it. Under Article 7, "value" means any consideration sufficient to support a simple contract. This includes a binding promise to be performed in the future. Thus, executory (not yet performed) as well as executed (performed) promises constitute "value" under Article 7.

4. The holder must purchase the document *in good faith* and must be *without notice of any defense or claim* of another person to it. A thief (or finder) of a bearer document is a holder, but cannot be in good faith (honest) because the thief knows he or she is claiming someone else's property. Furthermore, the thief is on notice of the true owner's claim to the document. However, if a thief is a holder and sells the document to an innocent person, that person can be a good faith holder who is without notice of the true owner's claim of ownership.

5. The negotiable document must be *negotiated* (transferred by delivery if a bearer document, or by delivery and indorsement if an order document) *in the regular course of business or financing*, and not, for example, by someone who does not reasonably appear to be in the business of trading in goods. Suppose that Joe, a postal employee, finds a bearer document made out for "50 boxcars of processed uranium" and sells the document to a metals dealer who knows that Joe is a mail carrier. It is not reasonable for the dealer to believe that Joe owns the document. The dealer will be denied the benefits of a due negotiation by anyone (such as the true owner of the uranium) who can prove that the negotiation by the mail carrier was outside the regular course of the metals-trading business.

What, again, are the benefits of a due negotiation? Essentially, there are two. First, the good faith purchaser receives from the seller of the document (1) title to (ownership of) the document and, consequently, the right to sell or otherwise dispose of it; and (2) title to the goods themselves—both free from many defenses or claims of other persons, for example, free from a previous owner's defense that the seller acquired the document by fraud [7-502]. Second, the good faith purchaser receives, as a result of the due negotiation, the direct obligation of the *issuer* (warehouse or carrier) to hold or deliver the goods according to the terms of the document, free from many of the issuer's own defenses. The issuer's defenses are discussed later in this chapter. All other transferees of negotiable documents (i.e., those failing to take a document by a "due negotiation"), and all transferees of *non*negotiable documents, are mere assignees who acquire only the rights, if any, of their transferors.

Typical Uses of Negotiable and Nonnegotiable Documents.   A business person needs to know how negotiable and nonnegotiable documents work in the actual distribution of goods so he or she can choose between the two kinds on the basis of business needs. Suppose that Sue, a wholesale seller of groceries, purchases 5000 cases of canned sardines to resell to supermarkets in her city. Having no storage facilities of her own, Sue deposits the sardines at Walt's Warehouse and is issued a nonnegotiable warehouse receipt (one made out "to Sue"). As a matter of routine record-keeping, Walt keeps a copy of the receipt so that his employees will know that the goods are to be delivered to Sue and no one else. If Sue instructs Walt to deliver the sardines to her, Walt will do so *without* requiring Sue to surrender the warehouse receipt. To prove he has delivered the sardines to the person entitled to them (here, Sue), all Walt needs to do is to have Sue "sign" for the goods when she receives them. Sue's signature, together with Walt's copy of the warehouse receipt, is proof of proper delivery.

But Sue does not want Walt to deliver the goods to her. She wants to *control* their delivery to the supermarkets for which the sardines are intended. Suppose Bert's Supermarket orders ten cases of sardines from Sue. Sue will write out a "delivery order" instructing Walt to release ten cases of sardines to Bert. Bert will pay Sue for the sardines, take the delivery order to Walt, and receive ten cases of sardines. Walt will require Bert to surrender the delivery order and sign for the ten cases so that Walt will have evidence that Sue gave the instruction and that Walt made a proper delivery. Sue still has the nonnegotiable warehouse receipt and the ability, therefore, to control the delivery of the other 4990 cases of sardines. Note, incidentally, that a delivery order is itself a document of title, and that Sue, not Walt, is its issuer. A delivery order is an example of a document of title that is "addressed to" a bailee.

Suppose instead that Sue had been issued a negotiable warehouse receipt (one made out "to bearer" or "to the order of Sue"). Sue could accomplish delivery of the ten cases to Bert by means of the negotiable warehouse receipt, but the delivery process would be awkward and slower. The reason is that Sue must *surrender* a negotiable document of title to Walt to receive the goods (or to have Bert receive them). Even though Sue wants only a partial delivery of the 5000 cases (here, ten cases), she still must actually deliver the document to Walt so that he can write on it that ten cases have been delivered. Thus, if Sue should later sell the negotiable document, a holder to whom it is duly negotiated will know that he or she is entitled only to 4990 cases. Negotiable documents are very suitable for transferring goods as a single unit to one buyer, but are inefficient for making partial deliveries to many different buyers.

Bailee's Obligations and Liabilities under Document. Regardless of whether a document of title is negotiable or nonnegotiable, the bailee (warehouse or carrier) issuing it has certain obligations and liabilities. However, some of these obligations and liabilities do vary according to whether the document is negotiable or nonnegotiable.

Warehouser's Obligation to Keep Goods Separate; Fungible Goods Exception. Ordinarily a bailee has a duty to return to the bailor the specific thing bailed or to dispose of it as the bailor instructs. Since many warehouses are large and very crowded, goods can easily be misplaced, and the warehouser might be unable to make a prompt delivery. To make locating goods easier and delivery more certain, the law requires that a warehouser keep separate from all other goods those covered by a particular warehouse receipt, unless the receipt provides otherwise [7-207].

There is an important exception for **fungible goods**. Goods are *fungible* if one unit (bushel of grain, barrel of oil) is, by nature or by usage of trade, the equivalent of any other unit of that size. Fungible commodities such as grain and oil often are purchased from many sellers and stored and transported in bulk. Because it would be impractical for a warehouse to keep each lot of fungible goods separate, they may be "commingled" (mixed or stored in one mass). A mass of commingled fungible goods, e.g., a mass of wheat or corn in a grain elevator, is owned in common by all the persons who contributed to the mass or who have acquired a share in it. The warehouser, e.g., the owner of a grain elevator, is liable to each owner of the mass for that person's share.

Obligation to Deliver to "Person Entitled under Document"; Excuse for Nondelivery. Unless excused by law, a warehouser or carrier must deliver goods to the person entitled to them by the terms of the document, and not to someone else [7-403]. Under a negotiable document, the "entitled person" is the holder. Suppose Sam delivers goods he owns to Carla, a carrier; that Carla issues a negotiable bill of lading to Sam; and that Sam intends to travel to the destination and pick the goods up when they arrive there. The negotiable bill will be made out "to bearer" or "to Sam or order," as Sam chooses. In either event, Sam is the holder as long as he possesses the bill of lading, and Carla must deliver the goods to him if he surrenders the bill and satisfies the bailee's lien (pays the shipping charges owed to the carrier).

Suppose the bill is made out "to bearer" and Sam sells the goods to Ben and delivers the bill to him. Ben is now the holder because he possesses a bearer document, and Ben is entitled to the goods.

May a finder or a thief of a bearer document be entitled to the goods? Suppose Sam loses the bearer document, Bill (a dishonest person) finds it, and before Sam can notify Carla Carrier of the loss, Bill takes the document to her and asks for the goods. Bill is the holder because he possesses a bearer document, and Bill appears to be entitled to the goods. If Carla *in good faith* delivers the goods to Bill, Carla cannot be held liable to Sam [7-404]. Carla acts in good faith if, as here, she lacks notice that Bill is not the true owner of the document. Bill's act of taking delivery will, of course, be wrongful as to Sam, and Sam will have a cause of action against Bill for damages or for the goods themselves.

Who is the holder of an order document of title? The answer depends on how the order document is indorsed. Suppose Sam's bill of lading is made out "to Sam or order." Then Sam sells the goods to Ben, indorses the bill "in blank" (i.e., merely signs his name on the back of the bill without naming anyone as indorsee), and delivers the bill to Ben. Ben is the holder because he possesses a properly indorsed "order bill" of lading, and Ben is entitled to the goods.

Since Sam's in-blank indorsement converts the order bill of lading into a bearer document, any finder or thief will be a holder. By making a "special" indorsement ("Deliver to Ben, [signed] Sam"), Sam can preserve the order character of the document and thereby make sure that only Ben will be the holder. Because Sam has identified Ben in the indorsement as the person to have the document, only Ben can be its holder, and only Ben is entitled to the goods. Now Ben must indorse the bill before anyone else can become the holder.

Under a nonnegotiable document (one issued "to Sam") the "person entitled under the document" is the person named in the bill to receive the goods *or* is someone to whom that person has issued a delivery order. Suppose Carla issues Sam a bill of lading made out "to Sam." Sam is the only person entitled to the goods. However, as explained earlier in this chapter, Sam can issue to Ben a delivery order (or assign the bill) and thereby instruct Carla to make a full or partial delivery to Ben. Ben thus becomes the person entitled to the goods.

In a number of situations the bailee is excused for failing to deliver the goods to the person entitled to them by the terms of the document, regardless of whether the document is negotiable or nonnegotiable. Four excuses are illustrated in the following paragraphs.

1. Delivery of the goods to a person with "paramount title," i.e., with superior ownership rights. Suppose Sue steals goods from Tom; delivers them to Walt, who issues Sue a negotiable warehouse receipt; and sells the goods to Brenda, indorsing and delivering the document to Brenda. In the meantime Tom, the true owner, learns where the goods are and talks Walt into releasing the goods to him. Then Brenda, a holder to whom the document was duly negotiated, presents it to Walt, who refuses to deliver any goods to her. Although Brenda is the person entitled under the document to receive the goods, Walt has no delivery obligation to her because Walt has delivered the goods to Tom who, because he is the true owner, has paramount title. The result would be the same if Walt, not knowing the situation, had by blind chance delivered the goods to Tom.

2. Damage to or loss of the goods for which the bailee is not liable. A tornado destroys a freight train and all the goods in it. The carrier is not liable because the loss was due to "an act of God," a source of loss beyond even a carrier's liability as an insurer.

3. A valid limitation of the bailee's liability. Carla Freight Lines, a common carrier, imposes a liability limit of $7 per pound for cloth it transports. Without declaring a higher value, Sam ships cloth containing gold thread. The cloth, worth $50 per pound, is ruined due to negligence of Carla's employees. Carla's liability is $7 per pound.

4. Rival claims to goods. As noted in Case 16.2, where two or more persons claim the same goods, the bailee is excused from delivery until the bailee has had a reasonable time to determine which of the rival claims is valid, or to bring a legal action to require the claimants to seek a court determination of their rights.

CASE 16.2   Bishop v. Allied Van Lines, Inc.
399 N.E.2d 698 (Ill. App. 1980)

Facts: Estelle Smiley owned $60,000 worth of household goods. She and her husband, R.V. Smiley, were named as joint shippers in a nonnegotiable bill of lading for the carriage and storage of the goods. After delivering the goods to the carrier, the Smileys began divorce proceedings. Mrs. Smiley then instructed Allied not to deliver the goods to either her or her husband until she gave further instructions. Later Allied delivered the goods to Mr. Smiley without receiving further instructions from Mrs. Smiley. She died, and her executor sued Allied for damages, alleging that Allied had made an improper delivery.

Question: Does Mrs. Smiley's estate have a cause of action against Allied for damages?

Answer: Yes. Allied's delivery to Mr. Smiley was improper.

Reasoning: The Smileys, as joint bailors under a nonnegotiable bill of lading that specified no consignee, were the persons entitled under the document to the goods. As *joint* bailors, they had the right, *acting together,* to control delivery of the goods. But Allied, knowing that Mrs. Smiley claimed the goods for herself, delivered them to Mr. Smiley alone. It is well known that a bailee is excused from delivery until he has had a reasonable time to determine the validity of adverse claims. By ignoring Mrs. Smiley's claim, Allied failed to observe reasonable commercial standards and therefore lacked good faith.

Liability for Bailee's Nonreceipt or Misdescription of Goods. Suppose that through mistake or fraud a warehouse (or a carrier) issues Sam a document of title without ever receiving goods from him, or issues a document that misdescribes goods, as where the document says, "5000 lb of lobster" but the warehouse (bailee) actually received 5000 lb of low-grade shark meat fit only for pet food. Then Sam sells the document to Ben, a good faith purchaser, who knows nothing of the warehouse's nonreceipt or misdescription. The warehouse is liable to Ben for any loss caused by the nonreceipt or misdescription [7-203; 7-301]. Good faith purchasers are protected in these circumstances *without regard* to whether the document is negotiable or nonnegotiable. However, if the document conspicuously and truthfully indicates that the issuer does not know whether the goods were received or conform to the description, the issuer is not liable to Ben. If the document says, for example, "contents, condition, and quality unknown," "this package said to contain ———," or "shipper's weight, load, and count," Ben is alerted to the nonreceipt or misdescription and should have looked into the situation before buying the document. Thus, the law protects warehouses and carriers who honestly do not know what was received and who give clear notice of that fact.

Liability for Altered or Forged Documents. Suppose Walt issues a negotiable or nonnegotiable warehouse receipt to Sam "for 50 typewriters" and without Walt's authority Sam alters the number to read "500" and sells the altered document to

Brenda. Brenda may enforce the receipt against Walt only in accordance with its "original tenor," i.e., in accordance with its original terms [7-208]. Walt is liable to Brenda for fifty typewriters. The result would be the same where a carrier issues a bill of lading that is later altered without the carrier's authority [7-306].

Suppose now that Sue steals a warehouse receipt form, makes it out to herself for fifty typewriters, and without delivering any typewriters to Walt's Warehouse, forges Walt's signature. Then Sue sells the forged document to Ben, who knows nothing of the forgery. Walt is not liable to Ben because he did not issue the warehouse receipt nor in any way authorize its issuance. The result is the same for any other forged document of title, whether negotiable or nonnegotiable.

Liability Where Document Is Lost or Missing.   Brenda purchases a properly issued document of title, but then it is lost, stolen, or destroyed. At Brenda's request, a court may order the bailee to deliver the goods to Brenda or to issue her a substitute document. The bailee may comply with the court's order without liability to anyone who might later present the missing document to the bailee and demand the goods [7-601]. If the missing document was negotiable, it might have been in bearer form when lost or stolen. To protect an innocent purchaser of a missing negotiable document, Brenda must "post security" (e.g., purchase a type of insurance) to indemnify (compensate) anyone who suffers loss as a result of buying the missing document. If the document was nonnegotiable, the court is permitted but not required to order Brenda to post security.

Conflicting Claims to Goods.   Occasionally a consignee, transferee, or even a holder to whom a document has been duly negotiated is not entitled to receive the goods and must seek a legal remedy from the transferor or someone else, or absorb the loss. Two examples follow.

Unauthorized Bailment.   Even good faith purchasers acquire no rights to goods that have been bailed with a carrier or a warehouse totally without the authority of the true owner [7-503]. Suppose Sue steals goods from Tom, stores them at Walt's Warehouse, and duly negotiates the warehouse receipt to Ben. Because a thief acquires no ownership rights in the stolen goods, Tom has "paramount title" and is entitled to the goods even if they have been delivered to Ben.

Change of Shipping Instructions under Nonnegotiable Bill of Lading.   Unless the bill of lading states otherwise, a carrier may, upon receiving proper instructions, deliver the goods to a person or destination other than that stated in the bill [7-303]. For example, a consignor on a nonnegotiable bill of lading is entitled to change the shipping instructions. Suppose Sam contracts to sell a printing press to Ben, delivers it to carrier Carla, and has the nonnegotiable bill made out "to Ben." Then Sam, in breach of his contract with Ben, sells the press to Howard and instructs Carla to deliver the press to Howard instead of Ben. Howard, if a buyer of the press in the ordinary course of business (i.e., if a good faith purchaser), is entitled to the press, and Ben is left to pursue Sam for a remedy.

TRANSFER OF TITLE AND RISK OF LOSS

The parties to a sales contract and their accountants often need to know exactly when title to (ownership of) goods passes from seller to buyer. Also, when goods are lost or damaged before reaching the buyer, the parties will need to know who must bear the risk of loss. The remainder of this chapter discusses how and when title and risk of loss are transferred from seller to buyer.

Transfer of Title   Accountants use the concept of title (ownership) as the basis for determining entries in the books of their clients. Consequently, the Article 2 title passage rules are especially significant to accountants whose clients deal in goods. On rare occasions, the parties to a sales contract will themselves want to know precisely when title to the goods passes from seller to buyer. Suppose that a state taxes goods and other personal property owned by its citizens. A citizen of such a state is not required to pay the tax until he or she actually owns the goods, i.e., until title passes. The exact time that a buyer receives title is governed by general rules of title passage contained in Article 2 of the UCC and discussed in the following paragraphs.

When Title Passes from Seller to Buyer.   Subject to two limitations, the parties to a sales contract may decide by explicit (clearly stated) agreement when and how title is to "pass" (be transferred) from seller to buyer. The limitations are: (1) The seller cannot pass title until the goods have been *identified to the contract*. That is, for title to pass, the goods must exist and must be designated as the ones intended for the particular buyer. (2) Any reservation of "title" by a seller who is extending credit to the buyer is to be considered as nothing more than the reservation of a "security interest" [2-401]. The unpaid seller's keeping such an interest does not prevent passage to the buyer of the basic rights of ownership commonly associated with the word title.

Where seller and buyer do not state when title is to pass, rules in Article 2 apply. Under those rules, if delivery is to be made *by moving the goods*, title passes when and where the seller completes performance with reference to *physical delivery* of the goods, even though a document of title is to be delivered at a different time and place [2-401]. So, if you order a sofa from a department store and the seller agrees to make a noncarrier delivery to you at your house, you get title to the sofa when the store completes the promised delivery.

But suppose you order a sofa from a manufacturer located in another state. Now the sofa will have to be delivered by a carrier; and the time at which the manufacturer "completes performance with reference to physical delivery" depends on whether you and the seller created a "shipment" or a "destination" contract. If, regarding delivery, the seller agreed merely to see to it that the sofa would be shipped, the seller has entered into a *shipment* contract, and title passes to you when the seller puts the sofa into the custody of the carrier. If, however, the seller specifically agreed to be responsible for actually getting the goods to the destination, he or she has entered into a *destination* contract, and title passes to you when the sofa actually arrives at the destination.

If delivery is to be made *without moving the goods*, other rules apply. Suppose you buy a sofa that the seller has stored in a warehouse in your city, and the seller is to make delivery by means of a document of title (warehouse receipt or delivery order). Title passes when and where the seller delivers the document to you. If no documents are to be delivered, title to identified goods passes at the time and place of contracting, as where you go to a department store, contract to purchase a sofa for cash or on credit, and take it home in your own vehicle.

When Title Revests in Seller. Normally a buyer has the right to inspect goods and to decide whether to accept or reject them. If, as in a shipment contract, the buyer receives title before seeing the goods and later rejects them, title "revests in" (goes back to) the seller regardless of whether the rejection was rightful or wrongful. Once the buyer accepts the goods, however, title will revest in the seller only if the buyer justifiably revokes acceptance—for example, after discovering a hidden defect. These revesting rules are intended to make clear who owns the goods when there is a dispute about their quality.

Transfer of Risk of Loss

Sometimes goods are lost, damaged, or destroyed without the fault of either buyer or seller. Yet one or the other will have to absorb the loss or try to collect from the person responsible for the loss, usually a carrier, warehouse, or insurer. The parties to a sales contract may decide for themselves which one will bear the risk of loss or how it will be shared. Where they remain silent as to risk, Article 2 assigns it by means of practical rules that tend to place the risk of loss upon the party (seller or buyer) who is likely to have actual control of the goods, who is likely to insure them as they move through the delivery process, or who is likely to be better able to prevent loss. Risk of loss is *never* assigned on the basis of who had title when the loss occurred, since a person can acquire title (legal ownership) long before learning of danger to the goods or acquiring sufficient control of them to take preventive measures.

The following rules apply where the parties to the sales contract are silent as to risk of loss. Some of the rules apply to situations involving a breach of contract; others apply to situations involving no breach.

Risk of Loss Where There Is No Breach of Contract. The risk of loss rules discussed here apply to situations involving goods shipped by carrier, goods held by a bailee, "pickup" and noncarrier delivery of goods, and goods subject to a right of the buyer to return them to the seller.

When goods are to be delivered by *carrier*, the assignment of risk depends on whether the parties have entered into a shipment or a destination contract. In a *shipment* contract, the risk of loss passes from the seller to the buyer when the seller properly delivers the goods to the carrier. In a *destination* contract, the risk passes to the buyer when the goods are presented at the stated destination in such a way as to enable the buyer to take delivery from the carrier [2-509(1)].

In commercial practice, the shipment contract, with its early risk-shifting feature, is considered the normal kind of contract for arranging a carrier delivery. A contract is a *shipment* contract where the buyer and seller agree merely that the goods are to be shipped, without stating that the seller is to be responsible for a safe delivery. For example, Ben telephones Sam the following order: "Please send five barrels of oil by express." Sam puts the barrels in the custody of a carrier. Ben and Sam have created a shipment contract because their words and actions have fallen short of putting the responsibility for a safe delivery on Sam. Sam is justified in feeling no further responsibility for the oil because, having put it in the custody of the carrier, he no longer controls it; his insurance probably no longer covers it; he might already have received payment; *and* he has no indication from Ben that Ben expects Sam rather than the carrier to guarantee the oil's safe arrival. For the less usual *destination* contract to arise—the kind that imposes risk of loss on the seller for the entire trip—the contract must contain specific language requiring the seller to remain responsible for the goods until they actually reach the buyer: "Please send five barrels of oil by express. I, Ben, will pay for them only upon their safe arrival."

Case 16.3 illustrates the difference in legal effect between a shipment and a destination contract.

CASE 16.3   Dana Debs, Inc. v. Lady Rose Stores, Inc.
319 N.Y.S.2d 111 (N.Y. Civ. Ct., N.Y. Co., 1970)

Facts: Dana Debs, a dress manufacturer in New York City, received a written order from Lady Rose Stores, Westbury, Long Island, for the purchase of 288 garments. The order instructed Dana Debs to "ship via Stuart" Express Co. Stuart Express picked up the shipment. Later Stuart informed the consignor Dana Debs that the entire shipment had been lost and that the bill of lading limited Stuart's liability to $1.00 per garment. Dana Debs then told the consignee Lady Rose of the loss and presented a bill for $1,756, the amount not paid by the carrier. Lady Rose refused to pay, and Dana Debs sued Lady Rose for $1,756.

Question: Must Lady Rose pay for the goods it never received?

Answer: Yes. Lady Rose must pay Dana Debs the $1,756.

Reasoning: Lady Rose Stores and Dana Debs created a "shipment" contract. Although Lady Rose chose the carrier, the transaction was a shipment contract because Lady Rose did not specifically require Dana Debs to remain responsible for the goods until they arrived at the destination. Lady Rose therefore acquired the risk of loss when Dana Debs put the goods into the custody of the carrier. To create the less usual destination contract, the parties must use language that clearly requires the seller to be responsible for the goods throughout the trip.

Seller and buyer can specify a shipment or destination contract in another way, by using standard shipping terms or instructions whose risk-of-loss consequences have been spelled out by Article 2. Suppose a St. Paul book manufacturer promises to ship 300 books to a New York buyer "FOB [free on board] St. Paul." Use of this expression creates a shipment contract, and the risk of loss shifts to the New York buyer when the seller puts the books into the possession of the carrier at St. Paul [2-319]. In contrast, a promise by the St. Paul seller to deliver books "FOB New York" would create a destination contract under which "the seller must at his own expense and risk transport the goods to that place and there tender delivery of them." Similarly, "FAS [free alongside a vessel at] the port of shipment" creates a shipment contract; and "FAS the port of destination" creates a destination contract.

The term *CIF* means that the price includes in a lump sum the *cost* of goods and *insurance* and *freight* to the named destination. The term *C&F* or *CF* means that the price includes the *cost* of goods and *freight* charges to the named destination. Despite the word "destination," these terms create a *shipment* contract [2-320]. If a New York buyer says to a St. Paul seller, "Ship 300 books CIF New York," the buyer in effect appoints the seller as an agent to purchase insurance and pay freight. By performing the CIF delivery obligations, the seller shifts the risk of loss to the buyer upon delivery of the goods to a carrier.

When goods are held by a *bailee* (warehouse or carrier) to be delivered *without being moved*, the risk of their loss may be passed from seller to buyer in any of three ways: (1) Risk of loss passes from the seller when the buyer receives a *negotiable* document of title covering the goods. (2) Where the buyer receives a *nonnegotiable* document of title, he or she has a reasonable time to present the document to the bailee. Until that reasonable time expires, the risk of the loss of the goods (*and* of any failure of the bailee to honor the nonnegotiable document) remains on the seller. (3) Sometimes goods are stored with a bailee who does not issue a document of title. Where there is no document of title, risk of loss passes from seller to buyer when the bailee is informed of *and acknowledges* the buyer's right to the goods [2-509(2)].

In *pickup* and *noncarrier deliveries,* the time that risk of loss shifts from seller to buyer depends on whether the seller is a merchant or a nonmerchant. Suppose that Bob, by telephone, buys a sofa from Sue. The parties are silent about risk of loss, but Sue says, "You may pick up the sofa any morning during the next three days." On the morning of the second day, Bob arrives to pick up the sofa only to learn that it was destroyed by fire the preceding night.

If Sue is a *merchant,* the risk is upon Sue, since the risk of loss does not pass from a merchant seller to the buyer until the buyer's *actual receipt* of the goods [2-509(3)]. This rule applies even though the buyer has made full payment and has been notified that the goods are at his or her disposal. The rule also applies where Sue is to make a noncarrier delivery to the buyer's premises. The reason for the rule is that a merchant is likely to have insurance coverage on goods as long as they remain in his or her possession, whereas the buyer is not likely to have insurance on goods not yet possessed.

If Sue is a *nonmerchant* seller, the risk is on Bob. Risk of loss passes from a nonmerchant seller to a buyer upon the seller's *tender* (offer) of delivery. The seller makes a tender of delivery by notifying the buyer that the goods are available to the buyer [2-503(1)]. Thus, where Sue is a nonmerchant, the risk of loss may pass to Bob *before* Bob actually receives the goods.

Some sales contracts give the buyer the right to return the goods to the seller even though the goods conform to the contract. There are two kinds of such sales. A seller may find the first kind, the "sale on approval," useful in breaking down sales resistance of reluctant consumers. Or a seller who wants to induce a merchant to stock a new product might resort to the second kind, the "sale or return."

A contract that grants a right to return conforming goods might not make clear which of the two kinds of sales was intended. Because the distinction is necessary to assign risk of loss, Article 2 provides a guide. If goods are delivered primarily for the buyer's use, the transaction is a *sale on approval,* and the risk of loss rests on the seller until the buyer accepts (i.e., approves) the goods [2-327].

If the goods are delivered primarily for resale, the transaction is a *sale or return,* and the risk passes from seller to buyer in accordance with the rules that apply to the particular delivery situation involved. Thus, where goods are shipped by carrier, the risk of loss passes from the seller to the buyer, either at the point of shipment or at the point of destination, depending on the kind of shipping terms used by the parties. If the buyer returns goods in accordance with the sale or return provision of the sales contract, the return is at the buyer's risk and expense.

Risk of Loss Where There Is Breach of Contract. The risk of loss usually falls totally or partially on the party who breaches a sales contract. Suppose a *seller* breaches by delivering defective goods. The risk of their loss remains on the seller until the seller *corrects* (cures) the defects (e.g., by replacing the goods) or until the buyer *accepts* them (takes them as his or her own) in spite of their defects. Where the buyer accepts goods, later learns of hidden defects, and then rightfully revokes the acceptance because of the defects, the buyer may *to the extent of any deficiency in his or her effective insurance coverage* treat the risk of loss as having rested on the seller from the beginning.

If the *buyer* breaches the contract before risk of loss has shifted to the buyer, the seller sometimes may, to the extent of any deficiency in his or her effective insurance coverage, treat the risk of loss as resting on the buyer for a commercially reasonable time before it normally would have shifted. Suppose Ben orders 500 radios from Sue for delivery by carrier at the end of 15 days, and Sue immediately *identifies* the 500 radios to be shipped to Ben. Ten days later Ben breaches the contract by canceling the order. Later on the day of the breach, the 500 radios are destroyed by fire, and just before the fire Sue's insurance expired. The risk of loss ordinarily would not pass to Ben until Sue puts the goods into the custody of the carrier for shipment to Ben. This has not occurred yet. However, because Sue *identified the goods to the contract* before Ben breached it, and because Sue had no insurance at the time of loss, the risk of loss is on Ben and Ben must pay for the radios in full. This is a much greater liability than the contract damages Ben would have to pay if the radios had not been destroyed.

TITLE OF GOOD FAITH PURCHASERS

As indicated earlier in this chapter, the law protects good faith purchasers of property, including good faith purchasers of goods. A person who buys stolen property acquires no rights in it because the thief had none. The true owner may recover the stolen property or its value from the purchaser, who, by possessing it, has committed the tort of conversion. But in many other circumstances the purchaser acquires ownership of property despite claims of prior owners.

To be entitled to take goods free from claims of aggrieved prior owners, a person must (1) be a "purchaser," (2) receive the goods in good faith, and (3) give value for the goods [2-403]. Good faith means honesty in fact in the transaction. If the purchaser is a merchant, good faith requires, in addition, conformance to reasonable commercial standards of fair dealing in the trade. In the law of sales, as in the law governing documents of title, a person gives value by giving any consideration sufficient to support a simple contract. Value therefore could consist of an executory (unperformed) promise.

The requirement that the protected person be a "purchaser" can be a source of confusion. In its ordinary sense "purchaser" means a person who buys something, and buying implies the giving of value. But the UCC adopts a broader, technical meaning of "purchaser." Under the UCC, a purchaser is a person who takes property by sale, negotiation, mortgage, *gift*, or any other voluntary transaction creating an interest in property. Thus, someone who receives a gift is a "purchaser," but is not a purchaser "for value" and consequently may lose the property to an aggrieved prior owner.

In two basic situations illustrated below, a good faith purchaser *for value* takes the goods free from the claims of prior owners: (1) where the seller acquired a "voidable" title from a prior owner, and (2) where a merchant-seller had no title but sold goods that were "entrusted" to him or her.

Where Seller Had Voidable Title

Suppose that Jane, a dealer in new and used garden equipment, fraudulently induced Tom to sell and deliver to her his garden tractor at a ridiculously low price. Tom intentionally transferred the tractor to Jane, but because of her fraud, she received only a voidable title. Consequently, Tom has a right to rescind (avoid, cancel) the contract and to get the tractor back from Jane. However, if Jane had sold the tractor to a good faith purchaser for value, Tom's only recourse would be a lawsuit against Jane for damages, and the purchaser would be entitled to the tractor itself, free from Tom's claim of fraud [2-403]. Thus, Jane, a person with *voidable* title, can confer on a good faith purchaser for value a better title than Jane had.

Where Goods Were Entrusted to Merchant-Seller

Suppose Jane's father loaned his own tractor to Jane, and without his knowledge she sold it to Bob, one of her customers. Jane's father has "entrusted" his tractor to Jane, a merchant. Any entrusting of goods to a merchant *who deals in goods of that kind* gives the merchant power to transfer all rights *of the entruster* to a "buyer in the ordinary course of business" [2-403]. Such a buyer is similar to a good faith purchaser for value and receives the same kind of protection. Here Bob may keep the tractor even though Jane had no title at all, but only possession resulting from the entrustment. Thus, as illustrated in Case 16.4, the law puts the risk of an unauthorized sale on the entruster, who is in a better position than the innocent purchaser to prevent loss.

CASE16.4   Carlsen v. Rivera
            382 So. 2d 825 (Fla. App. 1980)

Facts: Rivera leased a Mercedes Benz to James McEnroe who, Rivera knew, was the owner of an automobile dealership. Later, McEnroe fraudulently obtained title to the car in the name of his agency, Jimmy McEnroe Auto. McEnroe sold the car to Expo Rent-a-Car, Inc. Expo sold the car to Marlin Imports, Inc., which sold it to Carlsen. Eventually Rivera traced the car to Carlsen and sued Carlsen to recover possession of the car.

Question: Who is entitled to the car—Rivera or Carlsen?

Answer: Carlsen is entitled to the car.

Reasoning: Although McEnroe committed a type of theft by forging the title papers, he obtained possession of the car lawfully by means of the lease agreement. Thus, Rivera entrusted the car to McEnroe, a merchant who deals in goods of the kind that were entrusted. Accordingly, McEnroe had the power to transfer Rivera's ownership rights to Expo, a buyer in the ordinary course of business. Carlsen became a buyer in the ordinary course of business and is entitled to keep the car free from the claim of Rivera.

SUMMARY

This chapter has discussed the distribution of goods, transfer of title and risk of loss, and the title of good faith purchasers. Distribution of goods may involve some method of transporting goods, a place to store them, and the paperwork necessary to get them to the right person. Goods may be transported by common or private carrier. A common carrier serves the general public and has extensive liability for loss of or damage to the goods. A private carrier may choose with whom to contract and is liable as a bailee only, and not as an insurer.

Often, goods are stored in a public or private warehouse. Warehouses are liable as bailees for loss of or damage to goods during storage.

Documents of title are used to get goods from sellers to buyers. A document of title is a receipt, a contract of storage of carriage, and evidence of title to the goods. The two major kinds are the warehouse receipt and the bill of lading. Each may be negotiable or nonnegotiable. Negotiable documents differ from nonnegotiable ones in two main respects: what person is entitled to the goods, and what rights are acquired by a transferee of the document. The transferee of a nonnegotiable document is an assignee and receives only the rights that the transferor had. A holder of a negotiable document can receive more rights than the transferor had. A bailee has obligations and liabilities under a document of title, whether negotiable or nonnegotiable. Sometimes the bailee's obligations are excused, as where the bailee delivered the goods to a person with paramount title.

Sometimes a party to a sales contract needs to know when title to the goods passes from seller to buyer. If delivery is to be made by moving the goods, title passes when and where the seller completes physical delivery of the goods. If delivery is to be made without moving the goods, title passes when and where the seller delivers a document of title or, if no document is involved, at the time of contracting.

Where goods are lost or damaged, someone must bear the loss. Risk of loss is never assigned on the basis of who had title at the time of loss. Rather, rules of Article 2 assign the loss, mainly on the basis of who is in the better position to control or insure the goods. The risk-of-loss rules apply to situations involving goods shipped by carrier, goods held by a bailee, pickup and noncarrier deliveries, and goods subject to a right of the buyer to return them to the seller. Some of the rules apply where there is a breach of contract; others apply to situations involving no breach.

A good faith purchaser for value may take goods free from the claims of prior owners. Such a purchaser gets no rights in stolen goods, but does acquire ownership where the seller had voidable title or where a merchant-seller had been entrusted with the goods the purchaser bought.

REVIEW QUESTIONS

1. (a) How does the liability of a common carrier differ from the liability of a private carrier for loss of or damage to goods? (b) To what extent, if any, may a carrier limit its liability for loss of goods? (c) What liability does a warehouser have for loss of goods?

2. (a) Define "document of title." (b) What are its functions? (c) Explain the difference between a through bill of lading and a destination bill.

3. (a) What language would you use to create a negotiable document of title? A nonnegotiable document? (b) What are the two main differences in legal effect between a negotiable and a nonnegotiable document of title?

4. (a) What is required for a "due negotiation" of a document of title? (b) Explain whether a person who finds or steals a document of title can be its holder. (c) Explain whether a person who buys a stolen document can be a person to whom a document has been duly negotiated.

5. (a) What are the benefits of a due negotiation? (b) Under what circumstances would a nonnegotiable warehouse receipt be preferable to a negotiable one?

6. (a) Suppose a carrier releases goods to a person who has stolen the bill of lading. Is the carrier liable to the true owner of the document? Explain. (b) An earthquake breaks valuable antique bowls stored in a warehouse. Is the warehouser liable to the bailor? Why?

7. (a) Ben buys a document of title that has been altered to show a larger amount of goods than were left with the bailee. What is the bailee's liability to Ben? (b) Is the result different where the bailee left the document blank and someone later filled it in? Explain.

8. Under what circumstances will a good faith purchaser of a document *not* be entitled to the goods?

9. (a) What is the basis upon which the law assigns the risk that goods will be lost or damaged during delivery? (b) Does risk of loss pass from seller to buyer when the buyer receives title? Explain and illustrate.

10. (a) When does risk of loss pass under a shipment contract? Under a destination contract? (b) How do you know whether a contract is a shipment or a destination contract?

11. (a) When does risk of loss pass where goods are to be delivered without being moved? (b) When does risk of loss pass in a pickup or a noncarrier delivery? Why then? (c) When does risk of loss pass under contracts that give a buyer a right to return goods? (d) What effect does breach of contract have on passage of risk of loss?

12. (a) In the expression "good faith purchaser for value," why are the words "for value" necessary? (b) Illustrate the two basic situations in which a good faith purchaser for value takes goods free from the claims of prior owners.

CASE PROBLEMS

1. Fields, a cotton farmer, owned bales of cotton stored at Huntley's warehouse. Fields sold the warehouse receipts to Nowlin, a cotton buyer. Nowlin paid Fields with a check that "bounced" when Fields tried to cash it. At about this time Nowlin sold the warehouse receipts to a cotton processing company and immediately declared bankruptcy. Fields requested and received from a court an injunction restraining the cotton company from removing the cotton from the warehouse. The company appealed the granting of the injunction. If the appellate court decides that the company is entitled to the cotton, the court will "dissolve" the injunction. How could the company be entitled to the cotton?

2. Crawford sold two carloads of bulk fertilizer to Cunningham, who paid by check. Crawford delivered the fertilizer to M-K-T Railroad and received two nonnegotiable bills of lading. Cunningham promptly resold the fertilizer to Clock. A few days later Cunningham's bank returned the check to Crawford for lack of sufficient funds to cover it. The fertilizer was still in transit. Crawford certified to the railroad that he was the true owner and reconsigned the fertilizer to another customer. Having already paid Cunningham for the fertilizer, Clock sued the railroad and Crawford. Is the railroad liable to Clock? Is Crawford? Explain.

3. Hayward signed a contract to purchase a Revel Craft Playmate Yacht, on credit, from Postma. Postma was to install a number of accessories and deliver the boat to a slip on Lake Macatawa. Shortly after the boat arrived in the dealer's showroom, the boat was destroyed by fire. Neither Hayward nor Postma had insurance on the boat. However, the security agreement signed by Hayward provided that "buyer will at all times keep the goods fully insured against loss, damage, theft, and other risks." Was Hayward liable for the purchase price of the boat?

4. In September, Crump purchased from Lair a TV antenna and tower for $900, payable in monthly installments of $7.50 for 10 years. To secure the payments, Crump signed a contract stating that until the full purchase price was paid, title would remain with Lair, and Crump would not move the tower and antenna from his premises without the written consent of Lair. Lair installed the antenna system. The following June it was struck by lightning and severely damaged. Crump wanted to quit making payments. He argued that he had never been in possession of the antenna system because he was prohibited from moving it from his premises, that not being in possession he did not "receive" the system from Lair, and that therefore the risk of loss had not passed to him. Had Crump "received" the antenna system and, consequently, the risk of loss?

5. Klein, a wholesale jeweler, and Lopardo, a retail jeweler, had a long-standing business relationship whereby Klein would deliver jewels to Lopardo, who would sell the jewels to retail customers and pay Klein the agreed price. If unable to sell the jewels, Lopardo would return them to Klein. Approximately 10 days after Lopardo received two diamonds, they were stolen from his jewelry store. Who should bear the risk of loss?

CHAPTER 17

PERFORMANCE OF THE SALES CONTRACT

Chapter 15 discussed how the sales contract is created and what its terms are. Chapter 16 focused on how goods are distributed, when ownership passes to the buyer, and who must absorb any loss that occurs during and sometimes before shipment. This chapter deals with a related matter—specific acts of performance required of buyer and seller before they can be said to have fulfilled the obligations imposed by the sales contract. What these specific acts are for a particular contract depend in part on the kind of delivery process the parties agreed to.

As indicated in the preceding chapter, there are several ways of getting goods from seller to buyer. Although the legal principles that govern performance are similar for all of them, it will be helpful to consider for a moment the steps normally taken in carrying out a sale involving a delivery by carrier:

1. Bob (the buyer) orders a desk from Sue.
2. Sue identifies the desk to the contract (e.g., marks it "for Bob").
3. Sue begins physical delivery by putting the desk in the custody of the carrier. How this is done is discussed later in this chapter.
4. The desk arrives, and Bob inspects it.
5. If the desk has obvious defects, Bob rejects it.
6. Upon Bob's rejection, Sue attempts to "cure" (correct) the defects. If cure is timely, Bob must "accept" the desk or be liable for breach of contract.
7. If the desk arrives undamaged, Bob accepts it.
8. Where Bob accepts the desk and later discovers hidden defects, Bob revokes his acceptance and returns the desk to Sue.
9. If there is no basis for rejecting the desk, Bob pays the price, less any proper deductions for minor damage or shortages such as a missing drawer pull.

The steps of performance listed in the preceding paragraph, together with others to be discussed later in this chapter, may be involved in carrying out the obligations that a sales contract imposes on the seller and the buyer. The actual steps taken will depend on the kind of delivery process used and on the kinds of difficulties that the parties anticipated before contracting or that they face during performance.

The rest of this chapter focuses on the seller's obligation to deliver the goods, the buyer's obligation to accept and pay for the goods, and certain excuses for nonperformance that relieve both parties of their obligations.

PERFORMANCE: GENERAL CONCEPTS

Obligations of the Parties

Sellers and buyers "perform" by meeting the obligations they undertake by entering into a contract. In a sale of goods, the general obligation of the *seller* is to *transfer ownership* of the goods and *deliver* them as required by the contract. The obligation of the *buyer* is to *accept* the goods and *pay* for them as required by the contract [2-301]. The agreement of the parties, as supplemented or as limited by law, constitutes "the contract" by which the performance obligations of the parties are to be measured.

Meaning of "Tender"	Sellers and buyers meet their performance obligations by making a "tender" of performance. A **tender** is an offer of performance by one party that, if unjustifiably refused, places the other party in default and permits the tendering party to have remedies for breach of contract. For example, Bill orders a swing set from Sue to be delivered to his house on Tuesday. Late Monday night Bill decides to cancel the contract. Early Tuesday morning, Sue's truck arrives at Bill's house with the swing set in good condition. Sue has made a tender of delivery. If Bill refuses to accept the swing set, he will be in breach of the contract.
The Perfect Tender Rule	If the goods (or the seller's tender of delivery) fails *in any respect* to conform to the contract, the buyer may reject the goods (or the tender) [2-601]. This rule, called the "perfect tender rule," protects the buyer from having to track down missing documents, from having to accept faulty documents (such as a warehouse receipt that lacks a necessary indorsement), or from having to argue with the seller about the sufficiency of an incomplete performance (such as a truckload of cotton that is missing one bale). The protection provided by this rule is especially important to buyers who are geographically distant from sellers. However, to prevent buyers from taking undue advantage of the right to reject, the perfect tender rule has certain exceptions that are discussed later in this chapter.

SELLER'S OBLIGATION TO DELIVER

How Seller Meets the Delivery Obligation	A seller meets his or her obligation to deliver goods by making a tender of delivery. Tender of delivery requires that the seller (1) put and hold *conforming* goods at the buyer's disposition, and (2) give the buyer any notification reasonably necessary to enable the buyer to take delivery [2-503(1)]. Goods are "conforming" when they are in accordance with the obligations under the contract, including any warranty (assurance) as to the quality of or title to the goods. The seller's tender must be at a reasonable hour, and if the tender is of the goods themselves (as opposed to a tender of a document of title), the seller must keep the goods available for the period reasonably necessary to enable the buyer to take possession. Unless otherwise agreed, the buyer must furnish facilities reasonably suited to the receipt of the goods.
Tender Requirements for Common Types of Delivery	Specific acts required for an effective tender of delivery vary according to the kind of delivery agreed to by the parties to the sales contract or imposed by the UCC where the parties were silent as to delivery. Once the kind of delivery has been established, the specific acts required for an effective tender can be determined by applying the Code sections on tender. Tender requirements for some common types of delivery are discussed in the following paragraphs.

Delivery Involving No Carrier. Often delivery occurs at the seller's place of business. Suppose, for example, that Bob signs a contract to buy from Sue a particular motorboat from her stock of boats, that it is to be specially equipped from Sue's stock of accessories, and that the contract says nothing about the time and place of delivery. Sue must make delivery within a reasonable time [2-309]. Since Sue is a dealer who has a place of business, and since the boat and accessories are located there, the place for delivery is Sue's place of business [2-308]. Under Section 2-503(1), Sue may tender delivery by notifying Bob within a reasonable time that the boat is ready for pickup at her place of business.

Delivery might involve a bailee such as a warehouse. Where goods are in the possession of a bailee and are to be delivered without being moved, the seller can fulfill the tender obligation by offering a negotiable document of title covering the goods or by the seller's procuring the bailee's acknowledgment of the buyer's right to have the goods [2-503(4)]. *If the buyer does not object,* the seller can make a tender by offering a *non*negotiable document of title or a written instruction (such as a delivery order) to the bailee to release the goods to the buyer. Recall from Chapter 16, however, that a seller who tenders a nonnegotiable document or written instruction retains the risk of loss of the goods, and the risk that the bailee will not honor the document or instruction, until the buyer has a reasonable time to present it to the bailee. Furthermore, the bailee's refusal to honor the nonnegotiable document or written instruction *defeats* the seller's tender (i.e., the bailee's refusal means that the seller has made no effective tender). All documents required for making a tender must be in correct form.

Delivery Involving a Carrier.   Unless displaced by a contrary agreement, rules of Article 2 govern tender in common types of deliveries involving a carrier. Under a shipment contract (defined in Chapter 16), the seller fulfills his or her tender obligation by completing four steps: (1) putting conforming goods in the possession of a carrier, (2) making a reasonable contract for their transportation, (3) obtaining and promptly delivering or tendering in due form any document necessary to enable the buyer to obtain possession of the goods, and (4) promptly notifying the buyer of the shipment [2-504]. (The costs of shipping will be included in the price of the goods, or the buyer will pay the shipping charges separately.)

If the seller fails to notify the buyer of the shipment, or fails to make a proper contract for the transportation of the goods, the buyer may reject the goods—*but only if the seller's failure causes the buyer a material delay or loss* [2-504]. These rules relating to shipment contracts thus place upon the seller the responsibility for arranging suitable transportation, but relax the perfect tender rule to protect the seller from harmless error in making the arrangements. Suppose that Ben, a Michigan groceryman, orders 500 crates of grapefruit from Sue, a Florida grapefruit seller. Sue properly ships conforming grapefruit by rail to Ben, but forgets to notify Ben of the shipment. When the grapefruit arrives, the stationmaster immediately notifies Ben of its arrival. Ben suffers no harm from Sue's failure to notify him of the shipment and cannot reject the grapefruit.

Under a destination contract, the seller fulfills the tender obligation by completing three steps: (1) putting and holding conforming goods at the destination for the buyer's disposition, (2) giving the buyer any notification reasonably necessary to enable the buyer to take delivery, and (3) tendering any required documents in correct form [2-503(3)].

Seller's Cure of Improper Delivery   A seller may have a right to "cure" (correct) an improper tender or an improper delivery. Suppose Sue sells a power saw to Ben and promises delivery on or before June 1. Sue delivers the saw on May 25, but Ben rejects it because some parts are missing. Sue may give notice of her intention to cure the nonconforming delivery and then *within the contract time* may make a conforming delivery [2-508]. Even where Sue has taken back the nonconforming goods and refunded the purchase price, she may effect cure if she can do so *before the time for performance expires*. The time for performance is the time stated in the contract (here, June 1); if no time was stated, the time for performance is a reasonable time, as in Case 17.1 below.

Sometimes, to reduce the harmful effects of the buyer's surprise rejection of the goods, the UCC gives the seller the right to cure a defective tender *after* the time set for performance. Where a buyer rejects a nonconforming tender that the seller had *reasonable grounds to believe would be acceptable* with or without money allowance, the seller, upon notifying the buyer "seasonably" (in a timely manner), may have a further reasonable time to substitute a conforming tender. For example, suppose Brenda orders Brand X galvanized pipe from Sam for delivery at noon on November 1. At the appointed hour Sam delivers Brand Y pipe of the same kind and quality for the same price. If Brenda rejects the Brand Y pipe, and if Sam reasonably believed that the delivery of Brand Y pipe would be acceptable, Sam is entitled to a further reasonable time to cure the nonconformity.

CASE 17.1

Stephenson v. Frazier
28 UCC Rep. 12 (Ind. App. 1980)

Facts: Stephenson purchased a modular (mobile) home from Frazier, who was to install a septic system and construct a foundation as a part of the installation process. During installation, disputes arose as to the quality of the home and the foundation. Frazier admitted that the home had defects but insisted that the foundation was sound. When Frazier refused to alter the foundation, Stephenson ordered Frazier off the land and refused to allow any further installation work. Frazier responded with a letter stating he was "ready, willing and able" to install the septic system and repair the home. The letter did not mention the foundation. Stephenson brought suit to rescind (cancel) the contract.

Question: Was Stephenson entitled to rescind the contract?

Answer: Yes, if he did not improperly prevent Frazier's performance. As to the home, Stephenson improperly interfered, but rescission as to the foundation may have been rightful.

Reasoning: The home falls within the meaning of goods. The UCC grants a seller of goods the right to cure a defective performance upon notifying the buyer of the seller's intention to do so, if cure can be accomplished before the time set for performance has expired. Here Frazier had a reasonable time after delivery of the mobile home to complete installation. Because premature, Stephenson's interference was wrongful as to the home. However, the construction of the foundation, which is not within the meaning of "goods," is governed by the common law of contracts. Under that law, Stephenson had a right to rescind if Frazier (the seller) committed fraud in inducing, or materially breached, the contract. Whether Frazier did so is a question for the trial court to decide.

BUYER'S OBLIGATION TO ACCEPT AND TO PAY

Where the seller has properly tendered conforming goods, the buyer is obliged to accept them and pay the price. However, the buyer's obligations are conditioned on a right to inspect the goods. Where a tender of delivery does not conform to the contract, the buyer may have a right to reject the goods or revoke any acceptance he or she might have made and to recover any payment.

Meaning and Effect of Buyer's Acceptance

Acceptance of goods means that the buyer, in accordance with the contract, takes as his or her own the goods that the seller has appropriated (set aside) for the contract. The buyer may accept by words, action, or silence when it is time for the buyer to speak. Acceptance may occur in a variety of ways: for example, by the buyer's telling the seller that the goods are conforming or that he or she will take or retain them in spite of their nonconformity; by the buyer's failure to make an effective rejection; or by the buyer's doing some act inconsistent with the seller's ownership, such as reselling the goods or incorporating building materials into a building [2-606].

As illustrated by Case 17.2, the legal effect of acceptance is that the buyer becomes obligated to pay the contract price [2-607]. Moreover, a buyer who has accepted a defective tender is *barred from any remedy*, including a remedy for breach of warranty, unless the seller is *notified* of the defect within a reasonable time after it has been or should have been discovered. Notice is required so that the seller may take steps to cure a defective performance or, where defective goods are alleged to have caused harm, so that the seller may adequately prepare for negotiation or defense of a lawsuit. What constitutes "reasonable" notice depends on the facts of the case. An injured consumer who is unaware of the requirement to notify the seller may be allowed more time to give notice than a merchant would be.

CASE 17.2 Johnson v. Holdrege Cooperative Equity Exchange
293 N.W.2d 863 (Neb. 1980)

Facts: Johnson delivered 10,000 bushels of wheat to Holdrege. According to Johnson, Holdrege agreed to buy the wheat at market price plus a premium based on the actual protein content of Johnson's wheat. The alleged agreement was oral. Later, Holdrege refused to pay an "individual" premium (one based on the wheat that Johnson delivered) but offered instead a "station average" premium based on the average protein content of all wheat purchased during the season. Since Johnson's wheat had a higher than average protein content, Johnson brought suit for breach of contract. The trial court held that the UCC statute of frauds barred enforcement because the oral contract was for the sale of goods valued at more than $500.

Question: Was the oral contract (including the promise to pay an individual premium) unenforceable?

Answer: Not necessarily. Holdrege may have "accepted" the wheat and thus may have satisfied the statute of frauds.

Reasoning: The UCC provides that the buyer's acceptance of goods is one way to satisfy the statute of frauds. One way to "accept" goods is for the buyer to do any act inconsistent with the seller's ownership. Holdrege's testing the grain by single loads and commingling it with other wheat (making Johnson's wheat unrecoverable) were acts consistent with Holdrege's ownership, not Johnson's. Holdrege's altering the condition of Johnson's wheat by mixing it with grain of lower protein content also may be an act inconsistent with Johnson's ownership and may amount to an acceptance under the UCC. Whether acceptance occurred is a question for the jury. If it did occur, the contract, including the oral promise of the buyer to pay an individual premium, is enforceable.

Buyer's Right to Inspect the Goods

The buyer may make a reasonable inspection of the goods to see whether they conform to the contract. Usually, the right to inspect may be exercised before payment or acceptance. Accordingly, when the seller is required or authorized to send goods to the buyer, the buyer may take custody of the goods for the purpose of inspection without being considered to have accepted them. With rare exceptions, no agreement by the parties can displace the right of inspection [2-513, comment 1].

Even though the right to inspect usually may be exercised before payment, the buyer can be required by contract to pay first and inspect later. For example, unless otherwise agreed, CIF, COD ("collect on delivery"), cash against documents, and similar contract clauses require payment *before* inspection. Upon inspection after payment, the buyer may, of course, reject nonconforming goods and have appropriate remedies such as damages. And even where the contract requires the buyer to make payment before inspection, the buyer may withhold payment if the nonconformity is obvious without inspection [2-512]. The buyer is not required, for example, to pay for goods that obviously are not the goods ordered.

Buyer's Options on Improper Delivery

Within limits imposed by the Code, a buyer may reject an improper tender or an improper delivery of goods. In some situations the buyer may revoke acceptance of defective goods.

Rejection of Goods.   In general, a buyer may reject goods that do not conform to the contract. Specifically, the buyer may "(*a*) reject the whole; or (*b*) accept the whole; or (*c*) accept any commercial unit or units and reject the rest" [2-601]. A "commercial unit" is an amount of goods that in business practice is treated as a single whole for purposes of sale, and whose division would materially impair its value or character (e.g., a machine, a bale of cotton, a carload of wheat).

The rejection must be made within a reasonable time after delivery or tender of the goods, and the buyer *must seasonably* (in a timely manner) *notify* the seller of the rejection [2-602]. In addition, the buyer must specify the defects upon which he or she bases the rejection, if the defects are ascertainable by inspection [2-605]. The requirement that defects be specified is to protect the seller's right to cure any curable defects. A buyer who merely rejects a delivery without stating any real objections to it may be acting in commercial bad faith, seeking only to get out of a deal which has become unprofitable. Such conduct is not permitted. A buyer's failure to reject in accordance with Code rules results in acceptance and liability for payment.

The buyer's right of rejection is limited by important Code rules regarding installment contracts. An **installment contract** is one that requires or authorizes the delivery of goods in separate lots which are to be separately accepted. The buyer may reject a nonconforming installment (delivery of goods) *only if* the nonconformity *substantially impairs* the value of that installment *and cannot be cured* [2-612]. Suppose, for example, that Ben, a skilled furniture maker, uses 1000 board feet of high-quality walnut lumber each week. To meet his production needs he orders 10,000 board feet to be delivered in ten weekly installments of 1000 board feet each at 8:00 A.M. sharp each Monday morning. Sue, the seller, delivers the first three installments, but the fourth lot, delivered at 7:00 A.M. Monday morning, is so knotty that Ben cannot use it. Ben may reject the fourth installment because the nonconformity substantially impairs its value to him—but *only if* Sue cannot make a substitute delivery of conforming lumber by 8:00 A.M.

The installment-contract restriction on a buyer's right to reject goods is a second exception to the perfect tender rule. The purpose of the exception is to prevent a buyer from, for example, seizing on a trivial defect as an excuse to reject goods that are in fact substantially what was ordered. In a shipment contract, the goods ordinarily will be at the buyer's place of business when rejected. The seller might be hundreds of miles away. If the seller had to prove that the goods and their tender were perfect, considerable expense could be involved, and the buyer would be in a position to threaten rejection to force a lower price. To protect the seller, the Code therefore prohibits the buyer from rejecting goods unless the defect substantially impairs the value of the installment and cannot be cured. To protect the buyer, the Code permits the buyer to have damages for any defect, no matter how trivial.

Where one or more installments are so defective that they substantially impair the value of the whole contract (and cannot be cured), the buyer may cancel the contract (and have other remedies such as damages). However, if the buyer accepts a nonconforming installment without seasonably notifying the seller of cancellation, or brings suit as to past installments only, or demands performance of future installments, the buyer loses the right to cancel the breached contract (i.e., the buyer reinstates it).

An installment contract *may* require accurate conformity in quality as a condition to the seller's right to the buyer's acceptance, *but only if there is a real need* for such conformity. To be enforceable, a provision requiring accurate conformity in quality must have some basis in reason and must avoid imposing hardship by surprise. A requirement of strictly accurate conformity might be enforceable in a purchase of surgeon's tools or delicate parts for a space shuttle, but not in a purchase of waste logs to be processed into chipboard.

Revocation of Acceptance.   Suppose Ben accepts goods and later discovers they are defective. In two principal kinds of situations, Ben may have a right to revoke his acceptance of goods whose nonconformity substantially impairs their value to him [2-608]. He may revoke his acceptance (1) where he accepted the goods on the reasonable assumption that the substantial nonconformity would be cured, and it has not been seasonably cured; or (2) where his acceptance was reasonably induced either by the difficulty of discovering the substantial nonconformity before acceptance or by the seller's assurances that the defect would be cured. Ben may revoke as to the entire lot of goods accepted or as to any subdivision of the lot that constitutes a commercial unit. Revocation of acceptance must occur within a reasonable time after Ben discovers or should have discovered the substantial nonconformity. Ben may not revoke if the goods have undergone substantial change for reasons *other than* their own defects, such as Ben's failure to store them properly. Case 17.3 illustrates the meaning and legal effect of "substantial impairment."

CASE 17.3   Oberg v. Phillips
615 P.2d 1022 (Okla. App. 1980)

Facts: Oberg bought a new Chevrolet from Phillips and soon discovered numerous defects in engine performance, body, steering, paint, and accessories. During the first three months of Oberg's ownership, the car was in the seller's shop for 30 whole days and parts of 12 to 15 more days. After an unsuccessful repair session near the end of the first two months, Oberg gave Phillips a specific amount of time to repair the car. Seller did not comply. Oberg then, in writing, revoked his acceptance of the car and sued Phillips for breach of contract. Phillips contended that all of the defects were trivial and that Oberg therefore had no basis for revoking his acceptance.

Question: Did Oberg have a legal basis for revoking his acceptance?

Answer: Yes.

Reasoning: A buyer may revoke acceptance of defective goods if their defects substantially impair their value to the buyer and are not seasonably cured. Numerous uncorrected defects, even if each could be considered trivial, can have a cumulative effect that substantially impairs the value of the goods to the buyer. It is the combination of defects and the inability of the buyer to obtain proper adjustments within a reasonable time that constitutes a substantial impairment. Here there were dozens of defects and many unsuccessful attempts to cure them. The seller contended that it had the one-year warranty period to correct the defects. However, the right to cure is not a limitless one to be controlled by the will of the seller, but should approximate the expectations of both parties. Therefore, cure must be "seasonable," i.e., must be done within the time agreed or within a reasonable time.

Buyer's Obligation to Pay for Goods Accepted

Bob Buyer meets his obligation to pay the price by making payment in accordance with the contract. If the parties have not stated how payment is to be made, Bob may pay in any customary manner, unless the seller demands payment in legal tender (money) and gives any extension of time reasonably necessary to procure it [2-511]. This rule protects Bob from a surprise demand for cash. For the protection of sellers who accept checks, however, a buyer's payment by check is only a conditional payment and is defeated by refusal of the bank upon which the check was drawn to pay it.

If the parties have not stated the time and the place for payment, either of the following rules applies: (1) Payment is due at the time and place at which the buyer is to receive the goods; or (2) where delivery is to be made by means of documents of title, payment is due at the time and place at which the buyer is to receive the documents, regardless of where the goods are to be received. Both of these rules are subject to any right of the buyer to inspect the goods before payment.

If goods are lost in transit, and if the risk of loss has shifted to the buyer, the buyer is obligated to make payment at the time and place at which he or she was to receive the goods. Suppose that a foreign seller ships goods to a New York buyer under a CIF contract and they are lost at sea. A CIF contract places the risk of loss on the buyer when the seller properly puts the goods in the custody of the carrier. Because the buyer acquires the risk of loss when the carrier receives the goods, the buyer must pay for them despite their nonarrival and must rely on the insurance provided for in the CIF contract.

Where the parties have agreed to an extension of credit, the credit term governs the time, place, and manner of payment, to the extent that the credit term discusses these matters.

EXCUSE FOR NONPERFORMANCE OR SUBSTITUTE PERFORMANCE

If the performance of a contractual obligation becomes more burdensome than the obligated party anticipated, that party might ask to be excused from performance. In general, the parties to a contract are excused from their performance obligations when performance has been rendered impossible or unreasonably burdensome by circumstances beyond the contemplation of the parties at the time of contracting.

Excuse for Nonperformance   Article 2 adopts "commercial impracticability" as the main basis for excusing nonperformance of obligations under a sales contract. The article also provides rules that apply where an agreed method of payment or delivery fails and a substitute method is sought by the aggrieved (injured) party.

Commercial Impracticability.   Unless the seller has assumed a greater obligation, he or she is excused for delay in delivery or for nondelivery of goods if performance has been made impracticable by an unexpected occurrence of the type discussed in the next paragraph [2-615]. The seller is also excused if the agreed performance has been made impracticable because of an applicable foreign or domestic governmental regulation or order. Suppose that a manufacturer agrees to make and sell sophisticated electronics equipment to a buyer in a foreign country. If the foreign buyer's government later unexpectedly forbids importation of such equipment, the manufacturer is excused from performance.

The drafters of Article 2 explain the meaning of *commercial impracticability* as follows:

Increased cost alone does not excuse performance unless the rise in cost is due to some unforeseen contingency which alters the essential nature of the performance.

Neither is a rise or a collapse in the market in itself a justification, for that is exactly the type of business risk which business contracts made at fixed prices are intended to cover. But a severe shortage of raw materials or of supplies due to a contingency such as war, embargo, local crop failure, unforeseen shutdown of major sources of supply, or the like, which either causes a marked increase in cost or altogether prevents the seller from securing supplies necessary to his performance, is within the contemplation of this section [2-615, comment 4].

Where commercial impracticability only partially impairs the seller's capacity to perform, the seller must allocate production and deliveries among his or her customers in a fair and reasonable manner. Regardless of the degree of impairment, the seller will *not* be excused from performance unless he or she seasonably notifies the buyer that there will be a delay or nondelivery. If there is a partial impairment, the seller must also inform the buyer of any production or delivery quota to which the buyer is entitled.

In response to the seller's notice of a material delay or an allocation of goods, the buyer may, by written notification to the seller, elect to do one of the following: (1) terminate (and thereby discharge) any unperformed portion of the contract, or (2) modify the contract by agreeing to take the available quota [2-616]. The buyer may terminate the whole of an installment contract if the seller's deficiency substantially impairs the value of the whole contract. Where a seller is excused from performance because of unforeseen circumstances, the buyer is also excused, despite any agreement to the contrary.

The following case deals with the meaning of commercial impracticability.

CASE 17.4   Maple Farms, Inc. v. City School District
352 N.Y.S.2d 784 (N.Y. Sup. Ct. 1974)

Facts: Maple Farms agreed to supply the School District with milk for the school year 1973–1974. By December 1973, the price of raw milk was 23% higher than the price of raw milk in June when the contract was made. Maple Farms would lose $7,350 if required to supply milk at the December price. The School District refused to release Maple Farms from the contract. Faced with losses on similar contracts with other school districts, Maple Farms brought an action for a declaratory judgment, alleging that the performance of the contract was made impracticable by the occurrence of events not contemplated by the parties.

Question: Should Maple Farms be released from the contract?

Answer: No. Performance of the contract is not impracticable.

Reasoning: Performance of a contract will not be excused on the ground of commercial impracticability merely because loss will result from its performance. Performance is commercially impracticable where a totally unexpected circumstance arises. Here, Maple Farms should have foreseen the rise in the price of raw milk. Its president had ten years' experience in bidding on school district milk contracts and was or should have been aware of the following facts: (1) The price of raw milk had risen 10% during the year before this contract was signed. (2) There is a general inflation of prices in this country and always a chance of crop failure. (3) For many years the price of milk established by the Department of Agriculture has varied. Having reason to know these facts, and having failed to put an exculpatory (protective) clause into the contract, Maple Farms must be held to have assumed the risk of the price increase. Requiring Maple Farms to perform despite the losses is consistent with the School District's purpose in making the contract—to guard against fluctuation in the price of milk as a basis for the school budget.

Casualty to Identified (Specific) Goods.   Sometimes a contract is for sale of a specific item or lot of goods that is destroyed or damaged before the buyer actually receives it. Suppose Sarah Seller has on display a dozen Brand X refrigerators of a discontinued model. Eleven are green and one is yellow, and no others of that model are available to Seller. Bob Buyer makes clear that he needs the yellow refrigerator because it fits the color scheme of his kitchen. Bob buys the yellow refrigerator, but before Sarah can deliver it, it is destroyed by fire. Is Sarah liable to Bob for failure to deliver the yellow refrigerator?

The answer is "No." Where the contract requires for its performance specific goods that were identified when the contract was made, and the goods suffer casualty (damage) without fault of either party *before* the risk of loss passes to the buyer, then if the loss is *total*, the contract is *avoided*, i.e., neither seller nor buyer has any enforceable rights under the contract. If the loss is *partial*, the buyer may nevertheless demand inspection and at his or her option either treat the contract as avoided or accept the goods with due allowance from the contract price, but without any other right against the seller. Here, since the seller is a merchant, the risk of loss does not pass to the buyer until he or she actually receives the goods. Because the loss of the yellow refrigerator is total, Sarah Seller has no obligation to tender the refrigerator, and Bob has no obligation to pay for it. In contrast, if Bob had purchased *a* refrigerator of the discontinued model (instead of specifying the yellow one) Sarah would be obliged to tender a Brand X refrigerator and Bob would be obliged to accept it and make payment. However, if Sarah's entire stock of the discontinued model had been destroyed, she would be excused from performance on the ground of impracticability.

Excuse for Substitute Performance

Sometimes the parties to a sales contract agree to a particular method of delivery or payment. What happens if the agreed method of *delivery* fails—for example, if an agreed type of carrier becomes unavailable without the fault of either party? The parties are required to use a commercially reasonable substitute carrier, if one is available [2-614]. If there is no commercially reasonable substitute for the agreed method of delivery, both parties may be excused from their performance obligations on the ground of impracticability.

Where the agreed means or manner of *payment* fails because of domestic or foreign governmental regulation, the seller is required to make delivery only if the buyer provides a payment that is commercially a substantial equivalent. Suppose that

Sarah Seller contracts to sell refrigerators to a foreign buyer, and that the buyer's government devalues its currency to one-tenth the value it had at the time of contracting. Sarah Seller is entitled to a payment substantially equivalent to the payment agreed upon and may refuse delivery if the substantial equivalent is not forthcoming. Where the buyer has already taken delivery of the goods, payment in accordance with the regulation discharges the buyer's obligation unless the regulation is discriminatory, oppressive, or predatory.

The following case deals with a controversy over extra expense involved in a substitute method of delivery.

CASE 17.5 Jon-T Farms, Inc. v. Goodpasture, Inc.
21 UCC Rep. 1309 (Tex. App. 1977)

Facts: Jon-T agreed to sell 5,000 tons of grain sorghum to Goodpasture. Jon-T agreed to pay the cost of (a) transporting the sorghum from Jon-T's elevator to a nearby railhead and (b) loading it onto railroad cars. Due to a shortage of railroad cars, Jon-T could not complete deliveries on time. The parties then agreed that Goodpasture would use its own trucks to haul sorghum from Jon-T's elevator to Goodpasture's warehouse. Later, because of a sharp increase in the market price of sorghum, Jon-T refused to deliver any more sorghum at the original contract price. Goodpasture sued Jon-T for breach of contract. As a part of the damages claimed, Goodpasture sought $2,558.69 for use of its trucks in transporting 24 loads of the grain.

Question: Was Goodpasture entitled to the $2,558.69?

Answer: Yes.

Reasoning: Where the agreed method of transportation becomes unavailable, the seller must use and the buyer must accept delivery by any commercially reasonable substitute means. This the parties did by agreement. However, the UCC does not say who must bear any extra expense. Here, Jon-T must do so because the contract obliged it to ship the grain "FOB West Texas TCP Area." Goodpasture would not have incurred the transportation expense if Jon-T had performed according to the contract terms.

SUMMARY

The obligation of the seller is to transfer and deliver the goods, and that of the buyer to accept and pay for them. The seller meets the delivery obligation by making a tender of delivery. Tender requires that the seller put and hold conforming goods at the buyer's disposition and give the buyer any notice reasonably necessary to enable the buyer to take delivery.

Within limits imposed by the Code, the buyer may reject a tender that fails in any respect to conform to the contract. The seller has a right to cure an improper tender before, and sometimes after, the time for performance has expired. In an installment contract, the buyer may reject a nonconforming installment or cancel the contract only if the nonconformity substantially impairs the value of that installment or if the contract and the nonconformity cannot be cured.

The buyer's obligation to accept and pay is conditioned on his or her right to inspect the goods. Acceptance occurs in a number of ways, for example, where the buyer signifies that the goods are conforming. Upon acceptance, the buyer becomes obligated to pay the contract price. In two main situations, the buyer may revoke acceptance of nonconforming goods. Unless otherwise agreed, the buyer may pay by any customary means or any customary manner. The seller may require payment in money but must give any extension of time reasonably necessary for the buyer to procure such a payment.

The parties may be excused from their performance obligations if the agreed performance has been made commercially impracticable by an unforeseen occurrence that alters the essential nature of the performance. Where an agreed method of payment or delivery fails, the aggrieved party may be entitled to a substitute performance.

REVIEW QUESTIONS

1. In a contract for the sale of goods, what are the general performance obligations of the buyer and the seller?

2. (**a**) What is the meaning of tender? (**b**) What is the reason for the perfect tender rule?

3. (**a**) In general, how does a seller fulfill the seller's tender obligation? (**b**) What specific acts are required for a seller to fulfill the tender obligation in a shipment contract?

4. In what kinds of situations may a seller "cure" an improper tender or delivery?

5. (**a**) What constitutes acceptance of goods? (**b**) What is the legal effect of acceptance?

6. (**a**) How is the buyer's right to inspect goods related to his or her obligation to accept goods? (**b**) How does a COD clause in a sales contract affect the buyer's right to inspect the goods?

7. (**a**) In general, under what circumstances may a buyer reject the seller's tender of delivery? (**b**) With regard to an installment contract, under what circumstances may a buyer reject an installment? Cancel the whole contract?

8. In what two main situations may a buyer revoke acceptance of goods?

9. How does the buyer meet the obligation to pay: (**a**) Where the parties have not stated how payment is to be made? (**b**) Where the parties have not stated the time and place for payment?

10. Explain the meaning and legal effect of commercial impracticability as an excuse for nonperformance.

11. Explain how the concept of commercial impracticability could be applied to a situation involving casualty to identified goods, where the casualty occurs without the fault of either party to the sale of those goods.

12. (a) Explain what happens where it is not possible for the seller to use the agreed method of transporting the goods. (b) What happens where the buyer cannot pay in the agreed way because of governmental regulation?

CASE PROBLEMS

1. The Linscotts bought a double-width mobile home to be delivered and set up on a rural lot. Delivery and setup were completed in February, and the Linscotts moved in. They immediately encountered problems. The windows and storm windows were defective, the roof leaked, and the insulation was so inadequate that the furnace ran constantly without sufficiently warming the living areas. When spring arrived, the factory representative made some repairs. When summer arrived, he offered to install fiberglass insulation. The Linscotts refused to allow him to reinsulate unless he used foam core insulation. This request was refused and Smith, the seller, made no further effort to repair the home. In the fall and winter other troubles developed. Copper water pipes froze and burst, electrical service went out, a hot water heater burned out, kitchen cabinets came apart, the floor cracked, and an oven malfunctioned. The Linscotts sued Smith for damages. The trial court held that the Linscotts were not entitled to damages because they had improperly prevented Smith from curing the defects. The Linscotts appealed. Was the trial court in error? Explain.

2. In December 1964, Axion Corp. delivered a valve-setting machine to G.D.C. Leasing Corp. (GDC). In August 1965, GDC told Axion that the machine was useless and that GDC would not pay for it unless it would meet a "plus or minus 5 percent" specification. Axion agreed to take the machine back at GDC's expense and to repair it. In January 1966, representatives of GDC went to Axion's plant to conduct tests on the machine. Axion and GDC disagreed on whether the tests revealed a defect. In February 1966, GDC gave notice of rejection. Axion sued GDC for the price of the machine. Whether Axion was entitled to the price depended on whether GDC had accepted the machine. Did GDC accept the machine? If so, how?

3. Allen purchased a mobile home from Performance Motors, Inc. In litigation concerning her obligation to pay for the home, Allen listed a number of defects in manufacture. She testified that the home had never been leveled; that "you could see the ground through the floor"; that "when they were putting it up, I told those men, 'Now this is not right and I do not want it' "; that after the home was installed, she complained to the plaintiff's president continually "from September to the last day of December when he hung up on me and said Happy New Year"; that she ceased making monthly payments because of the plaintiff's failure to make the repairs necessary to place the trailer in a usable condition; and that she lived in the home from September to May when plaintiff repossessed it. (a) Did Allen accept the mobile home? (b) If Allen did accept it, did she revoke her acceptance? Explain.

4. Automated Controls, Inc. (ACI) agreed to design, manufacture, and sell to MIC Enterprises, Inc. (MIC) a system of solid-state electronic control boxes for use on center pivot "Blu-Max" irrigation machinery made by RVC, Inc., and distributed by MIC. ACI was to deliver six control boxes and a timer by January 1976 for field testing. By February 16, 1976, ACI could deliver only one box. Field testing was impossible with only one box. But, as ACI knew, timing was critical to MIC in coordinating the manufacture and marketing of the Blu-Max machines. Consequently, MIC placed an order for a quantity of the untested control devices to be delivered in 12 monthly installments. ACI delivered some, and MIC paid for them. However, after several attempts, ACI could not make the control boxes work, and in June 1976 MIC cancelled the contract. ACI sued MIC for breach of contract. Was MIC within its rights in cancelling the contract? Explain.

5. Mishara Construction Company (Mishara) was the general contractor for the construction of a housing project for the elderly. Transit-Mixed Concrete Corp. (Transit) agreed with Mishara to supply the ready-mixed concrete for the project. For several months Transit supplied concrete. Then a labor dispute disrupted work on the job site, and Transit stopped delivering concrete. Although work resumed on June 15, 1967, a picket line was maintained on the site until the completion of the project in 1969. Despite frequent requests by Mishara, Transit made no further deliveries of concrete. After notifying Transit of its intention, Mishara purchased the rest of its concrete requirements elsewhere. Mishara then sought as damages the additional cost of replacement concrete. During the litigation, Mishara contended that a labor dispute that makes performance more difficult never constitutes an excuse for nonperformance. Might such a labor dispute excuse Transit from performance? Under what circumstances?

CHAPTER 18

PRODUCT LIABILITY

Suppose that Ben, a commercial vegetable gardener, purchases a new garden tractor from Sue for $3000 cash. Due to a manufacturing defect, the engine explodes without warning the second time Ben uses the tractor, injuring Ben and a neighbor passing by on the sidewalk, and causing a fire that destroys the tractor and the neighbor's house. As indicated in the preceding chapter, Ben may revoke his acceptance of the tractor and recover the purchase price from Sue. If Sue is solvent, Ben is thus protected from the loss of the tractor itself. But what if Sue is insolvent? May Ben recover the value of the tractor from the manufacturer? Perhaps more important to Ben and his neighbor, who, if anyone, can they hold liable for the other losses—the personal injuries to themselves and the loss of the neighbor's house? These losses are substantial and may be far beyond Sue's ability to pay. Under the modern law of product liability both Sue *and* the manufacturer (among others) might be liable for the losses.

For a long time, however, manufacturers were not liable to people who did not buy goods directly from them. Centuries ago, goods produced for sale were relatively simple products, and buyers usually purchased them directly from the makers. Buyers were expected to examine the goods and judge for themselves whether the products were free from defects and fit for the buyers' purposes. The idea that the buyer must bear full responsibility for discovering defects and avoiding injury became the policy of the law: *Caveat emptor*, "Let the buyer beware." Under the law of that era, a person injured by a defective product could not maintain an action for damages unless he or she was "in privity of contract" (had a direct contractual relationship) with the seller. If purchases were made directly from the maker, as was usual, the buyer would be in **privity of contract** with the maker. If the buyer purchased an article from someone other than the maker, he or she had no right of action against the manufacturer.

Then, during the middle 1700s, came the industrial revolution. Machinery and power tools replaced hand tools. Large-scale industrial production led to mass advertising and complicated systems for distributing huge amounts of goods. Increasingly, goods were distributed in packaged form by "middlemen" who knew little about their quality. Products became vastly more complicated and dangerous. No longer could purchasers easily inspect goods and judge for themselves the merits of what they had bought. A seller's "puffery" (exaggerations used to make a sale) became dangerous because purchasers of unfamiliar products were no longer able to question the manufacturer personally or to recognize false statements if made. As industry developed, the doctrine of caveat emptor and the privity requirement made less and less sense.

Despite increased danger to the public from defective products, the courts were slow to discard the privity-of-contract requirement. As the use of middlemen increased, the privity requirement became a substantial barrier to the recovery of damages by injured consumers. Their contracts would normally be with retailers, not with manufacturers, and without privity of contract there could be no recovery of damages from the manufacturers who had produced the defective goods.

During the 1900s, the courts began to discard the privity-of-contract requirement. In the leading case of *MacPherson v. Buick Motor Co.*, Justice Cardozo stated the principle that the manufacturer of a product had a duty to make the product carefully and that this duty would be owed even to users other than the purchaser; that is, an injured person could have a cause of action against the manufacturer for negligence even though there was no contract between that person and the manufacturer.[1]

During recent decades, court decisions (like *MacPherson*) and legislation (especially the Uniform Commercial Code) have made dramatic changes in the law with respect to who should bear the cost of injury resulting from the use of defective products. The law has developed a number of theories of "product liability" that shift the burden of loss from the injured buyer, user, or bystander to the manufacturer, wholesaler, or retailer; and the privity requirement has been virtually abandoned. The most common causes of action available to the injured person are based on negligence, warranty, or "strict liability in tort." Frequently, the plaintiff alleges all three in the same complaint. If one cause of action does not fit the situation, the plaintiff might succeed with another.

The first part of this chapter is devoted to a brief discussion of negligence as a basis of product liability. The last two parts discuss warranties and strict liability as bases of product liability.

NEGLIGENCE AS A BASIS OF PRODUCT LIABILITY

Elements of Negligence A defendant is liable in negligence if the plaintiff proves that four traditional elements of negligence exist:

1. A duty of care on the part of the defendant. The duty arises where the defendant should foresee a risk of harm to others from his or her conduct.
2. A failure of the defendant to exercise due care, i.e., a failure to act reasonably in light of the foreseeable risk of harm to others.
3. A reasonably close causal connection between the failure to exercise due care and the resulting injury.
4. Actual loss to the plaintiff.

In negligence and other product liability cases, the defendant is usually a manufacturer, a distributor, or some other supplier of goods.

The courts have developed a number of tests to determine when a duty of care arises. A manufacturer producing "inherently dangerous" goods, such as explosives or poisons, has a duty to foresee possible dangers of various kinds and to take reasonable measures to prevent harm. Under the *MacPherson* decision a duty of care arises where a thing, if negligently made, may reasonably be expected to cause injury. Under other decisions, a duty of care arises if the goods are to be directly consumed, if the manufacturer can anticipate danger from normal use of a product, or if the manufacturer can anticipate danger from the use that actually occurred. Under the latter two tests, a manufacturer of a caustic drain cleaner could be liable for failing to explain how to use the cleaning material safely, or for failing to provide a

[1] 111 N.E. 1050 (N.Y. 1916). MacPherson had purchased a Buick from a retail dealer and was injured when a defective wooden wheel collapsed. MacPherson sued Buick Motor Co., alleging negligent failure to inspect the wheel. A judgment for MacPherson was affirmed by the New York Court of Appeals.

safety cap to protect children playing with the can. Retailers and other suppliers of goods have duties of care that correspond with the degree of danger they should foresee in their capacities as retailers or other suppliers.

Negligent conduct takes a variety of forms. Liability has been found for negligent design of a product; for negligent inspection or assembly of parts; for negligent inspection of a finished product; for negligent testing of a product before, during, or after production; and for negligent packaging. Other typical forms of negligence are failure to give adequate instructions for the use of a product, failure to warn of known dangers, and representations made negligently as to the effectiveness of a product.

Limited Usefulness of Negligence in Suits by Injured Plaintiffs

From the injured plaintiff's point of view, negligence as a theory of product liability may be useless in some situations. The plaintiff must prove that the defendant acted negligently. How could Bob Buyer prove that the defect in the garden tractor was the fault of the manufacturer? Acquiring proof of negligent design or of a negligent manufacturing process may require examination of the defendant's manufacturing facilities and processes. Defendants may be reluctant to provide necessary information, and compelling the provision of such information or otherwise acquiring it, if possible at all, can be costly.

Sometimes the required causal connection between a particular defendant and the plaintiff's injury cannot be proved. Establishing that a soft drink bottle exploded and injured a shopper does not constitute proof that any act of the bottle manufacturer caused the bottle to explode. The injury-causing condition might have occurred while the bottle was in the custody of the wholesaler or the retailer. In a proper case, the doctrine of *res ipsa loquitur* ("the thing speaks for itself") may place upon a defendant the burden of proving that he or she was *not* negligent. However, the doctrine is not universally available. Where it is available, the plaintiff must show (1) that the thing causing injury was in the defendant's exclusive control at the time of the alleged negligent act, and (2) that the accident was one that ordinarily does not happen in the absence of negligence. Suppose an airliner crashes on a clear, calm day. A court might be persuaded to apply the doctrine of *res ipsa loquitur* on the theory that the plane and its maintenance were in the exclusive control of the airline, and that commercial airline crashes normally do not occur in the absence of negligence by airline employees. If *res ipsa loquitur* applies, the defendant is presumed negligent and must carry the burden of proving it was not negligent.

Plaintiffs in negligence cases face another difficulty. They must deal with a variety of defenses commonly raised by defendants. These include contributory negligence, comparative negligence, and assumption of the risk. *Contributory negligence* occurs where the plaintiff's own negligence in using the product contributes to his or her own injury, as where the instructions for using caustic drain cleaner are vague, but contrary to instructions that are given, the plaintiff causes an explosion by using five times the recommended amount in hot water. In its strictest applications, contributory negligence bars the plaintiff from any recovery of damages. Under the doctrine of **comparative negligence,** the plaintiff's own negligence is taken into account in determining how much damages the plaintiff may recover. The award to the plaintiff is reduced in proportion to the percentage of harm attributable to the plaintiff's negligence. Under the doctrine of **assumption of risk,** a plaintiff who knowingly and voluntarily exposes himself or herself to an obvious danger ordinarily may not recover damages for any resulting injury. Using a new but obviously frayed rope for mountain climbing in a nonemergency situation would constitute assumption of risk.

To avoid the defenses and difficulties of proof that may be involved in negligence suits, the law now permits a plaintiff to base product liability on theories other than negligence.

WARRANTIES AS A BASIS OF PRODUCT LIABILITY

Originally, the term "warranty" meant a promise or agreement by the seller that (1) the thing sold had a certain level of quality, or (2) the seller had title to the thing and could confer ownership upon the buyer. Today, under the Uniform Commercial Code (UCC), warranties created by the seller's promises (or other "affirmations" of fact) are called "express" warranties. Article 2 of the UCC recognizes express warranties of title and express warranties of quality.

After the industrial revolution, courts began to impose warranty obligations upon the seller where, for example, the seller was *silent* about whether he or she intended to make a warranty. Warranties imposed by law are called "implied" warranties. Under Article 2, a seller can be subject to implied warranties of quality (1) where the seller says nothing about warranties, or (2) where the seller attempts to exclude implied warranties but fails to use properly the methods of exclusion required by the Code. Implied warranties are *in addition to* any express warranty that the seller might have made. Article 2 also imposes a warranty of title on most sellers who are silent about what ownership rights the buyer is to receive, but for the reason stated later in this chapter, this nonverbal title warranty is not classified as an implied warranty.

The main function of a warranty is to establish the characteristics of a thing (kind of ownership or level of quality) to which purchaser or some other person is entitled as a result of the existence of the warranty. In a sale of goods, a warranty may be the only practical source of remedy for loss due to a defect in the title to or the quality of the goods. A plaintiff is entitled to damages upon proof that (1) a warranty was made (or imposed by law), (2) the product does not conform to the standard of title or quality established by the warranty, and (3) the plaintiff suffered harm as a result of the breach of the warranty.

The first part of this chapter discusses two overlapping bodies of warranty law: Article 2 of the UCC (state law), and the Magnuson-Moss Warranty Act (federal law). These bodies of warranty law overlap because, although the federal Warranty Act applies to sales of "consumer products" and nullifies some warranty provisions of Article 2, the Warranty Act provides that other UCC warranty provisions continue to apply to sales of consumer products.

In the following discussion of UCC title and quality warranties, special attention is given to how warranties are made, what kind of ownership or level of quality is established by a warranty, how a seller may exclude warranties, and who, besides the buyer, is protected if a warranty is made.

UCC Warranties of Title **Nature and Scope of Title Warranties.** If a seller says to a buyer, "I own these goods free and clear," the seller has made an express warranty of title. But usually the parties to a sale are silent as to title. If the parties are silent, the Code imposes upon the seller a warranty that (1) the title conveyed shall be good, and its transfer rightful; and (2) goods shall be delivered free from any security interest or other lien of which the buyer at the time of contracting has no actual knowledge [2-312].

Sometimes goods are manufactured and sold in violation of trademark or patent rights. To protect the buyer the Code imposes upon a merchant seller regularly dealing in goods of the kind a warranty that the goods do not infringe upon the trademark or patent of any third person. However, if a buyer furnishes specifications for goods to be assembled, prepared, or manufactured by the seller, the buyer is responsible for avoiding infringement, unless buyer and seller have agreed to the contrary.

Exclusion or Modification of Title Warranties.   Sometimes goods are sold "as is" or "with all faults." Section 2-316(3) permits sellers to disclaim "all implied warranties" by the use of such expressions. Are these expressions sufficient to exclude the nonverbal warranty of good title, rightful transfer, and freedom from liens? The answer is "No." A person who buys something "as is" may be willing to take his or her chances as to the quality of the thing, but the buyer still expects to become the owner. To protect the buyer from an unexpected exclusion of the nonverbal warranty of title, Article 2 *limits the meaning of implied warranty to "implied warranty of quality."*

The nonverbal warranty of good title may be excluded or modified *only* by specific language or by circumstances that give the buyer reason to know that the seller does not have or claim ownership [2-312]. The "specific language" requirement could be met by the seller's statement that the seller does not warrant title, or that the seller warrants title only to a limited extent. However, the buyer is expected to recognize the fact that in certain circumstances sellers do not warrant title. For example, sales by sheriffs, executors, and foreclosing lienors are so out of the ordinary commercial course that their peculiar character is immediately apparent to the buyer. No personal obligation is imposed upon such a seller.

UCC Warranties of Quality   A warranty of quality establishes a level of quality to which goods must conform if the seller is to avoid liability for breach of warranty. The level of quality established by an express warranty is determined by the seller's statements or other representations. The level of quality established by an implied warranty is measured by the concept of "merchantability" or of "fitness for a particular purpose."

The Code permits a seller to disclaim all implied warranties or, if he or she wishes, to substitute for an implied warranty a less burdensome express warranty. Yet the nature of the marketing process, certain features of the Code, the Magnuson-Moss Warranty Act, and the growing tendency of courts to resolve warranty doubts in favor of consumers limit the opportunities for a seller to escape warranty liability altogether.

Express Warranties of Quality.   A seller may refrain from making express warranties, but they can arise in ways that the seller might not anticipate. Under Section 2-313, *any affirmation of fact or promise made by the seller to the buyer which relates to the goods and becomes part of the basis of the bargain* creates an express warranty. Any seller who advertises goods is subject to having advertising claims construed as factual, and some courts have held that a retail seller has adopted the statements made by the manufacturer, even though the retailer personally has said nothing concerning the goods.

Furthermore, under the Code an express warranty can arise without the use of words. *Any* description of the goods, including drawings and sketches, or *any sample or model* "which is made part of the basis of the bargain" creates an express warranty that the goods will conform to the description, sample, or model [2-313]. As long as business people make normal use of advertising, models, samples, and diagrams, express warranties are likely to be made.

An express warranty must rest on some statement or other affirmation of *fact*, not on mere opinion or "sales puffery" of the seller. Despite the strong movement away from caveat emptor, the buyer is expected to detect and discount such nonfactual sales talk as "a good coat, will wear very good," and "his father was the greatest living dairy bull." Statements made by sellers may range from those that are clearly opinion to those that are clearly fact. In the middle are statements that a court may have to interpret as either fact or opinion. The background against which a statement was made becomes important in interpreting it. Thus, a former garage mechanic who sold a used car to a nurse was held to have made an express warranty when he stated, "This is a car I can recommend . . . it is in A-1 shape."[2]

Under the Code's "basis of the bargain" test, postsale talk may, and often does, create an express warranty. Even though an affirmation is made after a contract has been entered into, the affirmation may create expectations that the product will do what the seller promised. For instance, a person who buys a packaged product and later reads descriptive information contained within the carton may be led to make a use of the product that he or she would not have made if the seller had remained silent. The statement should be regarded as an indicator of quality level and as an aspect of the bargain. Moreover, under the "basis of the bargain" test, assurances given when goods are delivered, and statements in advertisements read after the sale, could create express warranties.

Implied Warranties of Quality.   Unless warranties are properly excluded, the Code imposes an implied warranty of merchantability, or an implied warranty of fitness for a particular purpose, or both. The warranties differ with regard to who makes the warranties, how the warranties are made, what quality level is established by the warranties, and how the warranties may be excluded.

Implied Warranty of Merchantability.   A warranty that the goods shall be merchantable (fit for their *ordinary* purposes) is implied in a contract for their sale if the seller is a merchant who deals in goods of that kind [2-314]. A seller is a merchant if he or she deals in goods of the kind sold, or gives the appearance of having knowledge of the goods. Normally, a person making an isolated sale of goods is not a merchant and therefore is not subject to the implied warranty of merchantability. However, the nonmerchant seller of goods is required by the good faith provision of the Code to disclose any material hidden defects of which he or she has knowledge.

[2]*Wat Henry Pontiac Co. v. Bradley*, 210 P.2d 348 (Okla. 1949).

To be merchantable, goods must meet the minimum standards of merchantability set by the Code. Fungible goods must be of fair average quality within the description. All goods must pass without objection in the trade under the contract description; be fit for the ordinary purposes for which such goods are used; run of even kind, quality, and quantity within each unit and among all units; be adequately contained, packaged, and labeled as the sales agreement may require; and conform to the promises or affirmations of fact made on the container or label if any [2-314(2)].

Other attributes of merchantability may arise by usage of trade or through the development of case law. Goods usually are not "fit" for their ordinary purposes unless they can be used safely. The degree of safety required for a product to be considered merchantable is developed in the case law. Some courts hold that goods may be fit for their ordinary purposes even though a few persons suffer allergic reactions or other isolated injuries not common to ordinary people.[3] As illustrated by Case 18.1, the warranty of merchantability is not breached unless the goods fall below the required level of quality.

CASE 18.1   Williams v. Braum Ice Cream Stores, Inc.
15 UCC Rep. 1019 (Okla. App. 1974)

Facts: Williams purchased a "cherry pecan" ice cream cone from defendant's retail store. She broke a tooth on a cherry pit contained in the ice cream and sued the seller for damages, alleging breach of an implied warranty of merchantability. The trial court held that a cherry pit found in ice cream made of natural red cherry halves was a substance natural to such ice cream, and that the ice cream therefore was not defective.

Question: Did the seller breach the implied warranty of merchantability?

Answer: Perhaps. The trial court applied the wrong test of merchantability. Whether the ice cream was defective is a question for the jury.

Reasoning: Some courts hold that food is not defective, and there is no breach of an implied warranty, if the substance causing the injury is natural to the ingredients of the type of food served. Courts that apply this "foreign-natural" test find food defective only if it contains some foreign object such as a piece of metal. A better legal theory, and the one to be applied in this case, is the "reasonable expectation" theory. Natural substances that are generally not found in the style of food as prepared, e.g., cherry pits in highly processed ice cream, should be considered the equivalent of a foreign substance, since cherry pits and other unexpected natural substances can cause as much damage as foreign substances like a pebble. The ice cream was defective if the cherry pit was an object that the consumer would not reasonably expect to encounter.

[3]*Robbins v. Alberto-Culver Co.*, 499 P.2d 1080 (Kan. 1972).

Implied Warranty of Fitness for a Particular Purpose.   A warranty of fitness for a particular or special purpose is implied where, at the time of contracting, two circumstances exist: (1) The seller has reason to know any particular purpose for which the goods are required, and (2) the seller has reason to know that the buyer is relying on the seller's skill or judgment to select or furnish suitable goods [2-315]. Suppose that Carl Customer tells the owner of a sporting goods store that he will soon go on his first mountain climbing expedition and needs some good climbing shoes. The owner says nothing but produces a pair of climbing shoes that Carl quickly examines and buys. The seller has made an implied warranty of fitness for a partiuclar purpose. She knows the particular purpose for which Carl needs the shoes. Since she knows that Carl is a novice climber, she also has reason to know that Carl is relying on her to supply suitable shoes for that purpose. (The fitness warranty would be express if the owner had said "These shoes are just what you are looking for.")

The situation would be different if the owner had sold climbing shoes to "Cleats" Morton, a professional mountain climber with whom she had dealt many times before and who had always made his own choice of shoes, usually disregarding her advice. The seller would have no reason to believe that Cleats relied on her judgment. Therefore, an element necessary for an implied warranty of fitness to arise would be missing. Merchants and nonmerchants alike can be subject to an implied warranty of fitness.

An increasing number of judges hold that advertising can contribute to the existence of an implied warranty of fitness. A seller who advertises his or her product expects to persuade buyers that it is suitable for a certain purpose or purposes. Many sellers also expect to create "brand loyalty" by convincing the buyer that the seller's product is superior to the products of competitors. Sellers who engage in brand-loyalty advertising may well have reason to know of the buyer's particular purpose and of the buyer's reliance on the seller to provide suitable goods. The warranty could be implied even though the seller never meets the buyer.

CASE 18.2   Swan Island Sheet Metal Works, Inc. v. Troy's Custom Smoking Co.
619 P.2d 1326 (Or. App. 1980)

Facts: Troy asked Swan Island Sheet Metal Works to manufacture two gas-fired stainless steel crab cookers, to be modeled after a cooker that Troy's already owned. Troy explained to Bader, president of Swan Island, the use of the cooker and some of the special needs a crab cooker must satisfy. Bader informed Troy that Bader lacked knowledge of gas burners. Troy and Bader agreed that Swan Island would seek outside expert advice on the design of the burner. Swan Island could not duplicate the burner on the old cooker and instead installed a burner recommended by the expert. The cooker never worked properly. In a suit by Swan Island for the price of the cooker, Troy sought damages, alleging breach of an implied warranty of fitness for a particular purpose.

Question: Did Swan Island make and breach an implied warranty of fitness for a particular purpose?

Answer: Yes.

Reasoning: Swan Island knew the special needs a crab cooker must satisfy and knew that Troy lacked the expertise to build one. Although Bader made clear to Troy that Bader personally lacked knowledge of gas burners, Bader did agree to get expert advice. Troy relied on Swan Island to assemble the expertise necessary to select a suitable burner. Therefore the requirement that the buyer rely on the seller to furnish suitable goods was satisfied. Because the cooker never worked properly, the fitness warranty was breached.

Exclusion or Modification of Quality Warranties.   Once made, an *express* warranty is difficult to disclaim. Section 2-316(1) states a general principle that words or conduct creating an express warranty, and words or conduct negating warranty, shall be construed wherever reasonable as consistent with each other, but that "negation or limitation is inoperative to the extent that such construction is unreasonable." Suppose that Sam, a used car dealer, makes an express oral warranty in selling a used car to Brenda. If the contract that Brenda signs contains a disclaimer of "all warranties, express or implied," the disclaimer will be unenforceable. Sam has taken the trouble to make an express warranty calculated to capture Brenda's attention. To give effect to Sam's disclaimer of his own express warranty would be an unreasonable action.

What if Sam makes an express oral warranty, but the contract disclaims all warranties and further states that the writing is the final and exclusive expression of the agreement? Will the parol evidence rule of Section 2-202 prevent proof of the oral warranty? It might, but Brenda might be able to demonstrate that she did not agree that the writing should be considered final and exclusive. Under Section 2-202, the parties must agree. Litigation of the agreement issue is difficult because at its heart is the credibility of Brenda and Sam on a question of fact. The same is true about the question of whether Sam actually made the express warranty.

CASE 18.3   Century Dodge, Inc. v. Mobley
272 S.E.2d 502 (Ga. App. 1980)

Facts: Mobley purchased a new car from Century Dodge and later discovered that the car had been involved in an accident. The contract of sale described the car as "new" and contained a disclaimer of all warranties, express or implied. Mobley sued Century Dodge for damages, alleging breach of an express warranty. Century Dodge contended that it had disclaimed any express warranty.

Question: Was Century Dodge's disclaimer effective to exclude an express warranty that the car was new?

Answer: No.

Reasoning: Section 2-316(1) provides that contract language negating or limiting an express warranty is inoperative if the language of warranty and the language of limitation cannot reasonably be construed as consistent with each other. The car that Mobley purchased was described as new in the contract. It is unreasonable to allow an express warranty contained in a contract (the description of the car as "new") to be negated by a disclaimer of warranty in the same contract, since the two provisions are not consistent with each other.

The *implied* warranties of quality may be excluded in either of two main ways: (1) by the buyer's examining the goods or refusing to examine them, or (2) by the use of appropriate exclusionary language. If the buyer examines the goods (or a sample or model) before entering the contract, there is no implied warranty with regard to obvious defects. Nor is there an implied warranty as to obvious defects if the seller demands that the buyer examine the goods, but the buyer refuses. Making goods available for inspection does not constitute a demand. The seller must make clear that the buyer is assuming the risk of defects which the examination ought to reveal. Exclusion by examination applies only to obvious defects, not hidden ones; and it applies only to implied warranties, not to express warranties on which the buyer clearly indicates he or she is relying.

Except in certain situations governed by the Magnuson-Moss Warranty Act, a seller who wishes to disclaim implied warranties by using exclusionary language may do so in either of two ways: (1) All implied warranties may be excluded by using expressions such as "as is," "with all faults," or other language that in common understanding calls the buyer's attention to the exclusion of warranties and makes plain that there is no implied warranty [2-316(3)(a)]. (2) Implied warranties may also be excluded by complying with the provisions of Section 2-316(2). Under that subsection, an *implied warranty of merchantability* may be excluded orally or by a writing, but the exclusionary language must mention merchantability. If the disclaimer is written, the language of disclaimer must be conspicuous. Under the same subsection, an *implied warranty of fitness* can be excluded only by a conspicuous writing, but the exclusionary language may be general. A conspicuous general statement, such as "There are no warranties which extend beyond the description on the face hereof," is sufficient to exclude an implied warranty of fitness.

Strict compliance with the warranty exclusion provisions of the Code is not always sufficient to exclude an implied warranty. Some courts have held that certain attempts at exclusion are against public policy. In the pre-Code case of *Henningsen v. Bloomfield Motors*, 161 A.2d 69 (N.J. 1960), all automobile manufacturers doing business in New Jersey had adopted the same printed disclaimer of implied warranties and had substituted a "parts only" express warranty. Automobile buyers could not negotiate with the manufacturers for a more extensive warranty. The Supreme Court of New Jersey held that under these circumstances, an attempt by Bloomfield Motors to disclaim an implied warranty of merchantability was against public policy, and therefore invalid. As Case 18.4 illustrates, a few courts interpreting the Code have reached similar conclusions, usually on the ground that an attempted disclaimer is unconscionable. With regard to consumer products, the

Magnuson-Moss Warranty Act, discussed later in this chapter, prohibits or limits the exclusion of implied warranties where a warranty has been made in writing.

CASE 18.4　A & M Produce Co. v. FMC Corp.
186 Cal. Rptr. 114 (Cal. App. 1982)

Facts: Abatti decided to grow tomatoes. Although an experienced produce farmer, he had never grown tomatoes before. To pack the tomatoes, he purchased from FMC a "weight-sizer" machine for $32,000. Abatti was unfamiliar with such equipment. Because the machine failed to work properly, Abatti lost most of the crop and sued FMC for damages. The contract contained a written disclaimer of all warranties. The trial court awarded Abatti over $250,000 in damages on the ground that the disclaimer, though conspicuous, was unconscionable and that express or implied warranties had been breached.

Question: Was the trial court correct in holding that the disclaimer was unconscionable?

Answer: Yes.

Reasoning: The situation involved all the usual elements of unconscionability. There was evidence that Abatti was in fact surprised by the presence of the disclaimer on the reverse side of the contract form. Even if Abatti knew about and understood the disclaimer, he lacked power to bargain it out of the contract, since FMC is a large corporation and its sales representative had no authority to delete the clause. The disclaimer was commercially unreasonable. If it were given effect, FMC would in essence be guaranteeing nothing as to the machine's performance. A product's performance forms the fundamental basis for a sales contract. It is unreasonable to assume that a buyer would purchase a standardized mass-produced product from an industry seller without any enforceable performance standards. Lacking experience with weight-sizing machines, Abatti was forced to rely on the expertise of FMC in recommending necessary equipment. FMC was aware of this fact. The jury necessarily found that FMC expressly or impliedly guaranteed a performance level that the machine was unable to meet.

Cumulation and Conflict of UCC Warranties　In a sale of goods, a number of warranties may exist at the same time. For example, a *merchant* seller can be subject to a warranty of title, a warranty against infringement of a patent or a trademark, an implied warranty of merchantability, and an implied warranty of fitness for a particular purpose. In addition, any number of express warranties can be created, including express warranties of merchantability and fitness. To the extent that these express and implied warranties are consistent with one another, the buyer receives an accumulation of express and implied assurances. If a warranty of any kind is excluded, the seller remains subject to all other warranties that were made or imposed but that were not excluded.

Where there is a *conflict* of warranties, the intention of the parties to the sales contract determines which one is dominant. Section 2-317 states three tentative rules of construction for the guidance of the court: (1) Exact or technical specifications displace an inconsistent sample or model or general language of description. (2) A sample from an existing bulk displaces inconsistent general language of description. (3) Express warranties displace inconsistent implied warranties other than an implied warranty of fitness for a particular purpose.

Suppose that a building contractor is interested in a new type of high-strength building block. The contractor inspects a sample, reads the results of a laboratory test conducted by the manufacturer, and purchases from the manufacturer a large quantity of the blocks. The blocks conform in strength to the sample but not to the laboratory test results supplied to the buyer as part of the sales promotion. Which warranty prevails—the one arising from the sample, or the one arising from the test results? Under rule (1) in the preceding paragraph, the contractor is entitled to blocks that conform in strength to the specifications stated in the laboratory report.

Third-Party Beneficiaries of UCC Quality Warranties

Sometimes a defective product causes loss to someone other than the purchaser. The seller might admit that he or she made a warranty, but may argue that the warranty should extend only to the purchaser and not to others such as bystanders who might have been injured. Section 2-318 of the UCC gives certain "beneficiaries" the benefit of the same warranty or warranties that the buyer received in the contract of sale.

There are three alternative versions of Section 2-318: Alternatives A, B, and C. Although they have a common purpose—to give beneficiaries the same warranty the buyer received—they differ greatly as to who may be a beneficiary and as to the kinds of injury for which a beneficiary may receive a remedy.

Recall the situation described at the beginning of this chapter. A defective garden tractor engine exploded, injuring Ben and his neighbor and causing a fire that destroyed the tractor and the neighbor's house. Suppose that neither the manufacturer nor the retail seller excluded the implied warranty of merchantability. To whom, besides Ben, does the warranty of each seller run? The answer depends on which version of Section 2-318 is in effect in the state whose law applies to the situation. Most states (over thirty) have adopted Alternative A or some version of it. Some states have adopted Alternative B or C or some variation. California has not enacted the section, but relies instead on other consumer law.

Alternative A provides that "a seller's warranty whether express or implied extends to any natural person who is in the family or household of his buyer or who is a guest in his home if it is reasonable to expect that such person may use, consume or be affected by the goods and who is injured in person by breach of the warranty." This alternative permits recovery of damages only for personal injury, not for injury to property. Bystanders, nonfamily members, and guests in automobiles are unprotected, unless the court is willing to include them in the protected class by some process of interpretation. Ben's neighbor is not within the protected class.

Alternative B broadens the class of beneficiaries to whom a seller's warranty extends. The warranty "extends to any natural person [human being as opposed to a corporation] who may reasonably be expected to use, consume, or be affected by the goods and who is injured in person by breach of the warranty." Ben's neighbor could reasonably be expected to "be affected" by an exploding engine. Under

Alternative B the neighbor would be entitled to damages for personal injuries but not for loss of the house.

Alternative C is a variation of Alternative B. It differs from Alternative B in two ways. (1) Alternative C extends a seller's warranty to "any person" (not merely to a "natural" person) who may reasonably be expected to use, consume, or be affected by the goods. (2) Alternative C permits a beneficiary to recover damages for injury to property (as well as for injury to the person), unless the seller excludes or limits liability for injury to property. With regard to personal injury, a seller may not exclude or limit the operation of Alternative C. Under Alternative C, Ben's neighbor is entitled to damages for personal injuries and for the loss of the house if liability for property damage was not excluded by the sellers.

Limits on Usefulness of UCC Warranties to Injured Plaintiffs

Like other bases of product liability, warranty may be of little or no value to some persons injured by defective products. The UCC does not require a seller to make an express warranty, and the UCC permits the seller to exclude those imposed by law. Indeed, in transactions covered by the Code it is common practice for a seller to exclude implied warranties entirely and to substitute a much narrower express warranty, one limited, for example, to the replacement of defective parts. Even where there is an implied warranty, the amount of damages recoverable may be sharply limited by the sales contract. In contrast, contractual disclaimers or limitations of strict tort liability or liability for gross negligence or intentional torts ordinarily are not enforceable. Recall also that in many states an injured third party who is not a member of the buyer's family or a guest in the buyer's home has no warranty cause of action against the seller.

Injured persons may face another problem when suing for breach of warranty: a surprise running of the UCC statute of limitations. A statute of limitations imposes a fixed maximum time within which a person must bring suit, so that people are encouraged to bring their suits promptly, while evidence is still fresh and available. The UCC provides a rather generous amount of time for bringing suit—4 years, and more in some situations. However, the time for suing may be reduced to as little as *1* year by the original agreement of the parties. Moreover, the period, whatever its length, begins to run when the sales contract is breached—by, for example, the seller's breaching a warranty. With one exception, breach of a warranty occurs when the goods are *tendered to the buyer* (offered for delivery), "regardless of the aggrieved party's lack of knowledge of the breach" [2-725(2)].[4] Goods such as Ben's garden tractor may have hidden defects that do not become apparent until after the limitation period has expired. In such a situation, injured persons would be barred from any warranty remedy. In contrast, the limitations period that applies to a cause of action in *negligence* or *strict liability in tort* (usually 1 or 2 years) begins to run when the injury-causing condition *was or should have been discovered*. In tort, then, the period for suing may extend indefinitely, because the time that the defect reveals itself, not the time that the product was tendered for delivery, usually marks the

---

[4]The exception is that where a warranty "explicitly extends" to the future performance of the goods (e.g., the seller warrants the goods for 2 years), the UCC limitations period (1 to 4 years) does not commence until the time during the 2 years that the defect was or should have been discovered.

beginning of the period permitted for bringing suit. (For the protection of sellers, a few states specify that a suit in strict liability in tort must be brought within 6 to 12 years after the product was sold, regardless of whether the defect has been discovered by that time.)

"Consumer Product" Warranties under Federal Legislation

The UCC does not require warranties to be stated in language that is understandable by nonlawyers. Consequently, under the UCC many sellers have made warranties that are confusing, deceptive, or misleading, especially to consumers. To remedy the situation, Congress in 1975 enacted the **Magnuson-Moss Warranty Act.**[5]

Purpose and Scope of Magnuson-Moss Warranty Act. The act has two broad purposes: (1) to improve the adequacy of warranty information available to consumers, to prevent deception, and thereby to improve competition in the marketing of consumer products; and (2) to encourage warrantors to establish procedures for the informal settlement of disputes with consumers. The Federal Trade Commission (FTC) has the duty of developing appropriate rules and putting the Warranty Act into effect.

The Warranty Act applies only to consumer products. A **consumer product** is any item of tangible personal property that is distributed in commerce and is normally used for personal, family, or household purposes. "Consumer product" includes items intended to be attached to or installed in real property, such as a water heater. Although the Warranty Act applies to consumer products costing more than $5, the act permits the FTC to impose its rules on consumer products costing some higher amount that the FTC selects. The UCC continues to apply to warranties in sales of goods to be used for purely business purposes. Furthermore, the UCC may continue to supply warranties in sales of consumer products, since a supplier who makes a written consumer product warranty may not exclude UCC or other implied warranties arising under state law.

Chief Requirements of the Act. The Warranty Act does not require that a consumer product or any of its components be warranted. However, sellers who make a written consumer product warranty must comply with Warranty Act disclosure and labeling requirements.

Disclosure Requirements—Contents and Time of Disclosure. The Warranty Act requires the maker of a written consumer product warranty to disclose *fully and conspicuously* in a *single document* in *simple, understandable language* the items of information required by the FTC. The FTC requires the following information for products costing more than $15:

1. Where the written warranty is not to be extended to every consumer who owns the product during the term of the warranty, the identity of the person or persons (such as the "original owner") to whom the warranty *is* extended.
2. A clear description of the parts or product characteristics covered by the warranty and, where necessary for clarification, what is excluded from the warranty.

[5]15 U.S.C.A., secs 2301–2312.

3. A statement of what the warrantor (maker of the written warranty) will do to correct a defect, malfunction, or failure of the product to conform with the warranty, including the items or services the warrantor will pay for or provide. Also, where necessary for clarification, the items or services that the warrantor will *not* pay for or provide.
4. The time when the warranty term begins (if at a time other than the purchase date) and the duration of the warranty term.
5. A step-by-step explanation of how the consumer may obtain warranty service. If a consumer must fill out and return an owner's registration card, a warranty registration card, or the like to qualify for warranty coverage or service, the warranty must disclose this fact.
6. Information about any informal dispute settlement procedure, such as arbitration, used by the warrantor.
7. Any limitations on the duration of *implied* (e.g., UCC) warranties, together with the following statement: "Some states do not allow limitations on how long an implied warranty lasts, so the above limitation may not apply to you." A limitation on the duration of an implied warranty must appear on the face of the written warranty.
8. Any limitations or exclusions of damages, together with a statement that some states do not permit such limitations.
9. The following statement: "This warranty gives you specific legal rights, and you may also have other rights which vary from state to state."

If a written consumer product warranty is made, its text must be made readily available to the prospective buyer *prior to sale.* A seller may use a variety of methods for making the text available, as long as the information is conspicuous and access to it is easy. The seller may, for example, prominently display the text of the warranty at a counter and clearly indicate the products covered, maintain a clearly labeled binder containing copies of warranties for products sold in a department, or display packages of consumer products in such a way that the warranties printed on them are clearly visible. The requirement of presale warranty availability applies to all sellers of consumer products, including catalog, mail-order, and door-to-door sellers. Any supplier (such as a manufacturer) who makes a written product warranty must provide the seller (e.g., a retailer) with warranty materials—tags, stickers, signs, appropriately printed packaging, etc.—necessary for the seller to make the required presale disclosure.

Labeling Requirement—"FULL" v. "LIMITED" Warranty. In addition to the disclosures required by the FTC, the Warranty Act itself requires that any written warranty of a consumer product costing more than $10 must be clearly and conspicuously designated as either a "full warranty" or a "limited warranty," unless the warrantor is exempted from the designation requirement by a rule of the FTC.

A warranty is a "full warranty" (and can be so labeled) only if it meets four minimum standards or requirements imposed by the Warranty Act:

1. Where the product is defective or fails to conform to the written warranty, the warrantor must, without charge, remedy the product within a reasonable time.

2. Although a full warranty *may itself* be of limited duration (by use of language such as "FULL 12-MONTH WARRANTY"), the warranty may *not* impose any limitation on the duration of any *implied* (e.g., UCC) warranty on the product.
3. To be effective, any clause purporting to exclude or limit consequential damages for breach of warranty must conspicuously appear on the face of the warranty.
4. If the product (or a component part) contains a defect or continues to malfunction after a reasonable number of attempts by the warrantor to remedy defects or malfunctions in the product, the warrantor must permit the consumer to elect either a refund of the purchase price or a replacement of the product or part.

If the warrantor replaces a component part, the replacement must include installing the part without charge.

A full warranty (including one reading, for example, "FULL 12-MONTH WARRANTY") extends from the warrantor to any person who is a consumer with respect to the consumer product. The term "consumer" includes the buyer of a consumer product, any person to whom the product is transferred while its warranty coverage is in effect, and any other person, such as an injured bystander, who is entitled by the terms of the warranty or by state law to the benefit of the warranty.

A written consumer-product warranty that does not conform to the four minimum standards is a "limited warranty." A warranty is "limited" (and must be so labeled) if it, for example, requires the consumer (1) to fill out and return a warranty registration card to qualify for warranty coverage or service, or (2) to pay any costs of returning or remedying a defective product. A warranty that promises to replace defective parts but requires the purchaser to pay for installing them is a limited warranty. So is a 12-month warranty that protects the first purchaser but not a person to whom the product is transferred during the 12-month period.

Extent to Which the Act Supersedes the Code. The Warranty Act nullifies conflicting provisions of other warranty legislation. For example, the UCC permits the exclusion of implied warranties even where the seller has made a written warranty. Under the Warranty Act, a supplier who makes a written warranty may not disclaim or modify implied warranties. In two situations the act prohibits entirely the disclaimer or modification of implied warranties: (1) where the supplier makes a full warranty, and (2) where at the time of sale, or within 90 days thereafter, the supplier enters into a "service contract" with the consumer for the repair or maintenance of the consumer product. A service contract is a contract in writing to perform for a specified time services relating to the maintenance or repair (or both) of a consumer product. Where a supplier makes a *limited* warranty, implied warranties may not be disclaimed or modified as to content. But the supplier may limit the duration of implied warranties to the duration of a written warranty of reasonable duration, if the limitation is conscionable, is set forth in clear and unmistakable language, and is prominently displayed on the face of the limited warranty. In the sale of a consumer product these Warranty Act provisions prevail over the conflicting provisions of the Code.

Enforcement of Warranty Act Provisions. A person who has the benefit of a consumer product warranty may, if injured by a defective consumer product, bring suit in any state or federal court having jurisdiction and recover actual damages or have other remedies. However, where a warrantor sets up an informal dispute settlement procedure (e.g., arbitration) that conforms to FTC regulations, and the written warranty requires the consumer to use the procedure before going to court, the consumer is bound by this requirement.

Some defects produce so little monetary loss that the individual consumer may not find it worthwhile to bring suit even though the product is useless or caused injury. In such instances the consumer may choose to bring a class action against the warrantor, as is permitted by the Warranty Act, on behalf of all those harmed by the defective product.

To curb deception at the earliest possible moment, the Warranty Act empowers the Attorney General and the FTC to bring suit to enjoin (restrain) a warrantor from making a deceptive warranty or violating any prohibition of the act. In addition, a warrantor is subject to a $10,000 civil penalty if found by a court to be in violation of the Warranty Act or FTC regulations.

STRICT LIABILITY AS A BASIS OF PRODUCT LIABILITY

If negligence cannot be proved and the seller has made no warranty, an injured plaintiff may wish to rely on strict liability as a basis for recovering damages.

Nature and Scope of Strict Liability

Courts use the expression **strict liability** in two senses. In one sense, *strict liability* means a liability that flows from a breach of a warranty of quality. In another sense, the sense in which the expression is used in this chapter, *strict liability* means a liability imposed by tort law. "Strict liability in tort" is imposed when a defective product has caused injury or when injury results from a justifiable reliance on a material misrepresentation of the quality of a product. The liability is called "strict" because the plaintiff need not prove "fault" (negligence or fraud) on the part of the defendant. The liability is "in tort" because the existence of the liability does not depend on the existence of a warranty. Strict liability in tort usually cannot be disclaimed. The ability of sellers to disclaim or otherwise to avoid warranty liability for serious loss explains in large measure the rapid development of strict liability in tort as a basis for lawsuits.

Strict liability in tort has had its greatest growth since the early 1960s, when the leading case of *Greenman v. Yuba Power Products, Inc.*, 377 P.2d 897 (Cal. 1963) was decided. In that case, the plaintiff was injured while using a defective power tool that had been purchased by his wife. The court held, "A manufacturer is strictly liable in tort when an article he places on the market, knowing that it is to be used without inspection for defects, proves to have a defect that causes injury to a human being." Section 402A of the *Restatement of the Law, Second, Torts* contains similar language:

One who sells any product in a defective condition unreasonably dangerous to the user or consumer or to his property is subject to liability for physical harm thereby caused to the ultimate user or consumer, or to his property, if (a) the seller is engaged in the business of selling such a product, and (b) it is expected to and does reach the user or consumer without substantial change in the condition in which it is sold.

This rule applies although the seller has exercised all possible care in preparing and selling the product and even though the user or consumer has not bought the product from the seller.

Section 402B of the *Restatement* refers to situations not necessarily involving a defective product. By advertising, labels, or otherwise, a seller might make to the public "a misrepresentation of material fact concerning the character or quality of a chattel sold by him." A consumer of the chattel (or product) who justifiably relies on the misrepresentation and is thereby physically harmed may have a cause of action against the seller.

Reasons for Imposing Strict Liability; Procedural Benefits

The reasons most commonly offered for imposing strict liability include the following: (1) Users of complex or packaged goods are usually in no position to examine them at the time of purchase. Since much advertising is calculated to convince the public that goods may be used safely, users of defective goods are especially vulnerable to injury. So, when a defective product causes injury, the loss should be shifted from the individual to the manufacturer. (2) Manufacturers are in the best position to distribute loss due to defective products as a cost of doing business, either by raising prices or by procuring insurance. (3) Imposing strict liability will exert pressure on manufacturers to police their operations more carefully and to make fewer defective products. Also, some courts impose strict liability on everyone in the distribution chain so that the injured plaintiff will have a better chance of recovering damages. The manufacturer may be beyond the reach of the plaintiff but may be liable to a middleman who has been required to pay damages to the plaintiff.

Strict tort liability provides injured plaintiffs with procedural advantages similar to those of an action in warranty. The plaintiff may prevail essentially by proving (1) that the doctrine applies to the plaintiff's situation, (2) that the product had a defect when it left the defendant's hands and was unreasonably dangerous to the plaintiff (or that the plaintiff justifiably relied on the defendant's material misrepresentation), and (3) that harm to the plaintiff resulted. Ordinarily, contributory negligence of the plaintiff is not a defense to a suit based on strict liability in tort.

CASE 18.5 Martin v. Ryder Truck Rental, Inc.
353 A.2d 581 (Del. 1976)

Facts: Ryder Truck Rental leased a truck to Gagliardi Brothers, Inc. As a Gagliardi employee was operating the truck, its brakes failed. The truck struck a car that had stopped for a traffic signal. The impact caused the car to collide with another driven by plaintiff Martin. She was injured and her car was damaged. She sued Ryder for damages, basing her suit solely on the doctrine of strict liability in tort. The trial court held that the doctrine is not applicable to leases of goods.

Question: Is strict liability in tort applicable to leases of goods?

Answer: Yes.

Reasoning: The doctrine was developed originally for application against remote manufacturers for the protection of users and consumers. The reasons for applying strict tort liability to sales cases apply as well to this rental case. One such reason is that the cost of compensating injured persons should be borne by the person who placed the defective product in circulation. Also, imposing liability on the lessor regardless of fault will encourage the lessor to furnish safer vehicles.

Limits on Usefulness of Strict Liability to Injured Plaintiffs

Strict liability, like the other bases of product liability, is not universally available to injured plaintiffs. The courts of a very few states have refused to adopt the doctrine of strict tort liability. Some of these courts have stated that the decision to adopt strict liability is for the legislature. The courts of certain other states will not impose that doctrine if the plaintiff has suffered only property damage. These courts reserve strict liability for situations that involve serious personal injury, preferring to let most product liability matters be governed by warranty law. Moreover, the defendant in a strict liability suit usually may prevail by proving that the plaintiff knew of the defect, understood the danger, and voluntarily assumed the risk.

SUMMARY

A person injured by a defective product may sue in negligence, warranty, or strict liability in tort. A defendant is liable in negligence if he or she is subject to a duty of care, violates it, and causes harm to the plaintiff. The duty arises and can be violated in a variety of ways. However, negligence can be difficult to prove.

Article 2 of the UCC provides for warranties of title and warranties of quality. Quality warranties are classified as express or implied. Any affirmation of fact or promise that relates to the goods and becomes a part of the basis of the bargain creates an express warranty. The implied warranty of merchantability entitles the buyer to goods that are fit for their ordinary purposes. An implied warranty of fitness for a particular purpose entitles the buyer to goods that will serve that purpose. A seller may refrain from making express warranties and may exclude implied warranties. A number of warranties may exist at the same time. A warranty of quality made to a buyer extends also to certain third-party beneficiaries.

The Magnuson-Moss Warranty Act establishes special rules for written consumer-product warranties. These rules supersede conflicting rules of the UCC.

Strict liability in tort may be available to an injured person where the product is unreasonably dangerous to the user, or where the user has justifiably relied on the seller's misrepresentation of material fact concerning the nature of the product. One reason for strict liability is that sellers can best absorb loss and spread it as a cost of doing business.

REVIEW QUESTIONS

1. Why has the privity-of-contract requirement been abandoned in product liability cases?

2. Why might the law of negligence be of limited usefulness to injured plaintiffs? Illustrate.

3. What must a plaintiff prove to obtain damages for loss due to a breach of warranty?

4. (a) What ownership attributes may a buyer be assured of under a warranty of title? (b) How may nonverbal title warranties be excluded?

5. (a) How may an express warranty of quality be made? (b) What would be the best way to avoid the liability that can result from an express warranty? (c) Is this method of avoiding liability compatible with normal business practices? Why?

6. Compare the implied warranty of merchantability with the implied warranty of fitness for a particular purpose with regard to (a) method of creation, (b) quality level assured, and (c) method of exclusion.

7. Suppose a seller orally states, "I do not warrant these goods." What warranties, if any, exist?

8. Compare Alternatives A, B, and C of Section 2-318 with regard to the class of people protected; the kind of injury protected against.

9. Why might the law of warranty be of limited usefulness to an injured plaintiff? Illustrate.

10. (a) What are the chief kinds of requirements of the Magnuson-Moss Warranty Act? (b) How does a full warranty differ from a limited warranty? (c) How does the Warranty Act limit the right granted by Article 2 to exclude implied warranties?

11. How may the provisions of the Warranty Act be enforced?

12. (a) What are the two main situations in which strict liability may be imposed? (b) For injured plaintiffs, what are the procedural benefits of strict liability in tort? (c) Why might strict tort liability be of limited usefulness to injured persons?

CASE PROBLEMS

1. Associated Grocers delivered a pallet of produce to the back room of Thriftway Market. On top of the stack of produce was a cardboard box of Chiquita brand bananas. The bananas were unwrapped and the box contained breather holes. On the day of the delivery, Anderson, the produce manager, removed the box of bananas from the top of the stack. When he reached for a lug of radishes that had been under the bananas, a 6-inch "banana" spider leaped from some wet burlap onto his left hand and bit him. Not long afterward Anderson died. Assume that his death was caused by the bite of the spider. Is Associated Grocers liable to Anderson's estate for Anderson's death on the basis of (a) negligence, (b) the implied warranty of merchantability, and (c) strict liability in tort?

2. Holden Chemical Corp. ordered a set of rocker panels, an automobile part, from J. C. Whitney & Co. A rocker panel is a pressed steel panel approximately 6 inches wide, 60 inches long, and 1/16 inch thick. The ends are uneven and form sharp, angular projections. The panels were inserted in a long rectangular cardboard carton without any covering or sheathing, and the ends of the carton were sealed with adhesive tape. The package contained no warning that the ends of the rocker panels were unprotected. Earl Pugh, an employee of Holden Corp., seriously injured his thumb when he reached inside the package to remove the panels. Pugh had never before opened a package of this kind, and he had never seen a rocker panel as a part separate from an automobile. Pugh sued Whitney for breach of the implied warranty of merchantability. Had the warranty been breached?

3. Suppose that Mobley, in Case 18.3 of this chapter, had alleged that Century Dodge made and breached an implied warranty of merchantability in the sale of the car to Mobley. For whom should the court hold?

4. Harvey was injured, and his antique railroad pocket watch was broken, when an aluminum stepladder upon which he had been standing collapsed. The ladder had been manufactured by Whitelight Industries, Inc., and had been sold by Sears, Roebuck and Company to William White. The ladder had been loaned to Harvey through a series of other persons. Assume that the warranty of merchantability had been breached. (a) To what recovery, if any, would Harvey be entitled under Section 2-318, Alternative A? (b) Alternative B? (c) Alternative C?

5. Bob Buyer, a stockbroker whose hobby is gardening, purchased a new garden tractor from Sarah Seller for $3000 cash. Due to a manufacturing defect, the engine exploded without warning the second time Buyer used the tractor, injuring him and a neighbor passing by on the sidewalk and causing a fire that destroyed the tractor and the neighbor's house. By means of a full warranty the manufacturer promised to refund the purchase price or to replace the tractor if it proved to be seriously defective. Buyer and the neighbor seek compensation from the manufacturer for all their losses. The manufacturer contends that it is liable only to Bob Buyer and only for the value of the tractor. To whom is the manufacturer liable, and for what elements of damage?

CHAPTER 19

REMEDIES FOR BREACH OF THE SALES CONTRACT

A seller of goods expects to receive the price, and the buyer expects to receive goods that conform to the contract. If one party does not perform his or her contractual obligations, the other party may suffer inconvenience, monetary loss, or even a serious disruption of business. To minimize the difficulties that can result from a breach of a sales contract, Article 2 of the UCC provides a number of remedies for the seller and the buyer. These remedies are available upon a breach or a threatened breach of the performance obligations discussed in Chapter 17—the obligation of the seller to transfer and deliver the goods and the obligation of the buyer to accept and pay for them.

The first part of this chapter discusses the meaning of "breach of contract." The second and third parts discuss the remedies of seller and buyer for breach of contract and the extent to which the parties may limit remedies (e.g., the amount of damages) by means of the contract.

WHAT CONSTITUTES BREACH OF CONTRACT

Failure to perform obligations imposed by the sales contract, including any warranty obligations, constitutes a breach of the contract. For example, the seller might deliver the wrong kind of goods, unmerchantable or stolen goods, fewer goods than specified in the contract, or no goods at all. Or the seller might deliver the goods later than required by the contract, perhaps too late for the buyer to use them. The buyer might default (breach the contract) by refusing to accept goods that conform to the contract or by refusing to pay all or part of the price.

Often, the parties to a sales contract agree that their performances will be carried out at some future time, as where Sue sells Ben a car to be delivered and paid for 3 months from the date of the contract. But before the time scheduled for delivery, the buyer or the seller may express to the other party an intention not to go through with the contract. This refusal in advance to perform the contract is called a **repudiation** (or an **anticipatory breach**) of the contract. Such a repudiation gives the other party "reasonable grounds for insecurity," and the aggrieved (wronged) party has a right to "adequate assurance of due performance" [2-609].

The wrongdoer's failure to provide adequate assurance where such an assurance is warranted is also a repudiation of the contract. Upon a repudiation that will *substantially* impair the value of the contract to the aggrieved party, that party may suspend his or her own performance. Then the aggrieved party may await performance for a commercially reasonable time or take the remedial steps (such as canceling the contract) discussed later in this chapter [2-610]. However, the repudiating party (the wrongdoer) is free to retract the repudiation until the aggrieved party cancels the contract, materially changes his or her position, or otherwise indicates that he or she considers the repudiation final [2-611].

Suppose, for example, that Brenda has ordered 500 cabinets to be built by Sam and installed in Brenda's apartments before June 1, but on May 1 Sam's shop and many of the cabinets that have been built are seriously damaged by fire. Brenda has reason to doubt whether Sam can perform as promised, and she is entitled, upon making written demand, to an assurance of Sam's due performance. If Sam cannot make such an assurance—for example, by providing reasonable evidence of ability to perform despite the fire—Brenda may treat the contract as breached and get cabinets elsewhere. Similarly, Sam might have agreed to extend credit to Brenda only to learn soon afterward that she has failed to pay other creditors. Brenda's ability to produce reasonable evidence of creditworthiness and to give valid reasons for failing to pay the other creditors might constitute an adequate assurance of due performance to Sam. The defaulting party has a reasonable time, not to exceed 30 days, to give the assurance.

REMEDIES OF SELLER AND BUYER

The purpose of the UCC remedies for breach of contract is to put the aggrieved party in as good a position as he or she would have been in if the contract had been fully performed [1-106]. More specifically, the remedies discussed in this chapter are intended to protect three main interests of seller and buyer: the expectation, the reliance, and the restitution interests. The *expectation interest* is the gain that the nondefaulting party expected to make if the defaulting party had performed. The *reliance interest* is the interest the nondefaulting party has in recovering costs incurred in preparing for the hoped-for performance. For instance, the seller might have altered machinery solely to fill a special order for the buyer. The buyer might have made special arrangements to accommodate or sell goods that the seller promised but failed to deliver. The *restitution interest* is the interest the nondefaulting party has in recovering a benefit which that party conferred on the other party. The buyer might have made a prepayment on the price of the goods, or the seller might have made a partial delivery.

Remedies of the Seller Remedies are available to a *seller* where the buyer has breached the contract. The buyer breaches by (1) wrongfully rejecting goods, (2) wrongfully revoking acceptance of goods, (3) failing to make a payment due on or before delivery, or (4) repudiating as to all or part of the contract [2-703]. With respect to goods affected by the breach, the seller may do one or more of the following.

1. *The seller may withhold delivery of the goods* where, for example, the buyer repudiates the contract or fails to make a payment due on or before delivery. Furthermore, where the seller learns before the buyer receives the goods that the buyer is insolvent, the seller may refuse to make delivery except for cash and, as noted in the next paragraph, may stop delivery of goods already on their way to the buyer [2-702].
2. *The seller may stop delivery of goods in the possession of a carrier or other bailee* [2-705]. If the reason for stoppage is the buyer's insolvency, the seller may stop the delivery regardless of its size. But where the reason for stoppage is the seller's insecurity or something else not involving insolvency of the buyer, the right to stop delivery is limited to carload, truckload, planeload, or larger shipments. The reason for this limitation is to minimize the burden on carriers that would result if sellers were permitted to stop delivery of any shipment no matter how small. A seller making a small shipment to a solvent buyer of doubtful credit can protect himself or herself by shipping COD. Moreover, where stoppage occurs for

insecurity, the seller is merely suspending performance and awaiting the buyer's assurance of due performance. If the buyer makes the assurance, the seller is not entitled to resell or divert the goods.

3. As a preliminary to the remedy of resale or to an action for the price of the goods, *the seller may identify conforming goods to the contract.* If the goods are unfinished, the seller may either "complete the manufacture and wholly identify the goods to the contract, or cease manufacture and resell for scrap or salvage value, or proceed in any other reasonable manner" [2-704].

4. *The seller may resell the goods and recover damages* [2-706]. The resale must be made in good faith and in a commercially reasonable manner. Where the resale price is lower than the contract price, "the seller may recover the difference between the resale price and the contract price, together with any incidental damages . . . but less expenses saved in consequence of the buyer's breach." Incidental damages include (but are not limited to) any commercially reasonable expenses incurred in stopping delivery, transporting and caring for goods after the buyer's breach, and returning or reselling goods [2-710].

5. As illustrated by Case 19.1, *the seller may recover damage for nonacceptance or repudiation by the buyer.* The usual measure of damages is "the difference between the market price at the time and place for tender and the unpaid contract price, together with any incidental damages . . . but less expenses saved in consequence of the buyer's breach" [2-708(1)]. Suppose that Betty Buyer contracts to buy a large car from Dan Dealer for $12,000. Shortly before the time scheduled for delivery, a severe oil shortage develops, and Betty cancels the contract because she thinks the car will use more gasoline than she will be able to obtain. Because of the oil shortage, and despite his best efforts, Dan can resell the car for only $10,000. Dan is entitled to $2000 damages (the difference between the market price and the unpaid contract price), together with any incidental damages (such as interest or storage charges that accumulate while Dan attempts to find another buyer), but less any expenses that Dan saved because of Betty's breach (such as labor costs saved because the second buyer declined the undercoating and decorative painting ordered by Betty). Since the demand for large cars is weak, this measure of damages will "make the seller whole," i.e., will put him in as good a position as Betty's performance would have done.

   Sometimes, however, the measure of damages just described is inadequate to make the seller whole. In such a situation the measure of damages is the *profit* (including a reasonable amount for overhead) that the seller would have made from full performance by the buyer [2-708(2)]. Suppose that during a severe oil shortage Dan Dealer has access to an unlimited supply of small, efficient cars, with buyers lined up for blocks clamoring to buy at the full list price of $6000. If Betty Buyer contracts to buy one of the cars and later refuses to go through with the deal, Dan cannot make up the lost profit by reselling the car to the next buyer in line. Dan is in a position to sell an unlimited number of eagerly sought units, and Betty's default had reduced the number of sure sales by one. Dan is entitled to the profit he expected from Betty's contract—the list price ($6000) plus any incidental damages and a reasonable amount for his overhead expenses, but minus the cost of the car to him (perhaps $4500), and minus any expenses he saved as a result of Betty's breach.

6. When the buyer fails to pay the price as it becomes due, *the seller may recover the price of the goods.* This remedy is limited to (*a*) situations where the buyer has accepted the goods; (*b*) most situations where conforming goods have been lost or damaged after the risk of their loss has passed to the buyer; and (*c*) situations where goods identified to the contract cannot be resold at a reasonable price, for example, where furniture designed in compliance with a customer's order is so ugly that it can be sold only as scrap [2-709].

7. To the extent justified by the buyer's breach, *the seller may cancel the contract.*

8. In a few situations *the seller has a right to reclaim delivered goods.* For example, the seller may reclaim goods from the buyer where the contract requires payment on delivery, the goods were delivered, payment was demanded, and the buyer paid by a check that "bounced" [2-507]. However, the seller may *not* reclaim goods where the buyer has already transferred them to a good-faith purchaser for value.

The seller has a right of reclamation in another situation. Where the seller makes a credit sale and discovers that the buyer was insolvent when the goods were delivered, the seller may reclaim them from the buyer (but not from the buyer's good faith purchaser for value) *if* the seller makes written demand within 10 days after the buyer receives the goods [2-702].

CASE 19.1

Servbest Foods, Inc. v. Emessee Industries, Inc.
403 N.E.2d 1 (Ill. App. 1980)

Facts: Emessee contracted to buy 200,000 pounds of beef trimmings from Servbest at 52 1/2 cents per pound. Servbest delivered appropriate invoices and warehouse receipts to Emessee. The price of beef trimmings fell sharply. Emessee canceled the contract and returned the documents to Servbest. Servbest resold the trimmings at 20 1/4 cents per pound and sued Emessee for damages. Approximately four years after Emessee's breach and Servbest's resale of the trimmings, the court awarded Servbest $62,599.50 damages for breach of contract plus $727 as incidental damages and $13,152.46 in prejudgment interest. Emessee appealed.

Question: Was the trial court's award of damges proper?

Answer: Yes. The damages awarded were no more than necessary to make the seller whole.

Reasoning: One option open to an aggrieved seller is damages based on a resale of the goods. Here the seller made a timely and commercially reasonable resale and was entitled, as the trial court held, to the difference between the contract price and the lower resale price as damages. The seller was also entitled to incidental damages. The $727 was the cost of storing the meat until the seller could find a buyer and was a legitimate item of incidental damages. Finally, contrary to the buyer's argument, the award of prejudgment interest was proper. The amount due under the contract was capable of easy and exact computation, and the interest on that amount was correctly calculated.

Remedies of the Buyer

Remedies are available to a *buyer* where the seller has breached the contract. The seller breaches by (1) failing to make delivery, or (2) repudiating part or all of the contract. The seller is also in breach where (3) the buyer rightfully rejects the seller's tender, or (4) the buyer justifiably revokes acceptance [2-711]. With respect to goods affected by the seller's breach (including breach of a warranty), the buyer may do one or more of the following.

1. *The buyer may cancel the contract,* to the extent justified by the seller's breach.
2. *The buyer may recover so much of the price as has been paid and,* as explained later, *may have damages.*
3. *The buyer may "cover" and have damages* as to all the goods affected, whether or not the seller has identified them to the contract. The buyer *covers* by making or arranging in good faith a substitution of goods (from another source) for those due from the seller. The buyer may also recover from the seller as damages the difference between the cost of cover and the contract price, "together with any incidental or consequential damages . . . but less expenses saved in consequence of the seller's breach" [2-712]. *Incidental damages* resulting from the seller's breach include, for example, expenses reasonably incurred in inspecting, receiving, transporting, or caring for goods rightfully rejected, and expenses reasonably incurred in effecting cover. *Consequential damages* resulting from the seller's breach include "(a) any loss resulting from general or particular requirements and needs of which the seller at the time of contracting had reason to know and which could not reasonably be prevented by cover or otherwise; and (b) injury to person or property proximately resulting from any breach of warranty" [2-715].
4. *The buyer may recover damages for nondelivery* [2-713]. The measure of damages for nondelivery or repudiation by the seller is the difference between the market price, at the time when the buyer learned of the breach, and the contract price, together with any incidental and consequential damages, but less expenses saved as a result of the seller's breach. This remedy applies only when and to the extent that the buyer has not covered.
5. Where an insolvent seller identifies goods to the contract but fails to deliver them or repudiates the contract, *the buyer may obtain the identified goods* from the insolvent seller [2-502].
6. *The buyer may obtain specific performance.* "Specific performance may be decreed where the goods are unique or in other proper circumstances" [2-716]. The drafters of the Code explain specific performance as it relates to Article 2: "Specific performance is no longer limited to goods which are already specific or ascertained at the time of contracting. The test of uniqueness under this section must be made in terms of the total situation which characterizes the contract." Output and requirements contracts involving a particular source or market present the typical commercial specific performance situation. However, "uniqueness is not the sole basis of the remedy under this section, for the relief may also be granted 'in other proper circumstances,' and inability to cover is strong evidence of 'other proper circumstances'" [2-716, comment 2].
7. In a few situations *the buyer may have a right of replevin* [2-716]. **Replevin** is an action taken to acquire identified goods that the seller has wrongfully withheld from the buyer. Replevin is available where (a) the buyer is unable to effect cover after reasonable effort; (b) the circumstances reasonably indicate such an effort

will be useless; or (c) the seller has shipped the goods and has kept a security interest in them, and the buyer has made or tendered satisfaction of the security interest. Replevin and specific performance are similar in that the buyer seeks the goods themselves. But replevin is available only where the goods are identified to the contract, while specific performance is available as to unidentified goods.

A buyer may have other remedies in addition to those listed in the preceding paragraphs. For example, upon rightful rejection or justifiable revocation of acceptance, the buyer has a security interest in goods in his or her control for any payments the buyer has made on their price, and for expenses of handling and resale [2-711]. A buyer who has accepted goods and given timely notice of defects may recover damages for loss due to any nonconformity of tender [2-714]. (Recall from Chapter 17 that a buyer who has accepted a defective tender is *barred from any remedy*, including a remedy for breach of warranty, unless he or she notifies the seller of the defect within a reasonable time after it has been or should have been discovered.) Finally, upon giving proper notice to the seller, the buyer may "deduct all or any part of the damages resulting from any breach of the contract from any part of the price still due under the same contract" [2-717].

Case 19.2, which follows, illustrates the buyer's remedy of cover. Case 19.3 discusses some kinds of damages that may be available to an aggrieved buyer who cannot make a cover purchase.

CASE 19.2 Thorstenson v. Mobridge Iron Works Co.
208 N.W.2d 715 (S.D. 1973)

Facts: Thorstenson contracted to buy from Mobridge a Case 730 farm tractor and a mounted F-11 Farmhand loader with certain attachments. Nearly a year later Mobridge notified Thorstenson that there would be no delivery of the equipment ordered. Soon afterward Thorstenson made a "cover" purchase from a Case dealer of a similar but not identical 730 Case tractor equipped with an F-11 loader, at a price increase of $1,000. Thorstenson sued Mobridge for $1,000 damages, claiming that the cover purchase was reasonable. Mobridge contended it was an entirely different tractor from the one specified in the contract. The trial court directed a verdict for Mobridge, holding that Thorstenson had failed to introduce evidence of any damages sustained.

Question: Should the question of damages have been submitted to a jury?

Answer: Yes. The record of the trial reveals sufficient evidence of damages to require the issue to be submitted to a jury.

Reasoning: When a seller fails to make delivery, the buyer may "cover" and have damages. A buyer may cover by making any reasonable purchase of goods in substitution for those due from the seller. The goods need not be identical with those promised by the seller, nor must the goods be the cheapest available. The test of proper cover is whether the buyer acted in good faith and in a reasonable manner in procuring goods that were commercially usable as a reasonable substitute. Here a jury might find that the buyer acted reasonably in making the cover purchase.

CASE 19.3
Welken v. Conley
252 N.W.2d 311 (N.D. 1977)

Facts: Welken bought an A4T 1600 Minneapolis Moline tractor from the Conleys. As his down payment he traded in a used combine and received an allowance of $10,737.50. Welken immediately had difficulty with the clutch system of the new tractor and was not able to use it for his farming operations. The Conleys could not repair the tractor. They accepted its return and resold it. Because the Conleys could not provide an acceptable substitute for the defective tractor, Welken brought suit to recover the amount of his down payment—allegedly $10,737.50—and damages for travel and telephone expenses and substitute tractor rental fees incurred during negotiations with the Conleys. Welken won a jury verdict (which the judge reduced to $11,040.25), and the Conleys appealed, arguing that once the tractor was returned and accepted by them, Welken's only remedy was a return of his down payment. They also argued that there was no evidence to support the jury's verdict as to the value of the combine that served as the down payment.

Question: Was the award of damages proper?

Answer: Yes.

Reasoning: Under the UCC, rescission of a contract and damages for its breach are not mutually exclusive remedies. Welken rightfully revoked his acceptance of the tractor. Consequently, he was entitled under the UCC to cancel the contract and have damages for nondelivery, together with incidental and consequential damages. The record indicated that the Conleys resold the combine for $10,183, and thus there was evidence to sustain the jury's verdict as to the amount of the down payment. There was also evidence to substantiate the award to Wilken of $857.25 for travel, telephone calls, and tractor rental fees during the period when he was unable to obtain an acceptable substitute tractor.

AGREEMENTS CONCERNING, AND LIMITATION OF, REMEDIES

Under the UCC, reasonable agreements that modify or limit Code remedies will be given effect. Thus, seller and buyer may tailor their remedies to fit their special situation, as long as neither party takes undue advantage of the other.

Agreements Concerning Remedies   Like the general law of contracts, the UCC permits the parties to specify in the contract an amount of money (called "liquidated damages") that a defaulting party must pay for breaching the contract. A liquidated damages clause is enforceable only if the amount is reasonable in light of (1) the anticipated or actual harm caused by the breach, (2) the difficulty of proving loss, and (3) the impracticality of obtaining an adequate remedy without the clause [2-718]. A term fixing an unreasonably large amount as liquidated damages is void as a penalty. Similarly, a clause fixing an unreasonably small amount would probably be unenforceable because unconscionable.

Suppose that Bob Buyer, a rice farmer, is contracting to buy a large irrigation pump from Dan Dealer. If the pump fails and the crop is damaged, Bob might have difficulty proving the exact extent of his loss, since no one can predict with certainty how many bushels of rice would have been produced if the pump had not failed. But Bob might be able to negotiate a liquidated damages clause stating that Dan will pay a certain amount per acre if the pump fails and damages the crop. If the amount stated in the clause is a reasonable estimate of the anticipated loss, the clause will be enforceable. The amount will be reasonable if, for example, it is based on Bob's past rice production and gives Dan credit for any part of the crop that can be salvaged.

Suppose Bob makes a down payment on the pump, and the contract states that Dan may keep Bob's down payment as liquidated damages if Bob breaches the contract. Then Dan delivers a conforming pump and Bob wrongfully rejects it. Whether Dan may enforce the liquidated damages clause depends on whether the amount of the down payment is a reasonable estimate of Dan's loss. Dan is entitled to compensation for loss, but is not permitted to penalize Bob by enforcing a forfeiture clause. If the down payment is very small compared to the loss, Dan may keep it and have further damages [2-718]. If the down payment is substantially larger than the loss, Dan will have to make a partial refund.

Suppose now that Bob makes a down payment but the contract says nothing about liquidated damages or how the down payment will be treated if Bob breaches the contract. Then Dan delivers a conforming pump and Bob wrongfully rejects it. Under a UCC rule, Dan may, *without having to prove damages*, keep some or all of Bob's down payment. Dan may keep 20 percent of the total value of the contract up to a maximum of $500. However, Dan must return any excess to Bob unless he can prove that the damages due to Bob's breach exceeded the amount of down payment Dan is entitled to keep [2-718]. Bob contracted to pay $5000 for the pump and made a $1000 down payment. Upon Bob's breach Dan resold the pump for $5000. Dan may keep $500 of Bob's down payment but must return the other $500. Note that the UCC itself, not a clause in the contract, permits the aggrieved seller to keep the money, perhaps because the seller may have minor losses and costs of resale that are difficult to calculate.

Limitation of Remedies The remedies provided by Article 2 may be limited (or supplemented) by agreement of the parties. For example, the contract between Bob Buyer and the seller of the irrigation pump might have limited the seller's liability to replacement of defective parts. However, if the limitation is unconscionable, it will not be enforced. In transactions involving consumer goods, the limitation of consequential damages for personal injury is presumed to be unconscionable [2-719]. In other transactions the limitation of damages is not *presumed* to be unconscionable, but the aggrieved person may prove that the limitation was in fact unconscionable.

Sometimes a clause of limitation appears to be fair and reasonable, but because of the circumstances that actually arose, it "fails of its essential purpose" so that the buyer is left without a remedy. In such a situation the limitation is ineffective and the general remedy provisions of the Code apply. Case 19.4 illustrates how a clause of limitation deprived the buyer of the substantial value of the bargain.

To the extent described in Chapter 18, the Magnuson-Moss Warranty Act prohibits the exclusion of implied warranties where a supplier of a "consumer product" has made a full warranty. However, a conspicuous exclusion or limitation of consequential damages will be enforced if it appears on the face of the full warranty.

CASE 19.4

Wilson Trading Corp. v. David Ferguson, Ltd.
244 N.E.2d 685 (N.Y. 1968)

Facts: Ferguson bought yarn from Wilson. After knitting the yarn into sweaters and washing them, Ferguson discovered that the yarn had "shaded" so that the color of the sweaters varied. This defect rendered the sweaters unmarketable. Ferguson refused to pay for the yarn, and Wilson sued for the price. The sales contract provided: "No claims relating to excessive moisture content, short weight, count variations, twist quality or shade shall be allowed if made after weaving, knitting, or processing, or more than 10 days [after] the receipt of shipment." Holding that Ferguson had failed to comply with the notice provision of the contract, the trial court awarded Wilson a summary judgment for the price of the yarn. Ferguson appealed.

Question: Was the notice provision binding on Ferguson?

Answer: No.

Reasoning: Within limits, the parties to a contract may fashion their own remedies for its breach. But where an apparently fair and reasonable clause because of circumstances fails in its purpose or operates to deprive either party of the substantial value of the bargain, it must give way to the general remedy provisions of Article 2. The defendant alleged that the defect in the yarn was not reasonably discoverable before it was knitted into sweaters. If this was so, the time limitation clause leaves the buyer without a remedy. Therefore, the clause, insofar as it applies to defects not reasonably discoverable within the time limits established by the contract, must give way to the general Code rule that a buyer has a reasonable time to notify the seller of a breach of the contract.

SUMMARY

A party to a sales contract is entitled to a remedy if the other party breaches the contract. A party can default before the time set for performance by repudiating the contract. A party can be put in default by circumstances surrounding the sale that give the other party reasonable grounds for insecurity.

The purpose of UCC remedies is to put the aggrieved party in as good a position as the other party's full performance would have done. An aggrieved seller may withhold delivery of the goods, stop delivery of goods in the possession of a carrier, have an action for the price, or have other remedies. An aggrieved buyer may cancel the contract, "cover" and have damages as to the goods affected by the seller's breach, or have other remedies.

The remedies of Article 2 may be limited or supplemented by the agreement of the parties to the contract. An unconscionable limitation of remedies will not be enforced. Where a supplier of a consumer product makes a full warranty, the Warranty Act requires that an exclusion or limitation of consequential damages appear conspicuously on the face of the warranty.

REVIEW QUESTIONS

1. (a) Illustrate how a sales contract can be breached by the seller. By the buyer. (b) With regard to default, explain the significance of "reasonable grounds for insecurity." (c) What is "repudiation"? (d) Under what circumstances may an aggrieved party have a remedy for repudiation?

2. Remedies for breach of a sales contract are meant to protect the expectation, the reliance, and the restitution interests of nondefaulting parties. Define and illustrate each of these three interests.

3. (a) Under what circumstances may a seller recover the price of goods when the buyer fails to make payment? (b) Describe three other remedies of the seller.

4. (a) Explain the meaning and significance of "cover" as a buyer's remedy. (b) Describe three other remedies of the buyer.

5. (a) Under what circumstances will a liquidated damages clause be enforceable? (b) May a seller keep a defaulting buyer's down payment? Explain.

6. To what extent may a sales contract limit the remedies provided by Article 2?

CASE PROBLEMS

1. Weller agreed to manufacture ice scrapers and snow brushes, place Talon's name on them, and ship them directly to Talon's customers. Under the agreement, Weller extended $47,000 credit to Talon. After checking Talon's credit record, Weller's president tried to locate Talon's president, but his numerous phone calls were never returned. Weller became concerned about payment and demanded assurances of performance from Talon. Failing to receive them, Weller suspended shipments to Talon's customers for about 10 days. During this time Weller and Talon amended their agreement to give Talon more time to pay. Shipments resumed. Talon's debt increased to about $74,000. Weller sued for the amount owed. Talon argued that the amended agreement was not binding because Talon signed it under duress as a result of Weller's wrongful suspension of shipments. Weller contended that the suspension was rightful because Weller had reasonable grounds for insecurity. Was Weller's suspension of shipments to Talon's customers wrongful? Why?

2. CIS, a computer broker, agreed to deliver a satisfactory computer to the Huntington Beach Union High School District, and to do so by the end of July. CIS was unable to make delivery. Having allowed other bidders' offers to expire, the school district had to rebid the contract and pay a price almost $60,000 higher than CIS's contract price. The school district sued CIS for $60,000 in general contract

damages plus consequential damages of almost $10,000. The trial court awarded the school district the $10,000 but awarded only $12,000 in general damages on the ground that the second lowest bid in the original bidding exceeded CIS's by only that much. The school district appealed. Should the trial court's award of damages be upheld? Why?

3. Begley was injured in an accident when the brakes on his Jeep failed. In 1976 Begley sued Reliable Motor Company (the dealer) and American Motors Corporation (the manufacturer) for damages, alleging defects in the braking system and breach of warranty. Two years and 5 months later Reliable and AMC in turn sued the manufacturer of the brakes (Bendix Corporation) and the manufacturer of the brake fluid (Wagner Electric Corporation) for breach of warranty. Bendix and Wagner had no previous notice of Begley's suit. They denied liability, alleging unreasonable delay on the part of Reliable and AMC in giving notice of the breach of warranty. Should Bendix and Wagner be held liable to Reliable and AMC? Explain.

4. Lanier Fruit Co. agreed to pick and buy all fruit of merchantable quality in Varner's grove, about 22,000 boxes at $1.25 per box. The contract stated, "Should Buyer fail to comply with the terms and conditions herein enumerated, this contract shall . . . become null and void and the advance made to the Grower shall be retained by said Grower in full payment of liquidated damages." Lanier made an advance payment of $11,000, picked 12,000 boxes, paid Varner an additional $5000, and left 9500 boxes unpicked. Varner could not sell the unpicked fruit elsewhere. Varner sued Lanier for damages resulting from Lanier's breach of contract. The trial court held that the liquidated damages clause was binding and that Lanier therefore had no further liability to Varner. Varner appealed. Should the trial court's judgment be upheld? Why?

5. Brenda Buyer purchased two refrigerators, one for use in her home and the other for use in her business. On the face of each sales contract was the following clause in large type: "IF THIS REFRIGERATOR IS DEFECTIVE, SELLER'S LIABILITY SHALL BE LIMITED TO THE REPLACEMENT OF DEFECTIVE PARTS OR A REFUND OF THE PURCHASE PRICE AS THE SELLER ELECTS." The motors of both refrigerators were defective and shorted out, causing fires. The fire in Brenda's home damaged the kitchen and injured her. The fire at Brenda's place of business destroyed an expensive copier and injured her employee. The seller agreed to refund the purchase price but refused to pay any other damages. Brenda sued the seller for all damages caused by the defective refrigerators. What would be the result as to (**a**) the refrigerator in Brenda's home, and (**b**) the refrigerator in Brenda's place of business?

AGENCY

CREATION OF AGENCY; CONTRACT RIGHTS AND OBLIGATIONS OF PRINCIPAL AND AGENT

Years ago business was carried on by individual artisans in their homes and by small family-owned and operated shops. With the coming of the industrial revolution commerce vastly expanded and became more and more complex. The public wanted and expected an ever-increasing diversity of merchandise and services. To keep up with demand, manufacturers and shopkeepers stepped up production and hired others to work for them. As the size and complexity of commerce continued to grow, it became common practice for business owners to delegate responsibilities to others, sometimes conferring on subordinates the right to make managerial decisions. Very soon, as a result of this practice, many new kinds of legal problems arose. For example:

1. Under contract law, a contract, to be effective, must have the personal agreement of the parties who engage in it. But the world of commerce demands that others besides business owners be allowed to enter into valid contracts on the owner's behalf. Thus, how does the law permit Steve, the owner of a business, to give Jane the authority to bind the business by contract?

2. Under tort law, a person is not responsible for a tort committed by someone else. But social justice demands that an employer be responsible for a tort committed by an employee in the course of employment. On what basis can store owner Ralph be held liable if employee Dudley, while working in the store, commits a tort such as punching a customer in the nose?

To reach practical solutions for these types of problems, contract law and tort law are supplemented by the law of agency, which derives its name from the concept that one person may act as the legal *agent,* or representative, of another.

The law of agency is the subject of this and the two chapters which follow. This chapter discusses (1) the establishment of an agency relationship, and (2) the circumstances under which an individual (a **principal**) may be bound to a contract entered into by someone else (an **agent**) acting on the principal's behalf. The next chapter takes up the circumstances under which a principal may be liable for an agent's torts. The last chapter in this series examines the duties that parties to an agency (the principal and the agent) owe to each other and explains how the agency relationship is terminated.

ESTABLISHMENT OF AN AGENCY

Agency Defined

Agency is the relationship which exists when two persons or entities agree that one will perform work or services on behalf of, and under the direction or control of, the other. The one who performs the work or service is an **agent**; the one who directs or controls is a **principal**. As a result of that relationship, (1) the agent has the power to engage in contracts for the principal, and (2) the principal becomes legally liable for torts committed by the agent "within the scope of" (that is, in the course of) that employment.

The relationship need not be a formal one, and the business to be transacted need not be commercial. For instance, a principal–agent relationship is created when Helen, at Mary's request, stops by the nursery school on her way home from work, picks up Mary's son, and takes him to his home. Helen is performing a service at

Mary's direction (the request to pick up and deliver the child) and thus she has become the agent for Mary (the principal) for the duration of the errand.

Parties to an Agency

The Principal.   Any person capable of entering into a contract may be a principal; likewise, a business organization (a corporation, a partnership, etc.) or a federal, state, city, or other governmental entity, may be a principal. A minor, who under state law may legally engage in a contract, may be a principal; but, just as a minor (generally someone under 18 years of age) may disaffirm his or her contracts (see Chapter 10), a minor may disaffirm an agreement he or she has made to employ an agent.

There are three kinds of principals: (1) A disclosed principal, (2) a partially disclosed principal, and (3) an undisclosed principal.

Disclosed Principal.   Assume that John Smythe is employed to purchase horses for Purebred Farms. Smythe's business card is shown in Figure 20.1.

When Smythe gives his card to Adams, who sells horses, Adams knows that Smythe is acting for Purebred Farms. Therefore, Purebred Farms is a **disclosed principal** and Smythe is an agent for a disclosed principal.

Partially Disclosed Principal.   Alternatively, assume that John Smythe's card reads as shown in Figure 20.2.

When Adams reads this card he knows that Smythe is acting as an agent for someone, but Adams does not know who the principal is. In other words, only the fact that a principal stands behind Smythe is disclosed; the identity is not revealed. In such a circumstance, the principal is said to be **partially disclosed**, and Smythe is an agent for a partially disclosed principal. Of course, if Smythe reveals the name of his principal before making a contract with Adams, Smythe becomes the agent for a disclosed principal.

Undisclosed Principal.   Again, Smythe's business card may be in the form shown in Figure 20.3.

If Adams is handed this kind of card, he is led to believe that Smythe is acting for himself although Smythe may actually be acting for a principal. If Smythe is, in fact, acting for another, the principal is undisclosed, and Smythe is an agent for an **undisclosed principal**.

FIGURE 20-1
Disclosed principal.

John Smythe
Horse Buyer for
PUREBRED FARMS, INC.
Lexington, Kentucky

FIGURE 20-2
Partially disclosed principal.

John Smythe
Purchasing Agent
144 High Street
Lexington, Kentucky

```
                  John Smythe
              Horses Bought and Sold
                  144 High Street
                 Lexington, Kentucky
```

FIGURE 20-3   Undisclosed principal.

Some judges have expressed disdain for the business practice of using an agent for an undisclosed principal, asserting that an agent who fails to reveal that he or she is acting on behalf of someone else may take unfair advantage of the third party to the transaction. However, it is uniformly recognized that a principal legitimately may instruct the agent not to reveal his or her existence or identity. Doing business in this way many times has kept a wealthy principal from being unjustly gouged. As an example, the Rockefeller family bought property in the heart of New York City through agents who did not disclose to sellers the name of their famous principal. That property was then donated to the United Nations as the site for its headquarters.

The Agent.   A person who agrees to perform work or services under the direction or control of another (a principal) is an agent. A person or business organization may be an agent if he or she can comprehend the duties to be performed. An agent need not be a person legally capable of entering into a contract. Assume that a parent instructs a 6-year-old child to buy dog food and charge it to the parent's account. The child can legally carry out the instructions as the parent's agent and, on behalf of the parent, make a binding contract of purchase between the parent and the storekeeper.

Agents may be general agents, special agents, or gratuitous agents.

General Agent.   An agent whose duties involve a continuity of service is a **general agent**. For example, a woman permanently employed by a big chain store such as J.C. Penney, to find good locations in shopping centers where new stores can be opened, is a general agent. Similarly, a clerk who works in a store is a general agent for that store.

Special Agent.   A person employed to conduct a single transaction or a small group of related transactions is a **special agent**. The realtor whom you engage to sell your house is a special agent. The distinction between a general agent and a special agent rests upon the degree of continuity of the relationship rather than upon the extent of the agent's powers.

Gratuitous Agent.   It is not necessary for an agent to be paid for his or her services. An agent who receives no compensation is called a **gratuitous agent**. Such an agent may affect the legal relations of the principal with third parties to the same extent as an agent who is paid for his or her services. Thus, it may come as a surprise to learn that you may be liable as a principal for a friendly act of a neighbor or relative. For example, if you ask a friend to take your car to the service station for gas and on the way your friend carelessly injures someone, you may be liable to the victim for the tort your friend committed.

Agreement between Principal and Agent

Mutual Assent.   One party alone cannot establish a principal–agent relationship; both parties must in some way assent. To illustrate, assume that Arthur, formerly in the roofing business but now unemployed, wants very much to get a job with the Tip-Top Roofing Company. Without Tip-Top's knowledge or consent, Arthur goes around town telling building owners that he represents Tip-Top, attempting to sell them new roofing. He takes several orders which he brings to the Tip-Top Roofing Company. Is Arthur Tip-Top's agent? No. However, if Tip-Top assents to Arthur's actions and accepts the orders, then Arthur becomes Tip-Top's agent. We will shortly meet this concept again when ratification is discussed.

Similarly, a principal–agent relationship would *not* be established if the roofing company, endeavoring to borrow money from the bank, tells the banker that it expects an increase in business because it has hired Arthur, a super salesman. However, Arthur has not yet agreed to take the job. Tip-Top's statement to the bank has not created an agency between itself and Arthur. There must first be an assent by the agent. Mutual assent is required to create an agency.

Form of Agreement.   Except in special circumstances later discussed, no particular formality is needed to establish a principal–agent relationship, although when an important position is involved, it is common for the parties to enter into a written agreement, formalizing a contract of employment and setting out the agent's duties and the benefits to which the agent will be entitled. Usually, however, an agent is hired or employed by an informal oral understanding—for example, a storekeeper asks, "Can you start on Monday as a salesperson at $200 a week?" Fred answers, "Yes, that's fine." An agency contract is created.

Sometimes an agency is created by an oral request of the principal followed not by verbal assent but by action of the agent which demonstrates assent. For instance, Henry tells his neighbor, "Bob, when you go to the hardware store I'd appreciate your buying me a garden hoe. Charge it to my account." Bob does not reply but he buys the hoe. By his action, Bob became Henry's agent for that transaction and Henry is obligated to the hardware store to pay for the hoe.

Special Circumstances Requiring Written Agreement.   In certain circumstances an agency agreement must be in writing.

Real Estate Agency.   In some states a real estate agent is not entitled to a commission for finding a property buyer unless the property owner (the principal) and the agent have a written agreement for payment of a commission.

Equal Dignities Rule.   In most states when a principal authorizes an agent to enter into a *written* contract on behalf of the principal, the agent's authority to do so must also be in writing. This is the **equal dignities rule**. The rule applies particularly when the type of contract which the agent is to negotiate for the principal is required by the statute of frauds to be in writing (see Chapter 12). For instance, the statute of frauds of many states requires that enforceable contracts for the sale of goods above $500 must be in writing. Thus, if the state applies the equal dignities rule, an agent's authority from an artist to sell her $1000 painting must be in writing to be binding.

Direction or Control of Agent

As we have seen, an agency agreement involves the mutual understanding that the agent will act for the principal under the principal's direction or control. The words "direction" and "control" describe the degree of power that a principal may exercise over an agent. *Direction* means the right to tell an agent what to do but not how the agent will accomplish the task. *Control* is the right of a principal to tell an agent not only what to do but also how the physical task is to be performed.

Direction.   Examples of the kinds of agents to whom principals may give direction *without control* are:

Real estate agent: Joann (the principal) employs Parkway Realty (the agent) to sell her house. Joann tells Parkway what price and terms she wants. How Parkway finds and talks to potential buyers is entirely up to Parkway.

Auctioneer: Steven (the principal), owner of a valuable piece of sculpture, places it in the hands of auctioneers Sotheby-Parke-Bernet Inc. (the agent) for sale to the highest bidder, stating the minimum acceptable price. Sotheby decides for itself how the auction will be conducted.

Attorney-at-law: Ida (the principal), after recounting certain facts, asks Maxine, an attorney (the agent), to file a lawsuit on her behalf. What papers must be prepared and filed, and just how the suit is to be conducted are judgment decisions for Maxine to make.

Agents, like those in the examples above, over whom a principal may exert only direction, are *independent contractors*. An independent contractor is a person or business carrying on an occupation independent from the principal, hired only for a particular purpose and a limited time. An independent contractor is not on the permanent payroll of the principal, and may delegate to other people any of his or her duties except those which require the exercise of the agent's personal judgment. Thus, attorney Maxine, hired to conduct Ida's lawsuit, may have her clerks or assistants look up the law, write briefs, and prepare memoranda, but the actual lawsuit must be handled by Maxine herself (the agent) who was hired to carry on that activity.

Some independent contractors are not agents because they do not represent a principal to third parties. This type of independent contractor merely sells or furnishes a service to the principal. For example, you hire a roofing contractor at a fixed price to repair the roof of your house; or you employ a surgeon to remove your appendix. Not being agents, each is responsible to pay for any materials used or assistants hired, but each has no power to bind you in contracts with others.

Control.   Contrast the kind of agent to whom a principal gives direction but not control, with the following examples of agents who are under *both* direction and control of the principal:

Bank teller: Marge (the agent), is a teller in the City Bank (the principal). Everything Marge does in her job must conform to the explicit procedures set forth by the bank.

Airline pilot: Craig (the agent) who flies for Scheduled Airlines (the principal), must perform his duties in strict compliance with procedural directives from his supervisor, the chief pilot for the airline.

Salesperson: Edith (the agent), a traveling salesperson, is assigned a territory and must follow explicit instructions as to what territory to cover and what procedures to follow in selling the products of her employer (the principal).

An agent who must physically perform his or her duties subject to a principal's control is usually called an *employee*. Normally, an employee is given a salary, is employed for a considerable period of time, and uses the employer's tools or equipment in furtherance of the employer's business. An employee is hired to perform personally a particular job or service and cannot delegate the work to some other person except in an emergency when the principal cannot be reached.

How the terms *direction* and *control* are applied to a specific factual situation appears in the case which follows.

CASE 20.1   A. Gay Jenson Farms Co. v. Cargill, Inc.
309 N.W.2d 285 (Minn. 1981)

Facts: Warren Grain & Seed Company operated a grain elevator and purchased grain from local farmers. To finance its grain purchases, the Warren company borrowed large sums from Cargill, Inc. Under the arrangements they established, Cargill, Inc. almost daily told the Warren company how to run the business. The Warren company could not make plant repairs exceeding $5,000 without Cargill's approval; Cargill could at any time enter the Warren company's premises, had access to its books, and the Warren company used drafts and other business forms bearing Cargill's name. The Warren company ultimately was unable to pay its debts and one of the Cargill company officials took over and operated the Warren company. Warren company owed Jenson Farms two million dollars for grain it had bought. Jenson sued both the Warren Company and Cargill, Inc., claiming that Warren was merely an agent of Cargill, Inc., when the grain was purchased. Cargill denied that an agency existed, claiming that the arrangements were set up only as a means to protect Cargill's advancements of money to Warren.

Question: Was Warren Cargill's agent?

Answer: Yes, and thus Cargill is obligated to Jenson.

Reasoning: When Cargill directed Warren to follow its instructions as to how Warren was to carry on its business, Cargill consented to Warren being its agent. When Warren agreed to do business this way he consented to be an agent for Cargill. Although the parties did not call their relationship an agency, the managerial control assumed by Cargill and agreed to by both parties established in law a principal–agent relationship.

CONTRACT MADE BY AGENT FOR PRINCIPAL

An agent may engage in any work or service authorized by a principal provided the activity is not contrary to law. When an agent is authorized to contract with a third party on the principal's behalf, the contract the agent negotiates is between the principal and the third party and binds the principal to perform the contract, as shown in Figure 20.4.

Agent's Authority to Contract   An agent may bind a principal by contract if authority to do so (1) is communicated by the principal to the agent (the authority is then called *actual authority*); or (2) is made known by the principal to the third party to the transaction in which the agent is engaged (the authority is then called *apparent authority*; or (3) is given retroactively by the principal's approval of a contract which had been entered into by someone who, without authority, purported to act as an agent of the principal. This retroactive approval is called **ratification**.

Actual Authority.   Actual authority may be conferred by a principal on an agent either expressly or impliedly.

Express Authority.   If a principal tells an agent, either orally or in writing, what to do, this is the agent's **express authority** to act for the principal. For example, Sunrise Stables tells Brent, a horse trainer, to purchase for the stables a sound, five-gaited horse under 3 years old, and to pay no more than $2500 for it. What Brent is told to do and the limits of his authority have been clearly stated by the principal. Brent has express authority to buy the horse within the limits of his instructions, and when he has done so, Sunrise must pay for the horse.

Implied Authority.   Instructions, particularly if the services the agent will render cover an extended period of time, are usually expressed in more general terms than those Brent received in the above example. The principal's express words are implicitly extended to include inferences that the agent may reasonably draw from (1) the principal's words and actions, (2) the circumstances surrounding the agency, and (3) the customs of the trade and of the community where the service is to be performed. The sum of the express words plus the implications and inferences that the agent reasonably believes he or she possesses is the agent's **implied authority**. As was said by the court in *Fairfield Lease Corp. v. Radio Shack Corp.*, 256 A.2d 690 (Conn. 1961), "The law presumes that an employer intends his employees to have

FIGURE 20-4   Principal–agent–third party relationship.

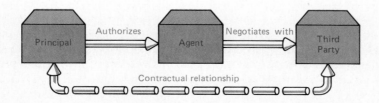

such powers as are reasonably necessary for him to carry on his work for the employer and such other powers as are reasonably necessary to carry into effect the powers thus implied." An example of implied agency powers would be the following: Clarice hires Bess "to manage my ladies' dress store." From that simple expression of authority Bess may reasonably imply that she has the power to do everything that is ordinarily necessary to operate a dress store in the town where it is located, such as the power to contract for newspaper and radio advertising, to hire and fire employees, to make emergency repairs to the store windows and fixtures, and to order and pay for merchandise a store of that kind usually sells in that community. However, Bess does not have the implied authority to make major changes in the fixtures in the store, to purchase a building into which the store could be moved, or to order men's clothing to be sold in the store. To have power to do these additional things, Bess must first secure further authority from Clarice.

Apparent Authority.   When a principal leads a third party to believe that a certain person is his or her agent, or that an agent has a particular degree of power, the authority the third party is led to believe the agent possesses is **apparent** or **ostensible authority**. The important factor in apparent authority is that it originates with, or, as might be said, is "set up" by the principal. A principal may manifest (make known in some way) apparent authority in a variety of ways, such as by a direct statement to the third party, or by permitting someone to have a business title, occupy a position, or perform duties which lead a third party reasonably to believe that the individual has power to act for the principal. Apparent authority is generated by the principal and does not spring from the statements of the agent alone. In the example in the previous paragraph it *appeared* to a wholesale representative who saw Bess in the store, acting as its manager, that she had the authority to purchase women's clothing for the store. Clarice, Bess' principal, because of that apparent authority, is bound by any contract Bess makes with those wholesale representatives.

If an agent really has the authority the third party believes the agent possesses, as in the above example, then apparent authority and actual (express) authority are both present—merely seen from different points of view. The agent is aware of his or her express and implied authority, while the third party observes only the agent's apparent authority.

Apparent authority may be an extension of an agent's actual authority. Assume that Joe works for a hardware store and has the authority to describe the merchandise he sells. One day, he is told by his employer, "A representative from the High-Klass Cookware Company is coming in to introduce and handle all the sales of the new High-Klass products, so refer all inquiries about them to her." Despite that limitation upon his authority, while the High-Klass representative is out on a coffee break, customer Shirley asks Joe if the pots are nonstick. Joe, eager to make a sale, replies that they are. The store, Joe's principal, is bound by the representation Joe made. It reasonably appeared to Shirley that Joe was authorized to describe the quality of the pots for sale in the store. The secret limitation on Joe's authority was not known to Shirley and she has a right to hold the store responsible for Joe's representations and can get her money back if food sticks to the pots.

Apparent authority may also exist after actual authority is no longer present. Assume Todd is a traveling salesperson for Write-O, a manufacturer of pens and pencils. Todd is fired, but Write-O neglects to get from him his sample kit and order books. A few days later, when he has no actual authority to make sales for Write-O, Todd, using his sample kit and order blanks, pretends to make sales of the company's pens and pencils. Todd keeps the deposit money he collects from the unsuspecting customers who reasonably view him as an agent of Write-O. Here, the principal is bound by the apparent authority, and must send pens and pencils to Todd's irate buyers who demand them.

Apparent authority may also be given to a person who never was an agent of the principal, creating what some courts hold to be an "ostensible agency." This is illustrated by the next case.

CASE 20.2

Weingart v. Directoire Restaurant, Inc.
333 N.Y.S.2d 806 (N.Y. 1972)

Facts: Weingart parked his Cadillac in front of the Directoire Restaurant. He gave the car keys to Douglas, who was standing at the entrance dressed in a doorman's uniform. Douglas gave Weingart a receipt and Weingart went into the restaurant to eat. When he finished he came out and handed the parking receipt to Douglas, but Douglas was unable to find Weingart's car. Weingart asserted that the restaurant should pay him the value of the automobile. The restaurant denied responsibility because Douglas was not its agent (employee); he was just parking cars on his own, expecting to receive tips.

Question: Was the restaurant liable for the loss of the car?

Answer: Yes. Weingart reasonably relied upon Douglas' appearance as the restaurant's agent.

Reasoning: Although Douglas was not actually an agent of the restaurant, the restaurant operators knew that Douglas stood at its door and acted as though he were the restaurant's parking attendant. The restaurant did nothing to prevent its customers from concluding that Douglas was its agent. Weingart reasonably relied upon Douglas' appearance when he gave him the car keys. The restaurant is liable for the loss of the car.

Ratification An agent's actual or apparent authority normally is manifested by a principal *before* the agent undertakes an authorized act or service. Ratification is the manifestation of authority by a principal *after* the act or service is performed. *Ratification* means the principal adopts or accepts an unauthorized act undertaken on his or her behalf. After ratification by the principal the transaction is treated as though it had been originally authorized. Ratification occurs when a principal, after having full knowledge of the facts, (1) accepts the benefits or the performance of an unauthorized agreement, or (2) fails in a timely fashion to repudiate an action purported to have been done on the principal's behalf, or (3) brings a legal action against the third party to enforce the unauthorized contract or agreement. If a principal ratifies an act, it is ratified in its entirety; the principal cannot adopt part of a transaction or agreement and deny the balance. The following case deals with ratification.

CASE 20.3   Perry v. Meredith
281 So. 2d 649 (Ala. 1980)

Facts: Perry, a candidate for public office, was short of funds and instructed his staff not to incur any debts on his behalf. Nevertheless, one of his staff, without authority, ordered campaign material to be printed by Meredith. After their receipt, the materials were used by Perry in his campaign but the printing bill was not paid. Meredith claimed that although the material was ordered without Perry's authority, Perry is obligated to pay the bill because he ratified the purchase.

Question: Did Perry ratify the purchase agreement?

Answer: Yes. His actions demonstrated his approval of the unauthorized agreement between his agent and Meredith.

Reasoning: Upon receipt of the material, Perry had full knowledge that it had been ordered by a member of his staff for use in his campaign. He knew that the material was not a donation. His *use* of the printed matter then constituted a ratification of the unauthorized printing order and he must pay the printer, Meredith, who was an innocent party to the transaction.

CONTRACT RIGHTS AND OBLIGATIONS OF PRINCIPAL, AGENT, AND THIRD PARTY

The contractual rights of the parties to an agency transaction differ when the agent acts with or without authority, and when the principal is disclosed, partially disclosed, or undisclosed.

Where Agent Acts Within Scope of Authority

When Principal Is Disclosed.   When an agent, acting within the scope of authority from a disclosed principal, contracts with a third party, the contract is as much a contract of the principal as it would have been had the principal personally entered into it. The agent is only a go-between; he or she is not a party to the contract (see Figure 20.4) and therefore not liable to the third party. The principal and the third party have contractual rights and duties directly to one another; each may require performance of the agreement by the other.

Since an agent is not a party to a contract between his or her principal and a third party, the agent for a disclosed principal can neither require performance nor be forced to make good a failure on the part of the principal to perform. An exception would, of course, occur if the third party and the agent agreed that the agent could be held responsible.

A principal's obligation under a contract made by an authorized agent is the subject of the following case.

CASE 20.4   **Pfluger v. Colquitt**
620 S.W.2d 739 (Tex. 1981)

Facts: Pfluger left two antique Cadillac automobiles with Williams, who restores classic cars. Colquitt offered to buy the cars. Williams replied that he would first have to secure Pfluger's permission. Pfluger orally agreed. Colquitt paid Williams by check and took possession of the cars but he did not receive their title certificates. Williams failed to turn the money over to Pfluger, and Pfluger demanded the return of the cars. Colquitt refused. Pfluger sued both Williams and Colquitt; Colquitt, in turn, demanded the certificates of title to the automobiles.

Question: Was Pfluger bound by Williams' sale?

Answer: Yes. Williams was Pfluger's agent.

Reasoning: When Williams sold the automobiles, he was acting as Pfluger's agent within the scope of his authority. The transaction had the same effect as if Pfluger had dealt personally with Colquitt because when a person acts through an authorized agent for a disclosed principal, that principal is bound as if he had himself acted. When Williams accepted Colquitt's check he did so as Pfluger's agent and the payment was the same as if it had gone directly to Pfluger. Williams, at that time, became responsible to Pfluger for the money. The fact that Williams did not pay Pfluger does not adversely affect Colquitt, who is an innocent party entitled to the certificates of title to the cars.

When Principal Is Partially Disclosed.   Unlike an agent for a disclosed principal, an agent for a partially disclosed principal is a party to the contract and both the agent and the partially disclosed principal are liable upon it. The reason for this is that when a principal is partially disclosed it is likely that the third party, when entering into an agreement, is relying on the reputation and credit of the known agent as well as the possible financial resources of the unknown principal. Accordingly, in the absence of agreement to the contrary, the partially disclosed principal *and* the agent may be required to perform the contract and are liable for its breach. For example, assume that a central purchasing agency which buys for a number of companies purchases a carload of tires from the Firestone factory without telling Firestone that Brown is the principal in this transaction. Firestone has never investigated Brown's credit rating but has investigated the credit rating of the central purchasing agency. Brown receives the tires but Firestone is not paid. Firestone, in making the sale, relies on the credit of the purchasing agency as well as that of the unknown principal. Therefore, both the purchasing agency and Brown are liable for the indebtedness.

Firestone can secure a judgment against both, but can collect the amount of its bill only once, of course.

If a third party fails to perform an agreement entered into with an agent acting for a partially disclosed principal, the rights of the parties are reversed and either the agent or the partially disclosed principal can require the third party to perform its part of the agreement.

When Principal Is Undisclosed.   The rights and obligations of the parties are slightly different when the agent does not reveal to the third party that he or she is representing a principal. In this case, the agent appears to be acting for himself or herself alone, and not as an agent at all. The agent, therefore, is a party to the agreement or contract in the role of principal, and thus can demand performance by the third party. By the same token, the third party can demand that the agent perform the contract or make compensation for any breach.

The interesting thing is that under agency law, even though the third party had no idea that someone else was involved in the transaction, that unknown "someone" (the undisclosed principal), is entitled to step forward and take advantage of the contract. Therefore, as in the case of a partially disclosed principal, either the undisclosed principal or the agent may require the third party to perform the contract or to make compensation for its breach. While giving this right to the undisclosed principal, agency law protects the third party by providing that the undisclosed principal cannot subject the third party to any greater liability than if the action had been brought by the agent. To clarify this concept, suppose that Henry, acting for undisclosed principal Paul, purchases a motorcycle for $1000 from the J. J. Company. Paul sues the J. J. Company to get back the $1000 because the machine is a "lemon." The company can "set off" a debt of, say, $200 that the agent, Henry, already owed the company, and need only reimburse the difference of $800 to Paul, the now-revealed principal in the transaction. This comes about because if Henry himself had brought the suit, the J. J. Company would have been entitled to apply, or "set off" the debt in this way.

Agency law further protects the third party in a transaction involving an undisclosed principal, by providing that neither the principal nor the agent can force a third party to perform a contract if the existence of the agency has been fraudulently concealed. This can occur in one of two ways: Either (1) the agent, when asked, denied the existence of the agency; or (2) if the undisclosed principal knew all along that the third party would not do business with that principal if the principal's identity had been disclosed.

It would be unfair to give an undisclosed principal a right against a third party without giving a parallel right to the third party against the undisclosed principal. Accordingly, if there is a failure of performance by the undisclosed principal or by the agent, the third party can hold either of them to the contract. This is called the "right of election." It would be natural for the third party to elect to hold responsible the one believed to have the most financial resources.

The following case illustrates the right of election and shows how the choice of "whom to elect to hold responsible" might possibly backfire, to the sorrow of the third party.

CASE 20.5

Bryans Road Building & Supply Co., Inc. v. Grinder
415 A.2d 615 (Md. 1980)

Facts: Grinder purchased goods on credit from Bryans without revealing that he was acting for a principal. The bill was not paid. When Bryans sued Grinder to collect payment, Grinder claimed that he had acted as agent for a corporation, an undisclosed principal, and so did not owe the debt. Bryans then added the corporation as a defendant to the suit as an undisclosed principal and sought payment from both the corporation and Grinder. Bryans secured a judgment against the corporation but the corporation did not have the resources with which to pay the amount owed. Bryans thereupon attempted to secure a judgment against Grinder. Grinder claims that Bryans had already made its election to hold the corporation liable and that therefore Bryans is not now entitled to a judgment against Grinder.

Question: After a third party secures a final judgment against a previously undisclosed principal, can it later secure a judgment against the agent of that principal to recover payment on the same indebtedness?

Answer: No. Securing a final judgment is an election.

Reasoning: If a third party contracts with an agent for an undisclosed principal, the agent or the undisclosed principal (when revealed), may be held on the contract debt, but the third party may not recover from both of them. Both the agent, Grinder, and his undisclosed principal may be joined as defendants in a single suit, but when a final judgment is taken against one of them, the third party elects to hold that one to the exclusion of the other. [A final judgment is a decision entered by a court upon an issue, usually following the verdict of a jury.]

liable ↓   *not liable* ↓

Where Agent Acts Outside Scope of Authority

When Principal Is Disclosed.   If an agent acts *outside* the scope of authority, either actual, implied, or apparent, and the principal does not ratify the agent's action, then the principal is *not* bound by the agent's act and the third party has no right of action against the principal. The third party, however, is not without a remedy. Assume that Tom, a mechanic for the Black Company, sees a truck Bill is selling at a very good price. Tom, believing his employer would want the truck, contracts in his employer's name to buy the truck. However, he had no authority to take that action. Unless the Black Company ratifies the purchase, it is not liable on the contract. Since the principal was disclosed, Tom is not personally liable on the contract to purchase the truck either. Bill, however, has a remedy (for whatever it may be worth). He can sue Tom for breach of Tom's implied warranty that he had authority to buy the truck for the Black Company.

When Principal Is Partially Disclosed.   An agent acting without authority for a partially disclosed principal is liable to a third party on a contract which the agent negotiated as though he or she were the principal. A partially disclosed principal is not liable on such a contract unless he or she ratifies it. For example, Judy contracts to buy a car, telling the seller that she is buying it "for a friend" without disclosing who that friend is. Since she has no authority from Steve, her friend, to take that action, then she is falsely acting as an agent for a partially disclosed principal. Unless Steve (the principal) ratifies the purchase, he is not liable on the contract, but Judy is bound by it and must pay for the car. Judy may also enforce the contract of purchase and have the car delivered to herself.

When Principal Is Undisclosed.   As in the case of a disclosed or partially disclosed principal, an undisclosed principal is not a party to a transaction entered into by an agent acting outside the scope of authority. The spurious agent of an undisclosed principal is, however, a principal in the transaction and is liable to, and has rights against, a third party with whom he or she has contracted.

SUMMARY

Agency is a consensual agreement whereby one person or entity (the principal) authorizes another (the agent) to act on the principal's behalf and subject to the principal's direction or control. Depending on the degree of control the principal has a right to exercise, the agent may be an independent contractor or an employee.

Anyone may be appointed an agent, but only an individual capable of entering into a contract may be a principal. The principal–agency relationship may be formally or informally established.

An agent has the power to bind a principal to legal obligations when acting within the scope of authority established by the principal. Authority may be actual or apparent (ostensible). Actual authority arises expressly, from the written or spoken words of the principal to the agent, or implicitly, from the agent's reasonable inferences. Apparent authority results from a manifestation by the principal to a third party that causes the third party reasonably to believe that an individual has authority to act for the principal. Apparent authority may be greater or less than an agent's actual authority. When a person without authority purports to act for another, the person for whom the unauthorized agent acts may ratify (affirm) the act.

If a third party knows a transaction is being conducted by an agent for a principal whose identity is revealed, the principal is a "disclosed principal"; if the principal's identity is not revealed, the principal is "partially disclosed." If a party to a transaction believes that the person with whom the business is being conducted is acting for himself or herself when, in fact, the person is acting for another, then the concealed other person is called an "undisclosed principal."

An agent acting within the scope of authority incurs no obligation on a contract entered into on behalf of a disclosed principal. The principal alone is responsible and may require performance by the third party.

When an agent, acting within the scope of authority, engages in a contract for an undisclosed principal, both the principal and the agent are parties to the contract. Either can require performance from the third party unless the agent fraudulently concealed the fact that he or she was acting for a principal. When the third party discovers the identity of the hitherto undisclosed principal, the third party elects whether to hold the principal or the agent responsible.

REVIEW QUESTIONS

1. (a) Why is agency a necessary subject in the study of business law, and why should a business person understand its concepts? (b) Define "agency."

2. What must parties do to create an agency?

3. (a) Who can be a principal? (b) Who can be an agent?

4. What is meant by the "equal dignities rule"?

5. In the law of agency, what do the terms "direction" and "control" mean?

6. What is the difference between an independent contractor and an employee? Give examples of each.

7. Distinguish between actual authority and apparent authority.

8. Contrast express authority and implied authority.

9. What is meant by "ratification"?

10. When an agent for an undisclosed principal makes a contract for that principal, and the principal fails to perform, can the agent be forced to perform the contract in the principal's place? Why or why not?

11. What are the rights of an undisclosed principal in a contract made in his or her behalf by an authorized agent?

12. What are the rights of the third party in a contract entered into by an agent who had acted without authority from an undisclosed principal?

CASE PROBLEMS

1. Winston went to the Uptown Hardware Store to buy a chain to use in a hoist. Winston told Peter, Uptown's salesperson, that the chain was to be used to lift a container weighing 2000 pounds. Peter showed Winston a chain and assured him that "it will do the job," although it was made to lift loads of no more than 1000 pounds. Winston bought the chain, and when he used it to lift the container, the chain broke and the container fell to the ground, breaking the glass it contained. Winston sued the hardware store for the value of the glass. Should Winston win his suit? Why or why not?

2. Art was the general manager of a radio station owned by State Broadcasting Company. It was Art's job to make all the purchases necessary in the day-to-day operations of the station. Art entered into a contract on behalf of the station by which the station agreed to buy, for 1 year, jingles and human interest stories to be used by the announcers to liven up their broadcasts. Two months later Art quit. State Broadcasting, upon learning of the contract, immediately canceled it, saying that Art had been specifically instructed never to buy any "canned" material for the station.

Did Art bind the station by the contract he had entered into? What is the basis for your answer?

3. Matt ordered a new car from Downtown Motors Co., which sold Ford cars, to be delivered with a special paint job. Matt left his 1-year-old Ford with Downtown as a trade-in, and paid the balance in cash. When Matt went to pick up the new car on the day of delivery, he discovered that Downtown was out of business and he was unable to find his traded-in car anyplace. Matt therefore demanded from the Ford Motor Company the new car that he ordered or payment for his trade-in. The Ford Motor Company replied that they would look into the matter. After some time had passed, Ford told Matt it had no responsibility. Do you agree? Why or why not?

4. Fred, a plumbing contractor who sometimes bought plumbing fixtures from Supply Company, purchased a number of articles of heating equipment at his wife's request and installed them in a house owned by his wife, Leah, in which they both lived. When the bill came from Supply Company, Fred did not pay it. The company sought to collect from Leah on the theory that she was the undisclosed principal in the transaction. The lower court held that Leah was not liable because the people at Supply Company intended to give credit only to Fred, with whom they had done business in the past and with whom they thought they were now dealing. The suit was therefore dismissed. Was the dismissal proper? Explain.

5. Lee, a member of the Modern Church, asked Paul, a printer, what it would cost to print the minutes of the church meetings. Paul quoted a price of $9 per page. Lee said that was satisfactory and instructed Paul to prepare proofs. Paul then prepared a sample of the printed minutes and delivered it to Lee. Paul heard nothing more from Lee although he called Lee's office several times. Paul ultimately learned that the printing contract had gone to another printer. Paul sued the church for the cost of the proofs and the profits that he would have made on the contract. At the trial it was established that the church had authorized Lee to do no more than to secure bids for the printing. Paul lost his suit against the church. He then filed suit against Lee. Lee claimed he was only an agent in the transaction and so was not liable. The court held that Paul could recover from Lee. Was the court correct? What is the basis for your answer?

CHAPTER 21

PRINCIPAL'S LIABILITY FOR AN AGENT'S TORTS

In the previous chapter we considered the circumstances under which an agent can bind a principal by contract. This chapter deals with the question, "If an agent commits a tort (a civil wrong, discussed in Chapters 3 and 4) while working for a principal, can the principal be held accountable to the injured party?"

A person who is injured through the tort of an agent may have causes of action against *both* the principal and agent. The agent is liable under *tort law* because everyone is accountable for his or her own wrongful actions. The principal may be liable under tort or agency law. Two illustrations should help to make this clear. (1) Thomas, the owner of a store, directs William, his employee, to throw out a disagreeable customer. William, being very literal-minded, physically throws the customer out of the store and onto the sidewalk, injuring him. (2) The same employer, Thomas, without making any attempt to find out if Eddie is a competent driver, hires Eddie to drive the company truck. A pedestrian is injured through Eddie's negligence the first time he drives the truck.

William and Eddie committed torts and are personally liable for the injuries they caused. In both situations the employer, Thomas, also has a liability. He is *directly* liable under tort law because in the first instance he *ordered* the wrong to be done when he told William to "throw the customer out." In the second example, he *negligently* put someone whom he should have known might injure others in charge of a truck. And at the same time, because the torts were committed by his employees (agents) in the course of their employment, Thomas the employer (principal) is indirectly (also called "vicariously") liable under agency law for damages the third parties sustained. More than likely, if either injured party files a lawsuit against William or Eddie and Thomas, it will be based upon both theories of law, but the injured party may be compensated only once for damages suffered.

This chapter does not deal with direct liability in tort; it deals solely with a principal's *indirect* (vicarious) liability for the tortious actions of an agent. Such indirect liability may arise (1) when the principal has the right to control how the agent physically performs his or her work, and physical injury to a third party results while the agent is acting within the scope of that employment; and (2) when a nonphysical injury results and the agent's unauthorized action was within the scope of his or her employment.

LIABILITY FOR TORTS RESULTING IN PHYSICAL INJURY

In the previous chapter we observed that principals have different degrees of authority over different kinds of agents. Principals have no right to control how independent contractor-type agents physically perform their work or services. Accordingly, a principal is *not* liable (except in special circumstances to be later discussed) for physical injury to a third party resulting from the tort of an independent contractor agent. For instance, you would not be liable for damages if your lawyer negligently has an accident on his way to the courthouse to file legal papers in your behalf.

Employers (principals) do, however, have the right to control the physical performance of their agents who are not independent contractors. Therefore, a principal *is* liable for the physical torts of such agents acting within the scope of their employment. It was under this principle of agency law that, in the examples at the beginning of this chapter, Thomas was liable for damages incurred by his employees, William and Eddie.

The employer's *right* to exercise control is the important element. The fact that an employer does not actually exercise control does not change the relationship between the employer and the agent. For example, Henry works as a janitor for Archer, who owns a four-story building. Archer has never given Henry instructions on where to hang his pail while washing windows. One day Henry drops a pail out of a fourth-floor window and it injures Lisa, walking below. Archer, although not personally at fault, is liable to Lisa for the injury Henry, his employee, caused while acting within the scope of his employment. It is immaterial that Archer did not exercise his right to control Henry's performance by giving specific safety instructions such as how to hang his pail. The important factor is that Archer had the *right* to do so because Henry was working for Archer.

"Master" and "Servant" Defined

As we have seen, a principal is liable for the physical torts of agents who are not independent contractors, but is *not* liable for the physical torts of independent contractor agents. Therefore, when a question of a principal's liability for an agent's torts arises, it is helpful to adopt some simple terminology to identify each of the two types of agents. Authoritative publications on agency law as well as court decisions call agents who are not independent contractors "servants." Their principals (employers) are called "masters." Independent contractor agents and their principals are called simply "agents" and "principals."

It would seem appropriate to use the more modern term "employee" rather than servant, but most courts have not taken this step. Accordingly, in this chapter we will follow court terminology and call employees "servants" and their principals "masters."

Doctrine of Respondeat Superior

The obligation of a master for the physical torts of a servant is known as **respondeat superior**, a Latin phrase meaning "Let the master respond." Respondeat superior does not apply to an independent contractor-type agent and would not have applied in the window-washing example, above, if Henry had run his own window-washing business and had simply contracted with Archer to clean his windows that day.

The following case illustrates how *right to control* is the key to respondeat superior.

CASE 21.1

L. M. T. Steel Products, Inc. v. Peirson
425 A.2d 242 (Md. 1981).

Facts: L. M. T. Steel Products, Inc., had a contract to install room partitions in a school. Webster, who worked "off and on" for L. M. T., was employed to superintend the work. Webster was given blueprints that he followed but he was not otherwise supervised on the job. He hired and supervised other installers who were paid by L. M. T. Webster was paid by the number of feet of partitions that were installed each week. He had no contractor's license.

Webster rode in his own car to a public telephone seven miles from the job site to telephone to L. M. T. On the way he collided with the Peirson automobile and Ms Peirson was injured. Peirson claims that Webster was L. M. T.'s servant. L. M. T. claims that Webster was an independent contractor.

Question: Under these facts, was Webster a servant or an independent contractor?

Answer: The jury found Webster to be a servant of L. M. T.

Reasoning: Of the various elements to be considered in determining the existence of a master–servant relationship, the most significant and decisive is the right to control the servant in the performance of his or her work. For an employee to be a servant an employer must have the ability to tell an employee what to do and how and when to do it. It is not the way in which, or how frequently, a master exercises his or her authority, but it is the *right* to do so that establishes a master–servant relationship.

Under the facts given here, Webster was the foreman on the job for L. M. T. and L. M. T. had the right to tell him what to do and how to do it. The workmen were paid by and were employees of L. M. T. and not of Webster. The jury found that L. M. T. had the right to exercise control over how Webster's work was to be done.

The doctrine of respondeat superior was first expressed in 1698 in an English case in which the judge said, " . . . whoever employs another, is answerable for him . . . The act of a servant is the act of his master, where he acts by authority of the master." (*Jones v. Hart,* Holt, K.B. 642 (1698).)

Judge Holt, in that old British case, gave no reasons for the conclusion he expressed, yet the doctrine of respondeat superior became firmly fixed in our law. Courts and legal writers over the years have given many reasons to justify this rule which makes an otherwise innocent person pay for another's fault. Among those reasons are:

1. A party who has the power to control another's acts should be held responsible for the results which follow.
2. Since a master gets the benefits of a servant's acts he or she should bear the burden of them.
3. Although a master may be without fault, the injured person may also be without fault, and as between two people equally free of fault, the one who initiates the affair should bear the loss.
4. Wrongful acts of servants in the course of employment are a cost of conducting business.
5. This liability is imposed on masters for the privilege of using the services of others.
6. To make masters liable tends to make them more careful in selecting their servants, and the public benefits.
7. The master has the "deeper pocket" out of which to pay a third party damages for any injury he or she sustains.

Under respondeat superior a master is responsible for the physical torts of a servant incurred in the scope of employment. Although this doctrine is simply stated, complex questions arise in its application. For example, it may be necessary to decide:

1. Was the wrongdoer a servant (employee) or a nonservant (independent contractor) agent?
2. Who is the responsible employer when an injury is caused by a servant who (with the permission of his or her master) is working temporarily for another employer?
3. Was the servant acting within the scope of employment when the injury was caused?

We will now consider these questions.

Was the Wrongdoer a Servant?   Since an employer need not exercise his or her right of control over an employee's physical actions, frequently it is not clear whether a master–servant or a principal–independent contractor relationship is present. Factors such as the following indicate, but do not conclusively establish, that an employee is a servant: The tools are supplied by the employer; payment is made by the hour, week, or month and not by the job; the work constitutes fulltime employment and is part of the employer's regular business; and the manner in which the work is done is dictated by the employer.

To illustrate the complex questions that can arise, consider these three hypothetical situations: (1) You volunteer to help your neighbor paint his fence. Even though you receive no money for your work, you are your neighbor's servant while you help him. Thus, he is liable to a third person for damages which may result if, in a fit of temper, you deliberately splash paint on someone or commit some other tort while working for him. (2) You occupy the front passenger seat of your car and allow your friend to drive because you have a headache. You are liable to any victim of your friend's negligent driving. (3) A physician who uses hospital facilities is not a servant of the hospital, but if he or she is on its paid staff as an intern or resident, the physician is then its servant and the hospital is liable for his or her malpractice.

Whose Servant Was the Wrongdoer?   An employer, to be held liable under respondeat superior, must be the master of the servant at the time the servant commits the tort. However, a servant may be temporarily "borrowed" by another employer and, while working for that employer, might commit a tort which injures a third party; or a servant may temporarily employ someone else (called a "subservant") to do the servant's work, and that subservant may commit a tort.

The Borrowed Servant Problem.   If an employer "lends" an employee to another employer, the first employer is the responsible master only if, at the time the servant commits a tort, that employer still retains an effective right of control over the servant. The question of "control" can be tricky. The following two examples illustrate this point.

1. Firefly Company, next to the Jones Moving Company, asks Jones to "lend"

Firefly an unskilled worker for 1 day because, due to the illness of one of its own employees, it is shorthanded on an important job. Jones (called the "general employer" in this type of situation) agrees and directs Mark, its employee, to go to the Firefly Company (called the "special employer," the borrower) and "do whatever they ask you to do." Jones Moving Company continues to carry Mark on its payroll. While temporarily working for Firefly, Mark negligently injures a third party. When the tort was committed, Firefly had control over Mark's physical actions in the performance of his work, all the tools and equipment belonged to Firefly, and the work was entirely for the benefit of Firefly. Therefore, Firefly, the special employer, is the responsible master.

2. The problem becomes more complicated where heavy equipment, such as a tractor earth-mover, along with its driver-operator, is rented out. The equipment is very valuable and the operator, a servant of the tractor owner, is specially trained. He must maintain the tractor and operate it at speeds and in the manner established by his employer (the general employer). But the person who rents the tractor (the special employer) directs the driver-operator where the machine is to be used, what earth to move, and where it should be piled. If the driver-operator, while complying with those instructions, drives the tractor negligently and destroys a third party's property, he or she is following the directions of the special employer, but is also working for and under the orders of the general employer with respect to the manner in which the machine is operated. In such situations the courts almost always hold that the general employer has not given up control and so is liable under respondeat superior for the servant's negligence.

The Subservant Problem.   A distinguishing characteristic of a servant's employment is that he or she has no authority except in an emergency to delegate work to others without the master's permission. If, without that permission, a servant gets someone else (a *subservant*) to perform his or her work, the servant is now the master of the subservant and has a master's liability under respondeat superior for any wrongful act the subservant may commit in the course of the work. The reason for this is that the servant has the *right to control* the subservant in the performance of his or her work. If the servant had been authorized by the employer to employ a subservant, then the principal would be liable as master for a tort the subservant committed in the scope of employment. For example, assume that Archie, a carpenter, works for a builder. One day Archie telephones his employer saying that he is sick and cannot get to the job but that his brother Bob will work in his place. The employer consents. While working on Archie's job, Bob is Archie's subservant. If, while working in Archie's place Bob negligently injures a passerby, Archie's employer is liable under respondeat superior to the injured person because the employer consented to a subservant doing the work.

Was the Servant in Scope of Employment?   For a master to be liable for the tort of a servant, the tort must be committed within the scope of employment. "Scope of employment" means that an act is (1) of the same general nature as the authorized work, (2) has a reasonable connection in time and place with such work, and (3) is intended by the servant as a part of his or her duties or results from authorized work.

If any of these elements is missing when a servant commits a tort, the doctrine of respondeat superior does not apply and the master is not liable under that doctrine.

Conscientious judges can disagree as to whether an act was of "the same general nature" as that which a servant was employed to perform, or had a "reasonable connection" in time or place with the employment, or was "intended by the employee" to serve the master, or "results from authorized work." Therefore, we can expect that different courts, while applying the same principles of law, may view differently what seem to be substantially similar facts. In case of doubt, the general tendency is for a court to find, or to support a jury's finding, that an act was within the scope of employment and therefore that respondeat superior applies.

Nature of the Work.   An act is in the scope of employment if it is of the kind usually carried on by the servant or by other servants engaged in similar work for the master, or is incidental to that work. For example, Paul hires Don to cut down trees and saw the timber into fireplace lengths. Paul tells Don which trees to cut down. Don erroneously cuts down a neighbor's tree. Paul is liable to the neighbor for Don's wrongdoing.

Time and Place of the Act.   For the doctrine of respondeat superior to apply, a servant's tortious act must have a reasonable connection in time and place with authorized work. Generally, going to and from work is not within the scope of employment and so a master is not liable if a servant drives negligently while rushing to get to work on time or if he falls asleep at the wheel while driving home after a hard day's work. But there are exceptions to this rule and the fact that the act occurs before or after normal working hours does not necessarily preclude the master's responsibility. For instance, an employer asks Bob, an employee, to mail a package at the post office *on his way home from work.* While driving to the post office Bob has an accident. Bob was within the scope of his employment. Had the accident occurred *after* Bob left the post office, he would no longer have been within the scope of employment.

Under the so-called "lunch hour rule," while a servant is away from the employer's premises for lunch—to go shopping or for other personal business—the servant is not within the scope of employment. However, if a lunch or coffee break is taken upon the employer's premises, or if the servant goes to a restroom provided by the employer, the employee remains within the scope of employment.

Often a servant is directed to drive a company vehicle on a prescribed route or between specific locations. If the servant does not follow instructions a **deviation** has occurred. If the deviation is slight, it is said that he or she is only on a **detour** and is still within the scope of employment, and the employer would be liable for a negligent act of the servant. If the deviation from the authorized route is great, the servant is said to be on a **frolic** of his or her own and outside the scope of employment, and the employer would *not* be liable for a negligent act of the servant. The courts have given no clear rule which would inform us just where a detour ends and a frolic begins. However, most courts hold that a servant reenters scope of employment when he or she is again reasonably near the authorized route and, within the time limits of the employment, again acts with intent to serve the master. The following four situations which could arise illustrate this problem.

1. Tom, a servant, is directed to take the company truck and deliver a crate to the freight office. Tom takes the normal or authorized route and on the way to the freight office he has an accident. Tom was clearly acting within the scope of his employment and, if he was negligent, the master is liable.

2. Tom delivers the freight. He then drives 2 miles farther away from his place of employment to visit his sister. He has an accident while turning into her driveway. At the time of the accident, Tom appears to be serving a purpose entirely of his own, unrelated to his employment. He is on a frolic of his own.

3. After a short visit with his sister, Tom begins to drive back to work. Before he reaches the vicinity of the freight office he has an accident. As Tom was not far from his authorized route, had intended to return to work and obviously was within his work hours, a court would hold Tom to be within his scope of employment when the accident occurred.

4. Tom, instead of taking the direct route to the freight office, takes a route a few blocks longer because he prefers the scenery along the way. Although Tom is satisfying a personal whim, the deviation is slight and a court would hold that he was engaged in a detour, still acting in furtherance of his master's business. Thus, he continues to be within the scope of employment while on that detour and his master would be liable if he had an accident. The following case applies that principle.

CASE 21.2 De Mirjian v. Ideal Heating Corp.
278 P.2d 114 (Cal. 1955)

Facts: Ideal Heating Corp. maintained a restroom where its employees could smoke, as smoking was not permitted in the work areas. Lupella, one of Ideal's employees, intended to go to the restroom to smoke. On the way, in order to fill his cigarette lighter, he opened the spigot of a drum of highly flammable paint thinner. A fire resulted which spread to premises next door occupied by De Mirjian. De Mirjian claims that Ideal is liable for the losses sustained.

Question: Was Lupella in the course of his employment when he started the fire?

Answer: Yes. Ideal is liable to De Mirjian.

Reasoning: An employer is responsible not only for the *negligent* act of an employee in the course of his or her employment, but also for a *wrongful* act committed as a part of, or in furtherance of, the employment.

Acts necessary to the comfort, convenience, health and welfare of an employee while at work, though strictly personal, do not take him or her outside the scope of employment. In a sense, these acts contribute to the accomplishment of the work. Acts such as smoking or going to the restroom are inevitable incidents of an employment. Therefore, when Lupella went to the restroom he was clearly within the scope of his employment. And when he attempted to draw some of the flammable liquid from the drum, *it was not such a material or substantial deviation from his authorized work as to amount to a departure from his scope of employment.* Lupella was, therefore, within the scope of employment when he started the fire and his employer became liable to De Mirjian.

Was the Act Intended to Serve the Master?   The last requirement for respondeat superior is that a servant's act must be undertaken with the intent to serve his or her master, or that the tort was connected with and grew out of the employment.

Negligent Acts.   Generally the requirement for respondeat superior is satisfied when a negligent act occurs during working hours at the prescribed place of work, or while driving along an assigned route, or while otherwise following the master's directions. Where a servant is on his or her employer's premises or upon a prescribed route, a servant is outside the scope of employment if the negligent act occurred while the servant was acting *solely* to satisfy his or her own purpose. For instance, assume that a factory maintains a parking lot for its visitors, but factory employees are not permitted to park in that lot. One morning Cy, an employee, is late for work so he parks in the visitors' parking lot, rushes into the factory where he punches the time clock, and returns to the parking lot to move his car to a street near the factory. While moving his car, and while still on factory grounds, Cy has an accident. At that time Cy was driving his car to satisfy his own purposes, so respondeat superior does not apply.

Frequently, a servant performs an act intended to serve the master which, at the same time, serves a private purpose of the servant as well. If the servant's intention to serve the master is a *substantial part* of the dual objective, the act *is* within the scope of employment. The following case considers such a situation.

CASE 21.3   Burger Chef Systems v. Gorvo
407 F.2d 921 (8th Cir. 1969)

Facts: Norris was employed by Burger Chef Systems. He had to go to the bank, slightly more than a mile away, to get change for the restaurant. After getting the change, he decided to drive about a mile farther along to a Kentucky Fried Chicken establishment to have lunch. However, a few blocks after leaving the bank he had an accident and the injured party claims damages from Burger Chef.

Question: Was Norris within the scope of employment at the time of the accident?

Answer: Yes. He was engaged in an activity for his master and for himself at the same time.

Reasoning: An employee who leaves his place of employment for lunch generally is not within the scope of employment. Here, however, the work that Norris was engaged in created the necessity for the travel. He was in the course of his employment even though he was, at the same time, serving a purpose of his own. The performance of Norris' personal business was not such a substantial deviation as to constitute an entire departure from his employment. Thus, notwithstanding the deviation, Norris was still engaged in the master's business and Burger Chef Systems was liable for his tort.

Intentional Acts. Thus far we have considered torts arising from *negligence* of a servant. A tortious act may also be committed *intentionally* by a servant during working hours at a place of employment. Whether such a tort can be said to have been intended to serve the master depends upon the circumstances under which it was committed. It may have been (1) because the servant believed he or she was carrying out the duties of employment, or (2) because of some personal animosity, or (3) because of a sudden outburst of anger due to the frustrations and pressures of the job.

When the commission of an intentional tortious act is reasonably within the duties of a servant, the action is within the scope of employment and the master is liable. For instance, assume that Horace is a security guard at a museum. He sees a stranger preparing to break into a case where gold nuggets are displayed. Horace seizes the man's arm. The man resists, and in the ensuing scuffle Horace breaks the man's arm. If a court rules that Horace used excessive force but that his actions were not unreasonable, the theory of respondeat superior still applies.

Quite a different legal conclusion results when the servant's act bears no relation to his or her duties, but takes place only because of personal animosity. For example, Bill, a lathe operator at the Square Deal factory, without the knowledge of his employers runs a football pool. During working hours he makes collections and pays off winners. Jim, who works at the factory next door, "invests" in Bill's pool. One day, during working hours, Jim goes to Bill's workplace and claims Bill is withholding winnings that should be paid. A fight results and Bill fractures Jim's jaw. Respondeat superior does not apply.

A third kind of intentional tort has characteristics of both the above-described wrongs. It is one committed by an employee in a sudden outburst of anger induced by exasperation, frustration, or disappointment caused by the pressures of the job. The courts take a very liberal view and hold that such a tort *is* within the scope of employment if it bears a relationship to the authorized work and is not so outrageous as to have been induced by purely personal motives. The following examples, taken from actual cases, should explain this principle.

• Paul played left center field for the Double Play Tavern's semiprofessional baseball team. In the ninth inning of the championship game the score was tied. The ball was hit to Paul in center field. Paul extended his glove to catch the ball and missed. A run was scored and the championship was lost. Paul, in disgust, threw the ball out of the ballpark and it struck a young woman walking on the street. The

Double Play Tavern, under whose name the team played and which supplied the team's uniforms and equipment, was liable for the resulting injury because the wrongful act was connected with, and grew out of, the duties of Paul's playing on the tavern's team.

• In the course of his employment, King parked his truck at a shopping center to load empty Coca-Cola bottles. Campanale drove up in another truck and asked King to move out of the parking space so that Campanale could park his truck there and make an urgent delivery. King refused to move his truck and Campanale punched him in the face. The act, although clearly wrongful and unauthorized, was committed by Campanale in an effort to overcome an obstacle in the way of his performance of his master's work. His employer was liable.

• Howard was a customer in a bar. He made unpleasant advances to a female customer. The bartender, who was behind the bar, told Howard that he "should not talk like that," picked up a pistol that he kept on hand, and shot Howard, wounding him. The court held that the bartender's action was utterly outrageous, out of all proportion to the necessities of the employer's business, and that the owner of the bar (the master) was not liable.

Liability When Duty Is Nondelegable

The duty to exercise care to protect the public from physical injury is not delegable when (1) the duty is statutory (that is, it is imposed by law), and (2) when the work involves an inherently dangerous or ultrahazardous activity (explained below). A principal is liable under such circumstances, not only when the work is performed by a servant but also when it is performed by a nonagent independent contractor.

Statutory Duties. If a statute (law) creates a nondelegable duty of care, the delegation of the duty does not free the principal from liability if injury to someone results from the activity. For example, a statute requires a railroad company to maintain proper signals at railroad crossings. The railroad company cannot escape liability if an independent contractor, hired by the railroad to cut down a tree near the signal, negligently causes a crossing signal to fail to work. The following case applies the nondelegable rule to a county in Minnesota.

CASE 21.4

Westby v. Itasca County
290 N.W.2d 437 (Minn. 1980)

Facts: Beavers had built a dam near a county road and caused water to back up. The county asked the State Department of Natural Resources to open the dam so that the water could flow. One of the department officers blasted open the dam. The operation left a lot of mud on the public road but the department officer did not post signs warning travelers about the road condition. Westby, driving along the road, suddenly ran into the muddy surface and suffered damage. He claimed compensation from the county. The county claimed freedom from liability because the road work had been done by an independent state agency.

Question: Was the county free from liability because an independent contractor did not post warning signs?

Answer: No. The county still had the duty to keep the road clear and to warn travelers of the danger.

Reasoning: A principal is liable for the negligent performance of a nondelegable duty by an independent contractor. Road maintenance by a city or county is such a duty. The presence of mud on the road and the need to warn the public of the danger was a natural result of the opening of the beaver dam. The county was liable for the failure of its independent contractor to take the necessary precautions.

Inherently Dangerous and Ultrahazardous Activities.   When an activity is inherently dangerous (that is, dangerous by its very nature), or ultrahazardous (extraordinarily dangerous), a principal has a duty to see that the public is protected from any harm that may result. These two activities differ in the degree of care required.

An *inherently dangerous* activity involves a high degree of risk but one which should not result in injury to the public if an equally high degree of care is exercised. For example, a department store hires a sign company to erect a large sign overhanging the sidewalk. The sign company must exercise more than ordinary care when erecting the sign to assure that passersby are not injured. If the sign company fails to do so and someone walking along the street is hurt, the department store (the principal), as well as the sign company (the nonagent independent contractor), is liable.

An *ultrahazardous* (also called *intrinsically dangerous*) activity is one where, even if a high degree of care is exercised in its performance, a risk to third parties still remains. Such an ultrahazardous activity would be, for example, exploding a large charge of dynamite near residences, or fumigating a restaurant with a poisonous gas.

LIABILITY FOR TORTS NOT RESULTING IN PHYSICAL INJURY

So far in this chapter we have considered a principal's liability for the torts of servant and nonservant agents which result in physical injury to third parties. We must now consider a principal's possible liability for another type of tort committed by agents—torts that do not result in physical harm—such as fraud, deceit, and defamation.

Basis of Principal's Liability When considering an employer's liability for such a tort, the distinction between a servant and nonservant agent ceases to apply. A principal may be liable if the tort is committed by either a servant or a nonservant agent in the course of a transaction authorized or apparently authorized by the principal. The basis for this liability is not respondeat superior but, rather, that when a principal appoints an agent and clothes that agent with actual or apparent authority to do something, the principal should be responsible for any misrepresentation or other nonphysical wrong the agent commits in the course of that activity, because the principal is the one who has set the entire affair in motion.

Assume, for example, that Tent City manufactures tents and sells them through a sales agency. The agency falsely represents to stores to which it sells that the canvas of which the tents are made is fireproof. Although Tent City did not authorize the sales agency to make such a representation, it must bear responsibility for the false statements because the making of statements concerning the character of the merchandise was within the apparent authority of the sales agency.

A principal's liability for the fraud of an agent, committed in the course of the agent's work, is the subject of the case which follows.

CASE 21.5   National Security Insurance Co. v. Beasley
406 S.2d 923 (Ala. 1981)

Facts: White was employed by National Security as an agent to sell its hospital insurance policies. White sold a policy to Ms Beasley and filled out the application for her. He marked "No" in the space after "arthritis" although she told him that she had been treated for that ailment. Beasley asked White if he was sure the company would honor her policy since it contained an incorrect answer and he answered, "Yes, what they [the company] don't know won't hurt them." Beasley paid the premium and three months later was hospitalized for an ailment due to her arthritis. The insurance company refused to pay the hospital bill because the policy did not cover preexisting medical problems. Ms Beasley claims that she is due payment of damages by the insurance company.

Question: Is an employer liable for damages resulting from an agent's misrepresentation in the course of the work?

Answer: Yes, an employer is liable.

Reasoning: A principal is liable for an agent's fraud committed without the principal's knowledge or consent if the agent's duties placed him or her in a position to deceive, and if the third party [Beasley] relied on the agent's apparent authority to make the misrepresentation. Here, White, the agent, was aware of Ms Beasley's history of arthritis when he filled out her application for insurance. White also knew that the policy did not cover hospitalization for preexisting illnesses. When he filled out the application form he was performing services for which he was employed. When he wrote an untruthful answer in the application and still proceeded to sell her the policy, he committed a fraud. Since the fraud was committed in the course of performing work of the kind White was employed to do, and since it occurred within the time and space limits of his employment, his principal, the insurance company, is liable for whatever damages were caused by the misrepresentation.

Remedies of Third Party

We have seen in Chapter 10 that where a contract is induced by the fraud of one of the parties, the other party has a choice of remedies. The third party may rescind the contract (declare it not binding) and recover whatever compensation had been paid, or may reaffirm (keep) the contract and bring a tort action in deceit (fraud) for damages. The same remedies are available to a third party against a principal when a contract is induced by the fraud of an agent acting within the scope of authority.

It follows that a principal is somewhat at the mercy of his or her agents in business affairs. Therefore, principals attempt to protect themselves from liability which might arise from fraudulent representations of their agents by inserting "disclaimer" or "exculpatory" clauses in the order blanks or contracts they furnish their agents. These clauses are designed to put a third party on notice that an agent is without authority to make representations binding the principal. Such a clause might read as follows: "It is hereby understood that there are no understandings, agreements, or representations between the parties other than those stated in this written contract."

This type of clause will protect a principal from liability for the deceit of an agent who acts beyond authority. However, a third party may still rescind a contract entered into by an agent who used fraud or deceptive practices while representing his or her principal. The reason for this is that under contract law a party who was fraudulently, or through other illegal means, induced to enter into a contract may rescind the contract.

If improper actions of an agent cause the principal to suffer a loss, the latter has a right of action against the agent to secure reimbursement for the loss sustained. Whether the principal will collect on the judgment depends, of course, upon the financial resources of the agent.

SUMMARY

A master is liable for physical harm caused by a servant who is within the scope of employment even though the servant is acting contrary to instructions. This rule is called respondeat superior.

In general, a servant is acting within the scope of employment if the act (1) is of the same general nature as, or is incident to, the authorized work; (2) is reasonably connected with the work in time and place; and (3) is intended by the servant to be a part of the work. A servant does not necessarily leave his or her scope of employment when there is a deviation from the prescribed work or specified route. A master *is* liable if a deviation is slight (then it is called a "detour"), but is *not* liable if a deviation is substantial (then it is called a "frolic"). If a deviation is a frolic by a servant, the courts do not agree as to when the servant reenters the scope of employment. The majority view is that reentry occurs when the servant reaches a point reasonably close to the authorized route, intending to re-engage in the work.

Courts recognize that a master may be liable for the willful torts of a servant if the intended act is connected with or grows out of the work the servant is employed to perform. But if the willful tort is of such a degree as to be outrageous, than it will be considered to have been personally motivated. In that event it is not within the scope of employment.

A principal (master or nonmaster) is liable for a servant's or nonservant's tort which does not involve physical injury if the act is committed in the course of the servant's or agent's employment or authority. Among such torts are fraud and defamation.

Principals attempt to protect themselves from liability from agents' frauds by having exculpatory statements printed on their order blanks and contract forms.

When (1) a statute imposes the duty of care, or when (2) the act out of which the tort arose is one which is inherently dangerous or ultrahazardous, a principal may be liable for a tort committed by an agent *or* by a nonagent independent contractor.

REVIEW QUESTIONS

1. Under what circumstances can both a principal and an agent be liable for a tort committed by the agent?

2. What is meant by a principal being vicariously liable for a tort?

3. What would you say is the basic reason why a principal should be liable for an agent's tort?

4. (a) What is the difference between a "master" and a "principal"? (b) What is the difference between a "servant" and an "agent"?

5. What is meant by the doctrine of respondeat superior?

6. How can you tell whether a person who commits a tort is or is not a servant? What tests will a court apply?

7. In what way does the time and place a tort is committed affect respondeat superior?

8. What is the "lunch hour rule"?

9. Distinguish between a "detour" and a "frolic."

10. Can a master ever be liable for a tort that is intentionally committed by a servant? Explain.

11. Under what circumstances can a principal be liable for a physical tort committed by an independent contractor?

12. (a) If an agent commits a tort which does not result in physical injury to a third party, can the principal be liable anyway? Explain. (b) Would your answer be different if the agent was not a servant? Explain.

CASE PROBLEMS

1. Gage, a skilled mechanic, was employed by Harry, a tractor dealer. Harry sent Gage to Robert's farm to repair a tractor. When Gage finished the repair, Robert asked him to look at the motor on Robert's water pump which "seemed to be acting up." Gage worked on the motor, then started it up. A part of the pump which he had failed to fasten flew out, hitting Ben, who was standing nearby. Assuming that Gage was negligent, is Gage, Harry, or Robert liable to Ben for the injury? Why?

2. Willy sold advertising for the *Oil Daily*. His duties required him to travel throughout several states soliciting business. Late one evening he was driving his own car to Dallas, Texas, the home office. On the way he drove 21 miles past Durant, Oklahoma. However, he felt too tired to continue on to Dallas that night, and returned to Durant. In Durant he could not find any accommodation, so ended up sleeping in his car. In the morning he started out again, taking another road to Dallas. He fell asleep while driving and collided with Ferdinand's car. Ferdinand, the plaintiff in the lawsuit, sued Willy's employer, *Oil Daily*. *Oil Daily* denied liability, claiming that Willy had deviated from his route and so he alone is liable for his negligence. Should the plaintiff recover in his suit against *Oil Daily?* What is the reason for your answer?

3. Baxter was employed by the Sho-Bar, owned by DuPree. Baxter's duties included supervising employees and seeing that customers were amused. At the conclusion of the last act of the show one night, Baxter, to amuse the customers, fired a pistol loaded with blank cartridges into the air. Then he suddenly pointed the pistol at the plaintiff and fired. The resulting explosion singed Ted, the plaintiff, and he sued DuPree. DuPree denied that Baxter was acting in the scope of his employment when he discharged the pistol. What test or tests should be applied to determine whether defendant DuPree is liable? How should such tests be applied to these facts?

4. Harry was hired by Ruth to be caretaker of an apartment house she owned. For some unknown reason, Harry shot one of the tenants in the building. Ruth continued to employ Harry and secured a lawyer to defend him in the criminal action which arose out of the incident. The injured tenant, Wesley, sued Ruth for the damages he sustained because of the shooting, claiming that Ruth had, by her actions, ratified Harry's wrongful act. The court found in favor of Ruth. Wesley appealed to a higher court. Should the judgment be sustained? Explain.

5. Gilmore was employed by Beacon Kitchenware Products to sell its "No Stickum" pots and pans. Gilmore was authorized to accept a deposit of 10 percent from the purchaser when taking an order. Gilmore was then supposed to send the order and deposit money to Beacon. The company would ship the merchandise to the purchaser, who was required to pay the balance due upon its receipt.

Gilmore sold a large order of kitchenware to Agnes, telling her that he could allow a 25 percent discount if she paid in advance. Agnes paid Gilmore the full purchase price less the discount. Gilmore, instead of sending the order and the money to Beacon, kept the money and destroyed the order form. When Agnes failed to receive the kitchenware she demanded that Beacon either deliver the merchandise or refund the money she had paid for it. Beacon replied that Gilmore no longer worked there, that he had acted illegally and outside the scope of his employment when he took Agnes' order, that Beacon never allowed discounts of the kind Gilmore had promised, that respondeat superior did not apply, and that Beacon was not obligated to Agnes in any way. Why would a court nevertheless hold Beacon responsible?

CHAPTER 22

OBLIGATIONS OF PRINCIPALS AND AGENTS TO EACH OTHER; TERMINATION OF AGENCY

I n the preceding two chapters we saw that an agent, when acting within the scope of his or her actual or apparent authority, has the power to bind the principal to a contract. We also examined the circumstances in which principals may be liable to third parties for torts committed by servants and nonservant agents. From that discussion it should be evident that an agent may impose unexpected and unwanted obligations on a principal. Therefore, the law provides that an individual, upon becoming an agent, must carry out his or her duties properly and in good faith. The principal, in turn, has definite obligations to the agent.

In this chapter we will examine the obligations of a principal and an agent to one another, and the remedies available to each if the other violates those obligations. In this discussion we do not need to distinguish between servant and nonservant agents because the obligations of a nonservant agent and a principal to each other are essentially the same as the obligations which exist between servant and master. Accordingly, we will simply use the terms "principal" and "agent." The chapter concludes with a discussion of the termination of the agency relationship.

You will observe that this entire chapter concerns the ethical obligations which underlie the principal-agent relationship. Those obligations move in both directions —from an agent to a principal and from a principal to an agent. As agency law governs all employment relationships, considerations of trust and confidence are applicable to all businesses and to all walks of life. It can be said, therefore, that because of the far-reaching and pervasive nature of agency obligations, everyone has the right to expect equally high standards of ethical treatment in all interpersonal relationships.

OBLIGATIONS OF AGENT TO PRINCIPAL

A person who agrees to act as agent for another occupies a fiduciary relationship to the principal. The term "fiduciary" is a Latin word, the root of which is *fides,* meaning "trust" or "confidence." In the context of the law of agency, this *fiduciary relationship* means that the principal has placed trust and confidence in the agent and relies upon him or her to act only in the principal's best interests. The agent, *whether paid or not,* assumes several obligations to the principal. Those obligations involve primarily the duty (1) to obey the reasonable instructions of the principal, (2) to perform the agency work personally, (3) to use at least normal care and skill, (4) to communicate pertinent information and account to the principal for money the agent receives, and (5) to act with loyalty toward the principal.

A principal's remedies against an agent who fails to fulfill his or her obligations depends upon the nature of the failure involved. If it is not serious, more than likely the principal would merely warn the agent to obey instructions in the future. If a serious breach of duty is involved, the agent may be discharged; and if, as a result of a breach the principal suffers financial loss, the principal may, through court action if necessary, obtain reimbursement and payment of damages.

Duty to Obey Reasonable Instructions

An agent has the duty to obey all *reasonable* instructions from the principal concerning the work the agent is employed to perform. Thus, when a construction worker (agent) is ordered to wear a hard hat or other protective clothing on the job, the instruction must be obeyed even if the agent sees no possibility of danger. The duty to obey reasonable instructions also means, conversely, that an agent must *not* do something in relation to the work which is contrary to the principal's orders. For example, a sales agent, instructed by her principal to accept only cash for the goods she sells, violates this duty of obedience if she accepts a check in payment for a sale. The duty is violated even if she is convinced that the check is good, that its acceptance would bring about a sale in which the principal would profit handsomely, and that if she does not accept the check the sale would be lost. If the agent accepts the customer's check in payment and it "bounces," she will be personally liable to reimburse her principal.

However, if an agent is not able to receive instructions from the principal in a genuine emergency, he or she may deviate from or even contradict instructions to the extent that the agent in good faith believes deviation is necessary to protect the principal's interests. For instance, suppose a refrigerator truck carrying perishable food breaks down at night out in the country. Jim, the truck driver, is unable to reach his employer, Foodland Stores, by telephone. Even though Jim has been specifically instructed not to purchase anything for his employer's account over $25, he assures a farmer who owns a tractor that Foodland Stores will pay $50 for towing the disabled truck to a garage for emergency repairs. Foodland Stores must compensate the tractor owner.

Duty to Perform Service Personally

In Chapter 20 we said that a servant does not have authority to delegate to others the performance of any of his or her duties without the express or implied assent of the principal (master) but must perform the work personally. On the other hand, a nonservant agent has the *implied authority* to delegate to others (subagents) the performance of so much of his or her work as does not involve the exercise of discretion (judgment). However, if the work does involve the exercise of discretion, the nonservant agent has the duty to perform it personally.

The following example should make clear the distinction between delegable and nondelegable duties. Assume that Dorothy, a real estate agent (a nonservant agent), is authorized by Homer (her principal) to buy Green Acres, a certain large estate, at the best price she can negotiate. Dorothy may delegate to subagents such jobs as finding out how much the current owner paid for Green Acres, whether there have been any recent offers for its purchase and, if so, for how much; and for what amounts comparable properties have recently been sold. However, Dorothy may not delegate decisions regarding such matters as to how much money to offer for the property or the terms under which payment would be made, nor may she delegate actual negotiations leading to the sale. Those duties involve the exercise of discretion and require the judgment and decision of the agent herself.

If Dorothy, without the principal's (Homer's) consent, gives Vernon (her subagent) the task of negotiating the actual purchase, Homer can, when he learns of the improper delegation, deny responsibility for any of Vernon's acts and may refuse to honor any agreement Vernon negotiated. On the other hand, if Homer *did know* that Dorothy's subagent handled the matter, and if he accepts the terms Vernon arranged, then Homer has ratified Vernon's actions and is bound by Vernon's agreement with the seller of the property.

Continuing this example, if Dorothy fails personally to perform her nondelegable duties, she may find that not only must she reimburse Homer for any loss he sustained, but that Homer also has the right to discharge her even if they had an agency contract extending into the future.

Duty to Use Reasonable Care and Diligence

Upon accepting employment, an agent impliedly assures the principal that he or she has the knowledge and skill to do the job and will use reasonable care and diligence in its performance. A principal is entitled to expect only that an agent has the degree of ability commonly possessed by others employed in the same kind of work in that locality, unless the agent holds himself or herself out to be an expert. For example, if Helen accepts a job requiring her to operate a computer, she impliedly represents that she has at least the average understanding of the computer language she will be using. Helen also impliedly represents that she will use the care and diligence that computer operators ordinarily demonstrate so that her employer can rely upon the accuracy of her work. An *expert* in any field must have the additional knowledge usually possessed by such an expert and must use an expert's care and diligence. An individual in a profession requiring extensive education and a special license from the state is generally considered to be an "expert." Thus, if an agent is, for example, an attorney, an accountant, or a surgeon, he or she owes clients and patients the duty to use the expert skill and diligence of other attorneys, accountants, and surgeons who have been admitted to those professions in that state.

The following case involves the practical application of the rule that an agent is obligated to use care and diligence.

CASE 22.1
Leamer Abstracting Co. v. Rosengartner
317 N.W. 2d 57 (Neb. 1982)

Facts: Rosengartner sold certain property to Morse. The Leamer Abstracting Company was employed by Rosengartner to prepare an abstract of title to the land and also the deed to Morse. The abstract Leamer prepared failed to disclose that a portion of Rosengartner's land had been taken by the state under a condemnation proceeding for a highway right-of-way and, in the deed Leamer prepared, the land was described as including the portion which had been taken by the state.

Question: Was the Leamer Abstracting Company liable to Rosengartner for any loss Rosengartner suffered?

Answer: Yes. The abstract company violated its obligation to use the care and diligence of an agent in that profession.

Reasoning: If an agent fails to exercise reasonable care, diligence, and judgment, the agent is responsible for any damages which result. An abstract company is employed to find and enumerate all matters which may affect the record title to a property. Here, Leamer, through lack of care and diligence, negligently failed to discover the transfer of the property to the state and prepared an incorrect deed. Therefore, Leamer is liable for any damage which resulted.

Duty to Communicate Notice and Information; Duty to Account

An agent is obligated to give a principal (1) all information relating to the agency of which the agent becomes aware, and (2) a strict accounting for all agency property and funds that came into his or her hands.

Duty to Communicate Notice and Information.   When an agent in the course of an agency receives any *notice* or learns of any *information* (written or oral) concerning matters he or she handles for the principal, it must be passed along to the principal. Furthermore, the law *assumes* that if an agent received such notice or information, it was conveyed to the principal. This assumption of the law holds true even if the agent in fact neglected to convey the notice or information. As a result, the rights and liabilities of the principal to any third party are the same as if the principal had personally received the notice or information. Two examples can clarify the application of this general rule.

1. Notice: Assume that Ben owns an apartment building. He leases an apartment to Agnes for 1 year. The lease, which expires on August 1, states that Agnes may extend the lease for another year at the same rent if she notifies Ben to that effect before June 30. On June 25 Agnes, when paying her rent to Fred, the agent who manages Ben's apartment building, tells him she is extending her lease for another year. Fred neglects to inform Ben of this notice; but since Ben's agent received it in the course of his duties, the law assumes that Ben, Fred's principal, also received the notice. As a result, Agnes' lease is extended at the same price even though Ben had expected to rent the apartment to a different tenant at a higher rental.

2. Information: Assume that Hiram, who owns Clearview Farm, instructs Mike, his agent, to buy a used tractor for the farm. George offers to sell Mike a tractor, saying "It's as good as new." Mike tests the tractor and discovers that it does not run well in reverse gear. However, believing that the machine is a "steal" at the price George asks and that it can easily be repaired, Mike buys it for the farm. After the tractor is delivered to Clearview, Hiram phones George and requests that he "take the machine back and return my money because something is wrong with the reverse gear." However, since Mike in the course of his duties acquired knowledge of the defect before buying the machine, the law assumes that Hiram, Mike's principal, had the same information. As a result, Hiram cannot use the tractor's defect as a basis for backing out of the purchase.

The following case further illustrates how a principal, to his detriment, may be charged with knowledge an agent receives in the course of work he performs as an agent.

CASE 22.2 Greensboro Housing Authority v. Kirkpatrick
289 S.E.2d 115 (N.C. 1982)

Facts: Greensboro Housing Authority contracted with Kirkpatrick to install the electrical system in a building under construction. Greensboro also employed architect Smith to inspect the work of all the building trades engaged in the construction. Smith regularly visited the job and saw how the electrical work was done. When the building was finished,

Smith filed a "Certificate of Completion" certifying that all work had been done in accordance with the plans and specifications. About a month later there was a fire at the building. It was determined that the fire had been caused by faulty electrical work. Greensboro demanded compensation from Kirkpatrick, the electrical contractor, because his work had not conformed to the plans and specifications.

Question: Was Greensboro, the principal, bound by the certification of its agent, Smith, that the electrical work was done satisfactorily?

Answer: Yes. The principal is bound by Smith's certification.

Reasoning: As a general rule, a principal is *presumed* to have knowledge of any information known to the agent concerning matters the agent is authorized to handle. Smith knew, or should have known, how Kirkpatrick performed his electrical contract. It is immaterial that the agent failed to tell his principal that the work was faulty. Therefore, Smith's knowledge of how Kirkpatrick performed the electrical work and Smith's acceptance of the work and certification that it met the plans and specifications, is imputed to his principal, Greensboro. In effect, Greensboro had agreed that the electrical contractor had performed his work satisfactorily.

There are two exceptions to the rule that a principal is presumed to have been given all information pertaining to an agency:

1. A principal is not presumed to have knowledge of any information the agent acquires in confidence. For example, assume that attorney Ruth, while representing client Fox, confidentially learns that he contemplates going out of business. Attorney Ruth may not reveal this information to Vortex, another of Ruth's clients, even though that information would be very valuable to Vortex.

2. A principal is not presumed to know that the agent is acting adversely to the principal. For instance, if an agent steals from his or her principal, the principal is not presumed to know of the theft. The principal is charged with knowledge of the wrong only after he or she actually learns of it.

Duty to Account.   An agent may, in the course of the agency, receive money or other property which belongs to the principal. Obviously, the agent must keep track of it all and return the money or property to the principal or otherwise account for its disposition.

Remedies for Failure to Communicate or to Account.   If an agent fails in his or her duty to transmit notice or information or to account to the principal, the principal may (1) demand (and ask a court to compel) reimbursement from the agent for any losses the principal sustained, (2) compel the agent to turn over any money or other property the agent wrongfully withheld, and (3) recover from the agent any profits the agent personally made from the use of the money or property. For example, Jerry, the rental agent for the Towers Building, has the duty to turn over to his principal every Monday all rents collected during the previous week. On Saturday,

Jerry uses the rent money collected from tenants to place bets at the racetrack. He is lucky and wins a large sum. On Monday Jerry must turn over to his principal not only all the rent money, but also the track winnings made by using that rent money to place bets. If Jerry had lost some or all the rent money on the horses, he would still be obligated to turn over the full amount he collected from the tenants.

Duty to Act Loyally to Principal

The most far-reaching obligation of an agent to a principal is the duty to be loyal (commonly called the "fiduciary duty"). The duty to act loyally means that in matters concerning the agency an agent must not, without the principal's knowledge, assume an interest or position adverse to the principal. For instance, an agent has a duty *not* to do any of the following *without disclosing the facts to the principal:* (1) engage in negotiations on behalf of both a principal and a third party to a transaction, (2) buy for himself or herself anything the agent sells for a principal or sell to the principal anything the agent owns, (3) make a secret profit from an agency transaction, (4) compete with the principal in a transaction in which the agent is supposed to be acting for the principal, or (5) disclose the principal's confidential information. Each of these situations will be discussed in turn.

Duty Not to Act for Principal and Third Party Simultaneously.   If an agent simultaneously acts for the principal and for the third party to a transaction, he or she is, in fact, acting at the same time for two principals who have conflicting interests. The agent is under the same obligation to each of the principals as if the agent were acting for only that principal alone. There is a strong possibility that any agent who serves conflicting interests, while meaning to be absolutely fair, will favor one principal over the other. Because this possibility exists, an agent may not act for principals on both sides of a transaction unless *both* principals know that fact and actually or impliedly consent to the dual representation.

If an agent, without full disclosure and consent of *both* principals, acts for principals on both sides of a transaction, either principal may (1) refuse to pay the agent or, if compensation has already been paid, secure its return regardless of the agent's honesty or the fairness of the agreement the agent negotiated, (2) either principal also may rescind any agreement negotiated by the agent, (3) recover from the agent any damages suffered because of the transaction, and (4) terminate the agency. If there was intentional wrongdoing by both the agent and one of the principals (a conspiracy), then that principal is also liable in damages to the unknowing principal. If neither of the principals know of the dual representation, then the remedies enumerated above are available to both of them.

Duty Not to Sell to or Buy from Principal.   An agent must not, without his or her principal's knowledge, buy from or sell to the principal. This is because if an agent who acts as *salesperson* for a principal were to buy the principal's property for himself or herself, and if a firm price had not been set by the principal, the agent would be in a position to buy at an unfairly low price. It would be equally unfair for the agent to buy such property through a family member or friend because it is a legal principle that a person may not do indirectly what may not be done directly. However, if a principal, without being influenced in any way by a selling agent, establishes the price at which an article is to be sold, the agent may purchase the property at the established price. Many stores go further and permit their employees (agents) to purchase store merchandise at a discount.

An agent who acts as a *buyer* for his or her principal may not, without the full knowledge and assent of the principal, sell his or her own property to that principal. In this situation, if the agent were to sell his or her own property to the principal, the agent would be in a position to charge an unreasonable price or sell an inferior article to the principal.

Even if an agent believes that he or she is treating the principal with the utmost fairness in a sale or purchase, the agent breaches the loyalty obligation unless the principal has full knowledge of the circumstances. In most states the transaction is voidable by the principal, but in some it may be rescinded only if some unfairness is present. In the following case an agent sold his own property to his principal.

CASE 22.3 Becker v. Capwell
527 P.2d 120 (Or. 1974)

Facts: Becker, relying on advice given him by Capwell, a real estate agent, bought certain property. Capwell had owned the property for some time before meeting Becker but he did not reveal this fact to Becker. Later, Becker discovered that he had purchased Capwell's property. Becker claims that Capwell violated his agency obligations and therefore that he, Becker, has a cause of action against him.

Question: Did agent Capwell violate his fiduciary duties?

Answer: Yes. Becker should be compensated for any loss he sustained.

Reasoning: A real estate agent stands in a fiduciary relationship with his or her clients. The agent therefore, must make a full, fair, and understandable explanation before having a client sign any contract, particularly if the agent sells his or her own property to the client. This Capwell did not do. Becker's remedies are (1) to rescind the contract of purchase and secure return of the money he paid, or (2) to keep the property and recover from Capwell so much of the price as exceeded the actual value of the property. If Capwell had purchased the property in order to sell it to Becker, his client, then Becker would have been entitled to recover the difference between what Capwell, the agent, paid for the property and what Becker paid Capwell for it. [In any event, Capwell is not entitled to any commission.]

Duty Not to Make a Secret Profit. An agent is not allowed to make a secret profit out of a transaction the agent conducts for his or her principal. The principal is entitled to all the benefits from a transaction conducted in his or her behalf. Two illustrations should make this clear.

1. Harry is authorized to sell Paul's car for $1500 and receive a commission of $150. Harry sells the car for $1750 and quietly keeps the extra $250 for himself. Paul, the

principal, is entitled to the $1500 for which he agreed to sell the car, *plus* the $250 profit Harry secretly made. In addition, Paul need not pay Harry any commission, for an agent is not entitled to payment for services in which there is a violation of the duty of loyalty.

2. Now assume Paul hires Harry to sell Paul's car for $1500 but this time Harry secretly tells Bob, a potential purchaser, that the price of the car is $1750 but that he will try to induce Paul to accept $1500 if Bob will split the difference ($125 to each) with him. On this basis, Bob pays Harry $1625. Harry gives Paul the $1500 true price of the car and keeps the remaining $125 for himself. In this situation, Paul, upon learning of his agent's double-dealing, may either rescind the sale (because Harry violated his fiduciary duties by acting as agent for both his principal, Paul, and for the third party, Bob), or Paul may elect to go through with the sale. In either event, Paul need not pay Harry any commission, and he also can recover the $125 "kickback" Harry received.

Duty Not to Compete with Principal.   An agent may not compete with his or her principal in a transaction conducted for the principal. For example, it would be an obvious breach of the duty of loyalty for a computer salesperson secretly to be selling a rival computer brand to the principal's potential customers.

The obligation not to compete may also be seen from another point of view: If an agent learns that a business opportunity exists in which the principal may be interested, he or she is obligated to inform the principal of this opportunity (see "Duty to Communicate Notice and Information," p. 356). If the agent does not inform the principal but, instead, takes advantage of the opportunity himself or herself, the agent has improperly competed with the principal. For example, Abner is an advance scout for a popular recording company. His duty is to discover new performers and arrange for their auditions at the recording studio with a view to possible recording contracts. Abner, hearing Lena sing, is certain that the young woman can become a very popular performer. Instead of sending Lena to his principal's studio, Abner becomes her manager and "sells" her to other recording companies. Clearly, Abner has seized for himself an economic opportunity that rightfully belonged to his principal. However, if Abner had told his principal about Lena, and the principal had decided not to put her under contract, then Abner would have been free to do so himself.

If an agent improperly takes advantage of an economic opportunity that should have been presented to the principal, the principal may do any or all of the following: (1) force the agent to turn the opportunity over to the principal, (2) secure an injunction against the agent to prevent continuance of the competition, (3) require the agent to turn over to the principal any profits made by the agent through his or her having taken advantage of the economic opportunity, and (4) fire the agent.

Duty Not to Use Confidential Information.   An agent must not use the principal's confidential information for his or her own benefit or for the benefit of a third party. Unlike the duties already discussed, this prohibition continues even after the agent ceases to work for the principal. Many companies require their employees to sign some type of "secrecy agreement"; but even without a secrecy agreement, any confidential information learned by an employee (agent) in the course of employment must not be disclosed without the principal's consent.

Confidential business information may take many forms, and usually involves lists of customers and trade secrets. A customer list is a compilation of names and addresses of potential purchasers of services or articles. A trade secret is any information, process, or procedure used in business which may give that firm some advantage over its competitors. For instance, how to "grow" silicon chips, or how to etch them with the finest lines for use in computers or other devices, or how to make a carburetor that develops high smog-free gas mileage, are trade secrets. However, an employee may use any skills acquired in a previous job and may also use information that can be secured from ordinary public sources, such as the Yellow Pages of the telephone book, trade journals, and the like, even if the names appearing there also appeared upon a former employer's confidential customer list.

OBLIGATIONS OF PRINCIPAL TO AGENT

When a principal–agent relationship is established, the principal assumes certain obligations to the agent. Some of these are expressed and others are implied from the relationship. Among the principal's obligations are (1) to compensate the agent for work or services performed unless it was understood that no payment would be made, (2) to continue the agent's employment for such period of time as had been agreed between them, and (3) to ensure that an employee-agent will be compensated for injuries sustained in the course of the employment.

Duty to Compensate Agent

A principal's duties to an agent center primarily around the obligation to compensate the agent for work or services rendered and to make such salary deductions and payments to the government as are required by law. This obligation does not exist, of course, if the agent is a *gratuitous agent,* that is, one who agreed to serve without pay. If the rate of compensation is not specified, then the customary pay scale within the community for such work or services is implied. All states have laws which provide for enforcement of the payment of wages and which impose penalties upon delinquent employers.

Duty to Continue Employment of Agent

The rule has been that if an agent is employed on a daily basis or for no fixed period of time, then there is no obligation upon the principal to retain the agent in the employment. However, recent cases are eroding this rule. With increasing frequency courts are holding that if an agent (servant or nonservant) accepts employment based on some assurance such as an advertisement that the job is "a career position" or that the agent will earn pension rights, the employer may not discharge the agent unless there is first some impartial determination that the discharge is justified.

If the principal agreed to employ the agent for a specified period, then the agent is entitled to that term of employment unless he or she is discharged *for good cause.* An employee discharged without cause has the right to receive the wages that would have been earned if the employment had continued as originally agreed. However, the employee's claim for unpaid wages is reduced by whatever he or she receives through any other employment during that period. For example, a professional football player, fired despite the fact that his contract has another year to run, becomes a television sports announcer. He is entitled to receive from the team management the difference between what he is paid as an announcer and the amount he would have received had he played out his contract.

Sometimes a principal promises "permanent employment." This does not mean he or she has agreed to employ the agent for the rest of the agent's life. It is understood to mean only that the principal will continue to employ the agent as long as his or her work is satisfactory and the employer's business conditions justify continuation of the job.

Duty to Compensate Agent for Injuries

At the beginning of this chapter we said that the obligations of a principal and of a nonservant agent (such as an attorney or a real estate agent) to each other are *generally* the same as the obligations between a master and a servant. However, unless a principal and a nonservant agent have specifically agreed otherwise, a nonservant agent is *not* entitled to be compensated for injuries sustained while performing services for the principal. A servant, however, *is* entitled, under workers' compensation laws, to be compensated for injuries sustained in the course of employment. Such laws are discussed in Chapter 43.

TERMINATION OF AGENCY

An agency relationship ends or terminates (1) according to the agreement of the parties at the inception of the agency, (2) by their subsequent mutual consent, (3) by the decision of just one of the parties, or (4) by operation of law.

Termination by Provision in Agency Agreement

When an agency is created for a specified purpose, such as to sell a certain property, it comes to an end when the purpose is accomplished. Similarly, if the parties had agreed at the inception of the agency that it would last for a certain period of time, the agency automatically comes to an end when that time arrives. For example, if Dick hires you to groom his show horses during the state fair, your employment ceases when the fair ends.

Termination by Mutual Consent

As an agency is created by mutual assent, it can be terminated at any time by mutual agreement. Thus, continuing the above example, if you and Dick agree that the horses need no further grooming for the last 2 days of the state fair, your employment can end earlier than you originally agreed.

Termination by Decision of One Party

An agency is a consensual agreement. Therefore, either the principal or the agent may terminate it by making known to the other either orally, in writing, or through actions, that the agency relationship no longer exists.

Even if the agency agreement provides that neither of the parties may, without the consent of the other, terminate it unless special circumstances arise, either party still has the *power* to terminate the agency relationship at any time. However, neither has the legal *right* to end it except for the agreed reasons. Therefore, if a principal or an agent improperly terminates the agency, he or she is liable to a suit for damages for the breach.

Termination by Operation of Law

An agency terminates automatically by operation of law upon (1) the death or permanent incapacity of either the principal or agent, (2) the loss by the principal or the agent of required qualifications, (3) the impossibility of performance of the agency purpose, (4) the illegality of the agency purpose, or (5) important changes in the circumstances of the parties or in the object of the agency.

Death or Permanent Incapacity. The general rule is that the death or permanent disability of a principal or agent terminates an agency. The reason for this is that an agency represents an active agreement between a principal and agent to accomplish some purpose. Therefore, when either dies or otherwise permanently cannot carry on the agency, the relationship comes to an end. The following case clarifies the definition of permanent incapacity in this context.

CASE 22.4 United States v. Price
514 F.Supp. 477 (S.D. Iowa, 1981)

Facts: Marie Reel directed Will Price to purchase "flower bonds" for her. Flower bonds are U.S. Government bonds which, when owned by an individual at the time of death, are accepted by the Government at face value in payment of federal estate taxes. Because they bear a low rate of interest, these bonds usually may be bought for less than their face value.

Soon after Price received these instructions, Marie suffered a stroke and fell into a coma. Nevertheless, Price bought the bonds with her money. Marie died two weeks later. When the bonds were tendered to the government in payment of her estate taxes, the government claimed that Price's agency authority was terminated when Marie suffered the stroke; that accordingly Price had no authority to use Marie's money to buy the bonds; and that they could not be used to pay her taxes. Marie's attending physician testified that until Marie died, her recovery continued to be a possibility.

Question: Was Price's agency terminated when Marie suffered the stroke?

Answer: No. Marie's incapacity, declared by her physician not to be permanent, did not terminate the agency.

Reasoning: A principal suffers permanent incapacity if he or she *never* again is able to act as a principal. The doctor testified that until her death, there was always the chance Marie would come out of the coma. Therefore, it cannot be said that her incapacity to act as a principal was permanent. Her death, not the coma, brought the agency to an end. Marie's estate is entitled to submit the flower bonds in payment of her estate taxes.

The rule that death or permanent incapacity of a principal brings an agency to an end may impose a hardship on an agent who contracts without knowledge of such a circumstance. For example, if you are an agent acting for Tom, your principal, you impliedly warrant (guarantee) to any third party that you have the authority so to act. If Tom has died and you do not know it, and you engage in a contract with a third party in Tom's behalf, you may be liable in damages to the third party for breach of your implied warranty.

Because of the harsh results that could follow the application of this rule, some states have passed laws which provide that, if neither the agent nor the third party knew that the principal had died, the agent's authority is not cut off by the death.

Loss of Qualification of Principal or Agent.   The failure of a principal or agent to obtain or to retain in effect a required license may result in the termination of an agency. For instance, if you hire Gerald as your lawyer to represent you in a legal matter and Gerald is later disbarred (not permitted to practice law), the disbarment automatically terminates Gerald's authority to represent you.

Impossibility of Performance of Agency Purpose.   An agent's authority terminates when it is impossible to accomplish the agency purpose. Thus, if you employ Harold to sell your classic car for $10,000, the total destruction of the car in a fire terminates Harold's authority to sell it.

Illegality of Agency Purpose.   A change of law that makes performance of the agent's duties illegal also terminates an agency relation. Suppose that Tally-Ho Amusement Company makes and sells slot machines. It employs Sally's consulting firm as its agent to manage the interstate sale of the machines. However, a new federal law makes transportation of slot machines across state lines illegal. Accordingly, the agency relationship with Sally's consulting firm is automatically terminated by operation of law.

Important Changes in Agency Circumstances.   An agent's authority terminates if the agent has notice of such important changes in either the circumstances of the principal or in the subject matter of the agency that a reasonable person should conclude that the principal no longer wishes the agency to continue. For instance, Carl lists his farm with a real estate agent for sale at a very low price. Before the property is sold, oil is discovered under land adjacent to Carl's. The entire community, including the agent, knows of the discovery and of the possibility that there is oil under Carl's land as well. Circumstances have changed so drastically that the agent's authority to sell the property has automatically terminated.

Notice to Third Parties of Termination of Agency

Notice When Termination Is by Act of Principal or Agent.   When an agency is terminated by one or both parties to an agency agreement, the principal should give prompt notice of the termination to all persons who may know of the agency. Failure to do so may leave the agent with *apparent authority* to continue representing the principal. (Apparent authority is discussed in Chapter 20.) Based upon this apparent authority, an agent, after termination of an agency, still has the power to bind his or her principal contractually to a third party who acts in reliance upon that apparent authority.

To illustrate, assume that Angus is employed by Prime Foundry to sell its widgets. Angus has sold widgets to the Jones Company in the past, and Prime has always shipped them in accordance with the orders Angus secured. Prime thereby clothed Angus with apparent authority to act for it in transactions with Jones. If Prime discharges Angus and terminates the agency, Angus still has the apparent authority to act as Prime's agent *and to bind Prime in transactions with the Jones Company* unless Jones in some way learns or is notified that the agency no longer exists. Thus, if Angus, after being fired, sells widgets to Jones and unscrupulously pockets a cash down payment, Prime is legally bound to ship the widgets to Jones. Of course, Prime can bring suit against Angus to recover the down payment, but how much simpler it would have been for Prime to have notified all its customers, including Jones, that Angus no longer represented the firm.

To end an agent's apparent authority when an agency is terminated by the parties, the principal should give actual notice of the termination to old customers and constructive notice to those who had not previously dealt with the principal. *Constructive notice* is given by placing a notice in a general circulation newspaper where the agency business operates, stating that the particular agency has been terminated.

Notice When Termination Is by Operation of Law.   The general rule is that when an agency terminates by operation of law, apparent authority automatically ceases without any notice being given to third parties.

SUMMARY

In return for the trust and confidence a principal places in an agent, the latter owes many duties to the principal. Besides the duty to obey reasonable instructions, to perform assigned work with reasonable care and diligence, and to account for all money owed the principal, an agent's primary obligation is the duty of loyalty to the principal. Loyalty involves dealing openly with one's principal, making full disclosure of all matters concerning the agency, and not adopting a position adverse to the principal. Therefore, an agent must not represent both a principal and a third party to a transaction without the consent of both those parties, nor may an agent become the third party to a transaction without the principal's knowledge. The same consideration also dictates that an agent must not directly or indirectly use to his or her own personal advantage, or otherwise disclose, any confidential information gained through the agency relationship.

When an agent violates his or her obligation to the principal, the principal has several remedies. Among them are to discharge the agent, to withhold compensation that would have been due if there had been no violation of duty, to secure the payment of any secret compensation or profit the agent may have made out of a breach of duty, and to secure damages for any loss suffered by the principal as a result of the agent's actions.

A principal's obligations to an agent involve paying compensation, permitting the agent to accomplish the work for which he or she was hired, and compensation if a servant-type agent is injured in the course of the work.

An agency agreement may be terminated at any time by either of the parties. An agency also terminates when its purposes have been accomplished; by operation of law if one of the parties dies, becomes permanently incapacitated, or ceases to be qualified to act; or if the agency purpose becomes illegal or impossible to accomplish.

An agent's apparent authority to act for a principal may continue after the agent's actual authority has come to an end. To terminate this apparent authority, a principal should give notice of termination to third parties.

REVIEW QUESTIONS

1. (a) What is meant by a fiduciary relationship? (b) If an agent acts without pay, does a fiduciary relationship exist between the agent and the principal?

2. (a) Why is an agent generally precluded from delegating to another his or her duty of performance? (b) Explain why this rule is not the same for agents and for servants.

3. How can an act of an unauthorized agent bind a principal?

4. What is the difference between "information" and "notice" in the law of agency?

5. (a) What is meant by an agent's duty of loyalty to a principal? (b) Give three examples of breach of loyalty.

6. Why is it improper for an agent to act at the same time for a principal and for a third party in a transaction?

7. How can there be a violation of a fiduciary duty when an agent whose duty it is to buy land for a principal, sells his own property to the principal at a fair price?

8. What obligations does a principal owe to his or her agent?

9. Give at least four bases upon which an agency may be terminated.

10. You, as Chris' agent, agree to buy a house from Mary. Neither you nor Chris knew Mary had been killed in an auto accident. What happens to the agreement you made and to the obligations each of you owes the other?

CASE PROBLEMS

1. Lola May was a motion picture actress. She was repeatedly late for rehearsals and many times could not be reached when she was needed for work. Her employer therefore gave Lola May a specific order to report to the studio every morning at 8:30 A.M., 5 days a week. Lola May did not report as directed 3 days in succession, saying that her presence was not required because she did not expect to be cast in any scenes on those days. She was forthwith discharged. Lola May brought suit for the wages due her for the unexpired period of her contract, claiming that the order was unreasonable. Would you say that her contract was or was not properly terminated? Discuss.

2. Helen bought a package tour to Las Vegas from a travel agency. The agency, in turn, booked Helen on a tour operated by another agency. At the airport, the agency leading the tour misdirected Helen's baggage. In addition, Helen was not given the type of hotel accommodations she had been promised. Helen says that she should be compensated for the inconvenience she suffered. If either travel agency is liable, would it be the one from which Helen purchased the tour or the agency which conducted the tour? Explain.

3. The San Antonio Company purchased certain land from Batson. Pursuant to the terms of the offer of purchase, Batson paid a real estate commission to Strehlow, the president of San Antonio. Batson later learned that Strehlow had merely used the San Antonio Company as a "front" so that he could buy the property for himself. Batson therefore filed suit to recover the commission he had paid Strehlow. Since Batson had sold the property at a price that was agreeable to him (Batson), and he voluntarily paid a normal real estate commission, can Batson now successfully require a refund of that commission? Explain.

4. The Department of the Interior periodically conducts a lottery for the sale of leases to lands that are potentially oil-productive. Clinker employed Southwest Oil Company as his agent to make the necessary filings so he could participate in the lotteries. After some months, Clinker won a lease. With the purchase of the lease, the services Southwest was required to perform for Clinker came to an end. Southwest offered to buy the lease from Clinker. Clinker asked whether other oil companies might also be interested in buying it and Southwest replied that it was possible. After further discussion, Southwest raised its offer and Clinker assigned the lease to it. Later, Clinker brought suit to cancel the assignment, claiming that Southwest had breached its fiduciary duty as an agent by not revealing all the relevant information as to the value of the lease when it purchased the assignment from him. The court held that the assignment should not be canceled. Do you agree? Explain.

5. Sarokhan had an irrevocable written contract with the Fair Lawn Memorial Hospital, appointing him its medical director for 10 years, giving him the sole authority to select the hospital professional staff. One year after entering into the agreement, the president of the hospital wanted Sarokhan to appoint certain doctors as assistant medical directors. Sarokhan refused, saying that under his contract he had the sole authority to make such selections. In response, the hospital notified Sarokhan that his association with the hospital was terminated. Sarokhan sued to prevent the hospital from terminating his services as medical director. The hospital answered that even if it did not have the right to cancel the contract, the hospital could terminate the contract any time it pleased, and that all Sarokhan could do would be to file a damage suit. Was the position of the hospital correct? Explain.

PART SIX

PROPERTY AND ESTATES

CHAPTER 23

NATURE OF PROPERTY; PERSONAL PROPERTY (INCLUDING BAILMENTS)

P roperty forms the foundation of any economic system. Private property constitutes the major portion of the foundation of a free enterprise economy. Property
law grew out of a need to protect the individual's creations and acquisitions, and is an
integral part of a free, competitive society. In recent years the institution of private
property has come under scrutiny, and many people have explicitly or implicitly
questioned the validity of private property. To understand the society in which we
live and to act intelligently in it, we need to know the nature and importance of
property, the most important legal principles relating to different types of property,
and the reasons underlying contemporary property law.

This chapter deals with the general nature and importance of property, particularly
private property, and with the most important aspects of the law of personal
property, including the subject of bailments. The next two chapters are devoted to
real property.

NATURE OF PROPERTY

Meaning of Property

The word "property" is used in two different senses. In one sense, property refers to
things owned, such as land, automobiles, and shares of stock in a corporation. Lay
persons customarily think of property in this sense. Sometimes the law also refers to
things as constituting property. For example, a California statute defines property as
"the thing of which there may be ownership."[1]

In its other sense, property means the exclusive right to use, possess, enjoy, and
dispose of a thing. Used in this sense, "property" refers not to a *thing* but to a
collection or bundle of *rights* in that thing. These rights are protected by law. This
second concept is the more fundamental one. Land and other physical objects can
exist where there is no law (e.g., rocks on the moon), but *property rights* can exist
only where there is law.

Classes of Property

Many laws apply only to certain specified classes or subclasses of property. The main
classes of property are tangible and intangible, real and personal, and public and
private.

Tangible and Intangible Property.   **Tangible property** consists of things that have a
physical existence, such as books, clothing, buildings, and land. **Intangible property**
consists of things that do not exist in physical form but that have economic value,
such as patents, copyrights, accounts receivable, and shares of stock.

To understand the concept of intangible property we need to observe an important
distinction. We know, for instance, that a stock certificate has a physical existence. It
can be seen, touched, endorsed by the owner, and transferred to a purchaser. But
the reason it has value and is accepted by others in the commercial world is that the
certificate represents an intangible property right—the right of ownership in a
corporation. In addition, if the stock certificate is lost or destroyed, it can be replaced
without loss of any right. A person is still a stockholder in a corporation even though
the certificate may have been totally destroyed in a fire. A stock certificate is simply

[1]Calif. Civ. Code, sec. 654.

evidence of ownership, and is not the property itself. The property consists of a bundle of rights that cannot be destroyed by fire.

Real and Personal Property. Real property consists of land, airspace above the land, and all things embedded in the land or firmly attached to it, such as minerals, trees, fences, and buildings. Personal property is all property that is not real property, and thus includes tangible things that are movable and intangible things that have economic value. However, the term "personal property" is often used in a more limited sense to mean only movable, tangible things, sometimes called "chattels."

It is possible for items to change in their classification from real to personal and from personal to real. For example, a tree is real property until it is severed from the land—either by a person cutting it down or by an act of nature, as by wind or flood. When the tree is severed it becomes movable and is reclassified as personal property. The reverse of this situation occurs when personal property becomes attached to land. For example, a building contractor takes movable items, such as lumber and bricks, and firmly affixes them to the land in constructing a house. The items are thereby converted to real property.

Public and Private Property. All property, whether tangible or intangible, real or personal, can be characterized as public or private. The essential difference is in designating who has the right to use, possess, enjoy, and dispose of the particular thing. Private property is that held by an individual or business entity primarily for personal or corporate benefit. Public property is that held by a governmental unit or agency, whether federal, state, or local. To illustrate: A national park and a city recreation center are classified as public property because a governmental unit holds the bundle of rights over the park or recreational center. By contrast, many football and baseball stadiums are held as private property; that is, a private individual or corporation holds the right to use, possess, enjoy, and dispose of the particular thing.

The following case illustrates one difference between public and private property.

CASE 23.1 Lloyd Corp. v. Tanner
407 U.S. 551 (1972)

Facts: Lloyd Corporation (Lloyd) owns a large modern retail shopping center in Portland, Oregon called Lloyd Center. Some 60 stores are located within the complex. The Center for some eight years had a policy, strictly enforced against the distribution of handbills within the complex. On November 14, 1968, Donald M. Tanner and others, distributed within the Center handbill invitations to a meeting to protest the draft and the Vietnam War. Security guards informed them that they were trespassing and would be arrested unless they stopped distributing the handbills. Suit was filed seeking an injunction to restrain Lloyd from interfering with Tanner's asserted right to distribute handbills in the shopping center. Lloyd appealed from the trial court's granting of an injunction.

Question: Did Tanner and others have a First Amendment right to distribute handbills on Lloyd's private property contrary to its wishes?

Answer: No. The First Amendment to the Constitution safeguards the rights of free speech and assembly by limitations on *state* action, not on action by the owner of private property used without discrimination for private purposes only.

Reasoning: Tanner and the others contended that the shopping center is open to the public, served the same purposes as a business district of a municipality, and therefore had been dedicated to certain types of public use. They argued that such a center has sidewalks, streets, and parking areas which are functionally similar to facilities customarily provided by municipalities. The court said, "property does not lose its private character merely because the public is generally invited to use it for designated purposes."

The judgment was reversed.

Legal Protection of Private Property

Private property is vital to the maintenance of a free, competitive society and governments recognize the need for laws to protect private property. The law provides protection from interference by others through the law of torts. (Much of the law covered in Chapters 3 and 4 is devoted to protection of private property.) For example, if someone intentionally enters another's land without consent or legal justification the owner may recover damages in a lawsuit for trespass. If one's personal property is improperly taken or destroyed, the owner may recover damages in a suit for conversion or trespass[2] to personal property. In addition, there are circumstances where the torts of negligence and fraud may be used to protect an owner whose property is damaged by another.

Private property is also protected against interference by the government. The United States Constitution provides in the Fifth and Fourteenth Amendments that neither the federal nor any state government shall deprive a person of his or her life, liberty, or *property* without due process of law. These provisions were added to the Constitution in the belief that the individual was entitled to protection from possible overreaching by the government.

Legal Restrictions on Private Property

Although the scope of this book does not permit a detailed discussion of legal restrictions on the use, possession, enjoyment, and disposition of private property, some mention should at least be made of the extent and importance of such restrictions. All states have health and safety laws regulating the use of property, motor vehicle laws, zoning ordinances, building codes, and the like. There are also federal rules and regulations to prevent undue pollution of the environment by property owners.

Part of the law of torts restrains a property owner from using property in such a way that it harms others. An owner can be held liable in damages to a person injured on or near the property due to an intentional or negligent act, and in some instances, even if the owner is without fault (see Chapter 24, "Duties of Owners").

There are many other legal restrictions on private property, and new restrictions

[2]See Chapter 3 for definition and discussion of conversion and trespass.

are being created at all levels of government. In today's world, the owner of private property must constantly keep abreast of new rules and regulations in order to plan his or her business transactions intelligently.

PERSONAL PROPERTY (INCLUDING BAILMENTS)

The most important aspects of the law of personal property involve the ownership and possession of such property. The rest of this chapter deals with the acquisition of ownership of personal property and with the temporary possession of such property by someone who is not an owner.

Acquisition of Ownership of Personal Property

A person can acquire ownership of personal property in various ways. We shall discuss in some detail the legal principles governing various methods and the background out of which these principles emerged.

Acquisition by Purchase.   Probably the most common method of acquiring ownership of personal property is by purchase from an owner. We are all consumers. We purchase goods daily in the marketplace from a variety of sellers. The legal principles relating to these transactions are so extensive that they cannot be treated here. Many of the principles are covered in Part Four of this book dealing with sales (Chapters 15 through 19). In addition, many rules presented in Part Three, which is devoted to the law of contracts, apply to sales transactions.

Acquisition by Gift.   Another common method of acquiring ownership of personal property is by gift. A simple definition of a gift is a voluntary transfer of property without consideration. The one who makes the gift is called the "donor," and the one who receives the gift is called the "donee."

Controversies sometimes arise as to whether a gift has actually been made. In such cases, the courts require that three elements must be present to establish a valid gift: (1) intent to make a present transfer; (2) delivery, or a satisfactory substitute; and (3) acceptance.

Intent to Make Present Transfer.   To have a valid gift, the donor must intend to make an unconditional present transfer of his or her rights. An unconditional transfer means one without conditions or strings attached. Statements such as, "Take it, it is yours," or "I want you to have this," are clear indications of the requisite donative intent. Where there is no clear indication of intent and a lawsuit results, the court must determine the intent.

Sometimes the law's requirements frustrate a donor's intention. Suppose that an elderly woman puts money in an envelope and writes on the outside, "To my nephew, John, upon my death." The aunt's intent obviously was to retain control over the money until death and to have the transfer occur at that time. There is no gift during the aunt's lifetime because a gift requires an unconditional *present* transfer. The desire to retain control over the money and to have the transfer occur at the time of death could be carried out only by a will. (Note: the words "To my nephew, John, upon my death" do not constitute a will. Under the statutes of most states, a will, to be valid, must meet certain formal requirements. One of these requirements is that the instrument must be signed.[3])

Delivery or Satisfactory Substitute.   The requirement of delivery is usually met by physically handing the object to the donee, thereby giving up control and possession of it. No gift occurs if the donor does not give up complete control and possession of the object. For example, if one person says to another, "I want you to have my watch," but continues to wear the watch, no gift is made.

In some situations it is impractical to physically deliver an item, and the law allows a *constructive* (sometimes called *symbolic*) delivery. "Constructive" means "just as if," or "the same as if" actual delivery is made. For example, giving the donee a key to a locker may under some circumstances be recognized as a gift of the contents. With intangible property, where physical delivery is impossible, a symbol may be given to the donee that will be sufficient to constitute a gift of the underlying interest. For instance, delivery of a savings account passbook is usually sufficient to pass ownership of the account to a donee.

In order to constitute a gift, delivery of an item need not necessarily be to the donee. Occasionally, a donor will turn over an item to a third person with instructions to deliver it to the donee or to hold it for the benefit of the donee. The question may then arise: Has the donor made an *unconditional* present transfer of his or her rights? The answer will depend upon the relationship of the third person to the donor.

Where the third person is an agent for the donor, there is no present transfer of rights. An agent owes a duty to follow the instructions of his or her principal. Thus, a donor who delivers an object to his or her own agent could have a change of mind at any time and get the object back. Where the donor delivers an item to an agent of the *donee,* the donor does not retain control and there is an unconditional present transfer of rights.

Frequently, the donor will execute a written conveyance of an object, that is, a statement transferring ownership to the donee. The delivery of such a document is as effective in transferring ownership as is physical delivery of the object. For example, the gift of an automobile or a boat is usually accomplished by the donor's signing and delivering the certificate of ownership to the donee. Ownership of securities, accounts receivable, and other intangibles is often transferred by means of a written form of assignment.

Acceptance.   There are few situations where an intended donee would not wish to receive a gift. However, it is fundamental that a person cannot be forced to accept something the person does not want. Some examples of items a person might not wish to accept as a gift are an automobile with an unpaid purchase price in excess of its current value, stock in a corporation on the verge of bankruptcy, and defective goods that require extensive repairs to be usable.

In most instances, though, a gift will result in a benefit to the donee. Therefore, in

[3]See Chapter 26 for discussion of the requirements of a will.

the absence of contrary evidence, the courts ordinarily will *presume* acceptance by the donee.

In the following case, the court discusses the three elements required to establish a valid gift.

CASE 23.2   **In re Estate of Stahl**
301 N.E.2d 82 (III. App. 1973)

Facts: Leonard Stahl (deceased) and his wife, Ursula, had executed a leasing agreement concerning a certain safe deposit box. The agreement gave co-renter status to the parties where previously, the box was solely in Leonard's name. Before Leonard died, he gave Ursula one of two keys, retaining the other for himself. He expressed a desire that Ursula have the contents of the box (certain government bonds). After Leonard died, Ursula filed a petition requesting the court to declare that the contents of the box belonged to her and not to the estate. The court found that the estate was entitled to the contents of the box. Ursula appealed.

Question: Did Leonard make a gift to Ursula of the contents of the box before he died?

Answer: No. The necessary elements for a valid gift were not present.

Reasoning: The prerequisites for a gift are present donative intent of the donor, delivery of the item to the donee, and acceptance of the gift by the donee. Here, delivery was not completed until after Leonard's death. At any time prior to his death he had the ability to withdraw the contents of the safe deposit box by virtue of the duplicate key. He did not make an "unconditional" present transfer. The court also noted that Leonard did not have the government bonds in the box reissued in Ursula's name and she did not enter the box until after his death.

The judgment was affirmed.

Acquisition by Will or by Descent.   When a person dies, with or without leaving a will, the deceased person's property passes to others, called "beneficiaries or heirs." The subject of wills and inheritances is discussed more fully in Chapter 26. Here, we will simply note that a common method of acquiring ownership of property is by inheritance from someone who dies.

Acquisition by Taking Possession.   A person may acquire ownership of a movable object that is unowned by taking possession of it. **Possession** in its literal sense means control or power over an object. Taking possession of a movable object in today's world, however, is not always sufficient to establish ownership. In an urban, industrial society, few objects are unowned. As stated above, ownership of personal property is usually established in other ways, but one of the primary methods recognized historically was taking possession of something in its natural state.

Wildlife.   There are many early court cases involving acquisition of ownership of wild animals, fish, and bees. Such acquisition often was necessary for survival in a frontier society. At times, more than one person claimed ownership of an animal. Obviously, some rule governing ownership rights in wild animals was required. The rule that emerged was that ownership of a wild animal was obtained by taking the animal into possession. This rule is still part of our contemporary common law. For example, if a person traps a wolf or mink, nets a fish, or shoots a wild deer, he or she thereby takes possession of the animal and acquires ownership.

Abandoned Property.   A contemporary application of the acquisition-by-possession principle may occur today in regard to abandoned chattels. Ownership of an abandoned item may be acquired by taking possession of it with intent to exclude others. For example, if someone finds a broken watch lying in a trash barrel, the person may acquire ownership of it by picking it up and exercising control over it to the exclusion of others. The finder must proceed cautiously, however, and first establish that the article has truly been abandoned. "Abandonment" is the intentional relinquishment of all rights in an object without transferring ownership to another person.

In the following case the court had to decide whether or not a painting had been abandoned.

CASE 23.3

Menzel v. List
267 N.Y.S.2d 804 (Sup. Ct. 1966)

Facts: Erna Menzel, a resident of Brussels, owned a painting by Marc Chagall. In 1941 the Nazis invaded Brussels and Mrs. Menzel fled the country, leaving the painting in her apartment. The Nazis seized the painting and left a certification of receipt indicating that the painting had been taken into safekeeping. After the war Mrs. Menzel searched for the painting but was unable to locate it, until in 1962 it was discovered in the possession of Albert A. List. He had purchased the painting from Perls Galleries which had bought it in July 1955 from Galerie Art Moderne in Paris. The whereabouts of the painting between 1941 and 1955 are unknown. Menzel sued List for return of the painting. The jury brought in a verdict for Menzel, and List moved to set aside the verdict.

Question: Did Menzel abandon the painting in 1941?

Answer: No. The painting was not abandoned by its owner.

Reasoning: Abandonment is a voluntary relinquishment with no intent to reclaim. Personal property temporarily abandoned at the approach of the enemy is not forfeited. The relinquishment here was not voluntary and from the history of the search for the painting, there was obviously a continuing intent to reclaim. The court stated that it was of no importance that Perls Galleries may have been a purchaser of the painting in good faith and for value without knowledge of the saga of Menzel. It is a basic principle that a thief conveys no title as against the true owner.

The motion to set aside the verdict was denied.

Lost and Mislaid Property.   A different rule of law applies to lost, as distinguished from abandoned, property. For instance, suppose Alice's dog wanders away from home and Ben finds and takes care of it. As a finder of lost property Ben acquires a legally protected right of possession against everyone except Alice, the owner. However, since the dog was *not unowned*, Ben does not acquire the rights of an owner.

The distinction between "lost" and "abandoned" property is not always easy to make. The test or guideline to apply is the intent of the owner. If the owner unconsciously or unintentionally gave up possession of the chattel, the item is said to be merely lost. If the owner has consciously given up possession, with the intent to relinquish ownership permanently, the item is thereby abandoned. A person's intent is not always obvious. Courts usually consider three factors to determine the intent of the owner in relinquishing possession: (1) location of the item, (2) value of the item, and (3) utility of the item. Trash barrels, public dumps, and roadside areas are all repositories for abandoned items. However, if an item of great value is found in any such place, the item has probably been lost by the owner without any intent to abandon it. If the item is unusable without the expenditure of a large sum of money for repair, it is probable that the owner chose to relinquish possession and ownership permanently.

Another distinction that sometimes is important in determining property rights is whether an item is lost or *mislaid.* An item is said to be lost when its disappearance results from something other than the owner's conscious conduct. For example, coins that fall through a hole in a person's pocket are not abandoned or mislaid, but lost. By contrast, an item is said to be mislaid if the owner intentionally placed it somewhere and later cannot remember, for the time being at least, where it was left.

In one respect, the law governing lost and mislaid objects is the same: In neither situation does a finder acquire ownership. The difference in legal effect concerns the right of possession. If the item was mislaid, the owner of the premises where the item was found is entitled to take possession. For example, suppose a customer places his or her sunglasses on a table while having a haircut and then leaves without them. The proprietor of the shop has a right of possession superior to that of a second customer who discovers the glasses. The rationale is that the owner logically can be expected to return to the premises as soon as he or she remembers where the item was left. On the other hand, if the item was lost, the finder is entitled to take possession and retain it against all persons except the rightful owner. For example, if sunglasses are found lying under a seat in a movie theater, the courts would most likely conclude that the item was lost, not mislaid, and the finder would be entitled to possession as against the theater owner.

In many states today the finder of a lost article can acquire full ownership of the item under proper circumstances. Usually, the statutes require the finder to take some steps to locate the owner, such as posting a public notice or advertising in a local newspaper. When a specified time has elapsed after the required steps have been taken, the statutes usually allow ownership to pass to the finder.

Bailments   The subject of bailments does not involve the acquisition of ownership of property. It concerns the *temporary* possession of personal property by one who is not the owner. We encounter bailments frequently in our daily lives and a knowledge of the law concerning bailments is important. For example, suppose you leave your stereo set with a merchant who agrees to repair it. The relationship is a bailment and there are rights and duties imposed by law upon you and the merchant.

Meaning of Bailment.   A **bailment** may be defined as the legal relationship resulting from the transfer of possession of personal property from one person (called the "bailor") to another person (called the "bailee") under such circumstances that the bailee has a duty to return the item to the bailor or to dispose of it as directed by the bailor.

Two points should be emphasized concerning this definition: (1) A bailment involves transfer of possession without transfer of ownership; where possession and ownership are both transferred, the transfer constitutes either a sale or a gift; and (2) the bailor need not be the owner of the property. If Ben, who has borrowed Adele's book, lends it to Carla, Ben is a bailor as to Carla. Even a thief may be a bailor.

The transfer of possession of property referred to in the definition above implies voluntary acceptance of the property. Thus, if goods come into a person's possession without the person's knowledge, he or she is not a bailee of the goods. If a person agrees to store an "empty trunk" for a neighbor, the person is not a bailee of an overcoat that the neighbor neglected to remove from the trunk.

Classes of Bailments.   Bailments may be classified as **gratuitous bailments** and **nongratuitous bailments**. Nongratuitous bailments are usually called "mutual benefit bailments" and are sometimes called "bailments for hire." Table 23.1 illustrates classification of bailments.

A gratuitous bailment is a bailment in which one of the parties receives a benefit in regard to the bailed article without being obligated to pay for the benefit. The examples in the right-hand column of Table 23.1 show that the party receiving the benefit is usually the bailor. However, in one situation (gratuitous loan of a thing) the bailee is the party who receives the benefit.

A mutual-benefit bailment is one in which each party is entitled to receive a benefit. Usually, the **bailor** receives a service with regard to the bailed article and the **bailee** receives compensation, as can be seen from the examples in the table. However, in one situation (hired use of a thing) the bailee receives the service and the bailor receives the compensation. And in one situation (a pledge or pawn) the bailment relation is not entered into for the purpose of giving or receiving a service with respect to the bailed item, but for the purpose of securing the payment of a debt or the performance of some other obligation.

A special bailment, as can be seen from Table 23.1, is one in which the bailee is an innkeeper (hotel, motel, etc.) or common carrier of goods (railroad, airline, etc.). The

TABLE 23:1 CLASSIFICATION OF BAILMENTS

Type of bailment	Example (E stands for bailee; R stands for bailor)
Gratuitous bailments For bailor's sole benefit:	
Gratuitous storage of a thing	E allows a neighbor, R, to store his or her car in E's garage without charge
Gratuitous carriage of a thing	E transports R's sofa without charging R for the service
Receiving possession of a thing for the purpose of gratuitously performing work on it	E offers to sharpen R's lawnmower if he or she will bring it to E's basement; R brings it and leaves it in E's basement
For bailee's sole benefit: Gratuitous loan of a thing	R lends his or her power saw to E
Mutual-benefit bailments Ordinary bailments for hire	
Compensated storage of a thing	R stores his or her furniture in a commercial warehouse
Receiving possession of a thing for the purpose of performing compensated work on it	R leaves his or her garment with Valet Shop to be cleaned and pressed
Hired use of a thing	E rents a car from the R Car Rental Co.
Pledge or pawn	R deposits stocks with his or her bank to secure a loan
Special bailments: bailments involving	
Innkeepers as bailees	R (hotel guest) leaves valuables in hotel safe
Common carriers of goods as bailees	R hires E (railroad) to transport merchandise

law governing special bailments is complex and varies greatly from state to state. It has been so affected both by federal and state statutes and by regulations of federal and state administrative agencies that it is not feasible to discuss in a volume of this size the contemporary law governing this type of bailment.

Creation of Bailments.   A bailment is a simple relationship, and its formation requires no ceremony. The relationship may exist even though there is no contract between the bailor and the bailee. The mere act of one person's transferring possession of personal property to another may result in a bailment relationship between them. The law then imposes certain duties on the parties and gives them certain rights. These rights and duties may be supplemented or modified by a written or oral agreement between the bailor and bailee.

One occurrence that deserves special attention is that of placing a car in a parking lot. Sometimes a bailment is created, while at other times a "lease" or "license" is created. The distinction between the two relationships is important if the owner's car is stolen or damaged while parked in the lot. A bailee of goods assumes certain duties toward the goods. (These duties are discussed in the next section.) One who merely leases a parking space to the car owner does not assume the duties of a bailee. Since a bailment results from the transfer of possession, the test to be applied is whether the driver has given up control over the vehicle. For example, if a student drives a car to school, parks the car in the student lot, locks the car, and takes the keys, a *lease* of space, not a bailment is created. The driver has not relinquished control over the car. On the other hand, if a person drives to a restaurant where an attendant parks the car, takes the key, and gives the owner a claim check, a *bailment* is created. The driver has given up control; possession has been transferred to the restaurant. Transfer of possession is all that is required. No formal documents need be signed and no particular words need be said.

The following case discusses some of the factors to be considered in determining whether or not a bailment exists.

CASE 23.4   **Broadview Apartments Co. v. Baughman**
350 A.2d 707 (Md. App. 1976)

Facts: Glenn H. Baughman was a tenant in the Broadview Apartments. He paid Broadview $15 a month to park his car in the Broadview Garage. The garage was beneath the apartment building and was enclosed. There was a security guard on duty twenty-four hours a day and each tenant had a key to the garage door. One night Baughman parked his car in his assigned spot, locked the car, and took the keys with him. When he returned the next day, his car was gone. It was never recovered. Mr. Baughman sued for the loss of his car. The trial court held that Broadview was a bailee of the car and, as such, was liable for the value of the missing car. Broadview appealed.

Question: Was there a bailment relation between Baughman and Broadview?

Answer: No. The parties did not create a bailment relation.

Reasoning: A bailment arises through the transfer of possession of goods. The court stated, "The courts have uniformly found a delivery of possession to the parking lot operators where the keys are surrendered with the car or where the car is parked by an attendant." Some other factors to be considered are: (1) whether there are attendants at the entrances and exits, (2) whether the car owner receives a claim check, (3) whether the parking lot is enclosed, and (4) whether the parking lot operator expressly assumes responsibility for the car. In this case the court said the evidence was insufficient to establish a bailment.

The judgment was reversed.

Bailee's Rights and Duties.   In a bailment relationship, possession of the bailed item passes to the bailee. Along with possession, the bailee acquires certain rights. In return, the bailee assumes certain duties to protect the bailor's interests.

Right to Possess the Bailed Property.   During the time a bailment relation exists, the bailee has a right to the exclusive possession of the bailed property. The right of possession is protected by the law of torts, which gives the bailee a cause of action for conversion against any person who wrongfully interferes. For instance, if Andrews leaves his pedigreed dog with Happy Valley Kennel while on his vacation and Brown steals the dog, Happy Valley has a cause of action in tort against Brown to secure return of the animal or to recover damages. The bailee's right of possession is protected even against the bailor. Suppose that Andrews rents his dog to Smith, to be used by Smith for hunting for a certain period of time, and Andrews returns unexpectedly and wrongfully interferes by retaking possession. Smith has a cause of action against Andrews.

Right to Use Borrowed or Rented Property.   Where the purpose of a bailment is the use of the bailed article, the bailee has the right to use the article in a fair and reasonable manner. For example, if George borrows his neighbor's drill and wood bit, he may use them to drill holes in wood. If George attempts to drill through metal or concrete, he is liable for any damage caused to the drill and bit. On the other hand, when the purpose of a bailment is for storage, the bailor does not contemplate any use of the goods and the bailee would be liable for *any* use made of them. For example, if Charles boards his horse at a stable and Donna, who works there, rides the horse in a parade, Charles has a cause of action against Donna.

Duty to Exercise Care.   Every bailee owes to the bailor some degree of care in the custody of the bailed article. The traditional view is that the degree of care depends on the type or class of bailment. In a mutual-benefit bailment, the bailee owes a duty of ordinary care; in a bailment for the sole benefit of the bailor, the bailee owes a duty of slight care; in a bailment for the sole benefit of the bailee, the bailee owes a duty of great care. People have criticized the traditional view because the amount of care required depends solely on the circumstances of who benefited from the bailment relation. In addition, juries find it difficult to draw any reasonably clear line of distinction between slight care and ordinary care, or between ordinary care and great care.

These criticisms of the traditional view have caused some courts to abandon the threefold standard of care and to substitute for it a single standard of care. The standard used by those courts is the degree of care that a reasonable person would exercise under all the circumstances of the case.[4] Among the more important circumstances are the value of the bailed article (jewelry, work of art); the nature of the article (whether easily portable or not, whether easily damaged or not); the facilities available to the bailee for taking care of the bailed article; the experience of the bailee (whether a professional bailee or not); the kind of community (metropolitan city or isolated rural town); and the presence or absence of any benefit to the bailee.

If the bailee is negligent and if the negligence is a contributing cause of damage to the bailor's goods, the bailee may be held liable to the bailor. In the absence of fault, the bailee is not liable. Unless the bailment agreement so provides, the bailee is not an insurer. Thus, if an earthquake or flood occurs and destroys property in the possession of the bailee, the bailee cannot be held liable. Let us suppose, however, that there is a hurricane warning. The bailee must now take reasonable precautions to protect the bailed property against this foreseeable, known risk, such as boarding up doors and plate glass windows. If the bailee does not do so and the goods are damaged, the bailee may be held liable for negligence.

In the event the bailor sues the bailee because goods were lost or damaged while in the bailee's possession, most courts would say that the bailee is *presumed* to be negligent and that the burden rests on the bailee to prove the precise cause of the loss or damage *and* to prove he or she acted in a reasonable and prudent manner. For example, suppose someone leaves furniture in storage at a warehouse and thereafter a piece is stolen. The presumption is that the storage company was negligent in failing to prevent the theft and is liable. However, if the company can prove that the goods were packed safely and that a night watchman patroled regularly, monitoring with closed-circuit television, a court might properly conclude the company had exercised the degree of care expected from a reasonable person and therefore was not liable to the bailor.

In the following case the court raised a presumption of negligence.

CASE 23.5   **Clark v. Fields**
219 N.E.2d 162 (Ill. App. 1966)

Facts: W. B. Fields was the bailee of an airplane. The plane was placed in his backyard, about 40 to 50 feet from his house and some 15 to 20 feet from a gulley where he customarily burned trash. One day Fields dumped some trash in the gulley and set it on fire. He was called into his house by his wife, leaving the trash fire smouldering. A short time later Mrs. Fields saw that the airplane was on fire and called to her husband. The plane was destroyed by the fire and the bailors, B. R. Clark and W. H. Jordan, sued for the fair cash market value of the airplane. The jury found for Fields and the bailors appealed.

Question: Should Fields have been liable to the bailors for the value of the airplane?

Answer: Yes. The bailee was liable to the bailors.

Reasoning: The court stated that where the bailor has shown that the goods were received in good condition by the bailee and were not returned to the bailor on demand, the bailor has

[4]Many of the principles discussed in this section are discussed more fully in Chapter 4.

created a presumption of negligence. Then, the bailee must show that the loss or damage was caused without his fault. Here, Fields did not introduce any evidence showing himself free from negligence.

The judgment was reversed.

Limitations on Liability. In some situations the liability of the bailee may be limited or even eliminated by agreement of the parties. The most common examples involve auto parking lots and checkrooms where claim checks or tickets are given to customers. The ticket usually contains language specifying a maximum amount of liability for damage to the bailor's property or disclaiming all liability. This situation is essentially one involving contract law, specifically the rules regarding communication of offers (see Chapter 7). Most courts hold that the bailee can limit liability only if the disclaimer is effectively communicated to the bailor. For instance, if a sign is posted with letters large enough for the average person to see upon entering the establishment, the bailor will be chargeable with *notice* of the terms posted. Ordinarily, the bailor will not be chargeable with notice of terms contained in small print on the back of a ticket stub. In many states, even if the disclaimer is properly communicated, the bailee will be liable for *willful* injury to the bailor's property. (See discussion of exculpatory clauses in Chapter 11, p. 159.)

When a bailor transfers possession of an item of great value, such as jewelry or a work of art, he or she should notify the bailee of that fact. In some states, such as California, the statutes limit the bailee's liability in case of loss to the *apparent* reasonable value of the chattel, unless the bailor had specifically notified the bailee of its unusual worth. And, of course, a bailee is not liable for loss of an item within a bailed chattel if the bailee was not aware and had no reason to be aware of the presence of the item.

Duty to Return the Property. In a bailment relation the bailee is obligated to return the bailed property at the termination of the bailment or to dispose of it as directed by the bailor.

A bailee may be liable for wrongfully delivering goods to someone other than the bailor or a person designated by the bailor. A bailee who delivers the property to the wrong person is liable to the bailor for the tort of conversion. The bailee may have been induced to deliver the bailor's property to someone through trickery, fraud, or simple mistake. The bailee's liability for misdelivery, however, is *absolute*, and is not based on negligence or bad faith.

Duty to Compensate Bailor in Rental Situations. In a mutual-benefit bailment of the type where the bailee hires the use of a thing, the bailee is obligated to compensate the bailor for that use. For example, a person who rents a trailer to haul goods must pay the bailor for the use of the trailer.

Bailor's Duties. When a bailment relationship is created, the bailor has certain rights, namely rights to performance of the duties listed in the preceding section, and the bailor owes certain duties with respect to the bailed property and to the bailee.

Duty to Protect Bailee from Defects in the Property.   Where the bailor knows that the bailee will be using the bailed item and will be exposed to a risk of harm from such use, the bailor must exercise due care to prevent harm to the bailee, the bailee's employees, and the bailee's property from a defect in the bailed property. This is merely an application of the basic tort law of negligence. If the bailor knows of a defect, he or she must disclose it to the bailee. For instance, if a person knows there is a loose belt on a power mower being loaned to a neighbor, the owner must inform the neighbor of the defect. Where great harm could occur from the use of a bailed item, the bailor is obligated to make an inspection of the article prior to relinquishing possession to the bailee. For example, a car rental agency should inspect a vehicle before it delivers the car to the customer-bailee. If the rental agency fails to make an inspection when an inspection would have disclosed a defect in the car, it may be held liable for an injury that later occurs as a result of the defect. Rental agencies have been held liable without fault under the law of product liability for injuries caused by a defect in the goods leased. (See Chapter 18, p. 301, especially Case 18.5.)

Duty to Compensate Bailee in Service Situations.   When the purpose of a bailment for hire (mutual benefit) is performance by the bailee of some service in connection with the bailed item, the bailor has a duty to compensate the bailee for the service. For instance, if a person leaves a car to be repaired at a commercial garage and the mechanic properly performs the service requested, the bailor has a duty to pay for that service. If the bailee is unable to collect for the services, the bailee has a cause of action against the bailor for breach of contract.

Often, the bailee has the privilege of retaining possession of the bailed chattel until his or her just charges are paid. This privilege of retaining possession until compensation is received is called a "possessory lien." In most states there are statutory procedures that enable an unpaid bailee who has a lien on bailed goods to advertise and sell them at public auction, after waiting a specified period of time for payment. The subject of possessory liens is discussed in more detail in Chapter 27, p. 443.

SUMMARY

Property law is fundamental to rational government. Private property is an essential part of a free enterprise economy. The word "property" is used in two different senses. In one sense, property refers to things owned. In its other sense, property means the exclusive right to use, possess, enjoy, and dispose of things. The main classes of property are tangible and intangible, real and personal, public and private. Tangible property consists of things that have a physical existence; intangibles do not exist in physical form but have economic value. Real property is land, airspace above land, and all things embedded in the land or firmly attached to it. Personal property is all property that is not real property. Public property is that held by a governmental unit or agency. Private property is that held by an individual or business entity.

The laws relating to personal property are an important part of the society in which we live. A person or firm may acquire ownership of personal property by purchase or by gift. The elements of a valid gift are an intent by the donor to make a present transfer; a delivery, or acceptable substitute; and an acceptance by the donee. To acquire ownership in an unowned chattel a person must take possession of it, that is, must exercise control over it. However, the individual must distinguish abandoned articles from lost and mislaid property. The finder of lost or mislaid property does not automatically acquire ownership rights. If the owner does not appear, title to lost property may pass in accordance with local statutes.

A bailment results from the transfer of possession, but not ownership, of personal property by one person (the bailor) to another person (the bailee). There are two major classes of bailments: (1) gratuitous bailments, where only one party receives a benefit from the bailment relationship; and (2) nongratuitous bailments, usually called "mutual-benefit bailments," (sometimes called "bailments for hire"), where each party receives a benefit.

Both parties to a bailment relationship have certain rights and duties. The bailee has the right to possess the bailed article and, when appropriate, the right to use it. The bailee has the duty to exercise reasonable care in the custody of the article, to return it to the bailor or to someone designated by the bailor, and, in one situation (hired use of a thing), to compensate the bailor. The bailor must exercise due care to protect the bailee from defects in the bailed item, and in commercial situations involving a service to the item, the bailor must compensate the bailee.

REVIEW QUESTIONS

1. (**a**) Discuss the two ways the word "property" is used in the law. (**b**) Define the following: tangible property; intangible property; real property; personal property; public property; private property.

2. How is private property protected under the law?

3. Give examples of how the law protects private property.

4. (**a**) Give examples of legal restrictions that the law places on the use, possession, enjoyment, and disposition of private property. (**b**) Why do you think the law imposes these restrictions?

5. (**a**) Define "gift." (**b**) What are the requirements for a gift of personal property?

6. (**a**) What does the term "donative intent" mean? (**b**) Indicate a method that a donor might utilize to make "delivery" of a musical composition. (**c**) Is acceptance of a gift by the donee usually a problem? Explain.

7. (**a**) How would a person take possession of a wild animal? (**b**) Do you think a person who traps a wild animal that has escaped from a circus acquires ownership of the animal? Why or why not?

8. (**a**) Distinguish between the following: abandoned and lost property; lost and mislaid property. (**b**) Why is it important to determine whether an article is abandoned, lost, or mislaid?

9. (**a**) What is a bailment? (**b**) How does it differ from a gift?

10. State whether you agree, partially agree, or disagree with the following statements, and why. (a) A gratuitous bailment is one in which the bailor receives a benefit in regard to the bailed article without being obligated to pay for the benefit. (b) A mutual-benefit bailment is one in which the bailor receives a service for which he or she is obligated to pay.

11. State whether you agree, partially agree, or disagree with the following statements, and why. (a) The bailee's right to the exclusive possession of the bailed property is good against everyone except the bailor. (b) A bailee has the right to use the bailed article in a fair and reasonable way.

12. (a) State and explain the duties a bailee owes to a bailor. (b) State and explain the duties a bailor owes to a bailee.

CASE PROBLEMS

1. On March 10, Juanita had a new certificate of registration to her car issued in the name of her friend, Gussie. The registration on the automobile was transferred because Juanita considered receiving welfare assistance, and she believed that such assistance would not be forthcoming as long as she owned a car. At the time of the transfer, she owed the finance company a balance of $1726.20. Gussie testified that she and Juanita had agreed that Gussie would assume the balance of payments due, but that if Juanita should return to work, Juanita would take the car back and make up to Gussie whatever payments she had made on the loan in the meantime. Gussie made six payments toward the loan, by making payments of $68 each directly to Juanita. At all times the actual custody and possession of the car remained with Juanita, who continued to use and operate the car. Had Juanita made a gift of her car? Explain your reasons for answer.

2. Harvey bought an automobile, paying $400 down and signing promissory notes for the balance due. He then gave his friend, Alene, a set of keys to the car and told her he was giving it to her. The next day he repeated the same thing in front of a neighbor and both parties stated before this witness that he had given Alene the automobile. Later that day Harvey was killed. The balance of the purchase price of the automobile was paid by insurance after his death. Does the administrator of Harvey's estate have the right to ownership of the car? Explain.

3. Thelma, an employee of Northwestern National Bank, found an unmarked envelope containing $1500 in currency on the floor of a passageway in the bank. The passageway extended from the vault where the safety boxes were to the section where booths were located for the convenience of safety vault patrons. The area was in the basement of the bank and was restricted to patrons who registered and presented a ticket to a guard. Thelma was employed as an attendant to assist vault customers, and at the time she found the money she was checking to see if anything had been left in the rooms where customers had gone for privacy. She immediately turned the envelope over to the bank. The owner of the money failed to appear and demand his or her property, and Thelma sued the bank for the $1500, claiming to be the finder of lost property. Was the property lost? State reasons.

4. Sampson was discussing the purchase of a car with Flack, a used car salesman employed by Birkeland. Sampson took one of Birkeland's cars for a trial drive and left his own car on the dealer's lot for appraisal and determination of trade-in allowance. Flack took Sampson's car from the lot and drove it several blocks to determine its condition. Upon returning to the lot he found the entrance to the lot blocked, and parked Sampson's car on the opposite side of the public street next to the lot. Sometime later an automobile being pursued by the police collided with Sampson's car and damaged it beyond repair. Are Birkeland and Flack liable for damages to Sampson's car? Why or why not?

5. Dumlao checked into the Franklin Park Hotel. He removed a great deal of clothing from the back seat of his car and then left the car to be parked by a hotel doorman. The hotel bell captain saw Dumlao remove a cosmetic case from the trunk of the car, but he could not see the trunk's other contents, nor was he told that any other items of personal property were in the car. An employee of Atlantic Garage picked up the car, pursuant to an arrangement between it and the hotel. When Dumlao checked out of the hotel 4 or 5 days later, the hotel was unable to deliver the car and could not account for its disappearance. It was later found, missing a cigarette lighter that had been left in the glove compartment, various articles of clothing left in the back seat of the car, and a $1000 set of drums left in the trunk. Is the Franklin Park Hotel liable for the loss of all these items? Why or why not?

CHAPTER 24

REAL PROPERTY: NATURE, ACQUISITION, AND OWNERSHIP

This chapter deals with several important aspects of the law of real property. To determine the rights and duties of parties in a transaction involving property, it is often necessary to classify the subject matter involved in the transaction as personal or real property. Some examples of areas of the law affected by such a classification are formal requirements for transfer, taxation, and succession at death. There are a number of statutes and court decisions that attempt to define and classify the physical elements of real property.

Real property may be owned by individuals, business firms, or governmental units or agencies. Anyone who contemplates acquiring real property should understand the various methods of acquiring ownership, types of ownership available, and rights and duties involved in owning real property.

The first part of this chapter discusses the physical elements customarily included in the term "real property." Special attention is given to the subject of fixtures. The last two parts of the chapter discuss acquisition and ownership of real property.

PHYSICAL ELEMENTS OF REAL PROPERTY

Land, Airspace, Subsurface

The term **real property** customarily includes the surface of the land, things attached to it, the airspace above, and materials below the surface. The surface includes things found in nature, such as water and soil; and things added by human effort, such as buildings and crops. Minerals, oil, and gas lie below the surface of the land. The law pertaining to each of these elements is complex and too extensive to be covered in a business law text.

Fixtures

General Nature of Fixtures.   A **fixture** is an article that was personal property but which has been attached to real property with the intent that it become permanently a part of the realty. Thus, a real property owner who takes building materials such as cement, lumber, and pipe and constructs a residence clearly intends to convert these items of personal property into real property. However, in some situations the affixing party's intent is not clear. If litigation results, the court has the difficult task of determining probable intent.

Tests of a Fixture.   To determine whether a particular item was intended to be a fixture, the courts have established several objective criteria. These criteria are not always given equal weight by the courts; the relative importance of each test depends on the circumstances of each case. The usual tests are (1) method of attachment, (2) adaptability to use, and (3) relationship of the parties.

Method of Attachment.   When someone attaches an item to land or to a building or other structure in such a manner that removing the item would injure it or the real property to which it is attached, the courts consider such attachment strong evidence that the item was intended to be a fixture. One can reasonably infer that items which are attached to a structure by cement or plaster are intended to remain permanently. Heating and air conditioning systems are generally installed in buildings in such a manner that to remove them would cause great injury, and therefore they usually are held to be fixtures.

The fact that an item is easily removable without injuring it or the real property suggests that the intent of the affixing party is to have the item remain personal property. However, ease of removal is not conclusive in determining whether an item was intended to be a fixture.

Adaptability to Use. An item of personal property that is beneficial or necessary to the ordinary use of the real property to which the item is attached, is likely to be held a fixture, even though the item may be easily removable. For example, doors, windows, and hot-water heaters are usually removable without injury, but courts normally hold such items to be fixtures. These items are necessary to the ordinary use of real property, and the courts infer that the affixing party must have intended the items to be a permanent part of the real property. Items custom-made for the particular premises, such as wall-to-wall carpeting and built-in kitchen appliances, are also normally held to be fixtures.

Relationship of the Parties. To determine the intent of the party who has attached an item to the property, courts also consider as evidence the relationship of the parties to each other. Thus, in litigation involving the right of a tenant to remove an item the tenant has attached to the landlord's real property, the courts will presume that the tenant intended to remove the item at the end of the lease period. Such items are usually held not to be fixtures because a tenant seldom intends to make a gift of personal property to the landlord.

Disputes often arise between the buyer and seller of real property as to whether certain items attached to the premises were intended to be removed by the seller or were intended to pass to the buyer as fixtures. Typical examples of items causing disputes are curtains, bookshelves, and television aerials. If the parties cannot agree and litigation results, the court will first apply the usual tests of method of attachment and adaptability to use. If doubt still exists, the court will generally favor the buyer and hold the disputed item to be a fixture. For example, a television aerial could be classed either as personal or real property, depending on the method of attachment (easy to remove) and the adaptability of its use (very beneficial). Most courts would probably declare it to be a fixture and would not allow the seller to remove it.

The following case involves a dispute between a business firm and a taxing agency.

CASE 24.1 Wilmington Suburban Water Corp. v. Board of Assessment
291 A.2d 293 (Del. Super. 1972)

Facts: Wilmington Water Corp. et al. are a group of companies that furnish water for commercial and residential uses within New Castle County. The County Board of Assessment taxed as real property various pipes, mains, and storage tanks used by the companies throughout the County. The companies appealed the decision of the Board, contending the equipment was personal property and not subject to taxation.

Question: Were the various pipes, mains, and storage tanks fixtures?

Answer: Yes. The equipment was intended to be a permanent part of the land.

Reasoning: The court discussed the usual tests to determine fixtures (mode of annexation, purpose or use of item, and relationship of the annexor to the property). The equipment was removable only with great difficulty. The items were intended to remain upon the land indefinitely or for a substantial period of time, since removal prior to termination of their useful life (approximately 30 years) would affect the water supply of the County. The water companies owned some land on which equipment was installed. Other land was held on 99-year leases.

The court held that the equipment was taxable.

ACQUISITION OF OWNERSHIP OF REAL PROPERTY

Acquisition by Private Individuals and Firms

Methods of Acquisition.   There are various methods of acquiring ownership of real property. In some situations an individual (or business firm) participates actively in a transaction to acquire ownership, as where a person contracts to purchase the property. In other situations one acquires ownership without active participation, as where a person inherits property.

Acquisition by Purchase.   The most common method of acquiring ownership of real property is to purchase it from the owner. The legal principles relating to purchase are presented in the contracts part of this text (Part Three). An oral agreement of purchase of real property is generally not enforceable under the statute of frauds (see Chapter 12). Almost invariably, a written contract is part of the real property purchase transaction. The contract may be a standard printed form with blanks filled in, or it may be a lengthy, specially drawn instrument containing many terms and conditions. In either event, one transfers ownership of real property by means of a written document, called a "deed," given by the owner to the purchaser. The various types of deeds are discussed later in this chapter.

Acquisition by Gift.   Another common method of acquiring ownership of real property is by gift. The three elements required to establish a valid gift of personal property were discussed in the previous chapter. The same elements (intent to make a gift, delivery to the donee, and acceptance by the donee) are required to establish a gift of real property. Since physical delivery of real property is impractical, the requirement of delivery is usually met by the owner's signing a deed and handing the deed to the donee or to the donee's agent.

Acquisition by Will or by Descent.   An individual or firm may acquire ownership of real property when someone dies. The owner of real property may have made a will, leaving the property to a named person or firm. If the owner dies without having made a will, the owner's real property passes to his or her heirs in accordance with the law of the state where the real property is located. (Wills and inheritance are discussed fully in Chapter 26.)

Acquisition by Adverse Possession.   Occasionally, an individual or firm acquires ownership of real property by **adverse possession**. The transfer of ownership occurs without the consent of the owner. It is an unusual method of acquisition, largely because compliance with the essential requirements is difficult. To acquire ownership of real property by adverse possession, the claimant must take possession of the property and prove that the occupation of the property was (1) open and notorious, (2) exclusive and hostile to the owner, (3) under claim of right or color of title, and (4) continuous for the statutory period. In some states the claimant must also pay all property taxes levied against the property during the statutory period.

"Open and notorious occupation" means that the adverse possessor must actually use the real property in such manner as to make his or her presence known. To establish "exclusive and hostile occupancy," the adverse possessor must be a trespasser.

In most states, the adverse possessor must have taken possession of the real property either under *claim of right* or under *color of title.* Claim of right means the claimant knows he or she is a trespasser, committing a wrongful act, but intends to establish ownership of the real property against all others. Color of title means the adverse possessor has some written document (usually a deed) or judicial decree that appears to transfer ownership but that is legally defective.

For an adverse possessor to acquire ownership of real property, the claimant must be in continuous possession for a minimum period specified by state law. The length of this period usually varies from 5 to 20 years.

In the following case the court discusses the requirement of "open and notorious occupation."

CASE 24.2

Hunt v. Matthews et al.
505 P.2d 819 (Wash. App. 1973)

Facts: Anna M. Hunt owned a parcel of land adjacent to a parcel owned by Biele and Brody, but they did not live on the adjacent parcel. For 11 years Anna maintained a lawn and a garden on a portion of the land owned by Biele and Brody. Anna filed suit alleging adverse possession of the area used by her. The trial court gave judgment for the defendants. Anna Hunt appealed.

Question: Were the actions of Anna Hunt sufficient to establish ownership by adverse possession?

Answer: No. The elements required for adverse possession were not satisfied.

Reasoning: The court stated, "Uninterrupted, open, notorious, hostile, and exclusive possession for 10 years is required." The claimant must give notice to the title holder that a challenge is being made. The acts "must be made with sufficient obtrusiveness to be unmistakable to an adversary, not carried out with such silent civility that no one will pay attention." Here the claimed area was a vacant lot. "Greater use of a vacant lot would be required to be notorious to an absentee owner than to one occupying the land who would observe an offensive encroachment daily. . . ."

The judgment was affirmed.

Transfer by Deed.   As stated earlier, the actual transfer of ownership of real property in a purchase or gift transaction is accomplished by deed. A deed is merely a written document used to transfer ownership from one person, the **grantor**, to another person, the **grantee**.

There are various types of deeds used in the United States to transfer ownership of real property. The more important types are the quitclaim deed, the grant deed, and the warranty deed.

The language in a **quitclaim deed** varies, but a typical wording is "Grantor hereby releases and quitclaims his interest to Grantee." The legal effect of a quitclaim deed is to transfer to the grantee whatever interest, if any, the grantor may have in the property. If a defect is discovered that results in loss or reduction of ownership of all or part of the real property, the grantee will have no recourse against the grantor.[1]

A **grant deed**, or special warranty deed, as it is called in some states, contains wording such as, "Grantor hereby grants and conveys" certain real property to the grantee. The legal effect of such a deed is to transfer the grantor's ownership to the grantee and to give the grantee some protection if, later on, a defect is discovered in the grantor's title. In many states a statute imposes upon the grantor implied covenants (promises) that (1) the grantor has not transferred the same real property or any interest in it to another grantee, and (2) the grantor has not encumbered the property. For example, if Carla grants to James ownership of timber growing on her land and later grants to Sally ownership of the entire real property, using a grant deed, Sally would have a cause of action against Carla for breach of implied covenant. A grant deed does not protect the grantee against all possible defects, however. Let us suppose that Carla does not have valid ownership of the property because she previously dealt with someone who gave her a forged deed. Neither James nor Sally could recover from Carla because she has not breached either of the implied covenants. In such a situation, the grant deed gives no more protection than does the quitclaim deed.

In most midwestern and eastern states, the **warranty deed** is the most common type of deed for the transfer of ownership of real property. In such a deed, the grantor expressly warrants (guarantees) to the grantee that ownership is transferred free from all defects or claims. Thus, in the previous example of a forged deed, both James and Sally would have a cause of action against Carla if she had given each of them a warranty deed.

Acquisition by Governmental Units and Agencies

Acquisitions by governmental units and agencies are increasingly significant in contemporary society. The size of government increases continually at all levels—federal, state, and local. As governmental units and agencies expand and new ones are created, a need to acquire real property for personnel, equipment, and supplies is created. In most instances, governmental units and agencies acquire property in the same way as do individuals and business firms. Typically, a governmental unit or agency bargains in the marketplace for the real property it desires, enters into a written contract of purchase, and receives a deed for the property.

There are three other ways in which governmental units and agencies may acquire ownership of real property: through eminent domain, dedication, or escheat.

---

[1]The grantee may have a cause of action on other grounds, such as fraud, however.

Acquisition through Eminent Domain.   **Eminent domain**, or "condemnation," as it is commonly called, is the right to take private property for public use without the owner's consent.[2] This right is limited by the Fifth and Fourteenth Amendments to the United States Constitution, which require that the owner of property taken through eminent domain be paid just compensation. There is a substantial body of statutes and court cases involving eminent domain. Only a very brief summary of the law on this subject can be presented here.

Before private property can be taken without the owner's consent, the acquiring agency must establish that the taking is for a public use. Early court cases recognized certain obvious public uses, such as streets, highways, military installations, public buildings, and reservoirs. The concept of public use has been steadily broadened over the years, and today courts rarely hold any contemplated use by a governmental unit or agency to be improper. Public use now includes urban renewal projects, automobile parking facilities, rapid-transit lines, and public recreation and entertainment facilities. The California supreme court has held that "public use" may include the acquisition of a professional football team by a city.

The right of eminent domain may be exercised not only by a governmental unit but also by a private corporation entrusted with performing a public service. For example, a private college can take property necessary for classroom expansion or student housing, and public utility corporations supplying gas, electricity, and telephone service can condemn property for utility lines and poles. In such instances, the corporation acts under delegation of power from the state or federal legislature.

Acquisition through Dedication.   Dedication of real property is a gift by the owner to a governmental unit or agency on the condition that the property be used for a designated public purpose. The designated purpose might be for a park, street, beach, or historical landmark. The gift can occur during the donor's life or upon his or her death. There is typically a statutory procedure which must be followed. The owner makes a formal offer to give certain real property to a city, state, or federal governmental unit or agency, indicating the use or uses to which the property may be put and any other conditions the unit or agency must meet. If the appropriate officials decide to accept the gift on the conditions stated, a statute or ordinance is formally passed, and the owner transfers the property to the governmental unit or agency. Thereafter, the government is responsible for maintaining and operating the facility.

In certain situations, a "common law" dedication can occur. If an owner of real property makes an offer, express or implied, to give ownership to the public and there is evidence of acceptance by the public, a dedication may take place without formal action. For example, if an owner freely allows the public to do such things as drive across the land, park cars on it, or have picnics on the land, a court may find that a common law dedication has occurred.

Acquisition through Escheat.   The state government may occasionally acquire ownership of real property by **escheat**. Earlier, it was pointed out that when a

---

[2]Technically, "eminent domain" and "condemnation" are not synonymous terms. *Eminent domain* is the right to take private property for a public use. *Condemnation* is the legal procedure by which this right is exercised.

property owner dies without making a will the property passes to his or her heirs. Let us suppose a decedent has made no will and has no heirs, that is, no spouse or blood relatives who can inherit the property under state law. When such a situation occurs, the ownership of the property passes to the state. Ownership is said to "escheat" to the state.

TYPES AND INCIDENTS OF OWNERSHIP OF REAL PROPERTY

Types of Ownership of Real Property

Various types of ownership of (also called "title to") real property are possible, but no state recognizes all of them. When given a choice, an individual (or firm) must decide which of the available types of ownership will best serve the person's needs or legal position.

Sole Ownership.   **Sole ownership**, the simplest form of ownership, is ownership by a sole individual, business firm, or governmental unit or agency. Where ownership is acquired by purchase or by gift, the grantor executes a deed naming the grantee to receive title. Appropriate descriptive words are normally added to the name of the grantee, such as "a single man," "a married woman," "a minor," or "a Delaware corporation."

Joint Tenancy.   If two or more individuals together acquire a parcel of real property, several types of ownership are available to them. Joint tenancy is not available in all states, but where available, it is one of the types of ownership most often selected by two or more purchasers who are closely related. In a **joint tenancy**, each cotenant owns an equal, undivided interest in the entire parcel of real property. To illustrate, if Arnold and Betty each buy contiguous 5-acre parcels of land, they are sole owners of their respective parcels and neither of them has an interest in the parcel of the other. But, if Arnold and Betty combine their resources and purchase one parcel of 10 acres as joint tenants, each of them owns an undivided one-half interest in the entire parcel.

The major characteristic of joint tenancy ownership is the "right of survivorship." If one of the joint tenants dies, the interest that he or she had in the property automatically passes to the surviving joint tenant or tenants. Thus, a deceased joint tenant's interest is not subject to disposition by will; nor does it pass to the person's heirs in the absence of a will.

A joint tenancy is "severed" (terminated) if any joint tenant conveys his or her interest to another. For example, if Arnold and Betty hold title as joint tenants and Arnold gives Clarence a deed transferring his one-half interest to Clarence, the joint tenancy is automatically severed. Thus, if Betty later dies, there is no right of survivorship and her one-half interest would pass to her heirs or beneficiaries named in a will.

In order for individuals to acquire ownership in joint tenancy by purchase or gift, the deed from the grantor would typically say, "to Arnold and Betty as joint tenants." If the individuals named in the deed are husband and wife, in some states their ownership is known as **tenancy by the entirety**. The characteristics of equal, undivided interests and right of survivorship are the same as those in joint tenancy.

There are some differences, however. A major difference is that neither spouse may convey an interest in a tenancy by the entirety without consent of the other spouse.

Tenancy in Common.   **Tenancy in common** is similar to joint tenancy in that two or more individuals acquire ownership and each cotenant has an undivided interest in the entire parcel of real property. Tenancy in common differs from joint tenancy in two respects. First, the interests of tenants in common need not be equal. Thus, one cotenant could own an undivided two-thirds interest in a parcel and the other cotenant own the remaining one-third interest. A second difference is that there is no right of survivorship. For example, if Arnold and Betty acquire ownership as tenants in common and Arnold dies, his undivided interest in the real property passes to his heirs or to beneficiaries named in his will.

To create a tenancy in common by deed, the deed would typically say, "to Arnold and Betty as tenants in common." In most states, it would be sufficient to say, "to Arnold and Betty," since the prevailing rule of law is that a conveyance to two or more persons will be *presumed* to create a tenancy in common in the absence of an express indication otherwise. This rule also applies when individuals acquire co-ownership by will or by descent. For example, if Charles dies, leaving a parcel of real property to his children, Dexter and Ephraim, in the absence of some express indication otherwise, the children would acquire ownership of the parcel as tenants in common.

In the following case the court had to decide whether a deed created a joint tenancy or a tenancy in common.

CASE 24.3   Zamiska v. Zamiska
296 A.2d 722 (Pa. 1972)

Facts: Mike Zamiska and George Zamiska were father and son. On December 26, 1957, Mike Zamiska executed a deed conveying the title in certain land to Mike Zamiska and George Zamiska "as joint tenants and as in common with the right of survivorship." Upon his father's death (without a will) on July 18, 1970, George claimed complete title in the land. Other children and grandchildren of Mike Zamiska, claiming the 1957 deed created only a tenancy in common in the grantees, instituted an action in equity asking the court to declare that George's ownership was limited to an undivided one-half interest. The court below ruled the deed created a joint tenancy in the grantees with the right of survivorship and entered a decree granting the defendant's [George Zamiska's] motion for judgment on the pleadings. This appeal followed.

Question: Did the 1957 deed create a joint tenancy or a tenancy in common?

Answer: The deed created a joint tenancy.

Reasoning: The court stated the general rule that there is a presumption that parties hold title as tenants in common unless a clear intention to the contrary is shown. The words in the deed "as joint tenants and as in common" create an ambiguity. However, the words following, "with the right of survivorship" remove the ambiguity and make it clear that the intention was to create a joint tenancy, with the passage of title to the survivor upon the death of the other.

Decree affirmed.

Community Property.   Community property is a type of ownership found only in eight states in the United States.[3] Historically, the area within these states was owned by France and Spain, both of which had adopted the civil law system of community property. The system was continued in the states later created out of this area. Each of the eight states has developed its own laws regarding community property, and the subject is too extensive to be covered in a business law text. However, we can make a few general observations.

Community property is usually defined in such a way as to include property acquired by a husband or wife during their marriage, except property acquired by gift, will, or descent. This type of ownership is similar to both joint tenancy and tenancy in common in that each person (spouse) owns an undivided interest in a parcel of property. As with joint tenancy, the interests in community property are always equal. As with tenancy in common, either spouse may make a will disposing of his or her one-half interest in community property. If a spouse dies without a will, his or her community interest generally will pass under state statutes to the surviving spouse. Any property owned by a spouse on the date of marriage and any property received by him or her thereafter by gift or inheritance is the *separate property* of that spouse.

Condominiums and Cooperatives.   In recent years, there has been a tremendous increase in the number of condominiums in the United States. A **condominium** type of ownership is utilized most often for residential purposes, but its use is rapidly expanding to office buildings and commercial property. Briefly stated, condominium ownership involves separate ownership of a unit in a multiunit building, combined with an interest in the common areas and the land. For example, if a grantee acquires ownership of a unit in a high-rise building, the grantee becomes the sole owner of that unit. In effect, the person owns a cube of airspace. Along with the ownership of that unit, the grantee acquires an undivided interest as tenant in common in the ground on which the building stands and in the "common areas" within the building, such as elevators, stairways, hallways, and recreation areas. In some planned communities, a condominium development may consist of a "campus" of buildings. In such developments, the common areas may include a clubhouse, swimming pool, golf course, and other recreational facilities.

The word "cooperative" is used in different senses. As used here, **cooperative** refers to a corporation which is organized for the sole purpose of owning and managing a multiunit building(s), such as an apartment house or an office building, and which sells shares of stock in the corporation. A purchase of shares of stock

[3]Arizona, California, Idaho, Louisiana, Nevada, New Mexico, Texas, and Washington.

carries with it the right to occupy a unit (apartment or office) in the building. Thus, the shareholder, unlike the purchaser of a condominium unit, does not own the particular unit of the building he or she occupies; all the units are owned by the cooperative. In legal effect, a unit in a condominium is real property, whereas a shareholder in a cooperative owns personal property.

Incidents of Ownership of Real Property

When an individual, firm, or governmental unit or agency acquires ownership of real property there are legal rights and duties that accompany the ownership. These rights and duties exist regardless of the method of acquisition of ownership or the type of ownership acquired.

Rights of Owners.   Ordinarily, an owner of real property has the exclusive right to use, possess, enjoy, and dispose of the land. The owner's rights extend into the subsurface and the airspace above the surface. The owner can cultivate the land, grow crops, build a house, or install a swimming pool. An owner may give permission to others to use the property or to take minerals from the subsurface, either for temporary periods or for long durations. An owner may use real property as security for a loan or may dispose of the property by gift, sale, or will.

Duties of Owners.   The rights of an owner of real property are not unlimited. There is a growing awareness of the rights of others, and the law imposes certain duties on every property owner. Occasionally property owners voluntarily assume duties through agreements with others.

Duties Imposed by Law.   One of the most pervasive of the duties imposed by law is the duty not to create a *nuisance.* For many years nuisance laws have prohibited landowners from maintaining anything on their premises that is injurious to the health of others, that is offensive to the senses, or that unreasonably interferes with the comfortable enjoyment of life or property. For example, the following things have been held to be nuisances under the circumstances involved: rock quarry, drop-forging shop, dilapidated wooden building, slaughterhouse, airport, emission of smoke or odors, obstruction of a street or river. In recent years, prosecutors have enforced nuisance laws more vigorously as a result of public demand to protect the environment from pollution. Liability generally is not based on intent or negligence of the owner, but is imposed by the courts even though the owner is without fault.

Another duty of the property owner is always to exercise *due care* in using and maintaining property to prevent injury to others. For example, an owner who invites guests to his or her house should remove a child's skates from the entry walk before guests arrive. This is an application of the tort law of negligence discussed in Chapter 4.

There are many local government regulations which impose duties on owners of real property. The power of local governments to impose these regulations is part of what is known as the "police power." *Police power* is the power to restrict the activity of persons in the interest of public health, safety, morals, and welfare. Such restrictions must not be unreasonable, arbitrary, or discriminatory. Zoning ordinances are enacted by city and county governments to regulate land use. These ordinances generally designate segregated zones or areas where land can be used for residential, agricultural, commercial, or industrial purposes. Zoning ordinances may also regulate the height, size, and appearance of buildings; the size of yards and open spaces; and the amount of off-street parking. Building and safety codes are enacted by city and county governments to regulate the construction, repair, or alteration of buildings. Most local governments have also enacted ordinances enabling the city or county to compel the property owner to move rubbish or weeds from his or her property, or to remedy unsafe or unsightly conditions on the property.

In the following case the court had to decide if a zoning ordinance was a valid exercise of a city's police power.

CASE 24.4   Bohannan v. City of San Diego
106 Cal. Rptr. 333 (Cal. App. 1973)

Facts: The City Council of San Diego adopted an ordinance regulating the architectural design of buildings and signs within an area surrounding a state park known as "Old Town." The ordinance required the use of materials and architectural styles in remodeling or repairing existing structures as were used and existed prior to 1871. Plaintiff owned a retail business in the zoned area and brought suit to declare the ordinance unconstitutional alleging that it violated free speech concepts and was not a valid exercise of the police power. The trial court found the purpose of the ordinance fell within the meaning of "general welfare" of the public and rejected plaintiff's claim. He appealed.

Question: Was the ordinance a valid exercise of the City's police power?

Answer: Yes. The ordinance was valid.

Reasoning: The court stated that "preservation of the image of Old Town as it existed prior to 1871 . . . as a visual story of the beginning of San Diego, and as an educational exhibit of the birth place of California, contributes to the general welfare. . . ." There was no showing that compliance with style requirements upon remodeling or repairing existing buildings would render them substantially less valuable. As to signs in the area, the ordinance regulates and restricts the use of signs for the purpose of preserving the historical atmosphere of the area. The ordinance was a proper exercise of the police power.

The judgment was affirmed.

Duties Created by Agreements.   In some situations, duties are imposed on the owner of real property by deed or contract. For example, when an individual acquires ownership of a parcel in a subdivision tract (including condominiums and cooperatives) he or she usually agrees as a condition of the purchase to assume certain obligations. Thus, each owner might be required to maintain his or her premises in a neat and safe condition at all times. Types of construction and architectural design within the tract are often controlled.

When the purchaser of real property finances all or part of the purchase price by borrowing from a private or institutional lender, certain duties are imposed for the protection of the lender. The borrower generally signs an agreement that includes, among other provisions, the obligation to pay all property taxes and assessments, maintain adequate insurance, keep the premises neat and sanitary, and not to resell the property without consent of the lender.

SUMMARY

The term real property customarily includes the surface of the land, things attached to the land, airspace above, and materials below the surface.

A fixture is an article that was personal property but which has been attached to real property with the intent that it become a permanent part of it. Controversies arise because the intent of the attacher is not always clear. In such cases, the courts apply three tests: (1) method of attachment, (2) adaptability of the item to the use of the real property, and (3) relationship of the parties.

Individuals and business firms can acquire ownership of real property in several ways. The most common ways are by purchase and by gift. In each instance, the grantor transfers ownership to the grantee by means of a deed. Other methods by which individuals and firms may acquire ownership of real property are by adverse possession; by will; and, in the case of individuals, by descent.

Governmental units and agencies—local, state, and federal—frequently acquire ownership of real property. In addition to acquiring ownership by the methods available to individuals and business firms, governmental units and agencies may acquire property by exercising the power of eminent domain. Under this power, private property may be taken for public use without the owner's consent. A governmental unit or agency may receive ownership of property by statutory or common law dedication. A state may acquire ownership of real property by escheat.

Various types of ownership of real property are possible. The list includes sole ownership, joint tenancy, tenancy by the entirety, tenancy in common, community property, condominiums, and cooperatives. The right of survivorship exists in a joint tenancy and tenancy by the entirety, but not in the other types of ownership.

Ordinarily, an owner of real property has the exclusive right to use, possess, enjoy, and dispose of the land, airspace, and subsurface. These rights are not unlimited, however; they are limited by duties to others imposed by law and by governmental regulation under the police power. In addition, many duties are assumed by purchasers of real property as part of a contract of purchase in a subdivision tract, or as part of a finance agreement with a lender.

REVIEW QUESTIONS

1. What physical elements does the term "real property" include? Give an example of each.

2. (**a**) Define a fixture. (**b**) What are the usual tests of a fixture? (**c**) Apply the tests to the following items: window screens, front door key, lawn statuary.

3. Explain why a real property purchase should be set forth in a written contract.

4. Describe how a grantor would go about making a gift of land to another.

5. (**a**) What must a claimant prove to acquire ownership of real property by adverse possession? (**b**) What suggestions could you make to a landowner to help prevent loss of ownership to an adverse possessor?

6. What are the essential differences between the following: quitclaim deed; grant deed; warranty deed.

7. List and explain the methods by which a governmental unit or agency can acquire ownership of real property.

8. (**a**) What are the distinctions between eminent domain and dedication? (**b**) What is the similarity between them? (**c**) Give an example of each of the two types of dedication.

9. (**a**) In which of the following types of ownership must the owners' interests be equal: joint tenancy, tenancy in common, community property. (**b**) If an owner died without making a will, who would acquire his or her interest in each of the three types of ownership listed?

10. Explain the difference between a condominium and a cooperative.

11. List and give examples of several important duties of landowners imposed by law.

12. Discuss the justification, pro and con, of impositions of deed restrictions by subdividers.

CASE PROBLEMS

1. A cable television company provides master television antennas at high, unobstructed points and transmits signals through a system of cables carried on utility company poles to the homes of subscribers to their service. At the terminal points, a cable is suspended from the utility pole to the subscriber's home. The cable then enters the home and with related wiring and equipment is fastened by clamps, screws, and bolts. The portion extending from the utility pole and into the house is called a "housedrop." The portion within the home is called the "interior house-drop." The cable company charges for installation and monthly service. If service is discontinued, the system is simply disconnected at the utility pole; nothing is removed. The company has no agreement whatever with the subscriber over what can be done with the equipment. The material and labor costs for installation of the housedrops are carried on the company's books as capital assets, and depreciation is taken as a deduction on its federal income tax returns. Should the interior housedrop portion be treated as a fixture owned by the subscriber or as property owned by the cable company? State the reasons for your answer.

2. In 1938 George and Amelia Popp executed and delivered a deed to Wachter conveying ownership of some 90 acres of land. Both parties agreed and understood that only land north of Rock Creek Road was intended to be transferred, but by mistake 11 acres of land south of the road were included in the deed. In 1941 Wachter conveyed the 90 acres to Lauf, and in 1955 Lauf conveyed the property to

Fitzpatrick. Meanwhile, in 1940 George Popp had died and his widow, Amelia, undertook to convey lands south of Rock Creek Road to Phelps in 1942, including the 11 acres mistakenly deeded in 1938. Phelps deeded to Siebeneck in 1944. Siebeneck fenced the entire area he considered he owned. Rock Creek Road was fenced as the north boundary line, in accordance with the deed description. He used the land for pasturing and feeding cattle continuously until 1962, when he deeded the farm to Boeckmann. All the deeds were promptly recorded following their execution and delivery. Through the years both sets of "owners" paid taxes on the 11 acres south of the road. Boeckmann filed suit against Fitzpatrick, the record owner, claiming that ownership of the 11 acres was acquired by Siebeneck by adverse possession and transferred to him. Who should win? Explain.

3. In 1950 Mrs. Ethel Nevins offered to buy a house for her younger sister, Carrie Johnson. A contract was entered into for the purchase of a home, and Mrs. Nevins paid the down payment of $1500. The seller executed a deed to Carrie Johnson, who then signed a deed conveying the property to Mrs. Nevins. The deed to Mrs. Nevins was held by her but not made public because she did not want her husband to know of the transaction. Carrie Johnson and her daughter lived in the home. The daughter was informed by her mother and by her aunt, Mrs. Nevins, that if her mother should die, the house would be hers. Carrie Johnson died in 1971, without leaving a will. After the death, Mrs. Nevins presented the 1950 deed signed by Carrie Johnson, and claimed ownership of the house. The daughter claims ownership by inheritance from her mother. Who owns the property? Give reasons.

4. State National owns the Reymond Building on the southwest corner of Third and Florida Streets in Baton Rouge. Attached to the north wall of the building is a canopy that projects over the sidewalk and extends several inches over Florida Street. The city claims ownership by dedication of the street and the airspace above it. A subdivision map dated 1837 shows Florida Street to be 64 feet wide. There is no evidence of a formal acceptance of the map by the city. Since 1837, this 64-foot strip has been considered as a main thoroughfare and has been used and maintained by the city. The street was originally 42 feet wide and there was an 11-foot sidewalk on each side of the street. The city initiated a downtown improvement program and after the construction of improvements by the city, the street measured 44 feet wide and each sidewalk measured 10 feet wide. The Reymond Building canopy did not project into Florida Street until the street was widened. Does the city own the street and can it compel State National to remove that portion of the canopy that now projects over the street? Explain.

5. Beulah Sharpe enrolled as a member of the Adam Dante health spa and paid for a 1-year membership. The premises contained an exercise area, a locker room, a shower room, and the "spa" area. The shower room and the spa area had tiled floors, and there were no mats on the floors. A small, inconspicuous sign read "Slippery When Wet." On her fifth visit to the spa, Mrs. Sharpe walked barefoot from the shower room past the steam room, sauna room, and sunken whirlpool to the swimming pool. After swimming, she spent a few minutes in the whirlpool and in the sauna room. Then she walked back toward the swimming pool to pick up a towel. Near the whirlpool her feet slipped from under her, and she was seriously injured. At the time of the accident there was no employee of Adam Dante in the spa area. Does Mrs. Sharpe have a cause of action against Adam Dante? Why or why not?

CHAPTER 25

INTERESTS IN REAL PROPERTY

The subject of interests in real property is important to almost everyone in contemporary society, including persons who do not own real property. The three major types of interests in real property are estates, easements, and liens. Estates in real property range from those involving full ownership to those involving considerably less than full ownership, such as tenancies. Easements and liens are both interests in the real property of *another*. Thus, two persons are always involved—one who owns the real property and one who owns the easement or the lien.

The first part of this chapter discusses the nature of estates and the different types of estates. Special attention is given to landlord-tenant relations. The last two parts of the chapter examine easements and liens.

ESTATES IN REAL PROPERTY

Meaning and Classification of Estates

The word **estate**, as used by lawyers, means an ownership interest in land. However, an ownership interest may vary from the absolute ownership of a title holder to the temporary possession of a tenant.

The usual classification of estates is based on duration of enjoyment. On that basis, estates are either *freehold* or *leasehold*. **Freehold estates** include those in which the duration of enjoyment is potentially infinite and those in which duration is measured by the life of a person. **Leasehold estates** include those in which the enjoyment is for a specified period of time and those in which the enjoyment is for an unspecified period not intended to be infinite.

Freehold Estates

There are two major types of freehold estates: **fee simple estates** and **life estates.** In either type the owner of the interest normally has the present right to use, possess, and enjoy the property.

Fee Simple Estates. The estate that owners usually acquire in real property is the fee simple, sometimes referred to as a *fee simple absolute*, or merely as a "fee." A person owning property in fee simple has the fullest type of ownership—the largest "bundle of rights" possible under the law. The owner has the exclusive right to possess and enjoy the property, sell it, give it away, lease it to another, or borrow against it. Upon the owner's death, a fee simple estate passes to the beneficiary or beneficiaries designated in the owner's will, or to his or her heirs if there is no will. This process of passing on a fee simple estate from generation to generation may continue indefinitely. There are no technical words required to transfer a fee simple estate from a grantor to a grantee. In most states any properly executed deed is presumed to transfer a fee simple estate, in the absence of specific words indicating that a lesser estate is intended.

Life Estates. A life estate is an estate the duration of which is measured by the life of a person. For example, a deed to "Alice for life" creates an estate that will automatically end when Alice dies. A deed to "Alice for the life of Ben" creates an estate that will end when Ben dies. In this latter example, if Alice dies before Ben, the unexpired portion of the life estate passes to Alice's heirs or to the beneficiaries under her will. During the existence of a life estate, the holder of the estate (called a "life tenant") has a great many rights. The life tenant can use, possess, and enjoy the property; sell his or her interest; give it to a donee; borrow against it; or lease it to someone and collect the rents.

Although a life tenant has many rights, he or she also has certain duties and obligations. The life tenant must keep all improvements on the property in good repair and must not use or treat the property in such a way as substantially to diminish its value. Any such abuse of the property is called "waste." Specific examples of waste are permitting the house or fences to fall into disrepair and removing timber, earth, or minerals unnecessarily. Normally, the life tenant must pay the annual taxes assessed against the property and pay interest on any mortgage or other encumbrance on the property. The reason the law imposes these duties on the life tenant is to protect the value of the property for the person who will take possession at the termination of the life estate.

Future Interests.   When a person's right to use, possess, and enjoy a parcel of property is to begin at some future time, he or she has what is called "a future interest." Of necessity, when a grantor creates a life estate a future interest is also created. Someone will succeed to the use and possession of the property upon termination of the life estate. There are several types of future interests recognized in the law as estates. A discussion of all types is beyond the scope of this text; however, we will discuss two major future interests: reversions and remainders.

Reversions.   When the owner of real property transfers a life estate to someone or leases the property to someone for a certain period, he or she gives up the present right of possession and enjoyment. When the life estate or lease terminates, someone will succeed to those rights. If the grantor reacquires the right of possession and enjoyment, he or she is said to own a **reversion.** For example, if Paul makes a deed conveying certain property to Betty "for her life" and makes no mention of who shall have possession and enjoyment when Betty dies, the general rule of law is that full possession and enjoyment will revert to the grantor. Thus, Paul has a reversion and is referred to as a "reversioner." Paul can transfer his future interest to another. If he dies before Betty, the reversion will pass to Paul's heirs or beneficiaries. When a life estate or lease terminates, the owner of the reversion will have all the rights of an owner of a fee simple estate.

Remainders.   A **remainder** is also an estate where possession and enjoyment of realty are to occur in the future, but the person who is to receive possession and enjoyment is someone other than the grantor or the grantor's heirs. For example, if Paul transfers certain real property to Betty "for her life, then to Carol," Carol acquires a remainder. She can transfer her interest in the property to another. If she dies before Betty without having transferred the remainder, it will pass to her heirs or beneficiaries.

As the following case illustrates, occasionally there is doubt as to whether the grantor intended to create a reversion or a remainder.

CASE 25.1

Root v. Mackey
486 S.W.2d 449 (Mo. 1972)

Facts: H. P. Snow was the owner of 280 acres of land. In 1927 he executed and delivered a deed to this land to two of his sons, Sam H. Snow and J. Edgar Snow. The grantor stated in the deed that he retained the right of possession of the land during his life and that, "in case of the death of either or both [of the grantees], the share of such deceased shall revert to the living brothers and sisters."

H. P. Snow died in 1933, leaving Sam and Edgar and five other children surviving him. Sam died in 1934. Edgar died in 1948, leaving several children surviving him. In order to get a court determination of where the title to the land was, the brothers and sisters of Sam and Edgar brought suit in the circuit court, naming the children of Edgar as defendants. The defendants claimed an interest in the land by inheritance from their father. The plaintiffs claimed that Sam and Edgar had had only a life estate and that upon the deaths of the life tenants, the remainder (referred to in the deed as the reversion) passed to them, as "the living brothers and sisters." The trial court, adopting plaintiffs' view, found that title in fee simple vested in (transferred to) the plaintiffs as remaindermen. The defendants appealed.

Question: Did the 1927 deed create a remainder or a reversion?

Answer: The deed created a remainder to Sam and Edgar's brothers and sisters.

Reasoning: Sam and Edgar had only life estates. The confusion was created by the grantor's use of the word "revert" upon their deaths. The court said the grantor did not use "revert" in its technical sense. To him it was his way of saying he intended title to the property to go to the living brothers and sisters.

Judgment was affirmed.

Leasehold Estates

not a transfer of ownership —

As previously noted, a leasehold estate is an estate in real property having a duration of a specified period of time or an unspecified period not intended to be infinite. The holder of a leasehold estate (called a "tenant" or "lessee") receives from the owner the exclusive right to possess and use certain premises during the leasehold period, or term. The owner of the property (called a "landlord" or "lessor") retains a reversion. He or she has all the other rights of a full owner and will normally regain the right to possess and use the premises at the end of the term. (*Premises* is a word used frequently in creating leaseholds and may mean land, a building, or part of a building with or without the land.)

There are four types of leasehold estates: tenancies for a fixed term, periodic tenancies, tenancies at will, and tenancies at sufferance. Each of these types is discussed below. The first three types normally come into existence by means of an agreement called a "lease."

Tenancies for a Fixed Term.   The most common type of leasehold estate is the **tenancy for a fixed term,** often referred to as an "estate for years," even though the duration of the tenancy may be for a single year or for a term shorter than a year.

Nature and Requirements of a Lease.   A lease has two aspects. In one of its aspects, a lease is a contract setting forth reciprocal rights and duties of the lessor and lessee concerning the use and possession of certain property. In its other aspect, a lease is a conveyance of an estate in real property from one person to another.

Although most people think of a lease as a written document, it need be in writing only if a statute so requires. Most states have a statute requiring leases for more than 1 year to be in writing.

No particular words are necessary to create a valid lease. However, certain items should be mentioned in any kind of a lease: (1) the identification of each of the parties; (2) a designation of the premises leased; (3) the rent to be paid, and the time and manner of its payment; and (4) the term of the lease, including a beginning and ending date.

Rights and Duties of Landlord and Tenant.   As previously noted, a lease sets forth the reciprocal rights and duties of the parties. The most fundamental right of the *landlord* is the right to receive the rental payments provided for in the lease. If the tenant defaults in payment, the landlord has a cause of action for the unpaid rent. If the tenant unlawfully remains in possession of the premises, the law provides one or more remedies by which the landlord may regain possession. The most fundamental right of the *tenant* is to have the exclusive possession of the premises for the agreed term, if the tenant fulfills his or her part of the bargain.

Leases usually include some provisions concerning rights and duties other than those relating to rent and occupancy. For example, some additional provisions customarily included in apartment leases are that the tenant is to pay all electric and gas bills for the apartment during the term of the lease; that the tenant is not to sublet the apartment or assign the lease without written consent of the landlord; that the tenant will deliver the premises at the expiration of the term in as good order and repair as when received, natural wear and tear excepted; and that the landlord or an agent shall have the right to enter the premises at any reasonable hour to examine the same and to make repairs. Leases of commercial and industrial properties, involving long terms and properties of great value, usually contain more provisions concerning rights and duties than do leases of residential properties.

Landlords and tenants are subject not only to the rights and duties set forth in a lease but also to those declared by the courts and those specified in statutes. For example, at common law the landlord had no duty to repair or maintain the premises occupied by the tenant during the term of the lease. Recently, there has been an important shift in the attitude of judges toward the rights of tenants of residential property, especially in large metropolitan communities. Stressing the contract aspect of leases, some courts have held that the lessor impliedly warrants (guarantees) the habitability of a dwelling. Thus, the landlord must maintain the premises in a habitable condition throughout the term of the lease. If the landlord fails to meet this obligation, the tenant may make necessary repairs and deduct the cost from the rent due. In some instances the tenant may stay in possession *without paying rent*. A number of state legislatures have responded to demands of tenant groups and have enacted statutes requiring the landlord of a building intended for residency to keep it in habitable condition, except for waste or dilapidations caused by the tenant. Generally, such statutes define "habitable" to include at least adequate plumbing, water supply, heating, and sanitation.

Periodic Tenancies.   A **periodic tenancy** is an estate in real property that is created for a specified period of time and that will continue for successive periods of the same length, until the tenancy is terminated. The period may be week to week, month to month, or any term the parties agree upon. Frequently, a periodic tenancy arises by inference from the conduct of the parties. Suppose, for example, that a landlord agreed to rent certain premises to a tenant, that no specified term was agreed upon, but that the tenant agreed to pay rent monthly. In the event of litigation, a court would normally hold that a month-to-month tenancy had been created.

A periodic tenancy continues indefinitely until the parties agree to terminate the tenancy, or one of the parties gives notice of termination. Requirements regarding the method and time of notice vary among the states. A common requirement is that notice must be given in writing in the same amount of time as the period of tenancy, but not to exceed 30 days. Under such a statute, 1 week's notice would be sufficient to terminate a week-to-week tenancy; and 30 days' notice would be sufficient to terminate a year-to-year tenancy. Generally, no reason for termination need be given by either party. However, in many states a landlord may not terminate a tenancy because the tenant reported dilapidations and building or health code violations to the authorities. Such a termination is called "retaliatory eviction." Neither may a landlord terminate a tenancy because the tenant withheld rent or deducted the cost of needed repairs from the rent due.

The following case sets forth the elements of the defense of retaliatory eviction.

CASE 25.2   Toms Point Apartments v. Goudzward
339 N.Y.S.2d 281 (N.Y. Dist. Ct. 1972)

Facts: The parties entered into a lease which expired August 31, 1972. The tenant (Goudzward) failed to vacate the premises and this proceeding was begun to evict her. At the trial the tenant raised the defense of "retaliatory eviction." She testified that she complained to the Attorney General's Office regarding the failure of the landlord to pay interest on rent security deposits and that she appeared at a hearing of the superintendent who was fired by the landlord.

Question: Was the landlord entitled to evict the tenant?

Answer: Yes. The tenant failed to establish the defense of retaliatory eviction.

Reasoning: The court said that *all* of the following must be present for the tenant to prevail: (1) the tenant must have exercised a constitutional right; (2) the grievance must be bona fide, reasonable, serious in nature, and have a foundation in fact; (3) the tenant did not create the condition complained of; (4) the grievance must be present when the eviction action commences; and (5) the overriding reason for the eviction is to retaliate against the tenant for exercising his constitutional rights. The court found that at the time the landlord commenced this action none of the original grievances existed. The tenants had collected the interest due them and the problem with the superintendent had been resolved.

Judgment in favor of the landlord.

Tenancies at Will. A **tenancy at will** is an estate in real property created by agreement of the parties that the tenant will have the exclusive right to possession for an indefinite period of time not intended to be infinite. Such tenancies arise only in limited circumstances. An example of the way in which tenancies at will arise is when the tenant is given possession while negotiations take place for a sale of the property or for a comprehensive written lease.

A tenancy at will can be terminated by either party, but many states require a landlord to give 30 days' written notice. The death of either the landlord or the tenant automatically terminates a tenancy at will. The tenant cannot assign a tenancy at will to another. Any attempt to do so would automatically terminate the tenancy.

Tenancies at Sufferance. A **tenancy at sufferance** typically arises when a tenant remains in possession after the expiration of a tenancy for a fixed term, without the landlord's consent. In most states the landlord can institute legal action to evict the tenant at sufferance without first giving notice of termination of the tenancy. The tenant would be liable for the reasonable rental value of the premises for the period he or she remains in possession after expiration of the tenancy for a fixed term. If the landlord accepts rent from a holdover tenant, a court very likely would hold that a periodic tenancy was created by the conduct of the parties. A landlord should therefore consider carefully legal consequences before accepting rent from a tenant at sufferance.

EASEMENTS

Meaning of Easement

An **easement** may be defined as the right to use or prevent the use of, the real property of another in a specific manner. An example would be the following: Edith grants to Fred, an adjoining landowner, the permanent right to drive his car over a designated portion of her land in order to get to and from the nearest public street. Fred has a right-of-way easement. His land is called the "dominant" tenement or parcel. Edith's land, the land subject to the easement, is called the "servient" tenement or parcel.

An easement is an interest in real property, but it is not an estate in real property.

We have seen that an estate is an interest that is, or may become, possessory. The owner of an easement does not have the right to possess the servient tenement but merely the right to use it, or to prevent the use of it, in a certain way. The easement for roadway purposes, mentioned above, entitles Fred to drive his car across Edith's land, but does not entitle him to fence it, cultivate it, or exercise the usual rights of an owner of an estate in real property.

Use and Maintenance of Easements

The owner of an easement may exercise the right to use, or prevent the use of, the servient tenement according to the purpose of the easement and the circumstances surrounding its creation. Where an easement is created by express grant, a properly drawn deed will indicate the specific purpose of the easement, such as using the land for a roadway, or for installation of power poles.

The owner of an easement has the right and the duty to maintain and repair installations connected with the easement. For example, an easement owner may grade and pave the surface designated in a roadway easement or, if the easement is for utility purposes, the easement owner may enter the servient property to repair and replace water lines or sewer pipes as needed. As the following case illustrates, the owner of the servient tenement may do as he or she wishes with the property so long as he or she does not unreasonably interfere with the use, enjoyment, and maintenance of the easement created.

CASE 25.3

Jordan v. Guinn
485 S.W.2d 715 (Ark. 1972)

Facts: Mr. and Mrs. Jordan owned a tract of land adjacent to property owned by Esther Guinn, plaintiff [appellee]. For many years there had been a roadway easement 20 feet wide running across the north side of the Jordans' property. The purpose of the easement was to give access to the Guinn property. Mr. Jordan erected a gate across the west end of the roadway and installed a fence across the east end of the roadway. Guinn brought suit against Mr. and Mrs. Jordan to require them to remove both the gate and the fence. The trial court directed their removal. Mr. and Mrs. Jordan appealed.

Question: Should the court have compelled removal of both the gate and the fence?

Answer: Yes. Both the gate and fence were unreasonable obstructions.

Reasoning: The court stated that the general rule was the owner of the servient estate may erect gates across an easement if they do not unreasonably interfere with the right of passage, when they are necessary for the preservation and proper and efficient use of the servient estate. There was no evidence that the gate and fence were placed across the way for any purpose relating to Jordans' use of the servient estate. In fact, the intent seemed to be to prevent its use as a means of ingress to and egress from the Guinn property.

The decree of the trial court directing removal was affirmed.

Termination of Easements	There are various ways in which an easement may be terminated or "extinguished." The most common method is by a deed from the owner of the easement to the owner of the servient tenement. Some of the other ways in which an easement may be terminated are by (1) abandonment; (2) merger, as where the same person becomes the owner of the easement and the servient tenement—for obviously a person cannot have an easement on his or her own land; (3) destruction of the servient property, as where the tenant in an apartment building has an easement in the common halls and stairways, and the building is destroyed by fire or earthquake; and (4) adverse possession, as where the owner of the servient tenement refuses to recognize the rights of the easement owner and, for the statutory period, occupies the property adversely to the easement owner's rights.

LIENS ON REAL PROPERTY

Meaning and Classification of Liens	In general, a **lien** is a claim or charge on property as security for the payment of a debt or for the performance of some other obligation. In one sense, a lien is a contingent claim held by a creditor. If the obligation is satisfied, there will be no interference with the debtor's right to use, possess, and enjoy his or her property. On the other hand, if the obligation is not satisfied, the lien holder may take steps (called "foreclosure") to sell the property and apply proceeds from the sale to the debt.
	There are two main classes of liens on real property: **voluntary liens**, which are created with the property owner's consent (mortgages, for example); and **involuntary liens**, which are created without the property owner's consent (mechanics' liens, for example). Only the most important voluntary and involuntary liens are discussed on the following pages.
Voluntary Liens on Real Property	**Mortgages.** A mortgage is the most common type of voluntary lien on real property. The mortgage device is used in connection with many different kinds of credit transactions. Usually, the device is used by a property owner as a means of borrowing a substantial sum of money needed for some personal or business reason. The property owner goes to a bank, borrows the money on a promissory note, and executes a mortgage on the owner's home or business property to secure the repayment of the money borrowed.

Nature and Requirements of a Mortgage.   As implied above, a real estate mortgage is an interest in real property given to secure the performance of some obligation. The two parties to a mortgage are called the "mortgagor" (the borrower or debtor) and the "mortgagee" (the lender or creditor). Under the statute of frauds, a mortgage transfers an interest in land and must be evidenced by a writing (see Chapter 12).

Rights and Duties of the Parties.   The *mortgagor* of real property retains the right to use, possess, enjoy, and dispose of the property. The mortgagor can lease the premises to another and collect rent. He or she can borrow further sums of money from other creditors and give subsequent mortgages to them. If the mortgagor transfers ownership of the property during life or if the property passes at death to his or her heirs or beneficiaries, the transferee takes the property subject to the mortgage. The typical mortgage instrument contains a list of duties to be performed by the mortgagor. Some of the duties customarily included are to repay money borrowed, to repay any future sums that may be advanced by the mortgagee, to keep the premises in good repair, to refrain from committing waste, to pay annual real property taxes, to pay any prior mortgage that may be on the property, and to maintain adequate fire insurance on improvements.

The *mortgagee* has the right to performance of all the mortgagor's duties. Under the typical mortgage instrument, the mortgagee has several duties. The mortgagee has a duty to lend money in accordance with the agreement of the parties. When the mortgagor pays back the loan, the mortgagee owes a duty to execute appropriate documents to remove the lien from the mortgagor's property. In the event foreclosure becomes necessary, the mortgagee owes a duty to act fairly and to follow the statutory procedure of the state. A mortgagee can transfer the mortgage to a third person and assign to such person the right to collect the debt secured by the mortgage. Upon the mortgagee's death, the mortgage passes to his or her heirs or beneficiaries. The transferee would be obligated to perform the mortgagee's duties mentioned above.

The following case illustrates the consequences of a mortgagor violating the terms of the mortgage.

CASE 25.4   Investors Savings & Loan Association v. Ganz
416 A. 2d 918 (N.J. Super. 1980)

Facts: Mr. & Mrs. Ganz (defendants) borrowed $50,000 from Investors Savings & Loan Association (plaintiff) to finance the purchase of a home. The loan was secured by a mortgage in favor of the plaintiff containing the following condition:

> And it is further agreed that, if the mortgaged premises are not used as the primary place of residence and are not occupied by the Mortgagor during the term of the mortgage loan, then and in such event, the aforesaid principal sum with accrued interest shall, at the option of the Mortgagee, become due and payable immediately, . . .,

In October 1979 plaintiff learned that the premises were not occupied by the defendants but were occupied by tenants. Plaintiff demanded that the balance due on the mortgage be paid in full. Defendants did not make this payment and the premises continued to be tenant-occupied. Plaintiff brought suit to foreclose the mortgage. Defendants filed an answer alleging that the acceleration clause and mortgage requirement that defendants reside in the mortgaged premises were unconscionable, inequitable, created a forfeiture, and thus were of no force and effect. Plaintiff moved for an order granting summary judgment.

Question: Was the occupancy provision in the mortgage enforceable?

Answer: Yes. The provision was not unconscionable or inequitable.

Reasoning: Historically the purpose of a savings and loan association has been to assist persons in acquiring a home in which to reside. Plaintiff argued that nonoccupying owners tend to

minimize property maintenance and upkeep and this leads to unreasonable depreciation of the property that jeopardizes the security on which the loan was made. The court
found the requirement of owner occupancy was not unjust and the fear of jeopardy to
the security was not unreasonable. Defendants freely and voluntarily entered into the
mortgage transaction.

Summary judgment was granted.

Foreclosure of a Mortgage; Right of Redemption.   If the mortgagor fails to perform
any of the listed duties, the mortgagee has the right to foreclose. **Foreclosure** is the
process by which the real property is sold and the proceeds from the sale applied to
the debt. The mortgagee may initiate a court proceeding to secure an order of sale.
After obtaining a court order, the sheriff or other officer of the court conducts a sale
by auction. At any time prior to the court's entering a decree of foreclosure, the
mortgagor can reinstate the mortgage by curing the default; ordinarily, that means
making up installment payments that have been missed. Normally, the mortgagor
also has a statutory **right of redemption** after a foreclosure sale takes place; that is, a
right for a limited time to repurchase the property by payment of the auction sale
price to the high bidder.

Trust Deeds.   About half the states recognize the trust deed as an acceptable
security instrument in real estate transactions. To the creditor (the lender), a trust
deed has several significant advantages over the mortgage, and in some states the
trust deed has virtually replaced the real property mortgage.

Nature of a Trust Deed.   A **trust deed** is a document by which a debtor transfers the
title to real property to a disinterested person (called a "trustee") to be held in trust as
security for the performance of an obligation, usually the payment of a debt. The
trustee is typically given the power to sell the property if the debtor defaults, and to
apply proceeds from the sale to the debt.
    Since mortgages and trust deeds perform a similar function, they necessarily have
many features in common. Most of the preceding discussion concerning mortgages
applies to trust deeds. However, while there are only two parties to a mortgage,
there are three parties to a trust deed: the *trustor* (the debtor), the *beneficiary* (the
creditor or lender), and the *trustee*. Although the trustee holds title to the real
property, it is a bare legal title, not a true ownership interest. In legal effect, the trust
deed is considered to be merely a lien on the real property. If the trustor meets his or
her obligations, there will be no interference with the use and possession of the
property. When the obligation is satisfied, the trustee will execute the necessary
documents to reconvey title to the trustor. However, if the trustor-debtor defaults on
an obligation, the holding of the title to the real property by the trustee becomes
important. The major difference between a mortgage and a trust deed relates to
foreclosure, as indicated in the following discussion.

Foreclosure of a Trust Deed.   Under the terms of the typical trust deed the trustee is
given the power to sell the property upon default by the debtor-trustor and to apply

proceeds from the sale to the debt. In most states that permit the trust deed device, the creditor-beneficiary (the lender) may elect to have the trustee use the same judicial procedure as for foreclosing a mortgage. However, the creditor ordinarily will elect to foreclose by having the trustee use the power of sale granted in the trust deed. The nonjudicial "power of sale" foreclosure by the trustee has certain advantages for the creditor: (1) It avoids the delay involved in getting a court order for a sale and the expenses of litigation; and (2) it allows the trustor no right of redemption after the sale.

To foreclose by power of sale, the trustee simply notifies all interested persons (the debtor, other lienholders) that the trustor has defaulted. After a short period of time allowed for reinstatement of the trust deed, the trustee advertises and conducts an auction sale. Since the trustor has no right of redemption, the purchaser can immediately take possession, make improvements, lease, or even sell the property.

Involuntary Liens on Real Property

There are a number of liens on real property that can be created without the consent or approval of the owner. The statutes concerning such liens are complex and vary widely among the states. We present here some general aspects of the more important involuntary liens.

Mechanics' Liens.   At common law, a person who was not paid for performing a service or supplying materials in improving someone's real property had a cause of action solely against the person who requested the service or materials. Today, nearly every state has a statute giving such a person a *mechanic's lien* on the property he or she helped to improve, provided the person takes the steps required to perfect a claim. The importance of having a lien on the property is that if the property owner does not pay the claimant, he or she can foreclose on the property.

The term *mechanic* is misleading. It does not apply to a person who works on machinery or automobiles; rather, it applies to all types of contractors, subcontractors, laborers, and material suppliers who perform services or supply materials for the improvement of real property. Suppose, for example, that Ann owns a house and that she enters into a contract with Carl, a general building contractor, to add a room to the house. Carl, in turn, enters into subcontracts with David, Fred, and Henry to do carpentry work, electrical wiring, and painting. Each subcontractor has employees who do the actual work under his or her supervision. Carl also contracts with Mary for the lumber and other materials to be used in the construction of the room. Each person mentioned in this example who is not paid for services or materials by the one he or she contracted with is entitled to a lien on Ann's property, provided the steps are taken as required by statute to perfect the lien.

The mechanics' liens statutes of the various states ordinarily require that a claim-of-lien form be filed or recorded in a specified government office within a limited time period. Some states require that notice of a possible claim be mailed to the property owner. In addition, the claimant ordinarily must initiate a civil action within a certain time period to foreclose the lien. The failure of a claimant to fulfill the statutory requirements will bar the claimant, in most instances, from obtaining the benefits of the mechanic's lien statute; however, such failure will not bar the claimant from pursuing contract law remedies against the party who requested the service or materials.

Attachment Liens.   In certain situations an unsecured creditor who has filed an action against a debtor may have the defendant's property seized by the sheriff under a **writ of attachment.** The purpose of the seizure is to hold the property pending the outcome of the suit. Where the property is real property, "seizure" consists of having the sheriff record the writ of attachment in the county recorder's office. Upon recording, a lien is created against the property. If the plaintiff-creditor later obtains a judgment in the civil action, and the defendant refuses to pay the amount of the judgment, the plaintiff can have the property sold by foreclosure. If the defendant-debtor prevails in the action, the attachment lien terminates. The United States Supreme Court has severely restricted the creditor's right to attachment, because attachment interferes with the debtor's constitutional right to use and dispose of his or her property *prior* to a court trial.[1]

Judgment Liens.   When one party to a lawsuit receives a judgment requiring the other party to pay a sum of money, the party receiving the judgment is thereafter called a "judgment creditor"; the party against whom the judgment is rendered is called the "judgment debtor." If the judgment debtor does not voluntarily pay the judgment, the judgment creditor may, under modern statutes, record the judgment in the county or counties in which the judgment debtor owns real property. When the judgment is recorded, it becomes a lien on any real property owned by the judgment debtor in the county. A **judgment lien** remains a lien on the property until the judgment is satisfied or rendered inoperative by the expiration of the statutory period.

Execution Liens.   A judgment creditor often must take coercive measures to enforce collection of a judgment. One method that may be available is to have the court issue a **writ of execution.** Such a writ is directed to the sheriff, ordering the seizure and sale of certain specified property of the judgment debtor. Details of the procedure vary among states, but usually the sheriff records a notice of execution in the county where the judgment debtor's real property is located. Recording the notice creates a lien on the described parcel of property. Unlike the judgment lien, recording a writ of execution does not create a lien on *all* the judgment debtor's real property in the county, just on the described parcel. The sheriff sets a time and place for foreclosure sale of the specific parcel, advertises, and conducts the sale in the same manner as that of a mortgage foreclosure sale.

Tax Liens.   A **tax lien** is a special type of involuntary lien against real property. It is a lien created by a governmental unit or agency to enforce collection of a tax. A wide variety of taxes exists in our contemporary society, imposed by various agencies ranging from local townships to the federal government.

   The most common tax lien in the United States is the real property tax lien. Generally, the taxing agency is given an *automatic* lien against the taxpayer's real property to secure payment of real property taxes. The state or local government is not required to file suit or have a trial prior to foreclosure. If the taxes are not paid within the statutory time period, the government can simply publish a notice in the

[1]*Sniadach v. Family Fin. Corp.*, 395 U.S. 337 (1969).

paper and conduct an auction sale. There is typically no redemption period after sale, and the high bidder receives a tax deed immediately.

When the federal government, a state, or local governmental taxing agency is attempting to collect an unpaid income tax, employment tax, sales tax, or other nonproperty tax, a lien on the taxpayer's real property is not automatically created. The governmental agency is usually required to record some type of delinquency notice in the county recorder's office. Recording the notice creates a lien. In order to sell the taxpayer's real property, the taxing agency generally must follow a procedure similar to that for foreclosing a mortgage. Often the taxpayer is given a redemption period after sale to recover his or her property.

SUMMARY

The subject of interests in real property is important to almost everyone in contemporary society, including persons who do not own real property. There are three main types of interests in real property: estates, easements, and liens. An estate in real property is an interest that is, or may become, possessory. Estates are either freeholds or leaseholds. The major freehold estates are the fee simple estate and the life estate. The owner of a freehold estate can sell it, give it away, lease it to someone, or borrow against it. The death of an owner of a fee simple estate does not terminate the estate. Upon the owner's death the estate passes to the owner's heirs or to the beneficiaries named in his or her will. A life estate automatically terminates at the death of the person whose life measures the estate.

If the owner of an estate in real property is not to exercise the right to use, possess, and enjoy the property until some future time, he or she has a future interest. There are two main types of future interests: reversions (where the right of future possession is retained by the grantor) and remainders (where the right of future possession is owned by someone other than the grantor). Leasehold estates are those in which a person acquires the right to exclusive possession of certain premises for a limited period of time. The most common types of leasehold estates are tenancies for a fixed term and periodic tenancies. The laws regarding landlord and tenant relations currently are undergoing analysis by state legislatures and the judiciary. Tenants in contemporary society have acquired more rights than stated in a lease, and landlords are required to assume a corresponding increase in duties.

An easement is an interest in real property, but it is not an estate in real property. An easement is the right to use, or to prevent the use of, the real property of another in a specific manner. Although an easement may give the easement holder a right to limited use of another's property, it does not give the holder the right to possess that property.

A lien is a claim or charge on property as security for an obligation. A creditor who holds a lien on real property has no right to possess or use the property. If the owner of the property does not satisfy his or her obligation to the creditor, the creditor can take steps to foreclose the lien. Foreclosure usually involves a sale of the property at auction and the use of as much of the proceeds as are needed to satisfy the creditor's claim.

Two major voluntary liens are the mortgage and the trust deed. A mortgage is a two-party document; a trust deed involves three parties. The steps in foreclosure differ greatly between them. Because of the differences, creditors prefer to acquire trust deeds in states that permit them, whereas debtors prefer to give a mortgage as security for an obligation. The major involuntary liens on real property are mechanics' liens, attachment liens, judgment liens, execution liens, and tax liens. The procedure for foreclosure of involuntary liens is similar to that for foreclosure of mortgages.

REVIEW QUESTIONS

1. (a) What is an estate in real property? (b) What is the essential difference between the following: freehold estate and leasehold estate; fee simple estate and reversion?

2. (a) What are the most important rights of landlord and tenant under a typical lease? (b) What duties does a landlord incur under the typical lease? (c) What duties does the tenant incur? (d) Why would an individual or firm be willing to assume these duties?

3. (a) How are the following tenancies created: periodic tenancy; tenancy at will; tenancy at sufferance? (b) How can each be terminated?

4. (a) What is an easement? (b) How does it differ from an estate in real property? (c) Define or explain: dominant tenement and servient tenement. (d) Why might it be important for you to know whether an easement exists before acquiring ownership of real property?

5. Describe the ways in which you could terminate an easement that is no longer desired.

6. (a) What is the nature and function of a lien? (b) Explain and give examples of the two main classes of liens.

7. (a) What functions do the mortgagor and mortgagee perform in a real estate transaction? (b) List the rights of each party under the typical mortgage. (c) List the duties of each party. (d) How can foreclosure of a mortgage be avoided if threatened?

8. (a) Who are the parties to a trust deed? (b) What functions does each perform in a business transaction? (c) Why would a lender rather have a trust deed than a mortgage?

9. (a) What is a mechanic's lien? (b) Why do you think the states enacted mechanics' liens statutes? (c) What remedy other than a mechanic's lien is available to an unpaid contractor, subcontractor, laborer, or material supplier who benefits someone's real property?

10. (a) Explain the differences between an attachment lien and an execution lien. (b) Give examples of common types of tax liens that the typical individual or business firm would encounter in today's world.

CASE PROBLEMS

1. W. O. Young had several children. In 1915 he executed a deed conveying to his two daughters, Bertha and Pearl, certain real property and providing as follows: "If either should marry or die, then the property shall belong to the other, and in case both Bertha and Pearl should get married or should die, the property shall revert to the estate of W. O. Young." W. O. Young died in 1918 without having made any other conveyance of the property and without making a will. Bertha Young died unmarried in 1921. Pearl Young died unmarried in 1969. Who now owns the fee simple estate in the real property? Explain the reasons for your answer.

2. In 1940 Mrs. Nitschke and her two children inherited a parcel of real property with a dry cleaning shop on it. The shop was occupied by Doggett under a series of written leases. In 1959, the children acquired the interest of Mrs. Nitschke in the property, but she continued to deal with Doggett concerning the leasing and payment of rents. In 1962 or 1963, after Doggett delivered a written lease form to her so that she could obtain the children's signatures, Mrs. Nitschke told him he did not need a written lease, and that he could have the property for the rest of his life for a rental of $85 per month. Doggett agreed to pay $85 a month so long as he remained a tenant. It is his intent to remain a tenant for the rest of his life. He has a life expectancy of 23 years. Does Doggett have a tenancy for a term or a tenancy at will? Explain.

3. The Missouri State Highway Commission instituted a condemnation proceeding connected with the widening of Lindbergh Boulevard. Damages in the amount of $14,500 were awarded by the commissioners for the land taken. The owners of the land did not accept this amount, and the Highway Commission filed suit in court. A Missouri statute requires the inclusion as parties defendant all persons who have a title appearing of record on the proper records of the county wherein the affected real estate lies. Southern Bank held a note secured by a deed of trust on the land. Is the Highway Commission required to include the trustee named in the deed of trust as a defendant and serve the trustee with a summons? Explain why or why not.

4. John and Mildred Hawthorne owned real estate on Summit Drive. They gave Assured Corporation a promissory note for $6600 and secured the note with a trust deed against the real estate. They defaulted, and Assured foreclosed on the real property. At the foreclosure sale Assured was the high bidder at $6224, which was the total of the balance due under the note plus interest, costs, and attorneys' fees. The Hawthornes had a statutory right of redemption by bidding the amount of the obligation but failed to exercise it. They sued Assured for $12,000, contending that the real estate was worth $38,000 and was subject to trust deeds totaling $26,000 and that Assured should have bid an amount equal to this equity in the property. Is the Hawthornes's contention valid? Explain.

5. The statutes in the state of Maine provide, among other things, that a mechanic's lien may be enforced by action against the owner of the property affected if filed within 90 days after the last of the labor, materials, or services are furnished, "and not afterwards." Bellegarde Custom Kitchens supplied materials used in the construction of a home for Jacques. Bellegarde filed an action in court 91 days after the last of the materials were furnished. The 90th day following the furnishing of the materials fell on Sunday. Did the fact that the deadline fell on Sunday excuse noncompliance with the mechanic's lien statute? Why or why not?

CHAPTER 26

ESTATES AND WILLS

Among the many rewards for success in the business world is the acquisition of real and personal property. People who are fortunate enough to accumulate assets must decide not only how best to manage those resources, but also how to dispose of all they own after death. It is only natural that a person should want to make provision for the distribution of his or her business interests and other property after death—or to know what would become of it if he or she fails to do so.

In legal terminology, a person who has died is a **decedent**. The property (estate) of a decedent passes into new hands in one of two ways, either (1) according to state inheritance laws when the decedent has left no valid will, or (2) according to the provisions of a will made by the decedent in his or her lifetime.

There is no general federal law concerning inheritance. State inheritance laws are essentially similar to one another but are not uniform throughout the country.

This chapter first considers inheritance when a person dies without leaving a valid will. Consideration is then given to how wills are made, modified, or revoked. Then a brief summary follows of the court process, called "probate," by which a court decides whether or not a will is valid and by which it controls administration of estates and distribution of their assets.

INHERITANCE WHEN THERE IS NO WILL

An individual who dies without leaving a valid will is called "an intestate." **Intestate** is also used as an adjective to describe the legal status in which the person died—that is, "he or she *died intestate*," meaning "died without leaving a valid will."

After all an intestate's debts have been paid, the remainder of his or her estate is distributed in accordance with state inheritance laws, also called laws of descent and distribution. In other words, the state decides who will receive an intestate's property (who will be the heirs).

Entitlement to Inherit from an Intestate

While there is little absolute uniformity in state laws, an intestate's property usually passes to others in the following order:

1. If a spouse (widow or widower) and one child survive the intestate, the spouse and the child each receives one-half of the estate.
2. If a spouse and more than one child survive, the children divide two-thirds of the estate and the spouse receives one-third.
3. If the intestate had no spouse when he or she died, but a child or children survive, they receive the entire estate.
4. If a spouse but no children survive the intestate, the spouse inherits the entire estate unless a member of the intestate's immediate family is also living. In that event, the spouse and immediate family member(s) usually each inherit one-half of the estate. "Immediate family" means the decedent's mother or father, if living, and if not, then his or her sisters and brothers and their children. This distribution often comes as a shock to a person who may have been married to the decedent for many years and helped to accumulate the assets which form the estate.
5. If the intestate leaves neither a spouse nor child, the estate passes to the intestate's immediate family members.
6. The last in order of eligibility are the closest living kin (blood relatives) of the

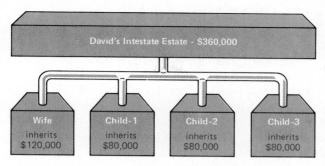

FIGURE 26-1   Distribution of intestate estate to spouse and children.

intestate who are not members of the immediate family. Kin includes such relatives as grandparents, uncles and aunts and their children, and more distantly removed *blood* relatives. Thus, for example, an uncle can inherit, but an uncle's wife cannot.

7. If none of the above classes of individuals survive, the intestate's estate *escheats*, that is, it becomes the property of the state.

The foregoing scheme of intestate descent and distribution can best be understood by analyzing two hypothetical situations. For the first, assume that David dies intestate. His estate, after all debts have been paid, is valued at $360,000. He is survived by his wife and by three children, Child 1, Child 2, and Child 3. He is also survived by a sister and a brother. The distribution of David's estate can be diagrammed as shown in Figure 26.1.

Since David left a wife and more than one child, one-third of the estate goes to the widow and two-thirds to the children, equally divided between them. The decedent's sister and brother inherit nothing because heirs in more preferred positions inherit the entire estate.

Now assume that Alice dies intestate, leaving no spouse or children. Alice does leave a sister, Donna, and a nephew and a niece, the children of her brother, Ben, who died some years ago. Ben's widow, Betty, is still living. Alice's estate of $360,000 will be distributed as shown in Figure 26.2.

FIGURE 26-2   Distribution of intestate estate to immediate family.

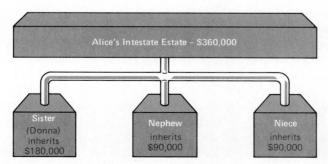

Here, a new principle of distribution is introduced, called the "right of representation." Since Alice's immediate family consisted only of one brother and one sister, her sister inherits half of the estate ($180,000) and her brother, Ben, if alive, would have inherited the other half ($180,000). But since Ben died before the intestate, Ben's children take his share of the estate "by representation." Thus, Ben's share is divided between his son (intestate's nephew) and daughter (intestate's niece), who each inherit $90,000. Have we forgotten Ben's widow, Betty? No, since she is not a blood relative of the intestate she is not an heir.

Inheritance of Intestate Estates in Special Situations

There are certain individuals to whom the regular order of distribution of intestate estates does not apply. Among them are an adopted child, an illegitimate child and a stepchild.

Adopted Child.   There is no uniformity among the states in the treatment of the inheritance rights of an adopted child. In a growing number of states an adopted child is treated for the purposes of inheritance as a natural child of the adoptive parents, and inheritance from a natural parent who dies intestate is entirely cut off.

Illegitimate Child.   All states recognize that an illegitimate child is an heir of its mother and also of its father if the child has been legitimized according to the law of the state. Some states also allow inheritance if a "parent and child relationship" existed between the child and father; in others, inheritance from an intestate father is possible if paternity is established by clear and convincing proof.

Stepchild.   The rights of a stepchild (half-blood) to inherit also vary. In most states a stepchild is treated equally with full brothers and sisters for inheritance purposes.

INHERITANCE WHEN THERE IS A WILL

What Is a Will?

A will is a declaration of a person's desires as to what should be done with his or her property after death. A person who makes a will is a **testator**, if male, or "testatrix" if female. As used in this chapter, "testator" refers to both.

A will, in addition to disposing of the testator's property, usually names an executor (whose functions are discussed as this chapter progresses) and may appoint a guardian for minor children.

Why Make a Will?

If an individual is satisfied with the way in which the state will distribute his or her business interests and property after death, then a will is not necessary. But if a person wants to favor one family member over another, to make a gift to someone other than blood relatives, or to leave something to a church or a favored charity, he or she must express these or any other desires by executing a will. Furthermore, a will also makes it possible to settle an estate, particularly one of appreciable size, with a minimum of delay. It follows that generally it is wise to make a will.

Requisites for a Valid Will

To make a valid will the testator must have (1) the requisite mental capacity (**testamentary capacity**), and (2) the intent to make a will (**testamentary intent**). In addition, the will must be in the form prescribed by law. If any of these requirements is absent, the decedent died intestate.

Testamentary Capacity.   Testamentary capacity has two elements: (1) attaining the statutory age (usually 18) *before the will is executed (signed)*; and (2) having the mental capacity required by law at the time of its execution.

Age.   If Tim makes a will when he is 16 years old, it is not a valid will; nor does it become valid when he reaches the statutory age. In order to have a valid will Tim must, when he reaches statutory age, execute (sign) a new will (or re-execute his old will) in the manner required by state law.

Mental Capacity.   Courts generally hold that a testator has the mental capacity to make a valid will if, at the time it is executed the testator *knew* that he or she was signing a will and had the *capacity* (1) to know the natural objects of his or her bounty, (2) to know the nature and extent of his or her property, and (3) to be able to make an orderly disposition of it.

Ordinarily, less mental capacity is required to make a will than to conduct business affairs. The maker may have a very low IQ, be very sick, very old, or may even be under a court-appointed conservator (a guardian of the business affairs of an individual) and still be legally competent to make a will. The liberal treatment given to testamentary capacity is apparent from the following case.

CASE 26.1   Matter of Estate of Congdon
309 N.W.2d 261 (Minn. 1981)

Facts   Mrs. Congdon had suffered a severe paralytic stroke and had developed aphasia, which caused her to have difficulty in reading, understanding what was said to her, and expressing herself, occasionally saying "No" when she meant "Yes." There was testimony, however, that after careful explanation, Mrs. Congdon was capable of understanding her will. Although she frequently forgot promises to charities, she remembered the names of her grandchildren, street names, and family history. She often played cards and beat most of her opponents.

A conservator was designated by a court to manage Mrs. Congdon's daily business affairs because she was not capable of handling them herself.

In this condition, Mrs. Congdon made a will. Her daughter contested its validity on the ground that Mrs. Congdon did not have testamentary capacity.

Question: Did these facts establish lack of testamentary capacity?

Answer: No. The will was valid.

Reasoning: Testamentary capacity is present if, when making a will, the testator understands the situation, the extent of his or her property, and the natural claims of others upon him or her and is able to hold these things in mind long enough to make a rational judgment. Testamentary capacity is a less stringent standard than the capacity to contract, and being under conservatorship does not prove that the person does not possess testamentary capacity. The facts are sufficient to establish testamentary capacity.

Testamentary Intent. **Testamentary intent** is the intention of a testator to direct the transfer of his or her property *effective upon death.* The distinction between an ordinary gift and a gift by will is readily seen by the following illustration. Alice hands her ring to Mabel, saying, "I'm giving you this ring as a token of my friendship." Alice has made a gift to Mabel, effective immediately, and Mabel now owns the ring. However, if Alice's *will* states in part, "I give my ring to Mabel," it has an entirely different legal effect. It is only the expression of a testamentary intention of what should be done with the ring after Alice's death. Until then, Alice remains the owner of the ring. She may change her mind and sell the ring, give it to someone else in her lifetime, or change her will to leave the ring to someone else after her death.

If an individual is induced through fraud, duress, or undue influence to execute a will or to make certain provisions within it, the will does not express the testamentary intent of the maker and it, or at least the wrongfully induced provision, is void. If the will or its improper provision is not revoked by the testator during his or her lifetime, the manner of its execution and the inducements exerted upon the testator are grounds for a contestant to object to the will's admission to probate.

Most courts will *presume* that undue influence was exercised against the testator if it is established (1) that a person in a confidential relationship with the testator, such as his or her doctor, lawyer, nurse-companion, or close family member, (2) counseled the testator concerning the preparation of his or her will, and (3) was a beneficiary under it, particularly if the will ignores other family members. Therefore, to prevent the gift from being declared void, a person in a confidential position who is a beneficiary under a will must prove that the gift was *not* the result of undue influence.

How a court views a claim that a testator was subjected to undue influence appears in the next case.

CASE 26.2   Estate of Paul Zech
285 N.W.2d 236 (S.D. 1979)

Facts   Paul Zech lived with and was cared for by his niece, Mary Tesch, and her husband, from 1967 to 1975 when he was moved to a nursing home. They visited him there frequently but it does not appear that any of his other relatives saw him. In 1970 a lawyer had come to the Tesch house and, after conference with Zech, prepared the latter's will which left the bulk of his property to the Tesches, who were not present when the will was signed. In 1977 Zech, then 83 years old, died. Other nieces and nephews contested the will, claiming that undue influence had been exerted by the Tesches.

Question: .Did the facts establish undue influence?

Answer: No, the will was not executed under undue influence.

Reasoning: The Tesches, being in a confidential relationship to Zech, had the burden of proving that they did not exert undue influence upon him.

To be undue, influence must be of such character as to destroy the free choice of the testator and substitute the desires of another. The testator must be susceptible and the other person must be disposed to influence him for an improper purpose. Neither of these conditions was present here.

Something more than mere opportunity is necessary to prove undue influence. Although the Tesches were in close proximity to Zech, there was no evidence that they did anything to influence the writing of his will. Although they benefited from it, the gift to them might have been a reward for their kindnesses. It was Zech's privilege to dispose of his property as he pleased.

The Tesches satisfied their burden of proving that they did not exert undue influence.

Execution of Wills

Laws governing the execution of wills must be strictly followed. If the rules are not observed, even if the intention of the testator is abundantly clear, the will is not legally valid and the maker dies intestate.

A will may be handwritten, typed, printed, engraved, or painted on paper or on any other kind of material. It may be in any language so long as the testator understands what he or she is signing. Normally, a will consists of all the sheets of paper intended by the testator to constitute the will. All the pages must be actually present when the will is signed. Usually, the pages are physically stapled or in some other way fastened together. If they are loose sheets there must be a logical continuity of thought in the text running from one page to the next.

The contents of another document, although not actually present when the will is signed, may nevertheless, in most states, be given effect as a part of the will if the document referred to (1) is in existence when the will is signed, (2) is identified in the will, and (3) is intended to be part of the will. This extension of the text of a will is called "incorporation by reference." For example, compare a will which states in part, "I give $1000 to each of the people named in a paper which will be found in my safe deposit box," with a will which states, "I give $1000 to each of the people named in a paper dated March 3, 1983 [a date prior to the execution of the will] which will be found in my safe deposit box." In the first instance the paper may or may not have been in existence before the will was executed and therefore it cannot be incorporated into the will by reference. In the second example, the will is dated after the date on the paper in the safe deposit box, thus showing that the paper was already in existence when the will was signed. In addition, the will properly identifies it; thus, the paper in the safe deposit box is incorporated into the will and is a part of it.

Some states authorize only **formal wills**, others recognize both formal and **holographic** (also called **olographic**) **wills**. A few states also authorize oral or **noncupative wills**. The latter involve personal property of limited value, usually made by soldiers or sailors under combat conditions. Because only formal and holographic wills are normally encountered, it is their execution we will consider.

Formal Wills.   Formal wills must be in writing, signed, and witnessed. Some states require, in addition, that such wills be dated and published.

Signing of Formal Wills.   A formal will must be signed by the testator. In some states the testator's signature must appear at the end of the will, but other states do not impose this requirement. As a general rule, it is not necessary that the signature be the testator's full name. Any name intended by him or her as a signature usually satisfies the statutes. So, signing with such a name as "Bubba Smith," or "Mommie," or just with initials have been held to be good signatures to wills. Despite this leniency of the courts, to sign a will with other than the true full name of the testator invites litigation and is a practice to be avoided.

If the testator is physically unable to sign his or her name, a mark such as "X," representing the signature, is acceptable. The testator's name is then usually written near the mark by someone else at the testator's request and in his or her presence. Thus, a paralyzed person can execute a valid will.

Witnessing of Formal Wills.   A testator's signature is not notarized but it must be witnessed. The witnesses add their signatures to the will in the presence of the testator and usually in the presence of each other. In the event of a will contest later, the witnesses may be called upon to testify as to whether the testator was mentally competent when he or she signed the will and whether any fraud, duress, or undue influence was exercised in their presence. Almost all states require two witnesses to the execution (signing) of a will; a few states require three.

Publishing and Dating of Formal Wills.   Some states require that witnesses be told that the paper being signed before them is a will. This declaration is called a "publication." However, in no state must the witnesses be informed of the contents of the will nor need it be given to them to read.

Not all states require that a will be dated, but it is, of course, good practice for a will to bear the date on which it is executed. In that way, later questions as to whether a particular will was the last one the testator executed, or whether it was signed when the testator was mentally competent may be minimized.

Holographic Wills.   A holographic will is one that is in the testator's own handwriting, signed by him or her, and dated but not witnessed. If there is a question as to the authenticity of a holographic will, it is established by comparing the handwriting in which the will is written with the testator's known handwriting. How this operates in practice was demonstrated in the lengthy court consideration of billionaire Howard Hughes' "Mormon will," which purported to be in his handwriting and which, after lengthy litigation, was held to be a forgery.

The liberal and growing view is that only the material parts of a holographic will must be in the testator's handwriting, and the balance may be printed or typed.

Codicils to Wills   Assume that Agatha executed a valid will on March 15, 1980. Later, she decides to add to the will a gift to her niece, Cathy, who was born after the will was written. Must Agatha write a new will? She may if she wishes, but that is not necessary. Instead, she may write a simple amendment, a **codicil**. Formal and holographic wills may have either formal or holographic codicils. Agatha's codicil might read something like this: "September 24, 1983. This is a codicil to my will executed by me on March 15, 1980. Paragraph 6(h) of that will is amended by adding, 'I give $2500 to my niece, Cathy.' [Signed] Agatha B. Doe." If the state recognizes holographic wills and the codicil is entirely in Agatha's handwriting and is signed and dated by her, she has executed a legally effective codicil. If the state does not permit holographic wills, Agatha's codicil becomes legally effective when she signs it before witnesses as required by the law of that state.

Limitations on Disposition by Will

It is generally said that a competent testator may make any disposition by will that he or she chooses. However, the law makes exceptions to this rule to favor the surviving spouse and children. In most states the law also imposes limitations upon the gifts that witnesses may receive through wills they witness.

Protection of Surviving Spouse.   All states have laws which are aimed at preserving to a surviving husband or wife some portion of the estate of the deceased spouse. These laws take three forms:

1. A few states apply the common law right of *dower.* Dower entitles a surviving wife to a life estate, free from the decedent's debts, in one-third of the real property that her husband had owned at any time during their marriage, and in which she had not, during the marriage, joined in a deed conveying it to someone else.
2. Because estates today frequently consist of both real and personal property, most states have broadened the rights of a surviving husband or wife. This is done by ensuring to the survivor a *fixed portion* of *all* the property, both real and personal, owned by the deceased spouse at the time of death. The portion assured the survivor, which varies among states, is called a "forced" or "elective" share.
3. Eight states—Arizona, California, Idaho, Louisiana, Nevada, New Mexico, Texas, and Washington—protect the interests of a surviving spouse by providing that all property, real and personal, acquired during the marriage through the efforts of *either* spouse, and the income from such property, is *community property.* Anything owned by either spouse before marriage or acquired after the marriage by some means other than his or her work, is separate property. Thus, money and property owned by Margaret before her marriage to Jim is Margaret's separate property; and property Jim inherited from his parents and money he won in a lawsuit for injuries sustained in an accident after his marriage to Margaret is all Jim's separate property.

Community property states allow a testator to dispose of his or her separate property to anyone he or she desires, but community property is treated differently. Each spouse owns an undivided one-half of all community property. Assume that in a community property state John and Helen are married. John starts a business with money he earned after their marriage. He owns and operates the business until his death. The business, having been acquired with money John earned after their marriage, is the community property of both John and Helen. John can dispose of one-half of the business by will to anyone he pleases. However, John cannot dispose of the other half because it belongs to Helen, being her share of their community property. If John dies without leaving a valid will, his half of the business will pass by succession to Helen and their children and, if they have no children, then according to the laws of the state in which the property is located.

Protection of Surviving Children. A parent may, if he or she so chooses, completely disinherit a child and give the child nothing whatsoever by will. But for a disinheritance to be legally effective it must be evident in the will that the testator *intentionally* gave the child nothing. Such an intention can be expressed by mentioning the child by name anywhere in the will but making no gift, or only some slight amount, to that child; or the intention may be expressed by a statement such as this: "I give nothing to my daughter, Ellen, because she is already amply provided for."

The unintentional omission of a child from a parent's will is called **pretermission**, and if the omission does *not* appear to be intentional, the child is said to be *pretermitted.* To protect a child who has been forgotten in a parent's will—that is, pretermitted—that child inherits from its deceased parent as though the parent had died intestate, but the will otherwise remains effective for all other beneficiaries. That the courts do not regard pretermission lightly is shown by the following case.

CASE 26.3

In re Estate of MacKay
433 A.2d 1289 (N.H. 1981)

Facts: James MacKay married Zatae Slack. They had one child, Virginia. Zatae and James were divorced and Virginia lived with her mother. Thereafter, there was little contact between father and daughter. James remarried and had four children by his second wife. James executed a will leaving his property to his second wife and four children. It provided, in part, that if his second wife did not survive him, the estate would go to the four children and, if they did not survive him, it would go to his heirs at law and next of kin. James died.

Virginia claimed that she was pretermitted and entitled to an intestate share of her father's estate. Her four half-brothers and half-sisters claimed that she was sufficiently referred to within the words "heirs at law" or "next of kin" and that, accordingly, she was not pretermitted.

Question: Is a gift by will to "heirs at law" or "next of kin" sufficient mention of the child as to preclude pretermission?

Answer: No. Virginia is pretermitted.

Reasoning: A child is pretermitted by a testator if it is not actually named or distinctly referred to in the will. A gift by will to a class which *may include children,* such as "heirs at law" or "next of kin" is not sufficient recognition. The will neither mentions nor refers to Virginia. She therefore is pretermitted and is entitled to an intestate share of her father's estate.

Witness as Beneficiary. To reduce the possibility of fraud and undue influence, in many states a person who is one of a required number of witnesses to a will and also one of its named beneficiaries is allowed to inherit no more than he or she would have received had the testator died intestate.

Devises and Bequests
The entitlement of the beneficiaries to receive their gifts depends upon the form in which the gifts are written.

Devises.   A gift of *real property*, called a **devise**, usually takes this form: "I give my house at 23 Park Road to my sister, Eileen." If the property had been disposed of by the decedent in his or her lifetime, and is not in the estate, Eileen, the beneficiary, gets nothing.

Bequests.   A **bequest** is the name given to a gift by will of *personal property*. Bequests are usually written in one of the four following forms:

1. "I give my gold watch to Al." This, like the devise of real property, is a *specific* bequest because it refers to a certain specified object. If the gold watch is not in the estate, Al gets nothing. Specific bequests are usually identified by the word "my."
2. "I give $500 to my sister, Dot." This is a *general* bequest of any $500 that can be found in the estate, either in cash or through the sale of real or personal property not otherwise the subject of gifts.
3. "I give Bea $500 payable from the money Tom owes me, but if he does not pay his debt, then it is payable from my general estate." A gift worded in this manner is a *demonstrative* bequest. If it cannot be satisfied out of the source designated, it is treated as a general bequest.
4. "I give my good friend, Joe, all the rest and residue of my estate." This is a *residual* devise or bequest. Joe is entitled to whatever remains in the estate after all specific, demonstrative, and general gifts have been paid. If nothing remains, Joe gets nothing.

The following case concerns a specific bequest.

CASE 26.4   **In re Estate of Nakoneczny**
319 A.2d 893 (Pa. 1974)

Facts: Michael Nakoneczny executed a will which, among other things, devised 3039 Preble Avenue to his son, Paul. However, during his lifetime Nakoneczyny sold the property. With most of the money he received from the sale, Nakoneczyny bought various bonds, and those bonds were in his estate when he died. However, the decedent had neglected to change his will. In the settlement of the estate his son, Paul, claims he is entitled to the bonds which his father purchased with the money from the sale of the Preble Avenue property.

Question: When a specific property is not in a decedent's estate, is the beneficiary of that property entitled, instead, to the money the decedent received from its sale?

Answer: No. A specific gift is extinguished when the subject of that gift is not in the testator's estate.

Reasoning: The beneficiary of a specific gift is entitled only to the specific thing that is bequeathed or devised to him or her. A gift of a particular piece of land is a specific devise. As the land was not in the testator's estate, Paul's gift was extinguished and he cannot follow the land into the bonds which were purchased with the proceeds from the sale of that land.

Revocation of Wills

A will is without legal effect until the testator dies. Until then, he or she may at any time *revoke,* that is, cancel the will. After a will has been revoked, it cannot be made effective again except by adding a codicil to it or, of course, by executing a new will containing the same terms.

A revocation can come about either by the intentional act of the testator or by operation of law.

Revocation by Act of Testator. A will may be revoked by a testator either (1) performing some physical act affecting the document, or (2) executing a later will which specifically revokes or is inconsistent with the earlier one.

Revocation by Physical Act. To revoke a will by physical act the testator must, *with the intent to revoke,* do something physical to the will which the state says constitutes a revocation, such as burning, tearing or obliterating it (making it unreadable), or drawing lines through the signature. Most states permit the *partial revocation* of a will by physical act affecting the part the testator wants to revoke. No witnesses are required for the physical revocation (or partial revocation) of a will.

Revocation by Later Instrument. A will may be revoked by the execution of a subsequent will or codicil which expressly revokes or is inconsistent with it. Usually, words to the following effect are used: "This will [codicil] revokes all prior wills and codicils made by me at any time." When more than one will is found after someone's death, and no express words of revocation are used in either one, confusion can readily result. It may be difficult to determine (1) which is the later will, (2) whether it is totally or only partially inconsistent with an earlier one, and (3) whether the testator intended the gifts of the later will to be in addition to the earlier ones or to be substituted for them. Therefore, when a testator desires to revoke a will in whole or in part and make new provisions, he or she should use words which clearly express that intent.

The reaction of a court to a questionable revocation of a will is dealt with in the next case.

CASE 26.5

In re Estate of Uhl
81 Cal. Reptr. 436 (Cal. 1969)

Facts: After Charles Uhl died in 1967 there was found among his effects a will that had been formally executed in 1946. No other will was found. The testator had made a number of notations on various bequests in the will and the following notation in the margin of the first page: "Revise whole mess." Among the questions presented at the time of probate of the will was the effect of the marginal notation.

Question: Did the marginal notation, "Revise whole mess," revoke the will?

Answer: No. The notation was not a statutory revocation.

Reasoning: A revocation of a will by physical act requires something which the statute recognizes as an act of revocation. The notation, "Revise whole mess," may have been only the expression of an intent to make a new will in the future, leaving the will upon which those words appear valid until the new will is written. This would seem to have been Uhl's intention since he retained the marked will until his death, did not cancel or destroy it, nor did he take any other action which would have amounted to a revocation.

Revocation by Divorce.   In some states a provision in a will which benefits a spouse is automatically (by operation of law) revoked upon divorce or annulment of the marriage. In other states a divorce must be accompanied by a property settlement to automatically revoke a provision for a spouse. And in still others even a divorce with a property settlement does not operate as a revocation unless, in the settlement, the right to inherit by will is expressly given up. Assume, for example, that in one of those states Henry's will provides: "I give to my wife, Helen, my house on Front Street." Subsequently, Helen and Henry are divorced, with a property settlement giving the house on Front Street to Henry. The divorce did not automatically revoke the will provision giving the house to Helen even though at the time of his death Henry was married to his second wife, Betty.

PROBATE

Probate is the name given to the legal process by which the validity of a will is established and both testate and intestate estates settled. Several functions are involved, among them determining (1) whether a will was legally executed, (2) who are the legal beneficiaries (if there is a valid will) or heirs (if the decedent died intestate), (3) what debts and taxes the decedent owes, and (4) how the debts should be paid and the estate distributed. Probate is especially important when there is real property in an estate because probate establishes the legal right of the beneficiary of real property to sell it.

Increasingly, particularly when an estate is small or consists only of personal property, statutes eliminate the necessity for formal probate and administration, and substitute a limited or informal proceeding. In this way beneficiaries and heirs may be saved considerable court costs and legal fees and more quickly come into possession of their gifts.

Admission of Wills to Probate

Until a will is *admitted to probate*, that is, found by the court to be valid, it has no legal effect. The probate process is begun by presenting the will to the court with proof of the circumstances of its execution as required by state laws.

If there are any objections to the probate of a will, these are heard by the court. Most states provide for a jury trial of the issues raised, and the ordinary rules of evidence apply. If it is determined that the testator executed a valid will, the court admits it to probate. If the court finds the will to be invalid, probate is refused and the decedent will have died intestate (unless, of course, another will is presented to the court and found to be valid). In either event, the estate is ready to be administered.

Probate Administration

Probate administration begins by the court appointing an *executor (executrix,* if female) for a testate estate, usually naming the individual or bank designated by the decedent in his or her will. For an intestate estate, the court appoints an *administrator* (or *administratrix*) who normally is the surviving spouse of the intestate or a member of his or her immediate family.

Functions of Executors and Administrators.   Executors and administrators, whose functions are essentially the same, are the personal representatives of the decedents for whose estates they have been appointed. Each *inventories,* that is, makes a list of, the assets of the estate, collects whatever money is owing the decedent, pays taxes and allowable claims, and distributes the remainder, if any, to the beneficiaries (under a will) or the heirs (under an intestate estate).

Carrying on Business.   A personal representative may, if the will so authorizes or the court approves, carry out the contracts of the decedent and make new contracts for the estate. However, if the representative, without authorization, carries on the decedent's business or makes contracts for the estate, he or she becomes personally liable for any losses.

Paying of Claims.   A primary duty of a personal representative is advertising for, considering, and paying claims filed against the estate. States dictate the manner and the time within which claims must be filed. If a claim is not filed within the time allowed, its payment is forever barred. In effect, this is a special statute of limitations which can be a trap for an unwary creditor who does not read the legal advertisements in the local newspapers. As might be expected, federal taxes are not barred by the limitation period.

Statutes also establish the order in which claims are paid. Certain kinds, such as the costs of administration, funeral expenses, costs of the decedent's last illness, and taxes have priority.

Obligations of Executors and Administrators.   An executor or administrator must care for and preserve the estate assets. He or she is a **fiduciary,**, meaning a person upon whom a special trust and confidence has been imposed. A representative is expected to act only with the best interests of the estate in mind and may not take any personal advantage of, or secure any personal gain from, estate business or assets. If a personal representative does not exercise the same care in managing the affairs of the estate as a prudent person would do in managing his or her own affairs, and if a loss results, the representative must personally make up that loss.

The representative is entitled to be compensated for his or her services. In some states compensation is upon a graduated scale, determined by the size of the estate. In other states the fee is negotiated and approved by the court. It is not unusual for a personal representative, particularly when a member of the decedent's family, to waive compensation.

Distribution of Estates.   After all costs, claims against an estate, and taxes have been paid, the personal representative accounts to the court and, with its approval, distributes the remaining money and property. In an intestate estate, distribution is made to the heirs according to the laws of descent and distribution and, in a testate estate, to the beneficiaries named in the will.

The personal representative is then discharged from his or her duties and the estate is closed.

SUMMARY

Property may be inherited (1) by heirs, under the rules of intestate succession, which apply when a person dies without leaving a valid will; or (2) by beneficiaries, according to the provisions of a properly executed will. If there is no will, the state fixes the portion of the estate each heir will receive. Primarily, a surviving spouse and children inherit an intestate's property. If neither spouse, children, nor immediate family survive, the closest blood relatives of the decedent divide the estate.

A will is not effective until the maker (the testator) dies. To make a valid will, a testator must have both testamentary capacity and testamentary intent. While a person must have a sound mind to make a will, it is not necessary that he or she have sufficient mental capacity to carry on business affairs. If a person in making a will is subject to fraud, duress, or undue influence, the maker is not expressing testamentary intent and the will is void.

A formal will must be in writing, signed, and witnessed. A holographic will (not authorized in all states) must, in at least all its essential parts, be in the testator's own handwriting, signed and, in most states, dated. A holographic will is not witnessed.

A testator may revoke a will by executing a new will or codicil which specifically revokes the earlier one or is entirely inconsistent with the earlier one. A will may also be revoked by physically affecting it in a manner defined by state statutes. In addition, a will may be revoked by operation of state law as a result of a subsequent marriage or divorce.

The validity of a will is proven in probate. A decedent whose will is admitted to probate (that is, the will is found to be valid) is said to have died testate. A decedent who dies without leaving a valid will is said to die intestate. When a will is admitted to probate, an executor is appointed to carry out its provisions. An administrator is appointed by the court to administer the estate of an intestate. Executors and administrators are the personal representatives of the decedents for whom they act. The personal representative takes charge of the assets of the estate, gives notice to creditors to file claims, pays valid claims filed within the period established by law, and then distributes the remaining assets among the heirs or beneficiaries.

REVIEW QUESTIONS

1. An individual dies without having made a will. The only surviving relatives are a sister and a sister-in-law. How much of the estate does each inherit?

2. Susan graduated from high school at 17 years of age. At that time she made a will dividing her estate between her favorite teacher and her parents. Susan becomes a well-known novelist. She dies at 35 years of age without ever having married. She did not revoke her will nor make any codicils to it. All her named beneficiaries survive her. How is Susan's estate divided?

3. Comment upon this statement: "If a person has the capacity to enter into a contract, he or she has the capacity to make a will."

4. Contrast a gift by will and one by deed.

5. What is a holographic will?

6. What is the difference between a codicil and a will?

7. What is meant by a pretermitted child? What effect does pretermission have on a will?

8. Distinguish between a specific, general, demonstrative, and residual bequest.

9. What is meant when someone says a will has been admitted to probate?

10. (**a**) What is the difference between an executor and an administrator? (**b**) What are the chief functions and obligations of each?

11. What is meant when it is said that a person occupies a fiduciary position?

12. (**a**) What are the ethical obligations of executors and administrators? (**b**) What is the reason they have such obligations?

CASE PROBLEMS

1. For many years Paul, a lifelong bachelor, and Mrs. Holmead, a widow about his own age, were constant companions. Paul made a will leaving the bulk of his estate to Mrs. Holmead and only a small bequest to his niece, his only relative. The niece claims that because of Mrs. Holmead's close friendship with her uncle, and the fact that Mrs. Holmead spent much time with him during his last illness, Paul's will was a result of her undue influence and therefore invalid. Do you agree? Explain.

2. After Mrs. Clara Thompson's death, an envelope was found among her papers on which was typed, "This envelope contains the will of Clara Thompson." Inside was a sheet of paper with the following, written entirely in Mrs. Thompson's handwriting: "After my death I give to . . ." followed by the names of several people, their relationship to Mrs. Thompson, and items of property to be given to each. Did the envelope and paper constitute a valid will? Explain.

3. John, who was not married, made a will in a state where two witnesses were required. The will was witnessed by his brother Carl and two other people. The total estate amounted to $60,000, and John's will left $30,000 to Carl. If John had died intestate Carl would have been entitled to one-third of his brother's estate. To how much of John's estate is Carl entitled?

4. In 1979 Lloyd executed a valid holographic will which stated in part, "I hereby revoke all wills and codicils heretofore made by me at any time but I still make the gifts set out in paragraph 7 of the will I made on March 3, 1966." Lloyd's 1966 will was typewritten and properly witnessed. The state where Lloyd lives recognizes holographic wills. Lloyd died. Were the gifts made by paragraph 7 of the 1966 will revoked or are they still effective? Explain.

5. Don died without a will, and was survived by Emma, his wife, and two grown sons of a former marriage. Emma was appointed administratrix. Without court approval, she took charge of and ran Don's business, then worth about $100,000. She did nothing to pay his creditors. After 20 months, during which time Emma paid herself a salary and other benefits, she closed the business, which was then on the verge of bankruptcy. The sons claim that Emma is liable to the estate for the money the business lost. Are they correct?

19) TONY EMPLOYED EVE TO REPRESENT HIM IN PURCHASING A BUILDING ON MAIN STREET FOR HIS BUSINESS. THE NEXT DAY, EVA LEARNED THAT ONE OF HER OTHER CLIENTS, BILL, WISHED TO SELL HIS BUILDING IN MAIN ST. BILL TOLD EVE THAT HE WAS GOING TO ASK $100,000 FOR THE BUILDING BUT WOULD ACCEPT AN OFFER OF 60000 OR MORE. EVE WOULD: (B) BE REQUIRED TO WITHHOLD THE INFORMATION ABOUT HOW MUCH BILL WOULD BE WILLING TO ACCEPT FOR THE BUILDING BECAUSE IT WAS ACQ. IN CONFIDEN

20) ROY AGREED TO ACT AS DONNA'S AGENT IN SELLING DONNA'S CAR. TWO WEEKS LATER, ROY AGREED TO ACT AS JANET'S AGENT IN PURCHASING A CAR. ROY MAY ARRANGE A SALE OF DONNA'S CAR TO JANET PROVIDED: (A) HE DISCLOSES THE FACT OF HIS DUAL AGENCY TO BOTH AND THEY AGREE THAT HE MAY ACT FOR BOTH OF THEM.

21 Yes, Sharon (agent) was hired to manage David's (principal) store. Hiring, firing and/store advertisement would be an *implied responsibility for Sharon*. It doesn't say like David had made a *written agreement*, regardless this is a *scope of authority*, *apparent* as Sharons title *indirectly* implied she could carry out the duties of a manager —

Yes. David made Sharon the manager of the video store and led the local newspaper believe that she had the *apparent* authority to buy advertising, and hire or fire employees on behalf of the store. Sharon has implied authority to make other decisions since they are reasonable inferred from her express authority as store manager —

PART SEVEN

SECURED TRANSACTIONS AND INSURANCE

CHAPTER 27

PURPOSE AND TYPES OF SECURED TRANSACTIONS; SURETYSHIP

In the cash societies of ancient times, the concept of credit was little known. Ordinarily, people accumulated wealth before expanding their businesses or undertaking new ventures. While waiting for capital to accumulate, they lost many business opportunities, and economic development was painfully slow. Then, gradually, people learned that they could borrow money to expand their businesses more quickly. As commerce and industry developed, credit came to be recognized as a valuable economic tool. Today credit is a basic element in the economy of the United States and in other economies throughout the world.

A person or business firm can receive credit in a variety of ways. If you want to buy a car but do not have the cash, you might get a loan from a bank. Or you might persuade the dealer to sell you the car "on time," on the understanding that you will make installment payments until the price is paid. Many credit purchases of goods and services involve the use of a credit card. Often people will simply deliver goods or render services and bill you later. In all these instances there has been an extension of credit.

However, credit extension involves a risk that the debtor will *default*, that is, fail to repay a loan or fail to make payment for property or services bought on credit. To reduce the risk of loss due to a debtor's default, a creditor may demand some sort of **security** from the debtor, i.e., some backup source of payment that will be available to the creditor if the debtor fails to pay.

This chapter discusses the kinds of security devices or arrangements commonly used in business, with major emphasis on the **secured transaction**. As used in this textbook, the term "secured transaction" means any contract between a creditor and a debtor that provides the creditor with a backup source of payment if the debtor breaks his or her promise to pay. Secured transactions are of two basic types: (1) those in which the creditor's backup source of payment is real or personal property called "collateral security" or, simply, "collateral"; and (2) those in which the creditor's security is the promise of some third person (a "surety") to pay the debt. The surety's promise is given or imposed by law *in addition to* the debtor's promise to pay.

Some forms of security, such as the *mechanic's lien* discussed in the first part of this chapter, are not truly contractual in nature. Rather, they are imposed by law in favor of certain creditors and therefore may exist without the knowledge of the debtor or creditor. Nevertheless, they are often viewed as a variety of secured transaction and are so treated in this chapter.

The first part of this chapter briefly surveys the kinds of security devices— noncontractual and contractual—commonly associated with credit extension. The second part focuses on suretyship, one kind of secured transaction.

PURPOSE AND TYPES OF SECURED TRANSACTIONS

Purpose of Secured Transactions

As already noted, a secured transaction (or other security device) serves to reduce the risk of nonpayment faced by a creditor who has made a loan or who has delivered property or rendered services expecting an agreed payment to be made later. How a secured transaction serves to reduce the risk can be seen by comparing an unsecured transaction with a secured one.

An *unsecured* creditor (one who extends credit without receiving any security) faces the maximum risk of nonpayment. For example, suppose Carl sells goods to Donna solely on the basis of her promise to pay later. Carl is an unsecured creditor and consequently has no right to repossess the goods if Donna fails to pay. Instead, to enforce his right to payment, Carl will have to sue Donna and obtain a judgment against her. If Donna refuses to honor the judgment, Carl will have to seek execution of it. To obtain execution, he must get a writ of execution from the court. The writ orders the sheriff or other proper officer to seize and sell any of the debtor's property located within the jurisdiction of the court and to apply the proceeds of the sale to the debt. Carl's obtaining judgment will be of little value if Donna has no assets, leaves the jurisdiction, or is discharged from her debts in a bankruptcy proceeding. Carl could "garnishee" (lay legal claim to) Donna's wages, but garnishment laws limit the percentage of wages he may take, and Donna might be unemployed or earn little.

Carl would substantially reduce his risk of nonpayment by insisting on a *secured* transaction—one that provides him with a backup source of payment he may resort to if Donna breaks her promise to pay. Suppose the contract of sale states that if Donna fails to make timely payment, Carl will have the right to repossess and sell the goods he sold her. Carl has reserved for himself a "security interest" in the goods. Upon Donna's default, Carl, as a secured creditor, will have not only a claim against Donna's *general* assets, but also first rights, as against Donna's other creditors, to *take possession of and to sell*, in satisfaction of the debt, the *specific* goods that are the subject of the secured transaction.

The main purpose of a secured transaction is to protect the creditor, but the debtor is to be treated fairly, too. Under modern security law, a defaulting debtor may lose the collateral and remains personally liable for any deficiency if the collateral is not valuable enough to cover the debt. But if the collateral is worth more than the amount of the debt, the debtor is entitled to any surplus proceeds realized upon the sale or other disposition of the collateral.

Types of Secured Transactions   Secured transactions can be classified in terms of the source of the backup payment available to the creditor upon the debtor's default. One of these sources is any real or personal property that is the subject of the transaction between the creditor and the debtor. Another source is the promise of a surety to pay the debtor's debt.

Where property is the collateral, the creditor acquires a *lien* (charge or claim) against the property. Some liens are imposed by law. Others are created by contract. So, security devices can also be classified in terms of how they arise—by law or by contract.

Liens Imposed by Law.   A transaction can be considered "secured" even though the parties to it made no agreement as to security. Instead, the law gives the creditor a security interest in the real or personal property involved.

Liens Imposed by Law on Personal Property.   Often a person (the bailor) hires someone (the bailee) to repair, ship, or store the bailor's personal property. Under court decisions or statutes, the bailee has a **possessory lien** on the property for the amount the bailor agreed to pay for the service, or, in the absence of a stated price, for the bailee's reasonable charges. The lien exists only as long as the bailee keeps possession of the property. If the bailee voluntarily gives the property back to the bailor without receiving payment, the lien is lost and the bailee becomes an unsecured creditor.

Suppose that Donna delivers her antique clock to Carl to clean and repair, agreeing to pay him $50 for the work. Carl performs as agreed, but Donna refuses to pay the bill. Carl has a lien on the clock for $50, as long as he keeps it in his possession. Many state statutes permit Carl to enforce his lien by selling the clock in the manner prescribed by the statute—usually by giving Donna notice of the sale and advertising it. If no such enforcement provision exists, Carl may have to "foreclose" his lien. To foreclose, Carl must get a judgment against Donna for the amount owed and have the clock sold at a judicial sale.

Suppose that Donna, having refused to pay for the repair work, breaks into Carl's shop after hours and takes the clock. Because Carl did not voluntarily give up possession, he still has his lien. The result would be the same if Donna had by fraud or duress induced Carl to give up the clock.

Suppose instead that Carl, having agreed to clean and repair the clock for $50, presents Donna with a bill for $200 when she arrives to pick the clock up. Donna "tenders" (offers) the $50 she agreed to pay, but Carl insists on $200. Carl's lien is terminated and his possession is now wrongful. Carl is now liable to Donna for conversion of her property.

Suppose now that Donna calls Carl to her house to repair a grandfather clock. He repairs it there and later sends Donna a reasonable bill. Donna refuses to pay Carl's reasonable charges. Since Carl never acquired possession of the clock, he has no lien on it and is therefore an unsecured creditor.

Possessory liens are classified as "specific" or "general." A **specific lien** (also called a "special" or "particular" lien) entitles the creditor to keep the property as security for only the one debt involved in the immediate transaction. A **general lien** entitles the creditor to keep the property until the debtor has paid all debts owed to the creditor as a result of the general course of business between the creditor and the debtor. For example, suppose Carl repaired Donna's watch last week and delivered it to her, but she has not yet paid the $40 they agreed to. Now she tenders (offers) the $50 she agreed to pay for today's clock repair but Carl wants to keep the clock until she also pays for the watch repair. Unless Carl and Donna agreed otherwise, his lien on the clock is "specific" and therefore is not effective as to the earlier debt. Donna's tender of the $50 terminates the specific lien, and she is entitled to possession of the clock. As to the $40 for the watch repair, Carl is an unsecured creditor. If Carl's lien against the clock had been "general," he would have been entitled to hold the clock until Donna also paid for the watch repair.

A bailor of personal property is interested mainly in the service to be performed in connection with the property and may not be aware that a possessory lien exists. Therefore, in ordinary business transactions it is unlikely that the parties will contract for a particular type of lien. Since possessory liens usually arise by operation of law rather than by contract, the law states (subject to a contrary agreement of the parties) who shall have a specific and who shall have a general possessory lien.

General liens, since they are more burdensome to debtors, are available automatically only to a few groups of business people. Attorneys-at-law, bankers, and factors (selling agents to whom their principals entrust goods for sale in the regular course of business), and sometimes a few others such as accountants, are granted general liens by law. Supposedly, these groups of people are more responsible than the usual run of business people and would not abuse the power conferred by a general lien. Under a general lien, an attorney, for example, could hold a client's papers or other property that comes into the attorney's possession until all amounts owed the attorney are paid, even if for a variety of separate debts.

In contrast, most bailees have only a specific possessory lien. These people include repairers and other artisans, common carriers, innkeepers, warehousers, finders of property for the return of which a specific reward is offered, a landlord who holds the property of a defaulting tenant, a landowner who seizes a thing doing damage to the land, and agisters (bailees who take possession of cattle for the purpose of feeding them).

Liens Imposed by Law on Real Property.   Real estate can be subject to a variety of liens—judgment liens, tax liens, and mechanics' liens, for example. A landowner who is a losing defendant in a lawsuit may have his or her property subjected to a judgment lien in favor of the winning plaintiff. Land is also subject to a lien in favor of the state or other governmental unit for unpaid taxes. The mechanic's lien, however, is more clearly an aspect of a secured transaction, since it is imposed in favor of a person who *under a contract* has performed labor or furnished materials for the improvement of the landowner's real estate. The lien itself is involuntary (because imposed on the debtor by law rather than being contracted for), but it provides the mechanic with a backup source of payment (the improved real estate) in the event of the landowner-debtor's failure to pay the debt.

The term "mechanic" is broader than it sounds. The statutes of most states grant a mechanic's lien to anyone who, under contract, furnishes labor, services, or materials for the improvement of land. Thus, carpenters, electricians, landscapers, concrete workers, brickmasons, lessors of equipment, general contractors, subcontractors, surveyors, suppliers such as lumberyards (often called "materialmen"), and many others fall within the meaning of mechanic. Ordinarily, labor and services must be performed, and materials must be delivered *and incorporated into the improvement*, before the mechanic, artisan, or supplier has a right to a lien against the property.

The procedure for obtaining and enforcing a mechanic's lien is governed by statute and varies from state to state. In general, however, the mechanic must give written notice (by certified mail, for example) to affected persons—e.g., landowner, general contractor, construction lender—that the mechanic has furnished labor, services, or material to improve the land. Then, after the mechanic completes the work, he or she must record a "claim of lien" in the courthouse of the county in which the improved land is located. The lien must be recorded within the time specified by the statute, e.g., 60 or 90 days after the work or contract has been completed. Upon complying with the statutory requirements, the mechanic has a lien against the property for the amount of the debt. Failure to comply means only that the mechanic is an unsecured creditor; the debt is still enforceable against the person who contracted for it.

Ordinarily, a mechanic has only a limited time to bring suit to enforce his or her lien—90 days after its creation, for example, or a longer time if the mechanic has extended credit. The time for enforcement is relatively short so that the landowner's title (ownership) will not be "clouded" (impaired) by the lien for an unreasonably long time. Mechanics' liens are enforced by a process of foreclosure. To foreclose, the mechanic must get a judgment for the amount due and a judicial order for the sale of the property.

The following case illustrates the circumstances under which a "materialman" may foreclose a mechanic's lien.

CASE 27.1   Johnson v. Smith
276 P. 146 (Cal. App. 1929)

Facts: Johnson supplied a contractor with hardwood flooring for installation in a house being built for the Smiths. The contractor who bought the flooring did not install it properly, and the Smiths' architect ordered it removed and other flooring laid in its place. After the contractor failed to pay for the hardwood flooring, Johnson brought suit to foreclose a mechanic's lien that he had acquired on the Smiths' house to secure payment for the flooring.

Question: Was Johnson entitled to foreclose his lien?

Answer: Yes.

Reasoning: A materialman is under no obligation to the owner of property to see that the contractor to whom the material is supplied complies with his contract. In the absence of bad faith the supplier may assume that the contractor is fulfilling his contract with the owner. Here the fault of the flooring lay entirely with the manner in which the contractor laid it; the flooring itself was not defective. The fact that the owner's agent (the contractor) may have rendered the flooring useless should not defeat the rights of the innocent materialman.

Liens and Other Security Created by Contract. Because they are so widely used, the secured transactions of greatest commercial significance are those created by contract in favor of lenders and sellers. Where real or personal property is the source of the backup payment, the secured transaction creates a contractual lien against the property, in favor of the lender or credit seller.

Secured Transactions in Personal Property. Vast amounts of consumer and business credit are secured by an interest in consumer goods, accounts receivable, negotiable instruments, inventory, equipment, and other forms of personal property. Secured transactions in personal property are so important commercially that they are the subject of Article 9 of the Uniform Commercial Code. These secured transactions are discussed in Chapter 28.

Secured Transactions in Real Estate. Few people have enough cash to buy houses, land, or commercial properties outright. In fact, it often is economically unwise to do so, since a cash purchase of real estate would divert financial resources that could be better applied to other consumer purchases or to other aspects of a business operation such as product development or the purchase of equipment. Three security devices are commonly used to finance the purchase of real estate—the **mortgage**, the **trust deed**, and the land contract. Mortgages and trust deeds are discussed in Chapter 25.

The **land contract**, called in some states a "contract for deed" or "installment land contract," is a long-term credit arrangement under which the seller commonly transfers some ownership rights to the buyer but retains a security interest in the property until it is paid for. Suppose Carla makes a credit sale of her house to Donald by means of a land contract. Depending on the terms of the contract, Donald will acquire the right to possess, use, and perhaps even sell the house, subject to a duty to pay Carla the agreed price plus interest in the manner spelled out by the contract. However, Donald will not receive a deed (document signifying full ownership) from Carla until he makes the final payment, perhaps several years later. In the meantime Donald is considered to be the "equitable" or "beneficial" owner, while Carla retains a sufficient interest, called "legal title," to enable her to have the property sold if Donald defaults.

Corporate Bonds.   A corporation issues (sells) bonds as one means of financing its activities. A **corporate bond** is the written promise of the corporation to pay a specific sum of money at a future time, plus interest, to the buyer or other holder of the bond. The corporate bond (as opposed to the similar but unsecured **debenture**) is backed up by a mortgage on some or all of the corporate property. Consequently, the purchaser of a corporate bond has not only the corporation's promise to pay but also a right against specific corporate property if the corporation fails to pay.

Contracts of Suretyship and Guaranty.   Rounding out our brief survey of security devices is the **contract of suretyship or guaranty**. In such a contract, the promise of the surety or guarantor is the creditor's source of backup payment if the debtor defaults. Usually the surety or guarantor simply makes a promise to pay, but sometimes that person commits specific property of his or her own to the undertaking.

Suppose, for example, that Dan wants to start a small retail business but lacks sufficient funds. He seeks a loan from a bank, but the bank refuses to make the loan unless he finds a creditworthy person who will cosign the promissory note he will give to the bank in exchange for the loan. Dan's wealthy cousin Sam is willing to cosign Dan's note. The note reads in part, "We, or either of us, agree to pay $10,000 to First Bank or its order one year from the date of this note. [Signed] Daniel Debtor and Sam Smith." As a cosigner of the note, Sam has the same kind of liability that Dan has, and when the note comes due, First Bank has the right to sue Sam for payment without first seeking payment from Dan. Sam is a *surety* and, like Dan, has "primary" liability to the bank. Now suppose that Dan is the only signer of the note just described, but that Sam signs a separate document reading, "If Daniel Debtor defaults in making scheduled payments on the $10,000 debt he owes First Bank, I will, upon notice of such default, pay any amount that Daniel Debtor still owes. [Signed] Sam Smith." Sam is a *guarantor*. Since Sam need not pay unless he receives notice of Dan's default, Sam's liability is "secondary."

Many states have abolished the distinctions between suretyship and guarantyship, preferring to treat all such contracts as variant forms of surety obligations, regardless of whether the backup promisor signed a separate document, and regardless of the kind of liability (primary or secondary) he or she undertook. California, for example, abolished the distinctions by statute in 1872. Several states have narrowed the distinctions by judicial decisions, and many remaining distinctions have been demonstrated to be invalid. The *Restatement of the Law of Security*, published in 1941 by the American Law Institute, treats the expressions "suretyship" and "guaranty" as synonyms. Accordingly, the discussion of suretyship in the next part of this chapter treats suretyship and guaranty as basically the same thing, although some of the guaranty terminology is defined because it is still used in some states.

SURETYSHIP

Nature, Creation, and Kinds of Suretyship

Nature of Suretyship.   By legal definition, a **surety** is a person who, by contract or by operation of law, is liable for the debt, default, or miscarriage of another. When Sam in the example above cosigned Dan's note, he became a surety because he contracted to be responsible for Dan's debt. Although the bank can look to either Dan or Sam for payment, as between Dan and Sam, Dan is the person with ultimate liability. Thus, the definition of suretyship found in the *Restatement of Security* applies: One person (Dan) has undertaken an obligation (debt to First Bank), and another person (Sam, because he cosigned) is also under an obligation to the obligee (bank) which is entitled to only one performance. And as between the two who are bound (Dan and Sam), one (Dan) rather than the other (Sam) should perform. Thus, if Sam is required to pay First Bank, Dan is liable to Sam.

First Bank is the *creditor,* also known as the *obligee.* Dan is the principal debtor, also known as the *obligor.* Sam is the principal debtor's *surety* and can also be viewed as First Bank's debtor.

A surety may be liable for the principal's *debt* (usually understood to mean an obligation to pay money). But a surety can be liable, too, for the principal's *default* (failure to perform a nonmoney obligation), as where Sam promises to make good any loss resulting from Dan's failure to perform Dan's contract to deliver oil; or for the principal's *miscarriage* (tort or crime), as where Sam agrees to make good to Dan's employer any losses resulting from Dan's embezzlement or other mishandling of the employer's funds.

Creation of Suretyship.   Suretyship usually is created by express contract, at the request of the creditor or the principal debtor. But suretyship also can arise without the knowledge of the parties, by operation of law. Recall from Chapter 13 what happens when a person assigns his or her rights under a contract and also delegates the duties he or she is required by the contract to perform. The delegator remains responsible as a surety for the performance of those duties if the delegatee fails to perform, unless the obligee (person to whom the duty is owed) releases the delegator.

As an example, suppose you are buying a house financed by Second Bank and you want to sell it to Julia before you have paid off the debt. Julia agrees to a purchase price of $50,000. You have a $30,000 mortgage indebtedness to the bank remaining. Julia pays you $20,000 and "assumes" the mortgage. Since you have delegated to Julia your duty to pay Second Bank the $30,000, you are now a surety for the $30,000 unless and until the bank releases you from liability. Your suretyship liability arises even though the bank might not know that Julia has assumed the mortgage and even though you might not realize that you are still liable to the bank. Upon assuming the mortgage, Julia becomes the principal debtor. So, if you must pay because she refuses or fails to pay, she is liable to you.

Suretyship can arise by operation of law in other unexpected ways. Suppose you drive negligently and injure Millie, another motorist. You have no insurance, but Millie is insured by Town Insurance Company. Both you and the insurance company are liable to Millie. The insurance company is liable on the basis of its contract to indemnify (compensate) her for loss, and you are liable because of your negligence. Probably the insurance company will pay Millie immediately and seek payment from you, since you are ultimately liable. Under the law you are the principal debtor and the insurance company is, in this instance, a surety. As such the insurance company has, like any other surety, a right of reimbursement against you, the principal debtor.

Kinds of Suretyship.   The precise obligation that a surety has is determined in part by the kind of suretyship that the surety undertook.

Gratuitous versus Compensated Suretyship.   Some sureties are paid for their services and some are not. Those who are not paid are called "gratuitous," "voluntary," or "accommodation" sureties because their main purpose in undertaking the surety obligation is to help out a relative or friend, and not to profit personally. **Gratuitous sureties** (accommodation sureties) *are*, in fact, contracting parties bound by their promises, but the consideration they receive consists of a "legal" benefit only—e.g., the creditor's promise to the surety to deal or to continue dealing with the principal debtor, as illustrated in Case 27.2. Any monetary or other actual benefit goes to the principal debtor and not to the accommodation surety.

Suppose, for example, that you make an installment purchase of a car, and at the request of the seller a friend or relative cosigns or guarantees your note without being paid to do so. The surety (your friend or relative) has made a contractual commitment binding on him or her. The consideration necessary for the contract of suretyship to arise is the seller's promise (made to the surety) to sell the car to you, in exchange for the surety's promise to pay if you do not. However, despite the fact that the surety receives consideration, the suretyship is called "gratuitous" because while you receive the car and the extension of credit in exchange for your own promise to pay, the surety receives only a "legal" benefit (the creditor's promise to deal with you) in exchange for the surety's promise to pay. Since a gratuitous surety receives little or no actual benefit from the contract, most courts will resolve any ambiguities, vagueness, or other doubts about the scope of the undertaking in favor of the gratuitous surety and against the creditor.

The opposite is true for **compensated sureties**, sometimes called "corporate" sureties. A person or firm undertaking a surety's obligation for hire usually will be held strictly to the contract, and any ambiguities, vagueness, or doubts as to the scope of the undertaking will be resolved in favor of the creditor and against the surety. This makes sense because the compensated surety usually is a company that, like an insurance company, estimates risks on an actuarial basis and charges the principal debtor a fee ("premium") that reflects the degree of risk.

The promise of a compensated surety to pay if the principal debtor does not is often called a "bond." There are many types of **surety bonds**, among them the following:

1. Bail, appearance, appeal, or judicial bond—various surety bonds associated with criminal or civil legal proceedings. A bail or appearance bond is the surety's promise to pay a specified sum to the court if the criminal defendant covered by the bond fails to show up for legal proceedings. An appeal bond is a surety's promise to cover the costs of appeal in a civil case. "Judicial bond" is a general term for any bond required by a court to guarantee, for example, the payment of costs connected with an appeal or the availability of a fund needed to satisfy a judgment.

2. Bid bond—a surety bond used in connection with public construction projects to protect the public agency (creditor) from loss if the bidder (principal debtor) withdraws the bid or, upon winning the right to the contract, refuses to enter into it.

3. Completion, contract, payment or performance bond—a surety bond guaranteeing, for example, that a contractor will complete a construction contract or pay for labor and materials.

4. Fidelity bond—a surety bond protecting an employer against loss due to embezzlement, larceny, or gross negligence by an employee.

5. Fiduciary bond—a surety bond required by a court to be provided by a trustee, executor, guardian, or other fiduciary to ensure proper performance of his or her duties.

6. License or permit bond—a suretyship bond required by state law before the state will issue a license or permit. The bond guarantees payment to an obligee for loss or damage resulting from operations of the licensee or permit holder.

CASE 27.2 Boise Cascade Corp. v. Stonewood Development Corp.
655 P.2d 668 (Utah 1982)

Facts: Boise Cascade furnished building materials to Stonewood Corp. on the basis of a guarantee agreement signed by Ronald Bennett and other officers of Stonewood. The agreement stated that "in consideration of $1.00, the receipt whereof is hereby acknowledged, and in further consideration that Boise Cascade sell and deliver goods to Stonewood," the signers unconditionally promise to pay any amount due and not paid. Stonewood defaulted, and Boise Cascade sued the guarantors for payment. The trial court awarded judgment to Boise Cascade, and Bennett appealed on the ground that he had never received the $1.00 recited as consideration for the guarantee.

Question: Was the guarantee binding on Bennett?

Answer: Yes.

Reasoning: It is not required that Bennett have received the $1.00 personally, as long as it was given. In any event, the extension of credit by Boise Cascade to Stonewood was, by itself, adequate consideration to support the guarantee.

Unconditional versus Conditional Suretyship.   Surety relationships can be classified according to the nature of the surety's promise or undertaking. In a traditional suretyship arrangement, e.g., cosigning a promissory note, the surety-cosigner makes an unconditional promise to pay and, like the principal debtor, is immediately liable to the creditor when the note is *due*. There is no requirement that the creditor first seek payment from the principal debtor. In another kind of unconditional suretyship called an *absolute guaranty*, the surety promises to pay or to perform *upon the default* of the principal debtor. Here, the surety has no liability until the principal debtor defaults; but if the debtor defaults, the surety is immediately liable. In a *conditional guaranty*, however, the creditor must do more than merely show that the principal debtor is in default. To hold the surety liable, the creditor must first make a reasonable attempt to exhaust the creditor's remedies against the debtor, for example by suing the principal debtor and having the judgment returned unsatisfied. What, precisely, is required to trigger a surety's liability is often a matter of contractual interpretation.

Cosuretyship versus Subsuretyship.   Sometimes two or more sureties will bind themselves on behalf of a single principal debtor. Depending on the circumstances, these sureties are in either a **cosurety** or a **subsurety** relationship. Cosureties must share the burden of the principal debtor's default. This is so because each cosurety has contracted to pay the full debt, and there is nothing in the situation that would justify a court in imposing the whole loss on one cosurety while freeing the others. In subsuretyship, however, there exists some circumstance that makes it fair for one surety alone to be ultimately responsible for payment.

Suppose Dan borrows $100,000 from Carla, and Sylvia cosigns the note at Dan's request. At the same time, at Carla's request, Sam (in writing) guarantees Dan's debt. Sylvia and Sam are cosureties. If Dan defaults, Sylvia and Sam must share the loss equally, unless they have agreed to share it in some different proportion. So, if Dan defaults and Carla compels Sylvia to pay the $100,000, Sylvia is entitled to a $50,000 payment, called "contribution," from Sam. Similarly, two or more accommodation signers of a note ordinarily are cosureties, and any one of them who is required to pay more than his or her share is entitled to contribution.

Suppose instead that, in the situation just described, Sylvia is the only surety, that Dan's debt is due, and Carla has told Sylvia that Carla will seek payment from Sylvia. Then Sylvia pays Sam to guarantee (in writing) Dan's payment, believing that Carla will delay suit against Sylvia because of Sam's guaranty. Sylvia is the "principal surety" and Sam is the "subsurety." Both are liable to Carla for Dan's default, but Sylvia's object in paying Sam to serve as surety was to protect herself from an existing liability. So, as between Sylvia and Sam, Sylvia is the one who ultimately should pay. In effect, Sam is surety for Sylvia. If Sam must pay Dan's debt, Sam, as subsurety, may hold Sylvia liable for the full amount.

Since the relationship between principal surety and subsurety is like the relationship between principal debtor and surety, subsuretyship will not be discussed further in this chapter.

Liability, Defenses, and Discharge of Surety

Liability of Surety.   In a suretyship created by contract there are as many as *three* contracts—one between the creditor and the principal debtor, one between the creditor and the surety, and one between the surety and the principal debtor. The liability a surety faces when a principal debtor defaults is determined by (*a*) the contract between the creditor and the principal debtor, (*b*) the contract between the creditor and the surety, and (*c*) other factors such as whether the surety has the benefit of any defenses when called upon to pay.

Usually the surety is responsible for precisely the performance, or any unperformed part of it, that the principal debtor promised the creditor—for example, to pay $10,000 plus 12 percent interest on July 17, or to deliver 50 tons of coal at the rate of 1 ton per week. Where the seller of mortgaged real estate becomes a surety by operation of law because the buyer assumed the seller's mortgage, the seller-surety is liable to the creditor for the amount of the assumed debt that remains unpaid. However, the contract between the surety and the creditor can *limit* the surety's liability, as where the surety promises, "If Dan defaults on his $10,000 obligation to you, I will pay $5000."

The surety-creditor contract can also *affect the timing* of the surety's liability (and, as discussed later in this chapter, the *defenses* available to the surety). A surety who simply adds his or her name (as cosigner) to the note of the principal debtor acquires an automatic contractual liability imposed by law. The law imposes upon the surety-cosigner an unconditional promise to pay when the note is due. If the cosigner fails to pay on that date, he or she is automatically in default, and the creditor may take the cosigner directly to court without even a polite request for payment. This is the nature of a cosigner's "primary" liability. Moreover, as far as the creditor is concerned, the debt undertaken by the cosigner is his or her own, since the cosigner has, by signing the note, said in effect, "I promise to pay the creditor the specified amount on the date stated in this note." In contrast, where a surety says, "I will pay Dan's debt if Dan doesn't pay when it is due," or "I will pay Dan's debt if it is uncollectible," the surety is obviously promising to pay the debt of someone else and has no liability until the creditor demonstrates that the debt is uncollectible. The creditor ordinarily will do this by getting a judgment against the debtor, attempting to collect on it, and having the judgment returned unsatisfied.

The case that follows addresses the problem that exists where the surety's maximum liability is less than the debt owed, and numerous creditors contend for the limited amount.

CASE 27.3   Homewood Investment Co. v. Moses
608 P.2d 503 (Nev. 1980)

Facts: Home Lumber and Supply Co. furnished over $16,000 worth of materials to Homewood. Homewood never paid. Home Lumber sued for the amount owed, and judgment was entered against Homewood and others, including United Pacific Insurance Co., in favor of Home Lumber. United had undertaken a $5,000 contractor's surety bond. United appealed from the judgment, alleging that since there were several other unpaid suppliers, Home Lumber was entitled to only a portion of the $5,000 bond amount.

Question: Was Home Lumber entitled to the full $5,000?

Answer: No.

Reasoning: A Nevada statute provides that claims of materialmen against a bond or deposit shall have equal priority, and if the bond is insufficient to pay all such claims in full, they shall be paid pro rata. Since there was evidence of other claims against United's bond, the trial court must determine Home Lumber's pro rata share.

Defenses and Discharge of Surety.   A surety may have the benefit of three kinds of defenses: (1) the surety's own contractual defenses, (2) some of the contractual defenses available to the principal debtor, and (3) special suretyship defenses that usually arise after the surety undertakes the obligation.

Surety's Own Contractual Defenses.   A person has no suretyship liability if no contract arose or if, where one did arise, the surety exercises a right to avoid it. No contract arose if, for example, the person alleged to be a surety lacked capacity to contract or received *no* consideration for his or her promise. (Recall that even a so-called 'gratuitous" surety receives consideration—the promise of the creditor to deal with the principal debtor.) A surety may avoid his or her contract where, for example, the creditor procured the surety's promise by fraud. Suppose First Bank seeks a fidelity bond to protect it from loss due to embezzlement of customers' funds by the bank's employees. First Bank knows, but does not reveal to the surety, that three of the bank's employees have been convicted of embezzlement. First Bank's fraud in concealing or knowingly failing to reveal material information gives the surety a ground for avoiding the contract.

Sometimes a surety may assert the **statute of frauds** as a defense. The statute of frauds comes into play where a surety agrees to answer for the debt, default, or miscarriage of another. Such an agreement is not enforceable unless it is in writing. Suppose Delbert is building himself a house on his own lot and is purchasing materials from Lumber Supply. Halfway through, Delbert fails to pay for some materials and Lumber Supply refuses to deliver any more until he persuades some creditworthy person to guarantee payment. At Delbert's request, Susan promises Lumber Supply on the phone that "If Del does not pay for materials when they are delivered, I will." Lumber Supply makes further deliveries, Del does not pay, and when called upon for payment, Susan refuses. Her promise is not enforceable because it was oral. However, if Susan's **main purpose** in making the promise had been to benefit herself, her oral promise would have been enforceable. Suppose Del, as a general contractor, is building the house for Susan on her lot. Here, Susan's main purpose in promising to pay Del's debt is to get her house built. Her oral promise to pay Del's debt is enforceable.

Principal Debtor's Contractual Defenses.   With some very important exceptions, the surety may assert against the creditor the defenses that the principal debtor could have asserted if there had been only the contract between debtor and creditor. The defenses that the surety *may* assert usually arise out of situations involving wrongdoing or default by the creditor. Suppose that the creditor fraudulently tricks, or by duress forces, the principal debtor into the contract of indebtedness. Most courts hold that a surety who did not know of the fraud or duress when agreeing to be a surety may assert the principal debtor's defense. Some courts hold that the surety may not do so unless the principal debtor first repudiates the contract because of the fraud or duress. Similarly, if the principal debtor received no consideration (e.g., the creditor did not make the promised loan or deliver the promised materials), the surety may assert that defense of the debtor and escape liability to the creditor.

In some situations the principal debtor has a defense that is unavailable to the surety. Suppose Sam cosigns a note so that his minor daughter Dora can buy a car. Dora wrecks the car and, as permitted under state law protecting minors, rescinds the contract. Sam does *not* have the benefit of Dora's defense of infancy. The fact that Dora might rescind and cause loss to the creditor-seller was the main reason the creditor required a surety in the first place, and Sam understood or should have understood this when he became surety. However, if Dora, instead of wrecking the car, had simply returned it the next day unused so that the creditor suffered no loss, Sam *would* be discharged from his suretyship obligation.

In a few other situations the surety is not protected by the debtor's defenses. Ordinarily the surety will be liable to the creditor despite the debtor's defense of insanity, bankruptcy, lack of corporate capacity to undertake the debt in question, or (where the debtor is a public agency) its assertion of sovereign immunity. Again, these are the kinds of risks that surety and creditor probably contemplated as the main reason for the suretyship. Case 27.4, however, illustrates a defense of the principal debtor that the surety *may* assert.

CASE 27.4 Domingues Motors, Inc. v. Lalonde
417 So. 2d 900 (La. App. 1982)

Facts: Deborah Lalonde made a credit purchase of a car from Domingues. Because of her small down payment, Domingues required security in addition to a security interest in the car itself and agreed to accept the written guaranty of Deborah's father, John. Domingues assigned the contract and the surety agreement to General Motors Acceptance Corp. (GMAC). About a year later, Deborah filed for bankruptcy. At GMAC's request, the trustee in bankruptcy took possession of the car and, without appraising it, transferred it to GMAC in full satisfaction of its claim. GMAC transferred the car to Domingues, which sold it at a private sale. The car did not sell for enough to cover the amount owed by Deborah. Domingues then sued John Lalonde for over $1,800, the amount of the deficiency. The trial court held in favor of John, and Domingues appealed.

Question: Was Domingues entitled to the amount of the deficiency?

Answer: No.

Reasoning: It is a strong policy of Louisiana law that a mortgage creditor may not collect a deficiency judgment from the debtor where the creditor provokes a sale of the mortgaged property without the benefit of appraisement (a just and true valuation of the property). This is for the protection of debtors. Such a sale likewise bars a deficiency judgment against the debtor's surety, since if the surety could be held liable and could in turn require the debtor to reimburse the surety, the debtor's protection would be lost.

Special Suretyship Defenses.   The purpose of the special suretyship defenses is to protect the surety where acts of others increase the surety's risk or reduce the likelihood that the surety can recover the amount that will have to be paid on behalf of the principal debtor. The existence of a special suretyship defense in a particular instance, or the extent of it, depends on a number of factors: (1) Did the surety consent to the change that affects the surety's liability? If so, the surety remains liable. (2) Was the harm (e.g., an increased chance that the surety will have to pay) "material"? If not, a compensated surety remains liable. The more common special suretyship defenses are discussed in the following paragraphs.

1. *Performance of the principal debtor's duty.* If the principal debtor, the surety, or some third person performs the debtor's duty, not only the debtor but also the surety is discharged from any further liability.

2. *Release of the debtor by the creditor.* Where the creditor releases the debtor from the debtor's duty, the surety is also discharged. A *release* is a legally binding contract to give up a right that the releasing person has against the person to be released.

3. *A tender (offer) of performance.* The surety is discharged where the principal debtor or the surety makes a proper tender of performance which the creditor wrongfully refuses. However, the principal debtor is *not* discharged, because he or she has received the benefit of the contract with the creditor and should have to perform by, for example, repaying a loan. But in fairness to the debtor who is trying to perform, the creditor's wrongful refusal of tender immediately stops the running of interest.

4. *Alteration of principal debtor's duty.* A surety is entitled to rely on the original terms of the contract between the principal debtor and the creditor. If those terms are changed without the consent of the surety in a way that increases his or her risk, an uncompensated (accommodation) surety will be completely discharged. However, a compensated surety will be discharged only if the increase in the surety's risk is material. If the risk increases, but not materially, the compensated surety is not discharged but his or her obligation is reduced to the extent of the loss resulting from the change in the contract between debtor and creditor. No surety is discharged where the unconsented-to modification can only benefit the surety.

Suppose, for example, that Dan leases a building from Carla for 2 years at a monthly rental of $500, and Sam agrees to pay the rent if Dan does not. Then Dan and Carla agree to reduce the rent to $450 per month. Sam is not discharged even if he is an uncompensated surety, since the change in Dan and Carla's contract can do nothing but benefit Sam. Sam is liable, of course, only for the lesser amount. But suppose that instead of changing the monthly rental, Dan and Carla agreed to extend the 2-year term by 1 hour. If Sam is an uncompensated surety, he is discharged because there is an increase, though a small one, in his potential liability for the rent. If Sam is a *compensated* surety, he will not be discharged as to the 2-year term unless the court holds that the 1-hour extension is material, a highly unlikely holding. Now suppose Dan pays the rent for the full 2 years but fails to pay the rent for the extra hour. Sam, though a compensated surety liable for the rent attributable to the 2-year term, is not liable for the hour's rent resulting from the minor modification.

Another type of alteration occurs where debtor and creditor make a legally binding agreement to extend the time for payment of the debt. Such an agreement immediately and completely discharges an *un*compensated surety who did not consent to it. However, a *compensated*, unconsenting surety is discharged only to the extent that he or she is harmed by the extension. Suppose Dora borrows $5000 from Calvin and signs a promissory note to repay the amount at the end of 6 months plus 10 percent interest. Sally guarantees Dora's note. Without Sally's consent Dora and Calvin then enter into a binding contract to extend the time of payment for 3 more months. If Sally is an uncompensated surety, she is immediately and completely discharged from liability. If she is a *compensated* surety, she is discharged only to the extent she is harmed by the extension. Sally would be harmed if called upon to pay the additional 3 months' interest that Calvin and Dora agreed to without Sally's consent. Moreover, if Dora became insolvent during the 3-month extension, Sally (even if she were a compensated surety) would also be discharged from liability to Calvin for the principal amount, because she agreed to bear the risk of Dora's insolvency for only 6 months, not 9.

Ordinarily, a legally binding agreement between debtor and creditor to increase the interest rate on a debt discharges an unconsenting surety. An agreement to *lower* the interest rate does not discharge the surety, who remains liable for the lowered amount.

5. *Surrender or impairment of collateral.* Sometimes a creditor has the benefit of a surety's obligation but also receives real or personal property from the debtor to secure the debt. The surety has a right to the benefit of the collateral. Therefore, where the creditor knows of the surety's obligation, the surety is discharged to the extent of any loss caused by the creditor's giving up the collateral or mishandling it in such a way as to reduce its value. Suppose Sarah is a surety where Clara lends $5000 to Dale who pledges (temporarily transfers possession of) 100 shares of his stock to Clara as additional security. The stock is worth $2000. Then, before Dale's debt is due and without Sarah's consent, Clara returns the stock to Dale. Sarah is discharged as to $2000 but remains liable as a surety for $3000.

Rights of Surety and Cosurety

Upon the default of the principal debtor, the surety becomes obligated to perform—e.g., pay the creditor—if there are no defenses the surety can assert. If required to perform, the surety has certain "rights" against the principal debtor. He or she may be entitled to exoneration, reimbursement, or subrogation, or to some combination of these. If there are cosureties, the surety who pays may be entitled, in addition, to "contribution" from the others.

Rights of Surety. **Exoneration** is the right of a surety to have a court of equity compel a capable but reluctant principal debtor to pay. The rationale for exoneration is that the surety should not have to suffer the inconvenience and expense of having to pay out of his or her own assets and then sue the principal debtor when the debtor has sufficient resources. The surety might choose exoneration rather than a suit for reimbursement where, for example, the surety's assets are real estate whose liquidation to pay the debt would cause undue hardship to the surety.

Upon the default of the principal debtor, the surety might simply pay the creditor and then sue the debtor for **reimbursement** (repayment). In general, a surety who has an obligation to perform for the debtor is entitled to be reimbursed by the debtor, but only after the surety actually pays the debt. The right of reimbursement exists regardless of whether the surety is a compensated or uncompensated one, and often the duty of reimbursement exists even though the principal debtor did not consent to the suretyship.

Where the surety undertook the suretyship with the consent of the principal debtor, the debtor has a duty of reimbursement based on an implied contract. Where the debtor has not consented to the suretyship, he or she nevertheless has a duty to reimburse the surety if the debtor is unjustly enriched because of the surety's performance. The unconsenting debtor will be unjustly enriched by the surety's performance where the debtor is bound to perform, has not performed, and has no defense. Suppose Dan signs a note for $5000 payable to Clara, for the purchase of an antique rug. At Clara's request but without Dan's knowledge, Shirley guarantees the note. The note falls due, Dan cannot pay, and Clara receives payment from Shirley, since the rug was stolen from Dan months ago and was not insured. Dan has a duty to pay Clara the $5000. Shirley, by making payment for Dan upon his default, has enriched him by discharging his duty to Clara, and Shirley is entitled to reimbursement despite the fact that Dan did not consent to the suretyship.

Sometimes the principal has *no* duty to reimburse the surety. For example, if the debtor has a defense that is good against the creditor and the surety pays, the surety (having no *legal compulsion* to pay) is a mere volunteer and is *not* entitled to reimbursement. Suppose Cora fraudulently induces Dan to sign a note for $10,000. Then, without Dan's knowledge Sue guarantees his note. The note falls due, Dan does not pay, and Cora receives payment from Sue who knew nothing of Cora's fraud. Sue is not entitled to reimbursement from Dan because he, as a result of his fraud defense, was under no obligation to pay and therefore could not have been enriched by Sue's payment. Her payment to Cora was simply unnecessary and cannot be charged to Dan. However, Sue may be able to recover her payment from Cora on the ground of Cora's unjust enrichment.

In a number of other situations the surety is not entitled to reimbursement from the principal debtor. For example, if the debtor has received a discharge in bankruptcy as to the creditor's claim, the discharge serves also to bar the surety's claim for reimbursement. If the debtor were required to pay the surety despite the discharge in bankruptcy, the discharge would not give the debtor the protection intended by the drafters of the bankruptcy law. Similarly, for the protection of persons who lack capacity to contract, a surety may not have reimbursement from a debtor whose obligation is void or has been avoided because of the debtor's lack of capacity.

A surety who satisfies the principal debtor's duty to the creditor acquires a right of **subrogation**, i.e., a right to be substituted for or to take over the rights of the creditor as against the principal debtor. The creditor might hold stock or other property as collateral security for the debt. The surety, as **subrogee**, is entitled to the collateral. The creditor might have obtained a judgment against the debtor and received payment of the judgment amount from the surety instead of having to execute the judgment. The surety, as subrogee, is entitled to stand in the shoes of the creditor and enforce the judgment against the debtor.

Rights of Cosurety.   A cosurety who performs the principal debtor's duty is entitled to **contribution** from the other cosureties. Suppose Dan defaults on his obligation to pay Candice $300,000 and there are three cosureties. If there was no agreement among the three as to how much each would be liable for upon Dan's default, the three must share the loss equally. If Simon, the first cosurety, is required to make full payment to Candice, Simon is entitled to a $100,000 contribution from each of the other two cosureties.

Suppose now that there are two cosureties. Simon agrees to be liable for $200,000 of Dan's debt, while Sheila agrees to be liable for $100,000. Then Dan pays $150,000 and defaults as to the other $150,000. Simon and Sheila must contribute in accordance with the proportion established by their agreements. Simon is responsible for two-thirds of the loss and Sheila for one-third. If Sheila must pay Candice the whole $150,000, Simon must contribute $100,000.

Suppose Dan owes Cora $60,000, and Sid, Sue, and Saul are equal cosureties. Dan is in default, and Cora releases Sid from liability. Sue and Saul are thereby discharged from liability as to the share of loss Sid would have had to absorb. Cora is entitled only to $40,000—$20,000 from Sue and $20,000 from Saul.

Like sureties, cosureties have rights of subrogation and exoneration. Cosureties are entitled to be subrogated to collateral held by the creditor, in proportion to the amount of their individual liabilities.

SUMMARY

The purpose of a secured transaction is to reduce the creditor's risk of nonpayment. Some security devices give the creditor a lien on real or personal property as the backup source of payment. The lien may be imposed by law or it may be created by contract. In suretyship, the source of backup payment is the surety's promise to pay if the debtor does not.

The law imposes liens on personal and real property in favor of persons who repair, store, improve, or otherwise render services in connection with the property. Liens created by contract include secured transactions in personal property, secured transactions in real estate such as mortgages and land contracts, corporate bonds, and contracts of suretyship. Contractual security devices are used to secure repayment of a loan or the purchase price of property or services.

A surety is responsible for the debt, default, or miscarriage of the principal debtor. The surety is liable for precisely the performance, or any unperformed part of it, that the debtor promised the creditor—unless the surety agreed to be liable only for a lesser amount, or unless the surety has a defense to payment. The surety may have the benefit of the surety's own contractual defenses, some contractual defenses that are available to the debtor, and special suretyship defenses such as an alteration of the debtor's obligation not consented to by the surety. If the surety is called on to perform, he or she may be entitled to exoneration, reimbursement, or subrogation. A cosurety who pays more than his or her share of the debt may be entitled also to contribution from the other cosureties.

REVIEW QUESTIONS

1. What practical advantage is there to being a secured creditor rather than an unsecured one?

2. (a) Under what circumstances will a bailee of personal property be entitled to enforce a possessory lien? (b) How does a "specific" possessory lien differ from a "general" one?

3. Under what circumstances may a person enforce a mechanic's lien against real property?

4. How does a "land contract" function as a security device?

5. Illustrate how suretyship can arise by operation of law.

6. How does a gratuitous surety differ from a compensated one? Is there any difference in legal liability? Explain.

7. What feature distinguishes a cosurety from a subsurety?

8. In defense to a claim that a surety is liable to the creditor, the surety may assert the surety's own contractual defenses. Give an illustration of such a defense.

9. A surety may assert some of the principal debtor's defenses but not all of them. Which ones may the surety *not* have the benefit of? Why?

10. Explain the purpose and give two illustrations of the special suretyship defenses.

11. What is "exoneration," and where is it likely to be sought?

12. (a) Under what circumstances may a surety have reimbursement from the debtor? *Not* have reimbursement? (b) Illustrate subrogation and contribution.

CASE PROBLEMS

1. Just before the beginning of the irrigation season Larry brings three portable irrigation pumps to Carl for their annual cleaning and repair. Carl completes the work and presents Larry with a bill for $150, the reasonable value of Carl's services. Larry is short on cash and needs the pumps right away. Carl releases two of them to Larry but holds the third one as security for payment of his bill. Larry contends that by releasing the first two pumps, Carl has lost his possessory lien on the third one as well. Does Carl have a possessory lien on the third pump? Explain.

2. Rockvoy was obligated on a promissory note to Pioneer Credit Company. Rockvoy failed to make payment, and Pioneer began foreclosure proceedings against Rockvoy's property. Rockvoy asked Pioneer to withhold execution on the judgment in exchange for a written guarantee signed by John Medalen, Rockvoy's father-in-law. Instead of paying the judgment, Rockvoy filed for bankruptcy. Pioneer then sought payment from Medalen. Medalen denied liability on several grounds, including lack of consideration for his signature. Did Medalen receive consideration for signing the guarantee? Why?

3. In 1970 Tilleraas received a $3500 student loan from Dakota National Bank (DNB). The loan was insured by the United States government under the Higher Education Act. Tilleraas defaulted on the loan on July 27, 1972. The government paid DNB's insurance claim on July 30, 1974, and was assigned title to the note. On June 14, 1980, the government sued Tilleraas for repayment. She alleged that the 6-year statute of limitations period began running on July 27, 1972 and had expired, barring the suit against her. The government contended the 6 years did not begin to run until July 30, 1974, and that its suit for reimbursement was therefore timely. Who is correct? Why?

4. Coffey and Sawyer worked for Applied Systems as program writer and computer operator, respectively. They left Applied Systems to go into business for themselves, converting to their own use several of Applied Systems' computer tapes and programs. In subsequent legal proceedings, Applied Systems was awarded a $25,000 verdict against Coffey and Sawyer; Applied Systems was awarded $25,000 against National Surety on its indemnity bond covering Coffey and Sawyer; and National Surety was awarded $25,000 against Coffey and Sawyer on its claim for reimbursement. Coffey and Sawyer appealed, arguing that the verdicts made them liable twice for the same wrong, since they would be liable both to Applied Systems and National Surety. Are Coffey and Sawyer correct? Explain.

5. Roscoe, Jr. bought a mobile home on credit, for about $22,000. Roscoe, Sr. guaranteed the buyer's performance. Western Coach, the seller, immediately assigned its rights under the sales contract. As part of Western's assignment of its rights, and unknown to the Roscoes, Western also guaranteed Roscoe, Jr.'s performance. Roscoe, Jr. sold the mobile home; the subsequent purchasers assumed the debt but defaulted. Eventually Western repossessed the home, which had been vandalized and stripped of its furnishings, and repaired and refurbished it. Western also made the delinquent payments on the home and paid back taxes that had accumulated. Western then sued Roscoe, Jr. and Roscoe, Sr. to recover the sums it claims to have spent on their behalf. (**a**) Under what theory of law might Roscoe, Jr. be liable to Western? (**b**) Under what theory might Roscoe, Sr. be liable to Western?

CHAPTER 28

SECURED TRANSACTIONS IN PERSONAL PROPERTY

As noted in the preceding chapter, vast amounts of consumer and business credit are secured by an interest in personal property—consumer goods, accounts receivable, inventory, equipment, and other "collateral"—possessed or owned by the debtor. Article 9 of the Uniform Commercial Code (UCC) governs secured transactions in personal property. This chapter focuses on how, under Article 9, a creditor may acquire a security interest in personal property and make that interest enforceable against the claims of rival creditors; who is entitled to the collateral (who has "priority") when two or more persons claim it upon the debtor's default; and how the secured party may dispose of the collateral if the debtor fails to pay.

Most rules of Article 9 apply regardless of whether the secured transaction involves consumer goods or business property. However, secured transactions in consumer goods (goods used or bought primarily for personal, family, or household purposes) are subject to a few special rules that are noted throughout the chapter.

PURPOSE AND COVERAGE OF UCC ARTICLE 9

Purpose of Article 9

Pre-Code Security Devices.   Before the industrial revolution, the courts refused to enforce against subsequent creditors any secured transaction in personal property that left the debtor in possession of the collateral. The reasoning was that a creditor who put a debtor into possession of unpaid-for property while retaining a "secret lien" on the property created an unwarranted danger for other lenders. Since credit purchases were unusual, these other lenders would naturally believe that the debtor owned free and clear all the property over which he or she had the usual owner's control. The security device preferred by the courts of that era was the **pledge**, in which the debtor gave possession of the collateral to the creditor in order to obtain a loan. Since the pledgee-creditor would possess the collateral until the loan was repaid, subsequent creditors would not be likely to overestimate the debtor's wealth and to extend unjustified credit.

The industrial revolution dramatically increased credit needs and forced the invention of new financing techniques. As industry developed, producers often lacked sufficient operating capital, even though they might own considerable equipment. The equipment could not be pledged because the owner needed to use it in the business. Lawyers therefore created some security devices intended to allow the borrower to use the collateral while the loan was being repaid. The most important pre-Code devices that emerged from these efforts were the chattel mortgage and the conditional-sale contract. Under the **chattel mortgage**, the debtor retained possession of the goods ("chattels") used as collateral but transferred to the creditor title to (ownership of) the chattel or, in some states, granted a lien on the chattel. Upon payment of the debt, title reverted (went back) to the debtor or the lien was discharged. Under the **conditional-sale contract** the buyer-debtor received possession of the goods from the seller, and the seller-creditor retained title until the buyer performed his or her part of the agreement. These two devices are still in general use.

A third security device, **field warehousing**, developed in response to a need for the financing of inventory. Inventory used as collateral was segregated in a fenced-off area of the borrower's (e.g., a manufacturer's) premises and placed under the control of an independent warehouser who acted on behalf of the lender (creditor). Then, as the debtor sold the inventory being used as collateral, the field warehouser would release the needed amounts and make sure that the creditor-lender received proper payment from the proceeds of the sale. Field warehousing is no longer a requirement for inventory financing, but it may be used as a policing technique by lenders who wish to keep close track of inventory being used as collateral.

Article 9 Reforms.   The pre-Code law of secured transactions had many shortcomings that made credit extension expensive and risky. Among them were: (1) a variety of security devices—chattel mortgages, trust receipts, factors' liens, etc.—each with its separate filing system; (2) courts that insisted on invalidating a security transaction if it did not fall clearly into the category the lender thought it did; (3) the expense of multiple filing as a hedge against a wrong guess; (4) undeveloped inventory and accounts receivable financing; and (5) different treatment by courts and legislatures of similar security devices, and even of devices of the same name.

The aim of Article 9 is to provide a legal framework for safe and efficient credit extension and thereby to make the law of secured transactions more uniform, predictable, and useful to business. This framework consists of four major elements:

1. The substitution of the single term **security interest** for the variety of expressions used in the past to describe the property right that the creditor sought to hold as security. Article 9 does not abolish the old security devices nor prohibit the use of the old terminology, but the old devices are no longer viewed as inherently different from each other. Instead, they are considered as variations of the same thing—an Article 9 secured transaction whose consequences are spelled out in the article. Thus, in the pledge, which is still widely used, possession of the debtor's property by the creditor is the security interest. In a conditional sale or chattel mortgage transaction, the debtor has possession and the creditor retains or receives "title" as the security interest. Note that the word "title" has two legal meanings that can be confusing. In the law of property, title often means full ownership of a thing—the right to possess, use, enjoy, and dispose of a thing by selling it, giving it away, or destroying it. But in the law of secured transactions, the "title" that a creditor holds to secure payment of a debt is of a very limited nature. Like any other security interest, the creditor's "title" gives the creditor a *limited* right to control or dispose of (e.g., sell) the collateral—a right that can be exercised only upon the debtor's default, and then only as to the amount of the debt still owed.

2. The substitution of a simplified public-notice filing system for the confusing and expensive pre-Code jumble of different files, records, and indexes for each type of security device.

3. A single system of priorities to resolve disputes where there are two or more conflicting interests in the same collateral, to replace the widely varying older state systems.

4. A uniform method of liquidating collateral (converting it into cash) after default, based on a commercially reasonable liquidation rather than the forced-sale provisions of many pre-Code statutes that caused economic loss to both creditor and debtor.

The Updating of Article 9.   Over the years, so many states changed Article 9 to suit themselves that it became less than uniform. In 1972 a revised Article 9 was published to replace the increasingly nonuniform 1962 version. Although basic secured transactions principles and techniques remain essentially unaltered, some significant changes were made. Today well over forty states have adopted the 1972 version. Consequently, references to Article 9 in this chapter are to the 1972 version of the article, unless otherwise noted. Because some states have not yet adopted the 1972 Article 9, differences between the two versions are pointed out where necessary for the purposes of this chapter.

Coverage of Article 9

Security Transactions Covered.   Except for certain classes of excluded transactions discussed later, Article 9 applies (1) to any transaction (regardless of its form) that is intended to create a security interest in personal property *or fixtures*, and (2) to any *sale* of accounts or chattel paper [9-102]. You may wish to glance ahead at Table 28.1, which lists and describes most of the types of personal property covered by Article 9.

The statement of Article 9's coverage raises two questions: (1) Fixtures are normally considered part of the real property to which they are annexed and for most purposes are subject to local real estate law. Why, then, does Article 9, which deals mainly with transactions in *personal* property, apply to the security aspects of fixtures? (2) Why does Article 9, which applies mainly to *credit* transactions, apply also to *sales* of accounts and chattel paper?

Fixtures begin life as goods and often move in interstate commerce until annexed to realty. If the security aspects of fixture transactions were governed by real estate law, fixture creditors who sell nationally would be uncertain of their rights to the collateral if the buyer defaulted, since state real estate laws vary greatly as to creditors' rights. Article 9 reduces the uncertainty by providing a single set of rules that govern those rights, both before and after the fixture is annexed to the real estate.

The answer to the second question requires a look at the nature of chattel paper and accounts and how their owners typically use them to raise money. **Chattel paper** is a writing, or writings, evidencing (1) a debtor's obligation to pay for goods he or she is buying on credit, and (2) the seller's security interest in those goods. Suppose you make a credit purchase of a home freezer from West Store. You sign a promissory note for the purchase price plus interest, and you sign a conditional sale contract giving West a security interest in the freezer. Together these two documents constitute chattel paper. In contrast, an *account* (often called an "account receivable") is any right to payment for goods sold or leased, or for services rendered, that is *not* evidenced by an instrument (e.g., a promissory note) or chattel paper. A charge account at West Store is an example. So, if you buy a camera at West's and simply "charge it," West is an unsecured creditor. Nevertheless, both the chattel paper and the account are property rights owned by West that it can use as collateral to raise money for its own business purposes such as buying new equipment or more inventory.

Suppose West has chattel paper from 100 customers like you. The total face amount is $100,000, but none of the paper is due for several months. To raise money for current business needs, West may either sell the paper outright or pledge it as collateral for a loan. If West sells it, the buyer will pay West a "discounted" amount, say $90,000, intending later to collect the full face amount plus interest from each customer. If West merely pledges the paper, West will be entitled to have it back later so that it can collect the face amount plus interest. But the problem is that in both transactions—sale and pledge—West receives money and gives up possession of the chattel paper. Because the transactions are so much alike, third persons such as West's other creditors or potential lenders may not know whether West still owns the paper. The difficulty is even greater where West sells the paper and is permitted to retain custody of it. To give fair warning to those third persons, a *buyer* of West's *chattel paper* must comply with the rules of Article 9—i.e., like a lender, a buyer of chattel paper must either file a financing statement or take possession of the chattel paper and thereby notify others who may later claim an interest in it that the buyer already owns it. A buyer of *accounts* ordinarily must file a financing statement, since there is little or no paper for the buyer to possess.

To permit the use of old security devices and the development of new ones, **security interest** is defined broadly as "an interest in personal property or fixtures which secures payment or performance of an obligation" [1-201(37)]. However, it is not always clear whether a transaction such as a sale, lease, or consignment (an entrustment of property by the owner to a bailee for care or sale) is a *secured* transaction. Under the Code, the intention of the parties determines whether a transaction is secured or not. For example, sellers of goods, in attempts to protect themselves from the claims of buyers' creditors, often characterize sales of goods as "leases." In a true lease (e.g., lease of a computer), the lessor retains title (ownership) and grants possession and usage rights to the lessee. The lessor intends to remain owner. In a security "lease," however, the intention of the "lessor" is not to remain the owner, but to sell the goods and reserve a right to retrieve them if payment is not made. Since the "lease" is intended to secure payment of an obligation, the seller must follow the rules of Article 9 to prevail over creditors of the buyer-"lessee." The Code provides that a lease is one intended for security if the parties agree that at the expiration of the lease the lessee shall become the owner of the property for no additional consideration or for only a nominal (insignificant) consideration.

Security Transactions Excluded.   Twelve kinds of transactions are excluded from Article 9 coverage. For example, assignments of wages as security for debts are excluded because such assignments present important social problems whose solution should be a matter of local regulation. Although most sales of accounts receivable are covered by Article 9, some are excluded because they have nothing to do with commercial financing—for example, sales of accounts or chattel paper as a part of a sale of the business out of which they arose. In other instances, such as in the use of life insurance as collateral, or in the creation and enforcement of mechanics' liens, the transaction is excluded because it is adequately covered by non-Code law.

ACQUIRING AND PERFECTING A SECURITY INTEREST

A business person's interest in the topic of secured transactions may center around what must be done to acquire a security interest or to grant one. Article 9 speaks in terms of "attachment" and "perfection." **Attachment** is the process by which debtor and creditor create a security interest and make it enforceable between themselves. **Perfection** is the process by which the creditor ("secured party") makes the security interest enforceable against third persons such as other creditors of the debtor who also claim an interest in the collateral.

Attachment of a Security Interest

Attachment Events. A security interest does not "attach" (arise), and therefore is not enforceable against the debtor, unless four attachment "events" have occurred.

1. The debtor and creditor must *agree* that a security interest is to be created [9-203]. The **security agreement** sometimes may be oral.

2. The creditor *must possess* the collateral *or* the debtor must sign a security agreement that "reasonably identifies" the collateral [9-203 and 9-110].

3. The *secured party must give value.* Otherwise, there will be no debtor's obligation to be secured. The secured party usually gives value by making a loan, selling goods on credit, or making a binding commitment to extend credit.

4. The *debtor must have rights* in the collateral. Under the terms of the security agreement, some or all the debtor's rights are held by the secured party as the security interest.

The attachment events may occur in any order. Attachment itself cannot occur earlier than the completion of the last event, but the parties to the security agreement can postpone the time of attachment.

Attachment Involving After-Acquired Property Clauses and Future Advances Provisions. Article 9 permits the use of an "after-acquired property clause" in commercial secured transactions (but sharply limits its use when the collateral is consumer goods).[1] By using such a clause, the creditor obtains a security interest in both present and future assets of the debtor instead of a security interest only in specific assets on hand at the creation of the secured transaction. If the other attachment events have occurred, the after-acquired property is subject to the security interest as soon as the debtor acquires rights in the property. Such a security interest is called a "floating lien." The floating lien is especially useful in inventory and accounts receivable financing because only one security agreement is needed to grant the creditor a security interest in a shifting mass of collateral.

The Code also permits the use of a "future advances" provision in the security agreement, so that the collateral put up by the debtor can secure future loans. Thus, without having to enter into a new security agreement for each new loan, the creditor safely and automatically gives value each time he or she extends new credit. Future advances provisions are especially useful where a creditor has agreed to make a large loan, but the debtor needs the money only a little at a time.

Perfection of a Security Interest

A secured party must do more than just enter into a security agreement with the debtor. For maximum protection from others who might claim the collateral, the secured party must *perfect* the security interest. Ordinarily, these competing claimants will be other creditors of the debtor, a buyer of the collateral from the debtor, or an artisan who has repaired or improved the collateral. Timely perfection of a security interest gives the secured party priority over most, but not all, of these competing claimants.

[1]The 1962 version of Article 9 also limits the use of the after-acquired property clause when the collateral is a farmer's crops. [9-204(4)(a)].

Methods of Perfection.   Perfection may be accomplished in three ways: (1) automatically at the completion of the attachment events, (2) by the secured party's taking possession of the collateral, or (3) by the filing of a financing statement in the public records. By looking ahead at Table 28.1, you will see which types of perfection may or must be used for particular types of collateral. A general discussion of perfection follows. A few specialized perfection rules are introduced later, in the section on priorities.

Perfection by Attachment Only.   Article 9 grants the status of perfection to a few security interests even though nothing more than attachment has occurred. For example, the Code exempts a "purchase money security interest" (PMSI) in most consumer goods from the general filing requirement.[2] (A **purchase money security interest** is one taken or retained by a seller of the collateral—or, sometimes, one taken by a bank or other lender—to secure all or part of the purchase price.) Credit sales of consumer goods are so numerous that requiring sellers to file a financing statement for each sale would impose an unreasonable burden on the market system. Since no physical notice-giving step, such as the secured party's taking possession, is required, the debtor-purchaser can, because of the seller's attachment-only perfection status, possess the consumer goods without endangering the seller's priority as against third persons who might claim the goods. However, as will be noted later in this chapter, the creditor-seller who perfects by attachment only is not fully protected and may lose the goods to a person who buys them from the debtor.

Motor vehicles and fixtures often are consumer goods, but attachment-only perfection usually is *not* available for them. Filing a financing statement (or compliance with a certificate of title statute) is required to perfect a security interest in a motor vehicle that is required to be registered; and in many states boats, trailers, and mobile homes also are subject to such a requirement. A "fixture filing" (discussed later) is required for perfecting a security interest in a fixture.

Perfection by Secured Party's Having Possession.   For most types of collateral, a security interest is perfected if the secured party possesses the collateral or if a third-person bailee possesses it on behalf of the secured party. The pledge and field warehousing involve perfection by possession. Usually possession is an alternative to filing, but for some collateral, possession is the required perfection method. For instance, because the public expects the possessor of money to own it, a security interest in money can be perfected only by the secured party's taking possession. A similar rule applies to instruments (documents) such as checks.

Perfection by Filing a Financing Statement.   Security interests in most kinds of property may be perfected by filing a **financing statement** in the public records. The financing statement gives notice to the public that the secured party claims a security interest in the collateral. A major reason for the use of public-notice filing is to allow debtors such as purchasers of business equipment to use the collateral while

---

[2]The 1962 Section 9-302(1)(c) exempts from the filing requirement "a purchase money security interest in farm equipment having a purchase price not in excess of $2,500." The 1972 revision of Article 9 removed this exemption.

TABLE 28.1 METHODS OF PERFECTING SECURITY INTERESTS

Type of collateral	Where defined	Perfection method	Where indicated
Account (receivable) Example: A buys goods or services, promising to pay later. The promise is an account if not evidenced by an instrument or chattel paper.	9-106	Filing required, but casual or isolated assignments need not be filed. See Section 9-104(f) for assignments not subject to rules of Article 9.	9-302(1)(e) and (g)
Chattel paper Example: A buys goods from B and signs a promissory note and security agreement. The note and agreement constitute chattel paper.	9-105(1)(b)	Filing or possession by secured party.	9-304(1); 9-305
Document (of title) Example: warehouse receipts, bills of lading, dock warrants, etc. May be negotiable or nonnegotiable.	1-201(15), (45) 7-201(2) 9-105(1)(f)	Filing or possession for negotiable documents. 21-day perfection status is available. For nonnegotiable documents, other rules apply.	9-304(1) 9-304(5) 9-304(3) and (5)
Instrument Example: Checks, drafts, notes, whether or not negotiable; investment securities.	9-105(1)(i)	Possession only, except where temporary perfection status is granted.	9-304(1), (4), (5)
General intangibles Example: Patents, copyrights, liquor licenses in some states.	9-106	Filing only.	9-302(1)
Goods	9-105(1)(h)	In general, filing or possession; 21-day perfection status is available.	9-302(1)(a); 9-305 9-304(5)
Consumer goods	9-109(1)	Attachment is sufficient for purchase money security interests in consumer goods. Filing or compliance with a certificate of title statute is required for motor vehicles, boats, trailers, etc. For other security interests in consumer goods, general rules apply.	9-302(1)(d) 9-302(3) 9-302(4); 9-305
Equipment	9-109(2)	Filing, usually.	9-302(1)(a); 9-305
Farm products	9-109(3)	Filing.	By implication from 9-109(3)
Inventory	9-109(4)	Filing, usually.	9-302(1)(a)

paying for it. However, for some classes of collateral, such as accounts and general intangibles, filing is the required method of perfection because the property cannot be physically possessed by the secured party in such a way as to give notice to the public of the secured party's interest.

To be legally effective as a notice to the secured party's rival creditors, the statement must be *signed by the debtor* and must include at least the following information: (1) the *names and addresses of the debtor and the secured party;* and (2) a *description of the item,* such as "one Buick automobile, serial number 1234," *or* a *statement of the type of collateral,* such as "all of the men's clothing at the Holiday Clothiers, 44 State Street, Your City." Where the collateral is closely identified with a particular parcel of land (e.g., crops, timber, minerals, fixtures), the financing statement must also contain a description of the land concerned [9-402(1)].

The amount of information required in the financing statement has been kept to a minimum because the reason for filing it is merely to give notice that the secured party may have a security interest in the collateral described. Potential rivals of the secured party, being able to see the financing statement in the public records, are expected to make further inquiry to determine the exact state of affairs between the secured party and the debtor.

The financing statement is not to be confused with a security agreement. A security agreement lays out the contract between the secured party and the debtor, usually in some detail. The financing statement is ordinarily a brief notice, filed in the public records, of the secured party's claim to the collateral. However, if a security agreement is in writing, contains the minimum information required for a financing statement, and is signed by the debtor, the security agreement itself may serve as a financing statement (i.e., may be filed), as may a *signed copy* of the security agreement.[3]

The proper place to file a financing statement can be determined only by reference to the relevant state's version of Section 9-401. A state's filing system may be "central" (e.g., one main office located in the state capital), or "local" (e.g., offices located in each township or county). Usually the filing system is some combination of central and local files, with security interests in such collateral as farming equipment and consumer goods to be filed locally, and security interests in inventory, industrial equipment, and accounts to be filed in the office of the Secretary of State. Thus, users of the filing system who normally need to acquire credit information on a statewide basis can do so efficiently, while credit information about purely local businesses can normally be found in the county or township where the debtor lives or, sometimes, where the goods are located.

If goods are or are to become fixtures, a *fixture filing* is required, and the proper filing place is the office where a mortgage on the real estate concerned would be filed or recorded. The fixture filing must describe the fixture and the real estate to which the fixture is to be annexed, and must say that the fixture filing document is to be filed in the real estate records.

Grace Periods. Frequently, practical business needs require that a secured party have extra time, called a "grace period," to file or otherwise perfect a security interest, or have the benefit of a temporary "attachment-only" perfection status. Suppose, for example, that First Bank has a field warehousing arrangement with Martha Manufacturer and Martha receives an order for warehoused goods to be

---

[3]Under the 1962 Article 9, only the debtor is required to sign the security agreement, but both the debtor and the secured party must sign the financing statement. Under the 1972 version, only the debtor need sign the financing statement and the security agreement.

specially processed by Martha and shipped immediately to the buyer. Normally, a secured party who perfects by taking possession of the collateral (or, like First Bank, has a field warehouser do so) *loses* perfected status upon *releasing* the collateral to the debtor. However, where, as here, collateral must be released to the debtor for storage, further processing, shipping, or similar routine business purposes, the secured party's security interest *remains* perfected for up to 21 days without filing [9-304(5)]. This rule causes the least disruption of ordinary business activities, minimizes filing fees for the secured party, and eases the burden of paperwork for the filing system. If the secured party needs a longer period of perfection, he or she must, before the 21-day period expires, either file a financing statement or take possession of the collateral.

Likewise, a security interest in the *proceeds* of a debtor's disposition of collateral remains perfected for a short time. Suppose Sue sells Dora a lathe on credit and files a financing statement. If Dora sells the lathe to Terri, Sue's security interest in the lathe continues for 10 days in any identifiable cash or noncash proceeds of Dora's sale [9-306]. After that time Sue's security interest becomes "unperfected" unless Sue, within the 10 days, makes a special filing with respect to the proceeds or takes possession of them.[4]

Sellers often make credit sales of and retain purchase money security interests (PMSIs) in *fixtures*, or in *collateral other than inventory* (e.g., business equipment such as a copier). Such sellers have 10 days after the fixture is annexed or the equipment is delivered to the debtor to perfect their PMSIs by filing a financing statement [9-313(4), 9-312(4)]. In the meantime their PMSIs are perfected by attachment only. Thus, suppliers may safely make early delivery and do the paperwork later. Case 28.1, which appears later in this chapter, deals with the question of when a grace period begins.

PRIORITIES AMONG CONFLICTING INTERESTS

Sometimes a debtor becomes insolvent and the collateral is not valuable enough to satisfy the claims of all creditors who allege an interest in it. Suppose, for example, that Dan has no money of his own but wants to open a hardware store. To finance the business, he gets a $50,000 start-up loan in January from First Bank. Dan's security agreement with First Bank has an after-acquired property clause granting First Bank a security interest in "all business assets that Dan presently owns and in any that he may hereafter acquire." In February Dan gets $20,000 additional start-up financing from Second Bank. Dan's security agreement with Second Bank also has an after-acquired property clause. In March, Dan buys a $3000 computerized cash register on credit from Computocash, and $10,000 worth of inventory on credit from Hardware Suppliers. Then, in late March, Dan's business fails. First Bank immediately claims all of Dan's business assets, which now consist of the unpaid-for cash register, the $10,000 worth of inventory bought on credit from Hardware Suppliers,

---

[4]The 1962 version of Article 9 requires the secured party to make an express claim to proceeds in the financing statement, if he or she wishes to reserve a right in them. The 1972 Article 9 removes the requirement by treating the original filing as an automatic filing with respect to proceeds.

and $5000 worth of shelving and other business equipment. Second Bank claims the same assets; Computocash claims the cash register; and Hardware Suppliers claims the inventory it sold Dan on credit.

We obviously have a dispute among Dan's creditors over who gets the collateral. The priorities provisions of Article 9 settle the dispute by spelling out who is entitled to the collateral. Most conflicts over the collateral fall into one of the five categories discussed below.

Priorities among Conflicting Security Interests in the Same Collateral

Where two or more secured parties claim the same collateral, which one will prevail depends on a number of factors. Of special importance are: (1) The *nature of the conflicting security interests.* Is one a purchase money security interest (PMSI), or are all of them non-PMSIs? (2) If one of the conflicting security interests is a PMSI, *what kind of collateral is involved?*

Priorities among Nonpurchase Money Security Interests. The general Code rule is that (1) conflicting security interests rank according to priority in time of filing or other perfection, and (2) so long as conflicting security interests are unperfected, the first to attach has priority [9-312(5)]. Suppose Ron owns free and clear an antique chest worth $5000. Then he gets a $5000 loan from Carla, who plans to take possession of the chest next week as security for the loan. In the meantime Ron gets another $5000 loan from First Bank, which takes and files a security interest in the chest before Carla takes possession of it. Since First Bank perfected its security interest first, it is entitled to the chest upon Ron's default. If Carla and First Bank both fail to perfect their security interests, Carla will prevail because her interest attached first.

Priority of a Purchase Money Security Interest. The after-acquired property clause so often put into security agreements by commercial lenders can cause serious difficulty for persons who sell goods to debtors on credit. Suppose that Third Bank makes a start-up loan to New Corporation, includes an after-acquired property clause in the security agreement, and files a financing statement; and that Northside Business Machines later sells New Corporation a cash register on credit. According to the terms of Third Bank's security agreement, the cash register, being after-acquired property, would now be subject to Third Bank's security interest. To protect sellers such as Northside, who extend credit and retain a security interest in the goods sold, and to encourage them to extend credit, Article 9 gives favored treatment to the seller's PMSI *if it is properly perfected.* By following the perfection rules for particular types of collateral, Northside will prevail (have first claim) as to the goods sold on credit, *despite* Third Bank's *earlier* filed security interest in after-acquired property. If Northside does not comply exactly with the PMSI perfection requirements, Third Bank has priority in the cash register.

Recall that a PMSI arises where a seller of goods retains a security interest in the goods to secure their purchase price. But *others than sellers* can also have a PMSI. Suppose you tell Second Bank you need a loan for new office furniture, the bank makes the loan and files a financing statement covering the furniture, and you actually use the loaned money to buy office furniture. Second Bank has a PMSI in the furniture even though Bank is not the seller, because it advanced you the purchase price. Note, however, that the bank would *not* have a PMSI (and would not have the favored status against other creditors that accompanies a PMSI) if you had used the loaned money for some other purpose such as buying a delivery truck. A nonseller who advances money to enable the debtor to purchase the collateral gets a *purchase money security interest* only "if such value is in fact so used" [9-107(b)].

Special rules for perfecting PMSIs are found throughout Article 9. These rules vary according to whether the PMSI is in consumer goods, inventory, collateral other than inventory, or fixtures. Purchase money perfection rules of major importance are discussed in the following paragraphs.

1. *Consumer goods.* The PMSI is perfected (and the credit seller gets priority over the debtor's other creditors) as soon as the PMSI attaches.

2. *Collateral other than inventory.* An example would be equipment for a retail store or a machine for a factory. The PMSI must be perfected by filing no later than 10 days after the debtor receives possession of the collateral.

3. *Inventory.* The purchase money secured party (e.g., the creditor-seller) must do two things before the debtor receives possession of the inventory. (*a*) The purchase money secured party must perfect the PMSI by filing a financing statement. (*b*) The secured party must give written notice, to record holders of conflicting security interests in the inventory (such as a bank with an after-acquired property clause), that the purchase money secured party "expects to acquire a purchase money security interest in inventory of the debtor" [9-312(3)].

Suppose Fifth Bank, under the future-advances provisions of a filed loan agreement, grants Doris loans to purchase inventory. If Doris is fraudulent or careless, she might keep the money she borrowed from the bank for inventory and purchase the inventory on credit, granting to her inventory seller a PMSI in the inventory. The requirement that the inventory seller give advance notice to Fifth Bank enables the bank to police Doris's inventory purchasing activities and thus to avoid possible loss. And the inventory seller, by complying with the Code requirements (filing to perfect and giving the required notice before delivering the inventory to Doris), gets protection from previously filed security interests of other secured parties and will therefore be more willing to extend credit.

4. *Fixtures.* The requirements for perfecting a PMSI in fixtures are discussed later under the heading Priorities of Security Interests in Fixtures.

Case 28.1 involves the question of how long a person has in which to perfect a security interest.

CASE 28.1   In re Automated Bookbinding Services, Inc.
471 F.2d 546 (4th Cir. 1972)

Facts: Automated Bookbinding Services received a loan from Finance Company of America (FCA), secured by a chattel mortgage covering Automated's equipment and after-acquired property. FCA perfected its security interest by filing a financing statement. Then Automated bought a new bookbinder on credit from Hans Mueller Corp. (HMC). HMC retained a purchase money security interest in the machine for the unpaid balance.

HMC was to install the machine. Fifteen cases of component parts arrived at

Automated's plant on several dates between May 26 and June 2, 1970. Installation was completed sometime between June 13 and June 19, 1970. On June 15, HMC filed a financing statement to perfect its PMSI. Later Automated filed a petition in bankruptcy. The referee in bankruptcy held that Automated had received possession of the binder on June 2 when the last crates were delivered, and that since HMC perfected its PMSI more than ten days later, HMC lost its purchase money priority. HMC argued that Automated did not receive possession until the machine was installed—on June 13 at the earliest—and that the June 15 filing was timely.

Question: Did HMC make a timely filing?

Answer: No. Therefore the bookbinder is subject to the claim of FCA because of its after-acquired property clause.

Reasoning: A PMSI has priority over conflicting security interests only if the PMSI is perfected within ten days after the debtor receives possession of the collateral. For the purpose of this perfection rule, "possession" means physical possession of the machine, regardless of whether it was actually installed. If the seller could postpone filing until all its contractual duties were completed, it could avoid the filing requirement indefinitely. This result would be contrary to the reason for the requirement, to assure prompt notice to competing creditors.

Priorities between Security Interests and the Interest of a Third-Person Purchaser

Sometimes the conflict is between the secured party and a purchaser of the collateral from the debtor. A buyer of goods in the ordinary course of business (e.g., a person who in good faith buys goods from a wholesale dealer or a retail store) takes the goods *free of* a security interest created by the seller in favor of the seller's creditor even though the security interest is perfected and the buyer knows of its existence [9-307(1)]. This rule applies primarily where the dealer has granted to his or her lender a security interest in inventory and then makes sales from the inventory. The rule is intended to encourage buyers to pay full market values by minimizing their fear of loss at the hands of unseen creditors. To be protected, however, the "buyer in ordinary course of business" must, by definition, be in good faith. If the buyer knows that the terms of the security agreement between the seller and the seller's creditor are being violated, the buyer does not come within the meaning of buyer in ordinary course of business, and he or she takes (the goods) *subject to* the security interest of the seller's creditor. Most good faith purchasers of chattel paper, negotiable instruments, and documents of title receive similar protection.

A dealer in consumer goods faces a serious problem when a consumer purchases the goods on credit and resells them to another consumer before paying the dealer for them. Suppose Camera Shop sells an expensive camera on credit to Joan for her personal use, that she sells the camera to her neighbor Fred before making any of the payments, immediately spends the money, and is now insolvent. If Camera Shop has retained a PMSI in the camera and has perfected the interest by *attachment only*, Camera Shop's PMSI gives it priority (first claim to the camera) over Joan's other creditors, but it provides *no* protection against Fred (and Fred may keep the camera) if he bought the encumbered camera "without knowledge of the security interest, for value and for his own personal, family or household purposes" [9-307(2)]. However, if Camera Shop had perfected the PMSI by filing before Joan resold the camera to Fred, Camera Shop would be protected from a claim of ownership by Fred or any other subsequent purchaser.

Priorities of Liens Arising by Operation of Law

Sometimes goods subject to a security interest are sent out for repairs or improvements. What if the repairer (bailee) remains unpaid? Will his or her lien have priority over the security interest? Section 9-310 gives priority to common law possessory liens and to most statutory possessory liens for materials or services furnished with respect to goods subject to a security interest, even though the security interest is perfected. Workers who repair or improve goods in the ordinary course of their business thus have the traditional bailee's lien on goods in their possession until their just charges have been paid, unless a statute granting the lien expressly subordinates it to a prior security interest.

Priorities of Security Interests in Fixtures

Article 9 governs the creation and priority of security interests in fixtures, but leaves the definition of "fixture" largely up to non-Code real estate law. However, "no security interest exists under this Article in ordinary building materials incorporated into an improvement on land" [9-313(2)]. The rights of materials sellers are governed by local real estate mechanics' lien laws.

The fixture priority rules are so numerous and complex that only some major ones are discussed here. The rules are best understood by examining the conflicts that they are intended to resolve. The usual conflict is between purchase money fixture financers and real estate financers. Real estate financers (mortgagees) argue that to offset building depreciation or otherwise to encourage real estate financing, the law should give real estate mortgagees first claim to any fixtures later annexed to the real estate. Fixture financers argue that unless they are allowed to repossess unpaid-for fixtures, fixture credit will diminish and the improvement of real estate will be slowed.

It is common for a fixture seller to have to contend with real estate claimants whose interests in the real estate arose *before* the fixture was annexed, as well as with real estate interests that arose *afterward*. As the following illustrations indicate, the sequence of events is one of several factors to consider in determining who has priority in a fixture.

Suppose Oscar buys a house or a commercial building and soon afterward discovers that he must replace the worn-out furnace. Oscar buys an expensive furnace "on time" from Frank, who reserves a PMSI in it. Then Frank installs the furnace in Oscar's building, which is subject to a recorded real estate mortgage in favor of Rachel. For Frank's PMSI in the furnace to prevail over Rachel's earlier recorded mortgage on the real estate, Frank must perfect his PMSI by a *fixture filing within 10 days* after the furnace is annexed.

Now suppose that the furnace is to be installed in a *new* house that Oscar is having built, and that Rachel is the construction financer. Rachel's **construction mortgage** will prevail over Frank's PMSI in the furnace if she takes two steps: (1) She must be sure that the furnace is installed (annexed) before the house itself is completed, *and* (2) she must record (file) the construction mortgage before the furnace becomes a fixture [9-313(6)]. By completing these two steps, construction financers who may have advanced money for major appliances as well as for the basic building can protect themselves from a surprise PMSI held by a fixture seller. Construction financers do not have this protection in the states still governed by the 1962 Article 9, since under that version a fixture financer acquires a "permanent" attachment-only priority over real estate interests existing at the time of annexation.

In many other fixture priority situations, the first creditor to file prevails. Suppose Oscar owns a house and buys a new furnace on credit from Frank. Frank retains a PMSI and installs the furnace. Then, before Frank makes a fixture filing, Rachel lends Oscar a large sum of money and takes as security a mortgage on Oscar's house. As compared to Frank, Rachel is a *subsequent* lender. Nevertheless, Rachel's mortgage prevails over Frank's PMSI in the fixture *if Rachel records her mortgage before Frank makes a fixture filing.* If Frank files first, *he* wins. The 1962 rule is similar. That is, to have priority over subsequent purchasers of the real estate or subsequent mortgage lenders such as Rachel, the fixture seller (Frank) must file first.

Priorities of Security Interests in Accessions and Commingled Goods

Accessions are goods installed in or affixed to other goods. For example, Orville owns a delivery truck, its engine burns out, and Orville's mechanic installs a replacement engine. The engine is an accession.

The following priority rule applies to accessions. If a security interest in an accession (Orville's replacement engine) *attaches before* the accession is installed or affixed, the security interest in the *accession* usually takes priority over the claims of all persons to the *whole* (Orville's truck) [9-314]. To prevail over subsequent purchasers and lenders, the accession financer must perfect the security interest in the accession, or the holder of the subsequent interest must have knowledge of the accession financer's interest, before the subsequent interest arises.

Suppose, for example, that Orville gives Thrifty Loan a security interest in the truck to secure a loan, and Thrifty files a financing statement. Then the engine burns out, Orville buys a replacement engine from Sam on credit, and Sam retains a PMSI before delivering the engine to Orville. Since Sam's PMSI attached before the engine was installed, the PMSI prevails over Thrifty's earlier perfected security interest.

Now suppose that Thrifty made the loan and took its security interest in the truck *after* Orville replaced the engine. To prevail over Thrifty, Sam must have *perfected* his PMSI in the engine (or Thrifty must have received knowledge of it) *before* Thrifty's interest arose (attached). This rule is for Thrifty's protection, since unless Thrifty has notice of the accession financer's (Sam's) claim before extending credit, Thrifty would extend credit believing that the new engine is part of its collateral.

Commingled goods are those that are combined with others to form a single mass or product. For example, flour, sugar, and eggs may be commingled into cake mix, or component parts may be assembled into a machine. Where goods subject to a perfected security interest are commingled with other goods so that their identity is lost in the mass, the security interest continues in the mass or product [9-315]. Where several such security interests continue in the mass, each of the various secured parties is entitled to a pro rata share of the mass. Suppose Egbert, Wheatley, and Sugarman sell eggs, flour, and sugar to Cake Mix Corp. and perfect their security interests. Then Cake Mix commingles the goods into a batch of cake mix. If Cake Mix fails to pay the suppliers, they have equal priority as to the mass, and each is entitled to share the batch of cake mix to the extent of that supplier's contribution to the mass.

Where component parts are assembled into a machine, a person who has a security interest in them must elect at the time of filing whether to treat them as accessions or as commingled goods. The difference is important, because upon the debtor's default a secured party may remove accessions (repossess them).

DEFAULT AND FORECLOSURE

Meaning of Default

Since "default" is not defined in the Code, the common law meaning of failure to perform a legal duty applies. Usually the duties of debtor and secured party are spelled out in the security agreement. Nonpayment by the debtor is the most common default, and the security agreement may identify additional events that constitute default. Examples are the debtor's unauthorized removal or sale of collateral, the debtor's failure to insure the collateral, the debtor's failure to furnish additional collateral if the value of the original collateral declines, the debtor's insolvency or bankruptcy, and loss or destruction of the collateral.

Rights and Duties of Secured Party upon Debtor's Default

When the debtor defaults, the secured party may enforce the security interest by taking possession of the collateral and (1) under certain circumstances *keeping* it in satisfaction of the debt, or (2) *disposing* of the collateral in some commercially reasonable way, e.g., by sale [9-501]. The secured party may also use any judicial procedure available under non-Code law (e.g., state execution or foreclosure laws).

Acquiring Control of the Collateral.   If the secured party does not already possess the collateral, he or she will need to acquire control of it. This can be done in a variety of ways. To collect accounts, the secured party may notify the debtor's account debtor (usually a purchaser from the debtor to whom the debtor has extended credit) to make payment directly to the secured party. As to collateral in possession of the debtor, the secured party has two basic options. (1) Unless otherwise agreed, the secured party may simply take possession of the collateral after default, if he or she can do so without breach of the peace. (2) The secured party may go to court to acquire possession (and *must* do so where a breach of the peace is threatened). In lieu of removing heavy equipment, the secured party may render it unusable (e.g., by removing a control device) and dispose of (e.g., sell) it on the debtor's premises.

What constitutes a breach of the peace varies according to the circumstances. Ordinarily, an objection by the debtor or a third party such as a custodian of the property involves a breach of the peace, since physical violence is a possible outcome. Breaking into the debtor's premises to get the collateral or posing as a police officer is also forbidden. But removing the collateral from a public street, a parking lot, or even the open parts of the debtor's premises is permitted, if done without objection by the debtor or a third party. As suggested by Case 28.2, mere lack of consent is not necessarily a peace-threatening objection.

CASE 28.2 Marine Midland Bank-Central v. Cote
351 So. 2d 750 (Fla. App. 1977)

Facts: Marine Midland had a purchase money security interest in a car sold to Cote. Cote was in default, and Altes, acting on behalf of Marine Midland, entered Cote's private property and removed the car from the open carport. Cote sued the bank for trespass and was awarded $2,500 in compensatory and $2,500 in punitive damages. Bank appealed.

Question: Did the bank's agent commit a trespass by entering Cote's property to repossess the car?

Answer: No.

Reasoning: Under the common law, as codified by the UCC, a secured party who is entitled to immediate possession of a thing is privileged to peacefully enter on the debtor's land even where, as here, the security agreement authorizes repossession but does not specifically authorize entry. This is a limited privilege and may be exercised only without breach of the peace. So, unless the parties agree otherwise, when a vehicle is covered by a valid security agreement providing that the creditor has a right to repossess the vehicle upon default, repossession of the vehicle from the debtor's unenclosed carport without threat or use of force is not a trespass.

Disposing of the Collateral.   After obtaining the collateral, the secured party will want to keep or dispose of it. The secured party's keeping it in satisfaction of the debt and thereby terminating the debtor's interest in it is called "strict foreclosure" and is appropriate where the value of the collateral is equal to or less than the amount of the debt. However, strict foreclosure is permitted only where the secured party gives written notice of intention to keep the collateral and the debtor does not object in writing. If the debtor makes timely objection to strict foreclosure, the secured party must dispose of the collateral. Disposal is required also where the collateral is *consumer goods* and the debtor has paid 60 percent of the purchase price or loan [9-505].

The secured party may dispose of collateral in any *commercially reasonable* way, whether by sale, lease, or otherwise [9-504]. A foreclosure sale may be public or private, as long as it is commercially reasonable. In any disposition, the secured party keeps the amount of proceeds necessary to cover the debt and foreclosure expenses. Any surplus goes to the debtor. However, as Cases 28.3 and 28.4 indicate, the debtor remains liable for any deficiency unless the secured party is denied the right to the deficiency because of the secured party's misconduct.

Largely to protect the debtor, Article 9 imposes disposition rules that cannot be changed by the security agreement. For instance, the secured party must exercise reasonable care to preserve collateral in his or her possession; the debtor has a right to redeem (buy back) repossessed collateral before it is disposed of; and the debtor is entitled to appropriate remedies if the secured party fails to comply with Article 9. However, after default, the debtor may waive some of these rights.

Prior dealings between the debtor and the secured party may affect the secured party's right to repossess and dispose of the collateral. Suppose Dan is late with some of his payments and Clark accepts them without protest. This pattern of conduct could reasonably cause Dan to believe that delay in making a future payment will not result in seizure of the collateral. Under such circumstances Clark may lose the right to repossess the collateral unless he first notifies Dan that late payments will no longer be tolerated.

CASE 28.3 In re Bishop
482 F.2d 381 (4th Cir. 1973)

Facts: The Bishops bought an outboard motorboat and trailer on credit. The seller assigned the Bishops' note and purchase money security agreement to Roanoke. The Bishops defaulted on the note. Roanoke repossessed the boat and trailer, sold them, and claimed a deficiency of more than $1,000. Then Mrs. Bishop filed a petition in bankruptcy. Roanoke sought a stay (suspension) of Mrs. Bishop's discharge in bankruptcy so that Roanoke could take action in state court to get a deficiency judgment against her. The referee denied Roanoke's request on the ground that Roanoke would not be entitled to a deficiency judgment because it had not complied with UCC provisions governing the sale of repossessed collateral.

Question: Was Roanoke disqualified from collecting the deficiency?

Answer: Yes.

Reasoning: Roanoke itself had purchased the boat at the sale and then resold it for $1,000 less than the indebtedness. A secured party *may* itself purchase the collateral, but only at a public sale. Here the sale was conducted on a nearby used car lot, there was no advertising or other notice to the public of the sale, and the only people present were Roanoke's representatives and two employees of the used car lot. Since this private sale was not likely to produce the full market value of the collateral, it was commercially unreasonable, and Roanoke was disqualified from collecting the deficiency.

CASE 28.4 Michigan Nat'l Bank v. Marston
185 N.W.2d 47 (Mich. App. 1970)

Facts: Marston purchased damaged automobiles and repaired and resold them. He obtained a $1,350 loan from Michigan National Bank to buy a fire-damaged convertible and gave the bank a security interest in the car without revealing its condition. Marston became disabled and went into bankruptcy without repaying the loan. The bank repossessed the car, which had accumulated $600 in storage charges. The bank tried to sell the car to three dealers, but only one—the garage owner who had stored the car—made an offer, for $500. The bank rejected the offer because the offeror was a poor credit risk. The bank then sued Marston for the amount of his note and received judgment against him on the ground that he had obtained the loan under false pretenses and therefore was not discharged from that debt. Marston appealed, contending that the bank was required to dispose of the collateral before suing for the amount of the note.

Question: Was the bank required to dispose of the car before suing for the amount of the note?

Answer: No.

Reasoning: The UCC requires only that the bank act in a commercially reasonable manner in disposing or attempting to dispose of collateral. Here the garageman's lien for storage charges was superior to the bank's lien and possibly was for an amount greater than the value of the car. Bank is not required to undergo further expense and increase the amount owed by a debtor already in default. Bank made reasonable efforts to sell the car. This is all that is required of the secured party in this instance.

SUMMARY

To make credit extension easier and safer, Article 9 substituted the term "security interest" for the variety of pre-Code descriptive terms, developed a simplified public-notice filing system, established a system of priorities for the states to use in common, and set up a uniform method of liquidating collateral after default.

The secured party receives maximum protection if the security interest is attached and perfected. Attachment is the process of creating a security interest and making it enforceable against the debtor. Perfection is the process of making the security interest enforceable against others than the debtor. Perfection occurs sometimes upon completion of the attachment events, but more commonly occurs by the secured party's taking possession of the collateral or filing a financing statement.

A perfected PMSI usually prevails over earlier perfected security interests. In most other conflict situations, the first to perfect or, if there is no perfection, the first to attach prevails. Similar priority rules apply to fixtures.

Upon the debtor's default the secured party has liberal repossession and disposition rights. However, the debtor is entitled to a commercially reasonable disposition of the collateral. The debtor is entitled to any surplus realized from disposition of the collateral, but remains personally liable for any deficiency unless freed from that liability by the secured party's misconduct.

REVIEW QUESTIONS

1. (a) Why are security interests in fixtures covered by Article 9 rather than by real estate law? (b) Why does Article 9 cover sales of accounts and chattel paper?

2. (a) What is the Code definition of *security interest?* (b) Distinguish between a true lease and a "lease" that creates a security interest.

3. What must be done for a security interest to attach?

4. (a) What is a floating lien? (b) What is the purpose of an after-acquired property clause? Of a future-advances provision?

5. Explain the legal consequence of perfecting a security interest.

6. (a) Why is a PMSI given priority? (b How may a PMSI in inventory be perfected? Why is the procedure relatively complex?

7. Naming the usual participants, illustrate each of the following: (a) Conflicting security interests in the same collateral. (b) Conflicting security interests in a fixture.

8. What is the meaning of default?

9. How may the secured party repossess collateral upon the debtor's default?

10. Is a sale required for a disposition of collateral to be commercially reasonable? Explain.

CASE PROBLEMS

1. NCR sold a cash register to Borgwald and filed a financing statement. Because NCR's clerk misspelled Borgwald's name, the financing statement was filed under the name of "Boywald." It was also filed under Borgwald's correctly spelled trade name. A year later Borgwald granted to Valley National Bank a security interest in personal property used in his business, including the cash register. The security agreement stated Borgwald's individual name but not the trade name. The bank properly filed a financing statement. Borgwald defaulted on the bank loan, and the bank claimed the cash register as part of its collateral. NCR protested, contending that its filing was sufficient to perfect its PMSI in the machine. Was NCR's filing sufficient to give it the protection of the filing statute?

2. Mar-K-Z Motors and Leasing Co. was primarily engaged in leasing automobiles, but it also sold automobiles no longer used in the leasing operation. In 1969 Mar-K-Z acquired a new Buick. The certificate of title issued by the Secretary of State showed that Mar-K-Z was the owner, that the car was a "lease unit," and that American National Bank had a lien on it for $6250. Mar-K-Z leased the car for a time, and after reacquiring possession of it sold it to Buttel. Mar-K-Z immediately quit making payments and did not pay the bank any of the proceeds of the sale. The bank sued Buttel to recover the car from him. Was the bank entitled to the car?

3. Mousel agreed in writing to sell his cattle to Daringer. Under the agreement, Mousel was to possess the cattle until they were paid for and he was to receive payment as "agister" for their care and feeding. Later Daringer borrowed $58,000 from State Securities to pay for the cattle, and State Securities took and perfected a security interest in them. Then Daringer defaulted on the loan. Under a state statute, an agister "shall have a first . . . lien upon [livestock] for the feed and care bestowed by him . . ., provided the holders of any prior liens shall have agreed in writing to the contract for the feed and care of the livestock. . . ." Mousel's reasonable charge was $18,523. State Securities contended that the cattle were not subject to Mousel's lien because State Securities did not agree in writing to the contract for their care. Whose lien should prevail?

4. Waters purchased a new Ford from Jones Ford, Inc., and signed a security agreement containing default and repossession provisions that could be exercised by the financer, Ford Motor Credit Co. Waters fell 2 months behind in his payments. FMCC, acting through its agent Seagren, repossessed the car by making a duplicate set of keys and driving the car from the parking lot of Waters' place of business. Waters sued FMCC for wrongful repossession of his car. Was the repossession wrongful?

5. Penrose Industries owned radio station WPEN. William and Harry Sylk, the chief officers of Penrose, pledged to Old Colony Trust Co. the stock of WPEN as security for a loan. Penrose defaulted. After giving the Sylks notice, Old Colony sold the stock at a private sale. The Sylks contended that the use of a private rather than a public sale was commercially unreasonable. Was the sale commercially unreasonable?

CHAPTER 29

INSURANCE

$\mathbf{E}$veryone faces the risk of economic or financial loss. Economic losses can occur in carrying on a business or in our personal lives. Losses, for example, can be caused by negligence, theft, vandalism, disease, labor disputes, or natural forces such as storms, floods, and earthquakes. Among the types of economic loss which can occur are damage to or total loss of physical property such as household furnishings, real estate, and business equipment and inventory; loss of income, future productive capacity, and business reputation (goodwill); loss of savings or other accumulated assets that must be used to pay expenses attending illness, injury, and death; loss of assets used to pay court-ordered judgments arising from injuries caused to others or damage to their property; and loss to a family or business of the valuable personal services of a decedent.

Preventing and reducing losses obviously concern business people. Insurance is an important topic to understand because it is one of several ways we may lessen the impact of economic losses. Insurance permits a business to shift risk of losses to an insurance company. Other techniques of "risk management," as it is called today, include risk control (loss prevention) and planned self-insuring (often done by large businesses).

This chapter deals with insurance because it is the primary means of transferring and distributing the risk of financial loss. We begin with a discussion of how insurance works, and then cover insurance against personal risk (life and health insurance), and insurance against risks to property (property and liability insurance).

HOW INSURANCE WORKS

The Purpose of Insurance

Transferring Risk.   The main purpose of insurance is to transfer risk from one person (either the insured person or the policyowner) to another (the insurer). This transfer of risk is accomplished by a two-party contract called an "insurance policy." In a typical insurance policy, in exchange for a payment called a "premium" an insurance company (the insurer) agrees with another party (usually the "insured") to assume a *named* risk that otherwise would have to be borne by the insured person or his or her family or business associates. The transfer of the risk from the insured to the insurer ordinarily occurs when the insurance contract is entered into. If the insured suffers a loss covered by the policy, the insurer pays money according to the policy's terms, usually to the insured or a third-person beneficiary. This payment is a compensation or reimbursement for actual loss, called "indemnity." Insurance is based on the *principle of indemnity*, that is, payment will be made to compensate for an actual loss. For example, suppose Alice Smith pays an insurer $100 to insure her expensive sportscar against fire or theft. If the car is destroyed by fire, the insurer will *indemnify* (reimburse) Alice by paying her the value of the car as of the time of the loss. Through insurance, Alice has traded the possibility of a heavy loss for a certain but lesser cost, the premium paid.

Meaning of "The Insured."   There are two types of insurance: property and liability insurance covering property risks, and life and health insurance covering personal risks. Generally, property insurance protects against the loss of property, and liability insurance protects against legal liability for damages caused by torts such as negligence. Life insurance protects against losses to third persons when someone dies. Health insurance protects against losses caused by illness or injury.

In *property and liability insurance,* "the insured" is any person protected by a policy from risk of loss. Suppose Alice Smith purchases automobile insurance covering liability for personal injuries resulting from negligent operation of her car. The insurance policy, if typical, will protect Alice and other licensed drivers to whom she might occasionally lend the car. All these persons are "insureds" under the policy and have the right to reimbursement (indemnity) from the insurer for amounts they are obligated to pay in settlement of claims covered by the policy.

Suppose Alice's employee drives Alice's car with her consent and negligently injures Ben Hitt. The employee is an "insured" under Alice's policy, and Ben has a claim against the employee for hospital bills, loss of income, and so on. As an insured, the employee gets reimbursement from the insurance company for any amount, up to the policy limit, he or she is required to pay Ben. The insurer might make payments directly to Ben without litigation, but Ben is not himself an insured under Alice's policy. Ben is only a claimant against an insured.

In *life insurance,* "the insured" is the person whose life is covered by the insurance contract. The death benefit specified by the policy will be paid to someone other than the insured—directly to a named third person called the "beneficiary" or to the insured's estate for distribution to others. In life insurance, as in some other kinds of insurance, the person insured will often not be a party to the insurance contract. Suppose that Alice Smith and Ken Jones are partners. Alice buys an insurance policy covering Ken's life and names herself as the policy's beneficiary. Alice and the insurance company are the contracting parties. Ken is the insured—meaning Ken is the person whose life is the subject of the insurance policy. Alice is the beneficiary as well as the "policyholder" and the "policyowner."

Spreading Risk through Pooling and Reinsurance.   Insurers spread the risks they have assumed by "pooling" and "reinsurance." **Pooling** treats a large number of individual risks of a certain kind as a single group or "pool" so that the total loss likely to be sustained by the pool of insured persons can be accurately estimated. Then individual losses are distributed among everyone in the pool by requiring them to pay the same premium per unit of coverage regardless of the amount of loss sustained by any one individual. The premium paid by an insured individual covers the insured person's share of predicted pool loss as well as administrative costs and any insurance company profit.

Reinsurance is a contractual arrangement in which an insurance company transfers (cedes) part of its total risks (not individual insurance contracts) to another insurance organization called a "reinsurer." The ceding company is somewhat like an individual who buys insurance, because the ceding company pays the reinsurer to assume part of a risk that the ceding company believes might be too great for it to bear alone. The reinsurer further distributes (spreads) the risk by pooling and further reinsurance.

Indemnity and
Insurable
Interest

The Indemnity Principle.   The principle of indemnity (compensation for actual loss) is based on the idea that insurance is a system for spreading losses and not for generating a profit for the insured. Therefore, in the event of casualty an insured person should be limited to reimbursement (indemnity) for loss actually suffered.

Suppose that Pam has identical medical insurance policies with two different insurers, that each policy will reimburse her for up to $5000 in hospital expenses in the event of her illness, that she becomes ill and incurs only $5000 in hospital expenses, and that each policy has a "coordination-of-benefits" clause. A coordination-of-benefits clause limits the insurer to paying for only a portion of a loss if other insurance also covers the same loss. Pam files a claim with each insurer for $5000 (for a total of $10,000). If she were allowed to collect the $10,000 she sought, she would receive $5000 profit, and premiums charged to all insured individuals would have to be large enough to provide that profit. Under the coordination-of-benefits clauses, Pam may collect only the amount of her loss and, moreover, *only a proportion* of her loss from each of the companies with which she had a policy. Since she has policies of identical coverage with two companies, she will collect $2500 from each company. Coordination of benefits is consistent with the concept that insurance should be a mechanism for reimbursing losses, not one for providing the insured with a profit.

The principle of indemnity is the basis of many legal rules governing insurance contracts such as the prohibition against the use of insurance contracts as gambling devices. However, the indemnity principle of reimbursement for actual loss only is less strictly applied to life insurance than to other kinds such as property, liability, and health insurance. Moreover, in some modern property insurance contracts, reimbursement for property losses is based upon *replacement cost* rather than an actual value of the property at the time of loss.

The Insurable Interest Requirement. The principle of indemnity is the source of the general requirement that a person who buys insurance must have an insurable interest in the property or life insured. An *insurable interest* is the financial stake that a person has in property or in someone's life or health. A person with an insurable interest usually will suffer financially if the insured property is damaged, or will lose an expected economic advantage if the insured person dies. For example, you have an insurable interest in your car but not in your neighbor's car. In property insurance, the following circumstances normally give rise to an insurable interest:

1. Ownership of, or other property rights in, property
2. Contract rights, such as in a contract for sale of goods
3. Potential legal liability to others

In a contract for the sale of goods, for example, a buyer obtains an insurable interest in the goods when they are *identified* to the contract (marked or otherwise designated as the subject of a particular contract for sale) even though the buyer might not yet have title to or possession of the goods. In property and liability insurance the insurable interest need exist only at the time of loss. This rule and the rules relating to identification of goods to a contract permit a person to make arrangements for insurance before acquiring property or being otherwise responsible for the loss of the property.

A person may obtain insurance on his or her own life. But to obtain valid insurance on the life of another, the person buying the insurance must have an insurable interest, that is, a financial stake in the other's life. This requirement is usually met when there is a close family relationship, where a person seeks to insure the life of his or her spouse or minor child to cover expenses resulting from that person's untimely death. Where an adult seeks to insure a parent's life, however, or the life of a brother, sister, uncle, niece, or other such family member, the courts tend to require something more than the family relationship itself (for example, an existing or potential financial interest) before holding that there is an insurable interest. (The courts differ as to whether an existing, or merely a possible, financial interest must be shown.) Where there is no family relationship, an actual financial interest is required. A creditor has an insurable interest in the life of his or her debtor (to the extent of the debt); a business entity has an insurable interest in the life of a key employee; and a partner may have an insurable interest in the life of his or her partner.

In life insurance, the insurable interest need exist only when the policy is taken out. By recognizing the validity of the policy even after the insurable interest ceases, this rule saves any cash values that might have accumulated. (Cash values accumulate for the policyowner in policies where the premium charged exceeds the amount set aside for claims, expenses, and profits of the insurer.) Also, the marketability of life insurance is improved by making clear to the public that policies will be paid if loss occurs.

The requirement of an insurable interest is useful for two main reasons:

1. The insurable interest is evidence that personal or business economic loss is likely and that the insurance contract is not just a gambling device for making a speculative gain. Insuring the life of a total stranger in the hope of making a large gain from a small investment in premiums involves no insurable interest and violates public policy, resulting in an unenforceable wagering contract. In contrast, insuring the life of your business partner may involve an expectation of economic loss to you if your partner dies. If a loss is expected, an insurable interest is present.

2. The presence of an insurable interest tends to reduce the possibility of an intentional loss or fraud for purposes of collecting insurance proceeds. If Edwin insures Jenny's car but has no insurable interest in it, Edwin might be tempted to destroy the car to collect the insurance. Determining whether an insurable interest exists can sometimes be difficult, as the following case illustrates.

CASE 29.1   **Butler v. Farmers' Insurance Company of Arizona**
616 P.2d 46 (Ariz. 1980)

Facts: In 1976, Butler unknowingly purchased a stolen 1967 Austin-Healy sports car for $3500. Two years later the Tucson police seized the car and returned it to its lawful owner. Butler had insured the car against loss, and he filed a claim with his insurance company for the car's value. Claiming Butler lacked an insurable interest, the insurer refused to reimburse him for the loss, offering instead to return his premiums. Butler sued the insurer for the car's value.

Question: Does a good faith purchaser of a stolen car have an insurable interest in that car?

Answer: Yes. Butler should recover from the insurer.

Reasoning:
An insurable interest is "any actual, lawful and substantial economic interest in the safety or preservation of the subject of the insurance, free from loss, destruction or pecuniary damage or impairment." Butler's interest in the car was both lawful and substantial because as a good faith purchaser of a stolen car he had a valid legal right to the car against everyone except the rightful owner. Also, Butler could have been liable to the true owner for the tort of conversion had the car been lost or damaged. Butler had a definite interest in maintaining the car in an undamaged condition.

The Insurance Contract

An insurance policy is a contract subject to the principles of contract law discussed in Chapters 6 to 14, but because of the specialized nature of insurance contracts, some particular aspects of contract law applying to insurance require consideration.

A Contract of Adhesion. Insurance is often a contract of adhesion because the typical purchaser has little or no power to negotiate the price or other terms of the insurance policy. The purchaser can choose the kind and amount of coverage, the beneficiary, and so on. But otherwise the purchase of insurance is usually a "take it or leave it" proposition with the terms of a very complex standard-form contract being imposed on the purchaser. Large businesses, however, have the bargaining power to purchase custom-tailored insurance.

As is pointed out in Chapter 6, contracts of adhesion have legitimate uses, and insurance is an example. If all terms of an insurance coverage had to be bargained individually, transaction costs would be too high. If insurers could not use standard-form contracts, the limits of an insurer's liability would be uncertain, making losses less predictable and premiums difficult to set. Yet, an unscrupulous insurance company can use the insurance contract of adhesion to take unfair advantage of purchasers. To preserve the advantages of standard-form insurance contracts while curbing their abuse, state administrative agencies control the content of insurance contracts, assuring fair treatment of policyholders, insureds, and beneficiaries. The courts interpret unclear policy terms against the insurance company which wrote the contract.

The Offer and Acceptance. The insurer's liability under an insurance policy usually arises immediately upon contract formation. Because this liability can greatly exceed amounts paid in premiums, both the insurer and the insured have a strong interest in knowing when an "offer" and "acceptance" have created an insurance contract.

Ordinarily, insurance policies are sold by a representative of the insurer, called an "agent." In property and liability insurance, the insurer may cancel a policy sold by an agent by giving a legally required notice to the insured and refunding any unearned premiums. Because the property and liability insurer may free itself from risks that have become unacceptable, the insurer gives its agents the authority to enter into binding contracts without consulting the company in advance about the merits of each individual contract. Often the agent may orally accept an applicant's offer and bill him or her later, and the property or liability applicant acquires immediate coverage subject to possible cancellation.

In contrast, the right of a life insurance company to cancel life insurance policies is sharply limited by law. Life insurance companies therefore prefer to check an applicant's health, and determine whether there is an insurable interest before issuing a policy. To give themselves time to make a proper investigation and to reserve to themselves the decision of whether to grant insurance coverage, life insurers often restrict their agents' authority to accept offers.

In life insurance, four common situations might lead to an offer and acceptance creating a life insurance contract.

1. A person fills out an application for insurance but does not pay the first premium. The applicant is inviting the insurer to make an offer. The company offers by presenting a policy for acceptance and the applicant accepts by paying the first premium.

2. A person offers by applying for insurance and paying the first premium. The insurer accepts by delivering the policy to the applicant or to the insurer's agent for unconditional delivery to the applicant.

3. A person offers by applying for insurance and paying the first premium. The agent immediately gives the applicant a "conditional receipt" making the insurance effective immediately (or as of a certain date) on condition that the applicant is found to be insurable. The insurer has accepted the applicant's offer. If the applicant is not insurable, there is no insurance coverage and the premium will be refunded. If the applicant was insurable, coverage occurs at the time stated in the conditional receipt, even though the applicant might, for example, die in an auto accident before insurability is determined.

4. The insurance company gives its agent authority to make temporary binding contracts. The agent accepts the applicant's offer by issuing either a "binding receipt" or a temporary insurance policy. The applicant has insurance coverage while the company decides whether or not to grant the requested coverage. The temporary coverage ends when the company issues a policy, when the applicant is denied insurance coverage, or at some other time set by the company or by law.

Assignment of Insurance Contracts.   For many reasons, people attempt to assign their insurance policies. A purchaser of real or personal property might want to be assigned the seller's fire insurance. A person might wish to sell or give away a policy of insurance on his or her life, or might wish to use the policy as collateral (security) for a loan. Some assignments of insurance are permitted and some are not.

Generally, contracts of property and liability insurance are treated as "personal" contracts and are *not* assignable without the consent of the insurer. This allows the insurer to screen out unacceptable risks. If, for example, a homeowner with a good safety record had an absolute right to assign his or her fire insurance policy to a homeowner with a record of serious fires, the assignor could, by assigning the policy, impose a heavier risk on the insurer than warranted by the premium the assignor paid.

Marine insurance (on a ship or its cargo while at sea) usually may be assigned without the consent of the insurer. In the transshipment of goods, there is a need to have a type of insurance that is readily transferable. The law will give effect to an assignment of marine insurance over the objections of the insurer unless the policy contains a clause restricting or prohibiting assignment.

Life insurance is more freely assignable than property and liability insurance, but assignability depends very much on the kind of situation involved. *After the death of the insured,* a life insurance policy is a promise by the insurer to pay money and as such is freely assignable. A policyowner, such as a creditor, could sell (assign) his right to collect under the policy despite any clause prohibiting assignment.

An assignment of a life insurance policy by the policyowner (transferring the right to control the policy) *during the lifetime of the insured* may or may not be enforceable. Although the courts favor free transferability of property, most courts enforce clauses prohibiting assignment by the owner during the lifetime of the insured. When there is no prohibition of assignment, ordinarily a person may assign a policy on his or her own life, thus making use of the property rights represented by the policy. These rights are (1) any cash values that might accumulate before the death of the insured, and (2) the face amount of the policy that will be paid upon the death of the insured (the "death benefit").

The rights of an assignee to the cash value may conflict with the rights of the named beneficiary, since a main function of the cash value is to provide funding for the beneficiary's death benefit. If the designation of beneficiary is *irrevocable* (no right to change the beneficiary has been reserved by the policy), the rights of the beneficiary prevail over those of the assignee. Where the beneficiary designation is *revocable* (can be changed), the assignee's rights usually are superior to those of the revocable beneficiary. By protecting the assignee, the law enables the policyowner to use the policy as collateral for a loan.

Duties, Defenses, and Rights of Insurers and Others

Duties of the Insurer.   An insurer has a duty to make prompt payment of valid claims. Statutes in some states provide for special remedies against insurers who unjustifiably fail to pay or are late in paying valid claims. These laws usually allow claimants to collect attorney's fees together with a monetary penalty. As Case 29.2 suggests, the statutes are especially useful in encouraging prompt payment of small claims.

CASE 29.2 Fresh Meadows Medical Associates v. Liberty Mutual Insurance Co.
400 N.E.2d 303 (N.Y. 1979)

Facts: An automobile passenger injured in a car accident had x-rays taken by Fresh Meadows Medical Associates. The bill was $70. The passenger assigned her claim for payment of the bill to Fresh Meadows, which requested payment from the responsible insurer, Liberty Mutual. The insurer refused to pay. Fresh Meadows, as required by statute, submitted the claim to arbitration seeking payment of the $70 plus its attorney's fees of $1650. Although the statute permitted the award of reasonable attorney's fees, Liberty challenged the amount. Fresh Meadows then asked for an additional $1200 for the attorney's work done to justify the original fee. The arbitrator awarded Fresh Meadows $70 for the bill and $2850 in attorney's fees. Liberty appealed.

Question: Did the arbitrator have the authority to award an amount for attorney's services in substantiating the original claim for attorney's fees.

Answer: Yes. The additional attorney's fees should be included in the award.

Reasoning: The intent of the statute in question is, where an insurer refuses to pay a valid claim forcing the claimant to hire an attorney, that the claimant should be reimbursed for the cost of obtaining payment from the insurer. If any part of the claimant's attorney's fees are excluded from the award and left for the claimant to pay, the purpose of the statute would be frustrated.

Liability insurers also have a duty to defend lawsuits against insureds and, where circumstances warrant, a duty to settle claims out of court. The insurer must defend, for example, where an injured person files a lawsuit against the insured, seeking compensation for the injury, and the insured's liability is covered by the policy. The insurer's duty to settle a claim out of court arises especially where the facts reveal a claim greatly in excess of the policy limits, the validity of the claim is not in serious doubt, and the claimant is willing to accept the policy maximum and to release the insured from liability for the excess. Where the validity of the claim is doubtful, the insurer is not required to settle out of court.

Duties of the Insured and Others. The insured and other claimants have a duty to present claims promptly. The insured must also assist and cooperate with the insurer in defending a lawsuit against the insured. Unless claims are promptly presented, the insurer cannot be held liable for payment. Reasonable policy requirements of notice and proof of loss within a set number of days after a loss are enforced by the courts to encourage prompt investigation and settlement of claims.

A duty to assist and cooperate arises under policies of liability insurance that require the insurer to defend the insured against tort claims. The insured is expected to notify the insurer promptly if suit is filed against the insured, and to attend hearings and trials, give evidence, help arrange a settlement, help obtain witnesses, refrain from interfering with legitimate defense and settlement efforts, and give any other reasonable assistance and cooperation connected with the trial. However, the insured may not be imposed on unreasonably. He or she does not breach the duty of assistance and cooperation by, for example, refusing to make an expensive trip unless reimbursed for travel expenses.

Defenses of the Insurer. Within limits, an insurer may use certain defenses such as concealment, breach of warranty, or misrepresentation to avoid paying a claim.

Concealment. Intentional failure by an insurance applicant to disclose a material fact is a "concealment" and is a good defense if the insurer granted coverage while unaware of the concealment. Examples are a driver's failure to reveal convictions for drunken driving when applying for automobile liability insurance, and a homeowner's failure when applying for fire insurance to reveal illegal storage of large amounts of gasoline in the basement. The essence of concealment is intentional nondisclosure of a material fact. The doctrine of concealment pertains more to property and liability insurance than to life insurance. Life insurance application forms are so detailed that an affirmative misrepresentation rather than concealment is likely to occur.

Breach of Policy Warranties.   A "warranty" in an insurance policy is a written statement, description, or undertaking by an insurance applicant assuring the insurer that certain facts are true. Suppose that Morton seeks to insure the contents of his warehouse against theft. The statement in the policy that "A watchman will be on duty at all times" is a warranty. At common law, breach of a warranty was a complete defense for the insurer regardless of the breach's importance. Thus, if on a Monday night there was no watchman on duty, the warranty was breached. If goods were stolen Tuesday night after the watchman returned to work, the insurer had a good defense despite the likelihood that the breach on Monday had nothing to do with the theft.

Because many insurers took advantage of this common law treatment of warranties to deprive insured persons of the coverage they expected, many states today have a statute providing that a breach of a warranty is a ground for avoiding the policy only if the breach is material, that is, only if the breach contributes significantly to the loss. In other states, the strict law of warranty is still in effect although courts have interpreted policies to protect those insured where possible. State statutes usually prevent life insurers from using breach of warranty as a defense to payment of death benefits.

Misrepresentation.   In the law of insurance, a "representation" is an oral or written statement of fact made by an applicant to induce an insurer to extend coverage. A misrepresentation is a false representation. An insurer who relies upon a material misrepresentation in issuing a policy may avoid the policy obligations. An applicant for life insurance makes a material (important) misrepresentation, for example, if she states she is in perfect health when in fact she has recently had a severe heart attack. The insurance company which relied on the misrepresentation in issuing a policy may rescind (cancel) the contract. If, through its own investigation, the insurer learned the true state of the applicant's health before issuing the policy, the insurer has not relied on the misrepresentation. But where there was no investigation, or where the insurer investigated but did not learn the truth, the insurer usually will be held to have relied on the applicant's misrepresentation. In most states the defense is good even though misrepresentation was unintentional.

Incontestability.   Most life and some health insurance policies contain a clause stating that the policy is "incontestable" after the passage of 1 or 2 years. *Incontestability* means that the insurer may not avoid the policy for concealment, breach of warranty, or misrepresentation. Most states require that an incontestability clause be included in life insurance policies to limit the use of insurer's defenses to the stated time. Incontestability clauses make life insurance more marketable.

Rights Contrary to Policy Provisions.   Insureds and other claimants may have rights that are inconsistent with the language of their policies. The older law of insurance enabled insurers to write insurance policies in such a restrictive way that insureds and other claimants often were deprived of expected benefits. Many denials of benefits were so surprising and harmful to claimants that the courts began interpreting policies in a way to control abuse and overreaching by insurers. For instance, instead of interpreting a description of insured property as a warranty (to which the property had to conform exactly to remain covered by the insurance), the courts came to treat a mere description as no more than an identification of the covered property, with no warranty significance. Thus, today a 1979 car might be inaccurately described as a 1980 model and yet be covered. Today, courts use many doctrines inconsistent with policy language to recognize rights of claimants. The use of these doctrines appears designed to deny the insurer any unconscionable advantage and to honor the reasonable expectations of applicants and beneficiaries.

PERSONAL RISKS: LIFE AND HEALTH INSURANCE

Life and health insurance policies protect against risks such as premature death, temporary and permanent disability, unemployment, and outliving one's financial resources. To a family, insurance can provide reimbursement for medical expenses, a replacement for income lost due to disability, and, at death, funds to cover the cost of the last illness, burial, unpaid debts, taxes, and similar expenses. Insurance can also provide surviving family members with funds to maintain their standard of living, to support and educate children, and to pay off a mortgage on the family residence.

A business firm can insure the lives of key personnel whose untimely death would create great financial hardship for the firm. Businesses can also use the protection that insurance provides to increase the availability of credit to the firm and to assure the continuation of business (where, for example, surviving partners need a large fund with which to buy out a deceased partner's share). Employee benefit plans created to attract and hold talented employees are often funded through insurance.

Determining how (or whether) to meet these family and business needs with insurance requires an understanding of the basic features of life insurance and health insurance.

Life Insurance   **Types of Life Insurance.**   Life insurance contracts fall into four basic classes: term life, whole-life, endowment life, and annuities. The first three classes enable a person to provide or to accumulate a fund for use or investment. These classes are associated with the risk of premature death. The fourth class of contract, the annuity, is a device for systematically *using up* (liquidating) an existing fund. An annuity protects against the risk of outliving one's financial resources. It is similar to a life insurance "settlement option" providing a periodic income. The topic of annuities is beyond the scope of this book, but settlement options are discussed later.

Term Life Insurance.   *Term life insurance* is a contract that furnishes life insurance protection for a fixed period or "term" (often 1 or 5 years) for an annual premium that remains the same throughout the term. The face value of the policy is payable only if death occurs during the term, and nothing is paid if the insured survives beyond the term. The purchaser of term insurance receives insurance protection only, and there is usually no buildup of cash values. The premium for term insurance is relatively low when compared to premiums for other types of life insurance for a given age and face amount, because term insurance usually does not provide coverage for people past 65 or 70 years of age. However, term insurance is often renewable, at increased premiums, until that age without proof of insurability. Where a person requires substantial amounts of "pure protection" and is not interested in maintaining coverage beyond retirement, term insurance may be the best choice.

Whole-Life Insurance. *Whole-life insurance* (also called "straight," "ordinary," or "lifetime" insurance) is a contract of "permanent" insurance, so called for two reasons. First, the insured is permitted (but not required) to pay premiums keeping the policy in effect for life. Second, even if the insured eventually stops paying premiums, there has been a buildup of cash values that can be used as premiums to keep the policy in effect for a further period of time. How long the policy will remain in effect after premium payment ceases, or at what face value, depends on the amount of the cash-value buildup.

Paying for whole-life insurance is almost always accomplished by means of "level-premiums." Suppose Jennifer pays a $500 annual premium for her whole-life insurance. The premium is "level" because the amount is fixed at $500 for the rest of the contract. In the early years of the policy, the premium paid by Jennifer and others in her age grouping is far more than is needed to pay claims and expenses that will arise from this group. The excess amount is invested by the insurer to fund the "cash surrender value" that whole-life policies accumulate. This amount will also be sufficient to pay the increasingly frequent claims that will arise in later years. Thus, a whole-life policy is insurance protection coupled with a forced-savings feature that finances, in advance, long-term insurance benefits for the policyowner and any beneficiary.

Because of the cash-value feature, a whole-life policy can be used as collateral for a loan (as can an endowment policy). Or, where the policyowner wishes to quit paying premiums before the policy is fully paid up, the cash value can be applied in a variety of ways to preserve a lesser degree of insurance coverage.

Endowment Insurance. *Endowment insurance* is a contract under which the insured pays premiums for a specified number of years called the "endowment period" and at the end of that time *receives the face amount of the policy.* If the insured dies before that time, the face amount is then paid to a beneficiary, as in other types of insurance.

An endowment policy operates in two ways: It is (1) a savings fund resulting from the accumulation and investment of part of the premium, and (2) term insurance whose face amount decreases as the endowment policy savings fund increases. At any time during the endowment period, the amount of the savings element plus the face amount of the decreasing term insurance equals the face amount of the endowment policy. An endowment policy develops a cash value, but its premiums are higher than for other life insurance policies, especially where the endowment period is relatively short.

Settlement Options. A life insurance policy "matures" when the insured person dies or when he or she survives the endowment period of an endowment policy. At the maturity of the policy, the "proceeds" (the face amount of the policy) are available to the person entitled to them under the terms of the policy, usually a beneficiary.

Exactly how the beneficiary will receive the proceeds depends on what "settlement option" (way of receiving the proceeds) is chosen. The insured may designate a settlement option. Often, however, the choice of settlement options is left for the beneficiary to make when the policy matures. The typical life insurance contract provides the following settlement options. The beneficiary may (1) receive a lump sum in cash; (2) leave the proceeds (principal) with the company, receive the interest in periodic payments, and withdraw principal from time to time; (3) have principal together with interest paid in equal installments over a fixed number of years; (4) have payments of a specified amount until principal and interest are exhausted; or (5) receive a specified income for the life of the recipient.

Health Insurance

Health insurance protects mainly against risks of temporary and permanent disability resulting from injury or illness. Policies and plans of health insurance vary greatly.

Basic Coverages. "Health insurance" encompasses two major categories of insurance protection: (1) disability income insurance, and (2) medical expense insurance. *Disability income insurance* provides periodic payments to the insured as a substitute for income lost as a result of illness or injury. Some disability income policies cover only those disabilities resulting from accidental injury. Others cover disabilities resulting from both accidental injury *and* sickness. The amount and duration of payments are carefully limited.

Medical expense insurance provides payments for medical care, which includes hospital expenses as well as surgical, nonsurgical, and nursing expenses. Medical benefits also are limited in amount and duration.

Health insurance policies typically exclude coverage of preexisting disabilities or health conditions and self-inflicted injuries. To prevent duplication of coverage and benefit payments, virtually all policies exclude coverage where the insured receives workers' compensation or other medical insurance benefits.

Types of Policies and Plans. People can acquire health insurance in so many ways that they may, without knowing it, have overlapping coverage and a higher than necessary health insurance cost. Health insurance can be acquired by means of individual policies, group policies, social security, and private noncommercial plans such as Blue Cross and Blue Shield.

Group health insurance is widely used and should not be confused with *individual* health insurance. Normally a person seeking individual insurance must provide evidence of insurability. But a company issuing group insurance (life or health, for example) insures every person in the group without regard to insurability of individuals. In group insurance, the insurer issues one detailed master contract to the group policyholder (often an employer) but only brief certificates to individual insureds such as employees. Also, many group policies are "experience-rated" in that the premium charged depends in part on the claims record of the group. Experience rating gives a group an incentive to keep claims at a minimum.

The following case illustrates the importance of a master contract to an individual covered by group health insurance.

CASE 29.3 Morrison Assurance Co. v. Armstrong
264 S.E.2d 320 (Ga. App. 1980)

Facts: Armstrong, a Morrison, Inc. (MI) employee, received workers' compensation benefits for an injury suffered on the job. MI also had a separate group insurance policy with Morrison Assurance Co. covering MI employees. The master policy issued to MI excluded benefits for any injury covered by workers' compensation. The group policy certificates, which were given to employees as a summary of the policy coverage, stated benefits would be excluded for job injuries "incurred in the course of working for an employer other than (MI)" if covered by workers' compensation. Because of her certificate's language, Armstrong thought she was entitled to benefits in addition to workers' compensation. The insurer denied liability stating Armstrong's claim was excluded under the master policy. Armstrong sued the insurer. The insurer appealed from the trial court's judgment in favor of Armstrong.

Question: When the limitations on coverage in a master group policy and an employee's policy certificate are different, which one controls?

Answer: The master policy controls. Armstrong should not receive benefits in addition to workers' compensation.

Reasoning: The primary contracting parties in group insurance are the employer and the insurer. The employee certificate holder is bound by the terms of the master policy. The certificate is evidence of coverage under the master policy. Here the certificate contains a disclaimer that it is not the whole contract and that the employee may inspect the master policy. Even though the master policy is not in the employee's possession, it controls the extent of policy coverage in this situation. This rule is so well established that to change it would require legislation.

PROPERTY RISKS: PROPERTY AND LIABILITY INSURANCE

Property Insurance

Nature of Property Insurance.   Property insurance indemnifies (compensates) a person who has an insurable interest in property (real or personal) for the property's loss or for the loss of its income-producing ability. Property insurance protects against loss from certain risks called "perils." A *peril* is a cause of loss such as fire, flood, theft, or vandalism.

Property insurance may be provided by means of either a "specified-perils" or an "all-risk" ("all-perils") contract. In a **specified-perils contract**, the insurer will compensate only for losses caused by the particular peril(s) specified in the contract. A farmer's insurance against hail damage to crops is an example of a specified-perils contract.

In an **all-risk contract,** the insurer will indemnify the insured for loss resulting from any peril except those specifically excluded by the contract. A homeowner's "personal property floater" is an all-risk contract because, despite certain exclusions and limitations, covered losses will be compensated for even though the particular peril was not spelled out in the contract. All-risk insurance is useful where the possible cause of property loss is difficult to predict.

The risk undertaken by a property insurer is subject to limits imposed by the policy. Many policies have a "deductible," and all policies contain clauses of exclusion. A **deductible** is a specified amount of loss that the insured must absorb before being entitled to payment from the insurer. Deductible amounts are common in automobile and homeowners' insurance. They serve to lower insurance costs (and premiums) by eliminating small claims. Clauses of exclusion confine the insured risk to manageable proportions. Damage resulting from an act of war is a typical exclusion.

A property loss may be "direct" or "indirect." A *direct loss* results from damage to the physical property itself. Collision damage to a taxicab is an example. An *indirect loss* only occurs as a consequence of a direct loss. Loss of income while a taxicab is out of service because of collision damage and the extra expense of renting a substitute vehicle are examples of indirect loss.

Types of Property Insurance.   The following summarizes the most representative kinds of property insurance available for protection against personal or business losses. Coverages are usually available on a single-peril, multiple-peril, "package," or all-risk basis. Some coverages are limited to direct losses, most encompass indirect losses, and a few (such as business interruption insurance) protect primarily against indirect losses.

Fire Insurance.   Fire insurance provides indemnity against losses to insured buildings, contents, ships in port, and so on, due to accidental fire. Loss due to a "friendly" fire may not be covered, as where, for example, a valuable object is accidentally tossed into a furnace. If a friendly fire escapes and becomes "hostile," the resulting damage is covered.

Automobile Insurance.   Automobile collision insurance covers loss to the insured vehicle from its collision with another object. Separate coverages are required for noncollision losses, such as bodily injury, liability to third persons, theft loss, and vandalism or storm damage.

Crime Insurance.   Crime insurance pays for losses caused by the criminal acts of others, such as burglary and other forms of theft.

Inland Marine Insurance.   Inland marine insurance originally provided protection for goods transported other than by ocean. It is often used today to cover a variety of transportation and nontransportation losses, whether or not incurred on waterways.

Accounts Receivable Insurance.   Accounts receivable insurance protects against an inability to collect an account because of damage to records that prove the existence of the account.

Business Interruption Insurance.   Business interruption insurance protects against losses due to an inability of a business to operate because of fire, flood, or other such hazards.

Liability Insurance

Nature of Liability Insurance.   A person or business faces two main types of liability for damages—liability for breach of contract and liability for a wide variety of torts. Liability insurance does *not* cover liability for breach of contract, nor does it cover losses resulting from other speculative activities such as trading in the stock market. Liability insurance protects only against tort liability. Tort liability falls into several somewhat overlapping categories. They include:

1. Liability for one's own torts—negligent driving, professional malpractice, false imprisonment of a suspected shoplifter, libel and slander, and so on.

2. Liability of an employer for torts committed by employees in the course of their employment, including many intentional torts.

3. Liability for loss resulting from defective products, whether based on negligence, breach of a warranty, or strict liability in tort.

4. Liability resulting from ownership of property. For example, the strict liability attending the ownership of hazardous property such as a reservoir, and liability to guests, business invitees, and certain trespassers for losses caused by negligently maintaining one's home or business premises.

Types of Liability Insurance.   Most of the tort risks listed above may be insured against, although insurers commonly exclude from coverage some intentional torts committed by the insured. A policy might exclude assault and battery committed by the insured. But where the insured is a journalist, the liability policy might cover the intentional tort of libel, since a charge of libel is a normal risk of journalism. The following kinds of liability insurance are typically available.

Employer's Liability Insurance.   One type of employer's liability insurance provides coverage for workers' compensation claims. Another type protects the employer against claims of persons other than employees—business invitees such as customers or sellers, for example.

Errors and Omissions Insurance.   Errors and omissions insurance protects the insured from liability to a customer resulting from the insured's error or oversight. An insurance salesperson, for example, might forget to include a requested coverage in a policy.

Malpractice Insurance.   Malpractice insurance protects professionals such as physicians, lawyers, and accountants from liability for negligence in the practice of their professions.

Fidelity Insurance.   Fidelity (guaranty) insurance protects against loss due to embezzlement and other dishonest acts of employees and other persons holding positions of trust.

Automobile Liability Insurance. Automobile liability insurance protects a motor vehicle operator or owner from liability to third persons as a result of the operation of the vehicle. About half the states have some form of "no-fault" automobile insurance law under which claims for personal injury (and, in Massachusetts, for property damage) must be made against the claimant's own insurance company, regardless of who was at fault. The aim of such laws is to reduce the cost of automobile insurance by reducing litigation and other expenses, but many no-fault laws are ineffective for this purpose because the right to litigate to recover for "pain and suffering" and other damages has been preserved, even for rather small claims.

Homeowners' Liability Insurance. Homeowners' liability insurance protects a homeowner from damage claims of invitees and others. These claims often arise because it is alleged the homeowner has negligently maintained the property or allowed a dangerous condition to exist (for example, faulty porch steps).

Subrogation and Coinsurance in Property and Liability Insurance

The two concepts of subrogation and coinsurance have special importance in property and liability insurance. An insurance company's right of *subrogation* is its right to be substituted as a claimant against a person responsible for loss. Subrogation applies mainly to liability insurance. Suppose that a teller in a bank embezzles funds from a customer's account and that the bank must make good the loss. At this point the bank has a right to recover the amount of the loss from the teller. If the bank has a policy of fidelity insurance, the insurance company must make good the loss. Upon payment of the bank's claim, the insurer acquires the right of the bank (is "subrogated to" the right of the bank) to collect the amount of the loss from the teller.

Coinsurance applies to the insuring of commercial property, and comes into effect when partial losses occur. A coinsurance clause is used by property insurers to prevent customers who underinsure their property from receiving disproportionately larger benefits than those who insure near the full value of their property.

A coinsurance clause works this way: The clause provides that if the owner insures property for at least a given percent of its value (usually 80 percent), then any loss will be paid in full up to the face amount of the policy. In contrast, if the owner insures the property for less than the required percentage, the owner must bear part of the loss and will recover from the insurance company only the amount indicated by the following formula:

$$\text{Recovery} = \text{actual loss} \times \frac{\text{face amount of insurance}}{80\% \times \text{actual cash value of property}}$$

For example, suppose Webster insures her $100,000 office building for only $20,000. If she sustains a fire loss of $20,000 she will recover only $5000 from the insurer, since recovery ($5000) equals:

$$\text{Actual loss (\$20,000)} \times \frac{\text{face amount of insurance}}{80\% \times \$100,000 \text{ (actual cash value of property)}} \quad \frac{(\$20,000)}{(\$80,000)}$$

In contrast, suppose Smith has insured his $100,000 office building for $80,000. The coinsurance requirement is met. If Smith sustains a $20,000 fire loss, it will be paid in full. People who insure residential property often are subject to a "replace-ment cost clause," which is similar in purpose to a coinsurance clause.

SUMMARY

Insurance is a contractual method of transferring risk from an insured to an insurer who distributes it by means of pooling and reinsurance. Since insurance is a system for distributing loss, an insured should not be allowed to profit in the event of casualty but, rather, should be limited to indemnity (compensation) for loss actually suffered. This principle of indemnity explains the requirement of an insurable interest, a financial stake that a person seeking insurance has in property or in someone's life or health.

An insurance policy is often a contract of adhesion. As such it is subject not only to ordinary rules of contract law, but also to legal controls commonly imposed on contracts of adhesion. Depending on the circumstances, an insurance contract may or may not be assignable.

An insurer has a duty to make prompt payment of valid claims, and liability insurers may have a duty to defend the insured in a lawsuit. Insureds have a duty to make prompt presentment of claims and to give reasonable assistance and coopera-tion in lawsuits. Within limits, the insurer may use the defenses of concealment, breach of a policy warranty, and misrepresentation.

Policies of life and health insurance protect against the risks of premature death, disability, unemployment, and outliving one's financial resources. The three basic types of life insurance contracts—term, whole-life, and endowment—provide or help a person accumulate a fund, whereas the annuity contract is used to liquidate an existing fund. Health insurance provides disability income and medical expense reimbursement. Group health or life insurance policies insure all in the group without regard to insurability of individuals, and the policies are experience-rated.

Property insurance protects against loss of property or its income-producing ability. Liability insurance protects against tort liability. Subrogation, the right to be substituted as a claimant against a person responsible for loss, applies mainly to liability insurance. Coinsurance is used to prevent persons who underinsure their property from receiving disproportionately larger benefits than those who insure near full property value.

REVIEW QUESTIONS

1. What are the two meanings of "the insured"?

2. (a) What is the principle of indemnity? (b) What is an insurable interest? (c) How is the principle of indemnity related to the requirement of an insurable interest?

3. (a) In property insurance, what circumstances create an insurable interest?

Why does the interest need to exist only at the time of loss? (b) In life insurance, what circumstances create an insurable interest? Why does the interest need to exist only when the policy is taken out?

4. Why are the rules of offer and acceptance of special importance in the formation of an insurance contract?

5. (a) Why is a contract of life insurance more freely assignable than a contract of property or liability insurance? (b When is the assignability of life insurance limited?

6. What are the general duties of the insurer? The insured?

7. (a) Describe the insurer's defenses of concealment, breach of a policy warranty, and misrepresentation. (b) What is the significance of incontestability?

8. How does the function of an annuity differ from that of life insurance contracts?

9. Describe the features of (a) term life insurance, (b) whole-life insurance, and (c) endowment insurance.

10. (a) What basic coverages does health insurance provide? (b) What exclusions from coverage do health insurance policies typically contain? (c) How does a group health (or life) insurance policy differ from an individual policy?

11. Explain the difference between a specified-perils and an all-risk (all-perils) contract of property insurance.

12. (a) What kind of liability does liability insurance cover? Not cover? (b) Explain the meaning and purpose of subrogation. Of coinsurance.

CASE PROBLEMS

1. Chadwick's car was badly damaged in a collision. The fair market value of the car just before the collision was $1650. Immediately afterward the salvage value was $100. Chadwick sought reimbursement from his insurer. The insurer's adjuster made five offers of settlement ranging downward from $1250 to $800. Chadwick then submitted a written demand for $1450. The insurer did not answer the letter or make a counterproposal. Chadwick sued the insurer for $1450 plus an amount for rental of a replacement car, storage costs for the damaged car, and attorney's fees. The jury returned a verdict in favor of Chadwick for $1550 in damages plus $800 for attorney's fees. The insurer appealed. Should the verdict in favor of Chadwick be upheld? Explain reasons for your answer.

2. A prisoner alleged that the sheriff's department of Nassau County, New York, negligently deprived him of medical care and that the deprivation aggravated injuries from which he suffered during imprisonment. The sheriff's department brought an action to determine whether its insurer had a duty to defend persons accused of negligence. The insurer denied that the alleged negligence constituted a covered "occurrence," defined in the policy as "an accident, including continuous or repeated exposure to conditions, which results in bodily injury or personal damage neither expected nor intended from the standpoint of the insured." Did the insurer have a duty to defend? Explain.

3. Customers of Diamond Tours brought suit against Diamond, alleging fraudulent misrepresentations by Diamond about a charter tour of Jamaica, West Indies.

Diamond had a professional liability insurance policy with American Home Assurance Company. The policy covered negligent acts, errors, and omissions of the insured. Diamond referred the suit to the insurer, which disclaimed coverage on the ground that the policy did not insure Diamond against its own fraud. The insurer then brought an action to confirm that fraud was not covered by the policy. Should the court decide in favor of the insurer? Explain.

4. Passenger Lisa Roberts was injured in an auto accident on October 27, 1978. The insurer, through its adjuster, sent a letter acknowledging the claim and stated that it would be processed when the enclosed forms were properly completed and returned. On December 28, 1978, Roberts' counsel forwarded to the insurer doctors' bills for $766 and copies of all required documents except the attending physicians' report form. At the end of January 1979 Roberts' counsel inquired about the failure to receive payment. The adjuster said there was no payment because he had not received the attending physicians' forms. Roberts' counsel stated that he had no duty to provide the forms and repeated this contention in two subsequent letters. On March 12, 1979, the insurer began to pay Roberts' claim. Thereafter, Roberts sued the insurer, seeking a penalty for the delay plus interest and an attorney's fee. She sued on the basis of a statute giving an insurer 30 days to make payment after receiving reasonable proof of loss. The insurer contended that Roberts had a duty to provide the physicians' forms and that because she had not done so, the delay was her fault. The trial court awarded her the amounts requested. Should it have done so? Why or why not?

5. Phillips applied for life insurance. The application asked the question: "Have you ever been told you had any of the following" listed diseases? Phillips answered "No" for each of the illnesses in the list. Phillips died, his widow sought payment of the face amount of the policy, and the insurer refused to pay. The widow brought suit against the insurer. The insurer produced evidence that Phillips had been treated for pulmonary emphysema, hemoptysis, chronic brain syndrome associated with the consumption of alcohol, hypertension, and epilepsy, along with other long-standing physical problems for which he had been hospitalized. The trial court awarded the insurer summary judgment on the ground of material misrepresentation. The widow appealed on the ground that Phillips spoke truthfully because he had never been told the names of any of the illnesses. Should the summary judgment for the insurer be upheld? Why or why not?

PART EIGHT

COMMERCIAL PAPER

CHAPTER 30

NATURE OF COMMERCIAL PAPER; NEGOTIABLE FORM; PERSONAL AND REAL DEFENSES

Business people use many kinds of commercial documents daily. These documents include, for example, warehouse receipts, delivery orders, bills of lading, and other documents of title used in the distribution of goods; security agreements, financing statements, and certificates of title to motor vehicles, needed to create and enforce secured transactions; and corporate securities such as stocks and bonds, sold to raise funds for business activities. These various documents serve primarily as evidence of ownership or indebtedness.

We turn now to another class of commercial documents, called "commercial paper" or "negotiable instruments," used mainly as a substitute for money or as a means of extending credit in terms of money. This chapter discusses the types and nature of commercial paper; the language ("form") required for an instrument (document) to be negotiable; and the main benefit that a purchaser of commercial paper receives—the right to have payment free from personal defenses of the person or firm that "issued" it (put it into circulation).

NATURE OF COMMERCIAL PAPER

Centuries ago merchants began to devise ways of paying for property and services without having to carry large sums of money. The **bill of exchange** (nowadays called a "draft") was used in Europe for this purpose as early as the fourteenth century. With the growth of banking, a special kind of draft called a "check" came into wide use. Today most business transactions are settled by check. Checks and other drafts serve as a temporary, safe, and efficient substitute for money. Another kind of commercial paper, the **promissory note**, is used primarily as a means to extend credit. In its simplest form, a promissory note is the written promise of a person (borrower or buyer) to pay a sum of money to another person (lender or seller) at some future date. Article 3 of the Uniform Commercial Code (UCC) governs commercial paper.

Types of Commercial Paper   Although all commercial paper may be classified as either a draft or a note, Article 3 lists four varieties of commercial paper—notes (often called "promissory notes"), certificates of deposit, drafts, and checks [3-104].[1] A certificate of deposit is a specialized type of note. A check is a specialized type of draft.

Promissory Notes.   Notes are the simplest kind of commercial paper because they involve only two parties. A note is a writing in which one party (the maker) promises to pay a sum of money to another party (the payee). A note may be either a **demand note** (i.e., payable on demand of the payee or other possessor called a "holder") or a **time note** (payable at a definite time after it is issued). A note may or may not bear interest, depending on the agreement of the parties. The principal and any interest may be payable in installments (e.g., a specified amount per month), or the principal and interest may be due all at once in a single payment. Figure 30.1 shows a simple form of a "single payment" time note.

[1]The hyphenated numbers in brackets refer to sections of the Uniform Commercial Code reprinted in the Appendix to this volume. The number "3-104" means "Article 3, section 104" and is commonly read as "Section 3-104."

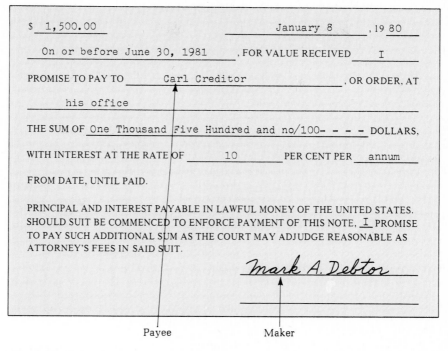

$ 1,500.00   January 8   , 19 80

____On or before June 30, 1981____, FOR VALUE RECEIVED   I

PROMISE TO PAY TO   Carl Creditor   , OR ORDER, AT

_____his office

THE SUM OF One Thousand Five Hundred and no/100- - - - DOLLARS,

WITH INTEREST AT THE RATE OF   10   PER CENT PER   annum

FROM DATE, UNTIL PAID.

PRINCIPAL AND INTEREST PAYABLE IN LAWFUL MONEY OF THE UNITED STATES.
SHOULD SUIT BE COMMENCED TO ENFORCE PAYMENT OF THIS NOTE, I PROMISE
TO PAY SUCH ADDITIONAL SUM AS THE COURT MAY ADJUDGE REASONABLE AS
ATTORNEY'S FEES IN SAID SUIT.

                                     Mark A. Debtor

Payee   Maker

FIGURE 30.1   A promissory note.

Certificates of Deposit.   A **certificate of deposit** ("CD") is an acknowledgment by a bank of receipt of money with an engagement (promise) by the bank to repay it, plus interest. The bank (broadly defined to include savings and loan associations and other business organizations legally empowered to engage in banking) is the maker. The payee, ordinarily an individual or business firm, deposits money with the maker and receives the CD which, because of the interest, may be attractive as an investment. There are two classes of CDs: **demand certificates** (payable on demand of the payee or other holder) and **time certificates** (often referred to as TCDs because they are payable at a definite time after they are issued). Figure 30.2 illustrates a TCD.

Drafts.   Drafts involve three parties. A **draft** is an order (command) by one person (the drawer) given to another person (the drawee) to pay a sum of money to a third person (the payee). The drawee can be any person or organization willing or obliged to obey the order. Suppose Ted's Pizza Shop owes Ann $500 for a new oven she delivered, and Ann owes Cora $500. When Cora demands payment, Ann might not have the cash, but if Cora agrees, Ann might "draw" a $500 draft on (write out a draft directed to) Ted's Pizza Shop with Cora as payee. Thus, Ann (the drawer) orders Ted's Pizza (the drawee) to pay $500 to Cora (the payee). Cora may now present the draft to Ted's Pizza for payment, and if Ted's Pizza "honors" (pays) it, two debts are settled at one time. A draft may be made out to the payee in a variety of ways—e.g., to the order of "bearer," some designated third person such as Cora, the Internal

SECURITY PACIFIC NATIONAL BANK

№ 100474

TIME CERTIFICATE OF DEPOSIT
Stated Maturity Date
Interest on 360-Day Year Basis

ISSUED AT Santa Barbara OFFICE Santa Barbara, CALIFORNIA, March 21, 19 79

THIS CERTIFIES THAT * * * * * *Paul A. Padilla* HAS/HAVE DEPOSITED IN THIS BANK,

* * * * * * *One thousand and no/100* * * * * * * * * * * DOLLARS, $1,000.00

PAYABLE Sept. 19, 19 79, TO * * * *Paul A. Padilla* * * * * * * * * * * * * * * * * OR ORDER UPON PRESENTATION AND SURRENDER OF THIS CERTIFICATE, PROPERLY ENDORSED, AT THE OFFICE OF ISSUE. THIS DEPOSIT BEARS SIMPLE INTEREST. INTEREST WILL BE COMPUTED FOR THE ACTUAL NUMBER OF DAYS ON A 360-DAY YEAR BASIS, AT THE RATE OF 6.00 PER CENT PER ANNUM, FROM DATE HEREOF TO MATURITY, BUT NO INTEREST WILL BE ALLOWED THEREAFTER. TO AVOID LOSS OF INTEREST, RENEW AT MATURITY.

NOT SUBJECT TO CHECK
NOT PAYABLE BEFORE MATURITY
NO INTEREST WILL BE PAID AFTER MATURITY

SPECIMEN

Mary L. Mahoney
AUTHORIZED SIGNATURE

080400 12-77 10 10Y

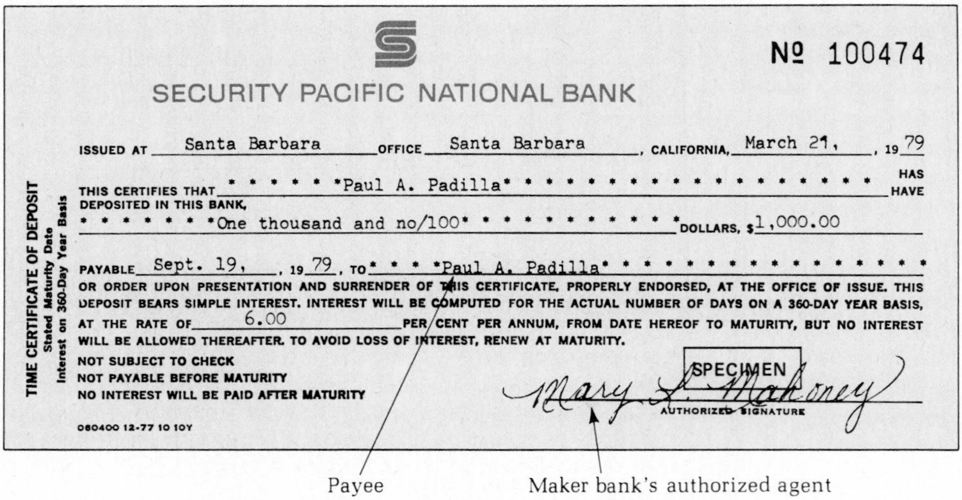

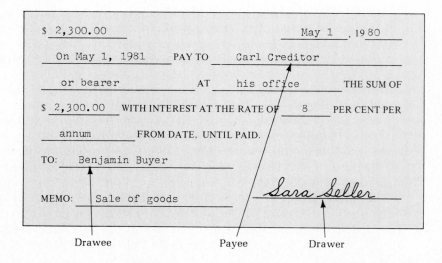

FIGURE 30.2 A time certificate of deposit (*by permission of Security Pacific National Bank*).

Revenue Service, First Church, or even the drawer herself. An interest-bearing draft is illustrated in Figure 30.3.

Drafts are either demand drafts or time drafts. A **demand draft** is payable literally on demand of the payee or other holder any time after issue. Although demand drafts often begin with the words "On demand pay" or "At sight pay," the language "Pay to . . ." is sufficient to indicate a demand draft. A **time draft** is payable at a specified time after issue. The time might be indicated merely by writing the date of issue on the draft and then filling in another blank with the future date on which payment is to

FIGURE 30.3 A draft.

$ 2,300.00 May 1, 19 80

On May 1, 1981 PAY TO Carl Creditor

or bearer AT his office THE SUM OF

$ 2,300.00 WITH INTEREST AT THE RATE OF 8 PER CENT PER

annum FROM DATE, UNTIL PAID.

TO: Benjamin Buyer

MEMO: Sale of goods

Sara Seller

be made, as in the draft illustrated in Figure 30.3. Or the time draft might say, instead, "Sixty days after date pay." A draft reading "Sixty days after sight [by the drawee] pay" is a time draft, but requires the "acceptance" of the drawee to fix the maturity date of the instrument. **Acceptance** is the drawee's written engagement (promise) to pay the draft when it falls due. Suppose Ann's draft drawn on Ted's Pizza Shop reads, "Sixty days after sight pay to the order of Cora Creditor $500." Cora then presents the draft to Ted's Pizza for acceptance. Ted, the owner of Ted's Pizza, will write "Accepted" across the face of the draft and will add the date and his signature. These acts constitute Ted's acceptance. Sixty days after acceptance, Cora is entitled to payment from Ted's Pizza.

From the time a draft is drawn, the drawee is customarily referred to as a "party" to the draft (a person with contractual liability for the face amount of the draft). However, a drawee is not truly a party unless and until he or she *accepts* the draft—that is, by signature agrees to pay it. Until then the drawee has no obligation "under the instrument" (i.e., is not bound by the terms of the draft) [3-401]. A drawee who accepts a draft is called the "acceptor" and at that time becomes personally liable to the payee (or to some other holder) for payment of the face amount. So, when Ann issued the draft to Cora, Ann was the only signer and therefore the only person liable to Cora for the face amount if Ted's Pizza refused to accept the draft. Then, when Ted's Pizza accepted the draft, Ted's Pizza also became liable to Cora as a signer (i.e., as a true party to the draft), and Cora has two sources of payment instead of one. If she decides to sell the draft now instead of waiting 60 days to collect it herself, the acceptor's signature gives the draft a greater value because, having two sources of payment, the purchaser faces a reduced risk of noncollection. The nature of a drawer's and an acceptor's liability is discussed further in Chapter 32.

Checks. A **check** is a draft drawn on a *bank* and payable on *demand* [3-104(2)(b)]. The drawer is a customer who has an account at a drawee bank. The payee may be any individual, firm, or organization named on the face of the check, whom the drawer wishes to receive payment. Typically, checks are made out on printed forms having blank spaces for the date of the check, the payee's name, the amount to be paid, and the drawer's signature, as in Figure 30.4. Checks are especially useful because they enable the drawer to make distributions from a single fund (the drawer's bank account) for paying debts and making gifts and purchases. And, because the checks issued by the drawer eventually "clear" the bank collection process and are returned to the drawer's bank and then to the drawer, he or she has a record of expenditures.

Although frequently issued as gifts, checks usually are issued as part of an "underlying" contract, e.g., as payment for goods or services. Thus, there usually are two contracts—the check and the underlying transaction. Suppose Ann buys a typewriter from Typeshop and issues a check in payment. The check is one kind of "formal" contract discussed in Chapter 6, and Ann, as a signer, is liable for the face amount to the payee (Typeshop) or to some other holder such as a business firm where Typeshop might have cashed Ann's check. Ann is also a party to the underlying "informal" contract (discussed in Chapter 6) between herself and Typeshop for the sale of the typewriter. Ann will be liable in damages to Typeshop if

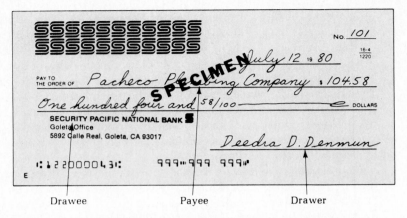

FIGURE 30.4   A check. (*by permission of Security Pacific National Bank*).

she breaches the underlying contract by, for example, stopping payment of the check without good reason.

Ordinarily, a check operates as only a conditional (not yet final) payment of the underlying obligation. The check does not become final payment until honored (paid) by the bank on which it was drawn. Until the check is honored, its issuer remains liable on the underlying transaction. However, the seller's taking a check as conditional payment *postpones* the seller's right to sue on the underlying obligation [3-802(1)(b)]. If the drawee bank dishonors the check, as where the drawer has insufficient funds or orders the bank to stop payment, the right of the seller to sue on the underlying obligation is "revived." Thus, where Ann pays by check and the drawee bank dishonors it, Ann is in breach of the underlying contract, and Typeshop now may sue her for damages.

When a bank draws a check on itself, the instrument is called a "cashier's check." When a bank draws a check on another bank in which the first bank has money on deposit, the check is referred to as a "bank draft."

A **traveler's check** is a three-party instrument purchased from a bank or other firm and carried by travelers instead of cash. The traveler is the drawer, and for purposes of identification must sign the traveler's check twice—once when the seller issues it and a second time when the traveler cashes it. The bank or other issuing firm is the drawee. When the drawee is a nonbanking firm such as American Express, the so-called traveler's "check" is not a check at all, but a draft subject to Code rules relating to drafts.

Negotiable Character of Commercial Paper

Understanding the negotiable character of commercial paper requires a preliminary look at some basic commercial paper concepts and practices, with a more detailed examination being reserved for later parts of this chapter and subsequent chapters. Three expressions are of special significance in the law of commercial paper: (1) "negotiable form," (2) "holder in due course," and (3) "personal and real defenses."

Meaning of Negotiable Form. To say that an instrument (note or draft) is "negotiable" or "negotiable in form" means simply that the writer of the instrument has used the language required by law for creating a negotiable instrument. For example, certain "magic words" called "language of negotiability" are required for an instrument to be a negotiable one. Precisely what those words are and why they must be used are discussed later in this chapter. It is sufficient for now to know that a note or draft is either negotiable or non-negotiable, depending on its *wording*; and that in certain situations (soon to be illustrated) a negotiable instrument can confer *greater rights* on its owner than can a non-negotiable instrument. Why a negotiable instrument confers greater rights requires a brief look at the meaning of "holder in due course" and "personal and real defenses."

Meaning of Holder in Due Course. Checks circulate from hand to hand as a substitute for money. Often, a check comes into the hands of a stranger to the drawer, as where the payee of a payroll check cashes it at a supermarket or liquor store. Similarly, notes may circulate among strangers. Notes (which usually bind their makers to a *future* payment) often are sold by their payees for *immediate* cash, as where you buy a car on credit and the dealer discounts (sells) your note to a buyer of commercial paper. Thus, commercial paper—issued by a maker or drawer to a payee—frequently comes into the hands of third persons who have no knowledge of the transaction between the original parties to the instrument. But sometimes the payee failed in the underlying transaction to perform a promised service, delivered defective goods, or in some other way gave the maker or drawer a *defense* to (legal reason for not making) payment. If proven in court, the defense will be good against the payee. But what are the rights of the innocent third person who cashed the check or bought the note? Here, holder-in-due-course status becomes important.

Negotiable instruments are useful in business primarily because innocent third persons, *if they qualify as holders in due course*, ordinarily may collect from the maker or drawer (or from others to be discussed in later chapters) the amount specified in the instrument even though the drawer or maker has a valid reason not to pay the payee. The third person qualifies as a holder in due course if the instrument is in *negotiable form*, if the payee *properly transferred ("negotiated")* the negotiable instrument, and if the third person receiving it has the *personal characteristics* required by law for holder-in-due-course status. Basically, the third person is a holder in due course if he or she took the negotiable instrument *for value, in good faith*, and *without notice of defenses*. These and other personal characteristics required for holder-in-due-course status are discussed in Chapter 31, as is the type of transfer called "negotiation." However, whether a holder in due course takes a negotiable instrument free from a defense depends, also, on the *kind* of defense it is—"personal" or "real." A holder in due course takes a negotiable instrument *free from personal* defenses, but *subject to real* defenses.

Meaning of Personal and Real Defenses. A personal defense is one involving wrongdoing or some other circumstance that the law says must remain a private matter between the immediate parties to a negotiable instrument (e.g., between the drawer of a check and the payee) instead of becoming a source of loss to a (third-person) holder in due course. The payee's delivering defective goods is a personal defense. In contrast, a *real* defense involves wrongdoing or some other circumstance of so serious a nature that the defense is good against even a holder in due course. Bankruptcy of the maker or drawer is a real defense. Personal and real defenses are discussed further in the last part of this chapter.

Significance of It All: Cashing a Check; Buying a Note.   Commercial paper is useful to the business community because holders in due course (and most of their transferees) can purchase it in relative safety, confident that it will usually be collectible despite disputes between the parties to the underlying transaction. Two examples follow:

1. John cashes his negotiable payroll check at a supermarket. Then Sam, the owner of the supermarket, presents John's check to the employer's bank for payment, only to learn that the employer has stopped payment of the check because John lied about the number of hours he worked during the week covered by the check. Sam immediately takes the dishonored check to the drawer (John's employer) for payment. The employer's *personal* defense to payment of the check (John's fraud) would be good against *John*, the payee, if John had kept the check and had himself sought payment from the employer after the bank dishonored the check. Sam, however, to whom John negotiated the check, is a holder in due course because he (Sam) paid for the check (by cashing it) and knew nothing of John's fraud when doing so. Therefore, Sam took the check free from the employer's personal defense. Accordingly, the employer must pay Sam the amount of the check and seek from John, the defrauding payee, any reimbursement (repayment) that might be due. The legal significance to Sam of holder-in-due-course status is that Sam takes the check free from the employer-drawer's personal defenses. One practical significance of Sam's holder-in-due-course status is that Sam, being free from personal defenses, will be more willing to cash checks for strangers than he would be if he had to absorb all losses.

2. You buy a car from Joe for use in your business. Joe expressly warrants that the car is in perfect running condition. Lacking cash, you pay for the car with your single-payment negotiable promissory note for $4000 plus 10 percent annual interest. The note is due 1 year from now. You will have to pay, in principal and interest, a total of $4400. Joe, the payee, could hold the note for a year and collect the $4400 from you; but he needs cash now, so he immediately discounts (sells) the note to Brenda, a buyer of commercial paper, for $4000. Thus, Joe has the $4000 he needs now, and Brenda has a chance to make a profit by collecting the $4400 in principal and interest from you when the note comes due.

A few days after these transactions, fire destroys your car because of a serious defect in its electrical system. The presence of the defect is a breach of Joe's warranty. You try to locate Joe but learn that he has left town permanently for parts unknown. At the end of the year, Brenda presents the note to you for payment. You refuse to pay because Joe's breach of warranty caused you the loss of the car. Unfortunately for you, the breach of warranty is a personal defense. Because Brenda became a holder in due course when she bought your note, she took it free from your personal defenses and is entitled to payment. You, the maker of the negotiable note, will have to absorb the loss if you cannot find Joe and make him pay.

As the preceding examples illustrate, a negotiable instrument can confer upon a holder in due course more than the usual contract rights, since unlike a transferee of an ordinary contract, a holder in due course of a negotiable instrument is free from personal defenses when attempting to collect payment.

If an instrument is *not* negotiable in form, its purchaser is merely an assignee (as opposed to a holder in due course) and therefore takes the instrument subject to *all* defenses, personal *and* real. (The law of assignments is discussed in Chapter 13.) Even a person who acquires a negotiable instrument from the payee might be only an assignee—for example, where the negotiable instrument was not transferred properly (i.e., was not "negotiated" as described in Chapter 31), or where the acquiring person does not qualify as a holder in due course.

A major practical significance of negotiability in the discounting of notes is that a holder in due course, being free from personal defenses of the maker, will tend to pay more for the note than if the purchaser were merely an assignee. Brenda in example 2 above probably would have paid Joe much less for your note if it had not been in negotiable form, because as an assignee she would be subject to *all* your defenses, personal as well as real, and therefore would face a much greater risk of noncollection.

Figure 30.5 shows a typical sequence of events in which (1) maker and payee enter into an underlying contract, (2) the payee sells the negotiable note to a holder in due course (HDC), and (3) HDC presents the note to the maker for payment. If the maker has a personal defense, HDC is nevertheless entitled to payment from the maker. If the maker has a real defense, HDC is *not* entitled to payment from the maker; however, as noted in Chapters 31, 32, and 33, HDC may be able to go back to the payee for payment.

Some people wrongly believe that a *non*negotiable instrument may not be

FIGURE 30.5   The legal significance of negotiability.

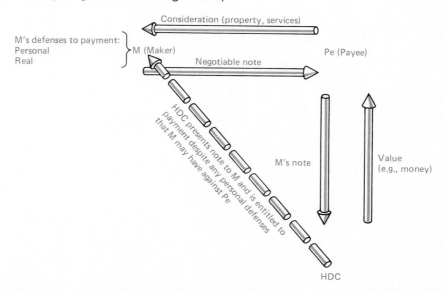

transferred from one person to another. However, the fact that an instrument is *negotiable* has relatively little to do with its *transferability*. True, a negotiable instrument is easy to transfer because, as the next chapter reveals, the mechanics of a "negotiation" (the special kind of transfer applicable to a negotiable instrument) are simple. But under the law of assignments discussed in Chapter 13, many ordinary contract rights are freely assignable (transferable), especially the right to a money payment. The main difference between a negotiable and a non-negotiable document lies in the number of defenses a good faith purchaser must face when seeking payment. A holder in due course of a negotiable instrument faces fewer defenses to payment than an assignee of a non-negotiable instrument faces.

Dual Nature of Commercial Paper

Commercial paper is, simultaneously, a contract and a type of property. Commercial paper is a *contract* because Article 3 imposes on *any signer* an "engagement" (promise) to pay the face amount, regardless of whether the signer knew he or she was making such a promise. People who indorse (sign) their payroll checks when cashing them probably do not realize that, by indorsing, they have *contracted* to pay the face amount if the drawer (employer) does not; but indeed they *have* so contracted—because Article 3 says so [3-413, 3-414].

As we have seen, the negotiable instruments that constitute commercial paper are not ordinary contracts. They are "formal" contracts that by law have been given special qualities so that they can serve better as a *substitute for money* (the main use of a check) and as a *means of extending credit* (the main use of a note). Negotiable instruments are "formal" because they conform to a particular form or style of language required by law. One of the special qualities resulting from their formal character is that the purchaser of a negotiable instrument can be a holder in due course, free from personal defenses of, for example, the maker or drawer. The purchaser of a non-negotiable instrument (an ordinary, "simple" or "informal" contract) can *never* be a holder in due course but is always a mere assignee, subject to all defenses.

Commercial paper is also a type of property that can be bought and sold. Recall from Chapter 28 that chattel paper, which consists of a promissory note and a security agreement, can itself be sold or pledged so that the business generating it can raise money before the note comes due. Also, many corporations issue commercial paper in the form of promissory notes, for short-term financing. A person who buys such paper from the corporation may, in turn, sell it like any other property. Since commercial paper is property, it is subject to some rules of property law. For example, delivery of a negotiable instrument is a requirement for conveying ownership of it to a donee (recipient of a gift) or to a buyer. And, as in the sale of goods, the law imposes warranties that may be available to a purchaser if the paper turns out to be defective in some respect. Warranties as they relate to commercial paper are discussed in Chapter 32.

Some Business Uses of Commercial Paper

Business people use commercial paper in numerous ways. For example, a person or firm usually buys a certificate of deposit as an investment, to collect the interest. While holding the CD, however, that person or firm might pledge it as collateral for a loan (Chapter 28 discusses the pledge) or might simply sell it to raise immediate cash for some personal or business purpose. The bank that issues a CD does so, of course, to attract funds to lend to its customers.

Often, the creation of commercial paper is only one step in a complex transaction involving many other documents. The following paragraphs describe some common business uses of notes and drafts and the role of negotiable instruments in complicated transactions.

Uses of Notes.   Promissory notes are used mainly as evidence of indebtedness in loan transactions and in credit sales of property or services. Typically, a borrower signs a note that bears interest on the principal amount. Principal and interest may be due in one lump sum at a fixed future time (or on demand); or principal and interest may be payable in installments, often equal monthly installments. Sometimes the maker agrees to pay the interest in installments and then make a final "balloon" (large) payment consisting of not only the final installment of interest, but also repayment of the principal. Frequently, lenders are willing to extend unsecured credit, solely on the basis of the borrower's personal note. Often, however, they will insist that some third person cosign the note as *surety* (discussed in Chapter 27), or that the note be secured by real estate or other property that the lender may sell if the borrower fails to repay the loan. (Secured transactions are discussed in Chapters 27 and 28.)

Notes frequently are used to finance the sale of goods on a secured basis. As indicated in Chapter 28, the *conditional sale contract* and the *chattel mortgage* are commonly used for this purpose. They consist essentially of a promissory note signed by the buyer as maker, together with a security agreement giving the seller the right to repossess the goods upon the buyer's default. Usually the notes are interest-bearing installment notes.

Uses of Drafts.   Businesses use drafts most often in financing the sale of goods. Drafts are especially useful for this purpose when buyer and seller are strangers, are located some distance from each other, and make use of a reliable intermediary to handle the transaction. Suppose that Sally Seller is in Boston, Bob Buyer is in San Francisco, and Seller has agreed to extend 60 days' credit to Buyer to purchase a machine to be used in his business. This transaction will require the use of a 60-day time draft. When Seller ships the machine, she obtains from the carrier a bill of lading. She then draws a time draft reading "To: Bob Buyer. Sixty days after sight pay to the order of Sally Seller $8200." This amount covers the price of the machine plus shipping costs. Seller attaches the bill of lading, an invoice (itemized account of the goods), a security agreement, and a financing statement to the draft and takes it to her bank in Boston. The Boston bank forwards the draft with the attached documents to its correspondent bank in San Francisco. The San Francisco bank notifies Bob Buyer that the draft has arrived. He accepts the draft and signs the security agreement and the financing statement. The bank then delivers the bill of lading to Buyer so he can claim the machine when it arrives. The bank arranges to have the financing statement filed and, depending on Sally Seller's instructions, either holds the time draft for collection at the end of the 60 days, sells the draft to a buyer of commercial paper, or sends it to Sally. Time drafts such as the one drawn by Seller on the purchaser of goods (here, Bob Buyer) and accepted by the purchaser are called "trade acceptances" and can be sold, or pledged as collateral for a loan.

NEGOTIABLE FORM

No purchaser of a note or draft can be a holder in due course unless the instrument is in negotiable form. If the instrument lacks negotiable form, even an innocent purchaser will be merely an assignee, subject to all defenses of the maker or drawer.

The UCC sets forth eight requirements that must be met for a note or draft to be in negotiable form:

1. The instrument must be in *writing*.
2. It must be *signed by the maker or drawer*.
3. It must contain a *promise or order* to pay.
4. The promise or order must be *unconditional* in character.
5. It must be payable in *money*.
6. It must be made out for a *sum certain*.
7. It must be payable either on *demand* or at a *definite time after its issue*.
8. It must be payable to the *order of the payee* or *to bearer* [3-104].

If any one of these eight requirements is not met, the instrument is not in negotiable form, and all transferees are assignees only.

Some types of commercial paper, such as checks, are extremely simple and easy to use. Other types, such as notes, can be quite complicated and lengthy because of the many protective clauses that a lender or seller will demand as a condition to making the loan or selling on credit. Sometimes the added language destroys negotiability, and sometimes even a preprinted check form is altered in such a way as to destroy negotiability. Thus we have two questions: (1) What minimum language is required for the creation of negotiable form? (2) Once negotiable form is created, what clauses or language may be added to the instrument without destroying negotiability?

Minimum Language Required for Negotiable Form

The minimum language required for an instrument to be negotiable varies somewhat according to whether the instrument is a demand or a time instrument. However, some wording is common to all commercial paper.

Unconditional Promise or Order to Pay.   To be negotiable, an instrument must contain language that clearly reveals the issuer's intention to be bound personally to make payment or to have a drawee pay. So, if the instrument is a note, it must contain the maker's *promise* to pay (e.g., "I promise to pay"; "I undertake to pay"). If the instrument is a draft, it must contain the drawer's *order* (command or instruction) to the drawee that the *drawee* is to pay (e.g., "Pay . . ."; "Pay to . . ."). A mere acknowledgment of debt ("IOU $50") is not a promise because there is no expression of the debtor's intention to pay the amount owed. The *intention to pay* must be *expressed*. Likewise, language such as "I wish you would pay" is not an order to pay but is merely an authorization or request.

The promise or order must be clear and definite; but for the instrument to be negotiable, and thus to circulate most freely or to bring the highest possible price, the promise or order must also be *unconditional* (without reservations; absolute). John's language, "I promise to pay Eva or order $100 *if* I receive from her one used typewriter by 5:00 P.M. Friday" is conditional (and the note in which the language appears is non-negotiable) because John has made his obligation to pay $100 dependent on Eva's delivering the typewriter. If Eva puts the note into circulation, every potential purchaser will have to investigate the underlying transaction to determine whether Eva delivered the typewriter. This burden of investigation is inconsistent with a major aim of commercial paper law—to remove as many doubts as possible about the collectibility of drafts and notes. The requirement that the promise or order be unconditional is discussed further in this chapter under the heading "Language That Destroys Negotiability."

Order or Bearer Language ("Language of Negotiability").   To be negotiable, an instrument must contain language expressing the issuer's intention (actual or presumed) that the instrument circulate freely. This language of negotiability can be either *order* language or *bearer* language, depending on the wishes of the parties. By using **order** language (e.g., "Pay *to the order of* Jean Jones" in a draft; "I promise to pay *to the order of* Jean Jones" in a note), the drawer or maker expresses a willingness for the payee to specify who will have the right to collect payment. By using **bearer** language (e.g., "Pay *bearer*" in a draft; "I promise to pay *bearer*" in a note), the drawer or maker expresses a willingness to pay *anyone* who is *in possession* of the instrument. The presence of bearer or order language assures any transferee (person who receives the instrument from the payee or other holder) that the issuer is willing to pay even a stranger.

In contrast, language such as "Pay Jean Jones" lacks the required order or bearer language (the instruction does not include the words "to the order of" or the word "bearer") and can cast doubt on whether the instrument was intended to circulate among strangers. The absence of order or bearer language results in a *non*-negotiable instrument. While a non-negotiable instrument is collectible under the law of assignments (if there are no real or personal defenses), not only the payee but also every transferee is subject to *any* defense, including any *personal* defense, that the maker or drawer has. So, if a drawer strikes out the words "to the order of" on a preprinted check form, he or she has created a non-negotiable check. In doing so, the drawer has preserved all personal defenses, but also has increased a purchaser's risk of noncollection and thus may have reduced the willingness of strangers to cash the check or to pay the full face amount for it.

Usually order or bearer language appears in a negotiable instrument because the issuer has simply filled out a preprinted form (such as a blank check) containing the language. Probably, most people neither know what language of negotiability is nor understand its significance. Nevertheless, language of negotiability is required by law for an instrument to be negotiable and, consequently, for a holder in due course to have the special benefit of being entitled to payment despite the personal defenses of the maker or drawer (or of other persons discussed in subsequent chapters).

Wording Indicating Instrument Is for a "Sum Certain" Payable in Money.   An instrument is *payable in money* if it gives the payee the right to be paid in the currency of any domestic or foreign government—dollars, marks, rubles, pesos, and so on. So, an instrument payable in wheat or corn cannot be negotiable. However, if the payee is given the option of demanding wheat *or* money, the instrument is payable in money. If the *drawer* or *maker* has the option of providing wheat or money, the instrument is *not* payable in money. The payment-in-money requirement allows a purchaser of the instrument to determine easily how much to pay for it, since calculations are made in some commonly accepted medium of exchange.

The requirement of a *sum certain* serves a similar purpose. If the sum is certain, a purchaser can determine quickly how much the maker or drawer owes, and therefore how much the purchaser should pay for the instrument. The sum is certain if the *purchaser* (or payee) can, *at the time set for payment,* determine *from the instrument itself without reference to any outside source* the amount then payable. Suppose Sue signs a note reading, "I promise to pay the bearer of this note, on demand, $500 plus 10 percent annual interest," and delivers the note to Joe, who discounts it to Ann. Since Sue cannot predict when Ann will demand payment, Sue has no way of knowing how much interest she will owe Ann. Despite this, the sum is certain because *Ann,* the purchaser, will be able to compute exactly how much Sue, the maker, owes at the moment Ann decides to demand payment. A provision in a note imposing a charge for late payment does not make the sum uncertain. Neither does a provision requiring the maker to pay reasonable attorney's fees for a collection suit upon the maker's default [3-106].

Signature of Maker or Drawer.   The signature of the maker or drawer is required for the obvious reason that payees and other holders must be able to prove whose legal commitment the instrument represents. A signature is any symbol used or adopted by a party (e.g., maker or drawer) with the present intention to authenticate the writing [1-201(39)]. So, a signature can be handwritten or typed, or it could be made by an agent for the agent's principal (and adopted by the principal), or it could consist of a trade name, an assumed name, a mark such as "X", or even a thumbprint.

The signature of a drawer or maker may appear in the body of the instrument, but normally appears at the end of the document. It is possible for the signature of the drawer or maker to appear on the reverse side of the instrument, but since such a placement is usually reserved for indorsements, it should be avoided for makers' and drawers' signatures because doubts could arise about who issued the instrument.

Wording Indicating Instrument Is Payable on Demand or at Definite Time **[3-109].**   To be negotiable, an instrument must be payable on demand or at a definite time so that a purchaser can determine with ease and certainty two things: (1) when the purchaser will have a right to payment, and (2) how much the drawer or maker will owe if the instrument bears interest. However, whether a *date* is required for negotiability depends on the other (nondate) language of the instrument, since definiteness can be provided in a variety of ways. Some *time* instruments do need a date for negotiability, as where the instrument reads, "60 days after *date* pay. . . ." No date is required, though, for a time instrument reading "60 days after *sight* pay" or "I promise to pay 60 days after *demand.*" In these instances payment is at a definite time because the payee or other holder knows from the wording exactly when he or she will be entitled to payment. Demand instruments, including checks, need no date to be considered payable at a definite time. The payee or other holder of a demand instrument knows when he or she will demand payment and thus can compute with precision how much the drawer or maker will owe if the instrument bears interest. The blank for the date in a check form is used by the drawer to record the date when the drawer *issued* the check; it is *not* used to set a date for payment, since the payee or other holder can demand payment of the check for a substantial time after date of issue. Usually, where no date for payment is stated, the instrument is a demand instrument, as where it reads, "I promise to pay . . . $100" [3-108].

Where payment is linked to an event that is uncertain as to time of occurrence, the instrument is not negotiable, and does not become negotiable even though the event has occurred [3-109]. For example, a note reading "payable 30 days after the death of my Uncle Abner" is non-negotiable because the time of Uncle Abner's death is uncertain.

Language That Destroys Negotiability

A note reading "On demand I promise to pay the bearer the sum of fifty dollars" is negotiable in form if signed by the maker—because the note contains an unconditional promise to pay and language of negotiability (the word "bearer"), and it states a sum certain payable on demand. Often, however, an instrument such as the note just described contains additional language. The additional language might have no effect on the negotiability of the instrument, or the addition might destroy negotiability. For example, additional language that *renders the sum uncertain* or the *time of payment indefinite* deprives the instrument of negotiability and limits its purchaser to the rights of an assignee. Likewise, although they are perfectly legal, words that condition the promise of the drawer or maker destroy negotiability because they may create doubts in the mind of a purchaser about the collectibility of the instrument, or may require a time-consuming investigation by the purchaser of the circumstances surrounding the transaction between maker and payee. Some common situations involving additional language are discussed in the following paragraphs.

Express Conditions. If the promise or order is expressly conditioned on the happening or nonhappening of an event, the instrument is non-negotiable. For example, a promise to pay "if the typewriter is delivered before June 4" is expressly conditioned on the happening of an event. An instrument containing such a promise is non-negotiable. The promise or order must be to pay in all events, not just on the occurrence of one event.

Words Referring to Another Agreement. The conditional or unconditional character of an instrument is determined solely by what is expressed on its face. If the instrument states that it is "subject to" or "governed by" another agreement, the promise or order is conditional. Suppose a note reads, "Subject to the terms and provisions of chattel mortgage No. 17 on file in the Amos County courthouse, I promise to pay bearer the sum of $1000." This note is non-negotiable because the holder must look to another agreement to learn the scope of the maker's promise. Placing such a burden on holders is contrary to the idea of free circulation and efficient collection. So, as illustrated by Case 30.1, the mere fact of subjecting the promise or order to the contents of an outside document destroys negotiability, regardless of what the outside document says.

However, it is common for people to make a notation on the face of a negotiable instrument for record-keeping purposes. If a check, draft, or promissory note merely *refers* to an underlying transaction, without making payment depend on the maker's or drawer's satisfaction with the underlying transaction, the reference does not make the order or promise conditional. Thus, a promise is not made conditional, and negotiability is not destroyed, by the statement that "This note is given for the purchase of goods as per contract of June 4, 19xx." Nor is a check rendered non-negotiable by the notation "For one red sofa."

CASE 30.1   **Holly Hill Acres, Ltd. v. Charter Bank of Gainesville**
314 So. 2d 209 (Fla. App. 1975)

Facts: Holly Hill bought real estate from Rogers and Blythe, signing and delivering as payment Holly Hill's promissory note, together with a mortgage on the land to secure the note. The note contained the following clause: "This note with interest is secured by a mortgage on real estate, of even date herewith, made by the maker thereof in favor of the said payee, and shall be construed and enforced according to the laws of the State of Florida. The terms of said mortgage are by this reference made a part hereof." Rogers and Blythe then transferred the note and mortgage to Charter Bank as security for a loan to them from the Bank. Holly Hill defaulted in its payments to Charter Bank. Bank sued Holly Hill to collect the amount due on its note. At trial, Holly Hill alleged that agents of Rogers and Blythe had used fraud to induce Holly Hill to purchase the real estate. Holding that Bank was a holder in due course, the trial court awarded a summary judgment against Holly Hill. Holly Hill appealed.

Question: Was Charter Bank entitled to a summary judgment?

Answer: No.

Reasoning: Contrary to the trial court's holding, Charter Bank was not a holder in due course, because Holly Hill's note was not negotiable in form. The note incorporated the terms of the mortgage document and made Holly Hill's promise subject to the terms of the mortgage. Consequently, Bank is a mere assignee who takes subject to any defense that Holly Hill can prove, including the personal defense of fraud in the inducement.

Words Limiting Source of Payment.   For an instrument to be negotiable, the maker or drawer must subject his or her *general credit* (total wealth) to liability for payment, as opposed to limiting payment to some fraction of his or her assets. This requirement is consistent with the idea of giving a holder maximum assurance of collectibility. A note reading "I promise to pay to the order of First Bank $3000 out of this year's wheat crop" is non-negotiable because the source of payment is a **particular fund** rather than the total assets of the maker. In contrast, an instrument reading "Pay $100 to the order of Paul Payee and charge the merchandise account" is negotiable. The instruction to charge the merchandise account is merely a bookkeeping instruction. The drawer has not expressed an intention to make the merchandise account the sole source of payment. If the drawer had said, "Pay *only out of* the merchandise account," the order would be conditional and the draft would be non-negotiable.

There are two exceptions to the rule that for an instrument to be negotiable, payment cannot be limited to a particular fund. First, short-term instruments issued by a government or governmental agency or unit are *not* rendered non-negotiable merely by the fact that payment is limited to a particular fund or to the proceeds of particular taxes or other sources of revenue. Second, an instrument issued by a partnership or unincorporated association limiting payment to "the entire assets" of the association is not rendered non-negotiable, despite the fact that the limitation is intended to protect the partners or members from their usual personal liability. The general credit of the association is still available for payment.

Case 30.2 illustrates the application of the particular fund doctrine.

CASE 30.2   Glendora Bank v. Davis
267 P. 311 (Cal. 1928)

Facts: Foothill Finance Corp. (FFC) sold auto accessories to Davis for $1,935. In payment, Davis gave FFC a note containing the following language: "Pay to Foothill Finance Corporation or order. This note is given in payment of merchandise and is to be liquidated by payments received on account of sale of such merchandise." FFC sold the note to Glendora Bank. Davis sold less than $200 worth of accessories before defaulting on the note. Bank sued Davis for the face amount, but the trial court held that Davis was liable for only $192.80. Bank appealed.

Question: Should Davis have been held liable for the full face amount of the note?

Answer: No.

Reasoning: The clause stating that the merchandise was to be paid for out of the proceeds of its sale makes the note a "promise to pay out of a particular fund." Consequently, the note is non-negotiable in form, Glendora Bank is only an assignee, and Bank takes the note subject to any personal defense that Davis has. The clause that deprives the note of negotiability also provides Davis with a personal defense. The only reasonable interpretation of the clause is that payment was to be made only out of receipts from the sale of the merchandise, a sale which might not take place at all or might take place to some, but to an uncertain, extent.

Language Not Affecting Negotiability

If a promise or order is unconditional, the sum is certain, and the time of payment definite, an instrument that has the minimum required language of negotiability may be negotiable despite the presence of certain additional language. Sometimes the added language *does* in fact affect time of payment or other qualities pertaining to negotiability, but is so beneficial that the UCC permits it and provides that it does not destroy negotiability. Other added language may or may not cause loss of negotiability. Some notable illustrations follow.

Acceleration Clauses.   Often the parties to a negotiable instrument provide for acceleration (early payment) of the instrument. The maker of a note might want to pay it off early to save on interest charges. The note might therefore read, "I promise to pay $1000 to First Bank or order, together with 12 percent annual interest, on or before May 1, 19xx." The "on or before" language is an acceleration clause favoring the maker. Because the *maker* may choose when to pay the note, the time of payment could be considered indefinite from the viewpoint of the holder. However, the acceleration clause is so beneficial to the maker, and causes the holder so little difficulty, that under the UCC its presence does not destroy negotiability.

The payee or other holder might also have the benefit of an acceleration clause, as where a holder is permitted to require early payment "if I deem myself insecure" (i.e., "if I come to doubt the ability of the maker or drawer to pay") or the instrument provides that it "shall become immediately due and payable upon any default in payment of interest or principal." The presence of such a clause does not affect negotiability. However, a holder who exercises an option to accelerate because of the holder's insecurity (fear of nonpayment) must have a good faith belief that the prospect of payment is impaired.

Confession of Judgment Clauses.   Sometimes an instrument contains a clause that authorizes the holder to have an attorney "confess judgment" (enter a judgment in court) against the maker or drawer if the instrument is not paid when due, even though failure to pay may be justified. The judgment cuts off every defense that the maker may have, and it also cuts off the maker's right to appeal the judgment. Confession of judgment clauses are so harsh that in most states they are void. However, the presence of such a clause in a negotiable instrument does *not* destroy negotiability *if* the clause can be exercised only after the maker's default. If the clause can be exercised at *any* time, its presence *does* destroy negotiability.

Rules for Interpreting Common Ambiguities

Like any other contract, a negotiable instrument may be so poorly written that it requires interpretation. The UCC states a number of rules of interpretation that the courts are to apply. These rules include the following:

1. Where a discrepancy exists between handwritten terms and typewritten or printed terms, handwritten terms control (prevail). Where a discrepancy exists between typewritten terms and printed terms, typewritten terms control.

2. Where the sum payable is expressed in words and also in figures, and the two expressions of amount differ, the sum payable is that expressed in words. However, if the words are ambiguous, the sum payable is that expressed in figures.

3. Where a provision for interest does not specify the rate of interest, the rate is the **judgment rate** at the place of payment. (A "judgment rate" is a rate of interest established by a state statute to be applied by the courts to judgments for damages where interest is an element of the damage award. The UCC adopts this rate for convenience and certainty.) If the instrument is dated, the interest will run from the

date of the instrument; if it is undated, the interest will run from the date the instrument was issued.

PERSONAL AND REAL DEFENSES

Most commercial paper is issued as payment by the maker or drawer for property or services received from the payee, or as evidence of a loan made by the payee to the maker. In all these underlying transactions, disputes can arise about the quality or sufficiency of the payee's performance. Even where the payee *performs* his or her part of the underlying transaction, the maker or drawer may nevertheless have a legal right, because of some other circumstance, to cancel the underlying contract. Thus, the maker or drawer of the negotiable instrument given in payment acquires *defenses* against having to pay the payee. But the payee might have transferred the instrument to a holder in due course who, having paid for it, naturally wants to collect from the maker or drawer. So the question is: Must the maker or drawer pay the holder in due course even though the maker or drawer has legal justification for canceling the transaction with the payee? The answer depends on whether the defense of the maker or drawer is *personal* or *real*.

As indicated earlier, the main benefit of being a holder in due course is that such a holder takes a negotiable instrument free of all rival claims to it and free from personal but subject to real defenses of all parties (signers). The "rival claims" just mentioned have to do especially with disputes about ownership that arise when an instrument is stolen or obtained by fraud. Such claims are discussed in Chapter 31. The remainder of this chapter concerns personal and real defenses. The discussion that follows involves defenses of makers and drawers. However, any party to a negotiable instrument (maker, drawer, acceptor, indorser) can have a real or personal defense to payment. Note, incidentally, that some conditions such as insanity and acts of wrongdoing such as fraud or duress can be either a personal or a real defense, depending on circumstances to be discussed later.

Personal Defenses As noted earlier in this chapter, a *personal* defense is one that the law says must remain a private matter between the immediate parties to a negotiable instrument, e.g., between maker and payee, instead of causing loss to a holder in due course. So, where a holder in due course seeks payment and the maker or drawer has only a personal defense, the maker or drawer must pay the holder in due course and initiate legal action against the payee for breach of the underlying contract, seek from the payee a voluntary repayment, or absorb the loss.

Personal defenses include the following:

1. *Payee's fraud, misrepresentation, duress, or undue influence in inducing the maker or drawer into the underlying transaction.* These defenses are discussed in Chapter 10, but one, fraud, needs special mention here. There are two kinds of fraud: *fraud in the inducement* (always a *personal* defense), and *fraud in the execution of the instrument* (which can be a *real* defense under the circumstances described later in this chapter).

Fraud in the inducement (illustrated in Case 30.3) gets its name from the fact that the payee induces (lures) the maker or drawer into voluntarily signing a negotiable instrument based on the payee's lie about the nature of the underlying transaction. For example, Sue fraudulently represents herself to John as a member of First Church seeking contributions for the church's missionary work. In fact, Sue does not belong to the church, and it has no missionary program. Not knowing this, John makes out a $100 check to Sue, who tells John she will indorse (sign) it over to the church. Instead, she cashes the check at a local supermarket and disappears with the money. The supermarket, a holder in due course, is entitled to payment from John free from his defense of fraud in the inducement.

The key factor in John's liability to the supermarket is that John *knew he was signing a check, signed it voluntarily, and put it into circulation.* John's negligence (failing to investigate Sue's representations and issuing the check to Sue instead of First Church) was great. A judge ruling in favor of the supermarket might point out that John was in a better position than the supermarket to detect the fraud and prevent loss. But some fraud in the inducement is so skillfully committed that it is undetectable; therefore its victims are blameless. Nevertheless, it is at least arguable that even blameless victims are in a better position than the holder in due course to prevent loss. This possibility of self-protection, together with the policy of enhancing the marketability of commercial paper, is the basis for the rule that all forms of fraud in the inducement, detectable or not, constitute merely a personal defense.

2. *Mistake* (discussed in Chapter 10) of the kinds that would justify the maker or drawer in rescinding (canceling) the underlying contract.

3. *Breach of warranty* (discussed in Chapter 18), especially in sales of goods.

4. *Failure of performance* (also called failure of consideration) such as inability or refusal to deliver property, discussed in Chapter 14.

5. *Nondelivery of the instrument.* Suppose that near the end of the month Dora makes out a payroll check to her employee Paul, intending to deliver it to him after the first of the next month. Before then Paul obtains possession of the check without Dora's knowledge and indorses it to Harry, a holder in due course. When Dora discovers that the check is missing, she stops payment on it. Then Harry presents the check to the drawee bank for payment. The bank refuses to pay, and Harry sues Dora, who contends she is not liable to Harry because she never delivered the check to Paul. If Paul himself had tried to cash the check at the bank, Dora's defense of nondelivery would be good. However, since nondelivery of a signed instrument is a *personal* defense, it is not good against Harry, the holder in due course.

Occasionally a maker or drawer delivers a negotiable instrument to the payee on the understanding (*not* expressed in the instrument) that the delivery will not become effective unless a specified event occurs (unless, for example, a particular service is performed), or on the understanding that the instrument is to be used for a special purpose. While the defenses of conditional delivery and delivery for a special purpose are good between the immediate parties, they are personal defenses and, as such, are not good against a holder in due course.

6. *Unauthorized completion of a signed instrument.* Suppose May signs a check naming Paul as payee but leaves the amount blank, instructing Paul to fill in the amount later for an amount not to exceed $100. He fills in the amount for $500 and

negotiates the check to Harry, a holder in due course. Harry is entitled to $500 from May, free from May's personal defense of Paul's lack of authority to complete the check for $500. By signing a check and permitting someone else to fill in the amount, May has created a trap for holders in due course and therefore should absorb any loss.

CASE 30.3 Mellon Bank v. Donegal Mutual Ins. Co.
29 UCC Rep. 912 (Pa. Ct. C.P. 1980)

Facts: McConnell made a claim against a person insured by Donegal Insurance Company. In settlement of the claim, Donegal drew a check for over $3,700 on Farmer's First Bank, naming McConnell as payee. McConnell cashed the check at Mellon Bank where he had an account and received the proceeds in cash. Mellon Bank presented the check to Farmer's for payment, but Farmer's refused to honor the check because Donegal had ordered Farmer's to stop payment on the ground that McConnell's insurance claim was fraudulent. Not being able to collect from the drawee, Mellon Bank sued Donegal, the drawer, for payment.

Question: Was Mellon Bank entitled to payment from the drawer?

Answer: Yes.

Reasoning: The check was a negotiable instrument, and Mellon Bank, having paid McConnell cash for the check without knowledge of the stop order, was a holder in due course entitled to payment free from the personal defenses of the drawer. Because Donegal's defense, that the payee made a fraudulent insurance claim, was only a personal defense, it is not good against a holder in due course. Donegal, as a signer of the check, must pay Mellon and seek any remedy from McConnell.

Real Defenses As noted earlier in this chapter, *real* defenses involve circumstances of such serious consequences to makers, drawers, and other signers of commercial paper that the policy of protecting holders in due course must yield to the need to protect signers. Unlike a personal defense, a real defense is good against any person, even a holder in due course. Article 3 identifies a number of real defenses [3-305].

Infancy (Minority). Infancy is a defense against a holder in due course "to the extent that it is a defense to a simple contract" under the law governing the underlying transaction. Recall from Chapter 10 that state law varies on matters such as the kinds of contracts a minor may rescind (cancel) and what the minor must do to be entitled to rescind. If state law permits a minor to rescind his or her contract (e.g., for the purchase of goods), minority (infancy) is a real defense as to any negotiable instrument the minor gave in payment. Suppose that the law of Mel's state permits minors to rescind their contracts for luxuries merely by returning the goods even though damaged. Mel, a minor, buys a camera (a luxury) and issues Camera Shop a check for $500 in payment. A short time later Mel damages the camera, rescinds the contract, and places a stop-payment order on the check. In the meantime Camera Shop has negotiated the check to Harriet, a holder in due course, who presents the check to Mel's bank and is refused payment. She then sues Mel for payment of the check. But because state law permits Mel to rescind the underlying transaction, Mel has, under the UCC, a real defense to payment of the negotiable instrument. By denying the holder in due course payment of the check, the UCC supports the local policy of protecting minors who elect to rescind the underlying contract. (As indicated in Chapter 32, Harriet may be able to compel Camera Shop to make good her loss, on the ground that Camera Shop breached a transfer warranty. Thus, as the law intended, Camera Shop ultimately would bear the risk of dealing with minors.)

Incapacity other than Minority; Duress; Illegality.   The defense of "other incapacity [than minority]" refers to incapacities such as insanity, drunkenness, and lack of corporate capacity to do business. They and the defenses of insanity and duress are described in Chapter 10. The defense of illegality is discussed in Chapter 11. Illegality occurs most often where a maker or drawer issues an instrument to pay a gambling debt in violation of a law prohibiting gambling, as in Case 30.4, or has signed a note carrying an interest rate that exceeds the rate permitted by the usury laws. All the defenses just mentioned may be real or personal, depending on state law.

State law often distinguishes between instances of relatively minor wrongdoing that render an obligation merely *voidable* (rescindable at the option of an affected party such as the maker of a note) and those instances of serious misconduct that render the obligation *void* (of no legal effect whatever). The defenses of illegality, duress, and nonminority incapacity are *real* defenses only if state law, because of the seriousness of the circumstance involved, "renders the obligation of the party a nullity" (*void*) [3-305(2)(b)]. Duress provides an example. Forcing a person to sign a negotiable instrument at gun point is the kind of duress that in all states renders the transaction void; the act of signing, though apparently creating a contractual obligation on the part of the signer, created no obligation at all because of the duress. In such a situation the drawer or maker has a real defense. However, in many states, forcing a person to sign a negotiable instrument under threat to prosecute the son of the maker for theft is a less serious form of duress that renders the maker's obligation under the instrument merely voidable and thus provides the maker with only a *personal* defense: one which is good against the wrongdoing payee if that person seeks payment, but not good against a holder in due course seeking payment.

Fraud in the Execution.   Fraud in the execution (signing) of a negotiable instrument occurs, for example, where a payee persuades a person to sign a negotiable instrument by misrepresenting it as some other kind of document, or by indicating that the paper being signed is a negotiable instrument but misrepresenting its contents. Sometimes called "fraud in the essence" or "fraud in the factum," fraud in the execution may be either a real or a personal defense, depending on the circumstances surrounding the signing. Fraud in the execution is a *real* defense if the payee or other wrongdoer "has induced the party to sign the instrument with neither knowledge nor reasonable opportunity to obtain knowledge of its character or essential terms" [3-305(2)(c)]. Suppose a trusted and faithful ex-employee of a blind person asks the former employer to sign a "letter of reference" that is in reality a check for $1000 made out to the ex-employee. Probably the ex-employee's fraud constitutes a *real* defense, good against even a holder in due course to whom the defrauder might negotiate the check. However, only a court can say with authority whether the blind drawer's defense is real or merely personal. If the drawer had reason to suspect wrongdoing by the former employee and had an opportunity to investigate but failed to do so, the defense is only a personal one even though the fraud concerned the nature of the document or its essential (important) terms.

Bankruptcy. One purpose of federal bankruptcy proceedings is to provide a hopelessly overburdened debtor with the opportunity for a fresh start, by means of a formal release from debt called a "discharge in bankruptcy." To give effect to the federal policy of debtor relief (and to the similar policy of state insolvency laws), Article 3 makes any discharge in insolvency proceedings (state or federal) a real defense, good against even a holder in due course of a negotiable instrument issued by the debtor [3-305(2)(d)].

Unauthorized Signature; Material Alteration. *Unauthorized signature* includes both a forgery and a signature made by an agent exceeding his or her actual *or apparent* authority. The defense is good even against a holder in due course, unless the alleged signer ratified the signature (approved the signature as his or her own after the signing) or is precluded (prevented) by law from denying it. For example, suppose the Drew Candle Company employs Ann as a bookkeeper. Ordinarily a bookkeeper has no authority to write checks for his or her employer, but Ann *is* authorized to draw checks on Drew's bank account provided they are cosigned by the controller. Ann draws a check payable to her friend Paul without securing the signature of the controller. Even if the check is negotiated to a holder in due course, Drew Company may assert the defense of unauthorized signature. However, Drew Company may be precluded from denying Ann's authority if it is careless in the handling of its checks, for example, if they are not kept in a secure place under proper supervision.

A *material alteration* (an unauthorized, significant change in the wording of a negotiable instrument) may be a partial real defense or no defense at all. It is no defense where the issuer assented (agreed) to the alteration or contributed to its making through negligence or other fault. For example, if the payee raises the amount of an instrument while the maker or drawer looks on, a holder in due course may collect the increased amount. Where the maker or drawer did not assent and was not at fault, that person has a real defense good against a holder in due course, but only to the extent of the alteration, since "a subsequent holder in due course may in all cases enforce the instrument according to its original tenor" [3-407]. Suppose Don draws a check for $200 payable to Pam. If Pam, without Don's knowledge or negligence, raises the amount of the check to $1200 and negotiates it to a holder in due course, Don may be held liable only for the original amount, $200.

CASE30.4   Sandler v. Eighth Judicial Dist. Court
614 P.2d 10 (Nev. 1980)

Facts: Sandler wrote checks on a Maryland bank account to Hutchings as payee to cover gambling losses incurred by Sandler. Hutchings negotiated them to Nevada National Bank. Being unable to collect from the drawee, Bank sued Sandler for the face amount. The trial court denied Sandler's request for judgment in his favor, and Sandler petitioned the appellate court for an order requiring the trial court to award judgment to Sandler.

Question: Was Sandler entitled to judgment in his favor?

Answer: Yes.

Reasoning: Nevada National Bank claims to be a holder in due course entitled to payment of the checks free from Sandler's defense. However, in the state of Nevada, checks drawn for the purpose of gambling are void and unenforceable under Nevada's statute. It provides that checks issued for gambling are "utterly void, frustrate, and of none effect." Because the statute makes the checks void, Sandler has a real defense that is good even against a holder in due course.

SUMMARY

Commercial paper serves as a substitute for money and as a means of extending credit because a holder in due course, unlike the purchaser of an ordinary contract, takes commercial paper (negotiable instruments) free from personal defenses of makers and drawers and other parties to it. Commercial paper is both a formal contract and a type of property that can be bought and sold. Whether in the form of a three-party draft or a two-party note, commercial paper has a variety of business uses.

For a person to have the favored status of holder in due course, commercial paper must be negotiable in form. An instrument will be negotiable if the maker or drawer uses certain minimum language prescribed by the UCC and avoids using additional language that renders the promise or order conditional or otherwise destroys negotiability. Most personal defenses, which are not good against a holder in due course, arise out of disputes about the quality or sufficiency of the payee's performance of an underlying transaction with the maker or drawer. Personal defenses include fraud in the inducement, breach of warranty in a sale of goods, nondelivery of the instrument, and unauthorized completion of a signed instrument. Real defenses, which are good even against a holder in due course, include infancy to the extent that it is a defense to a simple contract, serious forms of duress and illegality, fraud in the execution of the instrument, and unauthorized signature and material alteration.

REVIEW QUESTIONS

1. What are the two main functions of commercial paper?
2. What is the main function of a note?
3. How does a promissory note differ from a certificate of deposit?
4. (a) What is the basic function or use of a draft? (b) How does a demand draft differ from a time draft? (c) What is the meaning of "drawee"? "Acceptor"?
5. (a) What is the main use or practical value of checks? (b) What is the relationship between a check and an "underlying transaction"? (c) Explain or illustrate the meaning of the statement, "A check operates as only a conditional payment of the underlying obligation." (d) Explain whether a traveler's check is a check or a draft.
6. A negotiable instrument can confer upon a holder in due course more than the usual contract rights. Using the expressions "negotiable form," "holder in due course," and "personal and real defenses," explain or illustrate how this is so.
7. A negotiable instrument is, simultaneously, a contract and a type of property. Explain.
8. Explain how a draft may be used, together with other document, to finance the sale of goods.
9. What minimum language is required for an instrument to be in negotiable form? Is a date required? Explain.
10. (a) Give two illustrations of language that will destroy negotiability. (b) Give two illustrations of language that does not affect negotiability.
11. What is the difference between a personal and a real defense? Illustrate each kind.
12. Who can have a personal or real defense?

CASE PROBLEMS

1. Each of the names at the top of the note below was in the handwriting of the person named. Does the instrument meet the requirement that to be negotiable an instrument must be signed by the maker or drawer?

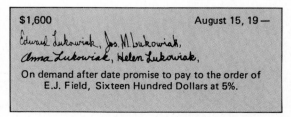

$1,600   August 15, 19—

Edward Lukowiak, Jos. M. Lukowiak,
Anna Lukowiak, Helen Lukowiak,

On demand after date promise to pay to the order of
E.J. Field, Sixteen Hundred Dollars at 5%.

2. Is the following installment note negotiable? Which two of the eight requirements for negotiability are in doubt?

May 5, 1977

I promise to pay to the order of Dr. Richard Rowe the sum of twenty dollars ($20.00) each month, beginning June 5, 1977, until I have paid four hundred and eighty dollars ($480.00). In case of death of maker, all payments not due at date of death are canceled.

John Doe

3. A contractor's note, properly dated and signed, read: "I promise to pay to the order of Paul Payee within the next sixty days the sum of five thousand dollars ($5,000) from the jobs now under construction." Is the note a negotiable instrument? Which of the eight requirements is in doubt?

4. Hank borrowed $50,000 from Jane so that he could establish his own hardware store. Jane required him to sign a promissory note for $50,000 payable to her order in ten annual installments plus 12% annual interest on the unpaid balance. The note stated, "This note shall immediately become due and payable with accrued interest whenever holder deems himself or herself insecure." Is this note negotiable? Which of the eight requirements is (are) in doubt?

5. Herb bought on credit a large-screen television set to use in the lobby of his motel. In payment he gave Maxine, the seller, a negotiable promissory note for $3000. She negotiated it to First Finance Corp., a holder in due course. When the note came due, First Finance sought payment from Herb, but he refused to pay on the ground that Maxine had lied to him about the performance characteristics of the TV set and that it had never worked satisfactorily. Assume that Maxine had lied as Herb said and that the TV set was worthless. Is First Finance entitled to payment from Herb? Why?

CHAPTER 31

NEGOTIATION OF COMMERCIAL PAPER; HOLDER-IN-DUE-COURSE STATUS

As noted in the preceding chapter, a holder in due course has a favored status in law. He or she takes commercial paper free from rival claims of ownership and free from the personal defenses of parties such as makers and drawers. An ordinary holder does *not* take an instrument free from defenses, but is, instead, a mere assignee of whatever rights his or her transferor had. The terms *holder* and *holder in due course* are discussed more fully later in this chapter.

For a person to be a holder in due course of a negotiable instrument, he or she (1) must take the instrument by a method of transfer called "negotiation," and (2) must possess the personal qualities required by law for holder-in-due-course status (must be a good faith purchaser). However, once the rights of a holder in due course have been established, they can be transferred to others by assignment. The first part of this chapter discusses the process of negotiation. The second part discusses the requirements for holder-in-due-course status and how a person may acquire the rights of such a holder without personally being one.

NEGOTIATION OF COMMERCIAL PAPER

"Issue" and "negotiation" are parts of the process of putting commercial paper into circulation. Ordinarily the maker or drawer will issue the paper to a payee. The payee may keep the instrument and later collect payment, or may instead negotiate the instrument to a third person. The third person becomes a *holder* if all requirements for a negotiation are met, and can be a *holder in due course* by meeting, in addition, the requirements for holder-in-due-course status.

Issue of an Instrument

Issue means the first delivery of an instrument by its maker or drawer to another person, usually the payee, with the intention of granting the payee rights in the instrument [3-102]. Upon issue, the payee is a holder of the instrument. So, when you make out a check and mail it to the gas company, you are *issuing* the check. The gas company becomes a *holder* when it receives (possesses) the check.

With respect to negotiable instruments, **delivery** means a voluntary transfer of possession [1-201(14)]. If Dora makes out a check to Paul, and he picks it up from Dora's desk without authority while Dora is out of her office, there is no delivery. Neither is there a delivery if Dora merely hands the check to her *own* agent with instructions to take the instrument to Paul. Delivery does not take place until the agent gives *control* of the instrument to Paul. Where a drawer or maker turns over an instrument directly to an *agent of the payee*, however, there is a delivery of the instrument.

An instrument can be issued even though the signer leaves lines blank for someone else to fill in [3-115]. Suppose Dora draws a check naming Paul as payee, leaves the lines for the amount blank, and gives the check to Paul with instructions to "fill in the amount I owe you." Because Dora signed the check and delivered it to Paul, it is issued even though it is an *incomplete instrument*. Issuing incomplete instruments is dangerous, but the practice is convenient and relatively frequent. Not to give effect to instruments completed by others than the issuers would unnecessarily raise doubts in the minds of holders in due course about the collectibility of such paper. However, an incomplete instrument cannot be enforced until completed [3-115(1)].

Sometimes the instrument is filled out for more than the amount authorized. The extent to which an unauthorized completion is binding on the issuer is discussed in Chapter 32.

Negotiation of an Instrument

Negotiation can occur in a variety of ways, depending on the kind of paper involved (bearer or order) and the wishes or needs of the parties. A surprising variety of people have the *power,* though not always the *right,* to negotiate commercial paper. Where commercial paper is negotiated by indorsement, the indorser has several types of indorsement from which to choose. These topics relating to negotiation are discussed in the following paragraphs.

Meaning and Methods of Negotiation. **Negotiation** is the transfer of a *negotiable* (properly worded) instrument in such a way that the transferee becomes a *holder.* (There can never be a negotiation unless the document is in *negotiable form.*) Basically, the word **holder** means a person *in possession* of *bearer* paper, or *in possession* of *order* paper that has been (1) *issued* to him or her, or (2) *transferred* to him or her and *properly indorsed* (signed) by the transferor. Thus, there are two methods of negotiation: (1) If the instrument is payable to *bearer,* it is negotiated by *delivery alone.* (2) If an instrument is payable to *order* (e.g., the drawer or maker has made the instrument out to a named payee), the instrument is negotiated by *delivery* (here, by the payee) *together with any necessary indorsement* (here, the payee's signature).

The term "order paper" refers not only to an instrument made out to the order of a named payee, but also to an instrument that is *indorsed* by a holder such as the payee *to* a named transferee. For example, Paul Payee indorses his payroll check (signs it on the back) as follows: "Pay John Jones (signed) Paul Payee." The check, which was order paper when issued to Paul, continues to be order paper because Paul, the transferor, named John as the transferee. Now, for John to negotiate the check to someone else, he too must indorse it.

What happens if the holder of order paper, wanting to negotiate it, delivers it but forgets to add his or her indorsement? In that event, there has been a mere *transfer* of the instrument, not a negotiation. The transfer constitutes an assignment of the transferor's rights. Until the indorsement is supplied, the transferee is merely an assignee and is subject not only to real defenses, but also to *any personal defenses learned of before the indorsement is supplied.* However, a transferee *for value* (i.e. a purchaser) is better off than an ordinary assignee. A transferee for value has "the specifically enforceable right to have [may have a court compel] the unqualified indorsement of the transferor" [3-201], and thus may become a holder in due course when the indorsement is supplied (if the transferee has the other qualities, such as good faith, necessary for holder-in-due-course status).

Who May Negotiate an Instrument. Any holder of commercial paper can negotiate it *and thereby enable a properly qualified transferee to become a holder in due course* (the type of good faith purchaser who takes a negotiable instrument free from personal defenses). With one exception discussed in Chapter 32, a person who lacks holder status cannot negotiate commercial paper. A transfer by a nonholder ordinarily is merely an assignment of whatever rights the nonholder may have.

However, if a transferor *is* a holder, that person has the power to negotiate the instrument even though the negotiation may be wrongful. This is because "holder" is defined broadly enough to include any person who is *or appears to be* the rightful owner of the instrument, as far as a prospective purchaser can tell from what is written on the face and on the back of the instrument. For example, any person in possession of paper made payable "to bearer" is a holder and can negotiate it, even though the possessor has stolen or found it. Order paper (such as a check made out to a named payee) that has been indorsed by the payee's merely signing it on the back (making an "in-blank" indorsement) is another form of bearer paper. Anyone in possession of it, even a finder or a thief, is a holder and can negotiate it [3-301].

Recall from the preceding chapter that lack of delivery is a personal defense of the *drawer, maker, or acceptor* that is not good against a holder in due course or an assignee who has received the rights of a holder in due course. As illustrated below, the same principle operates to deprive *payees and others in the chain of transfer* of the personal defense of nondelivery when a holder in due course seeks payment. However, where a negotiation was wrongful, whether for lack of delivery or for some other reason, the wronged party has a cause of action against the transferor who committed the wrong. Some illustrations of rightful and wrongful negotiations follow.

1. Dora draws a check payable "to bearer" and delivers it to Paul. Paul, the payee, is a holder because he is in possession of bearer paper. He is the rightful owner and may negotiate the check. Paul's transferee will be a holder in due course if the transferee has the required qualities.

2. Dora draws a check payable "to bearer" and delivers it to Paul. Paul is a holder. Then Paul loses the check and Fred finds it. Fred is now a holder because he is in possession of bearer paper. Fred has the power to negotiate the check and does so, even though Paul is the true owner and Fred's negotiation is wrongful as to Paul. Fred's transferee, Helen, a holder in due course, takes the check free from Paul's personal defense of nondelivery. Paul's only recourse is against Fred, for the tort of conversion.

3. Dora draws a check payable "to the order of Paul" and delivers it to him. Paul is a holder because he is in possession of an instrument drawn to Paul's order. Then Paul indorses the check by writing his name on the back (thereby converting the check to *bearer* paper) and lays the check on his desk, intending to take it to the bank the next day. That night Tom breaks into Paul's apartment and steals the indorsed check. Although Tom is a thief, he is a holder because he is in possession of properly indorsed order paper (which, because of the in-blank indorsement, is now bearer paper). As far as a prospective purchaser can tell from what is written on the check (Paul's name is in the "payee" blank and also on the back as an indorsement). Tom is the rightful owner. Tom negotiates the stolen check to Helen, a holder in due course who takes it free from Paul's personal defense of nondelivery. Paul's only recourse is against Tom, for the tort of conversion.

Legal Requirements for Indorsement

An **indorsement** is a signature, customarily found on the back of commercial paper, made by a person other than a maker, drawer, or acceptor—e.g., made by a payee or other transferor [3-402]. Like any other signer, an indorser is, in circumstances discussed later in this chapter, liable contractually for the face amount of the instrument. Often, the payee *must* indorse to negotiate the instrument, as where a check is made out to a named payee; and thus the payee will be liable for the face amount (unless the payee-indorser excluded contractual liability by using the "qualified" indorsement discussed later in this chapter).

Where an instrument is made out "to bearer," an indorsement is *not* required by law as part of the negotiation process. However, the transferee might insist on an indorsement anyway out of habit or because the transferee knows that the indorser, as a signer, has liability for payment. Contractual liability of indorsers and other parties to a negotiable instrument is discussed in Chapter 32.

To be effective, an indorsement must be written by or on behalf of the holder, since the holder is the proper person to transfer the instrument [3-202(2)]. An unauthorized signature, whether by a forger or by an agent exceeding his or her authority, is wholly inoperative as that of the purported (alleged) indorser [3-404]. An unauthorized indorsement provides the purported indorser (*and* the maker, drawer, or acceptor from whom payment is sought) with a real defense to payment—one that is good even against a holder in due course.

An instrument payable to the order of Al, Bob, *and* Cora is payable to all of them and may be negotiated only by the indorsements of all of them. An instrument payable to the order of Al, Bob, *or* Cora is payable to any one of them and therefore requires the indorsement of only one of them [3-116].

When an instrument is made payable to a person under a trade name (e.g., a check made payable to the order of "Ted's Pizza"), the holder may indorse by using the trade name, his or her own name, or both [3-203]. A person paying the instrument (e.g., a maker or drawee) or giving value for it (e.g., the payee's transferee) may require indorsement in both names. The same rules apply where the payee's name is misspelled. That is, the payee may indorse with either spelling or both spellings, and a transferee for value may require the payee to indorse by using both spellings.

Where an instrument is payable to the order of a corporation, the name of the corporation should appear in the indorsement. However, under case law interpreting the UCC, an indorsement such as "John Doe, Secretary-Treasurer" is legally sufficient as the indorsement of the corporation.

Types and Uses of Indorsements. Indorsements used to negotiate commercial paper can be described by the application of three sets of terms. An indorsement is either "in blank" or "special"; it is also either "unqualified" or "qualified"; it is also either "nonrestrictive" or "restrictive."

In-Blank or Special Indorsement. An indorsement *in blank* is so called because it does not specify who the transferee is to be. The payee or other indorser merely signs his or her name. Suppose a check is issued to the order of John Doe, who signs it on the back as in Figure 31.1. The check is indorsed "in blank." The legal effect of an indorsement in blank is to convert *order* paper to *bearer* paper. The check can now be further negotiated by delivery alone [3-204].

Keeping possession of or mailing bearer paper (such as a check indorsed in blank) involves serious risk because, as noted earlier in this chapter, any *possessor* of bearer paper, even a finder or a thief, can negotiate it [3-301]. If John indorses his check in blank and a thief negotiates it to a holder in due course, John is deprived of all rights

FIGURE 31.1

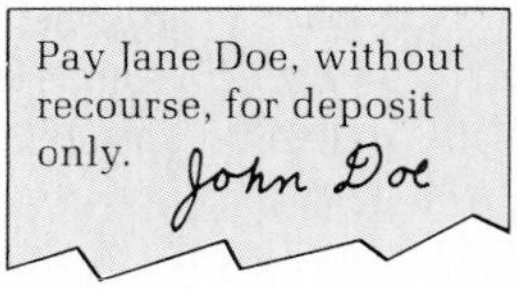

FIGURE 31.2

in the instrument, since a holder in due course takes it *free from all rival claims of ownership* [3-305(1)]. John's only recourse is to track down the thief.

John could protect himself from loss by using a "special" indorsement. A *special indorsement* specifies a person to receive payment. In Figure 31.2, the words "Pay Jane Doe, (signed) John Doe" is a special indorsement. Its legal effect is to continue the "order" character of the check. Thus, Jane's indorsement is required for further negotiation of the check. If it is lost or stolen before Jane indorses it, neither she nor John has much cause for worry. The drawee bank must follow John's instruction as to whom to pay. By his special indorsement John instructed the bank to pay Jane. If the drawee disregards that instruction by paying a forger, the *drawee* must absorb the loss or attempt to track down the person to whom payment was made. (Note that a thief who steals the check and forges Jane's indorsement is *not* a holder and cannot negotiate the check [3-404]. The thief's transferee is merely an assignee who acquires no rights in the instrument because the thief had none.)

Although words of negotiability must appear on the *face* of an instrument to make it negotiable in form, their presence in or absence from an indorsement does not affect the negotiability of the instrument. Indorsements simply give evidence of proper transfer and create liability on the part of indorsers; they neither create nor destroy negotiability of the instrument itself, no matter how they are worded.

Where an instrument is bearer paper on its face and carries no indorsement, the holder can protect against loss by using a special indorsement to convert the instrument into order paper. Suppose Jane draws a check payable to bearer and delivers it to Ann. Ann can protect herself against loss or theft by immediately naming herself the indorsee in a special indorsement: "Pay to the order of myself, (signed) Ann."

A holder may convert a blank indorsement into a special indorsement by writing appropriate words above the signature of the indorser. Suppose Rachel receives the instrument shown in Figure 31.3 below. It is payable to bearer because the last indorsement, that of John Doe, is in blank. Figure 31.4 shows how Rachel can convert the blank indorsement shown in Figure 31.3 into a special indorsement and therefore acquire the protection of order paper.

Unqualified or Qualified Indorsement.   One of the consequences of indorsing a negotiable instrument is that the indorser (payee of an order instrument or some other holder who signs an instrument to negotiate it) may be liable for the face amount of the instrument if others fail to pay. To escape the contractual liability for the face amount that the UCC imposes on a signer, the indorser must make a "qualified" indorsement. In Figure 31.2, by the use of the words "without recourse," John Doe makes a *qualified indorsement.* Unless an indorser qualifies his or her

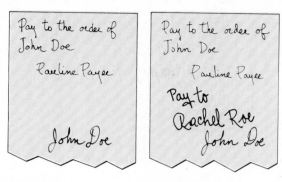

FIGURE 31.3   FIGURE 31.4

indorsement by use of "without recourse" or words of similar meaning, the indorsement is *un*qualified; and the indorser has the usual indorser's liability for the face amount of the instrument if it is not paid by the maker, drawer, acceptor, or some other indorser [3-414]. However, an indorser who routinely uses qualified indorsements (or conditional indorsements, discussed later) may undermine the marketability of his or her paper by suggesting the existence of more risk than there is.

Nonrestrictive or Restrictive Indorsement.   A *restrictive indorsement* specifies a particular use to which the indorsed instrument is to be put, or in some other fashion limits the way in which the indorsee may deal with the instrument [3-205]. If no restriction or limitation is stated in the indorsement, it is nonrestrictive, as in Figure 31.1. Most restrictive indorsements are enforceable, but some are not [3-206]. The following paragraphs illustrate the various kinds of restrictive indorsements.

1. *Indorsements purporting to prohibit further transfer of an instrument.* John Doe, a payee, indorses his paycheck as follows: "Pay Jane Doe only, and no one else. Further transfer is hereby prohibited, (signed) John Doe." This restrictive indorsement is *unenforceable*. Commercial paper cannot serve its function as a substitute for money if indorsers can prevent further negotiation. Jane may negotiate the check despite John's limitation, and so may Jane's transferee.

2. *Indorsement for deposit or collection.* John Doe, the payee of a check, indorses it "For deposit only, (signed) John Doe," delivers it to Ann, his bookkeeper, and tells her to deposit the check in his bank account. This restrictive indorsement, similar to the one in Case 31.1, is enforceable. Any person to whom Ann transfers the check, whether the bank or a supermarket at which Ann might attempt to cash the check, must pay or apply "consistently with the indorsement" any value given for the instrument [3-206(3)]. To the extent that Ann's transferee does so (i.e., sees to it that the funds are deposited in John's account), the transferee becomes a holder for value and may become a holder in due course by meeting the other requirements for holder-in-due-course status (such as good faith). If Ann's transferee does not make the payment in accordance with the instruction given in the restrictive indorsement, the transferee is liable to the indorser for any loss resulting from the transferee's failure to heed the restriction.

Suppose, for example, that Ann takes the check to Doe's bank, where she too has an account, and instead of following Doe's instructions, has the bank apply the proceeds of the check to a debt she owes the bank. Ann is acting wrongfully, and so is the bank. In ignoring Doe's restrictive indorsement, the bank has failed to apply payment consistently with Doe's indorsement, is not a holder for value, and cannot become a holder in due course of the check. Moreover, the bank has converted Doe's property and is liable to him for the amount of the check. The same would be true if the bank had disregarded an indorsement reading "For collection," "Pay any bank," or other words signifying a purpose of deposit or collection.

Any nonbank transferee would be required to observe Doe's restrictive indorsement, but not all banks within the banking system are required to do so [3-206(3)]. The bank where Ann deposited the check is a "depositary" bank. Depositary banks must obey restrictive indorsements (if they are enforceable). But other banks could be involved. If the check was drawn on a bank in another state, the depositary bank would have to forward the check to the out-of-state bank (called the "payor" bank), perhaps through one or more "intermediary" banks. Because intermediary and payor banks must handle checks in bulk, it is impractical for them to determine whether all restrictive indorsements have been heeded. Therefore, *intermediary and payor* banks are permitted to ignore all restrictive indorsements except those of the immediate transferors of such banks and those of persons presenting instruments for payment.

CASE 31.1   Rutherford v. Darwin
29 UCC Rep. 899 (N.M. App. 1980)

Facts: Darwin was a general partner of two partnerships—Rancho Village Partners (Village) and The Settlement, Ltd. (Settlement). Darwin had full authority to manage the funds of both partnerships with his signature alone. He received a money order for $300,000 made out to *Village* as payee. Darwin indorsed it "Deposit to the account of Rancho Village Partners, Ltd." Then he took it to First National Bank in Albuquerque (FNBIA) where both Village and Settlement had accounts, and had the amount deposited in *Settlement's* account. Within two weeks of the deposit, Darwin embezzled most of the $300,000 (wrongfully took Village's money for his own use). The other partners sued FNBIA for the embezzled amount and won a judgment. FNBIA appealed.

Question: Was FNBIA liable to the other partners for the embezzled amount?

Answer: Yes.

Reasoning: The words "Deposit to the account of Rancho Village Partnership, Ltd." constitute a restrictive indorsement. Section 3-206 of the UCC imposes on FNBIA the duty to pay the amount of the money order consistently with the restrictive indorsement. Since FNBIA's payment to Settlement was not consistent with the restrictive indorsement, FNBIA is liable for the loss.

3. *Conditional indorsement.* Occasionally, a holder of an instrument will indorse it over to a merchant as payment for goods or services on the condition that the merchant-indorsee deliver the goods or render the services before receiving payment. Suppose Jane Doe, the payee of a check, indorses it "Pay to Able Typewriters provided they deliver a typewriter to me as per contract dated June 4." This is a conditional indorsement because of Jane's expressed intention that Able will not collect payment unless Jane receives the typewriter. As it true of an indorsement for deposit or collection, transferees must make payment consistently with the indorsement. So, when Able presents the check to the drawee bank, that bank must determine whether Able delivered the typewriter to Jane. If the bank ignores the condition, i.e., makes payment to Able even though Jane received no typewriter, she may compel the bank to pay her the amount of the check even though the bank has already paid Able.

4. *Trust indorsement.* Sometimes an indorser wants the indorsee to hold or manage the proceeds of an instrument for the benefit of the indorser or someone else. Suppose Jane Doe is the payee of a note for $10,000 and wants that amount collected and held by Harriet for the benefit of Jane's daughter, Judy. Jane indorses the note thus: "Pay Harriet Holder in trust for Judy Doe." Harriet is a "fiduciary" and as such has a duty to collect payment and hold or manage it for the benefit of Judy. To qualify as a holder in due course, the *first taker* of the note from Harriet must be sure that Harriet applies the proceeds consistently with the indorsement [3-206(4)]. If Harriet transfers the note to Sam to pay a debt she owes Sam, there are two bad results for Sam. First, he is not a holder in due course (and takes the note subject to all defenses) because he knows that Harriet is applying the note to her own debt instead of collecting the amount for the benefit of Judy. Second, Sam is liable to the trust for the amount of the note.

But Sam's *transferee* can be a holder in due course even though the transferee makes payment to Sam personally and not for the benefit of Judy. Fiduciaries such as Harriet often have broad powers to sell assets of the trust for management purposes, and this fact is well known in business circles. Suppose Sam sells the note to Sara. Although *Sam* is liable to the trust for the proceeds of the sale (since he is the first taker from Harriet and knows she received his payment for her personal use), Sara is not prevented from being a holder in due course just because she knows Sam bought the note from a fiduciary. Such sales usually are legitimate. However, if Sara knows at the time she buys the note that its sale to Sam was in violation of Harriet's fiduciary duties, Sara cannot be a holder in due course.

Special Rules on Effectiveness of Indorsement. To increase the convenience and marketability of commercial paper, the Code provides that an indorsement is effective for negotiation only when it conveys the entire instrument or the entire unpaid residue [3-202]. Thus, an indorsement reading "Pay Ben one-half" is not effective as a negotiation. It operates only as a partial *assignment* of the indorser's rights. In some states, partial assignments are not enforceable. Where they are enforceable, the assignee of a fractional interest cannot personally qualify as a holder in due course, but will acquire whatever rights the transferor of the fractional interest had in it.

The same principle operates as to the transfer of an unpaid residue. Suppose Mary is the maker of a negotiable note giving her the right to pay the $5000 principal or any part of it "on or before March 1." In January she pays $1000 to Paul, the payee, who records the payment on the face of the note. If Paul indorses the entire remaining amount ($4000) over to Vicki, the transfer is a negotiation, and Vicki can be a holder in due course. A transfer of only part of the $4000 is merely an assignment of that part.

Sometimes a person negotiates an instrument in circumstances giving that person a right to rescind (cancel) the negotiation and to get the instrument back from the transferee [3-207]. Examples are:

1. *A negotiation by a minor or other person having a right to rescind for lack of capacity.* For example, Dora, an adult, makes a check out to Paul, a minor. Paul cashes the check at a supermarket or indorses it over to a friend as a gift. As long as the check remains in the possession of Paul's immediate transferee (supermarket or friend), Paul may rescind the negotiation and get the instrument back from the transferee.
2. *A negotiation obtained by fraud, duress, or mistake.* The wronged person may rescind the negotiation and retrieve the instrument from the immediate transferee.
3. *A negotiation made by a trustee in breach of a fiduciary duty owed to the beneficiary of the trust.* The beneficiary (or his or her legal guardian or other legal representative) may rescind the negotiation and retrieve the instrument from the immediate transferee.

However, although the transferor has a right to rescind the negotiation as to the immediate transferee, the negotiation is *effective* to transfer title to (ownership of) the instrument to the transferee [3-207(1)], and the transferee, even if a wrongdoer, has the power to negotiate the check further. So, if the instrument reaches the hands of a holder in due course *before* the aggrieved person (Paul in example 1 above) exercises the right to rescind, the aggrieved person loses the right to rescind the negotiation. Being thus freed from most claims and defenses of transferors, holders in due course are encouraged to accept and pay maximum value for commercial paper.

Suppose, for instance, that Paul, the payee-minor, negotiated Dora's check to Tom, and that before Paul could rescind the negotiation on the ground of minority, Tom cashed the check at Ferndale Auto Supply, which knew nothing of the transaction between Paul and Tom. Paul has lost the right to rescind the negotiation. Ferndale, a holder in due course, may keep the check and enforce it against Dora, the drawer. Nevertheless, though an aggrieved person loses the right to retrieve the instrument, he or she has a cause of action for damages against a wrongdoer such as an unfaithful trustee or, often, against the aggrieved person's immediate transferee.

Note that minority (infancy) is a complete (real) defense to payment where the minor is the *maker or drawer* of an instrument; but (for the protection of holders in due course) minority is, in effect, only a personal defense where a minor is *negotiating* an instrument issued by a person of full capacity. Yet, even a holder in due course cannot hold a minor contractually liable on his or her indorsement; so minority remains in some respects a real defense even in the process of negotiating instruments.

HOLDER-IN-DUE-COURSE STATUS

A holder (possessor of bearer paper or of properly indorsed order paper) may become a **holder in due course** (and take free from personal defenses) by doing three things: (1) giving *value* for the instrument, (2) taking it in *good faith*, and (3) taking it *without notice* of (*a*) defenses to payment, (*b*) rival claims of ownership, or (*c*) the fact (if true) that the instrument is overdue when received or has been dishonored [3-302(1)]. *Or*, where a holder does not qualify personally as a holder in due course, he or she might still acquire the *rights* of one by *assignment* from a holder in due course or from some other person who has acquired such rights. Either way (by qualifying personally or receiving superior rights by assignment), the holder takes the instrument free from any personal defenses that issuers and prior transferors may have. However, in certain consumer credit transactions, holders have been deprived of holder-in-due-course status by the Federal Trade Commission. The rest of this chapter deals with these aspects of holder-in-due-course status.

Requirements for Holder-in-Due-Course Status

Giving Value. To qualify as a holder in due course, the holder must give value for the instrument. So, if the payee of a negotiable instrument indorses and delivers it to a transferee as a gift, the transferee is not a holder in due course.

The *meaning of value in the law of commercial paper* differs sharply from its meaning in the law of sales and secured transactions. In sales and secured transactions, value means any consideration, including an executory (unperformed) promise, sufficient to support a simple (informal) contract. In the law of commercial paper, *value* means *performed* consideration [3-303(a)]. Suppose Mary Maker issues a negotiable note to Paula Payee, who transfers it to Hal Holder in exchange for his promise to paint Mary's house next week. Hal has given consideration for the note (has "bought" it), but has not yet given the required value for it because his promise has not yet been performed. When Hal does the painting, he will be a holder *for value*. If at that time he possesses the other qualities necessary for holder-in-due-course status, he will then be a holder in due course.

Suppose a different situation exists: Mary's note has a principal (face) amount of $2000 and Paula agrees to sell the note to Hal in exchange for $1000 to be paid at the time Hal receives the note, plus a used car to be delivered next week. Upon payment of the $1000, Hal is a holder for value (and perhaps a holder in due course) to the extent of the *performed* consideration ($1000). He will become a holder for value as to the rest of the note when he delivers the used car.

As indicated in the preceding illustrations, value can take the form of money, services, goods, or other property such as real estate. But value takes other forms as well. Some common business examples follow.

1. A bank's permitting a customer to withdraw money before a deposited item clears, as in Case 31.2 below. When a customer of a bank deposits for collection an "item" (check or other negotiable instrument), the bank credits the customer's

account with the amount of the item. Ordinarily the customer has no *right* to draw against the item until it "clears" (is collected by the bank). The bank's act of crediting the customer's account is, in effect, only a *promise* to give value—when the item clears. However, if the bank permits the depositor to draw against the item before it is collected, the bank gives value (and becomes a holder for value of the deposited item) to the extent to which the bank permits a precollection withdrawal of money.

2. Paying for commercial paper with a negotiable instrument. A holder takes an instrument for value by giving (in return for the negotiable instrument he or she receives) an entirely different negotiable instrument from the one the holder received. John sells Mary his certificate of deposit. Mary pays for it with a check. Mary is a holder for value.

3. Making a loan and receiving a negotiable instrument as security. Paul, the payee of a $5000 note, wants to borrow $2000 from Harriet. They agree that if Paul will indorse and deliver the note to Harriet for her to hold as security for the loan, she will lend him the $2000. The parties carry out the agreement. Harriet has given value for the note (to the extent of $2000) by making the loan.

CASE 31.2   **Falls Church Bank v. Wesley Heights Realty, Inc.**
256 A.2d 915 (D.C. App. 1969)

Facts: Wesley Heights Realty drew a check for $1400 to the order of its customer. The customer deposited the check in his account at Falls Church Bank and was given a provisional credit for $1400. Before the check cleared, Bank permitted the customer to withdraw $140. Then Bank discovered that Realty had stopped payment on the check. Bank reversed $1260 of the provisional credit. But because the customer had "skipped town" leaving no credits in his account on which to charge the $140, Bank sued Realty (the drawer of the check) for $140. The trial court awarded judgment to Realty, and Bank appealed.

Question: Was Bank entitled to have the $140 from Realty?

Answer: Yes. Bank was a holder in due course as to the $140.

Reasoning: As to the $140, Bank met all the requirements for holder-in-due-course status, including the giving of value. Under relevant sections of the UCC, a bank acquires a security interest in items deposited with it, to the extent that a provisional credit given to the depositor is drawn against. Furthermore, the depositary bank gives value to the extent that it acquires a security interest (here, for the withdrawn $140) in the item in question. Bank is a holder in due course as to the $140, and its claim against Realty cannot be defeated except by a real defense. Realty's defense was only a personal one.

Often a buyer of commercial paper pays the face amount of the instrument as value. If you cash your payroll check at a supermarket, you ordinarily will receive the face amount because the check is a demand instrument that the supermarket can immediately convert into cash. But to give value, a buyer of commercial paper *need not necessarily pay the face amount.* The seller of a *time* instrument (such as a time draft or a note payable at a future date) wants cash now for an instrument that cannot be collected until later. Because the purchaser expects a profit and faces a risk of noncollection, the seller ordinarily will have to accept a "discounted" (reduced) amount for the instrument—i.e., something less than its total "yield" (face amount plus any interest). By paying a discounted amount, the purchaser of a time note can profit by selling it or by personally collecting the total yield when the note comes due.

For example, Mary issues a note for $100 plus 15 percent annual interest to Pearl, payable 1 year from date. Then Pearl immediately sells the note to Hal for $95. Here the total yield is $115. Hal's payment of $95 will give him a profit of 21 percent. However, he must wait a year to collect and must take the chance that Mary will refuse or be unable to pay. In the meantime, any inflation will erode his profit. All courts are likely to hold that Hal has given value. If he otherwise qualifies as a holder in due course (e.g., takes Mary's note without notice of her personal defenses), he is entitled to collect $115 from Mary when the note comes due, unless she has a real defense.

What minimum amount must Hal pay before a court will hold that he has given value for Mary's note? Because there are so many elements of risk to assess, the courts will not look into the adequacy of the consideration (payment) and therefore do not impose any minimum amount. Rather, the buyer and seller of commercial paper are expected to make this economic judgment, and to do so in good faith. Suppose Hal pays only $20 for Mary's note. If Mary seldom pays her debts, Hal's paying $20 for her note could be a realistic assessment of risk. But if Mary has a good credit rating, a $20 payment for a $95 note could indicate that Hal believes Mary was cheated in her transaction with Pearl. Rather than rule that Hal's $20 payment did not constitute full value, however, the courts will consider whether Hal acted in good faith in making such a small payment.

Acting in Good Faith. To be a holder in due course, the holder must act in good faith when purchasing commercial paper. Under commercial paper law, "honesty in fact" [1-201(19)] is all that is required for a person to be in good faith. A holder will be considered dishonest (and lacking good faith) only if he or she (1) has actual knowledge of wrongdoing or defects concerning the paper, or (2) consciously ignores suspicious circumstances. The test of good faith that applies to commercial paper is "subjective." This means that a court will look at the actual experience, intelligence, and judgment of each individual when deciding whether that individual has acted honestly. An inexperienced person of low intelligence may be held to have acted in good faith in circumstances that should have aroused suspicion in a professional buyer of commercial paper.

Because good faith is a matter of individual honesty, it cannot be described fully. However, the following illustrations suggest the general nature of good faith.

1. Mary issues a check for $800 to Paul. Paul negotiates it for $50 to Hal, a person of normal intelligence and experience. Hal lacks good faith even though he knows of no actual wrongdoing or defect concerning the check. Hal should wonder why Paul, the payee, would accept $50 for a check that Paul could cash for $800 merely by presenting it to the drawee bank.

2. Paul is the payee of a payroll check that he procured from Mary, his employer, by fraudulently overstating the number of hours he worked during the pay period. Mary instructs her bank to stop payment. Paul negotiates the check to his own bank in another town. Paul's bank knows nothing of the stop order and pays him the face amount without making inquiry of the drawee bank. Paul's bank is acting in good faith despite its failure to inquire. If Paul's bank were required to inquire about stop orders on each of its thousands of daily transactions, there would be intolerable delays in processing checks and other commercial paper. Paul's bank is permitted to assume that a person who negotiates an instrument is acting honestly, unless the bank has knowledge of additional facts that should arouse its suspicions.

3. Paul's Roofing does house repairs, receives promissory notes from its customers, and discounts the notes to Paul's Finance Co., a financial subsidiary of Paul's Roofing. Paul is president of both companies. Paul's Roofing consistently defrauds its customers and does shoddy work, but Paul's Finance Co. denies knowledge of these practices and insists it is a holder in due course of the notes. In deciding whether Paul's Finance Co. has the good faith necessary for holder-in-due-course status, a court will consider the extent of the finance company's knowledge of the transactions that gave rise to the notes, as well as the closeness of the relationship between the finance company and the payee (Paul's Roofing) from whom it purchased the paper. A finance company that is controlled by (or controls) the payee or that buys great numbers of instruments from the payee at unusually large discounts is likely to be aware of questionable trade practices of the payee. Failure to investigate obviously suspicious circumstances can amount to bad faith.

Having No Notice of Defects.   To be a holder in due course, a good faith holder for value must also take the instrument *without notice* (1) that it is overdue, (2) that it has been dishonored, or (3) that there is a defense to payment or a rival claim of ownership [3-302].

Under the UCC, a person has notice of a fact when he or she has *actual knowledge* of it; has received *a notice such as a letter or spoken message* in time to take action to avoid loss; or from all the facts and circumstances known to him or her at the time in question has *reason to know* that the fact exists [1-201(25)]. Thus, the requirement of being without notice differs somewhat from the requirement of good faith. Mental awareness of wrongdoing or suspicious circumstances is required for a person to lack good faith. But to be *on notice* of a defense or other difficulty surrounding commercial paper, a person need only possess relevant information, whether or not that person has actual mental awareness of the difficulty.

Notice That Instrument Is Overdue [3-304(3)].   A negotiable instrument is overdue when the day of its maturity has passed and the instrument remains unpaid. An overdue instrument carries an increased risk of nonpayment, and a person who takes an instrument with notice that it is overdue falls short of the innocence required of holders in due course.

Whether a person has notice that an instrument is overdue depends greatly on whether the instrument is a time or a demand instrument, or on the terms (contents) of the instrument. The following illustrations involve *time* instruments.

1. In January, Mary issues Paula a note for $1000. The note states it is payable on

May 1. On May 20 Paula sells the note to Hal for $900. Hal can read and is alert mentally. Because the due date (May 1) appears on the note, and because Hal should know he is buying it on May 20, he is on notice that the instrument is overdue and should wonder why Paula is selling the note to him instead of collecting the amount from Mary. Hal cannot be a holder in due course.

2. In January, Mary issues Paula a note for $1000. The note states it is payable on May 1. It contains an acceleration clause which Paula may exercise "if Paula deems herself insecure." On April 3, Paula learns that Mary might not be able to pay the note on May 1. Feeling insecure, she exercises the clause (requires Mary to pay the $1000 early—on April 3); but after paying the note, Mary leaves it in Paula's possession. On April 16 Paula sells the note to Hal. If Hal knows or has reason to know that acceleration has occurred, he has notice that the instrument is overdue [3-304]. If he is without such notice, he can be a holder in due course entitled to Mary's payment even though she has already paid the note.

The purchaser of a *demand* instrument such as a check or a demand note has notice that it is overdue (and cannot be a holder in due course) if at the time of purchase the purchaser has reason to know that *demand has already been made,* or that the purchaser is taking the instrument more than a *reasonable time after* its issue. For *checks* drawn and payable within the United States and its territories, this reasonable time is *presumed* to be 30 days [3-304(3)(c)]. So, if Mary issues Paula a check on June 1, and Paula negotiates it to Hal on July 5, Hal has taken an overdue instrument and cannot be a holder in due course—unless he can "rebut" the presumption (prove that a longer time than 30 days was reasonable, given the circumstances he found himself in.)

Notice That Instrument Has Been Dishonored.

Dishonor is (1) a refusal by the maker of a note or the *drawee* of a draft to pay the instrument when it is due, or (2) a drawee's refusal to *accept* a *time* draft [3-507; 3-501, comment 3]. A holder who purchases an instrument with notice that it has been dishonored is taking risks beyond those normally associated with the taking of commercial paper, and does not deserve to have the special status enjoyed by a holder in due course. A holder could receive notice of dishonor by means of the letters "NSF" (meaning nonsufficient funds) stamped on the face of a check, or by information about dishonor received from some other source.

Notice of Defense or Rival Claim.

A holder who takes an instrument with notice of a *defense to payment* or of a *rival claim of ownership* cannot be a holder in due course. Examples follow.

1. Mary issues a check to Paula to pay for goods that Paula delivered to Mary. Hal, Paula's employee, knows that the goods are defective. Paula later negotiates Mary's check to Hal in lieu of his regular paycheck. Hal is on notice of Mary's defense (failure of consideration or breach of warranty) and cannot be a holder in due course. Case 31.3 further discusses what constitutes notice of a particular defense.

2. Paul indorses his paycheck in blank and places it on the dashboard of his car. On the way to the bank the check blows out the window. Hal sees the check land on the

ground and sees Fay Finder pick it up. Soon Fay negotiates the check to Hal. Hal is on notice of Paul's claim of ownership and cannot be a holder in due course.

A person can be on notice of a maker's or a drawer's defenses even though not aware of any particular wrongdoing by the payee. A purchaser cannot be a holder in due course if the instrument is *incomplete*, if the instrument is *irregular* on its face, or there are other defects. Examples of these sources of notice follow.

1. Mary signs and issues a check to Paul, but leaves the line for the amount blank. As Paul knows, she intended to fill the check out for $100. Paul so informs Hal and, without filling out the amount, negotiates the check to Hal for $100. Because Hal is the taker of an incomplete instrument, he is automatically on notice of any defenses Mary might have (e.g., failure of consideration or Paul's fraud), even though he has no knowledge of any particular defense [3-304(1)(a)].

2. Suppose that Hal, in the preceding illustration, fills in the amount of $100 in Lisa's presence and negotiates the check to her for $100. Lisa has taken a completed instrument. Her knowledge that an incomplete instrument has been completed does not, by itself, charge her with notice of a defense or claim. She must also have notice that the completion was improper [3-304(4)(d)].

3. Mary issues a note to Paul for $100. Paul crudely alters the amount to read $1000. The alteration is so obvious that it can be readily detected. This is an example of "irregular" paper. Because of the obvious irregularity, a purchaser is on notice of wrongdoing and cannot be a holder in due course. An instrument stamped "NSF" or "payment stopped" also is irregular.

4. Paula is trustee for Judy. Mary issues a check for $1000 "to the order of Paula for the benefit of Judy." Paula owes Hal a $1000 payment on her car and negotiates the check to Hal to pay her personal debt. Because the check reads "for the benefit of Judy," Hal is on notice that Paula has negotiated it in breach of her fiduciary duty. This is one of those "other defects," notice of which prevents Hal from being a holder in due course [3-304(2)].

CASE 31.3 Texico State Bank v. Hullinger
220 N.E.2d 248 (Ill. App. 1966)

Facts: Hullinger issued a check for $3,500 to Sledge. Sledge took it to Texico State Bank where he had an account and purchased a bank draft, using Hullinger's check as payment. The next day Hullinger stopped payment on the check. In the meantime Sledge sold the bank draft to a holder in due course, and Texico Bank (the issuer of the draft) eventually had to honor it. Bank, the holder of Hullinger's check, then demanded payment from Hullinger. He refused to honor his check on the ground that when Bank received the check from Sledge, it knew Sledge had a poor credit record. Bank sued Hullinger for $3,500. The trial court awarded judgment to Hullinger, and Bank appealed.

Question: Was the trial court's judgment for Hullinger in error?

Answer: Yes. Texico State Bank should have prevailed.

Reasoning: Sledge's poor credit record, even if proven with credible evidence, is irrelevant to the question of whether Bank was on notice of Hullinger's defense when Sledge purchased the bank draft. Even if he had a bad credit record, he still might have performed his part of the underlying transaction with Hullinger. Bank had no notice at the time it received Hullinger's check from Sledge of any defense such as Sledge's fraud or failure to perform a contractual duty. As a holder in due course, Bank was entitled to payment.

Rights of Holder through Holder in Due Course; Shelter Provision

When a holder in due course negotiates commercial paper, the transferee ordinarily acquires the rights of the holder in due course even if the transferee personally cannot qualify as one. Suppose Hal, a holder in due course of a note, negotiates it to Arnold as a gift. Since Arnold did not give value, he cannot qualify as a holder in due course. But he is an assignee of Hal's rights, and therefore acquires whatever right Hal had—here, Hal's right as a holder in due course to have payment free from personal defenses and rival claims of ownership. Arnold (and any other assignee of Hal's rights) is a holder "through" a holder in due course.

The UCC provision that gives holders through a holder in due course the same freedom from claims and defenses that a holder in due course enjoys is often referred to as the "shelter provision." The policy behind it is to provide the holder in due course a free market for the paper. Providing a free market is accomplished by allowing most holders who are merely assignees to collect payment free from claims and personal defenses, since those assignees will thus be inclined to pay full value to the holder in due course.

Figure 31.5 represents a series of negotiations (from Pe in the figure to H_1; from H_1

FIGURE 31.5   Shelter provision.

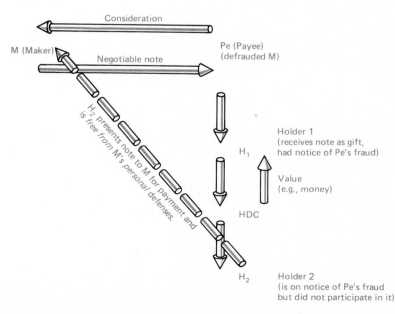

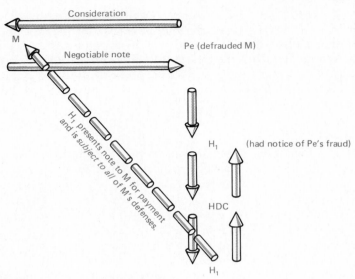

FIGURE 31.6   Shelter provision—a variation.

to HDC; and from HDC to H_2) in which H_2, though not personally a holder in due course, takes M's note from HDC *free from* M's personal defenses. However, some transferees of a holder in due course are disqualified from receiving holder-in-due-course rights. A transferee who has been a party to (participant in rather than merely on notice of) any fraud or illegality affecting the instrument, or who as a prior holder had notice of a defense or claim, cannot improve his or her position by taking from a later holder in due course. Attempts by prior holders to improve their positions by selling paper to a holder in due course and then receiving it back will be of no avail. In Figure 31.6, H_1 was not a holder in due course when he or she received M's note from Pe. H_1 is prohibited from improving his or her position by selling the note to HDC and buying it back. Consequently, H_1 takes the note *subject to* M's personal defenses.

Federal Changes Regarding Holder-in-Due-Course Status

In recent years, consumer groups have voiced strong opposition to holder-in-due-course status. They object to the idea that a maker or drawer of an instrument is not permitted to assert a legitimate defense, such as fraud in the inducement or breach of warranty, simply because the payee transfers a negotiable instrument for value to a third person. Especially upsetting is the impression that the courts have tended to resolve all doubts against consumers and in favor of finance companies whose relationships with payees are clearly suspect, thus permitting, if not encouraging, widespread fraud, shoddy work, excessive finance charges, and the like.

In the typical consumer credit transaction, the consumer's installment note is promptly transferred to a finance company, which purchases the note at a discount. A regulation of the Federal Trade Commission (FTC) requires that a consumer *credit* contract contain a prominently printed notice as follows:

NOTICE

ANY HOLDER OF THIS CONSUMER CREDIT CONTRACT IS SUBJECT TO ALL CLAIMS AND DEFENSES WHICH THE DEBTOR COULD ASSERT AGAINST THE SELLER OF GOODS OR SERVICES OBTAINED PURSUANT HERETO OR WITH THE PROCEEDS HEREOF. RECOVERY HEREUNDER BY THE DEBTOR SHALL NOT EXCEED AMOUNTS PAID BY THE DEBTOR HEREUNDER.

The presence of this notice preserves all claims and defenses that a consumer may have, even against a good faith purchaser for value without notice of any defenses. The "consumer" is a person who acquires goods or services for personal, family, or household use—for example, automobiles, home improvements, and health spa memberships. The regulation does not cover purchases of real estate or securities (e.g., stocks and bonds), or purchases over $25,000. It does not cover public utility services. Nor does it cover a consumer purchase where the consumer pays by check. The check is not a credit instrument and need not contain the notice.

A merchant may not circumvent the FTC regulation by arranging for the consumer to borrow money from a lender and pay cash to the merchant. The regulation provides specifically that when the merchant arranges for the loan, the credit instrument must contain the specified notice, and the lender has no greater rights against the consumer than the seller does. However, the lender is required to include the notice (and is therefore deprived of holder-in-due-course status) only where the merchant *refers* consumers to the lender or *is affiliated* with the lender by control or business arrangment.

SUMMARY

Any holder of commercial paper can negotiate it and thereby enable a properly qualified transferee to become a holder in due course. Bearer paper is negotiated by delivery; order paper by delivery plus any necessary indorsement. Depending on the needs of the parties, indorsements may be in blank or special, unqualified or qualified, and nonrestrictive or restrictive. A transferor of commercial paper has a right to rescind the negotiation, including any indorsement, but if the paper first gets into the hands of a holder in due course, the transferor cannot have the instrument itself back.

A holder may become a holder in due course by giving value for the instrument, taking it in good faith, and taking it without notice of defenses to payment, rival claims of ownership, or other problems surrounding its issuance and transfer. A holder who does not personally qualify as a holder in due course may receive the rights of one by assignment, under the shelter provision, the purpose of which is to assure a holder in due course of a market for the paper. In certain consumer credit transactions, holders have been deprived of holder-in-due-course status by the Federal Trade Commission.

REVIEW QUESTIONS

1. (a) How may negotiation of a bearer instrument be accomplished? Negotiation of an order instrument? (b) Suppose a person buys a negotiable order instrument, but the transferor forgets to indorse it. What is the legal position of the buyer?

2. (a) Who may negotiate an instrument? (b) What is the legal significance of negotiation?

3. For what purpose is each of the following indorsements used: (a) special, (b) qualified, and (c) restrictive?

4. Explain whether all banks are required to heed an indorsement for deposit or collection.

5. What might be the economic consequence of a person's always using qualified or conditional indorsements when indorsing checks or notes?

6. Explain the meaning of "value" as the term is used in the law of commercial paper.

7. (a) When is a check overdue? (b) When are other varieties of commercial paper overdue?

8. Illustrate (a) lack of good faith, (b) notice of dishonor, and (c) being on notice of a personal defense.

9. (a) Explain the rights and give an example of a holder through a holder in due course. (b) What is the purpose of the shelter provision? (c) What kinds of transferees may not benefit from the shelter provision?

10. Summarize the FTC regulation concerning commercial paper and explain the justification for the rule.

CASE PROBLEMS

1. Paul fraudulently induced Mary to issue him a note reading: "July 2, 19xx. Sixty days after date I promise to pay Paul the sum of seven hundred dollars ($700.00), together with interest at the rate of 8 percent per annum. Value received. (signed) Mary." The day after Paul received the note, he indorsed and sold it to Albert, who took it without notice of the fraud. Is Albert subject to Mary's defense of fraud? Why?

2. Thomas Jones, the payee of a negotiable instrument, transferred it to Frank White, who transferred it to Robert Grondahl, who transferred it to Arthur Benson, who transferred it to Kermit Smith. At the time of the transfer to Smith, it bore the indorsements shown in Figure 31.7. (a) Is Smith a holder of the instrument? Explain. (b) What difference does status as a holder make to Smith?

3. On May 16, 1969 the Bank of Hollywood Hills of Hollywood Hills, Florida, issued a cashier's check for $2000 payable to "Richard and Grace Grimaldi." Four days later Richard indorsed the check "Grace Grimaldi by Richard Grimaldi" and presented it to a teller of the Beach National Bank in Fort Myers Beach, Florida, where the Grimaldis had a joint account. The teller cashed the check and paid the full amount to Richard. On May 20 the cashier's check routinely arrived at the Bank of Hollywood Hills for payment. That bank refused to honor the check. Was it justified in refusing to honor the check? Explain.

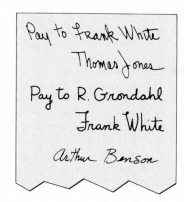

FIGURE 31.7

4. The payee of a check indorsed it "for deposit" and then delivered it for safekeeping to a "friend." The friend had a third person deposit the check in an account with a bank. The depositary bank sent the check to an intermediary bank for collection. That bank forwarded the check to the drawee bank, where it was paid. After the depositary bank received the payment, the third person withdrew the proceeds of the check and turned them over to the "friend," who then absconded. The depositary bank became insolvent, and so the payee sued the intermediary bank. Judgment for whom? Why?

5. The payee of a negotiable promissory note placed a special indorsement on it and transferred it to Gunther Gilmore. Gilmore transferred the note to Harold Horton but forgot to indorse it. Horton took the note for value, in good faith, and without notice that it was overdue, or that it had been dishonored, or that there was any defense against it. When Horton discovered that the note had not been indorsed to him, he requested and received his transferor's indorsement. (**a**) Could Horton be a holder in due course at the time he took the instrument? (**b**) Under what circumstances, if any, could Horton become a holder in due course at the time the instrument was indorsed to him?

6. Ferrante was a subcontractor on a job for which O. P. Ganjo, Inc., was a contractor. Ferrante proceeded so slowly with his plastering job that Ganjo became concerned that the subcontract might not be completed in time to allow Ganjo to complete its contract on time. When Ferrante was urged to speed up the work, he stated that he did not have funds enough to pay his workers. However, he said that he had a $3000 promissory note payable to his order that he had received on his last job. Ganjo agreed to discount the note for $2800, payable $1000 at the time of the transfer of the instrument, and the balance of $1800 if and when the transferor (Ferrante) completed the plastering job. Ferrante indorsed and transferred the note to Ganjo, and Ganjo paid the $1000 in cash. Before the plastering job was completed, Ferrante became involved in financial difficulties and departed for parts unknown. Ganjo sued the maker of the $3000 note, who proved he had a personal defense to the note. Was the Ganjo corporation a holder in due course? Explain.

CHAPTER 32

LIABILITY OF THE PARTIES; DISCHARGE

If you sign a promissory note to pay for goods, you expect to be (and are) liable for payment of the note in the absence of defenses assertable by you against the person presenting the note for payment. If you indorse your payroll check when cashing it, you might—to your surprise—be liable for the face amount if your employer's bank (the drawee) does not honor (pay) the check. You might receive a check containing a forged in-blank indorsement and make a gift of the check *without* signing it, and still have liability if the check proves uncollectible. Liability on a negotiable instrument, or in connection with its transfer and collection, can arise in a number of ways, both expected and unexpected.

A person who signs, transfers, or seeks payment of commercial paper may be subject to two kinds of liability: contractual liability and warranty liability. The Uniform Commercial Code (UCC) imposes *contractual* liability on most *signers* of commercial paper for the face amount of the instrument (including any interest). For example, if you issue a check, accept a draft in which you are named as drawee, or sign a promissory note, you will be liable contractually ("on the instrument") for the amount stated in the instrument. Likewise, when you indorse your paycheck to cash it, your indorsement, if unqualified, makes you contractually liable to the indorsee (e.g., bank or supermarket) and to any other transferee for the face amount if the drawee (your employer's bank) does not pay. Because commercial paper is not only a contract but also a type of property, the UCC imposes warranty liability too, on nonsigners as well as on signers. Breach of a warranty may occur when a person transfers or presents for payment an instrument (the property) that is defective in some respect, as where a signature has been forged. The UCC classifies commercial paper warranties as *transfer* or *presentment* warranties.

A person who pays the amount specified in a negotiable instrument, or who otherwise fulfills the contractual obligations imposed by the Code, is *discharged* (freed) from liability. A person may also be discharged from liability by the actions of others. Contractual liability of the parties, their discharge from liability, and liability for breach of warranty are the topics of this chapter.

Frequently a person who comes into possession of a negotiable instrument faces liability for the tort of conversion. **Conversion** is the wrongful exercise of dominion and control over the personal property of another, to the exclusion of the rights of the owner, or in a manner inconsistent with those rights. As noted in the preceding chapter, a person who steals or finds and sells bearer paper is a converter. A person who steals or finds order paper and forges an indorsement also commits conversion. So does a person who pays or buys an instrument containing a forged indorsement, even if this person has no knowledge of the forgery. And, as is noted in the next chapter, banks can commit conversion in a number of ways. In all instances of conversion, the converter is liable to the true owner for the face amount of the instrument [3-419]. However, although conversion is an important source of legal remedy for persons who have been wrongfully deprived of negotiable instruments, the main focus of this chapter will be the contractual liability of signers (and its discharge), and warranty liability. These latter two are the kinds of liability that contribute most to the value and usefulness of commercial paper.

CONTRACTUAL LIABILITY OF THE PARTIES

In commercial paper law, contractual liability is of two basic types—primary and secondary. So, a signer of commercial paper may be a **primary party** or a **secondary party**. The ultimate liability of primary and secondary parties is the same—to pay the face amount of the instrument. But, as is discussed below, the *timing* of primary liability differs markedly from that of secondary liability. Other circumstances than type of liability (primary versus secondary) affect the existence or order of contractual liability as among various signers. These include whether the signer is an accommodation party or a guarantor, and whether a signature was made by an agent or was forged.

Recall from Chapter 30 that the word *maker* means a person who issues a note or a certificate of deposit: *Drawer* means a person who issues a check or a draft. *Acceptor* means a drawee of a draft who signs the draft across its face and thereby agrees to pay it. As noted in Chapter 31, *holder* means a person who is in possession of bearer paper or properly indorsed order paper, and who therefore appears to be the rightful owner, entitled to payment or acceptance.

In commercial paper law, the term *maker* always refers to the issuer of a *note* (or a certificate of deposit). Therefore it is not correct terminology to call the *drawer* of a draft or check its "maker." Even so, this textbook uses the popular expression "to *make out* a check" (meaning "to write or *draw* a check"). The popular expression is not misleading because the kind of paper involved, a check (or draft), is named.

Liability of Primary Parties

The maker of a note or certificate of deposit (CD) and the acceptor of a draft or check are primary parties. Primary liability is *unconditional;* that is, a primary party is liable to the holder of the instrument for the face amount, and can be sued for it *immediately* when the instrument comes due, without the need for any further action by the holder [3-122]. Consequently, when sued, a primary party cannot delay the lawsuit on the ground of the holder's failure to make presentment (demand) for payment. However, as a practical matter holders normally try to collect payment from the primary party before bringing suit even though they are not required to do so.

When a draft or check is *issued,* there is no primary party (that is, no maker or acceptor). The drawer is a signer, but for the reason discussed in the next section of this chapter, is a *secondary* party. The drawee is not a signer, and unless and until there is acceptance, the drawee is not liable "on the instrument" (i.e., is not contractually liable for the face amount) to anyone. Of course, if the drawee accepts a draft, he or she becomes an acceptor and is then a primary party. "Certification" of a check by a drawee bank is a type of acceptance. Upon certifying a check, a drawee bank becomes a primary party, fully liable "on the instrument" without need for any further action by the holder. Other consequences of certification are discussed in Chapter 33.

Liability of Secondary Parties

The drawer of a check or draft and the indorser of any commercial paper are secondary parties. Liability of secondary parties differs from liability of primary parties mainly in the events that "trigger" liability and, as to indorsers, in how long liability lasts. How long liability lasts is discussed later in this chapter, in the section on discharge.

A primary party is immediately and unconditionally liable for the face amount when the instrument comes due. In contrast, a secondary party is liable (when the instrument is due) only if certain additional triggering "conditions" or events take place: **Presentment** (demand) for payment or acceptance; **dishonor** (refusal to pay an instrument or to accept a time draft); and, especially for indorsers, **timely notice of dishonor**. For instruments accepted or payable outside the United States—i.e., in international trade—a fourth triggering event, called "protest" may be required. A **protest** is a document or certificate of dishonor signed and sealed by a public official such as a United States consul or a notary public authorized to certify that the instrument was dishonored.

The fact that secondary liability is conditional can be seen in the following illustrations.

1. You issue (make out and deliver) a check to Paul to pay for a tennis racket. As drawer of the check, you are a signer, but the understanding between you and Paul is that he (or some transferee of the check such as Paul's bank) will present the check to your bank (the drawee) for payment, not to you. Paul understands that he will be entitled to have payment directly from you only if the bank does not pay. You, as drawer, are a secondary party because Paul (or a transferee) must *present* the check to the drawee for payment, undergo the unpleasant experience of having the check *dishonored,* and give you *notice of dishonor* before having the right to payment from you personally.

2. You work for Orange Groves, Inc., receive a paycheck for $300, indorse it in blank, and cash it at Ned's Supermarket. The understanding between you (the payee-indorser) and Ned is that Ned (or some transferee) will present the check to your employer's bank (the drawee) for payment. Ned can have payment from you only if (1) he *presents* the check to the drawee bank, (2) the bank *dishonors* the check, and (3) Ned gives you timely notice of dishonor. Thus, like the drawer of a check or draft, an indorser is a secondary party and is not liable for the face amount unless the conditions of presentment, dishonor, and notice of dishonor have been met.

The obligation of an indorser to pay upon the happening of the required conditions results from the indorser's "engagement" (promise) to pay imposed by the UCC [3-414(1)]. The holder of a dishonored instrument is entitled to payment from any indorser who has received timely notice of dishonor. But where one of several indorsers has paid, there may be a question as to whether the one who paid the holder may, in turn, have payment from some other indorser. Unless otherwise agreed among indorsers, the promise of an indorser is made only to *subsequent* indorsers (those signing later) and to the holder [3-414(2)]. Thus, liability of indorsers *to one another* is in relation to the order of signing. For example, Paul, the payee of a check, indorses and delivers it to Ben, who in turn indorses and delivers it to Cora. If Cora is unable to collect from the drawee bank, she may collect from Ben, who in turn may collect from Paul. But if Cora had skipped Ben and had received payment from Paul, Paul could not collect from Ben because Ben's engagement as an indorser is made to *subsequent* indorsers (Cora), not prior ones (Paul). Paul's only recourse is to the drawer of the check.

Presentment, dishonor, and notice of dishonor are so important in the collection of commercial paper that they require further discussion.

Requirement of Presentment.   *Presentment* is a demand for acceptance or payment of a negotiable instrument [3-504]. The demand is made by a holder upon the party expected to pay (i.e., the maker of a note or the drawee—including an acceptor—of a draft) or the party expected to accept (i.e., the drawee of a draft). Presentment may be made in person (for example, by the holder's taking a check directly to the drawee bank), by mail, or through a clearinghouse. A **clearinghouse** is a place where banks exchange checks and drafts drawn on each other and thereby settle their daily balances. A clearinghouse would be involved where, for example, the holder and the drawer of a check do their banking at different banks. The holder takes the check to his or her own bank for collection; the holder's bank sends the check to a clearinghouse; and the clearinghouse presents the check to the drawee bank (which also deals with that clearinghouse). If presentment is made by mail, the time of presentment is the time that the party who is to pay or accept receives the mail.

If a holder is slow to make presentment, secondary parties (indorsers and drawers) may be discharged (freed) from liability. As is discussed later in this chapter, a delay in presentment will discharge a *drawer* only in very rare circumstances. But unexcused delay always discharges *indorsers*.

Some instruments specify a date for presentment. A presentment after this date may discharge secondary parties. If no date is specified, the holder must make presentment within a "reasonable" time to avoid discharging secondary parties [3-503]. Where the holder of a draft seeks to avoid discharging the *drawer* (in those rare circumstances, discussed later, where discharge of a drawer is possible), the reasonable time for presentment is measured from the *date of the draft or its date of issue, whichever is later.* Where the holder seeks to hold an *indorser* liable, the reasonable time is measured from the *time of his or her indorsement.* What constitutes a reasonable time varies according to the circumstances. A court might allow more time if great distances or unreliable communications are involved than if distances are short and communication easy.

For an *uncertified check*—a check that has not been accepted ("certified") by the drawee bank—the reasonable time for presentment is presumed to be *30 days* with respect to the drawer's liability and 7 days as to an indorser's liability [3-503(2)]. These time limits are intended to encourage prompt presentment of checks so that the check clearing process will remain efficient. However, a holder may "rebut" (demonstrate the impropriety of) the presumption by proving that under the circumstances a longer time for presentment was reasonable.

Recall from the preceding chapter that a person who takes a check for value more than 30 days after issue is (presumed to be) on notice that the check is overdue. A slow taker therefore cannot be a holder in due course. The 30-day limit for presentment just discussed in this chapter is different. Here we are talking about a *timely* taker but a slow *presenter.* A person who takes a check for value within 30 days after its issue usually is a holder in due course. If that holder in due course fails to make timely presentment, he or she loses the liability of indorsers and *may* lose the liability of the drawer. But if the drawer remains liable, as is usual, the holder in due course takes the check free from the drawer's personal defenses despite loss of indorsers' liability due to slow presentment by the holder in due course.

Requirement of Dishonor.   *Dishonor* is a refusal or failure to pay or accept an instrument that the holder has properly presented for payment or acceptance

[3-507]. Dishonor of a note or certificate of deposit occurs if the maker refuses to pay on the due date. Dishonor of *any* draft or check occurs if the drawee or acceptor refuses to pay on the due date. A *time* draft (e.g., one payable at a specified date after issue, or one payable "60 days after sight") is dishonored if the holder presents it *for acceptance* before the due date and the drawee refuses to accept it [3-507(1)]. The holder of a time draft has a right to the drawee's acceptance so that the holder can know early whether the drawee is willing to pay when the due date arrives. However, a drawee's refusal to accept a *demand* draft (or to certify a check, which also is a demand draft) is not a dishonor, because the holder of a demand draft (one payable upon the holder's demand) is already entitled to payment in cash and does not face the uncertainty of payment facing the holder of a time draft that is not yet payable [3-501, comment 3]. Of course, a drawee's failure to *pay* a demand draft upon presentment is a dishonor.

A party to whom presentment is made has a right to assurances that the presentment for payment or acceptance is proper, though. So, return of an instrument for lack of a proper indorsement is not a dishonor [3-507(3)]. Moreover, the person to whom presentment is made may require exhibition of the instrument, identification of the presenter, evidence of the presenter's authority to make presentment for another person, and presentment of the instrument at the place, if any, specified in the instrument for payment or acceptance [3-505(1)]. If a required place for presentment has not been stated, the holder ordinarily must present the instrument at the business location or residence of the party who is to accept or pay.

Failure of the presenter to comply with any of these requirements invalidates the presentment; but the presenter has a reasonable time to comply, and the time for acceptance or payment runs *from* the time of the presenter's compliance [3-505(2)]. Thus, the person who is to accept or pay has the full time allowed by the Code to investigate the situation. Deferring acceptance of a time draft until the close of the next business day does not constitute dishonor [3-506(1)]. Nor is it a dishonor to defer payment of most commercial paper pending a reasonable examination to determine whether it is properly payable. However, if payment is not made by the close of business on the day of presentment, the instrument is dishonored [3-506(2)].

Requirement of Notice.   After an instrument has been dishonored, secondary parties (drawers and indorsers) must be given timely *notice of dishonor* if the holder (presenter) is to avoid discharging them from liability. Notice of dishonor must be given within time limits prescribed by the Code, usually 3 business days [3-508(2)]. Collecting banks have a shorter time to give notice of dishonor, up to 2 business days. The notice may be given in any reasonable manner, either orally or in writing. Unlike a presentment, a notice of dishonor sent by mail is given when *sent* even though it may never reach the secondary party.

Liability of Accommodation Parties   An **accommodation party** is a person who signs an instrument for the purpose of lending his or her name (credit) to another party to the instrument [3-415]. For example, suppose a person wishes to buy goods on credit and to give a promissory note in payment. The seller may refuse to extend credit if the buyer is a minor or has a poor credit rating. The seller may agree to sell the goods if another person (with good credit) will sign the note as an accommodation party.

Usually an accommodation party signs as either co-maker or indorser, but may sign in any other capacity, including co-drawer or acceptor. The contractual liability of an accommodation party to a holder and others depends on the capacity in which the party signs. A person signing as maker or acceptor has primary liability; a person signing a drawer or indorser has secondary liability (i.e., presentment, dishonor, and notice are required to establish liability).

An accommodation party has a signer's usual liability to a holder and others even though he or she received no consideration for signing. However, an accommodation party has no liability on the instrument to the party accommodated [3-415(5)]. An accommodation party who pays the instrument has a right of recourse against the party accommodated. For example, a father who cosigns a note so his son may buy a car, and who pays the note when the son defaults, may recover the amount from his son. As the following case illustrates, whether a person signs as an accommodation party or, instead, as a co-obligor (person equally liable) depends on the intention of the signers. An accommodation party has no liability on the instrument to the party accommodated; a co-obligor is liable (to the other co-obligor) for his or her share of the debt.

CASE 32.1   Grimes v. Grimes
267 S.E.2d 372 (N.C. App. 1980)

Facts: While Grimes and his wife were separated but still married, they co-signed a note for $27,600 payable to Lexington State Bank. After their divorce, Grimes paid the debt and sued his former wife for "contribution," the $13,800 that he alleged she was obligated for as co-maker. A North Carolina common law rule makes the husband, but not the wife, liable for a debt represented by a note signed jointly by husband and wife. On the basis of this rule the trial court awarded judgment for the wife. Grimes appealed.

Question: Was the wife liable to Grimes for one-half the amount of the note?

Answer: Yes, unless the wife can prove she was only an accommodation party.

Reasoning: The UCC has changed the common law rule relied on by the trial court. Under the UCC, where two or more persons sign a note as makers, they are jointly and *severally* (individually) liable. Because of the joint and several liability of co-makers, when one pays the whole amount of the note, that co-maker is entitled to contribution from the others. However, it is not clear in this case that the wife signed as a co-obligor. She alleges she signed only as an accommodation party. She has the right to show the true nature of her signing by means of parol evidence [discussed in Chapter 12]. If she was only an accommodation party, she is not liable for contribution.

Liability of Guarantor   A **guarantor** is a signer of commercial paper who adds "Payment guaranteed" or equivalent words to the signature. By such language a guarantor promises that if the instrument is not paid when due, he or she will pay it without the holder's having to resort to (make demand on) any other party [3-416(1)]. A *secondary* party who guarantees payment *waives* (gives up the right to) presentment and notice of dishonor, and thus acquires a liability that is indistinguishable from that of a co-maker.

A signer who adds "collection guaranteed" or equivalent words to the signature promises that if the instrument is not paid when due, he or she will pay it, but only if (1) the holder has first taken legal action to collect from the maker or acceptor, or (2) the holder can show that such legal action would be useless, for example, because the maker or acceptor is insolvent. A secondary party (indorser or drawer) who guarantees collection waives presentment and notice of dishonor [3-416(2)].

Accommodation parties and guarantors are *sureties*. Suretyship is discussed in Chapter 27.

Effect (on Liability) of Signatures by Agents and Forgers

Signature by Authorized Agent. Agents frequently are authorized to sign commercial paper on behalf of their principals. Suppose that Andy Agar is authorized to sign a negotiable instrument on Pam Pell's behalf and wishes to bind her as maker, drawer, acceptor, or indorser without binding himself on the instrument. The best way for Andy to do this is to sign the instrument

Pam Pell
By Andy Agar, Agent

Andy escapes liability as a signer because he has (1) named the person represented, and (2) shown that he signed his own name in a representative capacity [3-403].

If Andy uses forms of signature that do not do *both* of these things, he may be held personally liable for the face amount of the instrument. The following examples illustrate the dangers of an agent's signing incorrectly. In the examples Andy is authorized to sign a check for Pam, made out to Paul Payee in payment for goods delivered to Pam.

1. Andy merely signs his own name, "Andy Agar." Andy is liable on the instrument. If Paul sues Andy for payment of the check, Andy will *not* be permitted to use parol evidence (discussed in Chapter 12) to show that he intended to sign as agent for Pam. Pam is not liable to anyone *on the instrument* because her name does not appear on it. However, under agency law (discussed in Chapters 20, 21, and 22), Pam may be liable to Paul on the underlying transaction since she authorized it, as when Andy cannot pay the amount of the check.

2. Andy signs the check, "Andy Agar, Agent." Andy is liable on the check. However, parol evidence *is* admissible between the immediate parties (Andy and Paul) to prove that Andy was not intended to be liable. Andy's parol evidence is *not* admissible against a holder in due course; therefore Andy is liable to any holder in due course for the face amount. Pam is not liable on the check to anyone, since her name is not on it, but she may be liable to Paul on the underlying transaction, as in example 1 above.

3. Andy signs both names as follows:

Pam Pell
Andy Agar

Andy is liable on the check because he signed it, and Pam is liable on the check because she authorized Andy to sign her name. Parol evidence is admissible between the immediate parties (Paul and Andy) to show that Andy was not intended to be liable, but parol evidence is not allowed to defeat Andy's liability to a holder in due course.

Unauthorized Signature.   *Unauthorized signature* includes both a forgery and a signature by an agent without actual, implied, or apparent authority to sign the principal's name. An unauthorized signature is not binding on the person whose name is signed without authority unless that person *ratifies* (later approves) it or *is precluded* (prevented) by law from denying it as, for example, where the "signer's" negligence substantially contributes to the making of the unauthorized signature [3-404]. An unauthorized signature *is* effective, however, to impose on the actual signer (forger or agent) liability to persons who in good faith pay the instrument or take it for value.

How can a person be so negligent that his or her unauthorized signature will be binding? Many business people sign commercial paper by using a rubber stamp or a check-writing machine. If the owner of such a stamp or machine negligently gives unauthorized persons access to it, and the negligence substantially contributes to the making of an unauthorized signature, the owner will not be permitted to claim lack of authority as a defense when a holder in due course demands payment. The same is true where a drawee or other payor pays the instrument in good faith and in accordance with reasonable commercial standards of the drawee's or payor's business. If there is *no* negligence, the usual rule continues to apply—an unauthorized signature provides the "signer" with a real defense that is good against even a holder in due course.

Effect of Indorsement by Imposter or Dishonest Agent

As noted in Chapter 31, a person ordinarily must be a *holder* to negotiate commercial paper, but there is one exception to this rule. The exception applies where, for example, a principal has been induced by the fraud of a dishonest agent to sign a negotiable instrument made out to a fictitious payee. Suppose that an employer is induced by a dishonest agent to sign a payroll check made out to a nonexistent worker. Then the agent gets possession of the check, signs the name of the fictitious payee on the back of the check, and cashes it at a supermarket. The dishonest agent is not the payee. Ordinarily the agent would not be a holder, and the indorsement would be a forgery. However, UCC Section 3-405 specifically provides that the indorsement of such a dishonest person *is* effective as that of the payee. Thus, the dishonest agent has a Code-conferred holder status, and the supermarket can be a holder in due course entitled to payment. A similar principle applies where an imposter (person pretending to be someone else) tricks the issuer of a negotiable instrument into thinking the imposter is the intended payee.

Why should these particular dishonest people be given holder status? The reason is that the issuer of an instrument is in a better position than is a subsequent holder or a drawee to prevent the padding of payrolls and similar dishonesty, and to check the identity of imposters. An employer is expected to take reasonable care in supervising employees or to cover any loss by fidelity insurance. Although Section 3-405 may seem to encourage dishonesty, the persons who do the defrauding are still subject to criminal penalties for their dishonesty, to civil suits for damages, and, as signers, to liability on the instrument.

CASE 32.2   **Western Casualty & Surety Co. v. Citizens Bank of Las Cruces**
33 UCC Rep. 1018 (10th Cir. 1982)

Facts: Two employees of the state of New Mexico created a fictitious entity, the Greater Mesilla Valley Sanitation District. They fraudulently induced a state official to issue to the district a warrant (order to pay money) for $395,000. The employees presented the warrant to the drawee—Citizens Bank—which accepted, processed, and forwarded it to the Bank of New Mexico for payment. That bank, the fiscal agent for the state, honored the warrant. Having suffered the loss of the $395,000, the state called on Western Casualty, its surety on an employee bond, to pay $395,000 to the state. Western Casualty did so, and sued the banks to recover the amount paid. The trial court held that Western Casualty was not entitled to reimbursement from the banks.

Question: Was Western Casualty entitled to reimbursement?

Answer: No.

Reasoning: Here dishonest employees induced the employer to sign an instrument (the warrant) made out to a fictitious payee, intending the payee to have no interest in the instrument issued. Under UCC Section 3-405, the dishonest employees had holder status and the power to indorse the warrant to Citizens Bank. The employer (the state), instead of a subsequent holder or the drawee, must bear the loss. The employer had no basis for holding the banks liable, and neither does its surety, Western Casualty.

DISCHARGE FROM CONTRACTUAL LIABILITY

As a negotiable instrument is transferred from hand to hand, the liability of various signers—makers, drawers, acceptors, and unqualified indorsers—may be discharged (terminated) by a variety of methods. A signer may assert discharge as a defense in a lawsuit brought to compel the signer to pay the instrument. Most discharges are personal defenses, but a few are real defenses. This part of the chapter describes some common methods of discharge and the effect of discharge on the rights of a holder in due course.

Common Methods of Discharge

Payment.   A party who pays the amount of the instrument to a holder (and removes the instrument from circulation or cancels it by, for example, marking it "Paid") is completely discharged from liability on it [3-603(1)]. Discharge will not result, however, if the payment was made in bad faith, as where the person making payment knows that the holder acquired the instrument by theft. Nor will a payment that is inconsistent with a restrictive indorsement ordinarily result in discharge.

The discharge of a party who has no recourse on the instrument (no valid claim against any other party) usually results in the discharge of all other parties [3-601(3)]. Thus, if a maker or drawer pays a holder and is thereby discharged, all others such as indorsers and accommodation parties are discharged too.

Usually an instrument is given for the purpose of discharging some underlying obligation. For example, a tenant mails the landlord a check for a month's rent. Unless otherwise agreed, the underlying obligation (here, to pay rent) is not discharged until the check is actually paid [3-802]. However, the landlord's taking the check suspends the landlord's right to sue for nonpayment until the check is overdue or dishonored.

Fraudulent and Material Alteration.   After an instrument gets into circulation, it might be altered by a holder or by some other person. An *alteration* might consist of a deletion, an addition, or a substitution; or it might consist of the *completion* of an incomplete (but signed) instrument "otherwise than as authorized" [3-407].

An alteration may or may not discharge the party affected by it, depending on the circumstances surrounding the alteration. *No* alteration results in discharge of the affected party unless one of the following circumstances exists:

1. The alteration was made for a *fraudulent purpose*. This means a dishonest purpose. There is no fraudulent purpose where a blank is filled in with the honest but mistaken belief that the act is as authorized. Nor is there likely to be a fraudulent purpose where a holder substitutes a lower interest rate intending to benefit the maker.

2. The alteration was made by a *holder* of the instrument or by the holder's authorized representative. An alteration made by a "stranger" to the instrument has no effect on the liability of the parties. A holder who has not misbehaved should not be penalized for the midconduct of a stranger.

3. The alteration must be *material*. It is material if it changes the contract of a party in any respect. The addition of one cent to the amount payable, or an advance of one day in the date of payment, is material and will operate as a discharge *if* it is fraudulent. A change that does no more than correct an obvious error is not material.

The extent to which a party is discharged from liability on the ground of a fraudulent and material alteration (referred to hereafter as "material alteration") depends on the nature of the person seeking payment from the offended party. A party whose contract is changed by a holder's material alteration is completely discharged from liability to (1) the holder who made the alteration, and (2) any other person who is merely an assignee of the altered instrument—*unless*, for example, the affected party assented to the alteration [3-407(2)(a)]. However, even though material alteration is a real defense (one good against a holder in due course), material alteration is at most a *partial* real defense, and may be no defense at all. A holder in due course always may enforce the altered instrument against the affected party according to the original tenor (terms) of the instrument. And, where a signed but incomplete instrument has been completed, the holder in due course may enforce the instrument *as completed* [3-407(3)]. Furthermore, a holder in due course is entitled to enforce an instrument *as altered* (e.g., for a fraudulently raised amount) where the affected party's negligence (here, the maker's negligence) made alteration easy [3-406].

Suppose, for example, that Mary makes and delivers to Paul a note for $100 payable to Paul's order. Paul negotiates it to Art, who fraudulently raises the amount to $2100 and then negotiates the note to Ben. Mary and Paul are discharged from any liability to Art because Art's alteration was fraudulent and material. If Ben is *not* a holder in due course, Mary and Paul are liable to Ben for $100, the amount originally specified in the note. But if in preparing the note Mary negligently left spaces in which additional words or figures could easily be inserted, or if Mary consented to the alteration, Ben, if a holder in due course, may recover the full $2100 from Mary. Art, the defrauder, is liable to Ben for $2100 regardless of whether Ben is a holder in due course.

Where a holder makes an unauthorized *completion* of a signed, incomplete instrument and transfers it, the signer is discharged as to a mere holder, but is liable to a holder in due course for the amount of the instrument *as completed*. The loss should fall on the signer whose conduct (issuing a signed but incomplete negotiable instrument) has made the holder's fraud possible, rather than on the innocent purchaser. Suppose Dora issues a paycheck to Paul but leaves the amount blank for Paul to fill out for the amount she owes him, $200. Paul completes the check for $500. Dora is not liable on the instrument to Paul; but as to any holder in due course, Dora will be liable for $500.

Unexcused Delay. The liability of a secondary party (drawer or indorser) is conditioned on presentment, dishonor, and notice of dishonor, unless one or more of these acts is *excused*. Presentment or notice of dishonor might be excused where, for example, the secondary party from whom payment is sought waives (gives up the right to) presentment or notice, or where the holder by reasonable diligence cannot make presentment or give notice. However, any *un*excused delay in making presentment or giving notice of dishonor completely discharges an *indorser* from liability on the instrument, as Case 32.3 illustrates.

CASE32.3 Hane v. Exten
259 A.2d 290 (Md. App. 1969)

Facts: Mr. and Mrs. Exten were indorsers of an installment note dated August 10, 1964. The first monthly payment was due January 10, 1965. In late November 1965, Hane became the holder of the note. In April 1967, Hane demanded payment, but the maker did not pay. On June 7, 1967, Hane received judgment against the maker and against the Extens as indorsers. In subsequent litigation, Hane contended that the Extens should be held liable as indorsers for the amount of the note.

Question: Should the Extens be held liable as indorsers?

Answer: No.

Reasoning: Under Section 3-502, unless presentment or notice of dishonor is waived or excused, unreasonable delay discharges an indorser. Hane held the note (which was due when he acquired it) for almost 18 months before presenting it to the maker for payment. The trial court was correct in deciding that this delay was unreasonable. Moreover, Hane did not meet the Code's three-day requirement for giving the Extens notice that the maker had dishonored the note.

Though unexcused delay in making presentment completely discharges an indorser, it does not necessarily discharge a maker, drawer, or acceptor. Suppose, for example, that Dora, the drawer of a check made out to Paul, has on deposit with the drawee bank an amount sufficient to pay the check, that the drawee bank fails (becomes insolvent) 32 days after the check is issued, and Paul presents the check for payment 33 days after its issue. Thirty days after issue is presumed to be a reasonable time within which to present an uncertified check for payment [3-503]. Ordinarily, Paul's delay in presenting the check will be unexcused. In such a situation Dora, the drawer, may discharge her liability to Paul by *assigning in writing* to the holder (Paul) whatever rights regarding the deposited amount Dora might have against the insolvent bank [3-502]. Thus, where funds were available during the 30 days and the bank later failed, the holder must absorb any loss caused by the holder's unexcused delay in presenting the instrument for payment.

But a holder's delay in presenting commercial paper for payment is not enough, in itself, to discharge the liable party. If the bank (or other custodian of funds meant for payment) remains solvent, as most do, the maker, drawer, or acceptor remains liable on the instrument for the full time prescribed by the applicable statute of limitations, despite the holder's delay in seeking payment. The purpose of this rule is to avoid imposing loss on holders whose delay is harmless and to avoid unjustly enriching the drawer or other party who normally has received goods or other consideration for issuing the instrument.

Cancellation and Other Methods of Discharge.   Perhaps to make a gift or to pay a creditor, the holder of an instrument may discharge any party (e.g., indorser or accommodation maker) by canceling the instrument (i.e., by destroying or mutilating it) or by canceling the party's signature (i.e., by crossing out the signature) [3-605]. The holder's canceling a signature discharges the liability of the favored person, but the holder still owns (has title to) the instrument and may negotiate or collect it.

There are numerous other methods of discharging a party from liability on the instrument. These include the methods discussed in Chapter 13 that are recognized by the general law of contracts and apply to negotiable instruments as well: mutual rescission, novation, accord and satisfaction, and so on. So, a maker and a payee of a note may simply agree that the maker is no longer liable for payment. Other examples include a discharge in bankruptcy and, as noted in the next chapter, the discharge that may result from the certification of a check.

Effect of Discharge on Holder in Due Course

Generally, discharge of a party (maker, indorser, etc.) is a personal defense that is not good against a subsequent holder in due course who is without notice of it [3-602]. Suppose, for example, that Marty Maker pays Paul Payee the amount of a note before its maturity date and does not compel surrender of the note (remove it from circulation) or cancel it (e.g., by marking it "Paid"). A subsequent holder in due course to whom Paul sells the note may require Marty to pay again. However, a few discharges, such as a discharge in bankruptcy, are real defenses and are good even against a holder in due course.

WARRANTY LIABILITY

Because commercial paper is a type of property, the UCC imposes warranties (guarantees of the absence of certain defects) on sellers and other transferors of commercial paper. Sellers of commercial paper (transferors who receive consideration) make "transfer" warranties. Persons who present commercial paper for payment or acceptance make "presentment" warranties, and so does *any prior transferor* (e.g., a person who negotiates the instrument to the presenter), whether or not the prior transferor received consideration for the instrument.

Importance of Warranties

Warranty liability is important mainly because it often exists in the absence of contractual liability. The following, for example, have no contractual liability (i.e., no liability "on the instrument"): a qualified indorser; a person who negotiates an instrument without signing it; and an indorser who has been discharged because of the holder's unexcused delay in making payment. But signers and nonsigners alike have some degree of warranty liability and are liable for any actual damages resulting from their breach of a warranty, e.g., for selling a negotiable instrument that is defective in one of the ways discussed later in this chapter.

Warranty liability has several practical advantages, for wronged persons, over contractual liability. Among them are:

1. Presentment, dishonor, and notice of dishonor are not required for a suit in warranty.
2. The right to sue for breach of a warranty arises immediately upon discovery of the breach even though the time for payment may not yet have arrived.
3. Upon discovering breach of a warranty, a transferee may simply rescind the transfer by returning the instrument to the transferor and receiving back anything paid for it, instead of suing for damages. Often rescission for breach of warranty can be accomplished without a lawsuit.

Warranties of Sellers (Transfer Warranties)

Any person, including a thief, who transfers a negotiable instrument *and receives consideration for it* makes the five warranties discussed below. If the seller transfers the instrument without signing it (as in the transfer of bearer paper), the warranties run only to the nonsigning seller's *immediate* transferee. If the transfer is by indorsement, the warranties run to *any* subsequent holder who takes the instrument in good faith [3-417(2)].

Warranty Concerning Title.   A seller of a negotiable instrument warrants that he or she has good title to (ownership of) it or is authorized to obtain payment or acceptance on behalf of one who has a good title, and that the transfer is otherwise rightful. This warranty is breached when, for example, a finder or a thief of a bearer instrument sells it, or when there is a sale of an order instrument on which a necessary indorsement has been forged.

Warranty Concerning Signatures.   A seller of commercial paper warrants that all signatures are genuine or authorized. Thus, a seller's transferee may sue the seller or rescind the transfer if the signature of a maker, drawer, acceptor, or indorser is forged or unauthorized.

Warranty Concerning Alterations.   A seller of commercial paper warrants that the instrument has not been materially altered. Suppose Dan drew a check for $100 payable to the order of Pam; that she indorsed the check in blank and delivered it to Amy; and that Amy raised the check to $2100 and then negotiated it by delivery to Ben for $2100. As indicated earlier in this chapter, if Ben is a holder in due course, Pam and Dan are liable to Ben for $100, the original tenor of the instrument. But Ben also has a cause of action for breach of warranty against Amy. When Amy transferred the check to Ben and received consideration, she warranted that the check had not been materially altered. Her breach of warranty entitles Ben to recovery of actual damages: here, $2000 plus cost of litigation.

Warranty Concerning Insolvency Proceedings.   A seller of a negotiable instrument warrants that he or she has no knowledge of any insolvency proceeding instituted with respect to the maker, drawer, or acceptor.

Warranty Concerning Defenses.   The warranty concerning real and personal defenses—infancy, fraud in the inducement, and so on—varies according to the type of seller. A seller who transfers a negotiable instrument and makes an *unqualified indorsement*, or transfers without indorsement, warrants flatly that no defense of any party is good against him or her. But a seller who makes a *qualified* indorsement (one "without recourse") warrants only that he or she has *no knowledge* of a defense of any party. This less burdensome warranty is consistent with the qualified indorser's freedom from contractual liability, yet imposes warranty liability if the seller acts in bad faith by failing to reveal knowledge of, for example, some party's insolvency.

Warranties of Presenters and All Prior Transferors (Presentment Warranties)

Presenters' warranties run only to persons who pay or accept an instrument, i.e., only to a maker, drawee, or acceptor [3-417(1)]. These "presentment" warranties concern (1) title, (2) signatures, and (3) alterations. The presentment warranties are made by the person actually presenting the instrument for payment *and* are made by *all* prior transferors (sellers and nonsellers). Thus, if there is a breach of a presentment warranty, as where there is a forged indorsement, a payor (including an acceptor who pays) may have recourse against a rather large number of persons in addition to the actual presenter.

For example, suppose Dan issues a check to the order of Pam. Then a thief steals it, forges Pam's in-blank indorsement, and transfers the check to Amy as a gift. She transfers it without indorsement to Ben, who presents it to and receives payment from Dan's bank (the drawee). As noted in the next chapter, upon Dan's timely discovery of the forged indorsement (and his reporting it to the bank), the bank must recredit Dan's account with the amount of the check. However, having paid Ben, the drawee bank has a warranty cause of action against Ben, Amy, and the thief as a basis for recovering whatever money it paid out to Ben. Because of the forged indorsement, all three have breached the presenter's warranty that he or she "has good title to the instrument or is authorized to obtain payment or acceptance on behalf of one who has good title." A thief acquires no title by stealing, and therefore cannot confer title on anyone else. No one has breached the presentment warranty concerning signatures, though—not even the thief who forged Pam's signature: Unlike the *transfer* warranty concerning signatures (that "*all* signatures are genuine or authorized"), the *presentment* warranty concerning signatures is only that the presenter (or a prior transferor such as a thief) has no knowledge that the *maker's* or *drawer's* signature is unauthorized. Here, the unauthorized signature was that of Pam, the payee.

The presentment warranty concerning signatures has a further limitation. A holder in due course acting in good faith does *not* warrant lack of knowledge that the maker's or drawer's own signature is unauthorized. As between the two innocent parties, the maker or drawer is in the better position to verify his or her own signature before payment.

The case that follows explains why an accommodation indorser may have no warranty liability.

CASE 32.4   **First National Bank of Allentown v. Montgomery**
27 UCC Rep. 164 (Pa. Ct. Com. Pleas, 1979)

Facts: An insurance company issued a check for $685.28 to Willie Mincey, Jr. and MIC as co-payees. Without indorsing it, MIC forwarded it to Mincy. He indorsed it and tried to cash it at First National Bank (FNB). Because Mincy was not known to FNB personnel, FNB refused to cash the check. Mincey returned to the bank with his uncle, Montgomery, who was known to FNB. FNB agreed to cash the check if Montgomery would indorse it. He did so, and Mincey received the cash. Eventually the check was returned to FNB for lack of MIC's indorsement. For some reason not explained in the case, Mincey apparently was not entitled to payment and may not have been available for suit. FNB sued Montgomery for the amount of the check.

Question: Is Montgomery liable for the amount of the check?

Answer: No.

Reasoning: Montgomery is an accommodation indorser who received no consideration for his indorsement. As an indorser he has liability on the instrument, but only if it was dishonored. The check was not dishonored. The drawee merely returned the check for lack of proper indorsement (since MIC's was missing), an act that the UCC specifically states is *not* a dishonor. So, Montgomery is not liable on the instrument. Neither is he liable for breach of a warranty. For two reasons he made no *transfer* warranty: (1) He received no consideration for his indorsement. (2) He did not transfer the check. (Accommodated parties such as Mincey usually do the transfering.) Furthermore, Montgomery made no *presentment* warranty *to FNB.* Presentment warranties are made only to acceptors and to payors (drawees and makers). FNB was only a collecting bank, not a payor bank or acceptor, and therefore did not receive a presentment warranty.

SUMMARY

Most signers of commercial paper have contractual liability for the face amount of the instrument. The liability of makers and acceptors is primary; that of drawers and indorsers secondary. A primary party is liable immediately and unconditionally when the instrument is due. A secondary party is liable only if the triggering events of presentment, dishonor, and notice of dishonor take place or are excused. The nature of an accommodation party's liability depends on the capacity in which the party signs—maker, indorser, etc. A secondary party who guarantees payment has a liability like that of a co-maker.

To avoid liability as a signer, an agent should name the person represented and show that the agent has signed in a representative capacity. Ordinarily an unauthorized signature has no effect as that of the person whose name is signed, but it does serve as the signature of the person acting without authority. An indorsement made by an imposter or by a dishonest employee in a "padded payroll" case *is* effective to negotiate the instrument.

The liability of signers may be terminated by a variety of methods, including fraudulent and material alteration and unexcused delay in making presentment. Generally, discharge is a personal defense, but a discharge in bankruptcy is a real defense.

Since commercial paper is property, there can be warranty liability. The UCC imposes transfer and presentment warranties.

REVIEW QUESTIONS

1. (a) Distinguish between primary and secondary liability on an instrument. (b) Do all instruments have primary parties? Explain.

2. Explain the meaning and purpose of (a) presentment, (b) dishonor, and (c) notice of dishonor.

3. How long, and why, may acceptance or payment be delayed without the delay's being considered a dishonor?

4. What two things must an agent's form of signature do if the agent is to avoid liability on the instrument?

5. John Doe receives a check made payable to his order. A thief steals it, indorses it in Doe's name, and transfers it for value to Holder. (**a**) Is Doe liable on the instrument? Why? (**b**) Is the thief? Why?

6. Who is liable on an instrument made out to and indorsed by an imposter? Why?

7. (**a**) Under what circumstances will payment not discharge a maker, acceptor, or indorser of an instrument? (**b**) What effect does a person's taking a check have on the underlying obligation?

8. If an alteration discharges a party to the instrument, against whom will the discharge be effective? *Not* be effective?

9. (**a**) Whom does unexcused delay in making presentment discharge completely? (**b**) Under what circumstances will unexcused delay discharge a maker, drawer, or acceptor?

10. Explain or illustrate how the following transfer warranties are breached: warranty of title, warranty concerning signatures, and warranty against alterations.

11. How does a qualified indorsement affect the warranty concerning defenses?

12. How do presentment warranties differ from transfer warranties with regard to (**a**) who makes them, and (**b**) who receives them?

CASE PROBLEMS

1. Defendant executed and delivered to plaintiff a note dated July 14, 1967. In the body of the note appeared the words "Due and payable ten months and seventeen days after date of execution." In the upper left corner was the typed notation "Due June 1, 1968." About 6 months after the note became due, plaintiff gave it to his bank for collection. An officer of the bank, observing that the due date was incorrectly stated in the notation at the upper left corner, penciled in the date "5/31/68" above the typed date of June 1, 1968. Did this change constitute an alteration that precluded the payee from collecting the amount of the note from the maker? Explain reason for your answer.

2. Brannan created Sunrise Resources, Inc., for the purpose of investing in oil leases, and was seeking capital for that enterprise. Baird executed a note for $100,000 payable to the order of Brannan. The note was executed on a standard printed note form. Beneath his signature Baird wrote that the note was conditioned on Sunrise Resources, Inc., obtaining a minimum of $500,000 in subscriptions. Baird delivered the note to Brannan. Brannan cut off the conditional part of the note, and pledged the note as an apparently complete document to a bank as security for a loan. The bank sued on the note. Baird pleaded as a defense the material alteration of the instrument. Was the defense good? Explain.

3. John Doe issued the following draft to Paula Payee:

> February 1, 1979
> Thirty days after date, pay to the order of
> Paula Payee the sum of one thousand eight hundred
> dollars ($1,800.00). This draft is payable at
> First State Bank, Arrow Head, Arizona.
>   To: First State Bank
>   Arrow Head, Arizona   *John Doe*

On the date the draft was due, Doe had sufficient funds on deposit at First State Bank in Arrow Head, Arizona, to pay the draft. Three months later Doe withdrew the funds. Payee presented the draft at First State Bank on January 15, 1980. The bank dishonored the draft. Payee immediately sought payment from Doe. Doe refused to pay on the ground that Payee's delay in presenting the draft was unexcused and resulted in Doe's discharge. Was Doe discharged? Why or why not?

4. Martin Maker executed and delivered to Paula Payee a 30-day note for $195 Payable to the order of Payee. Payee indorsed the note in blank and "without recourse" and sold it to Alfred Anderson. Anderson indorsed the note in blank and "without recourse" sold it to Betty Brown. Brown, without indorsing the note, sold it to Harold Holder. After the due date of the note, Holder presented it to Maker for payment. Maker refused to pay, correctly stating that he had given the note to Paula Payee for a gambling debt and that a state statute made gambling instruments null and void. (**a**) Assume that Holder sued Brown for breach of warranty. Judgment for whom? (**b**) Assume that Holder sued Anderson for breach of warranty. Judgment for whom? (**c**) Assume that Holder sued Payee for breach of warranty. Judgment for whom? Give reason(s) for each answer.

5. Martin Maker executed a note payable to the order of Paula Payee. Payee lost the note. Fred Forger, the finder, forged Payee's indorsement and sold the note to Georgia Goodenough, who indorsed and sold the note to Harold Holder. Neither Goodenough nor Holder was aware of the forgery. Holder presented the note at maturity, and Maker paid it. Later Maker discovered that the signature on the instrument was a forgery. (**a**) Assume that Maker sued Holder for breach of warranty. Judgment for whom? (**b**) Assume that instead of suing Holder, Maker sued Goodenough for breach of warranty. What judgment? Explain.

CHAPTER 33

CHECKS; RELATIONSHIP BETWEEN BANK AND CUSTOMER

Millions of business firms and individuals have checking accounts and, consequently, continuing business relationships with banks. They issue checks drawn on accounts in their banks; and deposit for collection not only the checks they receive, but also drafts, matured bonds, interest coupons, and other instruments calling for payment in money. Banks refer to such instruments as "items."

Previous chapters dealt with many important aspects of checks—negotiable form; liability of drawers and indorsers; the requirements of presentment, dishonor, and notice of dishonor for triggering the liability of secondary parties; and so on. As noted in Chapter 30, a check performs a currency function; it is a substitute for money. Although a check is not normally used as a credit instrument (it cannot be payable in installments), it is freely transferable, and a transferee may purchase it (by "cashing" it for the holder) and become a holder in due course. Thus, the topics covered in Chapters 30 through 32, which apply to all negotiable instruments, govern the relationship of the parties to a check.

Additional laws, however, apply to checks and banks. For example, Article 4 of the Uniform Commercial Code (UCC), entitled "Bank Deposits and Collections," deals with the contractual relationship between a bank and its customers, especially its checking account customers. And federal law applies to the computer-controlled "electronic funds transfer" (EFT) systems now widely used as a substitute for paper checks. The first part of this chapter discusses the special nature of checks and the uses of certified checks. The remainder of the chapter discusses·(1) the rights and duties of banks and their checking account customers, and (2) the nature of computer-controlled EFT systems.

CHECKS

Special Nature of Checks

As noted in Chapter 30, a check is a particular kind of draft. Two features distinguish checks from other kinds of drafts: A check is always drawn on a bank, and a check is always payable on demand of the payee or other holder [3-104(2)].

Even a *postdated* check (one issued, say, on May 1 but dated May 5) is a demand instrument—but one that does not become effective (payable) until the stated date arrives [3-114(2)]. The postdating simply postpones the time at which the holder may demand payment. For the reason discussed later in this chapter, the drawee bank may not safely honor (pay) a postdated check until the stated day arrives, but then must honor the check upon the holder's demand unless there is some reason for dishonor such as insufficient funds in the drawer's account.

Figure 33.1 illustrates the relationship among the persons normally involved in issuing and cashing a check. Usually the drawer (Dr in Figure 33.1) issues a check to the payee (Pe) in payment for consideration such as goods or services sold to Dr by Pe. The exchange of the check for consideration is the "underlying" transaction (here, a contract) discussed in Chapter 30. After receiving the check from Dr, Pe may, for example, cash the check at a supermarket, cash it at Pe's own bank, or present it directly to the drawee bank for payment. Figure 33.1 shows Pe cashing the check at Pe's own bank (selling it, in effect) so that Pe's bank becomes a holder in due course (HDC) who takes the check free of the drawer's personal defenses. HDC will present the check (perhaps through a clearinghouse) to the drawee bank (De) for payment. In

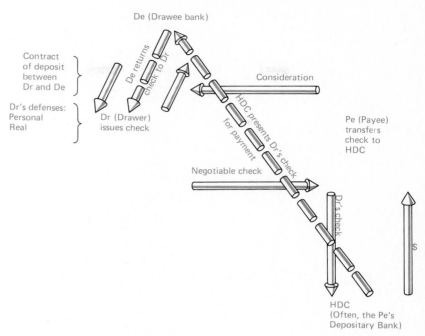

FIGURE 33.1   Issue, transfer, payment, and return of check.

accordance with the contract of deposit between Dr and De, De will pay HDC the amount of the check, take possession of the check, cancel it (mark it in a way that indicates payment has been made), and return it or otherwise make it available to Dr as a part of Dr's financial records.

A check is a depositor's order or instruction to the drawee bank to pay a specified amount from the Drawer's (depositor's) account. Unless otherwise agreed, a check does *not* operate as an assignment (present transfer) of funds in the account [3-409]. Rather, as Case 33.1 illustrates, the check is the customer's instruction to the bank to pay *when the payee or some other holder presents the check to the bank.* Since a check does not by itself transfer funds at the time of issue (and therefore does not confer on the payee or other holder any property right in the funds on deposit), the drawee bank is not liable *to the holder* for refusing to pay the check. However, the bank may be liable to the *drawer* (may be in breach of the contract of deposit) for refusing to pay. The bank's liability for wrongful dishonor (refusal to pay) is discussed later in this chapter.

CASE 33.1   Lambeth v. Lewis
150 S.E.2d 462 (Ga. App. 1968)

Facts: Lambeth brought suit on a check that had been issued to him as payee by a drawer who later died. Lambeth did not present the check to the drawee bank for payment, or otherwise negotiate it, during the drawer's lifetime. After the drawer's death the drawer's account was closed. Lambeth sued Lewis, the administrator of the drawer's estate, because Lewis was the representative of the drawer for the purpose of determining whether the estate was required to pay the check. The trial court awarded Lambeth the amount of the check, and Lewis appealed.

Question: Was the estate liable on the check?

Answer: No.

Reasoning: A check does not of itself operate as an assignment of the drawer's funds. It is only an order to pay and is not effective unless presented for payment. A check may be revoked (stopped) at any time by the drawer before it has been certified, accepted, or paid by the bank, and is revoked by operation of law 10 days after the death of the drawer where the drawee knows of the drawer's death. Because the check was revoked by the death of the drawer before Lambeth presented it, Lambeth cannot enforce the check itself. Instead, he will have to allege and prove that he performed an underlying transaction. If he can prove this, the estate will have to pay the amount determined to be owed, which might be less than the amount of the check.

Certified Checks

Recall from Chapter 30 that no one is contractually liable for payment of a negotiable instrument unless that person has signed the instrument. Therefore a drawee bank has no liability on a check when it is issued, and the payee or other holder must rely solely on the creditworthiness of the drawer (and of any indorser whose secondary liability has not been discharged) when deciding whether to cash a check or to receive it as payment for property or services. To reduce doubts of payees and subsequent holders about the collectibility of a check, the drawee bank may be willing to *certify* it.

Certification is the *acceptance* of a check by a drawee bank [3-411(3)]. A bank official certifies a check by stamping the word "accepted" or "certified" on its face and adding the date of certification and the official's signature. Upon certifying a check, the drawee bank becomes *primarily* liable for the face amount of the check [3-409(1); 3-413(1)]. Because the bank ordinarily charges (debits) the drawer's account for the amount of the check before certifying it, the certification is an assurance to the person seeking certification and to subsequent holders that the bank holds money to pay the check. But regardless of whether the bank actually debits the drawer's account, the bank makes an *independent* engagement (promise) to pay. Thus, the holder may rely on the credit of the drawee bank instead of the credit of individuals such as the drawer.

Unless otherwise agreed, a bank is under no obligation to either a depositor (drawer) or a third person (such as the payee) to certify a check [3-411(2)]. Usually, however, a bank is quite willing to certify a check, provided the drawer has sufficient funds to cover it. A bank may certify a check at the request of the bank's customer (the drawer) or at the request of the payee or other holder.

A *drawer* may, before issuing a check, seek certification at the request of the payee who is unwilling to rely on the credit of the drawer alone. For example, a transport company that moves household furnishings interstate usually insists on being paid with a certified check before unloading the furnishings. A drawer can use a certified check for moving personal funds too, by having the drawee bank certify a check made out to the drawer or to a bank at a new location. Because of the certifying bank's primary liability, a bank at the new location ordinarily will allow the drawer to make withdrawals from the new account immediately instead of requiring the drawer to wait until the certified check "clears." Where a bank certifies a check at the request of the drawer, the certification *adds* the primary liability of the certifying bank to the usual secondary liability of the drawer.

Sometimes the *payee or other holder* receives a check and then seeks certification from the drawee. This might happen, for example, where the payee or holder wants to take the check to a distant location and cash it there rather than cash it locally and carry the money. Where a bank certifies a check at the request of the payee or holder, the drawer and all prior indorsers are *discharged* from liability on the check [3-411(1)]. Thus, the certifying bank is *substituted* as the party liable for payment. The reason for discharging the drawer and prior indorsers is that the holder could have had cash merely by presenting the check for payment, and upon the holder's receiving cash the drawer and prior indorsers would have been discharged. The holder's act of procuring certification should not, and under the UCC does not, increase the liability of the drawer and prior indorsers beyond that which they originally had.

RELATIONSHIP BETWEEN BANK AND CUSTOMER

Contract between Bank and Customer
By opening a checking account, an individual or business firm enters into a contract with the bank (the "contract of deposit" noted in Figure 33.1). This contract imposes duties on the bank and on the checking account customer (the depositor). A major duty of the bank to the depositor is to make payments out of the depositor's account *only* in strict accordance with the depositor's *genuine* orders. Thus, the bank has absolute liability to the depositor for paying a forged or altered check and ordinarily may not charge (debit) the drawer's account for the amount of a forged check or for the amount by which an altered check has been raised. If the bank does charge the drawer's account under such circumstances, it usually must recredit the drawer's account for the amount of the improper payment.

The depositor owes two major duties to the bank: (1) to avoid negligence when drawing and issuing a check, and (2) to examine bank statements and canceled checks with reasonable care and to report forgeries and alterations promptly. If the depositor-drawer fails in these duties, the bank may be relieved of liability for an otherwise improper payment out of the drawer's account.

The technical complexities of banking operations are so great that it is not feasible to include in a printed contract all the rights and duties of the parties. Instead, many of these rights and duties are governed by provisions of the UCC. However, the bank and customer are free to vary by contract the effect of a Code provision, except that no agreement can disclaim a bank's responsibility for its own lack of good faith or its failure to exercise ordinary care [4-103].

Although it is not feasible to include in a printed contract all the terms of the contract, most banks require their checking account customers to sign a form, called a "signature card," that includes some of the principal contract provisions. Often the printed form deals with such matters as the bank's handling of items received from the customer for deposit or collection, the depositor's responsibility when the depositor requests the bank to stop payment on a check, and the service charges to which the account will be subject. If litigation involves a problem that is not governed by specific contract provisions or by statute, courts look to the common law and to banking usage for the solution.

Nature of Bank–Customer Relationship

There is a dual relationship between a bank and its checking account customer: that of debtor and creditor, in which the customer is the creditor; and that of principal and agent, in which the bank is the agent. When the customer deposits money in his or her account, the bank becomes the customer's debtor. In the event of the bank's bankruptcy, the customer is a general creditor of the bank. If a customer deposits a check or other item *for collection* (for the bank to present on behalf of the customer for payment), the bank is temporarily the customer's agent as to the particular item, until the bank collects the amount of the item for the customer. Then, upon collection of the item, the bank ceases being the customer's agent and becomes the customer's debtor as to the amount collected. A bank also acts as an agent for the customer in honoring checks that the customer has drawn against funds on deposit in the customer's account.

When Bank May Charge Customer's Account

When a bank honors a check properly drawn on the customer's account, or certifies a customer's check, it *debits* (charges) the customer's account for the amount of the check. However, there are several situations where the bank's right to charge the customer's account may be questioned.

Payment of Overdraft.   In the absence of some arrangement with the bank for permitting an overdraft (a check written on a checking account containing less funds than the amount of the check), the customer has no right to overdraw an account, and the bank has no obligation to pay an overdraft. If the bank chooses to honor an overdraft, it has a right to do so [4-401]. If the bank pays the overdraft, the customer must reimburse the bank.

In the ordinary checking account, the customer's obligation to repay an overdraft is not subject to interest charges. For the benefit of both customer and bank, many banks offer a special kind of checking account ("ready reserve checking account") that allows the customer to overdraw an account by a stated number of dollars. The amount of the overdraft in a "ready reserve" account is considered a loan, and the customer is charged interest.

Payment of Altered Check.   Where a holder in due course takes an instrument that has been altered, he or she may enforce the instrument according to its original tenor, i.e., for its original amount. The Code gives parallel protection to a drawee bank by providing that if the bank in good faith makes payment of an altered check, it may charge the customer's account according to the original tenor of the check [4-401(2)]. For example, if a customer issues a check in the amount of $100, a holder raises the amount to $2100, and the drawee bank pays the check in good faith, the bank may charge the drawer's account, but with only $100. However, the bank may charge the drawer's account with the *raised* amount if (1) the drawer's *negligence substantially contributed to the alteration*, and (2) payment by the bank was made in good faith and in accordance with reasonable commercial standards in the banking business [3-406].

Payment of Check Incomplete When Issued. A check containing a material omission, such as lack of an amount or lack of a named payee, will not be honored by the bank. However, the payee or holder of an incomplete check may fill in the missing information and present the check for payment. The UCC provides that if the bank in good faith makes payment of a completed item, it may charge the customer's account according to the manner in which the item has been completed [4-401]. Suppose that a customer signs a blank check and delivers it to the payee, telling that person to "fill it in for the amount I owe you," and the payee fills it in for twice the amount. If the bank in good faith pays the check, it may charge the drawer's account with the amount of the check as completed. Thus, as noted in Chapters 30, 31, and 32, the risk of loss is on the signer who, by issuing an incomplete instrument, made loss possible. The bank is protected even though it has knowledge of the completion —where, for example, the payee fills in the amount in the presence of a bank employee. However, the bank is *not* allowed to charge the customer's account if the bank is on notice that the completion was improper.

Payment of Stale Check. Banks generally call checks that are outstanding for 6 months or more "stale" checks. The drawee bank is not obligated to pay a check, other than a certified check, that is presented to it more than 6 months after the check is issued. If the bank chooses to honor a stale check, it may charge the customer's account, provided the payment is made in good faith [4-404].

Payment of Postdated Check. Postdating a check has no effect on its negotiability [3-114]. A taker of a postdated check therefore may be a holder in due course. However, if a holder presents the check to the drawee bank for payment before the specified date, it may properly refuse payment, and there is no dishonor to trigger the liability of secondary parties. The bank's refusal to pay before the stated date is proper because the bank could be held liable to its customer for paying a postdated check early, charging the customer's account, and thereby reducing the balance in the account to a point where currently payable checks are dishonored. A bank will *not* be held liable for paying a postdated check if the drawer's own negligence is the cause of the drawer's loss or if the drawer postdated the check for a fraudulent purpose.

Bank's Liability for Wrongful Dishonor

A bank is liable to its customer for damages caused by the *wrongful dishonor* of (refusal to pay) the customer's check [4-402]. Since a bank is liable only for a *wrongful* dishonor, it is not liable where it dishonors a check for the drawer's lack of funds, or for lack of a necessary indorsement, or for other good reasons. A bank is liable for wrongful dishonor only to the drawer-customer, for breach of the contract of deposit. A *payee or other holder* of a check who is harmed by the bank's wrongful dishonor has no right of recovery against the bank.

Wrongful dishonor includes intentional refusal to pay a check, brought about by mistake. Where the dishonor occurs through mistake, the bank's liability is limited to "actual damages proved," as Case 33.2 illustrates. The Code rejects the view that the wrongful dishonor of a check automatically defames the drawer by reflecting badly on his or her credit and therefore entitles the drawer to an award without proof that damage has occurred. The Code recognizes, however, that actual damages may include damages for an arrest or prosecution of the customer or other circumstances directly resulting from the wrongful dishonor.

CASE 33.2

Bank of Louisville Royal v. Sims
435 S.W.2d 57 (Ky. App. 1968)

Facts: Sims deposited with defendant Bank a $756 check drawn on an out-of-town bank. Ordinarily, Bank delayed crediting an account for three days so the out-of-town check would clear. But by mistake, Bank's employee placed a ten-day hold on Sims' check which, however, cleared within the usual time. Consequently, Bank wrongfully dishonored two small checks that Sims drew on her account after three days. Sims sued Bank and received a $631.50 judgment for the following items of damage: $1.50 for a telephone call; $130 for two weeks of lost wages; and $500 for "illness, harassment, embarrassment and inconvenience." Bank appealed.

Question: Should the trial court have awarded Sims $631.50?

Answer: No.

Reasoning: UCC Sec. 4-402 provides: "A payor bank is liable to its customers for damages proximately caused by the wrongful dishonor of an item. When the dishonor occurs through mistake, liability is limited to actual damages proved," including any consequential damages. Damages are "proximately caused" if they were reasonably foreseeable by the parties as the natural and probable result of the dishonor. Here, the nebulous items of damage alleged by Sims, including a case of "nerves," bore no reasonable relationship to the dishonor of her two checks and consequently could not be classified as "actual damages proved." The charge for the telephone call was a proper item of damages. The trial court should have awarded Sims a judgment for $1.50.

Stop-Payment Order   **Customer's Right to Stop Payment.**   Because a check is not an assignment of funds, but is a mere order to pay, it is subject to countermand by the person who ordered the payment. The Code recognizes the right of the customer to instruct the drawee bank not to pay a certain check by issuing a stop-payment order [4-403]. However, a drawer's stop order affects only the relationship between the drawer and the drawee. The stop order *does not* cancel the check itself. The check is a contract that binds the drawer, and the holder may bring suit on the check, against the drawer, when the bank dishonors the check by giving effect to the stop order. Whether the holder will prevail depends on the usual factors—for example, whether the holder is in due course or, if not, whether the drawer has a personal defense. Thus, as further explained later in this chapter in the section Bank's Rights after Improper Payment, a stop-payment order will protect the drawer in certain situations but not in others. Ordinarily there is a small charge to the customer for the bank's services in stopping payment.

Under the UCC, a stop-payment order may be given orally or in writing. Most states have adopted the UCC rule permitting oral stop orders. In those states an oral order is binding on the bank for 14 calendar days (one day in the District of Columbia) but must be confirmed in writing within that period to be binding for a longer time [4-403]. A written order is effective for 6 months, but may be renewed by the customer in writing. In some states (Arizona, California, Florida, Texas, and Utah), a stop order is not binding on the bank unless it is in writing (though the bank may honor an oral stop order if it wishes to do so).

To bind the bank, the stop-payment order must be received in time to give the bank a reasonable opportunity to act on the order before it has either certified or paid the check. After the bank has certified a check (and has charged the customer's account) the drawer can no longer stop payment. A certification is the bank's own engagement (promise) to pay, and it is not required to impair its own credit by refusing payment for the convenience of the drawer [3-403, comment 5].

Bank's Liability for Paying Stopped Check.   The drawee bank may be liable to the customer (drawer) for the loss resulting from the payment of a check contrary to a binding stop-payment order. It is no defense to the bank that it paid the check by mistake. Often a bank, by agreement with its customer, tries to limit or disclaim liability for paying a check contrary to a stop order. However, a bank may not by such an agreement absolve itself from liability for bad faith or for *negligently* paying a check contrary to a stop-payment order [4-103].

Bank's Right of Subrogation after Improper Payment.   Suppose a bank pays a check contrary to the drawer's (customer's) stop-payment order and charges the drawer's account. Then the drawer demands that the bank recredit the drawer's account for the amount of the check. The bank may or may not be required to do so. If the drawer's stop order has a valid basis, the drawee bank must recredit the drawer's account and seek payment from the person who in justice should make payment. If there was no legitimate basis for the stop order, the drawee is not required to recredit the drawer's account. These results follow from the fact that the drawee bank has a right of "subrogation" that at least partially protects the bank from loss due to its failure to honor the drawer's stop order. Consider the following examples of subrogation:

1. Mary issues a check to Pam to pay for totally defective goods Pam delivered. Mary issues to her bank (the drawee) a timely stop order, but when Pam presents the check to Mary's bank for payment, the bank ignores Mary's stop order and pays Pam the amount of the check, charging Mary's account. Since Mary has a defense to payment that is good against Pam (Pam delivered defective goods), the bank must recredit Mary's account. But under the UCC the bank is "subrogated" to (i.e.,

succeeds to or takes over) the rights of the *drawer* against the payee [4-407(c)]. This means that the bank "inherits" Mary's right to sue Pam for breach of the underlying transaction.

2. Suppose that, in the situation just described, Pam transferred Mary's check to Hal, a holder in due course; and that Hal, not Pam, received payment despite Mary's stop order. Under the UCC the bank also is subrogated to the rights of any *holder in due course* against the drawer [4-407(a)]. If the bank had honored the stop order, Hal (because he is a holder in due course) would still have a right to payment from Mary. She had only a personal defense against Pam, and a holder in due course takes an instrument free of personal defenses. Because the bank acquires Hal's rights by subrogation, the bank too would be entitled to payment from Mary free of her personal defense. So, the bank, having already charged Mary's account, need not recredit it; Mary's only remedy is against Pam.

3. Suppose Mary issues a check to Pam to pay for goods Mary *wrongly* believes are defective. Mary issues her bank a timely stop order, but when Pam presents the check to Mary's bank for payment, the bank ignores Mary's stop order and pays Pam the amount of the check, charging Mary's account. Mary demands that her bank recredit her account. The bank refuses. The bank is within its rights, since the bank, in paying despite the stop order, acquires any rights that the *payee* (Pam) has against the maker or drawer [4-407(b)]. Here, the goods are not defective and Mary has no valid defense against the payee. Thus, Pam has the right to Mary's payment and, by subrogation, so does the drawee bank. The bank, having already charged Mary's account, need not recredit it.

Case 33.3 provides another example of a bank's right of subrogation after improper payment of a check.

CASE 33.3   Southeast First National Bank v. Atlantic Telec, Inc.
389 So. 2d 1032 (Fla. App. 1980)

Facts: Atlantic made out a check to Genesis as payee, in payment for "soil inoculant" that Atlantic intended to resell to farm operators. Alleging that Genesis had breached its contract, Atlantic ordered Bank to stop payment of the check. Genesis presented the check for payment; despite the stop order, Bank paid the check; and Atlantic sued Bank for $13,000, the amount of the check. The trial court awarded judgment to Atlantic, and Bank appealed. Bank also appealed the trial court's dismissing Bank's third-party complaint against Genesis, which Bank wished to pursue if found liable to Atlantic.

Questions: Was Bank liable to Atlantic? Did Bank have a cause of action against Genesis?

Answer: Yes, to both questions.

Reasoning: Atlantic presented evidence that Genesis had breached the contract with Atlantic. Atlantic therefore had a defense to payment. Bank's failure to heed the stop order caused loss to Atlantic and made Bank liable to Atlantic. Bank, however, is subrogated to the rights of Atlantic against the payee and consequently may, as subrogee (successor), assert Atlantic's rights against Genesis for breach of contract.

Effect of Unauthorized Signature or Alteration

As noted earlier in this chapter, a bank ordinarily may not charge a customer's account for the amount of a check or other item containing an unauthorized signature or for the amount by which an altered check has been raised. A bank that pays (or certifies) such an item may be required to recredit the customer's account for the amount of the improper charge and to absorb any loss or collect the amount from someone else. However, the bank's liability may depend on whether the customer gave timely notice of unauthorized signatures or alterations.

Banks generally furnish their checking account customers with monthly statements of account accompanied by canceled checks and other items to support debit entries. Upon receiving such an account and supporting items (or being given reasonable access to them), the customer is under a duty to examine them promptly and carefully, and to give the bank *prompt* notice of any unauthorized signature or alteration [4-406(1)]. If the customer does not comply with the duties of inspection and prompt notice and the bank consequently suffers loss, the customer may not assert against the bank the customer's own unauthorized signature or any alteration [4-406(2)]. The bank would suffer loss, for example, where the customer's failure to give prompt notice of a forgery enabled the forger to "skip town" and avoid payment, or prevented the bank from suing the forger until he or she became insolvent.

If the customer can prove that the *bank* was negligent in not discovering an unauthorized signature or an alteration, the bank must recredit the customer's account for the amount of the unauthorized payment *even though the customer does not act promptly or is negligent* [4-406(3)]. However, the bank's liability, even for its own negligence, is subject to strict time limits. The customer must report *his or her own unauthorized signature or any alteration* within 1 year (60 days in the state of Washington) from the time the customer's statement is available to the customer. The customer must report an unauthorized *indorsement* within 3 years (1 year in California and Ohio) [4-406(4)]. Note that the times just mentioned are *outer limits* on the bank's liability for an improper charge. In reality, *unless the bank was negligent,* the customer has only a *reasonable* time to discover alterations and unauthorized signatures—not necessarily the full 1 or 3 years just discussed [4-406, comment 5].

Where a series of checks containing unauthorized signatures or alterations made by the *same wrongdoer* is paid by a non-negligent bank and charged to the customer's account over a period of time, the customer has less time than usual to detect and report the wrongdoing. Where the same wrongdoer makes a series of forgeries or alterations, the customer has a reasonable time *not exceeding 14 calendar days* to report the wrongdoing [4-406(2)(b)]. If the reasonable time (up to 14 days) expires, and the bank pays an unauthorized or altered item before receiving notice of earlier wrongdoing, the bank is not liable for the improper payments that occurred *between* the expiration of the reasonable time and the time that the bank received notice of the earlier wrongdoing.

Suppose, for example, that Carl's employee Amy skillfully forges Carl's signature on the 25th of each month to an extra monthly paycheck for 5 months in a row—May, June, July, August, and September. The bank pays all five checks in good faith, without negligence; and in late September Amy leaves town for parts unknown. On June 1, Carl received his bank statement and canceled checks for the month of May. They reveal the first forgery. The statements and canceled checks for the following months reveal the other forgeries. However, Carl waits until December 1 before inspecting any of the records. Then, on December 1 Carl discovers all five forgeries, reports them to the bank immediately, and demands that the bank recredit his account for the amount of all five checks. What are the rights of Carl and the bank?

1. As to the first check, Carl has a *reasonable* time to discover the forgery of his signature—up to the outer limit of 1 year. Six months might or might not be a reasonable time within which to discover the forgery. Whether Carl was reasonable in waiting that long is a question for a jury. If Carl's inspection and notice to the bank were "prompt," the bank must recredit Carl's account for the amount of the first check.

2. As to the other four checks, Carl is not entitled to a recredit. Because the five forgeries were made by the same wrongdoer (Amy), Carl is subject to the 14-day limit. Since he did not discover and report the first forgery within 14 calendar days after receiving the May statement, and did not give the bank notice of the first forgery before the bank paid Amy the amounts of the other forged checks, Carl must absorb the loss or take action against Amy for the amount of the last four checks.

Suppose now that Carl notified the bank of the first (the May) forgery on August 26, immediately after the fourth (the August 25th) forgery, but the bank paid the fifth (the September 25th) forged check anyway. If Carl's August 26 notice was prompt as to the May forgery, the bank must recredit his account for the May check, is not required to recredit the account for the next three checks (because Carl violated the 14-day rule), but must recredit the account for the fifth check because Carl gave notice of the earlier wrongdoing before the bank paid the fifth check, and gave the notice in time for the bank to act on it.

If a customer promptly discovers and reports an *altered* check on which the amount has been raised by a wrongdoer and paid in good faith by the bank, the customer is entitled to, at most, a *partial* recredit. A bank that makes a good faith payment of an altered check always may charge the customer's account according to the original tenor of the altered item [4-401(2)(a)]. And, where the customer has signed and issued an *incomplete* item, the bank may charge the account according to the tenor of the item *as completed*, unless the bank has notice at the time of payment that the completion was improper [4-401(2)(b)]. Moreover, a bank may charge a customer's account for the whole amount of an altered item if the *customer's own negligence* substantially contributed to the alteration *and* the bank paid the check in good faith and in accordance with the reasonable commercial standards of the bank's business [3-406]. The customer-drawer's leaving open spaces on the face of the check so that alteration is easy is one example of such negligence. Similarly, in situations involving indorsements by imposters or faithless employees (discussed in Chapter 32), a drawee bank that pays in good faith may charge the customer's account for the amount of the check and is not required to recredit the customer's account even after prompt discovery and notice [3-405].

Effect of Customer's Death or Incompetence

As stated earlier in this chapter, the bank acts as the agent of its customer in two ways: (1) When a customer deposits an item such as a payroll check for collection, the bank collects the amount on behalf of its principal, the customer. (2) When a customer deposits funds that the bank is to pay out on the customer's behalf, e.g., by honoring checks drawn by the customer, the bank acts as an agent in paying those funds. It is the general rule in agency law that the principal's death, or the adjudication of his or her incompetency, terminates the agency relationship and, consequently, the authority of the agent, even before the agent learns of the death or incompetency. However, if this rule were applied to banks, it would be completely unworkable. In view of the tremendous number of items handled, banks acting as agents could not possibly verify the continued life and competency of its customers. Accordingly, the UCC provides that neither the death nor the incompetency of a customer revokes the bank's authority to pay or collect an item, or to account for the proceeds of the collection, until the bank knows of the fact of death or of an adjudication of incompetence and has reasonable opportunity to act on it [4-405].

Furthermore, even though the bank knows of its customer's death, it may for 10 days after the date of death pay or certify checks drawn on, or prior to, that date. If there is any reason that such a check should not have been paid (such as fraud in the inducement), the executor or administrator of the decedent's estate may recover the payment from the payee or other holder of the check or, if there is a real defense, from a holder in due course. There is one *exception* to the provision that a bank may pay or certify a check within 10 days after the drawer's death. A bank may not do so if it was ordered to stop payment by a person claiming an interest in the account, such as a relative or creditor of the decedent.

Bank's Liability for Conversion

A bank can become liable for the tort of conversion in a variety of ways. *Conversion* is the act of handling or using someone else's personal property in a manner inconsistent with that person's ownership. A bank converts a negotiable instrument, and becomes liable to the wronged person for the face amount, in the following ways:

1. Refusing, on demand by the rightful owner (usually, the holder), to return a draft (or check) presented for acceptance.
2. Refusing, on demand by the rightful owner, to pay or to return to the owner an item presented for payment.
3. Paying an instrument on the basis of a forged indorsement.

Suppose Dora issues a check to the order of Paul. Then Tom steals the check, skillfully forges Paul's indorsement, and cashes the check at Dora's bank. Tom is both a thief and a converter. As a converter, Tom is liable to Paul for the amount of the check. Dora's bank is also a converter because it paid Tom on the basis of the forged indorsement and thereby acted in a manner inconsistent with Paul's ownership. As illustrated in Case 33.4, a bank can become a converter not only because of wrongdoing by a stranger such as Tom, but also because of its *own* customer's wrongdoing.

CASE 33.4   **National Bank of Georgia v. Refrigerated Transport Co.**
248 S.E.2d 496 (Ga. App. 1978)

Facts: United Account Systems (UAS) was employed by Refrigerated Transport Co. (RTC) to collect overdue accounts owed by RTC's customers, who made their checks out to RTC as payee. Without having authority to do so, UAS indorsed RTC's checks, deposited them in UAS's corporate checking account with National Bank of Georgia, and withdrew some of the funds. RTC won a judgment against the bank in conversion for the amount of the checks. Bank appealed, contending that its liability should be limited to the amount of money remaining in UAS's account at the time of suit.

Question: Was RTC entitled to the full amount?

Answer: Yes.

Reasoning: Under UCC section 3-419, a collecting bank that acts in good faith and in accordance with reasonable commercial standards applicable to the banking business is not liable in conversion to the true owner, when handling an item for a customer who is not the true owner, beyond the amount of any proceeds remaining in the bank's hands. However, here Bank failed to act in a commercially reasonable manner. When checks are offered for deposit into the checking account of one who is not the payee, the bank has a duty to determine whether the depositor has authority to make the deposit. Bank's failing to inquire about UAS's authority to indorse in the name of RTC was commercially unreasonable. Bank could not escape its duty of inquiry by relying on the word of its customer, UAS.

ELECTRONIC FUNDS TRANSFER

To reduce the daily burden of processing billions of paper checks and deposit transactions, banks are making increasing use of computer-controlled electronic funds transfer (EFT) systems. Most familiar to bank customers are the automated teller machines and the pay-by-phone bill-paying systems used in many parts of the country.

Automated teller machines, commonly located at banks, are operated by the customer's electronically encoded "debit card." When activated by the card, the machine will dispense prepackaged amounts of money and will debit (charge) the customer's account for the amount withdrawn. The card can also be used to transfer funds between the customer's saving and checking accounts. Teller machines accept deposits for the customer's account, but the actual crediting of the account is done after bank personnel have verified amounts, reviewed indorsements, and so on. *Pay-by-phone* bill-paying systems require the customer to authorize, in advance, a list of payees and amounts to be paid. Then the customer need only pick up a telephone, enter the proper identification data, and give payment instructions to the bank's computer. This kind of bill-paying system operates without the use of a debit card.

As in the use of paper checks, there are many opportunities for an unauthorized person to make improper use of a customer's debit card or to order improper payments by phone. There is also the problem of errors in record-keeping. Under the federal law governing EFT transactions, users of debit cards receive somewhat less protection from the wrongdoing of unauthorized persons than do users of paper checks. If a debit card is lost or stolen and used without the customer's permission, the customer is liable to the bank for a maximum of $50 worth of unauthorized use. The customer's loss is limited to $50 *only if* the customer gives the bank notice of the theft or loss within 2 business days. The customer's liability is a maximum of $500 if the 2-day notice requirement is not met; and if the customer does not give notice within *60* days, the customer's liability is unlimited. As to errors by the bank, they must be reported to the bank within 60 days after the customer receives a statement of account. Then the bank has 10 days to investigate and correct any errors.

SUMMARY

Since a check does not by itself transfer funds at the time of issue, the drawee is not liable to the payee or holder for refusing to pay it, but may be liable to the drawer for refusing to pay. A bank is not required to certify a check, but a certification at the request of the payee or a holder discharges the drawer and any prior indorsers.

A bank is the debtor of the customer as to money on deposit. But the bank is also the agent of the customer for purposes of collecting items and paying checks drawn by the customer. Many difficulties confront banks as they honor checks of their customers. These difficulties usually involve the payment of overdrafts, altered or forged checks, checks that were incomplete when issued, stale checks, and postdated checks. A bank is liable to the customer for damages caused by a wrongful dishonor, but in many situations a bank may charge the customer's account even though there was a valid stop order. Where a bank has no right to charge the customer's account, it may have a right of subrogation against the payee or a holder.

The bank may not charge the customer's account where there is an alteration or an unauthorized signature, but the customer must inspect bank statements and promptly notify the bank of any improper charges if it is to be held liable. A bank can be liable for the tort of conversion in a variety of ways. Where electronic funds transfer systems are in use, bank customers are liable in varying degrees for unauthorized use of lost or stolen debit cards. However, banks are fully liable, if properly notified, for their own EFT errors.

REVIEW QUESTIONS

1. What is the difference in legal effect between certification of a check at the request of the *holder* and certification at the request of the *drawer?*

2. When and why is the relationship between a bank and its checking account customer that of principal and agent?

3. Under what circumstances may a bank that has paid an altered check charge the customer's account with the altered amount?

4. Explain why a bank may be liable to its customer for paying a postdated check before the specified date.

5. (a) Explain and give an example of a wrongful dishonor. (b) How are damages measured when a check is dishonored by mistake?

6. (a) How may a stop order be made? (b) When must the order be received to be effective?

7. Explain in what way the following statement is inaccurate: "A bank by agreement with its depositor may absolve itself from liability for paying a check contrary to a stop order."

8. Suppose that a bank has paid a check in spite of a stop order and must recredit the drawer's account. Illustrate how the bank may be subrogated to the rights of the drawer.

9. List and give examples of situations where the payor bank may properly charge the customer's account for a check containing an unauthorized signature.

10. Where a customer's EFT debit card was lost or stolen and used without authorization, what is the customer's liability to the bank?

CASE PROBLEMS

1. Marvin Newman owed Belle Epstein $1200. In 1955 he gave her an undated check for $1200 as evidence of this debt. At time of issue the printed dateline read: "Detroit, Michigan," ——, 195—. Later, someone acting without authority dated the check by inserting "April 16" in the first blank, by writing a "6" over the printed "5", and by inserting a "4" in the second blank. Epstein indorsed the check and it was presented to the drawee bank and paid by it on April 17, 1964. Newman sued the bank for failure to exercise ordinary care in paying the check. At the trial he testified that he had paid all but $300 of the debt to Epstein and that she told him she had destroyed the check. He contended that the check was "on its face stale and altered," and that therefore it should not have been paid without consulting him. Judgment for whom? Why?

2. An uncle drew a $500 check payable to his nephew and had his bank certify it. He sent the check to his nephew, with a note saying that it was intended as a wedding gift and was not to be cashed until after he and his fiancee were married. An automobile accident caused the wedding to be postponed 7 months. After the wedding the nephew presented the check to the drawee bank, but the bank refused to pay on the ground that it did not pay stale checks without consulting the drawer. The nephew knew that his uncle had started on a round-the-world trip without leaving an address where he could be reached. Does the nephew have to wait until the uncle returns before he can collect on the check? Explain.

3. Plaintiff sued to recover damages for the wrongful refusal of drawee bank to honor her check. She claimed that by reason of the wrongful dishonor her credit had been injured, that she had been greatly humiliated and had endured great mental suffering, and that she had suffered a chill so severe that she had to be taken to her mother-in-law's home. She prayed (asked) for damages in the amount of $1000. The judge instructed the jury that if at the time the check was presented to the defendant, the plaintiff had in her bank to her credit sufficient funds to pay the check, and the defendant refused to honor it, they should find for her "a sum in damages as would fairly compensate her for any loss or impairment of credit she sustained, and for any humiliation or mortification of her feelings she had been subjected to." The jury awarded a verdict in the amount of $600 and there was a judgment on the verdict. On appeal the sole question was whether there was error in the instructions to the jury. Do you think there was error in the instructions? Explain.

4. On November 20 Owens wrote a check to the Extra Good Candy Co. in payment of Christmas candy bags to be delivered to his store on December 10. On November 21 Owens got a better buy, and telephoned the bank not to pay the candy company check. He meant to cancel the order for the candy, but forgot to do so. On November 27 the candy company indorsed the check to the W Wholesale Co. in payment of a bill. On December 5 the W Wholesale Co. presented the check to the drawee bank and received payment. Owens sued the bank. What decision? Why?

5. The A Corporation had a checking account in the X Bank. Baker, president of the A Corporation, was authorized to draw checks on the account. Callahan had been employed by the corporation for many years. She forged Baker's signature to several checks each month between July 1, 1960 and December 14, 1967, when A Corporation discovered the forgeries and notified the bank. The corporation sued the bank to compel it to credit the corporation's account with each of the forged checks.

The trial court, sitting without a jury, found that (**a**) the bank had been instructed to mail the monthly bank statements and canceled checks to the corporation's secretary, Callahan, and had done so; (**b**) the bank established that the corporation had failed to use reasonable care and promptness to examine the statements and checks; and (**c**) the corporation established lack of ordinary care on the part of the bank in paying the forged checks. What should be the judgment of the court? Defend your answer.

PART NINE

BUSINESS ORGANIZATIONS

CHAPTER 34

INTRODUCTION TO BUSINESS ORGANIZATIONS; FORMATION OF PARTNERSHIPS

If you decide to start a business, one of the first steps you must take is to decide what kind of business organization best suits your needs. The most common forms of business organization are sole proprietorships, general partnerships (including joint ventures), limited partnerships, and corporations. The form of organization you adopt will determine the degree of personal control you will be able to exercise over the business and the extent to which you will be personally liable to its creditors.

FORMS OF BUSINESS ORGANIZATIONS

When you are the **sole proprietor** (sole owner) of a business, the state exercises a minimum degree of control over the organization and operation of that business. A sole owner usually may engage in business merely by paying a license fee. The relationship between you and your employees is governed by the rules of agency (discussed in Chapters 20 through 22) and by any other applicable laws of the state in which the business is carried on, such as zoning ordinances and laws governing store closing hours. As sole owner you have full charge of the business and are personally liable for all its debts. You are also entitled to all the profits the business generates and they are treated as your personal earnings for income tax purposes. If you die while operating the business, your heirs will inherit it according to the laws that apply to wills and estates (explained in Chapter 26).

When you establish a business in which you share ownership and control with one or more other person or persons, you are forming a **general partnership**, a **joint venture**, or, perhaps, a **limited partnership**. The law provides how a partnership is formed and governs the rights, duties, and obligations of the partners.

If you form a *general partnership* you and your copartners manage the business jointly and each of you is personally liable for all its debts.

If you elect to establish a *joint venture* you are forming an organization that differs from a general partnership only in that its business is of a more narrow scope and duration, usually being designed to carry out a single undertaking. Laws governing general partnerships apply equally to joint ventures.

You may prefer to establish a form of partnership called a *limited partnership,* that is, one in which one or more of the partners manage the business (the general partners) while the other partners (the limited partners) merely invest in the enterprise and have only very limited rights in its management. If you are a general partner in a limited partnership you are personally liable for the firm's debts but limited partners do not have that liability. Limited partnerships are the subject of Chapter 36.

Instead of establishing a sole proprietorship or a business in one of the partnership forms, you may wish to organize a corporation. A **corporation** is a legal entity established by a charter from the state. It is the most common form of business organization and is particularly suited to large and complex business operations. The shareholders of a corporation are its owners; they participate in its earnings but are not personally liable for its debts. Corporations are discussed in detail in Chapters 37 through 40.

This chapter discusses the organization of general partnerships, partnership property, and the rights, duties, and powers of partners. Chapter 35, which follows, deals with termination of partnerships.

FORMATION OF PARTNERSHIPS

What Constitutes a Partnership

A general partnership is a voluntary association of two or more persons who carry on, as co-owners, a business for profit. (For the remainder of this chapter the single word "partnership" will be used to denote a general partnership). A partnership is a form of business organization that has an ancient lineage, having been used in classical Greek and Roman days. Except as may be provided by state law, a partnership is viewed only as a group or aggregate of people and not as a legal entity of itself. If a partner dies or leaves the organization, the partnership comes to an end. If the surviving or remaining partner or partners continue to carry on the business formerly conducted by the original partnership, the new organization is either a sole proprietorship (if only one of the former partners continues the business), or a new partnership (if more than one of the former partners continue it).

To ensure that the organization of partnerships and the rights and liabilities of its members are uniform and to enable a partnership to hold property in its own name as though it were a legal entity, the **Uniform Partnership Act (UPA)** has been adopted by almost all the states. However, the act does not completely cover all aspects of partnership law. For example, it is silent as to how a partnership may bring a lawsuit. Therefore, unless a state law otherwise provides, a partnership may not bring a lawsuit in its own name.

Requirements for Establishing a Partnership

To establish a partnership, the parties must agree to be associated in a business for profit, and they must be its co-owners. If, by an oral or written agreement parties establish a business relationship that lacks the requisites of a partnership, a partnership does not exist even though the parties may think they have established that form of business organization. To illustrate, suppose you and Harry organize an enterprise which you name Mariners Partnership. Your stated purpose is to encourage the development of the city marina as a recreational area. Since your association is not a business for profit, you have not formed a legal partnership even though you have given it that name, and thus partnership law will not apply to it.

An Agreement. The parties must have an understanding between themselves that they will operate a business *together*. Their agreement may be expressed either orally or in writing, or it may be implied from the parties' actions.

To prevent internal conflict concerning their rights and duties and to lessen the possibility of future litigation between themselves, individuals who form a partnership should reduce their agreement to writing. A well-drawn agreement will describe the business the firm will carry on, how it will be conducted, the functions of each of the partners, the money or property contributions each will make to the enterprise, and circumstances under which the partnership will come to an end. The agreement should also describe how the partnership assets and property will be disposed of if the business ceases or if one of the partners becomes permanently incapacitated or dies. Since a partnership agreement can be lengthy and complex, it is good policy for people who desire to form a partnership to enlist the help of a lawyer in writing the agreement.

If parties so conduct themselves in a business that the legal elements of a partnership are present, the existence of a partnership may be implied even though the parties do not know they have formed a partnership. For example, Arthur and

Ben decide to operate an automobile wrecking business. Each "puts up" some money and they agree to divide equally whatever profits the business earns. Even though they said that they were "not legal partners," they nonetheless have formed a partnership.

A Business for Profit.   The business the parties organize must be undertaken to make a profit. If that is the purpose of their enterprise and the other elements of a partnership are present, a partnership exists even if no profits are in fact earned.

The following case illustrates the principle that unless parties agree to establish a business for profit-making purposes, they have not formed a partnership.

CASE 34.1   Hispano Americano Advertising, Inc. v. Dryer
448 N.Y.S. 128 (N.Y. 1982)

Facts: Hispano Americano Advertising and Dryer, a lawyer, were not engaged in any business together. However, they had jointly occupied a suite of rooms in a building and had recently moved together into another building. A 5-year lease of the new suite was taken in Hispano's name. In a written agreement Hispano and Dryer referred to the lease as "our lease" and to "our respective share of the rent," with Dryer agreeing to pay two-thirds of the rent and utility charges. Dryer did not pay her share of the rent and Hispano brought suit to evict her. The question arose as to whether they occupied the premises as partners.

Question: When two parties who are not engaged in business together jointly occupy offices, are they partners?

Answer: No. They are not partners.

Reasoning: Although Hispano and Dryer jointly occupied a suite of offices and each paid a portion of the rent, no other business relationship existed between them. Therefore, they were essentially only "commercial room-mates." A partnership relationship requires the parties to be associated together for the purpose of carrying on a business for profit. This they were not doing and so a business organization called a partnership was not established.

Although a partnership is organized to make a profit, it may begin business with any capital or none at all. Its capital may be as varied as money, services, property of any kind, a patent, a license, a person's experience or know-how; or it might be merely the assumed value of a person's name or credit standing.

If a partnership agreement contains no statement of how the profits or losses of the firm will be shared among the partners, the provisions of the UPA will govern, and profits or losses will be shared *equally* regardless of the varying contributions each may have made to the firm's capital. The reason for this rule is that, in the absence of an understanding among the partners detailing a different division of profits or losses, the law presumes that the contributions of the partners were of equal *worth* to the partnership and therefore they should participate equally in its profits or losses.

Partners to Be Co-Owners.   To establish a partnership, the members must agree that each will be an owner of the business. Co-ownership involves sharing the *profits and losses* of the enterprise, but a person who receives a share of the profits is not necessarily a partner. For instance, Dad, Mary's father, lends Mary and Jim, who are partners, $5000 to assist them in their business. They all agree that no interest will be paid on the loan but, instead, Dad will receive a percentage of the profits the business earns until the loan is repaid. Dad is not a partner in the business; he is merely a *creditor*. Or, as another example, Mary and Jim hire Mabel to manage a store owned by their partnership. They agree that Mabel will receive as her compensation 25 percent of the store's profits. Mabel is an *employee* of the store and not a partner. In each of these illustrations there is no community of ownership by the three parties in the business itself.

Members of a Partnership

Who May Be a Member.   Any person who has the legal capacity to enter into a contract may enter into a partnership agreement. "Person," as defined in the UPA, includes individuals, partnerships, corporations (if authorized by their charters), and other associations. Therefore, a partnership may be one of the partners in another partnership.

Although a "person" may be legally qualified to be a partner, he or she can become a member of a partnership only with the consent of *all* the partners in the firm. The reason for this rule is that in a partnership each partner may become obligated to third parties by the actions of his or her copartners. Each member therefore must place great trust and confidence in all the copartners, and they have a fiduciary relationship to one another. For his or her own protection, therefore, each partner has the right to refuse admission of someone to the partnership either when the business is formed or later if a new member is proposed to be added to it. Assume that you and Ben are partners in a business. The partnership needs $50,000 additional capital; without it the business cannot continue. Charles offers to invest $50,000 in the firm provided he is made a partner (which would, of course, give him a voice in its management). You accept Charles' money. But this is not enough for Charles to become a partner; Ben must also agree. If Ben refuses, Charles does not become a partner and you must return to him the payment he made.

Minors as Partners.   Under ordinary contract law minors may enter into contracts. It follows that a minor can enter into a valid partnership agreement either with adults or with other minors. A minor has the same rights as other partners in managing the business, including the right to incur debts for the partnership and to share in its profits. But under contract law a minor may at any time during minority disaffirm ("get out of") his or her ordinary contracts. By the same token, a minor may disaffirm his or her agreement to be a member of a partnership and may withdraw from it without being liable for breach of contract.

If a minor disaffirms a partnership agreement, he or she is no longer personally liable to the partners and to partnership creditors. After disaffirmance, if the minor had not contributed the full amount of money or property he or she was supposed to put into the firm, the minor need not pay the balance. In some states, the money a minor had contributed can be used by his or her former partners to pay for any losses suffered by the partnership during the time the minor was a partner; in other states the minor's capital contribution must be returned to him or her without deducting for such losses.

If a minor does not disassociate himself or herself from the partnership before reaching majority, he or she then becomes personally bound for all liabilities incurred by the firm during the entire time of his or her association with it.

Types of Partners

General Partner.   All members of a general partnership are general partners. Unless otherwise established by their agreement, each partner has equal control over the operation of the partnership business and each is liable to any party who has a claim against the partnership. Under certain circumstances a partner may be a "dormant partner." Under other circumstances an individual, although not a true partner, may have partnership liabilities as a "partner by estoppel."

Dormant Partner.   A dormant partner (also sometimes called a "silent" or "secret partner") is a true member of the partnership although he or she has no dealing with the public. A dormant partner has all the rights and liabilities of a general partner but takes no part in its routine affairs, and the dormant partner's association with the firm is not generally known to the public.

Partner by Estoppel.   A partner by estoppel (also called an "ostensible partner") is really not a partner at all. The name is used under the following circumstances: If a person who is not a partner (1) represents himself or herself to a third party as being a partner in a certain firm, or (2) allows a member of that partnership to make such a representation, and (3) based upon that representation a third party extends credit to the partnership, then the individual thus falsely represented is called a partner by estoppel. Both the partnership *and the partner by estoppel* are liable to the third party who extended credit to the firm relying upon the impression that the individual—perhaps someone who is very wealthy or prominent in the community— is actually a member of the firm.

The following case shows how a problem involving a partner by estoppel may arise.

CASE 34.2   Anderson Hay and Grain Co. v. Dunn and Welch
467 P.2d 5 (N.M. 1970)

Facts: Welch, in order to lease a feed concession, had the monthly rental payments guaranteed by Dunn. In order to protect Dunn from any liability on his guarantee but not to establish a partnership between them, Welch gave Dunn the sole right to maintain the books and accounting records of the concession. A bank account was opened in the concession name and both Dunn and Welch signed checks on the account.

Anderson Hay and Grain, believing that Dunn was Welch's partner, and relying on his financial responsibility, extended credit to the concession. Whenever Anderson demanded from Dunn payment on the account, Dunn did not deny responsibility but signed and sent a check. Ultimately, Anderson's account was not paid and it sued Dunn and Welch as partners. Dunn denies liability because he is not a partner in the concession.

Question: Although Dunn is not actually a partner in the enterprise, is he a "partner by estoppel"?

Answer: Yes. Based on Dunn's course of conduct, relied upon by creditor Anderson, Dunn is a partner by estoppel.

Reasoning: A party becomes a partner by estoppel when he or she engages in, or consents to, a course of action which induces a reasonable and prudent person to believe that a partnership relationship exists and, on that reliance, extends credit. By his own actions Dunn allowed Anderson to believe he was a partner in the concession. Dunn paid its bills when payments were due; he wrote and signed checks on the firm's bank account; and he did not at any time tell Anderson that he was not a partner in the business. Here, Dunn became a partner by estoppel because Anderson, based on Dunn's conduct, relied upon him to be a partner when it extended credit to the concession. Therefore, Dunn, in addition to Welch, is liable for the debt.

PARTNER'S INTEREST IN PARTNERSHIP AND IN ITS PROPERTY

The UPA was designed to allow, among other things, a partnership to acquire and hold property in its own name. Under common law a partnership is not a legal entity. Its property is owned not by the partnership as such, but by the partners as individuals. The UPA does not go so far as to say that a partnership is a legal entity, but by allowing it to take title to and convey property by instruments in its own name, a partnership is given characteristics of a legal entity.

The UPA makes an interesting distinction between a partner's interest in the partnership in which he or she is a member and a partner's interest in the property that belongs to the firm.

Partner's Interest in the Partnership   Each partner's interest in a partnership is his or her share of the profits the firm earns and of its surplus when the business comes to an end. It is a partner's ownership share in the partnership and in the net value of all its resources, including its goodwill.

Assignment of Partnership Interest.   Any partner may sell or otherwise dispose of his or her interest in the partnership. Partner Ann, in order to raise some money may temporarily assign her partnership interest as security for a loan. (This would be a temporary assignment). If she decides to leave the partnership and retire or go into some other business, she may sell her partnership interest outright to whomever she chooses. (This would be a permanent assignment.) The *assignee* becomes entitled to receive the profits which Ann would have received and, upon the dissolution of the partnership the assignee is also entitled to receive the then value of the assigned interest. However, unless all the other partners agree to accept the assignee as a new *partner*, the assignee does *not* become a member of the firm. Unless made a member of the firm, he or she has no right to participate in its management nor to inspect the partnership books.

Heirs' Rights against Partner's Interest.   Under the UPA none of the property of a partnership becomes part of the estate of a partner who dies. However, his or her *interest in the partnership* is part of the estate. The partnership interest is considered to be personal property and is inherited according to the provisions of the deceased partner's will or, if the partner left no will, then according to the inheritance laws of the state. (Inheritance is discussed in Chapter 26.)

Creditors' Rights against Partner's Interest.   If you are a partner in a business and owe money on a personal debt in a state that applies the UPA, there is only one way the creditor can reach your partnership interest to enforce payment of your debt. The creditor must secure a **charging order** (an order in the nature of an attachment) from the court. On the basis of that order, the creditor then has a receiver appointed to collect and turn over to the creditor whatever partnership profits would otherwise be paid to you. The creditor, if unpaid, may foreclose the charging order (an action similar to foreclosure of a mortgage) and cause your interest in the partnership to be sold at a judicial (public) sale. You, your copartners, or the partnership itself can redeem (buy back) your partnership interest at any time before the sale by paying off your debt. But if your interest in the partnership is not redeemed, anyone may purchase it at the judicial sale. Of course the purchaser does not thereby become a partner in the firm. He or she becomes only an assignee of your interest with the limited rights of an assignee described above.

Partner's Rights in Specific Partnership Property   In those states which have adopted the UPA definition of partnership property, *partnership property* consists of (1) the real and personal property contributed by the partners to the firm's capital assets, (2) property acquired with partnership funds, (3) property created or manufactured by the partnership business, and (4) the profits the partnership earns.

Nature of Partner's Rights in Specific Partnership Property.   A member of a partnership is a *tenant in partnership* with his or her copartners in all partnership property. A tenancy in partnership is a new form of property holding created by the UPA. This form of property ownership sharply limits the ability of a partner to make personal use of specific partnership property such as its bank account, its vehicles, or its stock in trade (the articles or merchandise it sells). It gives a partner almost none of the rights to use, control, or sell partnership property that are usually associated with ownership. For all practical purposes the property is owned by the partnership rather than by the partners who comprise the firm. If a partner wants to make personal use of any specific partnership property, the consent of the other partners must first be obtained. For instance, assume that a partner has the right to use the firm's jet aircraft to call on customers and inspect the firm's distant operations. That partner has no right, without the consent of the other partners, to use the aircraft to take his or her family to a vacation resort when the plane is not needed for company business.

Partner's Right to Sell or Assign Specific Partnership Property.   Under a tenancy in partnership, a partner has no right to sell or assign any particular item of partnership property unless (1) all the partners consent, or (2) the sale or assignment is simply carrying on the partnership business in the usual way. For instance, say that a partnership buys six tickets to the Super Bowl, intending to give them to six of the firm's best customers for public relations purposes. Ross, one of the two partners in the firm, believing that as a partner he owns one-half of all partnership property, gives three of the tickets to his children. Ross did not "own" the tickets; they were partnership property and he had no right to appropriate them for his own use.

Heirs' Rights against Specific Partnership Property.   A partner's right in specific partnership property is not part of a deceased partner's estate and is not subject to a claim by the partner's spouse or by any other heir or beneficiary. The deceased partner's right in specific partnership property, such as particular automobiles, machines, or buildings, remains part of the firm's assets. However, the value of specific property is taken into consideration in determining the value of the deceased partner's interest in the partnership.

Creditors' Rights against Specific Partnership Property.   Just as a partner has no personal right to specific partnership property, his or her creditors have no right to attach such property. The only recourse a partner's creditor has is to secure a charging order against that partner's *interest in the partnership*. A case illustrating this limitation on a creditor follows:

CASE 34.3   Bohonus v. Amerco
602 P.2d 469 (Ariz. 1979)

Facts: Amerco secured a judgment against Bohonus, a partner in a firm, for an unpaid personal debt. Amerco then secured a charging order which directed that partnership property (its license to sell intoxicating liquor) be seized and sold to pay the judgment.

Question: Was the charging order properly issued?

Answer: No. It should have been directed against Bohonus's interest in the partnership, not against specific partnership property.

Reasoning: A charging order is an action against a partner's interest in a partnership. That interest is a partner's ownership right in the partnership as a whole and not an interest in any specific item of property. The value of the interest is a share in the value of all of the partnership property. Therefore, a charging order against a partnership interest indirectly reaches partnership property as a whole but cannot reach any particular item of partnership property. The charging order was improperly issued by the court.

Determining Whether Property Is Partnership Property.   Assume that the CTS partnership purchased an automobile from partner Charlie. Title to the car was left in Charlie's name. Charlie continued to use the car on his sales trips. He kept the car at his home (with the full consent of his partners, Tom and Sam). Charlie died owing $5000 to Jones for a personal loan. Now his creditor, Jones, claiming that the car belonged to Charlie, attempts to seize it as repayment for Charlie's debt. How can a court decide whether, in fact, Charlie or the CTS partnership is the true owner of the car?

In this and similar situations, the determining criterion is the *intent* of the parties. In the absence of a definite understanding between them, the partners' intent may be demonstrated by considering such factors as how the property is being used; who pays state and federal taxes, insurance premiums, and upkeep charges on it, and who, if anyone, has made insurance claims for its damage. Unless the contrary intention appears, property such as the auto in the above example, acquired with partnership funds, is presumed to be partnership property.

RIGHTS, DUTIES, AND POWERS OF PARTNERS

When you become a member of a partnership, you acquire certain rights and duties with respect to your copartners.

Rights of Partners

You and your partners have the right (1) to participate in the management of the firm, (2) to have access to its books, (3) to share in its profits, and (4) to be repaid for personal expenditures made by you on its behalf.

Right to Participate in Management.   Except as the partners may have otherwise agreed, each partner has an equal right with the other partners to manage the firm's business. If there is an odd number of partners and the question to be decided concerns an ordinary business matter, the decision of the majority controls. If the question is a major one, such as a proposed deviation from the partnership agreement or admission of a new partner, then the partners must arrive at a unanimous decision. If they cannot arrive at unanimity, any of the partners can bring a lawsuit to secure a court order to dissolve the partnership. If there is an even number of partners in the firm and they are deadlocked on a matter fundamental to the partnership, any partner may seek dissolution through court order, but if the disagreement concerns a matter of lesser importance they must in some way settle it among themselves.

The right to participate in the firm's management is not limited by the value or kind of contribution each partner may have made to the enterprise. For example, let us consider a partnership which consists of three people: Steve, who contributes $10,000 as his share; Edith, who contributes $2000 and her valuable business contacts; and Frank, who contributes only the use of a building he owns. Each of the partners, unless the partnership agreement provides otherwise, is entitled to an equal voice in managing the business. However, the partners may agree among themselves to limit the sphere of each one's activities. Thus, Steve will take sole charge of the partnership's engineering activities; Edith will be the firm's only purchasing agent; and Frank will be wholly in charge of the sale of its products. Such an internal arrangement will, of course, limit the managerial authority of each of the partners. But an agreed limitation on a partner's *functions* does not diminish his or her *legal power to act* for the partnership if a third party has no knowledge of the limitation. Suppose that one day Frank usurps Edith's function and purchases material normally used by the partnership and the party from whom the purchase is made does not know of the limitation on Frank's authority. Frank's act, even though contrary to the partners' internal agreement as to authority, is nevertheless binding upon the partnership.

Right of Access to Partnership Books.   The books of account of a partnership should be kept at the firm's principal place of business unless the partners agree they may be kept at some other location. Each partner has the right to look over the books at any reasonable time and to copy from them.

Right to Share in Profits.   In the example of the partnership of Steve, Edith, and Frank, unless the three agree otherwise, the individual partners are not entitled to compensation based upon the amount of service each performs for the enterprise. Instead, the compensation each receives will be a share of the partnership profits and, lacking an agreement to the contrary, it is presumed that each of the partners has an equal share in the business and is entitled to an equal share in its profits. This presumption of equality exists even though individual contributions to the firm may have differed considerably in amount and character.

If Frank, Edith, and Steve agree not to apply the presumption of equal sharing of the profits, they must set out in their partnership agreement what share each of them will receive. It may be that Frank as engineer and Steve as sales manager, will devote all their time to the partnership business while Edith, as purchasing agent, will work part-time. In such a case, the agreement would normally state the compensation each of the partners will receive in addition to his or her share of the profits.

Right to Be Repaid Personal Expenditures.   If Frank spends his own money to pay a partnership debt, he is entitled to reimbursement from partnership funds. If Edith advances her own personal funds when the partnership is in a temporary financial bind, she is entitled to repayment from the partnership. And when the partnership is dissolved, each of the partners is entitled to be repaid his or her capital contribution. Frank, who contributed only the use of a building, is entitled to get the building back when the partnership ceases to use it. If the partnership or a partner pays damages to a third party because of a tort committed by a partner, the one who paid may secure reimbursement from the wrongdoing partner.

The next case frequently appears in law books to illustrate (1) a partner's lack of entitlement to compensation for services rendered, and (2) his or her entitlement to repayment of advances made for the partnership's benefit.

CASE 34.4   Levy v. Leavitt
178 N.E. 758 (N.Y. 1931)

Facts: Levy joined Leavitt in a joint venture to purchase from the government a large quantity of bacon which they expected to sell immediately in Europe. Leavitt was to conduct the enterprise. After the bacon was delivered to the partners, the government at first refused to allow its shipment overseas, claiming that a World War I law restricted such exports. By the time the government finally permitted the exportation of the bacon, it had spoiled and had to be destroyed. Leavitt induced Congress to pass a special act permitting him to sue the government for the loss. Leavitt won his suit and the government paid the claim. Leavitt had advanced a considerable sum of money to the endeavor. In an accounting of the joint venture's affairs, Leavitt asserted he was entitled to payment for the reasonable value of his extraordinary services and also repayment, with interest, of money he advanced for the venture.

Question: In a state where the Uniform Partnership Act applies, (a) is a partner allowed compensation for extraordinary services furnished the partnership? and (b) is a partner due reimbursement with interest for money advanced for partnership purposes?

Answer: (a) In the absence of an agreement between the partners, a partner is *not* due payment for the value of extraordinary services performed for the firm. (b) A partner *is* due repayment of advances, with interest.

Reasoning: Partnership law applies to a joint venture. Unless partners agree otherwise, a partner's share of the profits is the only compensation due that partner for services rendered the firm despite the extraordinary character of the services. Therefore, Leavitt is not due compensation for his extraordinary endeavors on behalf of the partnership.

A payment made by a partner on behalf of the venture beyond what he or she agreed to contribute should be repaid with interest. Levy had the burden of proving that he and Leavitt intended that payments made by either of them for the partnership business would not draw interest. This Levy failed to prove. Therefore, the advancement made by Leavitt should be repaid to him, with interest.

Duties of Partners   Upon becoming a member of a partnership, each partner undertakes (1) to serve the partnership according to the terms of the agreement, (2) to share in the losses of the enterprise, and (3) to discharge fiduciary duties owing to his or her copartners. Any obligation or duty may be limited by the terms of the partnership agreement.

Duty to Serve Partnership.   Normally, a partner is required to put in full time on partnership affairs. When a partner fails to perform partnership services there may be varying consequences depending primarily upon whether the breach is or is not intentional. When, because of a passing illness or family crisis a partner temporarily fails to perform obligated services, he or she usually continues as a member of the partnership. On the other hand, a disability which renders a partner permanently unable to perform his or her required duties would be cause for a dissolution of the partnership. (Dissolution is discussed in detail in the next chapter.)

Duty to Share in Losses.   We have seen that each partner has a right to share with his or her partners in the partnership profits either equally or according to whatever ratio is established by the partnership agreement. Also, unless the partnership agreement specifies otherwise, each partner has the parallel duty to share in the losses of the business in the same ratio as he or she would have shared in its profits.

Each partner is personally liable for the firm's debts. In the partnership of Steve, Edith, and Frank, if Edith, as purchasing agent, buys a lathe from Smith but the partnership is unable to pay for it, Smith may secure a judgment against Steve or Frank or Edith or against two or all three of them. If the suit is against Edith alone and she is required to pay the partnership debt, she is entitled to be indemnified (paid back) out of partnership funds for any amount she has paid which is greater than her share of the debt. And if the partnership does not have funds with which to make repayment to her, then Steve and Frank are under the duty to contribute to her indemnification. This concept is more fully covered later in this chapter.

Fiduciary Duties.   Because of the nature of the partnership organization, each member is, at one and the same time, *a principal* in the partnership and, under the law of agency, *an agent* of the other partners. In these dual roles each member is obligated, under agency law, to act with the highest degree of good faith and loyalty toward his or her copartners. These obligations are called fiduciary duties.

Each partner, when acting as a principal in the firm or as an agent of his or her copartners, has the power to obligate the partnership or the copartners by (1) contract, (2) admissions or representations, (3) knowledge or notice, and (4) tortious or criminal acts.

Power of
Partner to
Obligate
Partnership
and
Copartners to
Third Parties

Power of Partner to Obligate by Contract.   A partner may obligate his or her partnership and copartners by contract (1) when specifically authorized by the partnership agreement, (2) when the other partners consent to the action, or (3) when the partner has apparent authority to enter into the contract. For example, four physicians in partnership own a building in which their offices are located. Normally, one of the physicians has no authority to sell the building. But if three copartners authorize the fourth to sell the building, a contract of sale entered into by the authorized physician is binding upon all the partners.

A partner has apparent authority to obligate a partnership and copartners by contract when it appears to the other party to the contract that the partner is carrying on the firm's business in the usual way. To illustrate, assume that John and Harry own and operate a commercial fishing boat. The fish they catch are sold to wholesale fish dealers. If John contracts with a dealer for the sale of a catch, John is carrying on the routine partnership business in the usual way and so has the apparent authority to sell the fish. If, however, John contracts for the sale of the boat, he is acting so far outside the way the partnership business is usually conducted that he is without apparent authority and the consent of his copartner is required to make the sale of the boat a legal, enforceable transaction. This is merely an application of the rule of apparent authority which we first met in the chapters discussing agency (Chapters 20, 21, and 22).

When partners have an agreement among themselves which limits the authority of a partner to act for the firm, a third party who has no notice of that limitation is not bound by the restriction on the partner's authority. For example, it is agreed among the partners who own Office Mart, a store selling office equipment, that Jayson, one of the partners, will make no purchase for the firm. Nevertheless, he contracts in the firm name to buy ten word processors that he is convinced Office Mart can sell at a profit. If the wholesaler of the word processors has no notice of the limitation on Jayson's authority, and he appears to be carrying on the partnership business in the usual manner, then the contract of purchase is binding upon the partnership and the other partners. If Office Mart fails to sell the word processors and the store suffers a loss, Jayson must reimburse the partnership or the partners in the amount of the loss because he breached his agreement with his copartners.

Power of Partner to Obligate by Admissions or Representations.   An admission or representation made by a partner while acting for the partnership obligates the firm and his or her copartners if the admission or representation pertains to the partnership business. For instance, partner Fred, after business hours, drives his own car to a store to buy material required by the partnership business the next day. On the way, Fred negligently drives his car into Sophie's car and damages it. Fred tells Sophie he is on partnership business and that the partnership will pay for the damage he has caused. This admission (representation) against the interest of the partnership may serve to establish liability of the firm and of its partners.

Power of Partner to Obligate by Knowledge or Notice.   Ordinarily, all partners are charged with knowledge of any matter relating to partnership affairs that comes to the attention of any of its members. For example, if one partner knows that an element in the lawn mower the partnership makes is defective and may cause the operator injury, all the members of the partnership are assumed to have that knowledge. However, there is an exception to this rule: Partners are not assumed to know when a copartner acts *adversely to* (that is, against the interests of) a partnership .Thus, if a partner steals partnership money, the copartners are not presumed to have knowledge of the theft.

All copartners are also legally bound by any *notice* received by a partner regarding a partnership matter. For example, the city of Broadview sends a notice to Arnold, a member of the New Horizon partnership, warning the firm that if a drainpipe which allows water to flood city land is not repaired within 30 days, the city will take action against the partnership. That notice is effective upon the partnership and all its partners when it is delivered to Arnold, notwithstanding the fact that he ignores the notice and neither takes action nor informs his copartners of its receipt. If the partnership suffers loss because of Arnold's inaction, Arnold may be required to compensate the partnership and his copartners for the loss sustained.

Power of Partner to Obligate by Tortious or Criminal Act.   Suppose Mary, one of three partners who own and operate The Beauty Shop, while giving a permanent wave to customer Virginia, carelessly uses the wrong chemicals (commits a tort) and thereby injures Virginia's scalp. Mary is liable to Virginia because everyone is liable for his or her own torts. The partnership and Mary's copartners are also liable because each partner is liable for the *tort* of a copartner committed within the scope of the partnership business. The case which follows illustrates this principle.

CASE 34.5   Martin v. Barbour
             588 S.W.2d 200 (Mo. 1977)

Facts: Doctors Barbour and Egle carried on a medical practice in partnership. Dr. Barbour
             operated upon Martin in a negligent manner and Martin sued both doctors for
             malpractice based upon Dr. Barbour's negligence.

Question: When doctors are partners, can the negligence of one be the basis of a malpractice
             suit against the other?

Answer: Yes, because each partner is an agent for his or her copartners.

Reasoning: Doctors Barbour and Egle were in partnership and partnership law applied to their
             actions in the course and scope of the partnership business. When physicians carry on a
             medical practice in partnership, an act done by one of them within the scope of
             partnership business is the act of each and all of them as fully as if each were present,
             participating in all that is done. Dr. Egle is therefore liable for Dr. Barbour's negligent
             treatment of the patient.

A *criminal act* generally is personal to the individual who commits it, reflecting his or her criminal intent. Therefore, ordinarily if a partner commits a crime, only that partner and not his or her copartners or the partnership is guilty of the wrong. However, some criminal offenses are statutory and regulatory in nature, requiring no criminal intent. Such offenses are commonly called *strict liability criminal offenses.* If a partner, in the course of partnership business, commits a strict liability offense, the partnership may be liable even though the wrongful act was not assented to by the other partners. Thus, if Martin, without the knowledge of his copartners, burns partnership garbage within the city limits in violation of a city ordinance which makes such an act punishable by a fine, the partnership is liable for Martin's wrongful act.

SUMMARY

There are many forms of business organizations. The most common are a sole proprietorship, a general partnership, and a corporation. The form of business organization adopted will depend upon the degree of personal control the organizer of the business intends to exercise and the degree of personal liability he or she is willing to assume.

A partnership is an association of persons who either formally or informally agree to carry on as co-owners a business for profit. The common law considers a partnership to be merely an aggregate or collection of persons who comprise the firm. Under the UPA, a partnership is treated as a legal entity for the purpose of owning and conveying real property. In most states, it may sue and be sued in its partnership name.

Any person who has the legal capacity to enter into a contract may become a partner. "Person" means a corporation or another partnership as well as a natural person. However, before anyone can join an existing partnership, all members of the partnership must consent.

Each partner has an equal right with his or her copartners to participate in the firm's management, to examine the firm's books, and to share in its profits. Unless otherwise agreed by all the partners, a partner does not receive, in addition to profits, compensation for his or her services to the partnership.

Every partner has a duty to serve the firm in accordance with the terms of the partnership agreement and to share in its losses as well as in its profits. A partner is both a principal and, at the same time, an agent of his or her copartners when acting within the scope of the partnership business, with the power to obligate the partnership and copartners to third parties both in contract and in tort. A partner therefore owes fiduciary duties to the other partners.

A partnership may purchase, hold, and sell real and personal property. Each partner owns partnership property as a tenant in partnership with the other members of the firm. As such, a partner does not have the right to use, control, or sell specific partnership property—rights that are usually associated with the ownership of property. A partner cannot sell specific partnership property unless it is in the regular course of the partnership business or is with the consent of the other partners. In addition to being a tenant in partnership, a partner owns an interest in the partnership. That interest is assignable and subject to the claims of a partner's judgment creditors.

REVIEW QUESTIONS

1. (a) What are the principal forms of business organizations? (b) Distinguish between them.

2. (a) What is a general partnership? (b) How many people compose a general partnership? (c) What is the maximum length of time a partnership can exist?

3. How is a partnership established?

4. (a) Comment upon this statement: "A partnership can exist even though the parties do not know they are doing business as a partnership." (b) Why is it important that they know whether or not a partnership exists?

5. Is the following statement true or false: "A person may participate in the profits of a business without being a partner in the business." Explain your answer.

6. What is the reason for the rule that a person cannot become a partner in a business unless all the partners already in the business give their consent?

7. Explain what is meant by a "partner by estoppel."

8. (a) Distinguish between an interest in a partnership and a partner's rights in specific partnership property. (b) How does a judgment creditor of a partner reach a partner's interest in a partnership to obtain payment of the judgment debt? (c) How does a creditor reach a partner's interest in specific partnership property?

9. Do all partners share equally in the profits a partnership makes? Explain.

10. Do all partners share equally in the losses a partnership suffers? Explain.

11. (a) What is meant by the fiduciary duties of a partner? (b) Why does a partner have fiduciary duties?

12. Under what circumstances can a partnership be liable for the torts of one of its partners?

CASE PROBLEMS

1. Roberts owned a building in which he ran a restaurant. He closed the restaurant but left on it a sign reading, "Roberts' Town and Country Restaurant." About a year later, Roberts rented the building, together with the sign and all the restaurant equipment, to Hanna, to operate a new restaurant there. The rent was to be a percentage of the gross receipts. A representative of Havelock Meats sold Hanna meat on credit. Hanna at first paid the meat bills but 3 months later absconded, leaving a large unpaid bill. The meat company demands payment from Roberts. Is Roberts obligated to pay the bill? Explain reason for your answer.

2. Hauke arranged with Frey to establish bowling alleys in a building which Hauke owned. It was agreed that Frey would act as the manager of the business and receive a salary from its revenues and that Hauke would receive a monthly sum for the use of the building. The bank account of the business was in their joint names and signatures of both Hauke and Frey were required to make a withdrawal. The contract for the purchase of the bowling equipment was signed by both Hauke and Frey. It was the intention of the parties to establish a corporation in which they would each own shares of stock. Before the corporation was organized, Hauke discharged Frey and brought an action to prevent Frey from interfering in any manner with the operation of the bowling alleys. In a case involving these facts, the court held in favor of Frey. Explain the basis for the court's decision.

3. Art, then 17 years old, entered into a partnership with Ben, aged 25. Each agreed to contribute $2500 to the partnership. Ben contributed his entire share, but Art contributed only $1000. The partnership began to do business, but Art refused to make any further contributions to the partnership capital. Instead, Art said that he was disassociating himself from the partnership and demanded the return of his $1000 contribution. Ben contended that Art had to pay into the partnership the balance of his agreed contribution amounting to $1500, and that he was liable to Ben for damages for breaking up the firm. Were Ben's contentions legally sound? Explain.

4. Salmon and Meinhard engaged in a joint venture to lease a certain building. Each contributed an equal amount to the venture. It was understood that Salmon would manage the building. When the lease was near its end, the owner of the property asked Salmon if he wanted a new lease of the building and of some adjoining property. Salmon, without telling Meinhard about the transaction, entered into the new lease in his own name. When Mainhard learned of the new lease, he demanded that it be held as an asset of the joint venture between himself and Salmon. Was Meinhard justified in making this demand? Explain.

5. Grice and Gabaldon were partners in the business of selling lots in a subdivision

the partnership owned. It was their practice for either of them to enter into contracts for the sale of lots without securing the concurrence of the other partner. Grice, without Gabaldon's knowledge, entered into a contract to sell one of the subdivision lots to Dotson. When Gabaldon heard of this he told Grice that he did not consent to the sale because the lot would be worth much more money after a projected road would be built and that, as the lot was specific partnership property, Grice had no authority to enter into the contract of sale without Gabaldon's consent. Dotson tendered to Grice the agreed purchase price but Grice told him that he could not accept the money because his partner, Gabaldon, would not sell the property. Dotson claims he is entitled to a deed to the property. Is he correct? Explain

CHAPTER 35

TERMINATION OF PARTNERSHIPS

A partnership usually comes to an end through a three-step process. The first step is the *dissolution* of the partnership. The second step normally is the *winding up* of its affairs. When the winding up is completed, the partnership *terminates* and ceases to exist. Sometimes a dissolution is not followed by a winding up of the business; instead, after an accounting of the interests of the partners, one or more of the partners continues the business.

The first two parts of this chapter deal with the dissolution of partnerships and the winding up of their affairs. The last part of the chapter deals with the circumstances under which the business of a dissolved partnership may continue without a winding up.

DISSOLUTION OF PARTNERSHIPS

A partnership is dissolved when the partners are no longer joined together as a business unit. Dissolution should not be confused with termination. When a partnership is dissolved it is not at that time terminated (ended); the partnership continues to be a business organization until its affairs are settled. For instance, if Sally and Vera are business partners and Vera quits the business and moves away, Vera has *dissolved* the partnership. But before it is *terminated* there must be an accounting of its affairs. This means that all the money due the firm must be collected and all its bills paid; any money left must then be divided between the partners according to law. Only then is the partnership *terminated*.

Dissolution may be brought about in several ways: (1) in accordance with a partnership agreement; (2) in violation of a partnership agreement; (3) by automatic operation of law; or (4) by court decree.

Dissolution in Accordance with Partnership Agreement

A partnership is dissolved in accordance with the partnership agreement when: (1) the prearranged term of the partnership has expired or its purpose has been accomplished; (2) all the partners agree to dissolve it, (3) a partner in a partnership at will brings it to an end, or (4) a partner has been expelled from the partnership in accordance with procedures set out in the partnership agreement.

Dissolution by Conclusion of Term or Accomplishment of Purpose.   It is common practice for partners, when they organize their partnership, to limit its life to a definite term. When the agreed period of time has elapsed, or its purpose is accomplished, or the specified event occurs, the partnership is dissolved. No court action is necessary.

Dissolution by Agreement of All the Partners.   Since a partnership is an association involving the voluntary agreement of its members, the partners may by unanimous assent at any time dissolve their association without regard to the term or purpose for which they established the partnership.

Most courts hold that a dissolution is not involved when a new member is admitted into an existing partnership because the original members have not ceased to be in business together. Any money or property contributed to the enterprise by the new member may be used to pay partnership obligations which arose before he or she became a partner, just as though the newly admitted member had been a partner when those obligations were incurred. However, the new partner is not *personally* liable (as are the old partners) to creditors who extended their credit prior to the new partner's admission to the firm. Only the old partners are liable to those creditors.

Dissolution by Act of a Partner in a Partnership at Will. A partnership at will is one in which the partnership agreement does not specify any date or circumstance for its dissolution. Since the agreement does not establish when the partnership will dissolve, any partner has the right to dissolve it at any time by withdrawing from it. The withdrawing partner does not breach the partnership agreement even if the firm is operating profitably and its dissolution results in a monetary loss to the other partners.

The dissolution of a partnership at will is discussed in the case which follows.

CASE 35.1   Paciaroni v. Crane
408 A.2d 946 (Del. 1979)

Facts: Paciaroni, Cassidy, and Crane formed a partnership to own and race for profit a horse called Black Ace. No time was specified for the duration of the partnership. Crane was to train the horse and to be in charge of its day-to-day supervision. After Black Ace had won about $100,000 he began to develop hoof trouble. Differences arose between the partners because Crane did not want to follow the advice of veterinarians. Crane made it clear to his partners that the partnership should be discontinued and the horse should be sold. The two other partners instructed Crane to turn the horse over to another trainer to be entered in additional races. Crane complied, but he retained the eligibility papers without which the horse could not be raced.

Paciaroni brought suit to dissolve the partnership and to force Crane to turn over the eligibility papers. Crane contends that the partnership has already been dissolved and he asks the court to direct the sale of the horse.

Question: Has the partnership been dissolved?

Answer: Yes. The parties by their actions have dissolved the partnership.

Reasoning: The partnership was at will. It was dissolved when Crane withdrew. Therefore, a court decree dissolving the partnership is not necessary. The dissolution did not terminate the partnership but it continues until the winding up of its affairs is completed. The parties are presently in the winding up stage of the partnership. [The court then held that in the winding-up, Paciaroni and Cassidy, after posting bond to protect Crane from loss in the event the horse suffers permanent injury, may enter Black Ace in the few remaining races for which he is eligible. If they do not furnish the bond, then the horse will be sold].

Dissolution by Expulsion of a Partner. A partnership agreement may specify the conditions under which a partner may be expelled from the firm. For example, it may provide that, after the unanimous agreement of the other partners, a partner who fails to perform his or her duties may be expelled. In case there is disagreement concerning the expulsion, a court decision is required before the partner can be expelled.

Partners cannot, by expelling a member of the firm, force the expelled partner to lose his or her investment in the business. The expelled partner is entitled to be paid in cash the value of his or her interest in the partnership, including the value of the firm's goodwill (its good reputation which attracts customers to buy its products, merchandise, or services). In this computation, the value of the expelled partner's share is reduced by any debts or obligations he or she owes the firm.

Dissolution in Violation of Partnership Agreement

Because a partnership is a voluntary association, any partner has the power to dissolve the association at any time despite the terms of the partnership agreement. The agreement merely puts limits on the *right* of a partner to exercise that power.

A partner may rightfully cause a dissolution by taking an action authorized by the partnership agreement as, for example, by retiring from the firm. A member may wrongfully cause a dissolution by acting contrary to the terms of the partnership agreement, as, for example, by withdrawing from the partnership before the dissolution date established in the agreement.

Wrongful Withdrawal of a Partner.   A partner who wrongfully causes a dissolution by withdrawing in contravention of the agreement is, like an expelled partner, entitled to receive payment for the value of his or her interest in the partnership. However, when a partner wrongfully withdraws, the value of the firm's goodwill is not included. As a breach of contract is involved, the outgoing partner is required to pay the remaining partners for any loss they suffer because of the wrongful withdrawal.

Assignment of Partnership Interest.   When a partner assigns his or her interest in a partnership, a dissolution does not automatically result because it does not necessarily follow that the partner has withdrawn from the performance of his or her partnership duties. For instance, suppose that partner Howard assigns his interest in a partnership to the Riverbend Bank as security for a loan. At the time of that assignment Howard normally continues to perform all his partnership duties. Under such circumstances, no dissolution of the partnership has occurred. However, if Howard sells his interest to go into business for himself, a dissolution in contravention of the partnership agreement results.

Dissolution by Operation of Law

Under certain circumstances the law dictates the dissolution of a partnership. The most important of these circumstances are the death of a partner, the bankruptcy of any partner, or the bankruptcy of the partnership.

Dissolution by Death of a Partner.   Most courts hold that if a partner dies and the partnership business is continued by the surviving partners without their entering into a new partnership agreement, the business is, in legal theory, conducted by a new partnership composed of the surviving partners. However, some of the more recent cases and several state statutes depart from this view. They give effect to partnership agreements which provide that a partnership may be continued by surviving partners without dissolution after a partner dies or leaves the firm. Such agreements usually also establish how the amount of money that may be due the estate of a deceased partner is to be computed and paid. Large partnerships such as stockbrokers, accountants, and lawyers, where a hundred or more members are not unusual, find this authority particularly useful. It obviates the possible need for frequent court actions and permits the partnership to continue to do business under its original firm name (which may have a definite value in the community and state) even though a partner whose name is part of the partnership name, is no longer living.

Dissolution by Bankruptcy. All of a bankrupt individual's assets (except for certain exemptions) are made available to pay his or her debt. To the extent those assets are not sufficient to discharge the debts, the bankrupt person is relieved from any additional obligations, including those arising out his or her membership in a partnership (see Chapter 44 which explains the Federal Bankruptcy Reform Act of 1978). Such a result is totally at variance with the fundamental partnership concept that all partners are equally responsible for the firm's obligations. Therefore, upon the bankruptcy of a partner, the partnership is automatically dissolved. A partnership is also automatically dissolved if the partnership itself is in bankruptcy.

Dissolution by Court Decree

There are a number of circumstances which do not automatically cause dissolution of a partnership by operation of law, but which may justify a court to decree dissolution on application of a partner. Among the causes for dissolution by court decree are (1) incapacity of a partner to perform his or her duties, (2) misconduct of a partner, (3) continuance of the business when continuance will result only in financial loss, or (4) any other circumstance that justifies a court in finding that dissolution is equitable.

Dissolution for Incapacity of a Partner. A partner's continuing mental or physical capacity to perform partnership duties may be questioned by the copartners. If a partner is declared insane by a competent court, his or her incapacity is clear. And if a partner is found by a competent physician to be permanently unable to perform required partnership tasks, the incapacity to act as a partner is equally clear. In either event the partnership should be dissolved. However, mental or physical incapacity may not be as clearly and easily established as in these two examples. It would be unfair to require partners to retain a member who is physically or mentally incapable of performing partnership functions. But it would be equally unfair to force a partner to leave a profitable business organization because of either a temporary disability or a more permanent disability which does not prevent performance of partnership duties. Therefore, when these questions cannot be settled amicably by all the partners, a competent court must review all available evidence and, on the facts in the case, decide whether or not to dissolve the partnership.

Dissolution for Misconduct of a Partner. On proper application, a court will order the dissolution of a partnership when a partner has been guilty of conduct which materially interferes with carrying on the partnership business. The misconduct must be such as to amount to a breach of the partnership agreement. If the misconduct is only, for example, an error of judgment resulting in slight loss to the partnership, or if one of the partners has a habit of losing his or her temper during discussions of partnership affairs, the misconduct is so trifling as not to warrant court action. But if a partner deals fraudulently with purchasing agents, refuses to explain or justify checks against the partnership account, or deals with customers in such a way that permanent injury to partnership business results and the firm's credit and goodwill are impaired, there is a valid basis for the firm's dissolution by court decree on the application of the innocent members of the partnership.

Dissolution for Unprofitable Business.   Since a partnership is an association designed to carry on a business for profit, a financially unsuccessful firm that fails to make a profit is usually voluntarily dissolved by the partners. However, one or more members may oppose immediate dissolution, demanding that the partners continue to carry on in the hope of a better future, or insisting that an attempt should be made to sell the business while it is still an active concern. In that event, the other partners may seek a court-ordered dissolution.

Dissolution for Other Circumstances.   If it is equitable (fair) to all parties concerned, a court may order the dissolution of a partnership under a number of circumstances other than those discussed above. Examples of such situations might be: (1) Partners Jean and Tom have irreconcilable differences concerning the amount of money their firm should spend on advertising or how its merchandise should be priced. (2) Partner Frank, without the knowledge of his partner Halsey and in his wife's maiden name, purchases a wholesale oil business from which the Frank-Halsey partnership buys large quantities of oil products. If Frank had told Halsey, as he should have done, that the oil business was for sale, Halsey would have wanted the partnership to purchase it. Taking personal advantage of a financial opportunity desirable to and within the capability of the partnership was a breach of Frank's fiduciary responsibility to his partner.

WINDING UP OF PARTNERSHIPS

The dissolution of a partnership brings to an end normal working relationships among partners. However, a partnership does not cease to exist when it is dissolved. Except under circumstances later to be discussed, it must first go through another step—its winding up—after which the partnership and its business come to an end. *Winding up* entails converting partnership assets into cash, collecting all moneys due the firm, paying its debts, and then distributing to the partners whatever funds remain.

Who Conducts the Winding Up; Compensation

If a partnership is dissolved because the partnership term has ended, its purpose has been accomplished, or the partners agree to its dissolution, all the partners are entitled to participate in the winding up. However, they usually entrust this duty to one of their number. If the partners cannot agree on how the winding up should be conducted, then upon application a court appoints a receiver to perform that function.

If a dissolution comes about because a partner has died and the surviving partners decide not to continue the business, the winding up is undertaken by a surviving partner. However, some state laws dictate that winding up must be performed by the personal representative of the deceased partner.

When a dissolution is ordered by a court decree, the court usually appoints a receiver to perform winding up duties.

Neither a partner who has caused a dissolution in contravention of a partnership agreement nor a partner whose bankruptcy caused a dissolution is entitled to take charge of the winding up.

When a dissolution is brought about by the death of a partner, the winding up partner is entitled to reasonable compensation for his or her services because the winding up under these circumstances is considered to be outside normal partnership affairs. But in all other circumstances a partner who engages in the winding up is entitled to compensation only if the other partners agree that it should be paid to him or her. A court-appointed receiver who conducts a winding up is entitled to be compensated.

The next case deals with the authority of a partner to conduct the winding up of a dissolved partnership.

CASE 35.2 Stark v. Utica Screw
425 N.Y.S.2d 750 (N.Y. 1980)

Facts: Stark and Henning entered into a partnership to act as sales representatives for various companies. Because of a dispute over accounting for commissions, the partnership was dissolved. Stark claimed that Utica Screw Company owed commissions to the dissolved partnership. Utica did not pay and Stark brought suit to collect the money. Utica, which was then employing Henning, claims that Stark is without authority to bring the suit as Henning, his former partner, did not join in it.

Question: Must a partner secure the consent of co-partners before taking action to wind up a dissolved partnership?

Answer: No. Any partner who has not wrongfully caused a dissolution has the power to conduct a winding up, either alone or with his or her co-partners.

Reasoning: Upon the dissolution of a partnership, if the partners do not designate who will be in charge of winding up, any partner who has not wrongfully caused the dissolution has the right to participate in its winding up and to do whatever is necessary to collect debts due the partnership. While the winding up partner is not entitled to payment for winding up the affairs of the firm, that partner is allowed payment for reasonable expenses incurred in performing such services. Stark, therefore, had the power, without Henning's permission, to commence action against Utica to collect an account which was due the partnership.

Winding Up Process A winding up entails liquidating the partnership business. In this process all debts owing to the partnership are collected, its assets converted to cash, its unfinished business completed, its liabilities discharged; and the person who conducts the winding up accounts for his or her activities. Finally, any remaining assets are distributed among the partners or, if the business suffered a net loss and only liabilities remain, each partner contributes a share to pay them off.

Collecting Debts.   An individual engaged in winding up must exert his or her best efforts to collect any debts due the partnership. If necessary, debts may be compromised, that is, a lesser amount may be accepted in full payment; and if all other collection methods fail, a suit may be filed against the debtor. Partnership funds may be used to pay necessary legal and accounting fees incurred during a winding up.

Completing Partnership Business.   During the winding up process (even if dissolution is brought about by the death of a partner), the winding up partner continues to carry out the terms of the firm's uncompleted contracts. However, the winding up partner is *not* authorized to engage in any new business for the partnership that is not related to the winding up process.

To illustrate, assume that you and Craig are in a partnership which builds houses under contracts with property owners. When Craig's sudden death dissolved the partnership, your firm had three houses under construction. Some materials are lying at the sites, many materials are on order, and additional materials will be needed to complete the buildings as contracted. You, as the winding up partner, may continue construction to complete the houses so that contracts with the property owners are fulfilled. You may hire the necessary workers, use the materials on the sites, pay for the materials on order, and buy the additional materials required to complete the work. While you may use partnership funds to pay all these costs, you are *not* authorized to bind the dissolved partnership by entering into any *new* contracts to perform additional construction. If you do enter into a new contract, you alone (not the dissolved partnership) will be obligated to fulfill it.

Converting Assets into Cash.   An important task in the winding up process is the conversion into cash of all partnership assets that will not be needed to fulfill outstanding contractual obligations. How the assets are best turned into cash depends upon the circumstances. Important considerations are whether the property is perishable, the season of the year, the warehousing charges that would be incurred if the property is held for any length of time, and so on.

The winding up partner or receiver acts in a fiduciary relationship to the partners and must act fairly. An account must be made of all partnership property and of every penny received from its disposition.

Paying Partnership Creditors.   During the winding up, creditors of the partnership are paid using the firm's funds and property to pay all its debts.

Making an Accounting.   After all the claims have been paid or the partnership funds are exhausted, the individual who conducts the winding up makes a full accounting, showing the total assets and debts of the firm at the date of the dissolution and at the conclusion of the winding up. After itemizing all receipts and disbursements, if partnership funds are exhausted and claims still remain unpaid, the accounting will show how much each partner is required to pay to satisfy the creditors. On the other hand, if a surplus remains after all creditors have been paid, the accounting will show how it will be distributed among the partners.

Partners' Powers Not Incident to Winding Up

Except in matters connected with winding up a partnership, dissolution terminates the authority of all partners to act for the business. However, although a partner has no *actual* authority, the dissolved partnership is still bound by a partner who takes it upon himself or herself to obligate the firm if he or she has *apparent* authority to take such action. A partner has apparent authority when a third party who has no notice of the dissolution believes that the partner's past authority to obligate the firm still continues.

A partner's apparent authority to obligate a partnership that is being wound up may be cut off by the other partner or partners. This may be done by giving either actual or constructive notice to third parties that the partnership has been dissolved.

Actual notice is notice given either orally or in writing to third parties. Sending registered or certified letters addressed to the third parties, with return receipts, is perhaps the most certain form of actual notice.

What constitutes *constructive notice* may differ from state to state. Generally, publication of a notice on more than one occasion in a newspaper of general circulation serving the area where the partnership did business, which states that the partnership has been dissolved, constitutes constructive notice even if the third party does not read the notice.

In the case which follows, a former partner is not liable to a creditor for goods sold to the partnership after the creditor is told that the partnership is in dissolution.

CASE 35.3 Sta-Rite Industries, Inc., v. Taylor
492 P.2d 726 (Ariz. 1972)

Facts: Sta-Rite Industries had been selling to a partnership consisting of Taylor and Hood. The partnership was dissolved and Taylor, intending to carry on the business himself, agreed to purchase Hood's interest. A short time later, but before the partnership was terminated, Taylor incurred a new indebtedness to Sta-Rite for the benefit of the continuing business. When the debt was not paid, Sta-Rite brought suit against Taylor *and Hood.* Hood claims that he is not liable because the debt was incurred after Sta-Rite's sales manager was told that the dissolution was in process and that Taylor was buying Hood's interest in the partnership.

Question: Is a creditor entitled to payment from a former partner for a debt incurred by the partnership after its dissolution and not connected with its winding up?

Answer: No, if the creditor, before extending such credit, had notice that the partnership had been dissolved.

Reasoning: A partner can bind a dissolved partnership to a third party who had previously extended credit to the partnership and who has no notice of the dissolution. In this case

Sta-Rite, before extending the credit, received notice that the partnership was in the process of dissolution and that Taylor was buying out Hood. Therefore, Sta-Rite did not rely on Hood's financial resources as a member of the partnership when extending credit in the sale and Sta-Rite cannot recover from Hood.

Settlement of Partnership Accounts

Order of Payment.   The liabilities of a dissolved partnership are paid in the following order:

1. Debts owing to partnership creditors other than to the partners themselves
2. Amounts owing to partners for loans or advances made to the partnership
3. Repayment to the partners of their capital contributions
4. Division of any remaining assets among the partners for their share of the profits

The partners may, by agreement, change the order of payment among themselves *provided* no creditor's priority of claim is affected.

Settlement of Accounts among Partners.   Unless a partnership agreement provides otherwise, partners: (1) share equally in the profits of the business even if their investments (capital contributions) in the partnership were unequal (see Chapter 34, page 601); or (2) if a dissolved partnership does not have enough assets to pay all of its creditors, each partner, regardless of the amount of his or her capital investment in the firm, must contribute toward paying off the partnership *losses*—either in equal shares or according to whatever formula the partners may have agreed upon for the sharing of profits.

The computation of how much each partner must contribute to make up partnership losses when partners, entitled to share equally in profits, have contributed different amounts to the capital of the firm, deserves illustration. Assume that partner Arnold made a capital contribution of $10,000; partner Baxter contributed $5000 and services; and partner Charles made no money contribution but agreed to devote expert knowledge to the firm. Assume further that the partners find that the partnership has paid all its bills except $2500 to creditor Judith and $1100 to partner Charles, who had loaned that amount to the business. The firm has no money or property to meet these obligations. Most courts would compute the partnership accounts of this firm as follows:

1. Obligations of firm:

To Judith:	$2,500	(for amount due)
To Charles:	1,100	(for loan to partnership)
To Arnold:	10,000	(for return of capital contribution)
To Baxter:	5,000	(for return of capital contribution)
To Charles	—	(no contribution made)
	$18,600	Total obligations

Since the partners had agreed to share equally in the profits, they must contribute equally to cover the losses. Therefore, Arnold, Baxter, and Charles must equally share the loss of $18,600 or $6,200 each.

2. Contributions required:

By Arnold: None (original contribution $10,000)
            Loss: $6,200; balance due Arnold, $3,800

By Baxter: $1,200 (original contribution $5,000)
            loss $6,200; balance due, $1,200

By Charles: $6,200 (no original money contribution)
            $7,400 Contributions required

Distribution of total contributions of $7,400:

To Judith: $2,500 (to pay creditor's bill)
To Charles: $1,100 (to repay loan)
To Arnold: $3,800 (partial return of contribution)

Proof that under this method of settling accounts all partners share equally the loss of $18,600:

Arnold loses $6,200 ($10,000 original contribution less $3,800)

Baxter loses $6,200 ($5,000 original contribution plus new contribution of $1,200)

Charles loses $6,200 ($6,200 new contribution)

A few courts (e.g., California) would distribute the loss only among partners Arnold and Baxter and assess no monetary contribution against Charles because Charles contributed services but no money to the partnership.

If any of the partners in the above example is unable to pay his or her share or refuses to do so, the other partner or partners must pay the whole amount—and then can attempt to recover from the nonpaying partner through a lawsuit.

Settlement of Accounts with Creditors.   Each partner is personally liable for all partnership obligations, that is, its debts, unperformed contracts, and tort claims. Each partner also probably has debts of his or her own for such things as credit card purchases, house mortgage payments, car payments, and so on. If a partner does not have sufficient resources with which to pay both the partnership debts and his or her own debts, and legal actions are brought against the partner, the question arises whether the personal creditors of the partner or the partnership creditors are entitled to be paid first out of the partner's funds. Here a formula informally called the "jingle rule" applies. Under that rule, a partner's *personal assets* are first used to pay *personal debts*, while *partnership assets* are first used to pay *partnership* debts.

Under the **Bankruptcy Reform Act of 1978**, the jingle rule does not apply when a partnership is in bankruptcy. In that event, partnership creditors can recover payment from the individual partners at the same time as the partners' personal creditors. To illustrate, assume that a partnership of Aaron and Ben is in bankruptcy and does not have assets with which to pay $6000 owing its creditors. Partner Aaron has no personal assets but partner Ben has personal assets of $4000 and owes Doris a personal debt of $2000. Since Aaron has no assets, Ben's $4000 must in some way be applied toward both the partnership debt of $6000 and his private debt to Doris of $2000. As these two debts are treated equally, Ben's $4000 is divided between the partnership creditors and Doris in the proportion each of the claims bears to the $8000 *total* debt. Therefore, the partnership creditors receive $3000 (six-eighths of Ben's $4000), and Doris receives $1000 (two-eighths of the $4000).

CONTINUATION OF PARTNERSHIP BUSINESS WITHOUT WINDING UP

The dissolution and winding up of a partnership always involves some measure of forced sale at which the property is sold for less than its true value or cost. Therefore, the partners who did not cause the dissolution are likely to be faced with financial loss if there is a forced liquidation of the business. The law attempts to protect innocent partners from such loss by permitting them to continue the business of a dissolved partnership without going through the winding up process when (1) the partnership is dissolved by expulsion or wrongful withdrawal of a partner, or (2) the partnership is dissolved by the retirement or death of a partner.

When a partnership business is continued without a winding up, there is no physical liquidation of the firm's assets but, instead, there is an accounting of all its assets and liabilities as of the *date of the dissolution*. Based on this accounting the value of each partner's interest in the firm is computed and the departing partner is paid.

The following case demonstrates the differing practical results which can follow when the value of a partner's share is determined as of the date of dissolution or as of the date when winding up is completed.

CASE 35.4 First National Bank of Kenosha v. Schaefer
283 N.W.2d 410 (Wis. 1979)

Facts: Ben died in 1969, owning real property in partnership with his brother, Arthur. For the next eight years there was litigation to determine the ownership of the property. During that time Arthur managed the property but made no attempt to sell it or to account to Ben's estate. In 1977 the court finally determined that the property belonged to the partnership. Arthur proposed to divide it by giving to Ben's estate 50 percent of the value of the property determined as of the date of Ben's death, *when the partnership was dissolved,* although the property had greatly appreciated in value between that date and the time the *winding up was completed.*

Question: If the business of a dissolved partnership is carried on by a surviving partner without the consent of the representative of the deceased partner, is the value of the partnership determined as of (1) the date of the dissolution, or (2) the date of the winding up?

Answer: The value of the partnership is determined as of the date the winding up is completed.

Reasoning: When a partner dies, the partnership is dissolved. However, it is not then terminated. Ordinarily, the surviving partner diligently winds up the partnership and its assets are then distributed. Here, the partnership business was continued and not wound up. If Ben's personal representative had consented to the continuance of the business *without a winding up,* then Ben's estate would have been entitled to one-half the value of the partnership *at the date of its dissolution.* On that date Arthur would have become the sole owner of the partnership business. However, Ben's representative did *not* consent to the continuation of the partnership business without a winding up. Therefore, during the eight years that elapsed since Ben died, Arthur must be considered to have been engaged in a "slow winding up" of the partnership. Accordingly, Ben's estate is due one-half of the value of the partnership when the winding up is completed. This will take into consideration the appreciated value of the property.

Continuance after Wrongful Withdrawal or Expulsion of a Partner

If a partnership is dissolved because a partner wrongfully withdraws from a firm or because he or she is expelled as provided for in the partnership agreement, the remaining partners may continue the partnership business without a winding up. In that event, the value of the departing partner's interest is determined by an accounting of the partnership affairs as of the date of the dissolution. The partner who caused the dissolution is entitled to be paid in cash for the computed value of his or her interest in the partnership, less the amount of any damages he or she may have caused the other partners. In that computation, a wrongfully withdrawing partner receives no credit for the value of the partnership goodwill.

Continuance after Retirement or Death of a Partner

Effect of Partnership Agreement. Partners may agree, either when the firm is organized or at some later time, that if one of their members retires or dies the surviving partner(s) may, *at that time,* decide whether to continue the business without going through a winding up, or to wind up and liquidate it. If they had so agreed and one of the members dies or retires, the surviving partner(s) may elect to continue the business. In that event, there is an accounting of the partnership affairs, including its goodwill, as of the date of the dissolution. The departing partner is paid his or her share and the continuing business is owned by the remaining partner(s). Or, if at that time the remaining partners elect not to continue the business, the partnership goes through a winding up.

A different situation exists if the partners have not previously agreed that the remaining partner(s) may continue the business without a winding up. In that event, when a partner retires or dies, the surviving or remaining partner(s) must secure the consent of the retiring partner or of the personal representative of the deceased partner to continue the business without a winding up. If that request is refused, then, despite the wishes of the remaining partners, the partnership must be wound up.

Payment of Value of Partner's Interest. When all the parties agree to continue a partnership business without a winding up, the departing partner or the representative of a deceased partner is entitled to receive in cash his or her share of the value of the partnership, including the value of its goodwill. However, the departing partner or the representative may instead, with the consent of the continuing partner(s), leave that share in the partnership business as an investment. In that event, the retiring partner or representative of the deceased partner must elect whether to receive *either* (1) interest upon the share left in the firm, *or* (2) so much of the profits of the continuing business as that share earned. This election to receive interest or profits may be made only one time.

To illustrate this principle, assume that Hazel retires from the Babcock Press partnership. She leaves her share in the firm and elects to receive the profits her investment earns. The following year the country is in a deep recession and Babcock Press makes no profit. Hazel may not then change her election and opt to receive interest on the money she has invested. Her election to receive profits instead of interest is binding for as long as her share remains in the firm.

The next case deals with a retired partner's right to receive a share of the profits of the continuing partnership.

CASE 35.5 Hilgendorf v. Denson
341 So. 2d 549 (Fla. 1977)

Facts: Hilgendorf and Denson were engaged in a real estate business as a partnership at will. The partnership was dissolved and Denson left to open her own business. Hilgendorf continued to operate the real estate business under the same name for six or seven weeks. During that time she accounted for and paid Denson one-half of all commissions the firm had earned up to the date of dissolution. Denson now claims that she is also due a share of all the commissions earned during the time Hilgendorf continued the business after its dissolution.

Question: If a partnership business is continued after dissolution and the retiring partner leaves no capital in the firm, is the retiring partner due any share of the profits of the continuing business?

Answer: No. A retiring partner who withdraws all of his or her interest from the firm, is due nothing more.

Reasoning: When a partnership is dissolved without a winding up, the retiring partner is entitled to have the value of his or her interest in the firm ascertained as of the date of the dissolution. The retiring partner may leave his or her interest in the firm and receive either: (1) the profits attributable to its use by the dissolved partnership, or (2) the interest on that share.

Denson was paid her share of all sums earned prior to the date of dissolution. After she retired she retained no interest in the continuing business. Therefore, there was no basis upon which she could be entitled to a portion of whatever profits the business made after its dissolution.

Rights against Original and Continuing Partnerships. When the business of a partnership is continued without a winding up of its affairs, the law assumes that the continuing business is carried on by a *new* partnership comprised of the remaining partners and such other persons as they may add. The creditors of the dissolved (original) partnership become creditors of the new (continuing) partnership. If a new member is added to the ongoing firm, his or her contribution to the capital of the firm may be used to pay partnership debts incurred *before or after* he or she joined the firm. The new member is not, however, liable *personally* for any partnership debts which were incurred before he or she joined the firm.

Rights against Departed and Continuing Partners. After dissolution, regardless of its cause and whether or not there is a winding up, each partner remains personally liable for all partnership obligations incurred while he or she was a member of the partnership. For example, Tom, a partner in the Acme Partnership died last April and the partnership is wound up. His estate (along with the other Acme partners) remains legally liable to pay partnership creditors for all debts incurred up to the time the winding up is concluded.

When there is a dissolution without a winding up, a partner who leaves the firm may, under circumstances such as the following, be charged twice for the same partnership debt. Suppose that at the time of Jim's retirement from the Sitco partnership (consisting of himself, Perry, and Todd), the firm's only debt is $3000 to Brown. Were it not for that debt, the value of Jim's interest in the partnership would be $11,000. However, taking that $3000 debt into consideration, Jim's interest is reduced by one-third of the amount of the debt, or $1000. Accordingly, when he leaves the partnership, Jim is paid $10,000. A year after Jim's retirement, Brown demands payment of his $3000. If the Sitco partnership cannot pay him, Perry and Todd (the partners who have continued the business) *and Jim* (because the debt existed while Jim was still a partner) must each contribute one-third ($1000) out of their own personal resources to discharge the Brown debt. Furthermore, if Perry or Todd (or both of them) cannot pay their own shares, Jim may find himself liable for $2000 or even for the entire debt of $3000.

To offset the possibility of the double liability which Jim now faces, partners often enter into what is called an "indemnification agreement" when a partner leaves the firm. By such an agreement the continuing partners agree to reimburse a departing partner for any amount he or she is later forced to pay to a creditor of the dissolved partnership. Sometimes a different device, called a *novation* (see Chapter 13, p. 198) is used. Under a novation agreement the creditor agrees not to hold the departing partner for the debt but to hold only the continuing partners responsible, and they agree to pay the creditor.

SUMMARY

When partners no longer carry on a business *together*, their firm is automatically dissolved. Following dissolution, the partnership may be either wound up, that is, liquidated, or the partnership business may be continued by the remaining partner(s) after an accounting of the interest of each partner. A partnership is dissolved (1) by the agreement of all the partners, as expressed in the partnership agreement or at a later date; (2) by the withdrawal of a partner in a partnership at will; (3) because of violation of the partnership agreement, such as by the wrongful withdrawal of a partner; (4) automatically by operation of law, as when a partner dies; or (5) by court decree for any reason a court finds proper.

A partnership does not cease to exist when it is dissolved, but ends when the winding up is complete—that is, when all money owing to the partnership has been collected, all its debts have been paid, and any remaining assets have been distributed to the partners. Depending upon the manner in which the partnership is dissolved, the winding up may be carried out by all the partners, by one or more of them, or by a receiver appointed by a court. In some states the law dictates that if the partnership has been dissolved because of the death of a partner, the winding up must be performed by the deceased partner's personal representative. If one of the partners caused the dissolution because of a wrongful act or because of personal bankruptcy, he or she may not conduct the winding up.

The person who conducts the winding up continues to carry out the terms of the firm's ongoing contracts but may not make any new contracts on behalf of the partnership except in connection with the winding up itself. After all debts owed to third parties are paid and contributions to capital are repaid, if any assets still remain they are divided among the partners in the same ratio as they share in the profits. If there are insufficient assets to pay all obligations, the partners must contribute from their own personal resources to share in the losses in the same ratio that they would have shared in the profits.

A withdrawing or retiring partner, or the personal representative of a deceased partner, must give his or her consent if the remaining partners want to continue the business after dissolution without a winding up. The departing partner (or personal representative of a deceased partner) must then elect whether to receive his or her share in the firm in cash or to leave that share in the business as an investment. If it is left in the business, he or she further must decide whether to receive interest on the money left in the business or to receive a share of the firm's profits.

Unless the partners have agreed otherwise, dissolution of a partnership for any cause does not free a withdrawing or retiring partner, or a deceased partner's estate from liability for debts of the firm which existed when that partner was still a member of the firm.

REVIEW QUESTIONS

1. Distinguish between "dissolution," "winding up," and "termination" of a partnership.

2. Does the addition of a partner to an existing partnership dissolve the partnership?

3. How is a partnership at will dissolved?

4. When a partner wrongfully withdraws from a firm, what happens to the capital contribution he or she made?

5. What is meant by the dissolution of a partnership caused by operation of law?

6. Assume a partner suffers a stroke and as a result is unable to walk. Discuss the effect of this unfortunate event upon a partnership of which this person is a member.

7. What is meant by winding up a partnership?

8. What effect, if any, does the dissolution of a partnership have on: (**a**) a debt owed to the partnership; (**b**) a contract to build a house which the partnership has half-completed; and (**c**) its rental obligation under an unexpired lease?

9. (**a**) At the conclusion of a winding up, what is the order in which partnership assets are distributed? (**b**) What action is taken if the assets are not sufficient to pay all the partnership debts?

10. When can a partnership business be continued without a winding up?

11. If the business of a dissolved partnership is continued without a winding up, does this mean that the original partnership is continuing the business? Explain.

12. When a partnership is continued without a winding up, what rights do the creditors of the dissolved partnership have?

CASE PROBLEMS

1. Hoppen and Powell entered into a partnership which was to last 3 years. It was agreed that Hoppen would work part-time for the partnership and receive a salary of $300 per month, and that Powell would work full-time for the partnership and receive $2000 per month. The partnership was successful and Hoppen demanded a salary equal to Powell's. The partners could not come into agreement and Hoppen brought suit to have the partnership dissolved, claiming that, under the circumstances, dissolution was proper and desirable. The court ordered the partnership dissolved and appointed a receiver to wind up its affairs. Powell states that the partnership agreement did not establish as a ground for dissolution the reason asserted by Hoppen and that therefore *Hoppen* has caused the dissolution in violation of the partnership agreement and is liable to the partnership in damages. Was Powell's contention correct? Explain reason for answer.

2. Anton and Baker formed a partnership to run a hardware store. Anton was to manage the business and Baker was to be a "silent partner." Baker contributed to the partnership the greater portion of its capital. During the first 5 years of the business, the store made considerable money. A large discount store was then built nearby and the partnership business began to diminish. For each of the next 3 years the partnership lost money. Baker asked Anton to liquidate the firm. Anton refused and Baker brought action to dissolve the partnership by court order because the firm was losing money. Anton protested, saying that Baker had received a generous return on his investment during the prior years, that the partnership was losing very little money, that he had plans for increasing its business, and therefore the partnership should not be dissolved. Do these facts establish a cause of action for dissolution of the partnership? Explain.

3. Charles and Myrtle were equal partners in the business of adjusting claims for fire losses for insurance companies. They dissolved the partnership by mutual agreement. Myrtle, who had possession of the partnership books, wound up the business. She claims compensation for her services and expenses in performing the winding up. Should Myrtle be paid from partnership assets (**a**) for her *expenses* in conducting the winding up? (**b**) for her *services* in performing the winding up? Explain.

4. Rasmussen and Thomas were partners. A disagreement arose between them as to the management of the partnership. Thomas brought a legal action to dissolve the firm and to secure the return of the capital contribution he made to the partnership. The court ordered the partnership dissolved and also ordered that the contribution Thomas made be returned to him immediately. Rasmussen argues that the court was not correct in directing the return of the contribution. Was Rasmussen or the court correct? Explain.

5. Paul and Ernest are in partnership. Their agreement makes no provision for the continuance of the partnership business if one of them should die. Ernest died, thereby dissolving the partnership. Paul wants to continue running the business without first liquidating its affairs. Ernest's personal representative demands that the partnership be wound up, saying that if Paul wants to carry on the business there must first be a regular winding up of the partnership affairs. Paul claims that as he had elected to continue the partnership he is only required to make a proper accounting of its affairs as of the date Ernest died, and therefore the personal representative is making an improper demand. Is Paul correct? Explain.

CHAPTER 36

LIMITED PARTNERSHIPS

In the last two chapters we saw that in a general partnership each partner is an owner of the business and is entitled to participate in its management. The partners share in the profits of the business and each is *personally* responsible for its debts. Because of these characteristics, a *general partnership* seldom attracts people with venture capital to become investors and partners in novel or possibly risky undertakings. Investors usually do not want to share in the management of a business and they abhor the possibility of having to pay the debts of a failed speculative venture.

To attract investors to speculative ventures such as the purchase of a herd of young cattle to be fattened and sold at a profit, the drilling of an oil well, or the purchase of land to be subdivided into saleable lots, a different kind of business organization is required. The law satisfies this need through a form of business organization called "limited partnership." Participation in a limited partnership may also furnish an investor with certain tax benefits.

The first two parts of this chapter examine the general function of limited partnerships and how such business organizations are formed. The last part deals with termination of limited partnerships.

FUNCTION OF LIMITED PARTNERSHIPS

A limited partnership is a partnership business organized to make a profit through the carrying out of a specified objective. It consists of one or more general partners and one or more limited partners.

Perhaps the best way to depict a limited partnership is through an illustration. Assume that Joan has read a play which she feels certain will be a Broadway hit but she does not have enough money to produce the play herself. She therefore decides to form a limited partnership to undertake its production. She will be the sole general partner and there will be twenty-five limited partners. Joan provides that individuals may become limited partners by each contributing (investing) $20,000 to the enterprise. She also provides that each month, beginning 4 months after the play opens, 85 percent of the net profits earned by the play will be distributed to the limited partners and the remaining 15 percent to Joan. She will manage the partnership and produce the show; the investors (limited partners) will have nothing to do with its management. Joan readily finds twenty-five investors who purchase the limited partnership interests, and a limited partnership is formed. The play is produced but Joan's high opinion of it is not shared by audiences and the play soon closes. Joan, meanwhile, has exhausted all the money she received from the limited partners and still owes money to the stage designer, the actors, and the theater owner. Because the enterprise was a limited partnership, Joan, the general partner, is personally responsible for all these unpaid debts. But though the limited partners had taken a risk and lost their investments, they have no personal liability to any of the creditors.

The **Uniform Limited Partnership Act**, as revised in 1976, establishes the legal foundation for limited partnerships, how they are organized, and the rights and duties of their members. Currently, only one state, Louisiana (which has its own pertinent laws), has not adopted either the original or the revised act. In this chapter, any reference to the Uniform Limited Partnership Act applies to the revised act and is identified merely as ULPA.

A limited partnership is distinct from an ordinary partnership but the two have many characteristics in common. In fact, the Uniform Partnership Act (UPA) applies to limited partnerships in matters where the ULPA is silent. The UPA states in Section 6(2), ". . . this act shall apply to limited partnerships except in so far as the statutes relating to such partnership are inconsistent herewith . . . "; and ULPA Sec. 1105 states, ". . . In any case not provided for in this Act the provisions of the Uniform Partnership Act govern." Therefore, if a question of law arises as to the rights of the general partners or as to the rights of the limited partners in a limited partnership, it may be necessary to take into consideration not only the provisions of the ULPA but also those of the UPA.

FORMATION OF LIMITED PARTNERSHIPS

Requirements for Formation

Need to File Certificate. In Chapter 34 we saw that to organize an ordinary (general) business partnership all that is required is the oral or written agreement of two or more people to be associated together as co-owners to carry on a business for profit. The organization of a limited partnership is more formal. Such a partnership comes into existence only when a proper *certificate*, signed by all the firm's general and limited partners, is filed as a public record, generally in the office of the secretary of state in the state where the partnership is formed. In addition, all the parties enter into an *agreement of limited partnership* but that agreement is not made a public record.

No minimum capitalization is required to establish a limited partnership. Its initial capital consists of the contributions (investments in the venture) made by the general and the limited partners, as enumerated in the partnership certificate.

Effect of Failure to File Certificate. If the parties engage in a business which purports to be a limited partnership without signing and filing a certificate, a limited partnership is not formed but, instead, the organization is considered to be an ordinary business partnership. In that event, all the members—those who had been designated as limited partners as well as those designated as general partners—are personally liable for the debts and obligations of the enterprise as though they were all general partners.

The case which follows involves an organization which purported to be a limited partnership but which filed no certificate of limited partnership as required by law.

CASE 36.1   **Heritage Hills v. Zion's First National Bank**
601 F.2d 1023 (9th Cir. 1979)

Facts: On July 2, 1975, Heritage Hills, a real estate development firm which purported to be a limited partnership, filed a petition in bankruptcy. However, at the time of that action no certificate of limited partnership for the organization was on file. Under Arizona law (where the bankruptcy petition was filed) and under the ULPA, a limited partnership does not come into existence until a certificate of limited partnership is filed. The bankruptcy petition was dismissed by the lower court on the ground that at the time it was filed there was no limited partnership named Heritage Hills and hence no entity existed to file the petition. The dismissal was appealed.

Question: (a) Does a limited partnership come into existence before a certificate of limited partnership is filed? (b) If not, does the organization have any status?

Answer: (a) No. A limited partnership is not formed until its certificate is filed; and (b) having failed to file the certificate, the organization is treated as a general partnership.

Reasoning: To be a limited partnership an organization must file a certificate of limited partnership. If one is not filed there is no limited partnership but the organization is not "a nothing"; it is seen by the law to be a general partnership [an ordinary business partnership]. The lower court, having had parties before it, should not have dismissed the bankruptcy petition because those parties, under the circumstances, were a general partnership improperly labeled a limited partnership.

The Limited Partnership Certificate

Contents of the Certificate.   The ULPA and state laws require that there be included in a certificate of limited partnership information which adequately reveals to third parties, among other things, (1) the business the partnership will conduct, (2) the period of time the partnership will exist, (3) its name and the names and addresses of its members, and (4) the contributions partners will make toward its capital.

Business of a Limited Partnership.   A limited partnership may carry on any business unless the statute under which it is organized provides otherwise. For example, approximately one-half of the states do not permit a limited partnership to engage in the banking or insurance business because of the limitation upon the liability of limited partners.

A limited partnership terminates at the time specified in its certificate. However, if the date of its termination is approaching and the objective of the business has not yet been reached, the partners may file an amended certificate which will establish a new date for termination.

Name of Limited Partnership.   The enterprise name must contain, without abbreviation, the words "Limited Partnership." The name may not be deceptively similar to the name of any other firm organized under the laws of that state. In addition, the limited partnership may not have the same name as the surname of one of its limited partners unless one of the *general* partners bears the same surname. For instance, if Henry Osborne is to be a limited partner, the business may not be named "Osborne Properties, a Limited Partnership" unless at the time the firm is organized one of the general partners is also named Osborne. The reason for this rule is that otherwise those doing business with the firm might improperly have the impression that Henry Osborne is actually a general partner and his financial resources (which might be considerable) are available to satisfy the firm's debts. However, if the partnership was named "Osborne Properties, a Limited Partnership" because Robert Osborne was a general partner, and *later on* Henry Osborne joins as a limited partner, the name "Osborne Properties . . ." may be retained.

If a general partner's name is incorporated in the name of a limited partnership and he or she leaves the firm which still continues in existence, the partnership need not change its name unless the partnership agreement so dictates.

Contributions to Limited Partnership's Capital. Both general partners and limited partners make contributions to the capital of the limited partnerships in which they are members. A contribution may be cash, property, or services performed, the value of which is stated in the limited partnership certificate.

For example, Peter conceives a limited partnership, does all the work required to bring it into existence, and is its sole general partner. He treats his services in putting the project together as his contribution to the firm's capital. (Although he could arbitrarily place a very high value upon those services, it is likely he would not do so because otherwise he would become entitled to such a large share of the profits that potential investors would not purchase limited partnership interests in his firm.) In organizing his enterprise Peter asks Ethel, a lawyer, to perform all the necessary legal services involved and she agrees to accept a limited partnership interest as her fee. The certificate will reveal that both Peter's and Ethel's contributions were services rendered and will state the value given to each of those services.

A promise, expressed in a promissory note or in some other form may constitute a contribution to a limited partnership. The amount or value of such a promise is stated in the partnership certificate. If a partner fails to make the promised contribution of cash, property, or services, then the partnership may by legal action force that partner to pay the value of the promised contribution in cash. If the partnership fails to act, a creditor of the firm may enforce the limited partner's obligation.

Figure 36.1 is an example of the form of a certificate of limited partnership.

The Limited Partnership Agreement

Form of Agreement. In addition to signing the certificate of limited partnership, all partners also enter into a limited partnership agreement. Normally, the agreement is in writing although it may be simply an oral understanding between the partners. The ULPA does not prescribe either its form or its content.

Content of Agreement. The partnership agreement covers matters concerning the relationship of the partners to the firm. It includes such things as the business a partner may transact with the partnership (for example, whether or not a partner may sell something to the partnership); the conditions under which an investor may acquire a limited partnership interest after the organization has already been established; and the right of a limited partner to vote on partnership matters (such as an amendment to the certificate or the admission of a new general partner).

An important part of the agreement is a provision governing how profits earned by the partnership will be divided (allocated) among the general and the limited partners. The agreement may allocate the profits (1) on the basis of the value of each member's contribution to the firm (not including promises of future contributions), or (2) by setting aside a certain portion of the total profits for the limited partners and

CERTIFICATE OF LIMITED PARTNERSHIP
OF
_____ [name]

We, the undersigned, desiring to form a limited partnership pursuant to the Uniform Limited Partnership Act as set forth in_____[cite statute] of the State of_____, do hereby certify:

1. The name of the firm under which the partnership is to be conducted is_____.

2. The character of the business intended to be transacted by the partnership shall be as follows:
_____

3. The location of the principal place of business shall be at_____.
[address], City of_____, County of_____, State of_____.

4. The name and place of residence of each general partner interested in the partnership are as follows:

Name	Place of Residence
_____	_____
_____	_____

The name and place of residence of each limited partner interested in the partnership are as follows:

Name	Place of Residence
_____	_____
_____	_____

5. The partnership shall exist for_____(specify period or an indefinite period] commencing
_____, 19

6. The amount of cash and a description and the agreed value of the other property contributed by each limited partner are as follows:_____.

7. The_____[additional contributions agreed to be made by each limited partner and the time at which or the events on the happening of which they shall be made are as follows:_____or limited partners may make such additional contributions to the capital of the partnership as may from time to time be agreed by all the partners].

8. The contribution of each limited partner shall be returned as follows:_____.

9. The share of the profits or the other compensation by way of income that each limited partner shall receive by reason of his contribution is as follows:_____shall receive _____[_____ percent (_____ %) of the profits of the partnership or_____ Dollars ($_____) per year or as the case may be]._____ [Repeat the above clause as necessary for each limited partner.]

10. The right of a limited partner to substitute an assignee as limited partner in his place, and the terms and conditions of the substitution, are as follows:_____.

11. The right of the partners to admit additional limited partners is an follows:_____.

12. The right of one or more of the limited partners to priority over other limited partners, as to contributions or as to compensation by way of income, and the nature of such priority, are as follows:_____.

13. The right of the remaining general partner or partners to continue the business on the death, retirement, or incapacity of a general partner is as follows:_____.

14. The right of a limited partner to demand and receive property other than cash in return for his contribution is as follows:_____.

In witness whereof, the undersigned have executed this certificate this____day of_____, 19_____.

[Signatures]

FIGURE 36.1 Form of a certificate of limited partnership. (*Reproduced from* American Jurisprudence Legal Forms, *second edition, with permission of the copyright owner, Lawyers Co-operative Publishing Company, Rochester, New York.*

the remaining portion for the general partner(s). The sum set aside for limited partners is then allocated among the limited partners in proportion to the contribution each has actually made to the firm. The sum set aside for general partner(s) is allocated in the same manner. If the agreement does not prescribe how profits will be allocated, they will be distributed as described in (1) above. Many matters concerning the operations of a limited partnership are not made a part of the partnership agreement because they are covered by the ULPA. For example, the act dictates where the partnership books will be kept and that they must be available for examination by all the partners, how the certificate may be amended, how an assignee of a limited partner may become a limited partner, and the circumstances under which the partnership may be dissolved.

General Partners

Who May Be a General Partner. Any person legally capable of engaging in a contract may be a general partner. A corporation, if its charter permits, or even another partnership, may be a general partner in a limited partnership.

There must be at least one general partner in any limited partnership. While there is no statutory limit to their number, usually there are fewer than three. A general partner may also make contributions as a limited partner in his or her partnership. In that event, that person is both a general partner and a limited partner in the same partnership. He or she then has the powers and is subject to the liabilities of a general partner and, except as may be provided in the partnership agreement, also has the rights of a limited partner.

Powers of General Partner. A general partner in a limited partnership has all the powers and is subject to all the same restrictions and liabilities as a partner in an ordinary business partnership. He or she is the manager and agent of the enterprise, conducting its business and executing, in the partnership name, any instrument required to carry on partnership affairs. Thus, a general partner may buy and sell partnership property without the knowledge or consent of the limited partners if such actions further partnership purposes and are in accord with the partnership agreement. However, a general partner's actions are limited to the purposes for which the partnership is established. If the general partner wishes to act beyond that authority, then all the partners (both general and limited) must first give their written consent. Thus, Steve, a general partner in an enterprise engaged in building a boating marina, has authority to purchase appropriate building materials, but if he wishes to buy a medical building in the partnership name, he must first obtain written consent from all the other partners.

A general partner may *personally* do business with his or her firm or lend the firm money if the transaction does not violate the partnership agreement. For example, Sue, a general partner, may contract with her firm to run its public relations campaign and to be paid for her services.

Admission of Additional General Partner. General partners may find it desirable to admit another general partner into an existing limited partnership. Because of the impact of such an action upon the business, the written consent of all the partners, both general and limited, must be secured before an additional general partner is admitted into the firm.

Compensation to General Partner.   A limited partnership agreement may provide for compensation to a general partner (in addition to a share of the profits) for managing the affairs of the partnership. There is no standard formula by which the rate of compensation to a managing general partner is determined. It may be fixed in a number of different ways as, for example, (1) a management fee representing a certain percentage of the partnership's annual income, (2) an agreed percentage of the total capital of the firm, or (3) only a reimbursement of money for reasonable expenses incurred in the management. In any event, whatever the arrangement, general partners try to arrive at compensation for themselves which will seem reasonable to investors when establishing their business.

Liability of General Partner to Third Parties.   Each general partner is personally liable to third parties for the debts and obligations of the firm. This liability is similar to the personal liability of partners in an ordinary business partnership (see Chapter 34).

A general partner is also liable to anyone who suffers a loss as a result of having relied upon a statement, known by the general partner to be false, in the certificate of limited partnership. For instance, you, as the general partner in a limited partnership, are *personally* liable to pay back a loan made by The National Bank to your partnership if, at the time the bank made the loan, it relied on a falsely inflated financial statement in your partnership certificate.

Obligations of General Partner to Limited Partners.   A general partner, being in full charge of the partnership business, must act with the highest good faith toward the limited partners as the latter have no option but to rely upon the integrity of the former. The general partner, therefore, owes a range of fiduciary duties to the limited partners, including the following:

1. Duty to serve the partnership to the best of his or her ability in an effort to accomplish the purposes for which the limited partnership was formed.
2. Duty to keep at the firm's principal place of business an adequate set of books reflecting the current financial condition of the partnership business and to render, on demand of a limited partner, full information about the partnership affairs.
3. Duty to account for any profit he or she may personally have made from the purchase or sale of partnership property.
4. Duty not to acquire for himself or herself a business opportunity which rightfully should be taken for the partnership.

This last duty can be illustrated by the following example: Peter is a general partner in Deep Pit Uranium Mines Limited Partnership which is engaged in acquiring sources of uranium ore. Peter learns that a prospector has filed a claim upon an ore deposit close to the Deep Pit properties. Peter purchases the prospector's claim and then sells it to the Deep Pit partnership, making a handsome profit on the transaction. If Peter had not been a general partner of Deep Pit, his sale to the partnership would have been acceptable, but under the assumed conditions, Peter could not buy the property and then sell it to the partnership because, as a general partner, he has a fiduciary obligation to give his firm the right to purchase the claim directly from the prospector at the lower price.

The next case is one in which it was claimed that a business venture was unsuccessful because the general partner did not properly carry out his fiduciary responsibilities.

CASE 36.2 Wyler v. Feuer
149 Cal. Rptr. 626 (Cal. 1979)

Facts: Wyler, as a limited partner, invested about $1.5 million in a limited partnership formed to produce a motion picture. Feuer, the general partner, was in charge of the film's production. The picture was not successful and Wyler sued Feuer charging, among other things, that the picture failed because Feuer, the general partner, did not use his expertise for the benefit of the partnership, thereby violating his fiduciary duty.

Question: Does a general partner breach his or her fiduciary duty to a limited partner when losses result from mistakes in business judgment?

Answer: No. An honest mistake in judgment is not a breach of fiduciary duty of a general partner.

Reasoning: A limited partner who makes a financial investment in a limited partnership thereby surrenders to the general partner the right to manage or control the partnership business. In carrying out managerial functions, the general partner is under a fiduciary duty to exercise good faith and fair dealing toward the other members of the partnership. A general partner is not liable for mistakes made in the exercise of honest business judgments when he or she has used the degree of care an ordinary prudent person would use. The alleged failure of Feuer to secure additional production financing, his use of an unknown French leading actress, or photographing the picture during the summer months when most Europeans go on vacation, coupled with the lack of attractiveness of the subject matter, did not demonstrate that Feuer had failed to conform to the standards demanded of him as a general partner. Therefore, Feuer did not breach his fiduciary responsibilities to the limited partner.

Causes for Termination of General Partner's Status.   Several circumstances cause a general partner to cease to be a member of the partnership.

Withdrawal of General Partner.   A general partner may at any time withdraw from the partnership by giving written notice to all the other partners. However, if the withdrawal violates the partnership agreement (as, for instance, if the general partner had agreed to serve for at least one full year but withdraws after only 6 months), then the general partner not only ceases to be a member of the firm but is also liable in damages for breach of his or her obligation to the limited partners.

Assignment of General Partner's Interest.   A general partner who assigns all of his or her interest in the partnership to some other person ceases to be a member of the partnership. If there are other general partners they continue the business; if he or she was the sole general partner, the limited partners may, if the agreement so provides, designate a new general partner to continue to operate the business. If no new general partner is designated, the limited partnership is terminated. Termination is discussed later in this chapter.

Removal of General Partner.   A general partner may be removed if the limited partnership agreement sets out the conditions under which that action can be taken. For example, if the agreement states that Brent, the sole general partner, can be replaced if he does not sell the firm's real estate within 18 months and Brent fails to sell it, then the limited partners may take advantage of that clause in the agreement and oust him.

Incompetency or Death of General Partner.   A general partner adjudged by a court to be mentally incompetent ceases to be a member of the firm; and, of course, one who dies ceases to be a member.

Bankruptcy of General Partner.   Unless otherwise provided in the certificate, a general partner ceases to be a member of a limited partnership if he or she (1) files a voluntary petition in bankruptcy, (2) is adjudged a bankrupt or insolvent, or (3) if the general partner is a corporation and a certificate is filed for that corporation's dissolution or for revocation of its charter.

Limited Partners

Who May Be a Limited Partner.   Any "person," including another partnership, a corporation if its charter permits, or a general partner, may be a limited partner.

In every limited partnership there must be at least one limited partner but the law sets no limit on the number there may be. The number of limited partners in a firm depends primarily upon the financial needs and the character of the business in which the partnership is engaged. Some limited partnerships, such as the many organized to drill for oil, or those that trade in real estate on a large scale, have hundreds of limited partners (investors) scattered all over the country. However, most limited partnerships are not nearly so huge or ambitious. Usually, fewer than 35 limited partnership interests are offered for sale because when that number is exceeded the firm is required to comply with stringent federal securities laws. The state in which the partnership is organized may also impose restrictions on the sale of limited partnership interests that exceed a number established by that state.

Admission of Additional Limited Partners.   The admission of an additional limited partner or partners may be advantageous to an existing limited partnership in order to augment its working capital. But because this action does not affect operations of the business (since limited partners normally have no voice in management), the limited partnership agreement may give authority to the general partners to admit new limited partners without the consent of the existing partners. However, if the firm's certificate does not specifically give this authority to the general partner(s) then the *written* consent of all the partners, both general and limited, is required before any new limited partner may be admitted.

Role of Limited Partner. While a limited partner is a *member* of a limited partnership, he or she is not a *partner* in the full sense in which that word is usually used. A limited partner is only an investor in the firm, receiving (if the firm is successful) income from that investment while having slight part in the management of the enterprise.

Like any stranger to the firm, a limited partner may be hired by the partnership as an employee or independent contractor. For example, Arnold, a limited partner, may be paid to superintend a construction job being carried on by the partnership; and Susan, another limited partner, may be hired as the chief of its accounting department. Unless prohibited by the partnership agreement, a limited partner may also transact business with the partnership as though he or she were not a member of the firm. So Ted, a limited partner whose own company sells air conditioning equipment, may sell his products to the partnership; Hazel, another limited partner, may buy a car from the partnership; and Lloyd, still another limited partner, may lend the firm money at interest. None of these or similar transactions will affect the limited partner's contribution to or status in the firm.

Unlike a general partner, a limited partner owes the partnership no fiduciary duties. For instance, John, a limited partner in the Full-Coverage Crop Dusting Limited Partnership, has bought an airplane of his own which he uses for commercial crop dusting. Even though Sun Burst Farms has been a long-time client of Full Coverage, John is not barred from attempting to take that client away from the partnership of which he is a member by offering Sun Burst Farms a better price to do their crop dusting himself.

Unlike a general partner, a limited partner, unless specifically designated to act as an agent for the partnership, has no authority to bind the partnership either by contract or by tortious conduct. Thus, Ann, a limited partner, cannot obligate the partnership to employ a roofer to fix a leak in the firm's roof unless she is authorized to do so by a general partner; and Henry does not make the organization in which he is a limited partner liable for a slander he commits against a competitor unless he was authorized by a general partner to make the slanderous statement.

Rights of Limited Partner.　The rights of a limited partner fall within four general categories: (1) to participate to a limited extent in the management of the partnership, (2) to share in its profits, (3) to secure information about the business, and (4) to assign his or her interest in the partnership or to withdraw from the firm.

Participating in Management.　The revised ULPA allows a limited partner to participate in certain of the firm's managerial functions without being considered to be exercising a general partner's control over the business. These functions are primarily:

1. To consult with and advise a general partner with respect to the partnership business;
2. To approve or disapprove an amendment to the partnership agreement; and,
3. To vote on: (*a*) the dissolution and winding up of the business; (*b*) the sale, lease, or other transfer, not in the ordinary course of business, of substantially all the partnership assets; (*c*) the incurring of partnership debt not in the ordinary course of business; (*d*) the change in the nature of the business; (*e*) the removal of a

general partner; and (f) any other matter authorized by the partnership agreement.

Sharing in Profits.   If you are a limited partner you are entitled to share in the allocation of partnership profits and in the distribution of its assets as provided in the partnership agreement.

Securing Information about the Partnership Business.   As a limited partner you are entitled to see and make copies of partnership records, including its tax returns and financial statements.

Assigning Limited Partnership Interest.   As a limited partner you may, at any time, assign (sell or give away) all or a portion of your limited partnership interest without causing a dissolution of the firm. If you assign all of your interest you cease to be a limited partner.

The person who acquires either all or part of your interest does not automatically become a limited partner. If the partnership certificate permits, you may designate such a person to be a limited partner in the firm. If the certificate does not give you that authority, then agreement of all the partners, both general and limited, must be secured to make the assignee a limited partner. If the assignee does not become a limited partner, he or she has the right to participate in the profits of the partnership and its assets in the event of dissolution, but does not have any of the other rights, as discussed above, of a limited partner.

Withdrawal or Death of Limited Partner.   If both the certificate and the agreement are silent on this subject and you, a limited partner, wish to withdraw, you may do so by giving not less than 6 months' written notice to each of the general partners. At the time of your withdrawal you will be entitled to receive cash reimbursement for the full amount of your contribution.

If a limited partner dies, his or her personal representative may exercise all the rights that the deceased limited partner had.

Limited Partner's Liability to Third Parties.   Normally, a limited partner's contribution, but not the limited partner *personally*, is liable for the firm's debts and obligations. The example at the beginning of the chapter, in which Joan was the producer of an unsuccessful play, illustrates this principle. There are two situations, however, in which a limited partner may incur personal liability for the firm's debts: (1) when a limited partner participates in the partnership's management, or (2) if no limited partnership certificate was filed.

Liability When Limited Partner Participates in Management.   If a limited partner takes part in the *control* of the business—that is, participates in *final decisions* affecting it—then the limited partner loses his or her personal immunity from liability and, along with the general partners, becomes personally liable for partnership debts. In the case that follows, the limited partners were held to have exercised the powers of a general partner and hence were personally liable to creditors of the firm.

CASE 36.3

Holzman v. De Escamilla
195 P.2d 833 (Cal. 1948)

Facts: Hacienda Farms, Limited, a limited partnership, was engaged in growing vegetables for the market. De Escamilla was the general partner and Russell and Andrews were the limited partners. Russell and Andrews went to the farm twice a week; they, together with De Escamilla, always conferred on what vegetables to plant and sometimes Russell and Andrews dictated what should be planted. The partnership had two bank accounts which required two signatures before a withdrawal could be made. De Escamilla could not withdraw any money without the signature of one of the limited partners. Russell and Andrews, without the knowledge or consent of De Escamilla, withdrew funds from one of the accounts. Later, Russell and Andrews forced De Escamilla to resign as manager of the farm and they appointed a new manager.

The partnership went into bankruptcy and Holzman, the appointed trustee, sued Russell and Andrews to force them to pay a partnership debt, claiming that they were liable because they had engaged in the control of the partnership.

Question: Should the limited partners be liable to the partnership creditors?

Answer: Yes, because they took part in the control of the partnership.

Reasoning: The Civil Code [the UPA] provides that a limited partner is not liable as a general partner to partnership creditors unless, in addition to the exercise of the rights and duties of a limited partner, he or she takes part in the control of the business. Russell and Andrews had done just that. They could refuse to sign checks for bills contracted by the general partner and thus they were able to limit his activities in the management of the business; they were active in dictating the crops to be planted; and they were able to require the general partner to resign as manager. Russell and Andrews, although limited partners, are liable to the creditors of the limited partnership.

Liability When No Limited Partnership Certificate Has Been Filed. Recall that on page 629 we observed that if an organization purporting to be a limited partnership fails to file its certificate of limited partnership, no limited partnership comes into existence. If, nonetheless, the organization engages in business, it is then considered in law to be a general partnership and all of its members—those designated limited partners as well as those designated general partners—are personally liable as general partners. Thus, if you purchase a limited partnership interest in a nonexistent limited partnership (because a certificate was not filed), believing you have no personal liability, you could find yourself responsible as a general partner for obligations the organization incurs.

You may protect yourself from this liability if, after discovering your mistake, you (1) cause an appropriate limited partnership certificate to be filed, or (2) withdraw from (renounce) any future participation in the profits or income of the enterprise. However, if a creditor had *already* transacted business with the partnership, actually believing in good faith that you were a general partner, then you can be held liable for a debt to *that creditor.*

TERMINATION OF LIMITED PARTNERSHIPS

A limited partnership, similar to an ordinary business partnership, goes through the steps of dissolution and winding up before it is terminated.

Bases for Dissolution

A limited partnership is dissolved when any of the following events occurs:

1. The time or the event specified in the certificate of limited partnership for dissolution has arrived.
2. All the partners in writing agree to the dissolution.
3. A general partner withdraws from the partnership, *unless* (a) the certificate provides that the business may be carried on by the remaining general partners (if any) and, if there are none, then (b) within 90 days after the general partner's withdrawal all the partners agree in writing to continue the business and to appoint one or more general partners.
4. The partnership is dissolved by court order. Any general or limited partner may apply to a court for an order to dissolve a limited partnership whenever it is no longer reasonably practical to carry on the business. Among the reasons for that conclusion may be that: (a) there is no profitable market for the products or services of the firm; (b) a limited partner has discovered that a general partner is acting fraudulently or in violation of his fiduciary obligations to the partnership; or (c) the sole general partner has withdrawn from the firm and the limited partners are unable to agree upon the appointment of a new general partner.

The right of a limited partner to secure the dissolution of a limited partnership by court action is the subject of the next case.

CASE 36.4   Block v. Dardanes
404 N.E.2d 807 (Ill. 1980)

Facts: Dardanes was the general partner and Block the limited partner in a limited partnership. The partnership purchased a restaurant which Dardanes was to manage. He was also to keep the partnership books and records. However, Dardanes seldom went to the restaurant and did not involve himself in its operation, having placed others in charge. Block requested income statements and an accounting but did not receive them. Block thereupon brought suit for an accounting and for the dissolution of the partnership.

Question: May a limited partner secure the dissolution of a partnership if the general partner refuses to furnish an accounting when it is reasonably demanded?

Answer: Yes. Such refusal is a ground for a judicial dissolution of a limited partnership.

Reasoning: A limited partner has the right to a formal accounting of the partnership affairs whenever the circumstances render it just and reasonable. Dardanes should have furnished an accounting when Block requested it. A decree of dissolution may be sought by a general or a limited partner under any of the numerous circumstances set forth in Section 32 of the Uniform Partnership Act [see Chapter 35] which section is applicable to limited partnerships. Particularly pertinent is that portion of Section 32 which allows a dissolution when a partner willfully or persistently commits a breach of the partnership agreement, as occurred in this case.

Winding Up

After its dissolution, a limited partnership is wound up by a general partner who has not caused the dissolution. If there is no general partner to conduct the winding up, then it may be performed by the limited partners or by some person, usually a receiver, designated by a court.

As in the winding up of an ordinary business partnership, the individual who conducts the winding up collects all debts owing to the partnership, sees that the partnership's existing contracts are performed, and turns its assets into cash.

Distribution of Partnership Assets

At the conclusion of the winding up, any remaining assets are distributed in the following order:

1. To the firm's creditors, including partners who are creditors.
2. To partners and former partners for distributions previously due to them and unpaid, except as otherwise provided in the partnership agreement.
3. To partners for the return of their contributions, except as otherwise provided in the partnership agreement.
4. Any remaining balance is distributed among the partners according to the partnership agreement formula.

The completion of the distribution terminates the limited partnership.

SUMMARY

A limited partnership (authorized by the ULPA) is a business organization different from an ordinary (general) business partnership, although the two have many elements in common.

A limited partnership is composed of at least one general partner and at least one limited partner. The general partner or partners manage and operate the partnership business. They have all the rights and liabilities of partners in an ordinary business partnership. The limited partners are investors in the firm, normally exercising no control over the management of its affairs. A limited partner is not personally liable for the firm's debts unless he or she participates in the control of the business.

A limited partnership may carry on any lawful business except as it may be restricted by state law. A limited partnership comes into existence when all the partners sign a certificate of limited partnership which is filed in the office of the secretary of state where the partnership is organized. The certificate furnishes general information such as personnel of the partnership, the contributions each makes to its capital, the purposes for which the partnership is formed, and the period of its existence. In addition, the parties either orally or in writing enter into a partnership agreement. The ULPA does not prescribe the content of the agreement. It usually deals with the authority of the general and limited partners and the distribution of the income and assets of the partnership between them.

Each limited partner and general partner makes a contribution of cash, property, or services to the capital of the partnership. If their agreement states no formula for the allocation of income, then the profits and losses are distributed in the same ratio as each partner's contribution bears to the total contributions received by the partnership.

Either a general partner or a limited partner ceases to be a member of the partnership upon assigning (selling or giving away) his or her entire partnership interest. In the event a general partner withdraws, the remaining general partner(s), if any, may continue to carry on the partnership business if the partnership certificate so provides. In the absence of such a provision, the limited partners may agree to continue the business with the remaining general partner(s). If no general partner remains, the limited partners may either appoint a new general partner or they may dissolve the partnership.

When a limited partnership is dissolved, it goes through a winding up process similar to the winding up of an ordinary business partnership. After the assets have been gathered together and turned into cash and all the creditors have been paid, the remaining assets are divided among the partners according to the formula set forth in the partnership agreement, and the partnership terminates.

REVIEW QUESTIONS

1. Why would a business person want to invest in a limited partnership?

2. (a) How is a limited partnership formed? (b) How does its formation differ from that of a general partnership?

3. What is a certificate of limited partnership? What, in general terms, is contained in this document?

4. If a required certificate of limited partnership is not filed, what is the result?

5. If a limited partner promises to make a contribution of $5000 to a limited partnership and fails to do so, (a) what rights, if any, does the partnership have with relation to that $5000? (b) What rights, if any, does a creditor have with respect to the contribution?

6. (a) What is a limited partnership agreement? In general terms, what might this agreement contain? (b) If there is a limited partnership agreement, must there also be a certificate of limited partnership? Explain.

7. What powers does a general partner exercise in a limited partnership?

8. How is a new general partner and how is a new limited partner admitted into a previously organized limited partnership?

9. Compare the liability of (**a**) general partners, and (**b**) limited partners, to third parties.

10. What are the obligations of a general partner to a limited partnership?

11. (**a**) What is the role of a limited partner in a limited partnership? (**b**) What are the rights of a limited partner in a limited partnership?

12. What is meant by limited partner participation in control of the partnership business and what is the result of such participation?

CASE PROBLEMS

1. Spira-Mart was a limited partnership. Its certificate showed that four of its limited partners were to contribute a total of $250,000 to the partnership. In fact, however, they had actually contributed a total of only $74,000. Suit was brought against Spira-Mart to force it to pay from the delinquent contributions an amount sufficient to discharge the claimant's judgment against Spira-Mart. Is the claimant entitled to this remedy? Explain.

2. Dixon was the general partner in a limited partnership which was developing a large land area. Dixon learned that certain adjacent acreage could be purchased. If the partnership bought the land (which it was financially able to do) it would be saved a considerable amount of money in its land development project. Dixon decided that the partnership should not buy the land, concluding that the price asked for it was too high. Six months later, finding that the land was still for sale, Dixon purchased it for himself and later sold it at a profit. The limited partners, in the partnership name, sued to force Dixon to pay to the partnership the profit he made on the transaction. Was the limited partnership entitled to that profit? Explain.

3. LNG, a limited partnership, refused to pay Gast money that Gast claimed was due him for back pay. Gast then sued not only LNG but also Garwin and Apt, two of the limited partners, for the amount owed. Gast asserted that Garwin and Apt, in addition to being limited partners in LNG, were employed by LNG as project and consulting engineers, that they received reports and attended meetings of the general partners where needs for additional capital investment were discussed, and so exercised control over the partnership management. LNG states that Garvin and Apt had no authority to control the business. Gast contends that the jury should hear evidence to the actual degree of participation Garwin and Apt exercised and that the jury should decide whether, under these facts, Garwin and Apt, or either of them, should be liable as general partners. Is Gast justified in making this demand? Explain.

4. Koch owned a limited partnership interest. Koch owed the bank, and an individual named Vechery, large sums of money. For an adequate consideration Koch assigned his limited partnership interest to Vechery. Later, the bank secured a judgment against Koch for the money he owed it. The bank now seeks to have the limited partnership interest that Koch assigned to Vechery made available to satisfy its judgment against Koch, claiming that the assignment was not effective because the assignee, Vechery, was not substituted as a limited partner in place of Koch. Was the assignment to Vechery effective even though he did not become a limited partner in the limited partnership? Explain.

5. In February, Graybar Electric Company extended credit to Blomquist Electric, a limited partnership in which Blomquist and Preston were the general partners and Lowe was the sole limited partner. Blomquist Electric had not filed the required certificate of limited partnership, but Graybar did not know this. Graybar knew, however, that Lowe was only a limited partner. In April, by letter to Graybar, Lowe renounced any interest in Blomquist Electric. Almost a year later Graybar, not having been paid and learning that no certificate of limited partnership had been filed, sued Preston, Blomquist, and Lowe for the unpaid bills. Graybar claimed that Lowe was liable as a general partner because no certificate of limited partnership was on file. Is Lowe liable to Graybar? Explain.

CHAPTER 37

FORMATION OF CORPORATIONS

A corporation is the most important form of business organization in the United States. Practically every large business is a corporate enterprise. Accordingly, it is essential for a student of business law to understand how corporations are organized and how they operate.

This chapter discusses the nature and formation of corporations. Subsequent chapters deal with corporate financing and management.

THE NATURE OF CORPORATIONS

Characteristics of a Corporation

A **corporation** is an artificial person created by a state or, infrequently, by an act of Congress. It is invisible and intangible and exists only as a creation of law. A corporation can perform only those functions authorized by law and by its charter. "Charter" is simply another name for the articles of incorporation—the document which, when filed in the manner provided by law, brings the corporation into existence.

A corporation has four basic characteristics: (1) It is a legal entity, (2) it may have a perpetual existence, (3) its ownership and control are separate from one another, and (4) its shareholders (the owners of the corporation) have a limited liability.

A Legal Entity.   The word "corporation" (from the Latin *corpus*) means *body*. A corporation is a distinct legal body with rights and obligations similar to those possessed by an individual. It can buy and sell property, have employees, borrow money, and sue and be sued. In addition, being a legal, although artificial person, it pays taxes, is subject to criminal prosecution, and is entitled to equal protection of the laws.

Perpetual Existence.   As the existence of a corporation does not depend upon the continuing membership of any particular person, a corporation generally has a perpetual existence. A few states, however, limit the lifetime of the corporations formed in those states, but those corporations can apply for renewal of their charters. Regardless of a corporation's permissible life span, a state may, in accordance with its laws, terminate a corporation's existence at an earlier time. In addition, its shareholders may, if a sufficient number concur, voluntarily dissolve the corporation, thereby bringing it to an end.

Separation of Ownership and Control.   A corporation is collectively owned by its shareholders—those who have acquired its shares of stock—but no particular number of shareholders is required. A corporation may have a single shareholder or may be owned by thousands of shareholders, as is true of many large corporations such as General Electric, or International Business Machines. Usually, an ownership interest is evidenced by a *stock certificate* stating the number and class of shares of the corporation's stock the shareholder owns. (Corporate stock is discussed in Chapter 38.) Stock certificates may be transferred from one owner to another without affecting the existence or the business of the corporation. To transfer a certificate an owner merely signs (indorses) and delivers the certificate to the person to whom it is transferred.

The shareholders elect a board of directors who establish and direct the policies governing the business affairs of the corporation. The directors elect or otherwise designate the officers of the corporation such as its president, vice president, secretary, and treasurer, who carry on its day-to-day business operations. The duties of corporation directors and officers are explained in Chapter 39.

Shareholders' Limited Liability. One of the principal reasons the corporate form of business organization is so popular is that its shareholders are not liable for the company's debts. A shareholder may lose all or part of his or her investment in the firm if the shares diminish in value, but that is the limit of the shareholder's potential loss. To illustrate this important concept, assume that the Winsome Corporation orders an expensive drill press from the Thompson Machine Tool Company. The money Winsome owes for the press is the obligation of the corporation and not of its shareholders. If Winsome does not pay for the press and Thompson sues for the money, the shareholders are not parties to the suit.

Shareholders do not own any of the corporation's property and they have no direct control over the management of the company. The shareholders are not the agents of the corporation in which they have invested and they owe it no fiduciary obligations. A shareholder may sue the corporation or be sued by it.

Types of Corporations

Any corporation may be placed into one or more of four general categories. It is either (1) a corporation for profit or one not for profit, (2) a public or a private corporation, (3) a domestic or a foreign corporation, or (4) a close (sometimes called a "closed" or "closely held") corporation.

Profit and Nonprofit Corporations. A *corporation for profit* is organized to carry on a business that is expected to make profits for the corporation and for its owners, the shareholders. The profits it makes are used, at the discretion of the board of directors, for business purposes of the firm, and may also be distributed to the shareholders as earnings on their shares of stock. Such a distribution is called a *dividend*. (Dividends are discussed in Chapter 38.)

A **nonprofit corporation** is formed for a charitable, religious, educational, or some similar purpose. Schools, hospitals, churches, and fraternal organizations are examples of nonprofit corporations. They are not required to pay taxes. Some nonprofit corporations issue stock, but most of them grant memberships instead. Although a nonprofit corporation may make money, it does not distribute those profits to its members. However, the corporate form protects members from personal liability which might otherwise arise out of its operations. For example, assume that the Community Church owns and operates the Heather School to teach basic skills to delinquent children. If the driver of the school's bus gets into an accident, the members of the church have no liability for any injuries a third party may have sustained.

Public and Private Corporations. *Public corporations* are formed to accomplish some objective for the public good. Incorporated cities are examples of public corporations formed by state legislatures. The United States Postal Service and the Federal Deposit Insurance Corporation (FDIC) which insures bank deposits, are examples of public corporations formed by Congress. Public corporations may be either profit-making or non-profit-making organizations. The Tennessee Valley Authority which manufactures and sells electric energy, and AMTRAK, which operates passenger railroad lines, are profit-making corporations, while others, such as incorporated cities and towns, are not for profit.

Any corporation that is not a public corporation is a *private corporation*. A private corporation such as one that distributes water, gas, or electricity carries on a business so closely tied to a public interest that it is subject to special regulations of state and federal agencies. Such a corporation is called a *quasi-public corporation*.

A private corporation may be organized for profit or nonprofit purposes. For example, the General Motors Corporation is a private corporation organized for profit-making purposes; the Henry Family Trust, Inc., which grants student scholarships, is a private corporation organized for charitable purposes.

All states have general corporation laws controlling how a private corporation may be formed and carry on its business. These laws set out, among other things: (1) the manner in which a corporation is organized, (2) the obligations of a corporation's directors, (3) the conditions under which a corporation may issue stock, and (4) the rights of the holders of shares of corporation stock.

Certain private corporations are subject to special federal and state laws. These are subchapter S corporations, professional corporations, and close corporations.

• *Subchapter S corporations.* A corporation of this name is an ordinary private corporation which complies with the provisions of subchapter S of the Internal Revenue Code. It may have no more than fifteen members who elect to be taxed as a partnership.

• *Professional corporations.* This type of organization is the incorporation of a professional practice such as that of a doctor, lawyer, or accountant, in order to obtain corporate tax benefits.

• *Close corporations.* A close corporation, frequently referred to as a "closed" or "closely held" corporation, has two basic characteristics: (1) Its shares are not traded (bought or sold on a stock exchange or security market), and (2) it is owned and managed by only a few people, usually friends or members of a single family. Many states have statutes which facilitate the formation of close corporations.

Domestic and Foreign Corporations.　A corporation is a *domestic* corporation in the state in which it is incorporated, but from the standpoint of every other state it is a *foreign* corporation. Thus, the Eastman Kodak Company, Inc., chartered in New York, is a domestic corporation in New York State regardless of where its shareholders live but it is viewed as a foreign corporation in every state other than New York. A corporation that is chartered in some country outside the United States is sometimes referred to as an *alien corporation* if it does business within the United States.

Corporations Distinguished from Partnerships　The basic differences between corporations and partnerships, the two most frequently used forms of business organizations, are summarized in Table 37.1. Examining the differences between the two forms of business organizations may be helpful in deciding which form is better suited to a particular business.

TABLE 37.1 COMPARISON OF CORPORATIONS AND PARTNERSHIPS

	Corporation	Partnership
Entity	A legal entity or "person," taxable as such.	Not a legal entity but has certain characteristics of one (see pp. 593, 597)
Creation	Created by the state upon application of organizers in required legal form.	Created by formal or informal agreement of its members (see p. 593)
Transferability of interest	Shares evidencing ownership are ordinarily transferred without consent of corporation or other stockholders.	All partners (co-owners of business) must consent to admission of new member to partnership (see pp. 595, 598)
Liability	Personal liability for corporate obligations limited to each stockholder's investment in shares.	Personal liability for partnership obligations goes beyond a partner's original investment in the business (see pp. 592, 598, 602–603)
Duration	Perpetual corporate life unless limited by statute or articles, but shareholders may dissolve the corporation.	Partnership life not perpetual (see pp. 610, 612)
Management	Stockholders' management authority generally limited to voting in elections of directors and on amendments to articles.	Partners manage business and act as agents of partnership unless otherwise provided in the partnership agreement (see pp. 600–612)
Purposes and powers	Limited to purposes and powers enumerated in articles and state corporation statute.	Purposes and powers determined by agreement of members, without state approval (see p. 593)

FORMATION OF CORPORATIONS

A corporation is formed in three stages: (1) the promotional or preincorporation stage, (2) the filing stage, and (3) the organizational stage.

The Promotional Stage

Before articles of incorporation can be filed with the state, much preliminary work must be carried on. The individual who is in charge is called a "promoter." The promoter may be organizing the corporation on his or her own behalf, or may have been hired by others to do so. The promoter, among other things, defines the business in which the new corporation will engage, hires legal counsel to prepare the articles of incorporation, and secures the agreement of individuals (usually three) to act as the incorporators of the enterprise and as its original board of directors. In addition, the promoter raises sufficient money to assure that the corporation can begin to do business. This money is usually raised through subscriptions to buy shares of stock of the company. After the corporation has been chartered and the subscriptions are paid for, shares of its stock are issued. The promoter also pays fees charged by the state for the filing of the articles of incorporation, and procures the necessary subscription agreement forms, stock certificates, corporate books, and the many other items and services that may be involved in the incorporation process.

Promoter's Liability for Preincorporation Contracts.   Assume that Robert, a promoter, purporting to act for the New World Corporation that has not yet been chartered, hired Archie, an architect, to make a feasibility study of certain land which will be developed by that corporation after it comes into existence. This is a preincorporation contract which Robert is making for the benefit of the corporation. If Robert promises personally to pay for the work, he will, of course, be required to pay Archie, but even if Robert made no such promise, if the corporation is not formed, then Robert, the promoter, must pay for the work he ordered.

Corporate Liability for Preincorporation Contracts.   As a general rule a newly formed corporation does *not automatically* become a party to a preincorporation contract made by a promoter on its behalf. The reason for this is that a corporation is a legal entity separate from its promoter with distinct rights and duties. Therefore, a new corporation is privileged to choose the preexisting contracts which it will assume and those it will reject.

A newly formed corporation can expressly or impliedly adopt a preincorporation contract. It *expressly* adopts such a contract by passing a resolution to that effect at a directors' or shareholders' meeting. It *impliedly* adopts a preincorporation contract by accepting the benefits of the contract or by performing according to its terms.

A newly formed corporation may also become a party to a preincorporation contract by entering into a *novation* agreement. Under such an agreement the other party to the contract accepts the corporation as a contracting party in place of the promoter and the promoter is discharged from any liability under the contract. (Novation was discussed in Chapter 13, p. 198.)

Fiduciary Duty of Promoters.   When a promoter performs preincorporation functions, he or she is not then the agent of the corporation because it is not yet in existence and a nonexistent principal cannot have an agent. Nevertheless, a promoter owes fiduciary duties to all those who participate in the firm's establishment and subscribe to its shares, to the corporation after it is organized, and to those who subsequently become its shareholders. These fiduciary duties include fair dealing and the exercise of good faith, including disclosure of all material facts concerning transactions the promoter undertook on behalf of the future enterprise.

A promoter's fiduciary obligation to a corporation he organized is illustrated in the case which follows.

CASE 37.1   Golden v. Oahe Enterprises, Inc.
             295 N.W.2d 160 (S.D. 1980)

Facts: Emmick, a promoter, organized Oahe Enterprises, Inc. He received from Oahe shares of
             its stock in exchange for shares of stock in CM, Inc., owned by him (Emmick) which he
             represented to be worth $19 per share, even though he knew it to be worth only $9.50
             per share.

             Golden purchased shares in Oahe Enterprises. Later, Oahe was dissolved and its
             assets were to be distributed among its shareholders. Golden claims that, because the
             CM shares Emmick exchanged for Oahe shares when that corporation was organized
             were overpriced, too many shares had been issued to Emmick and a fraud was
             committed upon the corporation and upon its shareholders.

Question: If a promoter transfers property at an inflated price to a corporation he or she organizes,
             does the promoter commit a fraud against the corporation?

Answer: Yes. The promoter thereby violates his or her fiduciary obligations.

Reasoning: Emmick was the promoter of Oahe. As such, he stood in a fiduciary relationship both to
             the corporation and to its shareholders. He was required to deal with them in good faith.
             When a promoter obtains a secret profit in a transaction he conducts with the
             corporation, he commits a fraud and is required to account to the corporation for the
             profit.

Subscriptions to Corporate Shares.   As part of the preincorporation process, a promoter usually solicits and secures subscriptions for shares of stock which will be issued by the corporation after it comes into being. A stock subscription is an offer to buy shares at the price set by the promoter. The subscriber is an *offeror.*

The solicitation of subscriptions to shares of stock of a corporation about to be organized, or for the purchase of shares of a newly organized corporation, conjures up visions of handsome profits. Therefore, solicitation of trusting investors to purchase such shares has been a fertile field for fraud by unscrupulous promoters. However, state and federal regulations have greatly reduced the incidence of fraudulent schemes by requiring promoters to secure permits before they may sell shares. To get these permits, government agencies require promoters to file sworn statements which fully disclose all prior transactions affecting the value of the proposed shares.

Revocation of Subscription.   A majority of courts look upon a subscription as a continuing offer that a subscriber-offeror may revoke at any time before its acceptance. A minority of courts hold that no subscription may be revoked unless *all* of the subscribers consent.

Acceptance of Subscription. The courts also disagree as to what constitutes acceptance of a preincorporation subscription. The majority view is that completion of the incorporation process of itself, without any other evidence of acceptance, amounts to an acceptance by the corporation of the subscriber's offer. Other courts require some act by the corporation to evidence its acceptance of a subscription to shares of stock, such as listing the subscriber as a shareholder in the company's stock records or physically issuing a stock certificate for the shares of stock.

Unless a state law dictates otherwise, the *form* in which a subscription agreement is written is not important. The following case is concerned with this principle.

CASE 37.2   Molina v. Largosa
465 P.2d 293 (Hawaii 1970)

Facts: Molina signed a subscription for the purchase of $2,000 worth of stock in a corporation to be called Specialties Unlimited, then being organized by Largosa, the promoter. The subscription form did not indicate the total intended capitalization of the corporation. Molina later paid Largosa the $2,000. The following month the articles of incorporation were filed. They showed that Molina had subscribed and paid $2,000 for 40 shares and that a total of $11,750 had been subscribed. The corporation soon ceased to do business.

Molina sued Largosa to get back the $2000 he (Molina) had paid, claiming that the subscription was not binding because it did not set out the total capital of the proposed corporation nor Molina's proportionate interest in it.

Question: Is there any particular form in which a stock subscription must be stated?

Answer: No, in the absence of a statutory requirement.

REasoning: When the articles of incorporation were filed, the corporation came into existence. The majority view is that the completion of the incorporation process amounts to the acceptance of the subscription. Here, in addition, there were actions indicating acceptance when the articles of incorporation showed that Molina was one of the shareholders and also Molina was later treated as a shareholder. Once Specialties Unlimited came into existence and the corporation accepted the subscription, the offer to subscribe could not be revoked.

The Filing Stage   State laws which set out the requirements to establish a corporation are not uniform. All states require the promoter or organizers of a corporation to draft and file a corporate charter (also called the "articles of incorporation"). However, states may differ in such things as the fees charged to incorporate, the taxes imposed upon active domestic corporations, the location of their principal offices, and their internal structure. Because of the differences in state laws, promoters of large corporations carefully select the states in which they will incorporate their ventures. Delaware, for example, is known as a state particularly friendly to corporations.

Drafting Articles of Incorporation.   The articles of incorporation, together with applicable laws of the state where the corporation is to be chartered, provide the legal framework within which a corporation must operate. The articles spell out the specific objectives of the incorporators and the rights of the company's stockholders. The articles of incorporation must also include such basic items of information as those in the following paragraphs.

Corporate Name.   Each new corporation must select a name which does not duplicate, or is not deceptively like, the name of another corporation chartered in that state. The word "Corporation," or "Incorporated," or the abbreviation of one of them must be included as part of the name.

Corporate Business.   All states require that the articles of incorporation set out the type or types of business which the company may engage in and the purpose for which it is organized. The Model Business Corporation Act [1] permits the purpose to be stated in such general terms as, "For the transaction of all lawful business for which corporations may be incorporated." Some states require a more particular statement of purposes, such as, "To carry on the manufacture, repair, and sale of personal property of every description in the state of Florida and elsewhere."

Corporate Life.   Some states require that the articles of incorporation state the term of years the enterprise may continue. For instance, such a statement might be, "the corporation shall have a perpetual existence," or "the corporation shall terminate and be dissolved in the year 2001."

Incorporators and Directors.   *Incorporators* are the individuals who sign and file in the office of the secretary of state the articles of incorporation, thereby making application for the grant of a corporation charter. In some states a single individual may be the incorporator of a company. The names and addresses of the incorporators and, in most states, the names and addresses of the members of the first board of directors must be set out in the articles.

Corporate Financial Structure.   The articles must also specify the classes of shares of stock (such as common stock and preferred stock, explained in the next chapter), and the number of shares in each class which the corporation is authorized to issue, together with any restrictions there will be on their transfer. An example of a restriction is the right of the corporation to be, if it so desires, the purchaser of any shares a shareholder desires to sell. This privilege is called the "right of first refusal."

---

[1]The Model Act was prepared by the American Bar Association to guide the states in modifying their general corporation statutes to meet business needs.

Signing Articles. The articles of incorporation must be signed by the minimum number of incorporators dictated by state law, and their signatures must be properly authenticated.

Filing Articles. After the articles of incorporation have been signed they must be sent, together with payment of filing fees, to the state office designated by law to receive and process them. In most states this is the office of the secretary of state. If the articles conform to state law, they are *filed.* The date of filing is the date the corporation comes into existence. This is also the date on which the corporation is said to be *chartered.* The secretary of state sends a certified copy of the articles to the incorporators and, in many states, that official also issues a Certificate of Incorporation. State law may require the corporation to file a certified copy of its articles of incorporation in the county in which the corporation's principal office is located.

The
Organizational
Stage

Once the corporation has been chartered, the organizational meeting of its incorporators is held. At that time, if the names of the original directors did not appear in the articles of incorporation, the incorporators elect the company's first board of directors.

The board of directors then holds its initial meeting. At that time the following actions are taken:

1. The board of directors prepares and adopts the corporation's *bylaws* (in some states it is the practice of the stockholders, instead of the board, to adopt the bylaws).

   Bylaws establish rules for the internal management of the company. They cover such matters as how and when the shareholders and the directors will hold their regular and special meetings; what notices are required and what constitutes a *quorum* at those meetings—that is, the minimum number of people who must be present to transact business. The bylaws also establish how vacancies on the board of directors will be filled, what officers the corporation will have and what will be their duties.

2. The board normally adopts a corporate seal having a design bearing the corporation's name and the word "SEAL." The seal can be impressed on official documents by some form of stamping device, usually hand-held. Most states require the corporate seal to accompany the signatures of corporate officers on documents affecting the title to real property. In addition, banks, government agencies, and others with whom the corporation does business, traditionally require the corporate seal to be affixed to certified copies of board of directors' resolutions authorizing the officers of the corporation to engage in important agreements.

3. The board elects company officers and fixes their salaries.

4. The board approves the form of the stock certificate the corporation will issue.

5. The board authorizes certain officers of the company, such as its president and its secretary, to issue its stock certificates in exchange for the paid subscriptions.

6. The board assumes the debts for specified preincorporation expenses and approves their payment.

7. The board performs other "housekeeping" functions such as providing for the

opening of a bank account and the selection of an office, factory building, or other appropriate place where the corporation will carry on its business.

8. The corporation secretary prepares the minutes of the first (and all subsequent) meetings of the shareholders and the board of directors. It is important that accurate minutes of all corporate meetings be maintained to establish proof of the authority of corporate officers to undertake important corporate activities such as the making of a bank loan or the buying and selling of real property.

LEGAL STATUS OF CORPORATIONS

Defectively Formed Corporations

A corporation organized without strict conformity to state incorporation laws is called a "defectively formed corporation." Such a corporation is open to several lines of attack. Its creditors may contend that the shareholders should be considered *partners* with unlimited liability for the debts of the enterprise rather than corporate stockholders with no such liability. Also, third parties may challenge the authority of a defectively organized corporation to enter into contracts, and debtors who are sued by such a corporation may challenge its capacity to sue.

A subscriber to the capital stock of a defectively formed corporation may claim that no payment is due upon a subscription he or she signed because the proposed corporation did not come into existence. Also, the state may claim that the organization's failure to comply with statutory requirements is cause to order forfeiture of its charter.

Compliance with Corporate Laws

When the validity of a corporation's existence is questioned in a lawsuit, a court will find that the organization is either (1) a de jure copoation, (2) a de facto corporation, (3) a corporation by estoppel, or (4) a sham corporation.

De Jure Corporations. A de jure corporation (meaning a legally organized corporation) is established when there has been complete or substantial compliance with the statutory requirements for a corporation. A de jure corporation has all the rights and benefits which flow from the corporation statutes.

De Facto Corporations. A de facto corporation (meaning a corporation "in fact") is established when a company carries on business as a corporation, having in good faith taken action to comply with the state corporation laws but, for some reason, has not properly complied. The state can, by an appropriate legal action, challenge the legal existence of a defectively formed corporation. If a court finds that the organization is a de facto corporation, a third party cannot successfully attack its corporate existence. The case which follows demonstrates how a de facto corporation may be formed.

CASE 37.3   Cantor v. Sunshine Greenery, Inc.
398 A.2d 571 (N.J. 1979)

Facts: On November 21, 1974, the corporate name Sunshine Greenery, Inc., was reserved by the Secretary of State for one Brunetti. On December 8, 1974, Brunetti and Sansoni signed the certificate of incorporation of Sunshine Greenery, Inc., and on the same day mailed it, accompanied by the required fee, to the Secretary of State to be filed. For some unknown reason, the certificate was not filed until December 18, 1974.

On December 16, 1974, Brunetti, signing as the President of Sunshine Greenery, Inc., entered into a lease with Cantor to rent certain property. On the following day, December 17th, Sunshine Greenery repudiated the lease and did not occupy the property. Cantor filed suit under the lease against both Sunshine Greenery and Brunetti. Brunetti claims that Sunshine Greenery was a *de facto* corporation on December 16th and therefore it alone, and not he personally, is liable on the lease.

Question: Can an organization become a *de facto* corporation before its certificate of incorporation is filed?

Answer: Yes, under appropriate circumstances.

Reasoning: Sunshine Greenery was not a *de jure* corporation on December 16, 1974, when the lease was signed. However, it had made a bona fide attempt to be incorporated before that date. In addition, there was an actual exercise of corporate powers by Sunshine Greenery when it executed the lease. The mere fact that there were no formal meetings or resolutions of the corporation does not prevent it from being a *de facto* corporation. The facts are sufficient to establish that a *de facto* corporation was in being when the lease was signed and therefore Brunetti is not personally liable on the lease.

Corporations by Estoppel.   A "corporation by estoppel" is not a type of corporation, it is merely a legal phrase meaning that, under the circumstances then present, a defectively formed corporation, or a third party who contracts with it, are *estopped* (prevented) from asserting in a legal action that the corporation was defectively formed. If a court finds that estoppel is present, both the defectively formed corporation and the other party are bound by the contract they entered into. For instance, assume that the Gamma Corporation is defectively formed. It enters into a contract to sell to Distributor a tank car of gasoline at 70 cents a gallon. Before delivery, the price of gasoline rises drastically. Gamma does not perform the contract, refusing to deliver the gasoline at the 70-cent price. When sued, Gamma claims that it is not liable for breach of the contract because the Gamma Corporation was defectively formed. A court would estop (prevent) Gamma from taking advantage of its own faulty organization. Instead, the court would characterize Gamma as "a corporation by estoppel" and hold it liable on the contract. The phrase "corporation by estoppel" applies only to the parties in a particular transaction.

Sham Corporations.   If a business holds itself out to be a corporation but it is neither a de jure corporation nor a de facto corporation, nor does the corporation by estoppel rule apply, then it is not a corporate entity at all. The shareholders of such a purported "corporation" as well as those who operate the business are personally liable to its creditors. If the "corporation" enters into a contract, the other party may challenge the "corporation's" authority to sue for a breach of the contract. Subscribers to the "corporation's" shares are relieved of their subscription obligations. The state may bring an action against the sham corporation, requiring it to forfeit its charter if one was issued to it in error, and to cease acting as a corporation.

Ignoring Corporate Existence

In certain situations, a court may reject the protection a corporate entity furnishes its shareholders and may hold them personally responsible for the actions of the corporation. This rejection of a corporate entity is called "piercing the corporate veil."

A court pierces the corporate veil to prevent a shareholder from committing a fraud, perpetrating a crime, or accomplishing some other wrongful purpose under the guise that the improper act is the action of the corporation. A court may take this action when the corporation is so dominated or controlled by a single individual or by very few individuals or by another corporation, that there is a unity of interest between them. Unity of interest may be evidenced by an intermingling of personal and corporate funds and other assets. A court will also "pierce the corporate veil" and hold the shareholder(s) liable on a corporation contract when the corporation carries on business with so little capital that it cannot meet its normal obligations. The legal theory a court applies in such a circumstance is that the shareholders are the corporation's "other self"—its alter ego. This doctrine is most frequently applied to one-person corporations.

In the following case the court "pierces the corporate veil" and holds a stockholder liable on a note executed by the corporation.

CASE 37.4 Rosebud Corporation v. Boggio
561 P.2d 367 (Colo. 1977)

Facts: Boggio owned all of the shares of 3M, Inc. He handled all its affairs and treated its assets as his own. 3M purchased a nightclub and restaurant from Rosebud Corp., paying for the property with a promissory note providing for future cash payments. Boggio, in his own name, later sold the nightclub, receiving cash and a note. Boggio kept the cash payment himself.

When no payments were made to Rosebud by 3M on its note, Rosebud sued both 3M and Boggio, claiming that the latter was the *alter ego* of the corporation.

Question: Can a stockholder be liable on a note that is executed in the corporate name?

Answer: Yes, if the stockholder is the *alter ego* of the corporation.

Reasoning: The *alter ego* doctrine applies where a corporation is used to protect a wrong, fraud, or crime. To establish the doctrine it must be shown that the corporate entity was merely an instrument used for the transaction of the stockholder's own affairs; that there was such a unity of interest and ownership that the distinction between the corporation and the owner ceases to exist; and that to permit the individual to be excused from an obligation on the basis that it is a corporate obligation would promote an injustice.

Under the facts here, to allow Boggio to hide behind the fiction that the note to Rosebud was the obligation only of the 3M Corporation would allow him to convert the proceeds from the sale of the corporation's property to his own personal use. Boggio is liable on the note to Rosebud as the *alter ego* of 3M, Inc.

Ignoring Existence of a Subsidiary Corporation

It is common practice for large, affluent corporations to own subsidiary corporations. Under appropriate circumstances, a court can ignore the separate corporate identity of the subsidiary and hold its parent corporation responsible for the debts or wrongs of the subsidiary. To bring about that result, a third party who seeks to have a court pierce the corporate veil of the subsidiary must prove (1) that there was unity of interest and ownership between the parent company and its subsidiary; and (2) that the subsidiary was used to promote a fraud or other illegality, *or* that the realtionship between the two corporations (the parent and its subsidiary) was designed to evade a statutory or contractual obligation.

Evidence proving unity of interest of a parent corporation and its subsidiary may be that the funds and accounting records of the two corporations are intermingled, that the same individuals act as directors of both corporations, that the capitalization of the subsidiary is not sufficient to meet its normal business needs, or that the two corporations do not represent themselves to the public as separate corporations.

A case in which a court ignored the distinction between a parent corporation and a subsidiary follows.

CASE 37.5

Shirley v. Drackett Products Co.
182 N.W.2d 726 (Mich. 1970)

Facts: "Vanish" is a toilet bowl cleaner manufactured by the Drackett Company, Inc. A wholly owned subsidiary of Drackett is the exclusive distributor of all Drackett's products. The two corporations have the same address; some officers and directors serve both companies; and there is some interchange of employees. Drackett's only source of revenue is generated by the sale of "Vanish" by the subsidiary.

Shirley purchased a can of Vanish and used it as directed. In the process she inhaled some of its fumes, became ill, and, as a result, will be permanently disabled. Shirley brought an action against the subsidiary for negligence and breach of warranty. She recovered a judgment for $100,000. The defendant appealed, claiming that any liability which exists is that of the parent manufacturing company.

Question: Can two corporations be seen as a single unit in determining liability for a defective product?

Answer: Yes, if the facts justify piercing the corporate veil.

Reasoning: As a general rule, a retailer or distributor is not liable for the negligent manufacture of a product. However, under the facts in this case, that rule is not applicable.

Where a corporation is so organized and so controlled as to make it a mere instrumentality or an agent of another corporation, its separate existence as a distinct legal entity will be ignored and the two corporations will be regarded as one. The facts present here deny to the defendant corporation the insulation from liability that ordinarily protects a retailer or distributor.

SUMMARY

A corporation for profit is the most widely used form of business organization in the United States. The chief characteristics of such a business corporation are: (1) It is a legal entity, (2) it may have a perpetual existence, (3) its control is separate from its ownership, and (4) the liability of its shareholders is limited to the amount of their capital investment. Shareholders elect a board of directors who establish company policies and elect the company's officers. The officers are in charge of the corporation's day-to-day affairs.

A promoter initiates the necessary actions and brings the interested parties together so that a corporation entity is formed. A promoter solicits subscriptions to the company's capital stock and owes fiduciary duties to those who agree to purchase shares. He or she also owes fiduciary duties to the corporation and its shareholders.

A corporation is not automatically liable on a promoter's preincorporation contracts. The company can become liable by either adopting the contract or undertaking to be party to the contract through a novation agreement.

An offer to purchase shares from an issuing corporation is called a "subscription." The completion of the incorporation process usually constitutes the acceptance of preincorporation subscriptions. A few courts require the corporation's acceptance of a subscription to be evidenced by some additional act.

A company is incorporated when its articles of incorporation are filed in the appropriate state office, usually the office of the secretary of state. When the articles are filed, the corporation's life begins. An organizational meeting is then held, at which time the shareholders elect a board of directors (if they have not already been named in the articles of incorporation). The directors adopt a set of bylaws for the company, elect its officers, and take such other actions, such as opening a bank account and selecting the place of business, as may be required to begin operations.

A corporation which complies with state laws governing incorporation is called a de jure corporation. If the company has in good faith attempted to comply with those laws but, despite the absence of full compliance, acts as a corporation, it is a de facto corporation. A business organization which acts as a corporation but is neither a de jure nor a de facto corporation is not a corporation at all and its members are personally liable for the debts and obligations of the enterprise. The state may force such a sham corporation to cease carrying on business as a corporation.

A court will disregard a corporate entity and hold its individual members personally liable if the interests of the corporation and the individuals are so united that a separation between them does not really exist.

REVIEW QUESTIONS

1. What is a corporation?
2. (a) What are the basic characteristics of a corporation? (b) What is another name for the owners of a corporation?
3. Distinguish between corporations and partnerships.
4. What are the obligations of a promoter upon contracts he or she enters into in the name of a corporation?
5. Why are promoters fiduciaries?
6. When can a subscriber to the capital stock of a corporation that is being organized revoke that subscription?
7. What is the difference between articles of incorporation and the charter of a corporation?
8. Distinguish between incorporators, directors, and officers of a corporation?
9. Distinguish between a de jure corporation, a de facto corporation, and a sham corporation.
10. Explain how the principle of corporation by estoppel acts to prevent injustice.
11. What is meant by piercing the corporate veil?
12. What does the alter ego doctrine mean?

CASE PROBLEMS

1. Maloney was the controlling stockholder of the Marlin Electric Company. He also served as one of its directors and as the president of the company. As president, he was in charge of the company's daily operations. He fixed his own salary, subject to the approval of the board of directors. Malony was killed while flying the company airplane on company business. His widow claimed that she was entitled to death benefits because Maloney was an employee killed while in the scope of his employment. The Aetna Casualty Company, which insured Marlin Electric Company, denied liability, claiming that Maloney was not an employee of the company because he owned most of its stock and "ran" the company and so could not also be one of its employees. Is the insurance company correct? Explain reason for your answer.

2. On May 1, Northwest Tech, Inc., entered into a 2-year lease with Heintze Corp., the building owner, for certain commercial space. The lease was signed by Norman Rippee, president of Northwest Tech, who was also the promoter of that corporation. The incorporation of Northwest Tech was not completed until July 15. The company paid the rent due for the first year, then moved out. Is Heintze entitled to recover the next year's rent from (a) Northwest Tech, Inc., or (b) Rippee, or (c) both? Explain.

3. Mrs. McDaniel, the owner of an 800-acre farm, was approached by ABC, Inc., about leasing her farm to a new corporation which ABC proposed to form. Mrs. McDaniel expressed interest and, with others, actively participated in the organizational meetings. The group agreed to commence spring planting on 200 acres of the McDaniel farm. However, after the planting they decided to abandon the idea of

forming the corporation. The company which supplied the seed used in the planting sued McDaniel for the unpaid seed bill, claiming that since she was part of the promoters' group, she was liable on the seed contract. Is the supplier correct? Explain.

4. Mr. and Mrs. Conway contracted to have their house remodeled by Trend Set Construction Company. Marilyn Samet signed as president of Trend Set. Trend Set did not complete the work, and the Conways sued Trend Set and secured a judgment for $10,747. The Conways discovered that no certificate of incorporation had been prepared, acknowledged, or filed for that corporation as was required by state law. The Conways then sued Samet individually, claiming that Trend Set Construction did not exist as a corporation and therefore Samet was liable on the contract she signed. Defendant Samet claimed that Trend Set was a de facto corporation because she had instructed her attorney to incorporate the company but he had failed to do so, and that she has no personal liability. (a) Is Trend Set a de facto corporation? Why or why not? (b) Is Samet individually liable on the contract? Why or why not?

5. Day contracted with Filmlab, Inc., for a franchise to use Filmlab's name and trademark to operate a film developing business. Dietel, Filmlab's director, vice president and principal stockholder, carried on those negotiations on behalf of his company. Later, Day discovered that Filmlab had not given him all the property rights he had bargained for. Day therefore sued Filmlab and Dietel for breach of contract. Day claims that because Dietel owned and controlled Filmlab and carried on the negotiations, there was such a joinder (joining) of interest that the court should "pierce the corporate veil" of Filmlab, Inc., and hold Dietal liable on the contract. Is Day's position correct? What factors should the court apply to Day's request, and what conclusion should the court reach?

CHAPTER 38

FINANCING OF CORPORATIONS

As explained in the preceding chapter, the money paid by the original members of a corporation for the purchase of shares of its stock forms the corporation's initial working capital. If the directors later decide to increase the corporation's capital, they may, within the limitations of the articles of incorporation (also called the "charter"), issue and sell additional shares. If the directors desire to issue a greater number of shares than are authorized by the corporation's charter, they may, with the consent of the shareholders in accordance with the corporation's bylaws, amend the articles of incorporation to authorize issuance of additional shares. When a corporation secures money from the sale of its stock, it is engaged in *equity financing*.

If the board of directors decides to secure financing from sources other than the sale of shares of stock, the sale of its property, or the sale of goods and services, they authorize the corporate officers to borrow money. This is usually done by means of short-term loans in the form of notes, or by long-term loans in the form of corporate bonds. When a corporation borrows money, it is engaged in *debt financing*.

Corporate shares of stock together with corporate bonds are called the "securities" of a corporation. This chapter discusses the nature of those securities and the process of equity and debt financing.

EQUITY FINANCING

The following is an example of equity financing. Arthur, Betty, Charles, and Doris form the Exeter Corporation and constitute its board of directors. Exeter's charter authorizes it to issue 5000 shares of stock. The directors, believing that $50,000 will be adequate for the corporation to begin business, authorize the sale, at $25 per share, of 2000 shares of the corporation's stock. Each of the four directors buys 500 shares. Thus, a total of 2000 shares are issued to make a working capital of $50,000; and 3000 shares remain unissued.

The corporation's business is successful and 2 years later the directors desire to expand the company. They authorize 800 more shares to be issued at $50 per share from the treasury stock of 3000 shares. Betty purchases 200 of these shares and George, a friend, buys the remaining 600 shares. With the $40,000 thus raised, the company can go ahead with its expansion plans. Now 2200 shares remain in the corporation's treasury and these may still be issued at the discretion of the board of directors.

Characteristics of Shares of Stock

A share of stock issued by a corporation represents a proportionate ownership interest, or *equity*, in a corporation. However, a share of stock does not confer upon the holder either the right to use, or the title to, any specific property owned by the corporation. A shareholder is one of the owners of the company, not one of its creditors.

The extent of a shareholder's ownership interest in a corporation depends upon the number of shares he or she owns relative to the total number of shares the corporation has issued. For example, on December 31, 1983, The General Electric Company, Inc., had issued 454,630,859 shares of common stock. Therefore, an individual who purchased 100 shares of GE stock on that date had an ownership interest of only one one-hundredth of the total number of shares.

Most small corporations and particularly close corporations (discussed in the preceding chapter) do not offer shares to the general public; a single shareholder or family often owns a majority or all the shares the corporation issues.

Entitlements of Shareholders.   The ownership of a share of stock typically gives the holder the right: (1) to receive *dividends* (a share of the corporation's profits), (2) to receive a proportionate share of the corporation's net assets in the event it is dissolved, (3) to exercise the powers given by law to shareholders (discussed in the next chapter), and (4) to transfer shares to another owner.

Stock Certificates.   Ownership of corporate shares normally is evidenced by a *stock certificate*. This is a serially numbered paper signed by authorized officers of the corporation, bearing the name of the corporation and the corporation's seal. The certificate states the number and class of shares it represents and the name of the owner or owners. On the reverse side are instructions for indorsing the certificate in order to transfer it to another owner.

A corporation's articles of incorporation may authorize it to issue one or more classes of shares. If more than one class is authorized, the articles name them and set out whatever preferences, limitations, and rights attach to each class. Among the classes of stock a corporation may issue are common stock, preferred stock, voting stock, nonvoting stock, par value stock and no-par value stock. Different classes of stock *within* any of these classifications may also be issued.

Shares of Common Stock.   If a corporation has only one class of stock, it is common stock. At shareholders' meetings the holders of common stock normally are entitled to vote in the election of the company's directors. Additional rights of shareholders are discussed in the next chapter.

Holders of shares of common stock receive dividends which may fluctuate in amount from year to year according to the decision of the board of directors. Those shareholders are entitled to receive dividends only after the holders of preferred classes of stock have been paid their dividends.

Shares of Preferred Stock.   Preferred shares, as their name implies, have "first call" upon the funds allocated by the board of directors for dividends to be distributed among the company's shareholders.

The holder of a preferred share is entitled to receive dividends of a fixed percentage of the share's value as established at the time it was issued. That percentage is printed on the face of the certificate. For instance, say you hold a share of Alabama Power Company 9.5 percent preferred stock which has a value of $100. Because it is a perferred share, your dividend will be paid before dividends are paid to holders of the company's common shares. You are entitled to receive a dividend of $9.50 each year from the profits of the Alabama Power Company for as long as you continue to own the share. However, unlike the holders of common stock who *do* elect the company's board of directors, the owners of preferred shares normally *do not* participate in the election of the board.

A corporation's charter may authorize the issuance of preferred shares in classes or in series which vary as to dividend entitlement, liquidation preferences, redemption, conversion, and voting rights (these terms are explained in succeeding paragraphs).

Promoters and directors of corporations may devise an almost endless variety of preferred shares. The three most common varieties are those which are (1) cumulative, (2) convertible, or (3) redeemable.

Cumulative Preferred Shares.   Holders of cumulative preferred shares, like ordinary preferred shareholders, have the right to receive payment of a fixed percentage dividend each year. However, holders of *cumulative preferred shares* have the additional advantage that if a dividend is passed (not paid) either because of a lack of funds or because the board of directors withholds the payment, the right to receive the "passed" dividend remains. When dividend money becomes available, the cumulative preferred shareholders are entitled to payment of both the current and the unpaid accumulated (cumulative) dividends before there is any distribution of current dividends to common shareholders or to the holders of shares which are not cumulative.

Convertible Preferred Shares.   A corporation may be authorized to issue *convertible preferred shares.* Such shares may be exchanged, usually at the option of the holder, for shares of another series or class, such as common shares, issued by the same corporation. This privilege may be of considerable value to a shareholder.

For example, assume that some years ago you had purchased 500 10 percent preferred shares of the Fixit Corporation, paying $17,500, and that each share is convertible into two shares of Fixit's common stock. At that time the Fixit common shares were selling for $10 each. But now the Fixit Company has become very successful and its common shares are selling for $20 per share. You therefore decide to exercise your conversion privilege and exchange your 500 shares of Fixit convertible preferred for 1000 shares of Fixit common. You may immediately sell those shares and receive $20,000. As your original investment was $17,500, you have made a profit of $2500 and, in addition, you received dividends of 10 percent upon the convertible preferred shares while you owned them. Remember, however, that when convertible preferred shares are issued there is no assurance that they will appreciate in value.

Redeemable ("Callable") Preferred Shares.   A corporation which issues *redeemable (or "callable") preferred shares* has the option to buy (or "call") them back, at a date and at a price, established when they are issued. The price and date when the company may (but is not obliged to) redeem the shares are printed on the certificates.

Voting and Nonvoting Shares.   Most states permit articles of incorporation to limit voting rights at shareholders' meetings to the holders of only certain classes of stock. If there is such a limitation, then usually that limitation is applied against the holders of preferred shares. Although the holders of common shares generally have the right to vote, common shares may be divided into classes, some of which have voting rights and other classes which do not.

Par and No-Par Value Shares.   *Par value* means the value given to each share in a class of shares as stated in the articles of incorporation, or the value assigned to such shares by the board of directors as their "par value" at the time of issuance. The par value is printed on the stock certificates.

In almost all states, shares may be issued without having an assigned par value if such action is authorized by the articles of incorporation and bylaws. Instead of a par value, the directors fix an arbitrary price for which the shares will be sold. This value is not printed on the stock certificates and they are called *no-par value* shares. The distinction between par value and no-par value shares is primarily the difference in the way the corporation enters in its books the receipts from their sale. Once the company has sold either par or no-par value shares, the price at which they may be traded (bought and sold, usually on the stock exchange) is determined by the forces of the marketplace.

Stock Options and Warrants

Stock Options.   A *stock option* is the right to purchase corporate shares at a fixed price at a stated future date. A corporation which issues a stock option anticipates that the option price of the shares at that future date will be lower than the amount the holder of the option would have to pay for the same security on the open market. A corporation may give stock options to its officers and other high-level employees to augment their salaries and to induce them to remain with the corporation. It is expected that, in return, the individual will work to increase the corporation's sales and profits.

A stock option may work in this way: the Formidable Company, Inc., wants James to join the company as its sales manager. To induce him to leave his current job, Formidable offers him a salary plus an option to purchase 1000 shares of Formidable common stock at $10 per share, the option to be effective 3 years from the date when James joins the corporation. When James accepts the position, Formidable's shares are selling on the open market (the stock exchange) for $10 per share. At the end of James' 3 years with the company the shares are selling for $20 each. At that time James has the right to take advantage of (exercise) his option. James can either buy the 1000 shares at the option price of $10 per share with his own money, or he may arrange a bank loan to buy the shares and then, if he wishes, immediately sell them for $20 a share, thereby making a profit of $10,000. If the price of Formidable's shares had not risen above the $10 per share option price within the option period, he would not, of course, have exercised his option and he would have lost nothing.

Stock Warrants.   To induce the public to buy its stock, a corporation may issue warrants. A warrant works in this fashion: Suppose the Cardboard Box Company, Inc., issues class A preferred shares at $15 per share. It gives to each purchaser of a share of that stock a *warrant*, a right to buy within a stated number of years one share of its *comon stock* at $10 per share. The common stock is selling for $5 a share when Mike buys shares of the class A preferred stock. If the common shares go up sufficiently in price during the option period Mike may either buy the common stock at the warrant price or sell the warrants at a profit. If the common shares do not enjoy a sufficient rise in price, Mike will not exercise the option and he loses nothing.

CORPORATE DISTRIBUTIONS TO SHAREHOLDERS

A person may buy shares in a company hoping they will go up in value so that they may be sold at a profit or may purchase shares in order to receive dividends. Dividends usually are paid in cash, but may be in property or in other shares of stock.

Of course, no one knows in advance whether any stock will go up or down in value or whether a corporation will pay dividends.

Distribution of Dividends

Amount of Dividends.   The amount of dividend a corporation pays upon each share of common stock is not fixed. Instead, the board of directors periodically, usually every 3 months, determines the amount of net profits available for distribution. (Occasionally a board may declare dividends payable from profits held in the treasury from earlier years.) From the sum determined by the board to be available, the dividends due on preferred shares are first allocated. The funds remaining are then divided equally among all the outstanding common shares. These dividends are paid to the common shareholders whose names are on the corporation's books on a certain date fixed by the board of directors. This is called the "record date." An extra dividend is occasionally declared by the directors at the end of the year if the corporation's profit warrants such a distribution.

Usually dividends are paid from only a part of the profits. The remainder is used for other corporate purposes, such as increasing its working capital, satisfying environmental protection laws, purchasing new plant and machinery, and extending product lines. However, the fact that profits are not paid out as dividends is not necessarily a disadvantage to the shareholders because the retained profits increase the company's worth and this, in turn, increases the per share value of its stock.

Stock Dividends.   A *stock dividend* is a dividend paid not in cash but in extra shares of stock. When a board of directors authorizes a stock dividend, it establishes the ratio of the number of shares that will be distributed to the number of shares already owned by the shareholders. To illustrate, assume that the Jolly Corporation's directors authorize a stock dividend on its common shares in the ratio of one for ten, and that Mary owns 100 shares of Jolly common stock. As a result, she receives a stock dividend of ten additional shares of the Jolly Corporation common stock. The directors may at the same time declare an ordinary dividend payable in cash.

A stock dividend does not increase the worth of Mary's interest in the corporation because her *proportionate* ownership interest in it remains unchanged. Her stock dividend, therefore, is not subject to income tax as she made no profit from its receipt; but when Mary *sells* her dividend shares, she must pay income tax on the profit from that sale.

A stock dividend in a growing company is welcomed by its shareholders because they acquire additional shares which may be profitably sold or upon which they may receive dividends.

Authority to Declare Dividends.   Most states give corporation directors the exclusive power, in their sound business judgment and discretion, to declare the amount and frequency of dividends on the company's common and preferred shares. However, dividends must be paid from the earnings of the corporation and not from its capital (funds derived from the sale of its securities). In making the judgment whether or not to declare a dividend, the directors must take into consideration the firm's working capital requirements and also the possible tax penalties that may be imposed if the firm retains earnings in excess of its anticipated needs.

If the directors with good judgment decide that the corporation did not earn sufficient money in a dividend period to make a distribution upon both its preferred and common shares, they may declare a dividend upon the preferred shares only. In that event holders of common shares receive no dividend payment.

In the case which follows, the court was asked by a stockholder to order a board of directors to declare a dividend.

CASE 38.1   **Zidell v. Zidell, Inc.**
560 P.2d 1086 (Or. 1977)

Facts: Arnold Zidell is a minority stockholder of Zidell, Inc., and of three other corporations operated as a group of family businesses. He formerly was employed by the corporations. They paid no dividends; instead, the stockholders were active in the firms and each received an adequate salary. After a disagreement, Arnold resigned his employment and was not reelected as a director.

Following his demand that the companies pay dividends, they did so, but Arnold contends that the dividends are unreasonably small. He now seeks to force the boards of directors of the four corporations to declare larger dividends. The essential basis for his demand is that the corporations have substantial retained earnings.

Question: May Arnold compel the corporation directors to increase the dividends?

Answer: No. The directors, in the exercise of their good judgment, may establish the amount of the dividends.

Reasoning: It is the duty of corporate directors to exercise good faith and fair dealing toward the stockholders. This duty is discharged if a decision as to dividends is made in good faith reflecting legitimate business purposes rather than the private interests of those in control. Here, the directors introduced evidence explaining that their conservative dividend policy was based upon the need for (a) expensive physical improvements to the company's property; (b) cash to buy an increased inventory; and (c) cash to cover bank loans. The size of the dividend therefore reflected legitimate purposes. Arnold did not sustain his burden of proof and his claim is dismissed.

Restrictions on Declaration of Dividends.   A corporation's charter may impose restrictions on the payment of dividends, or a corporation may agree by the terms of a loan or of a bond issue (discussed in a later paragraph) not to declare dividends on its common stock until the lenders or bondholders have been paid.

In addition, each state, to protect corporation creditors and stockholders, has laws requiring that dividends be distributed from a corporation's earnings and not from its capital. Payment of any dividend which would put a corporation in a position where it cannot pay its debts is uniformly prohibited.

Stock Splits   A stock split has elements in common with, but is not the same as, a stock dividend. The following illustrates a stock split. Suppose the Acorn Corporation's board of directors believes that the company's shares are being traded in the stock market at such a high price that sales of the shares have lagged. Acorn wants its shares to be actively traded because this attracts public recognition to the company, thereby benefiting the shareholders. The board, therefore, to make its shares attractive to purchasers, amends its articles of incorporation to reduce the par value of each share by splitting it into parts—such as in thirds—thereby increasing the number of shares issued. Each new share will now be worth one-third of the price of the original share.

For example, if Jane owns 500 shares of Acorn, Inc., and the stock is selling for $150 per share, Jane's stock has a total value of $75,000. When the directors split the stock "three for one," Jane receives a certificate for 1000 shares. She now owns 1500 shares of Acorn stock, three times as many as she owned before the split, each of which would now be worth $50. The total value of her Acorn shares is still $75,000.

A stock split is attractive to shareholders because (to continue the above example) if the market price of Acorn's shares had risen by $1 per share when Jane owned 500 shares she would have gained $500, whereas now that she owns 1500 shares, a rise of $1 per share means a gain of $1500. In addition, Jane will receive more dividends on the greater number of shares.

DEBT FINANCING

Means of Debt Financing

A corporation normally borrows money to carry on and expand its business. Its directors expect the borrowed funds to generate profits in excess of the interest the company must pay on the borrowed money. The process of corporate borrowing is called *debt financing*.

If a corporation intends to repay borrowed money within a short time, its authorized officers usually sign a promissory note for a bank loan. However, it is common for corporations to borrow money that does not have to be repaid for a number of years (usually 20). Such long-time obligations are undertaken by the issuance and sale of corporation bonds.

Issuance of Bonds

The laws of most states permit a board of directors to issue secured and unsecured corporate bonds without the approval of its stockholders, if so authorized by its articles of incorporation and bylaws.

Bond Indenture Agreement.   The terms of a bond issue are set out in an agreement, called a "bond indenture agreement," between the issuing corporation and a corporate trustee, usually a bank. The trustee acts as the representative of all the purchasers of the bonds, making sure that the terms of the indenture agreement are fulfilled. In accordance with the terms of the agreement, the corporation sells individual bonds to the public, usually in denominations of $1000 each, with interest payable semiannually. Thus, if you buy a 10 percent, 20-year, $1000 bond issued in 1985 by the Zero Corporation, and you do not sell it, you will be paid $50 every 6 months until the year 2005. Zero is obligated to repay to you the principal of the bond, $1000, on that date.

Many indenture agreements provide that the issuing corporation will deposit funds each year into a special account, called a "sinking fund," to be used to pay off the bonds. An indenture agreement may also provide that some of the bonds may be chosen by lottery each year and retired (paid off).

Unsecured Bonds.　An *unsecured bond* is called a "debenture." It is an unsecured promise of the issuing corporation to pay the interest on the bond as it becomes due and to pay the amount of the bond at its maturity. A holder of a debenture is an ordinary creditor of the issuing corporation. In the event the corporation is dissolved, the debenture holder has an unsecured claim against the corporate assets superior to any claim of the corporation's shareholders.

Just as a board of directors may issue callable preferred shares, they may issue bonds which are callable (redeemable) before their due date. The directors may also issue unsecured bonds which are convertible into another class of security. As is demonstrated in the following case, the holder of a debenture which is convertible into common shares has no assurance that the common shares will ever reach a price high enough to make the conversion profitable.

CASE 38.2　Kessler v. General Cable Corp.
155 Cal. Rptr. 95 (Cal. 1979)

Facts:　Kessler bought ten $1,000 Sprague Electric Company debentures. The bonds were convertible into Sprague common stock at the rate of 21.978 common shares for each $1,000 debenture. General Cable Corporation purchased a majority of the shares of Sprague's common stock. As a result, the stock ceased to be listed on the Exchange.

Kessler brought suit against both Sprague and General Cable claiming that, as the stock was no longer listed on the Stock Exchange, it would not increase in value; the conversion privilege would become meaningless; and he was thereby deprived of a valuable property right.

Question:　Has a convertible debenture holder any guarantee that the conversion will be of monetary value?

Answer:　No. The holder of a debenture has no guarantee that the bond can ever be profitably converted into stock.

Reasoning:　Convertible debentures are ordinarily sold at a lower rate of interest than non-convertible debentures. An investor who purchases a convertible debenture, in effect, gambles that the price of the shares to which the debenture may be converted will appreciate sufficiently in value to make its conversion profitable.

A debenture holder does not become a stockholder until the conversion takes place. He or she is merely a corporate creditor without any special status who has no basis on which to sue if the value of the conversion right is diminished. Therefore, although the debentures owned by Kessler may never reach the point at which it would be profitable for him to convert them into shares of common stock, neither Sprague Electric nor General Cable is obligated to Kessler in any amount other than that stated on the face of the bonds.

Secured Bonds.   A corporation may pledge any of its assets as security to guarantee repayment of a bond issue. Such security may be any specified asset, such as heavy machinery, buildings, railroad cars, or income of the corporation from specific sources. In the event a corporation defaults in paying a bond obligation, the trustee may cause the pledged assets to be sold to satisfy the bondholders' claims.

TRANSFER OF SECURITIES

Corporate securities, both shares of stock and bonds, are negotiable and may be freely transferred. This part of the chapter deals with how stocks and bonds may be transferred and how lost or stolen certificates may be replaced.

Stock Transfers

A certificate representing ownership of shares of stock normally is issued by a corporation to the named share owner. If you own 100 shares of stock in the Beta Corporation and you decide to sell them, you sign (indorse) the certificate for those shares in the space provided on its reverse side and either deliver it to the new owner or, more likely, deliver it to a stockbroker. The broker arranges for its sale. The certificate is sent by the new owner or by his stockbroker to the Beta Corporation, which issues a new certificate in the name of the new owner.

Shares Held in "Street Name."   It is not unusual for a purchaser of shares to instruct his or her stockbroker to buy the shares and to hold them subject to the purchaser's future instructions. In that event, the shares are held by the brokerage firm in its name and credited to the client's account. This arrangement is called "holding a security in a street (or nominee) name," and no certificate is issued to the client who placed the order.

Restricted Shares.   An individual's freedom to sell shares of stock may be limited by some contractual understanding, with, for example, a bank from which he pledges the shares as security for a loan. In addition, when shares are issued by a corporation to effect a merger, or a taking over of one company by another, the stock so issued is "restricted" and may not be sold for 2 years in accordance with the rules of the Securities and Exchange Commission (SEC).

For example, assume that Joe is the majority stockholder (owning 51 percent or more of the shares) in the Blue Streak Corporation, a closely held company. The Acme Corporation buys Blue Streak and merges the two companies. As part of the transaction, Acme pays Joe $1,000,000 in Acme stock. This stock is *restricted*, and cannot be sold by Joe for 2 years. After that time, Joe is free to dispose of the stock as he pleases.

Most courts hold that the owner of a majority of a corporation's shares is free to sell those shares at a premium price (a price over the normal market price) without being obliged to give the same opportunity to minority shareholders. However, this right does not exist if the majority shareholder, through such a sale, would commit a fraud or other act of bad faith against the corporation or against the minority shareholders. This view is expressed in the following case.

CASE 38.3   Zetlin v. Hanson Holdings, Inc.
421 N.Y.S.2d 877 (N.Y. 1979)

Facts: Hanson Holdings, Inc., owned a controlling interest in Gable Industries, Inc. Zetlin owned approximately two percent of Gable's outstanding shares. At a time when the shares of Gable Industries were selling on the open market for $7.38 per share, Hanson sold its shares to Flintkote Co. for approximately $22 per share. Zetlin claims that the controlling shareholder (Hanson Holdings) had no authority to sell its shares without giving minority shareholders the opportunity to sell their shares to the buyer at the same price.

Question: Is the owner of a majority of a corporation's shares free to sell those shares whenever and at whatever price he or she wishes?

Answer: Yes, provided no fraudulent act is involved.

Reasoning: Those who invest the capital necessary to acquire a dominant position in the ownership of a corporation have the right to control that corporation. For this reason controlling shares usually command a premium price. The premium is the amount the investor is willing to pay for the privilege of directly influencing the corporation's affairs.

As a rule, a controlling stockholder has the same right as any other stockholder to buy or to sell stock in the corporation. Absent a fraud or other act of bad faith, a controlling shareholder is free to sell his or her shares at a premium price and the purchaser is free to buy them.

Bond Transfers   Most bonds are issued (registered) in the names of their owners. Bonds, like stock certificates, are transferred by indorsement and delivery.

Some bonds are *coupon bonds* (also called "bearer bonds") and are not registered in the name of any owner. When an interest payment is due, the holder of such a bond cuts off ("clips") a little coupon attached to the bond and deposits it in a bank for collection. The coupon represents the interest due upon the bond on the date stated on the face of the coupon. An unregistered bond is transferred merely by delivering it to the transferee. Because of the ease with which profits from their sale can escape taxation, issuance of new unregistered bonds has been prohibited since July 1, 1983.

Lost or Stolen Certificates   If you lose or accidentally destroy a stock certificate registered in your name, or if it has been stolen from you, you may obtain a new one from the corporation which issued it. In order to do this you must, within a reasonable time after discovery of its loss, notify the issuing corporation that you are the true owner of the certificate and explain the circumstances of its loss.

The following case discusses the question of "reasonable time" within which an issuing corporation should be notified of the loss of a stock certificate.

CASE 38.4

Weller v. American Telephone & Telegraph Co.
290 A.2d 842 (Del. 1972)

Facts: In 1968 Mrs. Weller, a 94-year old widow, lived with Kenneth Jumper and his wife. Mrs. Weller gradually turned over her business affairs to Jumper. He told her that he was depositing her dividend checks in her bank and she believed him. In 1970 she discovered that Jumper had forged her signature on her AT&T stock certificates, had opened a trading account in their joint names with a stockbroker, and that, through the stockbroker, he had sold the stock to a bona fide purchaser.

Several weeks after discovering what had happened, Mrs. Weller notified AT&T and requested a replacement certificate. The corporation refused and Weller sued to recover the damages she had sustained.

Question: Is the owner of a stock entitled to recover a lost certificate from the issuing company?

Answer: Yes, if the owner notifies the corporation within a reasonable time after the loss is discovered.

Reasoning: Mrs. Weller was infirm and of advanced years and she had every reasonable right to trust Jumper whom she knew intimately. Under the circumstances Mrs. Weller did not act unreasonably when she did not check her bank accounts. Considering Mrs. Weller's condition and state of health, the fact that a few weeks elapsed before she gave the company notice of her loss, did not bar that notice from having been given in a "reasonable time." The corporation should therefore issue a replacement certificate for the same number of shares that were stolen, together with accrued unpaid dividends. [For repayment of the loss it had suffered, AT&T sued the brokerage company that had guaranteed Jumper's and Mrs. Weller's signatures in the sale of the stock.]

STATE AND FEDERAL CONTROL OVER ISSUANCE OF SECURITIES

A large body of law controls issuance of corporate securities that are to be sold to the public. For the most part the regulations are too technical for inclusion in a book presenting the basic principles of business law. We should recognize, however, that all states as well as the federal government have enacted laws designed to protect the public from fraudulent or overly speculative stock promotion schemes.

State Laws State statutes which control the issuance of securities, commonly known as *blue-sky laws*, prevent corporations from taking advantage of the public with schemes having no more foundation than "so many feet of blue sky." Although they differ in detail, these laws normally contain provisions which (1) require a corporate issuer to register proposed securities with a designated state agency, (2) require individuals who deal in securities to be licensed, (3) prohibit fraud in the sale of securities, and (4) impose severe penalties for submitting false or misleading data.

Federal Laws   The principal federal laws controlling the issuance of securities are the **Securities Act of 1933** and the **Securities Exchange Act of 1934**. The latter act created the Securities and Exchange Commission (SEC) which has broad rule-making powers. These acts regulate both the issuance of new securities by corporations and the sale or purchase of existing securities by investors. They also control the extent to which securities may be purchased on credit ("on margin").

The laws and SEC regulations require registration with the SEC of securities which are to be offered for public sale, and the periodic publication of informative reports by companies which have issued securities. A company report, available to the public, must include, among other things, its financial statements, and information about the company's management, business operations, outstanding securities and, in addition, any pertinent information furnished by its auditors.

The federal acts also impose civil and criminal penalties on directors, officers, and others—including the company's lawyers and accountants—who promote or participate in deceptive practices in connection with the purchase or sale of securities.

SUMMARY

When a corporation secures money from the sale of its stock, it is engaging in equity financing. Every corporation issues shares of common stock. It may, in addition, issue other kinds and classes of stock. Each share of stock may have a fixed value (par value) on the books of the company or it may be of no-par value. A share of stock represents a unit of ownership of the corporation.

Among a shareholder's rights are the right to receive a part of the company's net profits (the sums distributed are called "dividends") and the right to receive a proportionate share of its net assets if the corporation is dissolved. A shareholder is not a creditor of the corporation. Holders of preferred shares have a right to receive dividends before dividends are paid to holders of common shares. However, while common shareholders have the right to vote at stockholders' meetings, preferred shareholders generally do not have that right.

Cumulative preferred shares are those upon which a corporation is obligated to make good a past failure to pay the full amount of dividend to which those shares are entitled. Convertible preferred shares may be converted by the holder to some other designated class of shares issued by the same corporation.

Dividends are paid to shareholders from the net profits earned by a corporation, not from its capital. A dividend is usually paid in cash but it may be in stock or in other property of the corporation.

When a corporation borrows money, it is engaging in debt financing. In order to borrow money which may be repaid over a long period of time, a board of directors authorizes the issuance of bonds. Bonds may be backed by some security or they may be unsecured. Some bonds may also be convertible into another security of the same company or may be redeemable by the company before their maturity date.

Except under special circumstances, a corporation's securities are freely transferable by the indorsement of the holder. There are procedures whereby the owner of a lost or stolen stock certificate can secure its replacement.

Government laws and regulations control the issuance of corporate securities that are to be sold to the public. In order to prevent fraud, an issuer is required to furnish complete information about the security and the corporation which proposes to issue it.

REVIEW QUESTIONS

1. What is meant when it is said that a corporation is engaged in equity financing?

2. (a) If you own shares of the common stock of General Motors Corporation, is it correct to say that you are one of the owners of that corporation? Explain. (b) As a shareholder, do you have any voice in the policies of General Motors? Explain.

3. Explain the difference between shares of common stock and shares of preferred stock.

4. Explain the difference between cumulative preferred shares and noncumulative preferred shares.

5. Would you rather own cumulative preferred shares or noncumulative preferred shares? Why?

6. If you own a stock certificate which states in part that you may turn the shares back to the company and get other shares in exchange, what is the correct name for this type of security?

7. (a) If you own a stock certificate which states in part that the company may buy it back from you, what is the certificate called? (b) Would you rather own such a stock certificate or the one described in question 6?

8. What is meant by the par value of a share of stock?

9. (a) What are corporation dividends? (b) Out of what corporate funds are they paid? (c) Must a corporation pay dividends? Explain.

10. Comment upon this statement: "If a company splits its shares of stock in half, then the package of shares a shareholder owns is worth one-half as much as it was worth before the split."

11. (a) What is a corporate bond? (b) What is a bond indenture agreement?

12. Why does a person clip coupons?

CASE PROBLEMS

1. King owned preferred shares of the Edgerton Corporation. The corporation paid no preferred dividends for 5 years. Ultimately, being unable to pay its business obligations, a receiver was appointed to handle its affairs. The receiver asked all the corporation's creditors to file their claims. King filed a claim for unpaid accumulated dividends that had not been paid to him. Should the receiver consider King's claim? Explain the reason for your answer.

2. In May 1980, Sherman purchased 100 shares of the preferred stock of the Pepin Corporation. On May 1, 1983, its board of directors authorized the issuance of 20-year bonds. Under the bond indenture, the corporation agreed (**a**) to establish and maintain a sinking fund to provide for the retirement of a portion of the bonds before maturity, and (**b**) to declare no dividends on its common or preferred shares until there would be deposited in the sinking fund from the net profits of the corporation 10 percent of the total amount of the bond issue or until May 1, 1985, whichever comes first.

Sherman contends that the corporation has breached its obligation with respect to the preferred shares he owns because they are no longer preferred and have been reduced in value. He demands that Pepin pay him the value of his preferred shares (the amount he paid for them) in exchange for his surrender of the shares to the company. Is there merit in Sherman's contention? Explain.

3. Helen owned all the outstanding shares of Realty, Inc., except 2 percent which was held by Trust Bank. Helen ran the business. Each year over a period of years Realty earned a profit but it declared no dividends. When Trust Bank demanded that a dividend be declared, Helen replied that she believed in keeping money in the company treasury "for a rainy day." Can the bank force the board of directors, controlled by Helen, to declare a dividend? Explain.

4. In 1964 Sam agreed to buy Fine's shares in the Frontier Corporation. To make the purchase, Sam was to pay Fine, over a period of 2 years, $600,000 worth of Keller Corp. shares which Sam owned. As a part of their agreement, it was understood that the total number of Keller Corp. shares Fine would be entitled to receive could not exceed 30,000 and that this number would be "proportionately adjusted for any stock split." Sam made a down payment of 15,000 shares of Keller stock.

Before the 2 years had expired, Fine received a stock dividend of 3000 shares on the 15,000 shares Sam had paid him. Sam claims that the 3000 shares Fine received as a stock dividend should be credited against the purchase price. Fine denies this claim. Who is right, Sam or Fine? Explain.

5. Richard, the majority shareholder in Laurel, Inc., sold his shares to Steven at a price that was four times over their market price. Steven thereby assumed control of the business. Clagett was a minority shareholder in Laurel. He did not learn about the sale to Steven until some time later. Under the new management the Laurel shares went down in value. Clagett claims that if he had known of the impending change in management from Richard to Steven, he would have disposed of his shares. He also says that the fact that Steven so overpaid Richard for the shares makes it evident that Richard entered into a transaction which was a fraud upon the interests of Clagett and the other minority shareholders. Clagett therefore claims damages for the loss in value of the Laurel shares that Richard's actions generated. Does Clagett's claim have merit?

CHAPTER 39

MANAGEMENT OF CORPORATIONS

The management power structure of corporations may be described as a pyramid of delegated authority. At the top, the state creates the corporation and empowers it with all the authority contained in the articles of incorporation and the general corporation law. Next in the pyramid of authority are the shareholders who have the right to elect the directors and the ultimate power over the bylaws. The bylaws delegate authority to the directors and confer upon them the power to appoint or remove corporate officers. To facilitate the day-to-day operation of the business, directors adopt resolutions delegating specific duties and responsibilities to the officers. They, in turn, delegate particular duties to subordinate personnel.

A corporation's powers and potential liabilities for unauthorized or illegal acts are discussed in the first part of this chapter. The last part outlines respective powers, duties, and liabilities of directors and officers. Chapter 40 examines the managerial role of shareholders, their legal rights and remedies, and their potential liabilities.

THE CORPORATE ENTITY: POWERS AND LIABILITIES

The constitution and statutes of the state of incorporation establish the limits within which a corporation must operate. Its articles of incorporation cannot confer greater powers than those conferred on corporations by the state.

Sources of Corporate Powers

The term *corporate powers* refers to a corporation's legal capacity to carry out its business purposes. A corporation's powers may be express or implied.

Express Powers.   *Express powers* are powers granted in state statutes or specified in the articles of incorporation of the corporation. Corporation statutes set out the general powers which are traditionally granted to all business corporations, including the power to exist in perpetuity, to sue and be sued, to acquire or transfer real or personal property, to have a seal, and to make bylaws. The Model Business Corporation Act and the **Delaware statute** specifically includes a corporation's power to make gifts for charitable or educational purposes; to adopt profit sharing, pension, or stock option plans as incentive compensation for directors, officers, or employees; to be a partner or joint venturer; to guarantee obligations of others; and to indemnify against personal liability those directors, officers, and other agents who act for the corporation in good faith and without negligence.

Incorporators have wide discretion in drafting the articles of incorporation. All states require the articles to set forth the corporation's business purposes, but they may usually be stated in broad terms, such as "this corporation may engage in any lawful business." (See Chapter 37 for discussion of drafting and filing articles of incorporation.) The benefit of including such a broad statement in the articles is that the corporation may diversify its activities without continually amending the articles. For example, the modern-day "conglomerate" may engage in activities ranging from production of steel to drilling for oil to marketing farm machinery, all under the same "all-purpose" clause in its articles of incorporation.

Implied Powers.   Narrow interpretations of express powers can hamper a corporation's business operations. To prevent this, the courts developed the doctrine of implied powers, which gives corporations authority to do things that are reasonably necessary to carry out express powers and purposes. For example, many state statutes permit corporations to make gifts for charitable or educational purposes but are silent on the question of gifts for political purposes. In *Marsili v. Pacific Gas and Electric Co.* the California court allowed a gas and electric company to donate $10,000 to a campaign to defeat a ballot proposition in San Fransisco that would have raised the corporation's taxes significantly.[1] The court said that corporations have implied powers to do acts that are reasonably necessary to carry out their express powers. The ballot proposition would have adversely affected the business of the corporation.

Limitations on Corporate Powers

Limitations in Statutes.   All states have special statutes which protect the public by limiting the powers of particular kinds of corporations, such as banks, savings and loan associations, public utilities, and insurance companies. Thus, the articles of incorporation for such corporations may not contain an "all-purpose" clause. Instead, the articles would state a single purpose for the corporation such as "to engage in the banking business."

Most states have now enacted statutes which permit incorporation by professionals, such as doctors and lawyers, who have a similar responsibility to the public. Professionals often pursue their practices in corporate form in order to qualify for tax-deductible benefits, such as health insurance and retirement plans. As a general rule, incorporation does *not* give professionals the advantage of limited liability.

Limitations in Articles.   The articles may limit the broad powers granted to corporations in a general corporation statute. Such limitation may be necessary because of a special statute or because of voluntary corporate planning. For example, the articles may restrict a corporation to a particular business, or require the shareholders to approve certain transactions, such as the purchase of real property. These limitations on a corporation's power and authority guide the directors and officers who must use the shareholders' investment for the purposes stated in the articles. If the corporation later wishes to diversify or expand its powers, and it is legal under the state statutes to do so, the articles of incorporation would have to be amended. This procedure is discussed in the next chapter.

Effect of Ultra Vires Acts

"Ultra vires" means *beyond the powers* of a corporation. Thus, if the articles limit a corporation's purpose to manufacturing machine tools, a contract to purchase wood for the purpose of making yo-yos would be ultra vires. What is the legal effect of ultra vires acts?

The Ultra Vires Defense.   The idea that a corporation's acts or contracts could be ultra vires was first used in the courts by parties defending suits for breach of contract. The defending party (the corporation itself or the other party to the contract) would attempt to escape liability for contractual obligations by claiming that

[1]124 Cal. Rptr. 313 (1975).

the contract was ultra vires—outside the scope of the corporation's powers. It was argued that the corporation lacked legal capacity to contract ultra vires and that the contract was therefore void. This defense was often unrelated to the intent of the parties or to the merits of the case, and resulted in hardship to one party or the other. For example, a corporation could accept the benefits of a contract and then refuse to perform its side of the bargain on the ground that the contract was ultra vires.

Modern statutes do not recognize lack of corporate capacity to contract (ultra vires) as a defense in suits seeking to impose liability for breach of contract. The practical result is that a corporation may, in fact, contract in excess of its powers and the contract will be enforceable by either party.

Although a few courts still recognize the ultra vires defense, its applicability is generally limited to executory (wholly unperformed) contracts. Parties who have benefited from a partially performed contract are estopped from raising the ultra vires defense. Courts will not disturb a fully performed ultra vires contract.

Ultra Vires as Grounds in Direct Suits.   Most jurisdictions permit ultra vires acts to be used as grounds for "direct" suits. For example: The state attorney general may sue to enjoin or dissolve a corporation engaged in unauthorized business, or a shareholder may seek to enjoin the corporation's ultra vires acts. The corporation or a shareholder may bring an action to recover damages from directors and officers for acts already committed. An unusual application of these rules is presented in the following case.

CASE 39.1   Cross v. Midtown Club, Inc.
365 A.2d 1227 (Conn. 1976)

Facts: Samuel Cross was a member of The Midtown Club, Inc., a nonprofit, nonstock corporation. The certificate of incorporation set forth that the sole purpose of the corporation was "to provide facilities for the serving of luncheon or other meals to members." Cross sought to bring a female to lunch with him, and both he and his guest were refused seating. On three different occasions Cross submitted applications for membership on behalf of a different female. The applications were either ignored or rejected. Cross filed an action for declaratory judgment and sought an injunction against the board of directors, ordering the admission of his candidate to membership.

Question: Was the corporation's policy of not accepting women as members or as guests for lunch ultra vires?

Answer: Yes. The corporation exceeded its powers.

Reasoning: The corporation had the express power granted in its charter and those incidental powers which were necessary to effect its purpose, that being to serve lunch to its members. Since the club was not formed for the purpose of having an exclusively male luncheon club, it could not be considered necessary to its stated purpose for the club to have the implied power to exclude women. The court said, "Given the scope of the entry of women today into the business and professional life of the community and the changing status of women before the law and in society, it would be anomalous indeed for this court to conclude that it is either necessary or convenient to the stated purpose for which it was organized for this club to exclude women as members or guests." The actions and policies of the corporation and the board of directors were ultra vires.

Declaratory judgment was granted.

Corporate Liability for Torts

Corporate agents sometimes engage in acts which are legally within the corporation's powers (*intra vires*) but which, nevertheless, infringe on the legal rights of others. Such infringement may constitute a tort against an individual or a business firm. The various torts, intentional and unintentional, are discussed in detail in Chapters 3 and 4.

Under the agency law doctrine of respondeat superior, an injured party may hold the corporation liable for the torts of agents acting within the scope of employment. Respondeat superior is fully discussed in Chapter 21. The rules and rationales presented in that chapter apply to corporations and may impose vicarious liability on the corporate principal for acts of its officers and employees as agents.

DIRECTORS, OFFICERS, AND EMPLOYEES: POWERS, DUTIES, AND LIABILITIES

Powers of the Board of Directors

Many state statutes provide that "all corporate powers shall be exercised by or under authority of a board of directors." It is obvious, however, that in most corporations it is impossible for the directors to personally exercise corporate power and therefore the board delegates management to officers and employees. Although the board delegates the daily management of corporate affairs to designated corporate officers, this delegation does not diminish the directors' responsibility for corporate policy decisions.

Number of Directors. Ten states require a minimum of three directors[2] and twelve states require only one director.[3] The remaining states offer a compromise: Although there is a general requirement of three directors, the number of directors need not exceed the number of shareholders. Thus, if there is only one shareholder, there need be only one director. This trend reflects the growing importance of a close corporation owned by a single shareholder-director. The articles or bylaws must fix the number of directors but need not set out their qualifications.

Election and Removal of Directors by Board. Directors are elected by the shareholders, usually at the annual shareholders' meeting. Typically, directors serve

---

[2]Alabama, Colorado, Hawaii, Maryland, Mississippi, Montana, New Hampshire, North Dakota, Oklahoma, and Utah.
[3]Arizona, Delaware, Florida, Michigan, Missouri, New Jersey, New Mexico, Oregon, South Dakota, Texas, West Virginia, and Wisconsin.

a 1-year term, although it is permissible to provide for longer terms. A vacancy occurs if a director dies or resigns during his or her term. Ordinarily, it is not necessary to call a special shareholders' meeting to fill the vacancy. A majority of directors can elect a director to fill a predecessor's unexpired term. If the directors do so, they can fill vacancies until the next election of directors by the shareholders. Most statutes also permit the board to remove a director who has been declared insane or convicted of a felony. In addition, the holders of a majority of voting stock may remove a director at any time, with or without cause. This removal power tends to make directors responsive to the wishes of majority shareholders, particularly in closely held corporations.

Powers of Board.   The board of directors has the power to take any action related to managing the corporate enterprise which the articles or state statutes permit. The directors may also amend or repeal bylaws. As part of managing the ordinary business affairs of the corporation, the directors normally approve or ratify reports and authorize officers to take important actions (e.g., opening bank accounts, borrowing money, and signing contracts).

The board of directors has the power to fix its own compensation. Obviously, the directors have a conflict of interest in setting their own fees and must be careful not to set an excessive amount. Since directors meet only as needed (once a month, once a year), the compensation received is seldom very large. By contrast, corporate officers are full-time agents and often are entitled to receive large compensation packages.

Formal Actions of the Board

The directors usually meet as a board at regular intervals. The frequency of meetings depends on the size of the corporation. The directors of General Motors might meet every month; the directors of a closely held corporation might meet once a year.

Directors' actions are reflected in formal board resolutions. Resolutions can generally be adopted by a majority of the directors voting at any meeting at which a quorum is present. (A quorum normally consists of a majority of the number of directors specified in the articles or bylaws.) A director is not allowed to give a proxy, that is, the director may not designate someone else to cast a vote for him or her. Thus, if several directors are unable to attend a meeting, important action may be delayed.

Most statutes acknowledge the need for swift, informal action, especially in close corporations, by permitting the directors to adopt resolutions without a meeting by giving their unanimous written consent to a specified transaction or policy statement.

All resolutions are recorded in the corporate minute book.

Authority of Officers and Employees

Officers and employees are *agents* of the corporation. Directors are not agents of the corporation. They do not act on behalf of the corporation; they simply meet as needed to set policy and delegate management to corporate officers.

Election of Officers.   The directors elect (and remove) the corporate officers and fix their salaries. As a general rule, the bylaws provide for a president, one or more vice presidents, a secretary, and a treasurer and describe the general duties and authority of each officer. In addition, specific duties and responsibilities are assigned to the officers by the board. One person may hold more than one office but, in many states, the same person cannot be president and secretary.

Limitations on Authority of Officers and Employees.   As agents of the corporation, officers and employees negotiate contracts with third persons. The law of agency, discussed fully in Chapter 20, imposes liability on the corporation as a principal for contracts made by its agents within the scope of authority. The corporation is liable if the agent acted with express, implied, or apparent authority. The source of express authority of corporate officers is the corporate bylaws and resolutions adopted by the board. For example, bylaws usually provide that the president is the "chief executive officer of the corporation and has the power to enter contracts on behalf of the corporation." A corporate officer has implied power to bind the corporation and may do those things reasonably necessary to accomplish the task expressly delegated to him or her. Apparent authority involves conduct of the corporation that leads a reasonable third person to suppose that the agent has authority to enter into the particular transaction. The customary duties of the officer or employee will limit his or her apparent authority. For example, a third person may reasonably suppose that a president has the authority to enter a contract to purchase real estate for the corporation, but such a contract made by the treasurer cannot be argued to be within the scope of his or her apparent authority. It is basic agency law that the unauthorized acts of officers and employees can bind the corporation if it later ratifies such acts.

The following case discusses the actual and apparent authority of corporate officers.

CASE 39.2   Molasky Enterprises, Inc. v. Carps, Inc.
615 S.W.2d 83 (Mo. App. 1981)

Facts: Herbert and Emile Carp, president and executive vice-president, respectively, of Carps, Inc., applied for and received a personal loan of $267,000 from a bank. The bank required a promissory note to be signed by Herbert and Emile and to be guaranteed by another party. Herbert then co-signed the note in the name of the corporation. Herbert and Emile defaulted on the note. Molasky succeeded to the rights of the bank and made formal demand for payment on Carps, Inc. The corporation refused to pay, asserting that Herbert had no authority to co-sign the note on behalf of the corporation. Molasky filed suit alleging that Herbert was authorized to sign the note, or in the alternative that the corporation had ratified the transaction. The trial court rendered judgment for Carps, Inc. Molasky appealed.

Question: Did Herbert have authority to co-sign a personal note on behalf of the corporation? Did the corporation ratify the transaction?

Answer: No. Herbert did not have actual or apparent authority to sign the note on behalf of the corporation. There was no ratification.

Reasoning: The corporate minutes contained no authorization for Herbert or Emile to guarantee the payment of an indebtedness of officers. The president of a corporation is empowered to transact without special authorization from the board of directors all acts of an ordinary nature which are incident to his or her office by usage or necessity. The court said, "Authority to transact acts of an ordinary nature in the usual course of business does not include authority to sign accommodation paper or as security for a third person." The court rejected the allegation of apparent authority, stating that, "It is the conduct of the principal not the acts of the agent which create apparent authority." The board of directors did not ratify the unauthorized act in this case since there was no indication that there was a full disclosure of the facts to all members of the board and that they actually knew what had happened. The court said, "The first essential in ratification is that the principal have full knowledge of all the material facts at the time he is charged with having accepted the transaction as his own."

Judgment was affirmed.

Duties of Directors, Officers, and Employees

Directors are *not* corporate agents, but their basic duties are similar to those duties arising from the agency relation which officers and employees bear to the corporate principal.

Fiduciary Duty of Directors, Officers, and Employees. Directors, officers and employees owe a fiduciary duty to the corporation. State and federal statutes define fiduciary duty in broad terms, such as "loyalty, good faith, and fair dealing." Courts have used similar phrases, such as "honest conduct" and "independent judgment" to define the fiduciary duty. Directors and officers have been held liable to the corporation for breach of fiduciary duty where they acted for two principals in the same transaction, received secret compensation, or used confidential information for personal gain.

Conflicts of Interest. Conflicts of interest between a director, officer, or employee —and the corporation—arise in many ways. For example, a director may have an interest in a competing business, contract with an outside company owned by the director to furnish goods or services to the corporation, or use corporate funds or employees in an outside venture.

The view followed by Delaware, California, and the Model Act is that a contract between a corporation and one or more directors, officers, or employees is enforceable if:

1. The contract is "fair and reasonable to the corporation," or
2. The conflict is fully disclosed or known to the *disinterested* directors, or to the shareholders, and either body approves or ratifies the transaction without counting the vote or consent of the *interested* parties.

For example, suppose a corporation wishes to buy a parcel of land from a director. The agreement to purchase the land will be upheld if the price and terms are fair to the corporation. If the price or terms are not considered fair, the courts will still enforce the contract if there is a full disclosure and the disinterested directors approve the purchase. A contract that is neither fair nor approved by disinterested directors (or shareholders) is subject to rescission by the corporation.

The Corporate Opportunity Doctrine.   The corporate opportunity doctrine prohibits directors and officers from seizing business opportunities which may be of interest to the corporation. Although case law does not clearly define the elements of a corporate opportunity, an opportunity is generally held to belong to the corporation if:

1. A director or officer becomes aware of the opportunity in his or her corporate capacity, or
2. The corporation customarily deals in such an opportunity, or
3. It is developed with corporate capital, facilities, or personnel.

A clear example of the courts' application of the corporate opportunity doctrine is the following: Suppose a director of a washing machine manufacturing corporation learns that a supplier of washing machine parts is interested in selling its business. The director is not allowed to buy the parts business but must notify the corporation that the opportunity exists. In addition, since the director became aware of the opportunity in his or her corporate capacity, the director may not remain silent, then resign, and later purchase the parts business.

There are situations when a director or officer may take advantage of an opportunity presented during his or her term of office. A corporate opportunity is not usually held to exist if:

1. The corporation cannot obtain financing for the project, or
2. Involvement by the corporation would be ultra vires, or
3. The director or officer involved discloses his or her interest and a *disinterested* majority of directors votes against the proposal.

Such opportunities may be pursued by any director, officer, or employee.

The following case illustrates the corporate opportunity doctrine.

CASE 39.3   Morad, et al. v. Coupanas
361 So. 2d 6 (Ala. 1978)

Facts: Bio-Lab, Inc. was formed in 1972 and did business in Birmingham. It engaged in the business of acquiring blood plasma from paid donors and selling the plasma to biological manufacturing companies. Joseph Morad was president of the corporation. One of the purposes of creating Bio-Lab was to expand and open new offices in the state, including Tuscaloosa. By mid-1973 dissension had arisen, and in February 1974 Morad incorporated another plasma business, Med-Lab, Inc., that began operating in Tuscaloosa in September 1974. Morad served as president of both corporations. $44,000 had been required to establish Med-Lab. In 1974 Bio-Lab had only $24,300 available for this purpose. Bio-Lab had lost donors to Med-Lab and the two corporations sold 95% of their products to the same three biological manufacturing corporations. Coupanas, a shareholder in Bio-Lab Inc., filed suit individually and for the benefit of Bio-Lab, against Med-Lab, Morad, and others, alleging breach of fiduciary duty. The trial court rendered judgment for Coupanas and the defendants appealed.

Question: Did the formation of Med-Lab amount to a breach of duty by Morad?

Answer: Yes. Morad violated the corporate opportunity doctrine.

Reasoning: The court stated the law as follows: "If there is presented to a corporate officer or director a business opportunity which the corporation is financially able to undertake, is, from its nature, in the line of the corporation's business and is of practical advantage to it, is one in which the corporation has an interest or a reasonable expectancy, and, by embracing the opportunity, the self-interest of the officer or director will be brought into conflict with that of his corporation, the law will not permit him to seize the opportunity for himself." Here one of the purposes of Bio-Lab was to expand into new areas, including Tuscaloosa. The court also discussed the corporation's financial ability. In 1974 Bio-Lab had paid a "rather high" dividend of $20,000. If the dividend had not been paid, which is often done when a corporation wishes to expand, Bio-Lab clearly would have had the financial ability to expand. Further, there was no evidence that Bio-Lab could not have borrowed the necessary funds.

The judgment was affirmed that the stock of Med-Lab would be held for the benefit of Bio-Lab, Inc.

Liabilities of Directors and Officers

Directors and Officers who abuse the corporate powers entrusted to them are generally liable to the corporation for breach of the duty of obedience, due diligence, or loyalty. In addition, state or federal statutes impose civil or criminal liability on officers or directors for willful nonpayment of taxes, for violation of antitrust laws, and for illegal stock issues.

Liability for Ultra Vires Acts.   As stated earlier in this chapter, the corporation or a shareholder may hold directors, officers, and other agents liable for damages resulting from their ultra vires acts. Liability may be avoided in some cases if the directors or managerial agents acted in good faith or upon the advice of counsel, or if the shareholders ratify the ultra vires transaction.

Special Liabilities of Directors.   Directors are liable to the corporation for negligence. "Dummy" directors who fail to attend meetings, keep informed on corporate affairs, or review financial statements or legal opinions prepared by the corporation's accountants or attorneys, are liable for any injury which such omissions cause the corporation. However, courts have held that directors need only exercise ordinary care in the conduct of their duties. Thus, directors are not liable for an investment that turns bad, nor are they liable for keeping large amounts of cash in noninterest-bearing checking accounts, provided these actions would have been taken by "an ordinarily prudent person" in the management of his or her own affairs.

A growing number of state and federal statutes impose civil liability on directors who cause the corporation unlawfully to declare dividends, reacquire shares, or distribute assets in disregard of creditors rights.

The following case illustrates the liability of corporate directors and officers for negligence.

CASE 39.4   Speer v. Dighton Grain, Inc., et al.
624 P.2d 952 (Kan. 1981)

Facts: Walter Gormley was the manager of a newly formed grain elevator business. At the end of the first fiscal year the auditor's report showed that Gormley had written some $87,000 in corporate checks to himself. The record of grain shipment was inadequate and the inventory of grain on hand was short. The audit report contained recommendations for new procedures, including among other things, that two signatures be required on every check, that Gormley discontinue his unauthorized use of corporate funds, and that there be more frequent directors' meetings. None of these recommendations were followed. Gormley continued to use corporation money for his own personal use. After two years of operation, the doors of Dighton Grain, Inc. were closed, the corporation owing $400,000 to unsecured creditors. Walter Gormley was convicted of misappropriations from the business. Russell Speer, a creditor, sued the directors and officers of the corporation and obtained personal judgments against them. Defendants appealed.

Question: Were the directors and officers guilty of negligence? May a creditor recover a judgment against them?

Answer: Yes. The directors and officers were negligent. However, a creditor may not recover damages in this situation.

Reasoning: The court found the directors were guilty of gross negligence and mismanagement. The directors disregarded the auditor's report for over a year. Gormley remained in charge of the business and continued to use corporate funds. The standard of duty by which a corporate director's conduct is judged is "that measure of attention, care, and ability which the ordinary director and officer of corporations of this kind would be reasonably and properly expected to bestow upon the affairs of the corporation." However, the directors' negligence, the court said, "involves a breach of duty to the corporation for which only the corporation or someone suing on its behalf may recover. . . . There is no statutory authority authorizing suit by a creditor in the present case."

The judgments were reversed.

Special Liabilities of Officers.   A corporate officer who contracts in excess of his or her authority is personally liable to third parties for breach of implied warranty of authority. An officer who fails to disclose the corporate principal as a party to the contract may also be held personally liable by the third party. In agency law terminology, the officer is acting for an "undisclosed principal."

Defenses of
Directors,
Officers, and
Agents

In some situations a director who is sued by the corporation or a shareholder for an alleged wrong may assert the defense of "the business judgment rule." The business judgment rule holds that directors are not liable for errors in judgment if they act in good faith, without negligence, and in the best interests of the corporation. For example, a director would not be liable if he voted not to invest in what turned out to be a profitable venture, provided the director's vote was in good faith and without negligence. The law of most states protects directors who act in reliance on data, opinions, reports, or financial statements which a knowledgeable officer, employee, lawyer, public accountant, or board committee represents to be correct.

A corporate director or officer who is sued for an alleged wrong may spend large sums of money in attorney fees and court costs to defend the action. If the defense is successful, the defendant may seek "indemnification" (reimbursement) from the corporation. A corporation can indemnify directors, officers, employees, or other agents against personal liability in any proceeding resulting from any act or decision made, in good faith and without negligence, on behalf, or at the request of the corporation. In some instances the corporation may purchase insurance that provides limited indemnification. Insurance may be purchased to protect the director or officer (and the corporation) against the costs of lawsuits involving negligence. However, insurance companies do not insure against conduct involving bad faith, malice, dishonesty, or fraud. Shareholders may object to indemnification by the corporation or to the corporation paying the cost of insurance premiums from funds otherwise available for dividends. However, the protection afforded by these devices is often necessary to induce a responsible person to accept the position of director or corporate officer.

In the following case the court discusses a corporate officer's right to indemnification.

CASE 39.5

Wisener v. Air Express International Corporation
583 F.2d 579 (2nd Cir. 1978)

Facts: Wisener was president, director, and chairman of the board of Air Express International ("AEI"). Novo corporation negotiated to acquire AEI stock and relied on financial figures prepared without audit by Arthur Anderson & Co. The unaudited figures turned out to be seriously in error and Novo sued for fraud and violations of federal securities laws. The lawsuits were settled and withdrawn. Wisener claimed indemnity from AEI for his litigation expenses. The trial court denied relief, stating that Wisener was negligent in permitting Novo to rely on the interim figures when he knew or should have known of serious deficiencies in AEI's accounting system.

Question: Was Wisener entitled to indemnification?

Answer: Yes. Wisener may recover litigation expenses even though he may have not exercised ordinary care in dealing with Novo.

Reasoning: The court stated that the public policy of the State of Illinois favors, rather than disfavors, corporate indemnification of corporate officers. An Illinois statute reads, "To the extent that a director, officer, employee or agent of a corporation has been successful, on the merits or otherwise, in the defense of any action, suit or proceeding [against him or her by reason of being or having been a director, officer, employee or agent], . . . he shall be indemnified against expenses (including attorneys' fees) actually and reasonably incurred by him in connection therewith." It was contended that Wisener was not "sucessful" in the litigation, since the claims against him never proceeded to trial. The statute, however, refers to success "on the merits or otherwise," which the court held was broad enough to cover a termination of claims by agreement without any payment or assumption of liability.

The judgment was reversed and remanded for determination of the amount due Wisener for litigation expenses.

SUMMARY

A corporation's legal capacity is circumscribed by (1) express powers contained in state statutes or specified in the articles of incorporation, and (2) those *implied powers* which courts interpret as reasonably required to carry out express powers.

Statutes or articles sometimes restrict a corporation's powers. For example, a statute may deny to professional corporations the power to diversify, or the articles may prohibit the corporation from owning real estate.

The corporation, its officers, or its directors may be held liable for acts beyond the corporate powers (ultra vires). The corporation may also be held liable for acts within its legal powers (intra vires) if the conduct infringes on the legal rights of private persons. Under the doctrine of respondeat superior, the corporation is liable for torts which an agent commits within the scope of employment.

The shareholders exercise indirect control over corporate policies by electing or removing directors. Directors are elected for designated terms but may be removed with or without cause by a majority of the shares voted at a meeting called for that purpose.

Corporate affairs and policies are controlled by a board of directors, which derives its power from the articles and state statutes. The board of directors may act by formal resolution adopted by a majority of the directors voting at a regular or special meeting at which a quorum is present or by unanimous written consent without a meeting.

The directors elect officers, who carry out broad policies and assume the duties and authority prescribed in the bylaws and board resolutions. Directors and corporate agents (officers, employees, and others) owe the corporation a duty of loyalty. The *fiduciary duty* of loyalty includes an obligation to exercise honesty and independent judgment. A director may contract with his corporation if the contract is fair and reasonable, or if the conflict of interest is known to the *disinterested* directors or to the shareholders and either body approves the transaction without counting the vote or consent of the *interested* director(s). Under the *corporate opportunity doctrine*, fiduciaries cannot seize business opportunities which may be of interest to (and have not been rejected by) the corporation.

REVIEW QUESTIONS

1. Distinguish between: (**a**) a corporation's express and implied powers, and (**b**) the limitations placed on corporate powers by state statutes and by the articles of incorporation.

2. (**a**) What is the meaning of the term ultra vires? (**b**) Why have most states abolished the ultra vires defense? (**c**) In what three ways can the ultra vires concept be used in direct suits?

3. How are corporations affected by the doctrine of respondeat superior?

4. (**a**) How do statutory requirements affecting the size of the board of directors reflect the growing importance of close corporations? (**b**) How can the board of directors alter the composition of an existing board? (**c**) Give examples of powers that vest exclusively in the board of directors.

5. (**a**) What is the usual statutory requirement for a quorum of the board? (**b**) How does the minimum statutory requirement for approving a resolution at a board meeting differ from the usual requirement for adopting a resolution by written consent of the directors?

6. List the usual officers found in corporate bylaws.

7. (**a**) Describe the source(s) of express and implied authority of officers. (**b**) Under what circumstances does an officer have apparent authority?

8. What are the duties which directors and officers owe to the corporation?

9. Under what circumstances may directors and officers avoid personal liability for ultra vires acts?

10. Discuss some of the situations which can expose directors and officers to personal liability.

11. How does the business judgment rule serve to protect those who act on behalf of the corporation?

CASE PROBLEMS

1. Blue Cross applied to the commissioner of insurance for Connecticut for permission to purchase 100 percent of the common stock of American Professional Life Insurance Company. The commissioner denied the application, claiming that Blue Cross was not authorized by law to own and operate a life insurance company. Blue Cross's charter stated its purpose as: "to provide hospital, medical and other health care benefits as provided in . . . the General Statutes. . . ." The list of health care services in the statutes does not include life insurance coverage. Generally, hospital-medical service corporations are required to be formed exclusively for the purpose of providing hospital-medical services. The Connecticut statutes do grant the power to invest in shares and securities of other corporations. Was the commissioner correct in his decision? Explain your answer.

2. The bylaws of American Insurance, Inc., provided for a board of eight directors and a quorum of at least five directors. A contract with Management Corp. was reviewed and approved by unanimous vote of six directors present at a meeting of American's board. Three of the directors who voted were also on the board of Management; two of the three were the president and secretary, respectively, of both corporations. Upon further review, American found the contract to be against its best interests and served notice of termination on Management. Management sued American for breach of contract and $180,000 in damages. American claimed that the contract was voidable because it had not been authorized by a quorum of disinterested directors. Is Management entitled to recover from American? Explain reasons for your answer.

3. Glen's employment as president of Law Books, Inc., was "at will" and not for a stated term. In April he agreed to become president of a competitor on June 1. In May, Glen obtained confidential salary data on selected editors and other key personnel of Law Books, Inc., and in some cases personally assisted in their recruitment by the competitor. Glen quieted the fears of Law Books' directors by telling them that there was "no danger of a raid." Glen and 12 recruits resigned on May 30 and started working for Law Books' competitor the next day. Law Books sued Glen for breach of his fiduciary duty. Glen contended that his employment was "at will" and that, therefore, he did nothing wrong. Is Glen's contention correct? Give reasons.

4. Calvin and his sister, Thelma, were directors and controlling shareholders of Baseball Club, Inc., a close corporation. In 1961, the board voted to double Calvin and Thelma's salaries as president and vice president, which were increased to $75,000 and $50,000, respectively. The salaries of three employees who were related to them were also increased substantially. Gripe, a minority stockholder, challenged the increases as void for self-dealing and filed a suit which sought an injunction to restrain the corporation from paying the increased amount. Gripe did not present evidence showing the salary increases to be unreasonable. Should the court grant the injunction? Explain.

5. Abel and Brooks were directors, and president and vice president, respectively, of Quarry, Inc., a limestone mining business. The two men owned 100 percent of Quarry's outstanding shares, which they agreed to sell and transfer to Construction, Inc., as of October 20. On October 10, Brooks, on his own behalf, leased land which reports from Quarry's files showed to be suitable for a limestone quarry. Brooks did not tell Abel or Construction, Inc., about the lease. Construction acquired Quarry as a wholly owned subsidiary and elected new directors to serve on Quarry's board. The new board learned of Brooks's actions and authorized Quarry to file suit to compel Brooks to transfer the lease to the corporation. Should the court compel Brooks to transfer the lease to Quarry? Why or why not?

CHAPTER 40

SHAREHOLDERS' POWERS, RIGHTS, AND LIABILITIES

As we have seen in the previous chapter, the board of directors makes policy decisions for the corporation (what products to sell, which markets to enter). They delegate day-to-day operations to the officers and employees. However, the shareholders of a corporation also have an important role in its management: they have the power to elect and remove directors, amend the articles of incorporation, approve mergers, dissolve the corporation, purchase new issues of stock, examine the books, and bring lawsuits. The first part of this chapter discusses these powers and rights of shareholders. The last part of the chapter discusses shareholders' liabilities.

SHAREHOLDERS: POWERS AND RIGHTS

Powers of Shareholders; Extraordinary Transactions

As the owners of a majority of voting shares, the "majority" shareholders exercise *indirect* control over corporate activities and policies by electing and removing directors. Majority shareholders usually have the *direct* power to amend the articles, as well as the ultimate power to amend and repeal the bylaws.

In addition, shareholders exercise direct managerial power over extraordinary corporate transactions such as:

- Mergers or consolidations
- Sales or leases that dispose of substantially all corporate assets other than in the regular course of business
- Dissolutions
- Loans to directors
- Stock option plans benefiting officers and directors

The directors cannot complete such transactions without shareholder approval.

Election and Removal of Directors. Shareholders meet annually and elect directors by a majority of the shares voted. The directors hold office until the next such meeting or until their successors are elected and qualified. Shareholders have the power at common law to remove a director "for cause"—such as dishonesty or gross abuse of discretion. In California or New York, if a director is acting dishonestly or abusing his or her discretion and a majority of the shareholders are unwilling to act, the holders of 10 percent of the shares of the corporation may petition the court to remove the director for cause. Several states permit majority shareholders to remove directors with or without cause at a meeting called for that purpose.

Amendment of Articles. The shareholders may amend the articles (or "charter") for a variety of reasons. For example, the articles may be amended to change the corporation's name or purpose; the number or par value of authorized shares; or the relative rights and preferences of issued or unissued shares. The corporate charter can also be amended to create new classes of shares or to deny or grant the right to acquire additional shares to shareholders of any class.

Typically, the board of directors first proposes an amendment to the charter. Then, the board calls a meeting of the shareholders and mails to shareholders entitled to vote, proper written notice of the proposed amendment. If approved by a majority of shares voted at the meeting, articles of amendment (describing the amendment proceedings) are filed with the secretary of state.

Acquisitions by Merger, Consolidation, Share Exchange, Sale, or Lease.   Corporations can often expand quickly and economically by acquiring other corporations. There are various methods by which one corporation acquires another, and several methods require shareholder approval.

A **stock acquisition** occurs when the acquiring corporation buys at least a majority of the outstanding voting stock of the "target" corporation. When this is accomplished, the target corporation may be liquidated, merged, or kept as a subsidiary.

A **merger** occurs when an existing corporation acquires all the assets and assumes all the liabilities of another corporation which then ceases to exist. The *surviving* corporation usually exchanges its securities for the outstanding shares of the *disappearing* corporation. For example, some years ago Pan American World Airways acquired National Airlines. If you had been a stockholder in National Airlines your shares would have been exchanged and you would now be a stockholder in Pan Am.

A **consolidation** occurs when a new corporation is created for the express purpose of consolidating assets and liabilities of two or more constituent corporations which then cease to exist. Their outstanding shares are usually exchanged for securities issued by the consolidated corporation. For example, if corporation A and corporation B decide to consolidate, a new corporation, C is formed. Shareholders of A and B exchange their shares for shares of corporation C.

The statutes regulating mergers and consolidations are complex and vary from state to state. Shareholder approval is required in some form. For example, California requires approval by a majority of *all* classes of stock of *both* corporations.

A **share exchange** occurs when *all* of a target corporation's outstanding shares are exchanged for shares issued by another corporation, and both corporations continue to exist in a parent-subsidiary relation. Acquisition of a portion of another corporation's outstanding shares is not restricted. A share exchange requires that both corporations pass board resolutions and sign articles of exchange, but only the shareholders of the corporation to be acquired need approve the transaction.

A *sale, lease, or exchange of all—or substantially all—of a corporation's assets for a purpose not in the regular course of business* is an extraordinary transaction and requires approval by a majority of voting (common) shareholders of the selling corporation. For example, suppose a corporation has as its only asset a hotel and that the Hilton Corporation offers to purchase the hotel. If a majority of common stockholders approve the sale, the corporation simply exchanges its hotel for cash, a note, or stock of Hilton Corporation. The corporation may continue in existence with its assets consisting of the sale proceeds, or it may liquidate and distribute the proceeds to its shareholders.

Corporate Dissolutions.   Each year thousands of corporations quit doing business. Some are formally dissolved; others are not. A formal corporate dissolution can only occur in the following ways:

1. Legislative act of the state of incorporation.
2. Expiration of the period for which the corporation was formed.
3. Involuntary judicial dissolution by decree of an equity court—pursuant to suit by the attorney general to forfeit the corporate charter for causes such as nonpayment of taxes or abuse of corporate powers, or pursuant to suit by shareholders seeking to dissolve the corporation.
4. Action by a majority of incorporators prior to the issuance of shares or prior to the commencement of business.
5. Corporate action consisting of a resolution adopted by the directors, and approval by a majority of voting shares.

Shareholder action is involved in both voluntary and involuntary dissolutions. For example, in California 50 percent of voting (common) shares can dissolve a corporation at any time. The corporation may be profitable, yet the state law permits dissolution by the shareholders. The California statute regarding involuntary dissolutions is more restrictive. Holders of 33 ⅓ percent of voting (common) shares may petition the court for dissolution, but good cause must be shown. Good cause includes a deadlock among directors which threatens irreparable injury to the corporation; acts of those in control which are illegal, oppressive, or fraudulent; or corporate assets which are being misapplied or wasted. If good cause is shown, the court appoints a receiver to conduct the dissolution. The receiver will liquidate the assets of the corporation, pay all creditors, and distribute any surplus to shareholders.

Shareholders' Meetings

Annual and Special Meetings.   Most states require the bylaws to fix a time for the *annual shareholders' meeting*, the primary purpose of which is to elect the board of directors. If a place is not designated in the bylaws, meetings are held at the corporation's registered office. If a matter requires immediate attention (such as a merger proposal) and the next annual meeting of shareholders is some months away, a *special shareholders' meeting* may be called. As a general rule, a special shareholders' meeting may be called by the directors, by holders of 10 percent or more of the shares entitled to vote, or by the president of the corporation.

Every shareholder has a basic right to participate in shareholders' meetings by offering resolutions and by arguing and voting for or against resolutions presented. Shareholders have recently used such meetings as a forum in which to debate social policy issues, such as environmental control and nondiscrimination in employment.

Notice of Meetings and Waiver of Notice.   Most states require that shareholders eligible to vote at an annual or special meeting must receive timely written notice of the place, day, and hour of the meeting, *and* of the proposals they are to consider. A common provision is that notice of a meeting must be mailed at least 10 days in advance of the meeting. Actions taken at a meeting for which notice has not been properly given are not legally effective unless shareholders waive notice requirements by attending the meeting or by signing a written waiver of notice. The following case involves the waiver by a shareholder of the right to protest action taken.

CASE 40.1   Petition of Directors of Willoughby Walk Co-op
428 N.Y.S.2d 574 (N.Y. App. 1980)

Facts: The bylaws of Willoughby Walk Cooperative Apartments, Inc. prohibited a transfer of membership within 10 days preceding the annual stockholders' meeting. Five days prior to the 1979 annual meeting Mr. Garland Core-Shuler had his name added to that of his roommate, Virginia Shuler, on the stock certificate allotted to their apartment. At the meeting the petitioner, a shareholder and member of the board of directors, objected, but Core-Shuler was elected to serve on the board. Six months later petitioner filed suit to set aside the election, claiming Core-Shuler was an ineligible candidate.

The petition was denied and petitioner appealed.

Question: Was the election of Core-Shuler valid?

Answer: Yes. Core-Shuler was an eligible candidate. Further, the petitioner had waived his rights.

Reasoning: The bylaw provision establishes a "record date" for the purpose of determining which shareholders are entitled to notice or to vote. No reference is made to eligibility for election to the board. Any person who was a shareholder on the date of election was an eligible candidate. Petitioner waived any right to contest the election by participating in numerous board meetings for 6 months after the election. To overturn the election would necessitate vacating all board action taken since November 1979. This would be highly prejudicial to the interests of the shareholders.

The petition was denied.

Voting Rights of Shareholders

Although corporations may issue nonvoting stock, most common shares carry voting rights—usually one vote for each outstanding share. Unissued shares and treasury stock may not be voted. **Treasury stock** is stock that has been issued but later purchased by the corporation from the shareholder and held in inactive status.

Voting Eligibility. The corporate stock transfer books are closed as of a "record date" (usually a date between 10 to 50 days before a meeting) to determine the shareholders entitled to vote. Only holders of voting shares as of the record date have the right to vote at shareholders' meetings. The purpose of closing the stock transfer books is to allow the corporation to mail notice of the meeting and prepare a voting list. It would be impractical to allow stock transfers until the very day of the meeting.

Cumulative Voting. Each share of stock entitles the holder to one vote for each vacancy on the board of directors of the corporation. As a general rule, a majority of the shares voted at a meeting at which a quorum is present can elect all the directors. Cumulative voting permits a shareholder to accumulate votes and cast all his or her votes (shares owned × directors to be elected) for one candidate. Thus, dissenting minority shareholders who own a sufficient block of shares can vote cumulatively and elect one or more directors. For example, suppose a corporation has five directors to be elected and the stock is owned: Susan with 70 shares and Gary with 30 shares. Susan has 350 votes to cast (5 × 70) and Gary has 150 votes to cast (5 × 30). Gary may cast all his votes for one candidate and is assured of representation on the board since Susan must spread her votes over four or five candidates to maintain control.

Large, publicly held corporations often view dissent on the board as disruptive and avoid incorporating in states that require cumulative voting. A majority of states permit the articles to provide for cumulative voting, but no major industrial state, except California, gives shareholders an absolute right to cumulate votes in board elections.

Proxy Voting.　A shareholder can vote his or her shares in person or appoint another to do so. If another is appointed to vote, the authorization which the shareholder signs, is called a **proxy**. A few states permit oral proxies. Unless the proxy declares otherwise, its duration is limited to 11 months. Proxies can be limited to a particular transaction, but most proxies authorize the appointee to vote on all matters submitted to the shareholders.

Revocation of Proxies.　Proxies are governed by agency law rules. The proxyholder is an agent for the shareholder. As a general rule a proxy may be revoked at any time, just as any agency may be revoked. Revocation can occur in either of two ways: (1) The shareholder may change his or her mind and attend the meeting in person, or (2) the shareholder may sign a later proxy designating another person to cast the shareholder's vote.

Preemptive Rights

If the board of directors decides to issue new shares of stock, the issuance will affect the rights of existing shareholders to vote and receive dividends. For example, suppose Arnold owns 10 percent of the outstanding stock of a corporation and that the board of directors decides to issue a large block of new shares to Barbara. After the new issue Arnold's percentage of ownership will be reduced and he will receive a lesser percentage of future dividends. The impact of his votes in future elections also will be lessened.

The common law rule is that shareholders have a right to preserve their proportionate stock interests by purchasing shares of a new issue ahead of others. This concept of *preemptive rights* is designed to prevent the dilution of the existing shareholders' equity in a corporation when additional shares are issued. Thus, in the example above, a preemptive right would give Arnold the right to purchase up to 10 percent of the new stock issue in preference to Barbara. Only if Arnold and the other shareholders choose not to purchase additional stock, will Barbara be allowed to purchase shares. All states except New Hampshire recognize preemptive rights. In some states, including California, Delaware, New Jersey, Michigan, Massachusetts, and Pennsylvania, preemptive rights are recognized only if they are established in the articles.

Even if preemptive rights exist in a particular situation, there are several well-recognized exceptions. For example, a corporation may reissue treasury shares to an outsider without first offering the shares to existing shareholders. Most courts do not permit preemptive rights to be applied to shares issued for noncash consideration (as where a corporation receives property or services for its stock), to

698698   PART NINE: BUSINESS ORGANIZATIONS

shares issued as a result of merger or consolidation, or to shares issued pursuant to an incentive stock option plan for employees. The general consensus is that shareholders who have benefited from these types of acquisitions are not justified in claiming preemptive rights.

The size of the corporation often determines whether its charter should authorize preemptive rights. On the one hand, shareholders of close corporations may find that preemptive rights are crucial to voting control. On the other hand, most shareholders of publicly held corporations own only a small proportion of outstanding shares and compliance with preemptive rights would be expensive and time-consuming. The following case involves an interesting application of the preemptive rights rule.

CASE 40.2   Schwartz v. Marien
373 N.Y.S.2d 122 (N.Y. App. 1975)

Facts: Smith, Marien, and Dietrich each owned one-third (50 shares) of the outstanding stock of Superior Engraving Co. When Smith died in 1959, the corporation purchased his shares as treasury stock. When Marien died in 1961, his shares passed to his wife and three sons. Thereafter, Dietrich, his daughter Margaret Schwartz, and two of Marien's sons constituted the four-member board. When Dietrich died in 1968, the Mariens called a special board meeting and the third Marien son was elected to fill the Dietrich vacancy. The three Marien directors then voted to have the corporation sell one share of treasury stock to each of them. The three treasury shares gave voting control of the corporation to the Marien family (53 shares to 50 for Margaret Schwartz).

Schwartz sued the Marien brothers for breach of their fiduciary duty as directors and controlling shareholders.

Question: Was the board of directors correct in denying Margaret Schwartz the right to buy treasury shares to equalize the Dietrich holdings?

Answer: No. The board should allow preemptive rights in the absence of proof of special justification.

Reasoning: Ordinarily, preemptive rights do not attach to treasury shares. However, corporate directors owe a fiduciary duty to shareholders to treat all shareholders fairly and evenly. The burden of coming forth with proof of justification for their action shifts to the directors, where, as here, a prima facie case of unequal stockholder treatment is made out. The court said, "not only must it be shown that it was sought to achieve a bona fide independent business objective, but as well that such objective could not have been accomplished . . . by other means which would not have disturbed proportionate stock ownership."

Shareholders'
Right to Examine
Corporate
Books

Common Law Right of Inspection. Shareholders have a common law right to inspect corporate books and records for any proper purpose. As owners, shareholders have a right to inspect the records in order to determine the corporation's financial condition or the propriety of dividends, discover mismanagement, and obtain shareholders' lists to solicit proxies in opposition to management. Some courts limit inspection rights by holding that a proper purpose must be related to the shareholder's economic interest in the corporation. Thus, a shareholder's desire to express his or her social or political views is not a "proper purpose." If a shareholder is denied inspection rights, the corporation has the burden of proving the shareholder had an improper purpose. Rarely is such proof available. Examples of improper purpose include: aiding a competitor, discovering business secrets, or developing "sucker lists" for personal business purposes.

Statutory Right of Inspection. All states have statutes which supplement a shareholder's common law right of inspection. Each corporation must mail an annual financial statement to its shareholders. In the interim, if any of them makes a written request, the corporation must provide the most recent financial statement available. Books of account, minutes of shareholders' and directors' meetings, and shareholders' lists must be made available at the corporation's registered office.

Any corporate official who denies a proper demand for inspection is liable for a penalty equal to 10 percent of the value of a stockholder's shares. Most statutes attempt to reduce capricious demands by limiting the right of inspection to shareholders who have owned their shares for 6 months or to holders of 5 percent of outstanding shares. Delaware gives shareholders the right of inspection regardless of the size or duration of their holdings.

Shareholders' Rights of Action

Individual Suits and Class Actions. An *individual* shareholder can sue the corporation to enforce inspection rights, to enforce preemptive rights, or to enjoin ultra vires acts. A group of shareholders can collectively pursue individual causes of action arising out of the same transaction by bringing a *class* action against the corporation. The individuals joining in the suit commence the action in their own names and on behalf of "all others similarly situated." The benefit of a class action is that a large number of small claims are consolidated in one action, thus reducing the strain and expense placed on the court system. An example of a class action would be a shareholder suing to require the board of directors to declare a dividend. The amount of dividends payable to an individual is usually rather small and it would be intolerable to encourage thousands of shareholders to each file separate lawsuits for a few dollars. Class actions are not filed often as there are substantial costs involved. The individual who files the action must notify all members of the "class" that the suit has been filed and that they may take advantage of the proceeding. Other members of the class may join the action and may benefit from a final judgment by paying a pro rata share of litigation costs.

Shareholders' Derivative Suits. If a person wrongs a corporation so that the value of its shares is depreciated, each shareholder suffers a pro rata share of the damage. However, the shareholder(s) cannot recover the damage by filing suit in their own names. Such suits must be filed in the corporate name. This rule avoids a multiplicity of suits by individual stockholders and protects corporate creditors by returning funds to the corporation. All stockholders benefit equally because recovery by the corporation appreciates the value of all its shares.

If directors fail to act in situations involving harm to the corporation, one or more shareholders may act on behalf of the corporation by filing a *derivative* suit in its name. Harm to the corporation may be caused by an "insider" (officer, director, employee) or by an "outsider" (debtor, tortfeasor). The harm may consist of a breach of fiduciary duty, misapplication of corporate funds, or breach of a contract with the corporation. The damages recovered go into the corporate treasury, not to the shareholders individually.

In past years shareholders have used derivative suits to harass directors and officers with unwarranted accusations of mismanagement. These tactics have been used to intimidate management into making a lucrative out-of-court settlement or purchasing the complaining shareholder's stock at a favorable price. Abuse arising from such "strike" suits has led to restrictive statutes and court rules.

In order to file a derivative suit, a stockholder must show that several conditions have been met. (1) The shareholder owned his or her shares at the time of the wrongdoing. (2) The directors (and in some states, the shareholders) refused a demand to commence suit on behalf of the corporation. (3) The refusal by the directors was in bad faith (that is, not protected by the "business judgment rule"). As an alternative, the shareholder may show that a demand of the directors (or shareholders) to file suit would have been useless. For example, the shareholder may allege that the person who harmed the corporation dominates and controls the board of directors.

The court may require a shareholder who owns less than a prescribed percentage or dollar value of shares to give security sufficient to cover the litigation expenses of the parties. In the event of a favorable judgment, the shareholder can generally recover reasonable litigation expenses from the corporation, but is not compensated for his or her time.

The following case involves both a class action and a derivative suit.

CASE 40.3   Harff v. Kerkorian
324 A.2d 215 (Del. Ch. 1974)

Facts: The directors of Metro-Goldwyn-Mayer, Inc. declared a cash dividend on common shares in 1973. At that time, Philip and Stephanie Harff owned debentures which were convertible to MGM shares at the option of the holder. The Harffs brought a derivative action on behalf of the corporation and against its directors to recover the amount of the dividend paid. The complaint alleged that the dividend had damaged MGM's capital position and future prospects. The trial court dismissed the action on the ground that the Harffs were not MGM stockholders and, therefore, could not maintain the derivative suit.

The Harffs also brought a class action on behalf of all debenture holders against MGM and its directors.

The court granted summary judgment in favor of defendants. Plaintiffs appealed.

Question: Should either the derivative suit or the class action be allowed to proceed?

Answer: The class action should be permitted to proceed to trial on the merits, but the derivative suit must be dismissed.

Reasoning: The derivative suit must be dismissed since only one who was a stockholder at the time of the alleged wrong may maintain a derivative action. The holder of an option to purchase stock is not eligible. The class action rests upon a different footing. The court said, "unless there are special circumstances, e.g. fraud, insolvency, or violation of a statute, the rights of debenture holders are confined to the terms of the Indenture Agreement." Here, the class action alleged fraud by the directors which constituted a default under the Indenture Agreement.

A trial was ordered on the issue of fraud.

SHAREHOLDERS' LIABILITIES

One of the most important characteristics of doing business in the form of a corporation is the fact that a shareholder's liability is limited to his or her capital investment. However, there are exceptions to the rule.

As discussed in Chapter 37, creditors that prove abuse of the privilege of doing business as a corporation may "pierce the corporate veil" and hold a controlling shareholder liable for corporate debts. Special statutes may impose personal liability on shareholders.

One kind of statutory liability which is imposed very infrequently is liability for wages due corporate employees. For example, under New York law, the ten largest shareholders are jointly and severally liable for wages due employees of corporations whose shares are not publicly traded. Such statutes are contrary to the idea of limited liability and tend to discourage incorporation. Other liabilities which frequently arise are discussed in the following paragraphs.

Liability for True Value of Shares

Shares are sometimes issued for overvalued property. A majority of state statutes do not impose liability on the shareholder if there is no fraud and the directors value such property "in good faith." Of course, if the facts show fraud on the part of the shareholder or bad faith on the part of the directors, the shareholder is liable for the amount of any underpayment that results. Suppose a shareholder transfers a parcel of real estate valued at $75,000 to the corporation for capital stock valued at $100,000. If the transaction is negotiated "at arm's length," in good faith, a court will not hold the shareholder liable for the underpayment. However, if the directors and the shareholder have deliberately "watered" the stock, unpaid creditors of the corporation may require the shareholder to make further payment in cash.

In the absence of statute, courts use a variety of theories to impose liability on the stockholder. The end result, in most cases, is equivalent to the liability imposed on shareholders under the *true value* rule. This rule holds the shareholder liable to the corporation (or to its creditors) for the difference between the inflated value and the true value of the property. Stated another way, the shareholder must pay the difference between the true value of the property and the issuance price of his or her shares.

Liability for Unlawful Dividends and Distributions

Some statutes permit a corporation to recover from shareholders who know that a dividend or other corporate distribution is unlawful. The shareholder is liable to pay back the amount received as an illegal dividend. The amount returned to the corporation is then available to pay corporate creditors. If creditors are not fully satisfied from corporate funds, further recourse to shareholders would be available only if grounds exist to "pierce the corporate veil" or to take advantage of the "true value" rule.

Liability of Controlling Shareholders

Ordinarily, one shareholder does not owe a fiduciary duty to another shareholder. However, when a shareholder owns or controls a majority of the voting stock of a corporation, courts have imposed on the controlling shareholder a fiduciary duty to minority shareholders. The courts have not clearly defined the duties that controlling shareholders owe to minority stockholders. One problem area that arises frequently, especially in close corporations, involves injuries suffered by minority shareholders as the result of the sale of controlling shares. In a number of cases, the selling price of controlling shares has been found to include a premium which is paid for voting control of the corporation in excess of the fair market value of the stock. A growing number of courts will compel majority shareholders to disgorge the premium paid to them for control and will redistribute the amount of the premium ratably among *all* shareholders. As illustrated in the following case, courts will impose personal liability on controlling shareholders who use the corporate entity to sanction fraud, perpetrate a crime, circumvent a statute, accomplish a wrongful purpose, or promote injustice.

CASE 40.4 **DeBaun v. First Western Bank & Trust Co.**
120 Cal. Rptr. 354 (Cal. App. 1975)

Facts: The stock of Alfred S. Johnson, Inc. was owned as follows: First Western Bank and Trust Co. (Bank)—70 shares; DeBaun—20 shares; and Stephens—10 shares. Bank sold its shares to Raymond Mattison for $250,000, payable $50,000 down and the balance over 5 years, payment to be secured by the corporation's assets. Bank knew that it had an unsatisfied judgment against Mattison and Mattison's attorney referred Bank to courthouse records about other pending litigation. The courthouse records, which Bank failed to check, showed that Mattison had 38 unsatisfied judgments, 54 pending suits, and 18 tax liens. Mattison looted the corporation and it became insolvent. Pursuant to the security agreement, Bank sold the corporation's remaining assets for $60,000.

DeBaun and Stephens brought a derivative action against Bank to recover damages from its sale of controlling shares to Mattison. The trial court held Bank liable for $473,836 in damages (the corporation's net worth as of the transfer date plus 10 years of projected, after-tax earnings). Bank appealed.

Question: Is Bank liable as controlling shareholder for breach of duty to the minority shareholders?

Answer: Yes. Bank as controlling majority shareholder must exercise good faith and fairness to the corporation and the other shareholders.

Reasoning: Bank became aware of facts that would have alerted a prudent person that Mattison was likely to loot the corporation. Knowing that information could be obtained from the public records, Bank closed its eyes to that obvious source. In addition, Bank concealed from DeBaun and Stephens that the corporate assets were being pledged to secure Mattison's obligation to pay $200,000 to Bank. Bank knew that it was of doubtful legality to allow Mattison, as a shareholder, to secure his personal obligation with the corporation's assets.

SUMMARY

Shareholders exercise indirect control over corporate policies by electing or removing directors. Directors are elected for designated terms but may be removed with or without cause by a majority of the shares voted at a meeting called for that purpose. The shareholders may also amend articles to modify corporate purposes, or to alter the number, par value, rights, or classes of authorized shares. Other extraordinary transactions which require shareholder approval include merger, consolidation, sale, or lease of substantially all corporate assets *not* in the ordinary course of business, and voluntary dissolutions.

Shareholders exercise their powers by voting in annual or special meetings. Shareholders may offer resolutions and may argue and vote for or against resolutions offered by management. Proper notice of shareholders' meetings must be given unless waived in writing or by actual attendance.

A shareholder is entitled to one vote for each voting share held as of a fixed "record date" preceding a shareholders' meeting. Most statutes give minority shareholders greater influence by permitting their votes (shares owned × directors to be elected) to be cumulated for a single candidate. Agency law permits shares to be voted by proxy. A shareholder may revoke a proxy by attending the meeting in person or by executing a later proxy to another person.

Statutory recognition of preemptive rights (a shareholder's right to preserve proportionate stock interests and voting rights by buying shares of a new issue) may be limited or denied in the articles.

In addition to voting rights, shareholders have a right to:

- Inspect corporate books and records,
- Institute individual suits and class actions for the purpose of enforcing rights under a share contract, and
- Initiate derivative suits in the corporation's name to enforce its rights against third parties (if directors fail or refuse to do so).

Under certain circumstances, a shareholder may be held liable for unlawful dividends or distributions and for the "true value" of shares acquired in exchange for overvalued property. Minority shareholders may sue majority shareholders for breach of their fiduciary duty of due diligence and fair dealing. Controlling shareholder(s) of close corporations may also be liable for the sale of controlling shares in situations involving fraud or wrongful purpose.

REVIEW QUESTIONS

1. How do shareholders exercise their managerial power?

2. Why must shareholders approve amendments to the articles of incorporation?

3. What is the end result of a merger, consolidation, share exchange, and sale or lease of substantially all of a corporation's assets?

4. How does the statutory procedure for amending articles and affecting acquisitions protect the shareholders' power to exercise control over such transactions?

5. Distinguish between voluntary and involuntary dissolutions and give one example of each.

6. Statutory provisions covering annual shareholders' meetings generally: (**a**) require a time for such meetings to be fixed—in what instrument? (**b**) permit shareholders to compel such meetings—how and under what circumstances? (**c** permit special meetings to be called—by whom?

7. Under what circumstances is a shareholder deemed to have waived notice of a meeting?

8. (**a**) How are the voting rights of shareholders determined? (**b**) What is the effect of a "record date?"

9. How does cumulative voting benefit minority stockholders?

10. (**a**) What is a proxy? (**b**) How may a proxy be revoked?

11. Describe one or more situations in which a shareholder can be held personally liable to the corporation or its creditors.

CASE PROBLEMS

1. The stock of All Steel Pipe and Tube, Inc. was owned equally by Scott Callier and Leo Callier. Leo was president of the corporation and Scott was general manager. The board of directors appointed Scott and only the board could remove him from office. Over the years Scott and Leo had differences of opinion about various aspects of the business but corporation sales increased from $200,000 in 1970 to $25,000,000 in 1974. In 1975 Leo unsuccessfully tried to purchase Scott's shares of stock. In April they discussed a voluntary dissolution and liquidation of the corporation but no agreement could be reached. On April 30 Leo sent a telegram purporting to fire Scott. Thereafter, Scott stayed away and allowed Leo to run things alone. In May Leo closed down the business of All Steel. He formed a new corporation, Callier Steel Pipe and Tube, Inc. and hired forty of All Steel's previous employees. In June Leo filed an action to dissolve All Steel. Should the court grant the petition and order liquidation of the corporate assets? Explain reasons for your answer.

2. Beulah was president and Kenneth was secretary of Lafayette Distributors, Inc. In July 1970 an invalid board of director's meeting was held which purported to elect Kenneth as president and Joan as secretary. In January 1971 Kenneth called a shareholders' meeting to elect directors. The meeting resulted in the election of Kenneth, Joan, and Marie to the board. Beulah filed suit to have the shareholders' meeting declared void and the election invalidated. Beulah contended that since the

July 1970 directors' meeting was invalid Kenneth remained as secretary of the corporation and she remained as president. The secretary of a corporation has no power to call a shareholders' meeting. Did Kenneth have the authority to call the shareholders' meeting? Explain.

3. Lerman, a shareholder of Diagnostic Data, Inc. (DDI), gave notice that he intended to wage a proxy contest at the next annual shareholders' meeting. The bylaws provided for the annual meeting to be held on the third Thursday in June of each year. On April 21 DDI's board of directors met and adopted two changes in the corporation's bylaws. First, the bylaw fixing the annual meeting in June was repealed in favor of one which left the date to the discretion of the board. Secondly, a new bylaw was added requiring that the corporation be given certain personal and professional information concerning any candidate for the board of directors not less than 70 days prior to the shareholders' meeting. On August 1 the board met and fixed October 3 as the date for the annual meeting (63 days later). Lerman filed suit to have the bylaw amendments declared invalid. How should the court rule? Give reasons.

4. Pillsbury had no interest in the affairs of Honeywell, Inc., until he learned that Honeywell was manufacturing bombs for the Vietnam war. Pillsbury was opposed to the war and bought one share of Honeywell stock in order to make his views known to management and the stockholders. Pillsbury immediately demanded shareholders' lists and all corporate records dealing with weapons and munitions production. When Honeywell refused, Pillsbury sued to force disclosure. Should the court compel Honeywell to make the records available to Pillsbury for inspection? Why or why not?

5. Hornblower, Inc. was formed for the primary purpose of managing a Ramada Inn. Newton, Gubser, and Cohen each owned one-third of the stock in the corporation. Cohen and Gubser were the managing officers and directors of Hornblower, Inc. Cohen and Gubser later formed Hanover House, Inc. to operate the restaurant at the motel and to furnish and equip a 47-room addition to the motel. Newton brought a derivative suit claiming Cohen and Gubser paid themselves excessive management fees and salaries, misappropriated corporate funds and assets, paid expenses of Hanover House from Hornblower funds, and misappropriated business opportunities. Cohen and Gubser argued that Newton failed to allege any efforts made by Newton to obtain the action he desires from the directors. Should Newton's suit be dismissed? Explain.

6. Ed Ash and his wife, Fay, owned 74 percent of Lumber Corporation's stock. The corporation borrowed $240,000 from Ed in exchange for demand notes payable to Ed, who was board chairman and president of the corporation. Ed was very wealthy and never required substantial payments on the notes, but when Fay filed for divorce, Ed stated: "I'll run the corporation into the ground as long as Fay has an interest in it." That year, Ed enforced payment of $140,000 on the notes. He then used his influence to cause the corporation (which was left with a deficit of $120,000) to file a notice of election to dissolve. Fay filed a shareholder's derivative suit against Ed for breach of his fiduciary duty to the corporation and its shareholders. Is Fay entitled to judgment on behalf of the corporation? Give reasons.

PART TEN

GOVERNMENT REGULATION OF BUSINESS

CHAPTER 41

REGULATING BUSINESS CONDUCT, SCOPE, AND SIZE

A business is subject to regulation by the federal government and the government of any state in which it does business. No business person escapes the influence of *government regulators,* the government administrative agencies created to carry out statutes passed by legislatures. Much of the law controlling modern business is made by administrative agencies, rather than by legislatures or courts. An *administrative agency* is any government office, department, board, bureau, commission, or other office—other than legislatures and courts—having the power to determine or regulate private rights and duties by making rules and decisions. The term "administrative agency" does not refer to a specific type of government organization. Both the states and federal government set up many different kinds of administrative agencies to do specific jobs assigned to them. For example, the public utilities commission of your state is an administrative agency. So is your state's department of motor vehicles. Even a state's public universities are often considered administrative agencies. Examples of federal agencies include the Department of Labor (DOL), Internal Revenue Service (IRS), Environmental Protection Agency (EPA), and Consumer Product Safety Commission (CPSC). Many administrative agencies such as these are given limited powers to enforce their rules and decisions.

When administrative agencies have authority over businesses, they often are called "regulatory agencies" because they *regulate* (control or influence) how business is done. Regulatory statutes, rules, and decisions affect not only the conduct of business but also its scope and size. Many regulatory agencies have a more immediate impact on business than have courts and legislatures.

This chapter discusses how the federal and state governments regulate business activity, particularly through administrative agencies. The Federal Trade Commission is used to illustrate the workings of an administrative agency. The chapter also outlines some major examples of economic regulation and social regulation applying to most businesses. Finally, antitrust regulation is summarized. The chapters which follow discuss other examples of government regulation.

IMPACT OF GOVERNMENT REGULATION OF BUSINESS

To illustrate the impact of regulation of business, consider the hypothetical Gardner Company. It processes food and does business in four states. In creating and carrying on its business, the Gardner Company has been subject to the following regulation:

1. Before the corporation could exist, articles of incorporation had to be approved by the secretary of state of the "domicile" (home) state. Then the firm had to qualify in the "foreign" states (any state other than the domicile) before doing business there.
2. Before the corporation's stock could be sold to the public, registration of the stock issue (sale) was required under state blue-sky law and under federal securities law. A detailed registration statement containing a great deal of information about the business was filed with the federal Securities and Exchange Commission (SEC).
3. The firm had to acquire licenses for its food-processing activities from federal, state, and local authorities. To receive and keep the licenses, the Gardner Company had to submit detailed plans for the processing plant to various state

and federal agencies, make the plant facilities conform to health, safety, and fire codes, and allow frequent inspections of the plant and its operations.

4. The firm is required to file returns for the following taxes: state sales and use taxes, state and federal income taxes, state and federal unemployment taxes, and social security taxes. Gardner is also required to withhold income, unemployment, and social security taxes from employees' wages, and make its pension plan conform to state and federal laws.

5. Shortly after the Gardner Company opened for business, a labor union sought to organize Gardner's employees. Gardner is required by regulations of the National Labor Relations Board (NLRB) not to commit unfair labor practices.

6. In developing a testing program for job applicants, Gardner has faced charges of illegal discrimination in hiring in violation of the Equal Employment Opportunity Act.

7. The Federal Trade Commission (FTC) has proposed a consent order under which Gardner would agree to halt certain allegedly deceptive advertising practices. Beyond that, Gardner must make all its labeling and packaging conform to state and federal standards.

8. Gardner proposes to discharge food-processing wastes into a nearby river. Its waste disposal plan is opposed by local, state, and federal agencies, including the Environmental Protection Agency (EPA).

9. The Gardner Company wants to purchase a rival food-processing company. Either the Antitrust Division of the Justice Department or the Federal Trade Commission (FTC) may challenge this "merger" as being anticompetitive.

10. The Gardner Company wishes to purchase raw materials from a Russian supplier. The U.S. Customs Service informs the firm that those materials are subject to certain tariffs and quotas, and that no importation from the USSR will be permitted unless the firm first acquires a special import license from the U.S. State Department.

As can be seen, the Gardner Company, like many other businesses, is subject to extensive regulation.

NATURE OF GOVERNMENT REGULATION

Government Regulation: Federal and State

Government regulation refers to law meant to control or influence the conduct, scope, or size of business. Regulation in various forms has existed throughout the history of the United States. Most regulation is aimed at limiting the ways in which private business may operate, rather than at limiting the size of businesses directly.

As noted previously, both the federal government and the states regulate business. The federal government's power to regulate business comes largely from the commerce and taxing provisions of the United States Constitution. The *commerce clause* gives Congress the exclusive power to regulate *interstate commerce* ("Among the several States") and foreign commerce. The federal government may regulate any business activity which has a substantial effect on interstate commerce. Generally, federal law will "preempt" or take precedence over state law regulating the same business activity if there is any conflict between the two.

The U.S. Constitution delegates only some specific powers to the federal government and preserves for the states the remainder of governmental authority. The states' powers to regulate business are found mostly in their taxing authority and their "police powers" (powers to make law to promote the general welfare, safety health, and morals of the public).

A state may regulate local (intrastate) commerce having little or no effect on interstate commerce. A state may even regulate local business activity in a way that burdens interstate commerce so long as the burden is reasonable in light of the state's legitimate governmental purpose (for example, requiring the inspection of goods coming into the state to prevent the spread of disease). A state is *not* permitted to erect economic barriers to interstate commerce or to regulate by discriminating in favor of its own citizens or businesses over those from outside the state (for example, by banning the sale of out-of-state milk).

Constitutional Limitations on Regulation

Neither state nor federal regulation of business is permitted to infringe upon the liberties and rights guaranteed in the Constitution. Even when authorized by the federal commerce clause or by a state's police power, regulation will be invalidated if it conflicts with a protection found in the Constitution.

For example, an important safeguard is the First Amendment's protection of freedom of speech. In general, businesses are as protected as individuals from laws limiting their expression of *political* viewpoints. However, the First Amendment does not protect "commercial" speech, such as advertising to sell a product, as much as it protects "political" speech, such as the expression of opinions and ideas. Governments may place some limitations on commercial speech if it is necessary to achieve some proper governmental purpose, such as protecting the public's health. The health warning required in cigarette advertising is one example of government regulation of commercial speech. (Speech such as advertising which is misleading or which promotes unlawful activity is not protected by the Constitution.)

There are numerous other important constitutional protections which affect business. The Fourth Amendment prohibits unreasonable government searches and seizures, including most regulatory inspections of business premises without a search warrant if one is demanded by the business. The Fifth Amendment and the Fourteenth Amendment prohibit the government from depriving any person (including a corporation) of life, liberty, or property without due process of law. An extension of this safeguard prevents a business's property from being taken for public use unless the owner receives fair payment. Finally, the Equal Protection clause prevents the government from unfairly discriminating between similarly situated individuals or businesses. Thus, all similar car manufacturers should be subject to the same governmental rules of vehicle safety and pollution control. The law is not fundamentally fair if it treats businesses differently without adequate reason.

Role of Administrative Agencies in the Regulation of Business

The administrative agency is the primary method the government uses to regulate business. Whenever the Congress, courts, and the President cannot handle work that the government wishes to get done, an administrative agency is established to see that the job gets accomplished. The importance of administrative agencies is indicated by their number and by the wide scope of their duties and powers. There are literally thousands of federal, state, and local agencies in the United States. Virtually everyone is affected by agency regulation. Each of us uses electricity, natural gas, telephones, and gasoline, all of which are subject to state and federal regulation. Food, drugs, and many consumer products we purchase are subjects of government regulation designed to ensure their healthfulness or safety. Anyone injured on the job and seeking workers' compensation and anyone unemployed and seeking unemployment compensation or other government assistance will be affected by agency rules and regulations.

Like individuals, small business firms cannot escape regulation. Many trades and professions also are licensed and regulated by the states. Common examples are lawyers, beauticians, and building contractors. Large firms doing interstate business may be subject to a staggering amount of administrative regulation—federal, state, and local.

Where Administrative Agencies Come From.   Administrative agencies are created by statutes passed by legislatures, such as a city council, a state legislature, or the federal Congress. A city council, for example, may establish through a city ordinance an administrative body (perhaps called a development department) to review building plans, issue building permits, and inspect completed construction for building done within city limits. Similarly, an agency called a "zoning commission" may be created to make a general plan for land development in the city and to rule on requests for exceptions to the plan. The statute that creates the administrative agency and assigns its tasks is called "enabling legislation" because it enables or empowers an agency to act. Enabling legislation is often amended to reduce or increase the agency's responsibility and power. In fact, an agency is frequently assigned jobs to carry out by several different statutes enacted at various times. For example, since the creation of the Federal Trade Commission by the Congress in 1914, at least fourteen major statutes have delegated the FTC duties to be performed.

When Congress creates a federal administrative agency, the agency generally will become a part of one of the three constitutional branches of government—the executive, the legislature, or the courts. Some federal agencies such as the Federal Trade Commission and the Securities and Exchange Commission are said to be "independent" agencies. In practice, this usually means that the President lacks the power to fire the heads of the agency without cause. Thus, independent agencies are somewhat insulated from presidential control.

Most federal agencies are headquartered in or around our nation's capital, Washington, D.C. Many agencies also have regional offices in other major cities. Some agencies such as the Social Security Administration and the Internal Revenue Service must have offices throughout the United States in order to accomplish their work.

The head of an administrative agency is often called "secretary," "director," or "commissioner." Agency heads are normally appointed by the President, but many appointments require confirmation by the Senate. The agency heads and their immediate assistants are usually political appointments. Generally, political appointees may be fired at any time with or without cause unless they head an independent agency. However, most of the employees of federal administrative agencies are career employees hired by the civil service. The jobs of these employees do not depend upon which political party is in power. Therefore, most federal employees are protected from being fired without adequate cause.

Why We Need Administrative Agencies.   The President, Congress, and judges cannot possibly accomplish everything the public wants government to do. Neither do they have the expertise to do everything well. The increasing complexity of our modern life and economy demands expertness in every field the government regulates. Legislators and judges commonly are not experts in such technical and diverse fields as utility rates, public health, corporate finance, environmental protection, labor relations, and social insurance. However, an agency such as the Social Security Administration can develop the expertise necessary to properly administer a social insurance program. Moreover, by assigning the expert agency the job of determining how to achieve general goals defined in a statute, the Congress can free its time to deal with other problems. For this reason, agencies are often given some rulemaking authority.

An administrative agency can be an excellent substitute for the courts in resolving small cases. For example, an Internal Revenue Service decision that you owe more taxes than you have paid may well be resolved through an administrative appeal within the agency. Only the most difficult cases need to be heard by a court. Using an agency to make a decision will often be quicker, easier, and cheaper than using an alternative such as the courts. If all workers' compensation claims or eligibility for social security had to be determined by a court or a legislature, those programs would be impossible to administer.

In addition, an agency that deals with a particular social problem can provide the continuing attention the courts and legislature cannot. It can deal more uniformly and fairly with those affected by regulation than could our system of nationwide courts. And an agency often can prevent problems that could only be dealt with by courts after the fact. In creating the Securities and Exchange Commission (SEC), for example, Congress believed that it would be better to prevent fraudulent sales of stock than to have the courts give redress to people injured by fraudulent sales. Likewise, the Consumer Product Safety Commission can develop standards to prevent dangerous products from being sold. Without this preventive approach, consumers would have to risk being harmed and then, if harmed, pursue remedies under product warranty law or tort law (such as negligence).

What Administrative Agencies Do and How They Do It.   Through an enabling statute, a legislature gives an administrative agency the authority to act. The enabling legislation will often declare a general policy (for example, protecting competition in the marketplace) and set standards or guidelines for the agency to follow in performing the duties the legislature has assigned. In order to carry out their duties, agencies are empowered to engage in one or more of the following activities: investigating, rule making, prosecuting, adjudicating (including licensing and rate-making), administering, advising, and supervising.

The legislature must decide which of these powers an agency must have in order to get its job done. Some major regulatory agencies have a combination of legislative, executive, and judicial powers since they can make rules, prosecute violators, and impose orders after determining a violation has occurred. Although an agency may appear very powerful, it may not act beyond its delegated authority, nor may it act contrary to the Constitution. The President, Congress, and courts have adequate controls on each agency to prevent an abuse of power. These controls, or checks, include monitoring the agency's conduct, reducing or increasing its budget or statutory power, and judicial review of its actions.

The two most important jobs an agency can be assigned are rule making and adjudication.

Rule making. Administrative regulations are created through *rule making.* (The terms "rule" and "regulation" mean the same.) Rules are *procedural, interpretive,* or *legislative.*

Procedural rules set forth the process by which the public deals with the agency. For example, procedural rules would tell you how to apply for a license or government benefit, how to make a complaint, and how to appeal a decision within the agency.

Interpretive rules are the agency's expert opinion as to what the law it administers means. An interpretive regulation, being merely an opinion, is not considered law itself and is not legally binding on courts. However, courts often agree with the agency's interpretation of the statutes it administers.

Some agencies are authorized to make law by creating *legislative rules.* Congress has established special procedures federal agencies must follow in order to make legislative rules, that is, regulations with the force of law. Many of these special procedures are found in the **Administrative Procedure Act (APA)**. (Many states have similar administrative procedure acts.) The APA assures that the public and businesses affected by legislative rules will have notice that rules are being proposed and also will have an opportunity to comment on and criticize proposed rules before they become law.

If legislative rules are consistent with the Constitution, the agency's enabling legislation, and other requirements such as in the APA which Congress imposes, they are binding on everyone as if they had been enacted into law by Congress.

Generally, rules only apply to future activities and not to things that have happened in the past. It would be unfair to expect businesses or the public to obey rules that do not exist or that they have no notice of.

Adjudication. **Adjudication** is the method by which an agency issues an order, other than a regulation. **Orders** establish the rights or duties of people the agency regulates. An order might grant a license (for example, a license to operate a nuclear plant) or an order might determine that a business has violated the law in some way and require it to stop the violation.

Adjudication is the primary way an agency has of enforcing both the statutes Congress has assigned to it and the legislative rules the agency has made. An adjudication is often very similar to a court trial, with a hearing examiner or an administrative law judge presiding. Since the lawyers bringing an enforcement case and the judge deciding it are all employed by the agency, it is important for the agency carefully to separate these functions so that the other party receives a fair hearing. Once an administrative judge issues an order, it can be appealed within the agency and eventually to the federal courts. If a party refuses to obey the agency's order, the agency must ask a federal court to enforce it.

An Example of How Agencies Operate: The Federal Trade Commission.   Agencies vary greatly in the kind of work they do. Some agencies are given a narrow range of responsibilities. In contrast, the **Federal Trade Commission** is a large and complex agency charged with so many duties that its activities directly affect millions of people. Yet, in terms of the kinds of work it does, the FTC is representative of administrative agencies in general.

The FTC is an independent administrative agency created by Congress in 1914 and headed by five commissioners with overlapping 7-year terms. The commissioners, no more than three of whom may be members of the same political party, are nominated by the President and confirmed by the Senate. The President designates one commissioner to be chairman of the Commission.

The basic objective of the FTC is to prevent businesses from engaging in anticompetitive or anticonsumer practices. The FTC enforces the **Federal Trade Commission Act** (its enabling legislation) which prohibits the use of "unfair methods of competition" and "unfair or deceptive acts or practices" in or affecting commerce. Such prohibited conduct includes price-fixing, boycotts, illegal combinations of competitors, false and deceptive advertising, and other fraudulent marketing techniques. The FTC also has enforcement duties under numerous other acts of Congress, including the Clayton (antitrust) Act (preventing price discrimination and anticompetitive mergers), the Export Trade Act (supervising exporter associations), the Fair Packaging and Labeling Act (preventing deceptive packaging), the Consumer Credit Protection Act (assuring complete information on the cost of credit), the Fair Credit Reporting Act (preventing debt collectors from harassing consumers), and the Magnuson-Moss Warranty Act (assuring understandable warranty information is available to consumers).

In addition, the FTC must gather and make available to Congress, the President and the public, factual data concerning economic and business conditions. The FTC has extensive authority to demand information from businesses throughout the country.

The FTC uses adjudication and rule making on a continuing basis to correct problems within its jurisdiction. It prevents illegal business practices through **cease-and-desist orders** (prohibiting illegal conduct) and other means. Whenever possible the FTC encourages voluntary observance of the law, but if necessary formal complaints are filed in the agency court seeking a mandatory order against an offender.

Voluntary and Cooperative Action. Most law observance is achieved by voluntary and cooperative procedures. These procedures, discussed below, provide business with authoritative guidance and a measure of certainty as to what they may do under the laws administered by the FTC.

1. *Advisory opinions.* A business may seek an advisory opinion as to whether a proposed course of conduct will be permitted by the FTC. For example, may the business advertise or market a product in a certain unusual way without fear of being challenged by the FTC? An advisory opinion is binding on the FTC but may be canceled at any time. If the opinion is canceled, the requesting party must discontinue the conduct in question or face possible formal action by the FTC.

2. *Industry guides.* An industry guide is an interpretive rule without the force of law. It is merely an administrative interpretation of laws administered by the FTC expressed in language easily understood by the nonspecialist. An industry guide

enables the members of a particular industry, or business in general, to abandon questionable practices voluntarily and simultaneously. The FTC might, for example, attempt to establish some standards for the use of the word "diet" in the advertising and labeling of foods. If all industry members follow an industry guide, none will be put at a competitive disadvantage. Failure to comply with an industry guide may result in rule making or litigation (adjudication) to correct the problem.

3. *Trade regulation rules.* Trade regulation rules are legislative rules having the force of law. Trade regulation rules express the FTC's judgment concerning what the statutes it administers require. The rules may apply to all businesses in the nation, or they may be directed to particular industries, products, or geographical markets. A trade regulation rule will not be issued until the public and businesses to be affected have had ample opportunities to comment on the proposal. Although a trade regulation rule is binding on all to whom it is directed, an alleged violator has a right to a hearing on how the rule applies to him or her.

Litigation.   Cases before the FTC originate through informal complaints filed by consumers, competitors, Congress, or by federal, state, or local agencies. Complaints are screened to determine which ones warrant investigation. Also, the FTC itself may initiate an investigation to determine possible violation of the law it administers. Once an investigation is complete, the FTC staff may recommend (1) seeking an informal settlement of the case, (2) issuing a formal complaint, or (3) closing the matter by taking no further action.

If the FTC decides to issue a formal complaint, the alleged violator, who is called the "respondent," is served with a copy of the complaint and a copy of an order proposed by the FTC. Before a hearing on the matter takes place, the respondent may "consent" to the order. Under a **consent order** the respondent does not admit any violation of the law but agrees to discontinue the challenged practice.

If no agreement can be reached, the case is heard by an administrative law judge. After the hearing, the judge issues an initial decision which is appealable to the Commission (the five commissioners) or is reviewable by the Commission on its own initiative. If an initial decision is not appealed within the 30 days allowed (or if an adverse decision is upheld by the Commission upon appeal or review), a cease-and-desist order is issued. The respondent has 60 days after the order is served to appeal it to the appropriate United States court of appeal. The order becomes final if not appealed within the 60 days or if, upon appeal, it is affirmed by the proper courts.

Civil Penalty.   Violation of a final order to "cease-and-desist" subjects the offender to a suit by the federal government in a federal district court to collect a civil penalty of not more than *$10,000 for each day* the violation continues. Violations of other FTC orders (for example, consent orders and orders to make restitution or to place corrective advertising) as well as violations of a trade regulation rule are subject to the same civil penalties. The FTC does not have the authority to bring a criminal case. Criminal matters must be referred to the Justice Department for prosecution.

How and Why Courts Control Agency Activity.   Now that we have seen how agencies operate, it is important to understand how courts may review and overturn what agencies have done. The federal Administrative Procedure Act and similar state statutes contain common provisions regarding the proper scope of judicial review. Generally, a person aggrieved by a final decision of an agency is entitled to appeal to a court outside the agency. The proper court will remand, modify, or reverse an agency decision or conduct which violates the Constitution, exceeds the agency's authority, or is based on an error of law. The same result will occur if the agency followed an unlawful procedure, if the agency action is not supported by competent evidence, or if the agency otherwise acted arbitrarily or capriciously (without good reason).

When an agency action is challenged, a court must usually decide whether the agency acted unreasonably or whether there was substantial evidence to support its decision. The court's review does not include substituting its judgment for that of the agency. If the agency's action was arguably reasonable, the court will usually uphold the agency.

Some general points concerning judicial review are worth noting. A court will not review agency action until the person seeking the review has exhausted the possible administrative remedies within the agency. Exhaustion of remedies is not required for court review where the agency has acted obviously without authority or where the review is necessary to avoid irreparable injury to those affected by the agency action.

Many factors affect how closely a court scrutinizes the agency action under review. The experience of the agency and its professional reputation plays a part. Courts are less likely to upset agency action involving a highly technical subject than where the subject is one about which judges may more easily educate themselves. If administrative action was taken quickly, the judicial review will be more searching than where the agency action was more deliberate. Where the purpose of an agency is to discharge a function essential to the operation of government (such as collection of taxes), judicial review of its actions is usually less extensive than where the purpose of the agency is control of private business. Court review of administrative adjudication tends to be more searching than review of rule making.

The following case is an example of court review of the action of an administrative agency.

CASE 41.1 Industrial Union Department v. American Petroleum Institute
448 U.S. 607 (1980)

Facts: The Industrial Union Department of the Occupational Safety and Health Administration (OSHA) sets workplace exposure standards for "toxic materials" and "harmful physical substances." The exposure standard established for benzene, a chemical known to cause cancer, had previously been set at no more than 10 parts per million (ppm) in the air of a workplace. OSHA lowered the exposure standard to no more than 1 ppm, claiming that a lower standard was needed to reduce the incidence of leukemia caused by benzene exposure. OSHA had only assumptions, and no evidence, to back up its claim. The American Petroleum Institute challenged the agency's action in lowering the standard.

Question: May OSHA lower the workplace exposure standard for benzene without first determining that the old standard makes a workplace unsafe?

Answer: No. The old standard will remain in effect.

Reasoning: The law that permits OSHA to establish exposure standards requires the agency to determine that a place of employment is unsafe before an exposure standard may be issued. If a significant health risk is present, an exposure standard may be issued to eliminate or lessen the risk. Before lowering an existing standard, OSHA must show, as required by law, that the existing standard is not adequate to protect workers from a significant risk of harm. OSHA could not show that reducing the exposure standard from 10 ppm to 1 ppm would reduce health risks for workers. It merely assumed that lowering the standard would reduce the risks. Lowering the exposure standard must be based on reputable scientific evidence to support OSHA's belief.

TYPES OF ADMINISTRATIVE REGULATION

Government regulation can be divided into two general classifications: (1) regulation designed to achieve primarily an economic result, and (2) regulation designed to achieve primarily a social goal. Of course, all regulation has both economic and social consequences, and any given regulation may overlap both classifications.

Economic regulation includes bankruptcy law (Chapter 44); government control of the money supply through the Federal Reserve System; copyright, patent, and trademark protections; and antitrust law designed to encourage competition in our economy. Also included under economic regulation are the controls placed on specific industries, especially in transportation, communication, and utility businesses. Some examples are regulation of railroads and trucking by the Interstate Commerce Commission, of airlines by the Civil Aeronautics Board, and of television and radio broadcasting by the Federal Communications Commission.

Social regulation covers law designed to achieve a social or political goal, sometimes with little reference to its economic impact, whether good or bad. One example of social regulation is environmental law designed to achieve clean air and water, to discourage dumping of toxic wastes, to encourage recycling of resources, and to assure safe production and use of pesticides. Other examples of social regulation affecting business include consumer protection laws (Chapter 42), civil rights laws (especially those outlawing discrimination in employment), product safety laws (enforced by the Consumer Product Safety Commission and the Food and Drug Administration), and worker safety and health laws (enforced by the Occupational Safety and Health Administration). Although enacted to accomplish social ends, some social regulation actually governs economic relationships between parties covered by the regulation. Examples of this type of social regulation are consumer protection law, labor law (Chapter 43), and pension law, respectively meant to protect consumers, employees, and employee benefits.

Economic Regulation   For whatever reason it is created, all government regulation of business has economic consequences to both the businesses regulated and the public. However, a number of industries vital to the working of our economy are subject to economic regulation that it is believed will assist those industries. Such regulation is often meant to correct market failures or market problems. For example, economic regulation has been used to control "natural monopolies" such as public utilities, assure adequate service in transportation and energy, allocate limited space to airlines and broadcasters, and protect against costly bank failures. However, critics of economic regulation charge that regulation is burdensome and unnecessarily expensive because it often creates more inefficiency than an imperfect, unregulated market would. Some important examples of economic regulation are found in the areas of transportation, communication, finance, and energy.

Transportation Regulation.   Since its creation in 1887, the **Interstate Commerce Commission (ICC)** has become the primary regulator of interstate surface transportation, including trucks, trains, buses, inland waterway and coastal shipping, and freight forwarders. Generally, the ICC has the authority to issue certificates to carriers seeking to provide transportation for the public, as well as the authority to pass on the carriers' rates, adequacy of service, and mergers. The ICC attempts to assure that the carriers it regulates will offer the public reasonable services at fair rates. There have been recent actions in both the ICC and Congress to begin deregulating many aspects of surface transportation by allowing the free market to make decisions the ICC has until recently passed on.

Another area undergoing deregulation is the civil air transport industry, long regulated by the **Civil Aeronautics Board (CAB)**. Since the passage by Congress of the **Airline Deregulation Act of 1978**, the CAB's powers have gradually been reduced, giving it less authority to determine the routes airlines fly and the prices they charge. The board has also relaxed its requirements for the startup of new airlines, thus older airlines have recently seen increased competition. In the early 1980s, the CAB continued to make rules concerning compensation to passengers who are bumped from overbooked flights or who lose luggage. It has also considered banning smoking on short flights and in small planes. When the CAB is abolished on January 1, 1985, other agencies will be assigned its remaining functions.

Safety regulation of the air transport industry is the responsibility of the **Federal Aviation Administration (FAA)**, a part of the Department of Transportation. The FAA issues and enforces rules and minimum standards for manufacture, use, and maintenance of aircraft, and for certification of airports and pilots. The FAA also maintains our country's air traffic control and air navigation system.

Communication Regulation.   Created in 1934, the **Federal Communications Commission (FCC)** regulates all aspects of interstate communication. The scope of its regulation encompasses radio and television broadcasting, telephones and telegraph, cable television systems, two-way radio operations, and satellite communications. The FCC is generally responsible for overseeing the development and operation of an efficient and affordable nationwide communication system. The use of broadcast facilities to assist in civil defense and national defense is also part of its responsibilities. In addition, the FCC regulates communication services between the United States and overseas points by common carriers. Because the channels for airwave communication are limited, the FCC has traditionally granted licenses to radio and television operators based on policies established by the agency. Recently, however, the FCC decided to save money and labor by doing away with citizens' band (CB) radio licensing, while still policing against rule violations.

Finance Regulation.   The **Securities and Exchange Commission (SEC)** was established in 1934 to regulate the securities markets—the markets where the stocks and bonds of businesses are bought and sold. It is the SEC's job to see that the fullest possible disclosure is given to the investing public. The SEC also attempts to protect the interests of investors and the public by preventing fraud and manipulation of the financial markets by the unscrupulous. For example, the SEC may halt the sale of securities to the public when inadequate or inaccurate information has been provided. The Commission must approve most rules of the securities exchanges, and it also regulates many trading practices. In addition, the SEC has broad authority over brokers, dealers, and agents involved in securities transactions.

The **Federal Reserve System (FRS)** is also extremely important to the economic health of our country. Since 1913, the FRS has served as the central bank of the United States, making and administering credit and monetary policy. By regulating and supervising many banking functions, the Federal Reserve tries to preserve a sound banking industry able to meet the country's financial needs. Another agency, the **Federal Deposit Insurance Corporation (FDIC)**, assists in providing a stable banking industry by insuring the bank deposits in most banks.

Energy Regulation.   A continuing supply of energy is critical to the proper operation of the United States economy. The **Department of Energy (DOE),** and agencies within it such as the **Federal Energy Administration (FEA)** and the **Federal Energy Regulatory Commission (FERC),** have the primary responsibility for regulating the production and distribution of energy for our country. For example, the FERC sets rates and charges for the transportation and sale of natural gas, for the transmission and sale of electricity, and for the transportation of oil by pipeline. FERC also licenses hydroelectric power projects. FERC's authority even extends to controlling the price of energy produced and sold solely within one state, since such transactions can have an effect on interstate commerce. High intrastate energy prices in one state might cause energy shortages in other states.

The **Nuclear Regulatory Commission (NRC)** licenses and regulates nuclear energy. The NRC devises rules and standards for building and operating nuclear reactors. To protect the public health and the environment, the NRC is responsible for inspecting the activities of the companies it has licensed to ensure that they abide by the NRC's safety rules. Nuclear accidents such as the 1979 emergency shutdown of Three Mile Island in Pennsylvania indicate how important it is to have effective regulation of nuclear power.

Social Regulation

Much of the government regulation criticized by business in the past two decades as being too impractical or too expensive has been regulation designed to further social goals such as a clean environment, safe work places, and fair employment practices. Social regulation is not a new idea. For example, the *Food and Drug Administration* (FDA) was created in 1931 to protect the public's health. However, the 1970s saw the creation of a number of new agencies to promote social goals.

Environmental Regulation.   The **Environmental Protection Agency (EPA)** was established by Congress in 1970 to protect and enhance our country's physical environment. The EPA is assigned the task of working with state and local governments in controlling and reducing pollution in the areas of air, water, radiation, noise, solid waste, and toxic substances. The agency's responsibilities include doing research, monitoring pollution, setting pollution standards, and engaging in a number of enforcement activities. For example, in areas where air pollution is a serious problem, the EPA has threatened the cutoff of millions of dollars in federal aid unless the localities establish regular auto-emission testing programs.

The public is beginning to understand the risks posed to public health by toxic chemicals. The EPA's Office of Pesticides and Toxic Substances is charged with developing national strategies for controlling toxic substances and directing related enforcement activities. Its activities include the control and regulation of pesticides to ensure human safety and the establishment and monitoring of pesticide levels on foods. For example, the EPA recently suspended the use of the chemical EDB as a pesticide fumigant on food because its effect on humans is not fully known.

Health and Safety Regulation.   The **Food and Drug Administration (FDA)** is one of the oldest agencies whose activities are directed at protecting the public. Its mission is to guard the public's health against impure and unsafe food, drugs, and cosmetics. For example, when "starch blockers" became a popular fad diet aid in 1982, the FDA sought and obtained a court order that starch blockers were not food, but rather were untested drugs whose safety and effectiveness were unknown.

The **Consumer Product Safety Commission (CPSC)** was established in 1972 to protect the public from unreasonable risks of injury from consumer products. The CPSC requires manufacturers to report to it any products that contain substantial hazards and to correct or recall such products already on the market. The agency collects information on injuries caused by consumer products and operates an information clearinghouse. It also conducts product research and encourages voluntary development of safety standards for consumer products. When necessary, CPSC can create mandatory product safety standards and ban hazardous products. An example of a safety standard imposed by the CPSC is the "deadman control" currently required on walk-behind rotary lawn mowers. This safety feature must stop the mower blade within 3 seconds after the operator releases the mower handle. It is hoped this will significantly reduce injuries caused by power mowers.

The **Occupational Safety and Health Administration (OSHA)**, a part of the **Department of Labor (DOL)**, was created in 1970 to attend to the health and safety concerns of the American worker. OSHA develops, issues, and enforces occupational safety and health standards and rules. It may, for example, issue rules limiting worker exposure to hazardous chemicals, such as benzene, and to other hazardous substances, such as airborne asbestos and cotton dust. OSHA regularly conducts investigations and inspects work sites to determine employer compliance with its rules, and it may issue citations and propose penalties when it discovers safety or health violations.

The **National Highway Traffic Safety Administration (NHTSA)**, an agency within the **Department of Transportation (DOT)**, was also created in 1970. NHTSA's primary task is to regulate the safety of motor vehicles and tires. The agency has implemented a number of programs to reduce highway accidents and the severity of injuries caused by them. NHTSA may issue vehicle safety standards which require that vehicles have certain safety features, such as seat belts, air bags, or other passive restraints. It may also require that vehicles meet certain safety performance levels, such as having bumpers that can withstand a 2½-mile-per-hour collision without damage. The agency continuously investigates safety-related vehicle defects and has the authority to require a motor vehicle manufacturer to recall the vehicle to correct the defect. In the last decade, hundreds of thousands of cars have been recalled and repaired "voluntarily" by their manufacturers due to the work of this agency.

Employment Regulation.   The **National Labor Relations Board (NLRB)** (Chapter 43) administers the federal laws directly related to labor relations, including workers' rights to organize and bargain collectively.

The **Equal Employment Opportunity Commission (EEOC)** was created by the Civil Rights Act of 1964 to be responsible for compliance and enforcement activities relating to equal employment opportunity in the United States. The EEOC attempts to eliminate discrimination based on race, color, religion, sex, national origin, or age in hiring, promoting, firing, testing, training, and all other conditions of employment. In addition to investigating and attempting to resolve employee complaints of discrimination, the EEOC promotes voluntary action programs by employers, unions, and community organizations to encourage equal employment opportunity.

ANTITRUST LAW AND ITS ENFORCEMENT: EXAMPLE OF ECONOMIC REGULATION

Antitrust law is a prominent example of economic regulation applying to most businesses. The term "antitrust law" refers to a broad system of federal and state law that seeks to promote business competition and to discourage monopoly power. "Monopoly" literally means "a single seller." Monopoly power is defined as the power of a single large seller to use predatory (destructive) means in order to exclude competitors from a market or in order to fix prices at arbitrarily high levels. Underlying antitrust law is a fundamental precept of capitalism: Scarce resources can most efficiently be allocated to satisfy consumer wants at the lowest price through a competitive free enterprise system. Such a system is incompatible with monopoly power and the high prices that result from the abuse of such power.

Sherman Act: Purpose, Scope, and Enforcement

The **Sherman Act** was enacted in 1890 to outlaw joint business conduct which unreasonably restrains interstate or foreign commerce. Also prohibited is monopolizing or attempting to monopolize any part of interstate or foreign commerce. The Antitrust Division of the Department of Justice may bring both civil and criminal charges against Sherman Act violators. Maximum criminal fines of $1 million against corporations and $100,000 against individuals may be levied. Individuals are also subject to up to 3 years' imprisonment. Government civil suits seek to restrain violations by injunction. Individuals or businesses directly economically harmed by antitrust violations may bring civil damage suits and, if successful, collect treble (three times the actual) damages plus attorneys' fees and court costs.

Section 1 of the Sherman Act prohibits any *agreement* between at least two persons (individuals, businesses) to act together *to restrain trade*. Only agreements which *unreasonably* restrain trade are illegal under the Sherman Act.

Some types of agreement are always illegal and may not be justified or explained by the perpetrators. These agreements are said to be *per se illegal* or *per se unreasonable*. They include horizontal price-fixing (by direct competitors), vertical price-fixing (resale price maintenance through a chain of distribution as between a manufacturer and retailer), bid-rigging, horizontal market division (competitor agreements to allocate products, territories, or customers), agreements to limit production, and group boycotts to lessen economic competition.

Agreements that do not fall within a *per se* (automatically illegal) category are judged by the "rule of reason" test. In these cases a court must examine any economic justifications for the allegedly illegal agreement to see if they outweigh the agreement's anticompetitive effects. If the anticompetitive effects are not counterbalanced by procompetitive justifications, the agreement is declared unreasonable and therefore illegal.

Price-fixing is the most common violation of Section 1. Any private agreements establishing maximum prices, minimum prices, price ranges, bargaining prices, credit terms or otherwise adversely affecting competitive pricing can be considered *per se* illegal. The Supreme Court recently stated: "Price is the central nervous system of the economy, and an agreement that interferes with the setting of price by free market forces is illegal on its face."

CASE 41.2   Catalano, Inc. v. Target Sales
446 U.S. 635 (1980)

Facts: Catalano and other beer retailers in Fresno, California sued beer wholesalers in the area, seeking treble-damages for a violation of the Sherman Act Section 1. Catalano claimed that there was a horizontal conspiracy by the competing wholesalers to eliminate the industrywide practice of granting short-term credit. Catalano asked the court to declare the defendants' conduct to be a *per se* violation.

Question: Was a horizontal agreement among competitors to fix credit terms a *per se* violation of Section 1 of the Sherman Act?

Answer: Yes. Agreeing on credit terms is a type of price fixing.

Reasoning: A horizontal agreement to fix prices is illegal *per se*, regardless of the reasonableness of the price fixed. An agreement to terminate interest-free credit is tantamount to an agreement to eliminate discounts and thus is within the *per se* rule against price fixing.

There are three distinct offenses in Section 2 of the Sherman Act: (1) monopolizing, (2) attempting to monopolize, and (3) conspiracy to monopolize. The first two can be committed by the conduct of a *single firm* in acquiring a monopoly position or attempting to do so. In contrast, *conspiracies* to monopolize (like Section 1 violations) require the *joint conduct* of two or more persons to violate the law.

The most important of the three offenses is "monopolizing." Two elements must be proved to establish criminal or civil liability for monopolization: (1) the acquisition of *monopoly power*, that is, the power to control prices or exclude competitors in a relevant market; and (2) a *general intent* to monopolize, that is, deliberateness in acquiring monopoly power. Courts consider many factors in deciding whether a firm has monopoly power in a relevant market, but the most important is the size (percentage) of the firm's market share. In determining a relevant market, courts define the *product* involved (for example, all paint or only automotive paint) and the *geographic area* of effective competition in which the product, including interchangeable substitute products, is traded. The courts find general intent to monopolize present when a defendant has engaged in deliberate conduct the probable result of which is to obtain monopoly. This is often shown by predatory activities such as injuring or excluding competitors, erecting barriers to entry, adopting "predatory pricing" policies, or buying up competitors. The recent breakup of AT&T was agreed to in order to settle a monopolization case brought against it by the Antitrust Division of the Justice Department.

Clayton Act: Purpose, Scope, and Enforcement

Congress enacted the **Clayton Act** in 1914 to respond to criticisms leveled at Sherman Act enforcement. Small business had complained that the Sherman Act did little or nothing to stop anticompetitive practices in their beginning stages. It was thought that by prohibiting several kinds of anticompetitive business practices the Clayton Act could discourage or prevent monopolies in their *incipiency*. To do this, the Clayton Act deals with *probabilities*, not certainties. Thus, in each section of the act, the particular conduct under attack is declared unlawful if it *tends* "to substantially lessen competition." Section 2 of the Clayton Act (later amended and strengthened as the **Robinson-Patman Act**) generally prohibits price discrimination in the sale of commodities (goods). Also prohibited by the act are exclusive dealing and tying contracts (conditioning the sale of one product to the purchase of a second undesired product) (Section 3), anticompetitive business mergers (Section 7), and interlocking directorates (competing firms with common corporate directors) (Section 8). Because it deals only with probabilities, most violations of the Clayton Act are not criminal. The federal government through the Justice Department's Antitrust Division or the FTC may sue for civil remedies, usually injunctions, to correct violations. Private treble damage suits are also authorized where a plaintiff can show economic injury due to a Clayton Act offense affecting interstate commerce.

Federal Trade Commission Act: Purpose and Scope

Simultaneously with the passage of the Clayton Act in 1914, Congress enacted the Federal Trade Commission Act creating the FTC to provide day-to-day enforcement of the antitrust laws. The Commission was specifically charged with enforcement of the Clayton Act. Section 5 of the FTC Act gave the FTC broad authority to proceed against "unfair methods of competition" and "unfair or deceptive acts or practices." In enacting Section 5, Congress recognized the limitless ingenuity of business persons to circumvent existing laws by developing anticompetitive practices that were not specifically forbidden by the antitrust statutes. Therefore, the FTC was given comprehensive authority to prosecute any practice that it considered anticompetitive or unfair, subject to final review by the courts. In exercising this broad authority, the FTC considers whether the particular practice (1) offends public policy; (2) is immoral, unethical, oppressive, or unscrupulous; or (3) causes substantial injury to consumers, particularly with respect to their purchases of the necessities of life. Courts have also interpreted Section 5 as conferring upon the FTC the noncriminal power to enforce against any violation of the Sherman and Clayton Acts. Since 1914, many statutes have extended the FTC's jurisdiction into the area of consumer protection.

The following case is an example of the FTC's broad authority to curtail unfairness in the marketplace.

CASE 41.3   Atlantic Refining Company v. Federal Trade Commission
381 U.S. 357 (1965)

Facts: Atlantic Refining, an oil company, and Goodyear Tire Company agreed that Atlantic would "sponsor" the sale of Goodyear tires, batteries, and accessories to Atlantic's retail gasoline service station dealers. Goodyear made direct sales to Atlantic's dealers, but Atlantic carried on a joint sales promotion program with Goodyear, and Atlantic received commissions from Goodyear for all products purchased by Atlantic dealers. Atlantic, which leased service stations and equipment to dealers and sold them gas, used its economic power over its dealers to encourage them and to coerce them through threats to buy Goodyear products for resale. The FTC claimed this was an unfair method of competition by Atlantic in violation of Section 5 of the FTC Act. The evidence showed that prior to the Atlantic-Goodyear agreement Atlantic dealers preferred to buy tires and accessories from other manufacturers.

Question: Was the Atlantic-Goodyear agreement an unfair method of competition?

Answer: Yes. The effect of the agreement was to force Atlantic's dealers to buy Goodyear products.

Reasoning: Atlantic's economic coercion of its dealers to buy Goodyear products from which Atlantic made commissions had the effect of Atlantic agreeing with Goodyear to require its dealers to buy Goodyear products. This precluded the dealers from making their own choices about from whom to buy products. The agreement operated much like an unlawful tying scheme, where economic power in one market (as, service stations or gasoline) is used to curtail competition in another market (as, automotive accessories).

SUMMARY

Much law regulating business today is made by administrative agencies of the federal, state, and local governments. Government regulation refers to law controlling or influencing the conduct, scope, or size of business. The federal government regulates interstate commerce, and the states regulate mainly local commerce. When federal and state law conflict, federal law usually prevails. Regulation must not violate the rights protected by the Constitution.

Administrative agencies are used by government to regulate business by carrying out the policies created by statutes. The large number of agencies, the wide scope of their powers, and the great volume of their rules and decisions indicate that agencies have a great impact on modern business.

The trend toward administrative regulation developed due to the need for experts in certain fields of regulation as well as due to the public's demand for speedy, simple, and inexpensive legal procedures. Important also are the continuity and uniformity with which a problem may be addressed by an agency.

Agencies are assigned specific powers by enabling legislation, including, when necessary, the authority to investigate, make rules, prosecute, adjudicate, license, set rates, administer, advise, and supervise. Rules issued by an agency will be procedural, interpretive, or legislative. An adjudication by an agency will result in an order establishing the rights or duties of those regulated by the agency.

The Federal Trade Commission (FTC) is representative of how agencies operate. The FTC is assigned enforcement responsibilities under several statutes created by Congress. It attempts to achieve law observance by businesses through voluntary action such as advisory opinions and industry guides. When necessary, the FTC issues trade regulation rules and litigates to enforce the law, seeking civil penalties where appropriate.

The courts have the power to review the actions of administrative agencies and to overturn the result when an agency acts improperly.

Government regulation may be classified as economic regulation, social regulation, or both. Economic regulation is designed to achieve primarily an economic result, whereas social regulation is meant to accomplish a social goal. Regulation in the fields of transportation, communication, finance, energy, and antitrust are principal types of economic regulation. Important examples of social regulation include environmental protection, health and safety regulation, and regulation of employment practices.

Antitrust law, a prominent example of economic regulation applying to most businesses, seeks to promote business competition and to discourage monopoly power. Antitrust law is embodied in three statutes: the Sherman Act, Clayton Act, and Federal Trade Commission Act. The Sherman Act prohibits agreements and other joint conduct which unreasonably restrains trade. It also outlaws monopolizing, whether done jointly or by a single firm. The Clayton Act prohibits activities which *may* substantially lessen competition or lead to monopolies.

The Federal Trade Commission Act prohibits unfair methods of competition and unfair or deceptive acts or practices. The prohibited unfair conduct includes unethical, oppressive, or unscrupulous practices as well as the anticompetitive practices outlawed by the other two acts. The FTC enforces the FTC Act and the Clayton Act by seeking cease-and-desist orders from its administrative court. Using the federal courts, the Antitrust Division of the Justice Department enforces the Sherman Act and shares civil enforcement of the Clayton Act with the FTC. Violators of the Sherman Act may be criminally prosecuted.

REVIEW QUESTIONS

1. What is meant by the terms (**a**) administrative agency, and (**b**) regulatory agency?

2. Define government regulation.
3. Compare the powers of the federal government and the states to regulate business.
4. What are some constitutional limitations on government regulation?
5. What is meant by the term "independent agency"?
6. What are some important reasons for the trend toward administrative regulation?
7. What types of powers may an administrative agency be given?
8. Discuss how the FTC operates to enforce the laws under its jurisdiction.
9. How may courts "control" agency activity?
10. Explain what is meant by the terms "economic regulation" and "social regulation."
11. Give some examples of regulation affecting business.
12. Explain the purpose of antitrust law.
13. What activities are prohibited by the (a) Sherman Act, (b) Clayton Act, and (c) FTC Act?

CASE PROBLEMS

1. Under a federal agricultural statute designed to prevent surpluses and shortages of wheat, a farmer was alloted 11 acres upon which to grow wheat on his farm. He sowed and harvested 23 acres and was fined a civil penalty of $117 for the excess wheat he grew. The farmer sued to have this wheat marketing quota declared unconstitutional as it applied to him. He argued that since most of the wheat he grew was consumed as seed, feed, or flour on his own farm, the federal Constitution's commerce clause could not be used as a basis for regulating his production of wheat. The government argued that federal law could regulate the farmer as the excess wheat grown had an effect on the interstate market for wheat. Does the federal government have the authority under the commerce clause to regulate the quantity of wheat the farmer could grow? Explain your answer.

2. The New York Public Service Commission prohibited utilities in the state "from using [utility bill] inserts to discuss political matters, including the desirability of future development of nuclear power." The Commission's order prevented Consolidated Edison from expressing its opinions and viewpoints on controversial issues of public policy, such as the nuclear power issue, through inserts in monthly electric bills. Consolidated challenged the state regulation as a violation of the utility's freedom of speech guaranteed it in the First Amendment of the Constitution. The state Commission argued that it should be able to prohibit utilities under its regulation from using bill inserts to express political opinions because the utilities' customers receiving bills were a captive audience who should not be subjected to the utilities beliefs. Should a court uphold the right of a utility to express political opinions through bill inserts? Explain your conclusion.

3. The Federal Trade Commission issues a trade regulation rule making the use of sweepstakes in the marketing of products in interstate commerce an "unfair method of competition." A company which regularly uses sweepstakes to attract customers to

its products wishes to challenge the rule in federal court. May it do so? Why or why not?

4. Paper Companies was a group of ten manufacturing firms that accounted for 90 percent of the shipments of corrugated containers from plants in the southeastern United States. From 1955 to 1963, these firms regularly exchanged price information among themselves, but no formal agreements to adhere to a price schedule were made. When a seller requested and received price information from a competitor, it affirmed its willingness to furnish such information in return. After two competitors exchanged information, they would usually quote the same price to a buyer. The exchange had the effect of stabilizing prices of corrugated containers within a fairly narrow range. Did Paper Companies violate Section 1 of the Sherman Act? Explain the reasons for your answer.

5. Computer Giant Corporation, a large, profitable multinational company, has captured 90 percent of the home computer market in the United States in the last 2 years by driving some competitors out of business through selling its computers well below cost, and by purchasing most other competing firms which could afford to stay in the home computer market. Is Computer Giant monopolizing the home computer market? Explain.

CONSUMER PROTECTION

We are all consumers. Almost daily we purchase goods and services, sometimes paying cash and sometimes buying on credit. Often, we are induced to purchase items through advertising. The seller may give warranties or make representations about the nature or quality of the product being sold. If credit is extended to us, we are asked to sign an agreement containing provisions about installment payments, interest rates, and remedies in the event of default. Seldom do we have the advantage of consulting an attorney for advice at any stage of these transactions. An unscrupulous seller can, and occasionally does, defraud us. More often, we enter contracts that are unwise or beyond our means.

In recent years a body of law called "consumer law" has been developing to give protection to consumers. Historically, many areas of the law developed to give protection to particular groups of people. For example, the law of contracts and of sales were developed primarily for the benefit of merchants. The law of commercial paper arose primarily to help bankers and lenders in their dealings with business people. There were few laws created for consumers. Beginning in the 1960s and continuing throughout the 1970s a number of statutes were passed and regulations enacted which gave specific protection to the consumer.

This chapter discusses recent major developments in consumer protection through the regulation of advertising, sales to consumers, consumer credit, and consumer debt collection. These developments include court decisions (common law), statutes enacted by legislative bodies, and rules or regulations formulated by administrative agencies. Throughout the chapter references are made to other chapters in this text where additional law for the protection of consumers is discussed.

Although there is no universal definition of a "consumer transaction," many statutes use the phrase "a transaction made for personal, family, or household purposes." In this chapter we will use this phrase as the definition of consumer purchase or loan. For example, consumer law applies to the purchase of an automobile if the buyer intends to use the car for pleasure. If the buyer is a corporation purchasing a "company car" for its sales manager, consumer law will probably not apply.

REGULATION OF ADVERTISING

The consumer is bombarded with advertising throughout the waking hours. Sellers advertise their products and services in a variety of media, including television, radio, and newspapers. If an advertisement is false or misleading, the consumer may have legal recourse under state or federal law.

State Regulation of Advertising

A seller who falsely advertises his or her product may be liable in damages for the *common law tort of fraud.* In Chapter 3 we considered the tort of fraud (see pp. 46–49) and noted that in an action for fraud the plaintiff must prove five elements. The first element is a false representation of fact. It is often difficult for a plaintiff to prove that a defendant made a false statement of fact in advertising his or her product. Advertisers tend to use words such as "the best," "ideal," or "wonderful" to describe their product. Courts treat such statements as mere opinion or "puffing" and thus deny consumers the right to recover damages if they are disappointed. Only if the seller is considered an expert will the courts treat statements of opinion as actionable. Of course, if the seller makes a statement of fact which he or she knows is false, the buyer may recover damages for the tort of fraud or rescind the contract. For example, if the seller states that "this heater will heat your pool to 80° in less than one hour," and the seller knows or should know that this is impossible, the buyer has a cause of action.

It is possible that a consumer may have a cause of action under the Uniform Commercial Code (UCC) for *breach of a warranty*. In Chapter 18 we considered warranties as a basis of product liability (see pp. 287–297). If a seller of goods warrants the product fit for a certain purpose, the buyer may recover if damages are sustained because the product is defective. Advertising claims are often treated as express warranties. But, again, the courts are reluctant to impose liability on a seller who engages in mere "puffing" of his or her products without making statements of fact. In many sales transactions the UCC imposes an implied warranty of fitness or of merchantability. Often, consumers have been able to recover substantial damages in cases involving impure foods and defective prescription drugs. There are several problems for the consumer in recovering for breach of warranty, which were discussed in Chapter 18. One of the common problems arises when the seller sells goods "as is." Such language alerts the buyer that there is no express or implied warranty given for the product.

Federal Regulation of Advertising

The **Federal Trade Commission Act** charges the Federal Trade Commission (FTC) with the responsibility of regulating advertising in the United States. The act prohibits false advertising for foods, drugs, cosmetics, and devices, and prohibits "unfair or deceptive practices." Under powers given in the act, the FTC has enacted rules prohibiting false or misleading advertising in business. Proof of intent to deceive is not a prerequisite to finding a violation, as would be true under tort law. But, under FTC guidelines adopted in 1983, the FTC may prevent only advertising that has injured an average (i.e., reasonable) person. The FTC guidelines change prior rules where the FTC could prevent advertising that had the *capacity* to deceive the average person.

There is a major difference in consequences between the tort of fraud and the FTC rules. The FTC has the power to issue cease-and-desist orders to defendants, forcing them to stop false and misleading advertising, and the power to order corrective advertising. Corrective advertising requires the advertiser to inform the public that a previous advertisement was false or misleading and to supply the correct information to consumers.

A portion of the **Consumer Credit Protection Act**, commonly known as the "truth in lending act," or simply "truth in lending," regulates advertising in connection with certain consumer credit transactions. For example, "bait advertising" is prohibited. A creditor may not state that certain credit can be arranged or that a specific down payment will be accepted unless the creditor "usually and customarily" arranges credit in that amount or accepts down payments in that amount. Other parts of the Consumer Credit Protection Act require full disclosure in advertisements. We will discuss the disclosure provisions of the act later in this chapter.

Most states have adopted laws prohibiting deceptive advertising which are similar in scope to the regulations of the Federal Trade Commission and the Consumer Credit Protection Act. The following case illustrates "bait advertising" that violates one such state law.

CASE 42.1   McCormick Piano & Organ Co., Inc. v. Geiger
412 N.E. 2d 842 (Ind. App. 1980)

Facts: McCormick Piano & Organ Co., Inc. advertised in the newspaper a special sale price of $699 on Kimball Whitney Spinet pianos. The advertisement contained a drawing of a piano which was a composite of several more expensive models. The drawing bore a striking resemblance to a Crest Piano which sold for $1,500. The company vice-president acknowledged that the average person would not detect the discrepancies between the drawing and the Crest model. Dennis and Janice Geiger went to McCormick's showroom and remarked that the advertisement had caught their attention because the drawing matched the style of their furniture. The salesperson offered to sell a spinet piano to the Geigers but they rejected it, stating that it was not the same as the one depicted in the drawing. After several conversations, the salesperson advised the Geigers that she was unable to order the spinet piano from the factory. When Mrs. Geiger asked for the names of customers who had purchased the pianos advertised, the sales person became hysterical and exclaimed that she would not sell a piano to Mrs. Geiger if she were the last person on earth. Mr. and Mrs. Geiger filed suit alleging fraud and deceptive advertising in violation of Indiana law. The jury returned a verdict for the Geigers and McCormick appealed.

Question: Was McCormick guilty of deceptive advertising?

Answer: Yes. McCormick was deceptive and should be held liable.

Reasoning: The court stated that under the Indiana law a merchant commits a deceptive act when the merchant represents that the subject of a consumer transaction is of a particular "standard, quality, grade, style, or model," if it is not and the merchant knows or should reasonably know that it is not. The use of "bait-and-switch" advertising as a lure to sell other non-advertised products is exactly the kind of trade practice which the law is designed to prohibit. The court noted that a picture of the Kimball Whitney Spinet piano was available and that McCormick had placed an incorrect advertisement in the paper on a prior occasion.

The judgment was affirmed.

REGULATION OF SALES TO CONSUMERS

There are a number of state and federal statutes and regulations governing sales of goods and services. The common law of sales and of contracts provide some protection for consumers, but not nearly enough. As we have seen, Chapter 10 discussed various defenses to enforcement of a contract such as incapacity (minority, incompetency), duress, undue influence, fraud, and mistake. Chapter 11 presented certain situations where contracts are void because of illegality (usury, unconscionability). Chapter 12 pointed out that certain contracts are unenforceable unless evidenced by a writing (sale of goods over $500, contracts affecting an interest in land). Chapter 15 considered several sales concepts that may give protection to consumers (good faith purchaser, unconscionability). Also, Chapter 18 discussed product liability and express and implied warranties. Those chapters contain numerous provisions to protect purchasers of goods. In this part of this chapter we will examine the major state and federal laws giving consumers further protection in various types of sale transactions.

Sales of New Cars; "Lemon Laws"

In recent years a large number of states have enacted so-called "lemon laws" to protect consumers who purchase new cars for personal use. The statutes generally define a lemon as a car that in the first year after purchase has to be repaired four times for the same defect, or that is in the shop more than 30 days. When a dispute between a car dealer and a purchaser cannot be settled satisfactorily, the purchaser is entitled to an arbitration hearing (arbitration was discussed in Chapter 2). The arbitrator may order the car manufacturer to replace the car or refund the purchase price. If the consumer is not satisfied with the arbitrator's decision, he or she may file a lawsuit.

Home Solicitation Sales

A regulation of the FTC gives a consumer 3 days to rescind a home solicitation sale of consumer goods or services over $25. The purpose of the rule is to give the purchaser a "cooling-off" period to reflect on purchases made in the home. There are many instances of high-pressure salespeople inducing someone in his or her home to purchase an expensive vacuum cleaner or set of encyclopedia. Under the FTC rule the buyer does not have to give a reason for rescinding the sale. Of course, after the 3-day period expires the consumer may rescind only if one of the traditional contract law defenses exist (duress, undue influence, fraud). The FTC rule applies to both cash sales and credit sales. The rule does not apply to transactions in which the consumer requests the seller to visit the home for the purpose of repairing the consumer's personal property, nor to the sale of insurance. Many states have enacted statutes similar to the FTC rule, giving the consumer added protection.

Real Estate Lien Transactions

Under truth in lending legislation a consumer is given 3 business days to rescind a credit transaction involving a lien on his or her residence. At the time of the transaction the creditor must furnish the consumer with two copies of a notice of right to rescind. If the consumer decides to rescind within the 3-day period, no reason need be given; he or she simply mails a copy of the notice to the creditor.

The right of rescission applies to transactions creating both voluntary and involuntary liens (see discussion in Chapter 25). A typical example of the consumer's right to rescind occurs when a creditor makes improvements on the consumer's residence. If the consumer does not pay the creditor, or if subcontractors or suppliers are not paid in full, mechanics' liens are created. These liens are subject to the "cooling-off" period of 3 business days. After the 3 days expire the consumer may not rescind unless grounds exist under the law of contracts.

Truth in Lending covers transactions involving the usual single-family residence as well as a mobile home used as a consumer's principal dwelling. The right of rescission under the act does not apply to real estate or property other than the consumer's principal residence, such as vacation property. Also, the right does not apply to first mortgages (or trust deeds) created for the purpose of acquiring or constructing the consumer's residence. For example, suppose Dora borrows $50,000 from the bank in order to buy a home from Sam. Dora intends to live in the home. Bank requires Dora to execute a first mortgage on the home to secure the loan. Dora has no right of rescission under the Consumer Credit Protection Act.

There may be practical difficulties to exercising the right of rescission. A prerequisite to rescission is that the consumer must return or offer to return the consideration received from the creditor. No problem is encountered if the consumer has purchased goods that are removable from the residence. Suppose, however, that a consumer contracts to have custom-made carpeting installed in his or her residence and then has a change of heart and exercises the right to rescind within 3 days. A federal regulation provides that if return of the merchandise would be impractical or inequitable, the consumer must offer to pay its reasonable value.

In the following case the court discusses the consumer's duty to return the consideration given by the creditor.

CASE 42.2

Powers v. Sims and Levin
542 F.2d 1216 (4th Cir. 1976)

Facts: Mr. and Mrs. Powers negotiated a loan from Sims and Levin for $5,000. The proceeds were used to pay for improvements to their home but $3,304 was used to pay a previous loan to First Bank and to pay delinquent fire insurance premiums and real estate taxes. A dispute arose between the parties regarding the amount of monthly installments. Within the time period allowed under the Truth in Lending Act the Powers offered to rescind the loan and offered to return the home improvements. Sims and Levin responded that it would not agree to a rescission unless Mr. and Mrs. Powers also returned the $3,304 expended to pay debts. The Powers refused and brought suit under the Truth in Lending Act seeking rescission. The trial court granted summary judgment for the Powers. Sims and Levin appealed.

Question: Should the Powers be required to reimburse Sims and Levin $3,304 as a condition of rescission?

Answer: Yes. The Powers must return the $3,304 expended to pay their debts.

Reasoning: The court held that the offer to rescind was deficient. The consumer was required to return all home improvements and to reimburse the lender for money expended in satisfying the other indebtedness of the Powers. In demanding such reimbursement, the lender was insisting upon what was its legal due. What the Powers accomplished was not a rescission under the statute but an anticipatory breach of contract. The court reversed the trial court and conditioned the Powers' right of rescission upon their return to the lender of all funds spent by them in discharging the earlier indebtedness as well as the value of the home improvements.

Interstate Land Sales

A consumer who purchases unimproved land through the mail may receive protection under a federal statute known as the **Interstate Land Sales Full Disclosure Act**. The purpose of the act is to ensure that purchasers are informed at the outset of all material information pertaining to the land being purchased. Any seller of 100 or more lots in a common plan who uses the mails or any other means of communication in interstate commerce (television, magazines) must file a disclosure statement with the Department of Housing and Urban Development (HUD). The statement must inform prospective purchasers of material facts concerning future development, such as location of roads, water supply, schools, and shopping centers. This and other relevant information must be approved by HUD before land is offered for sale. When sales commence, the developer must give each purchaser a copy of the property report before signing any contract to purchase. A purchaser who does not receive the required report has the right to rescind the transaction. This right expires 2 years after the date the contract is signed. In addition, the act gives a purchaser the right for 7 days to rescind the transaction even though the developer has supplied the required report. After the 7 days the consumer may only rescind on traditional contract-law grounds.

Many states have enacted laws similar to the federal act giving protection to purchasers of real estate. The state statutes cover sales of land in subdivisions (including condominiums) where the developer does not advertise through the mail or other means of interstate communication.

Residential Real Estate Sales

The **Real Estate Settlement Procedures Act** (**RESPA**) is a federal statute enacted in 1975 which requires that purchasers of residential property be given certain information. The coverage of this law is broader than the Interstate Land Sales Full Disclosure Act. RESPA applies to "intrastate" sales as well as "interstate" sales. This statute also is broader than truth in lending legislation, which covers transactions in which liens are created against residences. RESPA applies to the purchase of a residence involving a "federally related mortgage loan." Such loans include first mortgages taken by most banks, savings and loan associations, and other lenders against property on which there is a one-to-four-family residential dwelling. RESPA applies even though the dwelling is not intended as the consumer's residence. Only the purchase of a residence is covered, not home improvements or repairs.

The typical example of a transaction covered by RESPA is the purchase of a single-family residence or condominium. The purchaser ordinarily applies for a mortgage loan from a bank or savings and loan association. RESPA requires the lender to give the applicant information setting forth the costs of "settlement" services. Such services usually include loan fees, escrow fees, title search and recording fees, among others. A major feature of RESPA is the Uniform Settlement Statement. The lender (or an escrow agent) must provide the borrower with a statement itemizing all charges imposed on both the seller and the buyer in the transaction. The statement lists such items as escrow fees, title insurance costs, and broker's commission.

REGULATION OF CONSUMER CREDIT

Consumer credit is vital to most Americans. Few of us pay cash for our purchases and we rely on the availability of easy credit almost daily. If a consumer is denied credit, the consequences can be severe. Laws have been enacted to ensure correctness of credit reports, absence of discrimination in granting credit, and accuracy in billing procedures. This part of the chapter discusses the major federal statutes the purpose of which is to protect consumer credit.

Consumer Credit Reports

The **Fair Credit Reporting Act** (**FCRA**) was enacted by the U.S. Congress in 1970. The purpose of the act is to ensure that consumer credit information is disseminated by credit reporting agencies in a fair and equitable manner with regard to confidentiality, accuracy, relevancy, and proper utilization of material.

Content of Reports.   Consumer credit reports usually contain information such as a person's occupation, marital status, income, outstanding lawsuits and judgments, location and amounts of bank accounts, and history of debt payments. Such information must of course be accurate. In addition, the FCRA requires consumer reporting agencies to avoid consumer reports containing obsolete information. An example of obsolete information would be the fact that a consumer filed bankruptcy proceedings over 10 years ago. Other adverse information over 7 years old is usually considered to be obsolete. The FCRA does not limit the kinds of information that can be included in reports. Certain credit reports contain information relating to a consumer's character or reputation. This information is acquired by interviews with neighbors, friends, or associates of the consumer. Under the FCRA, any adverse information regarding one's character or reputation in a report may not be used in another report unless the later report is prepared within 3 months, or the reporting agency reverifies the information.

Use of Reports.   The FCRA limits the use of consumer reports to qualified persons for certain purposes, primarily credit, insurance, or employment. The following are examples of ordinary transactions where a creditor may properly utilize a report from a credit reporting agency: A consumer applies for credit in order to purchase merchandise; an individual applies for insurance to be used for personal purposes; a person applies for employment; an individual applies to the state for a contractor's license. The agency that supplies consumer reports is responsible for verifying that only qualified users receive credit information. Users must certify the purposes to be made of the reports and must agree not to use the information for other purposes.

Rights of Consumers.   A significant achievement of the FCRA was to eliminate the anonymity involved when a consumer's credit application is rejected. A user of a consumer report who rejects a consumer for credit, insurance, or employment must supply the consumer with the name and address of the credit reporting agency. FCRA goes one step further: A creditor who does not use a reporting agency and denies credit to the consumer must make the nature of the information used available to the consumer upon request. The creditor need not disclose the source of information, however.

If a consumer credit reporting agency prepares a report containing inaccurate or obsolete information, the consumer may require the agency to investigate the matter. After the reinvestigation, if the agency refuses to correct its records, the consumer has the right to place in the agency's file a brief statement explaining the disputed information. The explanation must accompany any future consumer report containing the disputed information. In addition, the consumer may request that the explanation be given to any user who received a consumer report within the previous 6 months (2 years if the report was for employment purposes).

Discrimination in Credit Transactions

Under the **Equal Credit Opportunity Act** it is illegal for a creditor to discriminate against any applicant for credit on the basis of sex, marital status, age, race, color, national origin, religion, receipt of public assistance, or good faith exercise of legal rights under the Consumer Credit Protection Act. Thus, when a person applies for credit the creditor is prohibited from requesting information about the applicant's spouse, marital status, alimony or child support, child-bearing, race, or religion.

A consumer who is denied credit must be notified and must be given reasons for the denial. If a consumer can show a violation of the Equal Credit Opportunity Act by the creditor, either in acquiring the credit information or in evaluating the information, a suit may be filed for actual damages and punitive damages. The consumer may also ask for an injunction (a court order granting the credit applied for).

The following case involves an unusual allegation of racial discrimination.

CASE 42.3

Cherry v. Amoco Oil Co.
481 F. Supp. 727 (N.D. Ga. 1979)

Facts: Claire Cherry, a white female, applied for a gasoline credit card from Amoco Oil Company. Amoco rejected the application giving three factors: (1) level of income; (2) type of bank references; and (3) Amoco's credit experience in Cherry's immediate geographical area. The "immediate geographical area" was determined by the applicant's zip code. Cherry was a resident of a predominantly black zip code area of Atlanta. Cherry filed suit under the Equal Credit Opportunity Act, alleging racial discrimination. Amoco filed a motion to dismiss, arguing that Cherry was not a member of the race which she alleges was discriminated against.

Question: Should Cherry's suit be dismissed?

Answer: No. Cherry may proceed to trial and prove she suffered damages as a result of racial discrimination.

Reasoning: Under the Act, it is unlawful for a creditor to discriminate against "any" applicant on the basis of race. The statute does not say on the basis of "that applicant's" race or "his or her" race. The court stated that the Act will protect anyone affected or aggrieved by racially discriminatory behavior. In theory one might suppose that those "adversely affected" will always be members of the group having the particular characteristic upon which the discrimination is based, but in practical terms that is not necessarily so. Here, Cherry alleged that the rejection factor, "immediate geographical area," discriminates against blacks and non-blacks who happen to live in those neighborhoods.

The court denied Amoco's motion to dismiss.

Disclosure of Terms of Credit Transactions

For many years consumers were not told the rate of interest charged by creditors. Often, debtors were given statements showing only the amount and number of payments to be made. To remedy this situation, the Consumer Credit Protection Act, discussed previously, contains provisions that require creditors to disclose essential credit terms before entering into a consumer credit transaction. The requirements of the act are detailed and complex. Only the more important provisions are presented here.

The disclosure provisions of truth in lending apply to consumer credit transactions up to $25,000 and to the purchase of a home or mobile home by a consumer on credit, regardless of amount. The act does not require disclosure by every creditor, however. Truth in lending is directed at persons who regularly extend or arrange for extension of credit in the ordinary course of business, such as banks and loan brokers.

The type of disclosure made to the consumer under truth in lending depends upon which of two types of consumer credit transaction is involved—open end or closed end. Open end credit is typified by such plans as Visa, MasterCard, and the department store revolving account. The consumer engages in a series of credit transactions and has the option of paying in installments or paying in full. Closed end credit is illustrated by installment purchases of cars, furniture, and real estate. The consumer agrees to make specific payments over a fixed period of time.

Closed End Credit.   Disclosure in a closed end transaction must be made before the credit is extended. The purpose of this requirement is to promote "comparison shopping" for credit by the applicant. A creditor must disclose all "material" terms to the debtor, including the number, amount, due dates of payments, and the total of such payments. The consumer must be told of all finance charges to be made in the credit transaction. All other fees and charges imposed in the transaction must be itemized and disclosed to the debtor (as for example, late charges or prepayment penalties). Probably the most significant disclosure required of the creditor is the annual percentage rate. The debtor must be told the rate of interest he or she is paying, expressed as an annual percentage. Truth in lending does not regulate the interest a creditor may charge, the law simply requires the creditor to make a full disclosure to the consumer. As discussed in Chapter 11, there are state laws fixing maximum rates of interest that may be charged in various credit transactions.

The creditor in a closed end transaction must disclose any security interest acquired by the creditor. Security interest includes the lien of a real estate mortgagee (or trust deed beneficiary), a security interest under the UCC, a mechanic's lien, and an artisan's lien. The creditor must state whether after-acquired property will be subject to the security interest or if future indebtedness may be secured by any such property. There are two additional items of interest to the consumer in a credit real property transaction. First, the creditor must inform the debtor whether or not the mortgage debt is assumable (that is, whether a buyer from the debtor may take over the debt). Second, the creditor must give the consumer an estimate of required disclosures within 3 days after receiving the consumer's loan application. A final disclosure statement must be furnished at the time of closing of the transaction.

Open End Credit.   Open end credit involves a *series* of transactions by the consumer, and the option of the debtor to pay in installments or to pay in full. Two types of disclosures are required in open end credit transactions: an initial statement and periodic statements. The debtor is given an initial statement before the first transaction is made. The statement must disclose when a finance charge will be imposed, the method of determining the balance on which the finance charge is imposed, and the elements of the finance charge. In addition, the debtor must be informed of the conditions under which other charges may be imposed, or under which the creditor may acquire any security interest in any property, and must be told the minimum periodic payment required.

When a consumer begins to enter open end credit transactions (for example, purchasing goods using a MasterCard), periodic statements are mailed to the consumer. The statements list amounts and dates of all purchases, identification of each transaction, amounts credited to the customer's account, the amount of finance charge, and the annual percentage rate.

Credit Card Transactions

Open end credit transactions are often facilitated by the use of a credit card. When a dispute arises between a cardholder and a merchant, the dispute ordinarily will be settled by use of traditional common law principles or the UCC. However, the problem is complicated when the customer makes a purchase using a general bank credit card, such as Visa or MasterCard. There are *three* parties involved and the law of contracts or of sales does not provide an easy solution to such legal disputes.

Defenses of Consumer.   The Consumer Credit Protection Act (and several state laws) provides some relief for consumers in credit card disputes. Suppose, for example, that you purchase an electric toaster from a merchant, using a general bank credit card, and that the toaster is defective. If the merchant refuses to replace the toaster, you may assert certain rights. Under truth in lending legislation, after making a good faith effort to resolve the dispute with the merchant, you may notify the card issuer of the dispute. Then, you may refuse to pay the card issuer for the toaster if the sale is over $50 and either: (1) your billing address and the merchant's place of business are both in the same state; or (2) your billing address is within 100 miles of the merchant's place of business. The act permits consumers to assert any claims or defenses against the card issuer that could be asserted against the merchant in two other situations: The merchant is closely associated with the card issuer (same control or ownership); or the card issuer mailed promotional literature with its billing statement and urged the consumer to make a credit card purchase (e.g., gasoline credit card issuers promoting sales of merchandise).

Truth in lending legislation also protects credit card holders in the event of unauthorized use of the card. Suppose that your gasoline credit card is stolen and that the thief purchases four new tires for $300 using your credit card. Under the act your liability is limited to $50 if you receive no benefit from the unauthorized use of the credit card, and the user is one who had no "actual, implied, or apparent authority." (See Chapter 20 for discussion of authority.) You are liable up to $50 if the unauthorized use of the credit card occurred *before* you notified the card issuer that your credit card was stolen (or lost). Thus, in the example above, your maximum liability is $50.

In the following case the court discusses what is meant by "unauthorized use" of a credit card.

CASE 42.4   **Martin v. American Express, Inc.**
361 So. 2d 597 (Ala. Civ. App. 1978)

Facts: Robert A. Martin gave his American Express credit card to a business associate, E.L. McBride. Martin orally authorized McBride to charge up to $500 on the credit card. Prior to giving his card to McBride, Martin sent a letter to American Express asking them not to allow the total charges on his account to exceed $1,000. McBride later returned the credit card and disappeared, leaving an account that showed $5,300 was due. American Express sued Martin to collect the amount after Martin refused to pay. Martin claimed he was not liable beyond $50 because of McBride's "unauthorized use" of his credit card. The trial court granted summary judgment in favor of American Express. Martin appealed.

Question: Should Martin be held liable for the $5,300 charges incurred by McBride?

Answer: Yes. Martin should be liable for the full amount. McBride was authorized by Martin to use the credit card.

Reasoning: The court stated that the Truth in Lending Act limits a credit cardholder's liability to $50 when there is an "unauthorized use" of a credit card. Martin claimed that McBride acted beyond the scope of his authority. The court held that while McBride may have had no actual authority, he had apparent authority to incur charges even after ignoring Martin's directions by charging over $500 to the account. Consequently, Martin was responsible for any purchases made through the use of his card. The court also stated that a cardholder could not compel a credit card issuer to see to it that charges on a cardholder's account do not exceed a specified amount. Such a policy would place a difficult and potentially disastrous burden on the issuer. The unscrupulous and dishonest cardholder could allow his or her friends to use the card, run up hundreds of dollars in charges and then limit his or her liability to $50 by notifying the card issuer. The court held that the $50 limit applies where the card is obtained from the cardholder as a result of loss, theft, or wrongdoing. It does not apply where a cardholder voluntarily allows another to use his or her card and that person subsequently misuses the card.

The judgment was affirmed.

Billing for Credit Sales.   The **Fair Credit Billing Act** protects credit card customers who claim that an error exists in their billing statements. The act is designed to alleviate the frustration and fear felt by consumers trying to cope with the complexities of computer billing. Under the act a creditor who receives a claim of error has a maximum of 90 days to respond to the claim. Until the response is made, the creditor may not (1) take any action to collect the disputed amount; (2) restrict the use of an open end credit account, solely because the disputed amount has not been paid; or (3) report, or threaten to report, the disputed amount as delinquent. If the creditor's response is negative and is rejected by the consumer, the creditor may report the disputed amount as delinquent but must also report the dispute. The creditor must inform the consumer of any third party to whom the dispute was reported. The creditor also must advise the third party when the dispute eventually is resolved.

The act is perhaps not as effective as it might be. A creditor who violates its provisions forfeits the right to collect the disputed amount, but not to exceed $50 for each item claimed to be in error. Many creditors are no doubt tempted to forfeit the $50 rather than comply with terms of the act.

REGULATION OF CONSUMER DEBT COLLECTION

The consumer who defaults in payments to creditors faces a variety of collection techniques. Prior to filing lawsuits for collection, merchants and overzealous collection agencies often go beyond the accepted bounds of civilized conduct. As a result, courts and legislatures have given delinquent consumer-debtors certain rights and legal protections prior to suit. Once a lawsuit for collection has been initiated against a debtor, certain exemptions and defenses are available.

Collection Efforts Prior to Suit

Creditors may be classified in one of two ways: secured or unsecured. A *secured* creditor is one who has collateral which can be repossessed and sold (see Chapter 25 for discussion of liens on real property and Chapter 27 for discussion of liens on personal property). Upon default by the debtor, the secured creditor may foreclose without the expense and delay of filing a lawsuit. For example, a secured creditor who sells personal property to a consumer who then defaults may simply send someone out to repossess the goods (so long as this can be done without breach of the peace), resell the goods, and if the sale price is not adequate to pay the debt, pursue the debtor in court for the deficiency. The consumer has few rights under the UCC other than to insist that the creditor follow the prescribed procedure, including conducting a repossession sale that is commercially reasonable.

Unsecured creditors have few effective methods of debt collection without filing a lawsuit for breach of contract. They can send letters, make telephone calls, and visit the debtor to persuade him or her to pay the debt without the cost and stress of a lawsuit. In taking these actions, creditors must exercise care not to violate the consumer's rights.

Debtor's Rights under Common Law. There are several common law tort actions that consumer-debtors may file against an overzealous debt collector. These torts are discussed fully in Chapter 3 and only a brief reference will be made here. The tort of *infliction of mental distress* involves one who intentionally or recklessly causes severe mental suffering in another. Courts generally do not grant relief unless the defendant's conduct is extreme or outrageous. The debtor must prove: (1) that the debt collector acted with intent to cause mental suffering (or was "reckless"); (2) that the conduct "exceeded all bounds of decent behavior"; and (3) that the mental stress suffered was "severe." An elderly person, not in good health, who is subjected to midnight telephone calls, numerous personal visits, and threats of lawsuits might be successful in prosecuting a tort action against the debt collector. A healthy young person who endures the usual strain brought about by an aggressive collection agency probably is without a common law remedy.

In some circumstances a debtor may have an action for the tort of *defamation.* Defamation involves the unjustified publication of a false statement that tends to hold a person up to hatred, contempt, or ridicule. A debt collector may truthfully state that a consumer is delinquent and owes money to a creditor. Statements that are untrue regarding the debtor's character or debt-paying history may be defamatory. However, a debt collector charged with defamation often asserts *qualified privilege* as a defense. A defendant may communicate defamatory material to an interested person in order to protect some recognized interest. Thus, a debt collection agency may have a qualified privilege to communicate defamatory material to a debtor's employer, prospective employer, or prospective creditor.

The tort of *invasion of privacy* occasionally is of benefit to the beleaguered debtor. One type of invasion of privacy is unreasonably intruding upon one's physical solitude. Whether the debt collector is "unreasonable" depends upon the methods used to coerce payment from the consumer. It is unreasonable to enter a debtor's home without permission or to place a wiretap on his or her telephone. Another type of invasion of privacy is the public disclosure of private information about a person. A tort would be committed if a debt collector notified an unjustifiably large number of people that the debtor was delinquent in paying debts. The debt collector legitimately may notify the debtor's employer of a delinquency, but may not publish the debtor's name and other details in the newspaper.

Debtor's Rights under Federal Law. The **Fair Debt Collection Practices Act** was enacted by Congress to expand consumer protection beyond the common law. The FDCPA applies to professional debt collectors, but does not apply to lenders or creditors who collect their own debts. The actions of debt collectors are severely limited by the act. A debt collector may contact third persons only for the purpose of locating the debtor and may not volunteer that he or she is a debt collector. Even if asked, the debt collector may not tell a third party that the debtor owes a debt.

The FDCPA regulates contact between the debt collector and the debtor. A debt collector may not communicate with a consumer at any "unusual" time or place or at a time or place which should be known to be "inconvenient to the consumer." Ordinarily, this means a debt collector may not call or visit the debtor before 8:00 A.M. or after 9:00 P.M. The debt collector may not communicate under ordinary circumstances with a debtor who is represented by an attorney. The act also lists specific acts which are prohibited because they "harass, oppress, or abuse" the consumer. For example, a debt collector may not: (1) use or threaten to use violence or other criminal means; (2) use obscene, profane, or abusive language; or (3) publish a list of consumers who allegedly refuse to pay debts, except to a consumer reporting agency. In addition, a debt collector may not use any false, deceptive, or misleading representations, or use unfair or unconscionable means to attempt to collect a debt. The act lists a variety of specific prohibited actions under each of these provisions.

The following case illustrates several violations of the FDCPA.

CASE 42.5   Rutyna v. Collection Accounts Terminal, Inc.
478 F. Supp. 980 (N.D. Ill. 1979)

Facts: Josephine Rutyna, a 60-year old widow suffering from high blood pressure and epilepsy, incurred a debt for $56 to Cabrini Hospital Medical Group. She received a letter which stated: "You have shown that you are unwilling to work out a friendly settlement with us to clear the above debt. Our field investigator has now been instructed to make an investigation in your neighborhood and to personally call on your employer. The immediate payment of the full amount, or a personal visit to this office, will spare you this embarrassment." The letter was signed by a "collection agent." The envelope containing the letter showed a return address and the name "Collection Accounts Terminal, Inc." Upon receiving the letter Rutyna became very nervous, upset, and worried. She feared Collection Accounts Terminal would cause her embarrassment by informing her neighbors of the debt and about her medical problems. She filed suit for violations of the Fair Debt Collection Practices Act. Rutyna moved for summary judgment.

Question: Did the letter and envelope violate the provisions of the Fair Debt Collection Practices Act?

Answer: Yes. The Act was violated and the collection agent should be held liable.

Reasoning: The court held that the Act was violated in several respects. First, the Act provides that a debt collector may not harass, oppress, or abuse any person. The tone of the letter was one of intimidation. The threat of an investigation and resulting embarrassment to the debtor was clear. Second, the debt collector must not use any false, deceptive, or misleading representation. The letter threatened embarrassing contacts with Rutyna's employer and neighbors. The Act prohibits communication by the debt collector with third parties. Rutyna's neighbors and employer could not legally be contacted by the debt collector. The letter falsely represented, or deceived the recipient. Third, the envelope received by Rutyna had on it the debt collector's name and address. The Act prohibits unfair or unconscionable means to collect or attempt to collect any debt. Specifically, the Act bars use of "any language or symbol, other than the debt collector's address, on any envelope when communicating with a consumer . . . except that a debt collector may use his business name if such name does not indicate that he is in the debt collection business." Here, the business name Collection Accounts Terminal, Inc. indicated that it was in the debt collection business.

Judgment was entered in favor of Rutyna.

Collection Efforts after Suit   A creditor or debt collector who is unsuccessful at collecting a debt from a consumer by means of letters, telephone calls, or personal visits often resorts to filing a lawsuit against the debtor. Once a suit is filed there are various collection remedies available to the plaintiff, and various defenses and protections available to the defendant. We will discuss briefly the major remedies and exemptions available to protect consumers.

Debtor's Protection Regarding Garnishment. Garnishment is a creditor's remedy directed at a third person, called the "garnishee," who owes a debt to the consumer or has property of the consumer's. A garnishment is an order directing the garnishee to hold the debtor's property until the lawsuit is completed. Two common examples of garnishment are: (1) A creditor garnishes a debtor's savings account held by a bank or savings and loan association; and (2) a creditor garnishes the wages owed to a debtor by his or her employer. Garnishment is a remedy that usually occurs at the beginning of a lawsuit. The purpose of garnishment is to provide the creditor with a source to satisfy his or her debt after obtaining judgment. (See also the discussion of attachment in Chapter 25, p. 417.)

A provision of the Consumer Credit Protection Act protects most of the consumer's wages from garnishment. A creditor may garnish a maximum of 25 percent of the debtor's weekly disposable earnings or the amount by which the disposable earnings exceed thirty times the minimum hourly wage, whichever is *less*. *Disposable earnings* means salary less deductions required by law (withholding taxes, social security tax, and state disability usually). The 25 percent limitation is the maximum that can be reached by *all* the person's debtors, not just one. The act also protects the debtor by providing that no employee may be discharged because his or her earnings have been garnished for any one debt.

Debtor's Protection Regarding Execution. The major method of enforcing a civil judgment for damages is "execution." The successful creditor who knows where the debtor has specific property (real or personal) may have a writ of execution issued by the court. The writ directs the sheriff to take the property into custody and sell it to satisfy the creditor's judgment. However, all states have statutes which protect debtors by exempting certain property from execution. The provisions vary greatly but most states exempt a certain amount of life insurance owned by the debtor, some household furniture and appliances, tools of a trade, and an automobile under a certain value. Social security, veterans' benefits, and disability income are usually exempt from execution. A major exemption available to the consumer is the homestead exemption. California, for example, prohibits a creditor from seizing a debtor's equity in his or her principal residence up to $45,000 (if the debtor is the head of a family). "Equity" in this context means the value of the residence less outstanding liens (mortgages, mechanics' liens, taxes). The homestead exemption does not prevent secured creditors from exercising their right to foreclose; the exemption protects the consumer from *unsecured* creditors who wish to sell the residence by means of execution.

A consumer who is seriously overextended and faces a sea of creditors, each of whom is competing for the opportunity to seize the debtor's property, often takes advantage of federal bankruptcy law. The Bankruptcy Code is discussed in detail in Chapter 44. A major purpose of the bankruptcy law is to give debtors a "fresh start." One part of the Bankruptcy Code provides that most of a debtor's debts may be canceled while allowing him or her to retain a residence, automobile, and other exempt items deemed necessary for continued self-support. One provision of the code permits the debtor to choose between the exemptions provided by state law and the federal exemptions.

SUMMARY

In recent years courts, legislatures, and administrative agencies have developed a body of law called "consumer law," to protect consumers. A consumer transaction ordinarily is defined as one made for "personal, family, or household purposes." Thus, business purchases are not given the protection of consumer laws.

A consumer may have legal recourse against false or misleading advertising. False advertising may constitute the common law tort of fraud. However, it is often difficult to prove that the defendant made a false statement of fact in regard to a product rather than just a statement of opinion. Under the Uniform Commercial Code a seller may be liable for breach of warranty. In many sales transactions the UCC imposes an implied warranty of fitness or of merchantability. Under federal law the Federal Trade Commission may prohibit unfair or deceptive acts or practices. Most states have adopted laws similar in scope to the regulations of the FTC.

There are a number of state and federal statutes and regulations governing sales of goods and services. The common law of sales and of contracts, discussed earlier in this text, provides some protection for consumers. A regulation of the FTC gives a consumer 3 days to rescind a home solicitation sale of consumer goods or services in excess of $25. Under federal truth in lending legislation a consumer is given 3 business days to rescind a credit transaction involving a lien (voluntary or involuntary) on the consumer's residence. A prerequisite to rescission is that the consumer must return or offer to return the consideration received from the creditor, or its reasonable value. A consumer who purchases unimproved land through the mail receives certain protections under the Interstate Land Sales Full Disclosure Act. The developer must inform prospective purchasers of relevant information. There is a 7-day rescission period after sale. The Real Estate Settlement Procedures Act does not give a consumer the right of rescission but does require that purchasers of residences be given relevant information regarding settlement costs.

In recent years Congress has enacted several federal laws to protect the consumer who applies for or receives credit. The Fair Credit Reporting Act regulates the content and use of consumer credit reports. The act grants important rights to consumers whose applications for credit are rejected. The Equal Credit Opportunity Act protects credit applicants who are rejected on the basis of sex, marital status, age, race, color, national origin, religion, receipt of public assistance, or good faith exercise of legal rights under the Consumer Credit Protection Act. Truth in lending legislation requires creditors to disclose essential credit terms before entering into a consumer credit transaction. The type of disclosure required depends upon whether the credit transaction involved is open end or closed end. The act also provides some relief for consumers in credit card disputes. The consumer may assert claims or defenses against the card issuer that could be asserted against the merchant, and the consumer is not liable beyond $50 in the event of someone's unauthorized use of the credit card. The Fair Credit Billing Act protects credit card customers who claim that an error exists in their billing statements.

There are various state and federal laws which regulate debt collection. An overzealous debt collector may be liable for the common law torts of infliction of mental distress, defamation, or invasion of privacy. The Fair Debt Collection Practices Act severely limits the actions of debt collectors. If suit is filed to collect a debt, the Consumer Credit Protection Act protects the consumer's wages from garnishment. State laws protect much of the judgment debtor's property from execution.

REVIEW QUESTIONS

1. Define "consumer transaction" as used in modern statutes creating consumer protection.

2. (a) Explain why it is often difficult for a consumer to prove that false or misleading advertising constitutes the common law tort of fraud. (b) Give an example of false advertising that might come within the definition of fraud.

3. (a) What is the major difference between a consumer pursuing the common law tort of fraud and the Federal Trade Commission prosecuting unfair or deceptive acts? (b) Describe and give an example of "bait advertising."

4. (a) State the FTC "home solicitation" rule. (b) Explain the purpose of the rule. (c) Explain why the rule would or would not apply to the following transaction: At the request of a homeowner, a person repairs the owner's television set in the home and charges $40.

5. (a) State the general rule regarding rescission under truth in lending. (b) Give an example of a transaction that would be covered by the act. (c) Does a transaction involving a lien on a mobile home always come under the act? Explain. (d) Explain the prerequisite to a consumer's rescission under the act.

6. (a) What type of transaction is subject to the Interstate Land Sales Full Disclosure Act? (b) What is required of a developer under the act?

7. Explain the coverage and the purpose of the Real Estate Settlement Procedures Act.

8. (a) Describe a consumer credit report. (b) What uses of credit reports are permissible under the Fair Credit Reporting Act? (c) What is the responsibility of a credit report user under the act? (d) List the rights of a consumer under the act.

9. (a) What types of discrimination are prohibited under the Equal Credit Opportunity Act? (b) Do you think it would be illegal for a lender to deny credit to an applicant on the basis that the applicant is a college student? Explain.

10. (a) Describe the type of transactions covered by the "disclosure" provisions of the "Truth in Lending Act." (b) Must every lender make full disclosure? Explain and give an example of a creditor that would be exempt from the act. (c) Define open end credit and closed end credit. (**d**) List the major items that must be disclosed by a creditor in a closed end transaction.

11. In the event of a dispute between a consumer and a merchant in a credit card purchase, what rights does the consumer have against the credit card issuer?

12. (**a**) Define and give an example of a secured creditor. (**b**) Explain the rights of both the secured creditor and the debtor if the debtor defaults. (**c**) Describe the rights of an unsecured creditor before filing suit against a delinquent debtor.

13. List the major restrictions placed on debt collectors by the Fair Debt Collection Practices Act.

14. (**a**) Explain the remedy of garnishment. (**b**) What is the purpose of garnishment? (**c**) Explain the protection given to the debtor under the Consumer Credit Protection Act. (**d**) Explain the remedy of execution. (**e**) List the items of property usually exempted from execution.

CASE PROBLEMS

1. Singleton sold his used boat, motor, and trailer to Pennington. He stated that he had just had $500 worth of work done, making the boat and motor in "excellent condition," "perfect condition," and "just like new." These statements were false because the gear housing of the motor had been cracked and inadequately repaired. Singleton did not know the statements were false, nor did he make the statements recklessly because he had not experienced any difficulty with the boat after it was repaired. Pennington was required to spend $482 to repair the gear housing and sued Singleton for damages. (**a**) May Pennington recover damages for the common law tort of fraud? (**b**) Did Singleton's statements constitute a "deceptive business practice?" Explain reasons for your answers.

2. Hidden Valley Lakes, Inc. subdivided 215 acres of land in Mississippi into 379 lots. It mailed brochures to potential buyers and sold lots to persons in Tennessee, Arkansas, and Mississippi for recreational homes or second homes. The purchasers received property reports. The reports failed to state whether arrangements had been made by the developer to complete various recreational facilities (lake, sand beach, boathouses) and failed to state whether tests had been conducted to determine if the land was suitable for septic tanks. Did Hidden Valley Lakes, Inc. violate the Interstate Land Sales Full Disclosure Act? Explain.

3. Stephanie Rasor was a 53-year-old resident of Sandpoint, Idaho, a community of 5000 persons. She applied for health insurance with Bankers Life and they requested Retail Credit Company to prepare a consumer credit report on her. Retail conducted a brief investigation and prepared a report on November 8 which stated in part, "Rasor has had a reputation of living with more than one man out of wedlock in the past" and "her reputation has suffered because of out-of-wedlock living arrangements in the recent past." On November 14 Rasor applied for a Small Business Administration loan to construct an addition to a motel she operated. A credit report was requested from Retail. Retail made no new investigation but mailed a copy of the November 8 report. The information in the report was false and Rasor sued Retail for violation of the Fair Credit Reporting Act. Retail defended that the report was no longer a "consumer report" since it was used for business purposes and thus Retail should no longer be liable. Who should win the lawsuit? Give reasons.

4. Marcia Harris and Jerry Markham were engaged to be married. They signed a contract to purchase a residence and applied for a mortgage loan from Illinois Federal. Illinois Federal rejected their application because they were not married. In considering the application, Illinois Federal refused to aggregate the income of Marcia and Jerry. They filed suit alleging violation of the Equal Credit Opportunity Act. A section of the act requires mortgage lenders to consider the combined income of husbands and wives for purposes of extending mortgage credit. Did Illinois Federal violate the Act? Why or why not?

5. Jettie Ivey obtained a loan from HUD. HUD furnished her a "Truth in Lending Disclosure Statement" showing a total debt of $12,055.20 payable in 240 monthly payments. The first payment of $61.53 was due on February 1, 1970, and thereafter, 239 payments of $50.23 were due the first of each month. Ivey gave notice that she wished to rescind the transaction, claiming that HUD had made a material error in its disclosure statement and thereby violated the Consumer Credit Protection Act. The trial court agreed with Ivey, stating that the total of the 240 installments was $12,066.50, not $12,055.20 as shown on the statement. Was this a correct ruling? Explain.

6. Harriet E. Harvey was indebted to Fred Meyer, Inc. for $125. The debt was assigned to United Adjusters for collection. United sent a notice to Harvey on June 5, 1979 stating that she ignored her mail and her bills and lacked the common sense to handle her financial matters properly. On June 28 United filed suit against Harvey. She retained an attorney who, on July 26, filed a response to United's lawsuit. On December 17, 1979 and on January 3, 1980 United mailed notices to Harvey soliciting payment of the debt. Harvey filed suit alleging violations of the Fair Debt Collection Practices Act. Did United violate the act? Give reasons.

CHAPTER 43

EMPLOYMENT–LABOR LAW; WORKERS' COMPENSATION

Thus far we have been considering the general legal principles under which business is conducted. In that process we examined the basic rules by which businesses are established and the rights and obligations that accrue between business concerns and others with whom business is transacted. Only occasionally, as in Chapters 20 through 22, where we considered the law of agency, have we looked inward and considered the relationship between employers and employees in a business.

However else we may view ourselves in our relations with others, in the matter of earning a livelihood we generally fall into one of two categories: employers and employees. The relationship between them is established by an employment contract which is written, oral, or implied from the conduct of the parties. Employment contracts reflect the changing industrial climate of the country.

The expansion of the United States was accompanied by an extraordinary rise in the industrialization of the country. An individual employee who sought employment or who tried to better his or her working conditions had little bargaining power. The Thirteenth Amendment to the Constitution, which outlawed involuntary servitude, did not affect ordinary relations between employers and employees. An employer was free to hire an employee at as low a wage as the competitive forces of the marketplace would allow. Labor responded by banding together and forming powerful labor unions. Through the collective action of such organizations, with their ability to close a factory by calling strikes, employees won shorter working hours, higher wages, and improved working conditions.

It soon became evident that there should be laws applicable throughout the country that would govern relations between employers and employees. The resulting body of federal and state laws, administrative regulations, and opinions of the courts is given the general name of *labor law*. Labor law is so voluminous that its coverage here must be restricted to a brief overview. This chapter will consider only the following aspects of this broad subject: terms of employment, employers' obligation to maintain safe working places, labor management disputes, discrimination in hiring employees, and the rights of employees to receive compensation for injuries incurred on the job.

TERMS OF EMPLOYMENT

Who Is an Employee? In Chapter 22, the duties and obligations of employers to employees, and the reciprocal obligations of employees to employers, were discussed. That discussion is pertinent here because employees are individuals whose manner of performance and methods used are controlled by their employers who may detail precisely how the work is to be performed. For example, a lathe operator, an airline pilot, a bank teller, or a truck driver are all employees within the meaning of that word as used in the statutes discussed in this chapter. The word "employee" does not include a person who works as an independent contractor—that is, an individual who undertakes to furnish an end product or service to a purchaser of that product or service, such as someone who contracts to paint your house.

Minimum Wages and Hours of Employment

The Congress has established standards of (1) minimum wages that must be paid to employees, and (2) maximum hours that employees may be required to work without higher rates of pay. The **Fair Labor Standards Act**, enacted in 1938, established an allowable hourly wage for employment affecting interstate commerce, and directed that payment shall be 1½ times the hourly rate paid for each hour worked in excess of 8 hours per day and 40 hours per week. In addition, it prohibits child labor.

It is generally accepted that time spent in traveling to and from the workplace is not time for which wages are due, but just when compensable work does begin is sometimes in doubt, as reflected in the following case.

CASE 43.1   Marshall v. Gerwill, Inc.
495 F. Supp. 744 (Md. 1980)

Facts: Gerwill, Inc. operated a fleet of taxicabs. In computing the hours each driver worked, it was company practice not to include the time a driver took to clean out the cab in the morning and possibly to put gas in the vehicle. A driver's day began when he reported to the dispatcher that he was "ready to go." Each driver radioed in when going to lunch and when lunch was completed. Lunch time was not part of the work-day. When the last passengers were discharged, a driver radioed in and was immediately taken off work time even though driving back to the office consumed about eight minutes, and additional time was used to park the cab, to make out manifest sheets, and to turn in the daily receipts.

The time not counted as work at the start of the day and at the day's end was not counted by the employer in computing the driver's wages. The Secretary of Labor determined that, as a result, the minimum wage standards had not been met. Gerwill appealed.

Question: Was the time used by the driver to get his cab ready in the morning and to check in each evening a part of his work-day?

Answer: Yes, the time should have been considered in computing the minimum wage.

Reasoning: The minimum wage requirements established by Congress should be liberally construed. If the activity is in the interest of the employer, and if the employer benefited from it, then the activity constituted work for the employer.

Here, the cab drivers' activities were something more than merely preliminary to their work but were an integral part of it. Therefore, the Secretary of Labor was correct and the minimum wage law had not been complied with.

EMPLOYER'S DUTY TO PROVIDE A SAFE PLACE TO WORK

Legislative Requirement for Safe Workplace

Some hazards are associated with almost every workplace. For instance, certain work may require exposure to extremes of cold or heat, work processes may require artificial forced ventilation, a floor might be slippery, machinery may be unguarded, a carpet in front of a water cooler may be torn in such a way that the high heel of a woman's shoe might be caught in it, or the noise level in a workroom may be uncomfortably high. For years it was assumed that when an employee took a job, he or she accepted the workplace as it was, assuming any risk of injury that resulted. If an employee was not satisfied with the working conditions, he or she was free to leave. Today, this concept that an employee assumes all workplace risks, has changed. Now, pursuant to federal and state legislation, it is the responsibility of the employer to furnish all employees a place to work that is as safe as is feasible.

Federal Legislation.   All states have enacted laws establishing standards of safety which employers must maintain, but there is no uniformity among such laws. Therefore, Congress enacted the **Occupational Safety and Health Act of 1970 (OSHA)**. That act is intended to force employers to maintain safe and healthful working conditions for their employees. The Department of Labor has adopted far-reaching regulations in implementation of OSHA. For example, it has published rules establishing specifications for the construction of containers intended to hold hazardous substances; has fixed 12 inches as the minimum allowable width of extension ladders; and requires scaffolding rope to be capable of supporting six times the weight of the intended load.

The Department of Labor employs a large corps of inspectors to enforce compliance with OSHA's many and varied health and safety regulations. An employer's failure to comply may result in a large civil penalty, and in a case where death results from an accident under conditions of noncompliance, criminal charges may be filed against the employer.

To discourage the vindictive firing of a worker who reports a violation and files a complaint, such a worker is given the right to appeal his or her discharge to the Secretary of Labor who, in turn, is authorized to sue the employer and seek reinstatement of the worker with back pay.

State Legislation.   A number of states have had safety regulations for many years. These states have meshed their own system with the federal system. In addition to adoption of OSHA regulations, it is common for a state now to have an Occupational Safety and Health Standards Board and an Appeals Board, thus enabling employers to have access to local regulatory and judicial bodies.

Effect of Workers' Disregard of Rules	One of the oddities of human nature is that it is quite unpredictable. One would think that workers would follow regulations designed to assure their safety. But this is not always the case. What happens when a worker refuses to wear required safety glasses, or a face mask, or a hard hat? If an accident occurs because a worker disregards the rules, the employer is responsible. The following case deals with such a situation.

CASE 43.2

Getty Oil Co. v. Occupational Safety & Review Comm.
530 F.2d 1143 (5th Cir. 1976)

Facts: Robison was a responsible employee with thirty years experience. He was told by his superior at an oil refinery to install a pressure vessel, a procedure known throughout the industry to be hazardous. His superior discussed with Robison the work to be accomplished, repeatedly reminding him to pressure test the vessel before installing it. Notwithstanding the warnings, Robison tried to install the vessel without prior test and as a result he was killed. Robison's superior did not know that Robison had ignored his instructions. The employer was fined by the Occupational Safety and Health Administration for having failed to provide Robison with a place of employment free from recognized hazards likely to cause death.

Question: Under these facts has the employer violated OSHA regulations?

Answer: Yes. The employer could have discovered that Robison was embarking on the hazardous action and could have prevented him from taking his foolhardy action.

Reasoning: Under OSHA regulations an employer is required to discover and exclude from the workplace all reasonably preventable forms of hazardous conduct. By a small degree of effort the employer could have determined whether the necessary testing had been performed. Besides, there was opportunity to question Robison before he performed the attempted installation. The fine was properly imposed.

LABOR-MANAGEMENT DISPUTES

Many laws are concerned with the settlement of disputes between labor and management. Of particular importance are the **Wagner Act**, enacted in 1935, which created the National Labor Relations Board, and the **Labor-Management Relations Act** (also known as the **Taft-Hartley Act**), enacted in 1947.

The heart of the Wagner Act was Section 7, which originally provided that:

Employees shall have a right to self-organization, to form, join or assist labor organizations, to bargain collectively through representatives of their own choosing, and to engage in concerted activities for the purpose of collective bargaining or other mutual aid or protection.

The Taft-Hartley Act, which, among other things, carried forward labor's fundamental right to organize and to bargain collectively, placed limitations upon the right to strike and extended governmental control over the negotiation process in collective bargaining agreements.

The various labor laws, as amended, together with the holdings of the National Labor Relations Board (NLRB) and court decisions, define the relationship between employees, unions, and employers. Some laws also are concerned with the internal affairs of unions.

Right of Employees to Join Labor Unions

Labor laws guarantee to employees the *right* to join labor unions and, through their unions, to bargain collectively with their employers in matters concerning pay and working conditions. However, nineteen states have enacted "right to work" laws. These laws provide, in substance, that while an employee is free to join or not to join a union, an employee may *not be forced* to join a union as a condition either to get a job or to hold a job. In effect, "right to work" laws preserve to an individual the traditional freedom to contract for the sale of his or her services.

Right of Employees to Strike

Employees have the right to maintain a peaceful strike in conjunction with their demands for higher pay or changed working conditions. However, an agreement between an employer and a union may limit the right to strike.

Employees also have the right to establish peaceful picket lines communicating to the public the reason(s) for the strike, and to attempt (without resort to illegal means) to persuade potential customers not to purchase the employer's products. However, employees may not carry on a secondary boycott. A *secondary boycott* is the application by striking employees of economic pressure against another firm by whom they are not employed and with whom they have no dispute, in order to force that firm to stop doing business with their own employer. Such economic pressure would be, for example, picketing the premises of the secondary firm to induce its employees not to work, or passing out leaflets to its customers asking them not to purchase anything from the secondary firm. By the Taft-Hartley Act, Congress banned secondary boycotts to avoid embroiling neutrals in the labor disputes of third parties. Certain labor practices of employers and other labor practices of employees are no longer allowed. Those proscribed practices are called *unfair labor practices*.

Unfair Labor Practices

Unfair Practices by Employers. Among the unfair labor practices of employers are interfering with the relations between an employee and his or her union, encouraging or discouraging membership in a union, discharging an employee because he or she filed charges against the employer with a labor relations board, or refusing to engage in collective bargaining with a union.

Unfair Practices by Unions. A union may commit an unfair labor practice against either employees or employers. Examples of unfair labor practices of unions against employees are exacting an excessive or discriminatory initiation fee, attempting to coerce an employee in the way the employee votes in a labor election, or attempting to restrain an employee from crossing a picket line.

Examples of unfair labor practices by unions against employers are refusing to bargain, encouraging sabotage or other violence during a strike, or attempting to force an employer to pay for services not performed (sometimes called "featherbedding"). Featherbedding would be, for instance, requiring a radio station to pay standby musicians when the station actually broadcasts music only from phonograph records.

PROHIBITION OF DISCRIMINATION IN EMPLOYMENT

The acceptance of employment by an individual who wants to work and the hiring of a worker by an employer, are generally matters of negotiation between the two. Legislation has been enacted which tends to equalize the forces which each side can exert in such negotiations by prohibiting discrimination in employment.

Discrimination
Based on Race,
Color, Religion,
Sex, or
National Origin

When it ultimately became recognized that racial discrimination in employment is evil and should be stopped, the **Civil Rights Act of 1965** was enacted. In Title VII of that act, it is declared to be an unfair labor practice to fail or to refuse to hire, or otherwise in any way to discriminate against any individual with respect to pay, terms, conditions, or privileges of employment because of race, color, religion, sex, or national origin. It was also declared illegal to segregate or classify employees in such a way as to deprive any of them of employment opportunities.

The federal act does not do away with any laws a state may have enacted in this area. However, if corrective state action is not taken within a limited time, then the federal law may be invoked by action in the federal courts.

One of the problems in enforcing Title VII is that some actions taken by employers have the effect of being discriminatory even though they are not so intended. Such a problem was presented in the following case.

CASE 43.3

Griggs v. Duke Power Co.
402 U.S. 424 (Sup. Ct. 1971)

Facts: Duke Power required applicants for employment to present high school diplomas and to achieve successful scores on intelligence and mechanical comprehension tests. Many black applicants could not meet those requirements and they were denied employment. Duke Power contended that it did not intend to discriminate against the hiring of any portion of society and that it was following a state law which permitted the use of professionally developed tests that were not designed or intended to be used to discriminate.

Question: Can an impartial testing procedure bring about discrimination in employment?

Answer: Yes. Employment discrimination is present unless a business necessity for the test is shown.

Reasoning: A test may be given an applicant for a job if it measures the applicant's aptitude for a particular job but may not be given to determine an individual's qualifications in the abstract. If the tests are not shown to bear on the performance of the job for which the applicant is applying, and if they form the basis for exclusion of a particular class of people, it follows that the tests are being used to discriminate. Practices that are fair in form but discriminatory in operation cannot be excused.

This *Griggs* case was an important decision in the field of employment discrimination because it established the rule that the *impact* of an employer's action is the test by which a claim of discriminatory action will be judged.

In 1963 Congress prohibited employers from discriminating against employees on the basis of sex by paying one sex less than members of the opposite sex for equal work. Unequal pay is permitted, however, when based on some factor other than sex, such as (1) on a seniority or merit system, (2) on quantity of production (such as piecework), or (3) on the quality of production.

To apply the rule of equal pay requires a careful analysis of the work duties and skills involved rather than merely a comparison of job descriptions. For instance, male hospital orderlies and female practical nurses may have different duties requiring different skills, but if the general nature of the positions is the same, the skills may be held to be equal; accordingly, the pay scales of the two classes of employees would be the same. Similarly, male janitors and female maids may handle different equipment and perform different duties, but if the nature of their jobs and the degree of skill required are substantially the same, then equal pay may be required.

Discrimination Based on Age

The prohibition against discrimination because of age is designed to protect middle-aged workers—those from 40 to 69 years of age—from being cast adrift and younger workers hired in their places, perhaps at a lower wage. An employer may not because of age discriminate with respect to hiring, pay scales, conditions of employment, or job retention. In certain circumstances, however, an employer may take an action which, although in seeming violation of the law, is permissible. These exceptions permit the discharge of an employee within the protected age group where for good cause or for reasonable factors other than age there is a bona fide occupational qualification which the older worker cannot meet, such as a fire fighter whose strength and physical stamina are essential; or where, through the operation of an established seniority system a younger person, hired earlier than an older one, receives preference in job retention.

If an employee establishes that he or she has been discharged because of discrimination, the employer is required to reinstate the wronged worker and pay hin or her the amount of wages lost because of the employer's wrongful act.

It was formerly the practice for employers to ask on applications for employment, among questions deemed pertinent to the work, the age of the applicant. If such a question is now present on a job application form, a fertile field is present for a disappointed applicant to claim that the failure to be hired was based upon age and that therefore he or she should be given the job. Some employers advise a job applicant that a question concerning age on an application form should bear the notation, "This question *may*, but is not required to, be answered." Whether that device will protect an employer from having to respond to a claim of discrimination will depend upon the facts in the individual case.

Discrimination Based on Physical Handicap

Under federal law, certain persons who are handicapped may not be discriminated against with respect to a job for which they are otherwise qualified. That prohibition does not apply to all employers but only (1) to those performing services under government contracts, such as, for example, a firm having a government contract to build military aircraft or a post office; (2) to those private concerns which have received and are using federal funds, such as schools and hospitals; and (3) to public bodies receiving federal aid, such as city governments.

Many states have also enacted laws which prohibit employment discrimination against physically handicapped persons. In some states, the prohibition does not apply if the handicapped person is unable to perform the required work without endangering other employees.

WORKERS' COMPENSATION LEGISLATION

Necessity for Workers' Compensation Legislation

Around the turn of the twentieth century it was extremely difficult for a worker, injured at work, to recover damages from his or her employer. It was considered that a worker simply assumed the risks of the job and therefore could have no basis for complaint. In addition, the law imposed almost insurmountable hurdles to proving employer negligence. The employee could not recover if he or she suffered an accident that resulted from the workplace being unsafe, or from the negligent act of a fellow worker, or because the injured person had himself or herself contributed a degree of negligence which led to the injury. A worker's chances of recovering damages from his or her employer were slim indeed.

These injustices under the common law were remedied by a new system called the "workers' (formerly workmens') compensation law," devised in New York in 1903 and soon followed by other states. These laws are often termed the first social legislation in this country. In 1917 the Supreme Court of the United States determined that the principles underlying workers' compensation laws were constitutional. By 1920 all but six states had adopted workers' compensation laws; today all states have them.

Workers' Compensation Laws

Workers' compensation laws completely eliminate negligence or fault on the part of *either* the employer *or* the employee as an element of recovery for work-related injuries and diseases. The worker pays no part of his or her medical expenses. Instead, the employer, whether individual or corporate, is responsible for the cost of benefits paid to or provided for an injured or disabled worker. Some states have made insurance compulsory and a few have created state insurance funds to assure payments when the employer is insolvent.

An employee, covered by workers' compensation, who suffers an injury in the course of employment may not waive that compensation and, instead, elect to sue the employer in a court of law.

In addition to state workers' compensation laws, there are several federal laws which provide comparable benefits to workers engaged in specialized employments not covered by the state laws. Such workers are, for example, merchant seamen, longshoremen, federal employees, and railroad workers.

Source of Compensation.   The compensation paid to an injured employee, and the costs of medical treatment and job retraining (if the latter is necessary), are borne by the employer's insurance carrier. In the unusual circumstance that an employer has not purchased workers' compensation insurance, the employer remains liable to action in the civil courts by an injured employee. In that event, state laws generally are extremely favorable to the employee.

Basis for Receipt of Compensation.   To be entitled to workers' compensation, an injured worker need only establish that his or her injury or disease *arose out of and occurred in the course of employment*. To illustrate, assume that Jack works in a coal mine and develops black lung disease. Jack's work as a coal miner caused the illness to *arise,* and it was while he was in the mine during the *course of* that employment that he acquired the illness. Jack is entitled to workers' compensation although he failed to wear a prescribed face mask and even though the most modern exhaust fans operated in the coal-digging area.

A worker is entitled to compensation when a work-related injury is caused through the intentional or careless fault of someone else. The "someone else" could be a fellow worker, an outsider, or the employer.

It is not enough for the worker to be *present* at the workplace when an injury occurs, his or her presence must have been required. Suppose that on his day off Felix, a waiter, visits his friend, Mary, a cook, at the restaurant where he normally works. While in the restaurant kitchen a stove explodes and several people, including Felix, are injured. It is obvious that if anyone *working* in the restaurant is injured, that injury occurred in the course of employment. Felix, however, is in the same position as that of any customer in the restaurant: If the owner of the restaurant can be shown to have been negligent in the operation of the stove, Felix has a claim against the owner, but the claim would be under tort law, not under workers' compensation law.

The liberal attitude of courts in determining whether an injury is or is not work-related is reflected in the following case.

CASE 43.4 Industrial Indemnity Co., v. Industrial Accident Commission
95 Cal. App. 804 (Cal. 1950)

Facts: Eleanor Baxter tended bar at the Greenville Inn. While she was at the cash register making change, Katherine Walker, the wife of a man sitting at the bar, walked in, fired a pistol at her husband, and missed. The bullet ricocheted off the bar, struck Eleanor, and killed her. Eleanor's minor child sought to recover death benefits under the workers' compensation law.

Question: Did the victim's death arise out of her employment and in the course of her work?

Answer: Yes, her death occurred while she was performing her work.

Reasoning: Eleanor was in the bar because that was the place where she performed her duties. Even though the shooting was in no way related to her work, her employment brought her into a position of danger and her employer is liable. It is not essential that the risk be foreseeable nor that it be one peculiar to the employment. It is sufficient that her death occurred (arose) out of her being where her employment required her to be and occurred in the course of that employment. Therefore, Eleanor's daughter is entitled to recover the workers' compensation death benefit.

For workers' compensation purposes, "injury" is defined to include "disease." Therefore, any physical complaint which arises out of the workplace, whether it results in a disease (such as cancer or a severe allergy) or in any physical hurt such as the loss of a limb, is compensable under the workers' compensation law. Particularly difficult to link to the workplace is a mental disease or psychiatric disorder. Determination of the relation of such a condition to the claimant's work is the issue in the next case.

CASE 43.5   Wolfe v. Sibley, Lindsay & Carr Co.
330 N.E.2d 603 (N.Y. 1975)

Facts: Diana Wolfe was private secretary to John Gorman, the Security Director of a department store. Gorman was very nervous and upset about various aspects of his life and Mrs. Wolfe did all she could to allay his anxiety and tried to "boost his morale." Nevertheless, Gorman shot himself in his office and Mrs. Wolfe found his body lying in a pool of blood. Mrs. Wolfe became extremely depressed because of her feelings of guilt at not having been able to prevent the suicide. She remained at home, unable to work, was diagnosed as having an acute depressive reaction, and was hospitalized. After almost four months of hospitalization, during which she received intensive treatment, she returned to work and claimed workers' compensation.

Question: Is mental injury, precipitated by psychological trauma, compensable?

Answer: Yes. Mrs. Wolfe's psychic trauma, which arose out of and in the course of her employment, is compensable.

Reasoning: Workers' compensation is designed to shift the risk of loss of earning capacity caused by work-related accidents from the worker to the industry and ultimately to the consumer. In light of its beneficial and remedial character, the workers' compensation law should be construed liberally in favor of the employee.

Liability under the act is predicated on injury arising out of and in the course of employment. In this case there is no question concerning the relationship between the occurrence and the injury. The doctor stated that the discovery of her superior's body caused Mrs. Wolfe's condition. Psychological or nervous injury caused by psychic trauma is compensable to the same extent as physical injury. In a given situation one person may suffer a heart attack while another, as in this case, may suffer a depressive reaction. In either case the result is the same—the individual is incapable of functioning properly because of an accident and should be compensated under the Workers' Compensation Law.

Scope of Compensation.   Under workers' compensation laws, workers may be eligible for benefits relating to temporary and permanent disability, medical treatment, job retraining, and death.

Temporary and Permanent Disability.   Workers' compensation laws provide for both temporary and permanent compensation. Temporary benefits are paid during the time, including the healing period, when the worker is unable to work. This is to compensate the injured person for loss of wages. If there is a permanent residual disability, such as the loss of a leg or a lessened ability to engage in required heavy lifting, an additional sum of money is paid weekly for the balance of the worker's life as permanent disability compensation, the amount of which will depend upon the degree of disability. Compensation is allowed for aggravation of a preexisting injury or disease and for injury or disease which results from treatment for some other compensable occurrence.

Medical Treatment.   In some cases the most valuable benefit of workers' compensation is the availability of free medical treatment, including diagnostic tests, medicines, special nursing services, and artificial limbs or other prosthetics, for a lifetime, if necessary.

Job Retraining.   Another benefit, of more recent adoption in some states, is the furnishing of retraining for some other type of work if a worker's former job duties can no longer be performed because of an injury.

Death Benefits.   If the injury or disease that is related to work causes death, the dependents of the deceased worker may be entitled to death benefits.

Amount of Compensation.   The amount of compensation a disabled worker receives is fixed by statute or by a designated commission or other state agency. The amount of temporary disability compensation is less than the amount of the wages the worker lost because of the injury. The theory behind this is that if the compensation were the same as the lost wages, the worker might lose the incentive to return to work.

The rate of compensation for permanent disability is established by a fixed scale which places a value upon every type of injury. The money benefits do not represent damages, such as would be obtained in a personal injury action through the court system where such damages are based upon the court's evaluation of pain and suffering, loss of potential earnings, and expenses incurred by the accident. Payments under workers' compensation for permanent partial disability are measured by the person's diminished ability to compete in an open labor market. If the worker sustains a permanent disability, but is nonetheless able to work, he may do so without loss of workers' compensation benefits.

Figure 43.1 is an abbreviated representation of the benefits under workers' compensation, applicable in California in 1984. The coverage is typical of that provided by other state statutes.

Procedures under Workers' Compensation Laws

A workers' compensation case is begun by the filing of a claim with an office of the Workers' Compensation Commission. It is filed either by the claimant or by an attorney. Most claims are then processed administratively on the basis of the facts presented in the claim. If there is a dispute, such as whether an injury really occurred while the person was at work, there may be a trial before the Workers' Compensation Appeals Board. In either event, it is the purpose of the system to respond more quickly than the regular courts. This is particularly important in the case of a worker who, suddenly unable to work, is without earnings.

Coverage: Work-related injury or disease

Financed by: Employer

Amount and Duration of Benefits:

1. $84 to $196 per week:
   Temporary partial disability: up to 240 weeks.
   Temporary total disability: unlimited period.

2. $50 to $130 per week:
   Permanent partial disability.

3. $196 per week:
   Permanent total disability.
   For life, if disability is rated at 100%.

4. Death benefits according to number of dependents;
   e.g., two or more totally dependent, $85,000.

Medical Care: As needed. For life, if necessary.

Financed by: Employer, usually through insurance coverage.

FIGURE 43.1   Typical workers' compensation coverage.

Advantages of the Workers' Compensation System

The adoption of the workers' compensation system is attractive to employers because it specifies that a workers' claim for compensation is the *only* action that can be brought against the employer by an injured employee. Thus, the employer is shielded from large damage claims that might be demanded in a law suit in the regular courts.

At the same time, the workers' compensation system is advantageous for the worker because (1) the former defenses available in the law courts cannot be asserted against him or her by the employer, and (2) the system provides a speedy remedy with immediate cash payments and free medical treatment if there is no dispute as to the work-related nature of the injury or disease. If a worker's injury was caused by a third party (not an employee of the same employer) the worker retains his or her right to take legal action against the third party and at the same time to receive workers' compensation benefits. However, if the worker recovers damages against the third party, his or her employer (or the employer's insurance carrier) is entitled to be reimbursed from such funds to the extent the worker had received benefits under workers' compensation.

SUMMARY

Because of the unequal power that employers and employees can each exert in the fixing of wages and conditions of employment, a number of statutes have been enacted to protect employees. By the Civil Rights Act, Congress declared that it is an unfair labor practice to fail to hire or otherwise in any way to discriminate against an individual with respect to terms, conditions, rate of pay, or privileges of employment because of race, color, religion, sex, or national origin.

The Occupational Safety and Health Act of 1970 prescribes a multitude of rules designed to make the work places of all employees safe. Even though an employee intentionally disregards those rules, if the employer is in a position to know that the rules are not being followed, the employer is considered to be at fault.

By the National Labor Relations Act, as amended, Congress defined activities which are unfair labor practices.

Workers' compensation laws, separate and distinct from antidiscrimination acts, correct deficiencies of the common law which made it almost impossible for an employee to receive compensation for injury, disease, or death arising out of employment. Under the workers' compensation system an employee receives compensation for injury or disease arising out of, and in the course of, his or her work. Negligence on the part of either the employer or the employee is not considered in the handling of a compensation claim.

An employee does not file a lawsuit in order to be compensated. Payment is made by an administrative agency according to a schedule setting out a value for every type of injury and disease. Compensation is also paid when death results.

REVIEW QUESTIONS

1. Distinguish between a worker who is an employee and one who is an independent contractor.

2. A construction site is designated a "hard hat area." Because of the heat, neither the foreman nor any of the workers is wearing a hard hat. One worker is injured. Has there been a violation of OSHA rules?

3. Name three ways in which an employer, and three ways in which a union, may be guilty of an unfair labor practice.

4. Is there any law prohibiting a factory owner from hiring only persons from minority groups? Discuss.

5. You, as owner of a large drugstore, need to hire a cashier. You decide that, since the checkout counter is near the entrance to the store, you prefer to employ an attractive young woman for the position. (a) How could you word your advertisement in the newspaper to accomplish your purpose, and (b) what would be your position if a middle-aged man with several years of cashier experience applied for the job?

6. You want to hire a gardener. Among the applicants is a person with one arm. If you do not hire him have you violated one of the federal discrimination acts? Discuss.

7. Why do all states have workers' compensation laws?

8. John, solely through his own carelessness, drops a sledgehammer on his foot and breaks a toe. Does a workers' compensation law furnish him any relief?

9. Where is a workers' compensation claim filed?

10. What ethical considerations were behind the enactment of the laws outlined in this chapter? Discuss.

11. Do workers' compensation laws cast an undue burden upon American industry? Discuss.

CASE PROBLEMS

1. Partida owned a laundromat. He hired Mrs. Munoz to open the laundromat at 6 A.M. and to close it at 10 P.M. It required only about 2 hours each morning to clean up the facility. Partida also furnished Mrs. Munoz with living quarters adjoining the laundromat, separated from it only by a partition. During the day she also accepted laundry and attended to any trouble the customers might have with the machines. Representatives of the Secretary of Labor maintained that Mrs. Munoz should be paid for working a 16-hour day, with time-and-a-half pay for all time over 8 hours. Partida claims that Mrs. Munoz worked less than 8 hours a day and the rest of the time she "just kept her eyes on the place" from her adjoining living quarters. Is his position correct? Explain.

2. Alice, age 25, sought employment as a prison guard in a men's penitentiary for hardened criminals. Alice was rejected because she did not meet the height and weight requirements for guards and also because, as a woman, she was not eligible for the job. When challenged, the prison administration replied that the federal antidiscrimination law was not violated. Is Alice entitled to a court order requiring that she be hired? Explain.

3. A bus company refuses to hire applicants to be bus drivers if they are over 40 years of age and have had no bus-driving experience. However, the company retains in its employ drivers who reach that age. Is there any basis upon which the bus company's policy would *not* violate the law which proscribes discrimination in hiring based on age?

4. Piper was employed by Century Heating Company. He was sent out on a service call. Near the customer's house he tripped on a broken sidewalk and turned his ankle. He saw the company doctor, who said it was just strained, needed no treatment, and would soon be better. Instead, during the ensuing 2 weeks the ankle swelled up and Piper saw another doctor who found that Piper had broken his ankle and that, because it had not been properly attended to originally, would result in a permanent disability. Century Heating claimed that it was not liable for the disability because (**a**) the injury did not occur at Piper's place of work, and (**b**) it was caused by their doctor's malpractice which itself bore no relation to Piper's work. What chance does Piper have of securing workers' compensation for the permanent disability? Discuss.

5. William was employed by Homer. William had reported to the OSHA representative that the place where he worked was not safe. Homer was advised by his lawyer that William could not be fired for making the report and that Homer would have to find some other reason for discharging him. Homer then assigned William to disagreeable and dangerous duties, hoping that he would quit. While performing those duties William was injured. He now sues Homer in a court of law for the injury that he claims was suffered because Homer, out of spite, intentionally placed him in danger. Homer's lawyer claims that the suit must be dismissed and that if William has any action at all it is through workers' compensation channels. Is the lawyer correct? Explain.

CHAPTER 44

BANKRUPTCY

Anyone, even the largest corporation, can experience financial difficulty. If a business becomes so unprofitable that it cannot pay its debts, creditors naturally become concerned and can be expected to take steps to collect the amounts that the debtor owes. Often, however, the debtor has so few assets that the claims of creditors cannot be paid, or can be paid only in part. Thus, several legal questions arise: (1) What may an unpaid creditor do to enforce his or her right to payment? (2) Where the assets of a failing business are too few to pay all claims of creditors, how should those assets be distributed among the unpaid creditors? (3) Under what circumstances, if any, should a failing business or other debtor be discharged (freed) from liability for debts remaining after existing assets have been distributed? Depending on the circumstances, either state or federal law, or some combination of the two, provides the answers.

A creditor has a variety of ways under state law to enforce the obligation of a debtor who *can* pay but "defaults" (fails or refuses to pay a valid debt). Except as briefly described in the first part of this chapter, the methods of enforcement that creditors may use against solvent debtors are beyond the scope of this chapter. Rather, the emphasis is on the rights of creditors and debtors where a defaulting debtor is *insolvent* (unable to pay his or her debts when they become due). Where a defaulting debtor is insolvent, *state insolvency law*, discussed in the first part of this chapter, permits the debtor to make some arrangement with unpaid creditors for full or partial payment of debts. Or, the insolvent debtor or his or her creditors may be entitled to the benefits of *federal bankruptcy law* which, when resorted to, prevails over or displaces state insolvency law. **Bankruptcy**, the main topic of this chapter, is the process by which (1) a financially troubled debtor is declared by a bankruptcy court to be incapable of paying his or her debts; (2) the debtor's available assets are distributed to creditors as required by bankruptcy law; and (3) the debtor, if honest, is granted a discharge from liability for most of the remaining unpaid debts. The second part of this chapter discusses the nature of bankruptcy law and administration of debtors' estates. The third and fourth parts focus on three major kinds of bankruptcy proceedings: liquidation, business reorganizations, and repayment plans for debtors with regular income.

CREDITORS' RIGHTS AND DEBTOR RELIEF

The process of bankruptcy and the need for bankruptcy law can best be understood by examining briefly how financial difficulty can develop and how the rights of creditors and the needs of debtors may collide. Consider, for example, the history of Joe's financial failure.

Joe's Financial Failure

Upon his graduation from State University, Joe and his wife set up a retail art supply store. Having no funds of his own, he borrowed $100,000 from First Bank as a start-up loan for renting a store building and purchasing equipment and inventory. Needing more start-up financing, Joe borrowed an additional $20,000 from Second Bank; purchased a copier, a cash register, and a computer on credit from Bud's Business Machines; and purchased $5000 worth of art supplies on credit from Al's Art Supplies. Business was good. Joe opened several personal charge accounts with local department stores; bought a $100,000 home which he financed with a $90,000 mortgage from Third Bank at 15 percent annual interest; and opened two new stores that he financed in part with the profits from the first store and in part from unsecured loans from relatives. By now, Joe had 15 employees, two children in private schools, and a new Mercedes-Benz that he had bought on credit.

Then, as a result of a widespread economic recession, many businesses in Joe's city laid off their employees and schools cut back on their art programs. Joe's art supply sales dwindled to almost nothing. Within weeks, Joe's creditors—secured and unsecured—were seeking immediate payment, but Joe could not pay. Some of his creditors began calling him at odd hours of the night. One creditor, the veterinarian who had performed surgery on Joe's dog, repeatedly phoned Joe and his relatives, demanding immediate payment of Joe's account and threatening to inform Joe's country club that Joe was a "deadbeat" who should have his membership canceled. Bill collectors constantly hounded Joe, his wife, and even their children while at school. One night a bill collector accosted Joe in a parking lot and beat him, inflicting serious injuries. Attempting to check into a nearby hospital, Joe was turned away because he could not demonstrate ability to pay for medical services. The next day Joe sought financial counseling.

Carla, the financial counselor, pointed out several things to Joe about his financial difficulties:

1. Joe's plight was caused in part by his own mismanagement of his financial affairs and by a too-rapid business expansion, but there were other causes more or less beyond his control: for instance, the economic recession and the willingness of some lenders to extend credit without adequately checking Joe's ability to repay.
2. Nevertheless, all Joe's creditors have valid claims against Joe for payment. None had committed fraud or other wrongdoing when extending credit to Joe, and all are entitled to payment in full.
3. However, despite their valid claims, Joe's creditors are limited by law in what they may do by way of debt-collection activities. As discussed in Chapter 28, a secured creditor may peacefully repossess collateral and make a commercially reasonable disposition of it to satisfy the debt it secures, and usually may hold the debtor liable for any deficiency. As discussed in Chapter 27, unsecured creditors such as Joe's credit card and open account creditors must rely on Joe's promises to pay, since unsecured creditors have no claim to any specific property of Joe's. If Joe does not pay, an unsecured creditor must bring suit, receive a judgment for the amount owed, and rely on Joe's general assets, if any, as the source of payment.

But no creditor, secured or unsecured, may take debt-collection action that violates the debtor's rights under the law. For example, creditors who engage in overly vigorous collection activity risk liability to the debtor for defamation, invasion of privacy, intentionally causing emotional distress, or other torts discussed in Chapters 3 and 4. Under Article 9 of the Uniform Commercial Code (UCC), secured creditors must avoid a breach of the peace when repossessing collateral. Additional laws apply to *debt collectors* hired by Joe's creditors. Debt collectors may not engage in debt-collection activity that violates laws such as the federal Fair Debt Collection Practices Act [15 U.S.C.1692 et seq.]. The act prohibits a wide variety of objectionable collection practices: for example, threats of violence, the use of abusive language when trying to collect a debt, harassment by means of repeated telephone calls, or deception; and unfair methods of collection such as threatening to deposit a postdated check before the date of the check (and thereby intentionally causing other checks of the debtor to be dishonored).

4. Joe has a variety of options under state and federal law for attempting to pay his debts in full or in part, and under bankruptcy law may escape them altogether so that he can re-enter business with a "fresh start."

How Joe May Settle His Unpaid Debts

Arrangements under State Law.   Some of Joe's creditors received security interests in Joe's property when extending credit to him; but, as discussed in Chapter 28, if the collateral they claim is not sufficiently valuable to cover the amounts Joe owes them, even Joe's secured creditors will be unsecured in part. The temptation is great for unsecured creditors to protect themselves by exercising their rights under the state's "grab law"—i.e., law permitting an unsecured creditor to obtain a judgment against Joe for the amount owed and to "execute" the judgment by having Joe's unencumbered property, if any, seized and sold without regard to the welfare of Joe's other creditors. However, execution sales often produce low prices. Joe's creditors might be willing to forgo the cumbersome and wasteful execution process and consider alternative ways of receiving payment. Joe might suggest a composition or extension agreement. Or Joe might make an assignment for the benefit of creditors.

Composition and Extension Agreements.   Composition and extension agreements are contracts between a debtor and some or all of his or her creditors, by means of which debtor and creditors agree to substitute a less burdensome obligation for the debts ordinarily undertaken. In a **composition agreement**, the debtor agrees to pay the creditors some fraction (e.g., 20 percent) of the amount the debtor owes, in full settlement of the creditors' claims. Usually each creditor will receive the same percentage that all other creditors receive, in what is called a "pro rata" (equal percentage) distribution. However, the agreement may provide that some creditors —for example, those who are owed small amounts—will receive 100 percent of their claims. A creditor who chooses not to participate in a composition is not bound by it. Instead, the nonconsenting creditor may pursue the usual collection process and execute against the debtor's unencumbered assets even though such action prevents the debtor from carrying out the composition agreement.

In an **extension agreement**, the debtor agrees to pay the full amount of all debts (with or without interest), but the creditors agree to allow the debtor to pay over a greater time than originally agreed. Often, creditors grant extensions of from 1 to 3 years. Nonconsenting creditors are not bound by an extension agreement and may pursue the usual collection process as to amounts owed them.

Assignments for Benefit of Creditors.   A troubled debtor might choose to make a general assignment for the benefit of his or her creditors. A **general assignment** (also called an "assignment for the benefit of creditors") is a voluntary transfer by the debtor of all his or her available property to a person (the *assignee* or *trustee*) named by the debtor to (1) receive the debtor's property, (2) liquidate it (convert it into cash), and (3) distribute the cash to creditors in exchange for their promises to release the debtor from further liability. Under the terms of the assignment, each creditor covered by the assignment may receive a **pro rata** (equal percentage) **distribution**, or some creditors may receive a larger proportion of their claims than other creditors receive. Once a general assignment is made, no unsecured creditor may execute on or otherwise obtain rights to the assigned property, but is instead limited to whatever distribution the assignment document provides. However, creditors who did not assent to the assignment are not bound by its terms; consequently, the debtor's future earnings will be subject to the claims of unpaid nonconsenting creditors. Furthermore, as noted later in this chapter, a creditor who is unhappy with a general assignment may be able to upset it by commencing federal bankruptcy proceedings against the debtor.

Use of Federal Bankruptcy Law.   Instead of using procedures available under state law for resolving his financial difficulty, Joe (or his creditors) might seek the aid of federal bankruptcy law. The main advantage to Joe of a bankruptcy proceeding is the discharge from remaining unpaid debts that is available to him under the federal law. In contrast, under state law Joe remains liable to creditors (and subject to continuing executions against his property) unless contractually released from liability as, for example, by a composition agreement. For Joe's creditors a main advantage of a bankruptcy proceeding is the more evenhanded treatment they receive under federal law than they might receive under state law. For example, under federal law, creditors of a given class are entitled to a pro rata distribution. In contrast, under the insolvency laws of some states, debtors like Joe may "prefer" some creditors over others by paying the preferred creditors a larger percentage of their claims.

FEDERAL BANKRUPTCY LAW AND ADMINISTRATION

For most people, bankruptcy is a most unpleasant fact of business life. A person with a bankruptcy discharge on his or her credit record may have difficulty obtaining new credit. If a bankrupt business must close down, employees lose their jobs and may lose back wages and pension benefits. **General** (unsecured) **creditors** may be unable to collect unpaid debts. Tax authorities lose a source of revenue and may be unable to collect unpaid taxes. Customers must look elsewhere for goods and services, suppliers lose a customer, and proprietors and shareholders may lose all or most of their investment.

Yet, bankruptcy does have its positive aspects. Freed by their bankruptcy discharges from impossible burdens of debt accumulated for reasons beyond their control, competent business people may once again be good credit risks and productive citizens. Bankruptcy law also preserves employment by providing opportunities for a troubled business to stay in operation while it regains its financial health. And bankruptcy law reduces the potential for wasteful conflict among creditors by providing for an orderly and fair distribution of the debtor's remaining assets in the event of a liquidation proceeding. The nature of federal bankruptcy law and how its purposes are carried out are the subjects of the paragraphs that follow.

Purposes of Federal Bankruptcy Law

The United States Constitution gives Congress the power to regulate bankruptcies; and over the years since 1800, five different federal bankruptcy statutes have been in effect. The most recent one is the **Bankruptcy Reform Act of 1978**, referred to in this chapter as the **Bankruptcy Code**. The Bankruptcy Code, together with interpretive court decisions (and procedural bankruptcy rules and standards published by the United States Supreme Court), constitute our national bankruptcy law.[1]

Federal bankruptcy law has two main purposes: (1) to provide a fair and evenhanded basis for distributing a debtor's available assets among creditors, and (2) to free debtors from impossible burdens of debt and thus give them a fresh start so that they may more quickly return to productive business activities. One aspect of the fresh-start policy is the practice permitted by the Bankruptcy Code of allowing some firms to stay in business while they attempt to recover their financial health. Permitting financially distressed firms, especially large ones, to reorganize and stay in business tends to minimize the disruption of employment and to maintain the flow of goods and services to the public.

Basic Bankruptcy Procedure

Like any other judicial proceeding, bankruptcy follows a procedure specified by law. Although the procedure varies somewhat depending on who initiates it (debtor or creditors) or on the kind of relief sought (liquidation, reorganization, or repayment plan), the basic steps are as follows:

1. A person entitled to do so files a **petition** (in a federal bankruptcy court) requesting the bankruptcy judge to grant an "order for relief" with respect to a particular debtor alleged to be insolvent. An **order for relief** is a formal court ruling or declaration that the alleged debtor is insolvent (bankrupt). The filing of the petition results in an **automatic stay** (suspension) of most other legal action and nonjudicial collection activity affecting the debtor's estate (property), until the bankruptcy case is over or until the bankruptcy court vacates (terminates) the stay.
2. The debtor files with the bankruptcy court a listing of the debtor's assets and creditors.
3. Promptly upon entry (recording) of the order for relief, the bankruptcy judge appoints an *interim* (temporary) *trustee* to investigate the financial affairs of the debtor, to take control of the debtor's estate, to notify creditors of the bankruptcy proceeding, and to collect and distribute the debtor's *non*exempt property to the creditors as required by the Bankruptcy Code. Exempt property is property such as clothing and tools that an individual debtor may keep free from the claims of creditors.
4. Within a reasonable time after entry of the order for relief, the bankruptcy judge calls the *first meeting of creditors* (but is not allowed to preside at or attend it). The creditors may elect a permanent trustee. If they fail to do so, the interim

---

[1]In 1982 the United States Supreme Court declared the bankruptcy court system unconstitutional because the 1978 Bankruptcy Reform Act provides 14-year terms for bankruptcy judges with no protection against salary reduction instead of the lifetime judicial tenure and no salary reduction required by Article III of the Constitution. So, as of early 1984, the ability of the bankruptcy system to function properly is in doubt. However, the bankruptcy law itself, as stated in the Bankruptcy Code, was not ruled unconstitutional and is likely to remain substantially unchanged.

trustee serves as permanent trustee. The *debtor must attend* the creditors' meeting *and must submit to examination (questioning) under oath.*

5. Depending on the honesty of the debtor and on the kind of bankruptcy proceeding involved, the court grants the debtor a discharge from most debts remaining unpaid, approves a plan of business reorganization, or approves the debtor's plan for repayment of debts.

Role of State Law

Under the supremacy clause of the Constitution, the federal bankruptcy law prevails over conflicting state law. However, although Congress probably could preempt (displace) all state insolvency laws, it has chosen not to do so. The Bankruptcy Code looks to state law for resolution of a number of bankruptcy issues. Usually, the state law of property and of contracts will be followed for the purpose of determining, for example, what property the debtor owns. By express provision of the Code, state law may govern what property of the debtor (residence, tools, clothing, and so on) is exempt from claims of creditors. State insolvency law that does not defeat the purposes of the Bankruptcy Code will usually be allowed to stand.

Functions of Trustee and Judge

Bankruptcy is not merely a judicial proceeding. It also involves administration of the debtor's "estate," i.e., the debtor's property, for the benefit of the debtor and the creditors. Two officials have major responsibility for administering the estate: the trustee in bankruptcy and the bankruptcy judge.

The **trustee in bankruptcy** is responsible for collecting, liquidating, and distributing the debtor's estate. These tasks require the trustee to inspect the property and business of the debtor, to decide whether to adopt or reject executory (yet to be performed) contracts and leases, to operate the business of the debtor under certain circumstances, and to perform a variety of routine tasks relating to the administrative process. One of the trustee's major duties is to act on behalf of the general (unsecured) creditors. To discharge that duty, the trustee must guard the estate against unfounded claims of creditors, resist doubtful exemption claims of the debtor, and avoid (set aside) various transactions by means of which the debtor or others may have dissipated the estate. The trustee possesses extensive legal powers for carrying out these tasks. Many of the trustee's powers, especially the powers of avoidance, are discussed later in this chapter.

The **bankruptcy judge** has the usual judicial function of deciding any disputes that may arise during the bankruptcy process. Ordinarily the dispute will be between the trustee and a person affected by some act of the trustee in collecting and distributing the debtor's estate. The judge also has an administrative function—appointing trustees and supervising their activities in administrating debtors' estates.

Kinds of Bankruptcy Proceedings

The Bankruptcy Code is divided into eight odd-numbered "chapters." Chapter 7 deals with liquidation, also known as "straight" or "ordinary" bankruptcy. Chapter 11 deals with corporate reorganizations, and Chapter 13 covers plans for the adjustment of debts of individuals with regular income. Liquidation, corporate reorganizations, and Chapter 13 plans are discussed later in this chapter.

Most debtors—individuals, partnerships, or corporations—may *voluntarily* seek relief from debts or may be subjected to *involuntary* bankruptcy proceedings initiated by creditors. *Not* covered by the Bankruptcy Code are insurance companies, banks, savings and loan associations, credit unions, and similar organizations. Such organizations are regulated by administrative agencies under special state or federal statutes. Financial failure of regulated businesses is left to the regulatory agencies, which are considered to be better equipped than the courts to resolve such problems.

LIQUIDATION (STRAIGHT BANKRUPTCY)

The purpose of a Chapter 7 liquidation proceeding is to convert the debtor's nonexempt assets into cash, distribute it in accordance with the scheme of distribution provided by the Bankruptcy Code, and grant the honest debtor a discharge from most of the remaining debts.

Commencement of Straight Bankruptcy

Any "person" except a railroad or a regulated business of the type discussed earlier may file a **voluntary petition** to liquidate under Chapter 7. *Person* includes individuals, partnerships, and corporations, but not governmental units. Therefore, municipal corporations may not file under Chapter 7 and cannot be liquidated (but *can* have their debts "adjusted" under Chapter 9). The filing fee is $60 and may be paid in installments. No one is exempted from paying the fee.

Most persons who qualify for a voluntary liquidation may be subjected instead to an **involuntary liquidation proceeding**. However, farmers and charitable corporations may not be subjected to any kind of involuntary bankruptcy proceeding. A *farmer* is a person (individual, partnership, or corporation) whose gross income in the taxable year prior to bankruptcy was more than 80 percent from a farming operation owned or operated by that person.

A person cannot be declared an involuntary bankrupt unless three requirements or conditions have been met. First, the petitioning creditor or creditors must have claims totaling at least $5000 in unsecured debts. Second, where the number of creditors is twelve or more, three of them must join in the involuntary petition; otherwise, only one petitioning creditor is required. Third, the alleged debtor must have given the creditor or creditors a **ground for relief**. Under the Code there are two grounds for relief. One is that "the debtor is generally not paying such debtor's debts as such debts become due." The other is that the debtor has, within 120 days of the filing of the involuntary petition, made a general assignment (transfer of the debtor's property) for the benefit of creditors. Such an assignment is evidence of sufficient financial difficulty to warrant a bankruptcy proceeding.

Collection and Liquidation of Debtor's Estate

Collection and liquidation of the debtor's estate can involve considerable litigation. Issues for the court to decide may include what property belongs to the debtor's estate, what powers the trustee has to set aside transactions in order to acquire property for the estate, and what exemption claims by the debtor the trustee should honor.

Property of Debtor's Estate.   The debtor's estate consists of a broad range of property interests either owned by the debtor as of the commencement of the bankruptcy case or recoverable for the estate by the trustee from someone other than the debtor. Included in the estate are the following:

1. Property owned by the debtor as of the commencement of the bankruptcy case. A secured creditor's security interest does *not* become a part of the debtor's estate. A security interest in collateral is by its nature the property of the creditor. As illustrated by Case 44.1, only the debtor's "equity" (buildup of value) in the collateral is included in the debtor's estate. The trustee does, however, receive the collateral itself for purposes of administering the debtor's estate.
2. Any interest in property held by others than the debtor and recoverable by the trustee for the debtor's estate under various provisions of the Bankruptcy Code. An example is property that was fraudulently conveyed by the debtor on the eve of bankruptcy.
3. Certain property acquired by the debtor within 180 days after the date of the filing of the petition. This property includes inheritances, property acquired as a result of a divorce decree, and property acquired by the debtor as a beneficiary of a life insurance policy. (As noted later in this chapter, some or all of such property may later be exempted [freed from] the claims of creditors.)
4. Income from property of the estate. (Earnings from services performed by an *individual* debtor after the commencement of the case are *not* included in the debtor's estate.)

CASE 44.1 Collomb v. Wyatt
6 B.R. 947 (E.D.N.Y. 1980)

Facts: Collomb transferred the proceeds of a life insurance policy to the Wyatts as consideration for their promise to support her. The Wyatts used the money to purchase a
residence, to which they took legal title. Collomb resided there for a time. Then, alleging
that the Wyatts ceased to support her, Collomb brought suit in state court, claiming an
ownership interest in the real estate. The Wyatts filed a petition in bankruptcy. Under the
Bankruptcy Code the trustee acquires all legal or equitable interests *of the debtor* in the
property as of the commencement of the bankruptcy case. Collomb brought suit in the
bankruptcy court, claiming an interest in the real estate.

Question: Does Collomb have an interest in the real estate?

Answer: Yes.

Reasoning: The real estate purchased by the Wyatts was subject to a constructive trust in favor of
Collomb for the value of the life insurance proceeds. Under state law a constructive trust
creates a dual ownership of the property. The Wyatts had a legal title that gave them
the power to sell or otherwise deal with the property; but Collomb had an equitable
interest in it. Only those rights that the Wyatts (the debtors) had in the property pass to
the debtor's estate under the bankruptcy law. Thus, the debtors' *estate,* like the debtors
themselves prior to the filing of the bankruptcy petition, is under an equitable duty to
convey Collomb's interest to her.

Trustee's Power to Collect and Liquidate the Estate.   To administer the debtor's estate properly, the trustee in bankruptcy must gain possession, custody, or control of the property, regardless of who actually has the property. The "turnover" provisions of the Bankruptcy Code require people who have the debtor's property to deliver it to the trustee. In carrying out his or her duties, the trustee also has the benefit of (1) powers to use, sell, or lease property and to borrow money; (2) powers to assume or reject executory contracts and unexpired leases; and (3) powers to avoid a variety of transactions.

Power to Use, Sell, or Lease Property.   Often the trustee needs to use, sell, or lease property that is subject to the claims of persons such as secured creditors, or to borrow money in a manner that might threaten existing security or other interests. These acts may be necessary to preserve valuable property or to keep a business operation going. The trustee may use, sell, or lease encumbered (mortgaged) property as long as the security interest or lien is adequately protected. Consequently, the property may not be sold free and clear of an encumbrance unless, for example, the holder of the interest consents or the price received for the property is greater than the value of the interest.

Power to Assume Debtor's Contracts.   Subject to court approval, the trustee may assume, reject, or assign executory contracts and unexpired leases of the debtor. This power enables the trustee to reject improvident or burdensome transactions, to retain for the estate any beneficial transaction that is assumable under state law, and to assign (sell) any contract or lease that is assignable under state law. The trustee's rejection of an otherwise binding contract or lease constitutes a breach of it and gives the aggrieved party a claim against the debtor's estate.

Power to Avoid Fraudulent Transfers and Preferences.   The trustee has the power to avoid certain transactions entered into by the debtor. Among them are *fraudulent transfers* and *preferential transfers* (preferences). Such transfers are avoidable because they deprive the debtor's estate of assets to which it is entitled, or because they undermine a fundamental bankruptcy policy—equality of distribution among creditors.

The trustee may avoid any **fraudulent transfer** of the debtor's property made within 1 year before the filing of the petition in bankruptcy. Suppose, for example, that Dan is in financial difficulty and intends to file a voluntary petition in bankruptcy. But a week before doing so Dan transfers title to his $100,000 house to his sister for "safekeeping" until he receives a discharge in bankruptcy. Dan's transfer of the house is fraudulent as to his creditors.

The trustee may also avoid **preferential payments** or transfers (preferences). A transaction is a preference (and is therefore avoidable by the trustee) if the transfer (1) was made to a creditor in settlement of an *antecedent* debt (a debt owed before the debtor made the transfer), (2) was made "on or within" 90 days before the filing of the bankruptcy petition, (3) was made when the debtor was insolvent, and (4) conferred upon the creditor more than the creditor would have been entitled to receive in a bankruptcy liquidation case.

Preferences occur in a variety of ways. Sometimes, for example, a debtor faced with bankruptcy voluntarily pays a favorite creditor-supplier in full and leaves other creditors to share whatever remains. Sometimes a creditor pressures a debtor into making a preferential transfer. Frequently, the preference takes the form of a security interest given just before bankruptcy for an unsecured debt incurred a long time before the bankruptcy—where the extension of credit originally was intended to be unsecured. Preferences made within the 90-day period are vulnerable to the trustee's attack regardless of whether the creditor had reasonable cause to believe that the debtor was insolvent. Case 44.2 below discusses whether a payment by check occurred within the 90-day period.

The trustee has additional powers to avoid preferences made to "insiders," (i.e., the debtor's relatives, partners, directors, controlling persons, and so on). Preferences made to insiders within the 90-day period before bankruptcy are avoidable under the rule stated in the preceding paragraph. The trustee may also avoid preferences made to insiders between the beginning of the 90-day period and 1 year before bankruptcy *if* the insider had reasonable cause to believe that the debtor was insolvent at the time of the transfer.

Some transactions that appear technically to be preferences are not, and therefore they are not avoidable by the trustee. Suppose a supplier of inventory delivers goods to an insolvent retailer 30 days before the retailer's bankruptcy and, a few days later, receives full payment out of the proceeds from the resale of the goods. The supplier has extended unsecured credit and could be said to have received a preferential payment on account of an antecedent debt. However, the payment is not so treated under the Bankruptcy Code. The trustee cannot avoid an otherwise preferential payment of a debt incurred in the ordinary course of the debtor and creditor's business or financial affairs where the payment was made (1) in the ordinary course of business according to ordinary business terms, and (2) not later than 45 days after the debt was incurred.

A similar rule applies where a lender intends to make a secured loan to an insolvent debtor, but the execution of the security documents occurs a few days after credit is extended. Since the debtor actually received cash at nearly the time the documents were signed, the debtor's giving the lender a security interest is not a preference, and the trustee may not avoid the transaction. Such rules encourage suppliers and lenders to continue to do business with insolvent persons while there is a chance that they might recover their financial health. The rules do no harm to general creditors because the protected suppliers and lenders have not depleted the debtor's estate.

CASE 44.2   **Matter of Duffy**
3 B.R. 263 (S.D.N.Y. 1980)

Facts: Duffy leased a car from Avis Rent-A-Car System on a long-term basis. Duffy made no rental payments until July 30, 1979, when, after a conversation with an Avis representative, Duffy forwarded to Avis a check for $400 postdated to August 3, 1979. The check was honored by the drawee bank on August 6, which was 88 days before the debtor filed a Chapter 7 petition for relief in bankruptcy. Thus, the check was delivered to Avis more than 90 days before the filing, but was cashed within the 90-day period. The trustee challenged the $400 payment to Avis as a voidable preference. Avis denied that the payment occurred within the forbidden 90-day period.

Question: Did Avis receive payment within the 90-day period?

Answer: Yes.

Reasoning: A payment of a debt by check is a transfer of property within the Bankruptcy Code's broad definition of "transfer." But Duffy's payment did not occur when Duffy delivered the check to Avis. A check does not by itself vest in the payee any title to or interest in the funds held by the drawee bank. A check is simply an order to the drawee bank to pay the sum stated and does not constitute a transfer and delivery of the fund until it is paid. The date of the payment, and not the date of the delivery of the check is crucial in determining when the transfer occurred and, therefore, whether it was preferential.

The Debtor's Exemptions.   As a part of the fresh-start policy, the Bankruptcy Code permits an *individual* debtor to exempt certain property from the debtor's estate, i.e., to have it free from the claims of creditors. The Bankruptcy Code gives an individual debtor a choice between two exemption systems—state and federal—unless, as is permitted by the Code, the debtor's state has denied its citizens the right to elect the federal exemptions. States that choose to do this are said to have "opted out" of the federal exemption scheme. Well over thirty states have opted out, limiting their citizens to whatever exemptions the state laws provide.

Some states limit exemptions to no more than about $5000 worth of property. In other states the exemptible amount can exceed $100,000. The dollar value of the federal list lies between these extremes, consisting, for example, of $7500 equity in a residence, $1200 equity in one motor vehicle, ordinary household furnishings and personal apparel, $750 in books and tools of the debtor's trade, certain pension rights, and up to $4000 cash surrender or loan value of an unmatured life insurance contract on the life of and owned by the debtor.

Distribution of the Estate   Three kinds of creditors may be involved in the distribution of the debtor's estate: secured creditors, unsecured creditors called "priority" creditors, and other unsecured creditors called "general" creditors. The rights of the various kinds of creditors depend on rules governing proof of claim, allowability of claims, and priority of payments.

Proof of Claim.   The distribution process begins with the filing of a document called a "proof of claim." A proof of claim is prima facie evidence of the validity and the amount of the claim. Only unsecured creditors are required to file proofs of claim. A secured creditor whose secured claim exceeds the value of the collateral is an unsecured creditor as to the amount of the deficiency, and a proof of claim is required for the recovery of the deficiency. Where a proof of claim is required, it must be filed within 6 months after the first meeting of creditors. Unless a proof of claim is timely filed, a claim cannot be "allowed" even though the claim is otherwise valid.

Allowability of Claims.   Only "allowed" claims are eligible for payment out of the debtor's estate, and then, of course, allowed claims will be paid only to the extent that funds are available. What claims are allowed?

Upon the filing of a proof of claim, the claim is "deemed allowed" unless an interested party such as a creditor or the trustee objects to the allowance of the claim. If there is an objection, the bankruptcy court must decide whether the claim is to be allowed. Claims filed after the 6-month limit will not be allowed. Where the debtor has a defense to an alleged debt (e.g., fraud or failure of consideration), a claim for payment of the debt will not be allowed. The Bankruptcy Code lists other claims that will and will not be allowed.

Priority of Payments.   *Secured* creditors have property rights (security interests) that the trustee does not acquire. Consequently, secured claims are paid in full if the collateral is sufficiently valuable.

Next in line are the *priority* creditors, so called because the Bankruptcy Code gives them priority of payment over the claims of the general creditors. There are six classes of priority claims, which receive payment in the following order:

1. Claims for administrative expenses and expenses incurred in preserving and collecting the debtor's estate.
2. Claims of tradespeople who dealt with the debtor in the ordinary course of business after the filing of an involuntary petition but before the appointment of a trustee.
3. Claims of the debtor's employees for up to $2000 each in wages earned within 90 days preceding bankruptcy.
4. Some claims for contributions to employee benefit plans.
5. Claims of consumers for the return of up to $900 each in deposits paid to the debtor for goods not delivered or services not rendered.
6. Claims for taxes.

Finally, if any funds remain, the *general* creditors may receive a share of the debtor's estate. Where the amount of a secured claim exceeds the value of the collateral, the claimant is a general creditor as to the deficiency.

The principle of "pro rata" (equal percentage) distribution is applied throughout the Bankruptcy Code's general scheme of distribution. So, if funds are sufficient, the "first priority" claims are paid in full, and any excess is applied to the "second priority" claims. This process is repeated until the money runs out or all unsecured creditors are paid. Where funds are not sufficient to pay a class of claims in full, each claimant of that class receives the same percentage of his or her claim that the other claimants of that class receive, e.g., 10 percent.

Discharge; Nondischargeable Debts   Debtors who seek liquidation under Chapter 7 or 11, or who propose a Chapter 13 repayment plan, may receive a discharge from most debts that remain unpaid after the distribution of the debtor's estate or the performance of the plan. Most debtors are eligible for a discharge only once every 6 years. However, a wage earner or other debtor who is carrying out a Chapter 13 repayment plan may be eligible for discharge more frequently. The 6-year bar does not apply to a Chapter 13 debtor who pays 70 percent of the unsecured claims under a repayment plan that was proposed by the debtor in good faith and that represents the debtor's best efforts.

Grounds for Denying Discharge.   As illustrated by Case 44.3, a debtor who is eligible for a discharge will be denied a discharge for engaging in any of a variety of activities prohibited by the Bankruptcy Code. The grounds for denying discharge include the debtor's fraudulent transfer or concealment of property (within 1 year before filing a bankruptcy petition) with intent to hinder, delay, or defraud a creditor or an officer of the estate; unjustifiably concealing or destroying business records or failing to keep adequate business records; making a false oath, a fraudulent account, or a false claim in connection with the bankruptcy case; failing to explain satisfactorily any loss of assets or deficiency of assets to meet the debtor's liabilities; and refusal of the debtor to obey lawful orders of the court.

Nondischargeable Debts.   Although an individual debtor may receive a discharge, certain kinds of debts are not covered by the discharge and therefore remain binding on the debtor. Nondischargeable debts include the following:

1. Debts for certain taxes, e.g., where the debtor made a fraudulent tax return or a willful attempt at evasion of taxes.
2. Debts contracted on the basis of the debtor's false pretenses, false representations, or actual fraud. A materially false written financial statement can be the basis for denying discharge of the debt for which it was given (but not for denying a general discharge) where the debtor issued the statement with *intent to deceive* and the creditor *reasonably relied* on it.
3. Debts resulting from the debtor's embezzlement or larceny.
4. Debts arising from alimony, maintenance, or child support awards.
5. Debts arising from certain educational loans.

CASE 44.3   In re Mazzola
4 B.R. 179 (D. Mass. 1980)

Facts: The Mazzolas filed a Chapter 7 petition in bankruptcy. At the time of the filing, Dennis Mazzola was the sole stockholder of the Dennis M. Construction Co. and was engaged in the home construction business. Just before the filing, the LaVangies had been involved in bitter litigation with the Mazzolas over a claim of faulty home construction. The LaVangies obtained an attachment on two parcels of property owned by the Mazzolas. Within a few weeks, the Mazzolas had the attachment dissolved, sold the properties speedily, deposited the $14,000 received from the sale in the checking account of Dennis M. Construction Co., used the proceeds to pay the corporate creditors, abandoned their defense of the litigation with the LaVangies, and filed the petition in bankruptcy. The testimony in the bankruptcy court trial revealed several false answers in the Mazzolas' schedules and statement of affairs. Alleging that the Mazzolas made false oaths on their petition and transferred and concealed property within one year preceding the filing, the LaVangies seek to bar the Mazzolas' discharge.

Question: Should the Mazzolas be denied a discharge?

Answer: Yes.

Reasoning: The documents filed by the debtors contained numerous false statements. The issue with regard to the ultimate granting or denial of discharge is whether those false statements were knowingly and fraudulently made so as to fall within the prohibition of the Code. The explanations offered by Mr. Mazzola for the false statements are not credible. The present facts do not reflect mere mistake or inadvertence. Instead they reveal at the very least such a cavalier and reckless disregard for the truth as to cause the court to find fraudulent intent. The discharge is denied.

Discharge Hearing; Reaffirmation; Protection of Discharge.   Before an individual debtor may receive a discharge from unpaid debts, he or she must attend a **discharge hearing**. The Bankruptcy Code requires the hearing primarily to protect the debtor; therefore he or she must appear in person before the court to receive the discharge or to hear the reason why a discharge has not been granted.

A discharge in bankruptcy is not an automatic protection against having to pay the discharged debts. As many debtors have been shocked to learn, the discharge must be pleaded by the debtor as a defense to any action subsequently brought to enforce a discharged debt.

Perhaps because of a feeling of guilt, a discharged debtor might agree at the request of an unpaid creditor to pay a discharged debt. A debtor who thus reaffirms (agrees to pay) a discharged debt may be held to his or her promise despite the discharge. For a **reaffirmation agreement** to be enforceable, however, it must conform to requirements imposed by the Bankruptcy Code. The agreement must be made before the discharge is granted; the debtor must be given 30 days after the agreement becomes enforceable to rescind it; the court must have held the discharge hearing and warned the debtor of the consequences of reaffirmation; and the court must approve the agreement if it is a reaffirmation of a consumer debt.

The laws of some states seek to penalize discharged debtors for exercising certain of their discharge rights. In the case of *Perez v. Campbell*, 402 U.S. 637 (1971), for example, an Arizona financial responsibility law permitted suspension of the driver's license of an uninsured driver who failed to pay an automobile personal injury judgment that had been discharged in bankruptcy. The United States Supreme Court held, by a 5 to 4 vote, that the suspension provision of the Arizona law was in conflict with bankruptcy law and therefore was void under the supremacy clause of the United States Constitution. The Bankruptcy Code follows and expands on that case by providing, in essence, that a governmental unit may not penalize or discriminate against a debtor or the debtor's associates solely because of the debtor's failure to pay a discharged debt or because of the debtor's status as a debtor under bankruptcy law. Thus, the fresh-start policy of the Code prevails over the state policy of protecting favored creditors.

BUSINESS REORGANIZATIONS AND REPAYMENT PLANS

Business Reorganizations The main purpose of a Chapter 11 reorganization proceeding is to allow a financially troubled firm to stay in business while it undergoes a process of financial rehabilitation. Reorganization is essentially a process of negotiation in which the debtor firm and its creditors develop a plan for the adjustment and discharge of debts. The plan may provide for a change of management and even for the liquidation of the firm. However, a continuation of the business is the usual goal.

Most of the rules of bankruptcy law that apply to Chapter 7 liquidations apply also to Chapter 11 reorganizations. Most individuals, partnerships, and corporations eligible for Chapter 7 liquidation are eligible for Chapter 11 reorganization. Like Chapter 7 cases, reorganization cases may be voluntary or involuntary. And the requirements for forcing a debtor into involuntary liquidation apply to involuntary reorganizations as well. The trustee's powers, the law of fraudulent and preferential transfers, the grounds for denial of discharge, and many other aspects of bankruptcy law are the same or nearly the same for Chapter 11 cases as for Chapter 7 cases. Consequently, the discussion here is limited to topics of special significance to reorganization cases.

Role of Creditors' Committee.   As soon as practicable after the court enters an order for relief under Chapter 11, the court must appoint a committee of unsecured creditors to recommend a plan for reorganizing the debtor. Ordinarily, the committee will consist of the seven largest unsecured creditors willing to serve. At the request of a "party in interest" (e.g., a creditor or a shareholder or a committee of such persons), the court (1) may change the composition of the committee to make it representative of the various claims against the creditor, and (2) may appoint additional committees such as a committee of equity security holders (owners of stocks and bonds of the debtor if it is a corporation).

The principal tasks of the committee are to investigate the financial affairs of the debtor, to determine whether the business should continue to be operated, to determine whether to request the appointment of a trustee to displace the **debtor-in-possession** (the debtor or the management of a corporate debtor), and to consult with the debtor or trustee in the administration of the case. If the court appoints a trustee, the debtor's management is completely ousted. If no trustee is appointed, the debtor-in-possession continues the business under court supervision and has the duties of a trustee.

Plan for Satisfaction of Creditors' Claims.   The plan of reorganization determines how much creditors will be paid, whether the shareholders will retain any interest in the company, in what form the business will continue, and similar questions. To become effective, the plan must be *accepted* (consented to) by a certain percentage of affected creditors and shareholders and *confirmed* (approved and put into operation) by the bankruptcy court. Confirmation makes the plan binding, not only on the debtor but also on creditors, equity security holders, and others, whether or not their claims are "impaired" (e.g., not to be paid in full), and whether or not they have accepted the plan. Consent of an impaired class of claimants is *not* necessary for confirmation if the plan treats the impaired class in a manner that is "fair and equitable."

Continuing the Business. While the plan of reorganization is being developed and put into effect, the trustee (or debtor-in-possession) continues the business and tries to reduce business losses by selling unprofitable divisions of the company, reducing the work force, closing plants or stores where necessary, or rejecting or renegotiating burdensome contracts. Often these activities meet with strenuous objection, as where Continental Airlines sought in the early 1980s to reject its union contract with the Air Line Pilots Association in an effort to bring the company back to profitability. The bankruptcy court upheld the trustee's rejection of the union contract, as courts in similar cases are likely to do unless the power to reject contracts is used simply as a means of "breaking" a union.

Repayment Plans for Debtors with Regular Income

Chapter 13 of the Code permits an *individual* debtor to develop a repayment plan and, upon completion of payments under the plan, to receive a discharge from most remaining debts. Chapter 13 is available (on a voluntary basis only) to an individual (except a stockbroker or a commodity broker) who has regular income, unsecured debts of less than $100,000, and secured debts of less than $350,000. The debts must be owing and unpaid at the time of the debtor's application for relief.

Much of the bankruptcy law previously discussed applies to Chapter 13 cases. Especially notable are those provisions of the Code that prohibit governmental discrimination against debtors, restrict the enforceability of reaffirmation agreements, and provide exemptions for an individual debtor.

Typically, the plan proposed by the debtor will be either a composition or an extension plan. In a **composition plan** the debtor pays creditors less than 100 percent of their claims, on a pro rata basis for each class of claims. In an **extension plan** the debtor pays the full amount, but over a longer period than originally agreed. Payments under a plan (whether composition or extension) must be completed within 3 years after the court confirms the plan, or within 5 years if the court permits. Regardless of the kind of plan, the debtor must give the trustee control of the debtor's future income, the trustee makes payments of claims, and the debtor has the benefit of injunctive relief against creditors while the plan is being carried out. If the plan was a composition, the Chapter 13 discharge upon completion of the plan bars another discharge for 6 years unless the debtor has made 70 percent of the payments under the plan, the plan was proposed in good faith, and the plan was the best effort of the debtor.

SUMMARY

Under state insolvency law, an insolvent debtor may make an arrangement with unpaid creditors for full or partial payment of the debts. Or, the insolvent debtor or his or her creditors may be entitled to the benefits of federal bankruptcy law which, when resorted to, prevails over state insolvency law.

Federal bankruptcy law has two main purposes: (1) to provide for a fair treatment of competing creditors, and (2) to give overburdened debtors an opportunity to make a fresh start in business. The trustee in bankruptcy is responsible for collecting, liquidating, and distributing the estate. The bankruptcy judge supervises the activities of trustees and renders judicial decisions as the need arises.

The purpose of a Chapter 7 liquidation proceeding is to convert the debtor's nonexempt assets into cash, to distribute the cash in accordance with the scheme of distribution provided by the Bankruptcy Code, and to grant the honest debtor a discharge from most of the remaining debts. An individual debtor is entitled to exempt certain property from the estate. The claims of secured creditors are paid in full if the collateral is sufficiently valuable. To the extent funds permit, the remaining money is distributed to priority unsecured creditors and then to general creditors.

There are several grounds for a general denial of a discharge; and certain kinds of debts, such as alimony, are excepted from the discharge.

Business firms may be discharged from debts under Chapter 11, but its main purpose is to allow a financially troubled firm to reorganize and stay in business while it undergoes a process of financial rehabilitation. Chapter 13 permits individual debtors to develop a repayment plan and, upon completion of payments under the plan, to receive a discharge from most remaining debts.

REVIEW QUESTIONS

1. (a) What limits on debt-collection activity does the law impose on creditors? (b) How may an insolvent debtor settle his or her debts under state law?

2. To a debtor, what is the main advantage of federal bankruptcy law as opposed to state insolvency law? A main advantage of bankruptcy law to a creditor?

3. (a) What are the purposes of the federal bankruptcy law? (b) What are the basic steps involved in a bankruptcy proceeding? (c) How is federal bankruptcy law related to state law?

4. What are the main duties of the trustee in bankruptcy? Of the bankruptcy judge?

5. (a) What is the purpose of a Chapter 7 liquidation proceeding? (b) Who is eligible for a voluntary Chapter 7 proceeding? (c) Who may be subjected to an involuntary Chapter 7 proceeding? Under what circumstances?

6. (a) What two broad classes of property become part of the debtor's estate? (b) Does a secured party's security interest become part of the debtor's estate? Explain.

7. What fraudulent transfers may a trustee avoid?

8. Define "preference" and give an example.

9. Give an example of a claim that will not be allowed.

10. Illustrate the principle of pro rata distribution as applied to priority of payments.

11. List two grounds for denial of a discharge.

12. May a state suspend a driver's license because the driver failed to pay an automobile personal injury judgment that had been discharged in bankruptcy? Explain.

13. (a) What is the main purpose of a Chapter 11 business reorganization proceeding? (b) Explain the function of the creditors' committee. (c) How is the plan of reorganization made effective?

14. (a) With respect to Chapter 13 repayment plans for debtors with regular incomes, explain how a composition plan differs from an extension plan. (b) What is the source of funds for carrying out a repayment plan?

CASE PROBLEMS

1. Franklin filed a voluntary petition in bankruptcy. At that time she had debts of $100,000, and had the following property interests: (**a**) business equipment worth $5000, which was subject to a $3000 chattel mortgage in favor of her bank; and (**b**) an automobile worth $1000 that she intended to claim as exempt property. Five months after filing the petition, Franklin inherited $25,000 from her uncle. Three months later, at the death of another uncle, she received $50,000 as the beneficiary of an insurance policy on that uncle's life. In the meantime, after the filing of the petition, Franklin's business realized a net profit of $10,000, and Franklin earned $8000 as a consultant to another firm. The trustee in bankruptcy claimed for the debtor's estate all the property described above. To what property was the trustee entitled?

2. Bago Corporation, a manufacturer of industrial packaging, experienced financial difficulty as the result of a strike by its employees and eventually could not meet its debt service charges and other expenses. In an attempt to keep the company afloat, Thomas, its chief financial officer, made an unsecured loan of $10,000 to the company. Four months later the strike ended, but by then the market for industrial packaging had softened. Fearing that the company might fail, Thomas sought repayment of the loan. In settlement of the loan, the president of Bago Corporation paid Thomas $10,000 out of the proceeds of recent bag sales.

Six months after repayment of the loan, creditors of Bago filed a Chapter 7 petition and forced the company into bankruptcy. Liquidation of company assets produced sufficient funds to pay priority claims, but only enough to pay 10 percent of the claims of general creditors. Consequently, the trustee brought suit to avoid as a preferential transfer Bago's repayment of the $10,000 to Thomas. He defended on the ground that the repayment of the loan did not occur on or within 90 days before the filing of the bankruptcy petition and therefore could not be considered a preference. Was the repayment of the loan a preference?

3. In the bankruptcy situation described in the preceding problem, Bagging Suppliers, Inc., delivered on credit to Bago a load of packaging materials 60 days before the filing of the petition in bankruptcy. Ten days later, Bago paid Bagging Suppliers in full for the materials. The trustee sought to avoid the payment as a preference. Was the payment of Bagging Suppliers a preference?

4. In the liquidation of Blotto, Inc., the following creditors filed timely proofs of claim: (**a**) three employees who had not been paid their wages of $1000 each for 1 month preceding Blotto's bankruptcy; (**b**) 100 customers of Blotto, each of whom, prior to Blott's bankruptcy, had paid Blotto a $50 unsecured deposit on pen and pencil sets that Blotto never delivered; (**c**) Second Bank, to which Blotto owed $8000 secured by a valid, perfected security interest in collateral worth $4000; and (**d**) various administrative officials, lawyers, and accountants whose claims for their services totaled $5000. The trustee realized $14,500 upon liquidation of the debtor's estate. How much of its claim does each creditor or class of creditors receive?

5. In a Chapter 7 proceeding, Swanson received a discharge from her debts. General creditors received only 12 percent of their allowed claims. A week before the discharge was granted, Swanson signed a reaffirmation agreement with one of the general creditors, Hayes, a plumbing contractor who had sold Swanson an air conditioning unit on open account for Swanson's business. The agreement required Swanson to pay, in monthly installments, $3000 still unpaid for the air conditioner, a debt that was covered by the discharge. A week after signing the agreement, Swanson had second thoughts and sought to rescind the agreement. Hayes pointed out that the agreement was enforceable under state law. May Swanson rescind the reaffirmation agreement?

APPENDIX

Uniform Commercial Code*

ARTICLE 1: GENERAL PROVISIONS

Part 1: Short Title, Construction, Application and Subject Matter of the Act

§1-101. Short title. This act shall be known and may be cited as Uniform Commercial Code.

§1-102. Purposes; Rules of Construction; Variation by Agreement.

(1) This Act shall be liberally construed and applied to promote its underlying purposes and policies.

(2) Underlying purposes and policies of this Act are

(a) to simplify, clarify and modernize the law governing commercial transactions;

(b) to permit the continued expansion of commercial practices through custom, usage and agreement of the parties;

(c) to make uniform the law among the various jurisdictions.

*Copyright 1978 by The American Law Institute and the National Conference of Commissioners on Uniform State Laws. Reprinted with permission of the Permanent Editorial Board for the Uniform Commercial Code. The 1972 version of Article 9 and the 1977 version of Article 8 appear in this appendix.

(3) The effect of provisions of this Act may be varied by agreement, except as otherwise provided in this Act and except that the obligations of good faith, diligence, reasonableness and care prescribed by this Act may not be disclaimed by agreement but the parties may be agreement determine the standards by which the performance of such obligations is to be measured if such standards are not manifestly unreasonable.

(4) The presence in certain provisions of this Act of the words "unless otherwise agreed" or words of similar import does not imply that the effect of other provisions may not be varied by agreement under subsection (3).

(5) In this Act unless the context otherwise requires

(a) words in the singular number include the plural, and in the plural include the singular;

(b) words of the masculine gender include the feminine and the neuter, and when the sense so indicates words of the neuter gender may refer to any gender.

§1-103. Supplementary General Principles of Law Applicable. Unless displaced by the particular provisions of this Act, the principles of law and equity, including the law merchant and the law relative to capacity to contract, principal and agent, estoppel, fraud, misrepresentation, duress, coercion, mistake, bankruptcy, or other validating or invalidating cause shall supplement its provisions.

§1-104. Construction Against Implicity Repeal. This Act being a general act intended as a unified coverage of its subject matter, no part of it shall be deemed to be impliedly repealed by subsequent legislation if such construction can reasonably be avoided.

§1-105. Territorial Application of the Act; Parties' Power to Choose Applicable Law.

(1) Except as provided hereafter in this section, when a transaction bears a reasonable relation to this state and also to another state or nation the parties may agree that the law either of this state or of such other state or nation shall govern their rights and duties. Failing such agreement this Act applies to transactions bearing an appropriate relation to this state.

(2) Where one of the following provisions of this Act specifies the applicable law, that provision governs and a contrary agreement is effective only to the extent permitted by the law (including the conflict of laws rules) so specified:

Rights of creditors against sold goods. Section 2-402.

Applicability of the Article on Bank Deposits and Collections. Section 4-102.

Bulk transfers subject to the Article on Bulk Transfers. Section 6-102.

Applicability of the Article on Investment Securities. Section 8-106.

Perfection provisions of the Article on Secured Transactions. Section 9-103.

§1-106. Remedies to Be Liberally Administered.

(1) The remedies provided by this Act shall be liberally administered to the end that the aggrieved party may be put in as good a position as if the other party had fully performed but neither consequential or special nor penal damages may be had except as specifically provided in this Act or by other rule of law.

(2) Any right or obligation declared by this Act is enforceable by action unless the provision declaring it specifies a different and limited effect.

§1-107. Waiver or Renunciation of Claim or Right After Breach.
Any claim or right arising out of an alleged breach can be discharged in whole or in part without consideration by a written waiver or renunciation signed and delivered by the aggrieved party.

§1-108. Severability.
If any provision or clause of this Act or application thereof to any person or circumstances is held invalid, such invalidity shall not affect other provisions or applications of the Act which can be given effect without the invalid provision or application, and to this end the provisions of this Act are declared to be severable.

§1-109. Section Captions.
Section captions are parts of this Act.

Part 2: General Definitions and Principles of Interpretation

§1-201. General Definitions.
Subject to additional definitions contained in the subsequent Articles of this Act which are applicable to specific Articles or Parts thereof, and unless the context otherwise requires, in this Act.

(1) "Action" in the sense of a judicial proceeding includes recoupment, counterclaim, set-off, suit in equity and any other proceedings in which rights are determined.

(2) "Aggrieved party" means a party entitled to resort to a remedy.

(3) "Agreement" means the bargain of the parties in fact as found in their language or by implication from other circumstances including course of dealing or usage of trade or course of performance as provided in this Act, (Section 1-205 and 2-208). Whether an agreement has legal consequences is determined by the provisions of this Act, if applicable; otherwise by the law of contracts (Section 1-103). (Compare "Contract".)

(4) "Bank" means any person engaged in the business of banking.

(5) "Bearer" means the person in possession of an instrument, document of title, or certificated security payable to bearer or indorsed in blank.

(6) "Bill of lading" means a document evidencing the receipt of goods for shipment issued by a person engaged in the business of transporting or forwarding goods, and includes an airbill. "Airbill" means a document serving for air transportation as a bill of lading does for marine or rail transportation, and includes an air consignment note or air waybill.

(7) "Branch" includes a separately incorporated foreign branch of a bank.

(8) "Burden of establishing" a fact means the burden of persuading the triers of fact that the existence of the fact is more probable than its non-existence.

(9) "Buyer in ordinary course of business" means a person who in good faith and without knowledge that the sale to him is in violation of the ownership rights or security interest of a third party in the goods buys in ordinary course from a person in the business of selling goods of that kind but does not include a pawnbroker. All persons who sell minerals or the like (including oil and gas) at wellhead or minehead shall be deemed to be persons in the business of selling goods of that kind. "Buying" may be for cash or by exchange of other property or on secured or unsecured credit and includes receiving goods or documents of title under a pre-existing contract for sale but does not include a transfer in bulk or as security for or in total or partial satisfaction of a money debt.

(10) "Conspicuous": A term or clause is conspicuous when it is so written that a reasonable person against whom it is to operate ought to have noticed it. A printed heading in capitals (as: Non-Negotiable Bill of Lading) is conspicuous. Language in the body of a form is "conspicuous" if it is in larger or other contrasting type or color. But in a telegram any stated term is "conspicuous". Whether a term or clause is "conspicuous" or not is for decision by the court.

(11) "Contract" means the total legal obligation which results from the parties' agreement as affected by this Act and any other applicable rules of law. (Compare "Agreement".)

(12) "Creditor" includes a general creditor, a secured creditor, a lien creditor and any representative of creditors, including an assignee for the benefit of creditors, a trustee in

bankruptcy, a receiver in equity and an executor or administrator of an insolvent debtor's or assignor's estate.

(13) "Defendant" includes a person in the position of defendant in a cross-action or counterclaim.

(14) "Delivery" with respect to instruments, documents of title, chattel paper, or certificated securities means voluntary transfer of possession.

(15) "Document of title" includes bill of lading, dock warrant, dock receipt, warehouse receipt or order for the delivery of goods, and also any other document which in the regular course of business or financing is treated as adequately evidencing that the person in possession of it is entitled to receive, hold and dispose of the document and the goods it covers. To be a document of title a document must purport to be issued by or addressed to a bailee and purport to cover goods in the bailee's possession which are either identified or are fungible portions of an identified mass.

(16) "Fault" means wrongful act, omission or breach.

(17) "Fungible" with respect to goods or securities means goods or securities of which any unit is, by nature or usage of trade, the equivalent of any other like unit. Goods which are not fungible shall be deemed fungible for the purposes of this Act to the extent that under a particular agreement or document unlike units are treated as equivalents.

(18) "Genuine" means free of forgery or counterfeiting.

(19) "Good faith" means honesty in fact in the conduct or transaction concerned.

(20) "Holder" means a person who is in possession of a document of title or a certificated instrument or an investment security drawn, issued or indorsed to him or to his order or to bearer or in blank.

(21) To "honor" is to pay or to accept and pay, or where a credit so engages to purchase or discount a draft complying with the terms of the credit.

(22) "Insolvency proceedings" includes any assignment for the benefit of creditors or other proceedings intended to liquidate or rehabilitate the estate of the person involved.

(23) A person is "insolvent" who either has ceased to pay his debts in the ordinary course of business or cannot pay his debts as they become due or is insolvent within the meaning of the federal bankruptcy law.

(24) "Money" means a medium of exchange authorized or adopted by a domestic or foreign government as part of its currency.

(25) A person has "notice" of a fact when

(a) he has actual knowledge of it; or

(b) he has received a notice or notification of it; or

(c) from all the facts and circumstances known to him at the time in question he has reason to know that it exists.

A person "knows" or has "knowledge" of a fact when he has actual knowledge of it. "Discover" or "learn" or a word or phrase of similar import refers to knowledge rather than to reason to know. The time and circumstances under which a notice or notification may cease to be effective are not determined by this Act.

(26) A person "notifies" or "gives" a notice or notification to

another by taking such steps as may be reasonably required to inform the other in ordinary course whether or not such other actually comes to know of it. A person "receives" a notice or notification when

(a) it comes to his attention; or

(b) it is duly delivered at the place of business through which the contract was made or at any other place held out by him as the place for receipt of such communications.

(27) Notice, knowledge or a notice or notification received by an organization is effective for a particular transaction from the time when it is brought to the attention of the individual conducting that transaction, and in any event from the time when it would have been brought to his attention if the organization had exercised due diligence. An organization exercises due diligence if it maintains reasonable routines for communicating significant information to the person conducting the transaction and there is reasonable compliance with the routines. Due diligence does not require an individual acting for the organization to communicate information unless such communication is part of his regular duties or unless he has reason to know of the transaction and that the transaction would be materially affected by the information.

(28) "Organization" includes a corporation, government or governmental subdivision or agency, business trust, estate, trust, partnership or association, two or more persons having a joint or common interest, or any other legal or commercial entity.

(29) "Party", as distinct from "third party", means a person who has engaged in a transaction or made an agreement within this Act.

(30) "Person" includes an individual or an organization (See Section 1-102).

(31) "Presumption" or "presumed" means that the trier of fact must find the existence of the fact presumed unless and until evidence is introduced which would support a finding of its non-existence.

(32) "Purchase" includes taking by sale, discount, negotiation, mortgage, pledge, lien, issue or re-issue, gift or any other voluntary transaction creating an interest in property.

(33) "Purchaser" means a person who takes by purchase.

(34) "Remedy" means any remedial right to which an aggrieved party is entitled with or without resort to a tribunal.

(35) "Representative" includes an agent, an officer of a corporation or association, and a trustee, executor or administrator of an estate, or any other person empowered to act for another.

(36) "Rights" includes remedies.

(37) "Security interest" means an interest in personal property or fixtures which secures payment or performance of an obligation. The retention or reservation of title by a seller of goods notwithstanding shipment or delivery to the buyer (Section 2-401) is limited in effect to a reservation of a "security interest". The term also includes any interest of a buyer of accounts or chattel paper, which is subject to Article 9. The special property interest of a buyer of goods on identification of

such goods to a contract for sale under Section 2-401 is not a "security interest", but a buyer may also acquire a "security interest" by complying with Article 9. Unless a lease or consignment is intended as security, reservation of title thereunder is not a "security interest" but a consignment is in any event subject to the provisions on consignment sales (Section 2-326). Whether a lease is intended as security is to be determined by the facts of each case; however, (a) the inclusion of an option to purchase does not of itself make the lease one intended for security, and (b) an agreement that upon compliance with the terms of the lease the lessee shall become or has the option to become the owner of the property for no additional consideration or for a nominal consideration does make the lease one intended for security.

(38) "Send" in connection with any writing or notice means to deposit in the mail or deliver for transmission by any other usual means of communication with postage or cost of transmission provided for and properly addressed and in the case of an instrument to an address specified thereon or otherwise agreed, or if there by none to any address reasonable under the circumstances. The receipt of any writing or notice within the time at which it would have arrived if properly sent has the effect of a proper sending.

(39) "Signed" includes any symbol executed or adopted by a party with present intention to authenticate a writing.

(40) "Surety" includes guarantor.

(41) "Telegram" includes a message transmitted by radio, teletype, cable, any mechanical method of transmission, or the like.

(42) "Term" means that portion of an agreement which relates to a particular matter.

(43) "Unauthorized" signature or indorsement means one made without actual, implied or apparent authority and includes a forgery.

(44) "Value". Except as otherwise provided with respect to negotiable instruments and bank collections (Sections 3-303, 4-208 and 4-209) a person gives "value" for rights if he acquires them

    (a) in return for a binding commitment to extend credit or for the extension of immediately available credit whether or not drawn upon and whether or not a chargeback is provided for in the event of difficulties in collection; or

    (b) as security for or in total or partial satisfaction of a pre-existing claim; or

    (c) by accepting delivery pursuant to a pre-existing contract for purchase; or

    (d) generally, in return for any consideration sufficient to support a simple contract.

(45) "Warehouse receipt" means a receipt issued by a person engaged in the business of storing goods for hire.

(46) "Written" or "writing" includes printing, typewriting or any other intentional reduction to tangible form. As amended 1962 and 1972.

§1-201. General Definitions (1977 Amendments).

Subject to additional definitions contained in the subsequent Articles of this Act which are applicable to specific Articles or Parts thereof, and unless the context otherwise requires, in this Act:

* * *

(5) "Bearer" means the person in possession of an instrument, document of title, or certificated security payable to bearer or indorsed in blank.

* * *

(14) "Delivery" with respect to instruments, documents of title, chattel paper, or certificated securities means voluntary transfer of possession.

* * *

(20) "Holder" means a person who is in possession of a document of title or an instrument or a certificated investment security drawn, issued, or indorsed to him or his order or to bearer or in blank.

* * *

§1-202. Prima Facie Evidence by Third Party Documents.

A document in due form purporting to be a bill of lading, policy or certificate of insurance, official weigher's or inspector's certificate, consular invoice or any other document authorized or required by the contract to be issued by a third party shall be prima facie evidence of its own authenticity and genuineness and of the facts stated in the document by the third party.

§1-203. Obligation of Good Faith.
Every contract or duty within this Act imposes an obligation of good faith in its performance or enforcement.

§1-204. Time; Reasonable Time; "Seasonably".

(1) Whenever this Act requires any action to be taken within a reasonable time, any time which is not manifestly unreasonable may be fixed by agreement.

(2) What is a reasonable time for taking any action depends on the nature, purpose and circumstances of such action.

(3) An action is taken "seasonably" when it is taken at or within the time agreed or if no time is agreed at or within a reasonable time.

§1-205. Course of Dealing and Usage of Trade.

(1) A course of dealing is a sequence of previous conduct between the parties to a particular transaction which is fairly to be regarded as establishing a common basis of understanding for interpreting their expressions and other conduct.

(2) A usage of trade is any practice or method of dealing having such regularity of observance in a place, vocation or trade as to justify an expectation that it will be observed with respect to the transaction in question. The existence and scope of such a usage are to be proved as facts. If it is established that such a usage is embodied in a written trade code or similar writing the interpretation of the writing is for the court.

(3) A course of dealing between parties and any usage of trade in the vocation or trade in which they are engaged or of which they are or should be aware give particular meaning to and supplement or qualify terms of an agreement.

(4) The express terms of an agreement and an applicable course of dealing or usage of trade shall be construed wherever reasonable as consistent with each other; but when such

construction is unreasonable express terms control both course of dealing and usage of trade and course of dealing controls usage of trade.

(5) An applicable usage of trade in the place where any part of performance is to occur shall be used in interpreting the agreement as to that part of the performance.

(6) Evidence of a relevant usage of trade offered by one party is not admissible unless and until he has given the other party such notice as the court finds sufficient to prevent unfair surprise to the latter.

§1-206. Statute of Frauds for Kinds of Personal Property Not Otherwise Covered.

(1) Except in the cases described in subsection (2) of this section a contract for the sale of personal property is not enforceable by way of action or defense beyond five thousand dollars in amount or value of remedy unless there is some writing which indicates that a contract for sale has been made between the parties at a defined or stated price, reasonably identifies the subject matter, and is signed by the party against whom enforcement is sought or by his authorized agent.

(2) Subsection (1) of this section does not apply to contracts for the sale of goods (Section 2-201) nor of securities (Section 8-319) nor to security agreements (Section 9-203).

§1-207. Performance or Acceptance Under Reservation of Rights.
A party who with explicit reservation of rights performs or promises performance or assents to performance in a manner demanded or offered by the other party does not thereby prejudice the rights reserved. Such words as "without prejudice", "under protest" or the like are sufficient.

§1-208. Option to Accelerate at Will.
A term providing that one party or his successor in interest may accelerate payment or performance or require collateral or additional collateral "at will" or "when he deems himself insecure" or in words of similar import shall be construed to mean that he shall have power to do so only if he in good faith believes that the prospect of payment or performance is impaired. The burden of establishing lack of good faith is on the party against whom the power has been exercised.

§1-209. Subordinated Obligations.
An obligation may be issued as subordinated to payment of another obligation of the person obligated, or a creditor may subordinate his right to payment of an obligation by agreement with either the person obligated or another creditor of the person obligated. Such a subordination does not create a security interest as against either the common debtor or a subordinated creditor. This section shall be construed as declaring the law as it existed prior to the enactment of this section and not as modifying it. Added 1966.

Note: *This new section is proposed as an optional provision to make it clear that a subordination agreement does not create a security interest unless so intended.*

ARTICLE 2: SALES

Part 1: Short Title, General Construction and Subject Matter

§2-101. Short Title. This Article shall be known and may be cited as Uniform Commercial Code—Sales.

§2-102. Scope; Certain Security and Other Transactions Excluded From This Article. Unless the context otherwise requires, this Article applies to transactions in goods; it does not apply to any transaction which although in the form of an unconditional contract to sell or present sale is intended to operate only as a security transaction nor does this Article impair or repeal any statute regulating sales to consumers, farmers or other specified classes of buyers.

§2-103. Definitions and Index of Definitions.

(1) In this Article unless the context otherwise requires
 (a) "Buyer" means a person who buys or contracts to buy goods.
 (b) "Good faith" in the case of a merchant means honesty in fact and the observance of reasonable commercial standards of fair dealing in the trade.
 (c) "Receipt" of goods means taking physical possession of them.
 (d) "Seller" means a person who sells or contracts to sell goods.

(2) Other definitions applying to this Article or to specified Parts thereof, and the sections in which they appear are:
"Acceptance". Section 2-606.
"Banker's credit". Section 2-325.
"Between merchants". Section 2-104.
"Cancellation". Section 2-106(4).
"Commercial unit". Section 2-105.
"Confirmed credit". Section 2-325.
"Conforming to contract". Section 2-106.
"Contract for sale". Section 2-106.
"Cover". Section 2-712.
"Entrusting". Section 2-403.
"Financing agency". Section 2-104.
"Future goods". Section 2-105.
"Goods". Section 2-105.
"Identification". Section 2-501.
"Installment contract". Section 2-612.
"Letter of Credit". Section 2-325.
"Lot". Section 2-105.
"Merchant". Section 2-104.
"Overseas". Section 2-323.
"Person in position of seller". Section 2-707.
"Present sale". Section 2-106.
"Sale". Section 2-106.
"Sale on approval". Section 2-326.
"Sale or return". Section 2-326.
"Termination". Section 2-106.

(3) The following definitions in other Articles apply to this Article:
"Check". Section 3-104.

"Consignee". Section 7-102.
"Consignor". Section 7-102.
"Consumer goods". Section 9-109.
"Dishonor". Section 3-507.
"Draft". Section 3-104.

(4) In addition Article 1 contains general definitions and principles of construction and interpretation applicable throughout this article.

§2-104. Definitions: "Merchant"; "Between Merchants"; "Financing Agency".

(1) "Merchant" means a person who deals in goods of the kind or otherwise by his occupation holds himself out as having knowledge or skill peculiar to the practices or goods involved in the transaction or to whom such knowledge or skill may be attributed by his employment of an agent or broker or other intermediary who by his occupation holds himself out as having such knowledge or skill.

(2) "Financing agency" means a bank, finance company or other person who in the ordinary course of business makes advances against goods or documents of title or who by arrangement with either the seller or the buyer intervenes in ordinary course to make or collect payment due or claimed under the contract for sale, as by purchasing or paying the seller's draft or making advances against it or by merely taking it for collection whether or not documents of title accompany the draft. "Financing agency" includes also a bank or other person who similarly intervenes between persons who are in the position of seller and buyer in respect of the goods (Section 2-707).

(3) "Between merchants" means in any transaction with respect to which both parties are chargeable with the knowledge or skill of merchants.

§2-105. Definitions: Transferability; "Goods"; "Future" Goods; "Lot"; "Commercial Unit".

(1) "Goods" means all things (including specially manufactured goods) which are movable at the time of identification to the contract for sale other than the money in which the price is to be paid, investment securities (Article 8) and things in action. "Goods" also includes the unborn young of animals and growing crops and other identified things attached to realty as described in the section on goods to be severed from realty (Section 2-107).

(2) Goods must be both existing and identified before any interest in them can pass. Goods which are not both existing and identified are "future" goods. A purported present sale of future goods or of any interest therein operates as a contract to sell.

(3) There may be a sale of a part interest in existing identified goods.

(4) An undivided share in an identified bulk of fungible goods is sufficiently identified to be sold although the quantity of the bulk is not determined. Any agreed proportion of such a bulk or any quantity thereof agreed upon by number, weight or other measure may to the extent of the seller's interest in the bulk be sold to the buyer who then becomes an owner in common.

(5) "Lot" means a parcel or a single article which is the subject matter of a separate sale or delivery, whether or not it is sufficient to perform the contract.

(6) "Commercial unit" means such a unit of goods as by commercial usage is a single whole for purposes of sale and division of which materially impairs its character or value on the market or in use. A commercial unit may be a single article (as a machine) or a set of articles (as a suite of furniture or an assortment of sizes) or a quantity (as a bale, gross, or carload) or any other unit treated in use or in the relevant market as a single whole.

§2-106. Definitions: "Contract"; "Agreement"; "Contract for Sale"; "Sale"; "Present Sale"; "Conforming" to Contract; "Termination"; "Cancellation".

(1) In this Article unless the context otherwise requires "contract" and "agreement" are limited to those relating to the present or future sale of goods. "Contract for sale" includes both a present sale of goods and a contract to sell goods at a future time. A "sale" consists in the passing of title from the seller to the buyer for a price (Section 2-401). A "present sale" means a sale which is accomplished by the making of the contract.

(2) Goods or conduct including any part of a performance are "conforming" or conform to the contract when they are in accordance with the obligations under the contract.

(3) "Termination" occurs when either party pursuant to a power created by agreement or law puts an end to the contract otherwise than for its breach. On "termination" all obligations which are still executory on both sides are discharged but any right based on prior breach or performance survives.

(4) "Cancellation" occurs when either party puts an end to the contract for breach by the other and its effect is the same as that of "termination" except that the cancelling party also retains any remedy for breach of the whole contract or any unperformed balance.

§2-107. Goods to Be Severed From Realty: Recording.

(1) A contract for the sale of minerals or the like (including oil and gas) or a structure or its materials to be removed from realty is a contract for the sale of goods within this Article if they are to be severed by the seller but until severance a purported present sale thereof which is not effective as a transfer of an interest in land is effective only as a contract to sell.

(2) A contract for the sale apart from the land of growing crops or other things attached to realty and capable of severance without material harm thereto but not described in subsection (1) or of timber to be cut is a contract for the sale of goods within this Article whether the subject matter is to be severed by the buyer or by the seller even though it forms part of the realty at the time of contracting, and the parties can by identification effect a present sale before severance.

(3) The provisions of this section are subject to any third party rights provided by the law relating to realty records, and the contract for sale may be executed and recorded as a document transferring an interest in land and shall then constitute notice to third parties of the buyer's rights under the contract for sale.

Part 2: Form, Formation and Readjustment of Contract

§2-201. Formal Requirements; Statute of Frauds.

(1) Except as otherwise provided in this section a contract for the sale of goods for the price of $500 or more is not enforceable by way of action or defense unless there is some writing sufficient to indicate that a contract for sale has been made between the parties and signed by the party against whom enforcement is sought or by his authorized agent or broker. A writing is not insufficient because it omits or incorrectly states a term agreed upon but the contract is not enforceable under this paragraph beyond the quantity of goods shown in such writing.

(2) Between merchants if within a reasonable time a writing in confirmation of the contract and sufficient against the sender is received and the party receiving it has reason to know its contents, it satisfies the requirements of subsection (1) against such party unless written notice of objection to its contents is given within 10 days after it is received.

(3) A contract which does not satisfy the requirements of subsection (1) but which is valid in other respects is enforceable

(a) if the goods are to be specially manufactured for the buyer and are not suitable for sale to others in the ordinary course of the seller's business and the seller, before notice of repudiation is received and under circumstances which reasonably indicate that the goods are for the buyer, has made either a substantial beginning of their manufacture or commitments for their procurement; or

(b) if the party against whom enforcement is sought admits in his pleading, testimony or otherwise in court that a contract for sale was made, but the contract is not enforceable under this provision beyond the quantity of goods admitted; or

(c) with respect to goods for which payment has been made and accepted or which have been received and accepted (Sec. 2-606.)

§2-202. Final Written Expression: Parol or Extrinsic Evidence.

Terms with respect to which the confirmatory memoranda of the parties agree or which are otherwise set forth in a writing intended by the parties as a final expression of their agreement with respect to such terms as are included therein may not be contradicted by evidence of any prior agreement or of a contemporaneous oral agreement but may be explained or supplemented

(a) by course of dealing or usage of trade (Section 1-205) or by course of performance (Section 2-208); and

(b) by evidence of consistent additional terms unless the court finds the writing to have been intended also as a complete and exclusive statement of the terms of the agreement.

§2-203. Seals Inoperative.

The affixing of a seal to a writing evidencing a contract for sale or an offer to buy or sell goods does not constitute the writing a sealed instrument and the law with respect to sealed instruments does not apply to such a contract or offer.

§2-204. Formation in General.

(1) A contract for sale of goods may be made in any manner sufficient to show agreement, including conduct by both parties which recognizes the existence of such a contract.

(2) An agreement sufficient to constitute a contract for sale may be found even though the moment of its making is undetermined.

(3) Even though one or more terms are left open a contract for sale does not fail for indefiniteness if the parties have intended to make a contract and there is a reasonably certain basis for giving an appropriate remedy.

§2-205. Firm Offers.

An offer by a merchant to buy or sell goods in a signed writing which by its terms gives assurance that it will be held open is not revocable, for lack of consideration, during the time stated or if no time is stated for a reasonable time, but in no event may such period of irrevocability exceed three months; but any such term of assurance on a form supplied by the offeree must be separately signed by the offeror.

§2-206. Offer and Acceptance in Formation of Contract.

(1) Unless otherwise unambiguously indicated by the language or circumstances

(a) an offer to make a contract shall be construed as inviting acceptance in any manner and by any medium reasonable in the circumstances;

(b) an order or other offer to buy goods for prompt or current shipment shall be construed as inviting acceptance either by a prompt promise to ship or by the prompt or current shipment of conforming or nonconforming goods, but such a shipment of nonconforming goods does not constitute an acceptance if the seller seasonably notifies the buyer that the shipment is offered only as an accommodation to the buyer.

(2) Where the beginning of a requested performance is a reasonable mode of acceptance an offeror who is not notified of acceptance within a reasonable time may treat the offer as having lapsed before acceptance.

§2-207. Additional Terms in Acceptance or Confirmation.

(1) A definite and seasonable expression of acceptance or a written confirmation which is sent within a reasonable time operates as an acceptance even though it states terms additional to or different from those offered or agreed upon, unless acceptance is expressly made conditional on assent to the additional or different terms.

(2) The additional terms are to be construed as proposals for addition to the contract. Between merchants such terms become part of the contract unless:

(a) the offer expressly limits acceptance to the terms of the offer;

(b) they materially alter it; or

(c) notification of objection to them has already been given or is given within a reasonable time after notice of them is received.

(3) Conduct by both parties which recognizes the existence of a contract is sufficient to establish a contract for sale although the writings of the parties do not otherwise establish a contract. In such case the terms of the particular contract consist of those terms on which the writings of the parties agree, together with any supplementary terms incorporated under any other provisions of this Act.

§2-208. Course of Performance or Practical Construction.

(1) Where the contract for sale involves repeated occasions for performance by either party with knowledge of the nature of the performance and opportunity for objection to it by the other, any course of performance accepted or acquiesced in without objection shall be relevant to determine the meaning of the agreement.

(2) The express terms of the agreement and any such course of performance, as well as any course of dealing and usage of trade, shall be construed whenever reasonable as consistent with each other; but when such construction is unreasonable, express terms shall control course of performance and course of performance shall control both course of dealing and usage of trade (Section 1-205).

(3) Subject to the provisions of the next section on modification and waiver, such course of performance shall be relevant to show a waiver or modification of any term inconsistent with such course of performance.

§2-209. Modification, Rescission and Waiver.

(1) An agreement modifying a contract within this Article needs no consideration to be binding.

(2) A signed agreement which excludes modifcation or rescission except by a signed writing cannot be otherwise modified or rescinded, but except as between merchants such a requirement on a form supplied by the merchant must be separately signed by the other party.

(3) The requirements of the statute of frauds section of this Article (Section 2-201) must be satisified if the contract as modified is within its provisions.

(4) Although an attempt at modification or rescission does not satisfy the requirements of subsection (2) or (3) it can operate as a waiver.

(5) A party who has made a waiver affecting an executory portion of the contract may retract the waiver by reasonable notification received by the other party that strict performance will be required of any term waived, unless the retraction would be unjust in view of a material change of position in reliance on the waiver.

§2-210. Delegation of Performance; Assignment of Rights.

(1) A party may perform his duty through a delegate unless otherwise agreed or unless the other party has a substantial interest in having his original promisor perform or control the acts required by the contract. No delegation of performance relieves the party delegating of any duty to perform or any liability for breach.

(2) Unless otherwise agreed all rights of either seller or buyer can be assigned except where the assignment would materially change the duty of the other party, or increase materially the burden or risk imposed on him by his contract, or impair materially his chance of obtaining return performance. A right to damages for breach of the whole contract or a right arising out of the assignor's due performance of his entire obligation can be assigned despite agreement otherwise.

(3) Unless the circumstances indicate the contrary a prohibition of assignment of "the contract" is to be construed as barring only the delegation to the assignee of the assignor's performance.

(4) An assignment of the "the contract" or of "all my rights under the contract" or an assignment in similar general terms is an assignment of rights and unless the language or the circumstances (as in an assignment for security) indicate the contrary, it is a delegation of performance of the duties of the assignor and its acceptance by the assignee constitutes a promise by him to perform those duties. This promise is enforceable by either the assignor or the other party to the original contract.

(5) The other party may treat any assignment which delegates performance as creating reasonable grounds for insecurity and may without prejudice to his rights against the assignor demand assurances from the assignee (Section 2-609).

Part 3: General Obligation and Construction of Contract

§2-301. General Obligations of Parties.
The obligation of the seller is to transfer and deliver and that of the buyer is to accept and pay in accordance with the contract.

§2-302. Unconscionable Contract or Clause.

(1) If the court as a matter of law finds the contract or any clause of the contract to have been unconscionable at the time it was made the court may refuse to enforce the contract, or it may enforce the remainder of the contract without the unconscionable blause, or it may so limit the application of any unconscionable clause as to avoid any unconscionable result.

(2) When it is claimed or appears to the court that the contract or any clause thereof may be unconscionable the parties shall be afforded a reasonable opportunity to present evidence as to its commercial setting, purpose and effect to aid the court in making the determination.

§2-303. Allocation or Division of Risks.
Where this Article allocates a risk or a burden as between the parties "unless otherwise agreed", the agreement may not only shift the allocation but may also divide the risk or burden.

§2-304. Price Payable in Money, Goods, Realty, or Otherwise.

(1) The price can be made payable in money or otherwise. If it is payable in whole or in part in goods each party is a seller of the goods which he is to tranfer.

(2) Even though all or part of the price is payable in an interest in realty the transfer of the goods and the seller's

obligations with reference to them are subject to this Article, but not the transfer of the interest in realty or the transferor's obligations in connection therewith.

§2-305. Open Price Term.

(1) The parties if they so intend can conclude a contract for sale even though the price is not settled. In such a case the price is a reasonable price at the time for delivery if

(a) nothing is said as to price; or

(b) the price is left to be agreed by the parties and they fail to agree; or

(c) The price is to be fixed in terms of some agreed market or other standard as set or recorded by a third person or agency and it is not so set or recorded.

(2) A price to be fixed by the seller or by the buyer means a price for him to fix in good faith.

(3) When a price left to be fixed otherwise than by agreement of the parties fails to be fixed through fault of one party the other may at his option treat the contract as cancelled or himself fix a reasonable price.

(4) Where, however, the parties intend not to be bound unless the price be fixed or agreed and it is not fixed or agreed there is no contract. In such a case the buyer must return any goods already received or if unable so to do must pay their reasonable value at the time of delivery and the seller must return any portion of the price paid on account.

§2-306. Output, Requirements and Exclusive Dealings.

(1) A term which measures the quantity by the output of the seller or the requirements of the buyer means such actual output or requirements as may occur in good faith, except that no quantity unreasonably disproportionate to any stated estimate or in the absence of a stated estimate to any normal or otherwise comparable prior output or requirements may be tendered or demanded.

(2) A lawful agreement by either the seller or the buyer for exclusive dealing in the kind of goods concerned imposes unless otherwise agreed an obligation by the seller to use best efforts to supply the goods and by the buyer to use best efforts to promote their sale.

§2-307. Delivery in Single Lot or Several Lots.

Unless otherwise agreed all goods called for by a contract for sale must be tendered in a single delivery and payment is due only on such tender but where the circumstances give either party the right to make or demand delivery in lots the price if it can be apportioned may be demanded for each lot.

§2-308. Absence of Specified Place for Delivery.

Unless otherwise agreed

(a) the place for delivery of goods is the seller's place of business or if he has none his residence; but

(b) in a contract for sale of identified goods which to the knowledge of the parties at the time of contracting are in some other place, that place is the place for their delivery; and

(c) documents of title may be delivered through customary banking channels.

§2-309. Absence of Specific Time Provisions; Notice of Termination.

(1) The time for shipment or delivery or any other action under a contract if not provided in this Article or agreed upon shall be a reasonable time.

(2) Where the contract provides for successive performances but is indefinite in duration it is valid for a reasonable time but unless otherwise agreed may be terminated at any time by either party.

(3) Termination of a contract by one party except on the happening of an agreed event requires that reasonable notification be received by the other party and an agreement dispensing with notification is invalid if its operation would be unconscionable.

§2-310. Open Time for Payment or Running of Credit; Authority to Ship Under Reservation.

Unless otherwise agreed

(a) payment is due at the time and place at which the buyer is to receive the goods even though the place of shipment is the place of delivery; and

(b) if the seller is authorized to send the goods he may ship them under reservation, and may tender the documents of title, but the buyer may inspect the goods after their arrival before payment is due unless such inspection is inconsistent with the terms of the contract (Section 2-513); and

(c) if delivery is authorized and made by way of documents of title otherwise than by subsection (b) then payment is due at the time and place at which the buyer is to receive the documents regardless of where the goods are to be received; and

(d) where the seller is required or authorized to ship the goods on credit the credit period runs from the time of shipment but post-dating the invoice or delaying its dispatch will correspondingly delay the starting of the credit period.

§2-311. Options and Cooperation Respecting Performance.

(1) An agreement for sale which is otherwise sufficiently definite (subsection (3) of Section 2-204) to be a contract is not made invalid by the fact that it leaves particulars of performance to be specified by one of the parties. Any such specification must be made in good faith and within limits set by commerical reasonableness.

(2) Unless otherwise agreed specifications relating to assortment of the goods are at the buyer's option and except as otherwise provided in subsections (1)(c) and (3) of Section 2-319 specifications or arrangements relating to shipment are at the seller's option.

(3) Where such specifications would materially affect the other party's performance but is not seasonably made or where one party's cooperation is necessary to the agreed performance of the other but is not seasonably forthcoming, the other party

(a) is excused for any resulting delay in his own performance; and

(b) may also either proceed to perform in any reasonable manner or after the time for a material part of his own performance treat the failure to specify or to cooperate as a breach by failure to deliver or accept the goods.

§2-312. Warranty of Title and Against Infringement; Buyer's Obligation Against Infringement.

(1) Subject to subsection (2) there is in a contract for sale a warranty by the seller that
  (a) the title conveyed shall be good, and its transfer rightful; and
  (b) the goods shall be delivered free from any security interest or other lien or encumbrance of which the buyer at the time of contracting has no knowledge.

(2) A warranty under subsection (2) will be excluded or modified only by specific language or by circumstances which give the buyer reason to know that the person selling does not claim title in himself or that he is purporting to sell only such right or title as he or a third person may have.

(3) Unless otherwise agreed a seller who is a merchant regularly dealing in goods of the kind warrants that the goods shall be delivered free of the rightful claim of any third person by way of infringement or the like but a buyer who furnishes specifications to the seller must hold the seller harmless against any such claim which arises out of compliance with the specifications.

§2-313. Express Warranties by Affirmation, Promise, Description, Sample.

(1) Express warranties by the seller are created as follows:
  (a) Any affirmation of fact or promise made by the seller to the buyer which relates to the goods and becomes part of the basis of the bargain creates an express warranty that the goods shall conform to the affirmation or promise.
  (b) Any description of the goods which is made part of the basis of the bargain creates an express warranty that the goods shall conform to the description.
  (c) Any sample or model which is made part of the basis of the bargain creates an express warranty that the whole of the goods shall conform to the sample or model.

(2) It is not necessary to the creation of an express warranty that the seller use formal words such as "warrant" or "guarantee" or that he have a specific intention to make a warranty, but an affirmation merely of the value of the goods or a statement purporting to be merely the seller's opinion or commendation of the goods does not create a warranty.

§2-314. Implied Warranty: Merchantability; Usage of Trade.

(1) Unless excluded or modified (Section 2-316), a warranty that the goods shall be merchantable is implied in a contract for their sale if the seller is a merchant with respect to goods of that kind. Under this section the serving for value of food or drink to be consumed either on the premises or elsewhere is a sale.

(2) Goods to be merchantable must be at least such as
  (a) pass without objection in the trade under the contract description; and
  (b) in the case of fungible goods, are of fair average quality within the description; and
  (c) are fit for the ordinary purposes for which such goods are used; and
  (d) run, within the variations permitted by the agreement, of even kind, quality and quantity within each unit and among all units involved; and
  (e) are adequately contained, packaged, and labeled as the agreement may require; and
  (f) conform to the promises or affirmations of fact made on the container or label if any.

(3) Unless excluded or modified (Section 2-316) other implied warranties may arise from course of dealing or usage of trade.

§2-315. Implied Warranty: Fitness for Particular Purpose.

Where the seller at the time of contracting has reason to know any particular purpose for which the goods are required and that the buyer is relying on the seller's skill or judgment to select or furnish suitable goods, there is unless excluded or modified under the next section an implied warranty that the goods shall be fit for such purpose.

§2-316. Exclusion or Modification of Warranties.

(1) Words or conduct relevant to the creation of an express warranty and words or conduct tending to negate or limit warranty shall be construed wherever reasonable as consistent with each other; but subject to the provisions of this Article on parol or extrinsic evidence (Section 2-202) negation or limitation is inoperative to the extent that such construction is unreasonable.

(2) Subject to subsection (3), to exclude or modify the implied warranty of merchantability or any part of it the language must mention merchantability and in case of a writing must be conspicuous, and to exclude or modify any implied warranty of fitness the exclusion must be by a writing and conspicuous. Language to exclude all implied warranties of fitness is sufficient if it states, for example, that "There are no warranties which extend beyond the description on the face hereof."

(3) Notwithstanding subsection (2)
  (a) unless the circumstances indicate otherwise, all implied warranties are excluded by expressions like "as is", "with all faults" or other language which in common understanding calls the buyer's attention to the exclusion of warranties and makes plain that there is no implied warranty; and
  (b) when the buyer before entering into the contract has examined the goods or the sample or model as fully as he desired or has refused to examine the goods there is no implied warranty with regard to defects which an examination ought in the circumstances to have revealed to him; and
  (c) an implied warranty can also be excluded or modified by course of dealing or course of performance or usage of trade.

(4) Remedies for breach of warranty can be limited in accordance with the provisions of this Article on liquidation or limitation of damages and on contractual modification of remedy (Sections 2-718 and 2-719).

§2-317. Cumulation and Conflict of Warranties Express or Implied. Warranties whether express or implied shall be construed as consistent with each other and as cumulative but if such construction is unreasonable the intention of the parties shall determine which warranty is dominant. In ascertaining that intention the following rules apply:

(**a**) Exact or techinical specifications displace an inconsistent sample or model or general language of description.

(**b**) A sample from an existing bulk displaces inconsistent general language of description.

(**c**) Express warranties displace inconsistent implied warranties other than an implied warranty of fitness for a particular purpose.

§2-318. Third Party Beneficiaries of Warranties Express or Implied.

Note: *If this Act is introduced in the Congress of the United States this section should be omitted. (States to select one alternative.)*

Alternative A—A seller's warranty whether express or implied extends to any natural person who is in the family or household of his buyer or who is a guest in his home if it is reasonable to expect that such person may use, consume or be affected by the goods and who is injured in person by breach of the warranty. A seller may not exclude or limit the operation of this section.

Alternative B—A seller's warranty whether express or implied extends to any natural person who may reasonably be expected to use, consume or be affected by the goods and who is injured in person by breach of the warranty. A seller may not exclude or limit the operation of this section.

Alternative C—A seller's warranty whether express or implied extends to any person who may reasonably be expected to use, consume or be affected by the goods and who is injured by breach of the warranty. A seller may not exclude or limit the operation of this section with respect to injury to the person of an individual to whom the warranty extends. As amended 1966.

§2-319. F.O.B. and F.A.S. Terms.

(**1**) Unless otherwise agreed the term F.O.B. (which means "free on board") at a named place, even though used only in connection with the stated price, is a delivery term under which

(a) when the term is F.O.B. the place of shipment, the seller must at that place ship the goods in the manner provided in this Article (Section 2-504) and bear the expense and risk of putting them into the possession of the carrier; or

(**b**) when the term is F.O.B. the place of destination, the seller must at his own expense and risk transport the goods to that place and there tender delivery of them in the manner provided in this Article (Section 2-503);

(**c**) when under either (a) or (b) the term is also F.O.B. vessel, car or other vehicle, the seller must in addition at his own expense and risk load the goods on board. If the term is F.O.B. vessel the buyer must name the vessel and

in an appropriate case the seller must comply with the provisions of this Article on the form of bill of lading (Section 2-323).

(**2**) Unless otherwise agreed the term F.A.S. vessel (which means "free alongside") at a named port, even though used only in connection with the stated price, is a delivery term under which the selller must

(**a**) at his own expense and risk deliver the goods alongside the vessel in the manner usual in that port or on a dock designated and provided by the buyer; and

(**b**) obtain and tender a receipt for the goods in exchange for which the carrier is under a duty to issue a bill of lading.

(**3**) Unless otherwise agreed in any case falling within subsection (1) (a) or (c) or subsection (2) the buyer must seasonably give any needed instructions for making delivery, including when the term is F.A.S. or F.O.B. the loading berth of the vessel and in an appropriate case its name and sailing date. The seller may treat the failure of needed instructions as a failure of cooperation under this Article (Section 2-311). He may also at his option move the goods in any reasonable manner preparatory to delivery or shipment.

(**4**) Under the term F.O.B. vessel or F.A.S. unless otherwise agreed the buyer must make payment against tender of the required documents and the seller may not tender nor the buyer demand delivery of the goods in substitution for the doucments.

§2-320. C.I.F. and C.&F. Terms.

(**1**) The term C.I.F. means that the price includes in a lump sum the cost of the goods and the insurance and freight to the named destination. The term C.&F. or C.F. means that the price so includes cost and freight to the named destination.

(**2**) Unless otherwise agreed and even though used only in connection with the stated price and destination, the term C.I.F. destination or its equivalent requires the seller at his own expense and risk to

(**a**) put the goods into the possession of a carrier at the port for shipment and obtain a negotiable bill or bills of lading covering the entire transportation to the named destination; and

(**b**) load the goods and obtain a receipt from the carrier (which may be contained in the bill of lading) showing that the freight has been paid or provided for; and

(**c**) obtain a policy or certificate of insurance, including any war risk insurance, of a kind and on terms then current at the port of shipment in the usual amount, in the currency of the contract, shown to cover the same goods covered by the bill of lading and providing for payment of loss to the order of the buyer or for the account of whom it may concern; but the seller may add to the price the amount of the premium for any such war risk insurance; and

(**d**) prepare an invoice of the goods and procure any other doucments required to effect shipment or to comply with the contract; and

(**e**) forward and tender with commerical promptness all

the documents in due form and with any indorsement necessary to perfect the buyer's rights.

(3) Unless otherwise agreed the term C. & F. or its equivalent has the same effect and imposes upon the seller the same obligations and risks as a C.I.F. term except the obligation as to insurance.

(4) Under the term C.I.F. or C. & F. unless otherwise agreed the buyer must make payment against tender of the required documents and the seller may not tender nor the buyer demand delivery of the goods in substitution for the documents.

§2-321. C.I.F. or C. & F.: "Net Landed Weights"l "Payment on Arrival"; Warranty of Condition on Arrival. Under a contract containing a term C.I.F. or C. & F.

(1) Where the price is based on or is to be adjusted according to "net landed weights", "delivered weights", "out turn" quantity or quality or the like, unless otherwise agreed the seller must reasonably estimate the price. The payment due on tender of the documents called for by the contract is the amount so estimated, but after final adjustment of the price a settlement must be made with commercial promptness.

(2) An agreement described in subsection (1) or any warranty of quality or condition of the goods on arrival places upon the seller the risk of ordinary deterioration, shrinkage and the like in transportation but has no effect on the place or time of identification to the contract for sale or delivery or on the passing of the risk of loss.

(3) Unless otherwise agreed where the contract provides for payment on or after arrival of the goods the seller must before payment allow such preliminary inspection as is feasible; but if the goods are lost delivery of the doucments and payment are due when the goods should have arrived.

§2-322. Delivery "Ex-Ship".

(1) Unless otherwise agreed a term for delivery of goods "ex-ship" (which means from the carrying vessel) or in equivalent language is not restricted to a particular ship and requires delivery from a ship which has reached a place at the named port of destination where goods of the kind are usually discharged.

(2) Under such a term unless othewise agreed

(a) the seller must discharge all liens arising out of the carriage and furnish the buyer with a direction which puts the carrier under a duty to deliver the goods; and

(b) the risk of loss does not pass to the buyer until the goods leave the ship's tackle or are otherwise properly unloaded.

§2-323. Form of Bill of Lading Required in Overseas Shipment; "Overseas".

(1) Where the contract contemplates overseas shipment and contains a term C.I.F. or C. & F. or F. O.B. vessel the seller unless otherwise agreed must obtain a negotiable bill of lading stating that the goods have been loaded on board or, in the case of a term C.I.F. or C. & F., received for shipment.

(2) Where in a case within subsection (1) a bill of lading has been issued in a set of parts, unless otherwise agreed if the documents are not to be sent from abroad the buyer may demand tender of the full set; otherwise only one part of the bill of lading need be tendered. Even if the agreement expressly requires a full set

(a) due tender of a single part is acceptable within the provisions of this Article on cure of improper delivery (subsection (1) of Section 2-508); and

(b) even though the full set is demanded, if the documents are sent from abroad the person tendering an incomplete set may nevertheless require payment upon furnishing an indemnity which the buyer in good faith deems adequate.

(3) A shipment by water or by air or a contract contemplating such shipment is "overseas" insofar as by usage of trade or agreement it is subject to the commercial, financing or shipping practices characteristic of international deep water commerce.

§2-324. "No Arrival, No Sale" Term. Under a term "no arrival, no sale" or terms of like meaning, unless otherwise agreed,

(a) the seller must properly ship conforming goods and if they arrive by any means he must tender them on arrival but he assumes no obligation that the goods will arrive unless he has caused the nonarrival; and

(b) where without fault of the seller the goods are in part lost or have so deteriorated as no longer to conform to the contract or arrive after the contract time, the buyer may proceed as if there had been casualty to identified goods (Section 2-613).

§2-325. "Letter of Credit" Term; "Confirmed Credit".

(1) Failure of the buyer seasonably to furnish an agreed letter of credit is a breach of the contract for sale.

(2) The delivery to seller of a proper letter of credit suspends the buyer's obligation to pay. If the letter of credit is dishonored, the seller may on seasonable notification to the buyer require payment directly from him.

(3) Unless otherwise agreed the term "letter of credit" or "banker's credit" in a contract for sale means an irrevocable credit issued by a financing agency of good repute and, where the shipment is overseas, of good international repute. The term "confirmed credit" means that the credit must also carry the direct obligation of such an agency which does business in the seller's financial market.

§2-326. Sale on Approval and Sale or Return; Consignment Sales and Rights of Creditors.

(1) Unless otherwise agreed, if delivered goods may be returned by the buyer even though they conform to the contract, the transaction is

(a) a "sale on approval" if the goods are delivered primarily for use, and

(b) a "sale or return" if the goods are delivered primarily for resale.

(2) Except as provided in subsection (3), goods held on approval are not subject to the claims of the buyer's creditors until acceptance; goods held on sale or return are subject to such claims while in the buyer's possession.

(3) Where goods are delivered to a person for sale and such person maintains a place of business at which he deals in goods of the kind involved, under a name other than the name of the person making delivery, then with respect to claims of creditors of the person conducting the business the goods are deemed to be on sale or return. The provisions of this subsection are applicable even though an agreement purports to reserve title to the person making delivery until payment or resale or uses such words as "on consignment" or "on memorandum". However, this subsection is not applicable if the person making delivery

(a) complies with an applicable law providing for a consignor's interest or the like to be evidenced by a sign, or

(b) establishes that the person conducting the business is generally known by his creditors to be substantially engaged in selling the goods of others, or

(c) complies with the filing provisions of the Article on Secured Transactions (Article 9).

(4) Any "or return" term of a contract for sale is to be treated as a separate contract for sale within the statute of frauds section of this Article (Section 2-201) and as contradicting the sale aspect of the contract within the provisions of this Article on parol or extrinsic evidence (Section 2-202).

§2-327. Special Incidents of Sale on Approval and Sale or Return.

(1) Under a sale on approval unless otherwise agreed

(a) although the goods are identified to the contract the risk of loss and the title do not pass to the buyer until acceptance; and

(b) use of the goods consistent with the purpose of trial is not acceptance but failure seasonably to notify the seller of election to return the goods is acceptance, and if the goods conform to the contract acceptance of any part is acceptance of the whole; and

(c) after due notification of election to return, the return is at the seller's risk and expense but a merchant buyer must follow any reasonable instructions.

(2) Under a sale or return unless otherwise agreed

(a) the option to return extends to the whole or any commercial unit of the goods while in substantially their original condition, but must be exercised seasonably; and

(b) the return is at the buyer's risk and expense.

§2-328. Sale by Auction.

(1) In a sale by auction if goods are put up in lots each lot is the subject of a separate sale.

(2) A sale by auction is complete when the auctioneer so announces by the fall of the hammer or in other customary manner. Where a bid is made while the hammer is falling in acceptance of a prior bid the auctioneer may in his discretion reopen the bidding or declare the goods sold under the bid on which the hammer was falling.

(3) Such a sale is with reserve unless the goods are in explicit terms put up without reserve. In an auction with reserve, the auctioneer may withdraw the goods at any time until he announces completion of the sale. In an auction without

reserve, after the auctioneer calls for bids on an article or lot, that article or lot cannot be withdrawn unless no bid is made within a reasonable time. In either case a bidder may retract his bid until the auctioneer's announcement of completion of the sale, but a bidder's retraction does not revive any previous bid.

(4) If the auctioneer knowingly receives a bid on the seller's behalf or the seller makes or procures such a bid, and notice has not been given that liberty for such bidding is reserved, the buyer may at his option avoid the sale or take the goods at the price of the last good faith bid prior to the completion of the sale. This subsection shall not apply to any bid at a forced sale.

Part 4: Title, Creditors and Good Faith Purchasers

§2-401. Passing of Title; Reservation for Security; Limited Application of This Section.
Each provision of this Article with regard to the rights, obligations and remedies of the seller, the buyer, purchasers or other third parties applies irrespective of title to the goods except where the provision refers to such title. Insofar as situations are not covered by the other provisions of this Article and matters concerning title become material the following rules apply:

(1) Title to goods cannot pass under a contract for sale prior to their identification to the contract (Section 2-501), and unless otherwise explicitly agreed the buyer acquires by their identification a special property as limited by this Act. Any retention or reservation by the seller of the title (property) in goods shipped or delivered to the buyer is limited in effect to a reservation of a security interest. Subject to these provisions and to the provisions of the Article on Secured Transactions (Article 9), title to goods passes from the seller to the buyer in any manner and on any conditions explicitly agreed on by the parties.

(2) Unless otherwise explicitly agreed title passes to the buyer at the time and place at which the seller completes his performance with reference to the physical delivery of the goods, despite any reservation of a security interest and even though a document of title is to be delivered at a different time or place; and in particular and despite any reservation of a security interest by the bill of lading

(a) if the contract requires or authorizes the seller to send the goods to the buyer but does not require him to deliver them at destination, title passes to the buyer at the time and place of shipment; but

(b) if the contract requires delivery at destination, title passes on tender there.

(3) Unless otherwise explicitly agreed where delivery is to be made without moving the goods.

(a) if the seller is to deliver a document of title, title passes at the time when and the place where he delivers such documents; or

(b) if the goods are at the time of contracting already identified and no documents are to be delivered, title passes at the time and place of contracting.

(4) A rejection or other refusal by the buyer to receive or

retain the goods, whether or not justified, or a justified revocation of acceptance revests title to the goods in the seller. Such revesting occurs by operation of law and is not a "sale".

§2-402. Rights of Seller's Creditors Against Sold Goods.

(1) Except as provided in subsections (2) and (3), rights of unsecured creditors of the seller with respect to goods which have been identified to a contract for sale are subject to the buyer's rights to recover the goods under this Article (Section 2-502 and 2-716).

(2) A creditor of the seller may treat a sale or an identification of goods to a contract for sale as void if as against him a retention of possession by the seller is fraudulent under any rule of law of the state where the goods are situated, except that retention of possession in good faith and current course of trade by a merchant-seller for a commercially reasonable time after a sale or identification is not fraudulent.

(3) Nothing in this Article shall be deemed to impair the rights of creditors of the seller

(a) under the provisions of the Article on Secured Transactions (Article 9); or

(b) where identification to the contract or delivery is made not in current course of trade but in satisfaction of or as security for a pre-existing claim for money, security or the like and is made under circumstances which under any rule of law of the state where the goods are situated would apart from this Article constitute the transaction a fraudulent transfer or voidable preference.

§2-403. Power to Transfer; Good Faith Purchase of Goods; "Entrusting".

(1) A purchaser of goods acquires all title which his transferor had or had power to transfer except that a purchaser of a limited interest acquires rights only to the extent of the interest purchased. A person with voidable title has power to transfer a good title to a good faith purchaser for value. When goods have been delivered under a transaction of purchase the purchaser had such power even though

(a) the transferor was deceived as to the identity of the purchaser, or

(b) the delivery was in exchange for a check which is later dishonored, or

(c) it was agreed that the transaction was to be a "cash sale", or

(d) the delivery was procured through fraud punishable as larcenous under the criminal law.

(2) Any entrusting of possession of goods to a merchant who deals in goods of that kind gives him power to transfer all rights of the entruster to a buyer in ordinary course of business.

(3) "Entrusting" includes any delivery and any acquiescence in retention of possession regardless of any condition expressed between the parties to the delivery or acquiescence and regardless of whether the procurement of the entrusting or the possessor's disposition of the goods have been such as to be larcenous under the criminal law.

(4) The rights of other purchasers of goods and of lien creditors are governed by the Articles on Secured Transactions

(Article 9), Bulk Transfers (Article 6) and Documents of Title (Article 7).

Part 5: Performance

§2-501. Insurable Interest in Goods; Manner of Identification of Goods.

(1) The buyer obtains a special property and an insurable interest in goods by identification of existing goods as goods to which the contract refers even though the goods so identified are non-conforming and he has an option to return or reject them. Such identification can be made at any time and in any manner explicitly agreed to by the parties. In the absence of explicit agreement identification occurs

(a) when the contract is made if it is for the sale of goods already existing and identified;

(b) if the contract is for the sale of future goods other than those described in paragraph (c), when goods are shipped, marked or otherwise designated by the seller as goods to which the contract refers;

(c) when the crops are planted or otherwise become growing crops or the young are conceived if the contract is for the sale of unborn young to be born within twelve months after contracting or for the sale of crops to be harvested within twelve months or the next normal harvest season after contracting whichever is longer.

(2) The seller retains an insurable interest in goods so long as title to or any security interest in the goods remains in him and where the identification is by the seller alone he may until default or insolvency or notification to the buyer that the identification is final substitute other goods for those identified.

(3) Nothing in this section impairs any insurable interest recognized under any other statute or rule of law.

§2-502. Buyer's Right to Goods on Seller's Insolvency.

(1) Subject to subsection (2) and even though the goods have not been shipped a buyer who has paid a part or all of the price of goods in which he has a special property under the provisions of the immediately preceding section may on making and keeping good a tender of any unpaid portion of their price recover them from the seller if the seller becomes insolvent within ten days after receipt of the first installment on their price.

(2) If the identification creating his special property has been made by the buyer he acquires the right to recover the goods only if they conform to the contract for sale.

§2-503. Manner of Seller's Tender of Delivery.

(1) Tender of delivery requires that the seller put and hold conforming goods at the buyer's disposition and give the buyer any notification reasonably necessary to enable him to take delivery. The manner, time and place for tender are determined by the agreement and this Article, and in particular

(a) tender must be at a reasonable hour, and if it is of goods they must be kept available for the period reasonably necessary to enable the buyer to take possession; but (**b**) unless otherwise agreed the buyer must furnish facilities reasonably suited to the receipt of the goods.

(**2**) Where the case is within the next section respecting shipment tender requires that the seller comply with its provisions.

(**3**) Where the seller is required to deliver at a particular destination tender requires that he comply with subsection (1) and also in any appropriate case tender documents as described in subsections (4) and (5) of this section.

(**4**) Where goods are in the possession of a bailee and are to be delivered without being moved

(**a**) tender requires that the seller either tender a negotiable document of title covering such goods or procure acknowledgement by the bailee of the buyer's right to possession of the goods; but

(**b**) tender to the buyer of a non-negotiable document of title or of a written direction to the bailee to deliver is sufficient tender unless the buyer seasonably objects, and receipt by the bailee of notification of the buyer's rights fixes those rights as aginst the bailee and all third persons; but risk of loss of the goods and of any failure by the bailee to honor the non-negotiable document of title or to obey the direction remains on the seller until the buyer has had a reasonable time to present the document or direction, and a refusal by the bailee to honor the document or to obey the direction defeats the tender.

(**5**) Where the contract requires the seller to deliver documents

(**a**) he must tender all such documents in correct form, except as provided in this Article with respect to bills of lading in a set (subsection (2) of Section 2-323); and

(**b**) tender through customary banking channels is sufficient and dishonor of a draft accompanying the documents constitutes non-acceptance or rejection.

§2-504 Shipment by Seller. Where the seller is required or authorized to send the goods to the buyer and the contract does not require him to deliver them at a particular destination, then unless otherwise agreed he must

(**a**) put the goods in the possession of such a carrier and make such a contract for their transportation as may be reasonable having regard to the nature of the goods and other circumstances of the case; and

(**b**) obtain and promptly deliver or tender in due form any document necessary to enable the buyer to obtain possession of the goods or otherwise required by the agreement or by usage of trade; and

(**c**) promptly notify the buyer of the shipment.

Failure to notify the buyer under paragraph (c) or to make a proper contract under paragraph (a) is a ground for rejection only if material delay or loss ensues.

§2-505. Seller's Shipment under Reservation.

(**1**) Where the seller has identified goods to the contract by or before shipment:

(**a**) his procurement of a negotiable bill of lading to his own order or otherwise reserves in him a security interest

in the goods. His procurement of the bill to the order of a financing agency or of the buyer indicates in addition only the seller's expectation of transferring that interest to the person named.

(**b**) a non-negotiable bill of lading to himself or his nominee reserves possession of the goods as security but except in a case of conditional delivery (subsection (2) of Section 2-507) a non-negotiable bill of lading naming the buyer as consignee reserves no security interest even though the seller retains possession of the bill of lading.

(**2**) When shipment by the seller with reservation of a security interest is in violation of the contract for sale it constitutes an improper contract for transportation within the preceding section but impairs neither the rights given to the buyer by shipment and identification of the goods to the contract nor the seller's powers as a holder of a negotiable document.

§2-506. Rights of Financing Agency.

(**1**) A financing agency by paying or purchasing for value a draft which relates to a shipment of goods acquires to the extent of the payment or purchase and in addition to its own rights under the draft and any document of title securing it any rights of the shipper in the goods including the right to stop delivery and the shipper's right to have the draft honored by the buyer.

(**2**) The right to reimbursement of a financing agency which has in good faith honored or purchased the draft under commitment to or authority from the buyer is not impaired by subsequent discovery of defects with reference to any relevant document which was apparently regular on its face.

§2-507. Effect of Seller's Tender; Delivery on Condition.

(**1**) Tender of delivery is a condition to the buyer's duty to accept the goods and, unless otherwise agreed, to his duty to pay for them. Tender entitles the seller to acceptance of the goods and to payment according to the contract.

(**2**) Where payment is due and demanded on the delivery to the buyer of goods or documents of title, his right as against the seller to retain or dispose of them is conditional upon his making the payment due.

§2-508. Cure by Seller of Improper Tender or Delivery; Replacement.

(**1**) Where any tender or delivery by the seller is rejected because non-conforming and the time for performance has not yet expired, the seller may seasonably notify the buyer of his intention to cure and may then within the contract time make a conforming delivery.

(**2**) Where the buyer rejects a non-conforming tender which the seller had reasonable grounds to believe would be acceptable with or without money allowance the seller may if he seasonably notifies the buyer have a further reasonable time to substitute a conforming tender.

§2-509. Risk of Loss in the Absence of Breach.

(**1**) Where the contract requires or authorizes the seller to ship the goods by carrier

(**a**) if it does not require him to deliver them at a

particular destination, the risk of loss passes to the buyer when the goods are duly delivered to the carrier even though the shipment is under reservation (Section 2-505); but

(b) if it does require him to deliver them at a particular destination and the goods are there duly tendered while in the possession of the carrier, the risk of loss passes to the buyer when the goods are there duly so tendered as to enable the buyer to take delivery.

(2) Where the goods are held by a bailee to be delivered without being moved, the risk of loss passes to the buyer

(a) on his receipt of a negotiable document of title covering the goods; or

(b) on acknowledgement by the bailee of the buyer's right to possession of the goods; or

(c) after his receipt of a non-negotiable document of title or other written direction to deliver, as provided in subsection (4) (b) of Section 2-503.

(3) In any case not within subsection (1) or (2), the risk of loss passes to the buyer on his receipt of the goods if the seller is a merchant; otherwise the risk passes to the buyer on tender of delivery.

(4) The provisions of this section are subject to contrary agreement of the parties and to the provisions of this Article on sale on approval (Section 2-327) and on effect of breach on risk of loss (Section 2-510).

§2-510. Effect of Breach on Risk of Loss.

(1) Where a tender or delivery of goods so fails to conform to the contract as to give a right of rejection the risk of their loss remains on the seller until cure or acceptance.

(2) Where the buyer rightfully revokes acceptance he may to the extent of any deficiency in his effective insurance coverage treat the risk of loss as having rested on the seller from the beginning.

(3) Where the buyer as to conforming goods already identified to the contract for sale repudiates or is otherwise in breach before risk of their loss has passed to him, the seller may to the extent of any deficiency in his effective insurance coverage treat the risk of loss as resting on the buyer for a commercially reasonable time.

§2-511. Tender of Payment by Buyer; Payment by Check.

(1) Unless otherwise agreed tender of payment is a condition to the seller's duty to tender and complete any delivery.

(2) Tender of payment is sufficient when made by any means or in any manner current in the ordinary course of business unless the seller demands payment in legal tender and gives any extension of time reasonably necessary to procure it.

(3) Subject to the provisions of this Act on the effect of an instrument on an obligation (Section 3-802), payment by check is conditional and is defeated as between the parties by dishonor of the check on due presentment.

§2-512. Payment by Buyer Before Inspection.

(1) Where the contract requires payment before inspection non-conformity of the goods does not excuse the buyer from so making payment unless

(a) the non-conformity appears without inspection; or

(b) despite tender of the required documents the circumstances would justify injunction against honor under the provisions of this Act (Section 5-114).

(2) Payment pursuant to subsection (1) does not constitute an acceptance of goods or impair the buyer's right to inspect or any of his remedies.

§2-513. Buyer's Right to Inspection of Goods.

(1) Unless otherwise agreed and subject to subsection (3), where goods are tendered or delivered or identified to the contract for sale, the buyer has a right before payment or acceptance to inspect them at any reasonable place and time and in any reasonable manner. When the seller is required or authorized to send the goods to the buyer, the inspection may be after their arrival.

(2) Expenses of inspection must be borne by the buyer but may be recovered from the seller if the goods do not conform and are rejected.

(3) Unless otherwise agreed and subject to the provisions of this Article on C.I.F. contracts (subsection (3) of Section 3-221), the buyer is not entitled to inspect the goods before payment of the price when the contract provides

(a) for delivery "C.O.D." or on other like terms; or

(b) for payment against documents of title, except where such payment is due only after the goods are to become available for inspection.

(4) A place or method of inspection fixed by the parties is presumed to be exclusive but unless otherwise expressly agreed it does not postpone identification or shift the place for delivery or for passing the risk of loss. If compliance becomes impossible, inspection shall be as provided in this section unless the place or method fixed was clearly intended as an indispensable condition failure of which avoids the contract.

§2-514. When Documents Deliverable on Acceptance; When on Payment. Unless otherwise agreed documents against which a draft is drawn are to be delivered to the drawee on acceptance of the draft if it is payable more than three days after presentment; otherwise, only on payment.

§2-515. Preserving Evidence of Goods in Dispute. In furtherance of the adjustment of any claim or dispute

(a) either party on reasonable notification to the other and for the purpose of ascertaining the facts and preserving evidence has the right to inspect, test and sample the goods including such of them as may be in the possession or control of the other; and

(b) the parties may agree to a third party inspection or survey to determine the conformity or condition of the goods and may agree that the findings shall be binding upon them in any subsequent litigation or adjustment.

Part 6: Breach, Repudiation and Excuse

§2-601. Buyer's Rights on Improper Delivery. Subject to the provisions of this Article on breach in installment contracts

(Section 2-612) and unless otherwise agreed under the sections on contractual limitations of remedy (Sections 2-718 and 2-719), if the goods or the tender of delivery fail in any respect to conform to the contract, the buyer may

(a) reject the whole; or

(b) accept the whole; or

(c) accept any commercial unit or units and reject the rest.

§2-602. Manner and Effect of Rightful Rejection.

(1) Rejection of goods must be within a reasonable time after their delivery or tender. It is ineffective unless the buyer seasonably notifies the seller.

(2) Subject to the provisions of the two following sections on rejected goods (Section 2-603 and 2-604),

(a) after rejection any exercise of ownership by the buyer with respect to any commercial unit is wrongful as against the seller; and

(b) if the buyer has before rejection taken physical possession of goods in which he does not have a security interest under the provisions of this Article (subsection (3) of Section 2-711), he is under a duty after rejection to hold them with reasonable care at the seller's disposition for a time sufficient to permit the seller to remove them; but

(c) the buyer has no further obligations with regard to goods rightfully rejected.

(3) The seller's rights with respect to goods wrongfully rejected are governed by the provisions of this Article on Seller's remedies in general (Section 2-703).

§2-603. Merchant Buyer's Duties as to Rightfully Rejected Goods.

(1) Subject to any security interest in the buyer (subsection (3) of Section 2-711), when the seller has no agent or place of business at the market of rejection a merchant buyer is under a duty after rejection of goods in his possession or control to follow any reasonable instructions received from the seller with respect to the goods and in the absence of such instructions to make reasonable efforts to sell them for the seller's account if they are perishable or threaten to decline in value speedily. Instructions are not reasonable if on demand indemnity for expenses is not forthcoming.

(2) When the buyer sells goods under subsection (1), he is entitled to reimbursement from the seller or out of the proceeds for reasonable expenses of caring for and selling them, and if the expenses include no selling commission then to such commission as is usual in the trade or if there is none to a reasonable sum not exceeding ten per cent on the gross proceeds.

(3) In complying with this section the buyer is held only to good faith and good faith conduct hereunder is neither acceptance nor conversion nor the basis of an action for damages.

§2-604. Buyer's Options as to Salvage of Rightfully Rejected Goods.

Subject to the provisions of the immediately preceding section on perishables if the seller gives no instructions within a reasonable time after notification of rejection the buyer may store the rejected goods for the seller's account or reship them to him or resell them for the seller's account with reimburse-ment as provided in the preceding section. Such action is not acceptance or conversion.

§2-605. Waiver of Buyer's Objections by Failure to Particularize.

(1) The buyer's failure to state in connection with rejection a particular defect which is ascertainable by reasonable inspection precludes him from relying on the unstated defect to justify rejection or to establish breach

(a) where the seller could have cured it if stated seasonably; or

(b) between merchants when the seller has after rejection made a request in writing for a full and final written statement of all defects on which the buyer proposes to rely.

(2) Payment against documents made without reservation of rights precludes recovery of the payment for defects apparent on the face of the documents.

§2-606. What Constitutes Acceptance of Goods.

(1) Acceptance of goods occurs when the buyer

(a) after a reasonable opportunity to inspect the goods signifies to the seller that the goods are conforming or that he will take or retain them in spite of their non-conformity; or

(b) fails to make an effective rejection (subsection (1) of Section 2-602), but such acceptance does not occur until the buyer has had a reasonable opportunity to inspect them; or

(c) does any act inconsistent with the seller's ownership; but if such act is wrongful as against the seller it is an acceptance only if ratified by him.

(2) Acceptance of a part of any commercial unit is acceptance of that entire unit.

§2-607. Effect of Acceptance; Notice of Breach; Burden of Establishing Breach After Acceptance; Notice of Claim or Litigation to Person Answerable Over.

(1) The buyer must pay at the contract rate for any goods accepted.

(2) Acceptance of goods by the buyer precludes rejection of the goods accepted and if made with knowledge of a non-conformity cannot be revoked because of it unless the acceptance was on the reasonable assumption that the non-conformity would be seasonably cured but acceptance does not of itself impair any other remedy provided by this Article for non-conformity.

(3) Where a tender has been accepted

(a) the buyer must within a reasonable time after he discovers or should have discovered any breach notify the seller of breach or be barred from any remedy; and

(b) if the claim is one for infringement or the like (subsection (3) of Section 2-312) and the buyer is sued as a result of such a breach he must so notify the seller within a reasonable time after he receives notice of the litigation or be barred from any remedy over for liability established by the litigation.

(4) The burden is on the buyer to establish any breach with respect to the goods accepted.

(5) Where the buyer is sued for breach of a warranty or other obligation for which his seller is answerable over

(a) he may give his seller written notice of the litigation. If the notice states that the seller may come in and defend and that if the seller does not do so he will be bound in any action against him by his buyer by any determination of fact common to the two litigations, then unless the seller after seasonable receipt of the notice does come in and defend he is so bound.

(b) if the claim is one for infringement or the like (subsection (3) of Section 2-312) the original seller may demand in writing that his buyer turn over to him control of the litigation including settlement or else be barred from any remedy over and if he also agrees to bear all expense and to satisfy any adverse judgment, then unless the buyer after seasonable receipt of the demand does turn over control the buyer is so barred.

(6) The provisions of subsection (3), (4) and (5) apply to any obligation of a buyer to hold the seller harmless against infringement or the like (subsection (3) of Section 2-312).

§2-608. Revocation of Acceptance in Whole or in Part.

(1) The buyer may revoke his acceptance of a lot or commercial unit whose non-conformity substantially impairs its value to him if he has accepted it

(a) on the reasonable assumption that its non-conformity would be cured and it has not been seasonably cured; or

(b) without discovery of such non-conformity if his acceptance was reasonably induced either by the difficulty of discovery before acceptance or by the seller's assurances.

(2) Revocation of acceptance must occur within a reasonable time after the buyer discovers or should have discovered the ground for it and before any substantial change in condition of the goods which is not caused by their own defects. It is not effective until the buyer notifies the seller of it.

(3) A buyer who so revokes has the same rights and duties with regard to the goods involved as if he had rejected them.

§2-609. Right to Adequate Assurance of Performance.

(1) A contract for sale imposes an obligation on each party that the other's expectation of receiving due performance will not be impaired. When reasonable grounds for insecurity arise with respect to the performance of either party the other may in writing demand adequate assurance of due performance and until he receives such assurance may if commercially reasonable suspend any performance for which he has not already received the agreed return.

(2) Between merchants the reasonableness of grounds for insecurity and the adequacy of any assurance offered shall be determined according to commericial standards.

(3) Acceptance of any improper delivery or payment does not prejudice the aggrieved party's right to demand adequate assurance of future performance.

(4) After receipt of a justified demand failure to provide within a reasonable time not exceeding thirty days such assurance of due performance as is adequate under the circumstances of the particular case is a repudiation of the contract.

§2-610. Anticipatory Repudiation. When either party repudiates the contract with respect to a performance not yet due the loss of which will substantially impair the value of the contract to the other, the aggrieved party may

(a) for a commercially reasonable time await performance by the repudiating party; or

(b) resort to any remedy for breach (Section 2-703 or Section 2-711), even though he has notified the repudiating party that he would await the latter's performance and has urged retraction; and

(c) in either case suspend his own performance or proceed in accordance with the provisions of this Article on the seller's right to identify goods to the contract notwithstanding breach or to salvage unfinished goods (Section 2-704).

§2-611. Retraction of Anticipatory Repudiation.

(1) Until the repudiating party's next performance is due he can retract his repudiation unless the aggrieved party has since the repudiation cancelled or materially changed his position or otherwise indicated that he considers the repudiation final.

(2) Retraction may be by any method which clearly indicates to the aggrieved party that the repudiating party intends to perform, but must include any assurance justifiably demanded under the provisions of this Article (Section 2-609).

(3) Retraction reinstates the repudiating party's rights under the contract with due excuse and allowance to the aggrieved party for any delay occasioned by the repudiation.

§2-612. "Installment Contract"; Breach.

(1) An "installment contract" is one which requires or authorizes the delivery of goods in separate lots to be separately accepted, even though the contract contains a clause "each delivery is a separate contract" or its equivalent.

(2) The buyer may reject any installment which is non-conforming if the non-conformity substantially impairs the value of that installment and cannot be cured or if the non-conformity is a defect in the required documents; but if the non-conformity does not fall within subsection (3) and the seller gives adequate assurance of its cure the buyer must accept that installment.

(3) Whenever non-conformity or default with respect to one or more installments substantially impairs the value of the whole contract there is a breach of the whole. But the aggrieved party reinstates the contract if he accepts a non-conforming installment without seasonably notifying of cancellation or if he brings an action with respect only to past installments or demands performance as to future installments.

§2-613. Casualty to Identified Goods. Where the contract requires for its performance goods identified when the contract is made, and the goods suffer casualty without fault of either party before the risk of loss passes to the buyer, or in a proper case under a "no arrival, no sale" term (Section 2-324) then

(a) if the loss is total the contract is avoided; and

(b) if the loss is partial or the goods have so deteriorated as no longer to conform to the contract the buyer may nevertheless demand inspection and at his option either treat the contract as avoided or accept the goods with due allowance from the contract price for the deterioration or the deficiency in quantity but without further right against the seller.

§2-614. Substituted Performance.

(1) Where without fault of either party the agreed berthing, loading, or unloading facilities fail or an agreed type of carrier becomes unavailable or the agreed manner of delivery otherwise becomes commercially impracticable but a commercially reasonable substitute is available, such substitute performance must be tendered and accepted.

(2) If the agreed means or manner of payment fails because of domestic or foreign governmental regulation, the seller may withhold or stop delivery unless the buyer provides a means or manner of payment which is commercially a substantial equivalent. If delivery has already been taken, payment by the means or in the manner provided by the regulation discharges the buyer's obligation unless the regulation is discriminatory, oppressive or predatory.

§2-615. Excuse by Failure of Presupposed Conditions.

Except so far as a seller may have assumed a greater obligation and subject to the preceding section on substituted performance:

(a) Delay in delivery or non-delivery in whole or in part by a seller who complies with paragraphs (b) and (c) is not a breach of his duty under a contract for sale if performance as agreed has been made impracticable by the occurrence of a contingency the non-occurrence of which was a basic assumption on which the contract was made or by compliance in good faith with any applicable foreign or domestic governmental regulation or order whether or not it later proves to be invalid.

(b) Where the causes mentioned in paragraph (a) affect only a part of the seller's capacity to perform, he must allocate production and deliveries among his customers but may at his option include regular customers not then under contract as well as his own requirements for further manufacture. He may so allocate in any manner which is fair and reasonable.

(c) The seller must notify the buyer seasonably that there will be delay or non-delivery and, when allocation is required under paragraph (b), of the estimated quota thus made available for the buyer.

§2-616. Procedure on Notice Claiming Excuse.

(1) When the buyer receives notification of a material or indefinite delay or an allocation justified under the preceding section he may by written notification to the seller as to any delivery concerned, and where the prospective deficiency substantially impairs the value of the whole contract under the provisions of this Article relating to breach of installment contracts(Section 2-612), then also as to the whole,

    (a) terminate and thereby discharge any unexecuted portion of the contract; or

    (b) modify the contract by agreeing to take his available quota in substitution.

(2) If after receipt of such notification from the seller the buyer fails so to modify the contract within a reasonable time not exceeding thirty days the contract lapses with respect to any deliveries affected.

(3) The provisions of this section may not be negated by agreement except in so far as the seller has assumed a greater obligation under the preceding section.

Part 7: Remedies

§2-701. Remedies for Breach of Collateral Contracts Not Impaired.
Remedies for breach of any obligation or promise collateral or ancillary to a contract for sale are not impaired by the provisions of this Article.

§2-702. Seller's on Discovery of Buyer's Insolvency.

(1) Where the seller discovers the buyer to be insolvent he may refuse delivery except for cash including payment for all goods theretofore delivered under the contract, and stop delivery under this Article (Section 2-705).

(2) Where the seller discovers that the buyer has received goods on credit while insolvent he may reclaim the goods upon demand made within ten days after the receipt, but if misrepresentation of solvency has been made to the particular seller in writing within three months before delivery the ten day limitation does not apply. Except as provided in this subsection the seller may not base a right to reclaim goods on the buyer's fraudulent or innocent misrepresentation of solvency or of intent to pay.

(3) The seller's right to reclaim under subsection (2) is subject to the rights of a buyer in ordinary course or other good faith purchaser under this Article (Section 2-403). Successful reclamation of goods excludes all other remedies with respect to them. As amended 1966.

§2-703. Seller's Remedies in General.
Where the buyer wrongfully rejects or revokes acceptance of goods or fails to make a payment due on or before delivery or repudiates with respect to a part or the whole, then with respect to any goods directly affected and, if the breach is of the whole contract (Section 2-612), then also with respect to the whole undelivered balance, the aggrieved seller may

    (a) withhold delivery of such goods;

    (b) stop delivery by any bailee as hereafter provided (Section 2-705);

    (c) proceed under the next section respecting goods still unidentified to the contract;

    (d) resell and recover damages as hereafter provided (Section 2-706);

    (e) recover damages for non-acceptance (Section 2-708) or in a proper case the price (Section 2-709);

    (f) cancel.

§2-704. Seller's Right to Identify Goods to the Contract Notwithstanding Breach or to Salvage Unfinished Goods.

(1) An aggrieved seller under the preceding section may

    (a) identify to the contract conforming goods not already identified if at the time he learned of the breach they are in his possession or control;

(**b**) treat as the subject of resale goods which have demonstrably been intended for the particular contract even though those goods are unfinished.

(**2**) Where the goods are unfinished an aggrieved seller may in the exercise of reasonable commercial judgment for the purposes of avoiding loss and of effective realization either complete the manufacture and wholly identify the goods to the contract or cease manufacture and resell for scrap or salvage value or proceed in any other reasonable manner.

§2-705. Seller's Stoppage of Delivery in Transit or Otherwise.

(**1**) The seller may stop delivery of goods in the possession of a carrier or other bailee when he discovers the buyer to be insolvent (Section 2-702) and may stop delivery of carload, truckload, planeload or larger shipments of express or freight when the buyer repudiates or fails to make a payment due before delivery or if for any other reason the seller has a right to withold or reclaim the goods.

(**2**) As against such buyer the seller may stop delivery until

(**a**) receipt of the goods by the buyer; or

(**b**) acknowledgement to the buyer by any bailee of the goods except a carrier that the bailee holds the goods for the buyer; or

(**c**) such acknowledgement to the buyer by a carrier by reshipment or as warehouseman; or

(**d**) negotiation to the buyer of any negotiable document of title covering the goods.

(**3**)

(**a**) To stop delivery the seller must so notify as to enable the bailee by reasonable diligence to prevent delivery of the goods.

(**b**) After such notification the bailee must hold and deliver the goods according to the directions of the seller but the seller is liable to the bailee for any ensuing charges or damages.

(**c**) If a negotiable document of title has been issued for goods the bailee is not obliged to obey a notification to stop until surrender of the document.

(**d**) A carrier who has issued a non-negotiable bill of lading is not obliged to obey a notification to stop received from a person other than the consignor.

§2-706. Seller's Resale Including Contract for Resale.

(**1**) Under the conditions stated in Section 2-703 on seller's remedies, the seller may resell the goods concerned or the undelivered balance thereof. Where the resale is made in good faith and in a commercially reasonable manner the seller may recover the difference between the resale price and the contract price together with any incidental damages allowed under the provisions of this Article (Section 2-710), but less expenses saved in consequence of the buyer's breach.

(**2**) Except as otherwise provided in subsection (3) or unless otherwise agreed resale may be at public or private sale including sale by way of one or more contracts to sell or of identification to an existing contract of the seller. Sale may be as a unit or in parcels and at any time and place and on any terms but every aspect of the sale including the method, manner, time, place and terms must be commercially reasonable. The resale must be reasonably identified as referring to the broken contract, but it is not necessary that the goods be in existence or that any or all of them have been identified to the contract before the breach.

(**3**) Where the resale is at private sale the seller must give the buyer reasonable notification of his intention to resell.

(**4**) Where the resale is at public sale

(**a**) only identified goods can be sold except where there is a recognized market for a public sale of futures in goods of the kind; and

(**b**) it must be made at a usual place or market for public sale if one is reasonably available and except in the case of goods which are perishable or threaten to decline in value speedily the seller must give the buyer reasonable notice of the time and place of the resale; and

(**c**) if the goods are not to be within the view of those attending the sale the notification of sale must state the place where the goods are located and provide for their reasonable inspection by prospective bidders; and

(**d**) the seller may buy.

(**5**) A purchaser who buys in good faith at a resale takes the goods free of any rights of the original buyer even though the seller fails to comply with one or more of the requirements of this section.

(**6**) The seller is not accountable to the buyer for any profit made on any resale. A person in the position of a seller (Section 2-707) or a buyer who has rightfully rejected or justifiably revoked acceptance must account for any excess over the amount of his security interest, as hereinafter defined (subsection (3) of Section 2-711).

§2-707. "Person in the Position of a Seller".

(**1**) A "person in the position of a seller" includes as against a principal an agent who has paid or become responsible for the price of goods on behalf of his principal or anyone who otherwise holds a security interest or other right in goods similar to that of a seller.

(**2**) A person in the position of a seller may as provided in this Article withhold or stop delivery (Section 2-705) and resell (Section 2-706) and recover incidental damages (Section 2-710).

§2-708. Seller's Damages for Non-acceptance or Repudiation.

(**1**) Subject to subsection (2) and to the provisions of this Article with respect to proof of market price (Section 2-723), the measure of damages for non-acceptance or repudiation by the buyer is the difference between the market price at the time and place for tender and the unpaid contract price together with any incidental damages provided in this Article (Section 2-710), but less expenses saved in consequence of the buyer's breach.

(**2**) If the measure of damages provided in subsection (1) is inadequate to put the seller in as good a position as performance would have done then the measure of damages is the profit (including reasonable overhead) which the seller would have made from full performance by the buyer, together with any incidental damages provided in this Article (Section 2-710), due allowance for costs reasonably incurred and due credit for payments or proceeds of resale.

§2-709. Action for the Price.

(1) When the buyer fails to pay the price as it becomes due the seller may recover, together with any incidental damages under the next section, the price

(a) of goods accepted or of conforming goods lost or damaged within a commercially reasonable time after risk of their loss has passed to the buyer; and

(b) of goods identified to the contract if the seller is unable after reasonable effort to resell them at a reasonable price or the circumstances reasonably indicate that such effort will be unavailing.

(2) Where the seller sues for the price he must hold for the buyer any goods which have been identified to the contract and are still in his control except that if resale becomes possible he may resell them at any time prior to the collection of the judgment. The net proceeds of any such resale must be credited to the buyer and payment of the judgment entitles him to any goods not resold.

(3) After the buyer has wrongfully rejected or revoked acceptance of the goods or has failed to make a payment due or has repudiated (Section 2-610), a seller who is held not entitled to the price under this section shall nevertheless be awarded damages for non-acceptance under the preceding section.

§2-710. Seller's Incidental Damages.
Incidental damages to an aggrieved seller include any commercially reasonable charges, expenses or commissions incurred in stopping delivery, in the transportation, care and custody of goods after the buyer's breach, in connection with return or resale of the goods or otherwise resulting from the breach.

§2-711. Buyer's Remedies in General; Buyer's Security Interest in Rejected Goods.

(1) When the seller fails to make delivery or repudiates or the buyer rightfully rejects or justifiably revokes acceptance then with respect to any goods involved, and with respect to the whole if the breach goes to the whole contract (Section 2-612), the buyer may cancel and whether or not he has done so may in addition to recovering so much of the price as has been paid

(a) "cover" and have damages under the next section as to all the goods affected whether or not they have been identified to the contract; or

(b) recover damages for non-delivery as provided in this Article (Section 2-713).

(2) Where the seller fails to deliver or repudiates the buyer may also

(a) if the goods have been identified recover them as provided in this Article (Section 2-502); or

(b) in a proper case obtain specific performance or replevy the goods as provided in this Article (Section 2-716).

(3) On rightful rejection or justifiable revocation of acceptance a buyer has a security interest in goods in his possession or control for any payments made on their price and any expenses reasonably incurred in their inspection, receipt, transportation, care and custody and may hold such goods and resell them in like manner as an aggrieved seller (Section 2-706).

§2-712. "Cover"; Buyer's Procurement of Substitute Goods.

(1) After a breach within the preceding section the buyer may "cover" by making in good faith and without unreasonable delay any reasonable purchase of or contract to purchase goods in substitution for those due from the seller.

(2) The buyer may recover from the seller as damages the difference between the cost of cover and the contract price together with any incidental or consequential damages as hereinafter defined (Section 2-715), but less expenses saved in consequence of the seller's breach.

(3) Failure of the buyer to effect cover within this section does not bar him from any other remedy.

§2-713. Buyer's Damages for Non-Delivery or Repudiation.

(1) Subject to the provisions of this Article with respect to proof of market price (Section 2-723), the measure of damages for non-delivery or repudiation by the seller is the difference between the market price at the time when the buyer learned of the breach and the contract price together with any incidental and consequential damages provided in this Article (Section 2-715), but less expenses saved in consequence of the seller's breach.

(2) Market price is to be determined as of the place for tender or, in cases of rejection after arrival or revocation of acceptance, as of the place of arrival.

§2-714. Buyer's Damages for Breach in Regard to Accepted Goods.

(1) Where the buyer has accepted goods and given notification (subsection (3) Section 2-607) he may recover as damages for any non-conformity of tender the loss resulting in the ordinary course of events from the seller's breach as determined in any manner which is reasonable.

(2) The measure of damages for breach of warranty is the difference at the time and place of acceptance between the value of the goods accepted and the value they would have had if they had been as warranted, unless special circumstances show proximate damages of a different amount.

(3) In a proper case any incidental and consequential damages under the next section may also be recovered.

§2-715. Buyer's Incidental and Consequential Damages.

(1) Incidental damages resulting from the seller's breach include expenses reasonably incurred in inspection, receipt, transportation and care and custody of goods rightfully rejected, any commercially reasonable charges, expenses or commissions in connection with effecting cover and any other reasonable expense incident to the delay or other breach.

(2) Consequential damages resulting from the seller's breach include

(a) any loss resulting from general or particular requirements and needs of which the seller at the time of contracting had reason to know and which could not reasonably be prevented by cover or otherwise; and

(b) injury to person or property proximately resulting from any breach of warranty.

§2-716. Buyer's Right to Specific Performance or Replevin.

(1) Specific performance may be decreed where the goods are unique or in other proper circumstances.

(2) The decree for specific performance may include such terms and conditions as to payment of the price, damages, or other relief as the court may deem just.

(3) The buyer has a right of replevin for goods identified to the contract if after reasonable effort he is unable to effect cover for such goods or the circumstances reasonably indicate that such effort will be unavailing or if the goods have been shipped under reservation and satisfaction of the security interest in them has been made or tendered.

§2-717. Deduction of Damages From the Price The buyer on notifying the seller of his intention to do so may deduct all or any part of the damages resulting from any breach of the contract from any part of the price still due under the same contract.

§2-718. Liquidation or Limitation of Damages; Deposits.

(1) Damages for breach by either party may be liquidated in the agreement but only at an amount which is reasonable in the light of the anticipated or actual harm caused by the breach, the difficulties of proof of loss, and the inconvenience or nonfeasibility of otherwise obtaining an adequate remedy. A term fixing unreasonably large liquidated damages is void as a penalty.

(2) Where the seller justifiably withholds delivery of goods because of the buyer's breach, the buyer is entitled to restitution of any amount by which the sum of his payments exceeds

(a) the amount to which the seller is entitled by virtue of terms liquidating the seller's damages in accordance with subsection (1), or

(b) in the absence of such terms, twenty per cent of the value of the total performance for which the buyer is obligated under the contract or $500, whichever is smaller.

(3) The buyer's right to restitution under subsection (2) is subject to offset to the extent that the seller establishes

(a) a right to recover damages under the provisions of this Article other than subsection (1), and

(b) the amount or value of any benefits received by the buyer directly or indirectly by reason of the contract.

(4) where a seller has received payment in goods their reasonable value or the proceeds of their resale shall be treated as payments for the purposes of subsection (2); but if the seller has notice of the buyer's breach before reselling goods received in part performance, his resale is subject to the conditions laid down in this Article on resale by an aggrieved seller (Section 2-706).

§2-719. Contractual Modification or Limitation of Remedy.

(1) Subject to the provisions of subsections (2) and (3) of this section and of the preceding section on liquidation and limitation of damages,

(a) the agreement may provide for remedies in addition to or in substitution for those provided in this Article and may limit or alter the measure of damages recoverable under this Article, as by limiting the buyer's remedies to return of the goods and repayment of the price or to

repair and replacement of non-conforming goods or parts; and

(b) resort to a remedy as provided is optional unless the remedy is expressly agreed to be exclusive, in which case it is the sole remedy.

(2) Where circumstances cause an exclusive or limited remedy to fail of its essential purpose, remedy may be had as provided in this Act.

(3) Consequential damages may be limited or excluded unless the limitation or exclusion is unconscionable. Limitation of consequential damages for injury to the person in the case of consumer goods is prima facie unconscionable but limitation of damages where the loss is commercial is not.

§2-720. Effect of "Cancellation" or "Rescission" on Claims for Antecedent Breach. Unless the contrary intention clearly appears, expressions of "cancellation" or "rescission" of the contract or the like shall not be construed as a renunciation or discharge of any claim in damages for an antecedent breach.

§2-721. Remedies for Fraud. Remedies for material misrepresentation or fraud include all remedies available under this Article for non-fraudulent breach. Neither rescission or a claim for rescission of the contract for sale nor rejection or return of the goods shall bar or be deemed inconsistent with a claim for damages or other remedy.

§2-722. Who Can Sue Third Parties for Injury to Goods. Where a third party so deals with goods which have been identified to a contract for sale as to cause actionable injury to a party to that contract

(a) right of action against the third party is in either party to the contract for sale who has title to or a security interest or a special property or an insurable interest in the goods; and if the goods have been destroyed or converted a right of action is also in the party who either bore the risk of loss under the contract for sale or has since the injury assumed that risk as against the other;

(b) if at the time of the injury the party plaintiff did not bear the risk of loss as against the other party to the contract for sale and there is no arrangement between them for disposition of the recovery, his suit or settlement is, subject to his own interest, as a fiduciary for the other party to the contract;

(c) either party may with the consent of the other sue for the benefit of whom it may concern.

§2-723. Proof of Market Price: Time and Place.

(1) If an action based on anticipatory repudiation comes to trial before the time for performance with respect to some or all of the goods, any damages based on market price (Section 2-708 or Section 2-713) shall be determined according to the price of such goods prevailing at the time when the aggrieved party learned of the repudiation.

(2) If evidence of a price prevailing at the times or places described in this Article is not readily available the price prevailing within any reasonable time before or after the time described or at any other place which in commercial judgment

or under usage of trade would serve as a reasonable substitute for the one described may be used, making any proper allowance for the cost of transporting the goods to or from such other place.

(3) Evidence of a relevant price prevailing at a time or place other than the one described in this Article offered by one party is not admissible unless and until he has given the other party such notice as the court finds sufficient to prevent unfair surprise.

§2-724. Admissibility of Market Quotations. Whenever the prevailing price or value of any goods regularly bought and sold in any established commodity market is in issue, reports in official publication or trade journals or in newspapers or periodicals of general circulation published as the reports of such market shall be admissible in evidence. The circumstances of the preparation of such a report may be shown to affect its weight but not its admissibility.

§2-725. Statute of Limitations in Contracts for Sale.

(1) An action for breach of any contract for sale must be commenced within four years after the cause of action has accrued. By the original agreement the parties may reduce the period of limitation to not less than one year but may not extend it.

(2) A cause of action accrues when the breach occurs, regardless of the aggrieved party's lack of knowledge of the breach. A breach of warranty occurs when tender of delivery is made, except that where a warranty explicitly extends to future performance of the goods and discovery of the breach must await the time of such performance the cause of action accrues when the breach is or should have been discovered.

(3) Where an action commenced within the time limited by subsection (1) is so terminated as to leave available a remedy by another action for the same breach such other action may be commenced after the expiration of the time limited and within six months after the termination of the first action unless the termination resulted from voluntary discontinuance or from dismissal for failure or neglect to prosecute.

(4) This section does not alter the law on tolling of the statute of limitations nor does it apply to causes of action which have accrued before this Act becomes effective.

ARTICLE 3: COMMERCIAL PAPER

Part 1: Short Title, Form and Interpretation

§3-101. Short Title. This Article shall be known and may be cited as Uniform Commercial Code—Commercial Paper.

§3-102. Definitions and Index of Definitions.

(1) In this Article unless the context otherwise requires
   (a) "Issue" means the first delivery of an instrument to a holder or a remitter.
   (b) An "order" is a direction to pay and must be more than an authorization or request. It must identify the person to pay with reasonable certainty. It may be

addressed to one or more such persons jointly or in the alternative but not in succession.
   (c) A "promise" is an undertaking to pay and must be more than an acknowledgement of an obligation.
   (d) "Secondary party" means a drawer or endorser.
   (e) "Instrument" means a negotiable instrument.

(2) Other definitions applying to this Article and the sections in which they appear are:
"Acceptance". Section 3-410.
"Accommodation party". Section 3-415.
"Alteration". Section 3-407.
"Certificate of deposit". Section 3-104.
"Certification". Section 3-411.
"Check". Section 3-104.
"Definite time". Section 3-109.
"Dishonor". Section 3-507.
"Draft". Section 3-104.
"Holder in due course". Section 3-302.
"Negotiation". Section 3-202.
"Note". Section 3-104.
"Notice of dishonor". Section 3-508.
"On demand". Section 3-108.
"Presentment". Section 3-504.
"Protest". Section 3-509.
"Restrictive Indorsement". Section 3-205.
"Signature". Section 3-401.

(3) The following definitions in other Articles apply to this Article:
"Account". Section 4-104.
"Banking Day". Section 4-104.
"Clearing house". Section 4-104.
"Collecting bank. Section 4-105.
"Customer". Section 4-104.
"Depositary Bank". Section 4-105.
"Documentary Draft". Section 4-104.
"Intermediary Bank". Section 4-105.
"Item". Section 4-104.
"Midnight deadline". Section 4-104.
"Payor bank". Section 4-105.

(4) In addition Article 1 contains general definitions and principles of construction and interpretation applicable throughout this Article.

§3-103. Limitations on Scope of Article.

(1) This Article does not apply to money, documents of title or investment securities.

(2) The provisions of this Article are subject to the provisions of the Article on Bank Deposits and Collections (Article 4) and Secured Transactions (Article 9).

§3-104. Form of Negotiable Instruments; "Draft"; "Check"; "Certificate of Deposit"; "Note".

(1) Any writing to be a negotiable instrument within this Article must
   (a) be signed by the maker or drawer; and
   (b) contain an unconditional promise or order to pay a sum certain in money and no other promise, order,

obligation or power given by the maker or drawer except as authorized by this Article; and

(c) be payable on demand or at a definite time; and

(d) be payable to order or to bearer.

(2) A writing which complies with the requirements of this section is

(a) a "draft" ("bill of exchange") if it is an order;

(b) a "check" if it is a draft drawn on a bank and payable on demand.

(c) a "certificate of deposit" if it is an acknowledgement by a bank of receipt of money with an engagement to repay it;

(d) a "note" if it is a promise other than a certificate of deposit.

(3) As used in other Articles in this Act, and as the context may require, the terms "draft", "check", "certificate of deposit" and "note" may refer to instruments which are not negotiable within this Article as well as to instruments which are so negotiable.

§3-105. When Promise or Order Unconditional.

(1) A promise or order otherwise unconditional is not made conditional by the fact that the instrument

(a) is subject to implied or constructive conditions; or

(b) states its consideration, whether performed or promised, or the transaction which gave rise to the instrument, or that the promise or order is made or the instrument matures in accordance with or "as per" such transaction; or

(c) refers to or states that it arises out of a separate agreement or refers to a separate agreement for rights as to prepayment or acceleration; or

(d) states that is drawn under a letter of credit; or

(e) states that it is secured, whether by mortgage, reservation of title or otherwise; or

(f) indicates a particular account to be debited or any other fund or source from which reimbursement is expected; or

(g) is limited to payment out of a particular fund or the proceeds of a particular source, if the instrument is issued by a government or governmental agency or unit; or

(h) is limited to payment out of the entire assets of a partnership, unincorporated association, trust or estate by or on behalf of which the instrument is issued.

(2) A promise or order is not unconditional if the instrument

(a) states that it is subject to or governed by any other agreement; or

(b) states that it is to be paid only out of a particular fund or source except as provided in this section. As amended 1962.

§3-106. Sum Certain.

(1) The sum payable is a sum certain even though it is to be paid

(a) with stated interest or by stated installments; or

(b) with stated different rates of interest before and after default or a specified date; or

(c) with a stated discount or addition if paid before or after the date fixed for payment; or

(d) with exchange or less exchange, whether at a fixed rate or at the current rate; or

(e) with costs of collection or an attorney's fee or both upon default.

(2) Nothing in this section shall validate any term which is otherwise illegal.

§3-107. Money.

(1) An instrument is payable in money if the medium of exchange in which it is payable is money at the time the instrument is made. An instrument payable in "currency" or "current funds" is payable in money.

(2) A promise or order to pay a sum stated in a foreign currency is for a sum certain in money and, unless a different medium of payment is specified in the instrument, may be satisfied by payment of that number of dollars which the stated foreign currency will purchase at the buying sight rate for that currency on the day on which the instrument is payable or, if payable on demand, on the day of demand. If such an instrument specifies a foreign currency as the medium of payment the instrument is payable in that currency.

§3-108. Payable on Demand.
Instruments payable on demand include those payable at sight or on presentation and those in which no time for payment is stated.

§3-109. Definite Time.

(1) An instrument is payable at a definite time if by its terms it is payable

(a) on or before a stated date or at a fixed period after a stated date; or

(b) at a fixed period after sight; or

(c) at a definite time subject to any acceleration; or

(d) at a definite time subject to extension at the option of the holder, or to extension to a further definite time at the option of the maker or acceptor or automatically upon or after a specified act or event.

(2) An instrument which by its terms is otherwise payable only upon an act or event uncertain as to time of occurrence is not payable at a definite time even though the act or event has occurred.

§3-110. Payable to Order.

(1) An instrument is payable to order when by its terms it is payable to the order or assigns of any person therein specified with reasonable certainty, or to him or his order, or when it is conspicuously designated on its face as "exchange" or the like and names a payee. It may be payable to the order of

(a) the maker or drawer; or

(b) the drawee; or

(c) a payee who is not maker, drawer or drawee; or

(d) two or more payees together or in the alternative; or

(e) an estate, trust or fund, in which case it is payable to the order of the representative of such estate, trust or fund or his successors; or

(f) an office, or an officer by his title as such in which case it is payable to the principal but the incumbent of the office or his successors may act as if he or they were the holder; or

(**g**) a partnership or unincorporated association, in which case it is payable to the partnership or association and may be indorsed or transferred by any person thereto authorized.

(**2**) An instrument not payable to order is not made so payable by such words as "payable upon return of this instrument properly indorsed."

(**3**) An instrument made payable both to order and to bearer is payable to order unless the bearer words are handwritten or typewritten.

§3-111. Payable to Bearer. An instrument is payable to bearer when by its terms it is payable to

(**a**) bearer or the order of bearer; or

(**b**) a specified person or bearer; or

(**c**) "cash" or the order of "cash", or any other indication which does not purport to designate a specific payee.

§3-112. Terms and Omissions Not Affecting Negotiability.

(**1**) The negotiability of an instrument is not affected by

(**a**) the omission of a statement of any consideration or of the place where the instrument is drawn or payable; or

(**b**) a statement that collateral has been given to secure obligations either on the instrument or otherwise of an obligor on the instrument or that in case of default on those obligations the holder may realize on or dispose of the collateral; or

(**c**) a promise or power to maintain or protect collateral or to give additional collateral; or

(**d**) a term authorizing a confession of judgment on the instrument if it is not paid when due; or

(**e**) a term purporting to waive the benefit of any law intended for the advantage or protection of any obligor; or

(**f**) a term in a draft providing that the payee by indorsing or cashing it acknowledges full satisfaction of an obligation of the drawer; or

(**g**) a statement in a draft drawn in a set of parts (Section 3-801) to the effect that the order is effective only if no other part has been honored.

(**2**) Nothing in this section shall validate any term which is otherwise illegal. As amended 1962.

§3-113. Seal. An instrument otherwise negotiable is within this Article even though it is under a seal.

§3-114. Date, Antedating, Postdating.

(**1**) The negotiability of an instrument is not affected by the fact that it is undated, antedated or postdated.

(**2**) Where an instrument is antedated or postdated the time when it is payable is determined by the stated date if the instrument is payable on demand or at a fixed period after date.

(**3**) Where the instrument or any signature thereon is dated, the date is presumed to be correct.

§3-115. Incomplete Instruments.

(**1**) When a paper whose contents at the time of signing show that it is intended to become an instrument is signed while still incomplete in any necessary respect it cannot be enforced until completed, but when it is completed in accordance with authority given it is effective as completed.

(**2**) If the completion is unauthorized the rules as to material alteration apply (Section 3-407), even though the paper was not delivered by the maker or drawer; but the burden of establishing that any completion is unauthorized is on the party so asserting.

§3-116. Instruments Payable to Two or More Persons. An instrument payable to the order of two or more persons

(**a**) if in the alternative is payable to any one of them and may be negotiated, discharged or enforced by any of them who has possession of it;

(**b**) if not in the alternative is payable to all of them and may be negotiated, discharged or enforced only by all of them.

§3-117. Instruments Payable With Words of Description. An instrument made payable to a named person with the addition of words describing him

(**a**) as agent or officer of a specified person is payable to his principal but the agent or officer may act as if he were the holder;

(**b**) as any other fiduciary for a specified person or purpose is payable to the payee and may be negotiated, discharged or enforced by him;

(**c**) in any other manner is payable to the payee unconditionally and the additional words are without effect on subsequent parties.

§3-118. Ambiguous Terms and Rules of Construction. The following rules apply to every instrument:

(**a**) Where there is doubt whether the instrument is a draft or a note the holder may treat it as either. A draft drawn on the drawer is effective as a note.

(**b**) Handwritten terms control typewritten and printed terms, and typewritten control printed.

(**c**) Words control figures except that if the words are ambiguous figures control.

(**d**) Unless otherwise specified a provision for interest means interest at the judgment rate at the place of payment from the date of the instrument, or if it is undated from the date of issue.

(**e**) Unless the instrument otherwise specifies two or more persons who sign as maker, acceptor or drawer or indorser and as a part of the same transaction are jointly and severally liable even though the instrument contains such words as "I promise to pay."

(**f**) Unless otherwise specified consent to extension authorizes a single extension for not longer than the original period. A consent to extension, expressed in the instrument, is binding on secondary parties and accommodation makers. A holder may not exercise his option to extend an instrument over the objection of a maker or acceptor or other party who in accordance with Section 3-604 tenders full payment when the instrument is due.

§3-119. Other Writings Affecting Instrument.

(**1**) As between the obligor and his immediate obligee or any transferee the terms of an instrument may be modified or affected by any other written agreement executed as a part of the same transaction, except that a holder in due course is not affected by any limitation of his rights arising out of the separate written agreement if he had no notice of the limitation when he took the instrument.

(2) A separate agreement does not affect the negotiability of an instrument.

§3-120. Instruments "Payable Through" Bank. An instrument which states that is is "payable through" a bank or the like designates that bank as a collecting bank to make presentment but does not of itself authorize the bank to pay the instrument.

§3-121. Instruments Payable at Bank.

Note: *If this Act is introduced in the Congress of the United States this section should be omitted. (States to select either alternative.)*

Alternative A—A note or acceptance which states that it is payable at a bank is the equivalent of a draft drawn on the bank payable when it falls due out of any funds of the maker or acceptor in current account or otherwise available for such payment.

Alternative B—A note or acceptance which states that it is payable at a bank is not of itself an order or authorization to the bank to pay it.

§3-122. Accrual of Cause of Action.

(1) A cause of action against a maker or an acceptor accrues
   (a) in the case of a time instrument on the day after maturity;
   (b) in the case of a demand instrument upon its date or, if no date is stated, on the date of issue.

(2) A cause of action against the obligor of a demand or time certificate of deposit accrues upon demand, but demand on a time certificate may not be made until on or after the date of maturity.

(3) A cause of action against a drawer of a draft or an indorser of any instrument accrues upon demand following dishonor of the instrument. Notice of dishonor is a demand.

(4) Unless an instrument provides otherwise, interest runs at the rate provided by law for a judgment
   (a) in the case of a maker, acceptor or other primary obligor of a demand instrument, from the date of demand;
   (b) in all other cases from the date of accrual of the cause of action. As amended 1962.

PART 2: Transfer and Negotiation

§3-201. Transfer: Right to Indorsement.

(1) Transfer of an instrument vests in the transferee such rights as the transferor has therein, except that a transferee who has himself been a party to any fraud or illegality affecting the instrument or who as a prior holder had notice of a defense or claim against it cannot improve his position by taking from a later holder in due course.

(2) A transfer of a security interest in an instrument vests the foregoing rights in the transferee to the extent of the interest transferred.

(3) Unless otherwise agreed any transfer for value of an instrument not then payable to bearer gives the transferee the specifically enforceable right to have the unqualified indorsement of the transferor. Negotiation takes effect only when the indorsement is made and until that time there is no presumption that the transferee is the owner.

§3-202. Negotiation.

(1) Negotiation is the transfer of an instrument in such form that the transferee becomes a holder. If the instrument is payable to order it is negotiated by delivery with any necessary indorsement; if payable to bearer it is negotiated by delivery.

(2) An indorsement must be written by or on behalf of the holder and on the instrument or on a paper so firmly affixed thereto as to become a part thereof.

(3) An indorsement is effective for negotiation only when it conveys the entire instrument or any unpaid residue. If it purports to be of less it operates only as a partial assignment.

(4) Words of assignment, condition, waiver, guaranty, limitation or disclaimer of liability and the like accompanying an indorsement do not affect its character as an indorsement.

§3-203. Wrong or Misspelled Name. Where an instrument is made payable to a person under a misspelled name or one other than his own he may indorse in that name or his own or both; but signature in both names may be required by a person paying or giving value for the instrument.

§3-204. Special Indorsement; Blank Indorsement.

(1) A special indorsement specifies the person to whom or to whose order it makes the instrument payable. Any instrument specially indorsed becomes payable to the order of the special indorsee and may be further negotiated only by his indorsement.

(2) An indorsement in blank specifies no particular indorsee and may consist of a mere signature. An instrument payable to order and indorsed in blank becomes payable to bearer and may be negotiated by delivery alone until specially indorsed.

(3) The holder may convert a blank indorsement into a special indorsement by writing over the signature of the indorser in blank any contract consistent with the character of the indorsement.

§3-205. Restrictive Indorsements. An indorsement is restrictive which either

(a) is conditional; or

(b) purports to prohibit further transfer of the instrument; or

(c) includes the words "for collection", "for deposit", "pay any bank", or like terms signifying a purpose of deposit or collection; or

(d) otherwise states that it is for the benefit or use of the indorser or of another person.

§3-206. Effect of Restrictive Indorsement.

(1) No restrictive indorsement prevents further transfer or negotiation of the instrument.

(2) An intermediary bank, or a payor bank which is not the depositary bank, is neither given notice nor otherwise affected by a restrictive indorsement of any person except the bank's immediate transferor or the person presenting for payment.

(3) Except for an intermediary bank, any transferee under an indorsement which is conditional or includes the words "for collection", "for deposit", "pay any bank", or like terms (subparagraphs (a) and (c) of Section 3-205) must pay or apply any value given by him for or on the security of the instrument consistently with the indorsement and to the extent that he does so he becomes a holder for value. In addition such transferee is a holder in due course if he otherwise complies with the requirements of Section 3-302 on what constitutes a holder in due course.

(4) The first taker under an indorsement for the benefit of the indorser or another person (subparagraph (d) of Section 3-205) must pay or apply any value given by him for or on the security of the instrument consistently with the indorsement and to the extent that he does so he becomes a holder for value. In addition such taker is a holder in due course if he otherwise complies with the requirements of Section 3-302 on what constitutes a holder in due course. A later holder for value is neither given notice nor otherwise affected by such restrictive indorsement unless he has knowledge that a fiduciary or other person has negotiated the instrument in any transaction for his own benefit or otherwise in breach of duty (subsection (2) of Section 3-304).

§3-207. Negotiation Effective Although It May Be Rescinded.

(1) Negotiation is effective to transfer the instrument although the negotiation is

    (a) made by an infant, a corporation exceeding its powers, or any other person without capacity; or

    (b) obtained by fraud, duress or mistake of any kind; or

    (c) part of an illegal transaction; or

    (d) made in breach of duty.

(2) Except as against a subsequent holder in due course such negotiation is in an appropriate case subject to rescission, the declaration of a constructive trust or any other remedy permitted by law.

§3-208. Reacquisition. Where an instrument is returned to or reacquired by a prior party he may cancel any indorsement which is not necessary to his title and reissue or further negotiate the instrument, but any intervening party is discharged as against the reacquiring party and subsequent holders not in due course and if his indorsement has been cancelled is discharged as against subsequent holders in due course as well.

Part 3: Rights of a Holder

§3-301. Rights of a Holder. The holder of an instrument whether or not he is the owner may transfer or negotiate it and, except as otherwise provided in Section 3-603 on payment or satisfaction, discharge it or enforce payment in his own name.

§3-302. Holder in Due Course.

(1) A holder in due course is a holder who takes the instrument

    (a) for value; and

    (b) in good faith; and

    (c) without notice that it is overdue or has been dishonored or of any defense against or claim to it on the part of any person.

(2) A payee may be a holder in due course.

(3) A holder does not become a holder in due course of an instrument:

    (a) by purchase of it at judicial sale or by taking it under legal process; or

    (b) by acquiring it in taking over an estate; or

    (c) by purchasing it as part of a bulk transaction not in regular course of business of the transferor.

(4) A purchaser of a limited interest can be a holder in due course only to the extent of the interest purchased.

§3-303. Taking for Value. A holder takes the instrument for value

    (a) to the extent that the agreed consideration has been performed or that he acquires a security interest in or a lien on the instrument otherwise than by legal process; or

    (b) when he takes the instrument in payment of or as security for an antecedent claim against any person whether or not the claim is due; or

    (c) when he gives a negotiable instrument for it or makes an irrevocable commitment to a third person.

§3-304. Notice to Purchaser.

(1) The purchaser has notice of a claim or defense if

    (a) the instrument is so incomplete, bears such visible evidence of forgery or alteration, or is otherwise so irregular as to call into question its validity, terms or ownership or to create an ambiguity as to the party to pay; or

    (b) the purchaser has notice that the obligation of any party is voidable in whole or in part, or that all parties have been discharged.

(2) The purchaser has notice of a claim against the instrument when he has knowledge that a fiduciary has negotiated the instrument in payment of or as security for his own debt or in any transaction for his own benefit or otherwise in breach of duty.

(3) The purchaser has notice that an instrument is overdue if he has reason to know

    (a) that any part of the principal amount is overdue or that there is an uncured default in payment of another instrument of the same series; or

    (b) that acceleration of the instrument has been made; or

    (c) that he is taking a demand instrument after demand has been made or more than a reasonable length of time after its issue. A reasonable time for a check drawn and payable within the states and territories of the United States and the District of Columbia is presumed to be thirty days.

(4) Knowledge of the following facts does not of itself give the purchaser notice of a defense or claim

(a) that the instrument is antedated or postdated;

(b) that it was issued or negotiated in return for an executory promise or accompanied by a separate agreement, unless the purchaser has notice that a defense or claim has arisen from the terms thereof;

(c) that any party has signed for accommodation;

(d) that an incomplete instrument has been completed, unless the purchaser has notice of any improper completion;

(e) that any person negotiating the instrument is or was a fiduciary;

(f) that there has been default in payment of interest on the instrument or in payment of any other instrument, except one of the same series.

(5) The filing or recording of a document does not of itself constitute notice within the provisions of this Article to a person who would otherwise be a holder in due course.

(6) To be effective notice must be received at such time and in such manner as to give a reasonable opportunity to act on it.

§3-305. Rights of a Holder in Due Course.
To the extent that a holder is a holder in due course he takes the instrument free from

(1) all claims to it on the part of any person; and

(2) all defenses of any party to the instrument with whom the holder has not dealt except

(a) infancy, to the extent that it is a defense to a simple contract; and

(b) such other incapacity, or duress, or illegality of the transaction, as renders the obligation of the party a nullity; and

(c) such misrepresentation as has induced the party to sign the instrument with neither knowledge nor reasonable opportunity to obtain knowledge of its character or its essential terms; and

(d) discharge in insolvency proceedings; and

(e) any other discharge of which the holder has notice when he takes the instrument.

§3-306. Rights of One Not Holder in Due Course.
Unless he has the rights of a holder in due course any person takes the instrument subject to

(a) all valid claims to it on the part of any person; and

(b) all defenses of any party which would be available in an action on a simple contract; and

(c) the defenses of want or failure of consideration, non-performance of any condition precedent, non-delivery, or delivery for a special purpose (Section 3-408); and

(d) the defense that he or a person through whom he holds the instrument acquired it by theft, or that payment or satisfaction to such holder would be inconsistent with the terms of a restrictive indorsement. The claim of any third person to the instrument is not otherwise available as a defense to any party liable thereon unless the third person himself defends the action for such party.

§3-307. Burden of Establishing Signatures, Defenses and Due Course.

(1) Unless specifically denied in the pleading each signature on an instrument is admitted. When the effectiveness of a signature is put in issue

(a) the burden of establishing it is on the party claiming under the signature; but

(b) the signature is presumed to be genuine or authorized except where the action is to enforce the obligation of a purported signer who has died or become incompetent before proof is required.

(2) When signatures are admitted or established, production of the instrument entitles a holder to recover on it unless the defendant establishes a defense.

(3) After it is shown that a defense exists a person claiming the rights of a holder in due course has the burden of establishing that he or some person under whom he claims is in all respects a holder in due course.

Part 4: Liability of Parties

§3-401. Signature.

(1) No person is liable on an instrument unless his signature appears thereon.

(2) A signature is made by use of any name, including any trade or assumed name, upon an instrument, or by any word or mark used in lieu of a written signature

§3-402. Signature in Ambiguous Capacity.
Unless the instrument clearly indicates that a signature is made in some other capacity it is an indorsement.

§3-403. Signature by Authorized Representative.

(1) A signature may be made by an agent or other representative, and his authority to make it may be established as in other cases of representation. No particular form of appointment is necessary to establish such authority.

(2) An authorized representative who signs his own name to an instrument

(a) is personally obligated if the instrument neither names the person represented nor shows that the representative signed in a representative capacity;

(b) except as otherwise established between the immediate parties, is personally obligated if the instrument names the person represented but does not show that the representative signed in a representative capacity, or if the instrument does not name the person represented but does show that the representative signed in a representative capacity.

(3) Except as otherwise established the name of an organization preceded or followed by the name and office of an authorized individual is a signature made in a representative capacity.

§3-404. Unauthorized Signatures.

(1) Any unauthorized signature is wholly inoperative as that

of the person whose name is signed unless he ratifies it or is precluded from denying it; but it operates as the signature of the unauthorized signer in favor of any person who in good faith pays the instrument or takes it for value.

(2) Any unauthorized signature may be ratified for all purposes of this Article. Such ratification does not of itself affect any rights of the person ratifying against the actual signer.

§3-405. Impostors; Signature in Name of Payee.

(1) An indorsement by any person in the name of a named payee is effective if

(a) an impostor by use of the mails or otherwise has induced the maker or drawer to issue the instrument to him or his confederate in the name of the payee; or

(b) a person signing as or on behalf of a maker or drawer intends the payee to have no interest in the instrument; or

(c) an agent or employee of the maker or drawer has supplied him with the name of the payee intending the latter to have no such interest.

(2) Nothing in this section shall affect the criminal or civil liability of the person so indorsing.

§3-406. Negligence Contributing to Alteration or Unauthorized Signature.
Any person who by his negligence substantially contributes to a material alteration of the instrument or to the making of an unauthorized signature is precluded from asserting the alteration or lack of authority against a holder in due course or against a drawee or other payor who pays the instrument in good faith and in accordance with the reasonable commercial standards of the drawee's or payor's business.

§3-407. Alteration.

(1) Any alteration of an instrument is material which changes the contract of any party thereto in any respect, including any such change in

(a) the number or relations of the parties; or

(b) an incomplete instrument, by completing it otherwise than as authorized; or

(c) the writing as signed, by adding to it or by removing any part of it.

(2) As against any person other than a subsequent holder in due course

(a) alteration by the holder which is both fraudulent and material discharges any party whose contract is thereby changed unless that party assents or is precluded from asserting the defense;

(b) no other alteration discharges any party and the instrument may be enforced according to its original tenor, or as to incomplete instruments according to the authority given.

(3) A subsequent holder in due course may in all cases enforce the instrument according to its original tenor, and when an incomplete instrument has been completed, he may enforce it as completed.

§3-408. Consideration.
Want or failure of consideration is a defense as against any person not having the rights of a holder in

due course. (Section 3-305), except that no consideration is necessary for an instrument or obligation thereon given in payment of or as security for an antecedent obligation of any kind. Nothing in this section shall be taken to displace any statute outside this Act under which a promise is enforceable notwithstanding lack or failure of consideration. Partial failure of consideration is a defense pro tanto whether or not the failure is in an ascertained or liquidated amount.

§3-409. Draft Not as Assignment.

(1) A check or other draft does not of itself operate as an assignment of any funds in the hands of the drawee available for its payment, and the drawee is not liable on the instrument until he accepts it.

(2) Nothing in this section shall affect any liability in contract, tort or otherwise arising from any letter of credit or other obligation or representation which is not an acceptance.

§3-410. Definition and Operation of Acceptance.

(1) Acceptance is the drawee's signed engagement to honor the draft as presented. It must be written on the draft, and may consist of his signature alone. It becomes operative when completed by delivery or notification.

(2) A draft may be accepted although it has not been signed by the drawer or is otherwise incomplete or is overdue or has been dishonored.

(3) Where the draft is payable at a fixed period after sight and the acceptor fails to date his acceptance the holder may complete it by supplying a date in good faith.

§3-411. Certification of a Check.

(1) Certification of a check is acceptance. Where a holder procures certification the drawer and all prior indorsers are discharged.

(2) Unless otherwise agreed a bank has no obligation to certify a check.

(3) A bank may certify a check before returning it for lack of proper indorsement. If it does so the drawer is discharged.

§3-412. Acceptance Varying Draft.

(1) Where the drawee's proffered acceptance in any manner varies the draft as presented the holder may refuse the acceptance and treat the draft as dishonored in which case the drawee is entitled to have his acceptance cancelled.

(2) The terms of the draft are not varied by an acceptance to pay at any particular bank or place in the United States, unless the acceptance states that the draft is to be paid only at such bank or place.

(3) Where the holder assents to an acceptance varying the terms of the draft each drawer and indorser who does not affirmatively assent is discharged. As amended 1962.

§3-413. Contract of Maker, Drawer and Acceptor.

(1) The maker or acceptor engages that he will pay the instrument according to its tenor at the time of his engagement or as completed pursuant to Section 3-115 on incomplete instruments.

(2) The drawer engages that upon dishonor of the draft and

any necessary notice of dishonor or protest he will pay the amount of the draft to the holder or to any indorser who takes it up. The drawer may disclaim this liability by drawing without recourse.

(3) By making, drawing or accepting the party admits as against all subsequent parties including the drawee the existence of the payee and his then capacity to indorse.

§3-414. Contract of Indorser; Order of Liability.

(1) Unless the indorsement otherwise specifies (as by such words as "without recourse") every indorser engages that upon dishonor and any necessary notice of dishonor and protest he will pay the instrument according to its tenor at the time of his indorsement to the holder or to any subsequent indorser who takes it up, even though the indorser who takes it up was not obligated to do so.

(2) Unless they otherwise agree indorsers are liable to one another in the order in which they indorse, which is presumed to be the order in which their signatures appear on the instrument.

§3-415. Contract of Accommodation Party.

(1) An accommodation party is one who signs the instrument in any capacity for the purpose of lending his name to another party to it.

(2) When the instrument has been taken for value before it is due the accommodation party is liable in the capacity in which he has signed even though the taker knows of the accommodation.

(3) As against a holder in due course and without notice of the accommodation oral proof of the accommodation is not admissible to give the accommodation party the benefit of discharges dependent on his character as such. In other cases the accommodation character may be shown by oral proof.

(4) An indorsement which shows that it is not in the chain of title is notice of its accommodation character.

(5) An accommodation party is not liable to the party accommodated, and if he pays the instrument has a right of recourse on the instrument against such party.

§3-416. Contract of Guarantor.

(1) "Payment guaranteed" or equivalent words added to a signature mean that the signer engages that if the instrument is not paid when due he will pay it according to its tenor without resort by the holder to any other party.

(2) "Collection guaranteed" or equivalent words added to a signature mean that the signer engages that if the instrument is not paid when due he will pay it according to its tenor, but only after the holder has reduced his claim against the maker or acceptor to judgment and execution has been returned unsatisfied, or after the maker or acceptor has become insolvent or it is otherwise apparent that it is useless to proceed against him.

(3) Words of guaranty which do not otherwise specify guarantee payment.

(4) No words of guaranty added to the signature of a sole maker or acceptor affect his liability on the instrument. Such words added to the signature of one of two or more makers or acceptors create a presumption that the signature is for the accommodation of the others.

(5) When words of guaranty are used presentment, notice of dishonor and protest are not necessary to charge the user.

(6) Any guaranty written on the instrument is enforcible notwithstanding any statute of frauds.

§3-417. Warranties on Presentment and Transfer.

(1) Any person who obtains payment or acceptance and any prior transferor warrants to a person who in good faith pays or accepts that

(a) he has a good title to the instrument or is authorized to obtain payment or acceptance on behalf of one who has a good title; and

(b) he has no knowledge that the signature of the maker or drawer is unauthorized, except that this warranty is not given by a holder in due course acting in good faith

(i) to a maker with respect to the maker's own signature; or

(ii) to a drawer with respect to the drawer's own signature, whether or not the drawer is also the drawee; or

(iii) to an acceptor of a draft if the holder in due course took the draft after the acceptance or obtained the acceptance without knowledge that the drawer's signature was unauthorized; and

(c) the instrument has not been materially altered, except that this warranty is not given by a holder in due course acting in good faith

(i) to the maker of a note; or

(ii) to the drawer of a draft whether or not the drawer is also the drawee; or

(iii) to the acceptor of a draft with respect to an alteration made prior to the acceptance if the holder in due course took the draft after the acceptance, even though the acceptance provided "payable as originally drawn" or equivalent terms; or

(iv) to the acceptor of a draft with respect to an alteration made after the acceptance.

(2) Any person who transfers an instrument and receives consideration warrants to his transferee and if the transfer is by indorsement to any subsequent holder who takes the instrument in good faith that

(a) he has a good title to the instrument or is authorized to obtain payment or acceptance on behalf of one who has a good title and the transfer is otherwise rightful; and

(b) all signatures are genuine or authorized; and

(c) the instrument has not been materially altered; and

(d) no defense of any party is good against him; and

(e) he has no knowledge of any insolvency proceeding instituted with respect to the maker or acceptor or the drawer of an unaccepted instrument.

(3) By transferring "without recourse" the transferor limits the obligation stated in subsection (2) (d) to a warranty that he has no knowledge of such a defense.

(4) A selling agent or broker who does not disclose the fact that he is acting only as such gives the warranties provided in this section, but if he makes such disclosure warrants only his good faith and authority.

§3-418. Finality of Payment or Acceptance. Except for recovery of bank payments as provided in the Article on Bank Deposits and Collections (Article 4) and except for liability for breach of warranty on presentment under the preceding section, payment or acceptance of any instrument is final in favor of a holder in due course, or a person who has in good faith changed his position in reliance on the payment.

§3-419. Conversion of Instrument; Innocent Representative.
(1) An instrument is converted when
    (a) a drawee to whom it is delivered for acceptance refuses to return it on demand; or
    (b) any person to whom it is delivered for payment refuses on demand either to pay or to return it; or
    (c) it is paid on a forged indorsement.
(2) In an action against a drawee under subsection (1) the measure of the drawee's liability is the face amount of the instrument. In any other action under subsection (1) the measure of liability is presumed to be the face amount of the instrument.
(3) Subject to the provisions of this Act concerning restrictive indorsements a representative, including a depositary or collecting bank, who has in good faith and in accordance with the reasonable commercial standards applicable to the business of such representative dealt with an instrument or its proceeds on behalf of one who was not the true owner is not liable in conversion or otherwise to the true owner beyond the amount of any proceeds remaining in his hands.
(4) An intermediary bank or payor bank which is not a depositary bank is not liable in conversion solely by reason of the fact that proceeds of an item indorsed restrictively (Sections 3-205 and 3-206) are not paid or applied consistently with the restrictive indorsement of an indorser other than its immediate transferor.

Part 5: Presentment, Notice of Dishonor and Protest

§3-501. When Presentment, Notice of Dishonor, and Protest Necessary or Permissible.
(1) Unless excused (Section 3-511) presentment is necessary to charge secondary parties as follows:
    (a) presentment for acceptance is necessary to charge the drawer and indorsers of a draft where the draft so provides, or is payable elsewhere than at the residence or place of business of the drawee, or its date of payment depends upon such presentment. The holder may at his option present for acceptance any other draft payable at a stated date;
    (b) presentment for payment is necessary to charge any indorser;
    (c) in the case of any drawer, the acceptor of a draft payable at a bank or the maker of a note payable at a bank, presentment for payment is necessary, but failure to make presentment discharges such drawer, acceptor or maker only as stated in Section 3-502(1)(b).

(2) Unless excused (Section 3-511)
    (a) notice of any dishonor is necessary to charge any indorser;
    (b) in the case of any drawer, the acceptor of a draft payable at a bank or the maker of a note payable at a bank, notice of any dishonor is necessary, but failure to give such notice discharges such drawer, acceptor or maker only as stated in Section 3-502(1) (b).
(3) Unless excused (Section 3-511) protest of any dishonor is necessary to charge the drawer and indorsers of any draft which on its face appears to be drawn or payable outside of the states, territories, dependencies and possessions of the United States, the District of Columbia and the commonwealth of Puerto Rico. The holder may at his option make protest of any dishonor of any other instrument and in the case of a foreign draft may on insolvency of the acceptor before maturity make protest for better security.
(4) Notwithstanding any provision of this section, neither presentment nor notice of dishonor nor protest is necessary to charge an indorser who has indorsed an instrument after maturity. As amended 1966.

§3-502. Unexcused Delay; Discharge.
(1) Where without excuse any necessary presentment or notice of dishonor is delayed beyond the time when it is due
    (a) any indorser is discharged; and
    (b) any drawer or the acceptor of a draft payable at a bank or the maker of a note payable at a bank who because the drawee or payor bank becomes insolvent during the delay is deprived of funds maintained with the drawee or payor bank to cover the instrument may discharge his liability by written assignment to the holder of his rights against the drawee or payor bank in respect of such funds, but such drawer, acceptor or maker is not otherwise discharged.
(2) Where without excuse a necessary protest is delayed beyond the time when it is due any drawer or indorser is discharged.

§3-503. Time of Presentment.
(1) Unless a different time is expressed in the instrument the time for any presentment is determined as follows:
    (a) where an instrument is payable at or a fixed period after a stated date any presentment for acceptance must be made on or before the date it is payable;
    (b) where an instrument is payable after sight it must either be presented for acceptance or negotiated within a reasonable time after date or issue whichever is later;
    (c) where an instrument shows the date on which it is payable presentment for payment is due on that date;
    (d) where an instrument is accelerated presentment for payment is due within a reasonable time after the acceleration;
    (e) with respect to the liability of any secondary party presentment for acceptance or payment of any other instrument is due within a reasonable time after such party becomes liable thereon.

(2) A reasonable time for presentment is determined by the nature of the instrument, any usage of banking or trade and the facts of the particular case. In the case of an uncertified check which is drawn and payable within the United States and which is not a draft drawn by a bank the following are presumed to be reasonable periods within which to present for payment or to initate bank collection:

(a) with respect to the liability of the drawer, thirty days after date or issue whichever is later; and

(b) with respect to the liability of an indorser, seven days after his indorsement.

(3) Where any presentment is due on a day which is not a full business day for either the person making presentment or the party to pay or accept, presentment is due on the next following day which is a full business day for both parties.

(4) Presentment to be sufficient must be made at a reasonable hour, and if at a bank during its banking day.

§3-504. How Presentment Made.

(1) Presentment is a demand for acceptance or payment made upon the maker, acceptor, drawee or other payor by or on behalf of the holder.

(2) Presentment may be made

(a) by mail, in which event the time of presentment is determined by the time of receipt of the mail; or

(b) through a clearing house; or

(c) at the place of acceptance or payment specified in the instrument or if there be none at the place of business or residence of the party to accept or pay. If neither the party to accept or pay nor anyone authorized to act for him is present or accessible at such place presentment is excused.

(3) It may be made

(a) to any one of two or more makers, acceptors, drawees or other payor; or

(b) to any person who has authority to make or refuse the acceptance or payment.

(4) A draft accepted or a note made payable at a bank in the United States must be presented at such bank.

(5) In the cases described in Section 4-210 presentment may be made in the manner and with the result stated in that section. As amended 1962.

§3-505. Rights of Party to Whom Presentment Is Made.

(1) The party to whom presentment is made may without dishonor require

(a) exhibition of the instrument; and

(b) reasonable identification of the person making presentment and evidence of his authority to make it if made for another; and

(c) that the instrument be produced for acceptance or payment at a place specified in it, or if there be none at any place reasonable in the circumstances; and

(d) a signed receipt on the instrument for any partial or full payment and its surrender upon full payment.

(2) Failure to comply with any such requirement invalidates the presentment but the person presenting has a reasonable

time in which to comply and the time for acceptance or payment runs from the time of compliance.

§3-506. Time Allowed For Acceptance or Payment.

(1) Acceptance may be deferred without dishonor until the close of the next business day following presentment. The holder may also in a good faith effort to obtain acceptance and without either dishonor of the instrument or discharge of secondary parties allow postponement of acceptance for an additional business day.

(2) Except as a longer time is allowed in the case of documentary drafts drawn under a letter of credit, and unless an earlier time is agreed to by the party to pay, payment of an instrument may be deferred without dishonor pending reasonable examination to determine whether it is properly payable, but payment must be made in any event before the close of business on the day of presentment.

§3-507. Dishonor; Holder's Right of Recourse; Term Allowing Re-Presentment.

(1) An instrument is dishonored when

(a) a necessary or optional presentment is duly made and due acceptance or payment is refused or cannot be obtained within the prescribed time or in case of bank collections the instrument is seasonably returned by the midnight deadline (Section 4-301); or

(b) presentment is excused and the instrument is not duly accepted or paid.

(2) Subject to any necessary notice of dishonor and protest, the holder has upon dishonor an immediate right of recourse against the drawers and indorsers.

(3) Return of an instrument for lack of proper indorsement is not dishonor.

(4) A term in a draft or an indorsement thereof allowing a stated time for re-presentment in the event of any dishonor of the draft by nonacceptance if a time draft or by nonpayment if a sight draft gives the holder as against any secondary party bound by the term an option to waive the dishonor without affecting the liability of the secondary party and he may present again up to the end of the stated time.

§3-508. Notice of Dishonor.

(1) Notice of dishonor may be given to any person who may be liable on the instrument by or on behalf of the holder or any party who has himself received notice, or any other party who can be compelled to pay the instrument. In addition an agent or bank in whose hands the instrument is dishonored may give notice to his principal or customer or to another agent or bank from which the instrument was received.

(2) Any necessary notice must be given by a bank before its midnight deadline and by any other person before midnight of the third business day after dishonor or receipt of notice of dishonor.

(3) Notice may be given in any reasonable manner. It may be oral or written and in any terms which identify the instrument and state that it has been dishonored. A misdescription which does not mislead the party notified does not vitiate the notice. Sending the instrument bearing a stamp, ticket or writing

stating that acceptance or payment has been refused or sending a notice of debit with respect to the instrument is sufficient.

(4) Written notice is given when sent although it is not received.

(5) Notice to one partner is notice to each although the firm has been dissolved.

(6) When any party is in insolvency proceedings instituted after the issue of the instrument notice may be given either to the party or to the representative of his estate.

(7) When any party is dead or incompetent notice may be sent to his last known address or given to his personal representative.

(8) Notice operates for the benefit of all parties who have rights on the instrument against the party notified.

§3-509. Protest; Noting for Protest.

(1) A protest is a certificate of dishonor made under the hand and seal of a United States consul or vice consul or a notary public or other person authorized to certify dishonor by the law of the place where dishonor occurs. It may be made upon information satisfactory to such person.

(2) The protest must identify the instrument and certify either that due presentment has been made or the reason why it is excused and that the instrument has been dishonored by nonacceptance or nonpayment.

(3) The protest may also certify that notice of dishonor has been given to all parties or to specified parties.

(4) Subject to subsection (5) any necessary protest is due by the time that notice of dishonor is due.

(5) If, before protest is due, an instrument has been noted for protest by the officer to make protest, the protest may be made at any time thereafter as of the date of the noting.

§3-510. Evidence of Dishonor and Notice of Dishonor.

The following are admissible as evidence and create a presumption of dishonor and of any notice of dishonor therein shown:

(a) a document regular in form as provided in the preceding section which purports to be a protest;

(b) the purported stamp or writing of the drawee, payor bank or presenting bank on the instrument or accompanying it stating that acceptance or payment has been refused for reasons consistent with dishonor;

(c) any book or record of the drawee, payor bank, or any collecting bank kept in the usual course of business which shows dishonor, even though there is no evidence of who made the entry.

§3-511. Waived or Excused Presentment, Protest or Notice of Dishonor or Delay Therein.

(1) Delay in presentment, protest or notice of dishonor is excused when the party is without notice that it is due or when the delay is caused by circumstances beyond his control and he exercises reasonable diligence after the cause of the delay ceases to operate.

(2) Presentment or notice or protest as the case may be is entirely excused when

(a) the party to be charged has waived it expressly or by implication either before or after it is due; or

(b) such party has himself dishonored the instrument or has countermanded payment or otherwise has no reason to expect or right to require that the instrument be accepted or paid; or

(c) by reasonable diligence the presentment or protest cannot be made or the notice given.

(3) Presentment is also entirely excused when

(a) the maker, acceptor or drawee of any instrument except a documentary draft is dead or in insolvency proceedings instituted after the issue of the instrument; or

(b) acceptance or payment is refused but not for want of proper presentment.

(4) Where a draft has been dishonored by nonacceptance a later presentment for payment and any notice of dishonor and protest for nonpayment are excused unless in the meantime the instrument has been accepted.

(5) A waiver of protest is also a waiver of presentment and of notice of dishonor even though protest is not required.

(6) Where a waiver of presentment or notice of protest is embodied in the instrument itself it is binding upon all parties; but where it is written above the signature of an indorser it binds him only.

Part 6: Discharge

§3-601. Discharge of Parties.

(1) The extent of the discharge of any party from liability on an instrument is governed by the sections on

(a) payment or satisfaction (Section 3-603); or

(b) tender of payment (Section 3-604); or

(c) cancellation or renunciation (Section 3-605); or

(d) impairment of right of recourse or of collateral (Section 3-606); or

(e) reacquisition of the instrument by a prior party (Section 3-208); or

(f) fraudulent and material alteration (Section 3-407); or

(g) certification of a check (Section 3-411); or

(h) acceptance varying a draft (Section 3-412); or

(i) unexcused delay in presentment or notice of dishonor or protest (Section 3-502).

(2) Any party is also discharged from his liability on an instrument to another party by any other act or agreement with such party which would discharge his simple contract for the payment of money.

(3) The liability of all parties is discharged when any party who has himself no right of action or recourse on the instrument

(a) reacquires the instrument in his own right; or

(b) is discharged under any provision of this Article, except as otherwise provided with respect to discharge for impairment of recourse or of collateral (Section 3-606).

§3-602. Effect of Discharge Against Holder in Due Course.

No discharge of any party provided by this Article is effective against a subsequent holder in due course unless he has notice thereof when he takes the instrument.

§3-603. Payment or Satisfaction.

(1) The liability of any party is discharged to the extent of his payment or satisfaction to the holder even though it is made with knowledge of a claim of another person to the instrument unless prior to such payment or satisfaction the person making the claim either supplies indemnity deemed adequate by the party seeking the discharge or enjoins payment or satisfaction by order of a court of competent jurisdiction in an action in which the adverse claimant and the holder are parties. This subsection does not, however, result in the discharge of the liability

(a) of a party who in bad faith pays or satisfies a holder who acquired the instrument by theft or who (unless having the rights of a holder in due course) holds through one who so acquired it; or

(b) of a party (other than an intermediary bank or a payor bank which is not a depositary bank) who pays or satisfies the holder of an instrument which has been restrictively indorsed in a manner not consistent with the terms of such restrictive indorsement.

(2) Payment or satisfaction may be made with the consent of the holder by any person including a stranger to the instrument. Surrender of the instrument to such a person gives him the rights of a transferee (Section 3-201).

§3-604. Tender of Payment.

(1) Any party making tender of full payment to a holder when or after it is due is discharged to the extent of all subsequent liability for interest, costs and attorney's fees.

(2) The holder's refusal of such tender wholly discharges any party who has a right of recourse against the party making the tender.

(3) Where the maker or acceptor of an instrument payable otherwise than on demand is able and ready to pay at every place of payment specified in the instrument when it is due, it is equivalent to tender.

§3-605. Cancellation and Renunciation.

(1) The holder of an instrument may even without consideration discharge any party

(a) in any manner apparent on the face of the instrument or the indorsement, as by intentionally cancelling the instrument or the party's signature by destruction or mutilation, or by striking out the party's signature; or

(b) by renouncing his rights by a writing signed and delivered or by surrender of the instrument to the party to be discharged.

(2) Neither cancellation or renunciation without surrender of the instrument affects the title thereto.

§3-606. Impairment of Recourse or of Collateral.

(1) The holder discharges any party to the instrument to the extent that without such party's consent the holder

(a) without express reservation of rights releases or agrees not to sue any person against whom the party has to the knowledge of the holder a right of recourse or agrees to suspend the right to enforce against such person the instrument or collateral or otherwise discharges such

person, except that failure or delay in effecting any required presentment, protest or notice of dishonor with respect to any such person does not discharge any party as to whom presentment, protest or notice of dishonor is effective or unnecessary; or

(b) unjustifiably impairs any collateral for the instrument given by or on behalf of the party or any person against whom he has a right of recourse.

(2) By express reservation of rights against a party with a right of recourse the holder preserves

(a) all his rights against such party as of the time when the instrument was originally due; and

(b) the right of the party to pay the instrument as of that time; and

(c) all rights of such party to recourse against others.

Part 7: Advice of International Sight Draft

§3-701. Letter of Advice of International Sight Draft.

(1) A "letter of advice" is a drawer's communication to the drawee that a described draft has been drawn.

(2) Unless otherwise agreed when a bank receives from another bank a letter of advice of an international sight draft the drawee bank may immediately debit the drawer's account and stop the running of interest pro tanto. Such a debit and any resulting credit to any account covering outstanding drafts leaves in the drawer full power to stop payment or otherwise dispose of the amount and creates no trust or interest in favor of the holder.

(3) Unless otherwise agreed and except where a draft is drawn under a credit issued by the drawee, the drawee of an international sight draft owes the drawer no duty to pay an unadvised draft but if it does so and the draft is genuine, may appropriately debit the drawer's account.

Part 8: Miscellaneous

§3-801. Drafts in a Set.

(1) Where a draft is drawn in a set of parts, each of which is numbered and expressed to be an order only if no other part has been honored, the whole of the parts constitutes one draft but a taker of any part may become a holder in due course of the draft.

(2) Any person who negotiates, indorses or accepts a single part of a draft drawn in a set thereby becomes liable to any holder in due course of that part as if it were the whole set, but as between different holders in due course to whom different parts have been negotiated the holder whose title first accrues has all rights to the draft and its proceeds.

(3) As against the drawee the first presented part of a draft drawn in a set is the part entitled to payment, or if a time draft to acceptance and payment. Acceptance of any subsequently presented part renders the drawee liable thereon under subsection (2). With respect both to a holder and to the drawer

payment of a subsequently presented part of a draft payable at sight has the same effect as payment of a check notwithstanding an effective stop order (Section 4-407).

(4) Except as otherwise provided in this section, where any part of a draft in a set is discharged by payment or otherwise the whole draft is discharged.

§3-802. Effect of Instrument on Obligation for which It Is Given.

(1) Unless otherwise agreed where an instrument is taken for an underlying obligation

(a) the obligation is pro tanto discharged if a bank is drawer, maker or acceptor of the instrument and there is no recourse on the instrument against the underlying obligor; and

(b) in any other case the obligation is suspended pro tanto until the instrument is due or if it is payable on demand until its presentment. If the instrument is dishonored action may be maintained on either the instrument or the obligation; discharge of the underlying obligor on the instrument also discharges him on the obligation.

(2) The taking in good faith of a check which is not postdated does not of itself so extend the time on the original obligation as to discharge a surety.

§3-803. Notice to Third Party.
Where a defendant is sued for breach of an obligation for which a third person is answerable over under this Article he may give the third person written notice of the litigation, and the person notified may then give similar notice to any other person who is answerable over to him under this Article. If the notice states that the person notified may come in and defend and that if the person notified does not do so he will in any action against him by the person giving the notice be bound by any determination of fact common to the two litigations, then unless after seasonable receipt of the notice the person notified does come in and defend he is so bound.

§3-804. Lost, Destroyed or Stolen Instruments.
The owner of an instrument which is lost, whether by destruction, theft or otherwise, may maintain an action in his own name and recover from any party liable thereon upon due proof of his ownership, the facts which prevent his production of the instrument and its terms. The court may require security indemnifying the defendant against loss by reason of further claims on the instrument.

§3-805. Instruments Not Payable to Order or to Bearer.
This Article applies to any instrument whose terms do not preclude transfer and which is otherwise negotiable within this Article but which is not payable to order or to bearer, except that there can be no holder in due course of such an instrument.

ARTICLE 4: BANK DEPOSITS AND COLLECTIONS

Part 1: General Provisions and Definitions

§4-401. Short Title.—This Article shall be known and may be cited as Uniform Commercial Code—Bank Deposits and Collections.

§4-102. Applicability.

(1) To the extent that items within this Article are also within the scope of Articles 3 and 8, they are subject to the provisions of those Articles. In the event of conflict the provisions of this Article govern those of Article 3 but the provisions of Article 8 govern those of this Article.

(2) The liability of a bank for action or non-action with respect to any item handled by it for purposes of presentment, payment or collection is governed by the law of the place where the bank is located. In the case of action or non-action by or at a branch or separate office of a bank, its liability is governed by the law of the place where the branch or separate office is located.

§4-103. Variation by Agreement; Measure of Damages; Certain Action Constituting Ordinary Care.

(1) The effect of the provisions of this Article may be varied by agreement except that no agreement can disclaim a bank's responsibility for its own lack of good faith or failure to exercise ordinary care or can limit the measure of damages for such lack of failure; but the parties may by agreement determine the standards by which such responsibility is to be measured if such standards are not manifestly unreasonable.

(2) Federal Reserve regulations and operating letters, clearing house rules, and the like, have the effect of agreements under subsection (1), whether or not specifically assented to by all parties interested in items handled.

(3) Action or non-action approved by this Article or pursuant to Federal Reserve regulations or operating letters constitutes the exercise of ordinary care and, in the absence of special instructions, action or non-action consistent with clearing house rules and the like or with a general banking usage not disapproved by this Article, prima facie constitutes the exercise of ordinary care.

(4) The specification or approval of certain procedures by this Article does not constitute disapproval of other procedures which may be reasonable under the circumstances.

(5) The measure of damages for failure to exercise ordinary care in handling an item is the amount of the item reduced by an amount which could not have been realized by the use of ordinary care, and where there is bad faith it includes other damages, if any, suffered by the party as a proximate consequence.

§4-104. Definitions and Index of Definitions.

(1) In this Article unless the context otherwise requires

(a) "Account" means any account with a bank and includes a checking, time, interest or savings account;

(b) "Afternoon" means the period of a day between noon and midnight;

(c) "Banking day" means that part of any day on which a bank is open to the public for carrying on substantially all of its banking functions;

(d) "Clearing house" means any association of banks or other payors regularly clearing items;

(e) "Customer" means any person having an account with a bank or for whom a bank has agreed to collect items and includes a bank carrying an account with another bank;

(f) "Documentary draft" means any negotiable or non-negotiable draft with accompanying documents, securities or other papers to be delivered against honor of the draft;

(g) "Item" means any instrument for the payment of money even though it is not negotiable but does not include money;

(h) "Midnight deadline" with respect to a bank is midnight on its next banking day following the banking day on which it receives the relevant item or notice or from which the time for taking action commences to run, whichever is later;

(i) "Properly payable" includes the availability of funds for payment at the time of decision to pay or dishonor;

(j) "Settle" means to pay in cash, by clearing house settlement, in a charge or credit or by remittance, or otherwise as instructed. A settlement may be either provisional or final;

(k) "Suspends payments" with respect to a bank means that it has been closed by order of the supervisory authorities, that a public officer has been appointed to take it over or that it ceases or refuses to make payments in the ordinary course of business.

(2) Other definitions applying to this Article and the sections in which they appear are:

"Collecting bank". Section 4-105
"Depositary bank". Section 4-105.
"Intermediary bank". Section 4-105.
"Payor bank". Section 4-105.
"Presenting bank". Section 4-105.
"Remitting bank". Section 4-105.

(3) The following definitions in other Articles apply to this Article:

"Acceptance". Section 3-410.
"Certificate of deposit": Section 3-104
"Certification". Section 3-411.
"Check". Section 3-104.
"Draft". Section 3-104.
"Holder in due course". Section 3-302.
"Notice of dishonor". Section 3-508.
"Presentment". Section 3-504.
"Protest". Section 3-509.
"Secondary party". Section 3-102.

(4) In addition Article 1 contains general definitions and principles of construction and interpretation applicable throughout this Article.

§4-105. "Depositary Bank"; "Intermediary Bank"; "Collecting Bank"; "Payor Bank"; "Presenting Bank"; "Remitting Bank".

In this Article unless the context otherwise requires:

(a) "Depositary bank" means the first bank to which an item is transferred for collection even though it is also the payor bank;

(b) "Payor bank" means a bank by which an item is payable as drawn or accepted;

(c) "Intermediary bank" means any bank to which an item is transferred in course of collection except the depositary or

payor bank;

(d) "Collecting bank" means any bank handling the item for collection except the payor bank;

(e) "Presenting bank" means any bank presenting an item except a payor bank;

(f) "Remitting bank" means any payor or intermediary bank remitting for an item.

§4-106. Separate Office of a Bank.
A branch or separate office of a bank [maintaining its own deposit ledgers] is a separate bank for the purpose of computing the time within which and determining the place at or to which action may be taken or notices or orders shall be given under this Article and under Article 3. As amended 1962.

Note: (*The brackets are to make it optional with the several states whether to require a branch to maintain its own deposit ledgers in order to be considered to be a separate bank for certain purposes under Article 4. In some states "maintaining its own deposit ledgers" is a satisfactory test. In others branch banking practices are such that this test would not be suitable.*

§4-107. Time of Receipt of Items.

(1) For the purpose of allowing time to process items, prove balances and make the necessary entries on its books to determine its position for the day, a bank may fix an afternoon hour of 2 P.M. or later as a cut-off hour for the handling of money and items and the making of entries on its books.

(2) Any item or deposit of money received on any day after a cut-off hour so fixed or after the close of the banking day may be treated as being received at the opening of the next banking day.

§4-108. Delays.

(1) Unless otherwise instructed, a collecting bank in a good faith effort to secure payment may, in the case of specific items and with or without the approval of any person involved, waive, modify or extend time limits imposed or permitted by this Act for a period not in excess of an additonal banking day without discharge of secondary parties and without liability to its transferor or any prior party.

(2) Delay by a collecting bank or payor bank beyond time limits prescribed or permitted by this Act or by instructions is excused if caused by interruption of communication facilities, suspension of payments by another bank, war, emergency conditions or other circumstances beyond the control of the bank provided it exercises such diligence as the circumstances require.

§4-109. Process of Posting.
The "process of posting" means that usual procedure followed by a payor bank in determining to pay an item and in recording the payment including one or more of the following or other steps as determined by the bank:

(a) verification of any signature;
(b) ascertaining that sufficient funds are available;
(c) affixing a "paid" or other stamp;
(d) entering a charge or entry to a customer's account;
(e) correcting or reversing an entry or erroneous action with respect to the item. Added 1962.

Part 2: Collection of Items: Depository and Collecting Banks

§4-201. Presumption and Duration of Agency Status of Collecting Banks and Provisional Status of Credits; Applicability of Article; Item Indorsed "Pay Any Bank".

(1) Unless a contrary intent clearly appears and prior to the time that a settlement given by a collecting bank for an item is or becomes final (subsection (3) of Section 4-211 and Sections 4-212 and 4-213) the bank is an agent or sub-agent of the owner of the item and any settlement given for the item is provisional. This provision applies regardless of the form of indorsement or lack of indorsement and even though credit given for the item is subject to immediate withdrawal as of right or is in fact withdrawn; but the continuance of ownership of an item by its owner and any rights of the owner to proceeds of the item are subject to rights of a collecting bank such as those resulting from outstanding advances on the item and valid rights of setoff. When an item is handled by banks for purposes of presentment, payment and collection, the relevant provisions of this Article apply even though action of parties clearly establishes that a particular bank has purchased the item and is the owner of it.

(2) After an item has been indorsed with the words "pay any bank" or the like, only a bank may acquire the rights of a holder

(a) until the item has been returned to the customer initiating collection; or

(b) until the item has been specially indorsed by a bank to a person who is not a bank.

§4-202. Responsibility for Collection; When Action Seasonable.

(1) A collecting bank must use ordinary care in

(a) presenting an item or sending it for presentment; and

(b) sending notice of dishonor on non-payment or returning an item other than a documentary draft to the bank's transferor [or directly to the depository bank under subsection (2) of Section 4-212] (*see note to Section* 4-212) after learning that the item has not been paid or accepted, as the case may be; and

(c) settling for an item when the bank receives final settlement; and

(d) making or providing for any necessary protest; and

(e) notifying its transferor of any loss or delay in transit within a reasonable time after discovery thereof.

(2) A collecting bank taking proper action before its midnight deadline following receipt of an item, notice or payment acts seasonably; taking proper action within a reasonably longer time may be seasonable but the bank has the burden of so establishing.

(3) Subject to subsection (1) (a), a bank is not liable for the insolvency, neglect, misconduct, mistake or default of another bank or person or for loss or destruction of an item in transit or in the possession of others.

§4-203. Effect of Instructions. Subject to the provision of Article 3 concerning conversion of instruments (Section 3-419) and the provisions of both Article 3 and this Article concerning restrictive indorsements only a collecting bank's transferor can give instructions which affect the bank or constitute notice to it and a collecting bank is not liable to prior parties for any action taken pursuant to such instructions or in accordance with any agreement with its transferor.

§4-204. Methods of Sending and Presenting; Sending Direct to Payor Bank.

(1) A collecting bank must send items by reasonably prompt method taking into consideration any relevant instructions, the nature of the item, the number of such items on hand, and the cost of collection involved and the method generally used by it or others to present such items.

(2) A collecting bank may send

(a) any item direct to the payor bank;

(b) any item direct to any non-bank payor if authorized by its transferor; and

(c) any item other than documentary drafts to any non-bank payor, if authorized by Federal Reserve regulation or operating letter, clearing house rule or the like.

(3) Presentment may be made by a presenting bank at a place where the payor bank has requested that presentment be made. As amended 1962.

§4-205. Supplying Missing Indorsement; No Notice from Prior Indorsement.

(1) A depositary bank which has taken an item for collection may supply any indorsement of the customer which is necessary to title unless the item contains the words "payee's indorsement required" or the like. In the absence of such a requirement a statement placed on the item by the depositary bank to the effect that the item was deposited by a customer or credited to his account is effective as the customer's indorsement.

(2) An intermediary bank, or payor bank which is not a depositary bank, is neither given notice nor otherwise affected by a restrictive indorsement of any person except the bank's immediate transferor.

§4-206. Transfer Between Banks. Any agreed method which identifies the transferor bank is sufficient for the item's further transfer to another bank.

§4-207. Warranties of Customer and Collecting Bank on Transfer or Presentment of Items; Time for Claims.

(1) Each customer or collecting bank who obtains payment or acceptance of an item and each prior customer and collecting bank warrants to the payor bank or other payor who in good faith pays or accepts the item that

(a) he has a good title to the item or is authorized to obtain payment or acceptance on behalf of one who has a good title; and

(b) he has no knowledge that the signature of the maker or drawer is unauthorized, except that this warranty is not given by any customer or collecting bank that is a holder in due course and acts in good faith

(i) to a maker with respect to the maker's own signature; or

(ii) to a drawer with respect to the drawer's own

signature, whether or not the drawer is also the drawee; or

(iii) to an acceptor of an item if the holder in due course took the item after the acceptance or obtained the acceptance without knowledge that the drawer's signature was unauthorized; and

(c) the item has not been materially altered, except that this warranty is not given by any customer or collecting bank that is a holder in due course and acts in good faith

(i) to the maker of a note; or

(ii) to the drawer of a draft whether or not the drawer is also the drawee; or

(iii) to the acceptor of an item with respect to an alteration made prior to the acceptance if the holder in due course took the item after the acceptance, even though the acceptance provided "payable as originally drawn" or equivalent terms; or

(iv) to the acceptor of an item with respect to an alteration made after the acceptance.

(2) Each customer and collecting bank who transfers an item and receives a settlement or other consideration for it warrants to his transferee and to any subsequent collecting bank who takes the item in good faith that

(a) he has a good title to the item or is authorized to obtain payment or acceptance on behalf of one who has a good title and the transfer is otherwise rightful; and

(b) all signatures are genuine or authorized; and

(c) the item has not been materially altered; and

(d) no defense of any party is good against him; and

(e) he has no knowledge of any insolvency proceeding instituted with respect to the maker or acceptor or the drawer of an unaccepted item.

In addition each customer and collecting bank so transferring an item and receiving a settlement or other consideration engages that upon dishonor and any necessary notice of dishonor and protest he will take up the item.

(3) The warranties and the engagement to honor set forth in the two preceding subsections arise notwithstanding the absence of indorsement or words of guaranty or warranty in the transfer or presentment and collecting bank remains liable for their breach despite remittance to its transferor. Damages for breach of such warranties or engagement to honor shall not exceed the consideration received by the customer or collecting bank responsible plus finance charges and expenses related to the item, if any.

(4) Unless a claim for breach of warranty under this section is made within a reasonable time after the person claiming learns of the breach, the person liable is discharged to the extent of any loss caused by the delay in making claim.

§4-208. Security Interest of Collecting Bank in Items, Accompanying Documents and Proceeds.

(1) A bank has a security interest in an item and any accompanying documents or the proceeds of either

(a) in case of an item deposited in an account to the extent to which credit given for the item has been withdrawn or applied;

(b) in case of an item for which it has given credit available for withdrawal as of right, to the extent of the credit given whether or not the credit is drawn upon and whether or not there is a right of charge-back; or

(c) if it makes an advance on or against the item.

(2) When credit which has been given for several items received at one time or pursuant to a single agreement is withdrawn or applied in part the security interest remains upon all the items, any accompanying documents or the proceeds of either. For the purpose of this section, credits first given are first withdrawn.

(3) Receipt by a collecting bank of a final settlement for an item is a realization on its security interest in the item, accompanying documents and proceeds. To the extent and so long as the bank does not receive final settlement for the item or give up possession of the item or accompanying documents for purposes other than collection, the security interest continues and is subject to the provisions of Article 9 except that

(a) no security agreement is necessary to make the security interest enforceable (subsection (1) (b) of Section 9-203); and

(b) no filing is required to perfect the security interest; and

(c) the security interest has priority over conflicting perfected security interests in the item, accompanying documents or proceeds.

§4-209. When Bank Gives Value for Purposes of Holder in Due Course. For purposes of determining its status as a holder in due course, the bank has given value to the extent that it has a security interest in an item provided that the bank otherwise complies with the requirements of Section 3-302 on what constitutes a holder in due course.

§4-210. Presentment by Notice of Item Not Payable by, Through or at a Bank; Liability of Secondary Parties.

(1) Unless otherwise instructed, a collecting bank may present an item not payable by, through or at a bank by sending to the party to accept or pay a written notice that the bank holds the item for acceptance or payment. The notice must be sent in time to be received on or before the day when presentment is due and the bank must meet any requirement of the party to accept or pay under Section 3-505 by the close of the bank's next banking day after it knows of the requirement.

(2) Where presentment is made by notice and neither honor nor request for compliance with a requirement under Section 3-505 is received by the close of business on the day after maturity or in the case of demand items by the close of business on the third banking day after notice was sent, the presenting bank may treat the item as dishonored and charge any secondary party by sending him notice of the facts.

§4-211. Media of Remittance; Provisional and Final Settlement in Remittance Cases.

(1) A collecting bank may take in settlement of an item

(a) a check of the remitting bank or of another bank on

any bank except the remitting bank; or

(b) a cashier's check or similar primary obligation of a remitting bank which is a member of or clears through a member of the same clearing house or group as the collecting bank; or

(c) appropriate authority to charge an account of the remitting bank or of another bank with the collecting bank; or

(d) if the item is drawn upon or payable by a person other than a bank, a cashier's check, certified check or other bank check or obligation.

(2) If before its midnight deadline the collecting bank properly dishonors a remittance check or authorization to charge on itself or presents or forwards for collection a remittance instrument of or on another bank which is of a kind approved by subsection (1) or has not been authorized by it, the collecting bank is not liable to prior parties in the event of the dishonor of such check, instrument or authorization.

(3) A settlement for an item by means of a remittance instrument or authorization to charge is or becomes a final settlement as to both the person making and the person receiving the settlement

(a) if the remittance instrument or authorization to charge is of a kind approved by subsection (1) or has not been authorized by the person receiving the settlement and in either case the person receiving the settlement acts seasonably before its midnight deadline in presenting, forwarding for collection or paying the instrument or authorization,—at the time the remittance instrument or authorization is finally paid by the payor by which it is payable;

(b) if the person receiving the settlement has authorized remittance by a non-bank check or obligation or by a cashier's check or similar primary obligation of or a check upon the payor or other remitting bank which is not of a kind approved by subsection (1) (b),—at the time of the receipt of such remittance check or obligation; or

(c) if in a case not covered by sub-paragraphs (a) or (b) the person receiving the settlement fails to seasonably present, forward for collection, pay or return a remittance instrument or authorization to it to charge before its midnight deadline,—at such midnight deadline.

§4-212. Right of Charge-Back or Refund.

(1) If a collecting bank has made provisional settlement with its customer for an item and itself fails by reason of dishonor, suspension of payments by a bank or otherwise to receive a settlement for the item which is or becomes final, the bank may revoke the settlement given by it, charge back the amount of any credit given for the item to its customer's account or obtain refund from its customer whether or not it is able to return the items if by its midnight deadline or within a longer reasonable time after it learns the facts it returns the item or sends notification of the facts. These rights to revoke, charge-back and obtain refund terminate if and when a settlement for the item received by the bank is or becomes final (subsection (3) of Section 4-211 and subsections (2) and (3) of Section 4-213).

[(2) Within the time and manner prescribed by this section and Section 4-301, an intermediary or payor bank, as the case may be, may return an unpaid item directly to the depositary bank and may send for collection a draft on the depositary bank and obtain reimbursement. In such case, if the depositary bank has received provisional settlement for the item, it must reimburse the bank drawing the draft and any provisional credits for the item between banks shall become and remain final.]

Note: *Direct returns is recognized as an innovation that is not yet established bank practice, and therefore, Paragraph 2 has been bracketed. Some lawyers have doubts whether it should be included in legislation or left to development by agreement.*

(3) A depositary bank which is also the payor may charge-back the amount of an item to its customer's account or obtain refund in accordance with the section governing return of an item received by a payor bank for credit on its books. (Section 4-301).

(4) The right to charge-back is not affected by
(a) prior use of the credit given for the item; or
(b) failure by any bank to exercise ordinary care with respect to the item but any bank so failing remains liable.

(5) A failure to charge-back or claim refund does not affect other rights of the bank against the customer or any other party.

(6) If credit is given in dollars as the equivalent of the value of an item payable in a foreign currency the dollar amount of any charge-back or refund shall be calculated on the basis of the buying sight rate for the foreign currency prevailing on the day when the person entitled to the charge-back or refund learns that it will not receive payment in ordinary course.

§4-213. Final Payment of Item by Payor Bank: When Provisional Debits and Credits Become Final; When Certain Credits Become Available for Withdrawal.

(1) An item is finally paid by a payor bank when the bank has done any of the following, whichever happens first:
(a) paid the item in cash; or
(b) settled for the item without reserving a right to revoke the settlement and without having such right under statute, clearing house rule or agreement; or
(c) completed the process of posting the item to the indicated account of the drawer, maker or other person to be charged therewith; or
(d) made a provisional settlement for the item and failed to revoke the settlement in the time and manner permitted by statute, clearing house rule or agreement.

Upon a final payment under subparagraphs (b), (c) or (e) the payor bank shall be accountable for the amount of the item.

(2) If provisional settlement for an item between the presenting and payor banks is made through a clearing house or by debits or credits in an account between them, then to the extent that provisional debits or credits for the item are entered in accounts between the presenting and payor banks or between the presenting and successive prior collecting banks seriatim, they become final upon final payment of the item by

the payor bank.

(3) If a collecting bank receives a settlement for an item which is or becomes final (subsection (3) of Section 4-211, subsection (2) of Section 4-213) the bank is accountable to its customer for the amount of the item and any provisional credit given for the item in an account with its customer becomes final.

(4) Subject to any right of the bank to apply the credit to an obligation of the customer, credit given by a bank for an item in an account with its customer becomes available for withdrawal as of right

(a) in any case where the bank has received a provisional settlement for the item—when such settlement becomes final and the bank has had a reasonable time to learn that the settlement is final;

(b) in any case where the bank is both a depositary bank and a payor bank and the item is finally paid,—at the opening of the bank's second banking day following receipt of the item.

(5) A deposit of money in a bank is final when made but, subject to any right of the bank to apply the deposit to an obligation of the customer, the deposit becomes available for withdrawal as of right at the opening of the bank's next banking day following receipt of the deposit.

§4-214. Insolvency and Preference.

(1) Any item in or coming into the possession of a payor or collecting bank which suspends payment and which item is not finally paid shall be returned by the receiver, trustee or agent in charge of the closed bank to the presenting bank or the closed bank's customer.

(2) If a payor bank finally pays an item and suspends payments without making a settlement for the item with its customer or the presenting bank which settlement is or becomes final, the owner of the item has a preferred claim against the payor bank.

(3) If a payor bank gives or a collecting bank gives or receives a provisional settlement for an item and thereafter suspends payments, the suspension does not prevent or interfere with the settlement becoming final if such finality occurs automatically upon the lapse of certain time or the happening of certain events (subsection (3) of Section 4-211, subsections (1) (d), (2) and (3) of Section 4-213).

(4) If a collecting bank receives from subsequent parties settlement for an item which settlement is or becomes final and suspends payments without making a settlement for the item with its customer which is or becomes final, the owner of the item has a preferred claim against such collecting bank.

Part 3: Collection of Items: Payor Banks

§4-301. Deferred Posting; Recovery of Payment by Return of Items; Time of Dishonor.

(1) Where an authorized settlement for a demand item (other than a documentary draft) received by a payor bank otherwise than for immediate payment over the counter has been made

before midnight of the banking day of receipt the payor bank may revoke the settlement and recover any payment if before it has made final payment (subsection (1) of Section 4-213) and before its midnight deadline it

(a) returns the item; or

(b) sends written notice of dishonor or nonpayment if the item is held for protest or is otherwise unavailable for return.

(2) If a demand item is received by a payor bank for credit on its books it may return such item or send notice of dishonor and may revoke any credit given or recover the amount thereof withdrawn by its customer, if it acts within the time limit and in the manner specified in the preceding subsection.

(3) Unless previous notice of dishonor has been sent an item is dishonored at the time when for purposes of dishonor it is returned or notice sent in accordance with this section.

(4) An item is returned:

(a) as to an item received through a clearing house, when it is delivered to the presenting or last collecting bank or to the clearing house or is sent or delivered in accordance with its rules; or

(b) in all other cases, when it is sent or delivered to the bank's customer or transferor or pursuant to his instructions.

§4-302. Payor Bank's Responsibility for Late Return of Item.

In the absence of a valid defense such as breach of a presentment warranty (subsection (1) of Section 4-207), settlement effected or the like, if an item is presented on and received by a payor bank the bank is accountable for the amount of

(a) a demand item other than a documentary draft whether properly payable or not if the bank, in any case where it is not also the depositary bank, retains the item beyond midnight of the banking day of receipt without settling for it or, regardless of whether it is also the depositary bank, does not pay or return the item or send notice of dishonor until after its midnight deadline; or

(b) any other properly payable item unless within the time allowed for acceptance or payment of that item the bank either accepts or pays the item or returns it and accompanying documents.

§4-303. When Items Subject to Notice, Stop-Order, Legal Process or Setoff; Order in Which Items May be Charged or Certified.

(1) Any knowledge, notice or stop-order received by, legal process served upon or setoff exercised by a payor bank, whether or not effective under other rules of law to terminate, suspend or modify the bank's right or duty to pay an item or to charge its customer's account for the item, comes too late to so terminate, suspend or modify such right or duty if the knowledge, notice, stop-order or legal process is received or served and a reasonable time for the bank to act thereon expires or the setoff is exercised after the bank has done any of the following:

(a) accepted or certified the item;

(b) paid the item in cash;

(c) settled for the item without reserving a right to revoke the settlement and without having such right under statute, clearing house rule or agreement;

(**d**) completed the process of posting the item to the indicated account of the drawer, maker or other person to be charged therewith or otherwise has evidenced by examination of such indicated account and by action its decision to pay the item; or

(**e**) become accountable for the amount of the item under subsection (1) (d) of Section 4-213 and Section 4-302 dealing with the payor bank's responsibility for late return of items.

(**2**) Subject to the provisions of subsection (1) items may be accepted, paid, certified or charged to the indicated account of its customer in any order convenient to the bank.

Part 4: Relationship between Payor Bank and its Customer

§4-401. When Bank May Charge Customer's Account.

(**1**) As against its customer, a bank may charge against his account any item which is otherwise properly payable from that account even though the charge creates an overdraft.

(**2**) A bank which in good faith makes payment to a holder may charge the indicated account of its customer according to

(**a**) the original tenor of his altered item; or

(**b**) the tenor of his completed item, even though the bank knows the item has been completed unless the bank has notice that the completion was improper.

§4-402. Bank's Liability to Customer for Wrongful Dishonor.

A payor bank is liable to its customer for damages proximately caused by the wrongful dishonor of an item. When the dishonor occurs through mistake liability is limited to actual damages proved. If so proximately caused and proved damages may include damages for an arrest or prosecution of the customer or other consequential damages. Whether any consequential damages are proximately caused by the wrongful dishonor is a question of fact to be determined in each case.

§4-403. Customer's Right to Stop Payment; Burden of Proof of Loss.

(**1**) A customer may by order to his bank stop payment of any item payable for his account but the order must be received at such time and in such manner as to afford the bank a reasonable opportunity to act on it prior to any action by the bank with respect to the item described in Section 4-303.

(**2**) An oral order is binding upon the bank only for fourteen calendar days unless confirmed in writing within that period. A written order is effective for only six months unless renewed in writing.

(**3**) The burden of establishing the fact and amount of loss resulting from the payment of an item contrary to a binding stop payment order is on the customer.

§4-404. Bank Not Obligated to Pay Check More Than Six Months Old.

A bank is under no obligation to a customer having a checking account to pay a check, other than a certified check, which is presented more than six months after its date, but it may charge its customer's account for a payment made thereafter in good faith.

§4-405. Death or Incompetence of Customer.

(**1**) A payor or collecting bank's authority to accept, pay or collect an item or to account for proceeds of its collection if otherwise effective is not rendered ineffective by incompetence of a customer of either bank existing at the time the item is issued or its collection is undertaken if the bank does not know of an adjudication of incompetence. Neither death nor incompetence of a customer revokes such authority to accept, pay, collect or account until the bank knows of the fact of death or of an adjudication of incompetence and has reasonable opportunity to act on it.

(**2**) Even with knowledge a bank may for 10 days after the date of death pay or certify checks drawn on or prior to that date unless ordered to stop payment by a person claiming an interest in the account.

§4-406. Customer's Duty to Discover and Report Unauthorized Signature or Alteration.

(**1**) When a bank sends to its customer a statement of account accompanied by items paid in good faith in support of the debit entries or holds the statement and items pursuant to a request or instructions of its customer or otherwise in a reasonable manner makes the statement and items available to the customer, the customer must exercise reasonable care and promptness to examine the statement and items to discover his unauthorized signature or any alteration on an item and must notify the bank promptly after discovery thereof.

(**2**) If the bank establishes that the customer failed with respect to an item to comply with the duties imposed on the customer by subsection (1) the customer is precluded from asserting against the bank

(**a**) his unauthorized signature or any alteration on the item if the bank also establishes that it suffered a loss by reason of such failure; and

(**b**) an unauthorized signature or alteration by the same wrongdoer on any other item paid in good faith by the bank after the first item and statement was available to the customer for a reasonable period not exceeding fourteen calendar days and before the bank receives notification from the customer of any such unauthorized signature or alteration.

(**3**) The preclusion under subsection (2) does not apply if the customer establishes lack of ordinary care on the part of the bank in paying the item(s).

(**4**) Without regard to care or lack of care of either the customer or the bank a customer who does not within one year from the time the statement and items are made available to the customer (subsection (1) discover and report his unauthorized signature or any alteration on the face or back of the item or does not within 3 years from that time discover and report any unauthorized indorsement is precluded from asserting against the bank such unauthorized signature or indorsement or such alteration.

(5) If under this section a payor bank has a valid defense against a claim of a customer upon or resulting from payment of an item and waives or fails upon request to assert the defense the bank may not assert against any collecting bank or other prior party presenting or transferring the item a claim based upon the unauthorized signature or alteration giving rise to the customer's claim.

§4-407. Payor Bank's Right to Subrogation on Improper Payment.
If a payor bank has paid an item over the stop payment order of the drawer or maker or otherwise under circumstances giving a basis for objection by the drawer or maker, to prevent unjust enrichment and only to the extent necessary to prevent loss to the bank by reason of its payment of the item, the payor bank shall be subrogated to the rights

(a) of any holder in due course on the item against the drawer or maker; and

(b) of the payee or any other holder of the item against the drawer or maker either on the item or under the transaction out of which the item arose; and

(c) of the drawer or maker against the payee or any other holder of the item with respect to the transaction out of which the item arose.

Part 5: Collection of Documentary Drafts

§4-501. Handling of Documentary Drafts; Duty to Send for Presentment and to Notify Customer of Dishonor.
A bank which takes a documentary draft for collection must present or send the draft and accompanying documents for presentment and upon learning that the draft has not been paid or accepted in due course must seasonably notify its customer of such fact even though it may have discounted or bought the draft or extended credit available for withdrawal as of right.

§4-502. Presentment of "On Arrival" Drafts.
When a draft or the relevant instructions require presentment "on arrival", "when goods arrive" or the like, the collecting bank need not present until in its judgment a reasonable time for arrival of the goods has expired. Refusal to pay or accept because the goods have not arrived is not dishonor; the bank must notify its transferor of such refusal but need not present the draft again until it is instructed to do so or learns of the arrival of the goods.

§4-503. Responsibility of Presenting Bank for Documents and Goods; Report of Reasons for Dishonor; Referee in Case of Need.
Unless otherwise instructed and except as provided in Article 5 a bank presenting a documentary draft

(a) must deliver the documents to the drawee on acceptance of the draft if it is payable more than three days after presentment; otherwise, only on payment; and

(b) upon dishonor, either in the case of presentment for acceptance or presentment for payment, may seek and follow instructions from any referee in case of need designated in the draft or if the presenting bank does not choose to utilize his services it must use diligence and good faith to ascertain the reason for dishonor, must

notify its transferor of the dishonor and of the results of its effort to ascertain the reasons therefor and must request instructions.

But the presenting bank is under no obligation with respect to goods represented by the documents except to follow any reasonable instructions seasonably received; it has a right to reimbursement for any expense incurred in following instructions and to prepayment of or indemnity for such expenses.

§4-504. Privilege of Presenting Bank to Deal With Goods; Security Interest for Expenses.

(1) A presenting bank which, following the dishonor of a documentary draft, has seasonably requested instructions but does not receive them within a reasonable time may store, sell, or otherwise deal with the goods in any reasonable manner.

(2) For its reasonable expenses incurred by action under subsection (1) the presenting bank has a lien upon the goods or their proceeds, which may be foreclosed in the same manner as an unpaid seller's lien.

ARTICLE 5: LETTERS OF CREDIT

§5-101. Short Title.
This Article shall be known and may be cited as Uniform Commercial Code—Letters of Credit.

§5-102. Scope.
(1) This Article applies

(a) to a credit issued by a bank if the credit requires a documentary draft or a documentary demand for payment; and

(b) to a credit issued by a person other than a bank if the credit requires that the draft or demand for payment be accompanied by a document of title; and

(c) to a credit issued by a bank or other person if the credit is not within subparagraphs (a) or (b) but conspicuously states that it is a letter of credit or is conspicuously so entitled.

(2) Unless the engagement meets the requirements of subsection (1), this Article does not apply to engagements to make advances or to honor drafts or demands for payment, to authorities to pay or purchase, to guarantees or to general agreements.

(3) This Article deals with some but not all of the rules and concepts of letters of credit as such rules or concepts have developed prior to this act or may hereafter develop. The fact that this Article states a rule does not by itself require, imply or negate application of the same or a converse rule to a situation not provided for or to a person not specified by this Article.

§5-103. Definitions.
(1) In this Article unless the context otherwise requires

(a) "Credit" or "letter of credit" means an engagement by a bank or other person made at the request of a customer and of a kind within the scope of this Article (Section 5-102) that the issuer will honor drafts or other demands for payment upon compliance with the conditions specified in the credit. A credit may be either revocable or irrevocable. The engagement may be either an agreement to honor or a statement that the bank or other person is authorized to honor.

(b) A "documentary draft" or a "documentary demand for payment" is one, honor of which is conditioned upon the presentation of a document or documents. "Document" means any paper including document of title, security, invoice, certificate, notice of default and the like.

(c) An "issuer" is a bank or other person issuing a credit.

(d) A "beneficiary" of a credit is a person who is entitled under its terms to draw or demand payment.

(e) An "advising bank" is a bank which gives notification of the issuance of a credit by another bank.

(f) A "confirming bank" is a bank which engages either that it will itself honor a credit already issued by another bank or that such a credit will be honored by the issuer or a third bank.

(g) A "customer" is a buyer or other person who causes an issuer to issue a credit. The term also includes a bank which procures issuance or confirmation on behalf of that bank's customer.

(2) Other definitions applying to this Article and the sections in which they appear are:

"Notation of Credit". Section 5-108.

"Presenter". Section 5-112(3).

(3) Definitions in other Articles applying to this Article and the sections in which they appear are:

"Accept" or "Acceptance". Section 3-410.

"Contract for sale". Section 2-106.

"Draft". Section 3-104

"Holder in due course". Section 3-302.

"Midnight deadline". Section 4-104.

"Security". Section 8-102.

(4) In addition, Article 1 contains general definitions and principles of construction and interpretation applicable throughout this Article.

§5-104. Formal Requirements; Signing.

(1) Except as otherwise required in subsection (1)(c) Section 5-102 on scope, no particular form of phrasing is required for a credit. A credit must be in writing and signed by the issuer and a confirmation must be in writing and signed by the confirming bank. A modification of the terms of a credit or confirmation must be signed by the issuer or confirming bank.

(2) A telegram may be a sufficient signed writing if it identifies its sender by an authorized authentication. The authentication may be in code and the authorized naming of the issuer in an advice of credit is a sufficient signing.

§5-105. Consideration.
No consideration is necessary to establish a credit or to enlarge or otherwise modify its terms.

§5-106. Time and Effect of Establishment of Credit.

(1) Unless otherwise agreed a credit is established

(a) as regards the customer as soon as a letter of credit is sent to him or the letter of credit or an authorized written advice of its issuance is sent to the beneficiary; and

(b) as regards the beneficiary when he receives a letter of credit or an authorized written advice of its issuance.

(2) Unless otherwise agreed once an irrevocable credit is established as regards the customer it can be modified or revoked only with the consent of the customer and once it is established as regards the beneficiary it can be modified or revoked only with his consent.

(3) Unless otherwise agreed after a revocable credit is established it may be modified or revoked by the issuer without notice to or consent from the customer or beneficiary.

(4) Notwithstanding any modification or revocation of a revocable credit any person authorized to honor or negotiate under the terms of the original credit is entitled to reimbursement for or honor of any draft or demand for payment duly honored or negotiated before receipt of notice of the modification or revocation and the issuer in turn is entitled to reimbursement from its customer.

§5-107. Advice of Credit; Confirmation; Error in Statement of Terms.

(1) Unless otherwise specified an advising bank by advising a credit issued by another bank does not assume any obligation to honor drafts drawn or demands for payment made under the credit but it does assume obligation for the accuracy of its own statement.

(2) A confirming bank by confirming a credit becomes directly obligated on the credit to the extent of its confirmation as though it were its issuer and acquires the rights of an issuer.

(3) Even though an advising bank incorrectly advises the terms of a credit it has been authorized to advise, the credit is established as against the issuer to the extent of its original terms.

(4) Unless otherwise specified the customer bears as against the issuer all risks of transmission and reasonable translation or interpretation of any message relating to a credit.

§5-108. "Notation Credit"; Exhaustion of Credit.

(1) A credit which specifies that any person purchasing or paying drafts drawn or demands for payment made under it must note the amount of the draft or demand on the letter or advice of credit is a "notation credit".

(2) Under a notation credit

(a) a person paying the beneficiary or purchasing a draft or demand for payment from him acquires a right to honor only if the appropriate notation is made and by transferring or forwarding for honor the documents under the credit such a person warrants to the issuer that the notation has been made; and

(b) unless the credit or a signed statement that an appropriate notation has been made accompanies the draft or demand for payment the issuer may delay honor until evidence of notation has been procured which is satisfactory to it but its obligation and that of its customer continue for a reasonable time not exceeding thirty days to obtain such evidence.

(3) If the credit is not a notation credit

(a) the issuer may honor complying drafts or demands for

payment presented to it in the order in which they are presented and is discharged pro tanto by honor of any such draft or demand;

(b) as between competing good faith purchasers of complying drafts or demands the person first purchasing has priority over a subsequent purchaser even though the later purchased draft or demand has been first honored.

§5-109. Issuer's Obligation to Its Customer.

(1) An issuer's obligation to its customer includes good faith and observance of any general banking usage but unless otherwise agreed does not include liability or responsibility

(a) for performance of the underlying contract for sale or other transaction between the customer and the beneficiary; or

(b) for any act or omission of any person other than itself or its own branch or for loss or destruction of a draft, demand or document in transit or in the possession of others; or

(c) based on knowledge or lack of knowledge of any usage of any particular trade.

(2) An issuer must examine documents with care so as to ascertain that on their face they appear to comply with the terms of the credit but unless otherwise agreed assumes no liability or responsibility for the genuineness, falsification or effect of any document which appears on such examination to be regular on its face.

(3) A non-bank issuer is not bound by any banking usage of which it has no knowledge.

§5-110. Availability of Credit in Portions; Presenter's Reservation of Lien or Claim.

(1) Unless otherwise specified a credit may be used in portions in the discretion of the beneficiary.

(2) Unless otherwise specified a person by presenting a documentary draft or demand for payment under a credit relinquishes upon its honor all claims to the documents and a person by transferring such draft or demand or causing such presentment authorizes such relinquishment. An explicit reservation of claim makes the draft or demand non-complying.

§5-111. Warranties on Transfer and Presentment.

(1) Unless otherwise agreed the beneficiary by transferring or presenting a documentary draft or demand for payment warrants to all interested parties that the necessary conditions of the credit have been complied with. This is in addition to any warranties arising under Articles 3, 4, 7 and 8.

(2) Unless otherwise agreed a negotiating, advising, confirming, collecting or issuing bank presenting or transferring a draft or demand for payment under a credit warrants only the matters warranted by a collecting bank under Article 4 and any such bank transferring a document warrants only the matters warranted by an intermediary under Articles 7 and 8.

§5-112. Time Allowed for Honor or Rejection; Withholding Honor or Rejection by Consent; "Presenter".

(1) A bank to which a documentary draft or demand for payment is presented under a credit may without dishonor of the draft, demand or credit

(a) defer honor until the close of the third banking day following receipt of the documents; and

(b) further defer honor if the presenter has expressly or impliedly consented thereto. Failure to honor within the time here specified constitutes dishonor of the draft or demand and of the credit [except as otherwise provided in subsection (4) of Section 5-114 on conditional payment].

Note: *The bracketed language in the last sentence of subsection (1) should be included only if the optional provisions of Section 5-114(4) and (5) are included.*

(2) Upon dishonor the bank may unless otherwise instructed fulfill its duty to return the draft or demand and the documents by holding them at the disposal of the presenter and sending him an advice to that effect.

(3) "Presenter" means any person presenting a draft or demand for payment for honor under a credit even though that person is a confirming bank or other correspondent which is acting under an issuer's authorization.

§5-113. Indemnities.

(1) A bank seeking to obtain (whether for itself or another) honor, negotiation or reimbursement under a credit may give an indemnity to induce such honor, negotiation or reimbursement.

(2) An indemnity agreement inducing honor, negotiation or reimbursement

(a) unless otherwise explicitly agreed applies to defects in the documents but not in the goods; and

(b) unless a longer time is explicitly agreed expires at the end of ten business days following receipt of the documents by the ultimate customer unless notice of objection is sent before such expiration date. The ultimate customer may send notice of objection to the person from whom he received the documents and any bank receiving such notice is under a duty to send notice to its transferor before its midnight deadline.

§5-114. Issuer's Duty and Privilege to Honor; Right to Reimbursement

(1) An issuer must honor a draft or demand for payment which complies with the terms of the relevant credit regardless of whether the goods or documents conform to the underlying contract for sale or other contract between the customer and the beneficiary. The issuer is not excused from honor of such a draft or demand by reason of an additional general term that all documents must be satisfactory to the issuer, but an issuer may require that specified documents must be satisfactory to it.

(2) Unless otherwise agreed when documents appear on their face to comply with the terms of a credit but a required document does not in fact conform to the warranties made on negotiation or transfer of a document of title (Section 7-507) or of a certificated security (Section 8-306) or is forged or fraudulent or there is fraud in the transaction

(a) the issuer must honor the draft or demand for payment if honor is demanded by a negotiating bank or other holder of the draft or demand which has taken the draft or demand under the credit and under circumstances which would make it a holder in due course (Section 3-302) and in an appropriate case would make it a person to whom a document of title has been duly negotiated (Section 7-502) or a bona fide purchaser of a certificated security (Section 8-302); and

(**b**) in all other cases as against its customer, an issuer acting in good faith may honor the draft or demand for payment despite notification from the customer of fraud, forgery or other defect not apparent on the face of the documents but a court of appropriate jurisdiction may enjoin such honor.

(**3**) Unless otherwise agreed an issuer which has duly honored a draft or demand for payment is entitled to immediate reimbursement of any payment made under the credit and to be put in effectively available funds not later than the day before maturity of any acceptance made under the credit.

[(**4**) When a credit provides for payment by the issuer on receipt of notice that the required documents are in the possession of a correspondent or other agent of the issuer

(**a**) any payment made on receipt of such notice is conditional; and

(**b**) the issuer may reject documents which do not comply with the credit if it does so within three banking days following its receipt of the documents; and

(**c**) in the event of such rejection, the issuer is entitled by charge back or otherwise to return to the payment made.]

[(**5**) In the case covered by subsection (4) failure to reject documents within the time specified in sub-paragraph (b) constitutes acceptance of the documents and makes the payment final in favor of the beneficiary.]

Note: *Subsections (4) and 95) are bracketed as optional. If they are included the bracketed language in the last sentence of Section 5-112(1) should also be included.*

§5-115. **Remedy for Improper Dishonor or Anticipatory Repudiation.**

(**1**) When an issuer wrongfully dishonors a draft or demand for payment presented under a credit the person entitled to honor has with respect to any documents the rights of a person in the position of a seller (Section 2-707) and may recover from the issuer the face amount of the draft or demand together with incidental damages under Section 2-710 on seller's incidental damages and interest but less any amount realized by resale or other use or disposition of the subject matter of the transaction. In the event no resale or other utilization is made the documents, goods or other subject matter involved in the transaction must be turned over to the issuer on payment of judgment.

(**2**) When an issuer wrongfully cancels or otherwise repudiates a credit before presentment of a draft or demand for payment drawn under it the beneficiary has the rights of a seller after anticipatory repudiation by the buyer under Section 2-610 if he learns of the repudiation in time reasonably to avoid procurement of the required documents. Otherwise the beneficiary has an immediate right of action for wrongful dishonor.

§5-116. **Transfer and Assignment.**

(**1**) The right to draw under a credit can be transferred or assigned only when the credit is expressly designated as transferable or assignable.

(**2**) Even though the credit specifically states that it is nontransferable or nonassignable the beneficiary may before performance of the conditions of the credit assign his right to proceeds. Such an assignment is an assignment of an account under Article 9 on Secured Transactions and is governed by that Article except that

(**a**) the assignment is ineffective until the letter of credit or advice of credit is delivered to the assignee which delivery constitutes perfection of the security interest under Article 9; and

(**b**) the issuer may honor drafts or demands for payment drawn under the credit until it receives a notification of the assignment signed by the beneficiary which reasonably identifies the credit involved in the assignment and contains a request to pay the assignee; and

(**c**) after what reasonably appears to be such a notification has been received the issuer may without dishonor refuse to accept or pay even to a person otherwise entitled to honor until the letter of credit or advice of credit is exhibited to the issuer.

(**3**) Except where the beneficiary has effectively assigned his right to draw or his right to proceeds, nothing in this section limits his right to transfer or negotiate drafts or demands drawn under the credit.

§5-117. **Insolvency of Bank Holding Funds for Documentary Credit.**

(**1**) Where an issuer or an advising or confirming bank or a bank which has for a customer procured issuance of a credit by another bank becomes insolvent before final payment under the credit and the credit is one to which this Article is made applicable by paragraphs (a) or (b) of Section 5-102(1) on scope, the receipt or allocation of funds or collateral to secure or meet obligations under the credit shall have the following results:

(**a**) to the extent of any funds or collateral turned over after or before the insolvency as indemnity against or specifically for the purpose of payment of drafts or demands for payments drawn under the designated credit, the drafts or demands are entitled to payment in preference over depositors or other general creditors of the issuer or bank; and

(**b**) on expiration of the credit or surrender of the beneficiary's rights under it unused any person who has given such funds or collateral is similarly entitled to return thereof; and

(**c**) a charge to a general or current account with a bank if specifically consented to for the purpose of indemnity against or payment of drafts or demands for payment drawn under the designated credit falls under the same rules as if the funds had been drawn out in cash and then turned over with specific instructions.

(**2**) After honor or reimbursement under this section the customer or other person for whose account the insolvent bank has acted is entitled to receive the documents involved.

ARTICLE 6: BULK TRANSFERS

§6-101. Short Title.   This Article shall be known and may be cited as Uniform Commercial Code—Bulk Transfers.

§6-102. "Bulk Transfers"; Transfers of Equipment; Enterprises Subject to This Article; Bulk Transfers Subject to This Article.

(1) A "bulk transfer" is any transfer in bulk and not in the ordinary course of the transferor's business of a major part of the materials, supplies, merchandise or other inventory (Section 9-109) of an enterprise subject to this Article.

(2) A transfer of a substantial part of the equipment (Section 9-109) of such an enterprise is a bulk transfer if it is made in connection with a bulk transfer of inventory, but not otherwise.

(3) The enterprises subject to this Article are all those whose principal business is the sale of merchandise from stock, including those who manufacture what they sell.

(4) Except as limited by the following section all bulk transfers of goods located within this state are subject to this Article.

§6-103. Transfers Excepted From This Article.   The following transfers are not subject to this Article:

(1) Those made to give security for the performance of an obligation;

(2) General assignments for the benefit of all the creditors of the transferor, and subsequent transfers by the assignee thereunder;

(3) Transfers in settlement or realization of a lien or other security interests;

(4) Sales by executors, administrators, receivers, trustees in bankruptcy, or any public officer under judicial process;

(5) Sales made in the course of judicial or administrative proceedings for the dissolution or reorganization of a corporation and of which notice is sent to the creditors of the corporation pursuant to order of the court or administrative agency;

(6) Transfers to a person maintaining a known place of business in this State who becomes bound to pay the debts of the transferor in full and gives public notice of that fact, and who is solvent after becoming so bound;

(7) A transfer to a new business enterprise organized to take over and continue the business, if public notice of the transaction is given and the new enterprise assumes the debts of the transferor and he receives nothing from the transaction except an interest in the new enterprise junior to the claims of creditors;

(8) Transfers of property which is exempt from execution. Public notice under subsection (6) or subsection (7) may be given by publishing once a week for two consecutive weeks in a newspaper of general circulation where the transferor had its principal place of business in this State an advertisement including the names and addresses of the transferor and transferee and the effective date of the transfer.

§6-104. Schedule of Property, List of Creditors.

(1) Except as provided with respect to auction sales (Section 6-108), a bulk transfer subject to this Article is ineffective against any creditor of the transferor unless:

(a) The transferee requires the transferor to furnish a list of his existing creditors prepared as stated in this section; and

(b) The parties prepare a schedule of the property transferred sufficient to identify it; and

(c) The transferee preserves the list and schedule for six months next following the transfer and permits inspection of either or both and copying therefrom at all reasonable hours by any creditor of the transferor, or files the list and schedule in (a public office to be here identified).

(2) The list of creditors must be signed and sworn to or affirmed by the transferor or his agent. It must contain the names and business addresses of all creditors of the transferor, with the amounts when known, and also the names of all persons who are known to the transferor to assert claims against him even though such claims are disputed. If the transferor is the obligor of an outstanding issue of bonds, debentures or the like as to which there is an indenture trustee, the list of creditors need include only the name and address of the indenture trustee and the aggregate outstanding principal amount of the issue.

(3) Responsibility for the completeness and accuracy of the list of creditors rests on the transferor, and the transfer is not rendered ineffective by errors or omissions therein unless the transferee is shown to have had knowledge.

§6-105. Notice to Creditors.   In addition to the requirements of the preceding section, any bulk transfer subject to this Article except one made by auction sale (Section 6-108) is ineffective against any creditor of the transferor unless at least ten days before he takes possession of the goods or pays for them, whichever happens first, the transferee gives notice of the transfer in the manner and to the persons hereafter provided (Section 6-107).

§6-106. Application of the Proceeds.   In addition to the requirements of the two preceding sections:

(1) Upon every bulk transfer subject to this Article for which new consideration becomes payable except those made by sale at auction it is the duty of the transferee to assure that such consideration is applied so far as necessary to pay those debts of the transferor which are either shown on the list furnished by the transferor (Section 6-104) or filed in writing in the place stated in the notice (Section 6-107) within thirty days after the mailing of such notice. This duty of the transferee runs to all the holders of such debts, and may be enforced by any of them for the benefit of all.

(2) If any of said debts are in dispute the necessary sum may be withheld from distribution until the dispute is settled or adjudicated.

[(3) If the consideration payable is not enough to pay all of the said debts in full distribution shall be made pro rata.]

Note: *This section is bracketed to indicate division of opinion as to whether or not it is a wise provision, and to suggest that this is a point on which State enactments may differ without serious damage to the principle of uniformity.*

In any State where this section is omitted, the following parts of sections, also bracketed in the text, should also be omitted, namely:

Section 6-107(2) (e).
　　　6-108(3) (c).
　　　6-109(2).

In any State where this section is enacted, these other provisions should be also.

Optional Subsection (4)

[(**4**) The transferee may within ten days after he takes possession of the goods pay the consideration into the (specify court) in the county where the transferor had its principal place of business in this state and thereafter may discharge his duty under this section by giving notice by registered or certified mail to all the persons to whom the duty runs that the consideration has been paid into that court and that they should file their claims there. On motion of any interested party, the court may order the distribution of the consideration to the persons entitled to it.]

Note: *Optional subsection (4) is recommended for those states which do not have a general statute providing for payment of money into court.*

§6-107. The Notice.

(**1**) The notice to creditors (Section 6-105) shall state:

(**a**) that a bulk transfer is about to be made; and

(**b**) the names and business addresses of the transferor and transferee, and all other business names and addresses used by the transferor within three years last past so far as known to the transferee; and

(**c**) whether or not all the debts of the transferor are to be paid in full as they fall due as a result of the transaction, and if so, the address to which creditors should send their bills.

(**2**) If the debts of the transferor are not to be paid in full as they fall due or if the transferee is in doubt on that point then the notice shall state further:

(**a**) the location and general description of the property to be transferred and the estimated total of the transferor's debts;

(**b**) the address where the schedule of property and list of creditors (Section 6-104) may be inspected;

(**c**) whether the transfer is to pay existing debts and if so the amount of such debts and to whom owing;

(**d**) whether the transfer is for new consideration and if so the amount of such consideration and the time and place of payment; [and]

[(**e**) if for new consideration the time and place where creditors of the transferor are to file their claims.]

(**3**) The notice in any case shall be delivered personally or sent by registered or certified mail to all the persons shown on the list of creditors furnished by the transferor (Section 6-104) and to all other persons who are known to the transferee to hold or assert claims against the transferor.

Note: *The words in brackets are optional. See Note under § 6-106.*

§6-108. Auction Sales; "Auctioneer".

(**1**) A bulk transfer is subject to this Article even though it is by sale at auction, but only in the manner and with the results stated in this section.

(**2**) The transferor shall furnish a list of his creditors and assist in the preparation of a schedule of the property to be sold, both prepared as before stated (Section 6-104).

(**3**) The person or persons other than the transferor who direct, control or are responsible for the auction are collectively called the "auctioneer". The auctioneer shall:

(**a**) receive and retain the list of creditors and prepare and retain the schedule of property for the period stated in this Article (Section 6-104);

(**b**) give notice of the auction personally or by registered or certified mail at least ten days before it occurs to all persons shown on the list of creditors and to all other persons who are known to him to hold or assert claims against the transferor; [and]

[(**c**) assure that the net proceeds of the auction are applied as provided in this Article (Section 6-106).]

(**4**) Failure of the auctioneer to perform any of these duties does not affect the validity of the sale or the title of the purchasers, but if the auctioneer knows that the auction constitutes a bulk transfer such failure renders the auctioneer liable to the creditors of the transferor as a class for the sums owing to them from the transferor up to but not exceeding the net proceeds of the auction. If the auctioneer consists of several persons their liability is joint and several.

Note: *The words in brackets are optional. See Note under § 6-106.*

§6-109. What Creditors Protected; [Credit for Payment to Particular Creditors].

(**1**) The creditors of the transferor mentioned in this Article are those holding claims based on transactions or events occurring before the bulk transfer, but creditors who become such after notice to creditors is given (Sections 6-105 and 6-107) are not entitled to notice.

[(**2**) Against the aggregate obligation imposed by the provisions of this Article concerning the application of the proceeds (Section 6-106 and subsection (3) (c) of 6-108) the transferee or auctioneer is entitled to credit for sums paid to particular creditors of the transferor, not exceeding the sums believed in good faith at the time of the payment to be properly payable to such creditors.]

Note: *The words in brackets are optional. See Note under § 6-106.*

§6-110. Subsequent Transfers.

When the title of a transferee to property is subject to a defect by reason of his non-compliance with the requirements of this Article, then:

(**1**) a purchaser of any of such property from such transferee who pays no value or who takes with notice of such non-compliance takes subject to such defect, but

(**2**) a purchaser for value in good faith and without such notice takes free of such defect.

§6-111. Limitation of Actions and Levies.

No action under this Article shall be brought nor levy made more than six months after the date on which the transferee took possession of the goods unless the transfer has been concealed. If the transfer has been concealed, actions may be brought or levies made within six months after its discovery.

ARTICLE 7: WAREHOUSE RECEIPTS, BILLS OF LADING AND OTHER DOCUMENTS OF TITLE

Part 1: General

§7-101. Short Title. This Article shall be known and may be cited as Uniform Commercial Code—Documents of Title.

§7-102. Definitions and Index of Definitions.

(1) In this Article, unless the context otherwise requires:

(a) "Bailee" means the person who by a warehouse receipt, bill of lading or other document of title acknowledges possession of goods and contracts to deliver them.

(b) "Consignee" means the person named in a bill to whom or to whose order the bill promises delivery.

(c) "Consignor"means the person named in a bill as the person from whom the goods have been received for shipment.

(d) "Delivery order" means a written order to deliver goods directed to a warehouseman, carrier or other person who in the ordinary course of business issues warehouse receipts or bills of lading.

(e) "Document" means document of title as defined in the general definitions in Article 1 (Section 1-201).

(f) "Goods" means all things which are treated as movable for the purposes of a contract of storage or transportation.

(g) "Issuer" means a bailee who issues a document except that in relation to an unaccepted delivery order it means the person who orders the possessor of goods to deliver. Issuer includes any person for whom an agent or employee purports to act in issuing a document if the agent or employee has real or apparent authority to issue documents, notwithstanding that the issuer received no goods or that the goods were misdescribed or that in any other respect the agent or employee violated his instructions.

(h) "Warehouseman" is a person engaged in the business of storing goods for hire.

(2) Other definitions applying to this Article or to specified Parts thereof, and the sections in which they appear are:

"Duly negotiate". Section 7-501.

"Person entitled under the document". Section 7-403(4).

(3) Definitions in other Articles applying to this Article and the sections in which they appear are:

"Contract for sale". Section 2-106.

"Overseas". Section 2-323.

"Receipt" of goods. Section 2-103.

(4) In addition Article 1 contains general definitions and principles of construction and interpretation applicable throughout this Article.

§7-103. Relation of Article to Treaty, Statute, Tariff, Classification or Regulation. To the extent that any treaty or statute of the United States, regulatory statute of this State or tariff, classification or regulation filed or issued pursuant thereto is applicable, the provisions of this Article are subject thereto.

§7-104. Negotiable and Non-Negotiable Warehouse Receipt, Bill of Lading or Other Document of Title

(1) A warehouse receipt, bill of lading or other document of title is negotiable

(a) if by its terms the goods are to be delivered to bearer or to the order of a named person; or

(b) where recognized in overseas trade, if it runs to a named person or assigns.

(2) Any other document is non-negotiable. A bill of lading in which it is stated that the goods are consigned to a named person is not made negotiable by a provision that the goods are to be delivered only against a written order signed by the same or another named person.

§7-105. Construction Against Negative Implication. The omission from either Part 2 or Part 3 of this Article of a provision corresponding to a provision made in the other Part does not imply that a corresponding rule of law is not applicable.

Part 2: Warehouse Receipts: Special Provisions

§7-201. Who May Issue a Warehouse Receipt; Storage Under Government Bond.

(1) A warehouse receipt may be issued by any warehouseman.

(2) Where goods including distilled spirits and agricultural commodities are stored under a statute requiring a bond against withdrawal or a license for the issuance of receipts in the nature of warehouse receipts, a receipt issued for the goods has like effect as a warehouse receipt even though issued by a person who is the owner of the goods and is not a warehouseman.

§7-202. Form of Warehouse Receipt; Essential Terms; Optional Terms.

(1) A warehouse receipt need not be in any particular form.

(2) Unless a warehouse receipt embodies within its written or printed terms each of the following, the warehouseman is liable for damages caused by the omission to a person injured thereby:

(a) the location of the warehouse where the goods are stored;

(b) the date of issue of the receipt;

(c) the consecutive number of the receipt;

(d) a statement whether the goods received will be delivered to the bearer, to a specified person, or to a specified person or his order;

(e) the rate of storage and handling charges, except that where goods are stored under a field warehousing arrangement a statement of that fact is sufficient on a non-negotiable receipt;

(f) a description of the goods or of the packages containing them:

(g) the signature of the warehouseman, which may be made by his authorized agent;

(h) if the receipt is issued for goods of which the warehouseman is owner, either solely or jointly or in common with others, the fact of such ownership; and

(i) a statement of the amount of advances made and of liabilities incurred for which the warehouseman claims a lien or security interest (Section 7-209). If the precise amount of such advances made or of such liabilities incurred is, at the time of the issue of the receipt, unknown to the warehouseman or to his agent who issues it, a statement of the fact that advances have been made or liabilities incurred and the purpose thereof is sufficient.

(3) A warehouseman may insert in his receipt any other terms which are not contrary to the provisions of this Act and do not impair his obligation of delivery (Section 7-403) or his duty of care (Section 7-204). Any contrary provisions shall be ineffective.

§7-203. Liability for Non-Receipt or Misdescription.
A party to or purchaser for value in good faith of a document of title other than a bill of lading relying in either case upon the description therein of the goods may recover from the issuer damages caused by the non-receipt or misdescription of the goods, except to the extent that the document conspicuously indicates that the issuer does not know whether any part or all of the goods in fact were received or conform to the description, as where the description is in terms of marks or labels or kind, quantity or condition, or the receipt or description is qualified by "contents, condition and quality unknown," "said to contain" or the like, if such indication be true, or the party or purchaser otherwise has notice.

§7-204. Duty of Care; Contractual Limitation of Warehouseman's Liability.
(1) A warehouseman is liable for damages for loss of or injury to the goods caused by his failure to exercise such care in regard to them as a reasonably careful man would exercise under like circumstances but unless otherwise agreed he is not liable for damages which could not have been avoided by the exercise of such care.

(2) Damages may be limited by a term in the warehouse receipt or storage agreement limiting the amount of liability in case of loss or damage, and setting forth a specific liability per article or item, or value per unit of weight, beyond which the warehouseman shall not be liable; provided, however, that such liability may on written request of the bailor at the time of signing such storage agreement or within a reasonable time after receipt of the warehouse receipt be increased on part or all of the goods thereunder, in which event increased rates may be charged based on such increased valuation, but that no such increase shall be permitted contrary to a lawful limitation of liability contained in the warehouseman's tariff, if any. No such limitation is effective with respect to the warehouseman's liability for conversion to his own use.

(3) Reasonable provisions as to the time and manner of presenting claims and instituting actions based on the bailment may be included in the warehouse receipt or tariff.

(4) This section does not impair or repeal . . .

Note: *Insert in subsection (4) a reference to any statute which imposes a higher responsibility upon the warehouseman or invalidates contractual limitations which would be permissible under this Article.*

§7-205. Title Under Warehouse Receipt Defeated in Certain Cases.
A buyer in the ordinary course of business of fungible goods sold and delivered by a warehouseman who is also in the business of buying and selling such goods takes free of any claim under a warehouse receipt even though it has been duly negotiated.

§7-206. Termination of Storage at Warehouseman's Option.
(1) A warehouseman may on notifying the person on whose account the goods are held and any other person known to claim an interest in the goods require payment of any charges and removal of the goods from the warehouse at the termination of the period of storage fixed by the document, or, if no period is fixed, within a stated period not less than thirty days after the notification. If the goods are not removed before the date specified in the notification, the warehouseman may sell them in accordance with the provisions of the section on enforcement of a warehouseman's lien (Section 7-210).

(2) If a warehouseman in good faith believes that the goods are about to deteriorate or decline in value to less than the amount of his lien within the time prescribed in subsection (1) for notification, advertisement and sale, the warehouseman may specify in the notification any reasonable shorter time for removal of the goods and in case the goods are not removed, may sell them at public sale held not less than one week after a single advertisement or posting.

(3) If as a result of a quality or condition of the goods of which the warehouseman had no notice at the time of deposit the goods are a hazard to other property or to the warehouse or to persons, the warehouseman may sell the goods at public or private sale without advertisement on reasonable notification to all persons known to claim an interest in the goods. If the warehouseman after a reasonable effort is unable to sell the goods he may dispose of them in any lawful manner and shall incur no liability by reason of such disposition.

(4) The warehouseman must deliver the goods to any person entitled to them under this Article upon due demand made at any time prior to sale or other disposition under this section.

(5) The warehouseman may satisfy his lien from the proceeds of any sale or disposition under this section but must hold the balance for delivery on the demand of any person to whom he would have been bound to deliver the goods.

§7-207. Goods Must Be Kept Separate; Fungible Goods.
(1) Unless the warehouse receipt otherwise provides, a warehouseman must keep separate the goods covered by each receipt so as to permit at all times identification and delivery of those goods except that different lots of fungible goods may be commingled.

(2) Fungible goods so commingled are owned in common by the persons entitled thereto and the warehouseman is severally liable to each owner for that owner's share. Where because of overissue a mass of fungible goods is insufficient to meet all the receipts which the warehouseman has issued against it, the persons entitled include all holders to whom overissued receipts have been duly negotiated.

§7-208. Altered Warehouse Receipts.
Where a blank in a negotiable warehouse receipt has been filled in without authority, a purchaser for value and without notice of the want of authority may treat the insertion as authorized. Any other

unauthorized alteration leaves any receipt enforceable against the issuer according to its original tenor.

§7-209. Lien of Warehouseman.

(1) A warehouseman has a lien against the bailor on the goods covered by a warehouse receipt or on the proceeds thereof in his possession for charges for storage or transportation (including demurrage and terminal charges), insurance, labor, or charges present or future in relation to the goods, and for expenses necessary for preservation of the goods or reasonably incurred in their sale pursuant to law. If the person on whose account the goods are held is liable for like charges or expenses in relation to other goods whenever deposited and it is stated in the receipt that a lien is claimed for charges and expenses in relation to other goods, the warehouseman also has a lien against him for such charges and expenses whether or not the other goods have been delivered by the warehouseman. But against a person to whom a negotiable warehouse receipt is duly negotiated a warehouseman's lien is limited to charges in an amount or at a rate specified on the receipt or if no charges are so specified then to a reasonable charge for storage of the goods covered by the receipt subsequent to the date of the receipt.

(2) The warehouseman may also reserve a security interest against the bailor for a maximum amount specified on the receipt for charges other than those specified in subsection (1), such as for money advanced and interest. Such a security interest is governed by the Article on Secured Transactions (Article 9).

(3)

  (a) A warehouseman's lien for charges and expenses under subsection (1) or a security interest under subsection (2) is also effective against any person who so entrusted the bailor with possession of the goods that a pledge of them by him to a good faith purchaser for value would have been valid but is not effective against a person as to whom the document confers no right in the goods covered by it under Section 7-503.

  (b) A warehouseman's lien on household goods for charges and expenses in relation to the goods under subsection (1) is also effective against all persons if the depositor was the legal possessor of the goods at the time of deposit. "Household goods" means furniture, furnishings and personal effects used by the depositor in a dwelling.

(4) A warehouseman loses his lien on any goods which he voluntarily delivers or which he unjustifiably refuses to deliver. (As amended in 1966.)

§7-210. Enforcement of Warehouseman's Lien.

(1) Except as provided in subsection (2), a warehouseman's lien may be enforced by public or private sale of the goods in block or in parcels, at any time or place and on any terms which are commercially reasonable, after notifying all persons known to claim an interest in the goods. Such notification must include a statement of the amount due, the nature of the proposed sale and the time and place of any public sale. The fact that a better price could have been obtained by a sale at a different time or in a different method from that selected by the warehouseman is not of itself sufficient to establish that the sale was not made in a commercially reasonable manner. If the warehouseman either sells the goods in the usual manner in any recognized market therefor, or if he sells at the price current in such market at the time of his sale, or if he has otherwise sold in conformity with commercially reasonable practices among dealers in the type of goods sold, he has sold in a commercially reasonable manner. A sale of more goods than apparently necessary to be offered to insure satisfaction of the obligation is not commercially reasonable except in cases covered by the preceding sentence.

(2) A warehouseman's lien on goods other than goods stored by a merchant in the course of his business may be enforced only as follows:

  (a) All persons known to claim an interest in the goods must be notified.

  (b) The notification must be delivered in person or sent by registered or certified letter to the last known address of any person to be notified.

  (c) The notification must include an itemized statement of the claim, a description of the goods subject to the lien, a demand for payment within a specified time not less than ten days after receipt of the notification, and a conspicuous statement that unless the claim is paid within that time the goods will be advertised for sale and sold by auction at a specified time and place.

  (d) The sale must conform to the terms of the notification.

  (e) The sale must be held at the nearest suitable place to that where the goods are held or stored.

  (f) After the expiration of the time given in the notification, an advertisement of the sale must be published once a week for two weeks consecutively in a newspaper of general circulation where the sale is to be held. The advertisement must include a description of the goods, the name of the person on whose account they are being held, and the time and place of the sale. The sale must take place at least fifteen days after the first publication. If there is no newspaper of general circulation where the sale is to be held, the advertisement must be posted at least ten days before the sale in not less than six conspicuous places in the neighborhood of the proposed sale.

(3) Before any sale pursuant to this section any person claiming a right in the goods may pay the amount necessary to satisfy the lien and the reasonable expenses incurred under this section. In that event the goods must not be sold, but must be retained by the warehouseman subject to the terms of the receipt and this Article.

(4) The warehouseman may buy at any public sale pursuant to this section.

(5) A purchaser in good faith of goods sold to enforce a warehouseman's lien takes the goods free of any rights of persons against whom the lien was valid, despite noncompliance by the warehouseman with the requirements of this section.

(6) The warehouseman may satisfy his lien from the proceeds of any sale pursuant to this section but must hold the balance, if any, for delivery on demand to any person to whom he would have been bound to deliver the goods.

(7) The rights provided by this section shall be in addition to all other rights allowed by law to a creditor against his debtor.

(8) Where a lien is on goods stored by a merchant in the course of his business the lien may be enforced in accordance with either subsection (1) or (2).

(9) The warehouseman is liable for damages caused by failure to comply with the requirements for sale under this section and in case of willful violation is liable for conversion. As amended in 1962.

Part 3: Bills of Lading: Special Provisions

§7-301. Liability for Non-Receipt or Misdescription; "Said to Contain"; "Shipper's Load and Count"; Improper Handling.

(1) A consignee of a non-negotiable bill who has given value in good faith or a holder to whom a negotiable bill has been duly negotiated relying in either case upon the description therein of the goods, or upon the date therein shown, may recover from the issuer damages caused by the misdating of the bill or the non-receipt or misdescription of the goods, except to the extent that the document indicates that the issuer does not know whether any part or all of the goods in fact were received or conform to the description, as where the description is in terms of marks or labels or kind, quantity, or condition or the receipt or description is qualified by "contents or condition of contents of packages unknown", "said to contain", "Shipper's weight, load and count" or the like, if such indication be true.

(2) When goods are loaded by an issuer who is a common carrier, the issuer must count the packages of goods if package freight and ascertain the kind and quantity if bulk freight. In such cases "shipper's weight, load and count" or other words indicating that the description was made by the shipper are ineffective except as to freight concealed by packages.

(3) When bulk freight is loaded by a shipper who makes available to the issuer adequate facilities for weighing such freight, an issuer who is a common carrier must ascertain the kind and quantity within a reasonable time after receiving the written request of the shipper to do so. In such cases "shipper's weight" or other words of like purport are ineffective.

(4) The issuer may by inserting in the bill the words "shipper's weight, load and count" or other words of like purport indicate that the goods were loaded by the shipper; and if such statement be true the issuer shall not be liable for damages caused by the improper loading. But their omission does not imply liability for such damages.

(5) The shipper shall be deemed to have guaranteed to the issuer the accuracy at the time of shipment of the description, marks, labels, number, kind, quantity, condition and weight, as furnished by him; and the shipper shall indemnify the issuer against damage caused by inaccuracies in such particulars. The right of the issuer to such indemnity shall in no way limit his responsibility and liability under the contract of carriage to any person other than the shipper.

§7-302. Through Bills of Lading and Similar Documents.

(1) The issuer of a through bill of lading or other document embodying an undertaking to be performed in part by persons acting as its agents or by connecting carriers is liable to anyone entitled to recover on the document for any breach by such other persons or by a connecting carrier of its obligation under the document but to the extent that the bill covers an undertaking to be performed overseas or in territory not contiguous to the continental United States or an undertaking including matters other than transportation this liability may be varied by agreement of the parties.

(2) Where goods covered by a through bill of lading or other document embodying an undertaking to be performed in part by persons other than the issuer are received by any such person, he is subject with respect to his own performance while the goods are in his possession to the obligation of the issuer. His obligation is discharged by delivery of the goods to another such person pursuant to the document, and does not include liability for breach by any other such persons or by the issuer.

(3) The issuer of such through bill of lading or other document shall be entitled to recover from the connecting carrier or such other person in possession of the goods when the breach of the obligation under the document occurred, the amount it may be required to pay to anyone entitled to recover on the document therefor, as may be evidenced by any receipt, judgment, or transcript thereof, and the amount of any expense reasonably incurred by it in defending any action brought by anyone entitled to recover on the document therefor.

§7-303. Diversion; Reconsignment; Change of Instructions.

(1) Unless the bill of lading otherwise provides, the carrier may deliver the goods to a person or destination other than that stated in the bill or may otherwise dispose of the goods on instructions from

    (a) the holder of a negotiable bill; or

    (b) the consignor on a non-negotiable bill notwithstanding contrary instructions from the consignee; or

    (c) the consignee on a non-negotiable bill in the absence of contrary instructions from the consignor, if the goods have arrived at the billed destination or if the consignee is in possession of the bill; or

    (d) the consignee on a non-negotiable bill if he is entitled as against the consignor to dispose of them.

(2) Unless such instructions are noted on a negotiable bill of lading, a person to whom the bill is duly negotiated can hold the bailee according to the original terms.

§7-304. Bills of Lading in a Set.

(1) Except where customary in overseas transportation, a bill of lading must not be issued in a set of parts. The issuer is liable for damages caused by violation of this subsection.

(2) Where a bill of lading is lawfully drawn in a set of parts, each of which is numbered and expressed to be valid only if the goods have not been delivered against any other part, the whole of the parts constitute one bill.

(3) Where a bill of lading is lawfully issued in a set of parts and different parts are negotiated to different persons, the title of the holder to whom the first due negotiation is made prevails as to both the document and the goods even though any later holder may have received the goods from the carrier in good faith and discharged the carrier's obligation by surrender of his part.

(4) Any person who negotiates or transfers a single part of a

bill of lading drawn in a set is liable to holders of that part as if it were the whole set.

(5) The bailee is obliged to deliver in accordance with Part 4 of this Article against the first presented part of a bill of lading lawfully drawn in a set. Such delivery discharges the bailee's obligation on the whole bill.

§7-305. Destination Bills.

(1) Instead of issuing a bill of lading to the consignor at the place of shipment a carrier may at the request of the consignor procure the bill to be issued at destination or at any other place designated in the request.

(2) Upon request of anyone entitled as against the carrier to control the goods while in transit and on surrender of any outstanding bill of lading or other receipt covering such goods, the issuer may procure a substitute bill to be issued at any place designated in the request.

§7-306. Altered Bills of Lading.
An unauthorized alteration or filling in of a blank in a bill of lading leaves the bill enforceable according to its original tenor.

§7-307. Lien of Carrier.

(1) A carrier has a lien on the goods covered by a bill of lading for charges subsequent to the date of its receipt of the goods for storage or transportation (including demurrage and terminal charges) and for expenses necessary for preservation of the goods incident to their transportation or reasonably incurred in their sale pursuant to law. But against a purchaser for value of a negotiable bill of lading a carrier's lien is limited to charges stated in the bill or the applicable tariffs, or if no charges are stated then to a reasonable charge.

(2) A lien for charges and expenses under subsection (1) on goods which the carrier was required by law to receive for transportation is effective against the consignor or any person entitled to the goods unless the carrier had notice that the consignor lacked authority to subject the goods to such charges and expenses. Any other lien under subsection (1) is effective against the consignor and any person who permitted the bailor to have control or possession of the goods unless the carrier had notice that the bailor lacked such authority.

(3) A carrier loses his lien on any goods which he voluntarily delivers or which he unjustifiably refuses to deliver.

§7-308. Enforcement of Carrier's Lien.

(1) A carrier's lien may be enforced by public or private sale of the goods, in block or in parcels, at any time or place and on any terms which are commercially reasonable, after notifying all persons known to claim an interest in the goods. Such notification must include a statement of the amount due, the nature of the proposed sale and the time and place of any public sale. The fact that a better price could have been obtained by a sale at a different time or in a different method from that selected by the carrier is not of itself sufficient to establish that the sale was not made in a commercially reasonable manner. If the carrier either sells the goods in the usual manner in any recognized market therefor or if he sells at the price current in such market at the time of his sale or if he has otherwise sold in conformity with

commercially reasonable practices among dealers in the type of goods sold he has sold in a commercially reasonable manner. A sale of more goods than apparently necessary to be offered to ensure satisfaction of the obligation is not commercially reasonable except in cases covered by the preceding sentence.

(2) Before any sale pursuant to this section any person claiming a right in the goods may pay the amount necessary to satisfy the lien and the reasonable expenses incurred under this section. In that event the goods must not be sold, but must be retained by the carrier subject to the terms of the bill and this Article.

(3) The carrier may buy at any public sale pursuant to this section.

(4) A purchaser in good faith of goods sold to enforce a carrier's lien takes the goods free of any rights of persons against whom the lien was valid, despite noncompliance by the carrier with the requirements of this section.

(5) The carrier may satisfy his lien from the proceeds of any sale pursuant to this section but must hold the balance, if any, for delivery on demand to any person to whom he would have been bound to deliver the goods.

(6) The rights provided by this section shall be in addition to all other rights allowed by law to a creditor against his debtor.

(7) A carrier's lien may be enforced in accordance with either subsection (1) or the procedure set forth in subsection (2) of Section 7-210.

(8) The carrier is liable for damages caused by failure to comply with the requirements for sale under this section and in case of willful violation is liable for conversion.

§7-309. Duty of Care; Contractual Limitation of Carrier's Liability.

(1) A carrier who issues a bill of lading whether negotiable or non-negotiable must exercise the degree of care in relation to the goods which a reasonably careful man would exercise under like circumstances. This subsection does not repeal or change any law or rule of law which imposes liability upon a common carrier for damages not caused by its negligence.

(2) Damages may be limited by a provision that the carrier's liability shall not exceed a value stated in the document if the carrier's rates are dependent upon value and the consignor by the carrier's tariff is afforded an opportunity to declare a higher value or a value as lawfully provided in the tariff, or where no tariff is filed he is otherwise advised of such opportunity; but no such limitation is effective with respect to the carrier's liability for conversion to its own use.

(3) Reasonable provisions as to the time and manner of presenting claims and instituting actions based on the shipment may be included in a bill of lading or tariff.

Part 4: Warehouse Receipts and Bills of Lading: General Obligations

§7-401. Irregularities in Issue of Receipt or Bill or Conduct of Issuer.
The obligations imposed by this Article on an issuer apply to a document of title regardless of the fact that

(**a**) the document may not comply with the requirements of this Article or of any other law or regulation regarding its issue, form or content; or

(**b**) the issuer may have violated laws regulating the conduct of his business; or

(**c**) the goods covered by the document were owned by the bailee at the time the document was issued; or

(**d**) the person issuing the document does not come within the definition of warehouseman if it purports to be a warehouse receipt.

§7-402. Duplicate Receipt or Bill; Overissue.   Neither a duplicate nor any other document of title purporting to cover goods already represented by an outstanding document of the same issuer confers any right in the goods, except as provided in the case of bills in a set, overissue of documents for fungible goods and substitutes for lost, stolen or destroyed documents. But the issuer is liable for damages caused by his overissue or failure to identify a duplicate document as such by conspicuous notation on its face.

§7-403. Obligation of Warehouseman or Carrier to Deliver; Excuse.

(**1**) The bailee must deliver the goods to a person entitled under the document who complies with subsections (2) and (3), unless and to the extent that the bailee establishes any of the following:

(**a**) delivery of the goods to a person whose receipt was rightful as against the claimant;

(**b**) damage to or delay, loss or destruction of the goods for which the bailee is not liable [, but the burden of establishing negligence in such cases is on the person entitled under the document];

Note: *The brackets in (1) (b) indicate that State enactments may differ on this point without serious damage to the principle of uniformity.*

(**c**) previous sale or other disposition of the goods in lawful enforcement of a lien or on warehouseman's lawful termination of storage;

(**d**) the exercise by a seller of his right to stop delivery pursuant to the provisions of the Article on Sales (Section 2-705);

(**e**) a diversion, reconsignment or other disposition pursuant to the provisions of this Article (Section 7-303.) or tariff regulating such right;

(**f**) release, satisfaction or any other fact affording a personal defense against the claimant;

(**g**) any other lawful excuse.

(**2**) A person claiming goods covered by a document of title must satisfy the bailee's lien where the bailee so requests or where the bailee is prohibited by law from delivering the goods until the charges are paid.

(**3**) Unless the person claiming is one against whom the document confers no right under Sec. 7-503(1), he must surrender for cancellation or notation of partial deliveries any outstanding negotiable document covering the goods, and the bailee must cancel the document or conspicuously note the

partial delivery thereon or be liable to any person to whom the document is duly negotiated.

(**4**) "Person entitled under the document" means holder in the case of a negotiable document, or the person to whom delivery is to be made by the terms of or pursuant to written instructions under a non-negotiable document.

§7-404. No Liability for Good Faith Delivery Pursuant to Receipt or Bill.   A bailee who in good faith including observance of reasonable commercial standards has received goods and delivered or otherwise disposed of them according to the terms of the document of title or pursuant to this Article is not liable therefor. This rule applies even though the person from whom he received the goods had no authority to procure the document or to dispose of the goods and even though the person to whom he delivered the goods had no authority to receive them.

Part 5: Warehouse Receipts and Bills of Lading: Negotiation and Transfer

§7-501. Form of Negotiation and Requirements of "Due Negotiation".

(**1**) A negotiable document of title running to the order of a named person is negotiated by his indorsement and delivery. After his indorsement in blank or to bearer any person can negotiate it by delivery alone.

(**2**)

(**a**) A negotiable document of title is also negotiated by delivery alone when by its original terms it runs to bearer.

(**b**) When a document running to the order of a named person is delivered to him the effect is the same as if the document had been negotiated.

(**3**) Negotiation of a negotiable document of title after it has been indorsed to a specified person requires indorsement by the special indorsee as well as delivery.

(**4**) A negotiable document of title is "duly negotiated" when it is negotiated in the manner stated in this section to a holder who purchases it in good faith without notice of any defense against or claim to it on the part of any person and for value, unless it is established that the negotiation is not in the regular course of business or financing or involves receiving the document in settlement or payment of a money obligation.

(**5**) Indorsement of a non-negotiable document neither makes it negotiable nor adds to the transferee's rights.

(**6**) The naming in a negotiable bill of a person to be notified of the arrival of the goods does not limit the negotiability of the bill nor constitute notice to a purchaser thereof of any interest of such person in the goods.

§7-502. Rights Acquired by Due Negotiation.

(**1**) Subject to the following section and to the provisions of Section 7-205 on fungible goods, a holder to whom a negotiable document of title has been duly negotiated acquires thereby:

(**a**) title to the document;

(**b**) title to the goods;

(**c**) all rights accruing under the law of agency or estoppel, including rights to goods delivered to the bailee after the document was issued; and

(**d**) the direct obligation of the issuer to hold or deliver the goods according to the terms of the document free of any defense or claim by him except those arising under the terms of the document or under this Article. In the case of a delivery order the bailee's obligation accrues only upon acceptance and the obligation acquired by the holder is that the issuer and any indorser will procure the acceptance of the bailee.

(**2**) Subject to the following section, title and rights so acquired are not defeated by any stoppage of the goods represented by the document or by surrender of such goods by the bailee, and are not impaired even though the negotiation or any prior negotiation constituted a breach of duty or even though any person has been deprived of possession of the document by misrepresentation, fraud, accident, mistake, duress, loss, theft or conversion, or even though a previous sale or other transfer of the goods or document has been made to a third person.

§7-503. Document of Title to Goods Defeated in Certain Cases.

(**1**) A document of title confers no right in goods against a person who before issuance of the document had a legal interest or a perfected security interest in them and who neither

(**a**) delivered or entrusted them or any document of title covering them to the bailor or his nominee with actual or apparent authority to ship, store or sell or with power to obtain delivery under this Article (Section 7-403) or with power of disposition under this Act (Sections 2-403 and 9-307) or other statute or rule of law; nor

(**b**) acquiesced in the procurement by the bailor or his nominee of any document of title.

(**2**) Title to goods based upon an unaccepted delivery order is subject to the rights of anyone to whom a negotiable warehouse receipt or bill of lading covering the goods has been duly negotiated. Such a title may be defeated under the next section to the same extent as the rights of the issuer or a transferee from the issuer.

(**3**) Title to goods based upon a bill of lading issued to a freight forwarder is subject to the rights of anyone to whom a bill issued by the freight forwarder is duly negotiated; but delivery by the carrier in accordance with Part 4 of this Article pursuant to its own bill of lading discharges the carrier's obligation to deliver.

§7-504. Rights Acquired in the Absence of Due Negotiation; Effect of Diversion; Seller's Stoppage of Delivery.

(**1**) A transferee of a document, whether negotiable or non-negotiable, to whom the document has been delivered but not duly negotiated, acquires the title and rights which his transferor had or had actual authority to convey.

(**2**) In the case of a non-negotiable document, until but not after the bailee receives notification of the transfer, the rights of the transferee may be defeated

(**a**) by those creditors of the transferor who could treat the sale as void under Section 2-402; or

(**b**) by a buyer from the transferor in ordinary course of business if the bailee has delivered the goods to the buyer or received notification of his rights; or

(**c**) as against the bailee by good faith dealings of the bailee with the transferor.

(**3**) A diversion or other change of shipping instructions by the consignor in a non-negotiable bill of lading which causes the bailee not to deliver to the consignee defeats the consignee's title to the goods if they have been delivered to a buyer in ordinary course of business and in any event defeats the consignee's rights against the bailee.

(**4**) Delivery pursuant to a non-negotiable document may be stopped by a seller under Section 2-705, and subject to the requirement of due notification there provided. A bailee honoring the seller's instructions is entitled to be indemnified by the seller against any resulting loss or expense.

§7-505. Indorser Not a Guarantor for Other Parties.
The indorsement of a document of title issued by a bailee does not make the indorser liable for any default by the bailee or by previous indorsers.

§7-506. Delivery Without Indorsement: Right to Compel Indorsement.
The transferee of a negotiable document of title has a specifically enforceable right to have his transferor supply any necessary indorsement but the transfer becomes a negotiation only as of the time the indorsement is supplied.

§7-507. Warranties on Negotiation or Transfer of Receipt or Bill.
Where a person negotiates or transfers a document of title for value otherwise than as a mere intermediary under the next following section, then unless otherwise agreed he warrants to his immediate purchaser only in addition to any warranty made in selling the goods

(**a**) that the document is genuine; and

(**b**) that he has no knowledge of any fact which would impair its validity or worth; and

(**c**) that his negotiation or transfer is rightful and fully effective with respect to the title to the document and the goods it represents.

§7-508. Warranties of Collecting Bank as to Documents.
A collecting bank or other intermediary known to be entrusted with documents on behalf of another or with collection of a draft or other claim against delivery of documents warrants by such delivery of the documents only its own good faith and authority. This rule applies even though the intermediary has purchased or made advances against the claim or draft to be collected.

§7-509. Receipt or Bill: When Adequate Compliance With Commercial Contract.
The question whether a document is adequate to fulfill the obligations of a contract for sale or the conditions of a credit is governed by the Articles on Sales (Article 2) and on Letters of Credit (Article 5).

Part 6: Warehouse Receipts and Bills of Lading: Miscellaneous Provisions–

§7-601. Lost and Missing Documents.

(1) If a document has been lost, stolen or destroyed, a court may order delivery of the goods or issuance of a substitute document and the bailee may without liability to any person comply with such order. If the document was negotiable the claimant must post security approved by the court to indemnify any person who may suffer loss as a result of non-surrender of the document. If the document was not negotiable, such security may be required at the discretion of the court. The court may also in its discretion order payment of the bailee's reasonable costs and counsel fees.

(2) A bailee who without court order delivers goods to a person claiming under a missing negotiable document is liable to any person injured thereby, and if the delivery is not in good faith becomes liable for conversion. Delivery in good faith is not conversion if made in accordance with a filed classification or tariff or, where no classification or tariff is filed, if the claimant posts security with the bailee in an amount as least double the value of the goods at the time of posting to indemnify any person injured by the delivery who files a notice of claim within one year after the delivery.

§7-602. Attachment of Goods Covered by a Negotiable Document.

Except where the document was originally issued upon delivery of the goods by a person who has no power to dispose of them, no lien attaches by virtue of any judicial process to goods in the possession of a bailee for which a negotiable document of title is outstanding unless the document be first surrendered to the bailee or its negotiation enjoined, and the bailee shall not be compelled to deliver the goods pursuant to process until the document is surrendered to him or impounded by the court. One who purchases the document for value without notice of the process or injunction takes free of the lien imposed by judicial process.

§7-603. Conflicting Claims; Interpleader.

If more than one person claims title or possession of the goods, the bailee is excused from delivery until he has had a reasonable time to ascertain the validity of the adverse claims or to bring an action to compel all claimants to interplead and may compel such interpleader, either in defending an action for nondelivery of the goods, or by original action, whichever is appropriate.

ARTICLE 8: INVESTMENT SECURITIES

Part 1: Short Title and General Matters

§8-101. Short Title.

This Article shall be known and may be cited as Uniform Commercial Code—Investment Securities.

§8-102. Definitions and Index of Definitions

(1) In this Article, unless the context otherwise requires:

(a) A "certificated security" is a share, participation, or other interest in property of or an enterprise of the issuer or an obligation of the issuer which is

(i) represented by an instrument issued in bearer or registered form;

(ii) of a type commonly dealt in on securities exchanges or markets or commonly recognized in any area in which it is issued or dealt in as a medium for investment; and

(iii) either one of a class or series or by its terms divisible into a class or series of shares, participations, interest, or obligations.

(b) An "uncertificated security" is a share, participation, or other interest in property or an enterprise of the issuer or an obligation of the issuer which is

(i) not represented by an instrument and the transfer of which is registered upon books maintained for that purpose by or on behalf of the issuer;

(ii) of a type commonly dealt in on securities exchanges or markets; and

(iii) either one of a class or series or by its terms divisible into a class or series of shares, participations, interests, or obligations.

(c) A "security" is either a certificated or an uncertificated security. If a security is certificated, the terms "security" and "certificated security" may mean either the intangible interest, the instrument representing that interest, or both, as the context requires. A writing that is a certificated security is governed by this Article and not by Article 3, even though it also meets the requirements of that Article. This Article does not apply to money. If a certificated security has been retained by or surrendered to the issuer or its transfer agent for reasons other than registration of transfer, other temporary purpose, payment, exchange, or acquisition by the issuer, that security shall be treated as an uncertificated security for purposes of this Article.

(d) A certificated security is in "registered form" if

(i) its specifies a person entitled to the security or the rights it represents, and

(ii) its transfer may be registered upon books maintained for that purpose by or on behalf of the issuer, or the security so states.

(e) A certificated security is in "bearer from" if it runs to bearer according to its terms and not by reason of any indorsement.

(2) A "subsequent purchaser" is a person who takes other than by original issue.

(3) A "clearing corporation" is a corporation registered as a "clearing agency" under the federal securities laws or a corporation:

(a) at least 90 percent of whose capital stock is held by or for one or more organizations, none of which other than a national securities exchange or association, holds in excess of 20 percent of the capital stock of the corporation, and each of which is

(i) subject to supervision or regulation pursuant to the provisions of federal or state banking laws or state insurance laws,

(ii) a broker or dealer or investment company registered under the federal securities laws, or

(iii) a national securities exchange or association registered under the federal securities laws; and

(b) any remaining capital stock of which is held by individuals who have purchased at or prior to the time of their taking office as directors of the corporation and who have purchased only so much of the capital stock as is necessary to permit them to qualify as directors.

(4) A "custodian bank" is a bank or trust company that is supervised and examined by state or federal authority having supervision over banks and is acting as custodian for a clearing corporation.

(5) Other definitions applying to this Article or to specified Parts thereof and the sections in which they appear are:

"Adverse claim".	Section 8-302.
"Bona fide purchaser".	Section 8-302.
"Broker".	Section 8-303.
"Debtor".	Section 9-105.
"Financial intermediary".	Section 8-313.
"Guarantee of the signature".	Section 8-402.
"Intial transaction statement".	Section 8-408.
"Instruction".	Section 8-308.
"Intermediary Bank".	Section 4-105.
"Issuer".	Section 8-201.
"Overissue".	Section 8-104.
"Secured Party".	Section 9-105.
"Security Agreement".	Section 9-105.

(6) In addition Article 1 contains general definitions and principles of construction and interpretation applicable throughout this Article.

§8-103. Issuer's Lien. A lien upon a security in favor of an issuer thereof is valid against a purchaser only if:

(a) the security is certificated and the right of the issuer to the lien is noted conspicuously thereon; or

(b) the security is uncertificated and a notation of the right of the issuer to the lien is contained in the initial transaction statement sent to the purchaser or, if his interest is transferred to him other than by registration of transfer, pledge, or release, the initial transaction statement sent to the registered owner or the registered pledgee.

§8-104. Effect of Overissue; "Overissue".

(1) The provisions of this Article which validate a security or compel its issue or reissue do not apply to the extent that validation, issue, or reissue would result in overissue; but if:

(a) an identical security which does not constitute an overissue is reasonably available for purchase, the person entitled to issue or validation may compel the issuer to purchase the security for him and either to deliver a certificated security or to register the transfer of an uncertificated security to him, against surrender of any certificated security he holds; or

(b) a security is not so available for purchase, the person entitled to issue or validation may recover from the issuer the price he or the last purchaser for value paid for it with interest from the date of his demand.

(2) "Overissue" means the issue of securities in excess of the amount the issuer has corporate power to issue.

§8-105. Certificated Securities Negotiable; Statements and Instructions Not Negotiable; Presumptions.

(1) Certificated securities governed by this Article are negotiable instruments.

(2) Statements (Section 8-408), notices, or the like, sent by the issuer of uncertificated securities and instructions (Section 8-308) are neither negotiable instruments nor certificated securities.

(3) In any action on a security:

(a) unless specifically denied in the pleadings, each signature on a certificated security, in a necessary indorsement, on an initial transaction statement, or on an instruction, is admitted;

(b) if the effectiveness of a signature is put in issue, the burden of establishing it is on the party claiming under the signature, but the signature is presumed to be genuine or authorized;

(c) if signatures on a certificated security are admitted or established, production of the security entitles a holder to recover on it unless the defendant establishes a defense or a defect going to the validity of the security;

(d) if signatures on an initial transaction statement are admitted or established, the facts stated in the statement are presumed to be true as of the time of its issuance; and

(e) after it is shown that a defense or defect exists, the plaintiff has the burden of establishing that he or some person under whom he claims is a person against whom the defense or defect is ineffective (Section 8-202).

§8-106. Applicability. The law (including the conflict of law rules) of the jurisdiction of organization of the issuer governs the validity of a security, the effectiveness of registration by the issuer, and the rights and duties of the issuer with respect to:

(a) registration of transfer of a certificated security;

(b) registration of transfer, pledge, or release of an uncertificated security; and

(c) sending of statements of uncertificated securities.

§8-107. Securities Transferable; Action for Price.

(1) Unless otherwise agreed and subject to any applicable law or regulation respecting short sales, a person obligated to transfer securities may transfer any certificated security of the specified issue in bearer form or registered in the name of the transferee, or indorsed to him or in blank, or he may transfer an equivalent uncertificated security to the transferee or a person designated by the transferee.

(2) If the buyer fails to pay the price as it comes due under a contract of sale, the seller may recover the price of:

(a) certificated securities accepted by the buyer:

(b) uncertificated securities that have been transferred to

the buyer or a person designated by the buyer; and

(**c**) other securities if efforts at their resale would be unduly burdensome or if there is no readily available market for their resale.

§8-108. Registration of Pledge and Release of Uncertificated Securities.

A security interest in an uncertificated security may be evidenced by the registration of pledge to the secured party or a person designated by him. There can be no more than one registered pledge of an uncertificated security at any time. The registered owner of an uncertificated security is the person in whose name the security is registered, even if the security is subject to a registered pledge. The rights of a registered pledgee of an uncertificated security under this Article are terminated by the registration of release.

Part 2: Issue—Issuer

§8-201. "Issuer".

(**1**) With respect to obligations on or defenses to a security, "issuer" includes a person who:

(**a**) places or authorizes the placing of his name on a certificated security (otherwise than as authenticating trustee, registrar, transfer agent, or the like) to evidence that it represents a share, participation, or other interest in his property or in an enterprise, or to evidence his duty to perform an obligation represented by the certificated security;

(**b**) creates shares, participations or other interests in his property or in an enterprise or undertakes obligations, which shares, participations, interests, or obligations are uncertificated securities;

(**c**) directly or indirectly creates fractional interests in his rights or property, which fractional interests are represented by certificated securities; or

(**d**) becomes responsible for or in place of any other person described as an issuer in this section.

(**2**) With respect to obligations on or defenses to a security, a guarantor is an issuer to the extent of his guaranty, whether or not his obligation is noted on a certificated security or on statements of uncertificated securities sent pursuant to Section 8-408.

(**3**) With respect to registration of transfer, pledge, or release (Part 4 of this Article), "issuer" means a person on whose behalf transfer books are maintained.

§8-202. Issuer's Responsibility and Defenses; Notice of Defect or Defense.

(**1**) Even against a purchaser for value and without notice, the terms of a security include:

(**a**) if the security is certificated, those stated on the security;

(**b**) if the security is uncertificated, those contained in the initial transaction statement sent to such purchaser, or if his interest is transferred to him other than by registration of transfer, pledge, or release, the initial transaction

statement sent to the registered owner or registered pledgee; and

(**c**) those made part of the security by reference, on the certificated security or in the initial transaction statement, to another instrument, indenture, or document or to a constitution, statute, ordinance, rule, regulation, order or the like, to the extent that the terms referred to do not conflict with the terms stated on the certificated security or contained in the statement. A reference under this paragraph does not of itself charge a purchaser for value with notice of a defect going to the validity of the security, even though the certificated security or statement expressly states that a person accepting it admits notice.

(**2**) A certificated security in the hands of a purchaser for value or an uncertificated security as to which an initial transaction statement has been sent to a purchaser for value, other than a security issued by a government or governmental agency or unit, even though issued with a defect going to its validity, is valid with respect to the purchaser if he is without notice of the particular defect unless the defect involves a violation of constitutional provisions, in which case the security is valid with respect to a subsequent purchaser for value and without notice of the defect. This subsection applies to an issuer that is a government or governmental agency or unit only if either there has been substantial compliance with the legal requirements governing the issue or the issuer has received a substantial consideration for the issue as a whole or for the particular security and a stated purpose of the issue is one for which the issuer has power to borrow money or issue the security.

(**3**) Except as provided in the case of certain unauthorized signatures (Section 8-205), lack of genuineness of a certificated security or an initial transaction statement is a complete defense, even against a purchaser for value and without notice.

(**4**) All other defenses of the issuer of a certificated or uncertificated security, including nondelivery and conditional delivery of a certificated security, are ineffective against a purchaser for value who has taken without notice of the particular defense.

(**5**) Nothing in this section shall be construed to affect the right of a party to a "when, as and if issued" or a "when distributed" contract to cancel the contract in the event of a material change in the character of the security that is the subject of the contract or in the plan or arrangement pursuant to which the security is to be issued or distributed.

§8-203. Staleness as Notice of Defects or Defenses.

(**1**) After an act or event creating a right to immediate performance of the principal obligation represented by a certificated security or that sets a date on or after which the security is to be presented or surrendered for redemption or exchange, a purchaser is charged with notice of any defect in its issue or defense of the issuer if:

(**a**) the act or event is one requiring the payment of money, the delivery of certificated securities, the registration of transfer of uncertificated securities, or any of these on presentation or surrender of the certificated security, the funds or securities are available on the date set for paymnet or exchange, and he takes the security more than one year after that date; and

(b) the act or event is not covered by paragraph (a) and he takes the security more than 2 years after the date set for surrender or presentation or the date on which performance became due.

(2) A call that has been revoked is not within subsection (1).

§8-204. Effect of Issuer's Restrictions on Transfer. A restriction on transfer of a security imposed by the issuer, even though otherwise lawful, is ineffective against any person without actual knowledge of it unless:

(a) the security is certificated and the restriction is noted conspicuously thereon; or

(b) the security is uncertificated and a notation of the restriction is contained in the initial transaction statement sent to the person or, if his interest is transferred to him other than by registration of transfer, pledge, or release, the initial transaction statement sent to the registered owner or the registered pledgee.

§8-205. Effect of Unauthorized Signature on Certificated Security or Initial Transaction Statement. An unauthorized signature placed on a certificated security prior to or in the course of issue or placed on an initial transaction statement is ineffective, but the signature is effective in favor of a purchaser for value of the certificated security or a purchaser for value of an uncertificated security to whom such initial transaction statement has been sent, if the purchaser is without notice of the lack of authority and the signing has been done by:

(a) an authenticating trustee, registrar, transfer agent, or other person entrusted by the issuer with the signing of the security, of similar securities, or of initial transaction statements or the immediate preparation for signing of any of them; or

(b) an employee of the issuer, or of any of the foregoing, entrusted with responsible handling of the security or initial transaction statement.

§8-206. Completion or Alteration of Certificated Security or Initial Transaction Statement.

(1) If a certificated security contains the signatures necessary to its issue or transfer but is incomplete in any other respect:

(a) any person may complete it by filling in the blanks as authorized; and

(b) even though the blanks are incorrectly filled in, the security as completed is enforceable by a purchaser who took it for value and without notice of the incorrectness.

(2) A complete certificated security that has been improperly altered, even though fraudulently, remains enforecable, but only according to its original terms.

(3) If an initial transaction statement contains the signatures necessary to its validity, but is incomplete in any other respect:

(a) any person may complete it by filling in the blanks as authorized; and

(b) even though the blanks are incorrectly filled in, the statement as completed is effective in favor of the person to whom it is sent if he purchased the security referred to therein for value and without notice of the incorrectness.

(4) A complete initial transaction statement that has been improperly altered, even though fraudulently, is effective in favor of a purchaser to whom it has been sent, but only according to its original terms.

§8-207. Rights and Duties of Issuer With Respect to Registered Owners and Registered Pledgees.

(1) Prior to due presentment for registration of transfer of a certificated security in registered form, the issuer or indenture trustee may treat the registered owner as the person exclusively entitled to vote, to receive notifications, and otherwise to exercise all the rights and powers of an owner.

(2) Subject to the provisions of subsections (3), (4), and (6), the issuer or indenture trustee may treat the registered owner of an uncertificated security as the person exclusively entitled to vote, to receive notifications, and otherwise to exercise all the rights and powers of an owner.

(3) The registered owner of an uncertificated security that is subject to a registered pledge is not entitled to registration of transfer prior to the due presentment to the issuer of a release instruction. The exercise of conversion rights wtih respect to a convertible uncertificated security is a transfer within the meaning of this section.

(4) Upon due presentment of a transfer instruction from the registered pledgee of an uncertificated security, the issuer shall:

(a) register the transfer of the security to the new owner free of pledge, if the instruction specifies a new owner (who may be the registered pledgee) and does not specify a pledgee;

(b) register the transfer of the security to the new owner subject to the interest of the existing pledgee, if the instruction specifies a new owner and the existing pledgee; or

(c) register the release of the security from the existing pledge and register the pledge of the security to the other pledgee, if the instruction specifies the existing owner and another pledgee.

(5) Continuity of perfection of a security interest is not broken by registration of transfer under subsection (4) (b) or by registration of release and pledge under subsection (4) (c), if the security interest is assigned.

(6) If an uncertificated security is subject to a registered pledge:

(a) any uncertificated securities issued in exchange for or distributed with respect to the pledged security shall be registered subject to the pledge;

(b) any certificated securities issued in exchange for or distributed with respect to the pledged security shall be delivered to the registered pledgee; and

(c) any money paid in exchange for or in redemption of part or all of the security shall be paid to the registered pledgee.

(7) Nothing in this Article shall be construed to affect the liability of the registered owner of a security for calls, assessments, or the like.

§8-208. Effect of Signature of Authenticating Trustee, Registrar, or Transfer Agent.

(1) A person placing his signature upon a certificated security or an initial transaction statement as authenticating trustee, registrar, transfer agent, or the like, warrants to a purchaser for value of the certificated security or a purchaser for value of an uncertificated security to whom the initial transaction statement has been sent, if the purchaser is without notice of the particular defect, that:

(a) the certificated security or initial transaction statement is genuine;

(b) his own participation in the issue or registration of the transfer, pledge, or release of the security is within his capacity and within the scope of the authority received by him from the issuer; and

(c) he has reasonable grounds to believe that the security is in the form and within the amount the issuer is authorized to issue.

(2) Unless otherwise agreed, a person by so placing his signature does not assume responsibility for the validity of the security in other respects.

Part 3: Transfer

§8-301. Rights Acquired by Purchaser

(1) Upon transfer of a security to a purchaser (Section 8-313), the purchaser acquires the rights in the security which his transferor had or had actual authority to convey unless the purchaser's rights are limited by Section 8-302 (4).

(2) A transferee of a limited interest acquires rights only to the extent of the interest transferred. The creation or release of a security interest in a security is the transfer of a limited interest in that security.

§8-302. "Bona Fide Purchaser"; Adverse Claim"; Title Acquired by Bona Fide Purchaser.

(1) A "bona fide purchaser" is a purchaser for value in good faith and without notice of any adverse claim:

(a) who takes delivery of a certificated security in bearer form or in registered form, issued or indorsed to him or in blank;

(b) to whom the transfer, pledge or release of an uncertificated security is registered on the books of the issuer; or

(c) to whom a security is transferred under the provisions of paragraph (c) (d) (i), or (g) of Section 8-313(1).

(2) "Adverse claim" includes a claim that a transfer was or would be wrongful or that a particular adverse person is the owner of or has an interest in the security.

(3) A bona fide purchaser in addition to acquiring the rights of a purchaser (Section 8-301) also acquires his interest in the security free of any adverse claim.

(4) Notwithstanding Section 8-301(1), the transferee of a particular certificated security who has been a party to any fraud or illegality affecting the security, or who as a prior holder of that certificated security had notice of an adverse claim, cannot improve his position by taking from a bona fide purchaser.

§8-303. "Broker". "Broker" means a person engaged for all or part of his time in the business of buying and selling securities, who in the transaction concerned acts for, buys a security from, or sells a security to, a customer. Nothing in this Article determines the capacity in which a person acts for purposes of any other statute or rule to which the person is subject.

§8-304. Notice to Purchaser of Adverse Claims.

(1) A purchaser (including a broker for the seller or buyer, but excluding an intermediary bank) of a certificated security is charged with notice of adverse claims if:

(a) the security, whether in bearer or registered from, has been indorsed "for collection" or "for surrender" or for some other purpose not involving transfer; or

(b) the security is in bearer form and has on it an unambiguous statement that it is the property of a person other than the transferor. The mere writing of a name on a security is not such a statement.

(2) A purchaser (including a broker for the seller or buyer, but excluding an intermediary bank) to whom the transfer, pledge, or release of an uncertificated security is registered is charged with notice of adverse claims as to which the issuer has a duty under Section 8-403(4) at the time of registration and which are noted in the initial transaction statement sent to the purchaser or, if his interest is transferred to him other than by registration of transfer, pledge, or release, the initial transaction statement sent to the registered owner or the registered pledge.

(3) The fact that the purchaser (including a broker for the seller or buyer) of a certificated or uncertificated security has notice that the security is held for a third person or is registered in the name of or indorsed by a fiduciary does not create a duty of inquiry into the rightfulness of the transfer or constitute constructive notice of adverse claims. However, if the purchaser (excluding an intermediary bank) has knowledge that the proceeds are being used or the transaction is for the individual benefit of the fiduciary or otherwise in breach of duty, the purchaser is charged with notice of adverse claims.

§8-305. Staleness as Notice of Adverse Claims. An act or event that creates a right to immediate performance of the principal obligation represented by a certificated security or sets a date on or after which a certificated security is to be presented or surrendered for redemption or exchange does not itself constitute any notice of adverse claims except in the case of a transfer:

(a) after one year from any date set for presentment or surrender for redemption or exchange; or

(b) after 6 months from any date set for payment of money against presentation or surrender of the security if funds are available for payment on that date.

§8-306. Warranties on Presentment and Transfer of Certificated Securities; Warranties of Originators of Instructions.

(1) A person who presents a certificated security for registration of transfer or for payment or exchange warrants to the issuer that he is entitled to the registration, payment, or exchange. But, a purchaser for value and without notice of adverse claims who receives a new, reissued, or re-registered certificated security on registration of transfer or receives an initial transaction statement confirming the registration of transfer of an equivalent uncertificated security to him warrants only that he has no knowledge of any unauthorized signature (Section 8-311) in a necessary indorsement.

(2) A person by transferring a certificated security to a purchaser for value warrants only that:

(a) his transfer is effective and rightful;

(b) the security is genuine and has not been materially altered; and

(c) he knows of no fact which might impair the validity of the security.

(3) If a certificated security is delivered by an intermediary known to be entrusted with delivery of the security on behalf of another or with collection of a draft or claim against delivery, the intermediary by delivery warrants only his own good faith and authority, even though he has purchased or made advances against the claim to be collected against the delivery.

(4) A pledgee or other holder for security who redelivers a certificated security received, or after payment and on order of the debtor delivers that security to a third person makes only the warranties of an intermediary under subsection (3).

(5) A person who originates an instruction warrants to the issuer that:

(a) he is an appropriate person to originate the instruction; and

(b) at the time the instruction is presented to the issuer he will be entitled to the registration of transfer, pledge, or release.

(6) A person who originates an instruction warrants to any person specially guaranteeing his signature (subsection 8-312 (3)) that:

(a) he is an appropriate person to originate the instruction; and

(b) at the time the instruction is presented to the issuer

(i) he will be entitled to the registration of transfer, pledge, or release; and

(ii) the transfer, pledge, or release requested in the instruction will be registered by the issuer free from all liens, security interests, restrictions, and claims other than those specified in the instruction.

(7) A person who originates an instruction warrants to a purchaser for value and to any person guaranteeing the instruction (Section 8-312(6)) that:

(a) he is an appropriate person to originate the instruction;

(b) the uncertificated security referred to therein is valid; and

(c) at the time the instruction is presented to the issuer

(i) the transferor will be entitled to the registration of transfer, pledge, or release;

(ii) the transfer, pledge, or release requested in the instruction will be registered by the issuer free from all liens, security interests, restrictions, and claims other than those specified in the instruction; and

(iii) the requested transfer, pledge, or release will be rightful.

(8) If a secured party is the registered pledgee or the registered owner of an uncertificated security, a person who originates an instruction of release or transfer to the debtor or, after payment and on order of the debtor, a transfer instruction to a third person, warrants to the debtor or the third person only that he is an appropriate person to originate the instruction and at the time the instruction is presented to the issuer, the transferor will be entitled to the registration of release or transfer. If a transfer instruction to a third person who is a purchaser for value is originated on order of the debtor, the debtor makes to the purchaser the warranties of paragraphs (b), (c)(ii) and (c)(iii) of subsection (7).

(9) A person who transfers an uncertificated security to a purchaser for value and does not originate an instruction in connection with the transfer warrants only that:

(a) his transfer is effective and rightful; and

(b) the uncertificated security is valid.

(10) A broker gives to his customer and to the issuer and a purchaser the applicable warranties provided in this section and has the rights and privileges of a purchaser under this section. The warranties of and in favor of the broker acting as an agent are in addition to applicable warranties given by and in favor of his customer.

§8-307. Effect of Delivery Without Indorsement; Right to Compel Indorsement.

If a certificated security in registered form has been delivered to a purchaser without a necessary indorsement he may become a bona fide purchaser only as of the time the indorsement is supplied; but against the transferor, the transfer is complete upon delivery and the purchaser has a specifically enforceable right to have any necessary indorsement supplied.

§8-308. Indorsements; Instructions.

(1) An indorsement of a certificated security in registered form is made when an appropriate person signs on it or on a separate document an assignment or transfer of the security or a power to assign or transfer it or his signature is written without more upon the back of the security.

(2) An indorsement may be in blank or special. An indorsement in blank includes an indorsement to bearer. A special indorsement specifies to whom the security is to be transferred, or who has power to transfer it. A holder may convert a blank indorsement into a special indorsement.

(3) An indorsement purporting to be only of part of a certificated security representing units intended by the issuer to be separately transferable is effective to the extent of the indorsement.

(4) An "instruction" is an order to the issuer of an uncertifi-

cated security requesting that the transfer, pledge, or release from pledge of the uncertificated security specified therein be registered.

(5) An instruction originated by an appropriate person is:

(a) a writing signed by an appropriate person; or

(b) a communication to the issuer in any form agreed upon in a writing signed by the issuer and an appropriate person.

If an instruction has been originated by an appropriate person but is incomplete in any other respect, any person may complete it as authorized and the issuer may rely on it as completed even though it has been completed incorrectly.

(6) "An appropriate person" in subsection (1) means the person specified by the certificated security or by special indorsement to be entitled to the security.

(7) "An appropriate person" in subsection (5) means:

(a) for an instruction to transfer or pledge an uncertificated security which is then not subject to a registered pledge, the registered owner; or

(b) for an instruction to transfer or release an uncertificated security which is then subject to a registered pledge, the registered pledgee.

(8) In addition to the persons designated in subsections (6) and (7), "an appropriate person" in subsections (1) and (5) includes:

(a) if the person designated is described as a fiduciary but is no longer serving in the described capacity, either that person or his successor;

(b) if the persons designated are described as more than one person as fiduciaries and one or more are no longer serving in the described capacity, the remaining fiduciary or fiduciaries, whether or not a successor has been appointed or qualified;

(c) if the person designated is an individual and is without capacity to act by virtue of death; incompetence, infancy, or otherwise his executor, administrator, guardian, or like fiduciary;

(d) if the persons designated are described as more than one person as tenants by the entirety or with right of survivorship and by reason of death all cannot sign the survivor or survivors;

(e) a person having power to sign under applicable law or controlling instrument; and

(f) to the extent that the person designated or any of the foregoing persons may act through an agent, his authorized agent.

(9) Unless otherwise agreed, the indorser of a certificated security by his indorsement or the originator of an instruction by his origination assumes no obligation that the security will be honored by the issuer but only the obligations provided in Section 8-306.

(10) Whether the person signing is appropriate is determined as of the date of signing and an indorsement made by or an instruction originated by him does not become unauthorized for the purposes of this Article by virtue of any subsequent change of circumstances.

(11) Failure of a fiduciary to comply with a controlling instrument or with the law of the state having jurisdiction of the fiduciary relationship, including any law requiring the fiduciary to obtain court approval of the transfer, pledge, or release, does not render his indorsement or an instruction originated by him unauthorized for the purposes of this Article.

§8-309. Effect of Indorsement Without Delivery. An indorsement of a certificated security, whether special or in blank, does not constitute a transfer until delivery of the certificated security on which it appears or, if the indorsement is on a separate document, until delivery of both the document and the certificated security.

§8-310. Indorsement of Certificated Security in Bearer Form. An indorsement of a certificated security in bearer form may give notice of adverse claims (Section 8-304) but does not otherwise affect any right to registration the holder possesses.

§8-311. Effect of Unauthorized Indorsement or Instruction. Unless the owner, or pledgee has ratified an unauthorized indorsement or instruction or is otherwise precluded from asserting its ineffectiveness:

(a) he may assert its ineffectiveness against the issuer or any purchaser, other than a purchaser for value and without notice of adverse claims, who has in good faith received a new, reissued, or re-registered certificated security on registration of transfer or received an initial transaction statement confirming the registration of transfer, pledge, or release of an equivalent uncertificated security to him; and

(b) an issuer who registers the transfer of a certificated security upon the unauthorized indorsement or who registers the transfer, pledge, or release of an uncertificated security upon the unauthorized instruction is subject to liability for improper registration (Section 8-104).

§8-312. Effect of Guaranteeing Signature, Indorsement or Instruction.

(1) Any person guaranteeing a signature of an indorser of a certificated security warrants that at the time of signing:

(a) the signature was genuine;

(b) the signer was an appropriate person to indorse (Section 8-308); and

(c) the signer had legal capacity to sign.

(2) Any person guaranteeing a signature of the originator of an instruction warrants that at the time of signing:

(a) the signature was genuine;

(b) the signer was an appropriate person to originate the instruction (Section 8-308) if the person specified in the instruction as the registered owner or registered pledgee of the uncertificated security was, in fact, the registered owner or registered pledgee of such security, as to which fact the signature guarantor makes no warranty;

(c) the signer had legal capacity to sign; and

(d) the taxpayer identification number, if any, appearing on the instruction as that of the registered owner or registered pledgee was the taxpayer identification number of the signer or of the owner or pledgee for whom the signer was acting.

(3) Any person specially guaranteeing the signature of the originator of an instruction makes not only the warranties of a signature guarantor (Subsection (2)) but also warrants that at the time the instruction is presented to the issuer:

(a) the person specified in the instruction as the registered owner or registered pledgee of the uncertificated security will be the registered owner or registered pledgee; and

(b) the transfer, pledge, or release of the uncertificated security requested in the instruction will be registered by the issuer free from all liens, security interests, restrictions, and claims other than those specified in the instruction.

(4) The guarantor under subsections (1) and (2) or the special guarantor under subsection (3) does not otherwise warrant the rightfulness of the particular transfer, pledge, or release.

(5) Any person guaranteeing an indorsement of a certificated security makes not only the warranties of a signature guarantor under subsection (1) but also warrants the rightfulness of the particular transfer in all respects.

(6) Any person guaranteeing an instruction requesting the transfer, pledge, or release of an uncertificated security makes not only the warranties of a special signature guarantor under subsection (3) but also warrants the rightfulness of the particular transfer, pledge, or release in all respects.

(7) No issuer may require a special guarantee of signature (subsection (3)), a guarantee of indorsement (subsection (5)), or a guarantee of instruction (subsection (6)) as a condition to registration of transfer, pledge, or release.

(8) The foregoing warranties are made to any person taking or dealing with the security in reliance on the guarantee, and the guarantor is liable to the person for any loss resulting from breach of the warranties.

§8-313. When Transfer to Purchaser Occurs: Financial Intermediary as Bona Fide Purchaser; "Financial Intermediary".

(1) Transfer of a security or a limited interest (including a security interest) therein to a purchaser occurs only:

(a) at the time he or a person designated by him acquires possession of a certificated security;

(b) at the time the transfer, pledge, or release of an uncertificated security is registered to him or a person designated by him:

(c) at the time his financial intermediary acquires possession of a certificated security specially indorsed to or issued in the name of the purchaser;

(d) at the time a financial intermediary, not a clearing corporation, sends him confirmation of the purchase and also by book entry or otherwise identifies as belonging to the purchaser

(i) a specific certificated security in the financial intermediary's possession;

(ii) a quantity of securities that constitute or are part of a fungible bulk of certificated securities in the financial

intermediary's possession or of uncertificated securities registered in the name of the financial intermediary; or

(iii) a quantity of securities that constitute or are part of a fungible bulk of securities shown on the account of the financial intermediary on the books of another financial intermediary;

(e) with respect to an identified certificated security to be delivered while still in the possession of a third person, not a financial intermediary, at the time that person acknowledges that he holds for the purchaser;

(f) with respect to a specific uncertificated security the pledge or transfer of which has been registered to a third person, not a financial intermediary, at the time that person acknowledges that he holds for the purchaser;

(g) at the time appropriate entries to the account of the purchaser or a person designated by him on the books of a clearing corporation are made under Section 8-320;

(h) with respect to the transfer of a security interest where the debtor has signed a security agreement containing a description of the security, at the time a written notification, which, in the case of the creation of the security interest, is signed by the debtor (which may be a copy of the security agreement) or which, in the case of the release or assignment of the security interest created pursuant to this paragraph, is signed by the secured party, is received by

(i) a financial intermediary on whose books the interest of the transferor in the security appears;

(ii) a third person, not a financial intermediary, in possession of the security, if it is certificated;

(iii) a third person, not a financial intermediary, who is the registered owner of the security, if it is uncertificated and not subject to a registered pledge; or

(iv) a third person, not a financial intermediary, who is the registered pledgee of the security, if it is uncertificated and subject to a registered pledge;

(i) with respect to the transfer of a security interest where the transferor has signed a security agreement containing a description of the security, at the time new value is given by the secured party; or

(j) with respect to the transfer of a security interest where the secured party is a financial intermediary and the security has already been transferred to the financial intermediary under paragraphs (a), (b), (c), (d), or (g), at the time the transferor has signed a security agreement containing a description of the security and value is given by the secured party.

(2) The purchaser is the owner of a security held for him by a financial intermediary, but cannot be a bona fide purchaser of a security so held except in the circumstances specified in paragraphs (c), (d)(i), and (g) of subsection (1). If a security so held is part of a fungible bulk, as in the circumstances specified in paragraphs (d)(ii) and (d)(iii) of subsection (1), the purchaser is the owner of a proportionate property interest in the fungible bulk.

(3) Notice of an adverse claim received by the financial

intermediary or by the purchaser after the financial intermediary takes delivery of a certificated security as a holder for value or after the transfer, pledge, or release of an uncertificated security has been registered free of the claim to a financial intermediary who has given value is not effective either as to the financial intermediary or as to the purchaser. However, as between the financial intermediary and the purchaser the purchaser may demand transfer of an equivalent security as to which no notice of adverse claim has been received.

(4) A "financial intermediary" is a bank, broker, clearing corporation or other person (or the nominee of any of them) which in the ordinary course of its business maintains security accounts for its customers and is acting in that capacity. A financial intermediary may have a security interest in securities held in account for its customer.

§8-314. Duty to Transfer, When Completed.

(1) Unless otherwise agreed, if a sale of a security is made on an exchange or otherwise through brokers:

(a) the selling customer fulfills his duty to transfer at the time he:

(i) places a certificated security in the possession of the selling broker or of a person designated by the broker;

(ii) causes an uncertificated security to be registered in the name of the selling broker or a person designated by the broker;

(iii) if requested, causes an acknowledgment to be made to the selling broker that a certificated or uncertificated security is held for the broker; or

(iv) places in the possession of the selling broker or of a person designated by the broker a transfer instruction for an uncertificated security, providing the issuer does not refuse to register the requested transfer if the instruction is presented to the issuer for registration within 30 days thereafter; and

(b) the selling broker, including a correspondent broker acting for a selling customer, fulfills his duty to transfer at the time he:

(i) places a certificated security in the possession of the buying broker or a person designated by the buying broker;

(ii) causes an uncertificated security to be registered in the name of the buying broker or a person designated by the buying broker;

(iii) places in the possession of the buying broker or of a person designated by the buying broker a transfer instruction for an uncertificated security, providing the issuer does not refuse to register the requested transfer if the instruction is presented to the issuer for registration within 30 days thereafter; or

(iv) effects clearance of the sale in accordance with the rules of the exchange on which the transaction took place.

(2) Except as provided in this section and unless otherwise agreed, a transferor's duty to transfer a security under a contract of purchase is not fulfilled until he:

(a) places a certificated security in form to be negotiated by the purchaser in the possession of the purchaser or of a person designated by the purchaser;

(b) causes an uncertificated security to be registered in the name of the purchaser or a person designated by the purchaser; or

(c) if the purchaser requests, causes an acknowledgment to be made to the purchaser that certificated or uncertificated security is held for the purchaser.

(3) Unless made on an exchange, a sale to a broker purchasing for his own account is within subsection (2) and not within subsection (1).

§8-315. Action Against Transferee Based Upon Wrongful Transfer.

(1) Any person against whom the transfer of a security is wrongful for any reason, including his incapacity, as against anyone except a bona fide purchaser, may:

(a) reclaim possession of the certificated security wrongfully transferred;

(b) obtain possession of any new certificated security representing all or part of the same rights:

(c) compel the origination of an instruction to transfer to him or a person designated by him an uncertificated security constituting all or part of the same rights; or

(d) have damages.

(2) If the transfer is wrongful because of an unauthorized indorsement of a certificated security, the owner may also reclaim or obtain possession of the security or a new certificated security, even from a bona fide purchaser, if the ineffectiveness of the purported indorsement can be asserted against him under the provisions of this Article on unauthorized indorsements (Section 8-311).

(3) The right to obtain or reclaim possession of a certificated security or to compel the origination of a transfer instruction may be specifically enforced and the transfer of a certificated or uncertificated security enjoined and a certificated security impounded pending the litigation.

§8-316. Purchaser's Right to Requisites for Registration of Transfer, Pledge, or Release on Books.
Unless otherwise agreed, the transferor of a certificated security or the transferor, pledgor, or pledgee of an uncertificated security on due demand must supply his purchaser with any proof of his authority to transfer, pledge, or release or with any other requisite necessary to obtain registration of the transfer, pledge, or release of the security; but if the transfer, pledge, or release is not for value, a transferor, pledgor, or pledgee need not do so unless the purchaser furnishes the necessary expenses. Failure within a reasonable time to comply with a demand made gives the purchaser the right to reject or rescind the transfer, pledge, or release.

§8-317. Creditors' Rights.

(1) Subject to the exceptions in subsections (3) and (4), no attachment or levy upon a certificated security or any share or other interest represented thereby which is outstanding is valid

until the security is actually seized by the officer making the attachment or levy, but a certificated security which has been surrendered to the issuer may be reached by a creditor by legal process at the issuer's chief executive office in the United States.

(2) An uncertificated security registered in the name of the debtor may not be reached by a creditor except by legal process at the issuer's chief executive office in the United States.

(3) The interest of a debtor in a certificated security that is in the possession of a secured party not a financial intermediary or in an uncertificated security registered in the name of a secured party not a financial intermediary (or in the name of a nominee of the secured party) may be reached by a creditor by legal process upon the secured party.

(4) The interest of a debtor in a certificated security that is in the possession of or registered in the name of a financial intermediary or in an uncertificated security registered in the name of a financial intermediary may be reached by a creditor by legal process upon the financial intermediary on whose books the interest of the debtor appears.

(5) Unless otherwise provided by law, a creditor's lien upon the interest of a debtor in a security obtained pursuant to subsection (3) or (4) is not a restraint on the transfer of the security, free of the lien, to a third party for new value; but in the event of a transfer, the lien applies to the proceeds of the transfer in the hands of the secured party or financial intermediary, subject to any claims having priority.

(6) A creditor whose debtor is the owner of a security is entitled to aid from courts of appropriate jurisdiction, by injunction or otherwise, in reaching the security or in satisfying the claim by means allowed at law or in equity in regard to property that cannot readily be reached by ordinary legal process.

§8-318. No Conversion by Good Faith Conduct.   An agent or bailee who in good faith (including the observance of reasonable commercial standards if he is in the business of buying, selling, or otherwise dealing with securities) has received certificated securities and sold, pledged, or delivered them or has sold or caused the transfer or pledge of uncertificated securities over which he had control according to the instructions of his principal, is not liable for conversion or for participation in breach of fiduciary duty although the principal had no right so to deal with the securities.

§8-319. Statute of Frauds.   A contract for the sale of securities is not enforceable by way of action or defense unless:

(a) there is some writing signed by the party against whom enforcement is sought or by his authorized agent or broker, sufficient to indicate that a contract has been made for sale of a stated quantity of described securities at a defined or stated price;

(b) delivery of a certificated security or transfer instruction has been accepted, or transfer of an uncertificated security has been registered and the transferee has failed to send written objection to the issuer within 10 days after receipt of the initial transaction statement confirming the registration, or payment has been made, but the contract

is enforceable under this provision only to the extent the delivery, registration, or payment;

(c) within a reasonable time a writing in confirmation of the sale or purchase and sufficient against the sender under paragraph (a) has been received by the party against whom enforcement is sought and he has failed to send written objection to its contents within 10 days after its receipt; or

(d) the party against whom enforcement is sought admits in his pleading, testimony, or otherwise in court that a contract was made for the sale of a stated quantity of described securities at a defined or stated price.

§8-320. Transfer or Pledge Within Central Depository System.

(1) In addition to other methods, a transfer, pledge, or release of a security or any interest therein may be effected by the making of appropriate entries on the books of a clearing corporation reducing the account of the transferor, pledgor, or pledgee and increasing the account of the transferee, pledgee, or pledgor by the amount of the obligation, or the number of shares or rights transferred, pledged, or released, if the security is shown on the account of a transferor, pledgor, or pledgee on the books of the clearing corporation; is subject to the control of the clearing corporation; and

(a) if certificated,

(i) is in the custody of the clearing corporation, another clearing corporation, a custodian bank or a nominee of any of them; and

(ii) is in bearer form or indorsed in blank by an appropriate person or registered in the name of the clearing corporation, a custodian bank, or a nominee of any of them; or

(b) if uncertificated, is registered in the name of the clearing corporation, another clearing corporation, a custodian bank, or a nominee of any of them.

(2) Under this section entries may be made with respect to like securities or interests therein as a part of a fungible bulk and may refer merely to a quantity of a particular security without reference to the name of the registered owner, certificate or bond number, or the like, and, in appropriate cases, may be on a net basis taking into account other transfers, pledges, or releases of the same security.

(3) A transfer under this section is effective (Section 8-313) and the purchaser acquires the rights of the transferor (Section 8-301). A pledge or release under this section is the transfer of a limited interest. If a pledge or the creation of a security interest is intended, the security interest is perfected at the time when both value is given by the pledgee and the appropriate entries are made (Section 8-321). A transferee or pledgee under this section may be a bona fide purchaser (Section 8-302).

(4) A transfer or pledge under this section is not a registration of transfer under Part 4.

(5) That entries made on the books of the clearing corporation as provided in subsection (1) are not appropriate does not affect the validity or effect of the entries or the liabilities or

obligations of the clearing corporation to any person adversely affected thereby.

§8-321. Enforceability, Attachment, Perfection, and Termination of Security Interests.

(1) A security interest in a security is enforceable and can attach only if it is transferred to the secured party or a person designated by him pursuant to a provision of Section 8-313(1).

(2) A security interest so transferred pursuant to agreement by a transferor who has rights in the security to a transferee who has given value is a perfected security interest, but a security interest that has been transferred solely under paragraph (i) of Section 8-313(1) becomes unperfected after 21 days unless, within that time, the requirements for transfer under any other provision of Section 8-313(1) are satisfied.

(3) A security interest in a security is subject to the provisions of Article 9, but:

(a) no filing is required to perfect the security interest; and

(b) no written security agreement signed by the debtor is necessary to make the security interest enforceable, except as otherwise provided in paragraph (h), (i), or (j) of Section 8-313(1).

The secured party has the rights and duties provided under Section 9-207, to the extent they are applicable, whether or not the security is certificated, and, if certificated, whether or not it is in his possession.

(4) Unless otherwise agreed, a security interest in a security is terminated by transfer to the debtor or a person designated by him pursuant to a provision of Section 8-313(1). If a security is thus transferred, the security interest, if not terminated, becomes unperfected unless the security is certificated and is delivered to the debtor for the purpose of ultimate sale or exchange or presentation, collection, renewal, or registration of transfer. In that case, the security interest becomes unperfected after 21 days unless, within that time, the security (or securities for which it has been exchanged) is transferred to the secured party or a person designated by him pursuant to a provision of Section 8-313(1).

Part 4: Registration

§8-401. Duty of Issuer to Register Transfer, Pledge, or Release.

(1) If a certificated security in registered form is presented to the issuer with a request to register transfer or an instruction is presented to the issuer with a request to register transfer, pledge, or release, the issuer shall register the transfer, pledge, or release as requested if:

(a) the security is indorsed or the instruction was originated by the appropriate person or persons (Section 8-308);

(b) reasonable assurance is given that those indorsements or instructions are genuine and effective (Section 8-402);

(c) the issuer has no duty as to adverse claims or has

discharged the duty (Section 8-403);

(d) any applicable law relating to the collection of taxes has been complied with; and

(e) the transfer, pledge, or release is in fact rightful or is to a bona fide purchaser.

(2) If an issuer is under a duty to register a transfer, pledge, or release of a security, the issuer is also liable to the person presenting a certificated security or an instruction for registration or his principal for loss resulting from any unreasonable delay in registration or from failure or refusal to register the transfer, pledge, or release.

§8-402. Assurance that Indorsements and Instructions Are Effective.

(1) The issuer may require the following assurance that each necessary indorsement of a certificated security or each instruction (Section 8-308) is genuine and effective:

(a) in all cases, a guarantee of the signature (Section 8-312(1) or (2)) of the person indorsing a certificated security or originating an instruction including, in the case of an instruction, a warranty of the taxpayer identification number or, in the absence thereof, other reasonable assurance of identity;

(b) if the indorsement is made or the instruction is originated by an agent, appropriate assurance of authority to sign;

(c) if the indorsement is made or the instruction is originated by a fiduciary, appropriate evidence of appointment or incumbency;

(d) if there is more than one fiduciary, reasonable assurance that all who are required to sign have done so; and

(e) if the indorsement is made or the instruction is originated by a person not covered by any of the foregoing, assurance appropriate to the case corresponding as nearly as may be to the foregoing.

(2) A "guarantee of the signature" in subsection (1) means a guarantee signed by or on behalf of a person reasonably believed by the issuer to be responsible. The issuer may adopt standards with respect to responsibility if they are not manifestly unreasonable.

(3) "Appropriate evidence of appointment or incumbency" in subsection (1) means:

(a) in the case of a fiduciary appointed or qualified by a court, a certificate issued by or under the direction or supervision of that court or an officer thereof and dated within 60 days before the date of presentation for transfer, pledge, or release; or

(b) in any other case, a copy of a document showing the appointment or a certificate issued by or on behalf of a person reasonably believed by the issuer to be responsible or, in the absence of that document or certificate, other evidence reasonably deemed by the issuer to be appropriate. The issuer may adopt standards with respect to the evidence if they are not manifestly unreasonable. The issuer is not charged with notice of the contents of any document obtained pursuant to this paragraph (b) except to the extent that the contents relate directly to the appointment or incumbency.

(4) The issuer may elect to require reasonable assurance beyond that specified in this section, but if it does so and, for a purpose other than that specified in subsection (3)(b), both requires and obtains a copy of a will, trust, indenture, articles of co-partnership, by-laws, or other controlling instrument, it is charged with notice of all matters contained therein affecting the transfer, pledge, or release.

§8-403. Issuer's Duty as to Adverse Claims.

(1) An issuer to whom a certificated security is presented for registration shall inquire into adverse claims if:

(a) a written notification of an adverse claim is received at a time and in a manner affording the issuer a reasonable opportunity to act on it prior to the issuance of a new, reissued, or re-registered certificated security, and the notification identifies the claimant, the registered owner, and the issue of which the security is a part, and provides an address for communications directed to the claimant; or

(b) the issuer is charged with notice of an adverse claim from a controlling instrument it has elected to require under Section 8-402(4).

(2) The issuer may discharge any duty of inquiry by any reasonable means, including notifying an adverse claimant by registered or certified mail at the address furnished by him or, if there be no such address, at his residence or regular place of business that the certificated security has been presented for registration of transfer by a named person, and that the transfer will be registered unless within 30 days from the date of mailing the notification, either:

(a) an appropriate restraining order, injunction, or other process issues from a court of competent jurisdiction; or

(b) there is filed with the issuer an indemnity bond, sufficient in the issuer's judgment to protect the issuer and any transfer agent, registrar, or other agent of the issuer involved from any loss it or they may suffer by complying with the adverse claim.

(3) Unless an issuer is charged with notice of an adverse claim from a controlling instrument which it has elected to require under Section 8-402(4) or receives notification of an adverse claim under subsection (1), if a certificated security presented for registration is indorsed by the appropriate person or persons the issuer is under no duty to inquire into adverse claims. In particular:

(a) an issuer registering a certificated security in the name of a person who is a fiduciary or who is described as a fiduciary is not bound to inquire into the existence, extent, or correct description of the fiduciary relationship; and thereafter the issuer may assume without inquiry that the newly registered owner continues to be the fiduciary until the issuer receives written notice that the fiduciary is no longer acting as such with respect to the particular security;

(b) an issuer registering transfer on an indorsement by a fiduciary is not bound to inquire whether the transfer is

made in compliance with a controlling instrument or with the law of the state having jurisdiction of the fiduciary relationship, including any law requiring the fiduciary to obtain court approval of the transfer; and

(c) the issuer is not charged with notice of the contents of any court record or file or other recorded or unrecorded document even though the document is in its possession and even though the transfer is made on the indorsement of a fiduciary to the fiduciary himself or to his nominee.

(4) An issuer is under not duty as to adverse claims with respect to an uncertificated security except:

(a) claims embodied in a restraining order, injunction, or other legal process served upon the issuer if the process was served at a time and in a manner affording the issuer a reasonable opportunity to act on it in accordance with the requirements of subsection (5);

(b) claims of which the issuer has received a written notification from the registered owner or the registered pledgee if the notification was received at a time and in a manner affording the issuer a reasonable opportunity to act on it in accordance with the requirements of subsection (5);

(c) claims (including restrictions on transfer not imposed by the issuer) to which the registration of transfer to the present registered owner was subject and were so noted in the initial transaction statement sent to him; and

(d) claims as to which an issuer is charged with notice from a controlling instrument it has elected to require under Section 8-402(4).

(5) If the issuer of an uncertificated security is under a duty as to an adverse claim, he discharges that duty by:

(a) including a notation of the claim in any statements sent with respect to the security under Sections 8-408(3), (6), and (7); and

(b) refusing to register the transfer or pledge of the security unless the nature of the claim does not preclude transfer or pledge subject thereto.

(6) If the transfer or pledge of the security is registered subject to an adverse claim, a notation of the claim must be included in the initial transaction statement and all subsequent statements sent to the transferee and pledgee under Section 8-408.

(7) Notwithstanding subsections (4) and (5), if an uncertificated security was subject to a registered pledge at the time the issuer first came under a duty as to a particular adverse claim, the issuer has no duty as to that claim if transfer of the security is requested by the registered pledgee or an appropriate person acting for the registered pledgee unless:

(a) the claim was embodied in legal process which expressly provides otherwise;

(b) the claim was asserted in a written notification from the registered pledgee;

(c) the claim was one as to which the issuer was charged with notice from a controlling instrument it required under Section 8-402(4) in connection with the pledgee's request for transfer; or

(d) the transfer requested is to the registered owner.

§8-404. Liability and Non-Liability for Registration.

(1) Except as provided in any law relating to the collection of taxes, the issuer is not liable to the owner, pledgee, or any other person suffering loss as a result of the registration of a transfer, pledge, or release of a security if:

(a) there were on or with a certificated security the necessary indorsements or the issuer had received an instruction originated by an appropriate person (Section 8-308); and

(b) the issuer had no duty as to adverse claims or has discharged the duty (Section 8-403).

(2) If an issuer has registered a transfer of a certificated security to a person not entitled to it, the issuer on demand shall deliver a like security to the true owner unless:

(a) the registration was pursuant to subsection (1);

(b) the owner is precluded from asserting any claim for registering the transfer under Section 8-405(1); or

(c) the delivery would result in overissue, in which case the issuer's liability is governed by Section 8-104.

(3) If an issuer has improperly registered a transfer, pledge, or release of an uncertificated security, the issuer on demand from the injured party shall restore the records as to the injured party to the condition that would have obtained if the improper registration had not been made unless:

(a) the registration was pursuant to subsection (1); or

(b) the registration would result in overissue, in which case the issuer's liability is governed by Section 8-104.

§8-405. Lost, Destroyed, and Stolen Certificated Securities.

(1) If a certificated security has been lost, apparently destroyed, or wrongfully taken, and the owner fails to notify the issuer of that fact within a reasonable time after he has notice of it and the issuer registers a transfer of the security before receiving notification, the owner is precluded from asserting against the issuer any claim for registering the transfer under Section 8-404 or any claim to a new security under this section.

(2) If the owner of a certificated security claims that the security has been lost, destroyed, or wrongfully taken, the issuer shall issue a new certificated security or, at the option of the issuer, an equivalent uncertificated security in place of the original security if the owner:

(a) so requests before the issuer has notice that the security has been acquired by a bona fide purchaser;

(b) files with the issuer a sufficient indemnity bond; and

(c) satisfies any other reasonable requirements imposed by the issuer.

(3) If, after the issue of a new certificated or uncertificated security, a bona fide purchaser of the original certificated security presents it for registration of transfer, the issuer shall register the transfer unless registration would result in overissue, in which event the issuer's liability is governed by Section 8-104. In addition to any rights on the indemnity bond, the issuer may recover the new certificated security from the person to whom it was issued or any person taking under him except a bona fide purchaser or may cancel the uncertificated

security unless a bona fide purchaser or any person taking under a bona fide purchaser is then the registered owner or registered pledgee thereof.

§8-406. Duty of Authenticating Trustee, Transfer Agent, or Registrar.

(1) If a person acts as authenticating trustee, transfer agent, registrar, or other agent for an issuer in the registration of transfers of its certificated securities or in the registration of transfers, pledges, and releases of its uncertificated securities, in the issue of new securities, or in the cancellation of surrendered securities:

(a) he is under a duty to the issuer to exercise good faith and due diligence in performing his functions; and

(b) with regard to the particular functions he performs, he has the same obligation to the holder or owner of a certificated security or to the owner or pledgee of an uncertificated security and has the same rights and privileges as the issuer has in regard to those functions.

(2) Notice to an authenticating trustee, transfer agent, registrar or other agent is notice to the issuer with respect to the functions performed by the agent.

§8-407. Exchangeability of Securities.

(1) No issuer is subject to the requirements of this section unless it regularly maintains a system for issuing the class of securities involved under which both certificated and uncertificated securities are regularly issued to the category of owners, which includes the person in whose name the new security is to be registered.

(2) Upon surrender of a certificated security with all necessary indorsements and presentation of a written request by the person surrendering the security, the issuer, if he has no duty as to adverse claims or has discharged the duty (Section 8-403), shall issue to the person or a person designated by him an equivalent uncertificated security subject to all liens, restrictions, and claims that were noted on the certificated security.

(3) Upon receipt of a transfer instruction originated by an appropriate person who so requests, the issuer of an uncertificated security shall cancel the uncertificated security and issue an equivalent certificated security on which must be noted conspicuously any liens and restrictions of the issuer and any adverse claims (as to which the issuer has a duty under Section 8-403(4)) to which the uncertificated security was subject. The certificated security shall be registered in the name of and delivered to:

(a) the registered owner, if the uncertificated security was not subject to a registered pledge; or

(b) the registered pledgee, if the uncertificated security was subject to a registered pledge.

§8-408. Statements of Uncertificated Securities.

(1) Within 2 business days after the transfer of an uncertificated security has been registered, the issuer shall send to the new registered owner and, if the security has been transferred subject to a registered pledge, to the registered pledgee a written statement containing:

(a) a description of the issue of which the uncertificated

security is a part;

(**b**) the number of shares or units transferred;

(**c**) the name and address and any taxpayer identification number of the new registered owner and, if the security has been transferred subject to a registered pledge, the name and address and any taxpayer identification number of the registered pledgee;

(**d**) a notation of any liens and restrictions of the issuer and any adverse claims (as to which the issuer has a duty under Section 8-403(4)) to which the uncertificated security is or may be subject at the time of registration or a statement that there are none of those liens, restrictions, or adverse claims; and

(**e**) the date the transfer was registered.

(**2**) Within 2 business days after the pledge of an uncertificated security has been registered, the issuer shall send to the registered owner and the registered pledgee a written statement containing:

(**a**) a description of the issue of which the uncertificated security is a part;

(**b**) the number of shares or units pledged;

(**c**) the name and address and any taxpayer identification number of the registered owner and the registered pledgee;

(**d**) a notation of any liens and restrictions of the issuer and any adverse claims (as to which the issuer has a duty under Section 8-403(4)) to which the uncertificated security is or may be subject at the time of registration or a statement that there are none of those liens, restrictions or adverse claims; and

(**e**) the date the pledge was registered.

(**3**) Within 2 business days after the release from pledge of an uncertificated security has been registered, the issuer shall send to the registered owner and the pledgee whose interest was released a written statement containing:

(**a**) a description of the issue of which the uncertificated security is a part;

(**b**) the number of shares or units released from pledge;

(**c**) the name and address and any taxpayer identification number of the registered owner and the pledgee whose interest was released;

(**d**) a notation of any liens and restrictions of the issuer and any adverse claims (as to which the issuer has a duty under Section 8-403(4)) to which the uncertificated security is or may be subject at the time of registration or a statement that there are none of those liens, restrictions or adverse claims; and

(**e**) the date the release was registered.

(**4**) An "initial transaction statement" is the statement sent to:

(**a**) the new registered owner and, if applicable, to the registered pledgee pursuant to subsection (1);

(**b**) the registered pledgee pursuant to subsection (2); or

(**c**) the registered owner pursuant to subsection (3).

Each initial transaction statement shall be signed by or on behalf of the issuer and must be identified as "Initial Transaction Statement."

(**5**) Within 2 business days after the transfer of an uncertificated security has been registered, the issuer shall send to the former registered owner and the former registered pledgee, if any, a written statement containing:

(**a**) a description of the issue of which the uncertificated security is a part;

(**b**) the number of shares or units transferred;

(**c**) the name and address and any taxpayer identification number of the former registered owner and of any former registered pledgee; and

(**d**) the date the transfer was registered.

(**6**) At periodic intervals no less frequent than annually and at any time upon the reasonable written request of the registered owner, the issuer shall send to the registered owner of each uncertificated security a dated written statement containing:

(**a**) a description of the issue of which the uncertificated security is a part;

(**b**) the name and address and any taxpayer identification number of the registered owner;

(**c**) the number of shares or units of the uncertificated security registered in the name of the registered owner on the date of the statement;

(**d**) the name and address and any taxpayer identification number of any registered pledgee and the number of shares or units subject to the pledge; and

(**e**) a notation of any liens and restrictions of the issuer and any adverse claims (as to which the issuer has a duty under Section 8-403(4)) to which the uncertificated security is or may be subject or a statement that there are none of those liens, restrictions, or adverse claims.

(**7**) At periodic intervals no less frequent than annually and at any time upon the reasonable written request of the registered pledgee, the issuer shall send to the registered pledgee of each uncertificated security a dated written statement containing:

(**a**) a description of the issue of which the uncertificated security is a part;

(**b**) the name and address and any taxpayer identification number of the registered owner;

(**c**) the name and address and any taxpayer identification number of the registered pledgee;

(**d**) the number of shares or units subject to the pledge; and

(**e**) a notation of any liens and restrictions of the issuer and any adverse claims (as to which the issuer has a duty under Section 8-403(4)) to which the uncertificated security is or may be subject or a statement that there are none of those liens, restrictions, or adverse claims.

(**8**) If the issuer sends the statements described in subsections (6) and (7) at periodic intervals no less frequent than quarterly, the issuer is not obliged to send additional statements upon request unless the owner or pledgee requesting them pays to the issuer the reasonable cost of furnishing them.

(**9**) Each statement sent pursuant to this section must bear a conspicuous legend reading substantially as follows: "This statement is merely a record of the rights of the addressee as of the time of its issuance. Delivery of this statement, of itself, confers no rights on the recipient. This statement is neither a negotiable instrument nor a security."

ARTICLE 9: SECURED TRANSACTIONS; SALES OF ACCOUNTS AND CHATTEL PAPER

Part 1: Short Title, Applicability and Definitions

§9-101. Short Title. This Article shall be known and may be cited as Uniform Commercial Code —Secured Transactions.

§9-102. Policy and Subject Matter of Article.

(1) Except as otherwise provided in Section 9-104 on excluded transactions, this Article applies:

(a) to any transaction (regardless of its form) which is intended to create a security interest in personal property or fixtures including goods, documents, instruments, general intangibles, chattel paper or accounts; and also

(b) to any sale of accounts or chattel paper.

(2) This Article applies to security interests created by contract including pledge, assignment, chattel mortgage, chattel trust, trust deed, factor's lien, equipment trust, conditional sale, trust receipt, other lien or title retention contract and lease or consignment intended as security. This Article does not apply to statutory liens except as provided in Section 9-310.

(3) The application of this Article to a security interest in a secured obligation is not affected by the fact that the obligation is itself secured by a transaction or interest to which this Article does not apply.

Note: *The adoption of this Article should be accompanied by the repeal of existing statutes dealing with conditional sales, trust receipts, factor's liens where the factor is given a non-possessory lien, chattel mortgages, crop mortgages, mortgages on railroad equipment, assignment of accounts and generally statutes regulating security interests in personal property.*

Where the state has a retail installment selling act or small loan act, that legislation should be carefully examined to determine what changes in those acts are needed to conform them to this Article. This Article primarily sets out rules defining rights of a secured party against persons dealing with the debtor; it does not prescribe regulations and controls which may be necessary to curb abuses arising in the small loan business or in the financing of consumer purchases on credit. Accordingly there is no intention to repeal existing regulatory acts in those fields by enactment or re-enactment of Article 9. See Section 9-203(4) and the Note thereto.

§9-103. Perfection of Security Interests in Multiple State Transactions.

(1) Documents, instruments and ordinary goods.

(a) This subsection applies to documents and instruments and to goods other than those covered by a certificate of title described in subsection (2), mobile goods described in subsection (3), and minerals described in subsection (5).

(b) Except as otherwise provided in this subsection, perfection and the effect of perfection or non-perfection of a security interest in collateral are governed by the law of the jurisdiction where the collateral is when the last event occurs on which is based the assertion that the security interest is perfected or unperfected.

(c) If the parties to a transaction creating a purchase money security interest in goods in one jurisdiction understand at the time that the security interest attaches that the goods will be kept in another jurisdiction, then the law of the other jurisdiction governs the perfection and the effect of perfection or non-perfection of the security interest from the time it attaches until thirty days after the debtor receives possession of the goods and thereafter if the goods are taken to the other jurisdiction before the end of the thirty-day period.

(d) When collateral is brought into and kept in this state while subject to a security interest perfected under the law of the jurisdiction from which the collateral was removed, the security interest remains perfected, but if action is required by Part 3 of this Article to perfect the security interest,

(i) if the action is not taken before the expiration of the period of perfection in the other jurisdiction or the end of four months after the collateral is brought into this state, whichever period first expires, the security interest becomes unperfected at the end of that period and is thereafter deemed to have been unperfected as against a person who became a purchaser after removal;

(ii) if the action is taken before the expiration of the period specified in subparagraph (i), the security interest continues perfected thereafter;

(iii) for the purpose of priority over a buyer of consumer goods (subsection (2) of Section 9-307), the period of the effectiveness of a filing in the jurisdiction from which the collateral is removed is governed by the rules with respect to perfection in subparagraphs (i) and (ii).

(2) Certificate of title.

(a) This subsection applies to goods covered by a certificate of title issued under a statute of this state or of another jurisdiction under the law of which indication of a security interest on the certificate is required as a condition of perfection.

(b) Except as otherwise provided in this subsection, perfection and the effect of perfection or non-perfection of the security interest are governed by the law (including the conflict of laws rules) of the jurisdiction issuing the certificate until four months after the goods are removed from that jurisdiction and thereafter until the goods are registered in another jurisdiction, but in any event not beyond surrender of the certificate. After the expiration of that period, the goods are not covered by the certificate of title within the meaning of this section.

(c) Except with respect to the rights of a buyer described

in the next paragraph, a security interest, perfected in another jurisdiction otherwise than by notation on a certificate of title, in goods brought into this state and thereafter covered by a certificate of title issued by this state is subject to the rules stated in paragraph (d) of subsection (1).

(d) If goods are brought into this state while a security interest therein is perfected in any manner under the law of the jurisdiction from which the goods are removed and a certificate of title is issued by this state and the certificate does not show that the goods are subject to the security interest or that they may be subject to security interests not shown on the certificate, the security interest is subordinate to the rights of a buyer of the goods who is not in the business of selling goods of that kind to the extent that he gives value and receives delivery of the goods after issuance of the certificate and without knowledge of the security interest.

(3) Accounts, general intangibles and mobile goods.

(a) This subsection applies to accounts (other than an account described in subsection (5) on minerals) and general intangibles and to goods which are mobile and which are of a type normally used in more than one jurisdiction, such as motor vehicles, trailers, rolling stock, airplanes, shipping containers, road building and construction machinery and commercial harvesting machinery and the like, if the goods are equipment or inventory leased or held for lease by the debtor to others, and are not covered by a certificate of title described in subsection (2).

(b) The law (including the conflict of laws rules) of the jurisdiction in which the debtor is located governs the perfection and the effect of perfection or non-perfection of the security interest.

(c) If, however, the debtor is located in a jurisdiction which is not a part of the United States, and which does not provide for perfection of the security interest by filing or recording in that jurisdiction, the law of the jurisdiction in the United States in which the debtor has its major executive office in the United States governs the perfection and the effect of perfection or non-perfection of the security interest through filing. In the alternative, if the debtor is located in a jurisdiction which is not a part of the United States or Canada and the collateral is accounts or general intangibles for money due or to become due, the security interest may be perfected by notification to the account debtor. As used in this paragraph, "United States" includes its territories and possessions and the Commonwealth of Puerto Rico.

(d) A debtor shall be deemed located at his place of business if he has one, at his chief executive office if he has more than one place of business, otherwise at his residence. If, however, the debtor is a foreign air carrier under the Federal Aviation Act of 1958, as amended, it shall be deemed located at the designated office of the agent upon whom service of process may be made on behalf of the foreign air carrier.

(e) A security interest perfected under the law of the jurisdiction of the locatation of the debtor is perfected until the expiration of four months after a change of the debtor's location to another jurisdiction, or until perfection would have ceased by the law of the first jurisdiction, whichever period first expires. Unless perfected in the new jurisdiction before the end of that period, it becomes unperfected thereafter and is deemed to have been unperfected as against a person who became a purchaser after the change.

(4) Chattel paper.

The rules stated for goods in subsection (1) apply to a possessory security interest in chattel paper. The rules stated for accounts in subsection (3) apply to a non-possessory security interest in chattel peaper, but the security interest may not be perfected by notification to the account debtor.

(5) Minerals.

Perfection and the effect of perfection or non-perfection of a security interest which is created by a debtor who has an interest in minerals or the like (including oil and gas) before extraction and which attaches thereto as extracted, or which attaches to an account resulting from the sale thereof at the wellhead or minehead are governed by the law (including the conflict of laws rules) of the jurisdiction wherein the wellhead or minehead is located.

§9-103. Perfection of Security Interests in Multiple State Transactions (*1977 Amendments*).

* * *

(3) Accounts, general intangibles and mobile goods.

(a) This subsection applies to accounts (other than an account described in subsection (5) on minerals) and general intangibles (other than uncertificated securities) and to goods.

* * *

(6) Uncertificated securities.

The law (including the conflict of laws rules) of the jurisdiction of organization of the issuer governs the perfection and the effect of perfection or non-perfection of a security interest in uncertificated securities.

§9-104. Transactions Excluded From Article. This Article does not apply

(a) to a security interest subject to any statute of the United States to the extent that such statute governs the rights of parties to and third parties affected by transactions in particular types of property; or

(b) to a landlord's lien; or

(c) to a lien given by statute or other rule of law for services or materials except as provided in Section 9-310 on priority of such liens; or

(d) to a transfer of a claim for wages, salary or other compensation of an employee; or

(e) to a transfer by a government or governmental subdivision or agency; or

(f) to a sale of accounts, or chattel paper as part of a sale of the business out of which they arose, or an assignment of accounts or chattel paper which is for the purpose of collection only, or a transfer of a right to payment under a contract to an assignee who is also to do the performance under the contract or a transfer of a single account to an assignee in whole or partial satisfaction of a preexisting indebtedness; or

(**g**) to a transfer of an interest in or claim in or under any policy of insurance, except as provided with respect to proceeds (Section 9-306) and priorities in proceeds (Section 9-312); or

(**h**) to a right represented by a judgment (other than a judgment taken on a right to payment which was collateral); or

(**i**) to any right of set-off; or

(**j**) except to the extent that provision is made for fixtures in Section 9-313, to the creation or transfer of an interest in or lien on real estate, including a lease or rents thereunder; or

(**k**) to a transfer in whole or in part of any claim arising out of tort; or

(**l**) to a transfer of an interest in any deposit account (subsection (1) of Section 9-105), except as provided with respect to proceeds (Section 9-306) and priorities in proceeds (Section 9-312).

§9-105. Definitions and Index of Definitions.

(**1**) In this Article unless the context otherwise requires:

(**a**) "Account debtor" means the person who is obligated on an account, chattel paper or general intangible;

(**b**) "Chattel paper" means a writing or writings which evidence both a monetary obligation and a security interest in or a lease of specific goods, but a charter or other contract involving the use or hire of a vessel is not chattel paper. When a transaction is evidenced both by such a security agreement or a lease and by an instrument or a series of instruments, the group of writings taken together constitutes chattel paper;

(**c**) "Collateral" means the property subject to a security interest, and includes accounts and chattel paper which have been sold;

(**d**) "Debtor" means the person who owes payment or other performance of the obligation secured, whether or not he owns or has rights in the collateral, and includes the seller of accounts or chattel paper. Where the debtor and the owner of the collateral are not the same person, the term "debtor" means the owner of the collateral in any provision of the Article dealing with the collateral, the obligor in any provision dealing with the obligation, and may include both where the context so requires;

(**e**) "Deposit account" means a demand, time savings, passbook or like account maintained with a bank, savings and loan association, credit union or like organization, other than an account evidenced by a certificate of deposit;

(**f**) "Document" means document of title as defined in the general definitions of Article 1 (Section 1-201), and a

receipt of the kind described in subsection (2) of Section 7-201);

(**g**) "Encumbrance" includes real estate mortgages and other liens on real estate and all other rights in real estate that are not ownership interests.

(**h**) "Goods" includes all things which are movable at the time the security interest attaches or which are fixtures (Section 9-313), but does not include money, documents, instruments, accounts, chattel paper, general intangibles, or minerals or the like (including oil and gas) before extraction. "Goods" also includes standing timber which is to be cut and removed under a conveyance or contract for sale, the unborn young of animals, and growing crops.

(**i**) "Instrument" means a negotiable instrument (defined in Section 3-104), or a security (defined in Section 8-102) or any other writing which evidences a right to the payment of money and is not itself a security agreement or lease and is of a type which is in ordinary course of business transferred by delivery with any necessary indorsement or assignment;

(**j**) "Mortgage" means a consensual interest created by a real estate mortgage, a trust deed on real estate, or the like;

(**k**) An advance is made "pursuant to commitment" if the secured party has bound himself to make it, whether or not a subsequent event of default or other event not within his control has relieved or may relieve him from his obligation.

(**l**) "Security agreement" means an agreement which creates or provides for a security interest;

(**m**) "Secured party" means a lender, seller or other person in whose favor there is a security interest, including a person to whom accounts or chattel paper have been sold. When the holders of obligations issued under an indenture of trust, equipment trust agreement or the like are represented by a trustee or other person, the representative is the secured party;

(**n**) "Transmitting utility" means any person primarily engaged in the railroad, street railway or trolley bus business, the electric or electronics communications transmission business, the transmission of goods by pipeline, or the transmission or the production and transmission of electricity, steam, gas or water, or the provision of sewer service.

(**2**) Other definitions applying to this Article and the sections in which they appear are;

"Account". Section 9-106.
"Attach". Section 9-203.
"Construction mortgage". Section 9-313 (1).
"Consumer goods". Section 9-109 (1).
"Equipment". Section 9-109 (2).
"Farm products". Section 9-109 (3).
"Fixture". Section 9-313.
"Fixture filing". Section 9-313.
"General intangibles". Section 9-106.
"Inventory". Section 9-109 (4).

"Lien creditor". Section 9-301 (3).

"Proceeds". Section 9-306 (1).

"Purchase money security interest". Section 9-107.

"United States". Section 9-103.

(3) The following definitions in other articles apply to this Article:

"Check". Section 3-104.

"Contract for sale". Section 2-106.

"Holder in due course". Section 3-302.

"Note". Section 3-104.

"Sale". Section 2-106.

(4) In addition Article 1 contains general definitions and principles of construction and interpretation throughout this Article.

§9-105. **Definitions and Index of Definitions** (*1977 Amendments*).

(1) In this Article unless the context otherwise requires:

* * *

(i) "Instrument" means a negotiable instrument (defined in Section 3-104), or a certificated security (defined in Section 8-102) or . . .

* * *

§9-106. **Definitions: "Account"; "General Intangibles".** "Account" means any right to payment for goods sold or leased or for services rendered which is not evidenced by an instrument or chattel paper, whether or not it has been earned by performance. "General intangibles" means any personal property (including things in action) other than goods, accounts, chattel paper, documents, instruments, and money. All rights to payment earned or unearned under a charter or other contract involving the use or hire of a vessel and all rights incident to the charter or contract are accounts.

§9-107. **Definitions: "Purchase Money Security Interest".** A security interest is a "purchase money security interest" to the extent that it is

(a) taken or retained by the seller of the collateral to secure all or part of its price;

(b) taken by a person who by making advances or incurring an obligation gives value to enable the debtor to acquire rights in or the use of collateral if such value is in fact so used.

§9-108. **When After-Acquired Collateral Not Security for Antecedent Debt.** Where a secured party makes an advance, incurs an obligation, releases a perfected security interest, or otherwise gives new value which is to be secured in whole or in part by after-acquired property his security interest in the after-acquired collateral shall be deemed to be taken for new value and not as security for an antecedent debt if the debtor acquires his rights in such collateral either in the ordinary course of his business or under a contract of purchase made pursuant to the security agreement within a reasonable time after new value is given.

§9-109. **Classification of Goods; "Consumer Goods"; "Equipment"; "Farm Products"; "Inventory".** Goods are

(1) "consumer goods" if they are used or bought for use

primarily for personal, family or household purposes;

(2) "equipment" if they are used or bought for use primarily in business (including farming or a profession) or by a debtor who is a non-profit organization or a governmental subdivision or agency or if the goods are not included in the definitions of inventory, farm products or consumer goods;

(3) "farm products" if they are crops or livestock or supplies used or produced in farming operations or if they are products of crops or livestock in their unmanufactured states (such as ginned cotton, wool-clip, maple syrup, milk and eggs), and if they are in the possession of a debtor engaged in raising, fattening, grazing or other farming operations. If goods are farm products they are neither equipment nor inventory;

(4) "inventory" if they are held by a person who holds them for sale or lease or to be furnished under contracts of service or if he has so furnished them, or if they are raw materials, work in process or materials used or consumed in a business. Inventory of a person is not to be classified as his equipment.

§9-110. **Sufficiency of Description.** For the purposes of this Article any description of personal property or real estate is sufficient whether or not it is specific if it reasonably identifies what is described.

§9-111. **Applicability of Bulk Transfer Laws.** The creation of a security interest is not a bulk transfer under Article 6 (see Section 6-103).

§9-112. **Where Collateral Is Not Owned by Debtor.** Unless otherwise agreed, when a secured party knows that collateral is owned by a person who is not the debtor, the owner of the collateral is entitled to receive from the secured party any surplus under Section 9-502 (2) or under Section 9-504 (1), and is not liable for the debt or for any deficiency after resale, and he has the same right as the debtor

(a) to receive statements under Section 9-208;

(b) to receive notice of and to object to a secured party's proposal to retain the collateral in satisfaction of the indebtedness under Section 9-505;

(c) to redeem the collateral under Section 9-506;

(d) to obtain injunctive or other relief under Section 9-507 (1); and

(e) to recover losses caused to him under Section 9-208 (2).

§9-113. **Security Interests Arising Under Article on Sales.** A security interest arising solely under the Article on Sales (Article 2) is subject to the provisions of this Article except that to the extent that and so long as the debtor does not have or does not lawfully obtain possession of the goods

(a) no security agreement is necessary to make the security interest enforceable; and

(b) no filing is required to perfect the security interest; and

(c) the rights of the secured party on default by the debtor are governed by the Article on Sales (Article 2).

§9-114. **Consignment.**

(1) A person who delivers goods under a consignment which is not a security interest and who would be required to file under this Article by paragraph (3) (c) of Section 2-326 has

priority over a secured party who is or becomes a creditor of the consignee and who would have a perfected security interest in the goods if they were the property of the consignee, and also has priority with respect to identifiable cash proceeds received on or before delivery of the goods to a buyer, if

(a) the consignor complies with the filing provision of the Article on Sales with respect to consignments (paragraph (3) (c) of Section 2-326) before the consignee receives possession of the goods; and

(b) the consignor gives notification in writing to the holder of the security interest if the holder has filed a financing statement covering the same types of goods before the date of the filing made by the consignor; and

(c) the holder of the security interest receives the notification within five years before the consignee receives possession of the goods; and

(d) the notification states that the consignor expects to deliver goods on consignment to the consignee, describing the goods by item or type.

(2) In the case of a consignment which is not a security interest and in which the requirements of the preceding subsection have not been met, a person who delivers goods to another is subordinate to a person who would have a perfected security interest in the goods if they were the property of the debtor.

Part 2: Validity of Security Agreement and Rights of Parties Thereto

§9-201. General Validity of Security Agreement. Except as otherwise provided by this Act a security agreement is effective according to its terms between the parties, against purchasers of the collateral and against creditors. Nothing in this Article validates any charge or practice illegal under any statute or regulation thereunder governing usury, small loans, retail installment sales, or the like, or extends the application of any such statute or regulation to any transaction not otherwise subject thereto.

§9-202. Title to Collateral Immaterial. Each provision of this Article with regard to rights, obligations and remedies applies whether title to collateral is in the secured party or in the debtor.

§9-203. Attachment and Enforceability of Security Interest; Proceeds; Formal Requisities.

(1) Subject to the provisions of Section 4-208 on the security interest of a collecting bank and Section 9-113 on a security interest arising under the Article on Sales, a security interest is not enforceable against the debtor or third parties with respect to the collateral and does not attach unless

(a) the collateral is in the possession of the secured party pursuant to agreement, or the debtor has signed a security agreement which contains a description of the collateral and in addition, when the security interest covers crops growing or to be grown or timber to be cut, a description of the land concerned; and

(b) value has been given; and

(c) the debtor has rights in the collateral.

(2) A security interest attaches when it becomes enforceable against the debtor with respect to the collateral. Attachment occurs as soon as all of the events specified in subsection (1) have taken place unless explicit agreement postpones the time of attaching.

(3) Unless otherwise agreed a security agreement gives the secured party the rights to proceeds provided by Section 9-306.

(4) A transaction, although subject to this Article, is also subject to . . . . *, and in the case of conflict between the provisions of this Article and any such statute, the provisions of such statute control. Failure to comply with any applicable statute has only the effect which is specfied therein.

Note: *At * in subsection (4) insert reference to any local statute regulating small loans, retail installment sales and the like.*

The foregoing subsection (4) is designed to make it clear that certain transactions, although subject to this Article, must also comply with other applicable legislation.

This Article is designed to regulate all the "security" aspects of transactions within its scope. There is, however, much regulatory legislation, particularly in the consumer field, which supplements this Article and should not be repealed by its enactment. Examples are small loan acts, retail installment selling acts and the like. Such acts may provide for licensing and rate regulation and may prescribe particular forms of contract. Such provisions should remain in force despite the enactment of this Article. On the other hand if a retail installent selling act contains provisions on filing, rights on default, etc., such provisions should be repealed as inconsistent with this Article except that inconsistent provisions as to deficiencies, penalities, etc., in the Uniform Consumer Credit Code and other recent related legislation should remain because those statutes were drafted after the substantial enactment of the Article and with the intention of modifying certain provisions of this Article as to consumer credit.

§9-203. Attachment and Enforceability of Security Interest; Proceeds; Formal Requisites *(1977 Amendments).*

(1) Subject to the provisions of Section 4-208 on the security interest of a collecting bank, Section 8-321 on security interests in securities and Section 9-113 on a security interest arising under the Article on Sales, a security interest in not enforceable against the debtor or third parties with respect to the collateral and does not attach unless:

(a) the collateral is in the possession of the secured party pursuant to agreement, or the debtor has signed a security agreement which contains a description of the collateral and in additon, when the security interest covers crops growing or to be grown or timber to be cut, a description of the land concerned;

(b) value has been given; and

(c) the debtor has rights in the collateral.

* * *

§9-204. After-Acquired Property; Future Advances.

(1) Except as provided in subsection (2), a security agree-

ment may provide that any or all obligations covered by the security agreement are to be secured by after-acquired collateral.

(2) No security interest attaches under an after-acquired property clause to consumer goods other than accessions (Section 9-314) when given as additional security unless the debtor acquires rights in them within ten days after the secured party gives value.

(3) Obligations covered by a security agreement may include future advances or other value whether or not the advances or value are given pursuant to commitment (subsection (1) of Section 9-105).

§9-205. Use or Disposition of Collateral Without Accounting Permissible.

A security interest is not invalid or fraudulent against creditors by reason of liberty in the debtor to use, commingle or dispose of all or part of the collateral (including returned or repossessed goods) or to collect or compromise accounts or chattel paper, or to accept the return of goods or make repossessions, or to use, commingle or dispose of proceeds, or by reason of the failure of the secured party to require the debtor to account for proceeds or replace collateral. This section does not relax the requirements of possession where perfection of a security interest depends upon possession of the collateral by the secured party or by a bailee.

§9-206. Agreement Not to Assert Defenses Against Assignee; Modification of Sales Warranties Where Security Agreement Exists.

(1) Subject to any statute or decision which establishes a different rule for buyers or lessees of consumer goods, an agreement by a buyer or lessee that he will not assert against an assignee any claim or defense which he may have against the seller or lessor is enforceable by an assignee who takes his assignment for value, in good faith and without notice of a claim or defense, except as to defenses of a type which may be asserted against a holder in due course of a negotiable instrument under the Article on Commercial Paper (Article 3). A buyer who as part of one transaction signs both a negotiable instrument and a security agreement makes such an agreement.

(2) When a seller retains a purchase money security interest in goods the Article on Sales (Article 2) governs the sale and any disclaimer, limitation or modification of the seller's warranties. Amended in 1962.

§9-207. Rights and Duties When Collateral is in Secured Party's Possession.

(1) A secured party must use reasonable care in the custody and preservation of collateral in his possession. In the case of an instrument or chattel paper reasonable care includes taking necessary steps to preserve rights against prior parties unless otherwise agreed.

(2) Unless otherwise agreed, when collateral is in the secured party's possession

(a) reasonable expenses (including the cost of any insurance and payment of taxes or other charges) incurred in the custody, preservation, use or operation of the collateral are chargeable to the debtor and are secured by the collateral;

(b) the risk of accidental loss or damage is on the debtor to the extent of any deficiency in any effective insurance coverage;

(c) the secured party may hold as additional security any increase or profits (except money) received from the collateral, but money so received, unless remitted to the debtor, shall be applied in reduction of the secured obligation;

(d) the secured party must keep the collateral indentifiable but fungible collateral may be commingled;

(e) the secured party may repledge the collateral upon terms which do not impair the debtor's right to redeem it.

(3) A secured party is liable for any loss caused by his failure to meet any obligation imposed by the preceding subsections but does not lose his security interest.

(4) A secured party may use or operate the collateral for the purpose of preserving the collateral or its value or pursuant to the order of a court of appropriate jurisdiction or, except in the case of consumer goods, in the manner and to the extent provided in the security agreement.

§9-208. Request for Statement of Account or List of Collateral.

(1) A debtor may sign a statement indicating what he believes to be the aggregate amount of unpaid indebtedness as of a specified date and may send it to the secured party with a request that the statement be approved or corrected and returned to the debtor. When the security agreement or any other record kept by the secured party identifies the collateral a debtor may similarly request the secured party to approve or correct a list of the collateral.

(2) The secured party must comply with such a request within two weeks after receipt by sending a written correction or approval. If the secured party claims a security interest in all of a particular type of collateral owned by the debtor he may indicate that fact in his reply and need not approve or correct an itemized list of such collateral. If the secured party without reasonable excuse fails to comply he is liable for any loss caused to the debtor thereby; and if the debtor has properly included in his request a good faith statement of the obligation or a list of the collateral or both, the secured party may claim a security interest only as shown in the statement against persons misled by his failure to comply. If he no longer has an interest in the obligation or collateral at the time the request is received he must disclose the name and address of any successor in interest known to him and he is liable for any loss caused to the debtor as a result of failure to disclose. A successor in interest is not subject to this section until a request is received by him.

(3) A debtor is entitled to such a statement once every six months without charge. The secured party may require payment of a charge not exceeding $10 for each additional statement furnished.

Part 3: Rights of Third Parties; Perfected and Unperfected Security Interests; Rules of Priority

§9-301. Persons Who Take Priority Over Unperfected Security Interests; Right of "Lien Creditor".

(1) Except as otherwise provided in subsection (2), an unperfected security interest is subordinate to the rights of

(a) persons entitled to priority under Section 9-312;

(b) a person who becomes a lien creditor before the security interest is perfected;

(c) in the case of goods, instruments, documents, and chattel paper, a person who is not a secured party and who is a transferee in bulk or other buyer not in ordinary course of business, or is a buyer of farm products in ordinary course of business, to the extent that he gives value and receives delivery of the collateral without knowledge of the security interest and before it is perfected;

(d) in the case of accounts and general intangibles, a person who is not a secured party and who is a transferee to the extent that he gives value without knowledge of the security interest and before it is perfected.

(2) If the secured party files with respect to a purchase money security interest before or within ten days after the debtor recieves possession of the collateral, he takes priority over the rights of a transferee in bulk or of a lien creditor which arise between the time the security interest attaches and the time of filing.

(3) A "lien creditor" means a creditor who has acquired a lien on the property involved by attachment, levy or the like and includes an assignee for benefit of creditors from the time of assignment, and a trustee in bankruptcy from the date of the filing of the petition or a receiver in equity from the time of appointment.

(4) A person who becomes a lien creditor while a security interest is perfected takes subject to the security interest only to the extent that it secures advances made before he becomes a lien creditor or within 45 days thereafter or made without knowledge of the lien or pursuant to a commitment entered into without knowledge of the lien.

§9-302. When Filing Is Required to Perfect Security Interest; Security Interests to Which Filing Provisions of This Article Do Not Apply.

(1) A financing statement must be filed to perfect all security interests except the following:

(a) a security interest in collateral in possession of the secured party under Section 9-305;

(b) a security interest temporarily perfected in instruments or documents without delivery under Section 9-304 or in proceeds for a 10 day period under Section 9-306;

(c) a security interest created by an assignment of a beneficial interest in a trust or a decedent's estate;

(d) a purchase money security interest in consumer goods; but filing is required for a motor vehicle required to be registered; and fixture filing is required for priority over conflicting interests in fixtures to the extent provided in Section 9-313;

(e) an assignment of accounts which does not alone or in conjunction with other assignments to the same assignee transfer a significant part of the outstanding accounts of the assignor;

(f) a security interest of a collecting bank (Section 4-208) or arising under the Article on Sales (see section 9-113) or covered in subsection (3) of this section;

(g) an assignment for the benefit of all the creditors of the transferor, and subsequent transfers by the assignee thereunder.

(2) If a secured party assigns a perfected security interest, no filing under this Article is required in order to continue the perfected status of the security interest against creditors of and transferees from the original debtor.

(3)) The filing of a financing statement otherwise required by this Article is not necessary or effective to perfect a security interest in property subject to

(a) a statute or treaty of the United States which provides for a national or international registration or a national or international certificate of title or which specifies a place of filing different from that specified in this Article for filing of the security interest; or

(b) the following statutes of this state; [[list any certificate of title statute covering automobiles, trailers, mobile homes, boats, farm tractors, or the like, and any central filing statute*.]]; but during any period in which collateral is inventory held for sale by a person who is in the business of selling goods of that kind, the filing provisions of this Article (Part 4) apply to a security interest in that collateral created by him as debtor; or

(c) a certificate of title statute of another jurisdiction under the law of which indication of a security interest on the certificate is required as a condition of perfection (subsection (2) of Section 9-103).

(4) Compliance with a statute or treaty described in subsection (3) is equivalent to the filing of a financing statement under this Article, and a security interest in property subject to the statute or treaty can be perfected only by compliance therewith except as provided in Section 9-103 on multiple state transactions. Duration and renewal of perfection of a security interest perfected by compliance with the statute or treaty are governed by the provisions of the statute or treaty; in other respects the security interest is subject to this Article.

§9-302. When Filing is Required to Perfect Security Interest; Security Interests to Which Filing Provisions of This Article Do Not Apply *(1977 Amendments).*

(1) A financing statement must be filed to perfect all security interests[s] except the following:

* * *

(f) a security interest of a collecting bank (Section 4-208) or in securities (Section 8-321) or arising under the Article on Sales (see Section 9-113) or covered in subsection (3) of this section;

* * *

§9-303. When Security Interest Is Perfected; Continuity of Perfection.

(1) A security interest is perfected when it has attached and when all of the applicable steps required for perfection have been taken. Such steps are specified in Section 9-304, 9-305 and 9-306. If such steps are taken before the security interest attaches, it is perfected at the time when it attaches.

* **Note:** It is recommended that the provisions of certificate of title acts for perfection of security interests by notation on the certificates should be amended to exclude coverage of inventory held for sale.

(2) If a security interest is originally perfected in any way permitted under this Article and is subsequently perfected in some other way under this Article, without an intermediate period when it was unperfected, the security interest shall be deemed to be perfected continuously for the purposes of this Article.

§9-304. Perfection of Security Interest in Instruments, Documents, and Goods Covered by Documents; Perfection by Permissive Filing; Temporary Perfection Without Filing or Transfer of Possession.

(1) A security interest in chattel paper or negotiable documents may be perfected by filing. A security interest in money or instruments (other than instruments which constitute part of chattel paper) can be perfected only by the secured party's taking possession, except as provided in subsections (4) and (5) of this section and subsections (2) and (3) of Section 9-306 on proceeds.

(2) During the period that goods are in the possession of the issuer of a negotiable document therefor, a security interest in the goods is perfected by perfecting a security interest in the document, and any security interest in the goods otherwise perfected during such period is subject thereto.

(3) A security interest in goods in the possession of a bailee other than one who has issued a negotiable document therefor is perfected by issuance of a document in the name of the secured party or by the bailee's receipt of notification of the secured party's interest or by filing as to the goods.

(4) A security interest in instruments or negotiable documents is perfected without filing or the taking of possession for a period of 21 days from the time it attaches to the extent that it arises for new value given under a written security agreement.

(5) A security interest remains perfected for a period of 21 days without filing where a secured party having a perfected security interest in an instrument, a negotiable document or goods in possession of a bailee other than one who has issued a negotiable document therefor

    (a) makes available to the debtor the goods or documents representing the goods for the purpose of ultimate sale or exchange or for the purpose of loading, unloading, storing, shipping, transshipping, manufacturing, processing or otherwise dealing with them in a manner preliminary to their sale or exchange, but priority between conflicting security interests in the goods is subject to subsection (3) of Section 9-312; or

    (b) delivers the instrument to the debtor for the purpose

of ultimate sale or exchange or of presentation, collection, renewal or registration of transfer.

(6) After the 21 day period in subsections (4) and (5) perfection depends upon compliance with applicable provisions of this Article.

§9-304. Perfection of Security Interest in Instruments, Documents, and Goods Covered by Documents; Perfection by Permissive Filing; Temporary Perfection Without Filing or Transfer of Possession (1977 Amendments).

(1) A security interest in chattel paper or negotiable documents may be perfected by filing. A security interest in money or instruments (other than certificated securities or instruments which constitute part of chattel paper) can be perfected only by the secured party's taking possession, except as provided in subsections (4) and (5) of this section and subsections (2) and (3) of Section 9-306 on proceeds.

* * *

(4) A security interest in instruments (other than certificated securities) or negotiable documents is perfected without filing or the taking of possession for a period of 21 days from the time it attaches to the extent that it arises for new value given under a written security agreement.

(5) A security interest remains perfected for a period of 21 days without filing where a secured party having a perfected security interest in an instrument (other than a certificated security), a negotiable document or goods in possession of a bailee other than one who has issued a negotiable document therefor:

* * *

    (b) delivers the instrument to the debtor for the purpose of ultimate sale or exchange or of presentation, collection, renewal, or registration of transfer.

(6) After the 21 day period in subsections (4) and (5) perfection depends upon compliance with applicable provisions of this Article.

§9-305. When Possession by Secured Party Perfects Security Interest Without Filing.

A security interest in letters of credit and advices of credit (subsection (2) (a) of Section 5-116), goods, instruments, money, negotiable documents or chattel paper may be perfected by the secured party's taking possession of the collateral. If such collateral other than goods covered by a negotiable document is held by a bailee, the secured party is deemed to have possession from the time the bailee receives notification of the secured party's interest. A security interest is perfected by possession from the time possession is taken without relation back and continues only so long as possession is retained, unless otherwise specified in this Article. The security interest may be otherwise perfected as provided in this Article before or after the period of possession by the secured party.

§9-305. When Possession by Secured Party Perfects Security Interest Without Filing (1977 Amendments).

A security interest in letters of credit and advices of credit (subsection (2)(a) of Section 5-116), goods, instruments (other than certificated securities), money, negotiable documents, or chattel paper may be perfected by the secured party's taking possession of the collateral. If such collateral other than goods covered by a negotiable document is held by a bailee, the secured party is deemed to have possession from the time the bailee receives notification of the secured party's interest. A security interest is perfected by possession from the time possession is taken without relation back and continues only so long as possession is retained, unless otherwise specified in this Article. The security interest may be otherwise perfected as provided in this Article before or after the period of possession by the secured party.

§9-306. "Proceeds"; Secured Party's Rights on Disposition of Collateral.

"Proceeds" includes whatever is received upon the sale, exchange, collection or other disposition of collateral or proceeds. Insurance payable by reason of loss or damage to the collateral is proceeds, except to the extent that it is is payable to a person other than a party to the security agreement. Money, checks, deposit accounts, and the like are "cash proceeds". All other proceeds are "non-cash proceeds".

(2) Except where this Article otherwise provides, a security interest continues in collateral notwithstanding sale, exchange or other disposition thereof unless the disposition was authorized by the secured party in the security agreement or otherwise, and also continues in any identifiable proceeds including collections received by the debtor.

(3) The security interest in proceeds is a continuously perfected security interest if the interest in the original collateral was perfected but it ceases to be a perfected security interest and becomes unperfected ten days after receipt of the proceeds by the debtor unless

(a) a filed financing statement covers the original collateral and the proceeds are collateral in which a security interest may be perfected by filing in the office or offices where the financing statement has been filed and, if the proceeds are acquired with cash proceeds, the description of collateral in the financing statement indicates the types of property constituting the proceeds; or

(b) a filed financing statement covers the original collateral and the proceeds are identifiable cash proceeds; or

(c) the security interest in the proceeds is perfected before the expiration of the ten day period.

Except as provided in this section, a security interest in proceeds can be perfected only by the methods or under the circumstances permitted in this Article for original collateral of the same type.

(4) In the event of insolvency proceedings instituted by or against a debtor, a secured party with a perfected security interest in proceeds has a perfected security interest only in the following proceeds:

(a) in identifiable non-cash proceeds and in separate deposit accounts containing only proceeds;

(b) in identifiable cash proceeds in the form of money which is neither commingled with other money nor deposited in a deposit account prior to the insolvency proceedings;

(c) in identifiable cash proceeds in the form of checks and

the like which are not deposited in a deposit account prior to the insolvency proceedings; and

(d) in all cash and deposit accounts of the debtor in which proceeds have been commingled with other funds, but the perfected security interest under this paragraph (d) is

(i) subject to any right of set-off; and

(ii) limited to an amount not greater than the amount of any cash proceeds received by the debtor within ten days before the institution of the insolvency proceedings less the sum of (I) the payments to the secured party on account of cash proceeds received by the debtor during such period and (II) the cash proceeds received by the debtor during such period to which the secured party is entitled under paragraphs (a) through (c) of this subsection (4).

(5) If a sale of goods results in an account or chattel paper which is transferred by the seller to a secured party, and if the goods are returned to or are repossessed by the seller or the secured party, the following rules determine priorities:

(a) If the goods were collateral at the time of sale, for an indebtedness of the seller which is still unpaid, the original security interest attaches again to the goods and continues as a perfected security interest if it was perfected at the time when the goods were sold. If the security interest was originally perfected by a filing which is still effective, nothing further is required to continue the perfected status; in any other case, the secured party must take possession of the returned or repossessed goods or must file.

(b) An unpaid transferee of the chattel paper has a security interest in the goods against the transferor. Such security interest is prior to a security interest asserted under paragraph (a) to the extent that the transferee of the chattel paper was entitled to priority under Section 9-308.

(c) An unpaid transferee of the account has a security interest in the goods against the transferor. Such security interest is subordinate to a security interest asserted under paragraph (a).

(d) A security interest of an unpaid transferee asserted under paragraph (b) or (c) must be perfected for protection against creditors of the transferor and purchasers of the returned or repossessed goods.

§9-307. Protection of Buyers of Goods.

(1) A buyer in ordinary course of business (subsection (9) of Section 1-201) other than a person buying farm products from a person engaged in farming operations takes free of a security interest created by his seller even though the security interest is perfected and even though the buyer knows of its existence.

(2) In the case of consumer goods a buyer takes free of a security interest even though perfected if he buys without knowledge of the security interest, for value and for his own personal, family or household purposes unless prior to the purchase the secured party has filed a financing statement covering such goods.

(3) A buyer other than a buyer in ordinary course of business

(subsection (1) of this section) takes free of a security interest to the extent that it secures future advances made after the secured party acquires knowledge of the purchase, or more than 45 days after the purchase, whichever first occurs, unless made pursuant to a commitment entered into without knowledge of the purchase and before the expiration of the 45 day period.

§9-308. Purchase of Chattel Paper and Instruments.

A purchaser of chattel paper or an instrument who gives new value and takes possession of it in the ordinary course of his business has priority over a security interest in the chattel paper or instrument

(a) which is perfected under Section 9-304 (permissive filing and temporary perfection) or under Section 9-306 (perfection as to proceeds) if he acts without knowledge that the specific paper or instrument is subject to a security interest; or

(b) which is claimed merely as proceeds of inventory subject to a security interest (Section 9-306) even though he knows that the specific paper or instrument is subject to the security interest.

§9-309. Protection of Purchasers of Instruments and Documents.
Nothing in this Article limits the rights of a holder in due course of a negotiable instrument (Section 3-302) or a holder to whom a negotiable document of title has been duly negotiated (Section 7-501) or a bona fide purchaser of a security (Section 8-301) and such holders or purchasers take priority over an earlier security interest even though perfected. Filing under this Article does not constitute notice of the security interest to such holders or purchasers.

§9-309. Protection of Purchasers of Instruments, Documents and Securities *(1977 Amendments).*
Nothing in this Article limits the rights of a holder in due course of a negotiable instrument (Section 3-302) or a holder to whom negotiable document of title has been duly negotiated (Section 7-501) or a bona fide purchaser of a security (Section [8-301] 8-302) and such holders or purchasers take priority over an earlier security interest even though perfected. Filing under this Article does not constitute notice of the security interest to such holders or purchasers.

§9-310. Priority of Certain Liens Arising by Operation of Law.
When a person in the ordinary course of his business furnishes services or materials with respect to goods subject to a security interest, a lien upon goods in the possession of such person given by statute or rule of law for such materials or services takes priority over a perfected security interest unless the lien is statutory and the statute expressly provides otherwise.

§9-311. Alienability of Debtor's Rights: Judicial Process.
The debtor's rights in collateral may be voluntarily or involuntarily transferred (by way of sale, creation of a security interest, attachment, levy, garnishment or other judicial process) notwithstanding a provision in the security agreement prohibiting any transfer or making the transfer constitute a default.

§9-312. Priorities Among Conflicting Security Interests in the Same Collateral.

(1) The rules of priority stated in other sections of this Part and in the following sections shall govern when applicable: Section 4-208 with respect to the security interests of collecting banks in items being collected, accompanying documents and proceeds; Section 9-103 on security interests related to other jurisdictions; Section 9-114 on consignments.

(2) A perfected security interest in crops for new value given to enable the debtor to produce the crops during the production season and given not more than three months before the crops become growing crops by planting or otherwise takes priority over an earlier perfected security interest to the extent that such earlier interest secures obligations due more than six months before the crops become growing crops by planting or otherwise, even though the person giving new value had knowledge of the earlier security interest.

(3) A perfected purchase money security interest in inventory has priority over a conflicting security interest in the same inventory and also has priority in identifiable cash proceeds received on or before the delivery of the inventory to a buyer if

(a) the purchase money security interest is perfected at the time the debtor receives possession of the inventory; and

(b) the purchase noney secured party gives notification in writing to the holder of the conflicting security interest if the holder had filed a financing statement covering the same types of inventory (i) before the date of the filing made by the purchase money secured party, or (ii) before the beginning of the 21 day period where the purchase money security interest is temporarily perfected without filing or possession (subsection (5) of Section 9-304); and

(c) the holder of the conflicting security interest receives the notification within five years before the debtor receives possession of the inventory; and

(d) the notification states that the person giving the notice has or expects to acquire a purchase money security interest in inventory of the debtor, describing such inventory by item or type.

(4) A purchase money security interest in collateral other than inventory has priority over a conflicting security interest in the same collateral or its proceeds if the purchase money security interest is perfected at the time the debtor receives possession of the collateral or within ten days thereafter.

(5) In all cases not governed by other rules stated in this section (including cases of purchase money security interests which do not qualify for the special priorities set forth in subsections (3) and (4) of this section), priority between conflicting security interests in the same collateral shall be determined according to the following rules:

(a) Conflicting security interests rank according to priority in time of filing or perfection. Priority dates from the time a filing is first made covering the collateral or the time the security interest is first perfected, whichever is earlier, provided that there is no period thereafter when there is neither filing nor perfection.

(**b**) So long as conflicting security interests are unperfected, the first to attach has priority.

(**6**) For the purposes of subsection (5) a date of filing or perfection as to collateral is also a date of filing or perfection as to proceeds.

(**7**) If future advances are made while a security interest is perfected by filing or the taking of possession, the security interest has the same priority for the purposes of subsection (5) with respect to the future advances as it does with respect to the first advance. If a commitment is made before or while the security interest is so perfected, the security interest has the same priority with respect to advances made pursuant thereto. In other cases a perfected security interest has priority from the date the advance is made.

§9-312. Priorities Among Conflicting Security Interests in the Same Collateral (*1977 Amendments*).

(**7**) If future advances are made while a security interest is perfected by filing, the taking of possession, or under Section 8-321 on securities, the security interest has the same priority for the purposes of subsection (5) with respect to the future advances as it does with respect to the first advance. If a commitment is made before or while the security interest is so perfected, the security interest has the same priority with respect to advances made pursuant thereto. In other cases a perfected security interest has priority from the date the advance is made.

* * *

§9-313. Priority of Security Interests in Fixtures.

(**1**) In this section and in the provisions of Part 4 of this Article referring to fixture filing, unless the context otherwise requires

(**a**) goods are "fixtures" when they become so related to particular real estate that an interest in them arises under real estate law

(**b**) a "fixture filing" is the filing in the office where a mortgage on the real estate would be filed or recorded of a financing statement covering goods which are or are to become fixtures and conforming to the requirements of subsection (5) of Section 9-402

(**c**) a mortgage is a "construction mortgage" to the extent that it secures an obligation incurred for the construction of an improvement on land including the acquisition cost of the land, if the recorded writing so indicates.

(**2**) A security interest under this Article may be created in goods which are fixtures or may continue in goods which become fixtures, but no security interest exists under this Article in ordinary building materials incorporated into an improvement on land.

(**3**) This Article does not prevent creation of an encumbrance upon fixtures pursuant to real estate law.

(**4**) A perfected security interest in fixtures has priority over the conflicting interest of an encumbrancer or owner of the real estate where

(**a**) the security interest is a purchase money security interest, the interest of the encumbrancer or owner arises before the goods become fixtures, the security interest is perfected by a fixture filing before the goods become fixtures or within ten days thereafter, and the debtor has an interest of record in the real estate or is in possession of the real estate; or

(**b**) the security interest is perfected by a fixture filing before the interest of the encumbrancer or owner is of record, the security interest has priority over any conflicting interest of a predecessor in title of the encumbrancer or owner, and the debtor has an interest of record in the real estate or is in possession of the real estate; or

(**c**) the fixtures are readily removable factory or office machines or readily removable replacements of domestic appliances which are consumer goods, and before the goods become fixtures the security interest is perfected by any method permitted by this Article; or

(**d**) the conflicting interest is a lien on the real estate obtained by legal or equitable proceedings after the security interest was perfected by any method permitted by this Article.

(**5**) A security interest in fixtures, whether or not perfected, has priority over the conflicting interest of an encumbrancer or owner of the real estate where

(**a**) the encumbrancer or owner has consented in writing to the security interest or has disclaimed an interest in the goods as fixtures; or

(**b**) the debtor has a right to remove the goods as against the encumbrancer or owner. If the debtor's right terminates, the priority of the security interest continues for a reasonable time.

(**6**) Notwithstanding paragraph (a) of subsection (4) but otherwise subject to subsections (4) and (5), a security interest in fixtures is subordinate to a construction mortgage recorded before the goods become fixtures if the goods become fixtures before the completion of the construction. To the extent that it is given to refinance a construction mortgage, a mortgage has this priority to the same extent as the construction mortgage.

(**7**) In cases not within the preceding subsections, a security interest in fixtures is subordinate to the conflicting interest of an encumbrancer or owner of the related real estate who is not the debtor.

(**8**)) When the secured party has priority over all owners and encumbrancers of the real estate, he may, on default, subject to the provisions of Part 5, remove his collateral from the real estate but he must reimburse any encumbrancer or owner of the real estate who is not the debtor and who has not otherwise agreed for the cost of repair of any physical injury, but not for any diminution in value of the real estate caused by the absence of the goods removed or by any necessity of replacing them. A person entitled to reimbursement may refuse permission to remove until the secured party gives adequate security for the performance of this obligation.

§9-314. Accessions.

(**1**) A security interest in goods which attaches before they are installed in or affixed to other goods takes priority as to the goods installed or affixed (called in this section "accessions") over the claims of all persons to the whole except as stated in subsection (3) and subject to Section 9-315(1).

(2) A security interest which attaches to goods after they beocme part of a whole is valid against all persons subsequently acquiring interests in the whole except as stated in subsection (3) but is invalid against any person with an interest in the whole at the time the security interest attaches to the goods who has not in writing consented to the security interest or disclaimed an interest in the goods as part of the whole.

(3) The security interests described in subsections (1) and (2) do not take priority over

(a) a subsequent purchaser for value of any interest in the whole; or

(b) a creditor with a lien on the whole subsequently obtained by judicial proceedings; or

(c) a creditor with a prior perfected security interest in the whole to the extent that he makes subsequent advances

if the subsequent purchase is made, the lien by judicial proceedings obtained or the subsequent advance under the prior perfected security interest is made or contracted for without knowledge of the security interest and before it is perfected. A purchaser of the whole at a foreclosure sale other than the holder of a perfected security interest purchasing at his own foreclosure sale is a subsequent purchaser within this section.

(4) When under subsections (1) or (2) and (3) a secured party has an interest in accessions which has priority over the claims of all persons who have interests in the whole, he may on default subject to the provisions of Part 5 remove his collateral from the whole but he must reimburse any encumbrancer or owner of the whole who is not the debtor and who has not otherwise agreed for the cost of repair of any physical injury but not for any diminution in value of the whole caused by the absence of the goods removed or by any necessity for replacing them. A person entitled to reimbursement may refuse permission to remove until the secured party gives adequate security for the performance of this obligation.

§9-315. Priority When Goods are Commingled or Processed.

(1) If a security interest in goods was perfected and subsequently the goods or a part thereof have become part of a product or mass, the security interest continues in the product or mass if

(a) the goods are so manufactured, processed, assembled or commingled that their identity is lost in the product or mass; or

(b) a financing statement covering the original goods also covers the product into which the goods have been manufactured, processed or assembled. In a case to which paragraph (b) applies, no separate security interest in that part of the original goods which has been manufactured, processed or assembled into the product may be claimed under Section 9-314.

(2) When under subsection (1) more than one security interest attaches to the product or mass, they rank equally according to the ratio that the cost of the goods to which each interest originally attached bears to the cost of the total product or mass.

§9-316. Priority Subject to Subordination.
Nothing in this Article prevents subordination by agreement by any person entitled to priority.

§9-317. Secured Party Not Obligated On Contract of Debtor.
The mere existence of a security interest or authority given to the debtor to dispose of or use collateral does not impose contract or tort liability upon the secured party for the debtor's acts or omissions.

§9-318. Defenses Against Assignee; Modification of Contract After Notification of Assignment; Term Prohibiting Assignment Ineffective; Identification and Proof of Assignment.

(1) Unless an account debtor has made an enforceable agreement not to assert defenses or claims arising out of a sale as provided in Section 9-206 the rights of an assignee are subject to

(a) all the terms of the contract between the account debtor and assignor and any defense or claim arising therefrom; and

(b) any other defense or claim of the account debtor against the assignor which accrues before the account debtor receives notification of the assignment.

(2) So far as the right to payment or a part thereof under an assigned contract has not been fully earned by performance, and notwithstanding notification of the assignment, any modification of or substitution for the contract made in good faith and in accordance with reasonable commercial standards is effective against an assignee unless the account debtor has otherwise agreed but the assignee acquires corresponding rights under the modified or substituted contract. The assignment may provide that such modification or substitution is a breach by the assignor.

(3) The account debtor is authorized to pay the assignor until the account debtor receives notification that the amount due or to become due has been assigned and that payment is to be made to the assignee. A notification which does not reasonably identify the rights assigned is ineffective. If requested by the account debtor, the assignee must seasonably furnish reasonable proof that the assignment has been made and unless he does so the account debtor may pay the assignor.

(4) A term in any contract between an account debtor and an assignor is ineffective if it prohibits assignment of an account or prohibits creation of a security interest in a general intangible for money due or to become due or requires the account debtor's consent to such assignment or security interest.

Part 4: Filing

§9-401. Place of Filing; Erroneous Filing; Removal of Collateral.

First Alternative Subsection (1)

(1) The proper place to file in order to perfect a security interest is as follows:

(a) when the collateral is timber to be cut or is minerals or the like (including oil and gas) or accounts subject to subsection (5) of Section 9-103, or when the financing statement is filed as a fixture filing (Section 9-313) and the collateral is goods which are or are to become fixtures, then in the office where a mortgage on the real estate would be filed or recorded;

(b) in all other cases, in the office of the [[Secretary of State]]

Second Alternative Subsection (1)

(1) The proper place to file in order to perfect a security interest is as follows:

(a) when the collateral is equipment used in farming operations, or farm products, or accounts or general intangibles arising from or relating to the sale of farm products by a farmer, or consumer goods, then in the office of the .... in the county of the debtor's residence or if the debtor is not a resident of this state then in the office of the .... in the county where the goods are kept, and in addition when the collateral is crops growing or to be grown in the office of the .... in the county where the land is located;

(b) when the collateral is timber to be cut or is minerals or the like (including oil and gas) or accounts subject to subsection (5) of Section 9-103, or when the financing statement is filed as a fixture filing (Section 9-313) and the collateral is goods which are or are to become fixtures, then in the office where a mortgage on the real estate would be filed or recorded;

(c) in all other cases, in the office of the ......

Third Alternative Subsection (1)

(1) The proper place to file in order to perfect a security interest is as follows:

(a) when the collateral is equipment used in farming operations, or farm products, or accounts or general intangibles arising from or relating to the sale of farm porducts by a farmer, or consumer goods, then in the office of the ...... in the county of the debtor's residence or if the debtor is not a resident of this state then in the office of the ...... in the county where the goods are kept, and in addition when the collateral is crops growing or to be grown in the office of ...... in the county where the land is located;

(b) when the collateral is timber to be cut or is minerals or the like (including oil and gas) or accounts subject to subsection (5) of Section 9-103, or when the financing statement is filed as a fixture filing (Section 9-313) and the collateral is goods which are or are to beome fixtures, then in the office where a mortgage on the real estate would be filed or recorded;

(c) in all other cases, in the office of the ..... and in addition, if the debtor has a place of business in only one county of this state, also in the office of ...... of such county, or, if the debtor has no place of business in this state, but resides in the state, also in the office of ...... of the county in which he resides.

Note: *One of the three alternatives should be selected as subsection (1).*

(2) A filing which is made in good faith in an improper place or not in all of the places required by this section is nevertheless effective with regard to any collateral as to which the filing complied with the requirements of this Article and is also effective with regard to collateral covered by the financing statement against any person who has knowledge of the contents of such financing statement.

(3) A filing which is made in the proper place in this state continues effective even though the debtor's residence or place of business or the location of the collateral or its use, whichever controlled the original filing, is thereafter changed.

Language in double brackets is Alternative Subsection (3).

[[(3) A filing which is made in the proper county continues effective for four months after a change to another county of the debtor's residence or place of business or the location of the collateral, whichever controlled the original filing. It becomes ineffective thereafter unless a copy of the financing statement signed by the secured party is filed in the new county within said period. The security interest may also be perfected in the new county after the expiration of the four-month period; in such case perfected dates from the time of perfection in the new county. A change in the use of the collateral does not impair the effectiveness of the original filing.]]

(4) The rules stated in Section 9-103 determine whether filing is necessary in this state.

(5) Notwithstanding the preceding subsections, and subject to subsection (3) of Section 9-302, the proper place to file in order to perfect a security interest in collateral, including the fixtures, of a transmitting utility is the office of the [[Secretary of State]]. This filing constitutes a fixture filing (Section 9-313) as to the collateral described therein which is or is to become fixtures.

(6) For the purposes of this section, the residence of an organization is its place of business if it has one or its chief executive office if it has more than one place of business.

Note: *Subsection (6) should be used only if the state chooses the Second or Third Alternative Subsection (1).*

§9-402. Formal Requisites of Financing Statement; Amendments; Mortgage as Financing Statement.

(1) A financing statement is sufficient if it gives the names of the debtor and the secured party, is signed by the debtor, gives an address of the secured party from which information concerning the security interest may be obtained, gives a mailing address of the debtor and contains a statement indicating the types, or describing the items, of collateral. A financing statement may be filed before a security agreement is made or a security interest otherwise attaches. When the financing statement covers crops growing or to be grown, the statement must also contain a description of the real estate concerned. When the financing statement covers timber to be cut or covers minerals or the like (including oil and gas) or accounts subject to subsection (5) of Section 9-103, or when the financing statement is filed as a fixture filing (Section 9-313) and the collateral is goods which are or are to become fixtures, the statement must also comply with subsection (5). A copy of the security agree-

ment is sufficient as a financing statement if it contains the above information and is signed by the debtor. A carbon, photographic or other reproduction of a security agreement or a financing statement is sufficient as a financing statement if the security agreement so provides or if the original has been filed in this state.

(2) A financing statement which otherwise complies with subsection (1) is sufficient when it is signed by the secured party instead of the debtor if it is filed to perfect a security interest in

(a) collateral already subject to security interest in another jurisdiction when it is brought into this state, or when the debtor's location is changed to this state. Such a financing statement must state that the collateral was brought into this state or that the debtor's location was changed to this state under such circumstances; or

(b) proceeds under Section 9-306 if the security interest in the original collateral was perfected. Such a financing statement must describe the original collateral; or

(c) collateral as to which the filing has lapsed; or

(d) collateral acquired after a change of name, identity or corporate structure of the debtor (subsection (7)).

(3) A form substantially as follows is sufficient to comply with subsection (1):

Name of debtor (or assignor) . . . .
Address . . . .
Name of secured party (or assignee) . . . .
Address . . . .

1. This financing statement covers the following types (or items) of property:
(Describe) . . . .

2. (If collateral is crops) The above described crops are growing or are to be grown on:
(Describe Real Estate) . . . .

3. (If applicable) The above goods are to become fixtures on *(Describe Real Estate) . . . . . and this financing statement is to be filed [[for record]] in the real estate records. (If the debtor does not have an interest of record) The name of a record owner is . . . .

4. (If products of collateral are claimed) Products of the collateral are also covered.

(use whichever is applicable) {
. . . .
Signature of Debtor (or Assignor)
. . . .
Signature of Secured Party (or Assignee)

(4) A financing statement may be amended by filing a writing signed by both the debtor and the secured party. An amendment does not extend the period of effectiveness of a financing statement. If any amendment adds collateral, it is effective as to the added collateral only from the filing date of the amendment. In this Article, unless the context otherwise requires, the term "financing statement" means the original financing statement and any amendments.

(5) A financing statement covering timber to be cut or covering minerals or the like (including oil and gas) or accounts subject to subsection (5) of Section 9-103, or a financing statement filed as a fixture filing (Section 9-313) where the debtor is not a transmitting utility, must show that it covers this type of collateral, must recite that it is to be filed [[for record]] in the real estate records, and the financing statement must contain a description of the real estate [[sufficient if it were contained in a mortgage of the real estate to give constructive notice of the mortgage under the law of this state]]. If the debtor does not have an interest of record in the real estate, the financing statement must show the name of a record owner.

(6) A mortgage is effective as a financing statement filed as a fixture filing from the date of its recording if (a) the goods are described in the mortgage by item or type, (b) the goods are or are to become fixtures related to the real estate described in the mortgage, (c) the mortgage complies with the requirements for a financing statement in this section other than a recital that it is to be filed in the real estate records, and (d) the mortgage is duly recorded. No fee with reference to the financing statement is required other than the regular recording and satisfaction fees with respect to the mortgage.

(7) A financing statement sufficiently shows the name of the debtor if it gives the individual, partnership or corporate name of the debtor, whether or not it adds other trade names or the names of partners. Where the debtor so changes his name or in the case of an organization name, identity or corporate structure that a filed financing statement becomes seriously misleading, the filing is not effective to perfect a security interest in collateral acquired by the debtor more than four months after the change, unless a new appropriate financing statement is filed before the expiration of that time. A filed financing statement remains effective with respect to collateral transferred by the debtor even though the secured party knows of or consents to the transfer.

(8) A financing statement substantially complying with the requirements of this section is effective even though it contains minor errors which are not seriously misleading.

Note: *Language in double brackets is optional.*

Note: *Where the state has any special recording system for real estate other than the usual grantor-grantee index (as, for instance, a tract system or a title registration or Torrens system) local adaptations of subsection (5) and Section 9-403(7) may be necessary. See Mass. Gen. Laws Chapter 106, Section 9-409.*

§9-403. What Constitutes Filing; Duration of Filing; Effect of Lapsed Filing; Duties of Filing Officer.

(1) Presentation for filing of a financing statement and tender of the filing fee or acceptance of the statement by the filing officer constitutes filing under this Article.

(2) Except as provided in subsection (6) a filed financing statement is effective for a period of five years from the date of filing. The effectiveness of a filed financing statement lapses on the expiration of the five year period unless a continuation statement is filed prior to the lapse. If a security interest perfected by filing exists at the time insolvency proceedings are commenced by or against the debtor, the security interest remains perfected until termination of the insolvency proceedings and thereafter for a period of sixty days or until expiration of the five year period, whichever occurs later. Upon lapse the

security interest becomes unperfected, unless it is perfected without filing. If the security interest becomes unperfected upon lapse, it is deemed to have been unperfected as against a person who became a purchaser or lien creditor before lapse.

(3) A continuation statement may be filed by the secured party within six months prior to the expiration of the five year period specified in subsection (2). Any such continuation statement must be signed by the secured party, identify the original statement by file number and state that the original statement is still effective. A continuation statement signed by a person other than the secured party of record must be accompanied by a separate written statement of assignment signed by the secured party of record and complying with subsection (2) of Section 9-405, including payment of the required fee. Upon timely filing of the continuation statement, the effectiveness of the original statement is continued for five years after the last date to which the filing was effective whereupon it lapses in the same manner as provided in subsection (2) unless another continuation statement is filed prior to such lapse. Succeeding continuation statements may be filed in the same manner to continue the effectiveness of the original statement. Unless a statute on disposition of public records provides otherwise, the filing officer may remove a lapsed statement from the files and destroy it immediately if he has retained a microfilm or other photographic record, or in other cases after one year after the lapse. The filing officer shall so arrange matters by physical annexation of financing statements to continuation statements or other related filings, or by other means, that if he physically destroys the financing statements of a period more than five years past, those which have been continued by a continuation statement or which are still effective under subsection (6) shall be retained.

(4) Except as provided in subsection (7) a) filing officer shall mark each statement with a file number and with the date and hour of filing and shall hold the statement or a microfilm or other photographic copy thereof for public inspection. In addition the filing officer shall index the statements according to the name of the debtor and shall note in the index the file number and the address of the debtor given in the statement.

(5) The uniform fee for filing and indexing and for the stamping a copy furnished by the secured party to show the date and place of filing for an original financing statement or for a continuation statement shall be $ . . . . if the statement is in the standard form prescribed by the . . . . . and otherwise shall be $ . . . ., plus in each case, if the financing statement is subject to subsection (5) of Section 9-402, $ . . . . The uniform fee for each name more than one required to be indexed shall be $ . . . . The secured party may at his option show a trade name for any person and an extra uniform indexing fee of $ . . . . shall be paid with respect thereto.

(6) If the debtor is a transmitting utility (subsection (5) of Section 9-401) and a filed financing statement so states, it is effective until a termination statement is filed. A real estate mortgage which is effective as a fixture filing under subsection (6) of Section 9-402 remains effective as a fixture filing until the

mortgage is released or satisfied or record or its effectiveness otherwise terminates as to the real estate.

(7) When a financing statement covers timber to be cut or covers minerals or the like (including oil and gas) or accounts subject to subsection (5) of Section 9-103, or is filed as a fixture filing, [[it shall be filed for record and]] the filing officer shall index it under the names of the debtor and any owner of record shown on the financing statement in the same fashion as if they were the mortgagors in a mortgage of the real estate described, and, to the extent that the law of this state provides for indexing of mortgages under the name of the mortgagee, under the name of the secured party as if he were the mortgagee, thereunder, or where indexing is by description in the same fashion as if the financing statement were a mortgage of the real estate described.

Note: *In states in which writings will not appear in the real estate records and indices unless actually recorded the bracketed language in subsection (7) should be used.*

§9-404. Termination Statement.

(1) If a financing statement covering consumer goods is filed on or after . . . ., then within one month or within ten days following written demand by the debtor after there is no outstanding secured obligation and no commitment to make advances, incur obligations or otherwise give value, the secured party must file with each filing officer with whom the financing statement was filed, a termination statement to the effect that he no longer claims a security interest under the financing statement, which shall be identified by file number. In other cases whenever there is no outstanding secured obligation and no commitment to make advances, incur obligations or otherwise give value, the secured party must on written demand by the debtor send the debtor, for each filing officer with whom the financing statement was filed, a termination statement to the effect that no longer claims a security interest under the financing statement, which shall be identified by file number. A termination statement signed by a person other than the secured party of record must be accompanied by a separate written statement of assignment signed by the secured party of record complying with subsection (2) of Section 9-405, including payment of the required fee. If the affected secured party fails to file such a termination statement as required by this subsection, or to send such a termination statement within ten days after proper demand therefor he shall be liable to the debtor for one hundred dollars, and in addition for any loss caused to the debtor by such failure.

(2) On presentation to the filing officer of such a termination statement he must note it in the index. If he has received the termination statement in duplicate, he shall return one copy of the termination statement to the secured party stamped to show the time of receipt thereof. If the filing officer has a microfilm or other photographic record of the financing statement, and of any related continuation statement, statement of assignment and statement of release, he may remove the originals from the files at any time after receipt of the termination statement, or if he has no such record, he may remove them from the files at any time after one year after receipt of the termination statement.

(3) If the termination statement is in the standard form prescribed by the . . . . . , the uniform fee for filing and indexing the termination statement shall be $. . . . . , and otherwise shall be $. . . . . , plus in each case an additional fee of $. . . . . . . for each name more than one against which the termination statement is required to be indexed.

Note: *The date to be inserted should be the effective date of the revised Article 9.*

§9-405. Assignment of Security Interest; Duties of Filing Officer; Fees.

(1) A financing statement may disclose an assignment of a security interest in the collateral described in the financing statement by indication in the financing statement of the name and address of the assignee or by an assignment itself or a copy thereof on the face or back of the statement. On presentation to the filing officer of such a financing statement the filing officer shall mark the same as provided in Section 9-403(4). The uniform fee for filing, indexing and furnishing filing data for a financing statement so indicating an assignment shall be $. . . . . if the statement is in the standard form prescribed by the . . . . and otherwise shall be $. . . . . . . plus in each case an additional fee of $. . . . . for each name more than one against which the financing statement is required to be indexed.

(2) A secured party may assign of record all or part of his rights under a financing statement by the filing in the place where the original financing statement was filed of a separate written statement of assignment signed by the secured party of record and setting forth the name of the secured party of record and the debtor, the file number and the date of filing of the financing statement and the name and address of the assignee and containing a description of the collateral assigned. A copy of the assignment is sufficient as a separate statement if it complies with the preceding sentence. On presentation to the filing officer of such a separate statement, the filing officer shall mark such separate statement with the date and hour of the filing. He shall note the assignment on the index of the financing statement, or in the case of a fixture filing, or a filing covering timber to be cut, or covering minerals or the like (including oil and gas) or accounts subject to subsection (5) of Section 9-103, he shall index the assignment under the name of the assignor as grantor and, to the extent that the law of this state provides for indexing the assignment of a mortgage under the name of the assignee, he shall index the assignment of the financing statement under the name of the assignee. The uniform fee for filing, indexing and furnishing filing data about such a separate statement of assignment shall be $. . . . if the statement is in the standard form prescribed by the . . . . and otherwise shall be $. . . . . , plus in each case an additional fee of $. . . . . for each name more than one against which the statement of assignment is required to be indexed. Notwithstanding the provisions of this subsection, an assignment of record of a security interest in a fixture contained in a mortgage effective as a fixture filing (subsection (6) of Section 9-402) may be made only by an assignment of the mortgage in the manner provided by the law of this state other than this Act.

(3) After the disclosure or filing of an assignment under this section, the assignee is the secured party of record.

§9-406. Release of Collateral; Duties of Filing Officer; Fees. A secured party of record may by his signed statement release all or a part of any collateral described in a filed financing statement. The statement of release is sufficient if it contains a description of the collateral being released, the name and address of the debtor, the name and address of the secured party, and the file number of the financing statement. A statement of release signed by a person other than the secured party of record must be accompanied by a separate written statement of assignment signed by the secured party of record and complying with subsection (2) of Section 9-405, including payment of the required fee. Upon presentation of such a statement of release to the filing officer he shall mark the statement with the hour and date of filing and shall note the same upon the margin of the index of the filing of the financing statement. The uniform fee for filing and noting such a statement of release shall be $. . . . . if the statement is in the standard form prescribed by the . . . . . and otherwise shall be $. . . . . , plus in each case an additional fee of $. . . . . . . for each name more than one against which the statement of release is required to be indexed.

§[[9-407. Information From Filing Officer.]]

[[(1) If the person filing any financing statement, termination statement, statement of assignment, or statement of release, furnishes the filing officer a copy thereof, the filing officer shall upon request note upon the copy the file number and date and hour of the filing of the original and deliver or send the copy to such person.

[[(2) Upon request of any person, the filing officer shall issue his certificate showing whether there is on file on the date and hour stated therein, any presently effective financing statement naming a particular debtor and any statement of assignment thereof and if there is, giving the date and hour of filing of each such statement and the names and addresses of each secured party therein. The uniform fee for such a certificate shall be $. . . . . . . if the request for the certificate is in the standard form prescribed by the [[Secretary of State]] and otherwise shall be $. . . . . Upon request the filing officer shall furnish a copy of any filed statement or statement of assignment for a uniform fee of $. . . . . per page.]]

Note: *This section is proposed as an optional provision to require filing officers to furnish certificates. Local law and practices should be consulted with regard to the advisability of adoption.*

§9-408. Financing Statements Covering Consigned or Leased Goods. A consignor or lessor of goods may file a financing statement using the terms "consignor," "consignee," "lessor," "lessee" or the like instead of the terms specified in Section 9-402. The provisions of this Part shall apply as appropriate to such a financing statement but its filing shall not of itself be a factor in determining whether or not the consignment or lease is intended as security (Section 1-201(37)). However, if it is determined for other reasons that the consignment or lease is so intended, a security interest of the consignor or lessor which attaches to the consigned or leased goods is perfected by such filing.

Part 5: Default

§9-501. Default; Procedure When Security Agreement Covers Both Real and Personal Property.

(1) When a debtor is in default under a security agreement, a secured party has the rights and remedies provided in this Part and except as limited by subsection (3) those provided in the security agreement. He may reduce his claim to judgment, foreclose or otherwise enforce the security interest by any avialable judicial procedure. If the collateral is documents the secured party may proceed either as to the documents or as to the goods covered thereby. A secured party in possession has the rights, remedies and duties provided in Section 9-207. The rights and remedies referred to in this subsection are cumulative.

(2) After default, the debtor has the rights and remedies provided in this Part, those provided in the security agreement and those provided in Section 9-207.

(3) To the extent that they give rights to the debtor and impose duties on the secured party, the rules stated in the subsections referred to below may not be waived or varied except as provided with respect to compulsory disposition of collateral (subsection (3) of Section 9-504 and Section 9-505) and with respect to redemption of collateral (Section 9-506) but the parties may by agreement determine the standards by which the fulfillment of these rights and duties is to be measured if such standards are not manifestly unreasonable:

> (a) subsection (2) of Section 9-502 and subsection (2) of Section 9-504 insofar as they require accounting for surplus proceeds of collateral;
>
> (b) subsection (3) of Section 9-504 and subsection (1) of Section 9-505 which deal with disposition of collateral;
>
> (c) subsection (2) of Section 9-505 which deals with acceptance of collateral as discharge of obligation;
>
> (d) Section 9-506 which deals with redemption of collateral; and
>
> (e) subsection (1) of Section 9-507 which deals with the secured party's liability for failure to comply with this Part.

(4) If the security agreement covers both real and personal property, the secured party may proceed under this Part as to the personal property or he may proceed as to both the real and the personal property in accordance with his rights and remedies in respect of the real property in which case the provisions of this Part do not apply.

(5) When a secured party has reduced his claim to judgment the lien of any levy which may be made upon his collateral by virtue of any execution based upon the judgment shall relate back to the date of the perfection of the security interest in such collateral. A judicial sale, pursuant to such execution, is a foreclosure of the security interest by judicial procedure within the meaning of this section, and the secured party may purchase at the sale and thereafter hold the collateral free of any other requirements of this Article.

§9-502. Collection Rights of Secured Party.

(1) When so agreed and in any event on default the secured party is entitled to notify an account debtor or the obligor on an instrument to make payment to him whether or not the assignor was theretofore making collections on the collateral, and also to take control of any proceeds to which he is entitled under Section 9-306.

(2) A secured party who by agreement is entitled to charge back uncollected collateral or otherwise to full or limited recourse against the debtor and who undertakes to collect from the account debtors or obligors must proceed in a commercially reasonable manner and may deduct his reasonable expenses of realization from the collections. If the security agreement secures an indebtedness, the secured party must account to the debtor for any surplus, and unless otherwise agreed, the debtor is liable for any deficiency. But, if the underlying transaction was a sale of accounts or chattel paper, the debtor is entitled to any surplus or is liable for any deficiency only if the security agreement so provides.

§9-503. Secured Party's Right to Take Possession After Default.
Unless otherwise agreed a secured party has on default the right to take possession of the collateral. In taking possession a secured party may proceed without judicial process if this can be done without breach of the peace or may proceed by action. If the security agreement so provides the secured party may require the debtor to assemble the collateral and make it available to the secured party at a place to be designated by the secured party which is reasonably convenient to both parties. Without removal a secured party may render equipment unusable, and may dispose of collateral on the debtor's premises under Section 9-504.

§9-504. Secured Party's Right to Dispose of Collateral After Default; Effect of Dispositon.

(1) A secured party after default may sell, lease or otherwise dispose of any or all of the collateral in its then condition or following any commercially reasonable preparation or processing. Any sale of goods is subject to the Article on Sales (Article 2). The proceeds of disposition shall be applied in the order following to

> (a) the reasonable expenses of retaking, holding, preparing for sale or lease, selling, leasing and the like and, to the extent provided for in the agreement and not prohibited by law, the reasonable attorneys' fees and legal expenses incurred by the secured party;
>
> (b) the satisfaction of indebtedness secured by the security interest under which the disposition is made;
>
> (c) the satisfaction of indebtedness secured by any subordinate security interest in the collateral if written notification of demand therefor is received before distribution of the proceeds is completed. If requested by the secured party, the holder of a subordinate security interest must seasonably furnish reasonable proof of his interest, and

unless he does so, the secured party need not comply with his demand.

(2) If the security interest secures an indebtedness, the secured party must account to the debtor for any surplus, and, unless otherwise agreed, the debtor is liable for any deficiency. But if the underlying transaction was a sale of accounts, or chattel paper, the debtor is entitled to any surplus or is liable for any deficiency only if the security agreement so provides.

(3) Disposition of the collateral may be by public or private proceedings and may be made by way of one or more contracts. Sale or other disposition may be as a unit or in parcels and at any time and place and on any terms but every aspect of the disposition including the method, manner, time, place and terms must be commercially reasonable. Unless collateral is perishable or threatens to decline speedily in value or is of a type customarily sold on a recognized market, reasonable notification of the time and place of any public sale or reasonable notification of the time after which any private sale or other intended dispostion is to be made shall be sent by the secured party to the debtor, if he has not signed after default a statement renouncing or modifying his right to notification of sale. In the case of consumer goods no other notification need be sent. In other cases notification shall be sent to any other secured party from whom the secured party has received (before sending his notification to the debtor or before the debtor's renunication of his rights) written notice of a claim of an interest in the collateral. The secured party may buy at any public sale and if the collateral is of a type customarily sold in a recognized market or is of a type which is the subject of widely distributed standard price quotations he may buy at private sale.

(4) When collateral is disposed of by a secured party after default, the disposition transfers to a purchaser for value all of the debtor's rights therein, discharges the security interest under which it is made and any security interest or lien subordinate thereto. The purchaser takes free of all such rights and interests even though the secured party fails to comply with the requirements of this Part or of any judicial proceedings

    (a) in the case of a public sale, if the purchaser has no knowledge of any defects in the sale and if he does not buy in collusion with the secured party, other bidders or the person conducting the sale; or

    (b) in any other case, if the purchaser acts in good faith.

(5) A person who is liable to a secured party under a guaranty, indorsement, repurchase agreement or the like and who receives a transfer of collateral from the secured party or is subrogated to his rights has thereafter the rights and duties of the secured party. Such a transfer of collateral is not a sale or disposition of the collateral under this Article.

§9-505. Compulsory Disposition of Collateral; Acceptance of the Collateral as Discharge of Obligation.

(1) If the debtor has paid sixty per cent of the cash price in the case of a purchase money security interest in consumer goods or sixty per cent of the loan in the case of another security interest in consumer goods and has not signed after default a statement renouncing or modifying his rights under this Part a secured party who has taken possession of collateral must dispose of it under Section 9-504 and if he fails to do so within ninety days after he takes possession the debtor at his option may recover in conversion or under Section 9-507(1) on secured party's liability.

(2) In any other case involving consumer goods or any other collateral a secured party in possession may, after default, propose to retain the collateral in satisfaction of the obligation. Written notice of such proposal shall be sent to the debtor if he has not signed after default a statement renouncing or modifying his rights under this subsection. In the case of consumer goods no other notice need be given. In other cases notice shall be sent to any other secured party from whom the secured party has received (before sending his notice to the debtor or before the debtor's renunciation of his rights) written notice of a claim of an interest in the collateral. If the secured party receives objection in writing from a person entitled to receive notification within twenty-one days after the notice was sent, the secured party must dispose of the collateral under Section 9-504. In the absence of such written objection the secured party may retain the collateral in satisfaction of the debtor's obligation.

§9-506. Debtor's Right to Redeem Collateral.

At any time before the secured party has disposed of collateral or entered into a contract for its disposition under Section 9-504 or before the obligation has been discharged under Section 9-505(2) the debtor or any other secured party may unless otherwise agreed in writing after default redeem the collateral by tendering fulfillment of all obligations secured by the collateral as well as the expenses reasonably incurred by the secured party in retaking, holding and preparing the collateral for disposition, in arranging for the sale, and to the extent provided in the agreement and not prohibited by law, his reasonable attorneys' fees and legal expenses.

§9-507. Secured Party's Liability for Failure to Comply With This Part.

(1) If it is established that the secured party is not proceeding in accordance with the provisions of this Part disposition may be ordered or restrained on appropriate terms and conditions. If the disposition has occurred the debtor or any person entitled to notification or whose security interest has been made known to the secured party prior to the disposition has a right to recover from the secured party any loss caused by a failure to comply with the provisions of this Part. If the collateral is consumer goods, the debtor has a right to recover in any event an amount not less than the credit service charge plus ten per cent of the principal amount of the debt or the time price differential plus 10 per cent of the cash price.

(2) The fact that a better price could have been obtained by a sale at a different time or in a different method from that selected by the secured party is not of itself sufficient to establish that the sale was not made in a commercially reasonable manner. If the secured party either sells the collateral in the usual manner in any recognized market therefor or if he

sells at the price current in such market at the time of his sale or if he has otherwise sold in conformity with reasonable commercial practices among dealers in the type of property sold he has sold in a commercially reasonable manner. The principles stated in the two preceding sentences with respect to sales also apply as may be appropriate to other types of disposition. A disposition which has been approved in any judicial proceeding or by any bona fide creditors' committee or representative of creditors shall conclusively be deemed to be commercially reasonable, but this sentence does not indicate that any such approval must be obtained in any case nor does it indicate that any disposition not so approved is not commercially reasonable.

ARTICLE 10: EFFECTIVE DATE AND REPEALER

[omitted]

ARTICLE 11: EFFECTIVE DATE AND TRANSITION PROVISIONS

[omitted]

GLOSSARY

Abatement Generally, plea in abatement. A form of pleading which asserts that an action is without legal effect; if the plea is sustained, the entire action is ended. Also, in the law of wills, a required reduction or nonpayment of a gift stated in a will.

Acceleration clause A provision in a promissory note permitting the maker to make, or a holder to have, payment before the stated due date.

Acceptance An offeree's manifestation of assent to the terms of an offer, usually needed for a contract to arise. Also, *in the law of sales:* a buyer's act of taking as the buyer's own property the particular goods covered by a contract, whether by words or by action or silence when it is time to speak. Also, *in the law of commercial paper,* a drawee's act of writing the word "accepted" across the face of a draft (or the word "certified" across the face of a check), or signing on the face of the instrument, and thereby becoming a primary party to the instrument. Also, *in the law of bankruptcy,* an agreement by a class of creditors (or holders of ownership interests) to a plan for satisfaction of claims against the debtor's estate. A class accepts by means of a vote.

Accommodation party A person who signs an instrument for the purpose of lending his or her name (credit) to another party to the instrument.

Accord and satisfaction The reaching of a new agreement and the performance of it or the acceptance of it by both parties as a substitute for the original contract. Usually associated with settlement of a disputed claim.

Account receivable (account) A right to payment for goods sold or leased or for services rendered.

Acknowledgment Certification by a notary public as to the identity of a person who signs a document.

Adhesion contracts See *Contract of adhesion.*

Administrative agency A government office, department, board, bureau, or commission, (other than legislatures and courts) with power to make rules and regulations concerning private rights and duties.

Administrative law The law concerning the powers and procedures of administrative agencies, including the law governing judicial review of administrative action.

Administrative Procedure Act A federal law generally establishing the manner in which federal administrative agencies operate.

Administrator In estate or inheritance law: a person or entity, not designated by a decedent's will, appointed by a court to administer a decedent's estate.

Admitted to probate The determination of a court that a will is valid.

Affirmation (to affirm) The ratification of an act, statement, or promise. In the law, it is used primarily to express agreement to be held to a voidable transaction, as the affirmance or ratification of a minor's voidable contract or the ratification by a principal of an agent's voidable action on the principal's behalf.

After-acquired property clause A clause in a security agreement that gives a creditor a security interest in both present and future assets of the debtor instead of a security interest only in specific assets on hand at the creation of the secured transaction.

Agency A relationship in which one person acts for or represents another by the latter's authority; where one person acts for another either in the relationship of principal and agent, master and servant, or employer and employee.

Agent A person authorized by another to act for him or her; one entrusted with another's business.

Agreement See *Contract.*

Allowed claim In bankruptcy law, a valid claim against the debtor's estate. An allowed claim will be paid to the extent that funds are available.

All-risk contract An insurance policy which indemnifies the insured against property loss resulting from any peril except those specifically excluded by the insurance contract.

Amicus curiae. A "friend of the court", not a party to a law suit, who, with permission of a court, files a brief (usually in matters of broad public interest) suggesting a rationale for solution of a legal question.

Annuity A contractual device for systematically using up (liquidating) an existing fund; a type of contract sold by some life insurance companies.

Anticipatory breach of contract Repudiation of a contract obligation before performance is due.

Apparent authority The authority which, though not actually granted, the principal knowingly permits an agent to exercise or which the principal holds the agent out as possessing.

Appellant One who files an appeal. The various grounds for an appeal are discussed in Chapter 2.

Appellee The party opposite the appellant. Usually, the party who won at the trial level.

Arbitration A nonjudicial method of resolving civil disputes, informal and voluntary in most cases. Discussed in Chapter 3.

Arraignment The reading by a judicial officer of an information or indictment to an accused in a criminal case and asking how he or she pleads.

Articles of incorporation A legal document, filed with a designated state official, that meets the requirements of the state's incorporation statute before a person or persons can commence doing business as a corporation. The articles, sometimes called "corporate charter," provide the framework within which the corporation must operate.

Artisan A skilled craftsman, such as a plumber, mechanic, or tailor. An "artisan's lien" is the right of one who repairs goods of another to keep possession of the goods until the repair charges are paid.

Assignee A person to whom an assignment is made.

Assignment A transfer of rights, usually of contract rights.

Assignment for the benefit of creditors A voluntary transfer, under state law, by a debtor of all his or her available property to a trustee for distribution to the debtor's creditors in exchange for their promises to release the debtor from further liability. Also called a "general assignment".

Assignor The maker of an assignment.

Assumpsit A common law form of action to recover damages for breach of contract.

Attachment Seizure of a debtor's property, generally at the start of a lawsuit, through legal process to protect a creditor's claim.

Attachment of a security interest In the law of secured transactions, the name given to the process of creating (agreeing to) a security interest in personal property and of making it enforceable against the debtor.

Authority The power of an agent to affect the legal relations of a principal by acts done in accordance with the principal's manifestations of consent.

Authority by estoppel Authority that is not actual, but is apparent only, being imposed on the principal because the conduct of the principal has been such as to mislead a third party, so that it would be unjust to let the principal deny it.

Automatic stay A suspension of legal action. In bankruptcy law, a suspension of legal action (other than the bankruptcy proceeding itself) until the bankruptcy case is over or until the stay is vacated by the bankruptcy court.

Bail Security given to guarantee the presence of an accused at a criminal hearing or trial.

Bailment A transaction in which the possessor of personal property (bailor) puts someone else (bailee) in possession for a limited purpose, such as for repair or for storage.

Bankruptcy A process under federal law whereby the nonexempt assets of a debtor, incapable of paying his or her debts, are distributed to creditors and the debtor, if honest, is discharged from liability for most remaining unpaid debts.

Bearer document of title Similar to bearer commercial paper. See *Commercial paper*.

Bearer paper See *Commercial paper*.

Bequest A gift by will of personal property.

Bilateral contract A contract in which the parties make promises to each other. Cf *unilateral contract*.

Bill of exchange A draft.

Bill of lading A document of title issued by a railroad or other carrier that lists the goods accepted for transport and that sometimes states the terms of the shipping agreement. See *Document of title*. A *through bill* of lading is one issued by a carrier for transport of goods over its own lines for a certain distance, and then over connecting lines to the destination. A *destination bill* of lading is one to be issued at the destination point instead of the sending point so that the documents will be available when the goods arrive.

Bill of Rights The First Ten Amendments to the Constitution of the United States. The Bill of Rights confers a number of rights intended to protect individuals from governmental oppression.

Blue-sky laws State statutes that protect investors against fraudulent schemes by regulating the issuance, sale, and/or transfer of securities.

Board of directors One or more persons elected and authorized by the shareholders of a corporation to manage the corporation and its affairs.

Bona fide In or with good faith.

Bond With reference to corporate financing, a bond is a certificate or other evidence of debt that obligates the corporation to pay the bondholder a fixed rate of interest on the principal at regular intervals and to pay the principal on a stated maturity date.

Boycott A combination to abstain from or to prevent dealings with a person or organization as a means to influence the settlement of a labor dispute.

Breach The breaking of a promise, duty, or obligation, as a breach of contract.

Bribery Improperly attempting to influence an action, generally of a public servant, by offering money or other favors.

Bulk sale The sale of a whole stock in trade of a business.

Burden of proof In law, the degree of proof necessary to sustain a verdict or judgment; in criminal cases, beyond a reasonable doubt, in civil cases by a preponderance of the evidence.

Bylaws Self-made regulations or rules adopted by a corporation to regulate and govern its internal actions and affairs.

C&F (CF) An abbreviation meaning that the price includes in a lump sum the cost of goods and the cost of freight to the named destination.

CIF An abbreviation meaning that the price includes in a lump sum the cost of goods and the cost of insurance and freight to the named destination.

COD An abbreviation of "collect on delivery."

Call A demand of payment, either in installments or portions, made upon subscribers of shares by directors of a corporation. Also, a negotiable option contract under which the bearer has the right to buy a certain number of shares of stock at an agreed price before a fixed date.

Callable preferred shares Preferred shares which a corporation may "call back" or redeem at a fixed date and price established when they are issued.

Carrier An individual or a business firm engaged in transporting passengers or goods for hire. A *common carrier* offers its services to the public and must carry goods for all who apply, as long as there is room and no legal excuse for refusing. A *private carrier* carries goods only for those persons with whom the carrier chooses to contract.

Case law The accumulated body of court decisions that form an important part of the law of a particular subject.

Cash surrender value A dollar value of an insurance policy, generated from premium payments that exceed the amount needed to pay claims against and expenses of the insurer. The excess payments are retained and invested by the insurer, and the accumulation is held in a *legal reserve fund*.

Cause of action Legal basis for a lawsuit.

Caveat emptor A Latin phrase meaning "Let the buyer beware."

Cease-and-desist order A command from an administrative agency to stop a challenged practice. A cease-and-desist order is similar to an injunction.

Certificate of incorporation A document, issued by some states, that grants an organization permission to do business as a corporation.

Certified check A check that has been accepted by the drawee bank. See *Acceptance*.

Certiorari A formal request by a higher court to a lower court to transmit to it the record of a case so that it can be heard on appeal.

Chancery Equity. A *court of chancery* is a *court of equity*. See *Equity*.

Charging order A court order granting a creditor a right to a partner's interest in a partnership.

Charter An instrument by which the state creates a corporation and confers on it the right, power, and authority to do business under the corporate form. The term "charter" is sometimes used to refer to the articles of incorporation.

Chattel A term often used to refer to movable, tangible things which are not firmly attached to real property.

Chattel mortgage A writing evidencing a secured transaction in personal property, that is, a mortgage evidencing both a monetary obligation and a security interest in personal property. The debtor has possession of the property, but the creditor has, as his or her security interest, title to the property or, in some states, a lien (claim) against it.

Chattel paper A writing which evidences both a monetary obligation and a security interest in specific goods.

Civil law In the United States, that law under which a person (the plaintiff) may sue another (the defendant), for example, in a lawsuit involving a contract or tort, to obtain redress for a wrong committed by the defendant. The expression "civil law" is also used to describe those legal systems (e.g., the French) whose law is centered around a comprehensive legislative code.

Close corporation A corporation whose stock is held by one stockholder or by a relatively small group of stockholders who actively participate in management. The stock is generally subject to restrictions on transfer and is not publicly traded.

Codicil An amendment to a formal or holographic will.

Coinsurance A method used by property insurers to prevent customers who underinsure commercial property from receiving disproportionately larger benefits than those who insure near the full value of their property.

Collateral Something of value that can be converted into cash by a creditor if the debtor defaults.

Collusive bidding Bid-rigging. An aggreement for one of a group of bidders to make a low bid while the others refrain from bidding or bid higher amounts, to compare bids prior to submission, to create a bid depository where competitors compare bids and fix the bid price, or to split profits made by successful bidder.

Commercial impracticability A basis upon which a party to a contract may be excused from performance obligations. The essence of commercial impracticability is an unexpected occurrence which seriously impairs a party's ability to perform.

Commercial bribery Improperly attempting to gain advantage in a commercial transaction by offering money or other favors.

Commercial paper Negotiable instruments payable in money; negotiable drafts, checks, notes, and certificates of deposit.

Commercial unit An amount of goods that in business practice is treated as a single whole for purposes of sale, and whose division would materially impair its value or character (e.g., a machine, a bale of cotton, a carload of wheat).

Commingled goods Goods that are combined with others to form a single mass or product.

Common law In England, a body of law *common* to the whole population, produced primarily by the efforts of judges in various parts of England to harmonize their decisions with those of judges in other parts of the country.

Common stock A class of corporate stock that usually represents the voting control of a corporation. Such stock carries rights to dividends and, upon dissolution of the corporation, to corporate assets; but such rights are subordinate to the rights of preferred stock, if any.

Community property A system whereby husband and wife jointly own property earned by either during the marriage.

Compensatory damages Damages awarded to a plaintiff to compensate him or her for harm suffered, such as medical bills or lost profits. In tort cases, it includes general damages for embarrassment, pain, or suffering.

Complainant A party who brings an action in equity.

Complete integration See *Integration.*

Composition agreement An arrangement between a debtor and two or more creditors whereby the debtor agrees to turn his or her assets over to the creditors, and the creditors agree to accept their pro rata portions in full satisfaction of their claims.

Composition plan In bankruptcy law, a plan for the adjustment or settlement of debt in which the debtor pays creditors less than 100 percent of their claims on a pro rata basis for each class of claims. In contrast, under an *extension plan,* the debtor pays the full amount, but over a longer period than originally agreed.

Condition A qualification or limitation of a grant or of an agreement.

Conditional sale contract A contract evidencing a secured transaction in which a buyer of goods receives possession of them and the seller-creditor retains title to them until the buyer makes payment.

Confession of judgment clause A provision in a promissory note or other instrument authorizing the holder to have an attorney enter a judgment in court against the maker or drawer if the instrument is not paid when due, even though the failure to pay may be justified.

Confirmation In bankruptcy law, the act of the bankruptcy court in approving a plan of reorganization or some other plan for the adjustment or settlement of debt.

Conforming goods In the law of sales, goods that are in accordance with the seller's obligations under the contract of sale.

Conscious parallelism In antitrust law, uniform pricing or other business conduct by competitors not acting in concert, but who are aware of each other's actions.

Consent order An order of an administrative agency under which a person agrees to discontinue a challenged practice. Under a consent order the respondent does not admit any violation of law.

Consideration In contract law, a bargained-for legal detriment incurred in exchange for a promise.

Consignment A transfer of possession of property for the purpose of transportation or sale. The consignor retains title to (ownership of) the property.

Conspiracy An unlawful combination between two or more persons or corporations to do an illegal act or to accomplish a lawful end through illegal means; it may be a civil wrong *and* a criminal offense.

Construction As applied to a statute, the process of discovering and explaining the legal effect which the statute is to have. "Construing" a statute may involve interpreting unclear language, but it mainly involves such tasks as determining the purpose or policy of the statute, deciding how the provisions of a complex statute are related, and deciding to what specific people or things the statute applies.

Constructive notice A·notice, knowledge of which, pursuant to law, is charged to a party whether it was actually received or not; generally given by means of publication.

Constructive trust A device imposed by a court of equity to compel one who unfairly holds a property interest to convey that interest to another to whom it justly belongs.

Consumer goods Tangible personal property normally used for personal, family, or household purposes.

Consumer product As used in the Magnuson-Moss Warranty Act, any tangible personal property that is distributed in commerce and that is normally used for personal, family, or household purposes, including any such property intended to be attached to or installed in any real property.

Contempt of court Failure to comply with a personal order or direction of a court.

Contract A promise or set of promises for the breach of which the law gives a remedy or for the performance of which the law in some way recognizes as a duty. In the law of sales, a contract consists of the total legal obligation that results from the parties' agreement, as that agreement is affected by the UCC and by any other applicable rules of law. *Contract* should be distinguished from *agreement.*

Contract of adhesion A contract in which a party,

usually the buyer, has no meaningful choice with regard to some or all the terms of the contract, for example, an insurance contract.

Contract for sale *See Sale (of goods).*

Contract to sell *See Sale (of goods).*

Conversion Unauthorized and wrongful exercise of dominion and control over personal property of another, in a manner inconsistent with the rights of the owner.

Convertible preferred shares Shares of preferred stock which may be exchanged at the option of the holder for shares in another series or class issued by the same corporation.

Corporate opportunity doctrine A doctrine that prohibits a person who has a fiduciary relation to a corporation from seizing a business opportunity which rightfully belongs to the corporation.

Corporation A legal entity created by authority of a statute as an artificial person whose rights, obligations, and liabilities are separate and distinct from those of its shareholders.

Corporation by estoppel A legal phrase meaning that a defectively formed corporation is not permitted to assert as a defense to an action against it that the corporation was not properly formed.

Course of dealing In the law of sales, a pattern of prior business transactions (not just the performance of one transaction) which can establish a background for the interpretation of the immediate transaction.

Course of performance In the law of sales, the carrying out of a particular transaction. There can be no course of performance unless there are repeated occasions for performance, such as several deliveries of coal to be made pursuant to a single contract of sale.

Court of Claims A special court created by Congress for the purpose, among others, of hearing and determining contract claims against the United States.

Cover A buyer's arrangement for the purchase of goods in substitution for goods which the seller failed to deliver.

Cumulative voting A system, permitted by many state statutes, whereby a shareholder can cast all of his or her votes (shares owned multiplied by the number of directors to be elected) for one candidate.

Cure The act of correcting a defective tender or delivery of goods.

Damages Money compensation for a wrong; for example, a money payment for breach of a contract.

Dealer A person engaged in the business of buying goods or other property such as real estate for resale to final customers.

Dealer-merchant As used in this textbook, the kind of merchant who deals in goods of the kind involved in the transaction between the dealer-merchant seller and

the buyer. See *Merchant.*

Debenture An unsecured corporate bond.

Debtor-in-possession In a Bankruptcy Code business reorganization, the debtor or the management of a corporate debtor in possession of the firm.

Debtor's estate In the law of bankruptcy, the various property interests either owned by the debtor at the commencement of a bankruptcy case or recoverable for the estate by the trustee in bankruptcy from someone other than the debtor.

Deceit (action for deceit) An action at law based upon a misrepresentation or concealment by which one deceives another who has no means of detecting the fraud, to the injury and damage of such person. Used interchangeably with *fraud.*

Deductible A specified amount of loss that an insured must absorb before being entitled to payment from an insurer.

De facto corporation An organization that operates as a corporation, whose organizers have made an unsuccessful attempt in "good faith" to comply with the state enabling statute. Only the state can challenge the existence of a de facto corporation.

Defendant A party against whom a court action is brought.

Defense A circumstance or reason put forward by a defendant to defeat the claim of the plaintiff. In the law of commercial paper, defenses are personal or real. A *personal defense* is not good against a holder in due course. A *real defense* is good against anyone, including a holder in due course.

De jure corporation A corporation that has all the legal characteristics of a corporation and whose incorporators have substantially complied with the enabling statute of the state of incorporation.

Delegatee See *Delegation.*

Delegation The authorizing, by a person under a duty of performance, of another person to render the required performance. The person who does the authorizing is the *delegator.* The person authorized to carry out the performance is the *delegatee.*

Delegator See *Delegation.*

Demise As used in law, a transfer of real property or of an interest in real property. Usually in connection with a lease.

Demurrer A document, filed by the defendant in a lawsuit, by which the defendant challenges the court's jurisdiction or the legal sufficiency of the plaintiff's complaint. Usually a form of pleading which admits the facts alleged but asserts that they do not constitute a cause of action. Discussed in Chapters 1 and 2.

De novo From the beginning; a new start, as "trial de novo".

Derivative suit An action filed in the corporate name by one or more shareholders to enforce a corporate cause of action.

Destination bill of lading See *Bill of lading.*

Destination contract A contract in which the seller is required to make delivery at the point of destination.

Detour A slight deviation by an employee from a prescribed route while travelling on authorized work.

Devise A gift by will of real property.

Directed verdict A verdict entered for either the plaintiff or the defendant, not as a result of jury deliberation, but as a result of the judge ordering the entry. A directed verdict is ordered only if the facts are so clear that the jury could not reasonably reach a verdict for the other party. Discussed in Chapter 2.

Disaffirmance The setting aside or avoiding of a contract or obligation which can be avoided legally.

Discharge To extinguish an obligation, whether by performance or otherwise. The termination of a contractual obligation.

Disclaimer A denial, especially a denial that a warranty was made or is effective.

Discount In a general sense, to sell for less than face value. In banking, the taking of interest in advance.

Dishonor Refusal or failure to pay or accept a negotiable instrument that has been properly presented for payment or acceptance.

Dissolution In corporation law, the termination of a corporation by legislative act, by judicial decree, by voluntary action of the shareholders, or by expiration of the period of time for which the corporation was formed. With reference to a partnership, dissolution is a preparatory step to its termination (see Chapter 35).

Dividends Distribution from corporate assets (usually earned surplus), made on a pro rata basis to shareholders of a designated class of stock, as authorized by the corporation's board of directors. Also, *in the law of insurance*, the difference between (a) the premium charged for a policy plus earnings from investing the premium and (b) the lower amount justified by the actual loss and expense experience of the insurer. An insurance dividend may be viewed as a refund of a part of the premium initially charged for the insurance.

Dock receipt See *Document of title.*

Dock warrant See *Document of title.*

Document of title A writing that is treated as adequately evidencing that the person in possession of it is entitled to receive, hold, and dispose of the document and the goods it covers. Documents of title include *bills of lading, dock warrants, dock receipts, and warehouse receipts.*

Domestic corporation A corporation which is doing business in the state of incorporation.

Dormant partner A partner who does not represent the partnership to the public. Also called a *silent* or *secret* partner.

Double jeopardy A second prosecution after a prior prosecution for the same offense, transaction, or omission.

Dower The right of a widow to a portion of her deceased husband's estate. Most states now provide for a forced or elective share instead.

Draft A type of commercial paper commanding the drawee to pay a sum of money; a *time draft* is payable at a specified future time; a *demand draft* is payable on demand of the holder any time.

Drawee The person, bank, or firm that is ordered by the drawer of a draft or check to make payment to a payee.

Drawer The person, bank, or firm that issues a draft or check and thereby orders the drawee to make payment to the payee.

Due process The administration of law in accordance with rules and forms which have been established for the protection of private rights. *Procedural due process* requires a fair hearing or the right to one. *Substantive due process* requires that laws not be arbitrary, unreasonably discriminatory, or demonstrably irrelevant to the matter which the law purports to govern.

Duress Any wrongful or illegal coercion, by threat or other means, that overcomes the free will or judgment of a person and induces the person to do something he or she otherwise would not do.

Electronic funds transfer A process in which banking transactions are accomplished by means of computers.

Emancipation In contract law, a status whereby a minor enters contracts and assumes responsibility for his or her own support.

Embezzlement The wrongful appropriation of property by a person to whom it has been entrusted.

Enabling legislation A statute expressing in general terms the powers and purposes of an administrative agency.

Engagement In commercial paper law, a promise imposed by law.

Entrustment In the law of sales, the act of putting goods into the possession of a merchant who deals in goods of that kind.

Enforceable contract One for the breach of which the law gives a remedy.

Enjoin Prohibit. Ordinarily, a party files a lawsuit and requests the court to issue an injunction against the defendant; the injunction "enjoins" the defendant from certain conduct.

Equal dignities rule The requirement that an agent's authority must be in writing if his or her act requires a writing.

Equitable decree An order of a court of equity.

Equitable remedies The relief given by a court of equity.

Equity A body of law developed by the English Courts of Chancery to supplement the rigid common law of the time. The Courts of Chancery developed new remedies and flexible procedures for cases where the remedy at law (damages) was inadequate. The word equity implies fairness and a wise discretion in the formulation and application of equitable remedies. Also, an ownership interest in property.

Equity securities Shares of capital stock representing a shareholder's proportionate ownership interest in the corporation as a whole.

Estoppel A bar to alleging or denying facts in court.

Executed contract One that has been fully performed by both parties.

Execution (of judgment at law) The process of procuring a writ of execution from the clerk of court and having the sheriff seize the defendant's property and sell it to satisfy the judgment.

Executive committee In a corporation, a committee composed entirely of directors who are authorized by majority vote of the board of directors to make corporate management decisions (not involving extraordinary transactions) during intervals between board meeting.

Executor A person or entity designated by a testator in a will to carry out the testator's wishes concerning the disposition of the testator's property after his or her death.

Executory contract One in which neither party has rendered the promised performance.

Exemptions In bankruptcy law, property that an individual debtor may preserve free from the claims of creditors.

Exoneration An act freeing another from blame; the discharge of an obligation.

Experience rating In insurance, the process of adjusting the premium to reflect, for renewal years, the actual loss experience of the insured.

Ex post facto law A law imposing a criminal sanction upon a person for an act that, when committed, was not criminal. Ex post facto laws are unconstitutional.

Express authority The authority explicitly given by a principal to an agent, either in writing or orally.

Express contract One in which the terms of the contract are stated in words, either written or spoken.

Express powers In constitutional law, the powers specifically named by a constitution. The Constitution of the United States specifically grants certain powers (called "express" or "enumerated" powers) to the federal government. In corporation law, those powers set forth in articles of incorporation or in a statute.

Express warranty See *Warranty*.

Ex rel. Abbreviation for "ex relatione," meaning "upon relation" or information. Legal proceedings instituted by the attorney general (or other proper person) in the name and behalf of the state.

FAS Free alongside a vessel.

FOB (fob) Free on board.

Face value The nominal value of a security as expressed on its face, for example, the par value of a share of stock, or the amount due and payable on a bond, according to its terms.

Featherbedding The requirement, through union pressure, that an employer hire unnecessary employees, assign unnecessary work, or limit production.

Felony A serious criminal offense.

Fiction An assumption of law that something that is or may be false is true. It is a legal fiction to say that a corporation is a person.

Fictitious name A counterfeit, feigned, or pretended name taken by a person, differing in some essential particular from his or her true name; a name adopted to identify a business concern. Sometimes called a "dba" (doing business as).

Fiduciary A Latin word meaning trust or confidence.

Fiduciary relationship A relation between persons of such a character that trust and confidence are reposed in the other, who must exercise the utmost degree of fairness and good faith.

Field warehousing A secured transaction for the financing of business inventory. The inventory used as collateral is segregated in a fenced-off area of the borrower's premises and is placed under the control of an independent warehouse.

Financing statement A writing that is filed in the public records to give notice of the creditor's security interest in collateral.

Firm offer In the law of sales, a written offer in which the offeror, a merchant, promises to hold the offer open, usually for a certain period of time.

Fixture An article that was personal property but which has been attached to real property with the intent that it become a permanent part of the real property.

Floating lien A security interest in both present and future assets of the debtor instead of a security interest only in specific assets on hand at the creation of the secured transaction. Floating liens are created by the use of *after-acquired property clauses*.

Forced (elective) share The portion of a deceased spouse's estate to which the surviving spouse is entitled by law. Most states grant this rather than dower.

Foreclosure A procedure by which encumbered (mortgaged) property is sold upon the debtor's default, in satisfaction of the debt.

Foreign corporation A corporation that is doing business in a state other than the state of incorporation.

Formal contract A contract to which the law gives special effect because of the form used in creating it; for example, a negotiable instrument such as a check is a formal contract because to create a negotiable instrument, a person must use a particular form or style of language.

Four-corner rule In the law of commercial paper, the rule that whether an instrument is unconditional is to be determined solely by what is expressed on the face of the instrument.

Franchise A contract in which the owner (franchisor) of intangible property such as a trademark or trade name, authorizes another (franchisee) to use such property in the operation of a business within described territory.

Fraud An intentional, false representation or concealment of fact intended to induce another to act, justifiably relied on by the other to his or her injury.

Fraudulent transfer In bankruptcy law, a transfer of property by the debtor within 1 year preceding bankruptcy, where the debtor was insolvent when the transfer was made and where the debtor received less than a reasonable equivalent value for the transfer. A fraudulent transfer can also occur under circumstances other than those just described. Also called a *fraudulent conveyance*.

Frolic A substantial deviation by an employee from a prescribed route while travelling on authorized work.

Full warranty A written consumer product warranty that meets the four minimum standards or requirements of the Magnuson-Moss Warranty act.

Fungible Equivalent. Goods are fungible if by their nature or by usage of trade one unit is the equivalent of any other unit.

Future-advances clause A clause in a security agreement that permits the collateral of the debtor to be used to secure future loans.

Future goods Goods which are not both existing and identified to the contract for their sale.

Garnishment A legal procedure by means of which a creditor acquires money or other property of a debtor where the property is in the hands of some other person, such as a bank or an employer. "Property" includes a debt owed by a debtor, such as wages due from an employer.

General partnership (See *partnership*).

Going and coming rule A principal's freedom from liability for an employee's actions while the latter is going to or from work.

Good faith In the law of sales, honesty in fact in the conduct or transaction concerned. With regard to a merchant, good faith is honesty in fact and the observance of reasonable commercial standards of fair dealing in the trade.

Goodwill The expectation of a continuance of customers and profits enjoyed because of the manner in which a business has been conducted.

Grab law Law, usually state law, that permits unpaid creditors to seize and sell the property of the debtor.

Grace period Extra time to carry out a legal duty. In the law of secured transactions, an amount of time, beyond the usual time given, to file or otherwise perfect a security interest.

Graded rate In property insurance, a reduced premium rate that is applied when a person approaches insuring his or her property for full value. Graded rates reflect the fact that there are more partial than full losses and are a means, seldom used, for assuring that people who underinsure their property receive no more indemnity per dollar of premiums than do people who insure for full value.

Grantee One to whom a grant is made. In property law, the person to whom real property is granted and conveyed.

Grantor One who transfers property, or a right, to another (the grantee).

Gratuitous agent An agent who serves without pay.

Group insurance Insurance in which the insurer undertakes to insure every person in the group without regard to the insurability of individuals. The insurer issues one detailed *master contract* to the group policyholder, but only brief certificates to individual members of the group. Many group policies are experience rated.

Guarantor One who guarantees the obligation of another. In the law of commercial paper, a signer who adds "Payment guaranteed" or equivalent words to the signature and thereby promises that if the instrument is not paid when due, he or she will pay it without insisting on resort to any other party.

Hearsay evidence Statements, made in court by a witness, involving not personal knowledge or observation but mere repetition of what he or she has heard others say.

Heir Under modern law, a person who inherits from another real or personal property or an interest in such property. Formerly, one who inherits by virtue of the laws of descent and distribution.

Holder A person who is in possession of an instrument drawn, issued, or indorsed to him or to his order or to bearer or in blank.

Holder in due course A *holder* who takes an instrument for value, in good faith, and without notice that it is overdue or that it has been dishonored or that there is any defense against or claim to it on the part of any person.

Holographic will A will in the testator's own handwriting, signed and dated. Recognized in most states as a valid will.

Horizontal merger A combination of two firms at the same level, e.g., two manufacturers, two wholesalers, or two retailers.

Identification In the law of sales, the act of designating goods as the subject of a particular contract of sale.

Illusory Deceptive; an illusory promise appears to be promissory in its terms but actually promises nothing because the promissor retains the choice of performing or nonperforming.

Impairment In bankruptcy law, the adverse impact of a plan of reorganization that gives a claimant less than the full value of his or her claim or interest.

Implied contract One in which the terms of the contract are wholly or partly inferred from conduct or from surrounding circumstances.

Implied powers In constitutional law, powers that are not specifically named but which are necessary and proper for carrying out the express powers. In corporation law, powers not specifically set out in a statute or charter but necessary and proper for carrying out the corporation's express powers. In agency law, the implied authority of an agent.

Implied warranty See *Warranty*.

Incontestability An inability, imposed by law or by contract, of an insurer to avoid a policy for concealment, breach of warranty, or misrepresentation. Also, a non-contest clause in a will.

Incorporation The process (as established in state statutes) by which a corporation is formed.

Incorporator Person who organizes a corporation by signing and filing the articles of incorporation with the designated officer of the state.

Indemnification (to indemnify) The compensation or payment of a damage another sustains. In legal terms, it may also mean to give security against the possibility of future damage or loss; for instance, an insurance company undertakes to *indemnify* its policy holders against loss.

Indemnity Reimbursement for loss.

Indemnity principle The theory that in the event of casualty an insured should be limited to reimbursement (indemnity) for loss actually suffered, because insurance is a system for distributing losses and not for generating a profit for insureds. The principle is especially applicable in liability, property, and health insurance.

Independent contractor One who, exercising an independent employment, contracts to do certain work according to his or her own methods and without being subject to the control of an employer except as to the results to be accomplished.

Indictment An accusation in writing found and presented by a grand jury that a person named in the indictment has done some act or has been guilty of some omission which by law is a public offense.

Indorsement A signature customarily found on the back of commercial paper; made by a person other than a maker, drawer, or acceptor; and ordinarily resulting in secondary liability on the instrument. An indorsement is in-blank or special, nonrestrictive or restrictive, *and* unqualified or qualified. A *special indorsement* maintains the order character of an order instrument or gives order character to a bearer instrument. A *restrictive indorsement* specifies a use to which the proceeds of the instrument must be put. A *qualified indorsement* protects the indorser from liability on the instrument but not for liability for breach of warranty.

Informal contract One for which the law does not prescribe a particular form in order for the contract to be enforceable.

Information In criminal law, a formal accusation of crime similar to an indictment but preferred (made) by a competent prosecuting official, such as a district attorney instead of by a grand jury.

Infraction A minor wrong, usually not a criminal offense.

Inheritance Something obtained by operation of law from a person who dies without leaving a valid will and, under modern usage, by virtue of the provisions of a will.

Injunction An equitable remedy in which a court orders a person to do or to refrain from doing something.

In re In the matter of; regarding. The title of a judicial proceeding as, *In re Smith*, in which there are no adversary parties. Commonly used in bankruptcy and estate proceedings.

Insanity A mental derangement due to a disease of the mind. An insane person is without legal competence to enter into a contract or to make a will; proof of insanity may free an accused person from responsibility for a criminal act. Tests for insanity differ in contract law, probate law, and criminal law.

Insurable interest A financial stake in property or in someone's life that will justify the person who has that stake in insuring the property or life.

Insurance A contractual means of transferring and distributing the risk of financial loss.

Integration A written statement being the final expression of the parties to an agreement. *Complete integration:* a written complete and exclusive statement of all the contract terms. *Partial integration:* a written final expression only of the contract terms included in the writing, other contract terms existing outside the writing.

Inter alia Latin: Among other things.

Interlocking directorates A practice in which members on the board of directors of one corporation also serve as directors of other corporations.

Interpretation The process of discovering and explaining the meaning of any unclear language, for example, of a statute or a contract. See *Construction*.

Interpretive rule An administrative regulation, without the force of law, setting out the agency's opinion as to the meaning of the law it administers.

Interstate commerce Commercial intercourse, communication, transportation of persons or property between or among two or more states of the Union.

Inter vivos Between the living; from one living person to another. Where property passes by conveyance, the transaction is said to be inter vivos, to distinguish it from a transfer by will effective upon death.

Intestate Without making a will. Also, an intestate: a person who dies without leaving a valid will.

Intrastate Activity or territory that is wholly within a state of the Union.

Intra vires Within the power of a person or corporation; within the scope of express or implied powers or authority.

Ipso facto "By the fact itself; by the mere fact."

Issue A legal question to be decided by a court. Under the laws of *descent and distribution*, all persons who have descended from a common ancestor; also, the child or children of an individual and of their children. In the law of *commercial paper*, the act of putting a negotiable instrument such as a check into circulation; issuance of a negotiable instrument, a document of title, or some other commercial document.

Jingle rule The rule of partnership law that the creditors of partners have first claim to assets of the partners and that creditors of the partnership have first claim to the partnership assets. This rule has been modified by the Bankruptcy Code for situations to which the Code applies.

Joint and several liability The liability of the various defendants is joint and several when a plaintiff, at his or her option may sue and establish liability of persons separately, or sue all of them together. For example, if a plaintiff is a victim of a tort committed by several tortfeasors, they have joint and several liability and the plaintiff may sue only one, or elect to sue all of them.

Joint tortfeasors Includes: (1) persons who have acted together by agreement for the purpose of injuring another; and (2) persons who have acted independently but have caused a single indivisible injury.

Joint venture A business owned and managed by two or more persons to accomplish a single objective.

Judgment In law, the decision of a court.

Judgment creditor A party in whose favor a judgment for money is rendered.

Judgment debtor A party against whom a judgment for money is rendered.

Judgment nonwithstanding the verdict ("judgment n.o.v.") A judgment entered by the judge for the losing party in a jury trial, thus reversing the verdict of the jury. The trial judge will overrule the jury only if there is no substantial evidence to support their decision.

Jurisdiction The power of a court to hear and decide cases.

Jurisprudence The philosophy of law, or the science which treats of the principles of law and legal relations, a body of law.

Larceny The unlawful taking and carrying away of the property of another with the intent to deprive the owner of it permanently.

Law merchant The old law of merchants, developed to supplement the common law.

Lease A rental agreement in which the *lessor* conveys to the *lessee* the right to use the lessor's personal or real property, usually in exchange for a payment of money.

Laches See *Statute of limitations.*

Legacy A bequest (gift by will) of money.

Legal entity An entity, other than a natural person, existing in contemplation of law and having the legal rights and duties of a separate person, for example, a corporation.

Legal fiction See *Fiction.*

Legal reserve fund See *Cash surrender value.*

Legislative rule A regulation, promulgated by an administrative agency, having the force of law.

Letter of credit Promise by a bank or other person (the "issuer") made at the request of a customer of the issuer that the issuer will honor drafts or other demands for payment upon the customer's compliance with the conditions specified in the letter of credit; a letter of credit may be either revocable or irrevocable.

Level premium A life insurance premium fixed at a certain amount for the duration of the contract. The premium is larger than needed to pay claims and expenses during the early years of the contract. The excess is invested to provide funds to pay increasingly frequent future claims.

Libel Defamation expressed by print, writing, pictures, or signs.

Lien A claim or charge against property. A lien may be created by contract or imposed by law to secure, for example, the claims of mechanics or other artisans for work done on property, or to secure the claim of a government for unpaid taxes.

Limited partnership A partnership consisting of one or more general partners, responsible as ordinary partners, by whom the business is conducted, and one or more special partners, who are not liable for the debts of the partnership beyond the funds contributed, and who do not participate in the firm's management.

Limited warranty A written consumer product warranty that does not conform with the standards imposed by the Magnuson-Moss Warranty Act for a full warranty.

Liquidated damages An amount of money provided for as a remedy for breach of contract by the contract itself.

Liquidation proceeding A bankruptcy proceeding the object of which is to convert the debtor's nonexempt assets into cash, to distribute it in accordance with the scheme of distribution provided by the Bankruptcy Code, and to grant the honest debtor a discharge from most of the remaining debts.

"Long-arm" statute A statute conferring jurisdiction over out-of-state defendants.

Majority shareholders Shareholders who collectively own a majority of the voting shares of a corporation and who exercise control over the corporation by electing directors, amending articles, and making decisions on extraordinary transactions.

Mandamus "We command." A command issued by a court of competent jurisdiction to an inferior court, corporation, or person.

Master An employer who has the right to control the physical performance of an employee's (sevant's) work.

Master contract In group insurance, the detailed insurance policy held by the group policyholder, to be contrasted with the brief certificate held by each member of the group.

Mechanic's lien See *lien.*

Merchant In the law of sales, a person who deals in goods of the kind involved in the transaction. Also, a person who by occupation holds himself or herself out as having knowledge or skill peculiar to the practices or goods involved in the transaction, and a person to whom such knowledge or skill may be attributed by his or her employment of an intermediary who by occupation holds himself or herself out as having such knowledge or skill.

Merger In corporation law, the absorption of one corporation by another: the latter acquires all the assets and assumes all the liabilities of the "target" corporation which then ceases to exist.

Minor A person under the age at which the law recognizes a capacity to contract. The age of "majority," 21 at common law, is now 18 in many states.

Minority shareholders Shareholders whose collective voting rights are insufficient to elect a corporation's board of directors or otherwise control management decisions.

Miranda warning A statement by an arresting officer to an individual in custody as to his or her rights with respect to answering police questions.

Mirror image rule In the common (general) law of contracts, the requirement that for a contract to arise, the acceptance must correspond exactly to ("mirror") the offer. In the law of sales, the mirror image rule has largely been abandoned.

Misdemeanor A criminal offense less serious than a felony.

M'Naghten rule A test of insanity used in criminal cases by many courts; also known as the right and wrong test.

Monopoly power In antitrust law, the power to fix prices, exclude competitors, or control the market in a given geographical area.

Mortgage A secured transaction in real estate in which the creditor has an interest in the real estate to secure payment of the debt. See *Secured transaction, chattel mortgage.*

Motion to strike A request by a litigant that a court delete the whole or part of a pleading.

NLRB The National Labor Relations Board, established to hear disputes between labor and management.

Necessaries Suitable food, clothing, education, medical service, and place of residence in view of the rank, position, and mode of living of an individual.

Negotiable form The style of language required by law for creating a negotiable instrument or document.

Negotiable instrument A document such as a check or a promissory note which, because of its language, confers more than the usual rights of collection on a person who qualifies as or otherwise has the rights of a holder in due course. See *Commercial paper.*

Negotiation With reference to contracts, the exploring or discussing through oral or written communication of the terms and conditions of a contract preliminary to the making of a final contract. With reference to commercial paper, the *transferring* of a negotiable instrument to another.

Nolo contendere A plea to a criminal charge which neither admits nor denys guilt. Such a plea cannot be used as an admission of guilt for purposes of a related civil suit.

Nominal damages Usually $1.00. Awarded to a plaintiff who wins a case and receives a judgment but is unable to prove any harm or loss.

Nonconforming goods Goods that differ from what was ordered under a sales contract.

Nonconforming tender An offer of performance that differs from the performance called for by a sales contract. See *tender* and *performance.*

Nonprofit corporation A corporation that is formed for charitable, religious, educational, or fraternal purposes which are not profit-oriented. No part of income may be distributed to members, and assets can only be distributed to members when the corporation is dissolved.

No-par stock Authorized stock to which "no par" value is assigned by the articles of incorporation. Upon issuance, the directors fix the per-share subscription price, but the amount is not stated on the certificate.

Note A promissory note.

Notice A legal notification received by a party either directly or indirectly through an agent or as otherwise provided by law.

Novation The extinguishment of a party's obligation

(e.g. a debt) through an agreement between the old obligor, a new obligor, and the obligee for the substitution of the new obligor for the old one.

n.o.v. (non obstante veredicto) Notwithstanding the verdict. A judgment entered by order of a court for the plaintiff although there has been a jury verdict for the defendant.

Nullity Nothing; an act or proceeding which is of no legal force or effect.

OSHA The Occupational Safety and Health Act of 1970 which is implemented by the Department of Labor. The Act is intended to force employers to maintain safe and healthful working conditions.

Obligee A person to whom an obligation or duty is owed.

Obligor A person who owes a duty to someone else, that is, a person who has an obligation to perform.

Offer A statement or other conduct by which the offeror confers upon the offeree a legal power to accept the offer and thereby to create a contract.

Open term Some aspect or detail of a contract which the parties have not agreed upon but have, instead, left undecided.

Option An offer for which the offeree pays (or gives other valuable consideration) to keep the offer open for a stated period of time. Sometimes called *option contract*.

Order document of title Similar to order commercial paper. See *Commercial paper*.

Output contract A contract in which one party agrees to purchase the total production of the other party. Also, a contract in which the seller agrees to sell his or her total production to the other party.

Pari delicto Parties equally at fault.

Parol evidence rule The legal doctrine preventing the use of prior or contemporaneous oral statements or writings as evidence to contradict or change the terms of a signed integrated contract.

Partner A member of a general or limited partnership; may be either a general partner or a limited partner.

Partner by estoppel A non-partner who acquires a partner's liability to a third party who relied upon the non-partner's assertion (or the assertion of a member of a partnership) that the non-partner is in fact a partner. Also called ostensible partner.

Partnership A form of business organization owned and managed by two or more parties.

Par value stock Shares of corporation stock assigned a fixed value by the articles of incorporation; being the minimum price for which each share can be sold at the inception of a corporation. The par value is printed on each stock certificate.

Penal damages A harsh monetary penalty provided for by a contract, to coerce the performance of the contract. Penal damages clauses are not enforceable because the amount of damages provided for is not related to actual damages caused by breach of the contract.

Per capita Literally, "by the head." In inheritance laws, a method of distribution of the estate of a decedent where the persons designated are to receive equal shares, taking in their own right.

Per curiam By the court. Opinion of the whole court, as contrasted with an opinion written by one justice.

Perfection In the law of secured transactions, the process by which a security interest is made enforceable against subsequent lien creditors and certain other persons having a right in the collateral.

Perfect tender rule A rule of law, often relaxed by the UCC, that a buyer may elect to reject goods if the goods or the tender of delivery fails in any respect to conform to the contract.

Performance The carrying out of a legal obligation; the performance of a contract or a contractual promise.

Peril A cause of loss such as fire, flood, theft, or vandalism.

Per se In and of itself; inherently.

Personal defense See *Defense*.

Personal property floater A type of property insurance that applies to movable property, whatever its location.

Per stirpes A method of distribution of the estate of a decedent whereby heirs take the shares their respective deceased ancestor (e.g., parent, grandparent, etc.) would have taken if he or she had been living. Also called right of representation.

Piercing the corporate veil The process whereby a court disregards the separateness of the corporation from its shareholders and holds them liable for wrongful conduct that injures third parties.

Plaintiff A party who brings a civil suit.

Plea bargain A plea of guilty to a lesser charge in exchange for an agreed punishment or for the recommendation by the prosecutor to the judge of a lesser punishment than may have been imposed for the offense originally charged.

Pleading A formal statement in a lawsuit setting out a cause of action or defense.

Pledge A transaction in which a debtor gives possession of the debtor's personal property to the creditor as security for repayment of a loan.

Pooling A process of treating as a single group a large number of individual risks of a certain kind so that the total loss likely to be sustained by the group of insureds can be accurately estimated.

Possessory lien A lien (charge against property) that is effective only as long as the bailee retains possession of the property subject to the charge.

Power The ability to do any act; in agency law, the *authority* to do an act which the grantor might himself or herself lawfully perform; an authority by which one person enables another to do some act for him or her.

Predatory pricing In antitrust law, the prohibited practice of refraining from maximizing profits until competitors are driven out of the market.

Preempt To take exclusive control, as where the federal government, in accordance with the Constitution, expressly denies the states the right to regulate an activity, or enacts a comprehensive scheme of regulation which by implication precludes state regulation.

Preemptive right The right of a stockholder to preserve his or her proportionate stock interest by purchasing shares of a new issue ahead of others.

Preference In bankruptcy law, a transfer of property by the debtor that enables an unsecured creditor to receive a greater percentage of his or her claim against the debtor than the creditor would have received in a distribution of the debtor's assets pursuant to a Chapter 7 liquidation.

Preferential transfer See *Preference.*

Preferred stock A class of stock that has superior rights to dividends and, upon dissolution of the corporation, to corporate assets.

Presentment The act of producing a negotiable instrument and demanding its payment or acceptance.

Present sale See *Sale.*

Pretermitted In inheritance law, a child or other descendant not mentioned or provided for in an ancestor's will and who had not been otherwise provided for by the testator. Also, sometimes used to designate a spouse who is not provided for in a will.

Price discrimination In antitrust law, a practice whereby a seller charges two or more buyers different prices for an identical product or service.

Prima facie Latin phrase meaning, "on the face of it"; evidence sufficient to support a conclusion.

Primary party A signer of a negotiable instrument who is liable for payment immediately and unconditionally when the instrument comes due. To be contrasted with a *secondary* party, whose liability is conditional because it normally does not arise until after presentment, dishonor, and notice of dishonor.

Prime contract A contract between the government and a contractor. Such a contractor is a *prime contractor.*

Primogeniture An English system whereby the eldest son had the exclusive right to inherit the estate of his ancestor. Not used in the United States.

Principal In agency law, the party (disclosed, partially disclosed, or undisclosed) primarily responsible for an obligation incurred by an agent.

Priority claim In bankruptcy law, an allowed, unsecured claim that is, by statute, to be paid before claims of lower rank may be paid. The Bankruptcy Code lists six classes of priority claims.

Private corporation A profit or nonprofit corporation organized by individuals, as opposed to one formed by the government.

Private law Law dealing with the relationships among private persons and organizations.

Privity of contract A relationship that exists between contracting parties because of the contract. A person usually must be in privity of contract in order to bring suit on it. However, the absence of privity of contract between a manufacturer and a remote purchaser of goods is not ordinarily a good defense to a suit brought against the manufacturer by a plaintiff on the ground of negligence or breach of warranty.

Probate The act or process of proving the validity of a will; also, the name generally given to all proceedings within the jurisdiction of a probate court.

Procedural due process See *Due process.*

Procedural law That law which specifies the formal steps to be followed in enforcing or asserting rights, duties, privileges, or immunities. Also called "adjective" law.

Procedural rule An administrative regulation without the force of law, establishing the process by which the public may deal with the issuing agency.

Professional corporation A corporation which certain professional people such as doctors, lawyers, or accountants, may establish for their practices to obtain corporate tax benefits.

Promise A manifestation of intention to act or to refrain from acting in a specified way, so made as to justify a promisee in understanding that a commitment has been made.

Promissory estoppel A doctrine or rule of law that prevents (estops) a promissor from avoiding liability.

Promissory note A type of commercial paper in which the maker promises to pay the payee a sum of money at a future time or on demand, usually with interest.

Promoter A person who plans and takes necessary action, including soliciting subscriptions for the purchase of shares of stock, in organizing a corporation.

Promulgate To announce officially; to make known publicly as important or obligatory.

Proof of claim A document by which a creditor seeks payment from the debtor's estate, or from the estate of a deceased person.

Pro rata Proportionate.

Pro rata share Where funds are insufficient to pay a class of bankruptcy claims in full, the percentage of the claim that each creditor of that class will receive.

Protest A certificate of dishonor signed and sealed by an authorized public official such as a United States consul or a notary public. See *Dishonor.*

Proxy A person who is authorized by another person to represent or act for him or her at a meeting. With reference to corporations, a person authorized to vote a shareholder's shares at a shareholders' meeting. The term is used also to mean the writing that authorizes a person to vote the shares of another at a shareholders' meeting.

Public corporation A corporation created for governmental purposes by any agency or subdivision of state or federal government.

Public defenders Attorneys paid out of public funds to defend individuals who cannot afford to hire legal counsel in criminal cases.

Public law Law dealing with the organization of government and with the relation of the government to the people.

Puffing See *Sales puffing*.

Punitive damages Damages awarded against a defendant as punishment for outrageous conduct or to set an example for other wrongdoers.

Purchase-money security A security interest taken or retained by a seller or other financer in financing the purchase or leasing of the collateral.

Qualified indorsement See *Indorsement*.

Quasi Resembling, possessing some of the attributes of something else. An administrative agency may have a quasi-judicial and a quasi-legislative function. In its *quasi-judicial* function it hears and disposes of disputes in the manner of a court. In its *quasi-legislative* function it makes rules and regulations of relatively general application, in the manner of a legislature.

Quasi contract A restitutionary remedy for an obligation imposed by law, intended to prevent the unjust enrichment of a person upon whom a benefit has been conferred. See Chapter 6.

Quasi-judicial See *Quasi*

Quasi-legislative See *Quasi*.

Quasi-public corporation A profit corporation privately organized for purposes which affect the public interest to an extent requiring special state or federal regulation, for example, a bank or insurance company.

Quiet title A proceeding filed for the purpose of establishing one's ownership of property.

Quorum The number of qualified persons (usually a majority of the entire body) required to be present at a meeting in order to conduct business. With reference to corporations, the number of qualified persons (shares represented in person or by proxy) required to conduct business lawfully at a shareholders' meeting.

Ratable Proportional.

Ratification Confirmation of a prior act or promise.

Reaffirmation agreement An agreement by a debtor to pay a debt that has been discharged in bankruptcy.

Real defense See *defense*.

Recognizance In law, a personal assurance or promise to be present for trial, called giving one's own recognizance.

Redemption The exercise by a corporation of a right to buy back outstanding shares at a fixed price.

Reformation A contractual remedy in which a court rewrites or corrects a written contract so that it accurately reflects the bargain of the parties.

Reinsurance A contractual arrangement in which an insurance company transfers a part of the group risk it has assumed to another insurer called a reinsurer.

Release A legally binding contract to give up a right held by the releasing party.

Relevant market The geographic area of effective competition in which a particular product as well as other interchangeable products are traded.

Remand To send back; usually the sending back of a court record or case by a higher court to the court from which a decision, order, or judgment originated, for the purpose of having the originating court take the action dictated by the higher court.

Remedy A means, such as court action, by which a violation of a right is prevented or is compensated for; legal redress.

Reorganization In bankruptcy, a proceeding by means of which a financially troubled firm may stay in business while it undergoes a process of financial rehabilitation that may involve a discharge from the firm's debts.

Replevin An action taken to acquire possession of goods.

Requirements contract A contract in which one party agrees to purchase from the other party all the goods or services which the purchasing party needs in his or her business.

Resale price maintenance In antitrust law, the practice of a seller fixing the resale price terms of the buyer at a lower level in the chain of distribution. This practice is also known as *"vertical price-fixing."*

Rescission (to rescind) The setting aside or avoiding of a contract, transaction, or other obligation that can be set aside legally. Used primarily with reference to the avoidance of an agreement, such as the repudiation of a contract by one of the parties to it or a principal's repudiation of an unauthorized act by an agent undertaken beyond his or her authority.

Res ipsa loquitur A Latin expression meaning "the thing (or incident) speaks for itself." Under the doctrine of *res ipsa loquitur*, the defendant may be required to prove that he or she was *not* negligent where the injury-causing instrumentality was completely within the control of the defendant.

Respondeat superior A maxim meaning "Let the master answer." The doctrine under which a master (employer) can be held liable for the wrongful acts of his or her servant (employee) performed within the scope of employment.

Restitution In the law of contracts, compensation for or the return of partial performances. In general, the return of a thing.

Resulting trust A trust relationship imposed by a court of equity to carry into effect the presumed intentions of the parties.

Restrictive endorsement See *Indorsement.*

Reverse, to An order reversing, overthrowing or setting aside a judgment, order, or decree previously entered by a court.

Revocation Annulling, cancelling or rescinding an act, as to revoke a will.

Risk of loss In the law of sales, the danger that goods will be lost, stolen, destroyed, or damaged.

Revocation of offer The withdrawal of the offer by the offeror.

Rider An attachment to an insurance policy that modifies the contract in some way.

Rule of reason In antitrust law, the rule that conduct which unreasonably restrains trade is illegal.

Sale (of goods) The passing of title to goods from the seller to the buyer, in return for a consideration called the price. In a *present sale*, title passes at the time the sales transaction is entered into. In a *contract to sell*, title passes to the buyer at some future time. UCC Article 2 covers both present sales and contracts to sell. The term *contract for sale* includes present sales and contracts to sell.

Sale on approval A sale of goods in which the buyer is not obligated until the buyer accepts, that is, approves, the goods.

Sale or return A transaction in which the buyer of goods purchases them for resale but has a right to return to the seller any unsold goods.

Sales puffing Exaggeration and opinion (short of actual fraud) by a seller intended to induce a sale.

Sanction A punishment. However, sanction may also mean "approval."

Scienter A necessary element of the tort of fraud and deceit which requires the plaintiff to prove that at the time false representations were made, the defendant knew they were false. Scienter is a necessary element required to be proved in most violations of federal antitrust and securities laws.

Scope of employment The general nature and conditions of the work for which an employee is hired.

Seasonably In a timely manner.

Secondary boycott Economic pressure by employees of one firm against another firm with whom those employees have no dispute.

Secondary party See *Primary party.*

Secret lien A claim against the property of another person, the acquisition of which is unknown to the general public because the claim has not been filed in the public records or otherwise has not been made known to the public.

Secured transaction Any arrangement made by agreement of the parties for the purpose of providing a creditor with a backup source of payment if the debtor defaults. In a *surety* arrangement, a person or a firm makes a backup promise to pay the debt in the event that the debtor defaults. In a *secured transaction in personal property*, personal property is the collateral and may be sold in the event of the debtor's default.

Secured transaction in personal property See *Secured transaction.*

Security An investment in a common enterprise in which the investor usually profits solely from the efforts of others. If the investment is in a corporation, it is usually evidenced by a stock or bond certificate issued in bearer or registered form.

Security agreement An agreement between the debtor and the creditor that the creditor is to have a security interest in the collateral. Unless the creditor is to possess the collateral, the security agreement must be in writing.

Security interest Some interest in property, such as possession or title, which a creditor retains or acquires to secure the payment of a debt.

Separation of powers In constitutional law, the doctrine that each branch of government (judicial, legislative, executive) should be allowed to exercise its constitutional prerogatives without undue interference by the other branches.

Servant A person employed to perform work or services for another, whose physical conduct in the performance of the work or service and the means by which it will be accomplished are subject to the control of the person, (generally called a "master" or "employer") for whom it is being performed.

Set off The right of each party to a contract or litigation to require payment or performance from the other party based upon some other dealing with that party.

Settlement option Any of several ways of receiving the proceeds of a life insurance policy upon its maturity.

Shareholder A person who owns a proportionate ownership interest in a corporation; usually such ownership is evidenced by a stock certificate.

Share of stock An equity security that represents a proportionate ownership interest in a corporation and evidences the rights which the shareholder has in the management, profits, and assets of the corporation.

Shelter provision The provision of the Uniform Commercial Code that gives holders through a holder in due course the same freedom from claims and defenses that a holder in due course enjoys. The shelter provision reflects the principle that a person may assign whatever rights he or she has.

Shipment contract A contract in which the seller is

required or authorized to send goods to the buyer but is not required to deliver them at a particular destination.

Shop right privilege The right of an employer to use without payment of royalties an invention conceived by an employee in the course of employment or through use of the employer's facilities, the employee not having been hired to perform such work.

Shortswing transactions Those transactions under Section 16 of the Securities Exchange Act of 1934, in which a director, officer, or beneficial owner of more than 10 percent of any class of nonexempt securities buys and sells (or sells and buys) the company's securities within a 6-month period. The profits from such transactions belong to the corporation.

Slander Defamation expressed verbally; oral defamation.

Small claims court A court authorized to hear, in simplified proceedings, cases involving small sums usually no more than $500.

Special indorsement See *Indorsement.*

Specification A clear and accurate description of the technical requirements for a material, product, or service to be purchased, including the procedure for determining that the requirements have been met.

Specific lien A lien that entitles a creditor to retain possession of an item of property for only the one debt involved in the immediate transaction. Also called a *special* or *particular* lien.

Specific performance An equitable remedy under which a person is entitled to a contractual performance rather than to money damages for breach of the contract. Specific performance is granted where the remedy at law (damages) is inadequate.

Specified perils contract An insurance policy which indemnifies the insured against loss caused by specified perils.

Standing In antitrust law, a doctrine requiring the plaintiff to prove that the defendant's violation was a substantial or direct cause of the plaintiff's injury which can be measured with some certainty in money terms, and that the defendant's illegal act affected legally protected activities of the plaintiff.

Stare decisis Latin. To abide by, or adhere to. A doctrine that precedents set by decisions in previous cases are to be followed in later cases involving the same point unless there is a compelling reason to depart from precedent.

Stated capital That portion of the issuance price of the outstanding shares of stock that is set aside in the capital stock account.

Statute of frauds A law providing that certain classes of contracts are unenforceable unless in writing, signed by the party to be charged for its breach (or signed by his or her authorized agent).

Statute of limitations A statute prescribing time limita-

tions on certain described causes of action or criminal prosecutions; that is, declaring that no suit shall be maintained on such causes of action unless brought within a specified period of time after the right accrued. A statute of limitations applies to the remedy at law. In equity there is also a limit (called "laches") on the time that a person has to bring suit. Under the equitable principle of *laches*, suit is barred if not brought with a *reasonable* time.

Stock certificate A certificate issued by a corporation to a named person as owner of a given number of shares of stock in the corporation. The certificate is written evidence of the owner's proportionate equity interest in the corporation.

Stock split The issuance to a shareholder of additional shares of stock, without cost, at some ratio of new shares to old shares as established by the board of directors.

Stock subscription A contract whereby a person agrees to purchase a specified number and class of shares of a new stock issue.

Stop-payment order The instruction by a drawer of a check to the drawee not to pay a certain check.

Straight bankruptcy See *Liquidation proceeding.*

Strict liability in tort A liability imposed by the law regardless of the care or skill of the defendant, as, for example, when injury results from a defective product or from an ultrahazardous activity. The liability is called "strict" because the plaintiff need not prove fault (negligence or fraud).

Subchapter S corporation A corporation which complies with Sub-chapter S of the Internal Revenue Code. It may have no more than 15 members and is taxed as though it were a partnership.

Subrogation The act or process of substituting one person for another so that the first acquires the legal rights of the second. In the law of suretyship, a surety's right to be substituted for or to take over the rights of the creditor (whom the surety has paid) against the debtor. The surety who has the right of subrogation is called the "subrogee."

Substantial performance In contract law, a doctrine that permits a party to a contract to recover damages even if that party has not fully performed. To constitute substantial performance there must be only minor omissions from full performance.

Substantive due process See *Due process.*

Substantive law That law which is concerned with the recognition of rights, duties, privileges, and immunities (as contrasted with that law which is concerned with procedure).

Sum certain In the law of negotiable instruments, an amount payable that is sufficiently calculable for an instrument to be classified as a negotiable instrument.

Summary Short, abbreviated, as a summary hearing before an administrative agency.

Surety A person who, by contract or by operation of law, is liable for the debt, default, or miscarriage of another.

Tenancy in partnership The manner in which the legal title to partnership property is held.

Tender An offer of performance by one party to a contract which, if unjustifiably refused, places the other party in default and permits the party making the tender to exercise remedies for breach of contract.

Tender offer The offer by a corporation or person to purchase the shares of stock from shareholders of a "target corporation" in exchange for money or other securities. A tender offer is most commonly used to acquire voting control of the "target corporation."

Tenor In the law of negotiable instruments, the amount originally intended. Where the face amount of a stolen negotiable instrument has been raised without the consent of the maker, a holder in due course ordinarily may enforce the instrument only in accordance with its original tenor.

Testamentary capacity The capability to make a valid will.

Testamentary intent The intent to direct the transfer of property, effective upon death.

Testate With a will. A person who dies leaving a will is said to die testate.

Testator, Testatrix A person who makes a will.

Third-person beneficiary In the law of contracts, a person who is not a party to a contract but who is intended to receive benefits from it.

Through bill of lading See *Bill of lading*.

Time draft See *Draft*.

Title Ownership. In the law of secured transactions, "title" is often used to describe a security interest, an interest in property less extensive than ownership. See *Security interest*.

Tort A civil wrong, other than breach of contract, for which a court may award damages.

Trademark A word, symbol, device, or design affixed to or placed upon an article or its container to identify an article offered for sale.

Trade name A name used in trade to designate a particular business.

Trade regulation rule A legislative rule with the force of law promulgated by the Federal Trade Commission regulating business practices.

Transaction Any act of conducting business. Broader than the word *contract*, the word *transaction* includes "gift," "lease," "sale," "mortgage," and "bailment."

Traveler's check A three-party draft purchased from a bank or other firm and carried instead of cash.

Treasury stock Stock issued by a corporation but subsequently reacquired by the corporation.

Trial de novo A new trial held in an appellate court.

Trust An obligation arising out of a confidence reposed in a person, for the benefit of another, to apply property or services faithfully according to such confidence. A trust arises when property is given to one person with direction that it be used and applied for the benefit of another.

Trustee in bankruptcy A bankruptcy official responsible for collecting, liquidating, and distributing the debtor's estate.

Turnover In bankruptcy law, the act of delivering to the trustee in bankruptcy property that belongs to the debtor's estate.

Tying contract A contract in which a seller sells a product only on condition that the buyer also purchases a distinct second product which is not desired.

Ultrahazardous activity An activity that necessarily involves a risk of serious harm, which risk cannot be eliminated by the exercise of utmost care.

Ultra vires act A corporate act or action that is beyond the scope of authority and powers conferred upon the corporation by law or by the articles of incorporation.

Unconscionable Conduct (not necessarily amounting to fraud, misrepresentation, or duress) that results in the oppression or unfair surprise of one contracting party by the other.

Undue influence The overcoming of the free will of a person by unfair persuasion; usually involves misuse of a position of confidence or relationship.

Unenforceable contract One that the law will not enforce by direct legal proceedings but may recognize in some indirect way as creating some duty of performance.

Unilateral contract A contract in which one party makes a promise; the other party must perform an act to enforce the contract. Cf *bilateral contract*.

Uniform state laws A draft of law prepared by the National Conference of Commissioners on Uniform State Laws and submitted to all states for adoption. When adopted, such a law is amended to meet individual state needs.

Usage of trade In the law of sales, any practice or method of dealing having such regularity of observance in a place, vocation, or trade as to justify an expectation that it will be observed with respect to the transaction in question.

Usury The charging of any rate of interest in excess of that permitted by law.

Value In the law of *sales, secured transactions*, and *documents of title*, any promise or other consideration sufficient to support a simple contract. In the law of *commercial paper, performed* consideration.

Verification A person's statement, signed under penalty

of perjury, that facts recited in a document are true and correct.

Vertical merger A combination in which a firm at one level acquires a firm at a different level, e.g., a manufacturer acquiring a wholesaler.

Vertical price fixing See *Resale price maintenance.*

Vicarious act An act performed or exercised by one party for another. In agency law, an agent's or servant's act which may bind the principal or master.

Voidable contract One that a party may enforce or set aside (avoid) as that person wishes.

Void contract An attempt at contracting which never produced a contract because some essential contractual element was missing.

Vest To become established, to take effect; giving an immediate, fixed right of present or future enjoyment.

Wanton act A malicious and unjustifiable act; a heedless and reckless disregard for another's rights; careless of the consequences.

Warehouse A building or other enclosed area used to hold goods temporarily or for an indefinite time. A *public warehouse* stores goods for any member of the public who seeks and pays for the storage service. A *private warehouse* stores goods only for those persons with whom it chooses to contract.

Warehouser A person or firm engaged in the business of receiving and storing goods for hire.

Warehouse receipt See *Document of title.*

Warranty A guarantee; a statement, promise, or other representation that a thing has certain qualities or that the seller has title to the thing. Also, an obligation imposed by law that a thing will have certain qualities. In the law of sales, a *warranty of merchantability,* whether express or implied, assures the recipient that the goods are of fair, average quality. A sales *warranty of fitness for a particular purpose* assures the buyer that the goods are fit for the buyer's particular purpose. In the law of *commercial paper,* there are two kinds of warranties: transfer warranties and presentment warranties, see chapter 32.

Warranty of fitness See Chapter 18.

Warrant of merchantability See Chapter 18.

Warranty of title See Chapter 18.

Will In estate or inheritance law, a declaration of a person's wishes as to how his or her property will be disposed of, to take effect after death. Until death, a will is said to be ambulatory and may be revoked.

Winding up A necessary step after the dissolution of a partnership, during which the partnership assets are gathered in, all its debts are paid, and distribution of the remainder is made to the partners.

With reserve With regard to auctions, an expression indicating that the auctioneer, on behalf of the owner, reserves the right to withdraw the goods from bidding.

Without reserve With regard to auctions, an expression indicating that the owner of the goods will sell them to any bidder no matter how low the bid is, if a bid is made within a reasonable time.

Workers' Compensation Law Laws enacted in all states which establish systems for the payment of compensation to workers who are injured in, or suffer a disease as a result of, their employment.

Writ A writing, issued by a court or other competent tribunal and directed to the sheriff or to some other officer, for the purpose of carrying out an order or sentence of the court.

Writ of execution See *Execution.*

INDEX

CIF (shipping term), 260, 276
Civil Aeronautics Board (CAB), 720
(*See also* Antitrust law)
Civil law remedies (*see* Remedies, civil law)
Civil procedure, 24
Civil Rights Act of 1965, 756–757
Claims and counterclaims, 37
Clayton Act, 725
(*See also* Antitrust law)
Clearinghouse, 556
Coinsurance, 498–499
Collateral:
  acquisition on default, 476
    deficiency in, 478
    surplus in, 477–478
  disposition of, 477–479
  repossession of, 476–477
  types of, 442–468
Commercial impracticability, 276–278
Commercial paper:
  accommodation party, 557–558
  bearer paper, 517, 535–536
  bill of exchange, 506
  clearinghouse, 556
  confession of judgment clause, 522
  as contract, 514
  conversion of, 553, 583–584
  defenses to: personal, 511, 523–525
    real, 512, 525–529
  delivery of, 514, 532
    dual nature of, 514
    to holder in due course (*see* Holder in due course)
    issuance, 532
    liability of parties, 509–510
    meaning of, 506, 511
  demand note, 506
  discharge of, 561–565
  dishonor of, 556–557
  drafts, 507–508

Commercial paper, drafts (*Cont.*):
  acceptance of, 509, 515–516, 554
  (*See also* Checks)
  drawee and drawer of, 507
  forged or signed without authority, 559–561
  guarantor of, 558–559
  holder of, 506, 532, 533
  holder in due course (*see* Holder in due course)
  indorsement of: conditional, 539
    by imposter or dishonest agent, 560–561
    meaning of, 555
    qualified, 536–537
    requirements for, 534, 535
    restrictive, 537–539
    special, 535–536
  liability of parties to, 509–510, 514, 553–559
  liability when indorsement is forged, 559–561
  maker of, 506
  meaning of, 506
  negotiability of: language that destroys, 519–522
    meaning of, 511–514
    particular fund doctrine, 520–521
    requirements for, 511, 516–519, 521–523
    significance of, 511–514
  negotiation of: banks, role in, 538
    delivery, 532
    effect of, 533
    by holder, 533–534
    by indorsement, 534–541
    methods of, 532–541
    rescission of, 540
  notes, 506
  notice of dishonor, 555–557
  order paper, 517, 535–536
  payee of, 506, 507
  presentment of, 556, 566–568
  promissory note, 506

Commercial paper (*Cont.*):
  as property, 514
  protest of, 555
  shelter provision, 547–548
  transfer of, 511–514
  types of, 506–510
  uses of, 512–516
  value, meaning of, 541–543
  warranties on, 565–568
Commingling goods, 475–476
Community property, 399, 429
Comparative negligence, 56, 286
Complaint, 25
Composition agreement, 132, 768
Composition and extension agreement in bankruptcy, 768–781
Computer crimes, 77–78
Condemnation, 396
Conditional sale contract, 462
Condominiums, 399
Confession of judgment clause, 522
Consideration in contracts, 123
Consumer:
  credit to: closed and open end, 739
    Equal Credit Opportunity Act, 738
    reports, 737
  debt collection and, 742
  protection of: under Federal Warranty Act, 297, 299
    under Magnuson-Moss Warranty Act, 299
    (*See also* Warranty)
  truth in lending legislation, 734, 739
Consumer frauds, 79
Consumer Product Safety Commission (CPSC), 722
Contract law:
  meaning of, 224
  privity of contract, 284
  sales law modifications to, 231, 233–236, 239–240